MEDICINE IN THE LITIGATION PROCESS

Giovanna Roccamo, LL.B. • John H. Haydon, Q.C., B.A., LL.B.

Jacques A. Bouchard, M.D., F.R.C.S.C.
John Latter, M.D., F.R.C.P.C.
Howard Lesiuk, M.D., F.R.C.P.C.
Clare Stoddart, PH.D., C.PSYCH.
Robert W. Teasell, M.D., F.R.C.P.C.

•

Jacques A. Brunet, M.D., F.R.C.S.C.
Geoff Dervin, M.D., F.R.C.S.C.
Robert J. Feibel, M.D., F.R.C.S.C.
Alan Giachino, M.D., F.R.C.S.C.
Manfred Harth, M.D., F.R.C.P.C.
Robert M. Knights, PH.D., C.PSYCH.

©1999 Giovanna Roccamo and John H. Haydon

All rights reserved. No part of this publication may be reproduced, stored in a retrieval system, or transmitted, in any form or by any means, electronic, mechanical, photocopying, recording, or otherwise, without the prior written permission of the publisher.

This publisher is not engaged in rendering legal, accounting or other professional advice. If legal advice or other expert assistance is required, the services of a competent professional should be sought. The analysis contained herein represents the opinions of the authors and should in no way be construed as being official or unofficial policy of any governmental body.

This work reproduces official English language versions of Ontario Statutes and Regulations. As the Revised Statutes of Ontario, 1990 and many Ontario Regulations also have official French versions, the reader is advised that reference to the official French language material may be warranted in appropriate circumstances.

Canadian Cataloguing in Publication Data

Roccamo, Giovanna, 1959-
   Medicine in the litigation process

Includes bibliographical references and index.
ISBN 0-459-23829-9

1. Medical jurisprudence. 2. Evidence, Expert. I. Haydon, John H., 1935- II. Title.

RA1051.R62 1998   614'.1   C98-932609-8

The acid-free paper used in this publication meets the minimum requirements of the American National Standard for Information Sciences – Permanence of Paper for Printed Library Materials, ANSI Z39.48-1984.

One Corporate Plaza, 2075 Kennedy Road, Scarborough, Ontario M1T 3V4
Customer Service:
Toronto 1-416-609-3800
Elsewhere in Canada/U.S. 1-800-387-5164
Fax 1-416-298-5094

*I dedicate this piece of work to my husband, Eugene,
and children, Naomi, Marc, Mélanie and Morgan,
without whose love and support
this kind of undertaking simply could not be
conceived nor concluded.*

Giovanna Roccamo

*Lovingly dedicated to my wife, Doreen,
and children, Bruce, Geoffrey and Elizabeth.*

John Haydon

Forewords

This book will be indispensable to those undertaking actions for or against health service agencies, health service professionals and for those who have suffered personal injuries. At the outset the book sets out the statutes pertaining to all health professionals together with a general outline of the most pertinent statutory provisions. A thorough review is made of the records which are statutorily required to be kept by health professionals. This information itself will be extremely useful. It will help counsel to determine what records should be produced and what those records should contain. I think that it is the first time that in one book there has been such a thorough canvassing of the records required to be kept in a wide variety of care giving institutions from hospitals to psychiatric facilities.

The book provides as well a very comprehensive and helpful review of the *Work Safety and Insurance Act 1997* which replaces the *Workers' Compensation Act*. Here too the statutorily required records and what must be contained in those records is clearly set out. Further, the procedures that may be taken by workers appealing rulings is carefully reviewed. Lawyers working in this field will find this chapter to be very helpful.

The chapter dealing with access to health records provides an excellent review of the jurisprudence in this area. It begins with the Hippocratic oath and continues with a review of all the relevant cases. There is, of course, a conflict between the duty of the doctor to keep the records of a patient confidential and the right of patients and their legal advisers to review their own records and of courts to accurately assess damages in personal injury cases. The jurisprudence on this aspect again is carefully reviewed. There is a very helpful section which guides lawyers through the forms to be used by patients and their counsel in obtaining access to medical records. The protection that must be given to evidence put forward at coroners' inquests and reports given to authorities regarding problems with vision that will affect driving and that may make driving dangerous are all thoughtfully considered. The restricted use that may be made of reports concerning persons confined in psychiatric facilities is set out in the detail required by counsel.

As well, the discovery process is fully discussed and all aspects of the production of documents are reviewed. The rules of practice are set out together with all the relevant cases pertaining to them. The section on discovery contains a great deal of useful advice to counsel acting in personal injury claims. The relevant case law is thoroughly reviewed with the facts clearly set out and the reasons for judgment summarized and, where appropriate, quoted.

This book provides an excellent background for litigating personal injury claims. The pertinent legislation and the jurisprudence clearly demonstrate the never-ending search for a fair and just balance between the need to respect the privacy of the individual and the privacy interest in any reports dealing with that individual and the search for truth which must be the essence of any trial, particularly a civil claim seeking appropriate compensation for personal injuries. Quite simply, such litigation should not be undertaken without referring to this thorough and excellent text.

From the first advice to a client, through production of documents and discovery, to the preparation and conduct of a trial, this book provides invaluable instruction, guidance and assistance.

The Hon. Peter de Carteret Cory
The Supreme Court of Canada

This text undertakes an exhaustive review of the duties and obligations of health care professionals to maintain records and reports. It reviews all of the statutory obligations and outlines the steps necessary to obtain access to these records.

Trial counsel will find this work invaluable since it not only provides a source of reference but gives guidelines for effectively using these records and notes.

The final chapters will help counsel to determine how and when to retain an expert and more importantly, how to obtain a proper expert opinion. The text then goes on to provide a guideline for the preparation of the expert as witness, both in examination in chief and in cross-examination.

The authors have collaborated to produce an excellent resource which will prove indispensable for trial counsel and health professionals alike.

There is no other text available today which covers these topics in such depth and with such clarity.

Mr. Justice James B. Chadwick
Regional Senior Justice
Superior Court of Justice
Ottawa, Ontario

Preface

This book is intended to fill a void in Canadian legal publications that has been a source of irritation to many civil litigation lawyers, namely a book which addresses the legal and medical issues most commonly encountered in personal injury litigation. Until now, they have had to rely principally on American texts, which cover the subject amply, but have to be supplemented by further study of Canadian legal and medical literature to provide the perspective essential for persuasion in a court of law. This book represents an attempt to assemble legal and medical data in a form useful to the litigation practitioner in gaining a better understanding of these issues arising in his or her day-to-day practice.

Frequently lacking at any stage of counsel's experience is an understanding of the health professions generally, their members' training, their governance, their ethics, their standards of practice, and their statutory responsibilities. Like a lawyer, a physician spends many years in schools, colleges and universities, honing his or her skills. As a member of a self-regulating body dedicated to upholding and improving the high standards of care moulded by preceding generations, the health professional is bound to abide by codes of ethics pronounced by a College composed of his or her peers, and to conform with statutes and regulations promulgated by representatives of the public he or she has chosen to serve. This book, it is hoped, will assist in adding substance to the legal practitioner's perception of the health professional in the context of a lawsuit, which in turn may make more palatable and facile the task of preparing for and conducting the examination and cross-examination of the medical expert.

The judicial process is intended to be a quest for truth, and an important signpost on this quest may often be found in the health records of the patient whose injuries are in issue. If personal injury counsel, veteran and acolyte alike, are to serve their clients, they must routinely and purposefully direct their attention to the most likely repositories of health records. Among other things, this book strives to arouse a desire in personal injury counsel to take that extra step necessary to achieve the fullest possible disclosure within the framework of our civil justice system, consistent with the economic demands of prosecuting or defending the case.

Hand in hand with the development of a sense for locating probative medical records should be the accumulation of knowledge about the medical aspects of personal injuries and sequelae which are the subject matter of the litigation. It is difficult to spar with a medical expert on cross-examination unless counsel is as familiar as the expert on the narrow issues involved in a suit. Almost the only source of such medical information in Canada has been medical texts prepared expressly for health professionals, composed in a language which presupposes a fair degree of sophistication in medical matters, and presented in a style and organization far removed from the demands of litigation counsel. There is a need for literature which presents medical information in a language that is comprehensible to lawyers, and in a format suited to their tasks. The planners of this project have been, we believe, successful in assembling a thoroughly experienced group of medical experts to address this need. All are leaders in their respective fields, as well as being gifted in their ability to reduce complex medical data into terms and organization suited to the needs of personal injury counsel. Space and time demands made it impossible to address the entire lexicon of medical subjects, and the planners have attempted to limit treatment of medical subjects to only those areas most frequently encountered in personal injury litigation, which means a strong emphasis on traumatic injuries and those parts of the body most commonly affected by them. Perhaps, if response to this publication warrants it, the practising profession can look forward to additional literature on medical subjects, offering broader scope, more specialization, and greater depth.

It was with great sorrow that we learned of the death of Dr. Clare Stoddart, one of the contributors to this work, in August, 1997. Our periodic meetings of contributors were always enlivened by her cheerful presence and wise counsel. Her contribution was almost complete at the time of her untimely passing, and we are indebted to her partner, Dr. R.M. Knights, for applying the finishing touches.

A heartfelt thank you to Sabby Duthie, a former articling student of the Nelligan/Power firm and now a recently-called member of the legal profession, whose thorough research and assistance have buoyed Giovanna from start to finish of this at times daunting endeavour.

A special note of thanks is reserved for Diane Latter, who generously volunteered her expertise to edit the offerings of the medical contributors to this work, to avoid overlapping and to ensure that the treatment given by the various authors was uniform.

John H. Haydon
Giovanna Roccamo

Acknowledgements

The authors gratefully acknowledge the assistance given by the following persons, each in a different way, to prepare this book for publication. There are many duties associated with the publication of a work of this kind apart from authorship which must be selflessly performed by volunteers motivated only by their belief in the integrity of the project, and without which literary effort is impossible. For their dedication and energy given to these duties, we thank:

>Donna Bradbury
>Sabby Duthie
>Danielle H. Cayer
>Diane Latter
>Heather Morrison
>Dr. Gary G. Johnson

Publisher's Note

Court Name Changes in Ontario

The *Courts Improvement Act, 1996*, S.O. 1996, c. 25, Part IV, section 8 (in force April 19, 1999), renamed certain Ontario courts and court officials as follows:

Former names and titles	New names and titles
Ontario Court of Justice	Court of Ontario
Ontario Court (General Division)	Superior Court of Justice
Ontario Court (Provincial Division)	Ontario Court of Justice
Chief Justice of the Ontario Court of Justice	Chief Justice of the Superior Court of Justice
Associate Chief Justice of the Ontario Court of Justice	Associate Chief Justice of the Superior Court of Justice
Associate Chief Justice (Family Court) of the Ontario Court of Justice	Associate Chief Justice (Family Court) of the Superior Court of Justice
Chief Judge of the Ontario Court (Provincial Division)	Chief Justice of the Ontario Court of Justice
Associate Chief Judge of the Ontario Court (Provincial Division)	Associate Chief Justice of the Ontario Court of Justice
Associate Chief Judge-Co-ordinator of Justices of the Peace	Associate Chief Justice-Co-ordinator of Justices of the Peace
Accountant of the Ontario Court	Accountant of the Superior Court of Justice

Section 9(1) of the *Courts Improvement Act, 1996* also amended the *Courts of Justice Act* by adding section 1.1(1). Section 1.1(1) states that any reference in an Act, rule or regulation to a court or official by its former name shall be deemed, unless a contrary intention appears, to be a reference to the new name of that court or a new title of that official.

Section 10(1) of the *Courts Improvement Act, 1996*, provides that a reference in a court seal or printed court form to the former name of a court or title of an official does not prevent the form or seal from being used during the one year period following April 19, 1999. Section 10(1) applies only to court seals and printed court forms in existence on the date the changes to the names of the courts and titles of the officials became effective.

References to these Ontario courts and officials in this publication should be interpreted accordingly.

Table of Contents

Chapter 1 Health Profession Statutes

1.1 Introduction 1
1.2 *Regulated Health Professions Act, 1991* 3
1.3 Health Professions Procedural Code 5
    1.3.1 Prescription Period 7
1.4 The Health Profession Acts 7

Chapter 2 Statutory Duty to Create, Maintain and Preserve Health Records

2.1 Introduction 11
2.2 Record-Keeping under the Health Profession Acts 13
    2.2.1 *Medicine Act, 1991* 13
    2.2.2 *Chiropody Act, 1991* 14
    2.2.3 *Massage Therapy Act, 1991* 16
    2.2.4 *Optometry Act, 1991* 17
2.3 Record-Keeping under Medical Institutions Statutes 18
    2.3.1 *Public Hospitals Act* 18
2.4 General Statutes with Health Record Components 28
    2.4.1 *Child and Family Services Act* 29
    2.4.2 *Coroners Act* 34
    2.4.3 *Drug and Pharmacies Regulation Act* 35
    2.4.4 *Long Term Care Act, 1994* 38
    2.4.5 *Mental Health Act* 42
    2.4.6 *Vital Statistics Act* 52
    2.4.7 *Workers' Compensation Act; Workplace Safety and Insurance Act, 1997* 53

Chapter 3 Access to Health Records

3.1 Confidentiality of Health Records 61
3.2 Patient's Right to Access Own Personal Medical Records 65
3.3 Waiver of Right to Access Personal Medical Records by the Patient 67

3.4	Canadian Health Record Association		69
	3.4.1	Principles and Guidelines	69
	3.4.2	Position Statement re Patient Access to Health Records	76
	3.4.3	Code of Practice for Safeguarding Health Information	78
3.5	Legislation Regarding Access to Documents Containing Personal Medical Information		80
	3.5.1	*Long Term Care Act, 1994*	81

Chapter 4 Production of Health Records in a Personal Injury Action

4.1	Introduction		86
4.2	Health Records Not Producible in a Personal Injury Action		87
	4.2.1	*Child and Family Services Act*	87
	4.2.2	*Coroners Act*	88
	4.2.3	*Highway Traffic Act*	89
	4.2.4	*Human Rights Code*	90
	4.2.5	*Independent Health Facilities Act*	90
	4.2.6	*Mental Health Act*	91
	4.2.7	*Regulated Health Professions Act, 1991*, a health profession Act; *Drug and Pharmacies Regulation Act*	92
		Case Law	93
	4.2.8	*Workers' Compensation Act; Workplace Safety and Insurance Act, 1997*	93
4.3	The Discovery Process		96
	4.3.1	Affidavit of Documents	96
	4.3.2	Examination for Discovery of a Party	100
		Case Law	104
	4.3.3	Examination for Discovery of a Non-party	113
		Case Law	114
4.4	Order for Production of Documents from a Non-party		114
	Case Law		115
4.5	Court-ordered Medical Examination of a Party		
	Case Law		126
4.6	Trial		126
	Case Law		127
	4.6.1	Medical Records Under Section 35 of the *Evidence Act*	127
		Case Law	128
	4.6.2	Medical Reports Under Section 52 of the *Evidence Act*	129
		Case Law	130

	4.6.3	Medical Reports Under Section 53.03 of Ontario Rules of Civil Procedure........................... 134
		Case Law 135
	4.6.4	Medical Reports of Court-appointed Expert under Ontario Rules of Civil Procedure.................... 135
	4.6.5	Use of Photographic Film of Health Records at Trial... 136
4.7	Related Topics 137
	4.7.1	Incident Reports................................. 137
	4.7.2	Quality Assurance Programs........................ 138
	4.7.3	Deemed Undertaking.............................. 139
	4.7.4	Spoliation of Health Records....................... 141
	4.7.5	"Police Informer" Privilege 146
	4.7.6	Computerized Records 149
	4.7.7	*Freedom of Information and Protection of Privacy Act* and the *Municipal Freedom of Information and Protection of Privacy Act* 151
	4.7.8	Access by any Person to Information Concerning a Health Profession Member Maintained by Registrar of a College, under the Health Professions Procedural Code 153

Chapter 5 Statutory Duty to Report Personal Medical Information

5.1	Statutory Duty to Report Personal Medical Information 157
5.2	Duty to Warn 158
5.3	Statutes Containing "Duty to Report" Provisions 160
	5.3.1	*Child and Family Services Act*...................... 161
	5.3.2	*Coroners Act*.................................... 164
	5.3.3	*Health Protection and Promotion Act* 166
	5.3.4	*Highway Traffic Act*.............................. 172
		Case Law 173
	5.3.5	*Regulated Health Professions Act, 1991* 175
	5.3.6	*Vital Statistics Act* 176
	5.3.7	*Charitable Institutions Act* 177
	5.3.8	*Day Nurseries Act* 178
	5.3.9	*Homes for Retarded Persons Act* 178
	5.3.10	*Homes for the Aged and Rest Homes Act* 179
	5.3.11	*Mental Hospitals Act*............................. 180
	5.3.12	*Nursing Homes Act* 181
	5.3.13	*Private Hospitals Act* 182
	5.3.14	*Public Hospitals Act* 182

Chapter 6 Expert Evidence

- 6.1 Introduction.. 188
- 6.2 Opinion Evidence... 188
- 6.3 Why are Experts Needed?................................. 190
- 6.4 Qualifications of an Expert.............................. 191
- 6.5 Admissibility of Expert Opinion Evidence................ 193
  - 6.5.1 Relevance.. 193
  - 6.5.2 Necessity in Assisting the Trier of Fact......... 195
  - 6.5.3 The Absence of any Exclusionary Rule............. 197
  - 6.5.4 A Properly Qualified Expert...................... 197
- 6.6 Expert Opinion Based on Hearsay......................... 200
- 6.7 Ultimate Issue Rule..................................... 201
- 6.8 Novel Expert Opinion Evidence........................... 204
- 6.9 Duties and Responsibilities of an Expert Witness........ 210
- 6.10 Court-Appointed Experts................................. 214
- 6.11 Approaching the Right Expert Witness.................... 217
- 6.12 How to Locate the Expert Witness........................ 219
- 6.13 When to Choose an Expert Witness........................ 220
- 6.14 Remuneration for Expert Opinion......................... 221
  - 6.14.1 Professional Conduct............................ 222
  - 6.14.2 Payment for the Expert's Services............... 222
- 6.15 Expert Report... 223
  - 6.15.1 Rule 53.03...................................... 223
  - 6.15.2 Disclosure of Expert Report, Raw Data Drafts.... 224
  - 6.15.3 Why Such a Difference?.......................... 227
  - 6.15.4 Leave to File an Expert's Report................ 229
- 6.16 Ontario *Evidence Act* — Medical Reports................ 230
  - 6.16.1 Purpose of Section 52 of the Ontario *Evidence Act*..... 231
  - 6.16.2 Calling the Medical Practitioner to Testify..... 232
  - 6.16.3 Who has the Obligation to Secure the Attendance at Trial of the Medical Practitioner for Cross-examination?.............................. 233
  - 6.16.4 The Medical Practitioner is Unavailable for Cross-Examination............................... 235
- 6.17 Produce a Good Expert Report............................ 236
- 6.18 Format of the Expert Report............................. 241
- 6.19 Review the Expert Report................................ 242
- 6.20 Number of Experts Allowed to Testify.................... 243
- 6.21 Family Doctor-Patient Relationship...................... 244
- 6.22 Conclusion.. 245
- Appendix A... 246

Chapter 7 Preparing the Expert for Trial

- 7.1 Introduction 251
- 7.2 General Preparation 252
- 7.3 Theory of the Case 253
- 7.4 Expert Witness 254
- 7.5 Preparing an Expert to Provide the Expert Opinion 257
- 7.6 The Direct Examination 260
- 7.7 Qualifying an Expert Witness 260
- 7.8 The Heart of the Expert's Opinion 264
- 7.9 The Basis of the Expert's Opinion 264
  - 7.9.1 Build the Expert's Opinion Slowly 265
  - 7.9.2 Summarize each Stage of the Expert's Opinion 265
  - 7.9.3 The Hypothetical Question 265
  - 7.9.4 Demonstrative Aids 267
  - 7.9.5 Define Terms 271
  - 7.9.6 Show that Expert is Presenting a Mainstream Opinion .. 272
  - 7.9.7 Deal with any Weaknesses 272
  - 7.9.8 End of a Powerful Note 274
- 7.10 Cross-examination of Experts 274
- 7.11 Purposes of Cross-examination 274
- 7.12 Preparation for the Cross-examination of an Expert 275
- 7.13 Areas of Challenge on Cross-examination 277
- 7.14 Techniques of Cross-examination 280
- 7.15 Conclusion 282

Chapter 8 Head Injury

- 8.1 Introduction 285
- 8.2 Anatomy of the Brain and its Coverings 285
  - 8.2.1 The Skull 285
  - 8.2.2 Meninges (Coverings of the Brain) 286
    - 8.2.2.1 Introduction 286
    - 8.2.2.2 Dura Mater 286
    - 8.2.2.3 Arachnoid Mater 287
    - 8.2.2.4 Pia Mater 287
  - 8.2.3 The Brain 287
    - 8.2.3.1 Divisions of the Brain 287
      - 8.2.3.1.1 Introduction 287
    - 8.2.3.2 The Cellular Foundation of Neuroanatomy 288
      - 8.2.3.2.1 Introduction 288
      - 8.2.3.2.2 The Neuron 288
      - 8.2.3.2.3 Neuroglia 289

		8.2.3.3	The Cerebral Hemispheres	290
			8.2.3.3.1 Introduction	290
			8.2.3.3.2 Frontal Lobe	291
			8.2.3.3.3 Parietal Lobe	292
			8.2.3.3.4 Temporal Lobe	293
			8.2.3.3.5 Occipital Lobe	293
			8.2.3.3.6 Basal Ganglia	293
		8.2.3.4	The Diencephalon	293
			8.2.3.4.1 Thalamus	293
			8.2.3.4.2 Hypothalamus	294
			8.2.3.4.3 Subthalamus and Epithalamus	294
		8.2.3.5	The Brainstem	295
		8.2.3.6	The Cerebellum	296
	8.2.4	Blood Vessels of the Brain		296
		8.2.4.1	Arteries of the Brain	296
		8.2.4.2	Veins of the Brain	297
	8.2.5	The Ventricles of the Brain		298
8.3	Epidemiology of Head Injury			298
8.4	Pathophysiology of Head Injury			299
	8.4.1	Introduction		299
	8.4.2	Impact (Primary) Injuries		299
		8.4.2.1	Scalp Injuries	299
		8.4.2.2	Skull Fracture	300
			8.4.2.2.1 Classification	300
			8.4.2.2.2 Linear Skull Fractures	300
			8.4.2.2.3 Depressed Skull Fractures	301
			8.4.2.2.4 Basal Skull Fractures	302
		8.4.2.3	Cerebral Concussion	303
		8.4.2.4	Grey Matter Contusions	303
		8.4.2.5	Diffuse Brain Injury	303
	8.4.3	Secondary Injuries		305
		8.4.3.1	Intracranial Haematoma	305
			8.4.3.1.1 Epidural Haematoma	305
			8.4.3.1.2 Acute Subdural Haematoma	307
			8.4.3.1.3 Chronic Subdural Haematoma	308
			8.4.3.1.4 Traumatic Subarachnoid Hemorrhage	310
			8.4.3.1.5 Intracerebral Haematoma	310
		8.4.3.2	Raised Intracranial Pressure	310
			8.4.3.2.1 Introduction and Definitions	310
			8.4.3.2.2 Consequences of Raised Intracranial Pressure	314
			Ischemia	314

			Brain Shift and Herniation	315
			Cingulate Herniation	316
			Lateral Transtentorial (Uncal) Herniation	316
			Central Transtentorial Herniation	317

8.5 Acute Evaluation of the Head-Injured Patient 317
    8.5.1 Introduction 317
    8.5.2 History and Physical Examination.................. 318
    8.5.3 Diagnostic Imaging................................ 319

8.6 Acute Management of Severe Head Injuries 320
    8.6.1 Introduction 320
    8.6.2 Initial Resuscitation............................... 321
    8.6.3 Overall Management Goals 322
    8.6.4 Intracranial Pressure Monitoring 322
        8.6.4.1 Introduction 322
        8.6.4.2 Indications for Monitoring................ 323
        8.6.4.3 Choice of Monitor....................... 324
    8.6.5 Additional Monitoring Techniques 324
        8.6.5.1 Transcranial Doppler 324
        8.6.5.2 Jugular Venous Oxygen Saturation Monitoring............................... 324
    8.6.6 Treatment of Elevated Intracranial Pressure........... 325
        8.6.6.1 Guideline for Initiating Treatment 325
        8.6.6.2 Specific Therapeutic Measures 325
            8.6.6.2.1 Introduction.................... 325
            8.6.6.2.2 Sedation, Analgesia, and Neuromuscular Blockade.......... 325
            8.6.6.2.3 Head Elevation 326
            8.6.6.2.4 CSF Drainage................... 326
            8.6.6.2.5 Hyperventilation................. 326
            8.6.6.2.6 Mannitol 327
            8.6.6.2.7 Barbiturates..................... 327
            8.6.6.2.8 Corticosteroids 327
            8.6.6.2.9 Anti-seizure Prophylaxis.......... 328

8.7 Selected Special Topics in Head Injury 329
    8.7.1 Cerebral Concussion 329
        8.7.1.1 Introduction 329
        8.7.1.2 Definitions.............................. 329
        8.7.1.3 Immediate On Scene ("Sideline") Evaluation 331
        8.7.1.4 Management Recommendations 331
    8.7.2 Brain Death 333

		8.7.2.1	Introduction	333
		8.7.2.2	Guidelines	333

Figures 337

Chapter 9 Neuropsychology and Traumatic Brain Injury

9.1 The Neuropsychologist 350
9.2 Definition of Traumatic Brain Injury 351
    9.2.1 Glasgow Coma Scale 351
    9.2.2 Post-Traumatic Amnesia 351
    9.2.3 Post-Concussion Syndrome 352
    9.2.4 Post-Traumatic Stress Disorder 353
    9.2.5 Epidemiology 353
9.3 Neuropsychological Procedures 354
    9.3.1 Testing Procedures 354
        9.3.1.1 Interview and History 354
        9.3.1.2 Test Behaviour 355
        9.3.1.3 Test Administration 355
    9.3.2 Personality Variables which may Affect Test Performance 355
        9.3.2.1 Malingering 355
        9.3.2.2 Depression 356
        9.3.2.3 Pain 357
        9.3.2.4 Anxiety 357
    9.3.3 Commonly Used Tests 357
        9.3.3.1 Intelligence 358
        9.3.3.2 Attention and Concentration 358
        9.3.3.3 Memory and Learning 359
        9.3.3.4 Language 359
        9.3.3.5 Visuospatial and Visuoconstructive Abilities .. 359
        9.3.3.6 Sensory-Motor Abilities 359
        9.3.3.7 Executive Functions 360
        9.3.3.8 Personality Measures 360
    9.3.4 Test Results 361
        9.3.4.1 Test Interpretation 361
        9.3.4.2 Test Report 361
9.4 Sequelae of Traumatic Brain Injury 362
    9.4.1 Cognitive Sequelae 362
        9.4.1.1 Attention and Concentration 362
        9.4.1.2 Memory 362
        9.4.1.3 Learning 363
        9.4.1.4 Executive Functions 363
    9.4.2 Emotional and Behavioural Sequelae 363
        9.4.2.1 Fatigue 363

	9.4.2.2	Irritability	364
	9.4.2.3	Emotional Lability and Disinhibition	364
	9.4.2.4	Insensitivity or Lack of Empathy	364
	9.4.2.5	Anosognosia	364

9.5 Rehabilitation and Recovery 364
    9.5.1 Factors Related to Rehabilitation 364
    9.5.2 Rehabilitation Techniques 365
    9.5.3 Recovery — Age, Severity, Extent 365

Chapter 10 Spinal Injuries

10.1 The Role of Each Team Member 369
    10.1.1 Ambulance and Paramedics 370
    10.1.2 Trauma Team Leader 371
    10.1.3 Spinal Surgeon 371
    10.1.4 Rehabilitation Specialists 372
10.2 The Cervical Spine 372
    10.2.1 Anatomy 372
        10.2.1.1 Osseous Anatomy 372
        10.2.1.2 Intervertebral Discs 374
        10.2.1.3 Ligaments 375
        10.2.1.4 Muscles 375
        10.2.1.5 Nerves and Spinal Cord 376
            10.2.1.5.1 Cross Anatomy 376
            10.2.1.5.2 Neuronatomy 377
            10.2.1.5.3 Motor Tracts 377
            10.2.1.5.4 Sensory Tracts 377
    10.2.2 Biomechanics of the Neck 378
        10.2.2.1 The Occipito-Atlanto-Axial Complex
                (C0–C1–C2) 378
        10.2.2.2 The Subaxial Complex (C2 to T1) 378
        10.2.2.3 Concepts of Spinal Stability 379
        10.2.2.4 Common Injury Mechanism 380
    10.2.3 Evaluation of the Patient with a Cervical Injury 381
        10.2.3.1 History 381
        10.2.3.2 Physical Examination 382
    10.2.4 Soft Tissue Injuries 384
        10.2.4.1 Ligament Strain 384
        10.2.4.2 Muscle Strain 385
        10.2.4.3 Acceleration Injuries (Whiplash) 386
        10.2.4.4 Disc Disruption and Herniation 391
    10.2.5 Fractures and Dislocations 393
        10.2.5.1 Atlanto-Axial Fractures 393
        10.2.5.2 Flexion Instabilities 395

             10.2.5.3   Rotational Instabilities. 396
             10.2.5.4   Extension Instabilities 397
             10.2.5.5   Clay Shoveler's Fracture. 397
             10.2.5.6   Gunshot Injuries. 397
             10.2.5.7   Seat Belts and Airbags 398
             10.2.5.8   Treatment of Fractures/Dislocations 398
                        10.2.5.8.1 Brace Treatment 398
                        10.2.5.8.2 Halo Vest Treatment 398
                        10.2.5.8.3 Surgical Treatment 399
      10.2.6 Neurologic Injuries. 400
             10.2.6.1   Assessment 400
             10.2.6.2   Classification 401
                        10.2.6.2.1 Root Injuries 401
                        10.2.6.2.2 Incomplete Cord Lesions 401
                        10.2.6.2.3 Complete Cord Lesions 402
             10.2.6.3   Treatment and Rehabilitation 402
                        10.2.6.3.1 Initial Treatment 402
                        10.2.6.3.2 Definitive Treatment. 403
                        10.2.6.3.3 Rehabilitation and Long-Term
                                   Management. 403
             10.2.6.4   Complications. 410
                        10.2.6.4.1 Decubitus Ulcers (Pressure
                                   Sores) 410
                        10.2.6.4.2 Pulmonary 411
                        10.2.6.4.3 Contractures. 411
                        10.2.6.4.4 Infection of the Urinary Tract 411
                        10.2.6.4.5 Bowel Obstruction 411
                        10.2.6.4.6 Deep Vein Thrombosis 411
                        10.2.6.4.7 Automomic Dysreflexia 412
                        10.2.6.4.8 Heterotopic Ossification. 412
             10.2.6.5   Life Expectancy 412
10.3 The Thoracolumbar Spine 413
      10.3.1 Anatomy 413
             10.3.1.1   Osseous Anatomy. 413
             10.3.1.2   Intervertebral Discs 414
             10.3.1.3   Ligaments of the Thoracolumbar Spine 415
             10.3.1.4   Muscles of the Thoracolumbar Spine 416
             10.3.1.5   Neuroanatomy of the Thoracolumbar Spine . . . 417
             10.3.1.6   Location of Pain Fibers in the Spine 417
      10.3.2 Biomechanics and Pathophysiology of
             Thoracolumbar Injuries 419
             10.3.2.1   The Three-Column Concept 419
             10.3.2.2   Mechanism of Injury and Classification 420

10.3.3	Evaluation of the Patient....................................	420
	10.3.3.1	History	420
	10.3.3.2	Physical Examination	421
		10.3.3.2.1 Nonorganic Physical Signs.......	425
	10.3.3.3	Investigations.................................	426
	10.3.3.4	Missed Spine Fractures	427
10.3.4	Fractures and Dislocations of the Thoracolumbar Spine..		427
	10.3.4.1	Classification.................................	427
		10.3.4.1.1 Compression Fractures	427
		10.3.4.1.2 Burst Fractures...................	427
		10.3.4.1.3 Flexion-distraction Injuries.......	428
		10.3.4.1.4 Fracture-dislocation	428
	10.3.4.2	Treatment......................................	428
		10.3.4.2.1 Initial............................	428
		10.3.4.2.2 Pharmacologic Treatment	429
		10.3.4.2.3 Nonoperative Treatment	429
		10.3.4.2.4 Operative Treatment.............	429
	10.3.4.3	Outcome.......................................	431
10.3.5	Soft Tissue Injuries		434
	10.3.5.1	Disc Disruption and Herniation..............	434
10.3.6	Spondylolysis and Spondylolisthesis..................		439

Chapter 11 Injuries to the Extremities and Pelvis

11.1 General Principles...			469
11.1.1	Description of the Fracture........................		469
	11.1.1.1	Location	469
	11.1.1.2	Displacement............................	470
	11.1.1.3	Pattern	470
	11.1.1.4	Angulation...............................	471
	11.1.1.5	Closed versus Open	471
11.1.2	Principles of Immobilization		471
	11.1.2.1	Casts.....................................	472
	11.1.2.2	Braces...................................	473
	11.1.2.3	Traction	473
	11.1.2.4	Bedrest..................................	474
	11.1.2.5	Surgical Fixation........................	474
11.2 Injuries to the Pelvis and Lower Extremities.................			474
11.2.1	Pelvic Injuries		474
	11.2.1.1	Anatomy.................................	474
	11.2.1.2	Biomechanics of Pelvic Ring Injuries	476
	11.2.1.3	Classification............................	477
	11.2.1.4	Treatment................................	477

                11.2.1.4.1 Stable Pelvic Injuries 477
                11.2.1.4.2 Open Book Injuries.............. 478
                11.2.1.4.3 Lateral Compression Injuries...... 478
                11.2.1.4.4 Vertical Shear Fractures 478
                11.2.1.4.5 Open (Compound) Pelvic
                           Fractures 478
                11.2.1.4.6 Treatment of Hemorrhage
                           Associated with Pelvic Injuries ... 479
        11.2.1.5 Prognosis and Outcome.................... 479
    11.2.2 Fractures of the Acetabulum 481
        11.2.2.1 Anatomy................................. 481
        11.2.2.2 Mechanism of Injury 481
        11.2.2.3 Classification 481
        11.2.2.4 Diagnosis 482
        11.2.2.5 Treatment 482
        11.2.2.6 Prognosis............................... 483
                11.2.2.6.1 Return to Work 484
    11.2.3 Fractures and Dislocations of the Hip 484
        11.2.3.1 Introduction 484
        11.2.3.2 Anatomy................................ 485
        11.2.3.3 Dislocations of the Hip 486
                11.2.3.3.1 Anterior Dislocations of the Hip... 487
                11.2.3.3.2 Posterior Dislocations of the
                           Hip 488
        11.2.3.4 Fractures of the Femoral Neck............. 491
                11.2.3.4.1 Outcome of Femoral Neck
                           Fractures...................... 493
        11.2.3.5 Intertrochanteric Fractures of the Hip 495
                11.2.3.5.1 Outcome...................... 495
        11.2.3.6 Subtrochanteric Fractures of the Hip......... 496
    11.2.4 Fractures of the Femoral Shaft 497
        11.2.4.1 Classification 497
        11.2.4.2 Diagnosis 498
        11.2.4.3 Treatment 498
        11.2.4.4 Prognosis............................... 501
                11.2.4.4.1 Union Rate and Delayed Union ... 501
                11.2.4.4.2 Nonunion 501
                11.2.4.4.3 Deformities 501
                11.2.4.4.4 Knee Range of Motion.......... 502
                11.2.4.4.5 Return to Work 502
    11.2.5 Injuries about the Knee 502
        11.2.5.1 Fractures of the Distal Femur.............. 502
                11.2.5.1.1 Principles of Treatment 503

	11.2.5.2 Fractures of the Proximal Tibia.............	504
	11.2.5.2.1 Principles of Treatment..........	505
	11.2.5.3 Ligament Injuries of the Knee..............	507
	11.2.5.3.1 Collateral Ligaments............	507
	11.2.5.3.2 Cruciate Ligaments.............	508
	11.2.5.4 Knee Dislocations.......................	511
	11.2.5.5 Meniscal Injuries........................	512
11.2.6	Fractures of the Tibia.............................	513
11.2.7	Fractures and Injuries of the Ankle Joint.............	517
	11.2.7.1 Anatomy.................................	517
	11.2.7.2 Mechanisms of Injury.....................	518
	11.2.7.3 Classification of Ankle Fractures..........	518
	11.2.7.4 Treatment of Ankle Fractures..............	519
	11.2.7.5 Complications of Ankle Fractures...........	519
	11.2.7.6 Vertical Compression Fractures.............	521
	11.2.7.7 Ligamentous Injuries to the Ankle..........	522
	11.2.7.7.1 Injuries to the Syndesmotic Ligaments.....................	523
11.2.8	Injuries to the Foot..............................	524
	11.2.8.1 Introduction.............................	524
	11.2.8.2 Anatomy.................................	524
	11.2.8.2.1 Osteology.....................	524
	11.2.8.2.2 The Tarsus.....................	524
	11.2.8.2.3 The Metatarsus.................	526
	11.2.8.2.4 The Phalanges..................	526
	11.2.8.2.5 Sesamoid and Accessory Bones...	527
	11.2.8.3 Joint, Ligaments and Aponeurosis of the Foot.....................................	527
	11.2.8.3.1 Ankle Joint....................	527
	11.2.8.3.2 The Subtalar Joint.............	527
	11.2.8.3.3 Talonavicular Joint............	527
	11.2.8.3.4 The Calcaneocuboid Joint........	528
	11.2.8.3.5 The Cuneo-Navicular Joint.......	528
	11.2.8.3.6 The Tarsometatarsal Joints (Joint of Lisfranc)..................	528
	11.2.8.3.7 The Metatarsophalangeal Joints...	528
	11.2.8.3.8 The Interphalangeal Joints.......	528
	11.2.8.3.9 The Plantar Aponeurosis (Plantar Fascia)................	528
	11.2.8.4 Muscles of the Foot......................	529
	11.2.8.4.1 Extrinsic Muscles...............	529
	11.2.8.4.2 Intrinsic Muscles..............	529
	11.2.8.5 The Nerves of the Ankle and Foot..........	529

  11.2.8.6   Vascular System.......................... 530
       11.2.8.6.1 Arteries...................... 530
       11.2.8.6.2 Veins......................... 530
  11.2.8.7   Biomechanics............................ 531
  11.2.8.8   Evaluation of Foot Injuries................ 532
  11.2.8.9   Fractures of the Talus 532
       11.2.8.9.1 Blood Supply of the Talus........ 533
       11.2.8.9.2 Talar Head Fractures............. 533
       11.2.8.9.3 Talar Neck Fractures............. 533
       11.2.8.9.4 Prognosis and Complications of
              Talar Neck Fractures............. 535
       11.2.8.9.5 Fractures of the Body of the
              Talus.......................... 536
       11.2.8.9.6 Other Less Common Talar
              Fractures....................... 537
  11.2.8.10 Dislocations, Subluxations about the Talus.... 537
  11.2.8.11 Fractures of the Calcaneus 538
       11.2.8.11.1 Assessment..................... 541
       11.2.8.11.2 Special Tests 541
       11.2.8.11.3 Treatment..................... 542
       11.2.8.11.4 Prognosis 543
  11.2.8.12 Midtarsal Fractures 544
       11.2.8.12.1 Navicular Fractures.............. 544
       11.2.8.12.2 Cuboid Fractures................ 545
       11.2.8.12.3 Cuneiform Fractures............. 545
  11.2.8.13 Injuries to the Tarsometatarsal (Lisfranc's)
        Joints.................................. 545
       11.2.8.13.1 Anatomy...................... 545
       11.2.8.13.2 Mechanisms of Injury and
             Classification.................. 545
       11.2.8.13.3 Clincial Presentations........... 546
       11.2.8.13.4 Radiographic Findings 546
       11.2.8.13.5 Treatment..................... 547
       11.2.8.13.6 Prognosis 547
  11.2.8.14 Metatarsal Fractures....................... 548
  11.2.8.15 Dislocations of Metatarsophalangeal Joints ... 549
  11.2.8.16 Fractures and Dislocations of the Toes 550
       11.2.8.16.1 Fractures of the Great Toe
             (Hallux) 550
       11.2.8.16.2 Fractures of the Lesser Toes 550
       11.2.8.16.3 Dislocations of the Lesser Toe
             Joints 550
11.3 Injuries to the Upper Extremities........................... 550

- 11.3.1 Injuries to the Shoulder.......................... 550
  - 11.3.1.1 Introduction............................ 550
  - 11.3.1.2 Subluxations and Dislocations of the Glenohumeral Joint....................... 552
    - 11.3.1.2.1 Pathomechanics 553
    - 11.3.1.2.2 Diagnosis..................... 553
    - 11.3.1.2.3 Treatment 553
  - 11.3.1.3 Injuries to the Acromioclavicular Joint 555
    - 11.3.1.3.1 Anatomy 555
    - 11.3.1.3.2 Mechanisms of Injury 555
    - 11.3.1.3.3 Injury Types and their Management 555
    - 11.3.1.3.4 Complications................. 556
  - 11.3.1.4 Injuries to the Sternoclavicular Joint 557
    - 11.3.1.4.1 Anatomy 557
    - 11.3.1.4.2 Mechanisms of Injury, Diagnosis... 557
    - 11.3.1.4.3 Treatment 558
  - 11.3.1.5 Fractures of the Clavicle 558
    - 11.3.1.5.1 Anatomy 558
    - 11.3.1.5.2 Diagnosis and Classifications..... 558
    - 11.3.1.5.3 Treatment 558
    - 11.3.1.5.4 Complications................. 560
    - 11.3.1.5.5 Neurovascular Problems 560
  - 11.3.1.6 Fractures of the Scapula................... 561
    - 11.3.1.6.1 Incidence..................... 561
    - 11.3.1.6.2 Diagnosis..................... 561
    - 11.3.1.6.3 Treatment 561
  - 11.3.1.7 Fractures of the Proximal Humerus 562
    - 11.3.1.7.1 Introduction 562
    - 11.3.1.7.2 Classification 563
    - 11.3.1.7.3 Diagnosis..................... 563
    - 11.3.1.7.4 Treatment 563
    - 11.3.1.7.5 Prognosis..................... 565
    - 11.3.1.7.6 Complications................. 565
  - 11.3.1.8 Fractures of the Humeral Shaft............. 566
    - 11.3.1.8.1 Anatomy 566
    - 11.3.1.8.2 Diagnosis..................... 567
    - 11.3.1.8.3 Treatment 567
    - 11.3.1.8.4 Complications................. 568
  - 11.3.1.9 Rotator Cuff Tears........................ 569
    - 11.3.1.9.1 Introduction 569
    - 11.3.1.9.2 Pathomechanics 569
    - 11.3.1.9.3 Investigations 570

11.3.1.9.4 Treatment 570
11.3.1.9.5 Results of Surgical Treatment 571
11.3.2 Injuries to the Elbow and Forearm.................. 572
11.3.2.1 Anatomy and Biomechanics............... 572
11.3.2.2 Fractures about the Elbow in Adults 573
11.3.2.3 Injuries to the Mid-Forearm 575
11.3.2.3.1 Anatomy...................... 575
11.3.2.3.2 Injuries to the Forearm........... 575
11.3.2.3.3 Assessment.................... 577
11.3.2.3.4 Treatment.................... 577
11.3.3 Injuries to the Distal Forearm and Wrist.............. 581
11.3.3.1 Anatomy and Biomechanics............... 581
11.3.3.2 Fractures of the Distal Radius 584
11.3.3.2.1 Treatment of Distal Radial
Fractures 586
11.3.3.3 Fractures of the Scaphoid 587
11.3.4 The Hand... 590
11.3.4.1 Anatomy 590
11.3.4.2 Flexor Tendon Injuries 592
11.3.4.3 Extensor Tendon Injuries 593
11.3.4.4 Fractures of the Hand 593
11.4 Special Injuries and Complications 595
11.4.1 The Multiply Injured Patient........................ 595
11.4.2 The Open Fracture and the Mangled Extremity 598
11.4.2.1 Open Fractures.......................... 598
11.4.2.2 Mangled Extremities 602
11.4.2.3 Type III B Open Tibia Fractures 604
11.4.3 Complications of Injuries to the Musculoskeletal
System 607
11.4.3.1 Thromboembolism....................... 607
11.4.3.2 Pulmonary Embolism 608
11.4.3.3 Fat Embolism and Adult Respiratory
Distres Syndrome........................ 610
11.4.3.4 Leg Length Discrepancy and Fracture
Malunion............................... 612
11.4.3.4.1 Leg Length Discrepancy 612
11.4.3.4.2 Malunion 613
11.4.3.5 Nonunion (Pseudoarthrosis) 616
11.4.3.5.1 Classification................... 616
11.4.3.6 Infection 618
11.4.3.6.1 Osteomyelitis................... 618
11.4.3.6.2 Gas Gangrene (Clostridial
Myonecrosis) 621

              11.4.3.6.3 Necrotizing Fasciitis 622
        11.4.3.7 Compartment Syndrome................. 622
Tables 624
    Table 1: Injury Severity Score 624
    Table 2: Gustilo Classification........................... 625
    Table 3: Mangled Extremity Severity Score (MESS) 626
    Table 4: Cierny Clinical Staging System for Osteomyelitis..... 627
    Table 5: Treatment of Chronic Osteomyelitis of the Lower
             Extremity by Debridement and Microvascular
             Transplantation.................................. 628
Glossary 629
Figures.. 645

Chapter 12 Chronic Pain Disorders

12.1 Introduction 806
    12.1.1 The Problem...................................... 806
    12.1.2 Defining Chronic Pain............................. 807
    12.1.3 Clinical Classification Controversies................. 808
12.2 Specific Clinical Entities 809
    12.2.1 Whiplash Injuries................................. 809
        12.2.1.1 Mechanisms of Injury..................... 809
        12.2.1.2 Clinical Picture 810
    12.2.2 Nonspecificity of Chronic Soft Tissue Pain Disorders .. 811
    12.2.3 Myofascial Pain 811
    12.2.4 Fibromyalgia 812
        12.2.4.1 Clinical Criteria.......................... 812
        12.2.4.2 Questioning Clinical Criteria............... 813
    12.2.5 Relationship Between Fibromyalgia and Trauma 815
        12.2.5.1 The Argument Against 815
        12.2.5.2 The Argument For........................ 815
12.3 Recovery and Pathophysiology 817
    12.3.1 Recovery After Trauma............................ 817
    12.3.2 Evidence for an Organic Basis for Chronic Pain....... 817
        12.3.2.1 Evidence of a Central Neurological Origin
                 for Regional Pain 818
        12.3.2.2 Evidence of a Mechanical Origin for
                 Chronic Whiplash Injury Pain.............. 820
        12.3.2.3 Conclusions 820
    12.3.3 Are Psychological Factors Causative?................ 821
12.4 Disability Secondary to Chronic Pain Disorders 822
    12.4.1 Definitions: Impairment, Disability and Handicap 822
    12.4.2 The Rise in Chronic Pain Disability Claims........... 823

12.4.3 The Acute Medical Model and Chronic Pain
         Disorders 823
         12.4.3.1 The Search for Structural Abnormalities...... 824
12.4.4 Discordance Between Pain, Impairment, and
         Disability... 825
12.4.5 Assessment of Disability in Chronic Pain Disorders 826
12.4.6 Acceptance of Chronic Pain and Disability............ 829
12.4.7 Compensation and Secondary Gain in Disability....... 830
         12.4.7.1 Compensation and Chronic Pain 830
         12.4.7.2 Secondary Gain 831
         12.4.7.3 Secondary Losses......................... 832
12.4.8 Socioeconomic Factors and Disability................. 833
         12.4.8.1 Lower Socioeconomic Status and Risk of
                   Disability 833
12.4.9 The Work Environment 834
         12.4.9.1 Heavy Physical Work..................... 834
         12.4.9.2 Job Dissatisfaction....................... 835
12.4.10 The Shift to Managing Chronic Pain Disability Only .. 838
12.4.11 The Trend Towards Rejecting Chronic Pain
         Disability... 838
         12.4.11.1 The Report on Back Pain in the Workplace ... 838
         12.4.11.2 Quebec Task Force on Whiplash
                    Associated Disorders...................... 839
12.5 Future Conflict: Chronic Pain, Disability, and Society 839

Chapter 13 Reflex Sympathetic Dystrophy

13.1 Defining Reflex Sympathetic Dystrophy..................... 841
13.2 Role of the Sympathetic Nervous System in RSD 845
13.3 Concerns Regarding Definitions/Pathophysiology 847
13.4 The Role of Psychological Factors.......................... 847
13.5 Diagnosis... 849
       13.5.1 Clinical Diagnosis 849
       13.5.2 Nuclear Bone Scan............................ 849
       13.5.3 Radiological Studies........................... 850
       13.5.4 Sympathetic Blockade 850
13.6 Treatment... 850
       13.6.1 Physical Therapy 851
       13.6.2 Sympathetic Blockade 851
       13.6.3 Surgical Sympathectomy....................... 852
       13.6.4 Corticosteroids 852
       13.6.5 Calcitonin 853
       13.6.6 Hydroxyl Radical Scavengers 853
       13.6.7 Surgically Implantable Devices.................. 854

13.7 Prognosis 854
13.8 Summary.. 854

Chapter 14 Rehabilitation

14.1 Definition of Rehabilitation 855
    14.1.1 Impairment 856
    14.1.2 Disability 856
    14.1.3 Handicap... 856
    14.1.4 Possible Revisions of Classification Model 857
14.2 An Interdisciplinary Approach............................. 857
    14.2.1 Physiatrist... 858
    14.2.2 Physiotherapist..................................... 858
    14.2.3 Occupational Therapist 858
    14.2.4 Rehabilitation Nurse 859
    14.2.5 Social Worker...................................... 859
    14.2.6 Psychologist 859
    14.2.7 Speech-Language Pathologist...................... 860
    14.2.8 Nutritionist 860
    14.2.9 Leisure/Recreational Therapist..................... 860
    14.2.10 Vocational Counsellor............................ 861
    14.2.11 Child Life Worker/Specialist 861
    14.2.12 Teacher 861
14.3 Treatment Modalities in Rehabilitation..................... 862
    14.3.1 Therapeutic Heat and Cold......................... 862
    14.3.2 Acupuncture....................................... 863
    14.3.3 Massage 863
    14.3.4 Electrical Stimulation 864
    14.3.5 Other Modalities 864

Table of Cases

[All references are to section numbers.]

Axelrod, Re (1994), 16 O.R. (3d) 649, 24 C.B.R. (3d) 149,
   111 D.L.R. (4th) 540 (Ont. Gen. Div. [Commercial List]),
   affirmed (1994), 20 O.R. (3d) 133, 29 C.B.R. (3d) 74,
   17 B.L.R. (2d) 161 (Ont. C.A.) 3.1
Aynsley v. Toronto General Hospital, [1968] 1 O.R. 425, 66 D.L.R.
   (2d) 575 (Ont. H.C.), varied [1969] 2 O.R. 829, 7 D.L.R.
   (3d) 193 (Ont. C.A.), affirmed [1972] S.C.R. 435, 25 D.L.R.
   (3d) 241 (S.C.C.) 4.6.1
Badger v. Dowsett (1994), 21 Alta. L.R. (3d) 323 (Alta. Q.B.) 6.5.2
Baynton v. Rayner, [1995] O.J. No. 1617 .... 6.9
Bazzi v. Allstate Insurance Co. of Canada (1994), 4 M.V.R.
   (3d) 310, 28 C.P.C. (3d) 166 (Ont. Gen. Div.) 4.3.2
Bell Canada v. Olympia & York Developments Ltd. (1989),
   33 C.L.R. 258, 68 O.R. (2d) 103, 36 C.P.C. (2d) 193 (Ont. H.C.) 6.15.2
Bisaillon v. Keable, [1983] 2 S.C.R. 60, 4 Admin. L.R. 205,
   37 C.R. (3d) 289 (S.C.C.) 4.7.5
Black v. Royal Bank (1988), 33 C.P.C. (2d) 93 (Ont. Dist. Ct.) 4.6.1; 4.6.2
Briand v. Sutton (1986), (sub nom. Briand v. Sutton (No. 2))
   15 C.P.C. (2d) 36, 57 O.R. (2d) 629 (Ont. H.C.) 4.6.2; 6.16.2; 6.16.3
Brown & Williamson Tobacco Corp. v. Jacobson, 827 F.2d
   1119, 1135 (7th Cir. 1987) 4.7.4
Browne v. Dunn (1893), 6 R. 67 (U.K. H.L.) 7.14
Buckley v. Rice-Thomas (1554), 1 Plowd. 118 .... 6.2
Buttrum v. Udell, 57 O.L.R. 97, [1925] 3 D.L.R. 45 (Ont. C.A.) 6.20
C. (M.) v. M. (F.) (1990), 46 C.P.C. (2d) 254 (Ont. Gen. Div.) 6.15.4
Calvaruso v. Nantais (1992), 7 C.P.C. (3d) 254 (Ont. Gen. Div.) 6.15.2
Canada (Solicitor General) v. Ontario (Royal Commission of
   Inquiry into Confidentiality of Health Records) (1978), 21 O.R.
   (2d) 402, 6 C.P.C. 289 (Ont. Div. Ct.), varied (1979), (sub nom.
   Inquiry into Confidentiality of Health Records in Ontario, Re)
   24 O.R. (2d) 545, 13 C.P.C. 239, 98 D.L.R. (3d) 704 (Ont. C.A.),
   reversed 23 C.R. (3d) 338, 23 C.P.C. 99, 62 C.C.C. (2d) 193,
   [1981] 2 S.C.R. 494 (S.C.C.) 4.7.5
Can-Dive Services Ltd. v. Pacific Coast Energy Corp. (1994),
   31 C.P.C. (3d) 98, 1 B.C.L.R. (3d) 365 (B.C. S.C.) 6.15.2

Carew v. Loblaw's Ltd. (1977), 18 O.R. (2d) 660, 83 D.L.R. (3d)
603 (Ont. H.C.) 4.6.2; 6.16.3
Caron v. Chodan Estate (1989), 43 C.P.C. (2d) 255 (Ont. H.C.).......... 4.2.2
Catanzaro v. Doxtator (1988), 28 C.P.C. (2d) 42, 65 O.R. (2d)
199 (Ont. H.C.) 4.3.2
Children's Aid Society of Hamilton-Wentworth v. D. (S.) (1991),
35 R.F.L. (3d) 136, 83 D.L.R. (4th) 166 (Ont. U.F.C.)................. 6.4
Cook v. Ip (1985), 52 O.R. (2d) 289, 5 C.P.C. (2d) 81, 22 D.L.R.
(4th) 1 (Ont. C.A.), leave to appeal refused (1986), 55 O.R.
(2d) 288 (note) (S.C.C.) 4.3.2; 4.4
Coriale (Litigation Guardian of) v. Sisters of St. Joseph of Sault
Ste. Marie (1998), 41 O.R. (3d) 347 (Ont. Gen. Div.) 4.7.4
Couto v. Toronto Transit Commission (1987), 16 C.P.C. (2d)
241, 59 O.R. (2d) 406 (Ont. H.C.)..................................... 4.4
Daubert v. Merrill-Dow Pharmaceuticals Inc., 113 S.Ct. 2786 (1993) 6.8
Davie v. Edinburgh Magistrates, [1953] S.C. 34 (Scotland Ct. Sess.) 6.3
Dawes v. Jajcaj (1995), 15 B.C.L.R. (3d) 240, [1996]
3 W.W.R. 525 (B.C. S.C.) 4.7.4
Delgamuukw v. British Columbia (1988), 32 B.C.L.R. (2d) 156
(B.C. S.C.) 6.15.2
Draper v. Jacklyn (1969), [1970] S.C.R. 92 (S.C.C.) 7.9.4
Duguay v. Devoe (1988), 63 O.R. (2d) 499 (Ont. H.C.).................. 4.3.2
Ericsson Communications Inc. v. Novatel Communications Ltd.
(1996), 45 C.P.C. (3d) 94 (Ont. Gen. Div.).......................... 6.10
Etienne v. McKellar General Hospital (1994), 38 C.P.C. (3d)
342 (Ont. Gen. Div.) 6.16.4
Featherstone v. Grunsven, [1972] 1 O.R. 490 (Ont. C.A.)................. 6.10
Fedorczenko v. Jamieson (1986), 56 O.R. (2d) 252, 14 C.P.C.
(2d) 299 (Ont. H.C.) 4.3.2
Ferguson Estate v. Burton (1987), 50 M.V.R. 197 (Ont. H.C.) 5.3.4
Ferguson v. National Life Assurance Co. of Canada, 36 C.C.L.I.
(2d) 95, [1996] I.L.R. 1-3316 (Ont. Gen. Div.), affirmed
(1997), 102 O.A.C. 239 (Ont. C.A.) 6.11
Ferraro v. Lee (1974), 2 O.R. (2d) 417, 43 D.L.R. (3d)
161 (Ont. C.A.) 4.6.2; 6.16.1; 6.16.2
Fiege v. Cornwall General Hospital (1980), 30 O.R. (2d) 691,
117 D.L.R. (3d) 152, 4 L. Med. Q. 124 (Ont. H.C.).................. 4.7.1
Fillier v. Whittom (1995), 161 N.B.R. (2d) 241 (N.B. Q.B.),
affirmed (1995), 171 N.B.R. (2d) 92 (N.B. C.A.) 6.4
Flavelle v. Toronto Transit Commission (1985), 49 C.P.C.
209 (Ont. Dist. Ct.) 4.5
Fraser River Pile & Dredge Ltd. v. Empire Tug Boats Ltd.
(1995), 37 C.P.C. (3d) 119, 95 F.T.R. 43 (Fed. T.D.) 6.5.2
Frenette v. Metropolitan Life Insurance Co., 4 C.C.L.I. (2d) 1,
89 D.L.R. (4th) 653, 134 N.R. 169, [1992] I.L.R. 1-2823,
46 Q.A.C. 161, [1992] 1 S.C.R. 647 (S.C.C.) 3.3; 4.4
Frye v. United States (1923), 293 F. 1013 (U.S. D.C. Ct. App.) 6.8

Furlano v. Calarco (1987), 20 C.P.C. (2d) 279, 60 O.R. (2d)
  451 (Ont. H.C.) 4.3.2
G. (D.M.) v. G. (S.D.) (1990), 72 O.R. (2d) 774, 44 C.P.C.
  (2d) 52 (Ont. Master) 4.4
Gallo v. Gillham (1987), 15 C.P.C. (2d) 125, 58 O.R. (2d)
  115 (Ont. Master), affirmed 23 C.P.C. (2d) 109, 67 O.R.
  (2d) 734 (Ont. H.C.) 4.3.2
Gerula v. Flores (1995), 126 D.L.R. (4th) 506, 83 O.A.C.
  128 (Ont. C.A.) 4.7.4
Giroux v. Falusi (1992), 61 O.A.C. 317 (Ont. Div. Ct.) 4.4
Glowinsky v. Stephens & Rankin Inc. (1989), 38 C.P.C. (2d)
  102 (Ont. Master) 4.3.1
Goodman v. Rossi (1995), 12 C.C.E.L. (2d) 105, 37 C.P.C.
  (3d) 181, 24 O.R. (3d) 359 (Ont. C.A.) 4.7.3
Gorin v. Ho (1983), 38 C.P.C. 72 (Ont. Master) 4.3.2
Grant v. Dube (1992), 73 B.C.L.R. (2d) 288, [1993] 2 W.W.R. 41,
  12 C.P.C. (3d) 22 (B.C. S.C.) 6.8
Green v. Lawrence, [1996] 6 W.W.R. 378, 48 C.P.C. (3d)
  211 (Man. Q.B.) 6.5.1; 6.8
Greenwood Shopping Plaza Ltd. v. Neil J. Buchanan Ltd.
  (No. 1) (1979), 31 N.S.R. (2d) 135 (N.S. C.A.), reversed (sub nom. Green-
  wood Shopping Plaza Ltd. v. Beattie) [1980] 2 S.C.R.
  228, 10 B.L.R. 234 (S.C.C.) 6.15.2
Griffis v. Toronto Transit Commission (1985), 15 C.P.C.
  (2d) 119 (Ont. H.C.) 4.3.2
Halliday v. Wigmore (July 4, 1996), Doc. Vancouver
  B934746 (B.C. S.C.) 6.6
Halls v. Mitchell, [1928] S.C.R. 125, [1928] 2 D.L.R. 97 (S.C.C.) ... 3.1
Halteh v. McCoy (1974), 6 O.R. (2d) 512 (H.C.) 4.3.2
Hamilton v. Brusnyk (1960), 34 W.W.R. 172 (Alta. S.C.) 6.20
Harris v. Windsor Airline Limousine Services Ltd. (1985),
  6 C.P.C. (2d) 156 (Ont. H.C.) 6.16.3
Heppner v. Schmand (March 21, 1996), Doc. Campbell River
  S1026, S1530 (B.C. S.C.), additional reasons at (1996),
  24 B.C.L.R. (3d) 309, 2 C.P.C. (4th) 284 (B.C. S.C.),
  leave to appeal refused (1997), 29 B.C.L.R. (3d) 128
  (B.C. C.A. [In Chambers]), affirmed (November 19, 1998),
  Doc. Victoria VI02819 (B.C. C.A.) 6.9
Heywood v. Nash (1986), 18 C.P.C. (2d) 154 (Ont. H.C.),
  additional reasons at (1986), 18 C.P.C. (2d) 154 at 156
  (Ont. H.C.) 4.3.2
Highland Fisheries Ltd. v. Lynk Electric Ltd. (1989), 63 D.L.R.
  (4th) 493 (N.S. T.D.) 6.15.2
Hinton v. Engineering Products of Canada Ltd. (1986),
  16 C.P.C. (2d) 283 (Ont. Dist. Ct.) 4.7.4
Iler v. Beaudet, [1971] 3 O.R. 644 .... 4.6.2

Jonathan v. Gore Mutual Insurance Co. (1985), 6 C.P.C.
(2d) 300 (Ont. Dist. Ct.) 4.4
Josephine V. Wilson Family Trust v. Swartz (1993), 16 O.R.
(3d) 268, 23 C.B.R. (3d) 88 (Ont. Gen. Div.) 3.1
Kaptsis v. Macias (1990), 74 O.R. (2d) 189, 44 C.P.C. (2d)
285 (Ont. H.C.) 4.3.2
Kapulica v. Dumancic, [1968] 2 O.R. 438 (Ont. C.A.)...... 4.6.2; 6.16.2; 6.16.3
Karkanas v. Thomas (1986), 19 C.P.C. (2d) 303 (Ont. Dist. Ct.) 4.3.2
Kelliher (Village) v. Smith, [1931] S.C.R. 672 (S.C.C.)................... 6.2
Kelly v. Kelly (1990), 42 C.P.C. (2d) 181 (Ont. U.F.C.) 6.15.2
Khan v. College of Physicians & Surgeons (Ontario) (1992),
9 O.R. (3d) 641, 11 Admin. L.R. (2d) 147 (Ont. C.A.) 6.7
Kozak v. Funk (1995), [1996] 1 W.W.R. 107, 28 C.C.L.T.
(2d) 81 (Sask. Q.B.), appealed on different grounds to
Court of Appeal at (1997), [1998] 5 W.W.R. 232, 158 Sask.
R. 232, 153 W.A.C. (Sask. C.A.)............................... 6.5.1; 6.9
Levesque v. Comeau, [1970] S.C.R. 1010 (S.C.C.)..................... 6.5.2
Lonergan v. Morrissette (1993), 23 C.P.C. (3d) 186, 109 D.L.R.
(4th) 758 (Ont. Gen. Div.) 4.3.2
M. (A.) v. Ryan (1994), 98 B.C.L.R. (2d) 1, 32 C.P.C. (3d) 66,
[1995] 1 W.W.R. 677 (B.C. C.A.), leave to appeal allowed
(1995), 127 D.L.R. (4th) vii (note) (S.C.C.), affirmed
143 D.L.R. (4th) 1, 4 C.R. (5th) 220, 29 B.C.L.R. (3d)
133, [1997] 4 W.W.R. 1, 34 C.C.L.T. (2d) 1, [1997]
1 S.C.R. 157, 8 C.P.C. (4th) 1 (S.C.C.) 4.4
MacDonald Electric Ltd. v. Cochrane, [1955] O.W.N. 255 (Ont. H.C.)...... 6.10
Mackintosh v. Wright (1991), 9 O.R. (3d) 285 (Ont. Gen. Div.)............ 6.8
Majcenic v. Natale, [1968] 1 O.R. 189 (Ont. C.A.)...................... 7.9.4
Manufacturers Life Insurance Co. v. Dofasco Inc. (1989),
38 C.P.C. (2d) 47 (Ont. H.C.), additional reasons at (1989),
38 C.P.C. (2d) 47 at 53 (Ont. H.C.) 4.3.1
Marchand (Litigation Guardian of) v. Public General Hospital
Society of Chatham (October 3, 1996), Doc. 91-GD-16866
(Ont. Gen. Div.) 6.17
Marks v. Beyfus (1890), 25 Q.B.D. 494 (Eng. Q.B.) 4.7.5
Mather v. Turnbull (1991), 47 C.P.C. (2d) 180 (Ont. Gen. Div.)............ 4.4
Mazur v. Moody (1987), 14 B.C.L.R. (2d) 240 (B.C. S.C.).............. 6.17
McEachrane v. Children's Aid Society of Essex (County)
(1986), 10 C.P.C. (2d) 265 (Ont. H.C.) 6.15.1
McInerney v. MacDonald (1990), 66 D.L.R. (4th) 736
(N.B. C.A.), affirmed 7 C.P.C. (3d) 269, 12 C.C.L.T.
(2d) 225, [1992] 2 S.C.R. 138 (S.C.C.) 3.1; 3.2; 6.17
Micheli v. Sheppard (1994), 30 C.P.C. (3d) 297 (Ont. Gen. Div.).......... 4.3.2
Muir v. Alberta (1995), 32 Alta. L.R. (3d) 95, 41 C.P.C.
(3d) 386 (Alta. Q.B.).. 6.5.1; 6.5.2
Murdoch v. Low (1995), 168 A.R. 75 (Alta. Q.B.)...................... 6.10

National Justice Compania Naviera S.A. v. Prudential
  Assurance Company Ltd. (Ikarian Reefer), [1993] 2 Lloyd's
  Rep. 68, reversed [1995] 1 Lloyd's Rep. 455 (C.A.), leave
  to appeal to the House of Lords refused 6.9
Noonan v. Commercial Union Assurance Co. of Canada
  (1989), 36 C.P.C. (2d) 239 (Ont. Dist. Ct.), reversed in
  part (1989), 42 C.P.C. (2d) 1 (Ont. H.C.) 4.4
Orr v. Warren (1986), 18 C.P.C. (2d) 190, 59 O.R. (2d)
  286 (Ont. H.C.) 4.4
P. (L.M.) v. F. (D.) (1994), 22 C.C.L.T. (2d) 312, 34 C.P.C.
  (3d) 172 (Ont. Gen. Div.) 4.4
Pavao v. Pinarreta (1995), 40 C.P.C. (3d) 84 (Ont. Div. Ct.) 6.15.4
Perricone v. Baldassarra (1994), 7 M.V.R. (3d) 91 (Ont. Gen. Div.) 6.9; 6.17
Peter Kiewit Sons Co. of Canada v. British Columbia Hydro
  & Power Authority (1982), 36 B.C.L.R. 58, 26 C.P.C.
  221n, 134 D.L.R. (3d) 154 (B.C. S.C.) 4.3.2
Phillips v. Ford Motor Co. of Canada, [1971] 2 O.R. 637 (Ont. C.A.) 6.10
Piché v. Lecours Lumber Co. (1993), 13 O.R. (3d) 193,
  19 C.P.C. (3d) 200 (Ont. Gen. Div.) 6.15.3
Priore v. Hughes (1994), 28 C.P.C. (3d) 314 (Ont. Gen. Div.) 4.6.1
R. v. Abbey (1982), [1982] 2 S.C.R. 24, 39 B.C.L.R. 201,
  29 C.R. (3d) 193, [1983] 1 W.W.R. 251 (S.C.C.) 6.3; 6.5.2; 6.6
R. v. B. (R.H.), 29 C.R. (4th) 113, [1994] 1 S.C.R. 656 (S.C.C.) 6.7; 6.8
R. v. Béland, [1987] 2 S.C.R. 398, 60 C.R. (3d) 1 (S.C.C.) 6.5.4; 6.8
R. v. Beliveau (1986), 30 C.C.C. (3d) 193 (B.C. C.A.) 6.8
R. v. Bleta, [1964] S.C.R. 561, 44 C.R. 193 (S.C.C.) 7.9.3
R. v. C. (G.) (1996), 110 C.C.C. (3d) 233 (Nfld. C.A.) 6.8
R. v. Craig (1982), 1 C.C.C. (3d) 416 (B.C. C.A.) 7.9.6
R. v. Fisher, [1961] O.W.N. 94, 34 C.R. 320 (Ont. C.A.),
  affirmed [1961] S.C.R. 535, 35 C.R. 107 (S.C.C.) 6.3
R. v. French (1977), 37 C.C.C. (2d) 201 (Ont. C.A.),
  affirmed [1980] 1 S.C.R. 158 (S.C.C.) 6.7
R. v. Graat (1980), 30 O.R. (2d) 247, 7 M.V.R. 163,
  17 C.R. (3d) 55 (Ont. C.A.), affirmed [1982] 2 S.C.R. 819,
  18 M.V.R. 287, 31 C.R. (3d) 289 (S.C.C.) 6.7
R. v. Higgins (1979), 28 N.B.R. (2d) 20 (N.B. C.A.),
  leave to appeal refused (1979), 29 N.B.R. (2d) 450n (S.C.C.) 6.20
R. v. Howard, 69 C.R. (3d) 193, [1989] 1 S.C.R. 1337 (S.C.C.) 6.9; 7.13
R. v. J. (F.E.) (1990), 53 C.C.C. (3d) 64, 74 C.R. (3d) 269
  (Ont. C.A.) 6.8
R. v. Johnston (1992), 69 C.C.C. (3d) 395, 12 C.R. (4th) 99
  (Ont. Gen. Div.) 6.8
R. v. Khan, 79 C.R. (3d) 1, [1990] 2 S.C.R. 531, 59 C.C.C.
  (3d) 92 (S.C.C.) 6.16.4
R. v. Lavallee (1988), 65 C.R. (3d) 387 (Man. C.A.), reversed
  [1990] 4 W.W.R. 1, [1990] 1 S.C.R. 852, 76 C.R. (3d)
  329 (S.C.C.) 6.6; 6.8; 6.17

R. v. Leipert, 4 C.R. (5th) 259, [1997] 3 W.W.R. 457, [1997]
  1 S.C.R. 281 (S.C.C.) 4.7.5
R. v. Marquard, 25 C.R. (4th) 1, [1993] 4 S.C.R. 223 (S.C.C.) .. 6.5.4; 7.7; 7.13
R. v. Millar (1989), 49 C.C.C. (3d) 193, 71 C.R. (3d) 78
  (Ont. C.A.) 6.5.4
R. v. Mohan, 29 C.R. (4th) 243, [1994] 2 S.C.R. 9, 18 O.R.
  (3d) 160 (note) (S.C.C.) 6.5; 6.7; 6.8
R. v. Morin, 66 C.R. (3d) 1, [1988] 2 S.C.R. 345 (S.C.C.) 6.5.4
R. v. Olscamp (1994), 35 C.R. (4th) 37 (Ont. Gen.
  Div.) 6.5.1; 7.5; 7.13; 6.8; 6.9; 7.13
R. v. R. (D.), [1996] 2 S.C.R. 291, 48 C.R. (4th)
  368 (S.C.C.) 6.7
R. v. R. (W.D.) (1994), 35 C.R. (4th) 343 (Ont. C.A.) 6.5.4
R. v. Swietlinski (1978), 22 O.R. (2d) 604, 5 C.R. (3d)
  324 (Ont. C.A.), affirmed 18 C.R. (3d) 231, [1980]
  2 S.C.R. 956 (S.C.C.) 7.9.3
R. v. Warren, [1995] 3 W.W.R. 371, 35 C.R. (4th) 347
  (N.W.T. S.C.) 6.5.1
Ravenis v. Detroit General Hospital, 234 N.W.2d 411
  (Mich. App. 1975) 4.7.4
Regina v. Lewes Justices, ex parte Secretary of State
  for Home Dept., [1973] A.C. 3884 .... 4.7.5
Reichmann v. Toronto Life Publishing Co. (1988),
  28 C.P.C. (2d) 11 (Ont. H.C.), leave to appeal refused
  (1988), 29 C.P.C. (2d) 66 (Ont. H.C.) 4.7.3
Rice v. Sockett (1912), 27 O.L.R. 410, 8 D.L.R. 84
  (Ont. C.A.) 6.4
Rizzi v. Runtes, [1993] O.J. No. 1333, DRS 13291
  (Ont. Gen. Div.) 4.3.2
Sacilotto v. Crossman (1990), 49 B.C.L.R. (2d) 375
  (B.C. S.C.) 6.3
Schultz v. Galvin (1988), 27 C.P.C. (2d) 253, 65 O.R.
  (2d) 13 (Ont. H.C.) 4.3.2
Scime v. Guardian Insurance Co. of Canada (1988), 30 C.P.C.
  (2d) 149 (Ont. Dist. Ct.) 6.16.4
Sebastian v. Neufeld (1995), 41 C.P.C. (3d) 354 (B.C. S.C.) 6.9
Sengbusch v. Priest (1987), 14 B.C.L.R. (2d) 26 (B.C. S.C.) 6.5.2; 6.9; 6.13
Sevidal v. Chopra (1987), 45 R.P.R. 79, 41 C.C.L.T. 179,
  64 O.R. (2d) 169 (Ont. H.C.) 6.15.4
Sharpe Estate v. Northwestern General Hospital (1990),
  74 D.L.R. (4th) 43, 1 C.P.C. (3d) 104 (Ont. Master),
  affirmed (1991), 76 D.L.R. (4th) 535, 2 O.R. (3d) 40,
  46 C.P.C. (2d) 267 (Ont. Gen. Div.) 4.3.2
Shipman v. Antoniadis (1975), 8 O.R. (2d) 449 (Ont. C.A.) 7.9.4
Simpson v. Garbowsky (1983), 21 M.V.R. 153, 143 D.L.R.
  (3d) 260 (Ont. C.A.) 4.6.2

Slavutych v. Baker (1975), [1976] 1 S.C.R. 254, [1975]
  4 W.W.R. 620, 38 C.R.N.S. 306, 55 D.L.R. (3d) 224,
  2 N.R. 587, 75 C.L.L.C. 14, 263 (S.C.C.) 4.1; 4.3.2; 4.4
Smith v. Stewart (1991), 37 M.V.R. (2d) 140 (Ont. Gen. Div.) 4.3.2
Spencer v. Soanes (1994), 92 B.C.L.R. (2d) 129, 113 D.L.R.
  (4th) 567 (B.C. S.C.) 6.3
Spillane (Litigation Guardian of) v. Wasserman (1992),
  13 C.C.L.T. (2d) 267, 42 M.V.R. (2d) 144 (Ont. Gen. Div.),
  additional reasons at (April 1, 1993), 11625/86, 11629/86,
  (Ont. Gen. Div.); varied (1998), 41 C.C.L.T. (2d) 292
  (Ont. C.A.), which found the physicians
  five per cent responsible 5.3.4
St. Louis (Litigation Guardian of) v. Feleki (1990),
  75 D.L.R. (4th) 758 (Ont. Gen. Div.), affirmed (1993),
  107 D.L.R. (4th) 767 (Ont. Div. Ct.) 4.6
Stribbell v. Bhalla (1988), 32 C.P.C. (2d) 272 (Ont. H.C.) 4.6.2; 4.6.3; 6.16.1
Surrey Credit Union v. Willson (1990), 45 B.C.L.R.
  (2d) 310 (B.C. S.C.) 6.7; 6.9
Tamssot v. Belgrano (1987), 16 C.P.C. (2d) 189, 59 O.R.
  (2d) 57 (Ont. Master) 4.4
Tarasoff v. Regents of the University of California (1976),
  17 Cal. 3d 358, CA 131 Cal. Rptr. 14, 551 P.2D
  334 (CA S.C.) 5.2
Tecoglas Inc. v. Domglas Inc. (1985), 14 C.L.R. 88
  (Ont. H.C.) 6.15.4
Tilly v. Crangle (1981), 31 O.R. (2d) 641, 120 D.L.R.
  (3d) 563 (Ont. C.A.) 4.4
Toms v. Foster (1994), 7 M.V.R. (3d) 34 (Ont. C.A.) 5.3.4
Triumbari v. Bloch (February 3, 1987), Doc. 201620/83
  (Ont. Dist. Ct.), affirmed (1987), 20 C.P.C. (2d) 277 (Ont. H.C.) 4.3.2
Trovato v. Smith (1987), 15 C.P.C. (2d) 121 (Ont. Dist. Ct.) 4.3.2
Ure v. Fagnan, [1958] S.C.R. 377 (S.C.C.) 6.20
Vancouver Community College v. Phillips Barratt (1988),
  29 C.L.R. 268, 26 B.C.L.R. (2d) 296 (B.C. S.C.) 6.17
Vancouver Community College v. Phillips, Barratt (1987),
  27 C.L.R. 11, 20 B.C.L.R. (2d) 289 (B.C. S.C.) 6.15.2
Vieczorek v. Piersma (1987), 58 O.R. (2d) 583, 16 C.P.C.
  (2d) 62 (Ont. C.A.) 6.5.2
W. (T.) v. W. (K.R.J.) (1994), 111 D.L.R. (4th) 703,
  26 C.P.C. (3d) 45 (Ont. Gen. Div.) 4.3.2
W. (Y.) v. W. (L.) (1994), 28 C.P.C. (3d) 60 (Ont. Gen. Div.) 4.3.2
Walker Estate v. York-Finch General Hospital (1996),
  5 C.P.C. (4th) 240 (Ont. Gen. Div.) 6.5.1; 6.5.4
Walters v. Walters (1990), 45 C.P.C. (2d) 215 (Ont. Gen. Div.) 6.15.2
Watts v. Krause (September 19, 1994), Doc. Victoria
  92/2817 (B.C. S.C.) 6.7

Wells (Litigation Guardian of) v. Paramsothy (1996),
    32 O.R. (3d) 452 (Ont. Div. Ct.), leave to appeal refused
    (1997), 32 O.R. (3d) 452n (Ont. H.C.) 3.1; 4.3.2
Welsh v. United States, 844 F.2d 1239 (6th Cir. 1988) 4.7.4
Whitby v. Mount Sinai Hospital (1986), 13 C.P.C. (2d)
    274, 57 O.R. (2d) 219 (Ont. Master), affirmed (1987),
    24 C.P.C. (2d) 319, 67 O.R. (2d) 479 (Ont. H.C.) 4.3.2
White v. Chaumont (1996), 50 C.P.C. (3d) 156 (Ont. Gen. Div.) 6.16.3
Wilson v. College of Physicians & Surgeons (Ontario)
    (1981), 24 C.P.C. 52 (Ont. Div. Ct.) 4.2.7; 4.4
Wilton v. Brown (1993), 22 C.P.C. (3d) 249
    (Ont. Gen. Div.) 4.3.2; 4.7.3
Yewdale v. Insurance Corp. of British Columbia
    (1995), 3 B.C.L.R. (3d) 240 (B.C. S.C.), leave to
    appeal refused (1995), 3 B.C.L.R. (3d) 247 (B.C. C.A.) 6.3; 6.7; 6.9
Zailberg v. Kinsella (1985), 6 C.P.C. (2d) 124 (Ont. Dist. Ct.) 4.3.2; 4.5

Chapter 1

Health Profession Statutes

by John Haydon, Q.C., B.A., LL.B.

1.1 Introduction
1.2 *Regulated Health Professions Act, 1991*
1.3 Health Professions Procedural Code
    1.3.1   Prescription Period
1.4 The Health Profession Acts

1.1 INTRODUCTION

This book came into being on the premise that lawyers involved in personal injury litigation need and want to learn more about injuries most commonly encountered in negligence actions, and about the health professions generally. Ask almost any health practitioner involved in personal injury litigation, or any lawyer, and he or she will confirm that neither profession completely understands the role played by the other in the action. This and the ensuing four chapters has the modest aim of assisting lawyers to achieve a better understanding of the statutory and common law milieu in which health practitioners must work, with particular reference to the creation and dissemination of records containing personal medical information.

How can this objective be useful to counsel in the prosecution or defence of a personal injury action? Consider the following:

   (i) *Examination for discovery and documents discovery of the plaintiff*: From the defence point of view, discovery of the plaintiff is the most productive route to locating medical records pertaining to personal injuries in issue in the action. To capitalize on this opportunity, defence counsel must know what records should be available and where they are likely to be found. When discovery is thorough, counsel can compare information contained in documents received in the action from sources such as hospitals and treating physicians with information required to be kept by medical statutes or regulations. As well, counsel may tap into sources not often regarded as likely repositories of relevant personal medical information, such as records of rehabilitation or treatment facilities, of private hospitals or special-purpose institutions, of pain management clinics, of health professionals who have retired or died, to name just a few.

(ii) *Cross-examination of the medical witness at trial*: Preparation for the cross-examination of a medical witness at trial might begin by determining if the information contained in the health records he or she has furnished in the action represents all of the information required of him or her by law to be recorded or kept in the circumstances. A discrepancy may mean that medical records which should have been produced have not been produced, or were never made, either of which may offer suitable terrain from which to launch an attack on credibility. Also, the statutory duty of health professionals to report to public authorities certain medical conditions or events should be canvassed, as health professionals may be unaware of the considerable scope of this duty, as well as the exposure to personal liability afforded by failure to so report.

(iii) *Preparation of the medical witness for cross-examination at trial*: Counsel in a personal injury action has a duty to ensure that his or her medical witness is adequately prepared for cross-examination at trial. At the very least, the claimant's medical witness should be briefed on the importance of creating and preserving medical records of his or her patient which conform with pertinent medical statutes, of ensuring that his or her record keeping is meticulous and complete, and of producing all medical documents requested by opposite parties. Unlike an assault on a medical witness' professional opinion on medical issues, which can hardly be avoided in a hotly contested action, an attack on his or her record-keeping abilities, which has the potential for compromising a competent health professional's testimony, is a foreseeable risk which can be met with adequate preparation.

These chapters presume some understanding of the Ontario Rules of Civil Procedure dealing with the procurement of and the adduction into evidence at trial of health records. With regard to the latter, the Rules will be touched on only briefly, having been amply and well treated in current legal publications, and solely from the narrow perspective of medical matters arising in the course of discovery and trial.

1.2 REGULATED HEALTH PROFESSIONS ACT, 1991[1]

At this writing, the activities of the following health professionals in Ontario are governed by the *Regulated Health Professions Act, 1991*, namely:

- Audiology and Speech-Language Pathologists
- Chiropodists
- Chiropractors
- Dental Hygienists
- Dental Technologists
- Dentists
- Denturists
- Dieticians
- Massage Therapists
- Medical Laboratory Technologists
- Medical Radiation Technologists
- Physicians and Surgeons
- Midwives
- Nurses
- Occupational Therapists
- Opticians
- Optometrists
- Pharmacists
- Physiotherapists
- Psychologists
- Respiratory Therapists

Executive responsibility for the administration of the Act resides with the Minister of Health for Ontario. The object of the Act is to ensure that the health professions are regulated and co-ordinated in the public interest, that appropriate standards of practice are developed and maintained, that individuals have access to services provided by the health professions of their choice and are treated with sensitivity and respect in their dealings with health professionals, the Colleges of the regulated health professions, and the Health Professions Board.[2] The Act defines what "controlled acts" a health professional is authorized to undertake by virtue of his or her membership in a regulated health profession, i.e., counselling a patient in medical matters, performing procedures in the course of examination or

---

1   S.O. 1991, c. 18, as amended by S.O. 1993, c. 37; S.O. 1996, c. 1, Sched. G, s. 27.
2   *Ibid.*, s. 3.

treatment, prescribing medications and appliances, etc. It determines who may use the title "doctor". As of this writing, only Chiropractors, Optometrists, Physicians and Surgeons, Psychologists, and Dental Surgeons may use the designation.[3]

Separate statutes, known as health profession Acts, have been enacted for the administration of each health profession. These are identified at 1.3, below.

The following bodies are established by the *Regulated Health Professions Act, 1991*:

Health Professions Regulatory Advisory Council

This is an advisory body only, whose duties are to advise the Minister of Health on the following matters:

(a) whether unregulated professions should be regulated;
(b) whether regulated professions should no longer be regulated;
(c) suggested amendments to the Act, a health profession Act, or a regulation under any of those Acts;
(d) matters concerning the quality assurance programs undertaken by the Colleges of the health professions; and,
(e) any matter the Minister of Health refers to the Advisory Council relating to the regulation of the health professions.[4]

It is also the Advisory Council's duty to monitor the patient relations program of each of the Colleges of the health professions.[5] The Council is composed of at least five, and no more than seven, members appointed by the Lieutenant Governor in Council on the recommendation of the Minister of Health; the Lieutenant Governor in Council is required to designate one member to be the chair and one to be the vice-chair. Appointments are for terms of two years and a person may not be appointed if he or she is employed in the public service of Ontario or by a Crown agency as defined in the *Crown Agency Act*,[6] or is or has been a member of a Council or a College of a health profession.[7]

---

3   *Ibid.*, s. 33.
4   *Ibid.*, s. 11(1).
5   *Ibid.*, s. 11(2).
6   R.S.O. 1990, c. C.48.
7   *Ibid.*, ss. 7–9.

Health Professions Board

The Board's duties are to conduct the hearings and reviews and to perform the duties that are assigned to it under the *Regulated Health Professions Act, 1991*, or any other Act, such as:

(a) review of a decision of the Registration Committee of the College of a health profession relating to an application for registration;
(b) investigation of a complaint filed with the Registrar of a College of a health profession which has not been disposed of by the Complaints Committee within the time prescribed by the Code;[8]
(c) review of a decision of the Complaints Committee of a College.[9]

A proceeding before the Board is considered and determined by a panel of at least three members, one of whom is required to be the chair or a vice-chair, selected by the chair; a panel must have an uneven number of members, and three members of a panel constitute a quorum.[10] The Board is composed of at least 12 and no more than 20 members appointed by the Lieutenant Governor in Council on the Minister's recommendation; the Lieutenant Governor in Council is required to designate one member of the Board to be the chair and one to be the vice chair; the chair may from time to time designate additional members to be vice-chairs. Appointments are for terms not exceeding three years, and a person may not be appointed if he or she is employed in the public service of Ontario or by a Crown agency as defined in the *Crown Agency Act*, or is or has been a member of a Council or a College of a health profession.[11]

1.3   HEALTH PROFESSIONS PROCEDURAL CODE

The Health Professions Procedural Code is deemed by section 4 of the *Regulated Health Professions Act, 1991* to be part of each health profession Act. It establishes a College for each health profession, which is a body corporate without share capital with all the powers of a natural person,[12] i.e., the College of Physicians and Surgeons of Ontario. Under the Code, each College has the following objects:

---

8   *Ibid.*, Schedule 2, s. 21.
9   *Ibid.*, Schedule 2, s. 29.
10 *Ibid.*, Schedule 2, ss. 23, 25.
11 *Ibid.*, ss. 18–20.
12 *Ibid.*, Schedule 2, s. 2.

1. to regulate the practice of the profession in respect of which it was created, and to govern the members in accordance with the health profession Act, the Code and the *Regulated Health Professions Act, 1991*, and the regulations and by-laws;
2. to develop, establish and maintain standards of qualification for persons to be issued certificates of registration, which qualify them as members of the health profession in respect of which it was created;
3. to develop, establish and maintain programs and standards of practice to assure the quality of the practice of the profession in respect of which it was created;
4. to develop, establish and maintain standards of knowledge and skill and programs to promote continuing competence among the members;
5. to develop, establish and maintain standards of professional ethics for the members;
6. to develop, establish and maintain programs to assist individuals to exercise their rights under the Code and the *Regulated Health Professions Act, 1991*;
7. to administer the health profession Act, the Code and the *Regulated Health Professions Act, 1991* as it relates to the profession in respect of which it was created, and to perform the other duties and exercise the other powers that are imposed or conferred on the College;
8. Any other objects relating to human health care that the Council considers advisable.

Each College is required to have a Council to manage and administer its affairs; the number of Council members is determined under the health profession Act in respect of which the College was created; each Council member may be elected for a term of not more than three years, and may not be a Council member for more than nine consecutive years. A majority of the members of the Council constitute a quorum. Each College is required to establish the following committees:

1. *Executive Committee*, which supervises the activities of the College generally;
2. *Registration Committee*, which processes applications for registration as members of the health profession in respect of which the College was created;
3. *Complaints Committee*, which investigates complaints filed with the Registrar of the College regarding the conduct or actions of a member;
4. *Discipline Committee*, which holds hearings into specific allegations

of a member's professional misconduct or incompetence, in referral by the Executive Committee or Complaints Committee. It also holds hearings of applications for reinstatement made by a person whose certificate of registration has been revoked or suspended on the ground of professional misconduct or incompetence;
5. *Fitness to Practice Committee*, which holds hearings to determine if a member is incapacitated, on referral by the Executive Committee acting on the report of a board of inquiry appointed by it for the purpose. Incapacitated means a member is suffering from a physical or mental condition or disorder that makes it desirable in the interest of the public that the member no longer be permitted to practice or that the member's practice be restricted. It also holds hearings of applications for reinstatement made by a person whose certificate of registration has been revoked or suspended on the ground of incapacity.
6. *Quality Assurance Committee*, which appoints assessors to inspect the records and premises of a member to assess whether the member may have committed an act of professional misconduct or may be incompetent or incapacitated, in which event the Committee may disclose the name of the member and the allegations made against him or her to the Executive Committee.
7. *Patient Relations Committee*, which advises the Council on matters relating to the patient relations program of the College, particularly those relating to measures for preventing or dealing with sexual abuse of patients by members. It has responsibility for arranging for therapy and counselling for persons who, while patients, were sexually abused by members.

1.3.1 Prescription Period

Section 89(1) of the Code provides that no person who is or was a member of a College is liable to any action arising out of negligence or malpractice in respect of professional services requested of or rendered by the person unless the action is commenced within one year after the date when the person commencing the action knew or ought to have known the fact or facts upon which the negligence or malpractice is alleged.

1.4   THE HEALTH PROFESSION ACTS

Audiology and Speech-Language Pathology Act, 1991, S.O. 1991, c. 19
Chiropody Act, 1991, S.O. 1991, c. 20
Chiropractic Act, 1991, S.O. 1991, c. 21
Dental Hygiene Act, 1991, S.O. 1991, c. 22

Dental Technology Act, 1991, S.O. 1991, c. 23
Dentistry Act, 1991, S.O. 1991, c. 24
Denturism Act, 1991, S.O. 1991, c. 25
Dietetics Act, 1991, S.O. 1991, c. 26
Massage Therapy Act, 1991, S.O. 1991, c. 27
Medical Laboratory Technology Act, 1991, S.O. 1991, c. 28
Medical Radiation Technology Act, 1991, S.O. 1991, c. 29
Medicine Act, 1991, S.O. 1991, c. 30
Midwifery Act, 1991, S.O. 1991, c. 31
Nursing Act, 1991, S.O. 1991, c. 32
Occupational Therapy Act, 1991, S.O. 1991, c. 33
Opticianry Act, 1991, S.O. 1991, c. 34
Optometry Act, 1991, S.O. 1991, c. 35
Pharmacy Act, 1991, S.O. 1991, c. 36
Physiotherapy Act, 1991, S.O. 1991, c. 37
Psychology Act, 1991, S.O. 1991, c. 38
Respiratory Therapy Act, 1991, S.O. 1991, c. 39

The format of each Act is essentially the same. Each contains provisions dealing with:

1. the scope of the medical practice to be conducted by its members, and the activities in which the member is authorized to engage in the practice of his or her particular profession;
2. the name of the College incorporated by the *Regulated Health Professions Act, 1991*, to administer the affairs of the health profession, and the composition of its Council;
3. the titles which a member may use in the practice of his or her health profession;
4. authority to make regulations subject to the approval of the Lieutenant Governor in Council and with prior review by the Minister of Health, regarding
   (a) qualifications, selection and terms of office of Council members;
   (b) where permitted, regulating the compounding, dispensing, and sale of drugs, and the keeping of prescribed records, as well as the use of drugs that a member may use in the course of his or her practice.

The regulations enacted under each of the health profession Acts are also similar, and typically cover the following topics:

1. *Committee Composition:* The following committees are established,

as well as their officers, number of members, category of membership, and manner of appointment.

Executive Committee
Registration Committee
Complaints Committee
Discipline Committee
Fitness to Practice Committee
Quality Assurance Committee
Patient Relations Committee.[13]

2. *Election of Council Members:* In which are established the electoral districts for the election of members to the Council of each health profession, where applicable, as well as the rules and procedures for the election of members to each Council, which normally include the following:

Number of members to be elected
Election dates and terms of office
Eligibility to vote
Eligibility for election
Nomination procedure
Acclamation
Registrar's electoral duties
Number of votes to be cast
Tie votes
Recounts and election reviews
Disqualification of elected members
Filling of vacancies
Election or selection of academic members
Disqualification of academic members

3. *Professional Misconduct:* In which are set out acts of professional misconduct for the purposes of clause 51(1) of the Code, which commonly include all or some of the following, or variations thereof:

Giving information about a patient or client to a person other than the patient or client or his or her authorized representative except with the informed consent of the patient or client or his or her authorized representative or as required or allowed by law.

---

13 The function of each of these committees is discussed at 1.2, *supra.*

Failing to keep records as required.

Contravening the Act, the *Regulated Health Professions Act, 1991* or a regulation under either of them.

Failing, without reasonable cause, to provide a report or certificate relating to an examination or treatment performed by the member, within 30 days of a request from the patient or his or her authorized representative.

Failing to provide copies from a client or patient health record for which the member has primary responsibility, as required by regulation.

Failing to make arrangements with a patient for the transfer of the patient's records when,
    (a) the member ceases practice, or
    (b) the patient requests the transfer.

4. *Fees:* In which are prescribed what annual and other fees are to be paid by members and applicants in each health profession.

5. *Registration:* In which are prescribed the classes of certificates of registration for members of each health profession, and the requirements to qualify for same.

6. *Advertising:* In which are established the rules relating to advertising with respect to a member's practice.

7. *Records:* In which are set out records to be kept by a member in relation to his or her practice.

8. *Appointment of Non-Council Members to Committees:* In which are set out qualifications for appointment of non-council members to the committees of each health profession.

Chapter 2

Statutory Duty to Create, Maintain and Preserve Health Records

by John Haydon, Q.C., B.A., LL.B.

2.1 Introduction
2.2 Record-Keeping under the Health Profession Acts
    2.2.1 *Medicine Act, 1991*
    2.2.2 *Chiropody Act, 1991*
    2.2.3 *Massage Therapy Act, 1991*
    2.2.4 *Optometry Act, 1991*
2.3 Record-Keeping under Medical Institutions Statutes
    2.3.1 *Public Hospitals Act*
2.4 General Statutes with Health Record Components
    2.4.1 *Child and Family Services Act*
    2.4.2 *Coroners Act*
    2.4.3 *Drug and Pharmacies Regulation Act*
    2.4.4 *Long Term Care Act, 1994*
    2.4.5 *Mental Health Act*
    2.4.6 *Vital Statistics Act*
    2.4.7 *Workers' Compensation Act; Workplace Safety and Insurance Act, 1997*

2.1 INTRODUCTION

Doctors are not great note-takers. Any counsel who routinely views physicians' records in personal injury actions is often disappointed with the quality of the handwritten notes made by physicians in the course of examining and treating patients: quite apart from the illegibility of the notes (which can usually be overcome with the aid of secretaries who have mastered the art of deciphering lawyers' scribblings), physicians' notes may range from skimpy, to incomplete, to simply uninformative. The best note-takers are not necessarily the best physicians; indeed, it can be argued some of the best physicians are the worst note-takers, their very genius recoiling from such a mundane task. This is unfortunate, as a well-qualified physician who is vulnerable to attack for his or her record-keeping runs the risk of having his or her opinions' worth diluted in cross-examination at trial. Many physicians readily admit their weakness in record-keeping, pointing out that at medical school they were trained to be doctors, not clerks or administrators.

Even following graduation, health professionals receive sparse direction from their respective governing bodies concerning statutory duties to create and maintain health records. This is surprising, considering the likelihood these bodies would have provided input to the legislative process which created the duties, either as lobbyists or simply as persons from whom informed views were sought.

The creation and maintenance of proper health records by a health professional in the examination and/or treatment of a patient is important from a civil litigation standpoint for the following reasons:

1. any discrepancy between the contents of a medical record and the oral testimony at trial of the health professional who prepared the record is likely to be resolved in favour of the former, as the records are usually made at a time when litigation was not contemplated;
2. the weight to be given medical records at trial will be commensurate with their contemporaneity, thoroughness, and intelligibility.
3. The failure to include information in a medical record which is required to be kept by statute:

    (a) is a dereliction of duty which may provide opposing counsel with an opportunity to attack the health professional's credibility at trial; such an omission may constitute professional misconduct under the regulations made pursuant to his or her health profession Act, as well as contravene the code of ethics directed at the health professional by his or her College or professional organization;
    (b) in an action against the health professional, may give rise to an inference that the omitted information would have been unfavourable to the person responsible for its creation;
    (c) may directly constitute grounds for a negligence action against the health professional responsible for its creation, i.e., such an omission may hinder or prevent other health professionals later consulted from properly diagnosing or making decisions affecting the health of the patient;

4. medical records may be vital to refresh the recollections of health professionals and others present at the time of the event in question;
5. while good medical records may not be a warranty of good medical care, poor medical records are likely to cast a reflection on the quality of medical services rendered by their author.

2.2 RECORD-KEEPING UNDER THE HEALTH PROFESSION ACTS

Of the 21 health profession Acts, only four set out the precise information to be contained in the record made by a health professional for each patient, namely:

2.2.1 *Medicine Act, 1991* [1]

A member of the College of Physicians and Surgeons of Ontario is required to make records for each patient, containing the following:

1. the name, address, and date of birth of the patient;
2. if the patient has an Ontario health number, the health number;
3. for a consultation, the name and address of the primary care physician and of any health professional who referred the patient;
4. every written report received respecting the patient from another member of the health profession;
5. the date of each professional encounter with the patient;
6. a record of the assessment of the patient, including,

    (a) the history obtained by the member,
    (b) the particulars of each medical examination by the member, and
    (c) a note of any investigations ordered by the member and the results of the investigations.

7. a record of the disposition of the patient, including:

    (a) an indication of each treatment prescribed or administered by the member,
    (b) a record of professional advice given by the member, and,
    (c) particulars of any referral made by the member;

8. a record of all fees charged which were not in respect of insured services under the *Health Insurance Act*, which may be kept separately from the clinical record;

---

[1] S.O. 1991, c. 30.

9. any additional records required by regulation.[2]

In addition, a member is required to keep a daybook, daily diary or appointment record containing the name of each patient who is encountered professionally or treated or for whom a professional service is rendered by the member.

A member is required to retain the said records for at least ten years after the date of the last entry in the record, or until ten years after the day on which the patient reached or would have reached the age of 18 years, or until the member ceases to practice medicine, whichever occurs first.

A member who ceases to practice medicine is required, for records of family medicine and primary care, to:

1. transfer them to a member with the same address and telephone number, or,
2. notify each patient that the records will be destroyed two years after the notification and that the patient may obtain the records or have the member transfer the records to another physician within the two years.

No person may destroy records of family medicine or primary care except in accordance with the foregoing.

2.2.2 *Chiropody Act, 1991* [3]

A member of the College of Chiropodists of Ontario is required, in relation to his or her practice, to take all reasonable steps necessary to ensure that the following records, among others, are kept:

1. a daily appointment record that sets out the name of each patient whom the member examines or treats or to whom the member renders any service;
2. an equipment service record that sets out the servicing for every potentially hazardous piece of equipment used to examine, treat or render any service to patients;
3. a patient health record for each patient, which shall include:

    (a) the patient's name and address;
    (b) the date of each of the patients visits to the member;
    (c) the name and address of the primary care physician and any referring health professional;

---

2 O. Reg. 114/94, Part V, ss. 18, 19 [added O. Reg. 211/94].
3 S.O. 1991, c. 20.

(d) a history of the patient;
(e) reasonable information about every examination performed by the member and reasonable information about every clinical finding, diagnosis and assessment made by the member;
(f) reasonable information about every order made by the member for examinations, tests, consultations or treatments to be performed by any other person;
(g) every written report received by the member with respect to examinations, tests, consultations or treatments performed by other health professionals;
(h) reasonable information about all significant advice given by the member and every pre and post-operative instruction given by the member;
(i) reasonable information about every post-operative visit;
(j) reasonable information about every controlled act, within the meaning of subsection 27(2) of the *Regulated Health Professions Act, 1991*, performed by the member.
(k) reasonable information about every delegation of a controlled act within the meaning of subsection 27(2) of the *Regulated Health Professions Act, 1991*, delegated by the member;
(l) reasonable information about every referral of the patient by the member to another health professional, service or agency;
(m) any pertinent reasons a patient may give for cancelling an appointment;
(n) reasonable information about every procedure that was commenced but not completed, including reasons for the non-completion;
(o) a copy of every written consent.[4]

Every part of a patient health record must have a reference identifying the patient or the patient health record.

The member is personally responsible for all things recorded in relation to a patient, including all treatments, orders, advice, and referrals, and the member responsible and the author of the record should both be identified in the record.

Every patient health record is required to be retained for at least 10 years following:

1. the patient's last visit; or,
2. if the patient was less than 18 years old at the time of his or her last visit, the day the patient became or would have become 18 years old.

---

4   O. Reg. 203/94, Part III, ss. 13 to 16 [added O. Reg. 746/94].

2.2.3 *Massage Therapy Act, 1991* [5]

A member of the College of Massage Therapists of Ontario is required to take all reasonable steps necessary to ensure that the following records, among others, are kept:

1. A daily appointment record that sets out the name of each client whom the member examines or treats or to whom the member renders any service and the time of the appointment.
2. An equipment service record that sets out the servicing of equipment used to examine or treat clients or to render any service to clients.
3. A client health record for each client, to include the following:

    (a) the client's name and address;
    (b) the date, time and duration of each of the client's visits to the member;
    (c) the name and address of the primary care physician and any referring health professional;
    (d) any relevant medical history and a history of massage therapy;
    (e) particulars of every examination performed by the member and particulars of every clinical finding and assessment made by the member;
    (f) every written report received by the member with respect to the examinations, tests, consultations or treatments performed by any other person;
    (g) particulars of all advice given by the member;
    (h) particulars of every referral of the client by the member to another health professional;
    (i) particulars of every fee or other amount charged by the member;
    (j) a copy of every written consent;
    (k) a copy of every needs assessment;
    (l) a copy of any treatment plan;
    (m) particulars of the treatment applied at each of the client's visits to the member and the name of the member who applied the treatment.[6]

Every part of a client health record must have a reference identifying the client or the client health record, and every entry must be dated and the identity of the person who made the entry must be identifiable.

Every client health record shall be retained for at least 10 years following:

---

5   S.O. 1991, c. 27.
6   O. Reg. 544/94, Part III, ss. 7 to 11.

1. the client's last visit; or,
2. if the client was less than 18 years old at the time of his or her last visit, the day the client became or would become 18 years old.

A member shall ensure that any destruction of client health records is done in such a way as to maintain client confidentiality.

2.2.4   Optometry Act, 1991 [7]

A member is required, in relation to his or her practice, to take all reasonable steps necessary to ensure that the following records, among others, are kept:

1. A daily appointment record that sets out the name of each patient whom the member examines or treats or to whom the member provides any service.
2. A health record for each patient, to include the following:

   (a) the name and address of the patient and the name of the member who provided the service;
   (b) the date of each visit of the patient;
   (c) the name and address of any referring health professional;
   (d) the patient's health and oculo-visual history;
   (e) the clinical procedures used;
   (f) the clinical findings obtained;
   (g) the diagnosis, when possible;
   (h) every order made by the member for examinations, tests, consultations or treatments to be performed by any other person;
   (i) particulars of every referral to or from another health professional;
   (j) information about every delegation of a controlled act within the meaning of subsection 27(2) of the *Regulated Health Professions Act, 1991*, delegated by the member;
   (k) information about a procedure that was commenced but not completed, including reasons for non-completion;
   (l) a copy of every written consent to treatment.[8]

Every part of a patient health record must be dated and have a reference identifying the patient or the patient health record.

Every entry in the patient health record must be dated and the person who made the entry must be readily identifiable.

Every patient health record shall be retained for at least 10 years following:

---

7   S.O. 1991, c. 35.
8   O. Reg. 119/94, ss. 9-10 [added O. Reg. 749/94].

1. the patient's last visit; or
2. if the patient was less than 18 years old at the time of his or her last visit, the day the patient became or would have become 18 years old.

2.3 RECORD-KEEPING UNDER MEDICAL INSTITUTIONS STATUTES

While the complete list is larger, the following is a list of Ontario statutes relating to Ontario medical institutions most likely to be consulted with respect to procurement of health records in a personal injury action:

Charitable Institutions Act, R.S.O. 1990, c. C.9
Community Psychiatric Hospitals Act, R.S.O. 1990, c. C.21
Day Nurseries Act, R.S.O. 1990, c. D.2
Homes for Retarded Persons Act, R.S.O. 1990, c. H.11
Homes for Special Care Act, R.S.O. 1990, c. H.12
Homes for the Aged and Rest Homes Act, R.S.O. 1990, c. H.13
Independent Health Facilities Act, R.S.O. 1990, c. I.3
Mental Hospitals Act, R.S.O. 1990, c. M.8
Nursing Homes Act, R.S.O. 1990, c. N.7
Private Hospitals Act, R.S.O. 1990, c. P.24
Public Hospitals Act, R.S.O. 1990, c. P.40

All of the foregoing statutes contain provisions requiring persons connected with the institution in question to create and maintain records containing specific information with respect to each patient serviced. Space does not permit a review of information required to be kept for each institution listed; however, as the *Public Hospitals Act* is the most common source of health records pertinent to personal injury litigation, it will be useful, as well as illustrative, to set out its provisions relating to such records.

2.3.1 Public Hospitals Act

1. Order that patient be discharged to be made by attending physician or midwife or designate, where patient no longer in need of treatment in hospital.[9]

Where a patient is no longer in need of treatment in the hospital, the attending physician or midwife, or a member of the medical or midwifery

---

9   R.R.O. 1990, Reg. 965, s. 16(1), amended by Reg. 761/93.

staff designated by the physician or midwife, is required to make an order that the patient be discharged, and communicate the order to the patient.

2. Copy of medical certificate of death or report, as the case may be, to be filed in patient's medical record by attending physician, when patient dies in hospital.[10]

When a patient dies in a hospital, the attending physician is required to cause a copy of the medical certificate of death required by subsection 21(3) of the *Vital Statistics Act*[11] to be filed in the medical record pertaining to the patient; where by the said Act the coroner is required to complete the medical certificate of death and he or she does not provide the attending physician with a copy of the medical certificate of death, the attending physician is required to complete a report in Form 1 and cause a copy of the report to be filed in the patient's medical record.

3. Medical record for each patient of a public hospital to be kept by administrator; the medical record for a patient other than an out-patient to include specified information and documents.[12]

It is the duty of every administrator to ensure that a system is established for the keeping of a medical record for each patient of a public hospital, each entry to bear the date on which it was made and authenticated by the person or persons who authorized the entry. The medical record for a patient, other than an out-patient, must include:

1. the names of the attending physicians, dentists and midwives of the patient;
2. a history of the patient;
3. records of all medical, dental and midwifery examinations carried out on the patient in the hospital;
4. all diagnostic imaging hard copy records of the patient and reports made by a physician or dentist of the results of radiological examinations;
5. all videotapes of a patient's examinations or tests where the videotapes constitute the only hard copy of evidence of the examinations or tests, the results of the examinations or tests and reports made by a physician of the results of the examinations or tests;
6. all provisional and final diagnoses with respect to the patient;

---

10 *Ibid.*, s. 17.
11 R.S.O. 1990, c. V.4.
12 Reg. 965, *supra*, note 9, s. 19(1), (2), (4), amended by Reg. 761/93.

7. all orders for treatment or investigation with respect to the patient in the hospital;
8. records of all medical, dental and midwifery treatment carried out on the patient in the hospital;
9. all consents to treatment obtained in writing with respect to the patient;
10. all statements referred to in subsection 28(4) of R.R.O. 1990, Reg. 965, with respect to the patient;
11. all opinions required to be noted under subsection 25(5) of the *Health Care Consent Act, 1996* with respect to the patient;
12. progress notes with respect to the patient;
13. reports with respect to the patient of,

    (a) all consultations;
    (b) all investigative procedures;
    (c) all operations, anaesthesia and recoveries; and,
    (d) a post-mortem examination, if one has been performed, where the patient dies in the hospital;

14. discharge summaries;
15. orders for discharge with respect to the patient; and,
16. a death certificate where the patient dies in the hospital.

   4. Medical record of an out-patient to include specified information and documents.[13]

The medical records of an out-patient, other than an out-patient who visits the hospital solely for diagnostic procedures, must include:

1. the names of the attending physicians, dentists and midwives of the out-patient at each visit;
2. a history of the out-patient;
3. records of all medical, dental and midwifery examinations carried out on the out-patient in the hospital;
4. all diagnostic imaging hard copy records of the out-patient and reports made by a physician or dentist of the results of the radiological examination;
5. all videotapes of an out-patient's examinations or tests where the videotapes constitute the only hard copy evidence of the examinations or tests, the results of the examinations or tests and reports made by a physician of the results of the examinations or tests;

---

13 *Ibid.*, s. 19(5), (6).

6. all orders for treatment or investigation with respect to the out-patient in the hospital;
7. all consents to treatment obtained in writing with respect to the out-patient;
8. all statements referred to in subsection 28(4) of R.R.O. 1990, Reg. 965, with respect to the out-patient;
9. all opinions required to be noted under subsection 25(5) of the *Health Care Consent Act, 1996* with respect to the out-patient;
10. records of all medical, dental and midwifery treatment carried out on the out-patient in the hospital;
11. all reports of investigative procedures carried out on the out-patient in the hospital;
12. all diagnoses with respect to the out-patient; and,
13. a death certificate if the out-patient dies in the hospital.

The medical record of an out-patient who visits the hospital solely for diagnostic procedures need only include the orders for the procedures, any consent to the procedures obtained in writing and a record of the procedures.

> 5. Medical records or photographs thereof for patients and out-patients of a public hospital, to be retained for periods specified.[14]

A public hospital is required to retain its medical records or photographs[15] thereof for patients and out-patients, together with notes, charts and other material relating to patient care, as well as slides made for microscopic examination from tissue removed from a patient or an out-patient on which a report has been made (except for blood smears that are normal in the opinion of the person making the report on the slide), for the following periods of time:

(a) in the case of a patient who is 18 years of age or older, for at least 10

---

14 *Ibid.*, s. 20(2), (3).
15 *Ibid.*, s. 1. "Photograph" means a reproduction made by any process that makes an exact copy of the original, whether or not the copy is the same size as the original.
At s. 20(1), a hospital may photograph medical records and notes, charts and other material relating to patient care for the purpose of retaining the contents thereof in lieu of the original documents where the photographing of the documents is carried out in accordance with procedures established by the board after considering the recommendations of the medical advisory committee.

years after the date of discharge or death of the patient to whom the record or photograph relates;

(b) in the case of an out-patient who is 18 years of age or older, for at least 10 years after the date of the last visit or death of the out-patient to whom the record or photograph relates;

(c) in the case of a patient who is under 18 years of age, for at least 10 years after the 18th anniversary of the birth of the patient to whom the record or photograph relates; and

(d) in the case of an out-patient who is under 18 years of age, for at least 10 years after the 18th anniversary of the birth of the out-patient to whom the record or photograph relates.

6. Orders for treatment or for diagnostic procedure of a patient to be authenticated by physician, dentist or midwife giving treatment order, or by physician, dentist, midwife, or registered nurse in the extended class giving diagnostic procedure.[16]

Every order for treatment or for a diagnostic procedure of a patient is required be in writing and shall be dated and authenticated[17] by the physician, dentist or midwife giving the order. The order may be dictated by telephone to a person designated by the administrator of the hospital to take such orders, in which event the person to whom the order was dictated is required to transcribe the order, the name of the physician, dentist, midwife, or registered nurse in the extended class giving diagnostic procedure, who dictated the order, the date and the time of receiving the order, and to authenticate the transcription; the physician, dentist or midwife who dictated the order must authenticate the order on the first visit to the hospital after dictating the order.

7. Admitting note to be entered in patient's medical record within 24 hours of admission, setting out reason for admission, to be authenticated by member of medical or midwifery staff.[18]

Every board is required to ensure that procedures are established in the hospital such that, within 24 hours after each patient is admitted to the hospital, an admitting note is entered in the medical record of the patient

---

16 *Ibid.*, s. 24 as amended by 761/93, 45/98.
17 *Ibid.*, s. 1(1). "Authenticate" means to identify oneself as the author of a document or a record by personal signature or by any other means authorized by the board.
18 *Ibid.*, s. 25(1).

that sets out clearly the reason for admission of the patient, and is authenticated by a member of the medical or midwifery staff.

This requirement does not apply where a physician records, dates and authenticates a report of the findings of a physical examination and a provisional diagnosis of the patient within 24 hours after the patient is admitted to the hospital;[19] nor does it apply in respect of the repeat visits by a patient returning to the hospital from time to time for any treatment involving a series of visits for the same injury or illness.[20]

> 8. Record of medical history and report of findings of physical examination and provisional diagnosis of patient to be made by physician within 72 hours after admission.[21]

Every board is required to ensure that procedures are established in hospital that provide, within 72 hours after a patient is admitted to the hospital by a physician, that a physician,

(a) takes a medical history of the patient;
(b) gives the patient a physical examination;
(c) makes a provisional diagnosis of the patient's medical condition;
(d) records, dates and authenticates the history and a report of the findings of the physical examination and the provisional diagnosis of the patient.

This requirement does not apply in respect of a patient who is readmitted to the hospital with the same diagnosis within ten days after having been discharged,[22] nor in respect of the repeat visits by a patient returning to the hospital from time to time for any treatment involving a series of visits for the same injury or illness.[23]

> 9. Report of medical history, findings of physical examination and provisional diagnosis, and statement of proposed treatment of patient, to be made by attending dentist within 72 hours of admission where patient is admitted to hospital for treatment by a dentist.[24]

---

19 *Ibid.*, s. 25(2).
20 *Ibid.*, s. 25(5).
21 *Ibid.*, s. 25(3) as amended by 761/93.
22 *Ibid.*, s. 25(4).
23 *Ibid.*, s. 25(5).
24 *Ibid.*, s. 25(6).

Where a patient is admitted to a hospital for treatment by a dentist,[25] the attending dentist is required to, within 24 hours of the admission of the patient,

(a) take a dental history of the patient that relates to the reason for the treatment;
(b) make a dental and oral examination of the patient;
(c) make a provisional diagnosis of the patient's dental condition, and
(d) prepare, date and authenticate the history and a report of the findings of the examinations and the provisional diagnosis and a statement of the proposed course of dental treatment for the patient.

Where a patient is admitted to a hospital for dental surgery, the attending dentist is required to ensure that the said procedures, as well as those described in para. 8, above, have been carried out before surgery commences.[26]

> 10. Record of medical history and report of findings of physical examination and provisional diagnosis of patient, to be made by midwife within 72 hours after admission or prior to discharge (*whichever is earlier*), where patient is admitted to hospital by midwife.[27]

Where a patient is admitted to a hospital by a midwife, the attending midwife[28] is required, within 72 hours of admission or prior to discharge, if the patient is discharged within 72 hours of admission, to

(a) take a history of the patient;
(b) give the patient a physical examination;
(c) make a provisional assessment of the patient's condition; and
(d) record, date and authenticate the history and a report of the findings of the physical examination and the provisional assessment of the patient.

---

25 *Ibid.*, s. 1(1). "Attending dentist" means a member of the dental staff who attends a patient in the hospital; and "dentist" means a person holding a licence for the practice of dentistry under the *Health Disciplines Act*.
26 *Ibid.*, s. 25(7).
27 *Ibid.*, s. 25(8) as amended by Reg. 761/93.
28 *Ibid.*, s. 1(1). "Attending midwife" means a member of the midwifery staff who attends a patient in the hospital; and "midwife" means a member of the College of Midwives of Ontario.

11. Entries of specified information to be made in medical record of patient before administration of anaesthetic.[29]

No person may administer a general, spinal or epidural anaesthetic or an intravenous anaesthetic or a regional nerve block, other than a mandibular nerve block for a dental procedure, to a patient or an out-patient unless,

(a) a history of the present disability or disease and any previous medical history relevant to the disability or disease of the patient;
(b) the findings of a physical examination of the patient; and
(c) the results of any laboratory tests considered necessary by the attending physician or attending dentist with respect to the patient,

are entered in the medical record of the patient; and unless

(i) the anaesthetist has taken a medical history and made a physical examination of the patient sufficient to enable the anaesthetist to evaluate the condition of the patient and to choose a suitable anaesthetic; and
(ii) the anaesthetist has entered or caused to be entered on the anaesthetic record and has authenticated the data relevant to administering the anaesthetic for the proposed procedure from the patient's history, laboratory findings and physical examination,

except where the anaesthetist and attending physician are of the opinion that a delay for the purpose of complying with these requirements would endanger the life or a limb or vital organ of the patient, in which event the anaesthetist and surgeon are required, as soon as practicable, to jointly prepare and authenticate a statement that sets out that opinion.

12. Report to be prepared by anaesthetist who administers anaesthetic to a patient, showing specified information.[30]

Where a general, spinal or epidural anaesthetic or an intravenous anaesthetic or a regional nerve block, other than a mandibular nerve block for a dental procedure, is administered to a patient, the anaesthetist who administers the anaesthetic is required to prepare an anaesthetic report with respect to the patient that shows,

---

29 *Ibid.*, at s. 28(1), (2), (3) and (4) as amended by Reg. 588/93.
30 *Ibid.*, s. 28(5).

(a) the medications given to the patient in contemplation of anaesthesia;
(b) the patient airway, circuit and monitors used on the patient;
(c) the anaesthetic agents used, the methods of administration of the agents and the proportions or concentrations of all agents administered by inhalation to the patient;
(d) the names, quantities and times of all drugs given by injection to the patient;
(e) the duration of the anaesthesia on the patient;
(f) the estimated fluid loss of the patient;
(g) the quantities and type of all blood products and other fluids administered intravenously to the patient during the operation.
(h) the vital signs of the patient before, during and after anaesthesia.

> 13. Entry to be made on medical record of patient before surgeon performs surgical operation on a patient, containing statement of findings of physical examination of patient and diagnosis.[31]

No surgeon may perform a surgical operation on a patient unless the surgeon:

(a) performs a physical examination of the patient sufficient to enable the surgeon to make a diagnosis; and
(b) authenticates and enters or causes to be entered on the medical record of the patient, a statement of the findings on the physical examination and the diagnosis.

> 14. Written description of operative procedure, findings and diagnosis made during operation on patient, to be prepared by person qualified to do so, to be authenticated by the said person and by surgeon performing operation.[32]

Every surgeon who performs a surgical operation in a hospital is required to prepare or cause to be prepared by a person qualified to do so a written description of the operative procedure at the operation and findings and diagnosis made at the operation with respect to the patient, as the case requires, which written description shall be authenticated by the surgeon performing the operation and the person making the description.

---

31 *Ibid.*, s. 29(1).
32 *Ibid.*, s. 29(2) and (3).

15. (1) Report by laboratory of examination of tissues removed from patient during operation and curettage;
    (2) History of case and statement of findings of operation to be sent by surgeon with tissues to laboratory for examination.[33]

Where tissues are removed from a patient during an operation or curettage, the surgeon performing the operation or curettage is required to cause all tissues removed from the patient to be sent, together with a short history of the case and a statement of the findings of the operation, to a laboratory for examination and report; save that where the tissue removed is an arm, finger, foot, hand, hemorrhoid, lens, leg, prepuce, tonsil, toe, toenail, tooth, the tissue must not be sent to a laboratory unless the surgeon conducting the operation requests an examination and report on the tissue.

16. Record of specified information to be made by person taking blood from any person for use in a transfusion.[34]

Where blood is taken from any person for use in a transfusion, the person taking the blood is required to record or cause to be recorded:

(a) the name, address, blood-grouping and Rh factor typing of the person from whom the blood was taken;
(b) the date of taking of the blood;
(c) the amount of blood taken; and
(d) the result of any tests made on a sample of the blood taken for the transfusion.

17. (1) Report of officer of medical staff to be filed with secretary of the medical advisory committee where he or she assumes duty of investigating, diagnosing, prescribing for and treating patient in place of attending physician;
    (2) Report of secretary of medical advisory committee to superintendent concerning problem and action taken, if medical advisory committee concurs in opinion of officer of medical staff.[35]

Where the chief or president of the medical staff of a hospital, or the head of a department where the medical staff of a hospital is divided into medical departments, becomes aware that, in his or her opinion a serious problem exists in the diagnosis, care or treatment of a patient or out-pa-

---

33 *Ibid.*, s. 31.
34 *Ibid.*, s. 32.
35 *Public Hospitals Act*, R.S.O. 1990, c. P.40, s. 34.

tient, the officer is required to forthwith discuss the condition, diagnosis, care and treatment of the patient or out-patient with the attending physician, and, if changes in diagnosis, care or treatment satisfactory to the officer are not made promptly, he or she is required to assume forthwith the duty of investigating, diagnosing, prescribing for and treating the patient or out-patient, as the case may be, and shall notify the attending physician, the administrator and, if possible, the patient or out-patient that the member of the medical staff who was in attendance will cease forthwith to have any hospital privileges as the attending physician for the patient or out-patient. If the officer is unable to discuss the problem with the attending physician, he or she is required to proceed with his or her duties as if he or she had the discussion with the attending physician. The officer may delegate any or all of his or her foregoing responsibilities and duties to a member of his or her medical staff or of his or her medical department, as the case may be, but he or she remains accountable to the medical advisory committee[36] for the management of the patient by that member of the medical staff to whom any such responsibility or duty is delegated. The said officer is further required to inform two members of the medical advisory committee within 24 hours of his or her action, and is required to file a written report with the secretary of the medical advisory committee within 48 hours of his or her action.

Where the medical advisory committee concurs in the opinion of the officer who has taken the action that the action was necessary, the secretary of the medical advisory committee is required to forthwith make a detailed written report to the administrator of the problem and the action taken.

2.4 GENERAL STATUTES WITH HEALTH RECORD COMPONENTS

The following are some Ontario statutes of general application which require the creation and maintenance of health records of persons in circumstances specific to each statute. These statutes may be useful as a source of personal medical information in personal injury litigation, and should be considered where such health records pertaining to a claimant may relate to a matter in issue.

---

36 Under s. 36 of the Act, every hospital board is required to establish a medical advisory committee composed of such elected and appointed members of the medical staff as are prescribed by the regulations.

2.4.1 *Child and Family Services Act* [37]

Executive Responsibility: Minister of Community and Social Services

Statute Summary: The declared paramount objective of the Act is to promote the best interests, protection and well-being of children,[38] through the provision of the following services,[39] namely:

1. child development service, defined as a service for a child with a developmental[40] or physical handicap, for the family of a child with a developmental or physical handicap, or for the child and the family;
2. child treatment service, defined as a service for a child with a mental or psychiatric disorder, for the family of a child with a mental or psychiatric disorder, or for the child and the family;
3. child welfare service, defined as:

    (a) a residential or non-residential service, including a prevention service,
    (b) a service provided under Part III of the Act (Child Protection),
    (c) a service provided under Part VII of the Act (Adoption), or
    (d) individual or family counselling;

4. community support service, defined as a support service or prevention service provided in the community for children and their families;
5. foster care, defined as the provision of residential care to a child, by and in the home of a person who,

    (a) receives compensation for caring for child, except under the *Family Benefits Act*, the *General Welfare Assistance Act*, or the regulations made under either of them, and
    (b) is not the child's parent or a person with whom the child has been placed for adoption under Part VII of the Act,

    and "foster home" and "foster parent" have corresponding meanings.

6. residential service, defined as boarding, lodging and associated supervisory, sheltered or group care provided for a child away from the

---

37 R.S.O. 1990, c. C.11.
38 *Ibid.*, at s. 3. "child" means a person under the age of eighteen years.
39 *Ibid.*, at s. 3(1).
40 *Ibid.*, at s. 3(1). "developmental handicap" means a condition of mental impairment present or occurring in a person's formative years that is associated with limitations in adaptive behaviour.

home of the child's parent, and "residential care" and "residential placement" have corresponding meanings; and
7. young offenders' service, defined as a service provided under Part IV of the Act (Young Offenders), or under a program established under that Part.

Duty to Create: The statute imposes a duty to create the following records:

1. *Court-ordered assessment of child or parent or person having charge of child, by specified person, under Part III, Child Protection.*[41]

Under Part III of the Act, a society[42] may apply[43] to the Ontario Court (Provincial Division) or the Unified Family Court to determine whether a child is in need of protection.[44] Where a child has been found to be in need of protection, the court may order the child or a parent or a person, except

---

41 *Ibid.*, at ss. 40 and 54.
42 *Ibid.*, at s. 3(1). "society" means an approved agency designated as a children's aid society under subs. 15(2) of Part I [of the Act].
43 *Ibid.*, s. 40(1).
44 *Ibid.*, at s. 37(2), there are twelve criteria set out for determining if a child is in need of protection, including the following:

"(a) the child has suffered physical harm, inflicted by the person having charge of the child or caused by that person's failure to care and provide for or supervise and protect the child adequately;
(b) there is a substantial risk that the child will suffer physical harm inflicted or caused as described in clause (a);
(c) the child has been sexually molested or sexually exploited, by the person having charge of the child or by another person where the person having charge of the child knows or should know of the possibility of sexual molestation or sexual exploitation and fails to protect the child;
(d) there is a substantial risk that the child will be sexually molested or sexually exploited as described in clause (c);
(e) the child requires medical treatment to cure, prevent, or alleviate physical harm or suffering and the child's parent or the person having charge of the child does not provide, or refuses or is unavailable or unable to consent to, the treatment;
(f) the child has suffered emotional harm, demonstrated by severe,

  (i) anxiety,
  (ii) depression,
  (iii) withdrawal, or
  (iv) self-destructive or aggressive behaviour, and the child's parent or the person having charge of the child does not provide, or refuses or is unavailable or unable to consent to, services or treatment to remedy or alleviate the harm;

a foster parent, in whose charge the child has been or may be, to attend before and undergo an assessment by a specified person who is qualified, in the court's opinion, to perform medical, emotional, developmental, psychological, educational or social assessments and has consented to perform the assessment; the person performing the assessment is required to make a written report of the assessment to the court within the time specified in the order.

2. *Pre-adoption medical history of child proposed for adoption, to be prepared by adoption agency.*[45]

Every adoption agency that proposes to place a child for adoption is required, before placing the child, to prepare a report in a form approved by a Director that sets out the social and medical history of the child and of each person who is a parent of the child, and shall ensure the information contained in the said histories, except for any information that would identify the parents of the child, is shared in writing with the prospective adoptive parents prior to the adoption of the child. A copy of the report shall be filed:

(a) Where the Director's approval of the proposed placement is required, with the Director before the approval under section 142(2) of the Act is given or refused;
(b) Where the Director's approval is not required, with the Director when the placement is registered under section 141(6) or (7) of the Act, as the case requires.

3. *Daily log of each incident affecting health, safety or well-being of staff person or resident, to be maintained by licencee in each children's residence.*[46]

Every licensee is required to ensure that a daily log is maintained in

---

(g) there is a substantial risk that the child will suffer emotional harm of the kind described in clause (f), and the child's parent or the person having charge of the child does not provide, or refuses or is unavailable or unable to consent to, services or treatment to prevent the harm;
(h) the child suffers from a mental, emotional or developmental condition that, if not remedied, could seriously impair the child's development and the chid's parent or the person having charge of the child does not provide, or refuses or is unavailable or unable to consent to, treatment to remedy or alleviate the condition; . . ."

45 R.R.O. 1990, Reg. 70, s. 54.
46 *Ibid.*, s. 74.

each children's residence operated by the licensee, in which shall be included each incident that affects or that in the opinion of the licensee may affect the health, safety or well-being of a staff person in the residence or a resident.

4. *Cumulative record of each resident's medical and dental examinations and treatment, to be maintained by licencee of each children's residence.*[47]

Every licensee is required, with respect to each resident in a children's residence operated by the licensee, to maintain a cumulative record of each resident's medical and dental examinations and treatment while the resident is in the residence, which cumulative record shall be kept in the resident's case record.

5. *Record of medications given to each resident, to be kept by licensee of each children's residence.*[48]

Every licensee is required to ensure that with respect to each resident in each children's residence operated by the licensee a record is kept of all medications given to each resident, including the type of medication, the period for which it is prescribed, when each dose is to be given and is given and by whom each dose is given, except where the medication is self-administered in the situation described in 6, below.

6. *Self-medication plan for resident under 16 years of age to be kept in resident's record.*[49]

Where, in the opinion of the physician, a resident under 16 years of age will derive some benefit from the responsibility of administering the resident's own medication, a copy of the physician's written self-medication plan for that resident shall be kept in the resident's record.

7. *Case record for each resident, to be maintained by licensee of children's residence.*[50]

Every licensee is required to maintain a written case record for each resident in a children's residence operated by the licensee that includes, among other information,

---

47 *Ibid.*, s. 91(4) and (5).
48 *Ibid.*, s. 92(1) and (4).
49 *Ibid.*, s. 92(5).
50 *Ibid.*, s. 99(1).

(a) reports of all medical examinations and treatment given to the resident upon admission and while in the residence;
(b) the plan of care developed for the resident and particulars of any review of the plan of care or of the resident's status;
(c) reports of any serious occurrence involving the resident;
(d) where one of the following incidents occurs, the time of the occurrence, the name of the person reporting it and the person to whom the report was made, namely, where:

   (i) a resident dies;
   (ii) a resident is seriously injured;
   (iii) a resident is abused or mistreated;
   (iv) a resident is injured by a staff person in the residence or by the licensee;
   (v) a complaint is made by or about a resident that is considered by the licensee to be of a serious nature;
   (vi) a resident resides in a residence operated by the licensee in which a fire or other disaster occurs; or
   (vii) in addition to the matters set out in clauses (i) to (vi), any other serious occurrence takes place concerning a resident.

A written case record of a resident is required to be retained by the licensee for at least 20 years after the last entry in the record with respect to the resident or, where the resident dies, for at least five years after the death of the resident.[51]

8. *Statement from physician or approved individual regarding general health and specific illnesses or disabilities of foster parent applicant and family members.*[52]

No licensee shall approve a foster home to receive a child for foster care until the licensee or a person designated by the licensee, among other things, obtains a written statement from a physician or an individual approved by the local medical officer of health regarding the general health and specific illnesses or disabilities of the foster parent applicant and family members and whether or not they might interfere with the provision of foster care.

---

51 *Ibid.*, s. 99(2).
52 *Ibid.*, s. 118(1)(f).

2.4.2 Coroners Act [53]

Executive Responsibility: Solicitor General and Minister of Correctional Services

Statute Summary: The Lieutenant Governor in Council may appoint one or more legally qualified medical practitioners to be coroners for Ontario. In the ordinary course, a coroner or coroners will be appointed to an area in Ontario established by regulation by the Lieutenant Governor in Council, and the appointment and continuation in office of a coroner will be subject to the condition that he or she is ordinarily resident in the area named in the appointment.[54] The Lieutenant Governor in Council may also appoint a coroner to be the Chief Coroner for Ontario, who will supervise the activities of coroners in their duties and be responsible for the administration of the Act and its regulations.[55] Generally, a coroner will investigate the circumstances of the death of a person who has died,

1. as a result of,
   (a) violence,
   (b) misadventure,
   (c) negligence,
   (d) misconduct, or
   (e) malpractice;
2. by unfair means;
3. during pregnancy or following pregnancy in circumstances that might reasonably be attributable thereto;
4. suddenly and unexpectedly;
5. from disease or sickness for which he or she was not treated by a legally qualified medical practitioner;
6. from any cause other than disease; or
7. under such circumstances as may require investigation.[56]

The Act sets out numerous instances where untoward deaths are to be reported. If, as a result of the investigation, the coroner is of the opinion that an inquest ought to be held he or she is required to issue a warrant to hold an inquest, at which time a jury shall inquire into the circumstances of the death and determine,

---

53 R.S.O. 1990, c. C.37.
54 *Ibid.*, s. 3.
55 *Ibid.*, s. 4.
56 *Ibid.*, s. 10.

1. who the deceased was;
2. how the deceased came to his or her death;
3. when the deceased came to his or her death;
4. where the deceased came to his or her death; and
5. by what means the deceased came to his or death.[57]

The jury is not to make any finding of legal responsibility or express any conclusion of law in making its determination.[58]

Duty to Create: The statute imposes a duty to create the following records:

> *Report in writing of person who performs post mortem examination or analysis of a body at behest of coroner during an investigation or inquest.* [59]

A coroner may at any time during an investigation or inquest issue a warrant for a *post mortem* examination of the body, an analysis of the blood, urine or contents of the stomach and intestines, or such other examination or analysis as the circumstances warrant. The person who performs the *post mortem* examination is required to forthwith report his or her findings in writing only to the coroner who issued the warrant, the Crown Attorney, the regional coroner and the Chief Coroner, and the person who performs any other examination or analysis is required to forthwith report his or her findings in writing only to the coroner who issued the warrant, the person who performed the *post mortem* examination, the Crown Attorney, the regional coroner and the Chief Coroner.

2.4.3   Drug and Pharmacies Regulation Act [60]

Executive Responsibility: Minister of Health

Statute Summary: Generally speaking, a pharmacist may sell or dispense a drug to the following persons without prescription:

1. a person authorized under a health profession Act as defined in the *Regulated Health Professions Act, 1991*, to dispense, prescribe or administer drugs;[61]

---

57 *Ibid.*, s. 31(1).
58 *Ibid.*, s. 31(2).
59 *Ibid.*, s. 28.
60 R.S.O. 1990, c. H.4. (The former title of this statute was the "*Health Disciplines Act*"; the current title was created by S.O. 1991, c. 168, s. 47; proclaimed in force December 31, 1993).
61 *Ibid.*, s. 118(2).

2. a member of the College of Chiropodists of Ontario, the College of Dental Hygienists of Ontario, the College of Midwives of Ontario or the College of Optometrists of Ontario, a drug that the member may use in the course of engaging in the practice of his or her profession.[62]

Otherwise, no person is permitted to sell by retail any drug referred to in Schedule E, F, G or N, except on prescription given in such form, in such manner and under such conditions as the regulations prescribe.[63]

No person may establish or operate a pharmacy unless a certificate of accreditation has been issued in respect thereof under the Act.[64] Where the Accreditation Committee of the Ontario College of Pharmacists has reason to believe that a pharmacy or its operation fails to conform to the requirements of the Act and its regulations, or to any term, condition or limitation to which its certificate of accreditation is subject, it may refer the matter to the Discipline Committee of the College for a hearing and determination, which has the power to revoke or suspend a licence of accreditation, and impose a fine not exceeding $25,000.[65]

A corporation is not permitted to own or operate a pharmacy unless the majority of its directors are pharmacists, or a majority of each class of shares of the corporation is owned by and registered in the name of pharmacists.[66]

No person is permitted to operate a pharmacy unless it is under the supervision of a pharmacist who is physically present, and it is managed by a pharmacist so designated by the owner of the pharmacy.[67]

Only a pharmacist or an intern or a registered pharmacy student acting under the supervision of a pharmacist who is physically present is permitted to compound, dispense or sell any drug in a pharmacy, except for non-

---

62 *Ibid.*, s. 118(3).
63 *Ibid.*, s. 155.
64 *Ibid.*, s. 139.
65 *Ibid.*, s. 140 as amended.
66 *Ibid.*, s. 142, with the following exceptions:
 (a) a corporation operating a pharmacy on May 14, 1954;
 (b) the operation of a pharmacy by a non-profit corporation having as its objectives and providing health services by members of more than one health discipline;
 (c) shares registered in the name of the personal representative of a deceased pharmacist shall, for a period of four years be considered to be registered in the name of a pharmacist.
67 *Ibid.*, s. 146.

prescription drugs, duly packaged and labelled in accordance with the regulations under the Act.[68]

The owner or manager of a pharmacy is liable for every offence under the Act committed by any person in the employ of or under the supervision of the owner or manager with the owner's or manager's permission, consent or approval, express or implied, and every director of a corporation operating a pharmacy is liable for every offence under the Act committed by any person in the employ of the corporation with the director's permission, consent or approval, express or implied.[69]

Duty to Create: The statute imposes a duty to create the following records:

1. *Record of every purchase and sale of a drug to be kept by the manager of every pharmacy.*[70]

The manager of every pharmacy is required to keep or cause to be kept a record of every purchase and sale of a drug referred to in Schedule G or N,[71] in such form or manner as the regulations may prescribe.

2. *Information to be recorded on prescription before dispensing.*[72]

Every person who dispenses a drug pursuant to a prescription is required to ensure that the following information is recorded on the prescription,

> (a) the name and address of the person for whom the drug is prescribed;
> (b) the name, strength (where applicable) and quantity of the prescribed drug;
> (c) the directions for use, as prescribed;
> (d) the name and address of the prescriber;
> (e) the identity of the manufacturer of the drug dispensed;
> (f) an identification number or other designation;

68　*Ibid.*, s. 149.
69　*Ibid.*, s. 166(1).
70　*Ibid.*, s. 153.
71　*Ibid.*, s. 117(2) which states that a reference to Schedule A, B, C, D, E, F, G, or N is a reference to such Schedule established by the regulations; in this regard, see R.R.O. 1990, Reg. 551 and amendments.
72　*Ibid.*, s. 156(1) and (2).

(g) the signature of the person dispensing the drug and, where different, also the signature of the person receiving a verbal description;
(h) the date on which the drug is dispensed;
(i) the price charged.

The records described above are required to be retained for not less than two years.

Prescriptions in a pharmacy that ceases to operate as a pharmacy are required to be delivered to the persons, or agents of the persons, who presented the prescription, or to another pharmacy that is reasonably readily available to such person or his or her agent, or failing either, to the College.[73]

3. *Information to be marked on container in which drug is dispensed pursuant to a prescription.*[74]

The container in which the drug is dispensed pursuant to a prescription is required to be marked with,

(a) the identification number that is on the prescription;
(b) the name, address and telephone number of the pharmacy in which the prescription is dispensed;
(c) the identification of the drug as to its name, its strength and its manufacturer, unless directed otherwise by the prescriber;
(d) the quantity where the drug dispensed is in solid oral dosage form;
(e) the name of the owner of the pharmacy;
(f) the date the prescription is dispensed;
(g) the name of the prescriber;
(h) the name of the person for whom it is prescribed;
(i) the directions for use as prescribed.

2.4.4 *Long-term Care Act, 1994* [75]

Executive Responsibility: Minister of Health

Statute Summary: The main thrust of the Act is to ensure that a wide

---

73 *Ibid.*, s. 157(2).
74 *Ibid.*, s. 156(3).
75 S.O. 1994, C. 26, at s. 1(a) and (b).

range of community services[76] is available to people in their own homes and in other community settings, as an alternative to institutional care, and to provide support and relief to relatives, friends, neighbors and others who provide care for a person in the home. The Act was only proclaimed in force on March 31, 1995.[77] These community services are delivered by service providers.[78] The Minister may enter into an agreement with a First

---

76 *Ibid.*, at s. 2(3) to (7) incl. "community services" means:
   1. Community support services (meal services; transportation services; caregiver support services; adult day programs; home maintenance and repair services; friendly visiting services; security checks or reassurance services; social or recreational services; providing prescribed equipment, supplies or other goods; and services prescribed as community support services);
   2. Homemaking services (housecleaning; doing laundry; ironing; mending; shopping; banking; paying bills; planning menus; preparing meals; caring for children; assisting a person with any of the foregoing activities; training a person to carry out or assist with any of the said activities; providing prescribed equipment, supplies or other goods; and services prescribed as homemaking services);
   3. Personal support services (personal hygiene activities; routine personal activities of living; assisting a person with any of the foregoing activities; training a person to carry out or assist with any of the said activities; providing prescribed equipment, supplies or other goods; and services prescribed as personal support services);
   4. Professional services (nursing services; occupational therapy services; physiotherapy services; social work services; speech language pathology services; dietetics services; training a person to provide any of the foregoing services; providing prescribed equipment, supplies or other goods; and services prescribed as professional services).
77 Except for ss. 71 and 72, which are to come into force on proclamation.
78 *Ibid.*, at s. 2(1). "service provider" means:

   (a) the Minister of Health, who may provide community services directly or by establishing facilities for provision of community services;
   (b) an approved agency (an agency approved under s. 5(1) of the Act;
   (c) a person who provides a community service with assistance from the Minister of Health in the following manner: (i) payments for community services provided by others; (ii) financial assistance for operating expenditures incurred or to be incurred by others to provide community services; (iii) financial assistance to agencies for capital expenditures incurred or to be incurred by them to provide community services; or (iv) grants and contributions to provide community services and for consultation, research and evaluation regarding community services.
   (d) a person who provides a community service purchased by an approved agency.

Nation,[79] a group of First Nations, or an aboriginal organization, to provide community services for their respective constituents.[80]

The Act defines what documents are to be included in a "personal record"[81] of each person who receives a community service; however, it does not impose a duty on any person to create records with respect to such recipients, apart from those set out below. Part VIII of the Act sets out in considerable detail the persons to whom disclosure of the "personal record" is permitted.

Provision is made in the Act for the review of complaints by affected persons of decisions with respect to the provision of community services in approved agencies; the decision of an approved agency may be appealed to the Health Services Appeal Board, whose decision is final and binding.[82]

If a person suffers personal injuries as a result of the negligence or other wrongful act or omission of another, the Minister of Health is subrogated to the right of the injured person to recover the cost incurred or that will probably be incurred for approved services[83] received or to be received by the injured person as a result of the injuries.[84] Payment by the

---

79   *Ibid.*, at s. 2(1). "First Nation" means the council of the band, as defined in the *Indian Act (Canada)*.
80   *Ibid.*, at s. 9.
81   *Ibid.*, at s. 2(1). "personal record" means, in relation to a person, all recorded information, regardless of physical form or characteristics, that

   (a)   relates to the person,
   (b)   is recorded in connection with an application by the person to a service provider for a community service or in connection with the provision of a community service to the person by a service provider, regardless of whether the information is recorded by the service provider or by others,
   (c)   is in the custody or under the control of the service provider;
   and, at s. 2(2), it is provided that, for greater certainty, but without restricting the generality of the definition of "personal record", a person's personal record includes his or her plan of service and all assessments of the person that are in the custody or under the control of the service provider, whether recorded by the service provider or by others.

82   *Ibid.*, see Part IX, "Complaints and Appeals".
83   *Ibid.*, at s. 59(1). "approved services" means facility services provided by a long-term care facility and community services provided by a service provider;
     "facility services" means accommodation, care, services, programs and goods provided to residents of long-term care facilities;
     "long-term care facility" means a nursing home under the *Nursing Homes Act*, an approved charitable home for the aged under the *Charitable Institutions Act* or a home under the *Homes for the Aged and Rest Homes Act*.
84   *Ibid.*, s. 59(2).

Minister of Health for approved services does not affect the right of the injured person to recover the cost of those services; and the injured person may recover the amounts so paid by the Minister in the same manner as if those amounts had been paid or are to be paid by him or her,[85] in which event the injured person is required to notify the Minister of the proceeding and include a claim on behalf of the Minister for recovery of such costs, unless the Minister directs otherwise in writing;[86] any amounts so recovered shall promptly be paid to the Minister of Finance.[87] A release or settlement by the injured person does not bind the Minister unless the Minister has approved it.[88] The Minister may bring a court proceeding in his or her own name or in the name of the injured person for the recovery of such costs.[89] A liability insurer is required to notify the Minister of negotiations for settlement of every claim for the cost of approved services,[90] and may pay to the Minister of Finance an amount referable to a claim for the cost of approved services, and the payment discharges the obligation of the liability insurer to pay the amount to the injured person.[91] The Minister is not an insurer for the purpose of section 22 of the *Motor Vehicle Accident Claims Act*, and may be awarded payment from the Motor Vehicle Accident Claims Fund.[92]

As of this writing, only one regulation under the Act has been enacted, O. Reg 179/95, pertaining to conveyance of assets.

Duty to Create: The statute imposes a duty to create the following records:

1. *Assessment and plan of service to be developed for eligible person applying for community services provided by an approved agency.*[93]

    When a person applies to an approved agency for any of the community services that the agency provides or arranges, the agency is required to,

    (a) assess the person's requirements;
    (b) determine the person's eligibility for the services that the person requires; and

---

85   *Ibid.*, s. 59(3).
86   *Ibid.*, s. 59(7).
87   *Ibid.*, s. 59(8).
88   *Ibid.*, s. 59(9).
89   *Ibid.*, s. 59(6).
90   *Ibid.*, s. 59(10).
91   *Ibid.*, s. 59(11).
92   *Ibid.*, s. 59(12).
93   *Ibid.*, s. 22(1).

(c) for each person who is determined to be eligible, develop a plan of service to be provided to the person.

2. *Review of requirements and evaluation of plan of service of person receiving community service provided by an approved agency.* [94]

If a person is receiving a community service provided or arranged by an approved agency, the agency is required to,

(a) review the person's requirements when appropriate, depending on the person's condition and circumstances; and
(b) evaluate the person's plan of service and revise it as necessary when the person's requirements change.

2.4.5 *Mental Health Act* [95]

Executive Responsibility: Minister of Health

Statute Summary: The Act regulates the activities of every psychiatric facility in Ontario; a psychiatric facility is defined[96] to mean a facility for the observation, care and treatment of persons suffering from mental disorder,[97] and designated as such by the regulations. There are approximately 100 psychiatric facilities, identified by the regulations, located in population centres throughout the province. Advances in diagnosis and treatment of mental illness have brought about a better understanding of the subject; persons with mental illness are being diagnosed earlier and treatment is more effective than ever. Some of the advances in mental health services include:

- the introduction of modern chemotherapy, including major anti-psychotic and anti-depressant drugs;
- treatment in the community, with hospitalization as a last resort; this has significantly reduced the numbers of patients in psychiatric institutions;
- psychiatric services in Ontario now offer rehabilitation services, daycare, counselling services, residential accommodation, approved homes, sheltered workshops and volunteer programs;

---

94 *Ibid.*, s. 22(2).
95 R.S.O. 1990, c. M.7.
96 *Ibid.*, s. 1.
97 *Ibid.*, s. 1. "mental disorder" means any disease or disability of the mind.

- rights advisors are available in psychiatric facilities to advise patients of their rights.

There has been a steady growth in the accumulation of patient health records, with the result that stricter control over access has been made necessary through legislative change.

A person who is believed to be in need of the observation, care and treatment provided in a psychiatric facility may be admitted thereto as an informal or voluntary patient upon the recommendation of a physician. A voluntary patient consents to the admission, while an informal patient is admitted with the consent of another person who is entitled to give or refuse consent to treatment on his or her behalf under the *Health Care Consent Act, 1996*.[98] An involuntary patient is one who is admitted as a patient in a psychiatric facility on the authority of a certificate of involuntary admission, made by the attending physician if he or she is of the opinion that the person is suffering from a mental disorder of a nature or quality that likely will result in,

1. serious bodily harm to the person;
2. serious bodily harm to another person; or
3. imminent and serious physical impairment of the person.

An involuntary patient may be detained in a psychiatric facility for not more than two weeks under a certificate of involuntary admission; for not more than one additional month under a first certificate of renewal; for two additional months under a second certificate of renewal; and for three additional months under a third or subsequent certificate of renewal.[99]

A patient in a psychiatric facility is required to be discharged from a psychiatric facility when he or she is no longer in need of the observation, care and treatment provided therein.[100]

Forthwith on a patient's admission to a psychiatric facility, a physician must examine him or her to determine whether the patient is capable of managing property. If the physician determines that the patient is not capable of managing property, he or she is required to issue a certificate of incapacity, which is transmitted to the Public Guardian and Trustee, who will assume management of the patient's property.[101]

Much of the Act is taken up with the rights of patients in psychiatric facilities regarding such matters as access to the patient's medical records,

---

98 *Ibid.*, s. 1.
99 *Ibid.*, s. 20(4).
100 *Ibid.*, s. 34.
101 *Ibid.*, s. 54.

treatment decisions, and applications for review of the patient's status. The Act directs that certain matters of review be determined by the Board;[102] the matters of review over which the Board has jurisdiction include:

1. an application by a child who is 12 years of age or older but less than 16 years of age, who is an informal patient in a psychiatric facility and who has not so applied within the preceding three months, to inquire into whether the child needs observation, care and treatment in the psychiatric facility;[103]
2. an application by the officer in charge,[104] upon the advice of the attending physician, for authority to withhold all or part of the clinical record from a patient who is mentally competent;[105]
3. an application by a patient determined to be not mentally competent for the purpose of examining and copying his clinical record or consenting to the release of his clinical record to third parties, to inquire into whether the patient is not mentally competent;[106]
4. an application by a patient who is at least 16 years old, who has not appointed a representative to examine and copy his clinical record or to consent to the release of his clinical record to third parties and who is not mentally competent to do so, for the appointment of a representative for the said purposes;[107]
5. an application by an involuntary patient, or any person on his or her behalf, to inquire into his or her status as an involuntary patient;[108]
6. an application by a patient in respect of whom a certificate of incapacity has been issued to review the issue of his or her capacity to manage property.[109]

The Act applies to every psychiatric facility[110] in Ontario.

---

102 *Ibid.*, at s. 1. "Board" means the Consent and Capacity Board continued under the *Health Care Consent Act, 1996*.
103 *Ibid.*, s. 13.
104 *Ibid.*, at s. 1. "officer in charge" means the officer who is responsible for the administration and management of a psychiatric facility.
105 *Ibid.*, s. 36.4.
106 *Ibid.*, s. 36(14).
107 *Ibid.*, s. 36(2).
108 *Ibid.*, s. 39(1).
109 *Ibid.*, s. 60.
110 *Ibid.*, s. 1. "psychiatric facility" means a facility for the observation, care and treatment of persons suffering from mental disorder, and designated as such by the regulations.

Duty to Create, Maintain & Preserve Health Records 45

Duty to Create: The statute imposes the following duty to create records:

1. *Written report by senior physician as to mental condition of a person, to be made to a judge where the person has been ordered to attend psychiatric facility.*[111]

   The senior physician[112] is required to report in writing to a judge as to the mental condition of a person in the following circumstances:

   (a) where the judge, having reason to believe that a person who appears before him or her charged with or convicted of an offence suffers from a mental disorder, has ordered the person to attend a psychiatric facility for examination; or
   (b) where the judge, having reason to believe that a person in custody who appears before him or her charged with an offence suffers from mental disorder, has by order remanded that person for admission as a patient to a psychiatric facility for a period of not more than two months.

2. (1) *Application for psychiatric assessment by a physician of a person believed to be suffering from a mental disorder, which application is authority to detain the person for seven days in a psychiatric facility for observation.*[113]
   (2) *Written notice of the application to be given by the attending physician to the person who is the subject thereof.*[114]
   (3) *Certificate of involuntary admission to be completed and filed by the attending physician if he or she believes the person who is the subject thereof suffers from mental disorder.*[115]

   Where a physician examines a person and has reasonable cause to believe that the person,

   (a) has threatened or attempted or is threatening or attempting to cause bodily harm to himself or herself;
   (b) has behaved or is behaving violently towards another person or

---

111 *Ibid.*, ss. 21, 22 and 24.
112 *Ibid.*, at s. 1. "senior physician" means the physician responsible for the clinical services in a psychiatric facility.
113 *Ibid.*, s. 15.
114 *Ibid.*, s. 38.1.
115 *Ibid.*, s. 20(1).

has caused or is causing another person to fear bodily harm from him or her; or

(c) has shown or is showing a lack of competence to care for himself or herself,

and if in addition the physician is of the opinion that the person is apparently suffering from mental disorder of a nature or quality that likely will result in,

(d) serious bodily harm to the person;
(e) serious bodily harm to another person; or
(f) imminent and serious physical impairment of the person,

the physician may make application in the prescribed form for a psychiatric assessment of the person, setting out clearly:

(i) that the physician who signs the application personally examined the person who is the subject of the application and made careful inquiry into all of the facts necessary for him or her to form his or her opinion as to the nature and quality of the mental disorder of the person;

(ii) the facts upon which he or she formed his or her opinion as to the nature and quality of the mental disorder;

(iii) the distinction in the application between the facts observed by him or her and the facts communicated to him or her by others; and

(iv) the date on which he or she examined the person who is the subject of the application.

*The application is not effective unless it is signed by the physician within seven days after he or she examined the person who is the subject of the examination.

An application so completed is sufficient authority for seven days from and including the day on which it is signed by the physician to any person to take the person who is the subject of the application in custody to a psychiatric facility forthwith, and to detain him or her there, and to restrain, observe and examine him or her in the facility for not more than 72 hours.

The attending physician[116] of a person who is the subject of an application for assessment is required to promptly give the person a written no-

---

116 *Ibid.*, at s. 1(1). "attending physician" means the physician to whom responsibility for the observation, care and treatment of a patient has been assigned.

tice of the application or order,[117] which shall state the reasons for the detention and shall indicate that the person has the right to retain and instruct counsel without delay.

The attending physician, after observing and examining a person who is the subject of an application for assessment, is required to:

(a) release the person, if he or she is of the opinion that the person is not in need of the treatment provided in a psychiatric facility;
(b) admit the person as an informal[118] or voluntary patient, if the attending physician is of the opinion that the person is suffering from mental disorder of such a nature or quality that the person is in need of the treatment provided in a psychiatric facility and is suitable for admission as an informal or voluntary patient; or
(c) admit the person as an involuntary patient[119] by completing and filing with the officer in charge a certificate of involuntary admission if the attending physician is of the opinion both that the person is suffering from mental disorder of a nature or quality that likely will result in serious bodily harm to the person or to another person, or will result in imminent and serious physical impairment of the person, unless the person remains in the custody of a psychiatric facility and that the person is not suitable for admission as an informal or voluntary patient.[120]

If the attending physician has not so acted within 72 hours of detention in the psychiatric facility of the person who is the subject of the application, the officer in charge of the facility is required to release the person.[121]

3. *Completing and filing of certificate of involuntary admission by attending physician to change status of informal or voluntary patient to that of involuntary patient.*[122]

The attending physician may change the status of an informal or voluntary patient to that of an involuntary patient by completing and filing with the

---

117 *Ibid.*, s. 38.1.
118 *Ibid.*, at s. 1(1). "informal patient" means a person who is a patient in a psychiatric facility, having been admitted with the consent of another person under s. 24 of the *Health Care Consent Act, 1996*.
119 *Ibid.*, at s. 1(1). "involuntary patient" means a person who is detained in a psychiatric facility under a certificate of involuntary admission or a certificate of renewal.
120 *Ibid.*, s. 20(1).
121 *Ibid.*, s. 20(3).
122 *Ibid.*, ss. 19 and 20(5).

officer in charge a certificate of involuntary admission, but only after he or she has examined the patient and is of the opinion both,

> (a) that the patient is suffering from mental disorder of a nature or quality that likely will result in,
>
>> (i) serious bodily harm to the patient,
>> (ii) serious bodily harm to another person, or
>> (iii) imminent and serious physical impairment of the patient, unless the patient remains in the custody of a psychiatric facility; and
>
> (b) that the patient is not suitable for admission or continuation as an informal or voluntary patient.

4. *Completion of prescribed form by attending physician to permit involuntary patient whose authorized period of detention has not expired to continue as informal or voluntary patient.*[123]

An involuntary patient whose authorized period of detention has not expired may be continued as an informal or voluntary patient upon completion of the prescribed form by the attending physician.

5. *Written report of examination by senior physician of psychiatric facility of person charged or convicted of an offence, ordered to be examined by judge who believes he or she suffers from mental disorder.*[124]

Where a judge has reason to believe that a person who appears before him or her charged with or convicted of an offence suffers from mental disorder, the judge may order the person to attend a psychiatric facility for examination, following which the senior physician is required to report in writing to the judge as to the mental condition of the person.

6. *Written report of examination by senior physician of psychiatric facility of person in custody charged with an offence, ordered remanded by a judge for admission as patient to a psychiatric facility for period of not more than two months.*[125]

Where a judge has reason to believe that a person in custody who appears before him or her charged with an offence suffers from mental disorder, the judge may by order remand that person for admission as a patient to a psychiatric facility for a period of not more than two months, before

---

123 *Ibid.*, s. 20(7).
124 *Ibid.*, s. 21.
125 *Ibid.*, s. 22(1).

the expiration of which the senior physician is required to report in writing to the judge as to the mental condition of the person.

7. *Written notice in prescribed form by attending physician to patient determined to be not competent to appoint a representative, setting out powers and responsibilities of representative.*[126]

As soon as possible after determining that a patient who is at least 16 years old and has not appointed a representative under section 36.1 of the Act is not competent to appoint a representative, the attending physician is required to inform him or her of the right to apply to the Board for the appointment of a representative and shall give him or her a notice in the prescribed form setting out the powers and responsibilities of a representative.

8. *Written notice to be given to patient by attending physician who completes certificate of involuntary admission or certificate of renewal.*[127]

An attending physician who completes a certificate of involuntary admission or a certificate of renewal is required to promptly give the patient written notice and shall also promptly notify a rights adviser;[128] the written notice shall inform the patient:

(a) of the reasons for the detention;
(b) that the patient is entitled to a hearing before the Board; and
(c) that the patient has the right to retain and instruct counsel without delay.

9. *Written notice to be given to patient by physician who determines the patient is not mentally competent to examine a clinical record or consent to its disclosure to other persons.*[129]

A physician who determines that a patient is not mentally competent[130] to examine a clinical record or to give or refuse consent to its disclosure to other persons, is required to promptly give the patient a written

---

126 *Ibid.*, s. 36.2(2).
127 *Ibid.*, s. 38(1) and (2).
128 *Ibid.*, at s. 1(1). "rights adviser" means a person, or a member of a category of persons, designated by a psychiatric facility or by the Minister to perform the functions of a rights adviser under the Act in the psychiatric facility, but does not include a person involved in the direct clinical care of the patient to whom the rights advice is to be given.
129 *Ibid.*, s. 38(4).
130 *Ibid.*, at s. 1(1). "mentally competent" means having the ability to understand the subject-matter in respect of which consent is requested and able to appreciate the consequences of giving or withholding consent.

notice of the fact that indicates the patient is entitled to a hearing before the Board, and shall also promptly notify a rights adviser.

10. *Written notice of application to be given by attending physician to a person who is subject of application for assessment by Minister's order, authorized where Minister has reasonable cause to believe such person may be brought into Ontario suffering from mental disorder.*[131]

Where the Minister of Health has reasonable cause to believe that there may come or be brought into Ontario a person suffering from mental disorder of a nature or quality that likely will result in serious bodily harm to the person or to another person unless the person is placed in the custody of a psychiatric facility, the Minister by an order in the prescribed form may authorize any one to take the person in custody to a psychiatric facility, and the order is authority to admit, detain, restrain, observe and examine the person in the psychiatric facility. The Act does not impose any limit on the period of time the patient shall remain in the psychiatric facility under a Minister's order. The attending physician of a person who is the subject of an application for assessment is required to promptly give the person a written notice of the application or order, which shall state the reasons for the detention and shall indicate that the person has the right to retain and instruct counsel without delay.

11. *Statement of use of restraint on a patient to be entered in patient's clinical record.*[132]

The use of restraint on a patient is required to be clearly documented in the patient's clinical record by the entry of a statement that the patient was restrained, a description of the means of restraint and a description of the behaviour of the patient that required that the patient be restrained or continue to be restrained. Where a chemical restraint is used, the entry shall include a statement of the chemical employed, the method of administration and the dosage.

12. (1) *Note by physician, to be included in the patient's clinical record, of determination with reasons whether patient capable of managing property.*[133]
    (2) *Certificate of incapacity in prescribed form to be issued by physician on determining patient not capable of managing property.*[134]

---

131 *Ibid.*, ss. 32 and 38.1.
132 *Ibid.*, s. 53.
133 *Ibid.*, s. 54(1), (2) and (3).
134 *Ibid.*, s. 54(4).

Forthwith on a patient's admission to a psychiatric facility, a physician is required to examine him or her to determine whether the patient is capable of managing property. A patient's attending physician may examine him or her at any time to determine whether the patient is capable of managing property. After any such examination, the physician shall note his or her determination, with reasons, in the patient's clinical record.

If the physician determines that the patient is not capable of managing property, he or she is required to issue a certificate of incapacity in the prescribed form, and the officer in charge shall transmit the certificate to the Public Guardian and Trustee.

The foregoing does not apply if the patient's property is under guardianship under the Substitute Decisions Act, 1992.[135]

13. *Notice of continuance to be issued by attending physician on determining patient not capable of managing property, following examination of patient within 21 days before discharge from psychiatric facility.*[136]

Within 21 days before the discharge from the psychiatric facility of a patient with respect to whom a certificate of incapacity has been issued, the attending physician is required to examine him or her to determine whether the patient is capable of managing property. If the attending physician determines that the patient is not capable of managing property, he or she is required to issue a notice of continuance in the prescribed form, and the officer in charge shall transmit the notice to the Public Guardian and Trustee.

14. *Written notice to be given by attending physician to incapable person admitted to psychiatric facility, when physician proposes treatment of a mental disorder.*[137]

If a person who has been admitted to a psychiatric facility as a patient is 14 years old or older and if the persons attending physician proposes treatment of a mental disorder of the person and finds that the person is incapable with respect to the treatment within the meaning of the *Health Care Consent Act, 1996*, the attending physician is required to ensure that:

1. the person is promptly given a written notice indicating that he or she

---

[135] *Ibid.*, s. 54(6).
[136] *Ibid.*, s. 57.
[137] R.R.O. 1990, Reg. 741, as amended by O. Reg. 103/96; the section does not apply to exceptions noted at subs. 14(5).

has been found by the attending physician to be incapable with respect to the treatment; and
2. a rights adviser is promptly notified of the finding of incapacity.

2.4.6 Vital Statistics Act [138]

Executive Responsibility: The Minister of Consumer and Commercial Relations or such other member of the Executive Council to whom administration of the Act is assigned acts as the Registrar General under the Act.

Statute Summary: The Registrar General is responsible for maintaining a uniform system of registration of births, marriages, deaths, still-births, adoptions, divorces and changes of name in Ontario, as well as enforcement of the provisions of the Act.

Duty to Create: The statute imposes the following duty to create records:

1. *Registered deaths to be classified by Registrar according to classification of diseases in regulations.* [139]

The Registrar General [140] is required to cause all deaths registered under the Act to be classified according to the classification of diseases adopted by reference in the regulations.

2. *Medical certificate to be completed by legally qualified medical practitioner in attendance at still-birth, or a coroner, of cause of still-birth.* [141]

The legally qualified medical practitioner in attendance at a still-birth in Ontario or, where none is in attendance, a coroner is required to com-

---

138 R.S.O. 1990, c. V.4.
139 *Ibid.*, s. 3(3).
140 *Ibid.*, at s. 1. "Registrar General" means the Minister of Consumer and Commercial Relations or such other member of the Executive Council to whom the administration or this Act is assigned.
141 *Ibid.*, s. 18 (this section is repealed by S.O. 1994, c. 27, s. 102 (15), to come into force on proclamation; at this writing, it has not been proclaimed.)
At s. 1, "still-birth" is defined as the complete expulsion or extraction from its mother of a product of conception either after the twentieth week of pregnancy or after the product of conception has attained the weight of 500 grams or more, and where after such expulsion or extraction there is no breathing, beating of the heart, pulsation of the umbilical cord or movement of voluntary muscle.

plete a medical certificate in the prescribed form of the cause of the still-birth and to deliver it to the funeral director in charge of the body. The funeral director must then deliver the medical certificate, with other prescribed documents, to the division registrar of the proper registration division, who, if he or she is satisfied as to the correctness and sufficiency of the documents, shall register the still-birth by signing the medical certificate and other prescribed documents.

3. *Medical certificate of death in prescribed form to be completed and signed by legally qualified medical practitioner forthwith after the death of a person, stating cause of death.*[142]

Except in the case of an untoward death which must be reported to the coroner or a police officer pursuant to section 10 of the *Coroners Act*,[143] any legally qualified medical practitioner who has been in attendance during the last illness of a deceased person or who has sufficient knowledge of the last illness is required to forthwith after the death complete and sign a medical certificate of death in the prescribed form, stating the cause of death, and to deliver the medical certificate to the funeral director or other person in charge of the body.

2.4.7 *Workers' Compensation Act;* [144] *Workplace Safety and Insurance Act, 1997* [145]

The *Workplace Safety and Insurance Act, 1997*, replaces the *Workers' Compensation Act* with respect to accidents occurring after January 1st, 1998; accidents occurring before that date continue to be governed by the *Workers' Compensation Act*. Both statutes are considered below.

Workers' Compensation Act

Statute Summary: The declared purposes of the Act are[146]

1. to provide fair compensation to workers who sustain personal injury arising out of and in the course of their employment or who suffer from occupational disease and to their survivors and dependants;

---

142 *Ibid.*, s. 21(3). (This section is repealed by S.O. 1994, c. 27, s. 102(17), to come into force on proclamation at this writing, it has not been proclaimed.)
143 R.S.O. 1990, c. C.37.
144 R.S.O. 1990, c. W.11.
145 S.O. 1997, c. 16, Sched. A.
146 *Ibid.*, s. 1.

2. to provide health care benefits to those workers;
3. to provide for rehabilitation services and programs to facilitate the workers' return to work;
4. to provide for rehabilitation programs for their survivors;
5. to prevent or reduce the occurrence of injuries and occupational diseases at work;
6. to promote health and safety in workplaces.

Where personal injury is caused to a worker by accident arising out of and in the course of any employment to which the Act applies, the worker and the worker's dependants are entitled to benefits in the manner and to the extent provided therein. The benefits are to compensate the worker for, among other things:

- loss of earnings arising from disability,[147] including temporary total disability and temporary partial disability arising from injury.[148]
- non-economic loss and future loss of earnings arising from permanent impairment.[149]

In addition, benefits are available to dependants[150] of the worker.

Employers listed in Schedule 1 of the Act are liable to contribute to an accident fund, from which benefits are paid, and are not liable individually to pay compensation; whereas employers listed in Schedule 2 of the Act are liable individually to pay compensation and health care.[151]

The Act is administered by the Workers Compensation Board, which has the power to determine, among other things:

1. whether any industry or any part thereof falls within any of the classes included in Schedule 1 or 2;
2. the existence of, and degree of, disability or impairment by reason of any injury;

---

147 *Ibid.*, s. 1(1). "disability", in relation to an injured worker, means the loss of earning capacity of the worker that results from an injury.
148 *Ibid.*, ss. 36 and 37.
149 *Ibid.*, ss. 42 and 43. At s. 1(1). "permanent impairment", in relation to an injured worker, means impairment that continues to exist after maximum medical rehabilitation of the worker has been achieved.
150 *Ibid.*, at s. 1(1). "dependants" mean such of the members of the family of a worker as were wholly or partly dependent upon the worker's earnings at the time of his or her death or who but for the incapacity due to the accident would have been so dependent.
151 *Ibid.*, ss. 5 and 6.

3. the permanence of impairment by reason of any injury;
4. the amount of average earnings and the net average earnings of a worker;
5. the future loss of earnings by reason of any injury;
6. the existence of status, in relation to the worker, to claim;
7. the question whether personal injury or death has been caused by accident;
8. the question whether an accident arose out of and in the course of an employment.[152]

The Appeals Tribunal has exclusive jurisdiction to hear, determine and dispose of, among other things, all appeals from decisions, orders or rulings of the Board respecting the provision of health care, vocational rehabilitation or entitlement to compensation or benefits under the Act.[153]

The provisions of the Act are in lieu of all rights and rights of action, statutory or otherwise, to which a worker or members of his or her family are or may be entitled against the worker's employer.[154]

No employer listed in Schedule 1 and no worker of such an employer or dependant of such worker has a right of action for damages against any employer listed in Schedule 1, or any executive officer or any director or any worker of such employer, for an injury for which benefits are payable under the Act, where the workers of both employers were in the course of their employment at the time of the happening of the injury.[155] The worker of an employer in Schedule 2 or dependant of such worker or the employer of such worker maintaining a subrogated claim on behalf of the worker may not recover from the employer of the worker in Schedule 2 or an executive officer or director thereof any damages, contribution or indemnity caused by the fault or negligence of any of them.[156]

Where an accident occurs in circumstances where a worker or his or her dependant may have a cause of action against some person other than his or her employer, the worker or his or her dependants, if entitled to benefits, must elect whether to accept such benefits or to proceed with action against such other person.[157] If the worker elects to claim benefits, the employer (if the employer is individually liable to pay) and the Board (if compensation is payable out of the accident fund) are subrogated to the rights of the worker or his or her dependants.[158]

---

152 *Ibid.*, s. 69(2).
153 *Ibid.*, s. 86(1).
154 *Ibid.*, s. 16.
155 *Ibid.*, s. 10(9).
156 *Ibid.*, s. 10(12).
157 *Ibid.*, s. 10(1).
158 *Ibid.*, s. 10(4).

Duty to Create: The statute imposes the following duty to create records:

1. *Report of medical assessment by medical practitioner of worker entitled to compensation for non-economic loss.*[159]

   A worker who suffers permanent impairment as a result of an injury and claims compensation for non-economic loss is required to undergo a medical assessment after maximum medical rehabilitation is achieved. The medical practitioner appointed to conduct the medical assessment is required to promptly forward a copy of the medical assessment to the Board. The Board is required to send a copy of the medical assessment to the worker and to the employer who employed the worker on the date of the injury. A worker, an employer or the Board may, within 45 days after the medical assessment is sent, require a second medical assessment of the worker. The Board is required to send a copy of the second medical assessment to the worker and the employer.

2. *Report of medical assessment by medical practitioner on redetermination of degree of worker's permanent impairment on claim for non-economic loss.*[160]

   Not earlier than 12 months after the most recent decision by the Board respecting the degree of permanent impairment of the worker, the worker may apply to the Board for a redetermination of the degree of the worker's impairment,

   (a) if the Board has determined that the worker has a permanent impairment; and
   (b) if the worker has suffered a significant deterioration of condition that was not anticipated at the time of the most recent medical assessment under this section.

   The procedure to be followed for such second determination is the same as outlined for an initial determination in item 1., above, with modifications as the circumstances require.

3. *Report in respect of a worker to be furnished by specified persons as required by the Board.*[161]

   Every physician, surgeon, hospital official or other person attending, consulted respecting, or having the care of, any worker is required to fur-

---

159 *Ibid.*, s. 42.
160 *Ibid.*, s. 42(21) to (23).
161 *Ibid.*, s. 51(1).

nish to the Board from time to time such reports as may be required by the Board in respect of such worker.

4. *Report containing information concerning a worker to be provided by health professional who receives a request from worker or employer.*[162]

A health professional[163] who receives a request from a worker or the employer is required to provide each of them and the Board with a report containing the prescribed information, provided:

(a) the worker consents; and
(b) the prescribed requirements, if any, are satisfied.

Every such report is deemed to be a privileged communication of the person making it, and unless it is proved that it was made maliciously, is not admissible as evidence or subject to production in any court in an action or proceeding against the person providing it.

5. *Report of compulsory medical examination of worker by medical practitioner's at request of the chair or a vice chair of Appeals Tribunal.*[164]

The Appeals Tribunal has power to authorize the chair or a vice-chair to inquire into applications by way of appeal from decisions, orders or rulings of the Board respecting the provision of health care, vocational rehabilitation or entitlement to compensation or benefits under the Act, to determine whether an issue involves a decision of the Board upon a medical report or opinion and, if such is the case, the person making the inquiry may, before the appeal is heard by the Appeals Tribunal, require that the worker submit to an examination by one or more medical practitioners appointed under section 87(1) of the Act, who is required to report, in writing, to the Appeals Tribunal thereon.

Upon receiving the said medical report, the Appeal Tribunal is required to send a copy thereof to the parties to the appeal for the purpose of receiving their submissions thereon.

---

162 *Ibid.*, s. 51(2), (3), and (5).
163 *Ibid.*, at s. 51(6). "health professional" means a member of the College of a health profession as defined in the *Regulated Health Professions Act, 1991*.
164 *Ibid.*, s. 87(4) and (5).

Workplace Safety and Insurance Act, 1997

Statute Summary: The *Workplace Safety and Insurance Act, 1997*, replaces the *Workers' Compensation Act* with respect to accidents occurring after January 1st, 1998. The underlying purpose of the new Act remains the same, to provide benefits to workers and to the survivors of deceased workers who sustain personal injury in the course of their employment or suffer from an occupational disease, although new emphasis is placed on injury and disease prevention. The Workers Compensation Board is continued under the name Workplace Safety and Insurance Board,[165] and the Workers' Compensation Appeals Tribunal becomes the Workplace Safety and Insurance Appeals Tribunal.[166]

A worker who sustains a personal injury by accident arising out of and in the course of his or her employment is entitled to benefits under the insurance plan;[167] the benefits are to compensate the worker for, among other things:

- mental stress that is an acute reaction to a sudden and unexpected traumatic event arising out of and in the course of his or her employment.[168]
- chronic pain as defined in the regulations.[169]
- suffering from and impairment by an occupational disease that occurs due to the nature of one or more employments in which the worker was engaged.[170]
- loss of earnings as a result of the injury.[171]
- non-economic loss, if a worker's injury results in permanent impairment.[172]

In addition, benefits are available to dependants of a worker and to survivors of a deceased worker.

A worker employed by an employer listed in Schedule 1, the workers survivors and a Schedule 1 employer are not entitled to commence an action in respect of the worker's injury or disease against a Schedule 1 employer, or a director, executive officer or worker employed by any Schedule 1 employer.[173] A worker employed by an employer listed in

---

165 *Ibid.*, s. 159(1).
166 *Ibid.*, s. 173(1).
167 *Ibid.*, s. 13(1).
168 *Ibid.*, s. 13(5).
169 *Ibid.*, s. 14.
170 *Ibid.*, s. 15.
171 *Ibid.*, s. 43(1).
172 *Ibid.*, s. 46(1).
173 *Ibid.*, s. 28(1).

Schedule 2 and the worker's survivors are not entitled to commence an action in respect of the worker's injury or disease against the worker's Schedule 2 employer, or a director, executive officer or worker employed by the worker's Schedule 2 employer.[174]

When a worker or a survivor of a deceased worker is entitled to benefits under the insurance plan with respect to an injury or disease and is also entitled to commence an action against a person in respect of the injury or disease, the worker or survivor is required to elect whether to claim the benefits or to commence the action, in default of which he or she shall be deemed, in the absence of evidence to the contrary, to have elected not to receive benefits under the insurance plan.[175] If the worker or survivor elects to claim benefits under the insurance plan and if the worker is employed by a Schedule 1 employer or the deceased worker was so employed, the Board is subrogated to the rights of the worker or survivor in respect of the action.[176] A similar provision exists with respect to a worker or deceased worker who is or was employed by a Schedule 2 employer.[177]

Duty to Create: The statute imposes the following duty to create records:

(1.1) *Prescribed information to be given by health professional treating the worker to the Board concerning functional abilities.*[178]

When requested to do so by an injured worker or the employer, a health professional[179] treating the worker is required to give the Board, the worker and the employer such information as may be prescribed concerning the worker's functional abilities. The required information must be provided on the prescribed form.

(2.1) *Report of physician selected to perform examination of worker and assessment of extent of permanent impairment, to be given to the Board.*[180]

On a determination by the Board of the degree of permanent impairment suffered by a worker, the physician who is selected to perform a medical assessment of the worker after he or she reaches maximum medi-

---

174 *Ibid.*, s. 28(2).
175 *Ibid.*, s. 30(1) to (6), incl.
176 *Ibid.*, s. 30(10).
177 *Ibid.*, s. 30(11).
178 *Ibid.*, s. 37(3).
179 *Ibid.*, s. 2(1). "health professional" means a member of the College of a health profession as defined in the *Regulated Health Professions Act, 1991*; see list at 1.1, *supra*.
180 *Ibid.*, s. 47(5), (6), (7), (8), (9), (10) and (11).

cal recovery is required to examine the worker and assess the extent of his or her permanent impairment. When performing the assessment, the physician shall consider any reports by the worker's treating health professional. The physician is required to promptly give the Board a report on the assessment, and the Board shall give a copy of the report to the worker and to the employer who employed him or her on the date of the injury. The Board may request a physician to perform a second assessment of the worker if the Board considers the initial assessment or the report on it to be incomplete or inaccurate.The worker is entitled to request a redetermination of the degree of permanent impairment after 12 months have elapsed since the most recent determination by the Board, in which event the procedures that applied on the initial assessment with respect to the provision of a medical report apply with respect to the redetermination.

(3.1)   *Report of health professional to the Appeals Tribunal of examination of a worker, when an issue on an appeal concerns the Board's decision on a health report or opinion.*[181]

If the chair or a vice-chair of the Appeals Tribunal determines that an issue on an appeal concerns the Board's decision on a health report or opinion, the chair or vice-chair may require the worker to submit to an examination by a health professional (selected by the chair or vice-chair) and the worker shall do so. The health professional called upon by the Appeals Tribunal for assistance[182] is required to give the Appeals Tribunal a written report on his or her examination of the worker in question, and the tribunal shall give a copy of the report to the parties for the purpose of receiving their submissions on it.

---

181 *Ibid.*, s. 134(6) and (7).
182 *Ibid.*, at s. 134(1), the chair of the Appeals Tribunal may establish a list of health professionals upon whom the tribunal may call for assistance in determining matters of fact in a proceeding; at subpara. 4, the Appeals Tribunal may call upon a health professional on the list for assistance at any time before or during a proceeding.

Chapter 3

Access to Health Records

by John Haydon, Q.C., B.A., LL.B.

3.1 Confidentiality of Health Records
3.2 Patient's Right to Access Own Personal Medical Records
3.3 Waiver of Right to Access Personal Medical Records by the Patient
3.4 Canadian Health Record Association
    3.4.1 Principles and Guidelines
    3.4.2 Position Statement re Patient Access to Health Records
    3.4.3 Code of Practice for Safeguarding Health Information
3.5 Legislation Regarding Access to Documents Containing Personal Medical Information
    3.5.1 *Long Term Care Act, 1994*

3.1 CONFIDENTIALITY OF HEALTH RECORDS

The right in law to confidentiality of an individual's personal medical information circumscribes the duty imposed on others to preserve it. This duty was early recognized as a societal *caveat* in the Hippocratic oath, which required of medical men:

> Whatever, in connection with my professional service, or not in connection with it, I see or hear, in the life of men, which ought not to be spoken of abroad, I will not divulge, as reckoning that all such should be kept secret.

The Supreme Court of Canada recognized directly the right of a patient to have records containing personal medical information treated confidentially in the case of *Halls v. Mitchell*:

> Nobody would dispute that a secret so acquired [by a medical practitioner in the course of his practice] is the secret of the patient, and, normally, is under

his control, and not under that of the doctor. *Prima facie*, the patient has the right to require that the secret shall not be divulged; and that right is absolute, unless there is some paramount reason which overrides it. Such reasons may arise, no doubt, from the existence of facts which bring into play overpowering considerations connected with public justice; and there may be cases in which reasons connected with the safety of individuals or of the public, physical or moral, would be sufficiently cogent to supersede or qualify the obligations *prima facie* imposed by the confidential relation.

. . .

It is, perhaps, not easy to exaggerate the value attached by the community as a whole to the existence of a competently trained and honourable medical profession; and it is just as important that patients, in consulting a physician, shall feel that they may impart the facts touching their bodily health, without fear that their confidence may be abused to their disadvantage.[1]

The principle of confidentiality in the doctor-patient relationship was recently reviewed and affirmed by the Ontario Court (General Division) in *Wells (Litigation Guardian of) v. Paramsothy*.[2]

Furthermore, a breach of confidentiality may be actionable in circumstances where it could reasonably have been anticipated that the release of information would occasion compensable loss to a person. Many statutes in Ontario relating to health matters expressly state that a patient's health records are to be kept confidential by the individual or institution possessing them, usually subject to exceptions noted. Regulations made pursuant to the health profession Acts make it an act of professional misconduct for the member of a College to give information about a patient except with the informed consent of the patient or client or his or her authorized representative.[3]

An interesting wrinkle on the issue of a patient's interest in his or her health records was added in the case of *Josephine V. Wilson Family Trust v. Swartz*,[4] in which Blair J. had to deal with the competing interest of a creditor which sought to enforce its security interest under a duly registered general security agreement over the business assets of a dentist who had made an assignment in bankruptcy. The Court had to decide, among other things, whether the creditor's right to enforce its security could extend to the seizure and sale of the dental charts and patients' records as part of the sale of the goodwill of the dentist's practice. Blair J. considered

---

1 [1928] S.C.R. 125, [1928] 2 D.L.R. 97 (S.C.C.).
2 (1996), 32 O.R. (3d) 452 (Ont. Div. Ct.), leave to appeal refused (1997), 32 O.R. (3d) 452n (Ont. H.C.). See Ch. 4 at 4.3.3, Examination for Discovery of a Non-Party, Case Law, below, for case summary.
3 See Ch. 1 at 1.3, *supra*, for discussion of the health profession Acts.
4 (1993), 16 O.R. (3d) 268, 23 C.B.R. (3d) 88 (Ont. Gen. Div.).

as well-established the principle that a patient's medical records prepared by a physician, or a dentist for that matter, are the physical property of the physician, but that the information in the medical records "belongs" to the patient "in the sense that it is confidential and the patient is entitled to have access to and copy all of the information in the medical file, in the absence of an order to the contrary",[5] citing *McInerney v. MacDonald*.[6] He endorsed the characterization of the patient's interest in such information by Mr. Justice La Forest in the *McInerney* case through the fiduciary concept as "a trust-like 'beneficial interest'", and concluded:

> In my view, while the dental records may be the physical property of the dentist, they are property affixed with an inseverable trust of confidentiality in favour of the patient. Just as trust property is not property belonging to a bankrupt, the dental records are not property which belongs to the dentist for purposes of pledging as part of his or her 'undertaking, assets and property'.[7]
>
> . . .
>
> . . . there is a public interest in preserving and maintaining the doctor's ability to continue to have access to the information contained in the records in performance of the 'continuing care' obligations imposed by the regulations. These public interest factors override the business interest in facilitating financing by having the 'physical property' of the records available for that purpose.[8]

The matter was more recently considered by the Ontario Court of Appeal in *Axelrod, Re*[9] on appeal from an order of Ground J. permitting a creditor to enforce a security interest in dental records, patient files and records, given as security by a dental surgeon under a general security agreement. In this case, the security agreement specifically applied to the patient files, unlike *Swartz* where the issue in part was whether the general security agreement extended to cover the patient's charts and records. Ground J. had disagreed with the conclusion of Blair J. in *Swartz* that patient's files and records were property in which the bankrupt held a bare legal title but had no beneficial interest; he preferred the view they were property beneficially owned by the medical practitioner, but subject to common law and statutory rights of the patient with respect to maintaining confidentiality and with respect to access:

---

5 *Ibid.*, at (O.R.) 273.
6 [1992] 2 S.C.R. 138, 7 C.P.C. (3d) 269. See 3.2, below, for discussion of case.
7 *Supra*, note 5 at (O.R.) 275.
8 *Ibid.*, at 277.
9 (1994) 20 O.R. (3d) 133, 29 C.B.R. (3d) 74, 17 B.L.R. (2d) 161 (Ont. C.A.).

Property interests subject to certain restrictions or rights of third parties are capable of being charged. In my view, so long as such rights are preserved by the creditor realizing upon its security, that creditor ought not to be deprived of realization and enforcement rights granted pursuant to a security agreement.[10]

The order of Ground J. contained a provision which, among other things, permitted the creditor to take possession of the patient records for transfer to a duly licenced dentist, who was required to notify each patient that he or she had taken over the practice of the dental surgeon in question; if the patient wished to have the dental records transferred to another dentist, he or she was invited to call.

Arbour J.A., delivering the judgment of the Ontario Court of Appeal, agreed with the approach of Ground J., and stated:

> I see no difference between a dentist's entitlement to sell his or her practice, and a dentist's entitlement to pledge records. Both can be accomplished in a manner compatible with a dentist's professional responsibilities, as long as the dentist acts with the utmost good faith and loyalty in protecting the patient's confidence.
> ... This involves a duty on the part of the dentist who has pledged his or her patients' records, to seek and obtain the patient's consent to the transfer of files in execution of the security. This mirrors the duty a dentist would have if he or she were to sell his or her dental practice.[11]

Arbour J.A. concluded the provisions contained in the order reflected the best accommodation of the rights of the creditor and rights of the patients, and dismissed the appeal with this observation:

> Finally, I wish to add that the central interest advanced in this case, that is the interest of the patients, was not properly represented. By arguing that the GSA violated his patients' rights, the appellant was essentially attempting to avoid the consequences of the obligations which he willingly undertook. It would have been vastly preferable to have the patients' interests independently represented, possibly through notice of the proceedings to the Royal College of Dental Surgeons.[12]

---

10 *Axelrod, Re* (1994), 16 O.R. (3d) 649, 24 C.B.R. (3d) 149, 111 D.L.R. (4th) 540 (Gen. Div. [Commercial List]).
11 *Supra*, note 9 at (O.R.) 139.
12 *Ibid.*, at 141.

3.2 PATIENT'S RIGHT TO ACCESS OWN PERSONAL MEDICAL RECORDS

The recent decision of the Supreme Court of Canada, on appeal from the Court of Appeal of New Brunswick, in *McInerney v. MacDonald*,[13] considered the common law right of the patient to access medical records of his or her doctor. In that case, the plaintiff asked her doctor for copies of the contents of her complete medical file, apparently because of a difference of medical opinion between the doctor and earlier physicians who had treated the plaintiff. The doctor delivered copies of all notes, memoranda and reports she had prepared herself, but refused to produce copies of consultants' reports and records she had received from other physicians, stating that they were the property of those physicians and that it would be unethical for her to release them. The Supreme Court held that, while the personal medical records belong to the physician or health care institution that compiled it . . .,

> In the absence of regulatory legislation, the patient is entitled, upon request, to inspect and copy all information in the patient's medical file which the physician considered in administering advice or treatment. Considering the equitable base of the patient's entitlement, this general rule of access is subject to the superintending jurisdiction of the court. The onus is on the physician to justify a denial of access.[14]

Mr. Justice La Forest, who delivered the reasons for judgment of the Court, did not accept the principle that the patient's right to view his or her medical records should be based on an implied contractual term, on which the majority of the Court of Appeal for New Brunswick premised its decision;[15] nor the view that the patient's interest was "proprietary" in nature, as had been suggested by some textbook writers and case law.[16] He preferred to ground the patient's right in the fiduciary nature of the physician/patient relationship, from which certain duties arose on the part of the physician. He stated:

> Among these are the duty of the doctor to act with utmost good faith and loyalty, and to hold information received from or about a patient in confidence. . . . When a patient releases personal information in the context of the

---

13 (1990), 66 D.L.R. (4th) 736 (N.B. C.A.), affirmed 7 C.P.C. (3d) 269, 12 C.C.L.T. (2d) 225, [1992] 2 S.C.R. 138.
14 *Ibid.*, at (S.C.R.) 159.
15 *Ibid.*, at 146.
16 *Ibid.*, at 151.

doctor-patient relationship, he or she does so with the legitimate expectation that these duties will be respected.

> The physician-patient relationship also gives rise to the physician's duty to make proper disclosure of information to the patient; see *Reibl v. Hughes*, [1980] 2 S.C.R. 880, at p. 884, and *Kenny v. Lockwood*, [[1932] 1 D.L.R. 507, [1932] O.R. 141 at 155 (Ont. C.A.)]. The appellant concedes that a patient has a right to be advised about the information concerning his or her health in the physician's medical record. In my view, however, the fiducial qualities of the relationship extend the physician's duty beyond this to include the obligation to grant access to the information the doctor uses in administering treatment.[17]

And:

> As I see it, it is important that the patient have access to the records for the very purposes for which it is sought to withhold the documents, namely, to ensure the proper functioning of the doctor-patient relationship and to protect the well-being of the patient. If there has been improper conduct in the doctor's dealings with his or her patient, it ought to be revealed. The purpose of keeping the documents secret is to promote the proper functioning of the relationship, not to facilitate improper conduct.[18]

Hence, the fiduciary relationship gives rise not only to the physician's duty of disclosure, but to the very duty of holding any information from or about the patient in confidence; indeed, the former integrally flows from the latter:

> The duty of confidentiality that arises from the doctor-patient relationship is meant to encourage disclosure of information and communication between doctor and patient. In my view, the trust reposed in the physician by the patient mandates that the flow of information operate both ways.[19]

The decision is also useful in placing the development of the patient's right to access his or her medical records in an historical perspective; in this regard, Mr. Justice La Forest cited a number of textbook writers on the subject. He stated:

> Medical records continue to grow in importance as the health care field becomes more and more specialized. As L.E. Rozovsky and F.A. Rozovsky put it in *The Canadian Law of Patient Records* (1984), at pp. 73-74:
>
> > The twentieth century has seen a vast expansion of the health care serv-

---

17 *Ibid.*, at 149.
18 *Ibid.*, at 152.
19 *Ibid.*, at 153.

ices. Rather than relying on one individual, a physician, the patient now looks directly and indirectly to dozens and sometimes hundreds of individuals to provide him with the services he requires. He is cared for not simply by his own physician but by a veritable army of nurses, numerous consulting physicians, technologists and technicians, other allied health personnel and administrative personnel.

. . .

Medical records are also used for an increasing number of purposes. This point is well made by A.F. Westin, *Computers, Health Records, and Citizen Rights* (1976), at p. 27:

> As to medical records, when these were in fact used only by the physician or the hospital, it may have been only curiosity when patients asked to know their contents. But now that medical records are widely shared with health insurance companies, government payers, law enforcement agencies, welfare departments, schools, researchers, credit grantors, and employers, it is often crucial for the patient to know what is being recorded, and to correct inaccuracies that may affect education, career advancement or government benefits.[20]

The decision affirms the principle that a physician may refuse to disclose personal medical records if such disclosure will result in a real potential for harm either to the patient or to a third party.

> . . . the patient's general right of access to his or her records is not absolute. The patient's interest in his or her records is an equitable interest arising from the physician's fiduciary obligation to disclose the records upon request. As part of the relationship of trust and confidence, the physician must act in the best interests of the patient. If the physician reasonably believes it is not in the patient's best interests to inspect his or her medical records, the physician may consider it necessary to deny access to the information. But the patient is not left at the mercy of this discretion. When called upon, equity will intervene to protect the patient from an improper exercise of the physician's discretion.[21]

3.3 WAIVER OF RIGHT TO ACCESS PERSONAL MEDICAL RECORDS BY THE PATIENT

A patient may waive his or her rights expressly in writing, by authorizing the release of personal medical information. The Supreme Court of Canada recently considered such a situation in the case of *Frenette v. Metropolitan Life Insurance Co.*[22] In the case, Patrick Frenette completed an

---

20 *Ibid.*, at 146.
21 *Ibid.*, at 154.
22 89 D.L.R. (4th) 653, [1992] 1 S.C.R. 647, 4 C.C.L.I. (2d) 1.

application form for life insurance coverage with Metropolitan Life Insurance Co. ("the insurer"), which authorized the insurer to have access to Frenette's medical records "for the purposes of risk assessment and loss analysis." In due course, a policy was issued with a basic indemnity of $10,000 and a double indemnity rider in the case of accidental death; the rider excluded suicide and death from a fatal reaction to unprescribed drugs. Approximately three years later, Frenette's body was found floating in the Riviere des Prairies, where according to the coroner's estimate it may have been for five to seven days; an autopsy revealed that the probable cause of death was asphyxiation as a result of drowning. The insurer paid the basic indemnity of $10,000, but refused to pay the additional indemnity, on the ground that the cause of Frenette's death was suicide. An action was commenced by the beneficiary, Frenette's father, for the additional indemnity, and the insurer defended by alleging suicide, citing past chronic alcoholism and drug abuse, as well as earlier suicide attempts. Investigations conducted by the insurer indicated that, on the evening of his disappearance, the insured had been rushed to the emergency ward of Jean Talon Hospital for a possible drug overdose.

The insurer requested Frenette's medical records from Jean Talon Hospital, relying on the authorization contained in the insurance application form, which the hospital refused to honour because of its policy prohibiting the release of medical records, except where such original authorizations were signed by the beneficiary of the services within 90 days of the request. The insurer presented a motion to the Court for an order compelling the hospital to permit the insurer to examine and make copies of Frenette's entire medical record.

The motion was dismissed in the Court of Quebec and in the Quebec Court of Appeal; however, the Supreme Court of Canada allowed the appeal and upheld the insurer's entitlement to examine the records in question. It had no difficulty concluding that the terms of the authorization, "for the purposes of risk assessment and loss analysis", were clear and unambiguous, and did not require resort to the *contra proferentem* rule for interpretation. The parties intended the authorization to apply, firstly, to the initial investigation required for the formation of the insurance contract, and, secondly, to the investigation of the event which triggers the obligation of the insurer to indemnify the beneficiary. Consequently, the hospital, faced with the patient's express authorization, was obliged to release medical information which would enable the insurer to determine entitlement to the supplementary indemnity for accidental death according to the terms of the policy. The Court then considered how much information the insured was entitled to receive. It concluded the scope of disclosure depends on the wording used by the parties to the authorization and, in the case at hand, it meant access to the complete medical records of the insured.

L'Heureux-Dubé J., delivering the judgment of the Court, stated:

> Situations may arise, however, where no authorization has been given by the insured or beneficiary of the hospital services nor can any authorization be inferred from his acts, or where an authorization has been deemed insufficient, or again where a health care establishment has refused to release the records requested despite a valid express or implied authorization or a legislative provision allowing such access. In these circumstances, a party must have recourse to the courts for an order compelling the health care establishment to release such records. Presented with such a motion, a court must weigh the interests in conflict.
> ... In other circumstances, however, the right of privacy of the beneficiary of the hospital services may come into direct conflict with the public interest or the interest of justice. The courts have a duty to protect these interests as well and must therefore weigh the divergent interests at play.[23]

3.4 CANADIAN HEALTH RECORD ASSOCIATION[24]

The Canadian Health Record Association was founded in 1942, and was federally incorporated in 1949. The Canadian College of Health Record Administrators was federally incorporated in 1972 to deal with the educational standards and professional certification of the health record professional. Both bodies operate jointly under the acronym CHRA, to promote health information management. CHRA has 3,200 certified health record administrators and technicians across Canada, who are concerned with providing leadership and expertise regarding health record/information systems and management, patient access to health information, confidentiality, record security, record retention, data quality, analysis and utilization.

3.4.1 Principles and Guidelines

CHRA affirms that the health record is the property of the health facility which has compiled it, although an individual should have the right of protection of all information contained therein; further, computerized health information should be subject to the same security as is written information. CHRA has developed principles and guidelines for the guidance of all persons who access, process, maintain and use health information. It will be useful for lawyers to consider these principles and guidelines, abbreviated below, to understand what moves health record

---

23 *Ibid.*, at (D.L.R.) 674-75.
24 Extracts from Canadian Health Record Association publications are reproduced in the following pages with the kind permission of the Association.

custodians to conduct themselves as they do when confronted with requests for personal health information, as well as to prepare for examination-in-chief or to cross-examine these custodians at trial.

* * *

1. All individuals, facilities, organizations, etc., accessing, processing, maintaining and using health information shall:

    (a) develop and maintain written policies regulating access to, release of, transmittal and destruction of health information, consistent with any relevant legislation and regulations;

    (b) educate their employees with regard to maintaining confidentiality of information. In this regard, they should have their employees, as well as researchers, volunteers, students, and independent contractors (and their employees), handling health information, sign a "Pledge of Confidentiality" statement, in the form set out below:

PLEDGE OF CONFIDENTIALITY

I have read and reviewed the policies on confidentiality of health information of _____

(name of health facility)

I understand that all health information to which I may have access is confidential and is not to be communicated to anyone in any manner, except as outlined in the policies.

Signed:_____

Witnessed:_____

Date:_____

2. Health information shall be accessed or released only in the following circumstances:

 (a) **Direct Care Use** — when requested in writing by a physician or health facility responsible for the direct care of the individual.
 (b) **Individual Use** — when authorized in writing by the individual or his or her legally authorized representative, following review by the attending physician when appropriate.
 (c) **Secondary Use** — when requested by persons or agencies (such as lawyers, insurers, public health agencies, researchers, employers, and educational institutions) authorized in writing by the patient or his or her duly authorized representative.
 (d) **Legal Use** — when authorized by law, by government and law enforcement users, such as:

  - Courts of law and administrative tribunals;
  - for statistical purposes;
  - for immigration purposes;
  - for adjudication of compensation;
  - pursuant to search warrant being executed by police or other authority.

3. Requests for confidential information should be in writing; however, policies governing verbal/telephone requests shall conform to procedures established by the health facility.
4. Any authorization for release of information shall be an original and specific as to source, content, recipient, purpose and time limitations. Reproductions or original signatures shall not be accepted. The signature of a legally authorized representative shall be accepted:

 (a) when the person whose information is required is a minor as defined by provincial statute;
 (b) in case of death (authority to release health information prior to death is not valid after the patient's death);
 (c) in cases of certified mental incompetence.

Requests for the release of information should be accompanied by a consent or authorization in the form set out below, containing at least the information indicated:

CONSENT TO THE DISCLOSURE, TRANSMITTAL OR EXAMINATION OF A HEALTH RECORD

I,_____D.O.B._____
(print full name of person/patient and date of birth)

of _____

hereby consent to the disclosure or transmittal to or the examination by

_____ of the
(print name)

health record compiled in _____
(name of facility)

in respect of _____ D.O.B._____
(name of individual/patient and date of birth)

on _____.
(date of treatment/contact)

_____
(Signature)

_____   _____
(Witness)   (relationship, if other than person/patient)

Dated the _____day of _____, 19__

This authorization expires on _____

AUTHORIZATION FOR RELEASE OF INFORMATION

File No._____

To:_____
(name of institution/individual)

You are hereby authorized to release information from the health records of _____ concerning
(name of patient)
treatment received on _____ to
(dates of contact/hospitalizations)

_____
(name and address of third party)

Date:_____ Expiry Date of Consent:_____

Signed by:_____ D.O.B._____
patient/legal representative

Address: _____

Witness: _____

Address: _____
(Signature)

AUTHORIZATION MUST BE SIGNED BY THE PATIENT, OR BY THE LEGALLY AUTHORIZED REPRESENTATIVE IN THE CASE OF A MINOR

SPECIAL COMMENTS:

5. Information released to authorized persons shall not be available to any other party without further authorization, except for direct patient care. The provider of health information must advise the recipient that further disclosure by verbal interpretation, mechanical reproduction or by any other means, without further authorization, for any purpose other than direct patient care, is prohibited. In this regard, it is suggested that a form letter or notice be enclosed with the health information being sent, or a stamp containing appropriate text be affixed to each sheet of health information. The following are offered as examples.

LETTER OR NOTICE TO BE ENCLOSED WITH HEALTH INFORMATION (RELEASED)

To Whom it May Concern:

The enclosed information is being forwarded to you from our health records, which are the property of _____(insert name) _____. Such copies are released by us only to properly authorized persons, according to law and the policies of this _____(institution/individual)_____. In this way, we seek to uphold the trust vested in us by the individual who has entrusted details of their health to us and to ensure that the individual's wishes and best interests are served at all times.

It is not our intent that activities carried out on behalf of this individual be restricted in any way, but rather that the recipient be reminded of the necessity for similar vigilance. Accordingly, this information is released under the following conditions:

1. That it not be further copied, transmitted or disseminated without further specific authorization of the person concerned or of this (institution/individual).
2. That it be used only for the purpose as outlined in your request.
3. That it be destroyed by shredding when the original purpose has been served.

Your cooperation and compliance with the above is appreciated.

STAMPS	
SUGGESTED TEXT	*COMMENTS*
A. PRIVATE AND CONFIDENTIAL	
This document or any copy thereof may not be released, copied or published in whole or in part without further written consent of the patient.	Recommended as suitable for all third party requesters. (e.g. SECONDARY USERS). INDIVIDUAL USE.
B. This report is CONFIDENTIAL and for your information only. It is not for redistribution in any form and MUST NOT BE DUPLICATED.	Recommended as suitable for all purposes. NOTE: Does not address further authorization or destruction of material.
C. CONFIDENTIAL	Recommended as suitable for information being disseminated for direct care purposes (DIRECT CARE USERS)
D. PRIVATE & CONFIDENTIAL This document or any copy thereof may not be released, copied or published in whole or in part without written consent of (health facility/organization).	Recommended as suitable for all third party requesters (e.g. SECONDARY USERS, and for INDIVIDUAL USE).

6. Health information should be kept in secured areas and not left unattended in areas accessible to unauthorized individuals. While in active use, health information must be in the immediate care and control of designated persons only, and must be returned to the designated, secured area following active use.
7. When health information is sent to any service organization, there shall be a written contract (developed with legal advice) with the service organization, wherein the organization states:

    (a) that security of health of information will be ensured;
    (b) the methods by which the information will be processed and transported;
    (c) the number and types of individuals who will have access to the information, limiting these to those persons directly involved in processing;

(d) that information will not be released to any individual(s) other than the facility making the health information available;
(e) the means of disposal of the original documentation when the service has been completed, i.e., agreement to shred information in a confidential manner.

A service organization in this context refers to a firm or corporation, government or private, which will receive health information for such purposes as electronic data processing, medical transcription, archival storage, or for transporting or transmittal.

8. Health information shall be destroyed according to legislation and to the facility's specific written policies; the latter's policies shall specify:

(a) the method of destruction to be used, i.e., shredding, erasure of electronic media, etc.
(b) methods of routine destruction of daily accumulation of paper waste containing health information;
(c) periodic destruction of inactive or outdated records with particular attention to designating responsible personnel who will witness and/or attest to the destruction in writing.

For greater detail, the reader is referred to CHRA's publication entitled *Principles and Guidelines for Access to and Release of Health Information*.

3.4.2 Position Statement re Patient Access to Health Records

CHRA provides the following position statement to its members concerning patient access to health records.

* * *

1. **The CHRA supports the principle of patients having access to their own health records.**

   The facility or independent clinician who causes the health record to be compiled has the property right to that record.

   All health care facilities should establish policies and procedures governing patient access to health records in accordance with provincial legislation.

All requests for patient access to a health record should be in writing.

The request should contain sufficient information to positively identify the patient.

Provision of the reason for the request assists the facility to provide the most suitable assistance during patient access.

The patient cannot be coerced into giving a reason and has the right to refuse to give one.

Failure to give a reason should not, of itself, result in refusal of patient access.

Unless so specified in legislation, granting access to the health record does not automatically include provision of photocopies.

There should be time limits which allow for reasonable processing of the request without causing undue delay for the patient.

2. **All health professionals should communicate openly with their patients throughout the clinician/patient relationship.**

    It is the duty of all members of the health care team to keep the patient fully informed about his health.

3. **Access to a health record is more meaningful to a patient if such access is in the presence of a person who can explain medical terminology and hospital procedures.**

    All access to health records should be in presence of authorized staff to ensure that the integrity of the record is maintained.
    When acceptable to the patient, the authorized staff should provide interpretation, explanation or definition of medical terminology and hospital procedure.

4. **The patient may disagree with some of the information in his health record.**

    The patient must not be allowed to have the opportunity to alter, deface or remove any part of the health record.

    The patient should be permitted to append to the health record a written, signed, dated statement detailing any comments.

5. **Particular care should be taken when granting access to the health record of a minor or a person who is not mentally competent.**

   Legal guardianship of minors should be determined.

   The legal rights of other family members to the health information should also be established.

   Informed substitute consent should be obtained for patients who are not mentally competent.

6. **Granting a patient access to his health record may have the potential to result in harm to the physical or mental health of the patient or a third party.**

   The attending physician or authorized staff members should have the discretion to withhold information which is considered to have the potential result of harm to the physical or mental well-being of the patient or a third person.

   There should be an appeal mechanism when access is denied.

3.4.3   Code of Practice for Safeguarding Health Information

The CHRA has also prepared a code of practice for safeguarding health information for the guidance of persons who handle and have access to health information and records, which is set out below.

* * *

The underlying principle is that all health information related to an identified individual must be treated as confidential. This information may be written, verbal or in other form.

The primary purposes of the health record are:

- to document the course of an individual's health care, and
- to provide a means of communication amongst health care professionals for current and future patient care.

1. All individuals' institutions and organizations maintaining, handling or processing health information shall:

- have written policies regulating access to, release of, transmittal and destruction of health information;
- educate all their employees with regard to maintaining confidentiality of information, and have them sign a pledge of confidentiality. This procedure shall apply also to searchers, volunteers, contracted individuals and employees of firms and corporations performing contract work.

2. Health information shall be accessed or released only for:

   Direct care use — when requested by a physician or health care facility responsible for the direct care of the individual;
   Individual use — when authorized by the individual or his legally authorized representative;
   Secondary use — when requested by properly authorized persons or agencies;
   Legal use — when required by law.

3. Requests for confidential information should be in writing; however, policies governing verbal requests shall be as outlined by the individual institution.

4. Any authorization for release of information shall be an original and specific as to source, content, recipient, purpose and time limitations. Reproductions of original signatures shall not be accepted.

5. Information released to authorized persons shall not be made available to any other party without further authorization.

6. Health information and records shall be kept in a secured area and not left unattended in areas accessible to unauthorized individuals.

7. In research, individual confidentiality shall be maintained in the handling of information and any reporting or publication of findings.

8. When health information is sent to any service organization for processing, the contract shall include an undertaking by the recipient that confidentiality will be maintained.

9. The authorized destruction of health information shall be by effective shredding, burning or erasure.

10. Any misuse of health information shall be reported to the responsible authority.

Comment: The utility of having a code designed by an organization representing the custodians of health records is that it can be used as a standard against which the actual practices of health care facilities and even health professionals can be measured; and, further, the code can be used to prove custom and usage in this area.

3.5 LEGISLATION REGARDING ACCESS TO DOCUMENTS CONTAINING PERSONAL MEDICAL INFORMATION

Provincial legislatures have facilitated access to personal medical information by enacting legislation identifying specified persons other than the patient who are permitted to have access to patient health records, such as the patient's family members, guardians, personal representatives or substitute decision makers, government inspectors and certain health professionals and administrators having an interest in the patient's health or treatment, service providers, etc.; a sampling of such statutes likely to be useful in litigation include:

Child and Family Services Act, R.S.O. 1990, c. C.11
Coroners Act, R.S.O. 1990, c. C.37
Drug and Pharmacies Regulation Act, R.S.O. 1990, c. H.4
Health Care Consent Act, 1996, S.O. 1996, c. 2, Sched. A
Health Insurance Act, R.S.O. 1990, c. H.6
Health Protection and Promotion Act, R.S.O. 1990, c. H.7
Long Term Care Act, 1994, S.O. 1994, c. 26
Mental Health Act, R.S.O. 1990, c. M.7
Regulated Health Professions Act, 1991, S.O. 1991, c. 18
Workers' Compensation Act, R.S.O. 1990, c. W.11
Workplace Safety and Insurance Act, 1997, S.O. 1997, c. 16, Sched. A
Charitable Institutions Act, R.S.O. 1990, c. C.9
Community Psychiatric Hospitals Act, R.S.O. 1990, c. C.21
Day Nurseries Act, R.S.O. 1990, c. D.2
Homes for Retarded Persons Act, R.S.O. 1990, c. H.11
Homes for the Aged and Rest Homes Act, R.S.O. 1990, c. H.13
Independent Health Facilities Act, R.S.O. 1990, c. I.3
Mental Hospitals Act, R.S.O. 1990, c. M.8
Nursing Homes Act, R.S.O. 1990, c. N.7
Private Hospitals Act, R.S.O. 1990, c. P.24
Public Hospitals Act, R.S.O. 1990, c. P.40

Such provisions may be useful to personal injury counsel in a number of ways:

1. To marshall medical information with respect to a client which will support and lend credibility to his or her statements concerning symptoms and other sequelae of injury or disease;
2. to require opposing parties to take reasonable steps to obtain personal medical information concerning medical matters in dispute, in circumstances where reluctance to cooperate or other forms of obfuscation are encountered;
3. to identify non-parties who may possess or have access to personal medical information relevant to an issue in a civil proceeding, not otherwise available on request by the patient to whom they relate, with a view to compelling its production.

In addition, knowledge of such statutory enactments will assist medical persons to determine what authority, if any, they have to release personal medical information in their possession to persons requesting same.

The following examples from the *Long Term Care Act, 1994*,[25] illustrate how the subject is typically treated in current Ontario medical statutes.

3.5.1 Long-Term Care Act, 1994 [26]

Briefly, the Act is designed to ensure that a wide range of community health and social services is available to people in their own homes and in other community settings so that alternatives to institutional care exist.[27] This requires the creation and maintenance of health records for people receiving such services under the Act, no person may disclose a personal record, except as provided below:

1. A service provider[28] may disclose a personal record to:

    (a) any person,

        (i) if the person to whom the record relates is mentally capable, with the consent of the person to whom the record relates;

---

25 S.O. 1994, c. 26.
26 *Ibid.*, s. 32, as amended.
27 *Ibid.*, s. 1.
28 *Ibid.*, s. 2(1), "service provider" means,
    (a) the Minister of Health, if he or she is providing a community service under clause 4(a) or (b),
    (b) an approved agency,

(ii) if the person to whom the record relates is mentally incapable, with the consent of his or her substitute decision-maker, or

(iii) if the person to whom the record relates has died, with the consent of his or her personal representative.

(b) an employee of the service provider or an individual on contract with the service provider, if the disclosure is for the purpose of enabling the employee or individual to,

(i) assess or review the requirements of the person to whom the record relates for community services,

(ii) determine the eligibility of the person to whom the record relates for community services,

(iii) develop or revise a plan of service for the person to whom the record relates, or

(iv) provide a community service to the person to whom the record relates.

(c) the chief executive officer of a health facility that is involved in the direct health care, in the facility, of the person to whom the record relates, on the written request of the chief executive officer;

(d) a person involved in the direct health care, in a health facility, of the person to whom the record relates, without consent, if the delay required to obtain consent would result in the person to whom the record relates experiencing severe suffering, would prolong the suffering that he or she is already apparently experiencing or would put him or her at risk of sustaining serious bodily harm;

(e) if the person to whom the record relates has died, his or her personal representative;

(f) a lawyer acting on behalf of the service provider, or on behalf of an employee of the service provider, in connection with a proceeding or a possible proceeding by or against the service provider or the employee;

(g.1) a health practitioner, as defined in the *Health Care Consent Act, 1996*, who is determining whether the person to whom the record

---

(c) a person who provides a community service with the support of a payment under clause 4(d), financial assistance under clause 4(e) or (f) or a grant or contribution under clause 4(g), or

(d) a person who provides a community service purchased by an approved agency.

relates is capable with respect to a treatment for the purpose of that Act;

(g.2) an evaluator, as defined in the *Health Care Consent Act, 1996*, who is determining whether the person to whom the record relates is capable with respect to admission to a care facility, or with respect to a personal assistance service, for the purpose of that Act;

(h) a person who is entitled to have access to the record under section 83 of the *Substitute Decisions Act 1992*;

(i) the Minister of Health, if the disclosure is for the purpose of enabling the Minister to exercise a power under section 64 of the Act.[29]

If a service provider discloses a personal record to a person described in clause (g) above by giving the record or a copy of the record to the person for use outside the service provider's premises, the service provider is required, before giving the person the record or the copy, to remove therefrom the name or, or any means of identifying, the person to whom the record relates.

If a service provider discloses a personal record to a person described in clause (g) above by allowing the person to examine the record at the service provider's premises or by any other method of disclosure, the person,

(a) may not disclose the name of, or any means of identifying, the person to whom the record relates; and

(b) may not use or communicate the information or material contained in the record for any purpose other than research, academic pursuits or the compilation of statistical data.

---

29 *Ibid.*, at s. 64, the Minister of Health may collect, directly or indirectly, personal information within the meaning of section 38 of the *Freedom of Information and Protection of Privacy Act*, R.S.O. 1990, c. F.31, for the following purposes:
   1. Ensuring compliance with the Act, the regulations, an agreement made under clause 4(c) or a term or condition imposed by the Minister under this Act;
   2. Monitoring and evaluating community services provided by service providers;
   3. Monitoring and assessing the health, safety and well-being of persons applying for or receiving community services;
   4. Enforcing the right to which the Minister is subrogated under section 59 of the Act;
   5. Complying with federal-provincial cost-sharing requirements.

Chapter 4

Production of Health Records in a Personal Injury Action

by John Haydon, Q.C., B.A., LL.B.

4.1 Introduction
4.2 Health Records Not Producible in a Personal Injury Action
    4.2.1 *Child and Family Services Act*
    4.2.2 *Coroners Act*
    4.2.3 *Highway Traffic Act*
    4.2.4 *Human Rights Code*
    4.2.5 *Independent Health Facilities Act*
    4.2.6 *Mental Health Act*
    4.2.7 *Regulated Health Professions Act, 1991*, a health profession Act; *Drug and Pharmacies Regulation Act*
        Case Law
    4.2.8 *Workers' Compensation Act; Workplace Safety and Insurance Act, 1997*
4.3 The Discovery Process
    4.3.1 Affidavit of Documents
    4.3.2 Examination for Discovery of a Party
        Case Law
    4.3.3 Examination for Discovery of a Non-party
        Case Law
4.4 Order for Production of Documents from a Non-party
    Case Law
4.5 Court-ordered Medical Examination of a Party
    Case Law
4.6 Trial
    Case Law
    4.6.1 Medical Records Under Section 35 of the *Evidence Act*
        Case Law
    4.6.2 Medical Reports Under Section 52 of the *Evidence Act*
        Case Law

4.6.3 Medical Reports Under Section 53.03 of Ontario Rules of Civil Procedure
Case law
4.6.4 Medical Reports of Court-appointed Expert under Ontario Rules of Civil Procedure
4.6.5 Use of Photographic Film of Health Records at Trial
4.7 Related Topics
4.7.1 Incident Reports
4.7.2 Quality Assurance Programs
4.7.3 Deemed Undertaking
4.7.4 Spoliation of Health Records
4.7.5 "Police Informer" Privilege
4.7.6 Computerized Records
4.7.7 *Freedom of Information and Protection of Privacy Act* and the *Municipal Freedom of Information and Protection of Privacy Act*
4.7.8 Access by any Person to Information Concerning a Health Profession Member Maintained by Registrar of a College, under to the Health Professions Procedural Code

4.1 INTRODUCTION

The common law does not recognize privilege in the doctor/patient relationship as it does in the solicitor/client relationship, so that a physician may be compelled in a civil proceeding to divulge communications made to him or her arising from the relationship. There is movement towards the recognition in civil proceedings of a need to protect confidentiality in the psychiatric treatment of patients, and judges in a number of cases have, in given circumstances, refused access to a patient's psychiatric records, on the premise that disclosure would discourage the candour essential to promote a beneficial relationship. The movement has lacked momentum because of concern that the court cannot fully exercise its judicial function unless all relevant and probative evidence is before it, including psychiatric records.

As a general rule, any document which relates to a matter in issue in a civil proceeding is producible in that proceeding, except where prohibited by:

1. solicitor/client privilege — communications made directly between a solicitor and a client;
2. litigation privilege, i.e., communications between the client or his or

her solicitor and a third party which have come into existence for the dominant purpose of litigation;
3. new forms of professional privilege established by the Supreme Court of Canada in *Slavutych v. Baker*,[1] where it adopted four criteria as necessary to the establishment of privilege against the disclosure of a communication, derived from *Wigmore on Evidence*,[2] namely:

- the communication must originate in a confidence that they will not be disclosed;
- the element of confidentiality must be essential to the full and satisfactory maintenance of the relation between the parties;
- the relation must be one which in the opinion of the community ought to be sedulously fostered; and
- the injury that would inure to the relation by disclosure of the communications must be greater than the benefit thereby gained for the correct disposal of litigation.

4. statute or regulation prohibiting disclosure of personal medical information.

4.2 HEALTH RECORDS NOT PRODUCIBLE IN A PERSONAL INJURY ACTION

Only the last-mentioned category (4.) will be considered for the purposes of this section. While many statutes touching on medical matters prohibit the disclosure of documents containing personal medical information, except in specified circumstances, production of such documents is routinely ordered by the court in civil proceedings, citing that to do otherwise would hinder it in the exercise of its judicial function. However, some statutory prohibitions expressly prevent the disclosure of personal medical information in a civil proceeding, either absolutely or in limited circumstances. The following are examples.

4.2.1 *Child and Family Services Act*[3]

Court-ordered assessment of child or parent or person having charge of child, under Part III, Child Protection, is inadmissible in evidence except in limited circumstances.[4]

---

1 (1975), [1976] 1 S.C.R. 254, 55 D.L.R. (3d) 224, [1975] 4 W.W.R. 620, 38 C.R.N.S. 306.
2 3rd ed. 1961, vol. 8, para. 2285.
3 R.S.O. 1990, c. C.11.
4 *Ibid.*, s. 54.

Where the court[5] has found a child to be in need of protection under Part III (Child Protection) of the Act, and has ordered an assessment, the court, or where the assessment was requested by a party, that party, is required, at least seven days before the court considers the report at a hearing, to provide a copy of the report to,

1. the person assessed, provided that:

    (a) where the person assessed is a child less than twelve years of age, the child shall not receive a copy of the report unless the court considers it desirable that the child receive a copy of the report.
    (b) where the person assessed is a child twelve years of age or more, the child shall receive a copy of the report, except that where the court is satisfied that disclosure of all or part of the report to the child would cause the child emotional harm, the court may withhold all or part of the report from the child.

2. the child's solicitor or agent of record;
3. a parent appearing at the hearing, or the parent's solicitor of record;
4. the society caring for or supervising the child;
5. a Director, where he or she requests a copy;
6. where the child is an Indian or a native person, a representative chosen by the child's band or native community; and
7. any other person who in the opinion of the court, should receive a copy of the report for the purposes of the Act.

The report is not admissible into evidence in any other proceeding except,

1. an appeal in the proceeding under section 69 of the Act;
2. a proceeding under the *Coroners Act*;
3. a proceeding referred to in section 81 (recovery on child's behalf) of the Act.[6]

4.2.2 Coroners Act[7]

Answers given at inquest tending to criminate witness or establish liability to civil proceedings inadmissible in any trial other than a prosecution for perjury.[8]

---

5 *Ibid.*, s. 3(1). "court" means the Ontario Court of Justice or the Unified Family Court.
6 *Ibid.*, s. 54(8).
7 R.S.O. 1990, c. C.37.
8 *Ibid.*, s. 42(1).

A witness at an inquest is deemed to have objected to answer any question asked him or her on the ground that his or her answer may tend to criminate him or her, or may tend to establish his or her liability to civil proceedings at the instance of the Crown, or of any person, and no answer given by a witness at an inquest may be used or be receivable in evidence against him in any trial or other proceedings against him or her thereafter taking place, other than a prosecution for perjury in giving such evidence.

Consequently, a party to a civil action may not use the transcript of testimony given by an opposite party at a coroner's inquest to cross-examine the latter at trial as to credibility.[9]

4.2.3 Highway Traffic Act[10]

1. *Report prepared by legally qualified medical practitioner for Registrar inadmissible in evidence for any purpose in any trial except to prove compliance with Act.*[11]

Every legally qualified medical practitioner is required to report to the Registrar the name, address and clinical condition of every person 16 years of age or over attending upon the medical practitioner for medical services who, in the opinion of the medical practitioner, is suffering from a condition that may make it dangerous for the person to operate a motor vehicle. The report is privileged for the information of the Registrar only and is not open for public inspection, and the report is inadmissible in evidence for any purpose in any trial except to prove compliance with the Act.

2. *Report prepared by a member of the College of Optometrists of Ontario for Registrar is inadmissible in evidence for any purpose in any trial except to prove compliance with the Act.*[12]

Every member of the College of Optometrists of Ontario is required to report to the Registrar the name, address and clinical condition of every person 16 years of age or over attending upon such member for optometric services who, in the opinion of such member, is suffering from an eye condition that may make it dangerous for the person to operate a motor vehicle. The report is privileged for the information of the Registrar only and is not open for public inspection, and the report is inadmissible in evidence for any purpose in any trial except to prove compliance with the Act.

---

9   *Caron v. Chodan Estate* (1989), 43 C.P.C. (2d) 255 (Ont. H.C.).
10 R.S.O. 1990, c. H.8.
11 *Ibid.*, s. 203(3).
12 *Ibid.*, s. 204(3).

4.2.4 Human Rights Code[13]

1. *Member of Human Rights Commission not required to disclose information obtained in course of investigation under the Act.*[14]

No person who is a member of the Human Rights Commission shall be required to give testimony in a civil suit or any proceeding as to information obtained in the course of an investigation under the Act.

2. *Employee not required to disclose information obtained in course of person's employment in course of investigation under the Act.*[15]

No person who is employed in the administration of the Act shall be required to give testimony in a civil suit or any proceeding other than a proceeding under the Act as to information obtained in the course of an investigation under the Act.

4.2.5 Independent Health Facilities Act[16]

No requirement to disclose information obtained in course of person's employment or inspection or assessment under the Act.[17]

No person employed in the administration of the Act or who made an inspection or assessment under the Act shall be required to give testimony in a civil action or proceeding with respect to any information obtained in the course of the person's employment, assessment or inspection except in a proceeding under an Act or a regulation under an Act. Even in the event of the last-mentioned exception, an Ontario Court of Justice may exclude the public from proceedings to enforce any Act if the court is of the opinion that confidential information may be disclosed of such a nature, having regard to the circumstances, that the desirability of avoiding disclosure of that information in the interests of any patient or former patient to whom it relates outweighs the desirability of adhering to the principle that hearings be open to the public.[18]

---

13 R.S.O. 1990, c. H.19.
14 *Ibid.*, s. 30(1).
15 *Ibid.*, s. 30(2).
16 R.S.O. 1990, c. I.3.
17 *Ibid.*, s. 37(5).
18 *Ibid.*, s. 37(6).

4.2.6   Mental Health Act[19]

1. *Disclosure of patient's clinical record compiled in psychiatric facility not to be ordered unless Court satisfied that to do so is essential in the interests of justice.*[20]

Where the disclosure, transmittal or examination of all or part of a clinical record compiled in a psychiatric facility in respect of a patient is required of the officer in charge or a person designated in writing by the officer in charge by a summons, order, direction, notice or similar requirement in respect of a matter in issue or that may be in issue in a court of competent jurisdiction or under any Act, and the attending physician states in writing that he or she is of the opinion that the disclosure, transmittal or examination of all or part of the clinical record is likely to result in harm to the treatment or recovery of the patient, or is likely to result in injury to the mental condition of or bodily harm to a third person, no person shall comply with the requirement with respect to all or the part of the clinical record specified by the attending physician except under an order made by the court or body before which the matter is or may be in issue after a hearing from which the public is excluded, and that is held on notice to the attending physician. On such a hearing, the court may examine the clinical record and, if satisfied that such a result is likely, it shall not order the disclosure, transmittal or examination unless satisfied that to do so is essential in the interests of justice.

2. *Disclosure of patient information obtained in course of assessing or treating patient or in course of employment in psychiatric facility except on consent or on order of the Court following determination that disclosure is essential in the interests of justice.*[21]

No person is permitted to disclose in a proceeding in any court or before any body any information in respect of a patient obtained in the course of assessing or treating the patient, or in the course of assisting in his or her assessment or treatment, or in the course of employment in the psychiatric facility except

   (a) where the patient is mentally competent, with the patient's consent;
   (b) where the patient is not mentally competent, with the consent of,

---

19   R.S.O. 1990, c. M.7.
20   *Ibid.*, s. 35(6).
21   *Ibid.*, s. 35(9).

(i) the patient's representative appointed under section 36.1 or 36.2, or

(ii) the patient's substitute decision-maker; or

(c) where the court or, in the case of a proceeding not before a court, the Divisional Court determines, after a hearing from which the public is excluded and that is held on notice to the patient or (if the patient is not mentally competent) the person or representative referred to in the immediately preceding clause that the disclosure is essential in the interests of justice.

These exceptions do not apply to a proceeding before the Consent and Capacity Review Board continued under the *Health Care Consent Act, 1996*, under the *Mental Health Act*, or any other Act, or to an appeal from a decision of the said Board; nor to a proceeding before a court or any other body that is commenced by or on behalf of a patient and that relates to the assessment or treatment of the patient in a psychiatric facility.[22]

4.2.7 *Regulated Health Professions Act, 1991,* a health profession Act; *Drug and Pharmacies Regulation Act*[23]

1. *Matters coming to knowledge of persons in course of his or her duties under health profession-related statutes.*[24]

No person employed, retained or appointed for the purpose of the administration of the *Regulated Health Professions Act, 1991*, a health profession Act or the *Drug and Pharmacies Regulation Act* and no member of a Council or committee of a College shall be compelled to give testimony in a civil proceeding with regard to matters that come to his or her knowledge in the course of his or her duties.

2. *Records of proceedings under health-profession related statutes.*[25]

No record of a proceeding under the Act, a health profession Act or the *Drug and Pharmacies Regulation Act*, no report, document or thing prepared for or statement given at such a proceeding and no order or decision made in such a proceeding is admissible in a civil proceeding other

---

22 *Ibid.*, s. 35(11).
23 *Regulated Health Professions Act, 1991*, S.O. 1991, c. 18; *Drug and Pharmacies Regulation Act*, R.S.O. 1990, c. H.4.
24 *Regulated Health Professions Act, 1991, ibid.*, s. 36(2).
25 *Ibid.*, s. 36(3).

than a proceeding under this Act, a health profession Act or the *Drug and Pharmacies Regulation Act* or a proceeding relating to an order under section 11.1 or 11.2 of the *Ontario Drug Benefit Act*.

Case Law: *Documents prohibited from disclosure under Health Disciplines Act not producible in civil proceeding in circumstances:* Applicant had commenced application for judicial review, in which order sought in nature of prohibition prohibiting discipline committee of the respondent from proceeding with professional misconduct hearing arising from complaint against applicant; applicant brings application to compel production of all documents concerning deliberations of complaints committee of the College of Physicians and Surgeons of Ontario regarding decision made by the applicant not to administer an anaesthetic to a complainant. Respondent argued it was not required to produce material requested in view of section 65(1) and (2) of the *Health Disciplines Act, 1974*, which reads in part as follows:

> 65. (1) Every person employed in the administration of this Part . . . shall preserve secrecy with respect to all matters that come to his knowledge in the course of his duties . . . and shall not communicate any such matters to any other person . . .
> (2) No person to whom subsection 1 applies shall be required to give testimony in any civil suit or proceeding with regard to information obtained by him in the course of his duties, employment, inquiry or investigation except in a proceeding under this Part or the regulations or by-laws.

Held, dismissing the application, it was considered the provisions of section 65(1) were a bar to the application, and it was not believed the applicant had a positive right to the material before the complaints committee. Also, the material sought should not be disclosed for policy reasons and because the proceedings before the complaints committee were not under attack in the application for judicial review: *Wilson v. College of Physicians & Surgeons (Ontario)*.[26]

4.2.8 *Workers' Compensation Act; Workplace Safety and Insurance Act, 1997*

The *Workplace Safety and Insurance Act, 1997*, replaces the *Workers' Compensation Act* with respect to accidents occurring after January 1st, 1998; accidents occurring before that date continue to be governed by the *Workers' Compensation Act*. Excerpts from both statutes are set out below.

---

26 (1981), 24 C.P.C. 52 (Ont. Div. Ct.).

Workers' Compensation Act [27]

1. *Reports by specified persons concerning a worker, as required by the Board*[28]

Every physician, surgeon, hospital official or other person attending, consulted respecting, or having the care of, any worker is required to furnish to the Board from time to time such reports as may be required by the Board in respect of such worker.

Every such report and every other report made or submitted to the Board by a physician, surgeon, hospital, nurse, dentist, drugless practitioner, chiropodist or optometrist is for the use and purposes of the Board only, is deemed to be a privileged communication of the person making or submitting the same, and unless it is proved that it was made maliciously, is not admissible as evidence or subject to production in any court in an action or proceeding against such person.

2. *Report of health professional requested by worker or employer, containing information concerning a worker*[29]

A health professional[30] who receives a request from a worker or the employer is required to provide each of them and the Board with a report containing the prescribed information, provided:

(a) the worker consents; and
(b) the prescribed requirements, if any, are satisfied.

Every such report is deemed to be a privileged communication of the person making it, and unless it is proved that it was made maliciously, is not admissible as evidence or subject to production in any court in an action or proceeding against the person providing it.

Every such report and every other report made or submitted to the Board by a physician, surgeon, hospital, nurse, dentist, drugless practitioner, chiropodist or optometrist is for the use and purposes of the Board only, is deemed to be a privileged communication of the person making or submitting the same, and unless it is proved that it was made maliciously,

---

27 R.S.O. 1990, c. W.11.
28 *Ibid.*, ss. 51(1), 115.
29 *Ibid.*, ss. 51(2), (5), 115.
30 *Ibid.*, at s. 51(6), "health professional" means a member of the College of a health profession as defined in the *Regulated Health Professions Act, 1991*.

3. *Document, extract, report, material or statement obtained in performance of duties under the Act*[31]

Neither the Board, a member of the board of directors, officer or employee of the Board nor a person who is engaged by the Board to conduct an examination, test or inquiry or authorized to perform any function shall be required to produce in a civil suit to which the Board is not a party a document, extract, report, material or statement acquired, furnished, obtained, made or received in the performance of his, her or its duties under the Act.

The foregoing applies with necessary modifications to:

(a) the chair, vice-chair's and other members of the Appeals Tribunal, to all officers and employees of the Appeals Tribunal and any person engaged by the Appeals Tribunal to conduct an examination, test or inquiry, or authorized to perform any function under the Act;
(b) the officers and employees of the Office of the Worker Adviser;
(c) the officers and employees of the Office of the Employer Adviser.

Workplace Safety and Insurance Act, 1997[32]

1. *Information or material furnished, obtained, made or received in the performance of duties under the Act.*[33]

The Board and the persons named below are not required to produce, in a civil action in which the Board is not a party, any information or material furnished, obtained, made or received in the performance of the Boards or the persons duties under the Act:

    (a) Members of the board of directors of the Board.
    (b) The chair, vice-chairs and members of the Appeals Tribunal.
    (c) Employees of the Board or of the Appeals Tribunal.
    (d) Persons employed in the Office of the Worker Adviser or the Office of the Employer Adviser.
    (e) Persons who are engaged by the Board or the Appeals Tribunal to

---

[31] *Ibid.*, ss. 76(2), 88, 96(5), 97(4).
[32] S.O. 1997, c. 16, Sched. A.
[33] *Ibid.*, s. 180(2).

conduct an examination, investigation, inquiry, inspection or test or who are authorized by the Board or the Appeals Tribunal to perform any function.

(f) Health care practitioners providing information under section 37 of the Act.[34]

2. *Certain information provided to the Board concerning the worker.*[35]

Information provided under section 37[36] or section 47[37] of the Act is privileged and shall not be produced in any action or proceeding.

4.3 THE DISCOVERY PROCESS

4.3.1 Affidavit of Documents

In Ontario, the Rules of Civil Procedure require every party to an action to serve on every other party an affidavit of documents disclosing to the full extent of the party's knowledge, information and belief all documents relating to any matter in issue in the action that are or have been in the party's possession, control or power, whether or not privilege is claimed,[38] and, if privilege is not claimed, shall be produced for inspection if requested.[39] "Documents" are defined to include "a sound recording, videotape, film, photograph, chart, graph, map, plan, survey, book of account and information recorded or stored by means of any device."[40]

After an affidavit of documents has been served, counsel has a continuing obligation to serve a supplementary affidavit specifying the extent to which the affidavit of documents requires modification and disclosing any additional documents.[41]

---

34 *Ibid.*, s. 37(1), every health care practitioner who provides health care to a worker claiming benefits under the insurance plan or who is consulted with respect to his or her health care must promptly give the Board such information relating to the worker as the Board may require.
35 *Ibid.*, s. 180(4).
36 *Ibid.* Section 37 refers to information provided to the Board from health care practitioners and hospital or health facilities that provide health care to a worker claiming benefits, and from a health professional concerning a worker's functional abilities.
37 *Ibid.* Section 47 refers to information provided from a physician selected to examine a worker and assess the extent of his or her permanent impairment.
38 Rule 30.03, Rules of Civil Procedure, R.R.O. 1990, Reg. 194, and amendments.
39 Rule 30.02(1), (2).
40 Rule 30.01(1)(a).
41 Rule 30.07.

Medical documents for which production for inspection may be sought from the plaintiff in a personal injury action would include:

1. Records of examining and/or treating physician or other health practitioner (psychologist, chiropractor, physiotherapist, acupuncturist, etc.)[42]
2. Medical, clinical and health records of hospitals or other health institutions, clinics and homes in which plaintiff was a patient and has been examined and/or received treatment, including nurse's notes, medical orders, consultation reports, laboratory reports, diagnostic studies (including X-rays, EKG readings, EEG's, MRI's, scans, audiometric tests, thermographs), charts, letters, tapes, microfilm, laboratory tests and reports, computer generated data, progress notes, order sheets, medication sheets, consultation reports, specialists' reports and consent forms.
3. OHIP records.
4. No-fault insurer's records.
5. Disability insurer's records.
6. Curriculum vitae of health practitioner providing report.
7. Canada Pension Plan records.
8. Private pension plan records.
9. Health records required to be kept under certain non-medical statutes, i.e., *General Welfare Act; Family Benefits Act*, etc.

"*Matter in issue*": Relevancy to what is contained in the pleadings is the only test by which to judge whether a matter is in issue.[43] It is permissible for a party to produce documents with certain portions edited out, where the expunged portions are not relevant to the matters in issue,[44] subject nevertheless to the court's overriding jurisdiction to determine relevancy or the validity of a claim of privilege.[45]

"*Possession, control or power*": A document is deemed to be in a party's power if that party is entitled to obtain the original document or a copy of it and the party seeking it is not so entitled.[46] This means that not only documents which are in the personal possession of the party must be

---

42 For complete list of regulated health professions, see *Regulated Health Professions Act, 1991*, S.O. 1991, c. 18, at Schedule 1; also, see Chapter 1 at 1.1, *supra*.
43 *Glowinsky v. Stephens & Rankin Inc.* (1989), 38 C.P.C. (2d) 102 (Ont. Master).
44 *Manufacturers Life Insurance Co. v. Dofasco Inc.* (1989), 38 C.P.C. (2d) 47 (Ont. H.C.), additional reasons at (1989), 38 C.P.C. (2d) 47 at 53 (Ont. H.C.).
45 Rule 30.06(d).
46 Rule 30.01(1)(b).

produced for inspection, but also documents which may be in the possession of non-parties, such as no-fault insurers, employers, health practitioners, over which the party has control or power to compel their production because of his or her relationship to them.

"Disclosure" of documents: Disclosure is made by listing, and describing to the full extent of the party's knowledge, information and belief, every such document in an Affidavit of Documents which the party is required to deliver in the action.[47] Schedule A to the Affidavit of Documents form must describe such documents which the party does not object to producing; Schedule B describes such documents for which the party claims privilege, and the grounds for the claim; and Schedule C describes such documents that were formerly in the party's possession, control or power, whether or not privilege is claimed, together with a statement of when and how the party lost possession or control of or power over them and their present location.[48]

Adequacy of Affidavit of Documents: If counsel believes the affidavit of documents of an opposite party omits a relevant document or that a claim of privilege may have been improperly made, he or she may move for:

1. an order for cross-examination on the affidavit of documents;
2. an order for service of a further and better affidavit of documents;
3. an order for the disclosure or production for inspection of the document, or a part of the document, if it is not privileged; and,
4. inspection of the document by the Court for the purpose of determining its relevance or the validity of a claim of privilege.[49]

"Production for inspection" of documents: Production for inspection is effected by counsel making the document available to be inspected by opposing counsel at a mutually convenient time and place, usually at the office of the producing counsel. Typically, rather than insisting on a visual inspection of the original document in advance of examinations for discovery, opposing counsel are content to view copies of documents provided by producing counsel at the former's expense.

An affidavit of documents must be served by each party on every other party in an action within ten days after the close of pleadings.[50] As documents in a personal injury action tend to come to hand between the time of preparation and service of the initial affidavit of documents and the date

---

47 Rule 30.03(1).
48 Rule 30.03(2).
49 Rule 30.06.
50 Rule 30.03(1).

for examinations for discovery, counsel are advised to confront an opposing party with his or her affidavit of documents at the commencement of the examination for discovery, with a request that the party identify what, if any, additional documents should be added to the affidavit to make it contemporaneous. While a party is under a continuing obligation to disclose documents after service of the initial affidavit, the rules do not fix any time within which such disclosure must occur after coming into possession or control of the party.

Privilege may be claimed by a party in respect of documents disclosed under Schedule B of his or her affidavit of documents. While a party may not be required to disclose the contents of a document described in Schedule B, sufficient particulars must be disclosed to justify a claim of privilege. If insufficient particulars are provided, opposing counsel may ask pertinent questions on an examination for discovery to satisfy himself or herself on the point, such as when was the document prepared, by whom was it prepared, why was it prepared, why privilege is claimed, *etc*. If the answers elicited do not establish privilege or are inconclusive, an order may be obtained to compel disclosure or production for inspection of the document.[51]

A party who serves on another party a request to inspect documents in the proper form is entitled to inspect any document that is not privileged and that is referred to in the other party's affidavit of documents as being in the party's possession, control or power.[52] This means there is no requirement on a party served with such a request to produce for inspection documents that were formerly but are no longer in the party's possession, control or power, and which are required to be described in Schedule C of an affidavit of documents. There is a tendency for both sides in personal injury actions to heed Schedule C indifferently or not at all, and in many cases this attitude may not pose any threat to the integrity of the action. However, it is just this laxity which should exhort counsel for any party to invest a question or two concerning such documents when reviewing the affidavit of documents with the party being examined at discovery.

Personal injury actions commenced on or after March 11th, 1996, where the plaintiff's claim is exclusively for an amount of $25,000 or less, exclusive of interest and costs, are subject to the rules governing "simplified procedure".[53] Among other things, the simplified procedure requires that the affidavit of documents to be served in an action include a list of the names and addresses of persons who might reasonably be expected to have knowledge of transactions or occurrences in issue in the action unless

---

51   Rule 30.06(d).
52   Rule 30.04(1).
53   Rules 76.01(1), 76.02(1).

the court orders otherwise,[54] and a party may not call as a witness at the trial of the action a person whose name has not been so disclosed except with leave of the trial judge.[55]

It is still early to predict how this rule will be interpreted in its application to personal injury actions. It can be anticipated that injured plaintiffs will believe the rule to be satisfied if all witnesses they intend to call at trial are disclosed. However, the wording of the rule would suggest that a defendant may be entitled to disclosure of, among others, the names of all medical persons or institutions who or which have performed services relevant to the issues raised in the injured plaintiff's pleading. The fullest possible disclosure is important to the defence of a personal injury action because of the opportunity it provides to unearth health records which ameliorate or contradict the claimant's testimony or evidence tendered on his behalf. Although an examination for discovery is not permitted in an action under the simplified procedure,[56] a motion for an order permitting cross-examination on the affidavit of documents pursuant to Rule 30.06 is permitted and may be warranted, particularly if opposing counsel is uncooperative in responding to reasonable enquiries concerning disclosure.

4.3.2 Examination for Discovery of a Party

A party to be examined for discovery in an action is required to produce for inspection at the examination:

1. all documents in his or her possession, control or power that are not privileged;[57]
2. unless the parties otherwise agree, all documents listed in the party's affidavit of documents that are not privileged and all documents previously produced for inspection by the party;[58]
3. all documents and things in his or her possession, control or power that are not privileged and that the notice of examination requires the person to bring;[59]
4. where a party admits on an examination that he or she has possession or control of or power over any other document that relates to a matter in issue in the proceeding and it is not privileged, he or she shall pro-

---

54 Rule 76.04(1).
55 Rule 76.04(2).
56 Rule 76.05. Also not permitted under this Rule are cross-examination of a deponent on an affidavit filed on a motion and the examination of a witness before the hearing of a pending motion.
57 Rules of Civil Procedure, Rule 34.10(2)(a).
58 *Ibid.*, Rules 34.10(2)(a), 30.04(4).
59 *Ibid.*, Rule 34.10(2)(b), (3).

duce it for inspection at the examination, if available, and if not within two days thereafter.[60]

The court may at any time order production for inspection of documents that are not privileged and that are in the possession, control or power of a party.[61]

A party may on an examination for discovery obtain disclosure of the findings, opinions and conclusions of an expert engaged by or on behalf of the party being examined that relate to a matter in issue in the action and of the expert's name and address, but the party being examined need not disclose the information or the name and address of the expert where,

1. the findings, opinions and conclusions of the expert relating to any matter in issue in the action were made or formed in preparation for contemplated or pending litigation and for no other purpose; and,
2. the party being examined undertakes not to call the expert as a witness at the trial.[62]

The best tool to ferret out health records is the examination for discovery. On examination, an injured plaintiff must identify all the health professionals and institutions who or which have provided professional services since the accident or other event in issue, as well as for a reasonable period before. Through undertakings, the plaintiff may be compelled to use reasonable efforts to obtain the clinical notes and records of these sources as they relate to him or her, or alternatively an order for production may be obtained directly from a person who is not a party to the action, identified by the plaintiff, who has possession, control or power of such clinical notes and records. The clinical notes and records so produced may identify other health professionals and institutions possessing health records pertaining to the plaintiff, and so on.

The health records produced through the affidavit of documents and discovery will, in addition to being of help in evaluating the plaintiff's accident-related injuries for assessment purposes, contain statements or accounts of statements made by the plaintiff touching on every important issue in the action, including:

1. how the accident happened; and,
2. the symptoms of which the plaintiff has complained before and since the accident.

---

60 *Ibid.*, Rule 34.10(4).
61 *Ibid.*, Rule 30.04(5).
62 *Ibid.*, Rule 31.06(3).

These statements, reported to have been made by the plaintiff, afford an unparalleled opportunity to test the veracity of the plaintiff, through comparison for contradictions and inconsistencies with:

1. statements made by the plaintiff on his or her examination for discovery;
2. statements made by the plaintiff throughout the assembled clinical notes and records;
3. statements made by the plaintiff in other documents, such as the Motor Vehicle Accident Report, the report given by the plaintiff to his or her insurer (often required to be verified by the plaintiff's signature).

The importance of this documentary comparison cannot be overemphasized. It is not unusual for a plaintiff in a burst of frankness immediately following the accident to admit to the attending physician at the emergency department of the hospital that he or she was not wearing a seatbelt at the time of the accident, or to make some other inculpatory statement but, later, when the ramifications of such an admission in the context of a lawsuit have been brought to mind, state otherwise. Similarly, the plaintiff's recollection of the circumstances surrounding the accident may be sketchy when questioned immediately following the accident, but improve as time and opportunity present. A useful device in dealing with contradictions of this sort is to confront the examinee with each admission, in or out of sequence, asking if he or she did, on the occasion in question, make the statement to the author of the report. If he or she admits to making the statement, he or she should then be asked if the statement is true. At some point in the exchange, the plaintiff will have to admit that either he or she did not make the statement to the interviewer or was lying. In the former case, the physician making the report will usually stand by what is contained in his or her medical report at trial, and any dispute as to which is the more credible version will likely be resolved in favour of the disinterested physician. In both cases, the plaintiff's case is diminished. The same approach can be taken with regard to contradictions of any kind which appear in reports of statements made by the plaintiff.

If the plaintiff has been examined or treated by a member of a regulated health profession required to record certain health information concerning the patient under the regulations governing his or her profession, all of the prescribed records should be produced.[63] This is also the case where the plaintiff has received services from an institution required to keep health records under its governing statute and regulations.[64] The fail-

---

63 See Chapter 2 at 2.2, "Record-keeping Under the Health Profession Acts."
64 See Chapter 2 at 2.3, "Record-keeping Under Medical Institutions Statutes."

ure of a regulated health professional to keep prescribed health information concerning a patient may constitute professional misconduct under regulations governing his or her health profession, which may be useful for defence counsel to remember when considering a move to discredit a health professional in cross-examination at trial.

Undertakings: When requested by defence counsel, plaintiff's counsel routinely give undertakings to use reasonable efforts to obtain the clinical notes and records of any health professional visited by the plaintiff since the accident, or five or ten years before. Often the request will be for all the clinical notes and records created during the period the plaintiff has been a patient of the health professional, which in some cases can extend back to childhood. The authorities do not warrant such liberal undertakings on relevancy grounds alone, and plaintiffs' counsel are cautioned against providing an undertaking which goes beyond the immediate needs of the action. The principal reason is that such records may disclose medical conditions which have the potential of provoking great embarrassment, and even terror, in a client should they be disclosed to anyone, particularly in the course of a lawsuit where information can be made public, inadvertently or otherwise, during a trial. The writer recalls acting as defence counsel on a case brought by a plaintiff claiming damages for a minor whiplash injury, in which health records yielded information concerning a pre-accident abortion performed on the plaintiff, who had become pregnant by another man during a clandestine affair while married to her husband, with whom she was still living. In another case, in which the plaintiff claimed damages for a bone fracture in his foot, the health records detailed a lengthy history of sexual dysfunction, culminating in the surgical implanting of a penile device; the anguish of coping with the penile implant was faithfully recorded in agonizing detail. The actions were soon settled with offers which reflected the plaintiffs' concerns that such details might be made public. The defence was not looking for these records, which were patently irrelevant, and the broad undertakings which precipitated their production should never have been given by plaintiff's counsel. Furthermore, if prevailed upon by a plaintiff, the court may exclude documents or portions of documents which are not relevant or which should be excluded or at least protected from disclosure on other grounds.

In response to an undertaking to use reasonable efforts to produce clinical notes and records of a health professional, counsel will occasionally be informed that the health professional no longer practices medicine. Regulations made pursuant to some health profession Acts expressly require a member to retain patient health records for a minimum time period or until the member ceases to practice medicine, whichever occurs first; and if the member ceases to practice medicine he or she may have duties associated with the disposition of such records.[65] For example, regulations under the *Medicine Act, 1991*,[66] require a member of the College of Physicians and Surgeons of Ontario who ceases to practice medicine, with regard to records of family medicine and primary care, to:

1. transfer them to a member with the same address and telephone number; or,
2. notify each patient that the records will be destroyed two years after the notification and that the patient may obtain the records or have the member transfer the records to another physician within the two years.[67]

Case Law: The following are summaries of recent Ontario authorities which consider the obligation of a party to an action to produce documents containing personal medical information to an opposing party:

1. *Post-pleading events may narrow scope of relevance of issues pleaded for purpose of determining if documents should be produced:* Appeal by defendants from order dismissing motion for production of 32 sets of clinical notes and records of professionals who had seen the plaintiff since subject motor vehicle accident. Appeal dismissed. Although claim broadly pleaded in statement of claim, issues were narrowed through process of discoveries and exchanges of correspondence between counsel: *Micheli v. Sheppard.*[68]
2. *In ordering production of documents, court may restrict production or use of documents where issue of relevance arises:* Motion by female defendant to compel plaintiff to provide further and better affidavit of documents and to compel production of documents including, *inter alia*, medical records of physicians who had treated plaintiff during relevant period. In action plaintiff sued stepfather for damages for sexual assaults, and claimed damages against mother for failing to stop assaults which mother allegedly knew or ought to have known were occurring. Held, as mother's knowledge was central issue, it was important for her to discover what plaintiff had said about mother's conduct, knowledge or inactivity, or which exonerated her mother. Held, with respect to medical records of treating physicians, plaintiff ordered to request production of doctors' notes relating only to issue of complaint, non-complaint or exoneration of the defendant mother.

---

65 See Chapter 2 at 2.2, "Record-keeping Under the Health Profession Acts."
66 S.O. 1991, c. 30.
67 O. Reg. 114/94, Part V, s. 19, as amended by O. Reg. 241/94.
68 (1994), 30 C.P.C. (3d) 297 (Ont. Gen. Div.).

There is nothing in *Cook v. Ip*[69] which gives a right to the opposite party to production of the entire medical history of the party, however irrelevant it may be to the issues in the lawsuit. If an issue of relevance arises, the court may examine the records and may make an order restricting their production or their use. Also ordered, any record of negotiated settlement with the grandfather relating to the same issue. Balance of documents for which production sought to be sought by other means or by resort to Rule 30.10: *W.(T.) v. W.(K.R.J.)*.[70]

3. *Production of medical records will not be ordered on basis of possible credibility issue at trial; production will be ordered only if documents relevant to issues that are subject of trial:* Motion by testator's widow for production of all medical, psychiatric and counselling records for all medical treatment and counselling received by testator's daughter, in proceedings to probate a will, in which allegations were made of lack of testamentary capacity, undue influence and improper execution of will. On discovery, daughter made serious accusations of sexual abuse involving testator and testator's son. The medical records were demanded on basis that daughter's credibility would be in issue at trial. Held, dismissing motion, documents should be produced only if relevant; relevance means relevance to the issues that are the subject of the trial; while credibility is an important element in any factual issue, it is not itself an issue that would justify ordering the production of medical records of the kind here demanded in anticipation of possible volunteering of evidence irrelevant to the trial issues: *W.(Y.) v. W.(L.)*.[71]

4. If the defendant wishes to view and copy documents not in the plaintiff's possession, but within his or her control, a direction for such documents should be supplied, so that the defendant may pick those specifically relevant for copying, at his or her expense. Alternatively, the documents may be obtained by the plaintiff at the defendant's expense: *Bazzi v. Allstate Insurance Co. of Canada*.[72]

5. If the plaintiff has put in issue his entire medical and emotional health, production of all medical records will be ordered, whether or not there has been a medical report. *Cook v. Ip*[73] followed: *Lonergan v. Morrissette*.[74]

---

69 (1985), 52 O.R. (2d) 289, 22 D.L.R. (4th) 1 (C.A.), leave to appeal refused (1986), 55 O.R. (2d) 288 (note) (S.C.C.). See 4.4, Order for Production of Documents from a Non-party; Case Law; item 10., below, for case summary.

70 (1994), 111 D.L.R. (4th) 703, 26 C.P.C. (3d) 45 (Ont. Gen. Div.).

71 (1994), 28 C.P.C. (3d) 60 (Ont. Gen. Div.).

72 (1994), 28 C.P.C. (3d) 166, 4 M.V.R. (3d) 310 (Ont. Gen. Div.).

73 *Supra*, note 69. See 4.4, Order for Production of Documents from a Non-party; Case Law; item 10., below, for case summary.

74 (1993), 23 C.P.C. (3d) 186, 109 (4th) D.L.R. 758 (Ont. Gen. Div.).

6. Motion by defendant against plaintiff for production of pre-accident clinical notes and records of family physician of plaintiff; appeal from decision of Master who ordered production, subject to plaintiff's solicitors deleting portions considered irrelevant. Because of broad spectrum of medical complaints pleaded, production ordered without deletions, subject to relevance being determined at trial: *Wilton v. Brown*.[75]

7. *Production of medical information not to be ordered unless relevance established and it falls within reasonable period before accident:* Appeal by defendants from Master's order dismissing defendants' motion for, inter alia, additional medical information concerning the plaintiff. The defendants had obtained medical information about the plaintiff for ten years prior to the accident and wanted additional medical information (OHIP records and information from physician) for the preceding ten years, notwithstanding there was no evidence of any relevant problem during latter period. Held, dismissing the appeal, there was no reason for plaintiff to produce medical information requested as evidence established nothing relevant in plaintiff's medical condition during period in question, nor did it fall within reasonable period before accident: *Rizzi v. Runtes*.[76]

8. *In ordering production of documents, court may (i) impose terms of confidentiality and prohibition necessary to shield identity of persons from social stigma, and (ii) in appropriate circumstances, order that cost of production be at unrecoverable expense of requesting party:* Appeal from Master's order, requiring Canadian Red Cross Society (Third Party) to produce records relating to blood donors whose blood was given to deceased who had contracted AIDS and died following transfusions of blood supplied by Society, in action by deceased's estate. The Master's order compelled production of the blood donor records sought, but imposed terms of confidentiality for information received and prohibited plaintiff's counsel and his agents from contacting any donor identified without court order. The Society argued its whole operation of obtaining blood from volunteer donors depended on its keeping the record of each blood donor confidential, and in absence of confidentiality, the supply of volunteer blood would dry up, to the detriment of society. The court considered Wigmore's four fundamental conditions necessary to establish privilege against disclosure of communications adopted by the Supreme Court of Can-

---

75 (1993), 22 C.P.C. (3d) 249 (Ont. Gen. Div.).
76 [1993] O.J. No. 1333, DRS 93-13291 (Ont. Gen. Div.).

ada in *Slavutych v. Baker*,[77] and concluded no relationship of confidentiality ever existed between the Society and its individual blood donors. Further, with respect to condition (4), it concluded that without access to the Society's records the plaintiff was unlikely to be able to establish the causality necessary to succeed in the action, and to deny access would likely mean an end to the plaintiff's action. That result, when balanced with the potential effect of disclosure on the Society's blood programme, did not warrant protection from disclosure; the terms of confidentiality and the prohibition imposed by the Master provided the necessary shielding of donors and their families from social stigma. The Society also sought to bring itself within the exception to the general principle of disclosure considered in *Peter Kiewit Sons Co. of Canada v. British Columbia Hydro & Power Authority*,[78] namely, that production will not be ordered where it will require a party to incur enormous expense in what may be a futile search for something which does not exist. The Court held that a search could be conducted at plaintiff's unrecoverable expense as long as there was a chance, though slight, of success: *Sharpe Estate v. Northwestern General Hospital*.[79]

9. *Pre-accident health records will be ordered if pre-accident health relevant to issue in action:* Motion by defendant in personal injury action for order requiring plaintiff to produce clinical notes and records of physicians and hospital. Subject accident occurred in 1986; plaintiff's claim included damages for injuries to head, neck and back, as well as a claim for lessened enjoyment of life and loss of income. At examination for discovery, plaintiff stated he had been involved in 1973 motorcycle collision with van, when he suffered right leg fracture and struck his head against side of van; defendant seeking production of pre-accident clinical notes and records of physician who

---

77 *Supra*, note 1. The conditions are:
   (1) The communications must originate in a *confidence* that they will not be disclosed;
   (2) This element of *confidentiality* must be essential to the full and satisfactory maintenance of the relation between the parties;
   (3) The *relation* must be one which in the opinion of the community ought to be sedulously *fostered*;
   (4) The *injury* that would inure to the relation by the disclosure of the communications must be *greater than the benefit* thereby gained for the correct disposal of litigation.
78 (1982), 26 C.P.C. 221n, 36 B.C.L.R. 58, 134 D.L.R. (3d) 154 (S.C.).
79 (1990), 74 D.L.R. (4th) 43, 1 C.P.C. (3d) 104 (Ont. Master), affirmed (1991), 76 D.L.R. (4th) 535, 2 O.R. (3d) 40, 46 C.P.C. (2d) 267 (Ont. Gen. Div.).

had treated plaintiff and hospital where he received treatment arising from motorcycle accident. Defendant also sought production of clinical notes and records of neurologist who had provided report concerning plaintiff's injuries sustained in 1986 accident. Held, with respect to pre-accident clinical notes and records, they should be produced, because by including claim for compensation for lessened enjoyment of life and loss of income, plaintiff had put in issue his state of health prior to 1986 accident; and with respect to neurologist's clinical notes and records, they should also be produced, notwithstanding that the neurologist had prepared report which had been delivered to defendant, citing reasons of Cory J.A. in *Cook v. Ip*,[80] in support. Plaintiff also ordered to prepare supplementary affidavit of documents and re-attend at examination for discovery at his own expense to answer questions arising from such productions, if requested: *Smith v. Stewart*.[81]

10. Defendants provided with reports of two physicians retained by plaintiff to conduct examinations in contemplation of litigation, and now sought to obtain production of clinical notes and records. Held, per Rule 31.06(3), as long as medical reports contain findings, opinions and conclusions of expert, no requirement to produce clinical notes and records at discovery stage: *Kaptsis v. Macias*.[82]

11. Appeal by plaintiffs from order compelling plaintiff to produce to defendant pre-accident notes of treating physician. Appeal dismissed. *Cook v. Ip*[83] not limited to OHIP records; where plaintiff paints complaints with wide brush in pleadings so that pre-accident reports may be relevant at trial, defendant entitled to review pre-accident notes: *Catanzaro v. Doxtator*.[84]

12. *Protection from production of medical reports under Rule 31.06(3) does not extend to reports prepared by treating physicians:* Defendants sought order compelling production of medical report of physician who had treated plaintiff. Plaintiff's counsel refused to produce on ground that document privileged, as it was prepared in contemplation of litigation, per Rule 31.06(3). Production ordered as protection afforded under Rule extended to reports of experts retained to testify as experts only, and not to those of treatment givers. Defendants also

---

80 *Supra*, note 69. See 4.4, Order for Production of Documents from a Nonparty; Case Law; item 10., below, for case summary.
81 (1991), 37 M.V.R. (2d) 140 (Ont. Gen. Div.).
82 (1990), 74 O.R. (2d) 189, 44 C.P.C. (2d) 285 (H.C.).
83 *Supra*, note 69. See 4.4, Order for Production of Documents from a Nonparty; Case Law; item 10., below, for case summary.
84 (1988), 28 C.P.C. (2d) 42, 65 O.R. (2d) 199 (H.C.).

sought order compelling plaintiffs to request clinical notes and records of treating physicians, and to sign appropriate releases for this purpose. Motion refused on ground that documents not in possession, control or power of plaintiffs, per Rule 30.06, without prejudice to defendant's right to motion under Rule 30.10 (production from non-parties): *Duguay v. Devoe*.[85]

13. *Plaintiff's obligation to use "reasonable efforts" to obtain clinical notes and records of treating physicians considered:* Motion by defendant to compel production from plaintiff of clinical notes and records of treating physicians from date of accident; plaintiff refused at discovery to give "best efforts" undertaking to procure same; plaintiff also resisted production on ground of relevance. Held, plaintiff need only undertake reasonable efforts to obtain clinical notes, i.e., a letter of request to the doctor with a follow-up letter or phone call would be sufficient; if documents still not forthcoming, defendant then in position to move under Rule 30.10 (production from non-parties). On receipt of documents, plaintiff can make determination of relevance and, having done so, advise the defendant, who may assent or move for judicial determination. Defendant should pay attendant medical fees and reasonable photocopying charges, as plaintiff would not have incurred expense but for insistence of defendant: *Schultz v. Galvin*.[86]

14. *Court may refuse to order production of physician's clinical notes and records where physician's medical report has been delivered and there is no ambiguity, inconsistency or dispute of fact in report or other evidence:* Motion by defendant for production of clinical notes and records relating to both plaintiffs; male plaintiff had history of previous injuries, and differences noted in medical reports and testimony on his discovery. Female plaintiff neither complaining of prior injuries nor giving contradictory evidence. Male plaintiff ordered to

---

85 (1988), 63 O.R. (2d) 499 (H.C.).
86 (1988), 27 C.P.C. (2d) 253, 65 O.R. (2d) 13 (H.C.).
The *Duguay* case (see item 12, *supra*) and the *Schultz* case were decided within months of each other and without reference to the other. According to Stortini D.C.J. (L.J.S.C.) in the *Duguay* case, to require the plaintiff to request the clinical records from attending physicians "would be tantamount to a mandatory injunction sanctioned by drastic consequences", and that resort to Rule 30.10 (production from non-parties) is to be preferred; whereas, Kurisko L.J.S.C. in the *Schultz* case, demonstrates a strong preference for the reverse. In practice, the route followed in *Schultz* appears to have been adopted by the profession, probably because initial nervousness concerning release of physicians' clinical notes and records has abated; plaintiff's counsel are more disposed now to give "reasonable efforts" undertakings at discoveries if the relevance hurdle is overcome. From the defendant's viewpoint, the expense of the motion required under Rule 30.10 is avoided.

produce relevant clinical notes and records relating to pre-existing condition. Documents of post-injury treatment of female plaintiff not producible where report delivered and no ambiguity, inconsistency or dispute of fact in the report or other evidence. Appeal dismissed: *Gallo v. Gillham.*[87]

15. *A party's "control or power"* over documents considered: On defendant's motion to require plaintiff to produce clinical notes and records of treating physicians, order provided best practical solution was to require plaintiff to request that they be delivered to him. Appeal from decision dismissed; in reasons, Southey J. stated:

> There are many instances in which a party, through business or family relationships, has effective control or power over documents in the possession of another person, even though not legally entitled to compel delivery from the person having possession.

Consequently, the words "control" and "power" in Rule 30.02(1) should not be construed as limiting the obligation to those documents in respect of which a party is legally entitled to possession: *Triumbari v. Bloch.*[88]

16. *Plaintiff's clinical notes and records will be ordered if relevancy established; medical report not to be offered as alternative for defendant:* Appeal by defendant from order directing plaintiff to obtain from her family doctor a report *or* the clinical notes relating to her condition immediately preceding accident, as well as any prior neck injury. Statement of claim contained broad allegations of injury and its effects. Appeal allowed. The court would not agree with sweeping statements to effect that once personal injuries alleged a plaintiff's entire medical history in issue; criteria must be found by which to assess what part of medical history is relevant and what is not. Clinical records before and since accident ordered, but limited to medical conditions identified in statement or at examination for discovery.[89] *Furlano v. Calarco.*[90]

---

87 (1987), 15 C.P.C. (2d) 125, 58 O.R. (2d) 115 (Master), affirmed (1987), 23 C.P.C. (2d) 109, 67 O.R. (2d) 734 (H.C.).

88 (February 3, 1987), Doc. 201620/83 (Ont. Dist. Ct.), affirmed (1987), 20 C.P.C. (2d) 277 (Ont. H.C.).

89 The approach taken in this case and in *Trovato v. Smith*, below, leads to problem identified in *Wilton v. Brown, supra*, that discretion as to which information is to be produced will initially reside with plaintiff and possibly his or her physician, necessitating further procedures by defendant to pursue what he or she regards as relevant disclosure. It is suggested, in interest of promoting early settlement, that disclosure be as complete as possible, with finer points of relevance to be dealt with by judge at trial.

90 (1987), 20 C.P.C. (2d) 279, 60 O.R. (2d) 451 (H.C.).

17. Defendants sought from plaintiff production of clinical notes and records made by plaintiff's physicians. Order made directing plaintiff to seek clinical notes and records from doctors, which if produced would create responsibility in plaintiff to determine whether any of such documents relate to any matter in issue in the action. If any do so relate, then a supplementary affidavit of documents must be prepared by plaintiff, the documents produced, and the plaintiff will be obliged to re-attend for further examination for discovery in relation thereto. If defence not satisfied that supplementary affidavit of documents is accurate or complete, then defendant may turn to Rule 30: *Trovato v. Smith*.[91]

18. Motion by defendants to compel from plaintiff production of clinical notes and records of plaintiff's physician prior to accident. No issue was raised in pleadings or on facts presented relating to plaintiff's pre-existing condition. Order refused, although at some time in future issue may arise with respect to pre-existing condition, at which time circumstances may make it more appropriate to grant relief requested: *Karkanas v. Thomas*.[92]

19. Appeal from order dismissing portion of motion to compel plaintiff to produce clinical notes and records of her treating physicians, before and after accident. Following *Cook v. Ip*,[93] plaintiff ordered to produce all relevant documents she is able to obtain by requesting them from doctors involved; if not successful, defendant compelled to proceed under Rule 30.10: *Heywood v. Nash*.[94]

20. Appeal from order requiring plaintiffs to make best efforts to obtain clinical notes and records made by two physicians who had treated plaintiff, one of whom had prepared medical report. Appeal dismissed, following *Fedorczenko v. Jamieson*.[95] *Whitby v. Mount Sinai Hospital*.[96]

21. *Plaintiffs required to use reasonable efforts to obtain relevant medical records concerning plaintiff not in his possession:* Motion by defendants requesting order that plaintiffs use their best efforts to obtain clinical notes and records of medical doctors and summary of OHIP services. Basic issue was whether the new Ontario Rules of Civil Pro-

---

91 (1987), 15 C.P.C. (2d) 121 (Ont. Dist. Ct.).
92 (1986), 19 C.P.C. (2d) 303 (Ont. Dist. Ct.).
93 *Supra*, note 69. See 4.4, Order for Production of Documents from a Non-party; Case Law; item 10., below, for case summary.
94 (1986), 18 C.P.C. (2d) 154 (Ont. H.C.), additional reasons at (1986), 18 C.P.C. (2d) 154 at 156 (Ont. H.C.).
95 See below, note 97.
96 (1986), 13 C.P.C. (2d) 274, 57 O.R. (2d) 219 (Master), affirmed (1987), 24 C.P.C. (2d) 319, 67 O.R. (2d) 479 (H.C.).

cedure altered law under former Ontario Rules which held that a party could be ordered to make "reasonable efforts" to obtain documents in appropriate cases. On appeal from order dismissing motion, held that the words "in his possession, custody or power" in old Rule 347 were not substantially different than "in his or her possession, control or power" under new Rules 30.02(1) and 34.10(2), so that there is no difference with respect to the obligation to attempt to obtain documents in either case. Plaintiff ordered to use reasonable efforts to obtain OHIP summary, but appeal dismissed in other respects with leave to reapply on specific material: *Fedorczenko v. Jamieson*.[97]

22. Appeal from unsuccessful motion by defendants for production by plaintiff of clinical notes and records. Appeal allowed; plaintiff ordered to produce all relevant documents if she is able to obtain such by a request to the professionals involved: *Griffis v. Toronto Transit Commission*.[98]

23. Motion under Rule 33.04(2)(b) for order requiring plaintiff to produce and make available for inspection clinical notes and records of treating physicians. Held that, as the clinical notes and records of treating physicians are not "in the possession, power or control" of the plaintiff, no production would be ordered: *Zailberg v. Kinsella*.[99]

24. On discovery, in a personal injury action, the plaintiff has a duty to obtain and produce hospital and medical records for treatment he or she has received; it is insufficient merely to provide a written authorization permitting the defendant to obtain such records: *Gorin v. Ho*.[100]

25. *No privilege attaching to medical report provided by plaintiff's no-fault insurer to plaintiff's solicitor:* Appeal by defendant from an order refusing production of a medical report. The medical report was received by plaintiff's solicitor from the insurer of automobile in which plaintiff was a passenger when injured, which had procured same after plaintiff had applied for "no fault" insurance benefits (neither insurer nor owner of automobile were parties to the action). Appeal allowed, as report was not privileged. In his reasons, Galligan J. stated:

> The only possible basis upon which the plaintiff could refuse production of the medical report would be if it were protected by solicitor-client privilege. Unless it is covered by that privilege, there can be no reason why the plaintiff would not be obliged to produce it because it doubtless

---

97 (1986), 56 O.R. (2d) 252, 14 C.P.C. (2d) 299 (H.C.).
98 (1985), 15 C.P.C. (2d) 119 (Ont. H.C.).
99 (1985), 6 C.P.C. (2d) 124 (Ont. Dist. Ct.).
100 (1983), 38 C.P.C. 72 (Ont. Master).

contains relevant and material information to which the defendant otherwise would be entitled.

... I do not think the claim for privilege can be sustained because the report was not made at the request or suggestion of the plaintiff's solicitor, but was made at the instance of the Portage La Prairie Insurance Company. Also, the report was not made or procured for the purpose of any litigation. It was made for the purpose of assessing a claim for benefits under the "no-fault" provisions of the Portage La Prairie Insurance Company policy.

Halteh v. McCoy.[101]

4.3.3 Examination for Discovery of a Non-Party

The court may on motion order the examination for discovery of any person who there is reason to believe has information relevant to a material issue in the action, other than an expert engaged by or on behalf of a party in preparation for contemplated or pending litigation.[102] Before making such an order, the court must be satisfied, among other things, that:

1. the moving party has been unable to obtain the information from other persons whom the moving party is entitled to examine for discovery, or from the person the party seeks to examine;
2. it would be unfair to require the moving party to proceed to trial without having the opportunity of examining the person.[103]

The rules pertaining to production of documents on an examination for discovery would apply to such a person, including clinical notes and records, hospital records, etc.

The rule has not been used to any extent to examine medical experts for the reason that most medical records required for the prosecution or defence of a personal injury action will be producible under other rules, and also because the evidence of a person examined under the rule may not be read into evidence at trial.[104] However, the rule may be useful to examine a treating physician where an opposite party has no clear recollection of visits and the physician's clinical notes are incomprehensible, incomplete or unavailable. It is the appropriate rule to be employed when a party wishes to orally examine medical witnesses who have provided care to an

---

101 (1974), 6 O.R. (2d) 512 (H.C.).
102 Rules of Civil Procedure, Rule 31.10(1).
103 Rule 31.10(2).
104 Rule 31.10(5).

opposite party, and who may be called to testify at trial: see *Wells (Litigation Guardian of) v. Paramsothy*, below.

A party who examines a person orally under this rule is required to serve every party who attended or was represented on the examination with the transcript free of charge, unless the court orders otherwise;[105] which costs are not recoverable from another party unless the court expressly orders otherwise.[106]

Case Law: *Pre-trial access to speak with opposing party's health care professionals to be exercised through Rule 31.10, which permits pre-trial oral examination of non-parties:* Appeal from order in medical malpractice action dismissing defendant's motion to have unrestricted pre-trial access to speak with plaintiff's health care professionals to obtain disclosure of medical information. After discussing the historic common law recognition of confidentiality in the doctor-patient relationship, the Court reviewed authorities dealing with issue of disclosure of personal health information to opposing parties. It confirmed that in an action no privilege attaches to doctor-patient information, and that all medical information relating to the cause and extent of the injuries must be disclosed, subject to the Court's jurisdiction to exercise supervision and control over disclosure procedure where parties disagree. The procedure to be followed in this case was to be found in the Rules of Civil Procedure, specifically Rule 31.10, which, with leave, permits oral discovery of non-parties; this setting would respond to most of the concerns expressed in earlier authorities regarding extent of disclosure. Appeal dismissed: *Wells (Litigation Guardian of) v. Paramsothy*.[107]

4.4 ORDER FOR PRODUCTION OF DOCUMENTS FROM A NON-PARTY

The court has an inherent jurisdiction to ensure that it has all relevant material on the issue before it to enable it to reach a just conclusion and, in the absence of specific statutory prohibition, may order the production of medical records to determine the nature, extent and effect of the injuries which may have been suffered, and the appropriate measure of damages flowing from them.

If a person commences a civil action to recover damages for personal injuries sustained in an accident, his medical condition both before and af-

---

105 Rule 31.10(3).
106 Rule 31.10(4).
107 (1996), 32 O.R. (3d) 452 (Div. Ct.), leave to appeal refused (1997), 32 O.R. (3d) 452n (C.A.).

ter the accident are in issue to the extent that it is relevant to his or her accident-related injuries. In Ontario, an opposite party may move for inspection of a document that is in the possession, control or power of a person not a party and is not privileged where the court is satisfied that:

1. the document is relevant to a material issue in the action; and
2. it would be unfair to require the moving party to proceed to trial without having discovery of the document.[108]

If a party on his or her examination for discovery has undertaken to use reasonable efforts to obtain the clinical notes and records of medical persons who have examined or treated him or her with respect to his or her accident-related injuries, and such efforts have failed, this is the appropriate rule for an opposite party to employ against the medical person in question. Service of the Notice of Motion and supporting affidavit, which will attest to the plaintiff's consent through his or her undertaking, on the medical person will almost invariably result in production of the documents sought. Occasionally, a physician will refuse on the ground that the Canadian Medical Protective Association or other professional organization to which he or she may subscribe, would object; however, objections usually disappear when the patient's consent is established. Should the matter proceed to a hearing, the law is clear that a patient has a common law right to access the medical records of his or her physician.[109]

Case Law: The following are recent authorities which consider the application of this rule as it relates to production of documents containing personal medical information:

1. *Psychiatrist's patient records may be privileged in certain circumstances; and where privilege is warranted it may be necessary for the Court to qualify disclosure by imposing conditions designed to preserve balance between an opponent's right to access documents for litigation and the patient's right to confidentiality:* Appeal from order of British Columbia Court of Appeal permitting limited disclosure of psychiatrist's notes and records. The plaintiff claimed damages for mental distress, etc., arising from sexual relations she had with the defendant, a psychiatrist, in the course of treatment. In order to cope

---

108 Rule 31.10(1).
109 See 3.2, *supra*, "Patient's right to access own personal medical records." The regulations made pursuant to some health profession Acts expressly require a member to provide copies from a patient's health record upon request.

with these and other events, the plaintiff sought psychiatric treatment from another psychiatrist, Dr. Parfitt. On examination for discovery of the plaintiff, the defendant requested production of Dr. Parfitt's notes and records, which was refused. The defendant brought a motion before the Master to obtain disclosure of the notes and records from Dr. Parfitt. The B.C. *Supreme Court Rules*, provided in part as follows:

> 26(11) Where a document is in the possession or control of a person who is not a party, the court, on notice to the person and all other parties, may order production and inspection of the document . . .[110]

The Master found no blanket privilege existed for communications between patient and physician, and ordered that all documents be produced. The order was appealed and the matter was finally considered by Supreme Court of Canada. In her judgment, McLachlin J. (La Forest, Sopinka, Cory, Iacobucci and Major JJ. concurring), dismissed the appeal of the appellant (plaintiff) from the decision of the British Columbia Court of Appeal, which had ordered disclosure of Dr. Parfitt's reporting letters and notes recording discussions between her and the plaintiff, but did not order disclosure of Dr. Parfitt's personal notes, used by her to make sense of what the patient was telling her. The disclosure ordered had been subject to four conditions:

1. inspection was to be confined to the defendants solicitors and expert witnesses (the defendant was not to see them);
2. any person who saw the documents should not disclose their contents to anyone not entitled to inspect them;
3. the documents could be used only for the purposes of the litigation; and,
4. only one copy of the notes was to be made by the defendant's solicitors, to be passed on as necessary to the defendant's expert witnesses.

McLachlin J. considered that while the traditional categories of privilege did not include communications between a psychiatrist and his or her patient, it was accepted that the common law permitted privilege in new situations where reason, experience and application of the principles so dictated, as discussed in *Slavutych v. Baker*, namely:

> (a) the communication must originate in a confidence that they will not be disclosed;

---

110 B.C. Reg. 221/90.

(b) the element of confidentiality must be essential to the full and satisfactory maintenance of the relation between the parties;
(c) the relation must be one which in the opinion of the community ought to be sedulously fostered; and
(d) the injury that would inure to the relation by disclosure of the communications must be greater than the benefit thereby gained for the correct disposal of litigation.[111]

In her view, the orders made by the B.C. Court of Appeal supported the principles relating to privilege which she had attempted to set forth, and ought not to be disturbed.

McLachlin J. considered the distinction between absolute or blanket privilege, on the one hand, and partial privilege on the other:

> While the traditional common law categories conceived privilege as an absolute, all-or-nothing proposition, more recent jurisprudence recognizes the appropriateness in many situations of partial privilege. The degree of protection conferred by the privilege may be absolute or partial, depending on what is required to strike the proper balance between the interest in protecting the communication from disclosure and the interest in proper disposition of the litigation. Partial privilege may signify that only some of the documents in a given class must be produced. Documents should be considered individually or by sub-groups on a "case by case" basis.[112]

She observed in certain circumstances it may be necessary for the Court to examine documents to qualify the disclosure by imposing appropriate limits to preserve this balance: *M. (A.) v. Ryan*.[113]

2. Motion by defendants against plaintiff's family physician (general practitioner who practised psychotherapy) for production of clinical notes and records, in action for damages for sexual abuse brought against F., Children's Aid Society and provincial Crown. Pleadings put into issue the subject of plaintiff's mental and physical well-being, both before and after sexual abuse alleged. Production resisted because of physicians concerns of impact on plaintiff should his clinical notes be released, and because it is fundamental to psychotherapy process that patients feel free to disclose personal history, thoughts

---

111 *Supra*, note 1, derived from *Wigmore on Evidence*, vol. 8 (McNaughton rev. 1961) (Boston: Little Brown) para. 2285.
112 *Ibid.* at (D.L.R.) 227.
113 4 C.R. (5th) 220, 29 B.C.L.R. (3d) 133, [1997] 4 W.W.R. 1, 34 C.C.L.T. (2d) 1, [1997] 1 S.C.R. 157, 8 C.P.C. (4th) 1, 143 D.L.R. (4th) 1.

and feelings without threat of exposure or retaliation. A portion of the judgment in *M. (A.) v. Ryan* (B.C. C.A.) was cited, in which Southin J.A. states:

> . . . a defendant ought not to be deprived of an assessment of the loss he actually caused, founded on all relevant evidence. It would be as much a miscarriage of justice for him to be ordered to pay a million dollars when, if all the relevant evidence were before the court, the award would be for one-tenth that sum, as it would be for the injured person to feel compelled to retire from the field of battle because of a demand for documents containing intensely personal matters of little relevance.

There is no perfect balance to be struck between these competing considerations in this or any other case.[114]

Held, it would not be possible for defendants to properly evaluate the nature and quantum of the claim for damages, nor would it be possible for the trial judge to properly conduct an assessment of damages without having had access to the clinical notes and records of the family physician, to determine which aspects of the claims for damages are referrable to each defendant's conduct and which are referrable to other causes; production of all clinical notes and records of family physician ordered: *P. (L.M.) v. F. (D.)*.[115]

3. *Court may order production of psychiatrists medical records concerning plaintiff, if relevant, notwithstanding delivery of psychiatrist's report; no evidentiary privilege attaching:* Appeal from Master's order requiring plaintiff's psychiatrist to produce clinical notes and medical records, in action for damages for personal injuries resulting in lack of concentration, insomnia, nightmares, depression, etc. Psychiatrist had treated plaintiff before and since accident. Production resisted on ground that psychiatrist had provided report summarizing parts of treatment he considered relevant to personal injury claim, and that production would add to plaintiff's suffering and could cause set back. Counsel for psychiatrist argued, citing Supreme Court of Canada decision in *Frenette v. Metropolitan Life Insurance Co.*[116] new evidentiary privilege may be emerging whereby obligation to disclose patient's medical records subject to court's discretion, requiring court to balance competing interests, i.e., the interest in protecting the privacy of the patient to foster trust and open communication essential

---

114 (1994), 32 C.P.C. (3d) 66, 98 B.C.L.R. (2d) 1, [1995] 1 W.W.R. 677 (B.C. C.A.).
115 (1994), 22 C.C.L.T. (2d) 312, 34 C.P.C. (3d) 172 (Ont. Gen. Div.).
116 [1992] 1 S.C.R. 647, 134 N.R. 169, 46 Q.A.C. 161, [1992] I.L.R. 1-2823, 89 D.L.R. (4th) 653, 4 C.C.L.I. (2d) 1.

between doctor and patient, with the competing interest in applying principles of fundamental justice such as compellability, full disclosure of material facts, right to make a full defence, and search for truth by the defendants. Held, as plaintiff put both her physical and mental health in issue, records dealing with her physical and mental health, both prior and subsequent to the accident, were essential to determine whether injuries complained of were caused by the accident, were aggravated by the accident, or predate the accident; production of psychiatrist's records ordered; further, psychiatrist had not satisfied court on balance of probabilities that disclosure would be so traumatic to plaintiff's mental health that it outweighed defendant's interest in applying principles of fundamental justice: *Giroux v. Falusi.*[117]

4. *Exercise of court's discretion requires balancing of plaintiff's interest in confidentiality and defendant's interest in full disclosure of medical records, as well as interest of the non-party:* Motion by defendant against physicians and hospitals (non-parties) to compel production of medical records pertaining to plaintiff. The test for production of a document from a non-party differs from the obligation of a party to disclose documents: production from a non-party can only be ordered where the Court is satisfied that the document is relevant to a *material* issue in the action and that it would be *unfair* to require the moving party to proceed to trial without having discovery of the document. Production of clinical notes and records will not be ordered every time the request is made, especially when a report has been provided by the physician. Each case must be considered on its own merit, balancing the plaintiff's interest in the confidentiality of medical records, the defendant's interest in full disclosure of relevant materials, and the interest of the non-party. The broad nature of the plaintiff's claim was such that the whole medical history, past and present, was relevant. Production of medical records ordered, including the raw test data of a psychologist who had examined the plaintiff: *Mather v. Turnbull.*[118]

5. *Court has discretion to refuse production of relevant medical records in certain circumstances, i.e., where it would interfere with relationship between patient and psychiatrist:* Motion by husband against psychiatrist for order compelling production of medical records pertaining to wife, in matrimonial action in which wife pleaded psychiatric problems rendered her unable to seek independent employment. The court reasoned, notwithstanding relevance of records to issues in

---

117 (1992), 61 O.A.C. 317 (Div. Ct.).
118 (1991), 47 C.P.C. (2d) 180 (Ont. Gen. Div.).

action, order for production not automatic; court has discretion to refuse order. In refusing order, Master Cork stated:

> Here, I have clear and most emphatic evidence that any extension of the examination of the husband into the medical records of his wife's treatment by Dr. Johnston, will clearly have a most adverse effect on the wife not only now, but in the future, as it would appear that such examination affects the very foundation of the relationship between patient and psychiatrist, which is the base of the continuing future therapy thereafter. This is not at all a historical effect, but has a very real effect on the present as well as future attempts by Dr. Johnston to assist the wife hereafter.

He stated also that the further requirement in Rule 30.10(1)(b), relating to unfairness of requiring the moving party to proceed to trial without having discovery of the document, was not satisfied, in view of thorough series of reports on past, current and future problems of wife, which would render further probing a "fishing expedition" that would be most vexatious and harmful to the wife. Order refused: *G. (D.M.) v. G. (S.D.).*[119]

6. *Treating physician's clinical notes and records of plaintiff may be ordered notwithstanding delivery of medical reports:* Motion by defendant, *inter alia*, against treating physicians for production of medical records pertaining to pre-accident and post-accident treatment of plaintiff. Production from physician relating to pre-accident treatment refused for failure to establish relevance between pre-accident condition and alleged accident-related injuries and disability. Production from physicians relating to post-accident treatment of plaintiff refused in first instance, as all physicians named had prepared reports with respect to their treatment of plaintiff, which were in possession of defendant, and their notes would provide background material only; further, there was nothing to indicate that any of the reports was ambiguous or incomplete, or at odds with plaintiff's statements. On appeal, held medical records pertaining to post-accident treatment of plaintiff should be produced. Authority of *Tilly v. Crangle*[120] doubted; *Cook v. Ip*[121] cited with approval: *Noonan v. Commercial Union Assurance Co. of Canada.*[122]

---

119 (1990), 72 O.R. (2d) 774, 44 C.P.C. (2d) 52 (Master).
120 (1981), 31 O.R. (2d) 641, 120 D.L.R. (3d) 563 (Ont. C.A.).
121 *Supra*, note 69. See 4.4, Order for Production of Documents from a Nonparty; Case Law; item 10., below, for case summary.
122 (1989), 36 C.P.C. (2d) 239 (Ont. Dist. Ct.), reversed in part (1989), 42 C.P.C. (2d) 1 (Ont. H.C.).

7. *The extent to which the Court will order production of medical records will be determined by relevance.* Motion by defendant for production from OHIP of all medical records, medical reports, hospital records, microfische, computer print-outs and claim cards relating to plaintiffs, both before and after motor vehicle accident. *Cook v. Ip* did not state that all medical records are relevant or pertinent, but only that those which were relevant or pertinent should be available. The first question is whether the medical records requested are relevant, and the next question is whether it would be "unfair" to require the defendant to proceed to trial without the documents. Medical records would be relevant where they deal with any treatment for any injury or disease or condition which might reasonably be considered to still have some effect immediately before the accident in issue, which was not the case here. Furthermore, there did not seem to be any reasonable ground for suspecting plaintiffs suffered from any condition before period for which plaintiffs were prepared to authorize release of medical records, so that a request for documents prior to such period would be "fishing" and it would not be unfair that the defendant should proceed to trial without having them: *Tamssot v. Belgrano*[123]

8. *Pre-accident medical records and notes of physician concerning plaintiff to be produced if relevant, at expense of requesting party:* Appeal by defendant from order dismissing motion for leave to compel production for inspection of document in possession, control or power of non-party physician, who treated the plaintiff before motor vehicle accident in question. Appeal allowed: in view of pleadings and claims of female plaintiff, medical records and notes of physician before accident were relevant, particularly as physician did not care for plaintiff following accident. Defendant ordered to pay for costs incurred by physician in preparation of material requested: *Orr v. Warren.*[124]

9. *Physician's clinical notes and records of plaintiff to be produced to defendants unless plaintiff or physician can demonstrate production is unnecessary:* Appeal from order dismissing defendants' motion to compel production from treating physicians of clinical notes and records pertaining to plaintiff. Rules make it clear that it was intended a more onerous test be satisfied for the obtaining of documents from persons not parties to litigation under Rule 30.10, than from parties to the litigation under different rules. Following *Cook v. Ip,*[125] in per-

---

123 (1987), 59 O.R. (2d) 57, 16 C.P.C. (2d) 189 (Master).
124 (1986), 18 C.P.C. (2d) 190, 59 O.R. (2d) 286 (H.C.).
125 *Supra,* note 69. See item 10., below, for case summary.

sonal injury cases, where the question in issue is the nature and extent of the plaintiff's injuries, it would be an unusual situation where it would be fair to require the defendant to go to trial without production of the clinical notes and records requested. It is incumbent upon either the plaintiff or the doctors, if they oppose the motion under Rule 30.10, to produce some evidence to satisfy the Court that production of the documents is unnecessary. Clinical notes and records ordered produced: *Couto v. Toronto Transit Commission*.[126]

10. *In absence of specific statutory prohibition, a court may order all relevant material to enable it to reach a just conclusion:* Appeal from unsuccessful motion by defendant requiring OHIP to produce claim cards pertaining to plaintiff. The plaintiff at discovery gave an authorization to the defendant's solicitors permitting them to obtain copies of certain records, including claim cards pertaining to the plaintiff that were in the possession of the Ontario Health Insurance Plan, which refused to produce the records despite the authorization. In delivering the judgment for the Court, Cory J.A. stated the production of medical records was fundamental to a court's determination of the nature, extent and effect of the injuries which may have been suffered and the appropriate measure of damages flowing from them, and that in the absence of specific statutory prohibition a court is free to exercise its inherent jurisdiction to ensure it has all relevant material to enable it to reach a just conclusion. Speaking on behalf of the Court, he wrote:

> No doubt medical records are private and confidential in nature. Nevertheless, when damages are sought for personal injuries, the medical condition of the plaintiff both before and after the accident is relevant. In this case, it is the very issue in question. The plaintiff himself has raised the issue and placed it before the court. In these circumstances there can no longer be any privacy or confidentiality attaching to the plaintiff's medical records.

Cook v. Ip.[127]

11. *Hospital may impose safeguards on disclosure of medical information pursuant to request of patient or representative:* Motion for order directing defendant hospital to produce medical records pertaining to plaintiff; plaintiff's solicitor had requested records in writing, enclosing executed and witnessed authorization and direction to hospital, with original signature; hospital refused to produce records unless its own authorization form for the release of information was used, to be

---

126 (1987), 16 C.P.C. (2d) 241, 59 O.R. (2d) 406 (H.C.).
127 *Supra*, note 69.

signed, witnessed and returned. Under section 49(6) of the Hospital Management Regulation,[128] a Board may permit . . . a person who presents a written request signed by the patient . . . to inspect and receive information from a medical record and to be given copies therefrom. Held, in absence of more detailed legislation, it is in public interest in the confidentiality of medical records that the hospital should have the ability to impose reasonable safeguards on the disclosure of medical information. Motion dismissed: *Jonathan v. Gore Mutual Insurance Co.*[129]

12. *Documents prohibited from disclosure under* Health Disciplines Act *not producible in civil proceeding in circumstances:* Applicant had commenced application for judicial review, in which order sought in nature of prohibition prohibiting discipline committee of the respondent from proceeding with professional misconduct hearing arising from complaint against applicant. Applicant brought application to compel production of all documents concerning deliberations of complaints committee of the College of Physicians and Surgeons of Ontario regarding decision made by the applicant not to administer an anaesthetic to a complainant. Respondent argued it was not required to produce material requested in view of section 65(1) and (2) of the *Health Disciplines Act, 1974*, which reads in part as follows:

> 65.(1) Every person employed in the administration of this Part . . . shall preserve secrecy with respect to all matters that come to his knowledge in the course of his duties . . . and shall not communicate any such matters to any other person . . . (2) No person to whom subsection 1 applies shall be required to give testimony in any civil suit or proceeding with regard to information obtained by him in the course of his duties, employment, inquiry or investigation except in a proceeding under this Part or the regulations or by-laws.[130]

Held, dismissing the application, it was considered the provisions of section 65(1) were a bar to the application, and it was not believed the applicant had a positive right to the material before the complaints committee. Also, the material sought should not be disclosed for policy reasons and because the proceedings before the complaints committee were not under attack in the application for judicial review: *Wilson v. College of Physicians and Surgeons (Ontario).*[131]

---

128 R.R.O. 1980, Reg. 865, under the *Public Hospitals Act*, R.S.O. 1980, c. 410 (essentially the same as s. 22(6) of the current Hospital Management Regulation, R.R.O. 1990, Reg. 965).
129 (1985), 6 C.P.C. (2d) 300 (Ont. Dist. Ct.).
130 S.O. 1974, c. 47.
131 (1981), 24 C.P.C. 52 (Ont. Div. Ct.).

Comment: Most reported cases in Ontario dealing with production of documents containing personal medical information in civil actions under the Rules of Civil Procedure have been concerned with clinical notes, records, etc., in the custody of physicians, public hospitals and OHIP. Considering the many other repositories of such documents,[132] it is surprising so few reported cases are concerned with production of documents from them. This dearth may, in part at least, be due to lack of awareness of these sources by personal injury counsel.

4.5 COURT-ORDERED MEDICAL EXAMINATION OF A PARTY

The *Courts of Justice Act*[133] permits the Court, on motion, to order a party to undergo a physical or mental examination by one or more health practitioners, where the physical or mental condition of a party to a proceeding is in question.[134] Where an order is made the party examined is required to answer the questions of the examining health practitioner relevant to the examination, and the answers given are admissible in evidence.[135] The examining health practitioner is required to prepare a written report setting out his or her observations, the results of any tests made, and his or her conclusions, diagnosis and prognosis, and to forthwith provide the report to the party who obtained the order,[136] who in turn is required to forthwith serve the report on every other party in the action.[137]

The court's power to order a medical examination extends to any party whose physical or mental condition is in question in a proceeding; however, where the question of a party's physical or mental condition is first raised by another party in a proceeding, the court is not to make an order unless the allegation is relevant to a material issue in the proceeding and there is good reason to believe that there is substance to the allegation.[138] For example, if a plaintiff in a personal injury chose to make an issue of the defendant's medical condition, perhaps in relation to a liability issue,

---

132 Discussed in Chapter 2.
133 R.S.O. 1990, c. C.43, s. 105.
134 Section 105(1) defines a "health practitioner" as a person licensed to practise medicine or dentistry in Ontario or any other jurisdiction, a member of the College of Psychologists of Ontario, or a person certified or registered as a psychologist by another jurisdiction.
135 *Ibid.*, s. 105(5).
136 Rule 33.06(1).
137 Rule 33.06(2).
138 *Courts of Justice Act*, R.S.O. 1990, c. C.43, s. 105(3).

he or she would have to satisfy this rule before the court would order a medical examination of the defendant.

The Ontario Rules of Civil Procedure require the party to be examined to provide to the party obtaining such order at least seven days before the examination a copy of:

(a) any report made by a health practitioner who has treated or examined the party to be examined, other than a practitioner whose report was made in preparation for contemplated or pending litigation and for no other purpose, and whom the party to be examined undertakes not to call as a witness at the hearing; and

(b) any hospital record or other medical document[139] relating to the mental or physical condition in question that is in the possession, control or power of the party other than a document made in preparation for contemplated or pending litigation and for no other purpose, and in respect of which the party to be examined undertakes not to call evidence at the hearing.[140]

Regrettably, the rule is more frequently observed in the breach. From a defence point of view, the failure to insist on compliance may be disastrous, in that damaging medical reports or hospital records concerning the plaintiff may not only escape evaluation by the defence's medical experts, but may never see the light of day. To promote compliance, it is suggested that opposing counsel's attention be directed to the rule in a letter confirming the defence medical examination arrangements, accompanied by a specific request for provision of medical reports and hospital records. The precise wording of the section should be adopted to the extent possible so as to eliminate confusion should the matter surface at trial. One may speculate what sanctions are available to the trial judge when confronted with a party whose non-compliance has resulted in the disclosure at trial of a damaging report or record which should have been disclosed much earlier under this rule, but there can be no doubt about the cost in terms of the defaulting party's credibility.

The rules pertaining to a court-ordered medical examination apply to a physical or mental examination conducted on the consent in writing of the parties, except to the extent they are waived by the consent.[141] Almost

---

139 Rule 33.04(1) provides the meaning of "document" set out in Rule 30.01(1) applies; see 4.3.1, *supra*, for discussion of "document".
140 Rule 33.04(2).
141 Rule 33.08.

all medical examinations in civil actions are conducted on consent by arrangement between the parties.

Case Law:
1. Motion under Rule 33.04(2)(b) by the defendant for an order requiring the plaintiff in a personal injury action to produce medical documentation, including doctor's notes taken at the time of examination of the plaintiff preliminary to preparation of a report made by an unknown psychiatrist for the purpose of pending litigation; the defendant contended while the rule excluded privileged medical reports in respect of which an undertaking had been given not to call its author at trial the plaintiff was nevertheless required to provide information of observations made by a doctor of the plaintiff, history taken, diagnosis and prognosis made. Held that the defendant's contention would emasculate Rule 31.06(3), which exempted from disclosure the findings, opinions and conclusions of an expert engaged by a party being examined, as well as the expert's name and address, where the findings, opinions and conclusions were made in preparation of contemplated or pending litigation and the party being examined undertakes not to call the expert as a witness at the trial; Rule 33.04(2)(b) to be read as though the words "that is not privileged" appeared after "any hospital record or other medical document"; order for production of the psychiatrist's notes refused: *Flavelle v. Toronto Transit Commission.*[142]
2. Motion under Rule 33.04(2)(b) by defendants for an order requiring plaintiff to provide clinical notes of physicians who treated the plaintiff since the subject motor vehicle accident. Gibson D.C.J. held, dismissing the motion, that the clinical notes were "other medical documents" within the meaning of Rule 33.04(2)(b), but were not "in the possession, power or control" of the plaintiff, without prejudice to defendants' right to bring motion under Rule 30.10 (production from non-parties). In his reasons, Gibson D.C.J. felt different considerations applied to documents dealt with in earlier cases, other than those which applied to clinical notes and records of a treating doctor: *Zailberg v. Kinsella.*[143]

4.6 TRIAL

A party who requires the attendance of a person in Ontario as a witness at a trial may serve the person with a summons to witness form, re-

---

142 (1985), 49 C.P.C. 209 (Ont. Dist. Ct.).
143 (1985), 6 C.P.C. (2d) 124 (Ont. Dist. Ct.).

quiring him or her to attend the trial at the time and place stated in the summons; the summons may require the person to produce at the trial the documents or other things in his or her possession, control, or power relating to the matters in question in the action that are specified in the summons.[144] Having summoned a witness to attend at the trial and produce documents specified in the summons, the summoning party is not required to call the witness to testify in order to obtain production of his or her documents for inspection. If the witness has no objection to producing the documents, he or she may leave the documents with the court, so that either party may make use of them at trial, subject to a proper foundation being laid for their admissibility. This affords the defendant an opportunity, which might not otherwise exist, to have such documents available for cross-examination of the plaintiff's witnesses.

Case Law: *Defendants required to disclose details of discussions with plaintiff's physician provided without plaintiff's consent:* At the trial of a personal injury action, defendant's counsel disclosed that before trial defence representatives had interviewed some physicians who had treated plaintiff, without consent of the plaintiff and not pursuant to the Rules. On plaintiff's motion, defendants ordered to disclose the names of the attending or treating physicians from whom information was obtained and all the information obtained from them that differed in any substantial way from the information contained in the reports and documentation provided by the plaintiff to the defendants. The mere commencement of an action by a plaintiff for damages resulting from personal injuries does not waive the right to confidentiality arising out of the patient-physician relationship, or that the patient impliedly consents to the physician releasing information to the defendants: *St. Louis (Litigation Guardian of) v. Feleki*.[145]

4.6.1 Medical Records under Section 35 of the *Evidence Act*[146]

Any writing or record[147] made of any act, transaction, occurrence or event is admissible as evidence of such act, transaction, occurrence or event if made in the usual and ordinary course of any business[148] and if it was in the usual and ordinary course of such business to make such writing

---

144 Rule 53.04(1).
145 (1990), 75 D.L.R. (4th) 758 (Ont. Gen. Div.), affirmed on other grounds (1993), 107 D.LR. (4th) 767 (Ont. Div. Ct.).
146 R.S.O. 1990, c. E.23.
147 *Supra*, note 145, at s. 35(1), "record" includes any information that is recorded or stored by means of any device.
148 *Ibid.*, at s. 35(1), "business" includes every kind of business, profession, occupation, calling, operation or activity, whether carried on for profit or otherwise.

or record at the time of such act, transaction, occurrence or event or within a reasonable time thereafter, provided the party tendering the writing or record has given at least seven days notice of his or her intention to all other parties in the action; any party to the action is entitled to obtain from the person who has possession thereof production for inspection of the writing or record within five days after giving notice to produce the same.

The circumstances of the making of such a writing or record, including lack of personal knowledge by the maker, may be shown to affect its weight, but such circumstances do not affect its admissibility. Nothing in the section affects the admissibility of any evidence that would otherwise be admissible, or makes admissible any writing or record that is privileged.

Case Law:
1. *Documents sought must be sufficiently identified in Notice:* Motion by defendant made at trial of personal injury action, following close of plaintiff's case, for leave to introduce plaintiff's hospital records in evidence pursuant to section 35 of the *Evidence Act*. Held, notice must be sufficiently identified for the party receiving the notice to obtain a copy of the record from the person who has possession of it; order refused as the notice was so bereft of details that it was no notice at all within the meaning of the Act. Judge's discretion to waive notice, if there was one, was not exercised because of prejudice to plaintiff: *Priore v. Hughes.*[149]
2. *Medical opinion expressed in hospital record admitted under section 35 of* Evidence Act *may qualify as medical report under section 52 of* Evidence Act: Ruling sought at trial as to whether portions of hospital record constituted medical report within meaning of section 52[150] of *Evidence Act*. On consent, hospital records adduced by plaintiff were entered as evidence at trial; the records included document prepared by physician which contained a medical history of plaintiff, the results of a physical examination of plaintiff, and an opinion of the examining physician; the court construed the document as medical report within the meaning of section 52 of *Evidence Act*, and ordered plaintiff to produce any further medical reports of the physician.
(Note: *The plaintiff did not seek to adduce the hospital records or any portion thereof as a medical report under section 52; the court disregarded the notice requirement under section 52 because hospital records were entered "on consent", notwithstanding that the consent was given so that the records need not be proved by hospital medical librarian. Consequently, a plaintiff may be at some risk when he seeks to enter hospital records under section 35 of the* Evidence Act *in evi-*

---

149 (1994), 28 C.P.C. (3d) 314 (Ont. Gen. Div.).
150 See discussion at 4.6.2, below.

dence at trial which contain documents that qualify as a medical report under section 52); Black v. Royal Bank.[151]

3. *Persons who may qualify hospital records under section 35a of Evidence Act, without calling maker thereof:* In a malpractice action against hospital and physicians, any writing or record made of any act, transaction occurrence or event was admissible under section 35a of the *Evidence Act* as part of the hospital records without calling the maker, provided it is proved to have been made in the hospital routine and was made at the time or within a reasonable time thereafter. In his reasons, given at trial, Morand J. stated:

> It would be, it appears to me, more satisfactory if the custodian of the records were to be called to testify as to these records and as to the fact that they were made in the ordinary course of the business of the hospital. However, it is true that while this person is probably the best person to do it, documents may be proven by persons other than the people who actually have them in their custody, or other than the people who have actually produced them under certain circumstances . . .

Aynsley v. Toronto General Hospital.[152]

4.6.2 Medical Reports under Section 52 of the *Evidence Act*

A report obtained by or prepared for a party to an action and signed by a practitioner,[153] together with any other report of the practitioner that relates to the action, are, with the leave of the court and after at least ten days notice has been given to all other parties, admissible in evidence in the action.[154]

Unless otherwise ordered by the court, a party to an action is entitled, at the time that notice is given, to a copy of the report together with any other report of the practitioner that relates to the action.[155]

Except with the leave of the judge presiding at the trial, a practitioner who signs a report with respect to a party is not permitted to give evidence

---

151 (1988), 33 C.P.C. (2d) 93 (Ont. Dist. Ct.).
152 [1968] 1 O.R. 425, 66 D.L.R. (2d) 575 (Ont. H.C.), varied on other grounds [1969] 2 O.R. 829, 7 D.L.R. (3d) 193 (Ont. C.A.), affirmed on other grounds (1971), [1972] S.C.R. 435, 25 D.L.R. (3d) 241.
153 At s. 52(1), "practitioner" means:
    (a)   a member of a College as defined in subsection 1(1) of the *Regulated Health Professions Act*,
    (b)   a drugless practitioner registered under the *Drugless Practioners Act*,
    (c)   a person licensed or registered to practice in another part of Canada under an Act that is similar to an Act referred to in clause (a) or (b).
154 *Ibid.*, s. 52(2).
155 *Ibid.*, s. 52(3).

at the trial unless the report is given to all other parties in accordance with subsection (2).[156]

If a practitioner is required to give evidence in person in an action and the court is of the opinion that the evidence could have been produced as effectively by way of a report, the court may order the party that required the attendance of the practitioner to pay as costs therefor such sum as the court considers appropriate.[157]

This section of the *Evidence Act* should be read together with Rule 53.03 of the Ontario Rules of Civil Procedure, concerning service of an expert's report by a party who intends to call an expert witness at trial; see 4.6.3, below.

Case Law:
1. *Medical opinion expressed in hospital record admitted under section 35 of* Evidence Act *may qualify as medical report under section 52 of* Evidence Act: Ruling sought at trial as to whether portions of hospital record constituted medical report within meaning of section 52 of the *Evidence Act*. On consent, hospital records adduced by the plaintiff were entered as evidence at trial; the records included document prepared by physician which contained a medical history of plaintiff, the results of a physical examination of plaintiff, and an opinion of the examining physician; the court construed the document as medical report within the meaning of section 52 of the *Evidence Act*, and ordered plaintiff to produce any further medical reports of the physician.
(Note: *The plaintiff did not seek to adduce the hospital records or any portion thereof as a medical report under section 52; the court disregarded the notice requirement under section 52 because hospital records were entered "on consent", notwithstanding that the consent was admittedly so that the records need not be proved by hospital medical librarian. Consequently, a plaintiff may be at some risk when he seeks to enter hospital records under section 35 of the* Evidence Act *in evidence at trial which contain documents that qualify as a medical report under section 52.):* Black v. Royal Bank.[158]
2. *Medical expert may not be cross-examined with respect to opinions outside of his or her report filed at trial:* Ruling at trial as to scope of cross-examination of author of medical report filed at trial. The report of physician who conducted independent medical examination of plaintiff on behalf of the defendant was filed at trial by plaintiff, and

---
156 *Ibid.*, s. 52(4).
157 *Ibid.*, s. 52(5).
158 (1988), 33 C.P.C. (2d) 93 (Ont. Dist. Ct.).

so made part of the plaintiff's case; defendant sought to cross-examine the physician to elicit opinions on matters outside of opinions developed in report. Held, the physician was an expert whose evidence is caught by the provisions of both section 52 of the *Evidence Act* and Rule 53.03 of the Ontario Rules of Civil Procedure, requiring disclosure of expert opinions, and it is not appropriate that he be asked for an expert opinion that was not the product of his report. In his reasons, Osborne J. stated:

> I do not take the view that cross-examination must be contained within the four corners of the report. My judgment is that cross-examination cannot indirectly elicit from the witness expert opinions which should have been the subject matter of earlier disclosure. There was no such disclosure in this case, as required by Rule 53.03(1).

Stribbell v. Bhalla.[159]

3. *Report of medical expert not to be admitted unless author available for cross-examination by opposite party:* Objection made at trial of personal injury action by defendant to admission of medical report by plaintiff as evidence in the action, pursuant to section 52 of the *Evidence Act*, unless doctor made available to give oral evidence. Held, sustaining objection, that the right of opposing counsel to cross-examine is paramount, citing Kelly J.A., in *Kapulica v. Dumancic*, where he states:

> It follows from my understanding of the purpose of the amendment that, by tendering for admission a medical report which complies with the requirements of s. 50a, the party tendering it constitutes the medical practitioner who signs it his witness as fully as if he had produced him in Court and examined him under oath: consequently, that medical practitioner, if in the same trial brought into Court and placed in the witness-box, continues to be the witness of the party who tendered his report. He is subject to cross-examination not only upon his evidence given orally but also on the evidence given by means of the medical report in the same manner as he would have been if he had given oral testimony in the words of the report.[160]

Report admitted subject to doctor being available for cross-examination. Held further that:

---

159 (1988), 32 C.P.C. (2d) 272 (Ont. H.C.).
160 [1968] 2 O.R. 438 at 442 (C.A.).

> . . . the obligation is on counsel for the plaintiff to produce the medical practitioner in any instance where I exercise my discretion and sustain an objection to the filing of the report and permit the moving party to require the medical practitioner to give oral testimony.

Briand v. Sutton.[161]

4. *Physician statements relating to issue of liability contained in medical report does not qualify as evidence receivable under section 52:* Appeal by defendant from finding of liability made at trial of personal injury action; hospital admission notes containing report of physician to effect that plaintiff had been drinking heavily not admitted in evidence at trial pursuant to section 52 of *Evidence Act* because of defendant's failure to comply with notice requirements, and defendant not permitted to cross-examine physician. Held, that the part of the hospital admission notes containing statements relating to the issue of liability, as distinguished from physical injury, did not properly qualify as a *medical report* or as an annex to a medical report, and could not qualify as evidence receivable under section 52 even if requisite notice had been given. New trial ordered, as credibility of plaintiff's witnesses may have been materially affected by disputed evidence, and it was most important that trier of fact be provided with all relevant evidence bearing on cause of action: *Simpson v. Garbowsky.*[162]

5. *A party who elects to file a medical report in lieu of calling its author as a witness at trial must, in addition, file whatever documents had been received by him or her from the physician relating to the party:* Ruling on a point of evidence which arose in the course of a trial in a personal injury action; plaintiff's counsel elected to file as part of plaintiff's case one of two medical reports in his possession prepared by physician who had treated plaintiff. Held, having chosen to file one medical report pursuant to section 52 of the *Evidence Act*, plaintiff made physician who prepared report her witness for all purposes of the trial, and required plaintiff to file whatever documents had been forwarded by that physician which could be said to have been obtained by or prepared for a party to an action. It was not open to the plaintiff to file one such document without filing both. View affirmed that the adoption by a party of the procedure in section 52, by the filing of a medical report, obliges that party to have available the doctor who prepared the report for cross-examination, if required by the party adverse in interest: *Carew v. Loblaw's Ltd.*[163]

---

161 (1986), 15 C.P.C. (2d) 36, 57 O.R. (2d) 629 (H.C.).
162 (1983), 21 M.V.R. 153, 143 D.L.R. (3d) 260 (Ont. C.A.).
163 (1977), 18 O.R. (2d) 660, 83 D.L.R. (3d) 603 (H.C.).

6. *A party must elect whether to file medical report at trial or to call its author; he or she cannot do both, unless allowed to do so by the trial judge:* Appeal, *inter alia,* from ruling of trial judge at trial disallowing plaintiff to both file medical reports of plaintiff's physicians and to call the physicians as witnesses. Held, dismissing the appeal, that in the ordinary case a party cannot proceed both to file a medical report and call the author thereof as a witness, but must elect what course he will pursue; if the decision is made to proceed by way of filing the report, and if leave is granted, in most cases the doctor cannot be called by that party. Brooke J.A., in the reasons for judgment, stated:

> This section was not to provide for the introduction into evidence of a medical report when it was the intention of a plaintiff to call the doctor to give *viva voce* evidence; rather it was the intention of the Legislature to provide for the introduction into evidence of the medical report so that the party tendering it might be relieved from having to call the doctor to give evidence.
>
> . . . there will be situations where a party initially elects to file the report, and circumstances arise making it desirable that the trial Judge should permit or direct the doctor to be called as a witness. It may also happen — although much less frequently — that the doctor is initially called and in the view of the presiding Judge justice requires that his report should be filed. All of these situations call for the exercise of a judicial discretion by the trial Judge.

Ferraro v. Lee.[164]

7. *A physician who gives oral evidence at trial may not testify as to a new and substantial matter not disclosed in his report:* Ruling made at the trial of a personal injury action held that a medical report admitted under section 50a [now section 52] of the *Evidence Act* must substantially disclose the evidence the doctor will give orally. In his reasons, Zuber Co. Ct. J. stated:

> The doctor who gives oral evidence may obviously expand and amplify his report. As well, there may be cases where the condition of a litigant has worsened between the time the report was given and the time of trial, but in this case the variation would be one only of degree.
>
> . . . In this case, however, the reports fail to disclose a new and substantial matter. In my view, the plaintiff may not now adduce through Dr. Baranowsky evidence with respect to those new medical matters since they have not been disclosed in a report pursuant to subs. (3).

Iler v. Beaudet.[165]

---

164 (1974), 2 O.R. (2d) 417, 43 D.L.R. (3d) 161 (C.A.).
165 [1971] 3 O.R. 644 (Co. Ct.).

8. *An opposite party has an absolute right to cross examine medical practitioner who signed medical report tendered by a party and admitted in evidence at trial:* Appeal from ruling of trial judge at trial refusing defendant an opportunity to cross-examine medical practitioner who signed medical report tendered by plaintiff and admitted in evidence. Held, allowing the appeal and directing a new trial, the party tendering a medical report under section 50a [now section 52] of the *Evidence Act* constitutes the medical practitioner who signs it his or her witness as fully as if he or she had produced the medical practitioner in Court and examined him or her under oath, and is therefore subject to an absolute right of cross-examination, not only upon his or her evidence given orally, but also on the evidence given by means of the medical report in the same manner as he or she would have been if he or she had given oral testimony in the words of the report. Further, it is not a judicial exercise of the discretion of the trial judge's discretion to admit a medical report which includes a statement concerning the cause of the injury as opposed to the extent of the injury: *Kapulica v. Dumancic.*[166]

4.6.3 Medical Reports under Rule 53.03 of Ontario Rules of Civil Procedure

Rule 53.03[167] requires that a party who intends to call an expert witness at trial to, not less than 90 days before the commencement of the trial, serve on every other party to the action a report, signed by the expert, setting out his or her name, address and qualifications and the substance of his or her proposed testimony; and, further, a party who intends to call an expert witness at trial to respond to the expert witness of another party is required, not less than 60 days before the commencement of the trial, to serve on every other party to the action a like report. An expert witness may not testify with respect to an issue, except with leave of the trial judge, unless the substance of his or her testimony with respect to that issue is set out in,

(a) a report served under this rule; or

---

166 [1968] 2 O.R. 438 (C.A.).
167 Rule 53.03 was amended by O. Reg. 348/97; the amended rule, set out above, applies to all trials that commence on or after February 16th, 1998. The earlier rule provided that a party who intended to call an expert witness at trial was required to, not less than *ten* days before the commencement of the trial, serve on every other party to the action a report, signed by the expert, setting out his or her name, address and qualifications, and the substance of his or her proposed testimony.

(b) a supplementary report served on every other party to the action not less than 30 days before the commencement of the trial.

The judge may at the pre-trial conference, or the court may, on motion, extend or abridge the time provided for the service of a report or supplementary report under this rule.

Rule 53.03 should be read together with section 52 of the *Evidence Act* concerning service of an expert's report by a party who intends to call an expert witness at trial; see 4.6.2 *supra*.

Case Law: *Medical expert may not be cross-examined with respect to opinions outside of his or her report filed at trial:* Ruling at trial as to scope of cross-examination of author of medical report filed at trial. The report of physician who conducted independent medical examination of plaintiff on behalf of the defendant was filed at trial by plaintiff, and so made part of the plaintiffs case; defendant sought to cross-examine the physician to elicit opinions on matters outside of opinions developed in report. Held, the physician was an expert whose evidence is caught by the provisions of both section 52 of the *Evidence Act* and Rule 53.03, requiring disclosure of expert opinions, and it is not appropriate that he be asked for an expert opinion that was not the product of his report. In his reasons, Osborne J. stated:

> I do not take the view that cross-examination must be contained within the four corners of the report. My judgment is that cross-examination cannot indirectly elicit from the witness expert opinions which should have been the subject matter of earlier disclosure. There was no such disclosure in this case, as required by r. 53.03(1).

Stribbell v. Bhalla.[168]

4.6.4 Medical Reports of Court-Appointed Expert under Ontario Rules of Civil Procedure

On motion by a party or on his or her own initiative, a judge may, at any time, appoint one or more independent experts to inquire into and report on any question of fact or opinion relevant to an issue in the action;[169] the expert must be named by the judge and, where possible, shall be an expert agreed on by the parties.[170] The order must contain the instructions to

---

168 (1988), 32 C.P.C. (2d) 272 (Ont. H.C.).
169 Rule 52.03(1).
170 Rule 52.03(2).

be given to the expert, and the judge may make such further orders as he or she considers necessary to enable the expert to carry out the instructions, including, on motion by a party, an order for, *inter alia*, the physical or mental examination of a party under section 105 of the *Courts of Justice Act*.[171]

The expert so appointed is required to prepare a report, and send it to the registrar of the court, and the registrar shall send a copy thereof to every party.[172] The report is required to be filed as evidence at the trial of the action unless the trial judge orders otherwise.[173] The judge may direct the expert to make a further or supplementary report, which must also be sent to the registrar, who is required to send a copy thereof to every party.[174] Any party may cross-examine the expert at the trial.[175]

4.6.5 Use of Photographic Film of Health Records at Trial

Hospitals and other health institutions have for many years resorted to photographing their records with microfilm to reduce the time and expense involved in storing documents. The legislatures of each province have enacted some form of legislation permitting courts to admit microfilmed records as evidence at trials; in Ontario, section 34 of the *Evidence Act* provides:

34. (1) In this section,

"person" includes

(a) the Government of Canada and of any province of Canada, and a department, commission, board or branch of any such government,
(b) a corporation, its successors and assigns, and
(c) the heirs, executors, administrators or other legal representatives of a person;

"photographic film" includes any photographic plate, microphotographic film and photostatic negative and "photograph" has a corresponding meaning.

(2) Where a bill of exchange, promissory note, cheque, receipt, instrument, agreement, document, plan or a record or book or entry therein kept or held by any person,

(a) is photographed in the course of an established practice of such person of photographing objects of the same or a similar class in order to keep a permanent record thereof; and

---

171 Rule 52.03(3).
172 Rule 52.03(7).
173 Rule 52.03(8).
174 Rule 52.03(9).
175 Rule 52.03(11).

(b) is destroyed by or in the presence of such person or of one or more of the person's employees or delivered to another person in the ordinary course of business or lost,

a print from the photographic film is admissible in evidence in all cases and for all purposes for which the object photographed would have been admissible.

(3) Where a bill of exchange, promissory note, cheque, receipt, instrument, agreement or other executed or signed document was so destroyed before the expiration of six years from,

(a) the date when in the ordinary course of business either the object or the matter to which it related ceased to be treated as current by the person having custody or control of the object; or
(b) the date or receipt by the person having custody or control of the object of notice in writing of a claim in respect of the object or matter prior to the destruction of the object,

whichever is the later date, the court may refuse to admit in evidence under this section a print from a photographic film of the object.

(4) Where the photographic print is tendered by a government or the Bank of Canada, or a municipality as defined in subsection 31(1), subsection (3) does not apply.

(5) Proof of compliance with the conditions prescribed by this section may be given by any person having knowledge of the facts either orally or by affidavit sworn or affirmed before a notary public, and, unless the court otherwise orders, a notarial copy of any such affidavit is admissible in evidence in lieu of the original affidavit.

4.7 RELATED TOPICS

4.7.1 Incident Reports

It is the policy of most if not all hospitals in Ontario to prepare reports on untoward events or mishaps occurring on their premises, which may or may not involve a patient. These are usually referred to as incident reports. The reports are developed to enable the hospital to discover and eliminate situations of danger, as part of its risk management program, as well as to effect improvements in the delivery of services. Many hospitals have elaborate written procedures relating to the notification, investigation, and reporting of such incidents, as well as for the storage of the reports themselves, which may be kept in separate files. Where a patient is involved, the report may not be included in the patient's clinical record. Incident reports are not directly referenced in the list of medical records required to be kept by hospital administrators under the *Public Hospitals Act* and its regulations. A hospital's reluctance to disclose the existence of incident reports is understandable, considering the risk of negligence and libel actions posed by damaging admissions in the reports.

Consequently, when medical records are sought from a hospital or other medical institution, it is recommended that a request or motion for hospital records should contain a specific reference to incident reports involving the patient. In *Fiege v. Cornwall General Hospital*,[176] the trial judge required counsel to explain why the incident report was not included in the patient's medical record and produced with it, and rejected the hospital's argument that an incident report was not the subject of production because it was made in contemplation of litigation.

An incident report may be admissible in evidence at trial under section 35(2) of the *Evidence Act* ("business records") if made in the usual and ordinary course of the health facility's business and if it was in the usual and ordinary course of the health facility's practice to prepare incident reports at the time of or within a reasonable time after an occurrence.

4.7.2 Quality Assurance Programs

Many Canadian health care facilities administer quality assurance programs, designed to reduce claims by and improve service to patients. Such programs rely on frank disclosure by physicians and medical staff, and events which have generated claims against the hospital will in the normal course contain discussion and even assessments of professional conduct by the peers of those involved. This form of reporting may be contrasted with incident reports, which will typically contain the observations of those directly involved in the incident only, but without the benefit of peer assessment. Quality assurance program reports may be useful in the prosecution or defence of personal injury claims, and it is recommended when requesting records from a health care facility that specific reference should be made to documents pertaining to a patient which may be contained in such a report.

The *Health Professions Procedural Code*[177] requires the council of each college of a health profession or group of health professions to establish a Quality Assurance Committee,[178] to determine among other things if a member has committed an act of professional misconduct or may be incompetent or incapacitated. Section 36(3) of the *Regulated Health Professions Act, 1991*, provides that no record of a proceeding and no report of such a committee is admissible in a civil proceeding; however, no such

---

176 (1980), 4 L. Med. Q. 124, 30 O.R. (2d) 691 (H.C.).
177 Schedule 2 of *Regulated Health Professions Act, 1991*, S.O. 1991, c. 18.
178 *Ibid.*, s. 10.

statutory prescription exists with respect to quality assurance programs established by public hospitals and other health facilities.

4.7.3 Deemed Undertaking

Rule 30.1 of the Ontario Rules of Civil Procedure provides that all parties and their counsel are deemed to undertake not to use evidence obtained by documentary discovery, examination for discovery, and medical examination, among others, or information obtained from evidence from these sources, for any purposes other than those of the proceeding in which the evidence was obtained. The rule does not prohibit a use to which the person who disclosed the evidence consents, nor the use for any purpose of:

(a) evidence that is filed with the court;
(b) evidence that is given or referred to during a hearing;
(c) information obtained from evidence referred to in (a) or (b).

Additionally, the rule does not prohibit the use of evidence obtained in one proceeding or information obtained from such evidence to impeach the testimony of a witness in another proceeding.

The court may relieve against the undertaking if satisfied that the interests of justice outweigh any prejudice that would result to a party who disclosed evidence, and may impose such terms and give such directions as are just.

Before Rule 30.1 came into force on April 1, 1996, there existed, with some qualifications, an implied undertaking on the part of every party to civil litigation that discovery evidence, whether oral or documentary, would not be used for purposes collateral to the action. The rule followed a consideration of the implied undertaking by the Ontario Court of Appeal in *Goodman v. Rossi*.[179] In an earlier action, a plaintiff was suing her employer for wrongful dismissal; the employer produced documents including a report completed by the employer addressed to the Ministry of Consumer and Commercial Relations in compliance with the *Real Estate and Business Brokers Act*, stating the plaintiff had been terminated for reasons set out in the report, which the plaintiff regarded as defamatory. In a second action, the plaintiff sued the employer for damages for defamation arising from the statements made in the report, and the employer moved for an order permanently staying the action on the ground that the claim was based on evidence obtained by the plaintiff in the unjust dismissal case. In his reasons, Morden A.C.J.O., after limiting the issue to docu-

---

179 (1995), 37 C.P.C. (3d) 181, 12 C.C.E.L. (2d) 105, 24 O.R. (3d) 359 (C.A.).

ments obtained on discovery (as opposed to information obtained on examination for discovery), observed that in the latter part of the 19th century the English courts had recognized a general principal that a party obtaining documents on discovery had an obligation not to make them public or, more specifically, use them otherwise than for the purpose of the proceeding in which they were obtained; he states:

> ... the principle is based on recognition of the general right of privacy which a person has with respect to his or her documents. The discovery process represents an intrusion on this right under the compulsory processes of the court. The necessary corollary is that this intrusion should not be allowed for any purpose other than that of securing justice in the proceeding in which the discovery takes place.[180]

He affirmed the use of the rule for Ontario, and concluded any relief from the application of the rule should be dealt with in the form of a motion to the court by the party who obtained the document on discovery, for an order permitting use of the document in the manner sought,[181] and the test for granting relief was one which might tolerate some injustice to the discovered party if it was outweighed by a greater injustice to the discovering party if he or she could not make use of the discovered documents. In *obiter*, it was held the undertaking ceased to apply once the document had been read out in open court, unless the court otherwise ordered; it covered information the receiving party could not have otherwise obtained by legitimate means, and the obligation was in favour of the producing party only. The reasons expressly did not decide whether the rule would cover oral evidence given on examination for discovery, although Morden A.C.J.O. found it difficult to see why, as a matter of principle, the rule would not apply to this form of discovery, as had been held in *Reichmann v. Toronto Life Publishing Co.*[182]

The application of the rule to cases involving the disclosure of personal medical information was discussed tangentially in *Wilton v. Brown*, a successful appeal by the defendant from a Master's decision ordering the plaintiffs to produce the family physician's clinical notes and records after deleting portions considered irrelevant, and detailing why such deletions were made. Ordering production of the clinical notes and records without deletions, Wilkins J. stated:

---

180 *Ibid.*, at (C.P.C.) 190.
181 *Ibid.*, at 194.
182 (1988), 28 C.P.C. (2d) 11 (Ont. H.C.), leave to appeal refused (1988), 29 C.P.C. (2d) 66 (Ont. H.C.).

There is raised the concept of confidentiality. I would point out, however, there is ample authority to demonstrate that information obtained by counsel during the course of litigation is privileged and confidential information and that information obtained by counsel during the course of litigation may not be disclosed to others without leave of the court. That being the case, the general purpose of the public policy of confidentiality of medical records, is met by the duty imposed upon counsel not to divulge the information obtained in those medical records and to use those medical records only as may be required or permitted by the trial judge who will, at the appropriate time, determine whether or not they are properly admissible and relevant. The disclosure of such records in a personal injury case is for a strictly limited purpose and the documents remain confidential within the litigation. The only persons who would be entitled to see and review those records, aside from the solicitors and the court, might be the parties' experts whose purpose in reviewing such notes would be to assist the court as to the relevance by being able to accurately deal with them in their reports and opinions.[183]

4.7.4 Spoliation of Health Records

Health professionals and medical institutions create records containing personal medical information of patients which may be material to issues to be determined in a civil action. In many cases, statutes prescribe precisely what records must be kept, as well as by whom, where, and for what period they must be kept. Also, the codes of ethics adopted by the governing bodies of health professional groups for its members frequently refer to the duty to create and preserve medical records. Because the possessor of medical records may be in a position to influence the outcome of personal injury actions through their destruction or alteration, whether involving him or her, his or her employer, or others with whom no connection can be established, and whether or not litigation is pending or contemplated, the common law has developed sanctions to discourage such conduct.

The term *spoliation*, from the Latin *spolium* or *spoliatus*, describes any action, including destruction, alteration, or concealment of documents, which deprives the court or parties to a dispute of evidence. While the courts have long recognised a common law duty to preserve evidence which may be material to pending or contemplated litigation, there have been few reported cases in Ontario or elsewhere in Canada concerned with its breach. In the case of *Hinton v. Engineering Products of Canada Ltd.*[184] Mossop D.C.J. was confronted with a motion for leave to issue a third party claim against an adjuster and a consultant for damages for inten-

---

183 (1993), 22 C.P.C. (3d) 249 (Ont. Gen. Div.).
184 (1986), 16 C.P.C. (2d) 283 (Ont. Dist. Ct.).

tional spoliation of evidence. In the main action, the plaintiff was suing for damages arising from the explosion of a propane tank manufactured by the defendant; the plaintiff's adjuster had caused an examination to be conducted of the propane tank by a consultant, who thereupon destroyed the tank. He dismissed the motion because of likely prejudice and undue delay to the plaintiff, but in his reasons Mossop D.C.J. observed:

> On the motion before me, however, the question as to whether the facts support a claim arising from "intentional spoliation of evidence" and indeed whether such a cause of action exists or could be viable in law in Ontario was fully and ably argued before me. Had I granted the order sought in the notice of motion I would have considered and ruled on that question in the interests of expediency and economy. In view, however, of my decision under r. 29.02 the interesting legal question as to whether "intentional spoliation of evidence" constitutes a wrong for which there is a remedy in Ontario will have to be dealt with on another occasion.[185]

In *Gerula v. Flores*,[186] the Court of Appeal in a medical malpractice action awarded punitive damages against the defendant physician who had performed an operation on the plaintiff's back and erroneously operated on the wrong disc; the defendant physician altered the hospital records to conceal his error, and performed a second operation on the disc which should have been treated in the first place. While the bulk of the court's disapprobation was reserved for the defendant's conduct in having performed two operations, both of which in the circumstances were batteries against the plaintiff, it concluded that the defendant's alteration of the hospital records was an attendant circumstance in the appropriateness of an award of punitive damages for the first operation alone. The judgment of the court was delivered by Weiler J.A., who stated:

> The respondent's alteration of the preoperative diagnosis to indicate that he had always intended to operate at the L4-5 level and the alteration of the postoperative notes concealed reflect the fact that there had been no problem at the L4-5 level to begin with and that this operation was unnecessary. The respondent's acts were motivated by self-interest and were detrimental to the appellant's interest. As a result the appellant was unable to obtain a proper second opinion.
> The alteration to the notes flowed directly from the wrongful surgery in the first operation, which the trial judge found to be a battery. The alteration of the notes is an attending circumstance to be considered in the context of whether to award damages for the first operation and characterizes the re-

---

185 *Ibid.*, at 286.
186 (1995), 126 D.L.R. (4th) 506, 83 O.A.C. 128 (C.A.).

spondent's conduct as more than mere negligence. On the basis of these facts alone, an award of punitive damages would have been appropriate.[187]

In the recent British Columbia case of *Dawes v. Jajcaj*, the plaintiff, suing for damages for personal injuries sustained in a single vehicle accident, sought to exclude the report of an accident reconstruction expert retained by the defendant's insurer. The report concluded that the plaintiff was the driver of the automobile in which he was injured at the time of the accident. Exclusion was sought on the ground that the defendant's insurer had ordered the disposal of the vehicle in question following the expert's investigation, thereby depriving the plaintiff of any opportunity to conduct an independent examination of the vehicle and prejudicing the plaintiff's ability to counter the defence theory that the plaintiff was the driver. Boyd J., relying on American authorities, stated:

> . . . I do accept that in order to obtain the relief sought (exclusion of the expert reports), the Court must at least be satisfied that the object in issue was intentionally destroyed through bad faith and not as a result of mere negligence on the part of the party or his expert (*Brissette v. Milner Chevrolet Co.*, 479 S.W. 2d 176 (Miss. C.A., 1972)). As the Court pointed out in *State of Iowa v. Langlet*, 283 N.W. 2d 330 (Iowa S.C., 1979), at p. 333:
>
>> Spoliation involves more than destruction of evidence. Application of the concept requires an intentional act of destruction. Only intentional destruction supports the rationale of the rule that the destruction amounts to an admission by conduct of the weakness of one's case.
>
> And at p. 334:
>
>> Neither the rationale of the spoliation inference nor any authorities found support submission of the inference in the case of unintentional destruction.
>
> There is no suggestion here that Mr. Little took any steps to alter or destroy the vehicle. Rather, all blame is directed at the defendant's insurer and specifically Lamon, the adjuster. It is admitted that Lamon did not act maliciously or in bad faith. Lamon appeared and testified as a hostile witness under subpoena by the plaintiffs' counsel.
> . . . Finally, there is no evidence here of any reasonable possibility that the destruction of the vehicle has robbed the plaintiff of some evidence that would have been favourable to his claim. In the American Courts there is some authority for the proposition that in addition to proving bad faith, the complaining party must also show a reasonable possibility based on concrete evidence that access to the objects in issue would have produced such evidence (*Bright v. Ford Motor Co.*, 578 N.E. 2d 547, (Ohio App. 2 Dist.,

---

187 *Ibid.*, at (D.L.R.) 525-56.

1990)). While I am not persuaded that this latter condition precedent applies, its applicability or non-applicability is not determinative of the result.[188]

In the result, Boyd J. held the principle of spoliation did not arise so as to result in an order to exclude the expert reports.

In *Coriale (Litigation Guardian of) v. Sisters of St. Joseph of Sault Ste. Marie*,[189] Molloy J. permitted a plaintiff to plead "spoliation" as a distinct cause of action, compensable in damages. In the case, the plaintiffs sued the defendant hospital and doctors for damages sounding in negligence for their handling of the pregnancy of the plaintiff mother which resulted in brain damage, quadriplegia and speech impairment to the infant plaintiff. After action was commenced, the infant's litigation guardian learned that relevant hospital records were destroyed or missing, whereupon she applied successfully to the Master for an order permitting her to vary the statement of claim to add a claim based on the tort of spoliation. The defendants had argued that an independent tort of spoliation had never been recognized in Canada, and appealed the Master's order. In his reasons for dismissing the appeal, Molloy J. stated that while no Canadian court had recognized the existence of the independent tort of spoliation, well-established authority existed for the application of the doctrine of spoliation as a principle of evidence, namely that the destruction of evidence carries a presumption that the evidence destroyed would have been unfavourable to the party who destroyed it. He acknowledged that to plead and claim damages for the independent tort of spoliation was a developing area of the law in the United States, recognized in some states and declined in others. Following a review of Canadian authorities which had wrestled with this issue, he concluded:

> The only real issue is whether the plaintiffs are entitled to plead that the deliberate destruction of evidence by one or more of the defendants can constitute an independent basis for recovery by the plaintiffs. In my view, on the current state of the law, it cannot be said that such a claim is clearly untenable. It is far from plain and obvious that it cannot possibly succeed. Neither is it plain and obvious that spoliation can form the basis of an independent tort. This is a novel point of law which has yet to be explored to any extent in Canada and is still in its early stages of development in the United States. It is precisely in this sort of situation that the claim should be permitted to proceed to trial, so that the logic and necessity of such a tort can be tested against the reality of the facts in the case. It is, in my view, possible that the deliberate destruction of evidence could cause harm to a person for which he should

---

188 (1995), 15 B.C.L.R. (3d) 240, [1996] 3 W.W.R. 525 (S.C.).
189 (1998), 41 O.R. (3d) 347 (Ont. Gen. Div.).

receive an independent legal remedy regardless of whether he is successful on other causes of action.

The final sentence does advance incrementally the notion that spoliation may form the basis of an independent tort, although clearly the courts have considerable ground to cover before meaningful pronouncements on the issue can be made. The reasons of Molloy J. must be viewed in the context in which they are expressed, namely on a motion to amend a pleading under Rule 26.01, which reads:

> 26.01 On motion at any stage of an action the court shall grant leave to amend a pleading on which terms as are just, unless prejudice would result that could not be compensated for by costs or an adjournment.

In referring to the Rule, Molloy J. stated:

> The Rule is expressed in clear and mandatory language. The only factor which a court can take into account is the existence of prejudice that cannot be compensated for by costs or an adjournment. There is considerable judicial authority for the proposition that the merits of the proposed amendment are not to be considered in determining whether to grant leave to amend. . . . In *Atlantic Steel Industries Inc. v. CIGNA Insurance Co. of Canada* (1997), 33 O.R. (3d) 12 (Ont. Gen. Div.), Lax J. accepted that it is proper to refuse an amendment which discloses no reasonable cause of action or is untenable at law.

American jurisprudence has a well-developed body of law relating to the legal consequences of spoliation of records, from which the following principles can be deduced:

1. The Court may permit a jury to infer that the destroyed evidence would have been unfavourable to the person responsible for its safekeeping.[190]
2. The Court may give default judgment against a party responsible for the spoliated record.
3. The failure or neglect to maintain reasonable procedures which inhibits or prevents medical personnel from subsequently making proper diagnoses may provide cause of action to persons adversely affected.[191]

---

190 *Brown & Williamson Tobacco Corp. v. Jacobson*, 827 F.2d 1119, 1135 (7th Cir. 1987).
191 *Ravenis v. Detroit General Hospital*, 234 N.W.2d 411 (Mich. App. 1975): Two corneal transplant recipients commenced action for damages against hospital for its negligence in selecting eye donor, resulting in total loss of sight in affected eyes; trial judge concluded it was open for jury to find hospital negligent for failing to set up procedure which would have provided access to all relevant medical records of proposed donor by person responsible for determining suitability of cornea for transplant purposes.

4. The Court may instruct a jury that the onus of disproving elements of negligence shifts to a party responsible for a spoliated record where adverse inference due to missing documents is high.[192]
5. The Court may impose conditions or restrictions on admissibility of evidence tendered by party destroying or interfering with documents.

The Canadian law relating to spoliation of evidence, and in particular spoliation of records containing personal medical information, is in development. One can anticipate the American cases will play a significant role in the evolution of spoliation rules, as they have in other areas of Canadian law.

4.7.5 "Police Informer" Privilege

The common law privilege known as "police informer" privilege protects the identity of police informants from judicial scrutiny, and is briefly mentioned here as it applies to the protection afforded informants who disclose personal medical information to the police.

The matter came into recent prominence when the Ontario provincial legislature formed a commission under the direction of Mr. Justice Krever to inquire into alleged "leakage" of information from physicians and medical personnel without patient consent. The commission was formed because of a concern that a number of agencies, including metro, provincial, and national police investigative branches, private detective agencies, insurance companies investigative branches and other similar bodies, were obtaining personal medical information from health professionals, whether in the public employ or in private practice, by misrepresentation, deception or trick. The Commission was formed in 1977[193] and held a series of public inquiries in major centres in Ontario beginning April 20, 1978 and continuing until April 17, 1979, to ascertain if and to what degree this "leakage" was occurring.

Members of the RCMP testified that on numerous occasions they had obtained medical information from medical and non-medical personnel in Ontario hospitals without prior consent of the patient. These witnesses refused to divulge the names of those who had supplied them with the patients' records, arguing that there existed a police informer privilege which entitled them to refuse to identify their sources for the reason that the information was given upon assurance of confidentiality, and that disclosure of the sources would discourage future disclosures. Mr. Justice Krever ruled the RCMP were required to disclose the names of the people involved as no privilege operated to prevent such disclosures. The *Public*

---

192 *Welsh v. United States*, 844 F.2d 1239 (6th Circ. 1988).
193 By Order-in-Council O.C. 3566/77, as am. O.C. 1129/78.

Hospitals Act,[194] made it an offence to permit the removal, inspection or receipt of information from medical records, subject to certain exceptions. On a stated case known as *Canada (Solicitor General) v. Ontario (Royal Commission of Inquiry into Confidentiality of Health Records)* which went to the Divisional Court,[195] then to the Ontario Court of Appeal,[196] and ultimately to the Supreme Court of Canada,[197] it was finally decided that the police informer privilege as developed at common law and applied in judicial proceedings also applied by analogy to the proceedings of the inquiry, so that the RCMP were not required to disclose the names of physicians and medical personnel who had given medical information to the police without patient consent, regardless of any breaches of statutory duties of confidentiality by the physicians, or any other professional obligations. In effect, the existence of the informer privilege was confirmed, and its scope was extended from judicial proceedings to legislatively-empowered inquiries.

The subject of "informer privilege" was most recently visited by the Supreme Court of Canada in *R. v. Leipert*,[198] in which the Court was asked to determine if the trial judge erred in ordering production of a portion of a Crime Stoppers document containing particulars of an anonymous informer telephone call reporting that the accused was growing marijuana in his basement. It was the position of the accused, who was charged with cultivation and possession of marijuana for the purpose of trafficking, that, pursuant to his right under the *Canadian Charter of Rights and Freedoms*[199] to make full answer and defence, he was entitled to the document reporting the tip, which the Crown refused on the ground of informer privilege. The trial judge had ordered disclosure of the tip sheet after editing out references which, in his view, might lead to the informer's identity; the Crown appealed. In discussing the importance of informer privilege, McLachlin J., delivering the judgment of the Court, stated:

> A court . . . must begin from the proposition that informer privilege is an ancient and hallowed protection which plays a vital role in law enforcement. It is premised on the duty of all citizens to aid in enforcing the law. The discharge of this duty carries with it the risk of retribution from those involved in crime. The rule of informer privilege was developed to protect citizens who assist in law enforcement and to encourage others to do the same.[200]

---

194 R.S.O. 1970, c. 378.
195 (1978), 21 O.R. (2d) 402, 6 C.P.C. 289 (Div. Ct.).
196 (1979), 98 D.L.R. (3d) 704, 24 O.R. (2d) 545, 13 C.P.C. 239 (C.A.).
197 62 C.C.C. (2d) 193, 23 C.R. (3d) 338, 23 C.P.C. 99, [1981] 2 S.C.R. 494.
198 4 C.R. (5th) 259, [1997] 3 W.W.R. 457, [1997] 1 S.C.R. 281.
199 Part I of the *Constitution Act, 1982*, being Schedule B of the *Canada Act 1982* (U.K.), 1982, c. 11.
200 *Supra*, note 197 at (C.R.) 264.

The privilege prevents the disclosure, not just of the informant's name, but of any information which might reveal his or her identity. The Court acknowledged the special difficulty created by the anonymity of the informer, in that the Crown was thereby not in a position to determine if any part of the information given could reveal the informer's identity. In this circumstance, the Court concluded that the Crown was justified in claiming privilege for all of the information provided by the informer. This conclusion left the door open for the argument that circumstances could exist which would permit the Court to edit informant's information in the possession of the police. Referring to *Bisaillon v. Keable*,[201] McLachlin J. confirmed that while informer privilege developed in criminal proceedings, it applies in civil proceedings as well.[202]

In response to the Charter argument, the Court reasoned:

> In summary, informer privilege is of such importance that it cannot be balanced against other interests. Once established, neither the police nor the court possesses the discretion to abridge it.[203]

The only exception to the informer privilege is the "innocence at stake" exception, described in *Marks v. Beyfus*:

> ... if upon the trial of a prisoner the judge should be of opinion that the disclosure of the name of the informant is necessary or right in order to shew the prisoner's innocence, then one public policy is in conflict with another public policy, and that which says that an innocent man is not to be condemned when his innocence can be proved is the policy that must prevail.[204]

It would be a rare case where the identity of the informant would, of necessity, establish the innocence of an accused or, by extension, exculpate from liability a party to a civil suit, but the exception is noted for completeness.

While its application to criminal cases may be apparent, it is not so clear how this principle would fare in a civil proceeding. It is arguable a police officer should be required to disclose the identity of an informer if the party requesting same could satisfy the Court that disclosure would exculpate him or her from liability for the damages claimed.

For the privilege to arise, the communication must move from the informer to the recipient in the latter's capacity as an agent of the Crown, and in circumstances where it is clear the communication is made in con-

---

201 [1983] 2 S.C.R. 60, 4 Admin. L.R. 205, 37 C.R. (3d) 289.
202 *Supra*, note 197 at (C.R.) 266.
203 *Ibid.* at (C.R.) 266.
204 (1890), 25 Q.B.D. 494 at 498 (Eng. Q.B.).

fidence. Further, the identity of the informer must not be relevant to the disposition of the proceeding in which the privilege is claimed, and public policy must be best served by non-disclosure. A body of authorities has developed around each of these parameters.[205]

There is one significant difference between this variety of "Crown" privilege and the better-known solicitor/client privilege. In the latter, there is no question that the privilege belongs to the client, for whose protection it is given and who alone can waive it. The so-called Crown privilege exists for the protection of the informer, and the authorities suggest it belongs to the public, and cannot be waived by the Crown. It can be invoked by any party or witness in a proceeding,[206] and a Court must apply it even if it is not claimed.[207] The informer can effectively waive the privilege by identifying himself to the Court.

What may be needed in Ontario is legislation comparable to the *Access to Health Records Act*[208] in England, which would treat the confidentiality of personal medical information in a consistent and publicly recognized manner, so that health professionals would not have to resort to subterfuge in making medical records available to public authorities where the public interest clearly predominates, such as assisting the police in apprehending suspected criminals and locating missing family members, or in the promotion of medical research (provided patient anonymity is preserved). Fortunately, recent legislation affecting health professionals and medical institutions has extended availability of personal medical records for medical research.

4.7.6 Computerized Records

Computerization of health records has not produced any real problems for the civil litigator. Section 35(1) of the Ontario *Evidence Act*[209] describes "record" as including any information that is recorded or stored by means of any device, which is broad enough to cover information recorded and stored in a computer, and should be admissible in evidence if the criteria set out at section 35(2) are met.

Some Ontario statutes that require information to be in writing have been amended to provide for computerization. For example, regulations under the *Public Hospitals Act* require that every order for treatment or for

---

205 See generally, Dennis B. Evanson, "The Development and Power of the Informer Privilege: The Health Records Inquiry Case", (1983) Queen's L.J. 207.
206 *Regina v. Lewes Justices, ex parte Secretary of State for Home Dept.*, [1973] A.C. 388 at 407.
207 *Marks v. Beyfus* (1890), 25 Q.B. 494 (Eng. Q.B.).
208 1990, c. 23 (U.K.).
209 R.S.O. 1990, c. E.23.

a diagnostic procedure of a patient be in writing, subject to certain exceptions, and be dated and authenticated by the physician, dentist or midwife giving the treatment order or the physician, dentist, midwife or registered nurse in the extended class giving the diagnostic procedure order;[210] however, "writing" has been defined to include an entry in a computer and "authenticate" means to identify oneself as the author of a document or a record by personal signature or by any other means authorised by the board.[211] They also provide that where in the regulations or under by-laws of a hospital a notation, report, record, order, entry, signature or transcription is required to be entered, prepared, made, written, kept or copied, the entering, preparing, making, writing, keeping or copying may be done by such electronic or optical means or combination thereof as may be authorized by the board; and, further, the board is required to ensure that such electronic or optical means are so designed and operated that the notation, report, record, order, entry, signature, or transcription is secure from loss, tampering, interference or unauthorized use or access.[212]

Consequently, where computerized records are produced, it may be worthwhile to investigate what procedures, if any, were prescribed and followed to prevent tampering, unauthorized access, loss of data integrity, unauthorized alteration or purging of data. In this regard, the Canadian Health Record Association (CHRA) has prepared a publication entitled, "Security of Computerized Health Information", which contains its "Position Statement on Security of Computerized Health Information", as well as "Recommendations for Health Care Facility Policies and Procedures Regarding Security of Computerized Health Information". Under the latter heading, a health care facility is required to ensure, among other things:

- the physical protection of the system by guarding against threats from electrical failure/fluctuations, fire, flood and temperature variations.
- regular surveillance of the area, along with regular maintenance programs for physical protection of the system.
- locked and controlled access to computer facilities.
- transactions on the system are stored on "audit" tapes, so access can be tracked.
- documented manual systems to enable ongoing operation during a down period of the computerised systems.

---

210 R.R.O. 1990, Reg. 965, s. 24, as amended by Reg. 45/98. Under s. 1(1), the definition of "registered nurse in the extended class" means a member of the College of Nurses of Ontario who is a registered nurse and who holds an extended certificate of registration under the *Nursing Act*, 1991.
211 *Ibid.*, s. 1(1).
212 *Ibid.*, s. 34.

4.7.7 Freedom of Information and Protection of Privacy Act and the Municipal Freedom of Information and Protection of Privacy Act

The *Freedom of Information and Protection of Privacy Act*[213] is concerned with information under the control of provincial institutions. Executive responsibility for the provincial Act resides with the Chairman of the Management Board of Cabinet.[214] Administration of the Act is the responsibility of the Information and Privacy Commissioner,[215] as an officer of the legislature, appointed by the Lieutenant Governor in Council on the address of the Assembly.

In the Act, an "institution" means a ministry of the Government of Ontario, as well as any agency, board, commission, corporation or other body designated as an institution in the regulations,[216] i.e., the Review Committees established under the various health profession Acts, the Review Board under the *Mental Health Act*, the Workers Compensation Board, the Workers Compensation Appeals Tribunal.

The stated purposes of the Act is to provide a right of access to information under the control of institutions, as well as to protect the privacy of individuals with respect to personal information[217] about themselves held by institutions and to provide individuals with a right of access to that in-

---

213 R.S.O. 1990, c. F.31.
214 *Ibid.*, s. 3; see Order-in-Council 2733/87.
215 *Ibid.*, s. 4(1).
216 *Ibid.*, s. 2(1).
217 *Ibid.*, s. 2(1), "personal information" means recorded information about an identifiable individual, including:
   (a)   information relating to the race, national or ethnic origin, colour, religion, age, sex, sexual orientation or marital or family status of the individual;
   (b)   information relating to the education or the medical, psychiatric, psychological, criminal or employment history of the individual or information relating to financial transactions in which the individual has been involved;
   (c)   any identifying number, symbol or other particular assigned to the individual;
   (d)   the address, telephone number, fingerprints or blood type of the individual;
   (e)   the personal opinions or views of the individual except where they relate to another individual;
   (f)   correspondence sent to an institution by the individual that is implicitly or explicitly of a private or confidential nature, and replies to that correspondence that would reveal the contents of the original correspondence,
   (g)   the views or opinions of another individual about the individual; and
   (h)   the individual's name where it appears with other personal information relating to the individual or where the disclosure of the name would reveal other personal information about the individual.

formation.[218] It is only with this last mentioned aspect, the individual's right of access to personal information, that this section will be concerned.

The Act proceeds from the premise that every individual has a right of access to any personal information about him or her contained in a personal information bank or otherwise in the custody or under the control of an institution with respect to which he or she is able to provide sufficiently specific information to render it reasonably retrievable by the institution,[219] unless it falls within one of the exemptions listed in the Act. The exemptions are so comprehensive[220] that a request should be made only after ensuring the information sought is not exempted.

An individual may exercise this right of access by making a request in writing to the institution that he or she believes has custody or control of the personal information, identifying the personal information bank[221] or other location of the personal information. The head of the institution to which the request is made is required, within 30 days after the request is received, to give written notice to the person who made the request as to whether or not access to the personal information or a part thereof will be given; and, if access is to be given, to furnish such access. Where the head determines that another institution has custody or control of the personal information, the head is required, within 15 days after the request is received, to forward the request to the other institution and give written notice to the person who made the request that the request has been so forwarded. If the head considers that another institution has a greater interest in the personal information, the head may transfer the request and, if necessary, the personal information to the other institution, within 15 days after the request is received and give written notice of the transfer to the person who made the request. The request will be deemed to have been made to the institution to which it is so forwarded or transferred on the day the institution to which the request was originally made received it.

An appeal from the decision of a head of an institution may be made to the Commissioner by a person who has made a request for access to personal information, within 30 days after notice of the decision was given.[222] The Commissioner may authorize a mediator to investigate the circumstances of an appeal, and to try to effect a settlement of the matter under

---

218 *Ibid.*, s. 1.
219 *Ibid.*, s. 47(1).
220 *Ibid.*, see s. 49 for circumstances entitling a head to refuse to disclose personal information.
221 *Ibid.*, at s. 2(1), "personal information bank" means a collection of personal information that is organized and capable of being retrieved using an individual's name or an identifying number or particular assigned to the individual.
222 *Ibid.*, s. 50.

appeal.[223] Otherwise, the Commissioner is required to conduct an inquiry to review the head's decision[224] and to make an order disposing of the issues raised by the appeal.[225]

The *Municipal Freedom of Information and Protection of Privacy Act*[226] is concerned with information in the custody or control of municipal governments and other municipal institutions. It is the municipal counterpart of the provincial Act, and both Acts operate in substantially the same way.

It would be rare, in the course of a civil proceeding, that personal medical information about an individual would be pursued through these statutes, having regard to the courts considerable information gathering apparatus. However, they are mentioned for purposes of completeness and because situations may arise when resort to these statutes may be more convenient or less expensive than conventional means.

4.7.8 Access by any Person to Information Concerning a Health Profession Member Maintained by Registrar of a College, under Health Professions Procedural Code

Limited information concerning a health professional's professional status may be available to anyone by communicating with the Registrar of the College of which he or she is a member, under section 23(1)-(3.1) of the Health Professions Procedural Code,[227] which read as follows:

23. (1) The Registrar shall maintain a register.[228]
(2) The register shall contain,

    (a) each member's name, business address and business telephone number;
    (b) each member's class of registration and specialist status;
    (c) the terms, conditions and limitations imposed on each certificate of registration;
    (d) a notation of every revocation suspension of a certificate of registration;

---

223 *Ibid.*, s. 51.
224 *Ibid.*, s. 52.
225 *Ibid.*, s. 54.
226 R.S.O. 1990, c. M.56.
227 The Health Professions Procedural Code is Schedule 2 to *Regulated Health Professions Act, 1991*, S.O. 1991, 18; and is deemed by s. 4 of the said Act to be part of each health profession Act. For a list of health profession Acts, see Schedule 1 of the *Regulated Health Professions Act, 1991*, as well as Chapter 1, 1.3, Health Professions Procedural Code, *supra*.
228 *Ibid.*, at s. 1(1), "Registrar" means the Registrar of the College of a health profession.

(e) the result of every disciplinary and incapacity proceeding;
(e.1) where findings of the Discipline Committee are appealed, a notation that they are under appeal;
(f) information that a panel of the Registration, Discipline or Fitness to Practise Committee specifies shall be included; and
(g) information that is required to be kept in the register with the by-laws.

(2.1) When an appeal of findings of the Discipline Committee is finally disposed of, the notation added to the register under clause (2)(e.1) shall be removed.

(3) A person may obtain, during normal business hours, the following information contained in the register:

1. Information described in clauses (2)(a) to (c).
2. Information described in clause (2)(d) relating to a suspension that is in effect.
3. The results[229] of every disciplinary and incapacity proceeding completed within six years before the time the register was prepared or last updated,

    i. in which a member's certificate of registration was revoked or suspended or had terms, conditions or limitations imposed on it, or
    ii. in which a member was required to pay a fine or attend to be reprimanded or in which an order was suspended if the results of the proceeding were directed to be included in the register by a panel of the Discipline or Fitness to Practise Committee.

    3.1 For every disciplinary proceeding, completed at any time before the time the register was prepared or last updated, in which a member was found to have committed sexual abuse,[230] as defined in clause 1(3)(a) or (b), the results of the proceeding.
    3.2 Information described in clause (2)(e.1) related to appeals of findings of the Discipline Committee.
4. Information designated as public in the by-laws.

---

229 *Ibid.*, at s. 23(7), "result", when used in reference to a disciplinary or incapacity proceeding, means the panel's finding, particulars of the grounds for the finding, and the penalty imposed, including any reprimand.

230 *Ibid.*, at s. 1(3), "sexual abuse" of a patient by a member means,
　(a)　sexual intercourse or other forms of physical sexual relations between the member and the patient;
　(b)　touching, of a sexual nature, of the patient by the member.
　(c)　behaviour or remarks of a sexual nature by the member towards the patient.

Whether preparing to cross-examine a medical expert or preparing a medical expert for cross-examination at trial, counsel should consider launching an enquiry of the Registrar of the College of which the medical expert is a member for information available under this section.

(3.1) The Registrar may refuse to allow a person to obtain a member's business address and business telephone number if the Registrar has reasonable grounds to believe that disclosure of the information may jeopardize the member's safety.

Chapter 5

Statutory Duty to Report Personal Medical Information

by John Haydon, Q.C., B.A., LL.B.

5.1 Statutory Duty to Report Personal Medical Information
5.2 Duty to Warn
5.3 Statutes Containing "Duty to Report" Provisions
    5.3.1 *Child and Family Services Act*
    5.3.2 *Coroners Act*
    5.3.3 *Health Protection and Promotion Act*
    5.3.4 *Highway Traffic Act*
          Case Law
    5.3.5 *Regulated Health Professions Act, 1991*
    5.3.6 *Vital Statistics Act*
    5.3.7 *Charitable Institutions Act*
    5.3.8 *Day Nurseries Act*
    5.3.9 *Homes for Retarded Persons Act*
    5.3.10 *Homes for the Aged and Rest Homes Act*
    5.3.11 *Mental Hospitals Act*
    5.3.12 *Nursing Homes Act*
    5.3.13 *Private Hospitals Act*
    5.3.14 *Public Hospitals Act*

5.1 STATUTORY DUTY TO REPORT PERSONAL MEDICAL INFORMATION

The idea of a physician reporting to public authorities personal medical information imparted to him or her by a patient was almost unheard of 50 years ago, with the exception of observable maladies such as measles, scarlet fever, etc., which were highly contagious and frequently required the patient to be quarantined under the law. Until then, the prevailing attitude among members of the medical profession and the public at large was that physician/patient communications could and should be of no interest to anyone else. One can imagine the dilemma confronting the family physician who had diagnosed a socially unacceptable but communicable disease in a respected member of the community. His instincts told him the public, as well as those with whom the patient shared his or her household, should be informed if further contagion were to be avoided, but his professional sense of ethics, which sided with the public's view of the matter, was that such personal medical information must not leave the examining room. This ethical view was born in part of the notion that effective healing required the utmost candour and honesty on the patient's part, achievable only if the patient felt his or her disclosures would be held in the strictest confidence. The public's own distaste for discussion of personal medical matters was also a factor, and contrasts significantly with the public's fascination with such topics today. In time, the flood of medical information unleashed on the public by an expanding and crusading media generated discussion and, ultimately, changes in attitudes toward many hitherto taboo subjects, such as homosexuality, mental illness, sexually transmitted diseases, etc., and made a clash between the person's right to privacy and the public's right to know inevitable. Slowly, the edifice on which personal rights was built began to crumble, whereupon the paramountcy of the public's right to know ascended. Today, many laws exist on the statute books which formerly would have been regarded as a clear violation of the patient's right to privacy, particularly in the area of public health. Regulations under the *Health Protection and Promotion Act* specify 61 diseases as "communicable diseases", ranging from food poisoning to AIDS, which a physician is under a duty to report to a medical officer of health if he or she believes a patient is infected with an agent thereof. Laws which strike at the consumption of tobacco and alcohol are also the product of this change; no longer is the public prepared to assume the enormous financial burden of providing medical care and hospitalization for abusers of these substances. The high cost of treating the injured victims of motor vehicle accidents now requires every legally qualified medical practitioner to report to the Ministry of Transport particulars of a person who in his or her opinion is suffering from a condition that may make it dangerous for that person to operate a motor vehicle, in which event the Ministry may suspend the person's driving privileges.

5.2   DUTY TO WARN

The common law in Canadian jurisdictions is approaching the point of recognizing a duty on the part of a health professional to warn third parties put at risk by a patient's medical condition. This principle was considered in the 1976 Supreme Court of California decision of *Tarasoff v. Regents of the University of California*,[1] which acknowledged a duty on the part of a psychotherapist to take reasonable steps to prevent a dangerous mental patient from harming a third party. In that case, a student told a school psychologist he wanted to kill Tatiana Tarasoff. The psychologist told the supervising psychiatrist, who in turn notified the campus police. The police interviewed the student and let him go, and the chief of the department of psychiatry directed that no further action be taken. No-one warned Ms. Tarasoff or her parents of this peril. The student then killed Tarasoff, and her parents sued the university regents, the psychotherapists employed by the university hospital, and the campus police. In his reasons, expressed on behalf of the Court, Justice Tobriner described the duty as follows:

> In our view, however, once a therapist does in fact determine, or under applicable professional standards reasonably should have determined, that a patient poses a serious danger of violence to others, he bears a duty to exercise reasonable care to protect the foreseeable victim of that danger. While the discharge of this duty of due care will necessarily vary with the facts of each case, in each instance the adequacy of the therapists conduct must be measured against the traditional negligence standard of the rendition of reasonable care under the circumstances.[2]

The notion of requiring health professionals in Ontario to alert any person who might reasonably be at risk because of a patient's medical condition, whether psychological or physical, cannot be far behind.

While the common law has been slow to recognize a duty on a person to prevent another from causing harm to a third party, the courts have not failed to attach liability where the public interest so warranted. It is now common for the courts to impose liability on innkeepers where personal injury or death to a third party results from a motor vehicle collision caused by a driver who had earlier consumed alcoholic beverages on the innkeeper's premises so that it was apparent he would be a danger to others if allowed to drive. It is likely this liability will before long be visited on social hosts, as well.

There is a conflict between the duty of a health professional to warn a potential third party victim and the duty not to disclose personal medical information to anyone other than the patient or his or her authorized representative except with the consent of the patient or his or her authorized representative, or as required by law.[3] The courts must balance the right of

---

1   (1976) 17 Cal. 3d 358, CA 131 Cal. Rptr. 14, 551 P.2D 334 (CA S.C.).
2   *Ibid.*, at (Cal. Rptr.) 25.
3   The duty of confidentiality is discussed in Chapter 1.

the individual to confidentiality with society's right to know, so that harm to innocent persons can be avoided. In effecting that balance, a number of issues will have to be addressed:

1. what special relationship must exist for the duty to inform to arise?
2. to what extent must the potential victim be identifiable to give rise to liability?
3. when the duty to inform arises, what other steps must be taken to prevent unreasonable risk to others, i.e., reporting to authorities, controlling the patient by institutionalizing?
4. the nature and extent of the damage caused for which the Court will compensate a victim.

What complicates this problem is the fact that the duty to warn serves to destroy the honesty and trust that must characterize the relationship between physician and patient for it to be effective. If a patient believes, in his or her quest for a cure, that total frankness may bring notoriety, isolation, and even incarceration, he or she may gloss over reporting to the physician the very information needed to procure effective therapy. Similarly, if a physician is reluctant to subject a client to the consequences of the duty to warn, he or she may avoid drawing out facts necessary for correct diagnosis and treatment. Also, one must balance the cost to an already financially burdened law enforcement system of recording, investigating and acting upon such warnings, against the remote statistical risk of personal injury and death resulting from the failure to warn. Health professionals may protect themselves by purchasing additional insurance to cover the risks attendant on failure to warn.

5.3 STATUTES CONTAINING "DUTY TO REPORT" PROVISIONS

In Canada, all provinces have already introduced some type of legislation imposing a statutory duty on health professionals to report personal medical information where society's interests are considered paramount; some Ontario statutes are considered below.

One can foresee, particularly with the spread of human immunodeficiency virus (HIV) infection and acquired immune deficiency syndrome (AIDS), an increase in the number of civil actions by infected plaintiffs seeking redress from, among others, health professionals who have neglected or failed in their statutory duty to report or their common law duty to warn persons falling within the ambit of those likely to be infected by those already stricken, or both. The plaint of family members or friends, having the responsibility of caring for an AIDS-infected person during his or her final days of suffering but unaware of attendant risks, can be expected to receive a sympathetic ear from the trier of fact, whether judge or jury.

Why are these developments important to the personal injury lawyer? Any time there is a duty, statutory or otherwise, cast upon a health professional in relation to a patient's medical condition, the personal injury lawyer must consider the duty in the light of its possible relevance to a matter in issue in an action. A plaintiff's lawyer should consider whether the duty widens the net of potential tortfeasors. A defence lawyer should consider whether the duty exonerates his client, or enables him to shift responsibility for the plaintiff's condition elsewhere, to different persons or causes. Also, from the defence point of view, consideration must be given to the impact on an opposing expert's credibility which can result from disclosure at trial of a failure to observe a duty to report.

The following are excerpts from better-known medical statutes which contain provisions requiring health professionals and others involved in the administration of health facilities to report matters of medical concern to a third party.

5.3.1 *Child and Family Services Act*[4]

1. *Duty of every person who performs professional or official duties with respect to a child, to report suspicion of child abuse and information on which it is based.*[5]

Despite the provisions of any other Act, the following persons who, in the course of his or her professional or official duties, have reasonable grounds to suspect that a child is or may be suffering or may have suffered abuse are required to forthwith report the suspicion and the information on which it is based to a society;[6] namely, every person who performs professional or official duties with respect to a child, including:

 72(4) . . .
 (a) a health care professional, including a physician, nurse, dentist, pharmacist and psychologist;
 (b) a teacher, school principal, social worker, family counsellor, priest, rabbi, member of the clergy, operator or employee of a day nursery and youth and recreation worker;
 (c) a peace officer and a coroner;

---

4 R.S.O. 1990, c. C.11.
5 *Ibid.*, s. 72(1), (3), (4).
6 *Ibid.* At s. 3(1), "society" means an approved agency designated as a children's aid society under s. 15(2) of Part I (Flexible Services) of the Act.

(d) a solicitor; and
(e) a service provider and an employee of a service provider.

"To suffer abuse" means[7] where:

37(2) . . .
(a) the child has suffered physical harm, inflicted by the person having charge of the child or caused by that persons's failure to care and provide for or supervise and protect the child adequately;

. . .

(c) the child has been sexually molested or sexually exploited, by the person having charge of the child or by another person where the person having charge of the child knows or should know of the possibility of sexual molestation or sexual exploitation and fails to protect the child;

. . .

(e) the child requires medical treatment to cure, prevent or alleviate physical harm or suffering and the child's parent or the person having charge of the child does not provide, or refuses or is unavailable or unable to consent to, the treatment;
(f) the child has suffered emotional harm, demonstrated by severe,

   (i) anxiety,
   (ii) depression
   (iii) withdrawal, or
   (iv) self-destructive or aggressive behaviour, and the child's parent or the person having charge of the child does not provide, or refuses or is unavailable or unable to consent to, services or treatment to remedy or alleviate the harm;

. . .

(h) the child suffers from a mental, emotional or developmental condition that, if not remedied, could seriously impair the child's development and the child's parent or the person having charge of the child does not provide, or refuses or is unavailable or unable to consent to, treatment to remedy or alleviate the condition.

A child is defined in the Act as a person under the age of 18 years.[8]

2. *Duty of every person to report that a child may be in need of protection.*[9]

A person who believes on reasonable grounds that a child is or may be

---

7   *Ibid.*, s. 72(1).
8   *Ibid.*, s. 3 (Interpretation).
9   *Ibid.*, s. 72(2).

in need of protection[10] is required to forthwith report the belief and the information upon which it is based to a society.

3. *Duty of licensee to notify coroner of the death of resident of a children's residence.*[11]

Where a resident of a children's residence dies, the licencee who operates the residence in which the resident resides is required to notify a coroner, other than a coroner who is a physician that provides services to residents of a children's residence operated by the licensee, of the death of the resident.

4. *Duty of licensee to notify coroner of death of child while in receipt of foster care in foster home.*[12]

Where a child dies while in receipt of foster care in a foster home, the licensee who directly or indirectly operates the foster home is required, after consulting with the placing agency where the placing agency is not the licensee, to notify a coroner.

5. *Duty of licensee to report serious occurrences taking place concerning a resident of a children's residence.*[13]

Where,

    (i) a resident dies,
   (ii) a resident is seriously injured,
  (iii) a resident is abused or mistreated,
  (iv) a resident is injured by a staff person in the residence or by the licensee,
   (v) a complaint is made by or about a resident that is considered by the licensee to be of a serious nature,
  (vi) a resident resides in a residence operated by the licensee in which a fire or other disaster occurs, or
 (vii) in addition to the matters set out above, any other serious occurrence takes place concerning the resident,

---

10 *Ibid.* See s. 37(2) for definition of child in need of protection.
11 R.R.O. 1990, Reg. 70, s. 71(1).
12 *Ibid.*, s. 71(2).
13 *Ibid.*, s. 102.

the licensee is required within twenty-four hours of the occurrence to report the occurrence to,

(viii) a parent of the resident;
(ix) where applicable, the person who placed the resident and who has been involved in the plan of care for the resident,
(x) where applicable, the society that placed the resident, and,
(xi) a Director.

5.3.2 *Coroners Act*[14]

Duty of specified persons to notify Coroner of death of a deceased person in certain circumstances.[15]

A coroner must decide whether an inquest is to be held into the death of a person who has died in certain circumstances. To assist a coroner, the Act imposes a duty on the following persons to notify a coroner of the death, namely:[16]

1. Every person who has reason to believe that a deceased person died,[17]

    (a) as a result of,

    (i) violence
    (ii) misadventure
    (iii) negligence
    (iv) misconduct, or
    (v) malpractice;

    (b) unfair means;
    (c) during pregnancy or following pregnancy in circumstances that might reasonably be attributable thereto;
    (d) suddenly and unexpectedly;
    (e) from disease or sickness for which he or she was not treated by a legally qualified medical practitioner;
    (f) from any cause other than disease; or
    (g) under such circumstances as may require investigation.

2. The person in charge of the hospital, facility, institution, residence or home where a person dies while resident or an in-patient, in,

---

14 R.S.O. 1990, c. C.37.
15 *Ibid.*, s. 10.
16 *Ibid.*, s. 10.
17 In the circumstances indicated, a person may alternatively notify a police officer, who in turn is required to immediately notify a coroner.

(a) a charitable institution as defined in the *Charitable Institutions Act*;
(b) a children's residence under Part IX (Licensing) of the *Child and Family Services Act* or premises approved under subsection 9(2) of Part I (Flexible Services)of that Act;
(c) A home for retarded persons as defined in the *Homes for Retarded Persons Act*;
(d) a psychiatric facility designated under the *Mental Health Act*;
(e) an institution under the *Mental Hospitals Act*;
(f) a public or private hospital to which the person was transferred from a facility, institution or home referred to in clauses (a) to (e).
3. The person in charge of the home where a person dies resident in a home for the aged to which the *Homes for the Aged and Rest Homes Act* or the *Charitable Institutions Act* applies, or a nursing home to which the *Nursing Homes Act* applies.
4. The peace officer or officer in charge of the institution lock-up or place or facility, as the case may be, where a person dies while detained by or in the custody of a peace officer or while an inmate on the premises of a correctional institution, lock-up, or place or facility designated as a place of secure custody under section 24.1 of the *Young Offenders Act* (Canada).
5. The person in charge of the project, mining plant or mine where a worker dies as a result of an accident occurring in the course of the worker's employment at or in a construction, project, mining plant or mine, including a pit or quarry.
6. Paragraphs 2 and 3 above also apply where a person dies while,

(a) a patient of a psychiatric facility;
(b) committed to a correctional institution; or
(c) committed to secure custody or open custody under the *Young Offenders Act* (Canada),

but while not on the premises or in actual custody of the facility, institution or place of custody, as the case may be, as if the person were a resident of an institution named therein.

Where a coroner is informed that there is in his or her jurisdiction the body of a person and that there is reason to believe that the person died in any of the foregoing circumstances, the coroner is required to issue a warrant to take possession of the body and to view the body and to make such further investigation as is required to enable the coroner to determine whether or not an inquest is necessary.[18]

---

18 *Ibid.*, s. 15.

5.3.3 *Health Protection and Promotion Act*[19]

REPORTABLE AND COMMUNICABLE DISEASES[20]

1. Duty of specified regulated health professionals to report reportable disease, agent of communicable disease or reportable event, to medical officer of health.

    (i) A physician, a member of the Royal College of Dental Surgeons of Ontario, a member of the College of Nurses of Ontario, a member of the College of Optometrists of Ontario, or a member of the Ontario College of Pharmacists of Ontario, or a person registered as a drugless practitioner under the *Drugless Practitioners Act*, who, while providing professional services to a person who is not a patient in or an out-patient of a hospital, forms the opinion that the person has or may have a reportable disease[21] is required, as soon as possible after forming the opinion, to report thereon to the medical officer of health of the health unit in which the professional services are provided;[22]

    (ii) A physician who, while providing professional services to a per-

---

19 R.S.O. 1990, c. H.7.
20 The information required to be contained in reports of communicable or reportable diseases under ss. 25, 26, 27, 28, and 29 of the Act, is set out at R.R.O. 1990, Reg. 569.
21 *Ibid.* At s. 1, a "reportable disease" means a disease specified as a reportable disease by regulation made by the Minister of Health, which currently includes all communicable diseases covered by the Act (except chlamydia trachomatis, histoplasmosis, and toxoplasmosis), as well as the following:
   1.   Encephalitis, including, Primary, viral
          i.   post-infectious
          ii.   vaccine-related
          iii. Subacute sclerosing panencephalitis
          iv. Unspecified
   2.   Fungal systemic diseases,
          i.   Blastomycosis
          ii.   Histoplasmosis
   3.   Genital Chlamydia trachpmatis infections
   4.   Genital Herpes
   5.   Kawasaki disease
   6.   Lyme Disease
   7.   Herpes, neonatal
   8.   Polyneuritis, acute infective (Guillan-Barre syndrome)
   9.   Reye Syndrome
  10.   Toxocariasis
  11.   Congenital Toxoplasmosis
22 *Ibid.*, s. 25, as amended by S.O. 1998, c. 18, Sched. G, s. 55(2).

son, forms the opinion that the person is or may be infected with an agent of a communicable disease[23] is required, as soon as possible after forming the opinion, to report thereon to the medical officer of health of the health unit in which the professional services are provided.[24]

(iii) A physician who signs a medical certificate of death in the form prescribed by the regulations under the *Vital Statistics Act* where the cause of death was a reportable disease or a reportable disease was a contributing cause of death is required, as soon as possible after signing the certificate, to report thereon to the medical officer of health of the health unit in which the death occurred.[25]

(iv) Every physician is required to report to the medical officer of health the name and residence address of any person who is under the care and treatment of the physician in respect of a communicable disease and who refuses or neglects to continue the treatment in a manner and to a degree satisfactory to the physician.[26]

---

23 *Ibid.* At s. 1, "communicable disease" means a disease specified as a communicable disease by regulation made by the Minister of Health, which currently includes: Acquired Immunodeficiency Syndrome (AIDS); Amebiasis; Anthrax; Botulism; Brucellosis; Camplyobacter enteritis; Chancroid; Chickenpox (Varicella); Chlamydia trachomatis infections; Cholera; Cytomegalovirus infection, congenital; Diphtheria; Encephalitis, primary viral; Food poisoning, all causes; Gastroenteritis, institutional outbreaks; Giardiasis; Gonorrhoea; Haemophilus influenzae b disease, invasive:
    i.   Ebola virus disease,
    ii.   Marburg virus disease,
    iii. Other viral causes.
Hepatitis, viral:
    i.   Hepatitis A,
    ii.   Hepatitis B,
    iii. Hepatitis D (Delta hepatitis);
Influenza; Lassa Fever; Legionellosis; Leprosy; Listeriosis; Lyme Disease; Malaria; Measles; Meningitis, acute:
    i.   bacterial,
    ii.   viral,
    iii. other;
Meningococcal disease, invasive; Mumps; Ophthalmia neonatorum; Paratyphoid Fever; Pertussis (Whooping Cough); Plague; Poliomyelitis, acute; Psittacosis/Ornithosis; Q Fever; Rabies; Rubella; Rubella, congenital syndrome; Salmonellosis; Shigellosis; Syphilis; Trichinosis; Tuberculosis; Tularemia; Typhoid Fever; Verotoxin-producing E. coli infections; Yellow Fever; Yersiniosis
24 *Ibid.*, s. 26.
25 *Ibid.*, s. 30.
26 *Ibid.*, s. 34(1).

(v) A physician who provides medical services in a correctional institution, a place of secure custody, a detention facility or a place of temporary detention[27] and who is of the opinion that a person detained therein is infected or may be infected with an agent of a communicable disease is required to notify forthwith the medical officer of health of the health unit in which the institution is located.[28]

(vi) A physician, a member of the College of Nurses of Ontario, or a member of the Ontario College of Pharmacists, who, while providing professional services to a person, recognizes the presence of a reportable event and forms the opinion that it may be related to the administration of an immunizing agent is required, within seven days after recognizing the reportable event, to report thereon to the medical officer of health of the health unit where the professional services are provided.[29] In this section, an "immunizing agent" means a vaccine or combination of vaccines administered for immunization against diphtheria, tetanus, poliomyelitis, pertussis, measles, rubella, hepatitis B, rabies, Haemophilus influenzae b infections, influenza or a prescribed disease; and "reportable event" means:

(1) persistent crying or screaming, anaphylaxis or anaphylactic shock occurring within 48 hours after the administration of an immunizing agent;
(2) shock-like collapse, high fever or convulsions occurring within 3 days after the administration of an immunizing agent;
(3) arthritis occurring within 42 days after the administration of an immunizing agent;
(4) generalized urticaria, residual seizure disorder, encephalopathy, encephalitis or any other significant occurrence occurring within 15 days after the administration of an immunizing agent, or

---

27 *Ibid.*, s. 37(3):
"correctional institution" has the same meaning as in the *Ministry of Correctional Services Act*;
"detention facility" has the same meaning as in s. 205 of the *Municipal Act*;
"place of secure custody" means a place or facility designated as a place of secure custody under s. 24.1 of the *Young Offenders Act* (Canada);
"place of temporary detention" means a place or facility designated as a place of temporary detention under subs. 7(1) of the *Young Offenders Act* (Canada).
28 *Ibid.*, s. 37(1).
29 *Ibid.*, s. 38(3).

(5) death occurring at any time and following upon a symptom described in the preceding clauses.[30]

2. *Duty of administrator of a hospital to report entry in hospital patient records of reportable disease or agent of communicable disease to medical officer of health.*[31]

The administrator[32] of a hospital is required to report to the medical officer of health of the health unit in which the hospital is located if an entry in the records of the hospital in respect of a patient in or an out-patient has or may have a reportable disease or is or may be infected with an agent of a communicable disease, as soon as possible after the entry is made.

3. *Duty of superintendent of an institution to report entry in institution resident records of reportable disease or agent of communicable disease to medical officer of health.*[33]

The superintendent[34] of an institution[35] is required to report to the

---

30   Ibid., s. 38.
31   Ibid., s. 27(1).
32   Ibid., s. 21(2), "administrator", "hospital", "outpatient" and "patient" have the same meanings as in the *Public Hospitals Act*.
33   Ibid., s. 27(2).
34   Ibid. At s. 21(2), "superintendent" means the person who has for the time being the direct and actual superintendence and charge of an institution.
35   Ibid. At s. 21(1), "institution" means,

   (a)   "charitable institution" within the meaning of the *Charitable Institutions Act*;
   (b)   premises approved under subs. 9(1) of Part I (Flexible Services) of the *Child and Family Services Act*;
   (c)   "children's residence" within the meaning of Part IX (Licensing) of the *Child and Family Services Act*;
   (d)   "day nursery" within the meaning of the *Day Nurseries Act*;
   (e)   "facility" within the meaning of the *Developmental Services Act*;
   (f)   "approved home" and "home for retarded persons" within the meaning of the *Homes for Retarded Persons Act*;
   (g)   "home for special care" within the meaning of the *Homes for Special Care Act*;
   (h)   "home" within the meaning of the *Homes for the Aged and Rest Homes Act*;
   (i)   "psychiatric facility" within the meaning of the *Mental Health Act*;
   (j)   "approved home" and "institution" within the meaning of the *Mental Hospitals Act*;
   (k)   "correctional institution" within the meaning of the *Ministry of Correctional Services Act*;
   (l)   "detention facility" within the meaning of s. 205 of the *Municipal Act*;
   (m)   "nursing home" within the meaning of the *Nursing Homes Act*;

medical officer of health of the health unit in which the institution is located if an entry in the records of the institution in respect of a person lodged in the institution states that the person has or may have a reportable disease or is or may be infected with an agent of a communicable disease, as soon as possible after the entry is made.

4. *Duty of operator of a laboratory to report positive laboratory finding of reportable disease to medical officer of health.*[36]

The operator of a laboratory[37] is required to report to the officer of health of the health unit in which the laboratory is located each case of a positive laboratory finding in respect of a reportable disease, as soon as possible after the making of the finding.[38]

5. *Duty of health professional attending birth to report particulars of new-born child with reddened, inflamed or swollen eye to medical officer of health.*[39]

Every physician, public health nurse or other health care professional person who attended at the birth of the child and who is aware that an eye of the new-born child has become reddened, inflamed or swollen, within two weeks after birth of the child, is required to report in writing to the medical officer of health,

    (a) the name, age and home address of the child,
    (b) where the child is located, if not at home, and
    (c) the conditions of the eye that have been observed.

6. *Duty of physician, veterinarian, police officer or other person having information concerning animal contact that may result in rabies in persons to notify medical officer of health.*[40]

A physician, veterinarian, police officer or any other person who has

---

    (n) "private hospital" within the meaning of the *Private Hospitals Act*;
    (o) "place or facility designated as a place of secure custody" under s. 24.1 of the *Young Offenders Act* (Canada).

36 *Ibid.*, s. 29.
37 *Ibid.* At s. 29(3), "laboratory" has the same meaning as in s. 5 of the *Laboratory and Specimen Collection Centre Licensing Act*, R.S.O. 1990, c. L.1.
38 *Ibid.*, s. 29(1).
39 R.R.O. 1990, Reg. 557, s. 1.
40 *Ibid.*, ss. 2, 3.

information concerning any animal bite or other animal contact that may result in rabies in persons is required to notify the medical officer of health as soon as possible and provide the medical officer of health with the information. The medical officer of health who finds any person has been exposed to a rabid or suspected rabid animal so as to require anti-rabies treatment is required, in turn, to provide information, including details of exposure and treatment to the Manager of the Disease Control and Epidemiology Service of the Ministry of Health.

A medical officer of health is required to notify and furnish particulars to the nearest District Veterinarian of the Animal Health Division, Food Production and Inspection Branch, Agriculture Canada, as soon as possible, where the medical officer of health has reason to believe that an animal,

(a) is rabid; or
(b) has been in contact with another animal known or suspected of having rabies.

Where, after a laboratory examination, an animal is found to have been rabid or when there is clinical evidence of rabies, the medical officer of health is required to so inform,

(a) the owner or person who had been caring for the animal; and
(b) every person known to have been in contact with the animal during the infective stage of the disease and the person's attending physician.

Where an animal has bitten a person or is suspected of being rabid and has had contact with a person and the animal dies or is killed, the owner of the animal or the person having custody of the animal is required to notify the District Veterinarian of the Animal Health Division, Food Production and Inspection Branch, Agriculture Canada, to arrange for the collection of the head or carcass of the animal.

7. *Duty of laboratory director or veterinarian knowing or suspecting captive bird or poultry flock to be infected with agent of psittacosis or ornithosis to notify medical officer of health.*[41]

A director of a laboratory or veterinarian who knows or suspects that a captive bird or birds or a poultry flock is infected with the agent of psittacosis or ornithosis is required to notify the medical officer of health.

---

41 *Ibid.*, ss. 4, 5.

A medical officer of health who knows or suspects that a captive bird or birds or a poultry flock is infected with the agent of psittacosis or ornithosis is required, among other things, to notify the Manager of the Disease Control and Epidemiology Service of the Ministry of Health of the extent of the infection and the action being taken.

Where a bird or birds or a poultry flock is isolated by a medical officer of health pursuant to regulation,[42] the owner or person having the care and custody of the bird or birds or poultry flock is required to notify the medical officer of health as soon as possible if a bird dies during the isolation period and the bird or birds or poultry flock shall be retained and disposed of as directed by the medical officer of health.

5.3.4 *Highway Traffic Act*[43]

Report by specified health professionals to Registrar of Motor Vehicles of person suffering from condition that may make it dangerous for the person to operate a motor vehicle.

Every legally qualified medical practitioner is required to report to the Registrar of Motor Vehicles the name, address and clinical condition of every person 16 years of age or over attending upon the medical practitioner for medical services who, in the opinion of the medical practitioner, is suffering from a condition that may make it dangerous for the person to operate a motor vehicle.[44] Similarly, every member of the College of Optometrists of Ontario is required to report to the Registrar the same information with respect to every person 16 years of age or over attending upon the optometrist for optometric services who, in the opinion of the optometrist, is suffering from an eye condition that may make it dangerous for the person to operate a motor vehicle.[45] No action may be brought against a qualified medical practitioner or optometrist for complying with these provisions,[46] and the report is privileged for the information of the Registrar only and shall not be open for public inspection, and is inadmissible in evidence for any purpose in any trial except to prove compliance with the Act.[47]

---

42 *Ibid.* See s. 4(3), in which the medical officer of health, who knows or suspects that a captive bird or birds or a poultry flock is infected, is empowered to isolate or isolate and treat the bird or birds or poultry flock.
43 R.S.O. 1990, c. H.8.
44 *Ibid.*, s. 203(1).
45 *Ibid.*, s. 204(1).
46 *Ibid.*, ss. 203(2) and 204(2).
47 *Ibid.*, ss. 203(3) and 204(3).

Statutory Duty to Report Personal Medical Information 173

Case Law:

1. In the case of *Toms v. Foster*,[48] a motorcyclist and his passenger were seriously injured in a collision with an automobile operated by a driver, Foster, whose condition made it inadvisable that he be permitted to drive. A general practitioner and a neurologist who had attended on the driver before the accident were aware of his condition, but neglected to report pursuant to section 177 (now section 203) of the *Highway Traffic Act*. At trial, the jury found both physicians negligent in failing to report Foster's condition to the Ministry of Transportation and Communication, among other findings of negligence, and apportioned liability 20 per cent to the general practitioner and 10 per cent to the neurologist. In its judgment dismissing the appeal of the physicians as to liability, delivered *per curiam*, the Ontario Court of Appeal stated:

   > It appears from the evidence that had the doctors reported Foster's condition to the Registrar, an investigation would have been undertaken and Foster's licence probably suspended.
   >
   > The appellants argue that s. 177 does not give rise to a cause of action and evidence was tendered by medical experts that it was not the practice to report all incidents. That is, that somehow the medical practice overcame the statutory requirement. As we have indicated, we cannot accept that argument. If the burden is too onerous, it should be amended by the Legislature. We also think it is clear that the duty of doctors to report is a duty owed to members of the public and not just to the patient. It is clearly designed to protect not only the patient but people he might harm if permitted to drive.[49]

   For the time being, at least, the state of the law in Ontario will uphold a finding of liability made against a physician based on his or her negligence in failing to report pursuant to section 203 of the Ontario *Highway Traffic Act*.

2. In the case of *Spillane (Litigation Guardian of) v. Wasserman*,[50] the operator of an automobile suffered an epileptic seizure while driving and, struck and fatally injured a pedestrian. He was not taking all of the medication which had been prescribed for him on a regular basis, which failure resulted in the seizure. The driver had a long history of epileptic seizures, which he suffered on a regular basis without warn-

---

48 (1994), 7 M.V.R. (3d) 34 (Ont. C.A.).
49 *Ibid.*, at 37.
50 (1992), 42 M.V.R. (2d) 144, 13 C.C.L.T. (2d) 267 (Ont. Gen. Div.), additional reasons at (April 1, 1993), Doc. 11625/86, 11629/86 (Ont. Gen. Div.), varied (1998), 41 C.C.L.T. (2d) 292 (Ont. C.A.), which found the physicians 5 per cent responsible.

ing. Two physicians, who had treated the driver for his epileptic condition over the years, were found 40 per cent responsible for the accident. They had failed to run blood tests routinely on all drugs prescribed to check for compliance; they did not follow the minimum standards set out in notices sent out by the College of Physicians and Surgeons, and they had neglected to report his condition to the Registrar of Motor Vehicles, as provided by the *Highway Traffic Act* (Ont.).

3. In the case of *Ferguson Estate v. Burton*,[51] an epileptic driver lost consciousness while driving, resulting in death of driver of another automobile; the epileptic driver had not taken medication and was suffering from fatigue and stress. The personal representative of the deceased driver sued the epileptic driver and the owner of the automobile he was driving who, in turn, added the epileptic driver's family physician as a third party, alleging he was negligent on numerous grounds, including his failure to report the driver's medical condition pursuant to then section 177 of the Ontario *Highway Traffic Act*, requiring him to report to the Registrar of Motor Vehicles that the epileptic driver was suffering from a condition which might make it dangerous for him to operate a motor vehicle. The epileptic driver was found responsible for the accident at trial. The Court concluded, in applying section 177 of the Ontario *Highway Traffic Act*, that the family physician was entitled to take into account the effect of treatment on his patient, in forming his opinion as to whether a patient is suffering from a condition that may make it dangerous for the patient to operate a motor vehicle, and consequently was not under a duty to report. Further, the Court found the family physician was completely satisfied that the epileptic driver would follow his instruction regarding medication and the conditions under which he should not drive. In addition, there was no evidence that the epileptic driver's licence would have been suspended even if the family physician had made a report under the Act. Having concluded that the family physician had treated and advised the epileptic driver in accordance with the standard expected of an ordinary physician practicing at the relevant time, thereby satisfying the duty which he owed as a family physician to his patient, the Court felt there could be no breach of a duty to members of the public that could give rise to a right to contribution and indemnity in respect of the damages suffered by the plaintiff in the main action.

---

51 (1987), 50 M.V.R. 197 (Ont. H.C.).

5.3.5 Regulated Health Professions Act, 1991[52]

HEALTH PROFESSIONS PROCEDURAL CODE (deemed by section 4 of the *Regulated Health Professions Act, 1991*, to be part of each health profession Act):

1. *Duty of member of regulated health profession to file report of sexual abuse of a patient by another member of the same or a different College.*[53]

A member of a regulated health profession must file a report if the member has reasonable grounds, obtained in the course of practising the profession, to believe another member of the same or a different College has sexually abused a patient. A member is not required to file a report if he or she does not know the name of the member who would be the subject of the report.

The report must be filed in writing with the Registrar of the College of the member who is the subject of the report within 30 days after the obligation to report arises, unless the person who is required to file the report has reasonable grounds to believe that the member will continue to sexually abuse the patient or will sexually abuse other patients, in which case the report must be filed forthwith. The report must contain,

  (a) the name of the person filing the report;
  (b) the name of the member who is the subject of the report;
  (c) an explanation of the alleged sexual abuse;
  (d) if the grounds of the person filing the report are related to a particular patient of the member who is the subject of the report, the name of that patient; provided that the patient's name must not be included in a report unless the patient, or if the patient is incapable, the patient's representative, consents in writing to the inclusion of the patient's name.[54]

If a member who is required to file a report is providing psychotherapy to the member who would be the subject of the report, the report must also contain the opinion of the member filing the report, if he or she is able to form one, as to whether or not the member who is the subject of the report is likely to sexually abuse patients in the future.[55] A member who files

---

52   S.O. 1991, c. 18, of which Schedule 2 is the Health Professions Procedural Code.
53   Health Professions Procedural Code, s. 85.1(1), (2).
54   *Ibid.*, s. 85.3.
55   *Ibid.*, s. 85.3(5).

such a report is required to file an additional report to the same College if the member ceases to provide psychotherapy to the member who was the subject of the first report, which additional report must be filed forthwith.[56]

2. *Duty of operator of a facility where one or more members practice to file report of sexual abuse of a patient by member who practices at the facility.*[57]

A person who operates a facility where one or more members practise is required to file a report if the person has reasonable grounds to believe that a member who practices at the facility has sexually abused a patient. A person who operates a facility but who is not an individual shall be deemed to have reasonable grounds if the individual who is responsible for the operation of the facility has reasonable grounds. A person who operates a facility is not required to file a report if the person does not know the name of the member who would be the subject of the report.[58]

5.3.6 *Vital Statistics Act*[59]

1. *Duty of legally qualified medical practitioner or nurse who attends at the birth of a child to give notice of the birth in prescribed form to division registrar.*[60]

Every legally qualified medical practitioner who attends at the birth within Ontario of a child is required to give notice of the birth in the form prescribed by the regulations under the Act, by delivering or mailing the notice within two days after the day of birth to the division registrar of the registration division within which the child was born. Where no legally qualified medical practitioner is in attendance at the birth, the nurse[61] in attendance is required to give the notice of the birth.

---

56 *Ibid.*, s. 85.4.
57 *Ibid.*, s. 85.2.
58 *Ibid.* See s. 85.3 for particulars of report to be filed.
59 R.S.O. 1990, c. V.4.
60 *Ibid.*, s. 8.
61 *Ibid.* At s. 1, "nurse" includes any person, other than a legally qualified medical practitioner, who attends at the birth of a child. (This definition is repealed by S.O. 1994, c. 27, s. 102(1), to come into force on proclamation; as of this writing, it has not been proclaimed.)

2. *Duty of legally qualified medical practitioner in attendance at still-birth, or a coroner, to deliver medical certificate of cause of the still-birth to funeral director in charge of the body.*[62]

The legally qualified medical practitioner in attendance at a still-birth in Ontario or, where none is in attendance, a coroner is required to complete a medical certificate in the prescribed form of the cause of the still-birth and to deliver it to the funeral director in charge of the body. The funeral director must then deliver the medical certificate, with other prescribed documents, to the division registrar of the proper registration division, who, if he or she is satisfied as to the correctness and sufficiency of the documents, shall register the still-birth by signing the medical certificate and other prescribed documents.

3. *Duty of legally qualified medical practitioner to deliver medical certificate of death of deceased person to funeral director or other person in charge of the body.*[63]

Except in the case of an untoward death which must be reported to the coroner or a police officer pursuant to section 10 of the *Coroners Act*,[64] any legally qualified medical practitioner who has been in attendance during the last illness of a deceased person or who has sufficient knowledge of the last illness is required to forthwith after the death complete and sign a medical certificate of death in the prescribed form, stating the cause of death, and to deliver the medical certificate to the funeral director or other person in charge of the body.

5.3.7 *Charitable Institutions Act*[65]

Duty of physician for the institution to report contagious or communicable disease outbreaks to local medical officer of health.[66]

---

62 *Ibid.*, s. 18. At s. 1, "still-birth" is defined as the complete expulsion or extraction from its mother of a product of conception either after the twentieth week of pregnancy or after the product of conception has attained the weight of 500 grams or more, and where after such expulsion or extraction there is no breathing, beating of the heart, pulsation of the umbilical cord or movement of voluntary muscle.
63 *Ibid.*, s. 21(3).
64 R.S.O. 1990, c. C.37.
65 R.S.O. 1990, c. C.9.
66 R.R.O. 1990, Reg. 69, s. 15(4)(d).

The physician for the institution[67] is required to report any contagious or communicable disease outbreaks to the local medical officer of health in accordance with section 25 of the *Health Protection and Promotion Act*.

5.3.8 Day Nurseries Act[68]

Duty of operator to notify program adviser of "serious occurrence" in any day nursery or location where private-home daycare is provided.[69]

Every operator is required to ensure that a program adviser is notified of any serious occurrence in any day nursery operated by the operator or any location where private-home daycare is provided by the operator within 24 hours of its happening.

A "serious occurrence" is defined[70] to include:

(a) the death of a child while in attendance at a day nursery or in receipt of private-home care,
(b) any serious injury to a child while in attendance at a day nursery or in receipt of private-home daycare,
(c) abuse of a child within the meaning of the *Child and Family Services Act* by a staff member of a day nursery or person in charge of a location where private-home daycare is being provided or by any other person while the child is attending the day nursery or location where private-home daycare is being provided.

5.3.9 Homes for Retarded Persons Act[71]

Duty of person in charge of approved home or auxiliary residence to give notice of the death of a resident to a coroner.[72]

The person in charge of an approved home or auxiliary residence is required to give notice of the death of a resident to a coroner other than a

---

67 *Ibid.* At s. 14, a physician to each charitable institution shall be appointed by the board of directors of an approved corporation or a charitable institution, with the approval of the Minister of Community and Social Services, maintained by it to ensure that medical services are provided to each resident in accordance with his or her needs.
68 R.S.O. 1990, c. D.2.
69 R.R.O. 1990, Reg. 262, s. 35(b).
70 *Ibid.*, s. 1.
71 R.S.O. 1990, c. H.11.
72 R.R.O. 1990, Reg. 635, s. 10.

coroner who is the physician of an approved home appointed under section 12 of the General Regulation.[73]

5.3.10 Homes for the Aged and Rest Homes Act[74]

1. *Duty of administrator of a home to give notice of death of a resident to a coroner.*[75]

The administrator of a home or joint home is required to give notice of the death of a resident to a coroner other than a coroner who is the physician for the home in which the deceased resident was residing at the time of his or her death, in accordance with section 27 of the *Coroners Act*.

2. *Duty of municipality or municipalities or board maintaining and operating a home to report certain occurrences in the home to the Director.*[76]

The municipality, municipalities or board maintaining and operating a home shall report to the Director in full detail each of the following occurrences in the home, promptly after the occurrence in the form provided by the Minister of Health, namely:

(i) a fire;
(ii) an assault;
(iii) an injury in respect of which a person is taken to a hospital;
(iv) a communicable disease outbreak;
(v) a death resulting from an accident or an undetermined cause.

3. *Duty of medical director to report any incidence of reportable or communicable disease outbreaks to local medical officer of health.*[77]

The medical director[78] shall report any incidence of reportable or communicable disease outbreaks to the local medical officer of health in ac-

---

73 R.R.O. 1990, Reg. 635.
74 R.S.O. 1990, c. H.13.
75 R.R.O. 1990, Reg. 637, s. 5(t).
76 *Ibid.*, s. 25.1(1), (2).
77 *Ibid.*, s. 26(4), as amended by 372/94.
78 *Ibid.* At s. 1(1), "medical director" means the legally qualified medical practitioner appointed as physician for the home or joint home under s. 12(4) of the Act.

cordance with sections 25 and 26 of the *Health Protection and Promotion Act*.

5.3.11 Mental Hospitals Act[79]

1. *Duty of officer in charge of institution to report employee found to be suffering from active tuberculosis to medical officer of health, Workers' Compensation Board, and Minister of Health.*[80]

Every full-time or part-time employee of an institution (but not including an employee of an approved home) must receive an intra-dermal tuberculin test and x-ray film of the lungs within one week after the commencement of his or her employment, unless the employee presents the institution with satisfactory proof of the taking of such tests within one year preceding the commencement of his or her employment.[81]

No employee found to be suffering from active tuberculosis is permitted to work in the institution, and

   (i) the officer in charge[82] is required to report the case within 24 hours to the medical officer of health of the municipality in which the employee resides and to the medical officer of health in the municipality in which he or she is employed;
   (ii) the officer in charge is required to give to the Workers' Compensation Board and to the Ministry of Health written notice thereof, including a complete report of the medical findings within seven days of the time of diagnosis.

2. *Duty of medical practitioner to notify officer-in-charge of belief or suspicion that person admitted to an institution is suffering from tuberculosis.*[83]

A medical practitioner who believes or suspects that a person admitted to an institution is suffering from tuberculosis shall notify the officer-in-charge forthwith.

---

79 R.S.O. 1990, c. M.8.
80 R.R.O. 1990, Reg. 744, ss. 17, 18.
81 R.R.O. 1990, Reg. 744, s. 14.
82 *Mental Hospitals Act*, R.S.O. 1990, c. M.8, at s. 1,
   "officer in charge" means the officer of the Ministry of Health who is appointed as the superintendent or hospital administrator of an institution.
83 *Ibid.*, s. 23.

5.3.12 Nursing Homes Act[84]

1. *Duty by a person other than a resident to report to Director suspicion and information on which it is based that a resident has suffered or may suffer harm as result of unlawful conduct, improper or incompetent treatment or care or neglect.*[85]

A person other than a resident who has reasonable grounds to suspect that a resident has suffered or may suffer harm as a result of unlawful conduct, improper or incompetent treatment or care or neglect, must forthwith report the suspicion and the information upon which it is based to the Director. Even if the information on which a report may be based is confidential or privileged, the foregoing duty to report applies to a legally qualified medical practitioner or a member of a regulated health profession, and no action for the making of the report may be commenced against a practitioner or person who makes a report unless the person acts maliciously or without reasonable grounds for suspicion. The Act, insofar as it relates to the said duty to report, does not abrogate any privilege that may exist between a solicitor and the solicitor's client. The Director shall cause any such report to be investigated forthwith after receiving it.

2. *Duty to report death of resident in a nursing home immediately to a coroner and the resident's physician.*[86]

Where a resident dies in a nursing home, the resident's death must be reported immediately to,

   (i) a coroner by the person in charge in the nursing home at the time of the resident's death; and
   (ii) the resident's physician.

3. *Duty of licensee of nursing home to promptly report to Director in detail each of specified occurrences.*[87]

A licensee of a nursing home is required to report to the Director in full detail each of the following occurrences in the home, promptly and in the form provided by the Minister of Health:

---

84 *Nursing Homes Act*, R.S.O. 1990, c. N.7.
85 *Ibid.*, s. 25(7).
86 R.R.O. 1990, Reg. 832, s. 78.
87 *Ibid.*, s. 96, as amended by 373/94.

1. A fire.
2. An assault.
3. An injury in respect of which a person is taken to hospital.
4. A communicable disease outbreak.
5. A death resulting from an accident or an undetermined cause.

5.3.13 Private Hospitals Act[88]

1. *Duty of superintendent to report to Minister of Health the death of a patient in a private hospital resulting from pregnancy.*[89]

Where the death of a patient in a private hospital results either directly or indirectly from pregnancy, the superintendent is required within 24 hours to report the death upon the prescribed form to the Minister.

2. *Duty of legally qualified medical practitioner to notify superintendent of belief or suspicion that person admitted to hospital is suffering from tuberculosis.*[90]

Where any legally qualified medical practitioner believes or suspects that any person admitted to the hospital is suffering from tuberculosis, he or she is required to notify the superintendent forthwith.

3. *Duty of superintendent to give written notice and complete report of medical findings to Workers' Compensation Board where employee shows evidence of tuberculosis.*[91]

Where an employee shows evidence of tuberculosis, the superintendent is required to give written notice thereof and a complete report of the medical findings within seven days after the time of diagnosis to the Workers' Compensation Board.

5.3.14 Public Hospitals Act[92]

1. *Duty of physician or midwife who knows or suspects patient is or may become dangerous to notify administrator.*[93]

A physician or midwife who knows or suspects that a person being ad-

---

88 R.S.O. 1990, c. P.24.
89 R.R.O. 1990, Reg. 937, s. 16.
90 *Ibid.*, s. 28.
91 *Ibid.*, s. 33.
92 R.S.O. 1990, c. P.40.
93 R.R.O. 1990, Reg. 965, s. 14(1).

mitted to the hospital on the physician's or midwife's order is or may become dangerous to himself or herself or to other persons, is required to forthwith notify the administrator concerning the patient or registered nurse in the extended class.

2. *Duty of physician, dentist or midwife who knows or suspects patient suffering from infectious disease to notify specified persons.*[94]

An attending physician, attending dentist or attending midwife who knows or suspects that his or her patient is suffering from an infectious disease or condition is required to forthwith notify,

    (i) an infection control officer or nurse; and
    (ii) the administrator,

concerning the patient.

3. *Duty of administrator to notify specified persons of his or her belief that a member of the medical, dental or midwifery staff is unable to perform professional duties with respect to patient in public hospital.*[95]

Where an administrator believes that a person who is a member of the medical, dental or midwifery staff is unable to perform the person's professional duties with respect to a patient in the hospital, the administrator is required to notify the chief of staff or the chair of the medical advisory committee and, in the case of a member of the medical staff, the president or the secretary of the medical staff of the belief.

---

94 *Ibid.*, s. 14(2).
95 *Ibid.*, s. 18(3).

BIBLIOGRAPHY

1. Mairi Byrne, "Disclosure of Health Information to the Police: A Hospital Viewpoint" (1981) 2 Health Law in Canada 33.
2. John A. Campion and Diana W. Dimmer, *Professional Liability in Canada* (Toronto: Carswell, 1994).
3. *Canadian Health Facilities Law Guide* (North York: CCH, 1997).
4. Bernard M. Dickens, "Medical Records — Patient's Right to Receive Copies — Physician's Fiduciary Duty of Disclosure: *McInerney v. MacDonald*" [1994] 73 Can. Bar Rev. 234.
5. H.E. Emson, *The Doctor and the Law: A Practical Guide for the Canadian Physician* (Toronto: Butterworths, 1989).
6. Dennis B. Evanson, "The Development and Power of the Informer Privilege: The Health Records Inquiry Case" (1983) Queen's L.J. 207.
7. Kevin P. Feehan, "Legal Access to Patient Health Records/Protection of Quality Assurance Activities" (1991) 12 Health Law in Canada 3.
8. James L. Gilbert *et al.*, "Evidence Destruction — Legal Consequences of Spoliation of Records" (U.S. Reporter).
9. Howard S. Ginsberg, "Insurance — Life Insurance — Insurers Right of Access to Insureds' Medical Records: *Frenette v. Metropolitan Life Insurance Co.*" [1994] 73 Can. Bar Rev. 77.
10. K.G. Gray, *Law and the Practice of Medicine* (Toronto: Ryerson, 1955).
11. Justice E.L. Haines, "Confidentiality of Health Information and Court Disclosure" (1981) 2 Health Law in Canada 27.
12. Julie Hamblin and Margaret A. Somerville, "Surveillance and Reporting of HIV Infection and AIDS in Canada: Ethics and the Law" (1991) 41 University of Toronto L.J. 224.
13. Jeffrey F. Harris, "The Solicitor General for Canada et al. v. The Royal Commission of Inquiry into the Confidentiality of Health Records in Ontario; Opening the Files for the R.C.M.P." (1983) 12 Manitoba L.J. 399.
14. Brian D. Hoffman, "Privileged Communication and Court Disclosure: A Psychiatrist's Perspective" (1981) 2 Health Law in Canada 29.
15. Dr. Brian Hoffman, "Disclosure of Medical Information Without Consent: The Patient's Right to Confidentiality" (1992) 13 Health Law in Canada 156.
16. Deborah Jones, "Supreme Court decision forces CMA to revise policy on patients' right to records" (1992) 147(12) Can. Medical Assn. J. 1848.
17. Sandra B. Kidd, ed., *The Physicians' Legal Manual* (Toronto: Emond, Montgomery, 1996).

18. Dr. Robert MacMillan, "Confidentiality: A Physician/Bureaucrat's Perspective" (1992) 13 Health Law in Canada 150.
19. Dr. Samuel Malcolmson, "Access by Patients to the Clinical Record" (1992) 13 Health Law in Canada 160.
20. Ronald D. Manes and Michael P. Silver, *Solicitor-Client Privilege in Canadian Law* (Toronto: Butterworths, 1993).
21. Arnold Mann, *Medical Assessment of Injuries for Legal Purposes*, 4th ed. (Toronto: Butterworths, 1985).
22. T. David Marshall, *The Physician and Canadian Law*, 2d ed. (Toronto: Carswell, 1979).
23. Mary Marshall, "*Case Comment: R. v. Gruenke*" (1992) 13 Health Law in Canada 113.
24. Marilou McPhedran, "The Legal Assault on Physician-Patient Privilege" (1995) 153(10) Can. Med. Assn. J. 1502.
25. Wayne McKerrow, "Privileged Communication and Disclosure in Court" (1981) 2 Health Law in Canada 28.
26. Colin McNairn and Christopher Woodbury, *The 1996 Annotated Ontario Freedom of Information and Protection of Privacy Acts* (Toronto: Carswell, 1995).
27. Arthur J. Meagher, Peter J. Marr, and Ronald A. Meagher, *Doctors and Hospitals: Legal Duties* (Toronto: Butterworths 1991).
28. C. Mellor, "Position Paper: The Canadian Medical Association Code of Ethics, Annotated for Psychiatrists" (1980) 25 Can. J. of Psychiatry 432.
29. Tom Melville, "An Issue of Confidentiality: Widened Disclosure in the Clinical Context" (1987) 45 Toronto Faculty of Law Rev. 179.
30. Alan M. Mewett, "Medical Records of Rape Victims" (1994) 36 Crim. L.Q. 257.
31. John J. Morris, *Law for Canadian Health Care Administrators* (Toronto: Butterworths, 1996).
32. Ellen I. Picard, *Legal Liability of Doctors and Hospitals in Canada*, 2d ed. (Toronto: Carswell, 1984).
33. Daniel I. Reisler and Phillippa G. Samworth, "Production of Medical Records" (1985) 6 Advocates' Quarterly 257.
34. Gloria Ringwood, "Confidentiality: A Health Record Department Perspective" (1992) 13 Health Law in Canada 162.
35. Robert Roth and Stephen E. Firestone, "The Production of Clinical Notes and Records" (1987) 8 Advocates' Quarterly 477.
36. L.E. Rozovsky, *Canadian Hospital Law: A Practical Guide*, 2nd ed. [Canadian Hospital Association, 1979].
37. Lorne Elkin Rozovsky and Fay Adrienne Rozovsky, "*The Canadian Law of Patient Records*" (Toronto: Butterworths, 1984).
38. S.R. Seller, *The Law of Doctor and Patient* (London: Lewis, 1973).

39. G. Sharpe and G. Sawyer, *Doctors and the Law* (Toronto: Butterworths, 1978).
40. Barney Sneiderman, John Irvine, Philip H. Osborne, *Canadian Medical Law, An Introduction for Physicians and other Health Care Professionals* (Toronto: Carswell, 1989).
41. John Sopinka and Sidney N. Lederman, *The Law of Evidence in Civil Cases* (Toronto: Butterworths, 1992).
42. Thomas Stewart, "The Role of the Police in the Confidentiality of Health Records" (1981) 2 Health Law in Canada 31.
43. Noel Leigh Taylor, *Doctors and the Law* (London: Oyez, 1976).
44. Dennis Timbrell, "Perspectives on Confidentiality and Privacy" (1992) 13 Health Law in Canada 147.
45. R. Edward Turner, M.D., "Disclosure of Health Information to the Police: A Psychiatrist's Perspective" (1981) 2 Health Law in Canada 34.
46. Garry D. Watson and Craig Perkins, *Holmested and Watson: Ontario Civil Procedure* (Toronto: Carswell, 1993).

Chapter 6

Expert Evidence

by Giovanna Roccamo, LL.B.

6.1 Introduction
6.2 Opinion Evidence
6.3 Why are Experts Needed?
6.4 Qualifications of an Expert
6.5 Admissibility of Expert Opinion Evidence
    6.5.1 Relevance
    6.5.2 Necessity in Assisting the Trier of Fact
    6.5.3 The Absence of any Exclusionary Rule
    6.5.4 A Properly Qualified Expert
6.6 Expert Opinion Based on Hearsay
6.7 Ultimate Issue Rule
6.8 Novel Expert Opinion Evidence
6.9 Duties and Responsibilities of an Expert Witness
6.10 Court-Appointed Experts
6.11 Approaching the Right Expert Witness
6.12 How to Locate the Expert Witness
6.13 When to Choose an Expert Witness
6.14 Remuneration for Expert Opinion
    6.14.1 Professional Conduct
    6.14.2 Payment for the Expert's Services
6.15 Expert Report
    6.15.1 Rule 53.03
    6.15.2 Disclosure of Expert Report, Raw Data Drafts
    6.15.3 Why Such a Difference?
    6.15.4 Leave to File an Expert's Report
6.16 Ontario *Evidence Act* — Medical Reports
    6.16.1 Purpose of Section 52 of the Ontario *Evidence Act*
    6.16.2 Calling the Medical Practitioner to Testify
    6.16.3 Who has the Obligation to Secure the Attendance at Trial of the Medical Practitioner for Cross-examination?

    6.16.4 The Medical Practitioner is Unavailable for
           Cross-Examination
6.17 Produce a Good Expert Report
6.18 Format of the Expert Report
6.19 Review the Expert Report
6.20 Number of Experts Allowed to Testify
6.21 Family Doctor-Patient Relationship
6.22 Conclusion
Appendix A

6.1   INTRODUCTION

The courts are increasingly being asked to make decisions on complex and technical matters. Judges and juries do not possess the knowledge and the skills to arrive at these decisions alone, and depend on the assistance of expert witnesses to "teach" and assist the trier of fact in arriving at these decisions. There is no doubt that the expert witness is a vital player in the personal injury litigation process where the area of expertise relevant to personal injury litigation is highly technical and complex.

6.2   OPINION EVIDENCE

As a general rule, witnesses may not give opinion evidence. There are exceptions to this rule which Wigmore expressed as follows:

> First, all witnesses, whether testifying on observed data of their own or on data furnished by others, may state their inferences so far only as they have some *special skill* which can be applied to interpret or draw inferences from these data. Secondly, witnesses having *no special skill*, who have had *personal observation* of the matter in hand, may, as a result of their personal observation, have drawn inferences or made inferences or made interpretations which the tribunal could equally well make from the same data of personal observation, if laid before them; and thus if it is possible to detail these data fully for the tribunal, the witness' own inferences are superfluous. But there is also a *third* group in which exclusion must take place, though Courts seldom find it necessary to point out, namely, where the witnesses would detail the data of personal observation (and not only mere inferences), but the *tribunal has an equal opportunity* of personal observations, — as where the question is whether the accused in court has dark or light hair, or whether a house which has been viewed by the tribunal has three or six stories.[1]

---

1   J.H. Wigmore, *A Treatise on the Anglo-American System of Evidence* (3rd ed., 1940), Vol. vii, para. 1918.

Expert Evidence

Expert witnesses have long provided assistance to the courts. As long ago as 1553, Justice Saunders, in the Common Bench decision in *Buckley v. Rice-Thomas*, made the following observation:

> If matters arise in our law which concern other sciences or faculties we commonly apply for the aid of that science or faculty which it concerns. Which is an honourable and commendable thing in our law. For thereby it appears that we do not despise all other sciences but our own, but we approve of them and encourage them as things worthy of commendation. . . And in an appeal of mayhem the Judges of our law have used to be informed by surgeons whether it be a mayhem or not, because their knowledge and skill can best discern it.[2]

In an early decision on this subject, the Supreme Court of Canada in *Kelliher (Village) v. Smith*,[3] on appeal from the Court of Appeal of Saskatchewan, considered the use of expert evidence. In that case, the plaintiff was injured when he was operating a chemical fire extinguisher at a fire. The plaintiff sued the village for the damages that he sustained. The jury found that the plaintiff's injury was caused by the defendant's negligence in not having a fire extinguisher properly inspected and kept in perfect working order. The jury also held that the plaintiff was guilty of contributory negligence. The plaintiff appealed to the Court of Appeal; the court reversed the judgment of the lower court, and gave judgment to the plaintiff. At the Supreme Court of Canada, Mr. Justice Lamont, writing for the majority, held that no expert opinion evidence was required in order to form a correct judgment as to the plaintiff's acts, since the jury was capable of arriving at the decision without the assistance of an expert witness. Mr. Justice Lamont referred to the following excerpt from *Beven on Negligence*:[4]

> To justify the admission of expert testimony two elements must co-exist:
>
> (1) The subject-matter of the inquiry must be such that ordinary people are unlikely to form a correct judgment about it, if unassisted by persons with special knowledge.
> (2) The witness offering expert evidence must have gained his special knowledge by a course of study or previous habit which secures his habitual familiarity with the matter in hand.

---

2   (1554), 1 Plowd. 118 at 124.
3   [1931] S.C.R. 672.
4   *Ibid.*, at (S.C.R.) 683; at (D.L.R.) 141.

6.3 WHY ARE EXPERTS NEEDED?

The reason experts are allowed to provide their opinion is because of their knowledge, training and experience. This allows them to form opinions which the trier of fact is unable to form. Expert opinion is required to assist the trier of fact to evaluate the facts in order that a correct decision may be made. As Mr. Justice Dickson, as he then was, stated in *R. v. Abbey*:

> With respect to matters calling for special knowledge, an expert in the field may draw inferences and state his opinion. An expert's function is precisely this: to provide the judge and jury with a ready-made inference which the judge and jury, due to the technical nature of the facts, are unable to formulate. "An expert's opinion is admissible to furnish the Court with scientific information which is likely to be outside the experience and knowledge of a judge or jury. If on the proven facts a judge or jury can form their own conclusions without help, then the opinion of the expert is unnecessary." (Turner (1974), 60 Crim. App. R. 80, at p. 83, per Lawton L.J.).[5]

Where a trier of fact is able to arrive at a decision on a case based on the ordinary experience and knowledge of the trier of fact, an expert witness will not be allowed to testify.[6] In the decision of the British Columbia Supreme Court in *Spencer v. Soanes*,[7] the plaintiff sued for damages arising out of injuries alleged to have arisen in three motor vehicle accidents. The three actions were tried together. The defendants sought to tender a report of a psychologist. The psychologist subjected the plaintiff to a number of different psychological tests from which she concluded that "there is a significant nomogenic component to the plaintiff's complaints: the complaints of pain and disability are maintained by expectations of major financial gain through litigation." The plaintiff objected to the introduction of such a report on the ground that the psychologist's opinion was no more than an assessment of credibility, which was a matter for the court to decide. The court agreed with the plaintiff and held the psychologist's opinion to be inadmissible.

On the other hand, the plaintiff in *Sacilotto v. Crossman*[8] sought to introduce an economist's report setting out various earning capacity scenar-

---

5 [1982] 2 S.C.R. 24 at 42, 39 B.C.L.R. 201, 29 C.R. (3d) 193, [1983] 1 W.W.R. 251. See also *Davie v. Edinburgh Magistrates*, [1953] S.C. 34 (Scotland Ct. Sess) and *R. v. Fisher*, [1961] O.W.N. 94, 34 C.R. 320 (Ont. C.A.), affirmed [1961] S.C.R. 535, 35 C.R. 107.
6 See *Yewdale v. Insurance Corp. of British Columbia* (1995), 3 B.C.L.R. (3d) 240 (S.C.), leave to appeal refused (1995), 3 B.C.L.R. (3d) 247 (C.A.).
7 (1994), 113 D.L.R. (4th) 567, 92 B.C.L.R. (2d) 129 (S.C.).
8 (1990), 49 B.C.L.R. (2d) 375 (S.C.).

ios based on no injury, and others based on injuries that the plaintiff alleged he had suffered. The court admitted such evidence since it was useful and was outside the trial judge's general experience. Therefore, provided that the expert opinion is useful, it will be admitted. Regrettably, there are times when the courts are unsure as to whether or not expert evidence will provide assistance to them, and in such cases the courts may reject such evidence when it really should be admitted. As Sopinka, Lederman and Bryant point out in the *Law of Evidence in Canada*:

> Sometimes it is debatable whether the expert testimony would be of value or not. Rejection of expert evidence about whether a common English word used in the ordinary way was generic and what the word meant may be easily justified as not coming within a subject requiring any special study or experience. The courts, however, have allowed expert testimony about uncommon words or common words used in an unusual manner, as for example, drug slang. Curiously, however, courts have rejected expert evidence in some instances where one would have thought it would have been of value. For example, experts' evidence on the question of whether certain fire prevention facilities should have been provided was held to be inadmissible in a fatal accident action based upon a hotel keeper's negligence.[9]

In these instances, counsel will have to be vigilant in the review of rulings made by the courts in the admission of expert evidence and, indeed, tenacious enough to persuade the court as to the merits of allowing admission.

6.4 QUALIFICATIONS OF AN EXPERT

It is important to understand that an expert witness is an expert because of the special knowledge or skill that he or she possesses, and not because the expert is certified as a specialist by a body or association governing his or her profession, or possesses a certain number of qualifications. In *Rice v. Sockett*, Chief Justice Falconbridge wrote:

> The derivation of the term 'expert' implies that he is one who by experience has acquired special or peculiar knowledge of the subject of which he undertakes to testify, and it does not matter whether such knowledge has been acquired by study of scientific works or by practical observation; and one who is an old hunter, and has thus had much experience in the use of firearms, may be as well qualified to testify as to the appearance which a gun recently fired would present as a highly educated and skilled gunsmith.[10]

---

9   Sopinka, Lederman, Bryant, *The Law of Evidence in Canada* (Toronto: Butterworths, 1992) at 535.
10 (1912), 27 O.L.R. 410, 8 D.L.R. 84 at 85 (C.A.) quoting from *State v. Davis*, 33 SE. 449 (1899).

The New Brunswick Court of Appeal, on appeal from the New Brunswick Court of Queen's Bench in *Fillier v. Whittom*, considered what qualifications were required for a witness to be considered as an expert. In that case, the plaintiff sued the defendant for damages for injuries sustained in a motor vehicle accident. The lower court held that both drivers were at fault. The plaintiff appealed. One of the grounds of appeal was that the trial judge erred in qualifying an expert witness since he was not certified as a specialist by the College of Physicians. The Court of Appeal disagreed with the plaintiff, and held that the expert was qualified. The Court concluded:

> To become an expert for the purpose of giving opinion evidence at trial does not necessarily require a specific professional or occupational designation. Rather, it is the proposed expert's training and experience and the ability to relate that experience and training to the issue before the court in such a way that the evidence will assist the court in determining the issue before it that governs whether the witness should be permitted to give opinion evidence in his or her field.[11]

Children's Aid Society of Hamilton-Wentworth v. D. (S.),[12] a decision of the Ontario Unified Family Court, is another example of a case where a family practitioner was accepted as an expert in the diagnosis of child abuse, primarily because he had acquired a considerable amount of expertise in the field of child abuse through private study and practical experience.

Should there be any deficiency in an expert's expertise, this may affect the weight to be accorded the evidence by the trier of fact, but not its admissibility. As stated by Sopinka, Lederman and Bryant:

> The admissibility of evidence does not depend upon the means by which that skill was acquired. As long as the court is satisfied that the witness is sufficiently experienced in the subject-matter at issue, the court will not be concerned with whether his or her skill was derived from specific studies or by practical training, although that may affect the weight to be given to the evidence.[13]

---

11   (1995), 161 N.B.R. (2d) 241 (Q.B.), affirmed (1995), 171 N.B.R. (2d) 92 at 113 (C.A.).
12   (1991), 83 D.L.R. (4th) 166, 35 R.F.L. (3d) 136 (Ont. U.F.C.).
13   *Supra*, note 9, at 536.

6.5 ADMISSIBILITY OF EXPERT OPINION EVIDENCE

The Supreme Court of Canada in *R. v. Mohan*[14] reiterated the governing principles for admissibility of expert evidence. The admissibility of expert opinion evidence depends on the application of four criteria:

1. relevance;
2. necessity in assisting the trier of fact;
3. the absence of any exclusionary rule; and,
4. a properly qualified expert.

6.5.1 Relevance

As in the case of other evidence adduced at trial, the expert opinion evidence must meet the threshold requirement of relevancy. Relevance is a matter to be determined by a judge as a question of law. In order to determine if the expert opinion evidence is relevant, the following two questions must be considered:

1. Is the proposed expert opinion evidence logically relevant to an issue in the case? and,
2. A cost benefit analysis must be conducted in order to determine if the value of admitting the expert opinion evidence is outweighed by its cost. In other words, does the probative value of this expert opinion evidence outweigh any prejudicial effect? Would it involve an inordinate amount of time in adducing the expert evidence which is not commensurate with its value, or is the expert evidence misleading? In effect, expert evidence should not be admitted where there is a danger that it will be misused or will distort the fact-finding process, or will confuse the jury.

As Mr. Justice Sopinka put it:

> Evidence that is otherwise logically relevant may be excluded on this basis, if

---

14 [1994] 2 S.C.R. 9, 29 C.R. (4th) 243, 18 O.R. (3d) 160 (note) (S.C.C.). *Mohan* has been applied in a civil context consider the following cases: *Muir v. Alberta* (1995), 41 C.P.C. (3d) 386, 32 Alta. L.R. (3d) 95 (Q.B.); *Kozak v. Funk* (1995), [1996] 1 W.W.R. 107, 28 C.C.L.T. (2d) 81 (Sask. Q.B.) appealed on different grounds to Court of Appeal at (1997), [1998] 5 W.W.R. 232, 158 Sask. R. 232, 153 W.A.C. 283 (C.A.); *Walker Estate v. York-Finch General Hospital* (1996), 5 C.P.C. (4th) 240 (Ont. Gen. Div.); *Green v. Lawrence*, [1996] 6 W.W.R. 378, 48 C.P.C. (3d) 211 (Man. Q.B.).

its probative value is overborne by its prejudicial effect, if it involves an inordinate amount of time which is not commensurate with its value or if it is misleading in the sense that its effect on the trier of fact, particularly a jury, is out of proportion to its reliability. . . . The reliability versus effect factor has special significance in assessing the admissibility of expert evidence.[15]

In *R. v. Olscamp*,[16] the Crown intended to call expert opinion evidence in support of the complainant's testimony that she had been sexually abused. The Crown wanted the expert to provide an opinion on the general behavioural and psychological characteristics of child victims of sexual abuse, and then show that the complainant exhibited some symptoms consistent with sexual abuse. The defence argued against the admission of such expert evidence. Justice Charron concluded that the evidence lead was logically relevant, but was of little probative value. The evidence was of limited value primarily because the state of knowledge in the field of expertise offered failed to establish the behavioural symptoms as consistent with sexual abuse. The experts themselves were also not in agreement as to the profile of a victim of sexual assault. Justice Charron held that, although the expert's evidence was logically relevant to an issue in the case, the prejudicial effect outweighed the probative effect. She summarized her position:

> Although the proposed evidence is certainly logically relevant to an issue in the case, its probative value, for the reasons set out earlier, is extremely limited. On the other hand, its prejudicial value can be overwhelming. This trial will turn on a question of credibility. Although a distinction can be made between evidence going to credibility alone and this kind of evidence admitted in support of the complainant's testimony, the line is a very fine one. The admission of evidence "[d]ressed up in scientific language". . . in support of the complainant's testimony may well be given far more weight by the jury than it deserves and may even become determinative of the ultimate issue. The prejudicial effect of this evidence so far outweighs its low probative value that the matter cannot simply be left to be remedied by cross-examination and special instructions to the jury.[17]

In the Northwest Territories Supreme Court's decision in *R. v. Warren*,[18] the accused was charged with the murder of nine miners who died in an underground explosion at a mine. The accused gave a confession to the police. The defence sought to introduce the evidence of a psychologist to

---

15 *R. v. Mohan, ibid.,* at (S.C.R.) 21.
16 (1994), 35 C.R. (4th) 37 (Ont. Gen. Div.).
17 *Ibid.,* at (C.R.) 46.
18 [1995] 3 W.W.R. 371, 35 C.R. (4th) 347 (N.W.T. S.C.).

testify, based on assessments, tests or studies, that the confession made to the police was unreliable. Justice de Weerdt held that such expert evidence was inadmissible, since the tests had not been shown to be reliable. He concluded that there seemed to be little published research and the expert acknowledged "that the present status of the research in this area of psychometry is 'still in the toddler stage'." Justice de Weerdt summarized his thinking as follows:

> The evidence is misleading in the sense that its effect on the jury would be out of all proportion to its reliability. The tests have not been shown to be reliable as yet. Indeed, the contrary appears to be true. Any assessment based upon them must suffer likewise on grounds of unreliability. The probative value of the evidence is accordingly overborne by its prejudicial effect.[19]

6.5.2 Necessity in Assisting the Trier of Fact

Mr. Justice Dickson in *R. v. Abbey* expressed that expert opinion evidence would be admitted if it was "helpful" to the trier of fact.[20] Mr. Justice Sopinka in *Mohan* modified the helpful standard with a necessity requirement. He stated that the expert opinion evidence has to be more than "helpful." This was observed to set too low a standard for the admissibility of expert evidence. By using the necessity standard, courts can determine whether opinion evidence is necessary, in the sense that it provides information which is likely to be outside the experience and knowledge of the trier of fact.[21]

If the trier of fact is able to arrive at his or her own conclusions, based on the given facts of the case, without the assistance of anyone, then expert opinion evidence is unnecessary and hence inadmissible. For example, in *Fraser River Pile & Dredge Ltd. v. Empire Tug Boats Ltd.*,[22] the plaintiff commenced an action against the defendants for damages caused to their crane and a barge when the defendants were towing the barge on which the crane was mounted. A question arose before the trial division of the Federal Court of Canada, as to the admissibility of an affidavit of an expert witness. Justice Reed held that the affidavit was not admissible as expert opinion evidence since it was not necessary to assist the trier of fact in arriving at a decision. Justice Reed referred to the *R. v. Mohan* decision and made the following observation:

---

19 *Ibid.*, at (C.R.) 354.
20 *Supra*, note 5.
21 See *Muir v. Alberta supra*, note 14.
22 (1995), 37 C.P.C. (3d) 119, 95 F.T.R. 43 (Fed. T.D.). See *Sengbusch v. Priest* (1987), 14 B.C.L.R. (2d) 26 (S.C.).

In *R. v. Mohan*, Mr. Justice Sopinka discussed the dangers which can arise from expert evidence. He noted that it can confuse the fact finding process by dressing up evidence as being expert and therefore as carrying a weight which it does not deserve. . . .

I conclude, from this jurisprudence, that the criteria to be applied is whether the proffered evidence is necessary as expert opinion evidence in the context of the case in which it is proffered. Thus, it is not the subject matter of the opinion per se, nor the knowledge of the trier of fact apart from the evidence adduced in a given case which makes expert opinion necessary or unnecessary. *One has to assess whether it is necessary, in the light of all the evidence which is being given in a case, for an expert to be called to assist the trier of fact in drawing inferences.* (Emphasis added.)[23]

In this particular case, the expert offering the expert opinion was viewed by the court as having no more specialized skill or experience than the other witnesses. Also, the primary fact evidence in the case was relatively easy for the court to comprehend.

On the other hand, failure to call an expert witness, when one would ordinarily be expected, may lead the court to draw an adverse inference, such as evidence was not made available to the court because it would not have been favourable. The Supreme Court of Canada in *Levesque v. Comeau*[24] dealt with the dilemma all too often faced by counsel. There, the issue was whether the accident had caused the deafness of the plaintiff. The plaintiff called one expert, but none of the other examining or treating doctors were called. The Supreme Court of Canada, in a three-to-two majority, held that in such cases the court must presume that such evidence would have adversely affected the plaintiff's case. The Ontario Court of Appeal in *Vieczorek v. Piersma*[25] found sympathy with this reasoning. In this case, a husband and wife were both injured in an automobile accident. Both had medical problems prior to the accident. In an action for damages, they failed to call the physicians who had treated them before the accident. The Court of Appeal followed the *Levesque* decision and held that the jury should have been directed that they could, although they were not obliged to draw an adverse inference from the failure to call the treating physicians.[26] Where a judgment call is required to be made on a critical issue, counsel may consider erring on the side of caution and offer up the expert's evidence, in lieu of attracting a negative inference from the court.

---

23 *Supra*, note 14 at (S.C.R.) 124.
24 [1970] S.C.R. 1010.
25 (1987), 58 O.R. (2d) 583, 16 C.P.C. (2d) 62 (C.A.).
26 See also *Badger v. Dowsett* (1994), 21 Alta. L.R. (3d) 323 (Q.B.).

6.5.3 The Absence of any Exclusionary Rule

Expert opinion evidence can be excluded if another exclusionary rule of evidence which is separate and apart from the opinion rule itself, makes it inadmissible. For example, if the evidence is considered to be hearsay.[27] Another example may occur where the Crown will be excluded from adducing evidence of the accused's disposition and character, unless the accused has placed his or her character in issue.[28]

6.5.4 A Properly Qualified Expert

It is imperative to ensure that the expert witness presented is qualified to provide an expert opinion, otherwise the court may refuse to allow the expert to give evidence. Take for example, the decision of the Ontario Court (General Division) in *Walker Estate v. York-Finch General Hospital*,[29] where the court dismissed the plaintiffs' motion to qualify a CEO of a corporation as an expert witness. In that case, the plaintiffs commenced an action against the defendants for infecting the deceased plaintiff with HIV as a result of a blood transfusion. The plaintiffs sought to have a CEO qualified as an expert, with particular knowledge of world standards followed in the collection of human blood. The proposed expert had been the president and CEO of a corporation from 1982 to 1984, which conducted business as a commercial collector of human blood. The court concluded that the proposed expert was not qualified to provide such expert opinion evidence since the proposed expert was neither a medical doctor nor a scientist and was, therefore, unable to give medical or scientific evidence. The court found that the proposed expert had, during his time with the corporation, relied heavily on other doctors and scientists when making decisions; he had no education in blood banking; and his only experience in blood banking had been on the business side as CEO of the corporation.

It is important to ensure that the expert witness has been properly qualified as a person who has acquired special knowledge through study or practical experience that goes beyond that of a trier of fact.[30] It is counsel's duty to ensure that the expert witness whose evidence is adduced is properly qualified. However, a common problem often arises during testimony when an expert may venture forth into areas in which he or she has not

---

27 Please refer to 6.6, Expert Opinion Based on Hearsay, below, for a more detailed analysis of expert opinion based on hearsay evidence.
28 See *R. v. Morin*, [1988] 2 S.C.R. 345, 66 C.R. (3d) 1.
29 *Supra*, note 14.
30 *R. v. Béland*, [1987] 2 S.C.R. 398, 60 C.R. (3d) 1. See discussion at 6.4, Qualifications of an Expert.

been properly qualified. The Supreme Court of Canada, on appeal from the Ontario Court of Appeal, in *R. v. Marquard*[31] considered how an expert witness should be properly qualified. In that case, the appellant was charged with aggravated assault of her granddaughter. The granddaughter had suffered a severe facial burn. The Crown claimed that the grandmother had placed the child's face on a hot stove, while the defence argued that the burn was caused accidentally by the child playing with a lighter. The grandmother was convicted, she appealed the verdict on several grounds. One ground of appeal was that the trial judge erred in admitting opinion evidence given by experts outside their area of expertise. One expert was qualified as an expert in child abuse and paediatrics, but was not qualified as an expert in burns. However, she provided an opinion that the child had suffered a contact burn. Again, another expert was not qualified in the area of burns, but still provided an opinion in that area. Another expert, who was qualified to provide an opinion as to the nature or origin of burns, went beyond this area to provide an opinion on child abuse. Madam Justice McLachlin, writing for the majority, concluded that the trial judge had made no error in law in admitting the experts' evidence, and that while these experts possessed the special knowledge and skill beyond that of the trier of fact, the problem was that these experts were qualified more narrowly than their areas of expertise. Madam Justice McLachlin looked at the procedure required at trial in order to qualify an expert witness. She summarized the procedure as follows:

> Important as the initial qualification of an expert witness may be, it would be overly technical to reject expert evidence simply because the witness ventures an opinion beyond the area of expertise in which he or she has been qualified. As a practical matter, it is for opposing counsel to object if the witness goes beyond the proper limits of his or her expertise. The objection to the witness's expertise may be made at the stage of initial qualification, or during the witness's evidence if it becomes apparent the witness is going beyond the area in which he or she was qualified to give expert opinion. In the absence of objection, a technical failure to qualify a witness who clearly has expertise in the area will not mean that the witness's evidence should be struck. However, if the witness is not shown to have possessed expertise to testify in the area, his or her evidence must be disregarded and the jury so instructed.[32]

If counsel fails to make an objection, and it can be shown that the expert has some expertise to testify in the area, then the expert's evidence will not be automatically struck, but some consideration may be given to the issue of weight. For example, in the Ontario Court of Appeal's decision in *R. v.*

---

31 [1993] 4 S.C.R. 223, 25 C.R. (4th) 1. See also *R. v. Millar* (1989), 71 C.R. (3d) 78, 49 C.C.C. (3d) 193 at 218 (Ont. C.A.).

32 *R. v. Marquard, ibid.,* at (S.C.R.) 244.

R. (W.D.),[33] the accused appealed the decision of the trial judge for refusing to qualify an expert witness. The accused wanted to offer an expert in repressed memory of sexual assault victims and human memory. The trial judge refused to qualify him as an expert witness in the repressed memories of children and ruled as follows:

> Well there is no doubt that Dr. Yarmey is an expert in the field of memory in general. However, what you are attempting to do here is to qualify him as an expert in the field of repressed memories of an abused or a potentially abused person as a child. . . . I would like to see before I qualify the witness as an expert, as to some experience, either as a clinician or some articles written by him with respect to the particular subject matter.

The Ontario Court of Appeal held that the trial judge had erred when he refused to qualify the expert witness. The court followed *Marquard* and concluded that the expert had the relevant expertise in the area of memory recall and repressed memory in sexual abuse cases and commented as follows:

> Although Dr. Yarmey did not have any practical training in dealing with persons who had been sexually abused as children and he had not written in this area, these considerations went to the weight to be given to his evidence and not to the admissibility of his evidence.[34]

It is prudent, therefore, when qualifying an expert witness for counsel to note the following principles arising from the *Marquard* decision:

1. The proper practice is for counsel presenting an expert witness to qualify the expert in *all* areas in which the expert is expected to give opinion evidence.
2. It is for the opposing counsel to object if the witness goes beyond the proper limits of his or her expertise.
3. In the absence of an objection, a technical failure to qualify a witness who clearly has expertise in the area will not mean that the witness's evidence should be struck, although this may go to the weight of the evidence.
4. If the witness is not shown to have possessed expertise to testify in the area, his or her evidence must be disregarded and the jury so instructed.

---

33   (1994), 35 C.R. (4th) 343 (Ont. C.A.).
34   *Ibid.*, at (C.R.) 345.

6.6 EXPERT OPINION BASED ON HEARSAY

An expert opinion must be based on facts proven at trial. The expert should be in a position to state the reasons for his or her opinion and to support those reasons. There are elements of an expert's evidence which may be based on hearsay. For example, the expert may base his or her opinion on materials studied during the expert's academic training or on experience gained during his or her professional life. As Sopinka, Lederman and Bryantexplain:

> Although it has been asserted that the expert's opinion must be based upon either personal knowledge or facts presented at trial, it cannot be completely devoid of a hearsay element. Since the expert by definition possesses a special skill or knowledge in a material area superior to that of the court, the expertise is founded to a large extent upon hearsay data. An expert's opinion will be based on experience and education received. The latter is naturally comprised of the study and readings of works of authorities in the field and information and data culled from numerous sources.
> ... An expert's knowledge is made up of the distilled assertions of others not before the court. Recognition of this hearsay basis of expertise has been acknowledged by the Canadian courts for some time.[35]

In personal injury actions, there often arises the need to introduce expert evidence for example, from the field of psychology, psychiatry or neuropsychology. Such expert opinion evidence may be, to some extent, based on hearsay evidence derived from interviews with clients, friends and family members which may not be proved in evidence. The question, therefore, arises whether the expert opinion evidence is inadmissible because it is based on inadmissible hearsay evidence. This particular question was addressed by the Supreme Court of Canada in *R. v. Abbey*[36] and *R. v. Lavallee*.[37] The Supreme Court of Canada in *Abbey* iterated that an expert opinion based on second-hand or hearsay evidence is admissible if it is relevant. It will, however, be up to the trier of fact to decide how much weight should be attached to the testimony of the expert. The Manitoba Court of Appeal in *Lavallee*[38] interpreted *Abbey* as dictating that each and every fact relied upon by the expert must be independently proven and admitted into evidence before the entire opinion can be given any weight. Madam Justice Wilson of the Supreme Court of Canada in *Lavallee* clarified the ruling in *Abbey*, and cautioned that so long as there is some admis-

---

35 *The Law of Evidence in Canada, supra*, note 9, at 546.
36 *Supra*, note 5.
37 [1990] 1 S.C.R. 852, [1990] 4 W.W.R. 1, 76 C.R. (3d) 329.
38 (1988), 65 C.R. (3d) 387 (Man. C.A.).

sible evidence to establish the foundation for the expert opinion, the trial judge cannot instruct the jury to completely ignore the testimony, but must instruct the jury that, the more the expert relies on facts not proven in evidence, the less weight the jury may attribute to the opinion. Madam Justice Wilson clarified the ruling in *Abbey* as follows:

> *Abbey* does not, in my view, provide any authority for that proposition. The Court's conclusion in that case was that the trial judge erred in treating as proven the facts upon which the psychiatrist relied in formulating his opinion. The solution was an appropriate charge to the jury, not an effective withdrawal of the evidence. In my view, as long as there is some admissible evidence to establish the foundation for the expert's opinion, the trial judge cannot subsequently instruct the jury to completely ignore the testimony. The judge must, of course, warn the jury that the more the expert relies on facts not proved in evidence the less weight the jury may attribute to the opinion.[39]

An interesting example of where a court attached little weight to hearsay evidence, upon which the doctors based their expert opinion, is illustrated by the British Columbia Supreme Court's decision in *Halliday v. Wigmore*.[40] In that case, the plaintiff was involved in a motor vehicle accident. He sued the defendants for injuries sustained, including minor brain damage. The plaintiff's counsel provided to doctors (retained by the plaintiff) several witness statements attesting to the plaintiff's pre-accident health and personality and the changes that had taken place since the accident. The medical doctors used these statements to conclude that the plaintiff was suffering from a minor brain injury. However, there were a number of other doctors who had not seen these witness statements and had concluded that the plaintiff suffered no brain injury. During the trial it was discovered that these witness statements were inaccurate, misleading or simply not true. The court concluded that the expert opinion based on these statements should be given little weight.

6.7 ULTIMATE ISSUE RULE

In the past, it was held that an expert witness could not give an opinion on the very issue resting for determination on the trier of fact. The rationale for the "ultimate issue rule", as it has come to be known, is that, if the expert is allowed to draw conclusions based on the facts of the given case, then the function of the trier of fact is usurped. Other expressed concerns are that, if the expert is allowed to provide an opinion on the ulti-

---

39 *Supra*, note 37, at (S.C.R.) 896.
40 (July 4, 1996), Doc. Vancouver B934746 (B.C. S.C.).

mate issue before the court, then the jury may be impressed with the expert's credentials and knowledge, and may therefore attach greater weight to the expert's opinion than should be given.[41] There is also the concern that the trial would become a battle of the experts, with the trier of fact determining which opinion to accept.

Today, the reasons for invoking the ultimate issue rule have been largely abandoned or rejected in Canada. The Ontario Court of Appeal, in *R. v. Graat*,[42] considered the admissibility of non-expert opinion, and on the issue of the ultimate issue rule, Chief Justice Howland of the Court of Appeal wrote:

> In Canada, the ultimate issue doctrine may now be regarded as having been virtually abandoned or rejected. Where evidence has been rejected on the basis of the doctrine, such rejection can be explained on other grounds. In some instances the opinion evidence should be rejected because the trier of fact, whether judge or jury, is just as well qualified as the witness to draw the necessary inference. Accordingly, the non-expert testimony is superfluous, as it is of no appreciable assistance to the judge or jury. Alternatively, the admission of evidence on the ultimate issue can be justified on the basis that the witness is an expert and the judge and jury requires his assistance. . . . In *R. v. St. Pierre* (1974), 3 O.R. (2d) 642, 17 C.C.C. (2d) 489, this court held that the jury should have had the benefit of the evidence of a psychiatrist, who would have testified that whether the act of the accused constituted gross indecency depended upon the circumstances in which the act was committed. Even if the expert might be considered as usurping the jury's function, the court did not think that it was justified in excluding his evidence. In the final analysis, even with the benefit of the expert's evidence the jury still has to make the final determination of the issue, so that the expert is not really usurping the jury's function.[43]

Although expert opinion evidence which approaches an ultimate issue should no longer be rejected just because of the application of the ultimate issue rule, the concerns underlying the development of that rule must still be considered. These concerns are better met through the exercise of judicial discretion in determining whether the expert opinion evidence is reliable and necessary. Mr. Justice Sopinka in *Mohan*[44] stated that the closer the expert's evidence approaches an opinion on an ultimate issue the more

---

41 See *R. v. French* (1977), 37 C.C.C. (2d) 201 (Ont. C.A.), affirmed [1980] 1 S.C.R. 158.

42 (1980), 30 O.R. (2d) 247, 7 M.V.R. 163, 17 C.R. (3d) 55 (C.A.), affirmed [1982] 2 S.C.R. 819, 18 M.V.R. 287, 31 C.R. (3d) 289. See also *R. v. B. (R.H.)*, 29 C.R. (4th) 113, [1994] 1 S.C.R. 656 and *R. v. R. (D.)*, [1996] 2 S.C.R. 291, 48 C.R. (4th) 368.

43 *Ibid.*, at (C.R.) 70.

44 *Supra*, note 14.

such evidence should be scrutinized to determine whether it is reliable, and whether it is necessary for the trier of fact to have such evidence in order to arrive at a decision.

The Ontario Court of Appeal, on appeal from the order of the Divisional Court, in *Khan v. College of Physicians & Surgeons (Ontario)*,[45] dealt with the question of the ultimate issue rule. In this case, the discipline committee of the College of Physicians & Surgeons had found Dr. Khan guilty of professional misconduct in molesting a three-year-old girl. The Divisional Court quashed the finding of professional misconduct and directed a new hearing. One of the reasons for directing a new hearing was that the expert witness had answered the very question before the tribunal. On appeal, the court held that the expert opinion was admissible. Justice Doherty wrote:

> In my view, if the evidence of the expert witness is otherwise admissible, the fact that the opinion offered suggests the factual inference which should be drawn on the very factual issue in dispute does not necessitate the exclusion of that evidence.
> I readily acknowledge the potential danger of expert evidence going to the ultimate issue, particularly in cases involving allegations of sexual abuse against children. . . . Faced with the often intractable problem of trying to decide who is telling the truth in cases of alleged child abuse, the trier of fact may seek refuge in the apparent security and objectivity of the expert's opinion evidence. At the same time the value and the need for such evidence is strong in cases of child sexual abuse. . . .
> The protection against this danger lies not in a rule of automatic exclusion *but in the recognition of the trial judge's discretion to control the format in which the evidence is given.* (Emphasis added.)[46]

In the British Columbia Supreme Court's decision in *Watts v. Krause*,[47] the plaintiff had been injured in an automobile accident. At trial, the defendant sought to introduce an engineer's report that the plaintiff was not exposed to forces causing soft tissue injury. The plaintiff objected to the admission of such a report on the ground that the report went to the very issue that the trier of fact had to decide, namely whether the plaintiff was injured in the accident. The court admitted the report since it provided assistance on the effect of force upon the human body, a matter which was outside the jury's ordinary knowledge or experience.

Notwithstanding the application of judicial discretion in lieu of widespread or universal exclusion of expert evidence by reason of the ultimate

---

45 (1992), 9 O.R. (3d) 641, 11 Admin. L.R. (2d) 147 (C.A.).
46 *Ibid.*, at (O.R.) 666.
47 (September 19, 1994), Doc. Victoria 92/2817 (B.C. S.C.).

issue rule, the concerns underlying the rule remain strong, which may explain the confusion still surrounding it. As Justice Newbury, in *Yewdale v. Insurance Corp. of British Columbia*,[48] noted:

> The expert must not be permitted to displace the role of the trier of fact. Because of this, courts in the past resisted expert testimony going to the "ultimate issue". That clear rule has long since fallen by the wayside, but it still remains essential for the expert to state the facts he or she has assumed in the course of reaching the opinion, and if possible, to avoid making findings of fact on issues in dispute. Thus if the court does not find such facts or finds different facts, the weight of the expert's opinion can be assessed accordingly.

Robert White, in *The Art of Using Expert Evidence*,[49] gives valuable practical advice with respect to the ultimate issue rule. He writes:

> In short, if counsel pays careful attention to the fundamentals of expert evidence, they should not come into conflict with the "very issue" or "ultimate issue" rule, even if one exists. If notwithstanding the appropriate care, the objection is raised and appears to be taken seriously, there is an abundance of modern authority which states that the rule is not being applied or, if it is, that the exclusion is really based upon more fundamental principles which the court should be invited to address.[50]

6.8 NOVEL EXPERT OPINION EVIDENCE

With the advent of technology, new developments in medicine, and the growing use of social science and scientific evidence, the courts are required to carefully assess expert opinion evidence to ensure it is admissible. Mr. Justice Sopinka in *Mohan* stated:

> In summary, therefore, it appears from the foregoing that expert evidence which advances a novel scientific theory or technique is subjected to special scrutiny to determine whether it meets a basic threshold of reliability and whether it is essential in the sense that the trier of fact will be unable to come to a satisfactory conclusion without the assistance of the expert.[51]

---

48 *Supra*, note 6. See also *Surrey Credit Union v. Wilson* (1990), 45 B.C.L.R. (2d) 310 (S.C.).
49 Robert White, *The Art of Using Expert Evidence* (Aurora: Canada Law Book, 1997).
50 *Ibid.*, at 70.
51 *Supra*, note 14, at (S.C.R.) 25.

The Supreme Court of Canada, on appeal from the Manitoba Court of Appeal, in *R. v. Lavallee*,[52] was asked to determine whether the evidence on battered wife syndrome should have been admitted. In that case, the appellant killed her partner by shooting him in the back of the head. The defence introduced expert evidence on battered wife syndrome. The appellant was acquitted, but her verdict was overturned by a majority of the Manitoba Court of Appeal. At the Supreme Court of Canada, Madam Justice Wilson, writing for the majority, carefully examined the expert opinion evidence on the battered wife syndrome, and summarized her thinking as follows:

> Expert evidence on the psychological effect of battering on wives and common law partners must, it seems to me, be both relevant and necessary in the context of the present case. How can the mental state of the appellant be appreciated without it? The average member of the public (or of the jury) can be forgiven for asking: Why would a woman put up with this kind of treatment? Why should she continue to live with such a man? How could she love a partner who beat her to the point of requiring hospitalization? We would expect the woman to pack her bags and go. Where is her self-respect? Why does she not cut loose and make a new life for herself? Such is the reaction of the average person confronted with the so-called "battered wife syndrome". We need help to understand it and help is available from trained professionals.[53]

It is clear from Madam Justice Wilson's reasoning that expert evidence on battered wife syndrome was admissible since it was relevant and essential.

However, if the expert opinion evidence which is tendered is considered unreliable, the courts will hold such evidence to be inadmissible. In the Manitoba Queen Bench's decision in *Green v. Lawrence*,[54] a plaintiff sued the defendant police officer for injuries sustained in the course of an arrest. The plaintiff wanted to adduce the evidence of an expert witness who had expertise in scene reconstruction with a speciality in computer-generated sequential moving imaging. The expert had prepared a videotape of a computer-generated reconstruction of the scene. The videotape of the expert was offered both as an animated reconstruction of the scene, and as a demonstrative aid to assist the evidence of another expert, called to give evidence of the biomechanics of the plaintiff's injury and to give evidence as to the cause of the plaintiff's injury. The court was of the opinion that such expert evidence was scientifically unreliable because the video reconstruction included the expert's subjective evaluation of the case. The court noted the following deficiencies in the expert evidence:

---

52 *Supra*, note 37.
53 *Ibid.*, at (S.C.R.) 871.
54 *Supra*, note 14.

1. The expert's reconstruction included two anthropometric models of an adult man. The expert depicted the plaintiff as a "man" and the defendant was depicted as "man strong". The expert admitted that he used his own subjective judgment and that such a selection was not based on a scientific criteria. In this particular case, the issue of reasonable force was an issue, and the reconstruction did not depict an accurate picture.
2. The expert's subjective evaluation of the evidence was scientifically unreliable in showing the parties' movements and interaction.
3. The animation could not be used as a visual aid since the other expert did not assist in the preparation.

Difficulties often arise in cases where psychological testimony is offered and where such opinion lacks supportive scientific data. This concern arose in *R. v. Olscamp*,[55] where Justice Charron was faced with the question of whether to allow the Crown to call an expert witness to provide evidence to describe the general behavioural and psychological characteristics of child victims of sexual abuse, and then show that the complainant exhibited some symptoms consistent with sexual abuse. The defence objected to the admissibility of such evidence. Justice Charron sustained the objection of the defence and reasoned that the expert evidence was unreliable because of the lack of empirical data to support such an opinion. She concluded that the only consensus within the expert community was that there existed no valid profile on the basis of which one could identify a child who had been sexually abused. She also noted that the present state of knowledge in the field of sexual abuse was such that the soundness and reliability of any expert opinion purporting to characterize behavioural symptoms as consistent with sexual abuse cases could not be demonstrated. As Justice Charron summarized:

> While the proposed evidence is likely outside the experience and knowledge of the trier of fact, it is not yet within the experience and knowledge of the experts themselves with a sufficient degree of reliability to be useful.[56]

However, a number of courts have taken a less conservative or cautious approach. The Ontario Court of Appeal's decision in *R. v. J. (F.E.)*[57] held that

---

55 *Supra*, note 16.
56 *Ibid.*, at (C.R.) 46.
57 (1990), 53 C.C.C. (3d) 64, 74 C.R. (3d) 269 (Ont. C.A.). The British Columbia Court of Appeal in *R. v. Beliveau* (1986), 30 C.C.C. (3d) 193 (B.C. C.A.) also ruled that an expert in child abuse could express an opinion that certain behaviour, demeanour and other factors, such as consistency of story given to a number of persons, were consistent with the child having been sexually abused.

properly qualified expert opinion evidence about the general behavioural and psychological characteristics of child victims of sexual abuse is admissible for certain purposes. In this case, the accused was charged with sexual assault of his daughter. Shortly before the trial, the daughter wrote a letter to the Children's Aid Society recanting the charges of sexual abuse. The trial judge allowed the Crown to call a psychologist who testified that the letter was fairly typical of the recantations commonly seen among children who have been sexually abused, once they realize the problems that arise after the complaint. The Supreme Court of Canada, on appeal from Court of Appeal of British Columbia, in *R. v. B. (R.H.)*[58] also held that the use of experts to explain the behaviour of a person who has been systematically abused is one example of a matter on which experts may assist, provided that the expert can show to the court that the evidence tendered is relevant and reliable. It might be argued that the importance of the ruling in *R. v. Olscamp* may be minimized by observing that the expert clearly failed to satisfy Justice Charron that her opinion was based on reliable data.

The developments in the case law to this date seem to point to the conclusion, provided that the test for admissibility is otherwise met, i.e., the novel medical evidence is both relevant and reliable, that the expert's opinion will be accepted into evidence. The Ontario Court (General Division) in *R. v. Johnston*[59] dealt with the admissibility of novel scientific evidence, such as DNA profiling. In that case, the accused was charged with sexual assault, robbery and unlawful confinement of two children. The main issue in the trial was identification. The Crown sought to introduce evidence of identification through a scientific process of DNA profiling. Justice Langdon considered the judgment of Madam Justice Wilson, in dissent, in the Supreme Court of Canada decision in *R. v. Béland*[60] where Madam Justice Wilson considered the admissibility of novel scientific evidence and recommended that the adoption of relevancy and helpfulness should be the standard for the admissibility of such evidence.

Justice Langdon in *R. v. Johnston* provided a checklist of factors to determine whether novel scientific evidence is helpful or reliable. He summarized those factors as follows:

1. The potential rate of error.
2. The existence and maintenance of standards.
3. The care with which the scientific technique has been employed and whether it is susceptible to abuse.

---

58   [1994] 1 S.C.R. 656, 29 C.R. (4th) 113.
59   (1992), 69 C.C.C. (3d) 395, 12 C.R. (4th) 99 (Ont. Gen. Div.).
60   [1987] 2 S.C.R. 398, 60 C.R. (3d) 1.

4. Whether there are analogous relationships with other types of scientific techniques that are routinely admitted into evidence.
5. The presence of failsafe characteristics.
6. The expert's qualifications and stature.
7. The existence of specialized literature.
8. The novelty of the technique in its relationship to more established areas of scientific analysis.
9. Whether the technique has been generally accepted by experts in the field. . . .
10. The nature and breadth of the inference adduced.
11. The clarity with which the technique may be explained.
12. The extent to which basic data may be verified by the court and jury.
13. The availability of other experts to evaluate the technique.
14. The probative significance of the evidence.

A consideration of all of those factors should enable the court to decide if it is satisfied that the scientific technique in question exhibits a level of reliability sufficient to warrant its use in the court-room.[61]

Justice Langdon also recommended that the trial court reserve a residual discretion to reject evidence where the prejudicial effect outweighs its probative value.

Justice Langdon's reasoning was adopted by the British Columbia Supreme Court in *Grant v. Dube*,[62] where the plaintiff sued for damages for personal injuries arising out of a motor vehicle accident. The plaintiff in that case introduced a clinical psychologist's report which concluded that the plaintiff's pain was of a physical nature, and not psychological. The psychologist's conclusions were based on test results of electromyographic (EMG) activity. The defendant objected on the ground that the use of EMG measurements to determine if the pain was physical or psychological was novel scientific evidence, and was therefore not admissible. Justice Clancy followed *R. v. Johnston*[63] and rejected the defendant's argument and held that the test for the admissibility of scientific evidence was not whether or not it was recognized within the medical community, but whether such evidence was relevant, helpful and reliable.

The American courts have also had occasion to examine the admissibility of novel scientific evidence. Of particular note is the United States Supreme Court decision in *Daubert v. Merrill-Dow Pharmaceuticals Inc.*[64] This case involved a claim by parents against the chemical company that the children's serious birth defects had been caused by the mothers' prena-

---

61 *Supra*, note 59, at (C.C.C.) 415.
62 (1992), 73 B.C.L.R. (2d) 288, [1993] 2 W.W.R. 41, 12 C.P.C. (3d) 22 (S.C.).
63 *Supra*, note 59.
64 113 S.Ct. 2786 (1993).

tal ingestion of Bendectin, a drug marketed by the respondent. The District Court granted summary judgment to Merrill-Dow Pharmaceuticals based on expert reports that the drug failed to show a risk factor to pregnant women. The plaintiffs countered with their own expert evidence, but the District Court found such expert evidence to be inadmissible, since it was not generally accepted as reliable in the relevant scientific community. The District Court followed an earlier decision of the Court of Appeal of the District of Columbia in *Frye v. United States*[65] which held that for scientific evidence to be admissible, it was necessary to show that such expert scientific evidence was generally accepted in the relevant scientific community. On appeal, the United States Supreme Court in *Daubert* had the opportunity to reassess the principles surrounding the admissibility of novel scientific expert opinion evidence. The court there concluded that, in determining whether novel scientific expert evidence should be admitted, it should first be determined whether it is reliable and relevant, and it is not strictly determinative if it is not accepted by the relevant scientific community. The court provided four factors which the trier of fact may find of assistance in determining whether the novel expert opinion is reliable and relevant:

1. Whether the scientific theory can be tested.
2. Whether the scientific theory has been subjected to peer review and publication.[66]
3. Consider the potential rate of error and existence and maintenance of standards with respect to the particular scientific theory.
4. Whether or not the theory had obtained general acceptance within the scientific community.

Apparently, our courts have resolved any concerns as to the lack of scientific support or differences of opinion in such evidence by finding this a matter which may go to weight, and not to admissibility.[67] Take, for example, the Ontario Court (General Division) decision in *Mackintosh v. Wright*[68] where the plaintiff, who was involved in a motor vehicle accident, sought to introduce novel expert evidence in relation to the medical procedure known as thermography.[69] Justice Rapson admitted the expert evidence on thermography, and wrote:

---

65 (1923), 293 F. 1013 (U.S. D.C. Ct. App.).
66 Note that publication does not necessarily mean that a theory is reliable.
67 *R. v. C. (G.)* (1996), 110 C.C.C. (3d) 233 (Nfld. C.A.).
68 (1991), 9 O.R. (3d) 285 (Gen. Div.).
69 Thermography is a diagnostic tool which relies on the measurement of variation in skin temperature as an indication of underlying physiological abnormalities.

I am satisfied that thermography does not enjoy the same acceptance within the medical community as do X-rays and CAT scans, but that alone does not disqualify this procedure as evidence which the jury in this case should hear. . . . The fact that there is criticism of thermography goes to the weight, not the admissibility of the evidence. It would be wrong to deny the jury the opportunity to decide how much significance should be attached to this evidence.[70]

6.9 DUTIES AND RESPONSIBILITIES OF AN EXPERT WITNESS

To effectively present expert opinion evidence to the court requires not just an understanding of the basic rules of evidence, but an understanding of the duties and responsibilities of an expert witness when providing expert opinion. The courts have on several occasions outlined the parameters of these duties and responsibilities. These duties and responsibilities must be met whether the expert is preparing an expert report, or providing oral expert testimony in court. The following duties and responsibilities have been summarized, after a review of the relevant case law:[71]

1. Expert evidence presented to the court should be seen to be the independent product of the expert, and should not be influenced by the exigencies of the litigation.
2. The expert witness should provide independent assistance to the court through an unbiased opinion on matters within his or her expertise. It is important for an expert witness to provide expert opinion in an objective and professional manner. The failure of counsel to ensure that an expert is objective is a great concern of the courts.[72] This concern was expressed by Justice Preston in *Sebastian v. Neufeld*, where he wrote the following:

> In personal injury cases arising from motor vehicle accidents, the plaintiff and defence bars have, in recent years, developed "stables" of expert witnesses whose opinions predictably favour one side of the other in the

---

70 *Supra*, note 68 at 287.
71 See the British case of *National Justice Compania Naviera S.A. v. Prudential Assurance Company Ltd. (Ikarian Reefer)*, [1993] 2 Lloyd's Rep. 68, reversed [1995] 1 Lloyd's Rep. 455 (C.A.), leave to appeal to the House of Lords refused. Endorsed by the Canadian courts in such decisions as *Perricone v. Baldassarra* (1994), 7 M.V.R. (3d) 91 (Ont. Gen. Div.); *Baynton v. Rayner*, [1995] O.J. No. 1617 and *Kozak v. Funk*, *supra*, note 14. See also *R. v. Olscamp*, *supra*, note 16.
72 See *R. v. Howard*, [1989] 1 S.C.R. 1337, 69 C.R. (3d) 193.

litigation. There has been a tendency, of concern to this court, for experts to combine the role of expert and advocate. This is encouraged where experts approach their task with an unrestricted mandate and are given, by instructing counsel, material which is inadmissible but calculated to bias the expert in the formation of his or her opinion.[73]

In some cases, the courts may disapprove of an expert who does not present an objective opinion by awarding costs. For example, in the British Columbia Supreme Court's decision in *Heppner v. Schmand*,[74] the defendant in a personal injury action presented expert evidence from an engineer who testified that the low-impact accident could not be reasonably associated with the potential for injury to a normally fit person seated within the vehicle. The court found the opinion to be flawed and criticized the witness for "acting as an advocate, not as an independent expert." The plaintiff was successful in his claim and applied for an order for special or increased costs to reflect the court's disapproval of the way the engineer presented his expert evidence to the court. The court allowed the plaintiff's claim for special cost since the conduct of the engineer was "reprehensible and deserving of rebuke."

3. The expert witness should never assume the role of an advocate. The courts will not tolerate an expert who becomes an advocate. Expert witnesses are given the special privilege to testify as to their opinions. Such privilege should not be abused by the expert presenting arguments in the guise of expert evidence.[75] In the Ontario Court (General Division) decision in *Perricone v. Baldassarra*[76] the court was asked to determine whether the plaintiff's injuries fell within the statutory exceptions found in section 266(1) of the *Insurance Act*[77] which barred all actions for personal injury damage arising from motor vehicle accidents between June 22, 1990 and January 1, 1994, unless the injuries met the statutory exceptions. The court had before it several experts' reports, the clinical notes and records of the plaintiff's family physician, and transcripts of the examinations for discovery of the

---

73 (1995), 41 C.P.C. (3d) 354 at 358 (B.C. S.C.).
74 (March 21, 1996), Doc. Campbell River S1026, S1530 (B.C. S.C.), additional reasons at (1996), 2 C.P.C. (4th) 284, 24 B.C.L.R. (3d) 309 (S.C.), leave to appeal to C.A. refused (1997), 29 B.C.L.R. (3d) 128 (C.A. [In Chambers]), affirmed (November 19, 1998), Doc. Victoria V102819 (B.C. C.A.).
75 *Yewdale v. Insurance Corp. of British Columbia*, supra, note 6; *Surrey Credit Union v. Willson* (1990), supra, note 48; *Sengbusch v. Priest*, supra, note 22.
76 *Supra*, note 71.
77 R.S.O. 1990, c. I.8.

plaintiff. Despite the fact that the experts' reports before the court provided conflicting evidence, the court held that the plaintiff's injuries did not fall within the statutory exceptions found in section 266(1) of the *Insurance Act*. Justice E. Macdonald made the following observation about the expert's duty when preparing an expert report in light of conflicting evidence:

> On motions such as this, and in the face of apparent conflict among the experts' reports, it is important that the reports be viewed for what they truly are. In personal injury cases, there has developed a tradition of exchanging and relying on competing "expert" reports which, in my view, has eroded the legal basis for the acceptance of experts' reports into evidence either with or without cross-examination. These concerns about experts' reports have been expressed by Madam Justice Dunnet of this court in a recent speech. Experts are permitted to give hearsay evidence. The judge must render the ultimate decision based on the experts' reports *and other relevant evidence*. Once a judge is aware, as I am in this case, that an expert is hired by one of the parties to provide the court with an opinion that is supportive of that party's case, the judge must take this factor into account in weighing the credibility of the expert's report. When the report is overwhelmingly directed to advancing the position of the person engaging the expert's report, the report must be viewed accordingly.[78]

And Justice Macdonald further added:

> The consequences to the injured person are so serious that great care must be taken in the assembly and presentation of the expert's opinion. It is a role which is prescribed and, if the person rendering the evidence assumes the role of advocate, he or she can no longer be viewed as an expert in the legally correct sense; instead, he or she must be viewed as advocating the case of a party with the attendant diminishment in the credibility of the report. *Expert opinions guide the court but they do not determine the matters which are to be determined by the court.* (Emphasis added.)[79]

4. The expert should state the facts or assumptions that provide the basis for the opinion and must not omit material facts which detract from the opinion, as Justice McColl in *Surrey Credit Union v. Willson* stated:

> This type of evidence can take two forms, a statement of opinion based upon hypothetical facts or a statement of opinion regarding facts or as-

---

78 *Supra*, note 76 at 97.
79 *Ibid.*, at 99.

sumptions of facts concerning the case which have been communicated to him. In either case he is bound to communicate to the defendants the sources of those facts or assumptions of fact. They need not be (indeed in my view are not required to be) part of the opinion itself. What he cannot do is to make findings of fact himself. That is the exclusive role of the trial judge.[80]

He further added:

> All of the foregoing seems to have caused confusion in the minds of some experts as to the purpose of giving evidence, the nature of the opinion, its contents and how little or how much ought to be said. The reason for this is that the experts, usually having been retained by one of the disputants, are often misled or misinformed as to the true purpose and limitations of expert opinion. To add to this difficulty is the perception that because the law requires a person rendering an opinion to disclose the sources of his information or facts upon which the opinion is based, that the opinion itself should contain in minute detail those sources and assumptions. I do not understand that to be the case at all. What is required is that the expert must disclose those sources so that those who do not agree with the opinion will have the opportunity to test the reliability of the opinion itself or indeed to put to the expert facts or assumptions not previously known to the person offering the opinion which may alter, change or amend the opinion itself.[81]

5. An expert witness should state when a particular question or issue falls outside his or her expertise. The expert should stay within his or her stated area of expertise.
6. If insufficient data is available in order to properly research a particular part of the opinion, then that deficiency should be clearly stated and it should be indicated that any opinion reached is provisional.
7. An expert should be careful to distinguish between generally accepted scientific knowledge and personal professional opinion. It is important to ensure that the expert witness makes this careful distinction since it would then enable the trier of fact to properly evaluate and determine the reliability of the expert opinion evidence. Failure to do this may be exposed during cross-examination which will lead the trier of fact to place limited value on the expert's opinion. For example, Justice Charron in *R. v. Olscamp*[82] had before her an expert who purported to show that the complainant exhibited some symptoms consistent with sexual abuse. However, the expert provided evidence as if it was generally accepted scientific knowledge in her field, even

---

80 *Supra*, note 48, at 313.
81 *Ibid.*, at 314.
82 *Supra*, note 16.

though some parts of the evidence included her own personal opinions. Justice Charron found such testimony to be troubling and she stated:

> I was then prompted to ask her if the categorization she had been describing throughout was generally recognized in her profession or whether it was her own. It is only then that she said it was her own. I find this rather troubling since it should have been very obvious to Dr. Weiland that the validity of her methodology was seriously put in issue by the defence and it would be important to make a clear distinction between what may generally be accepted in the field and what was founded on her clinical experience alone.[83]

8. An expert witness, when using other works, studies or data in his or her particular field of expertise to support an opinion, should provide the specifics of such support, and should never make a general statement that support for the opinion can be found in other authorities.

9. An expert witness should ensure that when providing expert opinion the trier of fact is aware of the limits of such expertise. This is particularly so in cases where the expert witness is providing an opinion in the area of psychology where the scientific data is not conclusive. It is essential for the expert witness to acknowledge these limitations since they are best able to determine the limits on such evidence. Failing to make such qualifications may potentially misrepresent to the trier of fact the degree of scientific and medical validity of the expert's opinion.

It is the function of counsel to ensure that the expert whose evidence is adduced respects the role, duties and responsibilities of an expert witness. Otherwise, the risk remains that a court will attach little or no weight to the expert's testimony, which may lead to an unacceptable outcome in the litigation.

6.10 COURT-APPOINTED EXPERTS

Court-appointed experts are rare.[84] It is usually the case in an adversarial system that the parties hire the experts needed to assist their own

---

83 *Ibid.*, at (C.R.) 47.
84 There have been cases where the courts have exercised the discretion given under Rule 52.03 to appoint a court-appointed expert. For example in *MacDonald Electric Ltd. v. Cochrane*, [1955] O.W.N. 255 (H.C.) the court was asked to decide whether the televisions were faulty or not. The court appointed an expert to provide independent advice on the technical make-up of television sets. See also *Ericsson Communications Inc. v. Novatel Communications Ltd.* (1996), 45 C.P.C. (3d) 94 (Ont. Gen. Div.).

case. However, the Ontario Rules of Civil Procedure do provide the court with the discretion to introduce the evidence of a court-appointed expert.

Rule 52.03(1)-(2) provides that the court may appoint an expert:

> (1) On motion by a judge or on his or her own initiative, a judge may, at any time, appoint one or more independent experts to inquire into and report on any question of fact or opinion relevant to an issue in the action.
>
> (2) The expert shall be named by the judge and, where possible, shall be an expert agreed on by the parties.

The rest of Rule 52.03 deals with the remuneration of the expert, the expert report, cross-examination of the expert and the liability of the parties for remuneration of the expert.

The role of a court-appointed expert is no different from that of an expert that is retained by a party, namely to provide assistance to the trier in arriving at a correct decision and not to exercise the judicial function of the court. The Ontario Court of Appeal in *Phillips v. Ford Motor Co. of Canada*[85] looked at the matter of court-appointed experts, and Justice Evans, made the following comments about court-appointed experts:

> The expert is not a judicial officer charged with the responsibility of determining the matters in issue, nor is he a Court-appointed investigator empowered to advance possible theories and state, as conclusions of fact, opinions based on matters not advanced in evidence. While Rule 267 [predecessor to the current rule] permits the Court to obtain the assistance of experts in such way as it thinks fit, such assistance must be restricted to the purpose of better enabling the Court to determine from the evidence adduced the questions of fact in issue. In my opinion, Mr. McCaffrey totally misconceived his position and became, with the approval of the presiding Judge, a partisan advocate.[86]

In personal injury cases, the courts seem very reluctant to appoint a court-appointed expert. Justice Evans in *Phillips* identified some of those concerns:

> Our mode of trial procedure is based upon the adversary system in which the contestants seek to establish through relevant supporting evidence, before an impartial trier of facts, those events or happenings which form the bases of their allegations. This procedure assumes that the litigants, assisted by their counsel, will fully and diligently present all the material facts which have evidentiary value in support of their respective positions and that these disputed facts will receive from a trial Judge a dispassionate and impartial consideration in order to arrive at the truth of the matters in controversy. A trial is not intended to be a scientific exploration with the presiding Judge assuming the role of a research director; it is a forum established for the purpose of provid-

---

85 [1971] 2 O.R. 637 (C.A.).
86 *Ibid.*, at 661.

ing justice for the litigants. Undoubtedly a Court must be concerned with truth, in the sense that it accepts as true certain sworn evidence and rejects other testimony as unworthy of belief, but it cannot embark upon a quest for the "scientific" or "technological" truth when such an adventure does violence to the primary function of the Court, which has always been to do justice, according to law.[87]

The Alberta Court of Queen's Bench decision in *Murdoch v. Low*[88] is a good example of where the court refused to appoint a court-appointed expert in a personal injury case. In that case, the plaintiff was injured in two motor vehicle accidents which occurred several months apart. The defendant in the second accident claimed that the plaintiff's injuries were caused solely as a result of the first accident, while the defendant in the first accident claimed that the plaintiff's injuries were caused by a pre-existing condition. The plaintiff brought a motion for an order to compel the two defendants to share one independent medical examination or, alternatively, that the court appoint an expert. The court refused to restrict the defendants to one independent medical examination or to appoint a court-appointed expert, since each defendant had a separate or conflicting interest. Justice Veit provided the following reasoning as to why a court-appointed expert was not appropriate in this case:

> In other words, when the court appoints an expert, the judge can become a virtual party with a position to defend, and one with an unfair advantage over the litigants.
> A judge must therefore carefully limit her appointment of experts to the situations that call for such unusual measures. There is nothing in this case that attracts the exercise of such a discretion. The normal rules of the adversary process apply here.[89]

Unfortunately, Justice Veit does not indicate what is meant by limiting the appointment of court-appointed experts to situations that call for "unusual measures". It can be reasoned that in most cases it is better for the court not to be seen as interfering by appointing an expert, but to allow the adversary process to operate to resolve the matter at hand. However, in situations where the adversary system is not undermined, the courts may be prepared to appoint an expert. This was recently done in the Ontario Court (General Division) decision in *Ericsson Communications Inc. v. Novatel Communications Ltd.*[90] where one of the parties wanted to appoint an independent auditor to review the receipts and other related documents in order to determine the issue of damages on Novatel's counterclaim. The court

---

87 *Ibid.*, at (O.R.) 657.
88 (1995), 168 A.R. 75 (Q.B.).
89 *Ibid.*, at 78.
90 *Supra*, note 84.

agreed that this was an appropriate case in which to make an order to appoint an expert witness, so as to review the relevant documentation relating to the issue of damages. The court ruled:

> Rule 52.03(1) authorizes the court to, at any time, appoint an independent expert to inquire into, report on any question of fact or opinion *relevant* to an issue in the action.
> In my view this is an appropriate case to make such an order, the purpose of which is to review documentation relevant to the issue of damages. Notwithstanding the exercise may be mechanical in nature, it is nonetheless imperative it be done by qualified accounting firm with the ability to produce audited statements.[91]

A report prepared by the court-appointed expert becomes part of the record. Counsel are entitled to examine the expert report and to make any submissions on the report to the court.[92]

6.11 APPROACHING THE RIGHT EXPERT WITNESS

Once a determination has been made that an expert witness is required, then a careful search must be undertaken to locate the best one. Most medical practitioners are reluctant to get involved in litigation, and naturally prefer to devote their energies to the practice of medicine. This is understandable given the amount of time that an expert may be required to expend in preparation for, and during, trial. Therefore, it is essential for counsel to overcome this reluctance and to locate an expert witness who will work as a member of the litigation team. Picking the right expert is as crucial to the success of a case as planning the case strategy and marshalling the facts for trial.[93] Retaining the wrong expert, who fails to meet his or her duties and responsibilities as an expert witness, may lead to unexpected results. This was illustrated in the decision of the Ontario Court (General Division) in *Ferguson v. National Life Assurance Co. of Canada*.[94] In that case, the plaintiff worked as a bus driver and was insured for long-term disability by the defendant. The plaintiff was diagnosed with anxiety and depression. He applied for long-term disability benefits which he received for a period of four years. The insurance company then ar-

---

91 *Ibid.*, at 97.
92 *Featherstone v. Grunsven* (1971), [1972] 1 O.R. 490 (C.A.).
93 Wilder, J. Ross, "Choosing The Right Expert Witness" (Sprint 1990), Family Advocate 44.
94 [1996] I.L.R. 1-3316, 36 C.C.L.I. (2d) 95 (Ont. Gen. Div.), affirmed (1997), 102 O.A.C. 239 (C.A.).

ranged for the plaintiff to be assessed by a psychologist in Montreal. Based on this psychologist's report, the insurance company terminated the plaintiff's long-term disability benefits. Justice Bell found the psychologist to be "lacking in competence and objectivity." She found that the expert had already developed the hypothesis that the plaintiff was malingering, and had proceeded to look for factors that would confirm his hypothesis. She also observed that this particular expert was not familiar with the current text and education in his field.

When searching for the right expert witness consider the following factors:

1. Identify the type of expertise required. Careful identification of the key issues is critical. Once the issues are identified, then the particular type of expert required to provide assistance to the trier of fact in understanding each issue may be selected. After identifying the issues, it may still prove difficult to identify the type of expert required. This is not an uncommon scenario given the vast number of specialities in medicine, for example. Faced with this difficulty, and where one is representing the injured party, assistance may be sought from the family doctor who may provide direction and assistance as to what type of expert should be retained. Direction and assistance may also be obtained from the medical faculties of universities, colleges and professional associations, such as the Canadian Medical Association, or from provincial medical associations.

2. The expert retained should be qualified. He or she must possess the training and experience which demonstrates to the trial judge that the expert is qualified in the appropriate area. It is imperative that a full background check of the expert be conducted. A copy of the expert's curriculum vitae should be obtained and a close examination should be made of his or her academic and professional qualifications, as well as practical experience. Only at this stage, can a determination be made as to whether or not the expert is qualified to provide an opinion which will be of assistance to the trier of fact. For counsel to determine whether or not the expert is qualified requires an understanding of how members of the medical community become licensed and become experts in their field. This is especially so, for example, where a psychological expert is required. There are several specialties in psychology and there are no reliable indicators of what expertise is accepted within the profession.[95]

3. Retain an expert who can provide an objective and an independent ex-

---

95 See Donald Posluns, "An Introduction to Psychological Expert Testimony" (1981) 3 Adv. Q. 1-17.

pert opinion. The expert should not act as an advocate for the client. The expert should advance his or her opinion, and that is all.[96]
4. The expert retained should have no apparent conflict of interest. Obvious conflicts may include the following:

   a. close personal ties with either the client or the legal counsel;
   b. previous publications by the expert which conflict with the opinion that the expert is expected to provide; and
   c. if the expert witness is expected to make an inappropriate gain in providing the expert opinion.

5. The expert witness should have good communication skills with the ability to educate, not only counsel, but the court, in the particular area in which he or she has been called to provide expert opinion. The ability to translate complex technical information into simple clear language that the trier of fact can understand is vital. Should the expert witness use scientific jargon beyond the understanding of the trier of fact, then counsel runs the risk of confusing the trier of fact. It may even lead the trier of fact to consider whether the expert has a proper understanding of his or her field or whether the expert is trying to minimize weaknesses in his or her testimony.
6. The expert witness should have the ability to undergo intense cross-examination.
7. It is not prudent to hire a professional expert witness. Such a witness is an expert who spends most of his or her time assisting counsel and providing testimony in court. Professional expert witnesses are more likely to be viewed as unreliable by the trier of fact.
8. Retain an expert who is prepared to make the investment in time, in order to prepare a medical report and provide oral testimony in court.

6.12 HOW TO LOCATE THE EXPERT WITNESS

Actually finding a good expert who possesses the necessary attributes takes time and patience. Consider the following approaches to locate an expert witness:

1. Consult with other lawyers. Other lawyers may have used a particular expert in the past, who may have been very helpful, or not as helpful as expected.
2. Consult with medical universities, colleges and governing bodies such as the Canadian Medical Association, Ontario Medical Association,

---

96 See discussion at 6.9, Duties and Responsibilities of an Expert Witness.

and expert associations such as the Ontario Psychological Association.
3. Consult with local membership societies, such as the International Neurophysiologist Society and the National Academy of Neuropsychologists.
4. Consult with the client's family doctor. The family doctor is a valuable resource. The family doctor may be able to provide names of possible experts that may be of assistance. Where representing the injured party, consultation with the family doctor may lead to locating the right expert witness.
5. A review of medical literature and leading authorities may identify a particular expert.
6. There are various consulting firms that are in the business of finding an expert witness who is qualified to provide an expert opinion.
7. The Internet is also a very valuable source for locating an expert witness. It is especially useful in cases where one is attempting to locate an expert on a very obscure issue.[97]

6.13 WHEN TO CHOOSE AN EXPERT WITNESS

First, it is essential to determine if an expert witness is required. There is no point in retaining an expert witness and incurring that expense when the trial judge is likely to be able to arrive at a decision without the assistance of an expert. The courts are not sympathetic to counsel who increase the cost and time of litigation by calling unnecessary expert opinion. Justice McEachern of the British Columbia Supreme Court in *Sengbusch v. Priest*[98] made a critical comment when counsel provided expert opinion on matters of disability and employment opportunities, in addition to the evidence of the medical practitioners. Justice McEachern stated:

> . . . I regret the current tendency of counsel to increase the time and cost of litigation by the unnecessary use of opinion evidence.[99]
>
> He further added:
>
> In my view it is appropriate for the court to enforce reasonable limits upon the admissibility of opinion evidence. Too often, as in this case, persons with special training or experience are retained to construct scenarios or advance arguments in the form of an opinion when, with proper assistance from counsel, the court is able to analyze the evidence and reach a proper conclusion on

---

97 Mary McGugan, Can't find an expert witness? Try the Internet (September 20, 1996), The Lawyer's Weekly, at 9.
98 *Supra*, note 22.
99 *Ibid.*, at 36.

commonplace problems such as suitability for employment or calculations in personal injury, family matters or other areas of litigation.[100]

Once a determination has been made that an expert witness is required, one should be retained as early as possible in the litigation. Among the reasons for retaining an expert as early as possible are the following:

1. The expert can help evaluate the case and assist in determining whether legal action should be commenced.
2. The expert can prove to be a valuable source of information and can help advance the counsel's understanding of the medical and technical aspects of the case.
3. The expert can identify the strengths and weaknesses of his or her opinion and those of the opposing expert's opinion.
4. During the discovery process, the expert's assistance may prove invaluable. He or she may provide direction as to the issues that should be canvassed thoroughly during the discovery process, and what additional medical disclosure should be sought.
5. The expert is a valuable resource during preparation for trial and may assist in preparing areas for cross-examination of the opposing expert witness.
6. Most personal injury cases are settled before they reach the trial stage. On occasion, the assistance of an expert may prove to be valuable as guidance during settlement discussions as, for example, in providing for the future care of infants who sustain pre-birth injury and who are expected to develop a host of difficulties, with consequent medical and other needs over time.
7. In addition to the other reasons, litigation strategy may be enhanced by retaining an expert early, as the expert retained will not be available for retainer by the opposing side.

6.14 REMUNERATION FOR EXPERT OPINION

It is prudent for counsel to maintain a good working relationship with the expert retained. One of the most common problems affecting the relationship concerns the fee that the expert will be paid for the services that he or she renders either after preparing a medical report, assisting with the preparation of a case, or providing an oral expert opinion in court. Counsel should ensure that there is a clear understanding as to what the expert's fee will be from the outset, and who will be responsible for paying the fee.

---

100 *Ibid.*, at 40.

6.14.1 Professional Conduct

Rule 13 of the *Law Society of Upper Canada, Professional Conduct Handbook* provides that counsel is under an ethical duty to ensure that all financial obligations incurred, assumed or undertaken on behalf of the client are met, unless counsel has clearly indicated in writing that the obligation is not to be a personal one. Paragraph 6 of Rule 13 reads as follows:

> *Duty to meet Financial Obligations*
> 6.   In order to maintain the honour of the Bar, lawyers have a professional duty (quite apart from any legal liability) to meet financial obligations incurred, assumed or undertaken on behalf of the clients unless, before incurring such an obligation, the lawyer clearly indicates in writing that the obligation is not to be a personal one.

6.14.2 Payment for the Expert's Services

The expert is usually paid an hourly fee or a fixed amount. An expert should never be paid on a contingency basis. Such a practice is improper and will expose the expert, during cross-examination, as a witness who has an interest in the outcome of the litigation.

In determining the expert's fee the following factors may be taken into account:

1. The amount of time required to become familiar with the case, including the medical information, in order to prepare a useful expert's report;
2. The level of assistance that the expert is expected to provide through the entire litigation process, including the time to educate counsel on the medical and technical aspects of the case;
3. The experience of the expert;
4. The complexity of the case;
5. The amount of time required to prepare the expert's report;
6. The length of the expert's report; and
7. The amount of time spent by the expert in court.

Physicians are ethically and legally bound to ensure that they do not charge a fee that is excessive in relation to the services performed. Charging a fee that is excessive constitutes professional misconduct.[101] In prac-

---

101 See Reg. 856/93 made under the *Medicine Act, 1991*, S.O. 1991, c. 30 which defines professional misconduct at s. 1(1), para. 21 as:
Charging a fee that is excessive in relation to the services performed.

tice, however, the confidence counsel usually exhibits in the expert to appropriately fix a rate or fee for the service provided, is suggestive of the relatively few problems experienced in this area.

6.15   EXPERT REPORT

6.15.1   Rule 53.03

A party who intends to call an expert witness at trial is required, under the Ontario Rules of Civil Procedure, to serve every other party with a copy of the expert report not less than ninety days prior to trial. A party who intends to call an expert witness at trial to respond to the expert witness of another party is required to serve their expert report not less than sixty days prior to trial. Rule 53.03(1)-(2)[102] provides as follows:

> 53.03(1)   A party who intends to call an expert witness at trial shall, not less than 90 days before the commencement of the trial, serve on every other party to the action a report, signed by the expert, setting out his or her name, address and qualifications and the substance of his or her proposed testimony.
> (2)   A party who intends to call an expert witness at trial to respond to the expert witness of another party shall, not less than 60 days before the commencement of the trial, serve on every other party to the action a report, signed by the expert setting out his or her name, address and qualifications and the substance of his or her proposed testimony.

The purpose of the expert report is to disclose before trial what the evidence of the expert witness will consist of, and the factual basis upon which the opinion is provided. The rule is there to avoid the element of ambush and surprise. In the decision of *McEachrane v. Children's Aid Society of Essex (County)*,[103] the court had before it an expert report which gave the name of the expert, his address, his qualifications and presented the substance of his proposed testimony by merely listing the topics of his testimony. Justice Potts held that the expert report did not comply with Rule 53.03, and he wrote:

See also Regulations made under the *Drug and Pharmacies Regulation Act*, R.S.O. 1990, c. H.4, as amended by S.O. 1991, c. 18, s. 47, and the Health Professions Procedural Code, under the *Regulated Health Professions Act, 1991*, S.O. 1991, c. 18.

102   Ontario Rules of Civil Procedure, R.R.O. 1990, Reg. 194, Rule 53.03 amended by Reg. 348/97.

103   (1986), 10 C.P.C. (2d) 265 (Ont. H.C.). A decision made under an earlier version of Rule 53.03.

The whole point of allowing an expert report is to know what the evidence of the witness will consist of, and the factual basis upon which he proposed to give his proposed evidence.[104]

6.15.2 Disclosure of Expert Report, Raw Data and Drafts

The Ontario Rules of Civil Procedure require a party to serve a copy of the expert report at least ninety days before trial, or sixty days if the party is responding to the expert witness of another party.[105] Often, when the expert is produced to testify in court, a question arises as to whether he or she has waived a claim to privilege with respect to the remainder of the expert's file, namely the raw data, and any draft reports and written communications between counsel and the expert, such as a referral letter. In Ontario, the case law suggests that the expert's drafts should not be produced because they are privileged. However, in British Columbia, the tendency is to produce the expert's draft report, once he or she has been called to testify. The opposing views offered by the courts of these provinces exemplify the courts' struggle to achieve a balance between protecting litigation privilege, on the one hand, and on the other hand, ordering disclosure, in order that the expert's credibility and opinion can be fully tested.

In the British Columbia Supreme Court's decision in *Vancouver Community College v. Phillips, Barratt*,[106] the court concluded that once an expert becomes a witness, the party calling him or her has impliedly waived any litigation privilege with respect to any documents in the expert's possession. In that case, the plaintiff's counsel introduced into evidence a number of expert reports. Once the plaintiff's counsel had called an expert to testify, the defence moved for production of draft reports and other documents relevant to the litigation. Justice Finch provided the following reasons for allowing the defendant's motion:

> So long as the expert remains in the role of a confidential advisor, there are sound reasons for maintaining privilege over documents in his possession. Once he becomes a witness, however, his role is substantially changed. His opinions and their foundation are no longer private advice for the party who retained him. He offers his professional opinion for the assistance of the court in its search for the truth. The witness is no longer in the camp of a partisan. He testifies in an objective way to assist the court in understanding scientific, technical or complex matters within the scope of his professional expertise. He is presented to the court as truthful, reliable, knowledgeable and qualified.

---

104 *Ibid.*, at 270.
105 Ontario Rules of Civil Procedure, Rule 53.03, *supra*, note 102.
106 (1987), 20 B.C.L.R. (2d) 289, 27 C.L.R. 11 (S.C.).

It is as though the party calling him says: "Here is Mr. X, an expert in an area where the court needs assistance. You can rely on his opinion. It is sound. He is prepared to stand by it. My friend can cross-examine him as he will. He won't get anywhere. The witness has nothing to hide.[107]

Justice Finch added:

> I will attempt to summarize my view of the law. When an expert witness who is not a party is called to testify, or when his report is placed in evidence, he may be required to produce to counsel cross-examining all documents in his possession which are or may be relevant to matters of substance in his evidence or to his credibility, unless it would be unfair or inconsistent to require such production. Fairness and consistency must be judged in the circumstances of each case. If those requirements are met, the documents are producible because there is an implied intention in the party presenting the witness's evidence, written or oral, to waive the lawyer's brief privilege which previously protected the documents from disclosure.[108]

Justice Finch noted that before the expert's drafts can be produced, those drafts must be relevant to the inquiry. However, the threshold of relevance is low, since what is required is that all documents may be produced if they *are or may be relevant to the matters of substance or credibility*. However, in more recent decisions from the British Columbia courts, the threshold of relevance appears to have been raised before privilege will be deemed to have been waived.[109]

In the Ontario High Court decision in *Bell Canada v. Olympia & York Developments Ltd.*,[110] Justice Eberle rejected the view expressed by Justice Finch on the ground that Justice Finch's views were not consistent with solicitor-client privilege. In this case, the defence sought production of information supplied to the expert by the plaintiff's counsel. Among the documents sought were drafts of reports that were prepared by other experts. Justice Eberle came to the conclusion that a claim for privilege could not be said to have been waived simply by calling the expert to give evidence. In arriving at his decision, Justice Eberle specifically considered Justice Finch's reasoning in *Vancouver Community College* and he wrote:

---

107 *Ibid.*, at (B.C.L.R.) 296.
108 *Ibid.*, at 298.
109 Counsel would have to show that the document is required because they "likely affect" substance or credibility. See *Delgamuukw v. British Columbia* (1988), 32 B.C.L.R. (2d) 156 (S.C.) and *Can-Dive Services Ltd. v. Pacific Coast Energy Corp.* (1994), 1 B.C.L.R. (3d) 365, 31 C.P.C. (3d) 98 (S.C.).
110 (1989), 33 C.L.R. 258, 36 C.P.C. (2d) 193, 68 O.R. (2d) 103 (H.C.).

> Even if one were to go as far as Mr. Justice Finch has done in describing the implication behind the presentation of a witness at trial, I am of the opinion that the conclusion he reaches is at least doubtful.
> It appears to me to be a rather long step between offering a witness as credible and a conclusion that that dissolves the solicitor-and-client or litigation-purpose privilege, either or both of them.
> It seems to me that if his conclusion is valid, it would lead almost inevitably to the conclusion that a party who becomes a witness could well be in danger of cross-examination on communications passing between him and his solicitor.
> The privilege conceded in this case to have attached to the documents in question is not the privilege of the witness, the expert. It is the privilege of the client. It is perhaps an extension of the privilege which has traditionally been applied rigorously to the client himself, but it is not an independent privilege and remains the privilege of the client, not of the expert and not of the solicitor.[111]

And he further added, that production of the expert's draft reports is not essential in order to be able to test the credibility of the expert report:

> The facts upon which an opinion is based are normally to be found in the report itself. In any event, the facts must be proved or, if not, the opinion may be weakened. On the other hand, if, in coming to his opinion, an expert ignores relevant facts, his opinion may equally be weakened.
> If there are other relevant facts, it is for the opposing parties to prove them.
> None of these considerations, however, in my view, establish in any way the relevance of the material of which production is now sought. On this basis as well, it appears to me that the application for production is not well founded.[112]

In the Nova Scotia Supreme Court's decision in *Highland Fisheries Ltd. v. Lynk Electric Ltd.*,[113] the defendant retained an expert to investigate the cause of fire, and the plaintiff then sought production of the preliminary report that the expert had prepared. The defendant argued that the preliminary report was a privileged communication between a party and counsel, and that the implied waiver of privilege applied only to the expert report which was served on the plaintiff. Justice Richard followed the Nova Scotia Court of Appeal decision in *Greenwood Shopping Plaza Ltd. v. Neil J. Buchanan Ltd. (No. 1)*,[114] which provided that the waiver of privilege in the case of an expert extends to the expert report and the factual basis for

---

111 *Supra*, note 106 at (C.L.R.) 108.
112 *Ibid*.
113 (1989), 63 D.L.R. (4th) 493 (N.S. T.D.).
114 (1979), 31 N.S.R. (2d) 135 (C.A.), reversed [1980] 2 S.C.R. 228, 10 B.L.R. 234.

the opinions expressed in that report. Justice Richard also reviewed the *Bell Canada*[115] decision and the *Vancouver Community College*[116] decision, and concluded that the position taken by the Ontario courts and the Nova Scotia courts is to be preferred to the one taken by the British Columbia Supreme Court.[117]

In another decision from the Ontario courts in *Calvaruso v. Nantais*,[118] which did not involve the production of drafts but the production of an instructing letter sent to the expert from the plaintiff's counsel, Justice Brockenshire relied on the *Bell Canada* decision, and wrote:

> I reviewed the decision of Eberle in the *Bell Canada* case. This decision was on a motion at trial for production of a solicitor's instructing letter during cross-examination of an expert, but the principle is applicable here. The principle is that there still exists solicitor-and-client or litigation-purpose privilege, as one of the essential underpinnings of our system of administration of justice, which should not be lightly interfered with.[119]

6.15.3 Why Such a Difference?

One analysis which helps to explain the courts' difference in approach[120] may be made by examining the difference between solicitor-client privilege and litigation privilege. Solicitor-client privilege prevents the disclosure of any communication between a client and a solicitor, whether it is during, after or in contemplation of litigation. Litigation privilege, on the other hand, protects communications between the solicitor and a third party made for the purpose of actual or contemplated litigation. Robyn Bell submits that the approach taken by the British Columbia courts is more consistent with the purpose of the litigation privilege than the approach taken by the Ontario courts. She states:

> It is submitted that the case-law supporting production of drafts of an expert's report is more consistent with the limited purpose of the litigation privilege than the approach followed in *Bell Canada and Highland Fisheries*. In my view, Eberle J. and Richard J. failed to distinguish adequately between solicitor-client privilege and litigation privilege. The decision of Eberle J. is rooted in the desire of ensuring that a party has a sufficiently large sphere of privacy

---

115 *Supra*, note 110.
116 *Supra*, note 106.
117 See also *Kelly v. Kelly* (1990), 42 C.P.C. (2d) 181 (Ont. U.F.C.); *Walters v. Walters* (1990), 45 C.P.C. (2d) 215 (Ont. Gen. Div.).
118 (1992), 7 C.P.C. (3d) 254 (Ont. Gen. Div.).
119 *Ibid.*, at 255.
120 Bell, Robyn M., Drafts of Experts' Reports: How Far Does the Obligation to Produce Extend? (1992) 13 Adv. Q. 353.

so as to be able to obtain legal advice without the concern that such matters will have to be disclosed. This however is the purpose of solicitor-client privilege, not the litigation privilege which is aimed at protecting orderly trial preparation. That purpose is served by protecting from disclosure the reports of experts whom a party does not intend to call at trial. There is no disincentive to prepare one's case thoroughly, because negative reports obtained in the course of that preparation can, in effect, be "buried". Once an expert has been called to testify, however, disclosure of drafts of the reports should be made to permit proper adversarial preparation and to assist in the assessment of the credibility of the expert and the substance of his report. It should make no difference whether the drafts are in the expert's file or counsel's file. Both are under the power or control of the party calling the expert.[121]

Bell suggests that drafts of expert reports should be made available to the opposing side, subject to some safeguards for solicitor-client privilege. The arguments she makes are compelling, but they have yet to be accepted by the Ontario courts.

The issue of privilege attaching to an expert's file arose again in a recent decision of the Ontario Court (General Division) in *Piché v. Lecours Lumber Co.*,[122] where the court reviewed the two different approaches to disclosure of an expert's draft reports. In that case, an economist was qualified as an expert to give evidence in respect of the past and future income loss of the plaintiff. During cross-examination, the plaintiff sought production of the economist's file. The defendant refused to produce the file on the grounds of solicitor-client privilege. Justice Loukidelis reviewed the case law from both British Columbia and Ontario, and concluded that privilege over an expert's file is not lost by calling the expert as a witness. However, the privilege can be waived in respect of those facts or assumptions provided to the expert, if such facts or assumptions form the basis for the expert's opinion, and are not otherwise in evidence. Justice Loukidelis offered four guiding principles:

(1) Principles of waiver relating to a privilege claim for documents in an expert's file cannot be said to have been waived simply by calling that witness to give evidence.
(2) The privilege can be waived in respect of those facts or premises in the expert's file which have been used to base the expert's opinion and which came to the expert's knowledge from documents supplied to that expert.
(3) Whether there is a privilege or not can be ascertained by one of two ways. As in *Ocean Falls*, the judge can examine the documents or mate-

---

121 *Ibid.*, at 361.
122 (1993), 13 O.R. (3d) 193, 19 C.P.C. (3d) 200 (Gen. Div.).

rials for which privilege is claimed. Another way is for counsel, through cross-examination of the expert, to determine whether all or part of the file is privileged.

(4) As a general rule, if facts are supplied that are not found in other evidence or if certain assumptions are asked to be made in the instructing documents, privilege claimed for those facts or assumptions should be considered waived.[123]

6.15.4 Leave to File an Expert's Report

If the party intending to call an expert witness fails to serve the expert report not less than ninety days before trial, or sixty days before trial if responding to the expert witness of another party, then no expert witness may testify, except with leave of the trial judge, as provided in Rule 53.03(3).[124]

> 53.03(3) — An expert witness may not testify with respect to an issue, except with leave of the trial judge, unless the substance of his or her testimony with respect to that issue is set out,
> (a) a report served under this rule; or
> (b) a supplementary report served on every other party to the action not less than 30 days before the commencement of the trial.

Rule 53.08(1)(e) further adds:

> 53.08(1) — Where evidence is admissible only with leave of the trial judge under,
> . . . .
> (e) subrule 53.03(3) (failure to serve expert's reports)
>
> leave shall be granted on such terms as are just and with an adjournment if necessary, unless to do so will cause prejudice to the opposite party or will cause undue delay in the conduct of the trial.

The Ontario Divisional Court in *Pavao v. Pinarreta*[125] addressed the application of Rule 53.08(1)(e). In that case, the trial judge had failed to consider the rule when he denied the defendant's expert witness to provide expert opinion. The court ruled:

> Rule 53.08 is mandatory and requires the trial judge to grant leave on just

---

123 *Ibid.*, at (O.R.) 201.
124 Ontario Rules of Civil Procedure *supra*, note 102.
125 (1995), 40 C.P.C. (3d) 84 (Ont. Div. Ct.).

terms, unless there will be prejudice to the other party, or to do so will cause undue delay in the conduct of the trial.[126]

The court went on and further added:

> Once prejudice from allowing the testimony was not a factor, the mandatory application of the rule required that the evidence be allowed.

However, where failure to serve a report will cause unreasonable delay or would result in prejudice to the opposing party, the courts are reluctant to exercise their discretion to allow a party to deliver the expert's report outside the time provided by the Rule. Take the case in *C.(M.) v. M.(F.)*,[127] where Justice Keenan wrote:

> In this case there was no report at all. The purpose of the requirement of the preparation of a report by the expert witness is to give the other side information in advance with respect to the professional expert opinion. The advance notice will enable the other side to consult with other professionals and to prepare to meet the evidence. I cannot say that there would be any prejudice to the defendant if leave were granted on some terms but I can say that the time required for the preparation of the report and a response to it would cause an unreasonable delay. On that ground alone I would be inclined to refuse to give leave to call the evidence of the expert.

6.16   ONTARIO EVIDENCE ACT — MEDICAL REPORTS

Section 52 of the Ontario *Evidence Act*[128] sets out special rules which must also be observed if counsel wants to file a medical report that is prepared by a medical practitioner. Section 52 of the Ontario *Evidence Act* provides as follows:

> 52(2) — A report obtained by or prepared for a party to an action and signed by a practitioner and any other report of the practitioner that relates to the action are, with leave of the court and after at least ten days notice has been given to all other parties, admissible in evidence in the action.
> (3) Unless otherwise ordered by the court, a party to an action is entitled, at the time that notice is given under subsection (2), to a copy of the report together with any other report of the practitioner that relates to the action.

---

126 *Ibid.*, at p. 88. See also *Tecoglas Inc. v. Domglas Inc.* (1985), 14 C.L.R. 88 (Ont. H.C.); and *Sevidal v. Chopra* (1987) 45 R.P.R. 79, 41 C.C.L.T. 179, 64 O.R. (2d) 169 (H.C.).
127 (1990), 46 C.P.C. (2d) 254 at 260 (Ont. Gen. Div.).
128 R.S.O. 1990, c. E.23.

(4) Except by leave of the judge presiding at the trial, a practitioner who signs a report with respect to a party shall not give evidence at the trial unless the report is given to all other parties in accordance with subsection (2).

(5) If a practitioner is required to give evidence in person in an action and the court is of the opinion that the evidence could have been produced as effectively by way of a report, the court may order the party that required the attendance of the practitioner to pay as costs therefor such sum as the court considers appropriate.

Section 52, in effect, provides that a medical practitioner's expert report may be admitted in court, without counsel having to produce the medical practitioner to give oral testimony.

6.16.1 Purpose of Section 52 of the Ontario *Evidence Act*

As a result of section 52(2) and (4) of the Ontario *Evidence Act*, medical reports prepared by medical practitioners[129] can be accepted as evidence, without calling the medical practitioner. Section 52(5) ensures that medical practitioners are not called to court unnecessarily in cases where the expert's opinion could be effectively produced in a report by imposing costs on the party requiring the attendance of the medical practitioner. In effect, the Ontario *Evidence Act* provides that a party cannot proceed to file the report and call a medical practitioner, but must elect as to which is the appropriate course, and this was the view taken by the Ontario Court of Appeal in *Ferraro v. Lee*.[130] In that case, the plaintiffs, on appeal, argued that the trial judge had erred when he refused to allow the plaintiff to file both the medical reports and call the doctors as witnesses. The Court of Appeal disagreed with the plaintiff and held that no error in law had been committed. Justice Brooke, who delivered the judgment of the court, stated the following concerning section 52 of the Ontario *Evidence Act*:

> In construing this section regard must be had to its purpose, which was to do away with unnecessary surprise with respect to medical evidence, to dispense with the unnecessary attendance of medical practitioners at Court where the

---

129 Defined in s. 52(1):
In this section,
"practitioner" means,
  (a)   a member of a College as defined in subsection 1(1) of the *Regulated Health Professions Act, 1991*,
  (b)   a drugless practitioner registered under the *Drugless Practitioners Act*,
  (c)   a person licensed or registered to practice in another part of Canada under an Act that is similar to an Act referred to in clause (a) or (b).

130 (1974), 2 O.R. (2d) 417 (C.A.).

facts were such that their written medical reports would suffice in evidence to enable the fact-finding tribunal to adequately understand and apply medical diagnosis and opinion, but finally and most important, to assure that the control as to when such reports might be admitted in evidence remained with the trial Judge. This section was not to provide for the introduction into evidence of a medical report when it was the intention of a plaintiff to call the doctor to give *viva voce* evidence; rather it was the intention of the Legislature to provide for the introduction into evidence of the medical report so that the party tendering it might be relieved from having to call the doctor to give evidence.[131]

The same view was expressed by the court in *Stribbell v. Bhalla*,[132] where Justice Osborne, as he then was, wrote:

It seems to me that the policy underlying section 52 of the *Evidence Act* is reasonably clear. Section 52 was created to enhance the disclosure of medical evidence, to limit the expense related to the production at trial of medical evidence and to limit the inconvenience to which the medical profession would be exposed in attending at trial, waiting to give evidence and in giving evidence.[133]

Counsel should be aware of the cost consequences, provided in section 52(5) of the Ontario *Evidence Act*, of calling a medical doctor to provide *viva voce* evidence, when the expert report would have been sufficient.

6.16.2 Calling the Medical Practitioner to Testify

There are situations when it may be appropriate to present medical evidence at trial both by filing the practitioner's report, and through *viva voce* evidence. Such situations may arise where there exists a contradiction between the medical reports of the respective parties, or where the court may otherwise exercise its discretion to allow the medical practitioner to give *viva voce* evidence in the face of controversial evidence.[134]

A medical expert witness may be called to provide oral testimony, if counsel wishes to exercise the right of cross-examination. The Ontario Court of Appeal in *Kapulica v. Dumancic*[135] and in *Ferraro v. Lee*[136] provided that if leave is granted to file a medical report, then the opposite party has an absolute right of cross-examination. The court in *Kapulica*

---

131 *Ibid.*, at (O.R.) 419.
132 (1988), 32 C.P.C. (2d) 272 (Ont. H.C.).
133 *Ibid.*, at 270.
134 *Briand v. Sutton (No. 2)* (1986), 15 C.P.C. (2d) 36 (Ont. H.C.).
135 [1968] 2 O.R. 438 (C.A.).
136 *Supra*, note 130.

made the following comment about section 52(2) and (4) of the Ontario *Evidence Act*:

> The amendment is procedural: its effect is to provide an alternative method by means of which the Court may admit the evidence of a professional medical witness without the necessity of bringing that witness physically into Court and having his examination conducted in the face of the Court. The use of this alternative method in appropriate cases is beneficial to the litigants, to the Court and to the members of both the legal and medical professions. *It is not, however, designed to provide a means whereby expert medical testimony may be protected from the process of testing and refinement by cross-examination; nor is its purpose to deny the Court the benefit of an objective appraisal of the nature and extent of physical and mental disabilities reported upon and a reasonable statement of the observable data upon which the opinion is based.* (Emphasis added.)[137]

6.16.3 Who has the Obligation to Secure the Attendance at Trial of the Medical Practitioner for Cross-Examination?

The law is clear that when counsel elects to file the medical report, the medical practitioner who prepared the report remains the witness of the person who filed the report. However, a question may arise as to who has the obligation to bring the medical practitioner before the court for the purposes of cross-examination, when the opposite party expresses the wish to cross-examine the expert. Unfortunately, the authorities are divided on this particular question. Justice Kelly of the Ontario Court of Appeal in *Kapulica v. Dumancic*, in *obiter*, stated that it is the responsibility of the party who wishes to cross-examine the medical practitioner, to bring that practitioner before the court. However, Justice Holland of the Ontario High Court of Justice in *Carew v. Loblaw's Ltd.*[138] came to a different conclusion:

> In my view, once a party files a medical report that party becomes obligated to produce that doctor before the Court and for the purpose of cross-examination by the party adverse in interest, if so requested.

Justice Potts in *Briand v. Sutton*[139] similarly concluded that the obligation is on counsel relying upon the medical report to produce the medical prac-

---

137 *Supra*, note 135 at 442. Again, the Court of Appeal in *Ferraro v. Lee, supra*, note 130, stated that the opposite party has an absolute right to require that the author of the medical report attend for cross-examination.
138 (1977), 18 O.R. (2d) 660, 83 D.L.R. 603 at 663 (H.C.).
139 *Supra*, note 134. See *Harris v. Windsor Airline Limousine Services Ltd.* (1985), 6 C.P.C. (2d) 156 (Ont. H.C.), where the defendant wanted to cross-examine the plaintiff's medical practitioner, should the medical practitioner

titioner before the court. Justice Potts referred to the *obiter* comments of Justice Kelly in *Kapulica* and held that, since the comments were *obiter*, they were not binding on him. He further stated that the interpretation in section 52(5) (then 52(4)) was consistent with the expert being called by the plaintiff:

> The words of the section, "the party that required the attendance of the medical practitioner" are perfectly consistent with an interpretation that the party objecting simply requires the party who is tendering the report to make the medical practitioner available at the trial.[140]

This particular question was again canvassed by the Ontario Court (General Division) in *White v. Chaumont*,[141] where Justice Valin carefully reviewed the above decisions and concluded that, in determining which party has the obligation to secure the attendance of the expert, a careful analysis must be made of section 52 of the Ontario *Evidence Act*. This case involved an action for personal injury arising from a motor vehicle accident. At the beginning of the trial, the plaintiff sought leave to file medical reports. The defendants did not object to the filing of the reports but did request that the plaintiff secure the attendance of the authors of these medical reports for cross-examination. Justice Valin provided a sound and practical examination of section 52 and concluded that medical practitioners remain the witness of the party who filed his or her report, but that the defendants had the obligation to secure the medical practitioners for cross-examination:

> I return to where I began on this issue. The purpose of section 52 of the *Evidence Act* is to allow the introduction of a medical report in lieu of, and not in addition to, *viva voce* medical evidence. In the ordinary case, a party must elect between introducing the report and calling the doctor. When, as in this case, a party elects to file a medical report, he or she gives up the right to examine the author of the report in chief. However, such a decision fulfils the underlying policy of the section to lessen inconvenience to the medical profession, to save Court time, and to reduce the cost of the litigation. It should also be noted that the defendants did not request a defence medical examination of the plaintiff.
> The trial judge has a discretion as to whether to admit a medical report and, if so, whether to attach any conditions. This discretion must be exercised ju-

---

  tender a report. The defendant wanted a ruling as to what stage in the proceedings the physician should be cross-examined. Justice Anderson concluded that the medical practitioner, who tendered the report on behalf of the plaintiff, should be called as a witness before the plaintiff concluded his or her case.

140 *Supra*, note 134 at (C.P.C.) 40.
141 (1996), 50 C.P.C. (3d) 156 (Ont. Gen. Div.).

dicially. In the circumstances of this case, where the plaintiff seeks to adopt a procedure that would reduce the length of the trial and the cost of the litigation, I am of the view that it would be unjust to saddle the plaintiff with the cost of securing the attendance at trial of Dr. Laing and Dr. Chapman. *It is the defendants who wish to cross-examine them. They should bear the costs of the attendance of the doctors at trial.*[142] (Emphasis added.)

6.16.4 The Medical Practitioner is Unavailable for Cross-Examination

A problem may sometimes arise when counsel wishes to cross-examine an expert witness who is unavailable. Such a situation arose in the Ontario Court (General Division)'s decision in *Etienne v. McKellar General Hospital*.[143] In that case, the plaintiff sought to file two medical reports, notwithstanding that the medical practitioners who prepared the reports were not available for cross-examination. One of the practitioners had suffered a stroke and the other could not testify because he was located in the United States, and it was costly and inconvenient for him to testify. The court concluded that the two medical reports were not covered by section 52 of the *Evidence Act*, since the reports only dealt with the issue of liability, and not with the plaintiff's medical condition. The plaintiff then argued that the two expert reports should be admitted into evidence on the basis of the new rules of hearsay established by the Supreme Court of Canada in *R. v. Khan*,[144] and since they met the criteria of necessity and reliability. Justice Platana, after a review of the authorities, set out the circumstances where the expert report could be filed without the requirement to produce the expert for cross-examination:

1. Where the unavailability of the expert was sudden and unexpected in relation to the trial date;
2. Where the report was prepared at a crucial time in the development of the plaintiff's condition and there are no other experts who examined the plaintiff at that time;
3. Where the report was prepared by the main treating specialist who made personal observations known only to him at the time; and
4. Where the plaintiff's condition had not changed since the report was prepared such that it could have affected the opinion in the report.

Justice Platana considered the above guidelines and ordered that the expert reports not be admitted. He reasoned that the plaintiff had known about

---

142 *Ibid.*, at (C.P.C.) 160.
143 (1994), 38 C.P.C. (3d) 342 (Ont. Gen. Div.).
144 79 C.R. (3d) 1, [1990] 2 S.C.R. 531, 59 C.C.C. (3d) 92.

one of the expert's ill health and had ample time to get another expert report. Also, the two experts could not be described as main treating specialists, and the reports were not prepared at a crucial time in the action. Justice Platana concluded that there would be a greater prejudice to the defendant if these reports were filed without the ability to cross-examine, than any prejudice to the plaintiff by refusing to have the reports filed.

In the Ontario District Court's decision in *Scime v. Guardian Insurance Co. of Canada*,[145] the defence moved to introduce the report of a doctor who had died before trial. Justice Sullivan admitted the report as the doctor's examination had taken place at a crucial time in the development of the plaintiff's condition, and there were no other orthopaedic examinations which took place at or about the same time. Justice Sullivan stated that any prejudice to the plaintiff could be addressed in the weight accorded to the evidence by the court.

6.17 PRODUCE A GOOD EXPERT REPORT

The ability to draft an expert report which is clear, concise and easily understood by a lay person cannot be overemphasized. A good expert report may, in some cases, lead to an early settlement of a claim and hence avoid the expensive process of going to trial. Early retention of an expert witness provides the expert with the opportunity to fully understand the facts and issues in a case and to prepare a comprehensive written opinion. When an expert is preparing an opinion, he or she should be fully aware of their duties and responsibilities to the court. These duties and responsibilities are equally applicable when an expert is preparing a written opinion, since a medical report should generally provide information similar to that which would be received *viva voce*.[146]

The process of preparing a satisfactory expert report requires good communication between counsel and the expert. Whether or not an expert produces a good report may often depend on the instructions that counsel provides. Consider the following factors which should be taken into account when counsel instructs the expert to produce a report:

1. Ensure that the expert fully understands all the facts and issues in the case.
2. Provide the expert with a convenient assembly of material or brief confirming full disclosure of all pertinent information on the file. Disclosure of all relevant information to the expert is important, however unfavourable it may be to the case. Failure to provide all information to your expert may slant his or her opinion and lead the trial judge to attach little weight to it.

---

145 (1988), 30 C.P.C. (2d) 149 (Ont. Dist. Ct.).
146 See *Perricone v. Baldassarra, supra,* note 71.

3. Advise the expert that he or she is under a duty to ensure that an accurate expert report is prepared.
4. Provide the expert with clear, simple instructions as to what questions need to be addressed in the report. One of the reasons expert reports fall short of expectations is that counsel often fails to convey to the expert just what needs to be addressed by the opinion.
5. Provide instructions as to what the duties and responsibilities of an expert witness are,[147] and convey that it is the expert's obligation to be objective and independent. Objectivity and independence are compromised when counsel participates in the preparation of a report and the courts disapprove of such behaviour. In the British Columbia Supreme Court's decision in *Vancouver Community College v. Phillips Barratt*,[148] the expert retained by the plaintiff revised his report several times at the suggestion of the plaintiff's counsel. Justice Finch stated the importance of providing an independent and objective expert report:

> I in no way wish to condemn the practice of an expert's editing or rewriting his own reports prepared for submission in evidence or, for that matter, prepared solely for the advice of counsel or litigants. Nor do I wish to condemn the practice of counsel consulting with his experts in the pretrial process while "reports" are in the course of preparation. It is, however, of the utmost importance in both the rewriting and consultation processes referred to that the expert's independence, objectivity and integrity not be compromised. I have no doubt that in many cases these ends are achieved, and counsel and experts alike respect the essential boundaries concerning the extent to which a lawyer may properly discuss the expert's work product as it develops towards its final form.[149]

In *Marchand (Litigation guardian of) v. Public General Hospital Society of Chatham*,[150] a decision of the Ontario Court (General Division), Justice Granger strongly disapproved of experts providing an unsigned draft report for counsel's consideration. He wrote:

> During the trial, it became apparent that counsel adopted a practice of having the experts they retained submit an unsigned draft report for counsel's consideration. The retaining lawyer then discussed the report with the expert and after such discussion, a final report was submitted to

---

147 See the general discussion at 6.9, Duties and Responsibilities of an Expert Witness.
148 (1988), 29 C.L.R. 268, 26 B.C.L.R. (2d) 296 (S.C.).
149 *Ibid.*, at (B.C.L.R.) 305.
150 (October 3, 1996), Doc. 91-GD-16866 (Ont. Gen. Div.).

the retaining lawyer. This type of report preparation detracts from the perceived impartiality of an expert witness. I see no reason why experts cannot be requested to submit further reports to cover areas omitted in their initial report or to correct an opinion based on a misconception of facts. The procedure of asking an expert witness to submit his or her opinion for review and hence possible alteration leads to the inevitable perception that opinions can be purchased. In my view, this is a practice which should be discouraged.

Another way that the expert's objectivity and independence may be compromised is where the expert's report offers opinion which suggests legal argument. A good illustration of this can be found in the British Columbia Supreme Court's decision in *Mazur v. Moody*,[151] where the Honourable Chief Justice McEachern dealt with the admissibility of an accountant's report in a personal injury action. In finding the accountant's report inadmissible, the court offered the following reason:

> When I read the reports I concluded that the report of the chartered accountant is clearly inadmissible. It is an argument prepared after reviewing the plaintiff's income tax returns, the transcripts of his examination for discovery, the collective agreements and interviewing the plaintiff, the business agent of the union who was a witness, the union dispatcher, another employee of the union and a tax consultant, none of whom were witnesses.[152]

He further added:

> It is the function of counsel, possibly assisted by an aide memoire, to advance the plaintiff's claims based upon the evidence in understandable terms. It is not the province of expert witnesses, viva voce or by filing written reports, to construct scenarios that may or may not have any basis in reality and then to give in evidence an opinion about the amount of the plaintiff's loss.[153]

6. Advise the expert as to the admissibility of the expert report, and what should be avoided. For example, the expert should ensure that the opinion is not based on evidence which will not be before the court. Otherwise, as Madame Justice Wilson cautioned in *Lavallee*,[154] the trial judge will have to instruct the jury that, the more the expert relies on facts not proven in evidence, the less weight the jury may attribute to the opinion.

---

151 (1987), 14 B.C.L.R. (2d) 240 (S.C.).
152 *Ibid.*, at 243.
153 *Ibid.*, at 244.
154 *Supra*, note 37.

7. Good presentation of a medical report is important. The expert should be instructed to prepare a report which is easy to read. The use of headings, diagrams and a glossary of terms defined in layman's language enhances the comprehensibility. Instruct the expert that, long after he or she has provided an opinion, the judge may still refer to the written report to refresh his or her memory.
8. Instruct the expert that the report will be read by several people, such as other experts, other lawyers, the judge and jury and, of course, the client and, therefore, to ensure that the report is written in a manner that the intended reader can understand.
9. Arrangements should be made as to when the expert will deliver the report. Advise that he or she is under a duty to provide the report within a reasonable period of time. It constitutes a professional misconduct if a physician fails to provide a medical-legal report within a reasonable time.[155]
10. It is also important to instruct the expert of counsel's duty to disclose the expert report to the client. This is of a particular concern in cases involving brain injury or cases involving psychiatric evidence, where the findings of the report may be very disturbing to the client. There may be rare cases where the expert provides a report and specifically informs counsel not to disclose it to the client, for fear that it may cause injury or harm to the client. This is a very difficult situation to address. However, Rule 26 of the *Rules of Professional Conduct*[156] does lay down some guidelines:

    a. A lawyer who receives a medical-legal report from a physician that is accompanied by a proviso that it not be shown to the client, shall return the report immediately to the author, unless the lawyer has received specific instructions to accept the report on this basis.
    b. A lawyer who receives a medical-legal report from a physician containing opinions or findings which, if disclosed, might cause harm or injury to the client, should attempt to dissuade the client

---

155 See the regulation made under the *Medicine Act, 1991, supra,* note 101. Section 1(1), para. 17 defines professional misconduct as:
> Failing without reasonable cause to provide a report or certificate relating to an examination or treatment performed by the member to the patient or his or her authorized representative within a reasonabletime after the patient or his or her authorized representative has requested such a report or certificate.

Similarly the doctor's own code of ethics requires that the doctor provide the report within a reasonable time.

156 The Law Society of Upper Canada, *Professional Conduct Handbook*, Rule 26.

from seeing the report, but if the client insists, the lawyer is duty bound to produce it.

The commentary to Rule 26 provides that the expert and the lawyer should have a frank discussion as to what functions the report will serve, and the expert should be advised of the lawyer's duty to disclose the report to the client. Should the lawyer and the expert still continue to have reservations about the client seeing the report, the commentary suggests that the client should attend at the office of the expert to see the report, in order to be afforded the benefit of the expert's guidance in understanding the significance of the conclusions contained in the report.

Recent case law provides that a patient has a right to inspect and obtain a copy of his or her medical records. The leading decision in this area is the Supreme Court of Canada's decision in *McInerney v. MacDonald*,[157] where a patient requested that her doctor provide copies of all documents in her medical file, including documents received from five other physicians who had previously treated her. The doctor refused to produce copies of the documents originating from the other physicians and consultants, on the grounds that they were the property of those physicians, and that it would be unethical for her to release them. Mr. Justice La Forest held that the medical record belongs to the physician, institution or clinic that compiled it, but that the patient has a right to examine the record and to copy all the information contained in it, including consultation and reports obtained from other physicians. This case is significant not only because it rules that a client has access to his or her medical records, but also for the court's ruling on the nature of the relationship between a physician and a patient. Mr. Justice La Forest described the relationship between patient and doctor as follows:

> A relationship may properly be described as "fiduciary" for some purposes, but not for others. That being said, certain duties do arise from the special relationship of trust and confidence between doctor and patient. Among these are the duty of the doctor to act with utmost good faith and loyalty, and to hold information received from or about a patient in confidence. . . . When a patient releases personal information in the context of the doctor-patient relationship, he or she does so with the legitimate expectation that these duties will be respected.
>
> The physician-patient relationship also gives rise to the physician's duty to make proper disclosure of information to the patient; see *Reibl v. Huges*, [1980] 2 S.C.R. 880, at p. 884; and *Kenny v. Lockwood, supra*, at p. 155. The appellant concedes that a patient has a right to be advised about the information concerning his or her health in the physician's medical record. In my

---

157 [1992] 2 S.C.R. 138, 7 C.P.C. (3d) 269, 12 C.C.L.T. (2d) 225.

view, however, the fiducial qualities of the relationship extend the physician's duty beyond this to include the obligation to grant access to the information the doctor uses in administering treatment.[158]

6.18 FORMAT OF THE EXPERT REPORT

It is recommended that counsel instruct the expert as to how his or her report should be formatted. Counsel is in the best position to advise the expert as to what information the trier of fact requires in order to arrive at a decision. For example, the format of a medical report used in a personal injury action may be as follows:

- A pre-accident history of the client;
- The injuries sustained by the client as a result of the accident;
- The client's current health and complaints;
- Findings on physical examination;
- Results of any testing or investigation;
- Treatment prescribed;
- Diagnosis;
- Prognosis;
- Recommendations with respect to future treatment and investigation; and,
- Advice with respect to any limitations on the patient's work and activities of daily living.

The appropriate format for preparation of specific expert reports may, at times, be suggested by the expert. For example, Filgate and Snow offer guidance on the preparation of a neuropsychological report:[159]

> A comprehensive neuropsychological report will typically include a summary of the history obtained from records, information obtained from interview with the patient, information obtained from other interviews, a list of tests administered, a description of the test results and an interpretation of their meaning. Interpretation of the test results will usually include conclusions about the presence or absence of cognitive impairment, the presence or absence of brain dysfunction, the likelihood of the cognitive impairments being attributable to the brain dysfunction, the probable localization of the brain dysfunction, and the prognosis. In addition, there will generally be discussion of factors which may affect the interpretation of the findings, such as the patient's age, schooling, language and cultural background, emotional function-

---

158 *Ibid.*, at (S.C.R.) 149-50.
159 M.S. Macartney Filgate and W.G. Snow, "Forensic Neuropsychology" (1991) 12 Adv. Q. 83 at 94.

ing and motivation. The likely reliability of the test results and possible effects of medical and psychiatric problems should also be addressed. Finally, the relevance of the test results to practical matters will be summarized, including implications for daily living and self-care, vocational functioning, potential for education and training, needs for further medical and psychological investigation and/or treatment, and over all rehabilitation potential. In some cases, where improvement or deterioration in function over time is a possibility, recommendations for reassessment may be made.

Produced at Appendix A is a suggested guideline in the preparation of medical reports for presentation in court which may be of some assistance to the medical expert when he or she is preparing the expert report.[160]

6.19 REVIEW THE EXPERT REPORT[161]

Discuss the expert's opinion before it is reduced into a written form, being careful not to suggest its contents to the expert, or otherwise participate in its actual preparation. Doing so may avoid the difficulty faced when examining an incomplete or unhelpful report; one which may find its way before the courts if the expert is asked to divulge the contents of his or her file and any draft reports.[162] Once the expert report has been obtained, it is crucial that it be reviewed in detail. Determining the strengths and weaknesses of the report is important. Examine the contents in a timely fashion; it is a mistake to examine the report on the eve of trial. When reviewing the expert report, it may be helpful to consider the following questions:

- Does the expert report support the theory of the case?
- Did the expert fully understand the facts?
- Does the report reflect that the expert reviewed all the medical evidence in the case, including any unfavourable evidence?
- Did the expert make any assumptions; if so, which ones and are they defensible?
- Did the expert rely on any evidence which is unlikely to be before the trier of fact?
- What conclusions did the expert arrive at? How and why?
- Did the expert understand his or her duties to the court, i.e, is the expert report objective and independent?

---

160 Appendix A is included by permission of the Medico-Legal Society of Toronto.
161 See John A. Epp, "Avoiding Rookie Mistakes when using Experts in Canadian Courts" (1993), 14 Adv. Q. 185.
162 See the discussion at 6.15.2, Disclosure of Expert Report, Raw Data and Drafts.

- How will the report stand up under cross-examination?
- Is the report well presented? Will it be understood by the trier of fact?
- How will the expert report be interpreted by the opponent, the opponent's lawyer and the opposing expert?
- Is the expert report persuasive?

6.20 NUMBER OF EXPERTS ALLOWED TO TESTIFY

Section 12 of the Ontario *Evidence Act* provides as follows:

> 12. Where it is intended by a party to examine as witnesses persons entitled, according to the law or practice, to give opinion evidence, not more than three of such witnesses may be called upon either side without leave of the judge or other person presiding.

This section fails to clarify whether the limitation as to the number of experts applies to the entire proceedings, or to each issue. The Ontario Court of Appeal in *Buttrum v. Udell*[163] held that the statutory limit of three applied throughout the whole case, and did not extend to each issue arising in the case. The early decision in *Buttrum* suggests cause for concern for counsel in a personal injury action where there are often several issues relating to liability and damages, requiring that more than three expert witnesses be called to testify. Early thinking that limited the number of experts called has fortunately been supplanted by the Supreme Court of Canada, on appeal from the Alberta Court of Appeal, in *Ure v. Fagnan*,[164] where the Supreme Court of Canada was asked to interpret the relevant provisions from the *Alberta Evidence Act*,[165] which is quite similar in its wording to section 12 of the Ontario *Evidence Act*. The court held that the party was entitled to call three experts on each issue of the case, and was not limited to three for the whole proceeding. This interpretation makes eminent sense and is more in tune with the reality in many personal injury cases where the plaintiff may have a multitude of complaints, which may require a number of experts, certainly greater than three, to provide expert opinion to the court.

In the Alberta Supreme Court's decision in *Hamilton v. Brusnyk*,[166] the plaintiff called six expert witnesses. At the argument stage, the defendant objected to the number of expert medical witnesses that the plaintiff had called and argued that the plaintiff was limited to only three experts and

---

163 [1925] 3 D.L.R. 45, 57 O.L.R. 91 (C.A.).
164 [1958] S.C.R. 377. See also *R. v. Higgins* (1979), 28 N.B.R. (2d) 20 (C.A.), leave to appeal to S.C.C. refused (1979), 29 N.B.R. (2d) 450n (S.C.C.).
165 R.S.A. 1980, c. A.-21.
166 (1960), 34 W.W.R. 172 (Alta. S.C.).

that the court should disregard the evidence of the three who were last called to testify. The plaintiff argued that he was entitled to call three expert witnesses with regard to each particular injury or disability suffered by him if, according to modern medical practice, each fell within a different field or branch. The court agreed with the plaintiff and Justice Farthing stated:

> In my opinion it is very late in the day for counsel to argue that medicine is all one branch of learning. . . . If Mr. Whittaker's position is sound then the more extensive injuries the victim of an accident suffers, the more difficult will he or she find it to present evidence of them.[167]

6.21 FAMILY DOCTOR-PATIENT RELATIONSHIP

The family doctor is usually the primary contact for those seeking treatment for health problems. Once an individual is involved in a motor vehicle accident or some other traumatic incident, he or she normally comes under the care of the family doctor. Establishing a good working relationship with the client's family doctor can therefore prove to be most important. To fully understand the role that medical practitioners, particularly family doctors, can play in a litigation file requires an understanding of the legal obligations imposed on the physician, and the legal relationship between a physician and patient. As earlier observed, a medical practitioner is under a duty to ensure that a medical-legal report is provided on the request of legal counsel within a reasonable time. There are indeed other legal duties placed on medical professionals, most notably the duty to create and maintain accurate medical records which may enhance the presentation of evidence in litigation.[168]

These medical records are invaluable. They include, for example, detailed information pertaining to the client's diagnosis, treatment undertaken and prognosis. Where the family doctor instructed the client to undergo tests or x-rays those results should also be documented in the client's medical file. Where the client has been referred to other medical professionals their reports should also be included in the client's medical file.

Detailed medical records are a valuable tool, not only for the physician who is treating the client, but also for counsel. As a result of the medical records, a client who has been injured in an accident will obtain treatment that takes his or her medical history into account. After an accident, the physician is able to document the client's medical situation, noting developments in the client's condition. Properly maintained medical

---

167 *Ibid.*, at 174.
168 See Chapter 2 for a more detailed examination of this duty.

records are also invaluable when a medical expert is preparing his or her report.

Having detailed documentation of the client's injuries after a traumatic event will also assist counsel in assessing damages, and may also provide information pertinent to issues of liability, if the patient recounts the manner in which an accident took place. For counsel, these medical records are essential in providing a picture of the client's state of health both prior to and after the injury.

6.22 CONCLUSION

The success of a personal injury action depends on several factors. One crucial factor is the effective use of an expert witness. The expert witness is granted the privilege of providing an opinion to the court because of the knowledge and skills that he or she possesses. Without such evidence, the courts would be hampered in their ability to arrive at the right decision. For an expert witness to be effective requires that both counsel and the expert understand their respective roles, duties and responsibilities. Failure to reach this understanding cannot help but lead to undesirable consequences for the client.

APPENDIX A
GUIDELINES AND DETAILED OUTLINE FOR MEDICO-LEGAL REPORTS[169]

This appendix was prepared to assist the physician who has previously treated or examined a patient and who lacks experience in preparing a medico-legal report. It also contains a detailed outline of a medico-legal report recommended for civil court matters or arbitrations at the Ontario Insurance Commission but not for criminal court matters.

(a) Purpose of the Medico-Legal Report

The medico-legal report in civil personal injury matters is to help a judge or jury decide the appropriate amount of compensation for an injured person, for example, in cases of injuries, medical treatment, assaults, abuse cases, etc. in a motor vehicle injury case before the Ontario Insurance Commission, the purpose is to determine the entitlement of the patient or claimant to certain benefits (called "statutory accident benefits") including income replacement benefits, and medical and rehabilitation expenses.

It is essential that the report be full and frank. It must be prepared in a credible and competent manner to withstand intense scrutiny upon cross-examination. The medico-legal report should be objective. Therefore, the physician preparing it should not assume the role of advocate either for or against the patient's position. The content should be confined to relevant professional matters, and not include extraneous or subjective remarks.

(b) Guidelines on the Form of the Medico-Legal Report

A physician should submit the medico-legal report within 60 days after receiving a request to do so, under normal circumstances. Settlement of a case is not possible unless the medico-legal report is circulated to opposing parties well before trial. The physician should also be prepared to discuss any subsequent questions or clarifications about it with the lawyer. Usually, an additional fee is not charged as long as the discussion is reasonably related to the initial request. Remember that if a physician has not prepared a medico-legal report then he or she is not permitted to give evidence, except in special circumstances and by leave of the court.

The following are the *minimum* requirements:

---

[169] Included with the kind permission of the Medico-Legal Society of Toronto.

1. Physician's qualifications: The report must indicate that the physician is a "duly qualified medical practitioner holding a certificate authorizing practice within the Province of Ontario." While not legally obligatory, it is most desirable that the report contain a statement of the physician's qualifications such as year of graduation, fellowships, specialities, etc. If the physician does a significant amount of medico-legal work, a photocopy of his or her resume could be referred to in the report and appended to it.
2. Date and signature: It must be dated, and signed by a physician personally. It cannot be stamped or signed by the secretary on the physician's behalf.
3. Comments on liability: If specifically requested to comment on issues of liability, for example, where asked about the standards of medical practice in a medical malpractice case, then it is appropriate to do so.

However, in motor vehicle injury cases. It is unwise to give information bearing on liability. The physician should not, for example, state that the patient was stopped at a red light for ten seconds when he was suddenly hit from behind by a vehicle proceeding at a high speed. Rather, the physician may say that the patient stated that he was involved on a given day in a motor vehicle collision. The physician may say (if relevant) that the car was hit from behind. This does not preclude the physician obtaining, as part of the history, information to help understand the mechanism of injury or stating those aspects relevant to assessing injury.

4. Discussion of each examination to date: In a number of unreported court decisions the medico-legal reports were not accepted because they only dealt with some examinations.
5. Careful use of words throughout the report: Vagueness and uncertainty must be avoided when legitimately possible. Avoid vague expressions such as "it is possible that." Express the matter in terms of percentages if possible (for example, "there is a 10% chance of recurrence within five years").
6. Medical terminology for precision: However, it should also be explained in language which would be understood by judge or jury. Also, concepts unfamiliar to the general public should be explained, otherwise the physician (or some other physician) may be called to court to explain it.

(c) Detailed Outline for Medico-Legal Report

Many physicians may find this outline more detailed than the medico-legal reports they customarily submit, and consider the preparation of such a detailed report would make undue demands on their time. The Medico-legal Society has the opinion that such detailed medico-legal reports will not only increase the chance of settlement but also greatly reduce the number of physicians' court appearances. If a physician can avoid three hours at court, an extra hour spent in preparing the medico-legal report is obviously worthwhile. In any event, both lawyer and patient recognize that a superior medico-legal report involves considerable time, for which they will be prepared to pay. A well-written report may make a trial unnecessary or at least considerably reduce the time and expense incurred at trial.

The Medico-Legal Society suggests that the following outline be used as a checklist for most medico-legal reports in civil court lawsuits or arbitrations of the Ontario Insurance Commission:

1. The physician's qualifications (if the physician has not already submitted them in an earlier medico-legal report dealing with this patient).
2. The patient's name (preferably as indicated in the Statement of Claim).
3. The date, place and reason for the examination(s).
4. The history and symptoms related by the patient. If a physician is consulted as a specialist, then the medico-legal report should be confined to matters relevant to the condition upon which he or she is asked to report:

   (a) The patient's version of what he or she believes caused the condition (i.e., the mechanics of the injury — how it was caused, not who was at fault).
   (b) A complete list of the injuries or conditions complained of (whether they seem significant and relevant, or not, and whether the patient has recovered, or not).

5. Where known and relevant, a statement of a patient's previous health.
6. The physician's findings which do (or do not) corroborate each of the items of complaint, or which indicate the results of an injury which has not been noticed:

   (a) Physical examination and corroboration (spasm, limitation of movement, etc.) of complaint A, complaint B, etc.
   (b) Diagnostic examinations that corroborate complaint A, complaint B, etc. (for example, X-rays, EEG's).
   (c) Surveillance evidence, and the extent to which it was or was not of assistance in formulating the opinion.

7. The physician's diagnosis of each symptom complained of (and any other symptoms);

(a) A description of any diagnostic procedures undertaken by the physician or others with respect to each symptom or condition.
(b) Conclusions regarding diagnosis.

8. The causal connection(s) between the incident and the patient's complaints, which includes a professional opinion on the precipitating factor or "cause" of the condition. The court must know if the injury or condition for which damages are claimed was probably caused, aggravated or accelerated by the events complained about.

9. The treatment:

(a) Treatment recommended for symptom A, symptom B, etc.
(b) Whether or not any recommended treatment had been implemented. If not, why not, and the probable result.
(c) When requested, for example when an automobile insurance case is before the Ontario Insurance Commission, recommendations for any other future treatment or rehabilitation.

10. The degree of disability at the time of the examination:

(a) The extent of impair function which (i) should be treated, (ii) cannot be treated (this is very important if it exists), (iii) is unlikely to improve spontaneously, or (iv) will probably improve spontaneously.
(b) The pain, suffering, inconvenience and discomfort which the physician expects (i) the patient has suffered and (ii) will probably suffer (or not) in the future.

11. The prognosis:

(a) An opinion as to the probability of future recovery.
(b) An opinion as to the probable nature of any permanent impairment.
(c) The probable time within which maximum recovery can be expected.
(d) Having regard to the individual and his or her personal activities, the extent to which the latter should or will be curtailed.

Chapter 7

Preparing the Expert for Trial

by Giovanna Roccamo, LL.B.

7.1 Introduction
7.2 General Preparation
7.3 Theory of the Case
7.4 Expert Witness
7.5 Preparing an Expert to Provide the Expert Opinion
7.6 The Direct Examination
7.7 Qualifying an Expert Witness
7.8 The Heart of the Expert's Opinion
7.9 The Basis of the Expert's Opinion
    7.9.1 Build the Expert's Opinion Slowly
    7.9.2 Summarize each Stage of the Expert's Opinion
    7.9.3 The Hypothetical Question
    7.9.4 Demonstrative Aids
    7.9.5 Define Terms
    7.9.6 Show that Expert is Presenting a Mainstream Opinion
    7.9.7 Deal with any Weaknesses
    7.9.8 End of a Powerful Note
7.10 Cross-examination of Experts
7.11 Purposes of Cross-examination
7.12 Preparation for the Cross-examination of an Expert
7.13 Areas of Challenge on Cross-examination
7.14 Techniques of Cross-examination
7.15 Conclusion

7.1 INTRODUCTION

Personal injury cases that actually proceed to trial are few and far between. Despite the small number of matters that proceed to trial, preparation for trial should begin early. This is especially so in a personal injury action where careful documentation is required of the accident, the injuries sustained by the client, and the client's progress.

7.2   GENERAL PREPARATION

> Nothing so undermines the confidence of a court or jury in a lawyer as his constant groping and fumbling.
>
> John Appleman, ed.,
>
> *Successful Jury Trials 100 (1952)*

Preparation is the key to the success in presenting a persuasive version of a case to the trier of fact. Trial preparation requires, among other things, that counsel present the case in an organized manner. The presentation of the case may be strongly undermined if counsel appears to lack direction or change direction in managing the introduction of evidence at trial. Planning and managing the introduction of expert evidence at trial begins long before the trial date, and commences with careful creation of the trial brief.

It does not take long in a complex personal injury file to accumulate a voluminous brief. The brief must be organized in such a manner that allows counsel and the expert ready access to the material that will be presented to the court, during both the course of preparation and the trial. There is no single or standard method in which the trial brief should be organized, however, it should include the following:

- a brief summary of the theory of the case;
- pleadings;
- discovery summary with appropriate page references for possible examination on prior inconsistent statements;
- notes and documentation on jury selection (if applicable);
- an outline for argument and copies of relevant case law with respect to any preliminary motions;
- the opening statement;
- an outline for direct examination of each witness;
- an outline for cross-examination of each witness;
- closing argument including copies of relevant case law in support;
- an outline for argument in areas of anticipated evidentiary problems, which may become the subject of a *voir dire*;
- a list of documents to be submitted in evidence; and
- an exhibit sheet.

It is also recommended, where a large number of experts will give evidence at trial, that such materials, including the expert's reports, file and curriculum vitae, be incorporated into an expert's brief.

Leading trial writers, such as Mauet, Casswell and Macdonald in *Fundamentals of Trial Techniques*[1] and McElhaney in *Trial Notebook*[2] suggest that the trial brief be organized using the divider method or the trial notebook method. The divider method involves placing each part of the trial, such as opening statement, direct examination of particular witnesses, into a separate, labelled file divider. Mauet, Casswell and Macdonald describe the advantages and disadvantages of such a method as follows:

> The advantage of the divider method is that it is usually better suited to a long, complex case when the paperwork is so voluminous it cannot physically be organized and contained in a trial notebook. The disadvantages are primarily logistical. A divider method is only as reliable as counsel maintaining it. If a file is misfiled or its contents misplaced, it cannot be readily located and its utility is eliminated. If more than one counsel represents a party and shares the files, the possibilities of disruption are much greater.[3]

The notebook, on the other hand, is organized into a big binder containing each part of the trial with a table of contents.

7.3   THEORY OF THE CASE

Presenting a matter before the court in order that the court can make a favourable determination requires more than careful organization; it requires that counsel present the case in a persuasive manner. Persuasion is the key to trial advocacy. In order to persuade the trier of fact, it is imperative that counsel fully understands the case, addresses points of weakness and develops a theory. A theory of the case should be developed as early as possible, since it not only allows counsel to be able to present a persuasive case at trial, but will also direct counsel from the pleading stage through to trial.

The theory of the case allows counsel to provide an explanation to the court of why his or her client should be successful. Mauet, Casswell and Macdonald defined the theory of a case as follows:

---

1   T.A. Mauet, D.G. Casswell, G.P. MacDonald, *Fundamentals of Trial Technique*, 2nd ed. (Toronto: Carswell, 1995).
2   J.W. McElhaney, *McElhaney's Trial Notebook*, 3rd ed. (Chicago, Ill.: Section of Litigation, American Bar Association, 1994).
3   *Supra*, note 1 at 345.

A theory of the case is simply your position and approach to all the undisputed and disputed evidence, which will be presented at trial. You must integrate the undisputed facts with your version of the disputed facts to create a cohesive, logical position at trial. That position must remain consistent during each phase of the trial. At the conclusion of the trial your position must be the more plausible of "what really happened" to the jury.[4]

In effect, the theory of the case has to be logical, simple,[5] consistent and easy to believe. Once a theory of the case has been formulated, that does not mean that it remains rigid and immutable. As the case develops, and new facts come to light, the theory of the case may have to be modified in order to accommodate new facts. It is also important to acknowledge that one does not have to be limited to only one theory of the case. There may be a number of occasions when several theories of the case are advanced, in the alternative. As McElhaney, quoting from Irving Younger, remarked:

> One of the distressing things about the theory of the case is that you are permitted to have more than one. Through the magic of the law, they are even allowed to conflict. As Irving Younger says, at common law you are entitled to reply to a plaintiff who claims his cabbages were eaten by your goat:
>
> > You had no cabbages.
> > If you did, they were not eaten.
> > If they were eaten, it was not by a goat.
> > If they were eaten by a goat, it was not my goat.
> > And if it was my goat, he was insane.[6]

As a word of caution, one has to be careful where several theories are being advanced in the alternative, as there is the risk of confusing the trier of fact and providing no viable option as to "what really happened."

7.4 EXPERT WITNESS

The expert witness is qualified to give opinion evidence because of the special knowledge and skill that he or she has obtained through study or experience. In personal injury actions, the use of experts is common. Medical practitioners are commonly required to provide an opinion as to

---

4 *Supra*, note 1 at 349.
5 To ensure that the theory of the case is simple, Steven Lubet in his book, *Modern Trial Advocacy: Analysis and Practice* (NITA: Canadian Ed., 1995) stated that a good theory makes maximum use of undisputed facts. It relies as little as possible on evidence that may be hotly controverted, implausible, inadmissible, or otherwise difficult to prove.
6 *Supra*, note 2, at 49.

the injuries that the client has sustained, and the likelihood of recovery in the future. It is therefore only logical that the expert witness becomes a vital player in assisting counsel to advance the theory of the case. To be able to effectively use an expert witness requires an investment in time in preparing an expert witness to provide his or her testimony in court.

Counsel often make the erroneous assumption that expert witnesses are knowledgeable about providing expert testimony in court, and are fully aware of their duties and responsibilities when presented at trial. Unfortunately, this is often not the case. In most cases, counsel will be required to spend more time preparing an expert witness for the trial than other lay witnesses, and this is primarily because of the importance attached to the expert's testimony. Counsel should ensure that the expert is comfortable about testifying in court, and perhaps consider the following:

1. Ensure that the expert understands the duties and responsibilities of an expert witness when providing an expert opinion either in writing or in person.[7]
2. Unless an expert has provided testimony before, most will not be familiar with the process of how evidence is elicited. Failure to have even a basic understanding of the legal process may make the expert witness uncomfortable; therefore, counsel should inform the expert of the trial process and the part that the expert will be expected to play. The expert should be advised that his or her opinion will be elicited by a series of questions which will usually take the expert through the substance of his or her report. It should also be explained that, after those questions, the expert will then be cross-examined by opposing counsel. It is essential to explain that, after the cross-examination, there is then the opportunity, on reply, for the expert to clarify new parts of his or her testimony elicited during cross-examination. Advising the expert of the trial process allows the expert to concentrate on the opinion that will be provided to the court, rather than on the trial process itself.
3. If the expert is unfamiliar with the courtroom, recommend that he or she go attend to see an actual trial in progress. If this is not possible, it is helpful to show the expert around the courtroom where the trial will be conducted.
4. Advise the expert on how to testify in court and what is expected. Consider the following advice:

    (a) Instruct the expert that one should show deference to the court,

---

[7] See detailed discussion on duties and responsibilities of an expert witness in Chapter 6.

and this is achieved by respecting the trial procedure and providing the opinion in a truthful and respectful manner.

(b) Instruct the expert to answer the questions posed by counsel. The trier of fact will not look favourably upon an expert who is evasive and fails to answer the questions as posed.

(c) Instruct the expert to use non-technical language whenever possible. The trier of fact can easily become confused and not fully understand the expert's opinion. To present a persuasive case to the trier of fact requires that counsel ensure that the testimony presented by the expert is fully appreciated and understood by the trier of fact. Where technical terms have to be used, the expert should ensure that the terms are defined in order that the trier of fact can follow the expert's evidence.

(d) Instruct the expert not to answer questions which he or she does not understand. The expert should be instructed to advise counsel, asking the question, that the question was not understood. Counsel will then either repeat the question, or rephrase it.

(e) The expert should be instructed that, when answering a question, he or she should try to establish eye contact with the trier of fact, wherever possible. Advise the expert to refrain from seeking assistance from counsel that retained him or her, and refrain from discussing his or her evidence in the course of cross-examination.[8]

5. Consider the following additional advice that may be given to an expert witness in anticipation of his or her cross-examination:

(a) Instruct the expert never to argue with opposing counsel during a cross-examination, and to refrain from attacking the opposing expert witness. Arguments with opposing counsel may lead the trier of fact to conclude that the expert witness is more the advocate, than the expert.

(b) The expert should be instructed that there is no harm in conceding points made by opposing counsel during cross-examination, where no harm will be made to the theory of the case.

(c) Instruct the expert that whenever an objection is made, either during direct examination or cross-examination by counsel, the expert should not answer the question until the judge rules that the question should be answered.

(d) Instruct the expert to be wary of leading questions. The expert should carefully listen to the question. If a statement or an as-

---

8 Denis Power, Q.C., "Witnesses—Counsel's Obligations: "You mean I can't speak to my witness," " (Paper presented at the County of Carleton Law Association: Civil Litigation Updated November 27-28, 1987) [unpublished].

sumption is made in the question, which the expert does not accept, then the expert should make that clear to the court.

(e) The expert should be very wary not to respond to questions where the answer requires an opinion which goes beyond his or her area of expertise. If this is the case, the expert should be instructed to inform the court that the answer to the question lies outside his or her area of expertise.

7.5 PREPARING AN EXPERT TO PROVIDE THE EXPERT OPINION

Developing a theory of the case is essential to counsel in order to persuade the trier of fact to decide the case in his or her favour. Steven Lubet[9] suggests that the expert should also develop a theory of the opinion he or she will offer. Lubet suggests the following:

> An expert's theory is an overview or summary of the expert's entire position. The theory must not only state a conclusion, but must also explain, in common-sense terms, why the expert is correct. Why did she settle upon a certain methodology? Why did she review particular data? Why is her approach reliable? Why is the opposing expert wrong? In other words, the expert witness must tell a coherent story that provides the trier of fact with reasons for accepting, and, it is hoped, internalizing, the expert's point of view.[10]

It is not uncommon for counsel to spend more time preparing an expert witness than a lay witness. Such extensive preparation is required of an expert primarily because of the significance attached to the expert's testimony; it is even more important where the case can be categorized as a "battle of the experts." By the same token, expert witnesses are required to spend a considerable amount of time preparing, in order to provide an opinion which the trier of fact can accept.[11]

The following steps should be taken in order to prepare an expert witness for eventual examination at trial:

1. *Qualifications of the Expert:* The expert's qualifications and credentials are important. It is the qualifications that allow the expert to be able to provide an expert opinion to the trier of fact; therefore, time

---

9 Steven Lubet, *Modern Trial Advocacy Analysis and Practice* (NITA: Canadian Ed., 1995).
10 *Ibid.*, at 170.
11 This is one of the main reasons why counsel should ensure that they retain an expert witness who is willing to invest the required time in preparing his or her expert opinion.

should be spent carefully reviewing the expert's qualifications and credentials. Most experts are modest about their qualifications and may fail to emphasize some qualifications which, in the opinion of counsel, may enhance the credibility of the expert. A careful review prior to trial allows counsel and the expert to formulate questions for direct examination pertaining to the qualifications of the expert. On direct examination, counsel should highlight the expert's qualifications, rather than going through a painstaking list of every article that the expert wrote, or every speech or every exam that the expert may have done. Instruct the expert that opposing counsel may cross-examine the expert on his or her qualifications. It is also recommended that the expert prepare a written curriculum vitae of his or her credentials which can then be tendered as an exhibit at trial. This is particulary helpful when the trier of fact is making a decision, which may be weeks after the expert has testified. The resume also serves as a reminder that the expert is qualified to provide the expert opinion.

2. *Understand and Review the Expert's Opinion:* Counsel should fully understand how and why the expert arrived at his or her opinion. To be able to understand the expert's opinion, counsel should have enough knowledge of the area in which the expert will provide his or her expert opinion. This is essential since it is counsel who will be eliciting the expert's testimony by asking the relevant questions. If counsel does not understand the relevant area of the expert's opinion, then counsel will find it difficult to ask the right questions and will, therefore, fail to present a persuasive expert opinion to the court. Counsel should be familiar with all the leading literature in the area in which the opinion will be offered, as well as the literature that does not support the expert's opinion, especially if that literature is considered as leading authority. Failure to adequately research the leading authority may lead to the expert being discredited, as illustrated in the Ontario Court (General Division)'s decision in *R. v. Olscamp*,[12] where the defence was successful in discrediting the Crown's expert witness. The Crown's expert witness was called to provide an opinion on the general behavioural and psychological characteristics of child victims of sexual abuse, and then show that the complainant exhibited some symptoms consistent with sexual abuse. The defence was able to discredit the Crown's expert witness not only because she had no appreciation for her role as an expert witness, but also because she failed to acknowledge the medical literature and knowledge in this area.

3. *Review the Facts and Issues of the Case:* The expert and counsel should carefully review the facts and the issues in the case, as well as

---

12 (1994), 35 C.R. (4th) 37 (Ont. Gen. Div.).

the facts on which the opinion is based. If the opinion is based on facts which are not supported by the evidence presented, or if the expert witness has no appreciation of the facts of the case, it may lead the trier of fact to attach little weight to the expert opinion offered. Failure to understand the facts also opens the door for opposing counsel to attack the expert's opinion, as well as the credibility of the expert witness. In some cases, where the facts are in dispute, the expert may be required to provide his or her opinion based on a hypothetical question. If that is the case, counsel should ensure that such a question is well prepared and thought out. The hypothetical question should be reviewed with the expert in detail to ensure that the hypothetical question is the proper question to ask in order to elicit the desired expert opinion.[13]

4. *Review the Expert's Report:* Counsel and the expert should carefully review the expert's report to ensure that the oral opinion in court corresponds with the written report. If there have been any new developments since the drafting of the written report, these should also be examined to determine whether the expert's opinion requires modification and, if so, whether a supplementary expert report is required.[14]

5. *Review the Opposing Expert's Report:* As soon as counsel obtains a copy of the opposing expert's report, a copy of that report should immediately be forwarded to one's own expert. Counsel and the expert should carefully examine the opposing expert's report. It is critical that one's own expert understands the basis of the opposing expert's position, and is able to reconcile his or her own position, or is able to explain why the opposing expert's position should not be accepted. The expert's review of the opposing expert's report will also provide counsel with possible avenues for cross-examination.

6. *Conduct Practice Direct/Cross Examination:* It is recommended that the expert have an opportunity to review an outline of how the opinion will be elicited. If time permits, it may be a good idea to conduct a practice direct examination. This provides the expert with the opportunity to develop a road map for the presentation of his or her opinion to the trier of fact.

7. *Demonstrative Aids:* It is also important that counsel review with the expert the use of any demonstrative evidence. Counsel should fully understand and be familiar with the demonstrative evidence that will

---

13 See discussion at 7.9.3, The Hypothetical Question.
14 Rule 53.03(3) of the Ontario Rules of Civil Procedure, R.R.O. 1990, Reg. 194, as amended, provides that a supplementary report should be served on every other party to the action not less than 30 days before the commencement of the trial.

7.6 THE DIRECT EXAMINATION

Direct examination of the expert witness is the most important part of the trial process. This is the time when the expert witness has the opportunity to present his or her opinion in a persuasive manner to the trier of fact. It is during the direct examination that the expert has the undivided attention of the trier of fact and the opportunity to advance the theory of the case, and the theory of the opinion. Most leading writers have said that it is during direct examination that one wins a case.[16]

The purpose of a direct examination is to elicit from the expert, with the use of non-leading questions, the expert's opinion and to show the trier of fact that the expert is credible, and offers an opinion which should be accepted. Normally the direct examination of an expert witness proceeds as follows:

1. Introducing the expert witness;
2. Qualifying the expert witness;
3. The heart of the opinion itself;
4. Basis of the expert opinion;
5. Conclusion.

7.7 QUALIFYING AN EXPERT WITNESS

Direct examination should begin by introducing the expert witness. Every attempt should be made to personalize the expert. After introducing the expert witness, counsel must proceed to qualify the expert. It is important to qualify the expert in the areas in which he or she will provide an expert opinion. As Madam Justice McLachlin put it in *R. v. Marquard*:[17]

> The proper practice is for counsel presenting an expert witness to qualify the expert in all the areas in which the expert is to give opinion evidence. If this is done, no question as to the admissibility of their opinions arises.

---

15 See discussion at 7.9.4, Demonstrative Aids.
16 See Steven Lubet, *Modern Trial Advocacy: Analysis and Practice* (NITA: Canadian Ed., 1995) and J.A. Olah, *The Art and Science of Advocacy* (Toronto: Carswell, 1990) at 9-3.
17 [1993] 4 S.C.R. 223, 25 C.R. (4th) 1.

The normal practice is to elicit the expert's qualifications by asking short leading questions and non-leading questions. Asking one or two general questions, which requires the expert to provide his or her entire qualifications, is not recommended. Such a method may bore or confuse the trier of fact, and may even create the impression that the expert is immodest. Also, by following such a method, the expert may not provide his or her qualifications in a logical manner leaving the trier of fact unsure as to whether or not the expert is qualified to provide an opinion.

The better approach is for counsel to lead the expert through his or her qualifications, addressing the following areas:

1. expert's professional background;
2. academic achievements;
3. work experience;
4. professional associations;
5. publications or scholarly work; and
6. expertise relevant to the case at hand.

Addressing the above areas in a systematic order allows counsel to control the direct examination, and more importantly, highlights the relevant parts of the expert's qualifications. Consider the following example[18] of how a clinical neuropsychologist may be qualified in order to provide expert opinion on mild traumatic brain injury:[19]

Q. Dr. Smith, please state your full name and address?
A. James Smith and I live in Ottawa.
Q. What is your present profession?
A. I am a clinical neuropsychologist.
Q. What does a clinical neuropsychologist do?
A. Clinical neuropsychology treats the cognitive, emotional and behavioural effects of brain injury. The main focus being the effects of brain impairment on the individual and the ability of that individual to function in everyday life.[20]
Q. How long have you been a clinical neuropsychologist?
A. For 15 years.
Q. Where did you receive your undergraduate education?
A. At Carleton University.

---

18 Example applicable to qualifying other medical experts.
19 See Bruce Stern, *The Neuropsychologist in a Mild Traumatic Brain Injury Case: How to Conduct the Direct Examination* (June 1995) Trial.
20 M.S. Macartney Filgate and W.G. Snow, "Forensic Neuropsychology" (1991) 12 Adv. Q. 83.

Q. What was your major field of undergraduate study?
A. Psychology.
Q. When did you complete your undergraduate study?
A. In 1970.
Q. Where did you do your graduate training?
A. At Ottawa University.
Q. What did your graduate training consist of?
A. I followed a course of study for five years in order to obtain my doctoral degree in psychology.
Q. Did you do an internship?
A. Yes, following the degree I did a post-doctoral internship for a period of two years.
Q. What did your internship consist of?
A. It was a general internship in applied psychology. I worked under a neuropsychologist who dealt mostly with children and adults who suffer the effects of mild traumatic brain injury.
Q. Following the internship did you do further studies?
A. Yes, in order to become a registered psychologist I had to write further exams.
Q. When did you become a registered psychologist?
A. In 1977.
Q. Did you afterwards specialize in any particular field of psychology?
A. Yes, in clinical neuropsychology.
Q. What did you have to do to specialize in clinical neuropsychology?
A. I took a diploma in clinical neuropsychology with the American Board of Professional Psychology.
Q. What did this diploma entail?
A. I conducted five years of clinical practice in the area of brain dysfunction and I was also required to successfully complete further examinations.
Q. When did you obtain your diploma?
A. In 1982.
Q. Are you certified as a clinical neuropsychologist?
A. Yes.
Q. How long have you been certified?
A. Since 1982 in clinical neuropsychology, and 1977 as a registered psychologist.
Q. Are you licensed to practice in clinical neuropsychology?
A. Yes.
Q. Where are you licensed to practice?
A. In Canada and the United States.
Q. What professional organizations are you a member of?
A. I am a member of the American Board of Professional Psychology,

the Ontario Psychology Association and the Ontario Neuropsychologist Association.
Q. What are the requirements for membership?
A. To be a member of the Ontario Psychology Association you are required to be a certified psychologist, and for the American Board and the Ontario Neuropsychologist Association you need to have obtained a diploma in clinical neuropsychology.
Q. How long have you been a member in each of these Associations?
A. With the Ontario Psychology Association since 1977, and the American Board and the Ontario Neuropsychologist Association since 1982.
Q. Have you written any articles on mild traumatic brain injury?
A. Yes, I have written a number of general articles on mild traumatic brain injury as well as specific articles on the impact of traumatic events, such as motor vehicle accidents on the brain.
Q. Have they been published?
A. Yes, all my articles, except one, have been published.
Q. Where have they been published?
A. In the American and Canadian Journal of Psychology.
Q. In your practice, do you deal with a lot of cases dealing with mild traumatic injury?
A. Yes, I do.
Q. How many cases would that be in the last five years?
A. Approximately 200.

Once the expert has been qualified, counsel should offer the expert to the judge as qualified to provide expert testimony in the area concerned. Of course, opposing counsel has an opportunity to object to the expert being qualified. Some leading trial advocates recommend that where the expert's qualifications are inadequate one should not object to the expert being qualified, but should deal with those inadequacies under cross-examination.[21] However, where it is clear that the expert is not qualified at all to offer an expert opinion, then opposing counsel should object.[22]

Where an expert's qualifications are not in issue, opposing counsel may, before the expert's qualifications are elicited from the expert, inform the court that he or she does not object to the expert being qualified as an expert witness. However, it may be prudent and indeed helpful to the trier of fact to be fully informed of the depth of the expert's qualifications, thereby justifying a thorough review of the expert's credentials. In those cases, where the opposing counsel does not object, counsel should thank the opposing counsel, ask the court's indulgence to continue with the

---

21 John Epp, "Avoiding Rookie Mistakes When Using Experts in Canadian Courts" (1993) 14 Adv. Q. 185.
22 See the discussion at Chapter 6 at 6.5.4 on a properly qualified expert.

qualification of the expert, and continue with qualifying the expert witness. It is important that the trier of fact have the opportunity to hear of the expert's credentials, since the more impressive they are, the more likely it is that the trier of fact will attach greater weight to the testimony.

7.8 THE HEART OF THE EXPERT'S OPINION

Once the expert has been qualified, the next step is to elicit a summary of his or her opinion. By proceeding in this manner, the trier of fact is provided with the expert's opinion right from the start. For example, the trier of fact will know at the beginning that, in the expert's opinion, the plaintiff sustained the injuries as a result of the accident, rather than having to hear this towards the end, after the expert has testified as to why and how he or she arrived at that opinion. This direct approach also commands more immediate attention and provides the trier of fact with a basis for understanding how and why the expert arrived at his or her opinion. Some examples of the questions that may be asked to elicit the heart of the expert's opinion may be as follows:

Q. Will you please provide us with your expert opinion, based on a reasonable degree of neuropsychological certainty, as to what injuries Ms. Green suffered as a result of the motor vehicle accident?[23]

Q. Do you have an opinion as to whether Ms. Green's injuries were sustained as a result of the motor vehicle accident?

Q. Dr. Smith can you please summarize your opinion as to whether Ms. Green suffers from chronic pain syndrome?

7.9 THE BASIS OF THE EXPERT'S OPINION

The expert opinion should be presented in a logical manner which allows the trier of fact to understand and follow what the expert is saying. Presentation of an expert's opinion should not be rushed, and should provide the expert with the opportunity to explain complicated medical issues. If the trier of fact does not understand what the expert is saying, then counsel runs the risk of losing their interest, with potentially disastrous effects. Each counsel has his or her own style of presenting expert witnesses, however, there are some basic techniques[24] which counsel can employ which will enhance the presentation of the testimony. Those techniques are summarized below:

---

23 Stern, *supra*, note 19 at 66.
24 Steven Lubet, *Eight Techniques for Direct Examination of Experts* (December 1993) Trial at 16.

7.9.1 Build the Expert's Opinion Slowly

Most experts have never testified in court. When an expert is asked several open-ended questions to explain how and why he or she arrived at the opinion, the expert will likely provide his or her testimony in a manner that may be incoherent, difficult to understand and follow. In some instances, it is most effective to have the expert present the opinion as he or she would in a classroom setting and play the role of a teacher. The most effective way to present the expert's testimony is through short questions, in order to slowly build the expert's opinion. By presenting small segments of the expert's testimony to the trier of fact, one is allowing the trier of fact to follow and more clearly absorb the opinion. Asking short questions also allows counsel to control and highlight the important parts of the testimony. This cannot be done if the expert is asked to provide his or her expert testimony in response to one or two open-ended questions.

7.9.2 Summarize each Stage of the Expert's Opinion

Once the expert has provided his or her testimony on a particular point, counsel should seize every opportunity to have the expert summarize the evidence he or she provided and will continue to provide to the court. In most instances of direct examination, it is highly effective to inform the trier of fact where the next line of questioning is going by leading the expert into the area as follows:

Q. Now, Dr. Smith, am I correct in understanding that you conducted a psychological examination of Ms. X and that this examination revealed Ms. X's inability to concentrate for a long period of time?
A. Yes, that is correct.
Q. Now, Dr. Smith I want to examine what tests you conducted.

7.9.3 The Hypothetical Qestion

The expert opinion has to be supported by a factual foundation. The trier of fact should be aware of the factual basis of the expert's opinion. In some cases, the facts may be in dispute. Therefore, in order for him or her to render an expert opinion, a hypothetical question has to be put to the expert.

The Supreme Court of Canada, on appeal from the Ontario Court of Appeal, in *R. v. Bleta*[25] dealt with the use of hypothetical questions. In the

---

25 [1964] S.C.R. 561, 44 C.R. 193.

trial of the matter, the jury had acquitted the appellant. The Ontario Court of Appeal subsequently set aside the verdict and directed a new trial on the grounds that certain evidence given by a psychiatrist was inadmissible, since it was not elicited through a hypothetical question. Mr. Justice Ritchie, writing for the court, stated that the nature and foundation of the opinion, and the evidence upon which it is based, should be clearly indicated to the court, failing which the trier of fact may reject the expert opinion. As Mr. Justice Ritchie wrote:

> In commenting on what he described as "the orthodox and accepted theory of the hypothetical question in our law", the learned editor of Wigmore on Evidence, 3rd ed., summarized the matter in para. 672 at page 793 in the following language:
>> The key to the situation, in short, is that there may be two distinct subjects of testimony, — premises, and inferences or conclusions; that the latter involves necessarily a consideration of the former; and that the tribunal must be furnished with the means of rejecting the latter if upon consultation they determine to reject the former, i.e. of distinguishing conclusions properly founded from conclusions improperly founded.
>
> Provided that the questions are so phrased as to make clear what the evidence is on which an expert is being asked to found his conclusion, the failure of counsel to put such questions in hypothetical form does not of itself make the answers inadmissible.[26]

Where the expert does not have direct personal knowledge of the facts of the given case, or where the facts are in dispute the best way to establish the foundation of the expert's opinion is by asking a hypothetical question. As Mr. Justice Ritchie stated:

> The question of whether or not an accused person was in a state of automatism so as not to be legally responsible at the time when he committed the acts with which he is charged, is a question of fact, and indeed may be the most vital question of fact in a criminal case, and it is because the opinion of an expert witness on such a question can serve only to confuse the issue unless the proven facts upon which it is based have been clearly indicated to the jury that the practice has grown up of requiring counsel, when seeking such an opinion, to state those facts in the form of a hypothetical question. In cases where the expert has been present throughout the trial and there is conflict between the witnesses, it is obviously unsatisfactory to ask him to express an opinion based upon the evidence which he has heard because the answer to such a question involves the expert in having to resolve the conflict in accordance with his own view of the credibility of the witnesses and the jury has no way of knowing upon what evidence he based his opinion. Where, however,

---

26 *Ibid.*, at (S.C.R.) 566.

there is no conflict in the evidence, the same difficulty does not necessarily arise and different considerations may therefore apply.[27]

When asking an hypothetical question it is critical that the question is phrased in a clear manner so that the trier of fact can understand the basis of the expert's opinion.

The Ontario Court of Appeal in *R. v. Swietlinski*[28] agreed that where the facts are in dispute it is appropriate to ask an hypothetical question. The court provided the following comment:

> Defence counsel could then have asked the witness a hypothetical question, whether, assuming the truth of the facts in evidence referred to in the question, they were consistent with or supported the opinion he had formed from his examination of the appellant. Defence counsel did not, however, adopt this course.[29]

The use of hypothetical questions is a valuable trial technique which, if properly used, may help present a persuasive case to the trier of fact. The hypothetical question affords counsel the opportunity to reinforce a favourable version of the contested facts which supports the theory of the case. This is an opportunity for counsel to effectively advocate that his or her version of the facts should be accepted by the trier of fact.

7.9.4 Demonstrative Aids

"*A picture is worth a thousand words*", especially when an expert is providing an opinion on an area that is difficult to understand. In some cases, the use of visual aids may be essential in order for the trier of fact to understand the expert's opinion. As Goldstein put it:

> These lawyers know that it is better to show the trier of fact an object or event than to have a witness describe it. The wisdom of portraying events by means of visual evidence is readily apparent when one considers that the sense of sight contributes 85 per cent to a person's learning. The other four senses account for the remaining 15 per cent.[30]

---

27 *Ibid.*, at 564.
28 (1978), 22 O.R. (2d) 604, 5 C.R. (3d) 324 (C.A.), affirmed 18 C.R. (3d) 231, [1980] 2 S.C.R. 956.
29 *Ibid.*, at (C.R.) 365.
30 Elliott Goldstein, *Visual Evidence: A Practitioner's Manual* (Toronto: Carswell, 1991) at 1-2.

When presenting a case before the trier of fact, counsel is, in effect, trying to persuade the trier of fact that his or her theory of the case should be accepted. Visual aids should be used as a tool to persuade the trier of fact, and should be used as early on in the expert's direct examination as possible.[31] The trier of fact has a limited amount of time to incorporate and understand the information provided by the expert witness; therefore, every possible tool should be used to enhance early education and understanding in a complicated area of expert testimony. Also, if visual aids are used by an expert, the trier of fact is more likely to remember the testimony provided by that witness. Olah, in *The Art and Science of Advocacy*,[32] had the following to say about visual aids as a persuasive tool:

> What makes demonstrative evidence so persuasive? The answer is simple: demonstrative evidence permits the recipient to visualize what is given in oral testimony. It transforms complicated evidence into a simple, visual presentation. Demonstrative evidence graphically portrays and underscores the testimony being presented. It is highly compelling because it is vivid; it brings oral evidence alive. More importantly, the amount of information retained by the trier of fact is substantially increased when the information is conveyed by demonstrative evidence in conjunction with oral testimony.

Sopinka, in *The Trial of an Action*, clearly advocates the use of visual aids when presenting an expert witness:

> Arrange to have as much of the expert's evidence as possible illustrated by charts and diagrams. Have these marked as exhibits. Mr. Weir does this in his examination of Mr. Horn. In a jury trial these will be taken into the jury room. In the absence of notes of the expert's evidence, which a jury does not have, these exhibits will stand out from the other evidence.[33]

In personal injury cases, evidence that can be used to illustrate the oral testimony of a witness may consist of photographs, surveillance video, and anatomical charts. Such charts are extremely valuable in assisting the trier of fact to understand what injuries the plaintiff has sustained and how injury affects the operation of the human body. However, anatomical charts do have their limits. Such charts may contain information which is not relevant to the case in hand, or may be too detailed for the purposes of a particular case. In cases where specific information is required, one can

---

31 Roger G. Oatley, "Objectives of Examination-in-Chief of the Plaintiff's Chronic Pain Expert: How to Achieve Them" (1997) 19 Adv. Q. 188.
32 John Olah, *The Art and Science of Advocacy* (Toronto: Carswell, 1990) at 11-2.
33 John Sopinka, *Trial of an Action*, 2nd ed. (Toronto: Butterworths, 1993) at 68).

customize an anatomical chart which will then address the specific concerns in a given case. There is also the option of using anatomical models. An anatomical model is a three-dimensional aid, and can more accurately show what injuries were sustained in the accident and why.

Courts are open to the use of visual aids in order to enhance the understanding of complicated medical testimony, as reflected in the Ontario Court trial level's decision in *Majcenic v. Natale*.[34] In that case, the plaintiff sustained serious injuries when she was struck by the defendant's motor vehicle. Justice Haines, on the application of the plaintiff's counsel, dispensed with the jury on the basis that the medical evidence was so complex that he was satisfied that the jury members had little appreciation of it, and were more than likely confused. Justice Haines remarked:

> As this case proceeded the medical evidence became so complex that I was quite satisfied the jury had only the vaguest impression of the injury to the plaintiff's foot and were probably quite confused. As a result, on application of plaintiff's counsel I dispensed with the jury and continued the trial without their assistance. *I did so with reluctance especially since the complexities and confusion could have been removed by the appropriate use of anatomical charts and models and the precise use of medical terms.* (Emphasis added.)[35]

Justice Haines acknowledged that he had a better understanding of the medical evidence than the jury, primarily because he had the use of an atlas of anatomy. He further wrote:

> As the case proceeded I had before me my atlas of anatomy. As the doctors spoke of the various parts of the foot and the effect of the injury on the patient their evidence became more meaningful and took on a definite character that could not be gotten without an atlas of anatomy or model of the relevant bones.[36]

For a lay person, medical information may be very difficult to understand. A medical expert is invited to offer opinion evidence in order to assist the trier of fact in understanding the issues so as to arrive at a proper decision. The trier of fact will be unlikely to arrive at a decision if the expert fails to convey the necessary information in a form that can be understood. This was aptly acknowledged by Justice Haines:

---

34 [1968] 1 O.R. 189, appealed to the Court of Appeal where a new trial was ordered. The Court of Appeal made no comments concerning Justice Haine's comments about demonstrative evidence, except to say that it was in the trial judge's discretion as to how a trial should be conducted.
35 *Ibid.*, at (O.R.) 195.
36 *Ibid.*

> It is my considered view that if we are going to try these personal injury cases with a jury of laymen every proper aid to communication must be used to communicate to the jury the exact nature of that part of the anatomy involved, its use and injury. No lecturer to students would think of lecturing in anatomy without adequate anatomical charts and models. It seems to me that in genuine cases where such aids to communication are required they should be used in a modern trial. In response to my question why they had not been made available in the present case, I was informed by counsel that the opinion of Judges varies so greatly on the propriety of the use of anatomical charts and models that it was considered an unjustifiable expense to acquire and attempt to use them. While I appreciate that many Judges react in horror to reports of grinning skeletons, pathological specimens and other paraphernalia said to be used in some Courts south of the border, I am confident that our judiciary is fully capable of excluding evidence when its illustrative value is outweighed by its tendency to prejudice.[37]

In cases where the visual aids are likely to cause confusion in the mind of the trier of fact, or its prejudicial effect outweighs its probative value, then the trial judge has the discretion not to admit them. The prejudicial effect may outweigh its probative value in cases where the visual aids are not accurate, are likely to mislead the trier of fact, or are not relevant.

In the Ontario Court of Appeal's decision in *Shipman v. Antoniadis*,[38] on an appeal from an assessment of damages for personal injuries suffered by an infant plaintiff, the defendant claimed that the jury had awarded higher damages as a result of the introduction of an anatomical chart whose prejudicial effect outweighed its probative value. Such a chart was introduced by a medical witness to indicate the location of the liver, spleen and gall bladder and to illustrate the operative techniques that the surgeon had employed to repair the internal injuries suffered by the infant plaintiff. Justice Kelly, writing for the majority of the Court of Appeal, agreed that such an anatomical chart was "unnecessary for the understanding of the continuing permanent disabilities which form the most substantial part of the damages claimed by the plaintiff." However, Justice Kelly did not dismiss the use of visual aids and wrote:

> One may easily envisage injuries where, for the proper understanding of the disabling effect thereof, a jury might properly be asked to look at an anatomical diagram. One example of such a situation would be where limitation of movement of a hand was claimed to have resulted from injuries to muscles or tendons in the arm. A diagram showing the relationship of the injured tissue to the malfunction of the hand would be helpful to the jury in its under-

---

37 *Ibid.*, at 196.
38 (1975), 8 O.R. (2d) 449 (C.A.). See also *Draper v. Jacklyn* (1969), [1970] S.C.R. 92.

standing of a situation which did exist and might or would continue to exist. There the expert witness would properly be required to deal with that condition and its prognosis and could help the members of the jury by directing their attention to a drawing with reference to which they could better understand the condition. Another such example would be that of a malpractice action in which proof of the cause of action might require demonstration of the area which the treatment affected and wherein the negligence had occurred.[39]

The *Shipman* decision should not be used as an authority to frustrate the use of visual aids. As Goldstein put it:

> The Shipman case is not authority for the proposition that anatomical charts are inherently prejudicial and of negligible probative value and should, therefore, be inadmissible. Instead, Shipman says that when the use of an anatomical chart is unnecessary for the understanding of the continuing permanent disabilities of the plaintiff, the anatomical chart should not be admitted.[40]

Introducing the Visual Aid: Before a visual aid can be used in court, counsel has to lay a foundation for the use of such evidence. This foundation is laid as follows:

1. Show the demonstrative evidence to the expert and ask the expert to describe what the demonstrative evidence is.
2. At this stage, counsel should show the demonstrative evidence to the trier of fact and the opposing counsel as well.
3. Then have the expert review the demonstrative evidence and ask the question: "Based on your knowledge and experience is this anatomical chart an accurate and fair depiction of the subject matter?"
4. Then ask the expert whether or not the anatomical model or chart would clarify the testimony so that the trier of fact can better understand the expert's opinion.
5. Then counsel should tender the demonstrative aid in evidence and, if accepted, mark it as the next exhibit. Wherever possible, it may be a good idea to have duplicate versions of the demonstrative aid, since it would allow the trier of fact, and the opposing counsel, to follow the expert's testimony.

7.9.5 Define Terms

Whenever the expert witness uses complicated language, counsel should instruct the expert to define such terminology in simple, clear lan-

---

39 *Ibid.*, at (O.R.) 450.
40 *Supra*, note 30, at 16-5.

guage. As discussed earlier, when the expert is preparing the report, he or she should include an appendix with layman's definitions of complicated terminology.

7.9.6 Show that Expert is Presenting a Mainstream Opinion

In situations where the case involves a "battle of the experts", the way to enhance the expert's opinion in the eyes of the trier of fact is to show that the expert's opinion is supported by leading authorities.[41] The expert opinion should be presented in a way that shows that the expert has taken the mainstream view. One way to enhance the credibility of an expert witness is to refer to authoritative texts during the direct examination. The expert witness may use authoritative texts to support his or her opinion, but should be careful not to leave the impression that it is the writer of any one authoritative text that is actually providing the expert opinion. The British Columbia Court of Appeal in *R. v. Craig*[42] dealt with whether the witness had committed an error in law when the expert read a study done by another expert into evidence. The court held that an error was committed, and reasoned as follows:

> The difficulty is that the questions were put in a way which did not result in the witness saying in effect it is my opinion that the statistical likelihood of error is one in five thousand and supporting that opinion by reference to studies or work of other experts. Indeed, he said nothing on the question of a statistical likelihood of error but rather referred simply to a study done by another expert and in response to questions asked by Crown counsel simply repeated the opinion of that other expert. He did not adopt that opinion as supportive of his views and as an opinion with which he agreed. Thus the opinion of an expert who was not called as a witness was put before the jury. That was an error.[43]

7.9.7 Deal with any Weaknesses

It is always recommended that, if there are any weaknesses in an expert's opinion, counsel should deal with them during direct examination, when he or she is in control, rather than have opposing counsel expose them during cross-examination. Direct examination allows the expert to explain these areas, rather than have to meet with criticism during cross-examination. It is also during the direct examination that counsel should

---

41 Steven Lubet refers to this technique as "the concept of consensus", *supra*, note 9.
42 (1982), 1 C.C.C. (3d) 416 (B.C. C.A.).
43 *Ibid.*, at 419.

deal with any questions or concerns that the trier of fact may have. For example, in a case where the plaintiff is complaining about chronic pain or a pain condition unsupported by objective evidence, the trier of fact may be concerned about whether the expert was misled as to the plaintiff's injuries, especially where there are conflicting views in the medical community as to the basis of such complaints. Counsel should elicit such information to satisfy the trier of fact that the expert has not been misled by the plaintiff, and is in fact providing an opinion which is objective and based on medical findings. Roger Oatley, in his article "Objectives of Examination-in-Chief of the Plaintiff's Chronic Pain Expert"[44] provides an excellent illustration on how to deal with such concerns on a direct examination:

> Q. Doctor, in the course of reaching your opinion did you examine this x-ray?
> A. Yes I did. Joan's family doctor provided it to me and I looked at it when I assessed Joan last February.
> Q. Why was it ordered?
> A. It was ordered by Dr. Smith, Joan's family doctor, when he was trying to diagnose the source of the continuing pain and headaches.
> Q. What does it show us please, doctor?
> A. It shows us that the source of the pain must be injured soft tissues — the ligaments, nerves and muscles around the bones which we see on the x-ray.
> Q. Because this may be important doctor, would you please show us on the x-ray where these soft tissues are located?
> A. (doctor points to x-ray)
> Q. If I give you back our spine doctor, please show us where these soft tissues are located on the spine?
> A. (doctor refers to anatomical aid)
> Q. Doctor, why don't we see those soft tissues on the x-ray?
> A. None of our radiographic imaging techniques are so precise that soft tissues can be demonstrated. But it doesn't mean that they aren't there. We know they are there. Whether you use an x-ray, or its more sophisticated cousins, the CT scan, the MRI, the SPECT scan — the limitations are essentially the same. I expect that one day we'll have better imaging techniques, but we don't today.
> Q. If you can't see the soft tissues, doctor, why do you say the x-ray shows us they are injured?
> A. I know the basis of the patient's history and my objective examination that she is in pain, that her functioning is markedly impaired, and that she has suffered some sort of physical injury in this region of her body. This x-ray shows me on this basis that the soft tissues have been injured because I can see no bony injury.

---

44 *Supra*, note 31, at 193.

7.9.8 End on a Powerful Note

Counsel should try to end the expert's testimony in the manner it began, namely with a concise summary of the expert's opinion.

7.10 CROSS-EXAMINATION OF EXPERTS[45]

Lawyers often find the task of cross-examining an ordinary witness a daunting one. However, when the witness under cross-examination is an expert, the exercise is perhaps one of the most challenging tasks faced by any advocate.

Counsel can produce an effective cross-examination of an expert as long as he or she appreciates the purpose and techniques of cross-examination. It goes without saying that it is impossible to conduct an effective cross-examination without extensive preparation.

7.11 PURPOSES OF CROSS-EXAMINATION

Leading writers on trial advocacy, such as Thomas A. Moore,[46] Roger Salhany[47] and Thomas Mauet,[48] agree that there are two main purposes to cross-examination. The first is to elicit favourable testimony from the witness, and the second is to weaken the other side's case by discrediting the witness's testimony. In most cases, the best a counsel can achieve from a cross-examination of an expert is to elicit favourable testimony from the witness. Most leading trial authors acknowledge that it is difficult to "destroy" the expert's testimony. As Harvey Weitz suggests:

> Counsel need not "destroy" the expert's testimony (an unlikely event in any case) so long as he/she at least demonstrates disagreement with the opinions advanced or even distrust of the expert himself (e.g., through collateral impeachment). At a minimum cross-examination will provide the jury some reason for disregarding or disbelieving the expert or his testimony.[49]

---

45 The author wishes to acknowledge the assistance of Mr. John Nelligan of Nelligan Power; Mr. David Scott of Scott & Aylen; Mr. Adrian Hewitt of Hewitt Nesbitt Reid; Mr. Kenneth Radnoff of Radnoff Pearl Slover Swedko Dwoskin and Mr. Garret Cooligan of Cooligan Ryan in the preparation of this section of the book.

46 Thomas A. Moore, Cross-Examining the Defense Expert (May 1991) Trial at 49-52.

47 Roger Salhany, *Cross-Examination: The Art of the Advocate* rev. ed. (Toronto: Butterworths, 1991).

48 *Supra*, note 1.

49 Harvey Weitz "Cross-Examining the Expert at Trial" (February 1992) Trial at 55-58.

Writers on advocacy often suggest that when conducting a cross-examination one should always first try to elicit favourable testimony. Mauet, Casswell, Macdonald write:

> While you may utilize only one of the approaches with some witnesses, you should always consider eliciting favourable testimony from the witness before you attempt a destructive cross-examination. Why this order? At the end of the direct examination, most witnesses will have testified in a plausible fashion and their credibility will be high. The witness' inherent distrust of the cross-examiner will be minimal. This is the time to extract favourable admissions and information from the witness, since the witness' credibility will enhance the impact of the admissions. Such admissions will have less impact, and be less likely to occur, if you have previously attacked the witness.[50]

7.12 PREPARATION FOR THE CROSS-EXAMINATION OF AN EXPERT

When preparing to cross-examine an expert one has to ensure that thorough preparation has been undertaken. Counsel should never overlook the opportunity to use his or her own expert to assist with the preparation of the cross-examination of the opponent's expert. Consider the following preparation that may be required:

1. *Know the case:* Personal injury actions are complicated. Counsel needs to fully understand the facts and issues within the case. An effective cross-examination cannot be conducted where counsel does not fully appreciate the facts and the injuries that the plaintiff may have sustained. Most importantly, counsel should be guided at all times by the theory of the case when preparing and planning for the cross-examination of an expert.
2. *Know the area in which the expert opinion is offered:* To be able to conduct an effective cross-examination, counsel needs to know the area in which the expert is going to provide his or her opinion. While legal counsel are not skilled in the science of medicine, they are trained to test evidence given by witnesses. Therefore, it is expected that counsel will be knowledgeable enough to test the opinion of the expert. It is recommended that, to start, counsel read a generally accepted text on the injuries that the plaintiff has sustained in order to obtain a broad understanding of the area in which expertise is being offered. The counsel's own expert should also assist by directing counsel to more specific texts and literature and by educating counsel

---

50 *Supra*, note 1, at 203.

as to the area in which the opinion is sought. Knowing what the leading authorities say about a particular injury is very useful during a cross-examination, especially where the expert is providing an opinion that is not in the mainstream. It is important to acknowledge that counsel cannot obtain the level of knowledge that the expert possesses. This is understandable given that the expert has spent years studying and practising in his or her field. What counsel must ensure is that he or she knows as much, if not more, about the narrow area that concerns the case.

3. *Know who the expert is:* As with your own expert witness, careful examination should also be made of the opposing expert's curriculum vitae. Examine his or her education, continuing education, professional qualifications, and professional experience. The opposing expert may have a very impressive curriculum vitae, but if he or she has no qualifications or experience in the area where the expert testimony is being offered, then this would be a fertile ground for cross-examination. Counsel's own expert will not only be a valuable resource in discovering the weaknesses in the opponent's expert evidence, but will also be of assistance in exposing any weaknesses in the qualifications of the opposing expert.

4. *Examine the expert's prior publications:* Before counsel retains his or her own expert, counsel is well advised to review the expert's publications to ensure that the opinion will in no way be contradicted by previous publications or previous testimony. The same exercise must be undertaken with the opposing expert. Such information, if shared with a trier of fact, may help undermine the reliability of the opposing expert.

5. *Examine the expert's opinion:* Counsel should, with the assistance of his or her own expert, examine the opposing expert's opinion, and determine what the theory behind the opinion is; how the expert arrived at this opinion, and why. It is necessary to examine the factual basis of the opinion, and to consider whether the factual basis is flawed in any respect. If the opinion is seriously flawed, then counsel may have the opportunity to successfully challenge the opposing expert's opinion.

6. *Hypothetical question:* If the expert provides an opinion based on a hypothetical question, then this provides counsel with the opportunity to either attack the hypothetical question, or to put a more favourable version of the hypothetical question to the expert. This is a great opportunity for counsel to fashion a hypothetical question which supports counsel's version of the facts, and the theory of his or her case. Obtaining the assistance of one's own expert in eliciting the appropriate hypothetical question is recommended.

7. *Listen to the expert's direct-examination:* Preparation for the cross-examination of an opposing expert does not end when the trial commences; rather, it continues right up to the time that the first question is put to the expert on cross-examination. During the direct examination of an opposing expert, counsel should carefully listen to the opposing expert's opinion. A comparison should be made of the opinion offered and of the expert's written opinion. It may be that, if the expert misinterpreted a critical fact, or made an erroneous assumption, this may influence the strength of the expert's final opinion. It is always a good idea to have your own expert at the counsel desk assisting with the cross-examination of a critical opposing expert.
8. *Plan the cross-examination:* Counsel should plan the cross-examination. After researching the background of the expert, and analyzing the expert's opinion, counsel should design a plan for the cross-examination. Counsel must determine what areas, if any, of the expert's opinion need to be examined, and determine what approach should be taken on the cross-examination. Counsel should establish specific goals with respect to the cross-examination of each opposing expert so as to develop an appropriate plan for challenging the expert.

7.13 AREAS OF CHALLENGE ON CROSS-EXAMINATION

Counsel should never challenge the expert's conclusions directly. To do so is to risk providing the expert with an opportunity to disagree, and expound on the reasons why. Ian Blue expresses this caution:

> Never attack an expert's opinion directly. Always attack qualifications, assumptions, methodology, data limitations, certainty of conclusions and matters of professional debate. An expert will never concede that a conclusion is correct. Trying to obtain such a concession results only in protestations about the opinion's validity.[51]

There are several areas in which the expert's opinion can be challenged. Consider the following:

1. *Challenge the expert's credentials*—If the expert has limited credentials to provide an opinion in the area sought, then this should be exposed on cross-examination. For a successful cross-examination in this area, Mauet[52] suggests the following technique:

   > The cross-examination technique is to build up the witness' real expertise,

---

51 Ian A. Blue, "Cross-Examining the Expert" (1986) Adv. Q. 13 at 19.
52 *Supra*, note 1.

then show that this particular expertise is not directly applicable to the type of case on trial.

2. *Challenge the factual assumptions*—One way to attack an expert's opinion is by challenging the factual assumptions that he or she made in arriving at the opinion. If the expert took account of irrelevant facts, wrongly interpreted certain facts or failed, for example, to take account of certain facts, such as the plaintiff's complete medical history, then this gives the trier of fact reason to reject the expert's testimony. Cross-examination to test the basis of the expert opinion was approved by the Supreme Court of Canada in the *R. v. Howard* decision, where Mr. Justice Lamer wrote:

> Indeed, I agree with those judgments as they support the proposition that a cross-examination may be conducted to determine whether what the expert considered was relevant, whether there are matters relevant that were not considered and, of course, whether the expert might have arrived at his conclusion as *a result* of considerations irrelevant to his particular expertise. An expert may obviously be cross-examined to that effect, that is, whether relevant facts were ignored or disregarded, and whether irrelevant facts were taken into account, but only irrelevant facts supportive of the conclusion arrived at.[53]

If the expert witness has provided an opinion on the basis of an hypothetical question then this is counsel's opportunity to show that if the facts had changed, the expert's opinion would also be different. For example:

> Q. Dr. Green you offered your opinion based on the facts presented in the hypothetical question?
> A. Yes.
> Q. So if the facts were different from those presented in the hypothetical question, your opinion may differ?
> A. Yes.
> Q. Let's assume . . .

At this stage, counsel should present a hypothetical question which supports the counsel's version of the facts and the theory of his or her case.

3. *Challenge the methodology of the expert*—Witnesses who, for example, are experts in the field of psychology, such as neuropsychology and rehabilitation psychology, are often faced with a situation where

---

53 69 C.R. (3d) 193 at 202, [1989] 1 S.C.R. 1337.

there may be no general consensus in the community as to what psychological tests are reliable indicators. Also, there is often the concern that, even where experts conduct the same test, they arrive at different conclusions because of the different interpretation given to the test results. Counsel who are well prepared and knowledgeable about the tests that are required in order to arrive at an opinion are at an advantage during cross-examination in those areas. This is the opportunity for counsel to show that the expert's tests are not favoured by leading authorities, or that the interpretation of the expert is incorrect.

4. *Failure to take into account other factors*—After a traumatic event such as a motor vehicle accident, some victims develop post-traumatic stress disorders, or major depression, or various chronic pain disorders. In such cases, the question arises as to whether or not the expert ruled out other possible causes for a disorder. For example, counsel could challenge an expert's finding that the person developed post-traumatic stress following a motor vehicle accident by disclosing that, in fact, that person underwent a traumatic experience both before or at some date after the motor vehicle accident. The object is to consider whether the expert's opinion may be undermined by failure to consider other possible causes that might explain the plaintiff's complaints. If on cross-examination counsel can elicit from the expert that the plaintiff's complaints may also be due to such other causes, then counsel has made some headway towards discrediting that expert's opinion.

5. *Leading authorities do not support the expert's opinion*—One way to discredit an expert witness is to show that the expert's opinion contradicts leading authorities. The Supreme Court of Canada in *R. v. Marquard*[54] set down the proper procedure to be followed when examining an expert witness on another expert's work. The process was described by Madam Justice McLachlin as follows:

> The proper procedure to be followed in examining an expert witness on other expert opinions found in papers or books is to ask the witness if she knows the work. If the answer is "no," or if the witness denies the work's authority, that is the end of the matter. Counsel cannot read from the work, since that would be to introduce it as evidence. If the answer is "yes", and the witness acknowledges the work's authority, then the witness has confirmed it by the witness's own testimony. Parts of it may be read to the witness, and to the extent they are confirmed, they become evidence in the case.[55]

---

54 [1993] 4 S.C.R. 223, 25 C.R. (4th) 1.
55 *Ibid.*, at (S.C.R.) 251.

Where an expert acknowledges the work as authoritative, and a divergence of views between the expert's opinion and the leading authorities is thereby exposed, then this may lead the trier of fact to conclude that the expert's opinion should not be accepted. Take, for example, the case in *R. v. Olscamp*[56] where the Crown introduced the expert opinion to suggest that the general behavioural and psychological characteristics of child victims of sexual abuse were exhibited by the complainant and, were therefore, consistent with sexual abuse. The defence, during cross-examination, put to the expert articles written by other experts who confirmed that there is in fact little scientific evidence to enable one to identify a child who has been sexually abused. The court relied on opposing views in the articles to reject the opinion of the expert introduced by the Crown. Where an expert denies knowledge of leading work then this allows counsel to submit, in closing arguments, that the fact that this expert was unfamiliar with the leading authorities reflects a lack of expertise.

6. *Challenge the credibility of an expert*—The more credible an expert witness, the more likely that the trier of fact will accept the expert's opinion. When counsel decides to challenge the expert's opinion on this ground, he or she should be careful to ensure that the trier of fact does not view counsel as harassing or abusing the expert witness. To challenge an expert on this ground requires careful planning. The expert's credibility can be attacked on any one of the following grounds:

- the expert is biased;
- the expert has a financial gain in the outcome of the trial;
- the expert always provides the opinion for the same counsel or for one particular side; or
- the expert was paid an inordinate amount of money for the opinion offered.

7.14 TECHNIQUES OF CROSS-EXAMINATION

The first question that counsel should address is whether the opponent's expert witness should be cross-examined at all. In most cases, it is very difficult to get away without cross-examining the opposing expert witness. Harvey Weitz suggests that it is the rare instance where counsel does not take the opportunity to cross-examine an expert witness:

> Counsel cannot simply rely on his own expert as a counterweight; if such were the case, why not just flip a coin? — best two out of three wins. The

---

56 (1994), 35 C.R. (4th) 37 (Ont. Gen. Div.).

jury wants, and in fact needs, to see counsel challenge contrary opinions. Not only does the failure to challenge an opponent's expert lend tacit support to defendant's claim but it also provides opposing counsel with devastating ammunition for summation.[57]

Counsel should also be aware of the infamous rule in *Browne v. Dunn*,[58] namely that if one intends to call evidence later that contradicts a witness' testimony on a material point, then one should cross-examine the witness on that material point so that the witness has an opportunity to explain.

Consider the following techniques of cross-examination when cross-examining an expert witness:

1. *Ask the questions to which an answer is known*—This rule is very often broken by counsel, primarily because counsel feel that they simply must cross-examine and, therefore, end up asking questions to which they do not know the answer. When cross-examining an expert this rule should be complied with, otherwise counsel may unwittingly fortify the expert opinion of the opposing party. There may be some situations where counsel may be able to ask the question to which an answer is unknown, if counsel is not concerned about the response provided. However, such situations are likely to be rare.

2. *Be in control*—It is very easy to lose control when cross-examining an expert. An expert has extensive knowledge and experience in the field in which he or she is testifying. It is familiar ground. Counsel should maintain control by asking simple leading questions which keep the expert under control. A leading question suggests a particular answer. By asking such leading questions, counsel can dictate the areas of focus. It is a mistake for counsel to use technical and complicated questions, as this may not only confuse the trier of fact, but it may also give the expert the opportunity to provide further explanation supporting their own opinion. The expert can quickly seize the opportunity and take control.

3. *Maintain respect*—It is important to remember that the expert on the stand is a professional and should be afforded the appropriate respect.

4. *Listen to the expert*—This seems very basic, but in most cases counsel who conduct a poor cross-examination are those who fail to listen to the answers supplied by the witness. One of the reasons why this happens is because counsel is not thinking about what the witness is going to say, but is more concerned about what the next question will be. This rule is probably more important when cross-examining an expert, since counsel should be paying close attention to any inconsis-

---

57 "Cross-examining the Expert at Trial", *supra*, note 49.
58 (1893), 6 R. 67 (U.K. H.L.).

tencies in the expert's opinion and listening for any signs of equivocation or qualification in the testimony. Also, if counsel is not careful, the expert may make a comment which supports his or her opinion, which may not be addressed in subsequent cross-examination.

5. *Do not repeat the direct examination*—The biggest mistake that counsel make is to ask the expert to repeat his or her opinion. One of the purposes of cross-examination is to elicit testimony that supports one's theory of the case, not that of the opponent.
6. *Once you obtain favourable testimony, do not have the expert repeat it*— It is very easy to get excited when counsel elicits favourable testimony when cross-examining an expert witness. However, the moment of excitement can soon be lost if counsel repeats the favourable testimony, or has the expert repeat it, because then the expert is provided with an opportunity to explain. It is wiser to avoid this scenario. Counsel will have ample opportunity to repeat such favourable testimony during closing argument.
7. *Never argue with the witness*—This rule should always be respected when cross-examining an expert witness. It should be borne in mind that this particular witness is an expert who purports to be fully knowledgeable in the area in which the opinion is offered. Should counsel argue with an expert, it is very likely that counsel will lose the argument and, also, that the trier of fact will not be favourably disposed to the argument or counsel.
8. *End on a powerful note*—To make the cross-examination effective, the lawyer should ensure that the cross-examination ends on a winning note.

7.15 CONCLUSION

Preparation is the secret to the successful outcome of a litigation. It is ill advised to underestimate the appropriate time required to prepare an expert witness. In some cases, expert witnesses may not be willing to invest a large amount of their time in preparing for trial. Should that be the case, counsel should instruct the expert that, without the proper preparation, the expert's testimony may not be as helpful as was hoped, and the expert may be attacked or discredited while giving evidence. If counsel is successful in presenting the expert's opinion in a persuasive manner, and the expert witness has been thoroughly prepared for cross-examination, then the expert witness will have served his or her function.

Chapter 8

Head Injury

by Howard Lesiuk, M.D., F.R.C.P.C.

8.1 Introduction
8.2 Anatomy of the Brain and its Coverings
    8.2.1 The Skull
    8.2.2 Meninges (Coverings of the Brain)
        8.2.2.1 Introduction
        8.2.2.2 Dura Mater
        8.2.2.3 Arachnoid Mater
        8.2.2.4 Pia Mater
    8.2.3 The Brain
        8.2.3.1 Divisions of the Brain
            8.2.3.1.1 Introduction
        8.2.3.2 The Cellular Foundation of Neuroanatomy
            8.2.3.2.1 Introduction
            8.2.3.2.2 The Neuron
            8.2.3.2.3 Neuroglia
        8.2.3.3 The Cerebral Hemispheres
            8.2.3.3.1 Introduction
            8.2.3.3.2 Frontal Lobe
            8.2.3.3.3 Parietal Lobe
            8.2.3.3.4 Temporal Lobe
            8.2.3.3.5 Occipital Lobe
            8.2.3.3.6 Basal Ganglia
        8.2.3.4 The Diencephalon
            8.2.3.4.1 Thalamus
            8.2.3.4.2 Hypothalamus
            8.2.3.4.3 Subthalamus and Epithalamus
        8.2.3.5 The Brainstem
        8.2.3.6 The Cerebellum
    8.2.4 Blood Vessels of the Brain
        8.2.4.1 Arteries of the Brain
        8.2.4.2 Veins of the Brain
    8.2.5 The Ventricles of the Brain

8.3 Epidemiology of Head Injury
8.4 Pathophysiology of Head Injury
    8.4.1 Introduction
    8.4.2 Impact (Primary) Injuries
        8.4.2.1 Scalp Injuries
        8.4.2.2 Skull Fracture
            8.4.2.2.1 Classification
            8.4.2.2.2 Linear Skull Fractures
            8.4.2.2.3 Depressed Skull Fractures
            8.4.2.2.4 Basal Skull Fractures
        8.4.2.3 Cerebral Concussion
        8.4.2.4 Grey Matter Contusions
        8.4.2.5 Diffuse Brain Injury
    8.4.3 Secondary Injuries
        8.4.3.1 Intracranial Haematoma
            8.4.3.1.1 Epidural Haematoma
            8.4.3.1.2 Acute Subdural Haematoma
            8.4.3.1.3 Chronic Subdural Haematoma
            8.4.3.1.4 Traumatic Subarachnoid Hemorrhage
            8.4.3.1.5 Intracerebral Haematoma
        8.4.3.2 Raised Intracranial Pressure
            8.4.3.2.1 Introduction and Definitions
            8.4.3.2.2 Consequences of Raised Intracranial Pressure
                Ischemia
                Brain Shift and Herniation
                Cingulate Herniation
                Lateral Transtentorial (Uncal) Herniation
                Central Transtentorial Herniation
8.5 Acute Evaluation of the Head-Injured Patient
    8.5.1 Introduction
    8.5.2 History and Physical Examination
    8.5.3 Diagnostic Imaging
8.6 Acute Management of Severe Head Injuries
    8.6.1 Introduction
    8.6.2 Initial Resuscitation
    8.6.3 Overall Management Goals
    8.6.4 Intracranial Pressure Monitoring
        8.6.4.1 Introduction
        8.6.4.2 Indications for Monitoring
        8.6.4.3 Choice of Monitor
    8.6.5 Additional Monitoring Techniques

             8.6.5.1 Transcranial Doppler
             8.6.5.2 Jugular Venous Oxygen Saturation Monitoring
      8.6.6 Treatment of Elevated Intracranial Pressure
             8.6.6.1 Guideline for Initiating Treatment
             8.6.6.2 Specific Therapeutic Measures
                      8.6.6.2.1 Introduction
                      8.6.6.2.2 Sedation, Analgesia, and Neuromuscular Blockade
                      8.6.6.2.3 Head Elevation
                      8.6.6.2.4 CSF Drainage
                      8.6.6.2.5 Hyperventilation
                      8.6.6.2.6 Mannitol
                      8.6.6.2.7 Barbiturates
                      8.6.6.2.8 Corticosteroids
                      8.6.6.2.9 Anti-seizure Prophylaxis
8.7 Selected Special Topics in Head Injury
      8.7.1 Cerebral Concussion
             8.7.1.1 Introduction
             8.7.1.2 Definitions
             8.7.1.3 Immediate On Scene ("Sideline") Evaluation
             8.7.1.4 Management Recommendations
      8.7.2 Brain Death
             8.7.2.1 Introduction
             8.7.2.2 Guidelines
Figures

8.1 INTRODUCTION

The appropriate management of a head-injured patient is based on an understanding of the normal structure, or anatomy, of the central nervous system, the normal function, or physiology, of the central nervous system, and the derangements of normal structure and function, that is, pathology and pathophysiology, that are the direct consequences of head injury. It is therefore essential to begin this chapter by providing a review of normal anatomy and physiology of the brain and environs before proceeding to a discussion of head injury and its management.

8.2 ANATOMY OF THE BRAIN AND ITS COVERINGS

8.2.1 The Skull

For its protection, the brain is encased in a bony vault, the skull. The skull not only provides a case for the brain but also provides cavities for the special sense organs (sight, hearing, smell, taste, and balance). It also provides openings for the passage of air and food.

The skull consists of a series of bones, most of which are united at immovable joints termed sutures. The bones of the skull may be divided into the bones of the cranial cavity, and the bones of the face and nasal cavities. The bones of the cranial cavity include the paired parietal and temporal bones as well as the frontal, occipital, sphenoid, and ethmoid bones [Figures 1 and 2]. The bones of the face and nasal cavities include the maxilla, zygoma, palatine, nasal, lacrimal, inferior concha, vomer, and mandibular bones [Figures 1 and 2].

8.2.2 Meninges (Coverings of the Brain)

8.2.2.1 Introduction

The brain (like the spinal cord) is a very delicate structure remarkably susceptible to injury, with a limited capacity for self-repair. It needs great protection. For this reason, in addition to being encased in a bony vault, it is covered by a series of three membranes or meninges, which incorporate a fluid cushion. The outermost membrane, called the dura mater ("hard mother"), is a leathery fibrous covering much thicker than the delicate membranes which lie beneath it. For this reason it is known as the thick membrane or pachymeninx. The innermost membrane, the pia mater ("pious or faithful mother," so named because it faithfully follows every contour of the brain), is a thin translucent membrane of tissue tightly adherent to the surface of the brain that precisely follows each brain contour. Between the dura and the pia, is the arachnoid mater ("spider like mother" because of its delicate, reticular, web-like structure). The arachnoid mater and pia mater are both composed of thin translucent fibers and are known collectively as the thin membranes or leptomeninges. Unlike the pia, the arachnoid skips over the grooves (sulci) of the brain.

8.2.2.2 Dura Mater

The dura consists of an inner and an outer layer, with the outer (periosteo) layer tightly adherent to the inner surface of the skull rich in blood vessels and nerves. There is an inner meningeal layer of dura. In various places within the skull the two layers become separated by large venous channels known as the dural venous sinuses, which provide the major pathways for drainage of venous blood out of the brain [Figure 3]. The inner layer of the dura features four inwardly projecting folds: the falx cerebri, the falx cerebelli, the tentorium cerebelli, and the diaphragma sellae. These folds subdivide the bony cranial vault into compartments that communicate with each other [Figure 4].

The dura mater, or dura for short, is normally tightly adherent to the inner surface of the skull. In situations of injury, the meningeal blood vessels travelling through the dura can become lacerated. This can result in bleeding into the potential space between the dura and the inner surface of the skull, which strips the dura away from the inner surface of the skull and results in accumulation of a blood clot known as an epidural or extradural haematoma.

The combination of the shape of the base of the skull and the enfolding of the dura serves to divide the cranial vault into three compartments known as the anterior cranial fossa, middle cranial fossa, and posterior cranial fossa [Figure 4B].

8.2.2.3 Arachnoid Mater

The arachnoid is adjacent but not adherent to the inner surface of the dura. This creates a second potential space that can accumulate blood clots in situations of trauma. This space between the inner surface of the dura and the outer surface of the arachnoid is known as the subdural space. The arachnoid itself consists of an outer layer adjacent to the dura which is separated from the pia mater which is tightly adherent to the outer surface of the brain itself. Between the arachnoid and the pia is a space known as the subarachnoid space. This space is normally filled with cerebral spinal fluid (CSF). The subarachnoid space is bridged by a web-like meshwork of arachnoid fibers known as the arachnoid trabeculae, which give the arachnoid its name. There is free flow of CSF around and between the arachnoidal trabeculae [Figure 5].

8.2.2.4 Pia Mater

The pia intimately follows the brain surface. Any blood vessel penetrating the brain surface is surrounded by a pial cuff. This further anchors the pia and makes it for practical purposes undetachable from the brain.

8.2.3 The Brain

8.2.3.1 Divisions of the Brain

8.2.3.1.1 Introduction: During embryonic development, the brain and spinal cord are formed from a primitive tubular structure known as the neural tube. The cells, which are to form the nervous system, surround a small central canal that is filled with cerebrospinal fluid. In the spinal cord, this rather primitive arrangement of nervous system tissue surrounding a small central fluid-filled cavity persists throughout life. However, at the head end, where the brain will form, the tubular structure first develops three primary fluid filled expansions or vesicles. From top to bottom, these are known as the prosencephalon or forebrain vesicle, mesencephalon or mid-brain vesicle, and rhombencephalon or hindbrain vesicle. The fluid-filled cavities of these vesicles are destined to develop into the cerebrospinal fluid-forming ventricular system of the adult brain. The embryonic brain tissues surrounding these fluid filled cavities are destined to divide, migrate, and specialize to form the structures that constitute the adult brain. The prosencephalon develops into a telencephalon or endbrain and a diencephalon or interbrain. The telencephalon further develops into the large paired cerebral hemispheres that constitute the bulk of brain tissue in the adult. The diencephalon comes to lie deep in the centre of the brain surrounded by the cerebral hemispheres. The mesencephalon remains a relatively simple structure and gives rise to the midbrain. The rhombencephalon develops into a metencephalon, which gives rise to the pons, a myelencephalon that gives rise to the medulla oblongata, and the cerebellum. The midbrain, pons, and medulla, taken together, constitute what anatomists refer to as the brain stem. As the nerve tissue is developing, the ventricular system filled with cerebral spinal fluid and lying deep within the brain structures is similarly developing. The paired lateral ventricles are formed deep within the cerebral hemispheres from the cavity of the paleencephalon. The third ventricle forms from the cavity of the diencephalon. The fourth ventricle forms from the cavity arising from the rhombencephalon and is thus associated with the brain stem. The final adult relationships of these divisions of the central nervous system are summarized in Figure 6.

8.2.3.2 The Cellular Foundation of Neuroanatomy

8.2.3.2.1 Introduction: As in all biologic structures, the basic building block of the central nervous system is the cell. There are several varieties of cells that make up the central nervous system. Most well known to the general public are the neurons whose complex interconnections and cell-to-cell communication capabilities form the basis of nervous system function. Less well known are the supporting cells of the nervous system, called glia, which include astrocytes, oligodendroglia, and microglia. These cells provide scaffolding and maintenance functions necessary to normal nervous system activity. Lastly there are a variety of other cellular types such as the appendimal cells that line the ventricles, the endothelia cells, muscle fibers, and connective tissue cells that make up the blood vessels, and a variety of cells that make up the meningeal coverings of the brain.

8.2.3.2.2 The Neuron: Neurons are very different from other cell types being characterized by their specialization for conduction of impulses, their sensitivity to oxygen deprivation, and the ominous fact that with rare exceptions, they cannot divide to provide replacement cells when damage occurs.

A generic neuron is composed of a cell body, containing the nucleus and a variety of metabolic machinery, which produces the fuel and the chemicals necessary to support the neurons signalling activity. The most striking feature of neurons however, is the specialized elongated processes extending upward and away from the cell bodies that neurons have developed to receive stimuli from other neurons and in turn send stimuli to other neurons. Those processes that are primarily concerned with receiving stimuli from surrounding neurons are referred to as dendrites. They tend to be multiple and relatively short. Axons are generally concerned with transmission of a stimulus to another nerve cell. Their length can be extremely variable ranging from a few microns to more than a meter. A schematic of a generic neuron is shown in Figure 7.

The site of contact between the process of one neuron and a second neuron is known as a synapse. Information is transmitted between neurons at synapses. Each neuron may synapse with up to thousands of other neurons. At a synapse rather than simple conduction of an electrical impulse from one neuron to another, there is a unique and more complicated method of conveying the signal. When the electrical impulse reaches the synaptic portion of the transmitting neuron, it causes the release of a chemical substance into the synapse. The chemical substance is called a neurotransmitter. There are hundreds of different types of neurotransmitter chemicals. The neurotransmitter chemical travels across the synapse to the receiving neuron membrane. There it interacts with a receptor molecule in the membrane. When it binds to the receptor molecule, it causes a change internally in the receiving neuron that can either tend to produce or inhibit the production of electrical signals within the receiving neuron. In this way, the information sharing between neurons can be much more complicated and varied and a simple binary on/off signal.

The axons of nearly all neurons are covered with a fatty white substance called myelin. This may be crudely thought of as a form of insulation for the axon. The myelin greatly enhances the speed at which electrical signals can travel down the axon.

8.2.3.2.3 Neuroglia: Neuroglia or glial cells outnumber the neurons by almost 10:1 within the nervous system.

Astrocytes or astroglia are named because of their star-shaped appearance with certain types of chemical stains under the microscope. They have many processes extending from their cell bodies. Astrocytes are thought to be involved with four basic supporting functions: structural scaffolding, scar formation as part of the limited repair process that takes place following injury, assistance in isolating synaptic junctions from each other, and a major contribution to the so-called blood brain barrier. Given the delicate balance of body salts and other chemicals that are necessary to the maintenance of proper nervous system signalling, it is perhaps not surprising that there is very restricted access to the nervous system by substances travelling in the blood stream. This greatly restricted access is referred to as the blood brain barrier. It is created by several factors. One factor is that the small capillary blood vessels of the brain do not have the usual pores between the cells that make up the capillaries. These pores, found in capillaries elsewhere in the body, are responsible for the free passage of many substances out of the blood stream and into the surrounding tissue. This is not allowed to take place in the brain. In addition, astrocyte processes surround and envelope the capillaries providing a second line of defense against unwanted substances getting into the nervous system.

Oligodendroglias are named for their relative lack of processes. Oligodendroglias are responsible for producing and maintaining the myelin insulation that surrounds the axons of neurons.

Microglia are scavenging janitorial cells that migrate into areas of injury to ingest, digest, and remove damaged material.

8.2.3.3 The Cerebral Hemispheres

8.2.3.3.1 Introduction: The average adult brain weighs approximately 1400 grams constituting about 2% of the total body weight. It has a gelatinous consistency. The largest component of the brain is formed by the two large cerebral hemispheres, which are illustrated from their outside or lateral surface in Figure 8, and from a mid-line viewpoint in Figure 9. As can be seen from these figures, the surface of the brain is not smooth, but rather is convoluted into elevations know as gyri and depressions known as sulci or fissures. These convolutions are a means of increasing the effective surface area of the brain. This is important to increase the size of the cerebral cortex. The cerebral cortex is the outer layer of so called gray matter, which contains the cell bodies of the cortical neurons that are the basis of most of the more complex functions of the nervous system. This layer of gray matter is several millimeters thick. Underneath it lies the so-called white matter. It is white because of the myelin covering the nerve fibers projecting from the neuron cell bodies of the cortex. Thus to summarize, the cortex contains cell bodies and the white matter contains the insulated fibers that interconnect the cell bodies. The cerebral hemispheres also contain deep collections of cell bodies that are not visible on the surface. These are known as the basal ganglia, which can be thought of as areas that provide preprogrammed subroutines for rapid coordinated motor activity.

There are several consistent sulci or grooves that are used by anatomists and physicians to subdivide the cerebral hemisphere into frontal, parietal, occipital, and temporal lobes. The lobes are named in relation to the bones of the skull that overlie them, although the correspondence is not exact. Thus we have frontal, parietal, occipital, and temporal lobes of the brain. The most prominent grooves that aid in making the division on the brain surface, are the central sulcus of Rolando, which divides the frontal from the parietal lobe, and the lateral sulcus of Sylvius, which divides the frontal and, to a lesser extent, the parietal lobe from the temporal lobe. Both of these grooves are illustrated in Figure 8, which also includes a crude sketch outlining the lobe divisions.

Different nervous system activities are localized in different areas of the cortical surface. For example, visual information is initially processed in areas of the occipital lobe, where as in contrast the most posterior (closest to the back) portion of the frontal lobe controls motor (muscular) activity. Some areas of the brain surface have quite well understood and characterized functions whereas the function of other areas is much more nebulous, obscure, and poorly understood. Our understanding has been best for those functions that can be modelled on the basis of a simple circuit diagram with a few neurons with limited, clear-cut, well-defined connections to a few other neurons. This type of circuit model works quite well for modelling many aspects of the motor control system or the basic sensory reception system. However, many areas of brain function defy analysis on the basis of simple circuit modelling. In these areas, everything appears to connect to everything else, forming an absolute maze of interconnections, and it is difficult to conceive how useful information transfer can take place. Some progress in recent years has been made in understanding this type of confusing meshwork in terms of information transfer in nonlinear, near-chaotic systems. A discussion of this is well beyond the scope of this chapter.

Neuroscientists have long known that sensory information tends to be received and processed in the more posterior or rearward portions of the nervous system, whereas motor control information tends to come from the more anterior or frontward portions of the nervous system. In addition, the vast majority of nerve pathways cross at some level of the nervous system (often in the brainstem). As a result of this, the right side of the brain tends to receive from and send to the left side of the body and vice versa. Lastly, information to and from the upper parts of the body are often distributed to areas lower on the cortical surface than information going to or from lower parts of the body. As a result of all these considerations, a useful, if somewhat ironic rule of thumb is that information processing in the nervous system takes place reversed: right for left, back to front, and upside down.

8.2.3.3.2 Frontal Lobe: The large frontal lobe makes up almost one-third of a cerebral hemisphere. The most well defined area of frontal lobe function occurs in the primary motor cortex, which is confined to the precentral gyrus just in front of the central sulcus of Rolando. The motor control neurons along this gyrus (known as the motor strip) are organized according to the distribution of their control with respect to the body. That is, all of the neurons that control the head are grouped together, those that control the hand are grouped together, and so on. The arrangement is such that one can draw out a rather distorted humanoid figure, termed a homunculus, over the surface of the motor strip, which illustrates the control areas in the body corresponding to a given area of motor strip [Figure 1A]. It is a rather distorted figure because those areas which need very fine and extensive motor control such as the face and hand, occupy much greater areas of the motor cortex than those areas which do not need much fine control such as the trunk of the body.

In front of this and other related motor areas is the frontal eye field, which contributes to coordinated eye movement.

In the dominant (for almost all right-handers and almost all left-handers the left) hemisphere, the motor speech area of Broca is located. This is just in front of the motor strip low in the frontal lobe just above the lateral fissure.

The most anterior aspects of the frontal lobe and its under surface have important but less well-defined functions concerning memory, emotion, and intellectual functions.

8.2.3.3.3 Parietal Lobe: The parietal lobe features two major areas. The first is a strip of cortex immediately behind the central sulcus that divides the parietal from the frontal lobe. It parallels the motor strip and has an analogous function for sensation. It is where the basic general sensations of touch, pain, temperature, and vibration receive their higher level processing. The sensory neurons of this cortical area are organized in a fashion analogous to the neurons of the motor strip; that is, there is an equivalent sensory homunculus.

Behind the primary sensory cortex is the sensory association cortex, which receives the input from the primary sensory cortex and integrates it with input from other areas including the visual cortex, auditory cortex and memory area. Damage in this region impairs the ability to recognize complex objects by feel alone. Neurologists test for this by drawing numbers in the palm of someone's hand. Ability to recognize the drawn number by feel is known as graphesthesia. Alternately, an object such as a key or pen may be placed in the hand to be identified by feel. The ability to do so is called stereognosis.

The parietal cortex in the dominant hemisphere also aids language processing, and damage to this area can lead to a variety of speech disturbances including difficulty naming objects and disturbances that may effect the ability to process written language as opposed to spoken language.

8.2.3.3.4 Temporal Lobe: The temporal lobes contain the primary auditory cortex in which higher processing of sound takes place. In addition, groups of neurons deep within the temporal lobe have important functions in memory and emotion. Most of the temporal circuitry tends to be duplicated on both sides of the brain, so that the consequences of damage on one side are far less severe than the consequences of damage on both sides.

There is, as in the other lobes, a dominant temporal lobe. This features speech reception areas adjacent to the primary hearing centers. Damage to these areas can prevent the understanding of words. The person may still be able to speak, but the speech output, although smooth and regular, may contain distorted or nonsense words.

8.2.3.3.5 Occipital Lobe: The occipital lobe is primarily concerned with visual processing, containing both the primary visual processing cortex and visual association cortex which further refines visual information and integrates it with other incoming sensory information as well as memory.

8.2.3.3.6 Basal Ganglia: These deep collections of gray matter (neuronal cell bodies) cannot be seen from the brain's surface and can only be visualized by cutting into the brain. The basal ganglia are among the areas with myriad connections to many other centres. Thus simple circuit analysis is of limited benefit in describing their function. They have great influence over motor activity, and disease or damage to these areas can produce tremors and other forms of uncontrolled or improperly controlled movement.

8.2.3.4 The Diencephalon

The diencephalon, or inner brain, is strategically located at the core of the cerebral hemispheres at the site where they are linked to the brain stem. Less than one-fortieth of the size of the cerebral hemispheres, the diencephalon contains many important motor and sensory links as well as control nuclei (collections of neurons) concerned with many basic body regulatory functions. Four regions of the diencephalon have been recognized and have been named the thalamus, subthalamus, hypothalamus, and epithalamus.

8.2.3.4.1 Thalamus: The thalamus is a compact but complex collection of nuclei (groups of neurons serving a common function). These nuclear groups relay information between the cerebral cortex and the rest of the nervous system (and thereby the rest of the body) as well as providing important coordinating and regulating activities to the function of the cerebral cortex.

The functions of the thalamus may be grouped into four basic roles:

1. As a sensory relay station. All sensations except smell are relayed to the cortex through the thalamus. The cortex in turn feeds back information to and through the thalamus. It is likely that conscious awareness of many sensations such as pain, touch, pressure, and temperature are achieved in the thalamus.
2. As a motor relay system.
3. A role in regulating general level of neural activity. The thalamus modulates sleep-wake cycles and normal cortical rhythms.
4. As a mediator of emotion, behaviour, and higher intellectual function.

8.2.3.4.2 Hypothalamus: This tiny 4-gram structure is the main control area for the subconscious, automatic regulation by the nervous system of the activity of internal organs such as the gastrointestinal tract, heart, and related organs, as well as for control of the bodies hormonal systems. To elaborate, the hypothalamus is the main control centre for both the sympathetic nervous system which induces a wide variety of responses that optimize the ability to respond to danger. For example, the pupils dilate to gather in more light, the heart beats faster, and respiration increases in depth and frequency. In contrast, the hypothalamus also regulates the parasympathetic nervous system, which is concerned with digestive and recuperative functions. Hypothalamic releasing factors control all of the major endocrine glands and are responsible for maintenance of an appropriate hormonal milieu. The hypothalamus directly releases antidiuretic hormones, which regulate the reabsorption of water by the kidneys. The hypothalamus contains centres that are concerned with both hunger and a feeling of fullness, so that it is important to eating behaviours. Temperature-regulating centres are also found in the hypothalamus, and injury to this area can be accompanied by erratic fluctuations in body temperature. The hypothalamus has a role in regulating sleep. The hypothalamus regulates cardiovascular function, affecting the heart rate and the amount of blood output from the heart, blood pressure, and respiration. Lastly, the hypothalamus has a role in expression of emotion. Emotions of fear and rage in particular are under the influence of hypothalamic nuclei.

8.2.3.4.3 Subthalamus and Epithalamus: The collection of nuclei referred to as the subthalamus is fundamentally concerned with motor control systems. That is, they have a role in regulating the coordinated activity of multiple muscle groups that is necessary to produce any complex and coordinated movement. Disorders of this area can result in uncoordinated and uncontrollable movements of various parts of the body.

The epithalamus consists of the pineal gland and the habenular nuclei. The pineal gland is a small cone-shaped structure lying just above the surface of the back of the midbrain. Its function has intrigued scientists and philosophers since antiquity. Descartes referred to the pineal as "The seat of the soul." In lower animals, the pineal has light receptors and is associated with changes in behaviour with day/night cycles. Even in man, it is speculated that the pineal may retain some influences over body rhythms that fluctuate with day/night cycles, monthly cycles, and seasonal cycles. In addition, the pineal secretes the hormone melatonin. This hormone is felt to trigger the body's time clock: making people sleep in the evening when it is time to go to bed. As such, it has been touted without conclusive proof as a treatment for jet lag. Practitioners of alternative medicine have suggested roles in aging, proper function of the immune system, and seasonal affective disorder.

The habenular nuclei link other areas of the diencephalon with the brain stem and appear to have some role in regulation of autonomic function.

8.2.3.5 The Brainstem

From top to bottom, the brainstem is made up of the midbrain, the pons and the medulla. These are in fact continuous with each other, as can be seen in Figure 9. They can be analyzed functionally as a unit.

Functionally the brainstem components may be divided into: cranial nerve nuclei, ascending pathways, descending pathways, the reticular formation, the unconscious proprioceptive system, and periventricular gray matter.

There are twelve paired cranial nerves (they are paired, as there is a left and right-sided nerve in each case). Two of the cranial nerves, the olfactory nerve (for smell) and the optic nerve (which carries visual information from the retina of the eye to the visual processing areas of the brain), arise from the cerebral hemispheres. The remaining ten arise from the brainstem. These cranial nerves do for the head and neck what the peripheral nerves coming out of the spinal cord do for the rest of the body. That is, they carry descending motor information from the brain to the muscles of the face and neck, ascending sensory information from the skin and deep structures of the head, face and neck, and autonomic information to the blood vessels and glands of the head and neck. In addition, two of the paired cranial nerves, the facial and glossopharyngeal nerves, carry taste from the tongue and the paired vestibulocochlear nerves carry hearing from the ear and balance and equilibrium information from the balance organs of the inner ear.

Also within the brainstem, tending to lie more towards the front of the brainstem, are descending motor fiber pathways. These carry motor control information coming from higher brain centres to be distributed to all of the rest of the body. Analogously, in the more rearward or posterior regions of the brainstem, lie ascending fiber paths that carry sensory information from the rest of the body to higher brain centres.

The reticular formation is an ill-defined and very complex network of neurons and interconnecting fibers lying within the very core of the brain stem. The ascending pathways from the reticular formation are vitally important in controlling overall activation of the brain and therefore the level of arousal wakefulness and consciousness of the person. Damage to this small but vital area can produce coma.

The unconscious proprioceptive systems in the brainstem help to connect the impulses arising from the balance organs of the inner ear with fine movement coordinating centres and balance centres of the cerebellum (see below). This system contributes to unconscious, reflexive maintenance of appropriate head and eye position during rapid and complex head and body movements.

The periventricular gray matter is concerned with unconscious automatic nervous system control of internal organs and glands, as well as aspects of the transmission of pain signals to higher centres.

8.2.3.6 The Cerebellum

The cerebellum is a vital modulator of motor activity. It integrates feedback coming from the balance organs of the inner ear and the sensory systems so as to permit complex and finally coordinated motor activities to proceed smoothly. It is needed to maintain appropriate posture, muscle tone, and balance. It is also needed for finely controlled and coordinated movements, both of the trunk and of the limbs. Voluntary movement can occur without the activity of the cerebellum, but the resulting movements will be clumsy, disorganized, and excessive. Damage to the cerebellum, for example, can result in an unsteady, wide-based, staggering gait of the sort people typically associate with alcohol intoxication. This phenomenon is known as ataxia.

8.2.4 Blood Vessels of the Brain

8.2.4.1 Arteries of the Brain

The brain receives its arterial supply from the branch of four vessels that travel up the neck and enter the base of the skull. There are two large arteries, the internal carotid arteries, that travel up the anterior (front) aspect of the neck and two smaller vertebral arteries that travel up the posterior (back) aspect of the neck. The internal carotid arteries arise from the common carotid arteries at about the angle of the jaw. At this point the common carotid artery on each side divides into an internal carotid artery branch going to the brain and an external carotid branch which divides into further branches that supply blood to the scalp and face.

After travelling through the base of the skull, and twisting and turning through the cavernous sinus, the internal carotid artery enters the intercranial compartment at the base of the brain and contributes to an important arterial circle known as the Circle of Willis (see below). It gives off several small branches and then divides into its large terminal branches the anterior cerebral artery and the middle cerebral artery. There is a carotid artery on each side, and therefore an anterior and middle cerebral artery on each side. The middle cerebral artery, which is the largest branch, supplies most of the lateral surface or convexity of the cerebral hemisphere. The anterior cerebral artery supplies the front half of the medial or midline surface of the cerebral hemisphere.

The two smaller vertebral arteries travel up into the skull through the largest channel in the base of the skull, the foramen magnum. They travel along the front or anterior surface of the brainstem, and soon do something unique to arteries in the body. That is, they join together to form one larger artery, called the basilar artery. The basilar artery completes the journey up the front surface of the brainstem, giving off branches to the brainstem and cerebellum along the way, and divides into its terminal branches the two posterior cerebral arteries, one for each side. The posterior cerebral arteries participate in the Circle of Willis, and then supply blood to the occipital portion of the cerebral hemispheres, particularly along the medial or midline surface.

The Circle of Willis is a vitally important series of interconnections forming an arterial circle at the base of the brain. It was first noted and described by Sir Christopher Wren, the architect who designed St. Paul's Cathedral in London. Sir Thomas Willis, the British royal physician, who was a colleague and contemporary of Wren's, received Wren's description with interest and published the information, rather taking the credit for it. The importance of the Circle of Willis is that it forms a series of interconnections between arteries at the base of the brain. In the event that one of the major arteries becomes blocked before it reaches the Circle of Willis, the interconnections allow one or more of the other three major arteries to take over and continue to supply blood to the entire brain. Connecting the internal carotid arteries with the posterior cerebral arteries by means of two so-called posterior communicating arteries, one on each side, form the Circle of Willis. Connecting the two anterior cerebral arteries with a single anterior communicating artery that crosses the midline joining the two then completes the circle. This is illustrated clearly in Figure 10B.

8.2.4.2 Veins of the Brain

The venous drainage from the brain is illustrated in Figure 10C. There are superficial sets of veins that drain the surface of the brain, and a deep set that drain the interior of the brain. The venous blood ultimately drains out through the base of the skull at the back of the posterior fossa through the jugular foramen and thereby into the jugular veins of the neck. The venous drainage of the brain is unusual in comparison with other parts of the body in that in most areas of the body, the veins closely follow the arteries. In the brain, in contrast, the veins take a rather separate course to the arteries. The other unusual feature is that the major draining veins are large venous channels within folds of the dura known as dural venous sinuses. The largest of these is the superior sagittal sinus that lies in the midline travelling from front to back just inside the inner surface of the skull, in the cleft between the two cerebral hemispheres.

8.2.5 The Ventricles of the Brain

The ventricles are fluid-filled cavities which lie deep within the brain. The cavities are filled with a clear fluid called cerebrospinal fluid. The fluid is secreted by the ependymal cells, which line the ventricles, and also with tufts of cells found within the ventricles known as choroid plexus. The ventricular system is shown in schematic form in Figure 10D.

As can be seen from the figure, each cerebral hemisphere contains a C-shaped lateral ventricle. Each of the lateral ventricles connects with a single midline third ventricle by means of a short narrow passageway; the interventricular foramen of Monro. Thus, there are two foramina of Monro, one for each lateral ventricle. The third ventricle is the ventricle of the diencephalon. It connects through a long narrow passage known as the aqueduct of Sylvius to the fourth ventricle, which is the ventricle of the brainstem. From the fourth ventricle, the cerebrospinal fluid passes out through three small passageways to fill the subarachnoid space lying over the surface of the brain and spinal cord. Thus, the cerebrospinal fluid provides a fluid cushion to encase and protect the brain and spinal cord.

Ultimately, the cerebrospinal fluid is reabsorbed into the venous system. This largely takes place through a series of what may be roughly termed microscopic filters that protrude from the subarachnoid space into the large venous channel known as the superior sagittal sinus. These multiple microscopic filters are known as arachnoid villi.

8.3 EPIDEMIOLOGY OF HEAD INJURY

Trauma is the most common cause of death in people under the age of 45 years. Head injury is the most heavily weighted predictor of outcome in the trauma population. Road traffic accidents account for around 60% of head injuries in adults and a greater percentage in children. Falls are a common cause of head injury in the elderly and the very young. Assaults have generally been associated with head injuries to young adult males, but there has been growing recognition of the significance of child abuse as a cause of head injury in children and particularly infants. In infants less than 1 year of age with serious head injuries, some studies have reported that as many as 90% may be non-accidental.

8.4 PATHOPHYSIOLOGY OF HEAD INJURY

8.4.1 Introduction

In gaining an understanding of what is happening in the head-injured patient, it is useful to divide the injury process into things that happen at the moment of impact, known as impact, injuries or primary injuries, and other processes that are more slowly developing, taking minutes, hours, days, or even weeks to manifest themselves. These latter are known as secondary injuries. Although this provides a useful framework for discussion, it must be recognized that there is overlap and interplay between these factors. The information regarding altered function in the setting of trauma can be further usefully organized by classifying the derangements that occur beginning at the outer surface of the head and progressing layer by layer to and through the interior.

8.4.2 Impact (Primary) Injuries

8.4.2.1 Scalp Injuries

The scalp is a surprisingly thick protective covering for the skull and the underlying nervous system. It measures between a quarter- and a half-inch in thickness in most areas. It is important both for physical protection of the underlying tissues and as an exceptionally distinctive body part often vital to a person's self image and sense of physiologic well-being.

The potential for serious scalp injuries to be life-threatening was recognized as early as the time of the ancient Egyptians, as evidenced by their written records of such injuries and their consequences. The scalp is extremely rich in blood vessels. This confers the advantage of relative resistance to infection, but it must be recognized that major and even life-threatening hemorrhage can occur with extensive scalp injuries. A second potentially life-threatening aspect to the scalp injury is the potential for infection of underlying tissues if the integrity of the scalp cannot be promptly re-established to act as a barrier to microorganisms.

Injuries to the scalp can include lacerations (cuts) as well as contusions (bruises). Bleeding can take place between the deep layers of the scalp and the skull so that haematoma (blood clot) formation is possible between the scalp and skull. Although serious blood loss by such haematoma formation in the absence of external bleeding cannot occur in the adult, it can occur due to such haematoma formation in infants.

The goals of management of scalp injuries are straightforward. The first priority is rapid and safe coverage of the underlying structures. One must convert a dirty wound to a clean one, and an open wound to a closed one. Durable cover must be established and where possible, normal contour and the best possible cosmetic result must be arrived at. These goals become progressively more difficult to achieve as the injury becomes progressively more extensive. It can be an especially difficult management problem where there has been actual extensive loss of scalp tissue. In this case complex procedures involving rotation of scalp tissue from other areas of the scalp into the area of injury or even transplantation of tissue from other areas of the body may be necessary to achieve closure. In these more complex cases, consultation with a plastic surgeon is often prudent.

8.4.2.2 Skull Fracture

8.4.2.2.1 Classification: Skull fractures may be classified as linear (a simple crack in the bone without separation or displacement of the fractured pieces) or depressed. Each type may be further classified as open (also known as compound; this implies an overlying laceration which means the fracture is in communication with the outside air raising the possibility of contamination and infection) or closed. Lastly, fractures may occur over the vault of the skull or along the base of the skull, the latter being referred to as basal skull fractures.

8.4.2.2.2 Linear Skull Fractures: Linear skull fractures that are simple, nondisplaced cracks in the bone are markers of a substantial transfer of energy to the head at the time of impact. In population studies, head-injured patients who had sustained skull fractures were more likely as a group than those without skull fractures as a group to have sustained a serious intercranial injury. However, there is a very poor correlation in any individual case. Thus, many patients with linear skull fractures do not harbor serious intercranial injuries, and conversely many patients who do harbor serious intercranial injuries do not have skull fractures. This is a point worth dwelling on, because the issue of whether or not to obtain plain skull radiographs in a head-injured patient has been the subject of both medical and medical/legal controversy for a number of years. Many large studies have been conducted regarding this subject. They have all demonstrated an extremely poor correlation between the presence or absence of skull fracture and the subsequent presence or absence of a serious intercranial injury. Modern neurosurgical thinking regarding this is that plain skull radiographs are rarely indicated in the head-injured patient. If the clinical impression of a possible significant intercranial injury is formed, definitive imaging, usually in the form of CT, should be performed rather than plain skull radiographs. With regard to treatment, linear nondepressed closed skull fractures rarely require specific treatment. These nondisplaced cracks will heal on their own in 6 to 8 weeks. Activities are generally restricted during that period of time to avoid situations where further trauma to the area, such as might occur in contact sports, is avoided.

Open linear skull fractures should have the associated overlying laceration cleaned and closed.

There is a rare exception to the lack of need for specific treatment in the setting of a closed linear skull fracture. This is the rare situation of the so-called growing skull fracture of childhood. This is a rare condition that occurs in the setting of skull fracture in the toddler to early school-year age group. It occurs because this is a period of rapid brain growth. If there is a linear skull fracture, and the fracturing has created a tear in the dura, the normal pulsations of the cerebral spinal fluid transmitted to the fracture edges because of the dural tear, can act as a subtle jackhammer gradually causing the fracture edges to progressively separate, leading to an enlarging defect in the skull. For this reason, some practitioners have suggested that surveillance radiographs be obtained in follow up with children in this age group who sustain skull fractures. If a growing defect is disclosed, early surgical intervention to prevent continued growth of the defect is warranted.

8.4.2.2.3 Depressed Skull Fractures: A skull fracture is generally defined as significantly depressed if the outer surface of one of the bone fragments has been driven inward to the extent that it lies below the level of the inner surface of the surrounding intact skull. This type of fracture is associated with a direct contact injury of fair severity involving a rigid object such as a baseball bat or steel bar. There is often an associated laceration of the overlying scalp, so that many of these are open. There is also, because of the sort of circumstances under which such injuries arise, a fairly high incidence of contamination of the tissue underlying the laceration with external debris. Because a fragment has been driven in, there may also be tearing of the coverings of the brain or laceration of the brain surface itself.

If the fracture is open, operative treatment is usually recommended to permit cleaning of any debris from underlying tissues and to permit removal of any lacerated, devitalized tissue. When the fracture is closed, the main indication for surgical intervention is for cosmetic reasons. A divot in the skull in a highly visible area such as the frontal region is extremely unsightly and psychologically distressing to the patient and should be corrected. A number of older textbooks and articles have suggested other reasons for elevating closed depressed fractures that have not proven to be valid. These include:

1. Improvement of an associated neurologic deficit. This is predicated on the belief that the fracture fragment pressing on the underlying brain tissue is the cause of the deficit. This is almost certainly never the case. Rather, laceration or contusion of the brain surface at the moment of impact has caused the underlying deficit. Elevating the fracture fragment will have no influence on the recovery of that deficit.
2. Prevention of post-traumatic epilepsy. Again, the underlying cause of the post-traumatic epilepsy is generally an injury to the underlying cortex that occurred at the moment of impact. Subsequent elevation of the fracture fragment will have no influence on this.

In summary, closed depressed fractures do not require treatment unless they create a cosmetically unacceptable skull deformity.

8.4.2.2.4 Basal Skull Fractures: Like linear fractures of the vault of the skull, basal skull fractures are a marker of a substantial energy transfer to the skull. Most often, the point of impact is somewhere over the vault of the skull and the fracture in the base has been created by transmission of force by a relatively thick vault to a relatively thin area of the base. Like linear fractures of the vault, they are in most cases, small nondisplaced cracks in the bone of the base of the skull. In the setting of very serious injuries, more extensive disruptions of the skull base may occur.

A distinctive feature of basal skull fractures is the potential for leakage of cerebrospinal fluid. This occurs when there is a fracture of the skull base either along the floor of the anterior cranial fossa above the nasal cavity, or a fracture of the temporal bone, which extends into the ear canal. If there is an associated tearing of the dura and arachnoid, cerebrospinal fluid can leak out through the fracture and out the nose or the ear. Because of the associated trauma, the normally clear cerebrospinal fluid is often blood tinged in these circumstances. The fracture itself does not require specific treatment but the cerebrospinal fluid leak indicates that there is a communication between the outside and the intercranial compartment. This represents a risk for infection. Fortunately, in most instances, the leak will seal spontaneously within a few days. In those rare instances where it does not, some form of surgical intervention becomes necessary to stop the leak and seal the communication to prevent ongoing risk of infection.

One controversial area in the management of basal skull fractures with cerebrospinal fluid leaks is the use of prophylactic antibiotics to reduce the risk of intercranial infection. In most cases, prophylactic antibiotics are not useful; in one prospective trial, it was found that the frequency of infection did not decrease, but that the infections more often occurred with antibiotic resistant organisms as a result of the use of prophylactic antibiotics. The one exception to this may be in the severely injured patient where a plastic catheter is inserted into the fluid filled cavities in the centre of the brain (the ventricles) to drain cerebrospinal fluid. Several authors have reported that incidence of infection is markedly increased with the combination of a ventricular catheter and basal skull fracture with cerebrospinal fluid leak. Some authors have suggested that in this particular situation, prophylactic antibiotics may be worthwhile.

8.4.2.3 Cerebral Concussion

This topic is discussed below in the selected topics in head injury.

8.4.2.4 Gray Matter Contusions

We now skip over injuries to the meninges because these are discussed in association with the overlying skull injuries or with the discussion of the intracranial haematomas under the secondary injuries section. This brings us to the surface of the brain itself, and the issue of gray matter contusions.

This bruising and scuffing of the cortical surface of the brain occurs in the setting of so called acceleration-deceleration injuries. This type of situation is seen in motor vehicle accidents and bad falls. The entire head is either suddenly brought to a stop or suddenly jerked into motion. The brain floating in its fluid cushion literally rattles back and forth inside the skull as a result. As the brain slides rapidly back and forth over a distance of perhaps only a few millimeters it tends to become scuffed and bruised where it comes in contact with the roughest or sharpest inner surfaces of the skull. The skull is rather rough over the orbital plates of the anterior fossa base so that the inferior frontal lobes tend to become contused. In addition, the inner surface of the skull is sharp over the sphenoid wing area so that the anterior temporal lobes can become contused or lacerated. This type of injury occurs at the moment of impact and, unfortunately, there is no specific treatment for this type of tissue damage. As we will see this type of injury can form the substrate for blood clot formation within the brain tissue and specific intervention may be required for that development which is appropriately discussed under secondary injuries.

8.4.2.5 Diffuse Brain Injury

This type of injury occurs in the setting of severe head trauma, usually a high-speed road traffic accident, in which there is severe prolonged acceleration or deceleration of the head. The patient is generally unconscious from the moment of impact.

The injury is primarily located in the white matter. There is widespread shearing of axons within the white matter. There may also be shearing of tiny capillaries. The deep hemispheric structures such as the corpus callosum and the white matter at the junction of the brainstem and diencephalon are not infrequently affected with potentially disastrous long-term consequences. The direction and nature of the head movement during the injury is vitally important. Injuries associated with lateral movement of the head are generally worse than those associated with front back movements of the head and those with a rotational component are perhaps worst of all.

As a result of the disruption of white matter axons and capillaries there is often associated diffuse brain swelling.

This type of injury can be dangerously disarming to the unwary physician. Although widespread microscopic damage has occurred, there is relatively little to be seen on a computed (CT) scan or magnetic resonance image (MRI). Early in the course of events the scan may be normal tomography, or there may be a few tiny punctate hemorrhages scattered through the cerebral tissue, particularly in the white matter as markers of the associated capillary damage, but most importantly as markers of the severe forces which have been brought into play. Depending on the severity of the injury, diffuse swelling of the brain tissue may be seen to a variable degree on the diagnostic images. This type of injury is one of the factors that make it very difficult to accurately predict outcome following a head injury. Although there has been widespread microscopic disruption of white matter fiber paths, the diagnostic images may appear relatively normal, giving false reassurance about the severity of the injury. The clinician must be alert to the subtle signs of this type of injury and must be cautious in attempting to predict the actual severity of the injury that has occurred. It is worth re-emphasizing that the CT or MRI changes may be subtle and, when abnormalities are present, tend to be result of tiny capillary hemorrhages associated with brain swelling of secondary injuries that will be discussed in following sections. Figure 11 is a CT scan from a head-injured patient showing the tiny hemorrhages that may be the only manifestation visible of this sort of injury.

There is not specific treatment for the shearing injury and management must focus on dealing with the swelling, the associated elevations in intracranial pressure and the metabolic consequences of these (this will be discussed below).

The prognosis from such injuries is extremely variable and difficult to predict early on. However, the more severe cases are often associated with poor outcomes such as persistent vegetative states or severe mental and physical handicaps.

8.4.3 Secondary Injuries

8.4.3.1 Intracranial Haematoma

8.4.3.1.1 Epidural Haematoma: Normally the dura is closely applied to the inner surface of the skull. It is also rich in blood vessels and there are a number of quite substantial arteries travelling through the dura to supply blood to it. An epidural haematoma is a blood clot developing in the potential space between the inner surface of the skull and the outer surface of the dura. To form, the bleeding has to strip the dura away from the inner surface of the skull to convert this potential space into a real space. It is perhaps not surprising then that the more vigorous bleeding that occurs with arterial disruption (as opposed to slower lower pressure venous bleeding) is the most common cause of epidural haematoma. In adults, over 90% of epidural haematomas are associated with skull fracture. Typically, the fracture lacerates one of the arteries of the dura setting of the bleeding that will create the haematoma. Less commonly, venous channels in the skull produce such bleeding. The most common location for an epidural haematoma is in the temporal region. This occurs because the skull is very thin in the temporal region and prone to disruption by injury in that region and, one of the largest arteries travelling through the dura, the middle meningeal artery lies immediately under the skull in this region.

Epidural haematomas are relatively uncommon in comparison with other intracranial bleeding and haematoma formation, which we will discuss below. It has been estimated that of those admitted to hospital with head injury the occurrence of epidural haematomas is between 1% and 3%. Epidural haematomas are uncommon in the elderly and the very young. The elderly are less likely than young adults to be involved in the sort of trauma that causes such haematomas, and, in addition, as one ages the dura becomes progressively more adherent to the inner surface of the skull. It then becomes less likely that the torn blood vessel will generate bleeding of sufficient force to strip the tightly adherent dura away from the inner surface of the skull. In young children, the skull is much more deformable and less prone to fracturing and lacerating underlying blood vessels.

In contrast to the acute subdural haematomas, which we will discuss below, epidural haematomas are less frequently associated with an immediate severe underlying brain injury. Therefore, the prognosis for good recovery is much better as long as the haematoma is diagnosed and evacuated in a timely fashion before it becomes so large that the pressure it exerts on the underlying brain causes irreversible injury. An epidural haematoma is a true surgical emergency; the bleeding is often arterial and brisk and the haematoma may be expanding rapidly. Rapid decompression of the underlying brain is key to achieving a good outcome.

The classic textbook description of an evolving extradural haematoma, faithfully taught to each medical student, features a brief period of unconsciousness at the time of injury, followed by recovery of consciousness to normal or near normal levels (known as the "lucid interval") followed by subsequent progressive deterioration in brain function. The initial loss of consciousness is said to be due to the cerebral concussion, which occurs at the movement of impact. The patient recovers from the concussion and regains consciousness. The bleeding has already started, though, and as the haematoma enlarges, putting increasing pressure on the brain, progressive deterioration then occurs. In fact, such a classic story featuring the archetypal "lucid interval" is seen in less than 40% of patients with epidural haematoma. In the rest, the initial concussive effect or the subsequent lucid interval may be omitted. The hallmark of an epidural haematoma as with other intracranial haematomas is based on the fact that these are focal lesions affecting the particular area of brain tissue they are adjacent to, or located in more distant areas of the brain. The general guide that is used is that the right cerebral hemisphere controls the left side of the body and the left cerebral hemisphere controls the right side of the body, thus an epidural haematoma forming on the right hand side will tend to cause progressive paralysis on the left side of the body. It cannot be emphasized enough that the hallmark of appropriate clinical thinking in the management of head injuries is to be on the lookout for focal brain dysfunction, such as paralysis on one side but not the other. The reason for this is that focal brain dysfunction may indicate a focal lesion which may be a mass lesion such as a haematoma and may be a lesion that requires emergent surgery.

The management of epidural haematoma consists of rapid diagnosis generally by CT scan followed by rapid surgical removal of the haematoma with control of bleeding.

One long-standing controversy in the management of epidural haematoma has been the potential role of drilling an exploratory series of holes in the skull of the patient in the Emergency Room before a CT scan is taken. This is to save the time of CT scanning and transfer to the Operating Room. The side the holes are drilled on initially is based on the clinical evaluation of the patient (for example, the side opposite the paralysis). This type of heroic procedure is fraught with uncertainties, however. The clot is not always on the side you would expect it to be on and the clot may not be extradural or even subdural but rather within the brain tissue itself, and this will not be disclosed without diagnostic images. In most large medical centres where such drilling procedures could be undertaken, CT images are available within 5 to 10 minutes after the decision to obtain them. This provides definitive diagnosis of the location of any and all mass lesions present and will, in many cases, actually result in less delay in definitive treatment than fiddling about with drill holes in the Emergency Room. The exception may be the deteriorating patient in a remote centre where definitive diagnosis is hours away and the patient will literally be dead by that point if nothing is done.

In summary, definitive management of epidural haematoma is based on rapid diagnostic imaging followed by rapid surgical removal of the haematoma and control of bleeding. An acute epidural haematoma as visualized on a CT scan is illustrated in Figure 12.

Prognosis for recovery from epidural haematoma is, as we shall see, better than that for an acute subdural haematoma, discussed below. This is likely due to the lesser likelihood of severe underlying brain injury in association with epidural haematoma than with acute subdural haematoma. In most large series the mortality from epidural haematomas is still substantial at about 20 to 30%. However, Hooper found that with rapid diagnosis and early surgery, that figure could be reduced to about 10%. The mortality and morbidity tends to be related to the patient's neurologic status immediately prior to surgical intervention.

8.4.3.1.2 Acute Subdural Haematoma: Acute subdural haematomas are unfortunately a common concomitant of severe head injury. They are certainly seen with substantially greater frequency than are epidural haematomas. The incidence of subdural haematoma in association with head injury has been estimated between 1 to 22%, depending on the criteria used to define head injury. Figures closer to the higher end of the range are generally found when one considers severe head injuries. Acute subdural haematomas are associated with high mortality and morbidity. This is because they are associated with substantial energy transfers to the head and brain and there is often a severe underlying brain injury from the moment of impact, so that even rapid evacuation of the haematoma does not result in a good outcome.

One large study found that outcome was dependent on age of the patient and the time interval between moment of impact and definitive surgical treatment of the subdural haematoma. Patients over 60 and patients in whom treatment was delayed for more than 4 hours from the moment of impact did worse. In this group the mortality approached 100%. Overall the mortality is close to 80%, making this an extremely poor prognosis lesion.

Acute subdural haematomas are associated with the substantial traumatic situations necessary to provide the levels of force and energy transfer required to produce them. Thus severe falls, severe blows to the head, and especially motor vehicle accidents are the common substrates of these dangerous injuries. They are seen more commonly in men than women, likely because substantial trauma is seen more commonly in men than in women.

A CT scan image of an acute subdural haematoma is illustrated in Figure 13. As can be seen from this and Figure 12, illustrating an acute extradural haematoma, an acute blood clot appears essentially white on a CT scan. This is in contrast to the chronic subdural haematomas we will discuss below wherein the liquified blood often appears a darker shade of gray then the surrounding brain tissue.

The majority of acute subdural haematomas are caused by tearing of veins on the surface of the brain or bridging between the surface of the brain and the inner surface of the dura. The bleeding is taking place underneath the dura so that it is not restrained by the adherence of the dura to the skull, as was the case with epidural haematomas. Although the venous bleeding is less vigorous than the arterial bleeding typically associated with epidural haematomas, because of this lack of restraint a very large clot can accumulate in quite short order. What ultimately restrains growth of the clot is dangerously rising pressure inside the head as the brain is badly compressed by the clot.

Typically, patients with acute subdural haematomas are deeply unconscious from the moment of impact. There is rarely any sort of lucid interval as is described with epidural haematomas. Definitive management features rapid diagnosis generally by CT imaging, urgent surgical evacuation, and then management of the underlying brain injury and associated swelling as will be discussed in sections below.

8.4.3.1.3 Chronic Subdural Haematoma: Chronic subdural haematomas provide a marked contrast in almost every respect to acute subdural haematomas. They tend to be associated with relatively minor trauma as opposed to the severe traumas associated with acute subdural haematomas. Indeed, in almost half the cases a clear history of the trauma that caused the subdural haematoma cannot be obtained. By definition these haematomas present clinically greater than 2 weeks following the inciting traumas. These chronic subdural haematomas are overwhelmingly more common in the elderly population. This is because, as we age, our brains atrophy or shrink. The skull, of course, does not change in size. The shrinking brain, therefore, pulls away from the inner surface of the skull and dura. Bridging veins between the surface of the brain and the inner surface of the dura are put on the stretch. With some minor trauma the atrophied brain can rattle back and forth within its confines. This can lead to a small tear developing in the already stretched bridging veins. The haematoma accumulates slowly as intermittent slow, low-pressure bleeding takes place from the small injury to the vein. Because the blood is accumulating slowly, it has time to liquify as it develops, therefore, instead of having the grape jelly consistency of an acute blood clot, these chronically accumulating blood clots tend to be liquid of varying viscosity depending on the exact age of the haematoma. Nonetheless, as they continue to grow, the pressure insidiously builds up on the surrounding brain. Because the pressure builds slowly, and in the typical elderly patient the brain is atrophied, the haematomas can achieve quite substantial size before symptoms occur and the patient presents to medical attention.

Figure 14 illustrates a chronic subdural haematoma of substantial size compressing the brain of the elderly patient in whom it occurred.

The clinical presentation is variable. Subdural haematoma is known to physicians as the "great mimic". This is because the presentation of a subdural haematoma can mimic the presentation of many other neurologic conditions. The haematoma may present with slowly, even insidiously, progressing neurologic deficits over weeks or even months with such features as slowly progressive weakness, speech disturbance, and memory loss or personality change. This presentation mimics that of a slowly growing tumor. In other cases the deficits can come and go transiently or fluctuate considerably, mimicking transient ischemic attack or stroke. Most importantly, the patient may present without a focal neurologic deficit despite the focal nature of the lesion. It is not uncommon for these elderly patients to present with a progressive dementing process. Subdural haematoma must be considered in an elderly patient who is becoming demented because it is one of the truly reversible causes of dementia.

Diagnosis is based on appropriate clinical suspicion leading to diagnostic imaging. Either CT or MR imaging will generally reveal the haematoma. With CT imaging one must be aware of the rare occurrence of an isodense subdural. The CT pictures of acute haematomas reveal that acute blood on a CT scan is generally white in appearance (a lighter shade of gray than the adjacent brain). In contrast the CT image of the chronic subdural haematoma indicates that chronic blood is dark (a darker shade of gray than the adjacent brain). It, therefore, stands to reason that in the transition between acute blood and chronic blood the blood passes through a phase where it is the same shade of gray as the adjacent brain, indeed this is true and it generally occurs between 7 and 14 days following a hemorrhage. This situation is known as an isodense subdural haematoma because the density and, therefore, the shade of gray of the haematoma is the same as the adjacent brain, making it difficult to distinguish from the adjacent brain. Under these circumstances, someone reading the CT who is not on the look out for this entity may be deceived into believing there is no haematoma, assuming that it is just simply part of the brain tissue. It should be emphasized that with modern, late generation CT scanners and their great sensitivity to even subtle variations in tissue density, a true isodense subdural haematoma is, in practical terms, a rare cause of diagnostic confusion.

Definitive treatment is surgical evacuation of the haematoma. Because the blood is liquified, this can be accomplished through a relatively small brain hole drilled in the skull rather than requiring a much bigger opening of the skull as is necessary with the acute haematomas.

In contrast to the dismal prognosis associated with acute subdural haematomas, about 75% of patients who suffer a chronic subdural haematoma return to a premorbid level of function following evacuation of the haematoma, and overall mortality is not more than 10%.

8.4.3.1.4 Traumatic Subarachnoid Hemorrhage: We are continuing in our discussion of secondary injuries to move closer to the brain tissue itself. We have discussed bleeding into the epidural space and subdural space and now come to the subarachnoid space. Subarachnoid hemorrhage is associated in the minds of physicians with rupture of cerebral aneurysms. Indeed, cerebral aneurysms are the most common cause of non-traumatic or spontaneous subarachnoid hemorrhages. However, the most common cause of subarachnoid hemorrhage overall is trauma. The hemorrhage occurs in the CSF-filled subarachnoid space. The bleeding generally consists of a relatively thin layer of blood over the surface of the brain. The blood itself does not occupy a significant volume and surgical intervention to remove the blood is neither feasible nor worthwhile. The hemorrhage serves simply as a marker of a substantial blow to the head and a warning to be vigilant to a possible diffuse brain injury and associated brain swelling. One must also consider the possibility if the circumstances are appropriate that the hemorrhage may in fact have been due to rupture of an aneurysm which then caused the patient to become unconscious and become involved in some sort of trauma such as a motor vehicle accident. If this is a possibility, diagnostic imaging, usually cerebral angiography, is suggested to look for an underlying aneurysm.

8.4.3.1.5 Intracerebral Haematoma: Intracerebral haematomas are, of course, blood clots that develop right within the substance of the brain tissue as a result of injury to blood vessels within the brain itself. They typically develop after a delay of hours to several days. In one series, only 20% of the intracerebral haematomas were present on the initial CT, whereas 35% had developed within 24 hours and over 80% by 72 hours. Thus there must be a mechanism by which delayed bleeding occurs in the majority of cases. The overall incidence of intracerebral haematoma is estimated at around 20% of those with severe enough injuries to undergo CT scanning. The mechanism of formation of acutely developing intracerebral haematomas is most well understood. The first mechanism is a direct injury to the skull typically with fracture fragments causing direct pain injury. The brain is lacerated and the bleeding which will lead to formation of the intracerebral haematoma starts. This has been termed a coup injury. The second mechanism of formation of acute haematomas has been termed a countercoup injury. As a result of acceleration and deceleration of the head, the brain rattles around inside the skull. The motion of the brain relative to the inner surface of the skull causes injury where the skull is rough (affecting the inferior frontal lobes) or sharp (affecting the anterior temporal lobes). This is as was discussed under gray matter contusions. The mechanism of delayed hemorrhage is less well understood, but the proposed mechanisms generally involve injury to the walls of blood vessels leading to their delayed rupture and hemorrhage.

An example of a large intracerebral hemorrhage on CT scan is shown in Figure 15.

The clinical presentation of patients with intracerebral haematomas varies widely with the location and size of the haematoma as well as the rapidity of its development. The more rapidly developing ones tend to present with more severe and extensive symptoms as the brain has less time to adapt and accommodate to the extra material within the extracranial compartment. Some combination of focal deficit depending on the location of the lesion and alteration in level of consciousness is generally found. The effects of the increasing pressure within the intracranial compartment and the mechanical distortion of brain tissue are discussed below in the sections on consequences of raised intracranial pressure.

The management of intracerebral haematomas is somewhat more complicated than the management of epidural or subdural haematomas, where rapid surgical removal is almost always undertaken. With intracerebral haematomas, the desire to remove the haematoma and thereby relieve pressure on the surrounding brain must be tempered by the fact that surgical intervention is going to require incision, mechanical manipulation, and associated surgical traumatization of the brain tissue itself. This is particularly true if the haematoma is situated deep within the brain tissue away from the surface. In these cases, the damage that might potentially be done by the surgical intervention has to be weighed against the damage done by leaving the haematoma in place. Management decisions must be individualized, but as general guidelines haematomas that are larger than 3 cm in greatest dimension, and those that are close to the surface and/or located in areas of the brain where surgical disruption is known to be relatively safe, are evacuated, whereas smaller, deep seated, and/or haematomas that are situated in vitally eloquent areas of brain are more likely to be managed without surgical evacuation. In any case, there is progressive neurologic deterioration due to the mass effect of the haematoma "causing increased intracranial pressure and mechanical distortion of the brain," surgical intervention must be considered if the extent of brain injury and disruption is not so bad as to render such intervention futile.

The prognosis with such lesions is quite variable depending on the size and location of the lesion and the presence of other forms of intracranial injury. As will be discussed below, the neurologic status of the patient is a major predictor of outcome. Overall, mortality from these lesions are in the 25% range.

8.4.3.2 Raised Intracranial Pressure

8.4.3.2.1 Introduction and Definitions: A major contributor to cerebral tissue damage following a head injury is the development of dangerously elevated levels of pressure within the intracranial compartment. The brain is a unique organ in this respect; for its protection it is floated in a fluid cushion and then encased in a rigid box, the skull. Unfortunately, when injury occurs there may be blood clot formation, tissue swelling, or changes in the calibre of the blood vessels which increase the volume of material within the rigid box. In other areas of the body there is not this rigid constraint on increased volume and swelling, and therefore pressure does not rise; but because in the case of head injury we are dealing with this rigid closed container, relatively small changes in intracranial volume can produce potentially disastrous rises in intracranial pressure. Elevated intracranial pressure is damaging because it can impair blood flow to the point that tissues starve for vital nutrients and also because it can cause serious mechanical distortion of the tissue, particularly if the cause of the pressure rise is a focal mass. These issues will be discussed in more detail in the next section. To understand the factors that can contribute to rises in intracranial pressure in head injury, it is necessary to understand what are the normal intracranial contents, what factors can cause these normal contents to change in size, and what mechanisms of compensation exist. The normal contents of the intracranial compartment include about 1200 mL of neurons and glial cells, including the intracellular fluid associated with these, about 100 mL of intracellular fluid, about 100 mL of blood, most of it in the dural venous sinuses, and about 100 mL of CSF in the ventricles and the subarachnoid space.

Normal intracranial pressure in the adult is 6 to 12 mm Hg (by comparison the mean blood pressure in the major arteries of the body is approximately 90 mm Hg). If the brain tissue starts to swell or an abnormal material (such as a tumor or a blood clot) accumulates in the intracranial compartment, either some of the other material must exit or the pressure will rise. The normal compensatory mechanisms to buffer against pressure rises are for some of the CSF to be squeezed out into the spinal compartment or for some of the blood in the larger venous sinuses to be squeezed out. Obviously, there is only a limited amount of these materials that can be shifted before these compensatory mechanisms fail.

As a result of these compensations and their subsequent failure with continuing increases in intracranial volume, there is a curvilinear relationship between intracranial pressure and intracranial volume. This is illustrated in Figure 16. As can be seen in this figure, as volume is added to the cranial compartment the pressure initially rises slowly, because the compensatory mechanisms are able to buffer the pressure rise; however, at a point at which the pressure has risen to around 20 mm Hg the compensatory mechanisms are exhausted and with further small changes in volume the pressure rises dramatically and dangerously. It is for this reason that management goals with regards to intracranial pressure generally attempt to keep the pressure at or below 20 mm Hg.

Knowing the factors that change the volume of the normal components of the intracranial compartment (particularly the volume of blood in the blood vessels) forms the basis on which management interventions are decided; one attempts to modify those factors so to encourage reduced blood volume and reduced intracranial pressure. It is a general rule of thumb that any factor which increases cerebral blood flow will increase cerebral blood volume and, thereby, intracranial pressure. Therefore, many of the intracranial pressure management strategies aim at reduction in cerebral blood flow. We will review these in a moment, but first it is important to recognize that one cannot go too far in this direction. It is possible to reduce the intracranial pressure by severely reducing cerebral blood flow, but the severe reduction in cerebral blood flow will cause tissue ischemia and tissue damage. Compromises must be sought.

Having understood this, let us now look at the factors which influence cerebral blood flow (CBF), cerebral blood volume (CBV), and intracranial pressure (ICP). The first of these, and an extremely important one, is the amount of oxygen in the blood. This is usually measured as a partial pressure of oxygen in the blood or pO_2. A normal pO_2 for a healthy individual might be in the range of 80 to 90 mm Hg. As the oxygen in the blood becomes depleted (the critical point is a pO_2 of around 60-mm Hg), the metabolic demands of the brain tissue require that CBF go up. As a result, under conditions of lack of oxygen or hypoxia, CBF, CBV and ICP all rise rapidly. Interestingly, once a normal oxygen level in the blood is achieved, raising the oxygen level further by giving the patient enriched oxygen concentrations does not affect CBF and ICP a great deal.

Another major determinate of CBV, CBF and ICP is the level of carbon dioxide in the blood. This is also measured as a partial pressure with a normal pCO_2 being 35 to 45 mm Hg. It is very easy for pCO_2 to rise to abnormally elevated levels in the head-injured patient for as level of consciousness declines there is a tendency for respirations to become slower and shallower. As they do, less carbon dioxide is excreted through the lungs and the CO_2 level in the blood rises. ICP is directly proportional to the CO_2 level in the blood, so that as CO_2 rises so does the intracranial pressure. Conversely, it is possible to lower intracranial pressure by driving down the pCO_2 to lower than normal levels. This is easily accomplished by placing a tube into the patient's trachea and connecting the patient to a mechanical ventilator device. However, caution must be exercised; as noted above, what is happening as pCO_2 goes down is that CBF is being reduced, and this in turn is responsible for the decline in intracranial pressure. It is possible to go too far and reduce the cerebral blood flow to dangerously low levels where the tissue becomes ischemic. When to drive down the pCO_2 and how much is an area of controversy and one that is evolving in management of these patients.

A third important determinant of intracranial pressure is the acid base status or pH of the tissue. It is the pH of the extracellular fluid that is important and this has a complex relationship with the pH in the blood stream so that it is difficult to give simple rules for the effects of pH changes in the blood on intracranial pressure. Suffice it to say that conditions of tissue acidosis (low pH), such as can occur in the trauma setting when there is shock, can contribute to tissue acidosis and elevation of intracranial pressure. This is obviously best avoided and rapidly corrected when present.

Cerebral metabolic demand is also a major determinant of intracranial pressure. Obviously, as brain activity increases, the need for nutrients from the blood stream increases, so that cerebral blood flow, cerebral blood volume and intracranial pressure will all increase too. In the setting of head injury one wishes to minimize cerebral metabolic demand. Factors that increase cerebral metabolic demand are agitation, fever, and seizures. These are to be avoided. Actually lowering the metabolic demand by sedating a patient can be of benefit in certain circumstances but the sedative drugs can make evaluation of the patient's brain status more difficult. An appropriate balance between these conflicting priorities must be struck in the individual case. There will be further discussion of this under the management section. Inducing mild hypothermia, that is, lowering the body's temperature, has also been considered a potentially useful means of lowering cerebral metabolic demand and intracranial pressure. This too is presently a controversial and evolving management option. It is certainly effective in reducing intracranial pressure, but there may be significant detrimental effects in the form of suppression of the immune defense system and increased incidence of infections.

8.4.3.2.2 Consequences of Raised Intracranial Pressure:

- *Ischemia*—As discussed, one of the major ways in which raised intracranial pressure causes brain tissue injury, is by impeding the flow of blood to the brain tissue, so that the continuing need for oxygen and glucose is not met. A failure to meet the metabolic demands of tissue due to insufficient blood flow to the tissue is termed ischemia. The brain is a remarkably metabolically active organ. A tremendous amount of energy is expended on a continuing basis by the brain to maintain the appropriate concentration of electrically charged particles on either side of the cell membranes. The brain is so metabolically active that although it constitutes less than 2% of the total weight of the body, it consumes about 20% of the blood flow through the body and 25% of the oxygen used by the body. Unlike many other organs, which can survive for many minutes or even hours without blood flow, permanent brain injury begins within a few minutes of having its blood supply cut off. It is, therefore, not surprising that lack of blood flow to areas of the brain due to head injury and elevations in intracranial pressure can have rapid disastrous consequences for the brain tissue and the patient.

One of the most interesting and exciting areas of research into treatment of head injury concerns a variety of investigations into the metabolic consequences of ischemia at the cellular and even the molecular level coupled with investigations into potential interventions that might ameliorate these harmful metabolic consequences. An extensive discussion of these research areas is beyond the scope of this chapter but it certainly has been shown that dozens of known metabolic pathways are seriously disturbed. Researchers have documented excess entry of calcium ions into cells with consequent activation of enzyme systems that chew up the cell membrane, intracellular proteins, and even the cell's DNA. Many signalling systems within the cell become deranged and inappropriate messages are generated, some of which may activate suicide programs within the cell.

- *Brain Shift and Herniation*—An enlarged intracranial mass, whether it is a tumor, an infection, damaged swollen brain tissue itself, or an intracranial hemorrhage, will displace, distort, and compress surrounding brain tissue. The mechanical displacement and distortion can become so severe that it produces direct tissue injury. In addition, the brain that is being compressed and distorted will seek some means of escape from this. The situation was eloquently described by Fred Plum and Jerome Posner in their classic monograph *The Diagnosis of Stupor and Coma.*

  > Sooner or later, however, nearly all masses enlarge so much, either through their own growth or the edema added to their periphery that the surrounding brain can no longer accommodate them. The surrounding cerebral structures shift across the midline or downward toward the base of the brain; the shear bulk of the shifting tissues compresses new regions, and these, in turn, begin to swell and shift. Eventually, the brain, thus progressively increased in volume, has no choice but to squeeze into the only available supratentorial exit, the tentorial notch.

Thus, as noted by Plum and Posner, when pressure develops on the cerebral hemispheres, portions of them will shift across the midline (subfalcene herniation) and, ultimately, portions of the cerebral hemispheres will try to squeeze out through the defect in the tentorium cerebelli into their only escape route available, the posterior fossa, which is already occupied by the brainstem and cerebellum. Unfortunately, this displacement or herniation by portions of the cerebral hemispheres over the edge of the tentorium cerebelli rapidly begins to put dangerous pressure on the brainstem, the cranial nerves, coming out of its upper portion, and the associated blood vessels. If this situation is not rapidly corrected irreversible damage to the brainstem with consequent persistent coma or death will occur. This situation is illustrated in Figure 17. As can be seen in this figure, there are three major herniation syndromes that can result from brain shift in the supratentorial compartment and from the supratentorial compartment to the posterior fossa. These are identified by their end stages: cingulate herniation, central transtentorial herniation, and lateral transtentorial (uncal) herniation.

- *Cingulate Herniation*—In this situation the expanding hemisphere causes the cingulate gyros along the medial aspect of the hemisphere to herniate (become abnormally displaced) under the edge of the fold of dura hanging between the two hemispheres, the falx cerebri. The danger of this herniation pattern is that it compresses blood vessels travelling in the region, in particular the anterior cerebral arteries and the internal cerebral veins. Compression of the anterior cerebral arteries can result in bilateral dysfunction of the more medial aspects of the motor strip, thus causing paralysis in both legs. The venous compromise can further exacerbate the swelling process.
- *Lateral Transtentorial (Uncal) Herniation*—Uncal herniation typically occurs when an expanding mass lesion in the lateral aspect of the supratentorial compartment causes the inner inferior edge of the temporal lobe (the uncus) to herniate over the edge of the tentorium cerebelli and to start compressing the lateral aspect of brainstem. This results in compromise of three important structures that produce the clinical syndrome that results from such compression. The first structure is the third cranial nerve on the side of the herniation. The third cranial or oculomotor nerve is responsible for constriction of the pupil of the eye as well as for eye movements that involve turning of the eye inwards and either up or down. The pressure on the nerve typically produces a dilated pupil and sometimes deviation of the eye outwards. The second structure compressed is the posterior cerebral artery. Continuing pressure on this can lead to injury to the visual processing areas of the occipital lobe and to certain motor relay areas. The third area that can be compromised are the motor fibers travelling down from the cerebral hemisphere to the brainstem in the so-called cerebral peduncles. Pressure on these produces paralysis on the side opposite. Fourth, if the pressure continues to build and the central

core of the brainstem becomes affected, level of consciousness progressively declines and signs of progressive brainstem failure such as alterations in breathing pattern, alterations in brainstem reflexes (see the section below on evaluation of the head-injured patient), and alterations in heart rhythm and blood pressure appear. To summarize, the clinical presentation of uncal herniation features a dilated pupil on the side of the compression, paralysis on the side opposite the compression, possible visual cortex damage in survivors and in the face of continuing progression, progressive brainstem failure.

In about 10 to 15% of cases the pressure of the herniating brain tissue squeezes the same structures on the opposite side of the brainstem, up against the sharp edge of the tentorial cerebelli on the opposite side. This produces a constellation of symptoms, which is identical to what is produced by direct pressure but with the sides reversed. This is called Kernahan's notch phenomenon after the physician who described it. It can lead to confusion in the absence of diagnostic imaging as to which side the pressure is really coming from. It is one more confounding factor that makes the concept of Emergency Room drilling of holes without diagnostic imaging a tenuous concept.

- *Central Transtentorial Herniation*—In this herniation syndrome, pressure increases from top to bottom progressively on the central core of the brainstem early. There is early change in the level of consciousness; irregular respirations are also an early phenomenon. The findings seen in the lateral herniation syndrome (pupillary dilation on one side and paralysis on the opposite side) are less often seen in the central herniation syndrome. Rather, the pupils often dilate together; a very ominous sign that the upper brainstem is in grave danger of immediate irreversible injury. Similarly, motor abnormalities (paralysis and/or abnormal reflex movements) often develop with a relative symmetry on both sides.

8.5 ACUTE EVALUATION OF THE HEAD-INJURED PATIENT

8.5.1 Introduction

Prompt, accurate evaluation of the head-injured patient by a knowledgeable, skilled physician is key in arriving at an appropriate assessment of the nature of the injury and proceeding with interventions as required to minimize secondary injury and consequent effects of the trauma. The evaluation is most commonly carried out at the same time as initial resuscitation and stabilization measures are being instituted. A skilled multidisciplinary trauma team can be of great benefit in completing this process efficiently and thoroughly. As will be reviewed in the management section that follows, the first steps of the encounter with the patient follow the ABC (airway, breathing and circulation) protocol that has been established as standard initial care of the traumatized patient in advance trauma life support literature. Thus, the examiner initially ensures that an adequate, unobstructed airway is present, that the patient is either breathing or has respiratory support, and that the circulation with respect to heart rate and blood pressure are adequate or being appropriately treated. Once these initial steps are taken, one can proceed to more definitive evaluation of the structural and functional integrity of the nervous system.

8.5.2 History and Physical Examination

Gathering of historical details must take place contemporaneously with resuscitation, stabilization, and other evaluative efforts. In many cases, particularly if the patient is unconscious, limited historical information only will be readily available. Nonetheless, it can be extremely helpful to have information concerning the circumstances of the injury, whether observers of the transfer from accident scene to hospital have noted any change in neurologic status, and even background history regarding background diseases, sensitivities, and medications. Knowledge of the details and mechanism of injury may be useful.

Initial physical examination includes a quick survey for external signs of trauma, incorporating the general surveys of the entire patient recommended by the advanced trauma life support literature, but also focusing on evidence of trauma to the head, neck, and spine. Deformities, swellings, lacerations, and contusions should be identified. The examiner should be alert for leakage of spinal fluid from the nose or ear or bruising around the eyes or behind the ears, which may be indicative of basal skull fracture.

Then an evaluation of nervous system function is in order. Of vital importance is the overall level of consciousness and responsiveness. Normally, patients should be awake and alert, and should be able to answer simple questions and follow simple commands, moving all limbs with strength and vigor when asked. They should indicate that they can perceive sensations in all areas of the body. Reflexes such as the biceps jerk, triceps jerk, knee jerk, and ankle jerk should be symmetric throughout. The undersurface of the feet should be gently stroked to elicit the so-called plantar reflex. This normally involves a downward curling of the toes. In cases where there is higher brain dysfunction, the toes may extend towards the head and fan out. This abnormal reflex should be sought routinely in the evaluation of the head injured patient.

In addition, evaluation should be made of reflex responses that are controlled by the brainstem and the cranial nerves that emerge from the brainstem. Thus, the patient should be evaluated for spontaneous conjugate eye movements. If there are no spontaneous eye movements and one is certain that the cervical spine is not stable, the head may be moved to see if there is reflex eye turning in the direction opposite to which the head is turned. This is termed a Doll's eye reflex. The cornea of each eye should be lightly touched with a cotton swab or tissue to elicit the blinking response mediated by the trigeminal and facial cranial nerves. Finally, the back of the throat should be stimulated to evaluate the gag response mediated by the glossopharyngeal and vagus nerves.

In integrating this information it is useful to complete the patient's score on the Glasgow Coma Scale or GCS. A very active neurotrauma group in Glasgow, Scotland devised this scale. It has been in use for many years because it provides useful reproducible information about a patient's progress, be it improvement or deterioration, and in addition is useful in making some prediction about long-term prognosis. The initial Glasgow Coma Score following resuscitation does have a high correlation with ultimate outcome. The Glasgow Coma Score can range from 3 for a patient who is completely unresponsive and unconscious to a level of 15 for an entirely normal individual. Scores of 13 to 15 are considered mild head injuries, 8 to 12 moderate, and less than 8 severe. Those with scores of 6 or less have a dismal prognosis. Anyone with a score of 8 or less may be considered comatose. The scale is summarized in Figure 18. It is based on the patient's response spontaneously to voice and, if necessary, to painful stimuli in three areas. The three areas are eye opening, verbalization and motor responses. The minimum score for unresponsiveness in each category is 1 rather than 0.

The hallmark of appropriate care of the head-injured patient is to continue to re-evaluate the patient at regular intervals to determine if the patient's status is improving, stable or ominously worsening. One is constantly searching for not only changes in responsiveness but also for focal neurologic deficits, recalling that a focal deficit may be caused by a focal lesion, which may require surgical intervention.

8.5.3 Diagnostic Imaging

The first-line diagnostic imaging method of choice for the head-injured patient is CT scanning. Plain skull radiographs show only the bony structures. They do not reveal the brain tissue at all nor will they show bleeding within the cranial compartment. They will show bony fractures, but as discussed in the section on fractures, this information in isolation rarely alters clinical management.

Magnetic resonance imaging does offer enhanced demonstration of soft tissue contrasts over CT. It tends to show bone edges less well. The enhanced soft tissue contrasts demonstrated by MR are, however, not often of advantage in the setting of trauma. The acute setting, the relative slowness of an MR scan, the confined space, and the need to exclude metallic objects from the environment, limit its role. It is currently generally reserved for a small minority of cases where there is diagnostic uncertainty following the CT image.

Angiography may be used in selected cases where there is concern regarding injury to blood vessels. Other, newer modalities such as single photon emission CT (SPECT), positron emission tomography (PET) and neuromagnatography have not, thus far, found routine application in the management of traumatic brain injury.

8.6 ACUTE MANAGEMENT OF SEVERE HEAD INJURIES

8.6.1 Introduction

Despite extensive medical literature on head injuries with tens of thousands of published articles over many years on manifestations and management, survey of U.S. centres in 1995 revealed a remarkable degree of variability in management strategies from centre to centre. In response to this variability the major North American Surgical Societies struck a committee and organized a 2-year effort to develop evidence-based guidelines for the management of severe head injury. These guidelines were based on an exhaustive review of available literature dating back over 30 years. The available evidence for various management strategies was classified on the basis of their statistical validity into three classes. Class I studies are prospective, randomized, placebo-controlled trials (PRCTs) that are properly designed and performed without an unacceptable number of protocol errors; Class II studies include the PRCTs that do not meet the above criteria as well as non-randomized, prospective controlled trials and large prospectively collected observational studies; Class III studies included flawed Class II studies as well as case series, case reports, and reviews of expert opinion.

The recommendations generated were ranked as standards (based on Class I studies; unfortunately there were relatively few Class I studies and, therefore, relatively few standards that could be formulated), guidelines (based on Class II studies) and options (based on Class III studies). Standards represent "the management method to use in the absence of extenuating circumstances." Guidelines represent "the management method that is probably the best choice in the majority of applicable situations." Options represent "a suggested management method without proven superiority over other applicable methods." Unfortunately the majority of recommendations were at the guideline or option level. In the following discussion, the recommendations of this committee are incorporated.

8.6.2 Initial Resuscitation

The initial resuscitation of the head-injured patient plays a vital role in the subsequent outcome. Critically important is the prompt and efficient management of the so-called ABCs of resuscitation; the airway, the breathing and the circulation. In one study it was found that as many as 60% of patients with significant head injuries presented to the Emergency Room with dangerously low oxygen levels in the blood (defined as an arterial pO_2 of less than 60 mm Hg). The same study found that 15% of patients with significant head injury presented with systemic shock (defined as a mean arterial pressure of less than 60 mm Hg). Other studies have demonstrated that low oxygen in the blood or hypoxemia as well as low blood pressure or hypotension severely aggravate the brain injury and result in a much poorer prognosis. The combination of hypoxemia and hypotension is extremely bad with the effects being synergistic in a very negative way.

Therefore, prompt establishment of an adequate airway, and of proper oxygenation and ventilation is necessary. People with a Glasgow Coma Score of 8 or less will likely not protect their airways and are at substantial risk for aspiration of gastric contents into the lungs, hypoventilation with hypoxemia and dangerous elevations of carbon dioxide level. Therefore, in this group of patients placement of an endotracheal "breathing" tube should strongly be considered. Placement of such a tube can be very stimulating and can lead to a dangerous spike in the intracranial pressure if the pressure is already elevated to critical levels. For this reason, consideration should be given to having the intubation carried out by an expert anesthetist using established neuroanesthetic techniques. One also has to consider the potential for a cervical spine injury in the setting of significant head injuries, and the spinal column must be considered unstable until proven otherwise. During the course of the intubation this will necessitate at least gentle immobilization of the neck, and in selected circumstances, a fiberoptic visualization device to facilitate the intubation might be required (another reason to consider utilizing the services of an experienced neuroanesthetist). It is recommended that ventilatory support and supplemental oxygen be provided as necessary to maintain the arterial pO_2 at least 60 mm Hg and preferably better (in the range of 80-90 mm Hg).

With regard to the circulation, measures such as the administration of appropriate intravenous fluids and where necessary blood pressure-elevating drugs should be carried out to maintain the systolic blood pressure over 90 mm Hg as a first goal and then to raise the mean blood pressure to 90 mm Hg. Ultimately, the management of blood pressure in the severely brain-injured will be carried out to feed back information from intracranial pressure monitoring devices as will be discussed below.

The application of brain-specific treatments (for example, hyperventilation or osmotic diuretics, which will be discussed below) should usually await CT scan information and intracranial pressure recording. The exception is the patient demonstrating specific clinical manifestations of elevated intracranial pressure or progressive neurologic deterioration not attributable to extracranial sources.

8.6.3 Overall Management Goals

Generally, overall management goals are:

1. Maintain adequate airway, breathing and circulation with adequate oxygenation (pO_2 greater than 60 mm Hg) and blood pressures (mean arterial pressure or MAP of approximately 90 mm Hg or better).
2. If necessary, surgically remove any space-occupying lesions (such as intracranial haematoma) and clean and repair lacerations, depressed skull fractures, etc.
3. Control intracranial pressure.
4. Provide intensive supportive care to prevent metabolic disturbances such as low blood sodium levels.
5. Be vigilant for, take measures to prevent, and promptly treat complications affecting other body systems such as pneumonia, blood clots forming in the large leg veins (deep vein thrombosis), urinary tract infection, or pressure sores.
6. Provide adequate nutritional support.

8.6.4 Intracranial Pressure Monitoring

8.6.4.1 Introduction

We have discussed above, the potentially disastrous consequences of significantly elevated intracranial pressure, including brain tissue ischemia as well as brain shift and herniation. Therefore, it is not surprising that in the setting of severe head injury, it would be advantageous to monitor and control the intracranial pressure.

An important concept in the interpretation of intracranial pressure readings is the concept of cerebral perfusion pressure (CPP). This concept evolves from the consideration of the question "what determines the amount of blood flow to the brain tissue?" This is really a question of fluid mechanics and the answer comes from that field. The cerebral blood flow is determined by the pressure driving blood flow through the cerebral vessels divided by the resistance to flow of the blood vessels which depends largely on their calibre. The pressure driving flow through the blood vessels is known as the cerebral perfusion pressure. It is the pressure on the in flow or arterial side minus the pressure on the outflow or venous side. The pressure on the in flow side is the mean arterial pressure or MAP. The pressure on the venous side, as it turns out, is the same as the intracranial pressure. Thus we may write the equation CPP = MAP - ICP. In the normal brain, the blood vessels will adjust their internal calibre to vary the blood vessel resistance so that the amount of cerebral blood flow remains constant over a fairly wide range of perfusion pressures. This phenomenon is known as autoregulation. Unfortunately, a head injury extensively disrupts the autoregulation mechanism, often for a prolonged period of time. Under these circumstances the amount of cerebral blood flow is directly dependent on the cerebral perfusion pressure and maintaining an adequate cerebral perfusion pressure becomes critically important. A normal cerebral perfusion pressure reflects a normal mean arterial pressure (90 mm Hg) minus a normal ICP (roughly 10 mm Hg); thus a normal cerebral perfusion pressure is approximately 80 mm Hg. When the cerebral perfusion pressure drops below 60 mm Hg, the cerebral blood flow begins to drop to dangerously low levels. A cerebral perfusion pressure of less than 40 mm Hg is frankly inadequate and will lead to progressive tissue damage.

Thus when we are confronted with an elevated ICP, our goal must be more extensive than to "fix the abnormal number." When we make an intervention to try and lower ICP we must anticipate what effect our maneuver will have on cerebral blood flow by changing either the cerebral perfusion pressure or the cerebrovascular resistance.

8.6.4.2 Indications for Monitoring

The guidelines for intracranial pressure monitoring promulgated by the committee established by the Joint Section on Neurotrauma and Critical Care of the American Association of Neurological Surgeons and the Congress of Neurological Surgeons are:

Intracranial pressure (ICP) monitoring is appropriate in patients with severe head injury with an abnormal admission CT scan. Severe head injury is defined as a Glasgow Coma Scale Score (GCS) of 3 to 8 after cardiopulmonary resuscitation. An abnormal CT scan of the head is one that reveals haematomas, contusions, edema, or compressed basal cisterns (these are the prominent subarachnoid spaces around the upper brainstem at the base of the brain).

ICP monitoring is also appropriate in patients with severe head injury with a normal CT scan if two or more of the following features are noted at admission: age over 40 years, unilateral or bilateral motor posturing, systolic blood pressure less than 90 mm Hg.

ICP monitoring is not routinely indicated in patients with mild or moderate head injury, however, a physician may choose to monitor ICP in certain conscious patients with certain traumatic mass lesions.

8.6.4.3 Choice of Monitor

The "gold standard" for intracranial pressure monitoring has long been, and remains a ventricular catheter. This is a flexible plastic catheter placed through the brain tissue into the cerebrospinal fluid-filled ventricles deep within in the brain. This type of monitoring device offers the most accurate measurement of ICP. It also permits treatment of ICP by drainage of cerebrospinal fluid. It is, of course, invasive, requiring placement of a foreign body, which passes through the brain tissue. It is associated with an approximately 2% risk of intracerebral hemorrhage occurring at the time of placement. In addition, because it creates a portal from the outside to the intracranial compartment, it creates a risk of subsequent infections. The infection rate for ventricular catheters is in the 10% range. Infection risk rises progressively with the length of time the catheter has been in place.

A marginally less invasive catheter is the Camino fiberoptic intraparenchymal catheter. This is passed just into the superficial brain tissue, is smaller in diameter than a ventricular catheter, and carries with it a somewhat lower risk of hemorrhage and infection but only marginally so. It does not permit cerebrospinal fluid drainage.

Previously monitoring devices have been placed in the subarachnoid space, subdural space and epidural space; although considered less invasive, they have, over the years, proven to be unreliable and inaccurate. They are no longer recommended.

8.6.5 Additional Monitoring Techniques

8.6.5.1 Transcranial Doppler

An ultrasound device can be used to measure noninvasively the velocity of blood flow in the large blood vessels at the base of the brain around the Circle of Willis. Such measurements can give some indication of the state of blood flow. An increased flow velocity may indicate either narrowing of the cerebral blood vessels or increased cerebral blood flow in normal vessels. There are a variety of changes that have been described with rising intercranial pressure, which are beyond the scope of this chapter. Transcranial Doppler has not yet found a place as a standard monitoring method in the care of the head-injured patient, because of the unreliability of the measurements and the difficulty in interpreting their clinical significance. However, this is an area where treatment methods are evolving.

8.6.5.2 Jugular Venous Oxygen Saturation Monitoring

A fiberoptic catheter can be introduced into the jugular vein in the neck and advanced upwards to the region of the jugular bulb at the skullbase. In this position, it can measure the partial pressure of oxygen in the venous blood leaving the brain on that side (pvO_2). The difference between the oxygen saturation on the arterial side, paO_2 and that on the venous side pvO_2 gives a measure of oxygen extraction by the tissue. The greater a percentage of oxygen being extracted by the tissue, the more marginal cerebral profusion is in relation to the metabolic demands of the tissue. Thus, low pvO_2 readings correlate with inadequate cerebral profusion and risk of cerebral damage. This method can be usefully coupled with intercranial pressure readings to evaluate whether interventions to lower ICP are improving cerebral blood flow as would be hoped, or whether the interventions are in fact inappropriate and are reducing the ICP at the expense of dangerously reduced profusion of the brain.

This method is not in standard use in neurosurgical intensive care units as yet, but this is yet another area that is evolving as this text is written.

8.6.6 Treatment of Elevated Intracranial Pressure

8.6.6.1 Guideline for Initiating Treatment

Normal intracranial pressure in the adult is 6-12 mm of mercury. Intracranial pressure treatment should be initiated at an upper threshold of 20-25 mm of mercury. It is suggested that a cerebral profusion pressure (CPP = MAP - ICP) should be maintained at or above 70 mm of mercury.

8.6.6.2 Specific Therapeutic Measures

8.6.6.2.1 Introduction: What follows is a discussion of general measures used to treat elevated ICP. The presumption is that any specific lesions which require surgical intervention, such as intracranial haematomas, will have been removed and, as was discussed previously.

8.6.6.2.2 Sedation, Analgesia, and Neuromuscular Blockade: Adequate sedation and analgesia are a cornerstone of modern intensive management of severe head injury. A comatose patient is not necessarily insensitive to pain. The pain and agitation that can be associated with related injuries, with the stimulation of having an endotracheal breathing tube placed, and with other related ICU maneuvers can substantially increase cerebral metabolic rate, the demand for cerebral blood flow, the cerebral blood volume, and hence the ICP, as has previously been discussed. To prevent that, judicious use of analgesic and sedative medications is appropriate. One should always remember, in the patient who is breathing spontaneously rather than being supported with a mechanical ventilator, that narcotic analgesics could depress respiratory drive. Diminished ventilation can be dangerous as it can lead to elevated levels of carbon dioxide in the blood, which causes dilation of cerebral blood vessels and increased ICP.

Neuromuscular blockade is the use of curare-like drugs to induce temporary, generalized muscular paralysis. It may be a useful adjunct to sedative and analgesic agents in minimizing the effects of inappropriate cerebral agitation. However, it has the disadvantage of limiting the neurologic examination (with induced protomuscular paralysis, even an otherwise normal patient would be incapable of eye opening, speech, or any other motor response). In addition, neuromuscular blockade offers neither sedation nor analgesia, and may mask the clinical manifestations of pain or agitation. It is profoundly distressing for a patient to be paralyzed and wide-awake. Generally, short-acting, quickly reversible blockade agents should be used.

8.6.6.2.3 Head Elevation: The relatively simple maneuver of elevating the head of the bed promotes venous drainage out of the head, and is felt by some to retard edema formation (this is analogous to elevating a swollen limb). However, it also reduces cerebral profusion pressure. Thus, although increasing head elevation generally reduces ICP, it is possible in some cases to unacceptably lower the cerebral profusion pressure and the cerebral blood flow thereby creating a situation of tissue ischemia and exacerbating the tissue damage. Imperial application of head elevation by angling the head of the bed at 15 to 30 degrees above horizontal has traditionally been applied in neurosurgical units. A more rational application of this therapy would be based on measuring cerebral profusion pressure and ideally some measure of adequacy of cerebral blood flow, such as jugular venous oxygen saturation. These latter adjuncts to guiding head elevation are not in standard use at this time, but this is an evolving area of treatment.

8.6.6.2.4 CSF Drainage: Drainage of cerebrospinal fluid has one of the most favourable benefit-to-risk ratios of any therapeutic maneuvre that can be carried out for elevated ICP. It is only an option if a ventricular catheter has been placed to monitor ICP.

8.6.6.2.5 Hyperventilation: The use of a mechanical ventilator to induce hyperventilation (that is, cause the patient to breathe faster and deeper than normal) has been a standard treatment for raised intracranial pressure for many years. However, in recent years, the use of this therapy has become increasingly controversial. Hyperventilation by reducing the pCO_2 in the blood causes cerebral vasoconstriction and reduces ICP. However, the vasoconstriction reduces cerebral blood flow and can potentially be causing or worsening cerebral ischemia. Current management guidelines suggest that hyperventilation should not be used prophylactically. In addition, when used for the treatment of documented elevated ICP, it should generally be reserved for ICP problems that are refractory to treatment modalities with a more favourable benefit-to-risk ratio such as establishment of an adequate CBP, CSF drainage, sedation, analgesia, and neuromuscular blockade, and mannitol. When hyperventilation is used, the pCO_2 level should only be reduced moderately to the range of 30 to 35 mm of mercury (normal being 35 to 35 mm of mercury).

8.6.6.2.6 Mannitol: Mannitol is a so-called osmotic diuretic. When administered intravenously, it draws fluid from surrounding tissues into the blood stream leading to increased excretion of fluid by the kidneys. Mannitol has been found effective in reducing raised ICP following severe head injury. Intermittent administration is probably more effective than continuous infusion. Effective doses range from 0.25 to 1.0g/kg body weight administered at intervals of approximately 6 hours. Mannitol can lead to serious disturbances of the serum osmolarity. Osmolarity should be monitored and kept below 320 mosm/L to avoid participating kidney damage. The placement of a bladder catheter to drain the increased urine volume and monitor urine output is mandatory. Steps should be taken to ensure that the diuretic effect does not lead to dehydration.

8.6.6.2.7 Barbiturates: These anesthetic agents are powerful central nervous system depressants. They have been shown to be of benefit in reducing elevated ICP refractory to other treatment methods. They appear to exert their effect primarily by reducing cerebral metabolism and consequently cerebral blood flow. Thus, not only do they lower ICP but they also have a generally favourable effect on the ratio of cerebral blood flow to cerebral metabolic demand.

Barbiturates have a number of profound and potentially serious side effects, which make them a treatment of last resort. Firstly, they depress central nervous system function profoundly. A deep barbiturate-induced coma is indistinguishable clinically from brain death. Thus, when barbiturates are on board to a significant degree, the clinical neurologic evaluation of the patient is useless. Secondly, barbiturates depress respiratory drive, so that mechanical ventilatory support is mandatory. Thirdly, barbiturates depress vascular tone and heart pump function. Low blood pressure may be induced which can obviously be harmful to cerebral profusion and it may be necessary to use powerful cardiac stimulant drugs to counteract this. Lastly, and some feel most importantly, barbiturates substantially depress the function of the immune defense system and increase the risk significantly of serious and potentially life-threatening infections.

8.6.6.2.8 Corticosteroids: Highly potent synthetic analogues of steroid hormones produced by the adrenal cortex have been used for over 30 years to reduce brain edema in a variety of situations. They have proven most effective in reducing swelling (edema) due to accumulation of fluid in the extra cellular space resulting from leaky capillary vessels of the sort seen most typically in association with tumors. They have been relatively ineffective at reducing the intracellular so-called cytotoxic edema of the sort associated with head injuries. In addition, their anti-insulin effects tend to elevate blood glucose. In the setting of possible ischemia, elevation of blood glucose can lead to increased tissue acidosis and tissue damage. Also, these corticosteroids suppress immune system function and increase the risk of infection.

Because the benefit-to-risk ratio is not favourable in the setting of head injury for corticosteroids, their use in the head-injured patient is not currently recommended.

8.6.6.2.9 Anti-Seizure Prophylaxis: Following head injury, the risk of post-traumatic seizures (PTS) is significant. Post-traumatic seizures are classified as early if they occur within 7 days of the injury and late if they occur after 7 days. In a variety of head injury studies, the incidents of early PTS vary between 4% and 25% and of late PTS between 9% and 42% in untreated patients.

It is desirable to prevent both early and late PTS. However, it is not desirable to use medications with potentially serious neurologic and other side effects if they are ineffective at preventing such events.

A number of risk factors have been identified for the development of post-traumatic seizures. These include a Glasgow Coma Scale score of less than 10, cortical contusion, depressed skull fracture, intracranial haematoma, and penetrating head wound. In addition to above, the best risk factor for the development of late PTS is the occurrence of an early PTS.

The use of prophylactic anticonvulsants has not been demonstrated to reduce the incidence of late post-traumatic seizures. Therefore, the prophylactic use of currently available anticonvulsants is not recommended for preventing late PTS (they have not been shown to be of benefit and they have well-described significant potential side effects). However, prophylactic anticonvulsants have been shown to reduce the incidence of early PTS. The prevention of early PTS has not been clearly demonstrated to improve outcome following severe head injury. However, such prophylaxis is physiologically rational treatment. The presence of a seizure increases cerebral metabolic demand by some 300% over baseline levels. This increase in metabolic demand can certainly compromise cerebral tissue severely and damage it if cerebral profusion is marginal as may be the case in situations of severe head injury. Therefore, the use of prophylactic anticonvulsants during the initial treatment of severe head injuries is a reasonable option.

8.7 SELECTED SPECIAL TOPICS IN HEAD INJURY

8.7.1 Cerebral Concussion

8.7.1.1 Introduction

The following definitions and management guidelines are based on the recommendations of the Quality Standards Subcommittee of The American Academy of Neurology, promulgated to promote appropriate management of concussion in the setting of athletic competition, which is a very common background to the occurrence of concussion. The sub-committee's report appeared as a special article published in the journal *Neurology* in March 1997.

8.7.1.2 Definitions

Concussion is a trauma induced alteration in mental status that may or may not involve loss of consciousness. Confusion and amnesia are the hallmarks of concussion. The confusional episode and amnesia may occur immediately after the blow to the head or several minutes later. Close observation and assessment of the (patient) over some period of time is necessary to determine whether evolving neuropathologic change associated with concussion will lead to a confusional state, or to the development of memory dysfunction. A history of recent head trauma outside the sport setting, such as a motor vehicle accident, should be considered in the evaluation of an athlete with concussion.

Frequently observed features of concussion include:

1. A vacant stare or befuddled facial expression.
2. Slowness in answering questions or following instructions. Either the response required is verbal or motor.
3. Easy distractibility, confusion, and inability to focus attention.
4. Disorientation to identity, location, or day and exact date.
5. Slurred or incoherent speech.
6. Gross observable incoordination such as stumbling, inability to walk a straight line, or inability to tightrope walk.
7. Emotional lability.
8. Memory deficits, such as repeatedly asking the same question that has already been answered, or the inability to memorize and recall three of three words or three of three objects after five minutes.
9. Any period of loss of consciousness.

Symptoms of concussion may be divided into early categories, which occur within minutes to hours of concussion, and late categories, which occur days to weeks following concussion. Early symptoms include: headache, dizziness or vertigo, lack of awareness of surroundings, and nausea or vomiting. Late features of concussion include: persistent low grade headache, lightheadedness, poor attention and concentration, memory dysfunction, easy fatigability, irritability and low frustration tolerance, intolerance of bright lights or difficulty focusing vision. Intolerance of loud noises. Ringing in the ears, anxiety, depression, sleep disturbance.

Practitioners of sports medicine have established a concussion grading scale, which has proven useful in determining severity and planning appropriate management.

Grade I Concussion:

1. Transient confusion.
2. No loss of consciousness.
3. Concussion symptoms or mental status abnormalities on examination resolve in less than 15 minutes.

Commentary by the Committee: "Grade I concussion is the most common, yet the most difficult form to recognize. The athlete is not rendered unconscious and suffers only momentary confusion (e.g., inattention, poor concentration, inability to process information or sequence tasks) or mental status alterations. Players commonly refer to this state as having been dinged or having their bell rung."

Grade II Concussion:

1. Transient confusion.
2. No loss of consciousness.
3. Concussion symptoms are mental status abnormalities on examination lasting more than 15 minutes.

Commentary by the Committee: "With Grade II concussions, the athlete is not rendered unconscious but experiences symptoms or exhibits signs of concussion or mental status abnormalities on examination that last longer than 15 minutes (e.g., poor concentration or post-traumatic amnesia). Any persistent Grade II symptom (greater than one hour) warrants medical observation."

Grade III Concussion:

1. Any loss of consciousness.

8.7.1.3 Immediate on Scene ("Sideline") Evaluation

1. Test orientation to time, place, person, and situation (circumstances of injury).
2. Test concentration; the patient should be able to repeat a five-digit number backwards and name the months of the year in reverse order.
3. The patient should be able to name the teams involved in the athletic contest, should be able to recall three of three words and three of three objects at zero and five minutes after being given the names of the three words and objects. The patient should also be able to recall the details of the contest and recent newsworthy events.
4. External provocative tests. A 40-yard sprint, five push-ups, five sit-ups, and five knee bends. Any appearance of associated symptoms is abnormal; such as headaches, dizziness, nausea, unsteadiness, photophobia, blurred or double vision, emotional lability, or mental status changes.
5. Neurologic tests. The pupils should be checked for symmetry and reaction to light. Coordination should be checked by the rapidity with which the patient can touch his nose and the examiner's finger, back and forth in a rapid fashion. The ability to tandem walk (like walking a tightrope) should also be evaluated and normal. The balance should be normal and unswaying with the eyes closed, and feet together, and the arms outstretched. The patient should be able to bring his outstretched index finger in from the side and touch his nose accurately on both sides.

8.7.1.4 Management Recommendations

Grade I Concussion:

1. Remove from contest.
2. Examine immediately and at five-minute intervals for the development of mental status abnormalities or post-concussive symptoms at rest and with exertion.
3. May return to contest if mental status abnormalities or post-concussive symptoms clear within fifteen minutes.
4. A second Grade I concussion in the same contest eliminates the player from competition that day with the player returning only if asymptomatic for one week at rest and with exercise.

Grade II Concussion:

1. Remove from contest and disallow return that day.

2. Examine on-site frequently for signs of involving intracranial pathology.
3. A trained person should examine the athlete the following day.
4. A physician should perform a neurologic examination to clear the athlete for return to play after one full asymptomatic week at rest and with exertion.
5. CT or MRI scanning is recommended in all instances where headache or other associated symptoms worsen or persist longer than one week.
6. Following a second Grade II concussion, return to play should be deferred until the athlete has had at least two weeks symptom free at rest and with exertion.
7. Terminating a season for that player is mandated by any abnormality on CT or MRI scan consistent with brain swelling, contusion, or other intracranial pathology.

Grade III Concussion:

1. Transport the athlete from the field to the nearest Emergency Department by ambulance if still unconscious or if worrisome signs are detected (with cervical spine immobilization, if indicated).
2. A thorough neurologic exam should be performed emergently, including appropriate neuroimaging procedures when indicated.
3. Hospital admission is indicated if any signs of pathology are detected or if the mental status of the athlete is abnormal.
4. If findings are normal at the time of the initial medical evaluation, the athlete may be sent home. Explicit instructions will help the family or responsible parties observe the party over a period of time.
5. Neurologic status should be assessed daily thereafter until all symptoms have stabilized or resolved.
6. Prolonged unconsciousness, persistent mental status alterations, worsening post-concussion symptoms, or abnormalities on neurologic examination require urgent neurosurgical evaluation or transfer to a trauma centre.
7. After a brief (seconds) Grade III concussion, the athlete should be withheld from play until asymptomatic for one week at rest and with exertion.
8. After a prolonged (minutes) Grade III concussion, the athlete should be withheld from play for two weeks at rest and with exertion.
9. Following a second Grade III concussion, the athlete should be withheld from play for a minimum of one asymptomatic month. The evaluating physician may elect to extend that period beyond one month, depending on clinical evaluation and other circumstances.
10. CT or MRI scanning is recommended for athletes whose headache or other associated symptoms worsen or persist longer than one week.

11. Any abnormality on CT or MRI consistent with brain swelling, contusion, or other intracranial pathology, should result in termination of the season for that athlete, and return to play in the future should be seriously discouraged in discussions with the athlete.

8.7.2 Brain Death

8.7.2.1 Introduction

As the Canadian Medical Association has noted in its position paper on the Guidelines for Diagnosis for Brain Death, published in the Journal of the Canadian Medical Association in January of 1987, "The development of techniques for the ventilatory and circulatory support of critically ill patients has created a need for new definitions of death. Although irreversible cessation of circulatory and respiratory functions acceptably defines death, irreversible cessation of brain function is also equivalent to death even though the heart continues to beat while the patient is on a respirator."

Since the 1960s a variety of medical centres and medical societies have promulgated guidelines for the diagnosis of brain death. The goal has always been to establish criteria that define, with certainty, a situation of irreversible cessation of brain function. In general, these criteria have been similar, based primarily on the clinical evaluation of the patient, and have been proven reliable in large clinical studies. In one New York study, over 800 patients were followed in the Intensive Care Unit subsequent to a diagnosis of brain death, and were supported to the limits of technology. None of the patients survived and none made any neurologic recovery.

The guidelines below are those endorsed by the Canadian Medical Association upon the advice and consensus of its affiliated neurologic societies. These guidelines were published as a position paper in the *Journal of the Canadian Medical Association* on January 15, 1987.

8.7.2.2 Guidelines

Brain death must be determined clinically by an experienced physician in accord with accepted medical standards. Thus, the guidelines described below are based on current medical information and experience. As knowledge advances, it can be anticipated that further revisions will become necessary. Because of the major consequences of the diagnosis of brain death, consultation with other physicians experienced in the relevant clinical examinations and diagnostic procedures is usually advisable.

The clinical diagnosis of brain death can be made when all the following criteria have been satisfied.

1. An etiology has been established that is capable of causing brain death and potentially reversible conditions have been excluded (see Comment 2, below).
2. The patient is in deep coma and shows no response within the cranial nerve distribution to stimulation of any part of the body. No movements such as cerebral seizures, dyskinetic movements, "decorticate" or decerebrate posturing arising from the brain are present (see 1a, below).
3. Brainstem reflexes are absent (see 1b, below).
4. The patient is apneic when taken off the respirator for an appropriate time (see 1c, below).
5. The conditions listed above persist when the patient is reassessed after a suitable interval (see 2, below).

Comments: Although the purpose of this document is to state general principles and recommend guidelines rather than to outline a set of rules, certain features of the guidelines merit more detailed explanation.

1. *Cessation of brain function.* The clinical absence of brain function is defined as profound coma, apnea and the absence of brainstem reflexes.
   (a) *Coma.* The patient should be observed for spontaneous behaviour and response to noxious *stimuli*. In particular, there should be no motor response within the cranial nerve distribution to stimuli applied to any body regions. There should be no spontaneous or elicited movements (dyskinesis, "decorticate" or decerebrate posturing or epileptic seizures) arising from the brain. However, various spinal reflexes may persist in brain death.
   (b) *Brainstem reflexes.* Pupillary light and corneal, vestibulo-ocular and pharyngeal reflexes must be absent. The pupils should be midsize or larger and must be unreactive to light. Care should be taken that atropine or related drugs that could block the pupillary response to light have not been given to the patient. The vestibulo-ocular reflexes should be tested with caloric stimulation while the head is 30° above the horizontal. In adults, a minimum of 120 ml of ice water should be used. Grimacing or any other motor response to pharyngeal or tracheal suctioning is incompatible with brain death.
   (c) *Apnea.* Apnea was originally defined as lack of respiration when the patient was disconnected from the respirator for 3 minutes. This failed to consider whether an adequate $PaCO_2$ level was present to trigger respiration. The $PaCO_2$ threshold for respiratory

stimulation in comatose patients may be elevated to as high as 50 to 55 mm Hg, and many patients on respirators have low $PaCO_2$ levels that rise slowly (e.g., 2 to 3 mm Hg/min) when the respirator is stopped. In patients who fulfil the other clinical criteria of brain death, apneic oxygenation, described below, is a safe way of testing respiratory activity.

If blood gas determinations are available, the $PaCO_2$ should be 405 mm Hg before testing for apnea begins. The patient should be preoxygenated (but not hyperventilated) with 100% oxygen for 10 minutes before testing. The respirator is then disconnected for 10 minutes while, to prevent hypoxemia, 100% oxygen is delivered at 6 L/min through an endotracheal cannula. This should produce a sufficient rise in $PaCO_2$ to serve as a respiratory stimulant.

If blood gas determinations are not available, an adequate test of brain-stem responsiveness to hypercarbia can be provided by ventilating the patient for 10 minutes with a 95%oxygen/5% carbon dioxide mixture before the 10-minute apneic oxygenation. In patients with severe respiratory disease, it is advisable to obtain the opinion of a respiratory physician to determine the safety and validity of this test for apnea.

Testing for apnea without passive oxygenation is not recommended. In addition to its potential deleterious effects on the brain, the resultant hypoxemia can occasionally cause complex movements of the limbs and trunk, presumably owing to spinal cord ischemia, that could be confused with reflex movements of cerebral origin.

2. *Irreversibility.* Cessation of brain function is determined to be irreversible when potentially reversible causes have been excluded and the changes are judged to be permanent. Drug intoxication (particularly of barbiturates, sedatives and hypnotics), treatable metabolic disorders, hypothermia (core temperature less than 32.2C), shock and peripheral nerve or muscle dysfunction due to disease or neuromuscular-blocking drugs must be excluded.

Re-evaluation is essential to ensure that the nonfunctioning state of the brain is persistent and to reduce the possibility of observer error. Depending on the etiology, the interval between such examinations may be as short as 2 hours or as long as 24 hours; observation for at least 24 hours is usually recommended to confirm brain death due to anoxia/ischemia (e.g., postcardiac arrest). In situations where brain death is declared for purposes of organ transplantation, local regulations may stipulate specific intervals for reassessment.

Special Circumstances:

1. *Infants and children.* Brain death has not been sufficiently well studied in neonates, infants and young children to determine whether the clinical criteria listed above apply to these groups.
2. *Inability to apply the clinical criteria.* Some clinical situations such as uncertainty regarding etiology, inability to examine one or both eyes due to trauma, middle ear injuries, cranial neuropathies or severe pulmonary disease may preclude the valid application of the listed clinical criteria. In these circumstances, the only reliable means of confirming brain death is the absence of cerebral perfusion determined by cerebral angiography or radionucleide scintigraphy.

Laboratory Tests: Although brain death can be established reliably by clinical criteria alone, special tests can be used to support and in some instances supplement the clinical diagnosis. The electroencephalogram assesses cerebral cortical function. Electrocerebral inactivity is confirmation of brain death only if all the clinical criteria apply, and if established techniques are followed to ensure proper sampling of cortical activity. Visual, auditory and somatosensory evoked responses or other tests may eventually prove to be useful, but, at present, there are no standard guidelines for their use in assessing patients with suspected brain death.

The absence of intracranial perfusion, demonstrable by cerebral angiography or radionucleide scintigraphy, is reliable evidence of brain death. The mean arterial pressure should be greater than 80 mm Hg when cerebral perfusion is assessed. If cerebral angiography or radionucleide scintigraphy is used to determine the absence of cerebral perfusion, the procedure should be performed by an appropriately qualified specialist.

The above set of guidelines was prepared by a subcommittee of the Canadian Congress of Neurological Sciences and has been approved by the membership of the Canadian Neurological Society, the Canadian Neurosurgical Society, the Canadian Association for Child Neurology and the Canadian Society of Clinical Neurophysiologists.

Head Injury   337

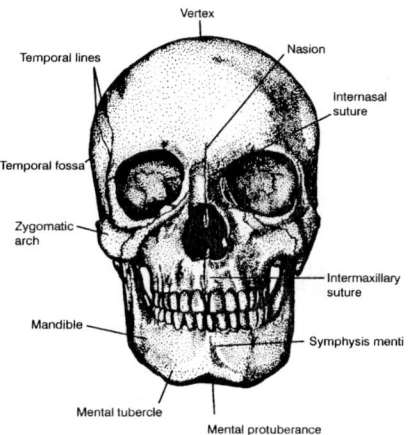

Figure 1
Frontal veiw of skull.

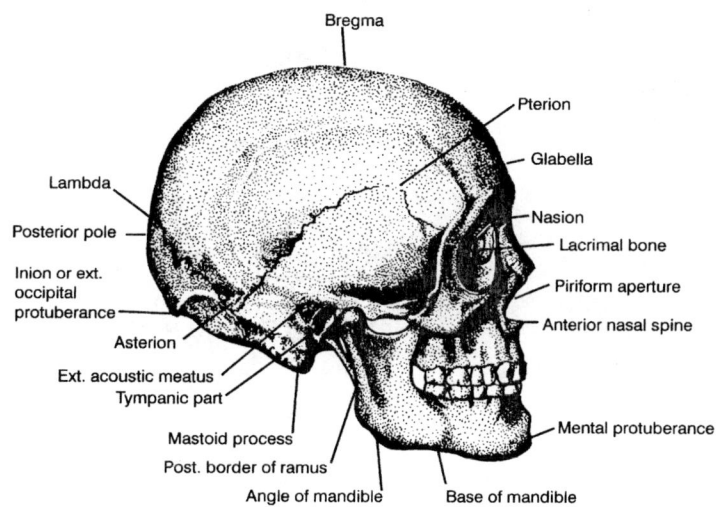

Figure 2
Lateral (side) view of skull.

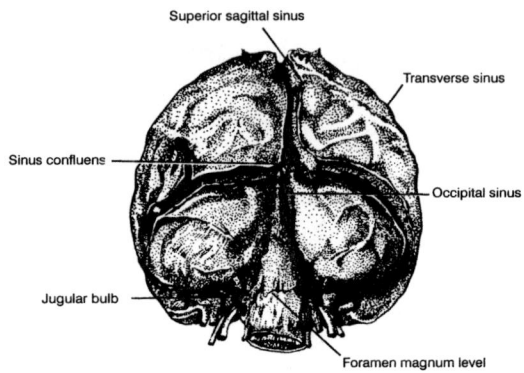

Figure 3
Posterior (back) view of the dura covering the brain. The large venous channels travelling through the dura and known as the dural sinuses have been cut open.

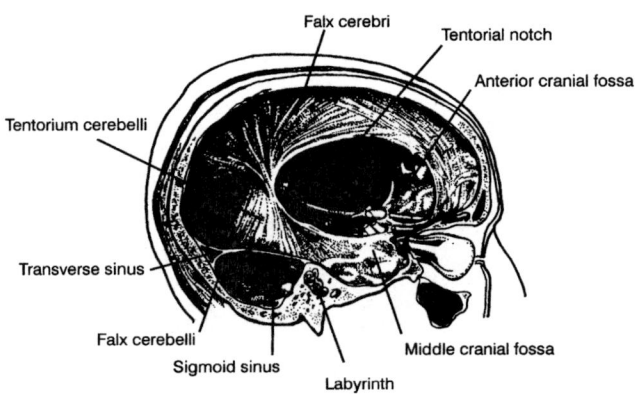

Figure 4A
Lateral (side) view of head cut away to show the infoldings of the dura that subdivide the brain case into compartments.

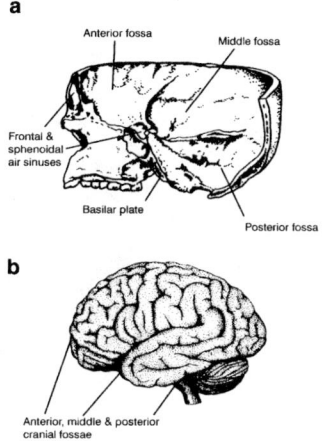

Figure 4B
Relationships between the inner surface of the skull (a) and the related brain regions (b).

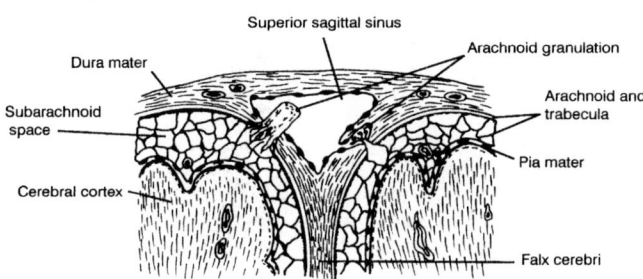

Figure 5
The layers of the meninges which cover the brain.

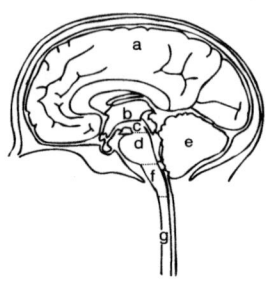

Figure 6
The divisions of the central nervous system:
(a) Cerebral hemisphere   (e) Cerebellum
(b) Diencephalon   (f) Medulla
(c) Midbrain   (g) Spinal cord
(d) Pons

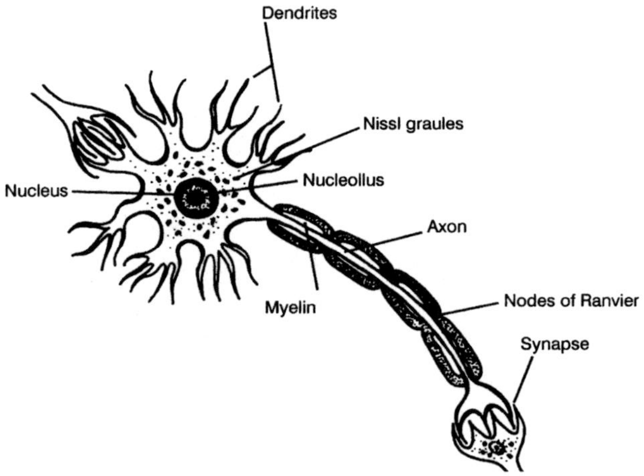

Figure 7
A typical neuron.

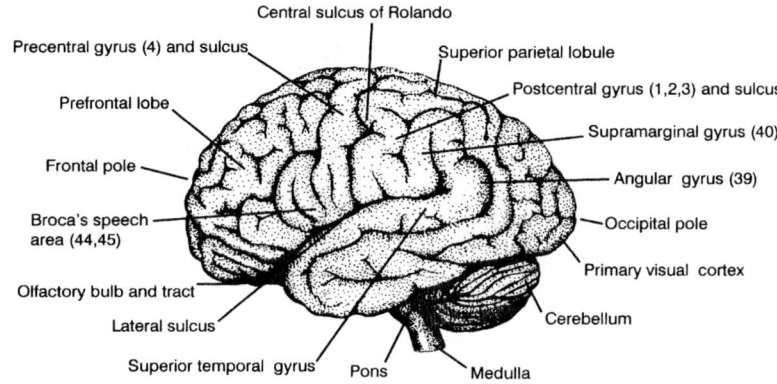

Figure 8
Lateral (side) view of brain.

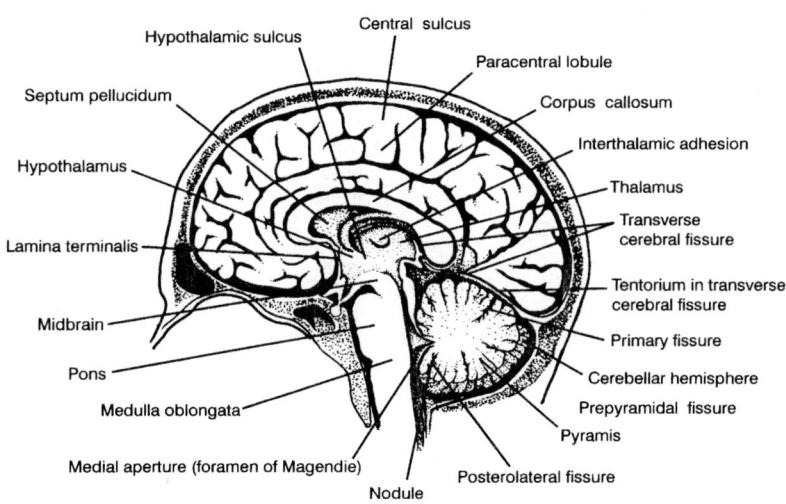

Figure 9
Medial (side view of midline surface) of brain.

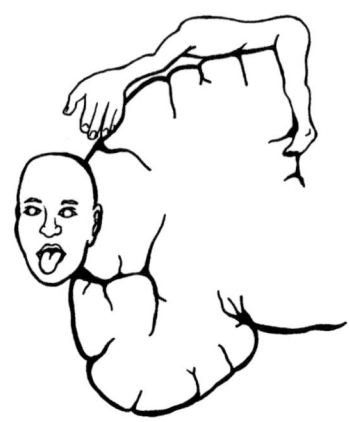

Figure 10A
The motor homunculus.

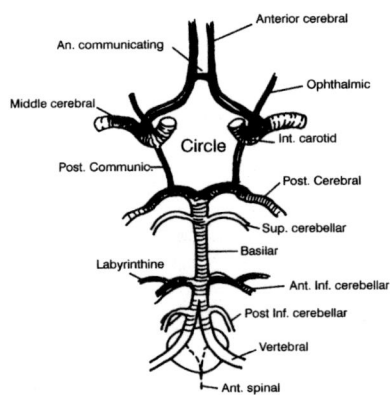

Figure 10B
The arterial supply to the brain.

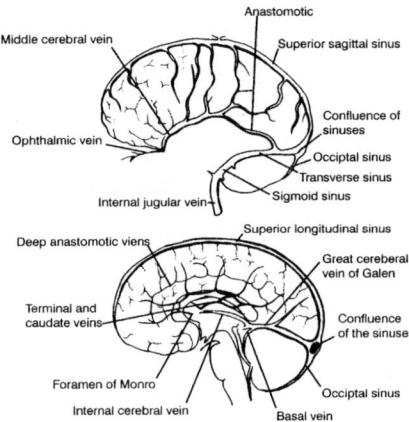

Figure 10C
The venous drainage of the brain.

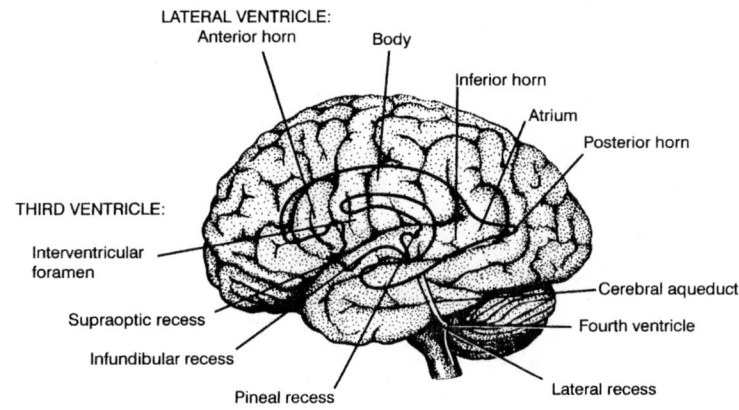

Figure 10D
The ventricles (lateral view).

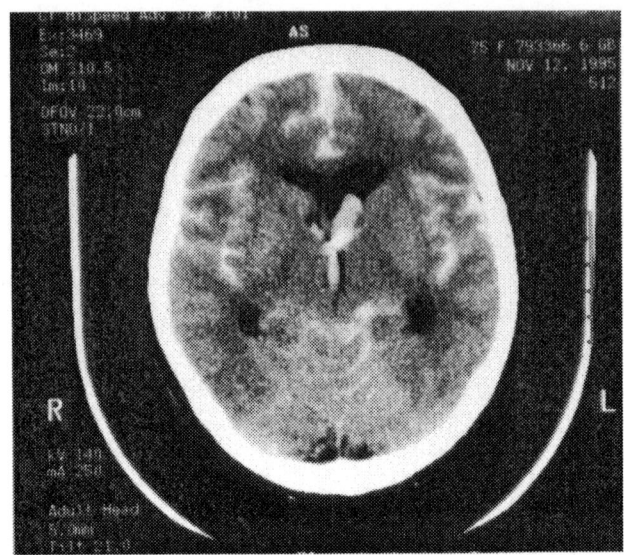

Figure 11
CT Scan of a patient with a diffuse axonal injury showing punctate hemorrhages.

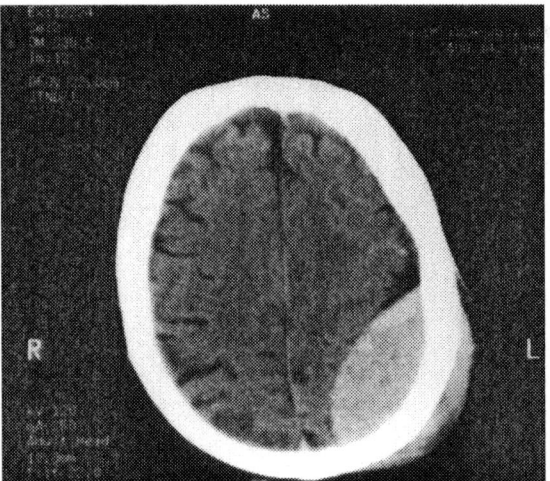

Figure 12
Acute epidural haematoma. Note the large light grey collection of blood inside the skull on the side of the image marked L and towards the bottom of the image. it is biconvex in shape and compresses the underlying darker grey brain tissue substantially. Outside the skull, there is a small collection of light grey blood within the scalp, marking this as the area where the blow to the head occurred.

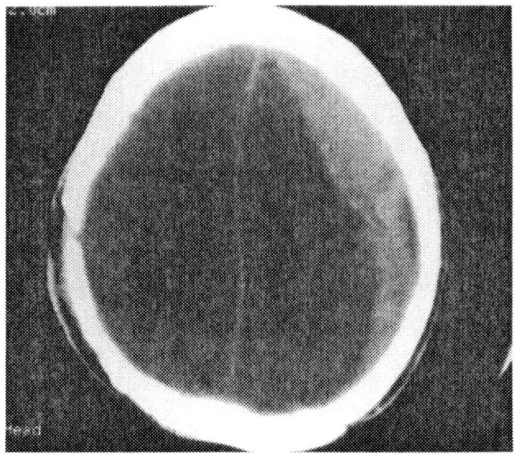

Figure 13
Acute subdural haematoma. Note the large light grey collection of blood inside the skull on the right side of the image. It extends over almost the whole hemisphere of the brain and compresses the underlying darker grey brain tissue substantially. In contrast to the previously illustrated epidural haematoma, the inner surface of the subdural haematoma tends to be flat or concave as it is here rather than convex.

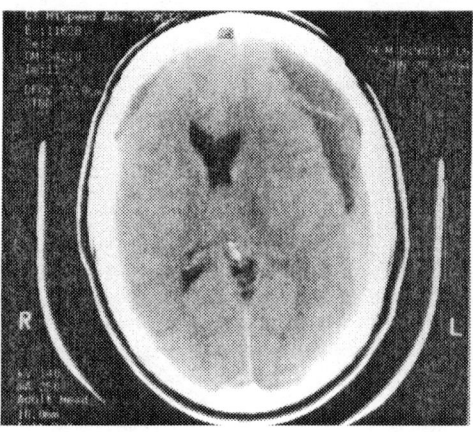

Figure 14
Chronic subdural haematoma. Note the large collection of blood inside the skull on the side of the image marked L. The portion of the collection towards the front of the brain (towards the top of the image) is darker than the underlying brain. This indicates blood that has been present for some time (generally more than 7 days, sometimes much more). The portion of the collection towards the back of the brain is a lighter shade of grey indicating it is more recently developed. Lastly note that there is a very small dark grey collection on the opposite side (marked R) towards the front.

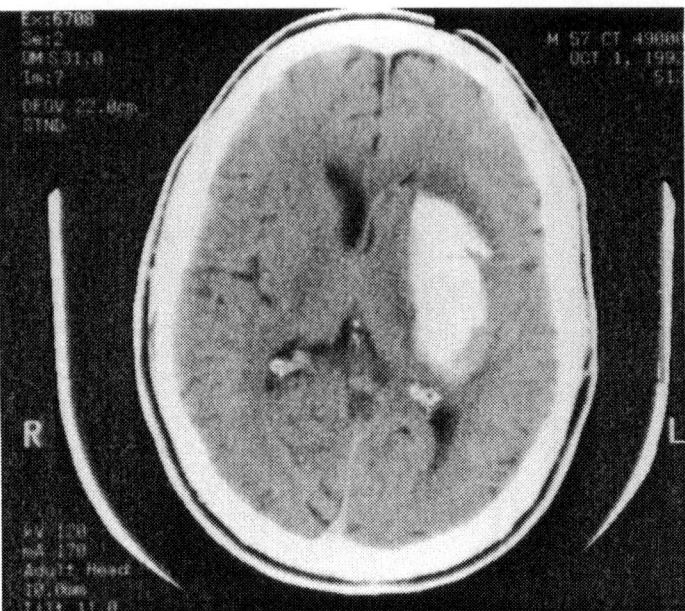

Figure 15
Acute Intracerebral haematoma (large).

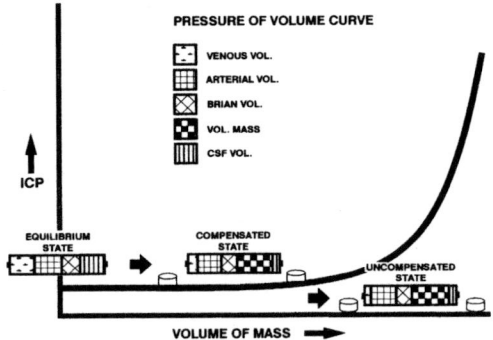

Figure 16
Intracranial pressure versus volume curve. (ICP = intracranial pressure).

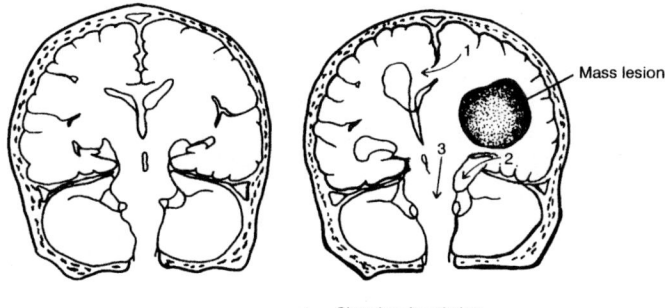

1 = Cingulate herniation
2 = Lateral Transtentorial herniation
3 = Central transtentorial herniation

Figure 17
Intracranial shifts and herniations.

The Glasgow Coma Scale

Eye Opening:
Spontaneous	4
To Voice	3
To Pain	2
None	1

Best Verbal Response:
Oriented	(To Person, Place, and Time)	5
Confused	(Attempts to answer but gives incorrect answers)	4
Inappropriate	(Using words but not attempting to answer questions)	3
Incomprehensible	(Not using words just moans and groans)	2
None		1

Best Motor Response:
Obeys		6
Localizes	(Can locate and push away noxious stimulus)	5
Withdraws	(Withdraw limb from noxious stimulus)	4
Abnormal Flexion	(a.k.a. decorticate posturing; stereotyped flexion in arms and extensions in legs either spontaneously or in response to noxious Stimulus)	3
Abnormal Extension	(a.k.a. decerebrate posturing; stereotyped extension in arms and legs either Spontaneously or in response to noxious stimulus)	2
None		1

Figure 18
The Glasgow coma scale.

Chapter 9

Neuropsychology and Traumatic Brain Injury

by Clare Stoddart, PH.D., C.PSYCH.
with the assistance of Robert M. Knights, PH.D., C.PSYCH.

9.1 The Neuropsychologist
9.2 Definition of Traumatic Brain Injury
    9.2.1 Glasgow Coma Scale
    9.2.2 Post-Traumatic Amnesia
    9.2.3 Post-Concussion Syndrome
    9.2.4 Post-Traumatic Stress Disorder
    9.2.5 Epidemiology
9.3 Neuropsychological Procedures
    9.3.1 Testing Procedures
        9.3.1.1 Interview and History
        9.3.1.2 Test Behaviour
        9.3.1.3 Test Administration
    9.3.2 Personality Variables which may Affect Test Performance
        9.3.2.1 Malingering
        9.3.2.2 Depression
        9.3.2.3 Pain
        9.3.2.4 Anxiety
    9.3.3 Commonly Used Tests
        9.3.3.1 Intelligence
        9.3.3.2 Attention and Concentration
        9.3.3.3 Memory and Learning
        9.3.3.4 Language
        9.3.3.5 Visuospatial and Visuoconstructive Abilities
        9.3.3.6 Sensory-Motor Abilities
        9.3.3.7 Executive Functions
        9.3.3.8 Personality Measures
    9.3.4 Test Results
        9.3.4.1 Test Interpretation
        9.3.4.2 Test Report

9.4 Sequelae of Traumatic Brain Injury
   9.4.1 Cognitive Sequelae
      9.4.1.1 Attention and Concentration
      9.4.1.2 Memory
      9.4.1.3 Learning
      9.4.1.4 Executive Functions
   9.4.2 Emotional and Behavioural Sequelae
      9.4.2.1 Fatigue
      9.4.2.2 Irritability
      9.4.2.3 Emotional Lability and Disinhibition
      9.4.2.4 Insensitivity or Lack of Empathy
      9.4.2.5 Anosognosia
9.5 Rehabilitation and Recovery
   9.5.1 Factors Related to Rehabilitation
   9.5.2 Rehabilitation Techniques
   9.5.3 Recovery — Age, Severity, Extent

9.1 THE NEUROPSYCHOLOGIST

Clinical neuropsychology is an applied science concerned with the relationship between brain and behaviour. Neuropsychological assessments are generally used in the evaluation of individuals who are known or suspected of having focal or diffuse brain dysfunction such as occurs in traumatic brain injury (TBI). From a legal perspective, these are primarily the result of motor vehicle accidents but may also occur in work-related accidents such as falls. The neuropsychologist may be asked to determine whether or not a brain injury has occurred and also the effects of impairment on the individual's future rehabilitation and vocational options. A neuropsychological assessment is frequently required in cases of minor traumatic brain injury where more subtle changes in higher cognitive functions may not be detected in a mental status examination, and neurodiagnostic tests such as the electroencephalogram (EEG) and neuroimaging tests such as the computerized tomography (CT) and magnetic resonance imaging (MRI) have revealed normal findings. It is possible to have no physical findings on these tests and still demonstrate impaired adaptive and behavioural skills.[1]

Neuropsychological assessment is based on a knowledge of the functional neuroanatomy of the brain and relies on the extensive use of stand-

---

[1] Bigler ED, Snyder JL. Neuropsychological Outcome and Quantative Neuroimaging in Mild Head Injury. *Archives of Clinical Neuropsychology.* 1995; 10(2):159-174.

ardized tests to investigate brain-behaviour relationships. The clinical neuropsychologist, as a psychologist, is a member of a regulated health profession governed by the College of Psychologists of Ontario. A clinical neuropsychologist should have training in neuroanatomy, neuropathology, clinical neurology, psychological assessment, and psychopathology. In addition, he/she should have 1 year of practice supervised by a clinical neuropsychologist, and (in the author's opinion) in order to testify in court, at least a second year of practice in the field.

9.2 DEFINITION OF TRAUMATIC BRAIN INJURY

9.2.1 Glasgow Coma Scale

The term traumatic brain injury is used in this chapter as preferable to the term "head injury" as the latter does not specifically imply damage to the brain per se, as might occur in superficial scalp lacerations. The most commonly accepted definition of the severity of brain injury is the Glasgow Coma Scale,[2] which is a brief rating completed by an emergency nurse or physician of the patient's responsiveness to questions of visual, vocal and motor instructions. The total score is 15 and scores below 5 rated severe, 6 to 11 rated moderate, and those 12 to 15 as mild injury. The other estimates of severity, obtained from the patient when interviewed and from medical records, refer to the period of loss of memory, or clouded and confused recall.

9.2.2 Post-Traumatic Amnesia

It is essential to provide an estimate of the length of retrograde amnesia (loss of memory for events preceding the accident) and post-traumatic amnesia (PTA), that is, loss of memory for events immediately following the accident. The period of post-traumatic amnesia is sometimes used as an indicator of the severity of the brain trauma. A PTA duration of greater than one week is associated with a severe traumatic brain injury (TBI), 1 to 7 days with a moderate TBI, and less than 24 hours with a mild TBI.

Individuals who have persistent cognitive emotional and physical complaints beyond the expected time of recovery from a minor trauma or where there is no substantial evidence of brain trauma may be suffering from a post-concussion syndrome (PCS) or a post-traumatic stress disorder (PTSD).

---

2   Teasdale G, Jennet B. Assessment of Coma and Impairment of Consciousness: A Practical Scale. *Lancet* 1974; 2:81-84.

9.2.3 Post-Concussion Syndrome

In some persons involved in accidents a concussion can occur without the head actually striking anything, such as in a whiplash injury.[3] This is due to the acceleration/deceleration phase of the injury which causes microscopic stretching and tearing or shearing of some axon fibers, and is often related to rotational forces which are greatest at the surface of the brain in the frontotemporal areas. These individuals may be diagnosed as suffering from a post-concussion syndrome (PCS), although there is considerable overlap between this term and "minor head injury" in some textbooks.[4]

The symptoms of PCS may occur in any area of functioning and the cluster of symptoms vary among individuals. The most common complaints are considered to be in three different domains — cognitive, somatic and affective/behavioural. The cognitive signs are: difficulty in attention and concentration, memory for new information (as well as retrograde and PTA), slowed information processing, and loss of abstract thinking. The somatic symptoms, which are somewhat unique to TBI, include: hearing, visual, smell and taste disturbances, dizziness, and sleep disorders. Headache and fatigue are common (40–80%) but are less diagnostic since they often occur in controls (20-40%). Affective and behavioural symptoms include disinhibition, emotional lability, depression, loss of libido, and the need to dwell on past events.

PCS symptoms, such as decreased concentration, may not become apparent until the individual attempts to return to work, when the cognitive demands are greater than when not working, and the individual must now function in a distracting environment. It has sometimes been assumed that due to the delay in reporting these symptoms, these complaints are less genuine or not directly related to the brain trauma. In addition, in the early stages following a motor vehicle accident in which an individual has sustained physical injuries, they and their caretakers are more concerned with abilities such as walking independently than with more subtle cognitive deficits. The delay in reporting these symptoms may lead to an erroneous assumption that the symptoms are due to such factors as ongoing litigation or secondary gain.

---

3 Evans RW. Some Observations on Whiplash Injuries. *Neurology Clinics.* 1992; 10(4):975-997.

4 Rutherford WH. (1989) Postconcussion Symptoms: Relationship to Acute Neurological Indices, Individual Differences, and Circumstances of Injury. In: Levin HS, Eisenberg HM, Benton AL, eds. *Mild Head Injury.* Oxford: Oxford University Press, 1989.

9.2.4 Post-Traumatic Stress Disorder

The extent of PTSD which occurs is dependent on a number of psychosocial variables and the personality characteristics, displayed by the person, which existed prior to the head injury. PCS is most evident immediately following the injury and tends to decrease over time, whereas PTSD tends to occur when a person has recovered from the immediate effects of the trauma and is in the recovery phase.

The most common symptoms of PTSD also may occur in a variety of areas of functioning, but tend not to include as many somatic symptoms. There are often cognitive complaints of difficulty in concentration and attention as well as memory problems, but the majority of symptoms are affective/behavioural in nature. These include: anxiety, reliving the event, avoidance of thoughts or feelings or situations that recall the event, apathy, loss of affect, fatigue, and sleep problems.

In PTSD the accident becomes a focus for the person's difficulties and the added stress and anxiety may render the person incapable of returning to his/her regular home and/or employment responsibilities. There is an overlap in the syndromes of PCS and PTSD, but the difference is considered to be that PCS results from a specific cluster of symptoms which has a neurologic basis, while PTSD occurs as a function of the trauma situation and the person's inability to cope with additional life stressors.

9.2.5 Epidemiology

It is estimated the rate of motor vehicle accidents is approximately 100 per 100,000 persons and one-quarter of these are rear-end collisions resulting in a whiplash injury.[5] The most common TBI patient is male (two to three times the female rate) between 16 and 34 (40–60%), single (approximately 60%) with less than 12 years of education (approximately 50–70%). Motor vehicle accidents are most common in the young adult age group while falls are more common in children and the older age group. Alcohol is estimated to be a factor in 50 to 70% of accidents. Seat belt use has dramatically reduced the frequency and severity of motor vehicle injury by two to three times. Most persons with mild TBI make good recoveries (50–90%) and the patients seen by neuropsychologists are a minority group who do suffer debilitating symptoms.

---

5 Evans, *supra*, note 3, at 975-997.

9.3 NEUROPSYCHOLOGICAL PROCEDURES

9.3.1 Testing Procedures

9.3.1.1 Interview and History

In order to complete a neuropsychological assessment of a traumatically brain injured patient, a thorough interview and history is required in order to determine the individual's pre-trauma level of functioning and identify the possible contribution of pre-existing conditions such as neurologic, psychiatric, and learning disorders or substance abuse. This information should be corroborated by any previous medical, educational, or occupational records. It is also important to obtain information from significant others, as the brain-injured individual may not himself be aware of any changes in functioning. This lack of self-awareness, or denial, is the result of the neurologic dysfunction rather than a psychological defense mechanism, but may cause significant problems for the patient who insists that nothing is wrong with him. The individual may also have memory problems which preclude his ability to provide a coherent history. The individual with an alleged head injury should be questioned regarding his ability to recall the accident itself, including events immediately preceding and following the accident. This can provide important information related to the severity of the brain injury and aid in differential diagnosis. Patients who are able to provide a detailed coherent account of the accident itself are unlikely to have suffered a traumatic brain injury, and reports of nightmares, or flashbacks related to the accident are more typical of a post-traumatic stress disorder (PTSD). Sbordone's book on *Neuropsychology for the Attorney*[6] is a very comprehensive review of most of the topics discussed in this chapter.

9.3.1.2 Test Behaviour

Behavioural observations of the patient during the interview and testing procedures in both structured and unstructured settings also form an important component of the neuropsychological assessment. This provides information related to motivational factors, such as anxiety or depressed mood, which have an effect on their test performance. It may also reveal inconsistencies between observed functional abilities, such as locating the psychologist's office and remembering the correct appointment times, and severely impaired performance on formal memory assessment procedures. This inconsistent behaviour-test performance raises the consideration of possible malingering.

---

6   Sbordone RJ. *Neuropsychology for the Attorney.* Orlando, FL: Paul M. Deutsch Press, 1991.

9.3.1.3 Test Administration

The tests are always administered in a standardized fashion according to the instructions in the test manual. Each test has normative data for age and, where appropriate, sex and education. There are reliability data and research studies of the performance of normal and brain-injured, on the tests described.[7]

The neuropsychological evaluations are comprehensive and therefore expensive. A typical assessment requires 5 to 8 hours of testing time, then 5 to 12 hours of test scoring, data interpretation and report writing. A feedback interview explaining the meaning of the test results is typically given to the patient and/or relevant spouse or care taker.

Neuropsychological procedures are unique in that there is a consideration of real life cognitive capacities of the person to be able to maintain normal family interactions, to return to employment, and to handle everyday skills, such as driving. For many individuals, driving ability is crucial for their employment and must be carefully considered.

9.3.2 Personality Variables which may Affect Test Performance

9.3.2.1 Malingering

The possibility of faking or conscious or unconscious malingering during the test performance is of great concern to both the neuropsychologist and the attorney.[8] The frequency of malingering is considered to be low. Snow[9] estimated the frequency in neuropsychological settings to be between 5 and 20%. Malingering behaviour is usually detected by an experienced neuropsychologist. The signs during the interview include inaccurate history details, an attitude of "martyred gloom", arriving late, and family member taking an active part in the interview process. The most predominant feature is the person's conviction that they are unable to work, which is discordant with their assessed disability or observed everyday activities. During the testing these persons demonstrate a lack of interests in the tests, provide unusual responses, and fake selectively. They may show normal IQ scores but do poorly on sensorimotor measures. There are tests of malingering which are designed to be very easy so that doing

---

7 Spreen O, Strauss E. *A Compendium of Neuropsychological Tests.* New York: Oxford University Press, 1991.
8 Reitan RM, Wolfson D. *Detection of Malingering and Invalid Test Scores.* Tucson AZ: Neuropsychological Press, 1997.
9 Snow, WG. *Implications of Base Rates for the Diagnosis of Malingering.* Poster presented at the International Neuropsychological Society Annual Meeting, San Diego, February 1995.

poorly is a deliberate attempt to fail. For example on a forced choice technique they tend to score below chance levels.

Tests of malingering are given when the tester observes the patient is not motivated to try hard, since most patients want to do well and find the tests challenging. Patients with and those without litigation and compensation claims, have similar symptoms which improve with time, and present a similar pattern of cognitive abilities. They do not generally produce greater neuropsychological deficits.[10] There is, however, a minority with more subjective complaints and litigation pending may increase the level of stress. The end of litigation does not end or cure the patient's problems nor does the resolution result in a return to work for many claimants.

9.3.2.2 *Depression*

Depression is a common finding in an individual with a TBI due to a reaction to loss of functional abilities and loss of self-esteem. In addition it may be caused directly by brain dysfunction. For example, damage in the frontotemporal region, diffuse white matter, the limbic system and neurotransmitter systems have all been implicated as possible physiological causes of depression. Frequently depressive symptoms are not apparent until some time after the TBI, in which case they are generally considered to be psychologically based due to a reaction to losses. Individuals with mild head injury are often particularly prone to depression as they experience frustration stemming from their inability to walk and talk appropriately and may appear to the lay person as if nothing is wrong. This may result in a return to work too soon after the injury, and subsequent difficulties in the work situation leading to experiences of failure and increasing the likelihood of a reactive depression.

Due to the frequent co-occurrence of depression and head injury it should be considered as a possible confounding factor in evaluating the results of a neuropsychological assessment. Individuals who are clinically depressed typically present as unmotivated. They show a slowed speed of psychomotor response and tend to do worse on more effortful tasks. Responses to verbal questions are frequently minimal and drawings are sketchy showing a lack of attention to detail. Other individuals, particularly those suffering from an emotional reaction to circumstances, may report a high number of subjective complaints of memory and concentration problems but do well on these measures on the highly structured testing situation. Differentiation between depression and TBI is frequently important from a legal perspective and presents a challenge to the neuropsychologist. It is sometimes necessary to conduct reassessments when an

---

10   Rutherford WH, *supra*, note 4.

individual has been treated for his/her depression either with medication or psychotherapy or a combination of both.

9.3.2.3 Pain

Chronic pain is discussed in more detail in another chapter in this book. Individuals who have sustained a traumatic brain injury particularly in a motor vehicle accident may also suffer from chronic pain, headaches, low back pain and myofascial pain. The severity of pain and the location of pain may have an effect on the individual's neuropsychological test performance and should be taken into account in the interpretation of the test results.

Information regarding pain symptoms may be obtained from the clinical interview, behavioural observations of the patient and personality measures such as the MMPI-2. The most common cognitive deficits associated with chronic pain are inattention and impaired concentration. Chronic pain patients do not show localized or lateralized findings in neuropsychological functioning.

9.3.2.4 Anxiety

As is the case with depression, elevated levels of anxiety are frequently seen in individuals who have sustained a TBI. This may be the result of neurological deficits, but also may be seen as a reaction to the individual's increased awareness of their neuropsychological and physical deficits. Individuals who have been made aware of their cognitive deficits may also begin to show a chronic self doubt of the correctness of their responses or actions. This can lead to further social isolation and avoidance of social situations which in turn increases the level of emotional distress.

Individuals who are observed to have high levels of anxiety during the assessment procedures may respond well to more detailed discussion procedures or require that the assessment be conducted in a number of shorter sessions. The role of anxiety in the individual's test performance may be determined by the overall pattern of neuropsychological test results as some tests are known to be particularly sensitive to the effects of anxiety. If anxiety is considered to have affected the test results this would be indicated in the Neuropsychological Report.

9.3.3 Commonly Used Tests

A neuropsychological assessment includes a comprehensive battery of tests designed to evaluate the individual's ability in a wide variety of brain-behaviour relationships. The choice of tests may be determined by factors such as the severity of the traumatic brain injury and the individual neuropsychologist's personal orientation. The areas of abilities assessed, however, should include measures of intelligence, attention, concentration, memory and learning, visuospatial abilities, language, sensory-motor skills, and executive functions such as planning, self-monitoring and problem-solving. Measures of academic abilities and personality/emotional functioning are also frequently included.

The tests briefly described below will provide the attorney with a working knowledge of the abilities measured by these commonly used tests and will show how the pattern of results is used to evaluate variables such as severity, location, diffuseness, and chronicity of the lesion. The best and most comprehensive text that includes a description of neuropsychological tests and test techniques is provided by Lezak.[11]

9.3.3.1 Intelligence

Most neuropsychologists use the Wechsler Adult Intelligence Scale (Revised) as the commonly used standardized measurement of intellectual functioning. This test provides a Verbal I.Q., Performance I.Q., and an overall, or Full Scale, I.Q. These scores are summary scores derived from the five verbal subtests and six performance or nonverbal subtests. In neuropsychological assessment, the examiner may be more interested in the pattern of the individual subtest scores. For example, overlearned verbal measures such as Vocabulary are frequently preserved in brain injury and may be used as an indication of premorbid level of functioning, whereas timed performance subtests such as Digit Symbol, a paper-and-pencil coding test, are frequently lowered following a TBI. It is also important to remember that the standardized intelligence test, such as the WAIS-R, was not specifically developed to determine brain-behaviour relationships and that significant cognitive deficits resulting from brain trauma may not necessarily result in a lowering of I.Q. scores.

9.3.3.2 Attention and Concentration

Assessment of attention and concentration forms an important part of the neuropsychologist's evaluation. Deficits in attention and concentration may compromise performance on other measures, and problems with sustained attention and concentration are typically seen in TBI patients with significant diffuse axonal injuries. Tests used to evaluate attention and concentration should include measures of basic attention, such as digit span, but also tasks requiring alternating or divided attention such as Trails B, a visuomotor tracking task, requiring alternating between numbers and letters and the Consonant Trigrams task, a measure of sustained attention and

---

11 Lezak MD. *Neuropsychological Assessment.* Oxford: Oxford University Press, 1995.

concentration requiring the recall of stimulus material following a distractor task.

9.3.3.3 Memory and Learning

The most commonly used standardized measure of memory functioning is the Wechsler Memory Scale-Revised. This test includes both a Verbal and a Visual Memory Index, measuring the immediate recall of information in each modality, and also a Delayed Recall Index measuring recall of both types of information following a time delay. Decay of information over time is a frequent sequela following a traumatic brain injury. Measures of learning through repetition and sensitivity to distractor tasks may provide information important in future rehabilitation, such as whether the individual learns best in the verbal or visual modality or shows increased sensitivity to distraction. Examples of these tests are the California Verbal Learning Test, the Rey Auditory Verbal Learning and the Rey Visual Design Learning Test.

9.3.3.4 Language

Language assessment should include measures of confrontation naming such as the Boston Naming Test, and measures of verbal fluency or word-list generation (how many words can be generated beginning either with a particular letter or from a specific semantic category). In cases where the patient's language impairments have been more severely affected, specific aphasia batteries may be employed such as the Western Aphasia Battery.

9.3.3.5 Visuospatial and Visuoconstructive Abilities

Visuospatial abilities are assessed by various drawing tasks, including reproducing the Rey Complex Figure, and individual performance subtests of the WAIS-R, which require visuospatial conceptualization and integration, such as Block Design and Object Assembly.

9.3.3.6 Sensory-Motor Abilities

A neuropsychological assessment should also include measures of sensory-motor functioning. Sensory tests include measures of finger localization, in which the patient must identify with his eyes closed which finger has been touched, and fingertip number writing, in which the patient must identify which of four numbers have been written on each of the five fingers. Motor skills may be assessed through measures of finger-tapping, which measures the patient's ability to rapidly depress a lever attached to a counter with his index finger, grip strength, and fine motor coordination. These motor and sensory tests are administered bilaterally, that is, to each hand, and may be used to provide information to determine the laterality (side of the brain) that has been damaged. Neuropsychological measures of sensory-motor functioning may provide useful functional information related to the individual's ability to resume tasks such as assembly work requiring fine motor coordination. In addition, these measures form an important part in providing information regarding whether the damage is primarily to the left or right hemisphere, as both sensory and motor information are represented contralaterally in the cerebral hemispheres. That is, information from the right body side is mediated by the left hemisphere and vice versa, information from the right body side is mediated by the left hemisphere. Interpretation of these findings should take into account that impaired performances may be attributable to peripheral nerve damage or orthopaedic injuries.

9.3.3.7 Executive Functions

Measures of executive functions generally include tasks requiring abstract reasoning, problem-solving, planning and organization, and self-regulation and monitoring. Impaired verbal abstract reasoning may be seen on the similarities subtests of the WAIS-R, where the patient must state how two objects are related. Interpretation of proverbs is also sometimes used as a measure of verbal abstract reasoning; however, this is highly dependent on the individual's educational level and cultural background. The Wisconsin Card Sorting Task is frequently used as a measure of nonverbal problem-solving skills. This test requires deductive reasoning to generate the concepts involved in the task, and it also requires mental flexibility as the patient must be able to modify his method of responding on the basis of feedback from the examiner.

9.3.3.8 Personality Measures

Assessment of personality functioning may be included in a neuropsychological assessment. The most widely used personality inventory is the Minnesota Multiphasic Personality Inventory (MMPI-2). This test was not designed to determine brain damage and caution should be used in interpreting the results in an individual with a traumatic brain injury. For example, an individual may endorse items reflecting a wide variety of vague physical symptoms which are directly related to the brain injury or other injuries sustained in the accident rather than imagined physical problems. The MMPI-2 does, however, contain validity scales which can provide information as to whether or not the individual is malingering. It may also reveal significant emotional problems which need to be taken into account in evaluating the individual's performance on neuropsychological tests.

9.3.4 Test Results

9.3.4.1 Test Interpretation

Of paramount importance to the attorney is the interpretation of the pattern of tests results presented by the neuropsychologist. The tests are standardized, but the validity of interpretation is dependent on the skill and experience of the neuropsychologist. In evaluating brain-behaviour relationships, not only is the level of performance or quantitative analysis used (usually a measure of severity), but also: qualitative indicators, pathognomonic signs, right-left differences, and change in test scores over time. The pattern of abilities and deficits often indicates how diffuse the damage is, the extent of the lesion, the location of the lesion, and the potential for recovery. The pattern of neuropsychological tests is different for focal versus diffuse brain damage. Cerebral contusions may result in focal damage, in which case the neuropsychological impairments demonstrated are generally consistent with tasks mediated by the site of injury. For example, frontal lobe damage is often associated with difficulty in executive functions. Temporal lobe injury is associated with memory problems. Damage to the left hemisphere of the brain is typically associated with language impairments (expressive or receptive aphasia), verbal memory deficits, decreased verbal fluency, impairments in reading and writing, and right-sided motor and sensory deficits. In addition, the individual with primarily left-hemisphere damage may demonstrate difficulty in processing information that is analytic, discrete, and sequential in nature. When the individual presents with marked language problems this is usually immediately evident to family members and caregivers. However, when damage is primarily to the right cerebral hemisphere, the cognitive impairments may not be so readily obvious, particularly initially in the structured setting of the hospital. Individuals with damage to the right hemisphere may demonstrate difficulty in copying designs, making constructions, discriminating patterns, visual memory deficits and left-sided sensory-motor impairments. In addition, individuals with right-hemisphere damage may have difficulty in information processing that requires perceiving the global gestalt or seeing the overall picture. In view of the fact that these individuals display intact language abilities and may show preservation of social skills, the severity of their impairments may be underestimated or overlooked if a complete neuropsychological assessment is not conducted.

9.3.4.2 Test Report

The neuropsychological test report regarding a traumatic brain injured client should include a discussion of most of the following points:

1. The examiner's estimate of the reliability of the test results, which

commonly include comments on cooperation and effort, fatigue, and possible malingering.
2. The level of intellectual functioning and a comment on the severity of brain damage (e.g. mild, moderate, severe) and the probable change in score from pre-injury, based on the history information, to post-injury performance.
3. The pattern of abilities and deficits in the areas of attention/concentration, memory & learning, language, visuospatial, sensory and executive abilities and their implications for returning to previous activities.
4. Comments on whether the lesion is diffuse or localized, and if localized, which hemisphere and if possible the area and extent. The location of lesion will differentially affect abilities as previously described.
5. The need for reassessment, since recovery is most accurately measured after two or three testings in the 2 years after injury.
6. The prognosis with respect to personal and family adjustment and the probable return to previous employment capabilities.
7. Comments on any limitations to be imposed with respect to driving a motor vehicle.

9.4 SEQUELAE OF TRAUMATIC BRAIN INJURY

9.4.1 Cognitive Sequelae

9.4.1.1 Attention and Concentration

Deficits in attention and concentration are frequently found in an individual who has suffered a TBI. The nature of the deficits will vary according to the severity of the brain injury and the length of time since the injury. Problems with sustained attention and concentration affect the individual's ability to maintain attention on a task over time, or be able to keep track of more than one thing at a time. These abilities are particularly important in a work setting where the employee may have difficulty functioning in a distracting environment. Problems with attention and concentration also affect the individual's ability to remember recent conversations or instructions causing distress in both social situations and work environments.

9.4.1.2 Memory

While memory complaints are frequent in traumatically brain-injured patients, estimates range from 40 to 80%, it is important to determine the nature of reported difficulties in memory. Individuals with less severe injuries will normally display problems in recalling new information or memory for day-to-day events since the accident, while they show preservation of their ability to recall events prior to the accident. Neuropsychological assessment can provide information not only to differences between whether auditory or verbal information has been selectively affected, but also to the stage in the memory process in which the individual may be experiencing difficulty. Problems may arise with the initial encoding or processing information, the storage or consolidation in memory, or in the subsequent retrieval.

9.4.1.3 Learning

Limitations in learning abilities have important implications for possible further retraining or rehabilitation for the traumatically brain-injured. Information regarding the best possible learning strategies may be obtained from comparing the individual's performance on different neuropsychological tests. For example, the use of verbal versus visual learning, limiting the amount of information presented at one time or teaching more appropriate ways of encoding information through the use of categorical cues can be recommended.

9.4.1.4 Executive Functions

Deficits in these areas are generally attributable to frontal lobe dysfunction and are common sequelae of a traumatic brain injury, secondary to contusions or diffuse axonal shearing. Impairments may be manifested in mental flexibility, self-monitoring, problem-solving, planning and organization, and initiation. Deficits in these areas are not only the most difficult to treat, but are also frequently confused with psychiatric/emotional problems. For example, the individual with difficulties in initiation, or being able to get started on a task, may be considered as "lazy" by family members. A lack of self-awareness may make it difficult to engage the patient's participation in a rehabilitation programme. An individual with frontal lobe dysfunction may show a marked tendency to perseverate, or get stuck in a specific way of responding. This may be evidenced as mental inflexibility, being unable to perceive an alternative solution to problem-solving, or displayed as stereotypical repetitive behaviour.

9.4.2 Emotional and Behavioural Sequelae

9.4.2.1 Fatigue

Fatigue is one of the most common behavioural sequelae of traumatic brain injury. In part, this may be attributable to disturbances in sleep patterns, but may also reflect the fact that many activities which were once automatic now require deliberate effort to accomplish.

9.4.2.2 *Irritability*

Increased irritability or decreased frustration tolerance is a frequent complaint of TBI patients and their families. For example, they will report having a "short fuse" or getting easily annoyed with their children for minor incidents. This, in part, reflects the individual's difficulty with self-monitoring or being unable to control their emotional behaviour.

9.4.2.3 *Emotional Lability and Disinhibition*

An individual who has suffered a TBI may have significantly impaired ability to monitor his/her emotional behaviour. This may take the form of inappropriate angry outbursts, or laughing or crying for apparently little reason. Inappropriate social behaviour may also be seen in more frequent use of swear words, or inappropriate sexual behaviour.

9.4.2.4 *Insensitivity or Lack of Empathy*

Individuals with a TBI frequently have difficulty in being able to perceive a situation from another's point of view and may present as more egocentric or self-concerned than they were prior to the injury. The lack of insight may lead to significant problems in relationships and result in social isolation and marriage breakdown.

9.4.2.5 *Anosognosia*

Anosognosia or denial of disability, is the lack of ability to perceive the severity of one's condition and is a real neurologic deficit generally associated with damage to the right parietal lobe or the frontal lobes. This may lead to significant difficulties in dealing with insurance companies or under cross examination in court, because the individual's lack of insight leads him to a denial of cognitive impairments. It can also significantly affect the ability of the patient to benefit from a rehabilitation program as the individual fails to perceive the need for treatment.

9.5 REHABILITATION AND RECOVERY

9.5.1 Factors Related to Rehabilitation

Professionals generally agree that treatment of the brain-injured patient is efficacious and important for recovery. Therapy by speech, occupational, and rehabilitation professionals should be conducted as soon as possible after the injury. The exact mechanisms of recovery by the brain are not well understood but they are characterized by: 1) reduction of edema, or brain swelling due to water content, in the short term, usually over days; 2) the capacity of the brain for adaptation or reorganization in some physiological way, although how this occurs is not readily explained; and 3) in the long term, the individual's ability to compensate or adjust to his or her lost skills. The available evidence at the present time, indicates that the major factor in recovery is influenced primarily by the severity of injury and then to subsequent personal and environmental factors.

9.5.2 Rehabilitation Techniques

There is enough research evidence in the area of the remediation of brain-injured patients to indicate real and positive effects. The various types of therapy include those directed to the remediation of speech, memory, visual imagery techniques, verbal expressive and receptive strategies, behavioural shaping, attentional deficits and cognitive rehabilitation. The efficacy of strategies of "substitution" and "compensation", are used in speech therapy, memory training techniques such as "written or electronic memory books" and "cueing" are often used by rehabilitation therapists, and are generally considered helpful by professionals in the area. Visual imagery training involves the use of the "peg method" in which the association is established between the list of items which are to be remembered and the "peg" list which consists of a previously learned list of words. The peg words are selected on the basis of phonetic and rhyming similarity. An alternative to using peg words is to use peg locations or to use the "link method", which involves sequencing from one "peg" to the next.

Verbal strategies are usually related to motivation, retrieval techniques, relaxation, rehearsal and repetition. Behavioural prosthetics refer to apparati that are available in electronic circuitry devices. Diaries, wrist watches with alarms, and pagers with a vocal reminder are all available and reasonably priced.

Training of attentional and concentration processes are typically divided into alertness, selective attention and vigilance. The general goals are the elimination of errors, increasing the speed of performance and reducing the level of complexity of task. An Orientation Remedial Module program is available from Ben-Yishay[12] and Bracy[13] has published a number of computer training programs.

9.5.3 Recovery — Age, Severity, Extent

The neuropsychological assessment, because it is comprehensive and standardized, provides an excellent basis for evaluating change in level of functioning after brain injury. Ideally, the patient should have three

---

12 Ben-Yishay. *Working Approaches to Remediation of Cognitive Deficits in Brain Damaged Persons.* New York: NYU Medical Center, 1980.

13 Bracy, OL, Computer Assisted Rehabilitation Therapy. J Cog Rehab 1992: 10(3):28.

neuropsychological assessments, one soon after the brain injury, one at 6 months and then 2 years later. Most patients show improvement; however, some remain stable and a few deteriorate due to brain atrophy, which is revealed by their test scores. Unfortunately, some patients become dysfunctional due to psychogenetic factors. It is, of course, extremely important for all persons involved in a litigation procedure to have acquired all school and occupational records available prior to, and subsequent to, the trauma in order to independently assess any changes that may have occurred.

Recovery is often difficult to evaluate due to complicating factors such as pain and depression. Post-traumatic stress syndrome, related to an accident, is another reaction which leads to personal inability to function at previous levels and is often disruptive to marital, family and occupational adjustment.

Recovery from post-concussion symptoms has been shown to be dependent on a number of variables, including socioeconomic status, family and social support systems, higher educational level, and the absence of pre-existing psychopathology such as substance abuse.

In conclusion, it is recommended that an evaluation of the patient's functional capacity be obtained by a detailed and extensive personal history and cognitive and neuropsychological assessments in order for the court to make reasonable and realistic judgments regarding rehabilitation.

Chapter 10

Spinal Injuries[†]

by Jacques A. Bouchard, M.D., F.R.C.S.C.[*]
and John Latter, M.D., F.R.C.P.C.[**]

10.1 The Role of Each Team Member
    10.1.1 Ambulance and Paramedics
    10.1.2 Trauma Team Leader
    10.1.3 Spinal Surgeon
    10.1.4 Rehabilitation Specialists
10.2 The Cervical Spine
    10.2.1 Anatomy
        10.2.1.1 Osseous Anatomy
        10.2.1.2 Intervertebral Discs
        10.2.1.3 Ligaments
        10.2.1.4 Muscles
        10.2.1.5 Nerves and Spinal Cord
            10.2.1.5.1 Gross Anatomy
            10.2.1.5.2 Neuroanatomy
            10.2.1.5.3 Motor Tracts
            10.2.1.5.4 Sensory Tracts
    10.2.2 Biomechanics of the Neck
        10.2.2.1 The Occipito-Atlanto-Axial Complex (C0–C1–C2)
        10.2.2.2 The Subaxial Complex (C2 to T1)
        10.2.2.3 Concepts of Spinal Stability
        10.2.2.4 Common Injury Mechanism
    10.2.3 Evaluation of the Patient with a Cervical Injury
        10.2.3.1 History
        10.2.3.2 Physical Examination
    10.2.4 Soft Tissue Injuries
        10.2.4.1 Ligament Strain

[†] Jacques A. Bouchard, is author of that portion of the Chapter comprised in 10.1 to 10.2.6.2 and 10.3 onward. John Latter is author of 10.2.6.3 to 10.2.6.5 inclusive.
[*] Associate Professor, Division of Orthopaedic Surgery, University of Ottawa.
[**] Professor in Head, Section of Physical Medicine and Rehabilitiation, University of Manitoba.

                10.2.4.2 Muscle Strain
                10.2.4.3 Acceleration Injuries (Whiplash)
                10.2.4.4 Disc Disruption and Herniation
        10.2.5 Fractures and Dislocations
                10.2.5.1 Atlanto-Axial Fractures
                10.2.5.2 Flexion Instabilities
                10.2.5.3 Rotational Instabilities
                10.2.5.4 Extension Instabilities
                10.2.5.5 Clay Shoveler's Fracture
                10.2.5.6 Gunshot Injuries
                10.2.5.7 Seat Belts and Airbags
                10.2.5.8 Treatment of Fractures and Dislocations
                        10.2.5.8.1 Brace Treatment
                        10.2.5.8.2 Halo Vest Treatment
                        10.2.5.8.3 Surgical Treatment
        10.2.6 Neurologic Injuries
                10.2.6.1 Assessment
                10.2.6.2 Classification
                        10.2.6.2.1 Root Injuries
                        10.2.6.2.2 Incomplete Cord Lesions
                        10.2.6.2.3 Complete Cord Lesions
                10.2.6.3 Treatment and Rehabilitation
                        10.2.6.3.1 Initial Treatment
                        10.2.6.3.2 Definitive Treatment
                        10.2.6.3.3 Rehabilitation and Long-Term Management
                10.2.6.4 Complications
                        10.2.6.4.1 Decubitus Ulcers (Pressure Sores)
                        10.2.6.4.2 Pulmonary
                        10.2.6.4.3 Contractures
                        10.2.6.4.4 Osteoporosis
                        10.2.6.4.5 Infection of the Urinary Tract
                        10.2.6.4.6 Bowel Obstruction
                        10.2.6.4.7 Deep Vein Thrombosis
                        10.2.6.4.8 Automomic Dysreflexia
                        10.2.6.4.9 Heterotopic Ossification
                10.2.6.5 Life Expectancy
10.3 The Thoracolumbar Spine
        10.3.1 Anatomy
                10.3.1.1 Osseous Anatomy
                10.3.1.2 Intervertebral Discs
                10.3.1.3 Ligaments of the Thoracolumbar Spine
                10.3.1.4 Muscles of the Thoracolumbar Spine

            10.3.1.5 Neuroanatomy of the Thoracolumbar Spine
            10.3.1.6 Location of Pain Fibers in the Spine
    10.3.2 Biomechanics and Pathophysiology of Thoracolumbar Injuries
            10.3.2.1 The Three-Column Concept
            10.3.2.2 Mechanism of Injury and Classification
    10.3.3 Evaluation of the Patient
            10.3.3.1 History
            10.3.3.2 Physical Examination
                    10.3.3.2.1 Nonorganic Physical Signs
            10.3.3.3 Investigations
            10.3.3.4 Missed Spine Fractures
    10.3.4 Fractures and Dislocations of the Thoracolumbar Spine
            10.3.4.1 Classification
                    10.3.4.1.1 Compression Fractures
                    10.3.4.1.2 Burst Fractures
                    10.3.4.1.3 Flexion-distraction Injuries
                    10.3.4.1.4 Fracture-dislocation
            10.3.4.2 Treatment
                    10.3.4.2.1 Initial
                    10.3.4.2.2 Pharmacologic Treatment
                    10.3.4.2.3 Nonoperative Treatment
                    10.3.4.2.4 Operative Treatment
            10.3.4.3 Outcome
    10.3.5 Soft Tissue Injuries
            10.3.5.1 Disc Disruption and Herniation
    10.3.6 Spondylolysis and Spondylolisthesis
    Figures

10.1 THE ROLE OF EACH TEAM MEMBER

Spinal injuries most commonly occur as a result of motor vehicle accidents or as a result of falls from a height. In some parts of North America, penetrating injuries such as gunshot wounds frequently cause spinal injury. The assessment and treatment of these injuries are complex and require a team effort. The stages of management are the following:

1. Safe extraction of the patient from site of accident and transport to the emergency room;
2. Emergency room stabilization of the patient and evaluation of the injuries;
3. Definitive treatment of the spinal injury—acute care hospitalization;
4. Rehabilitation to regain independence; and
5. Discharge to the community and reintegration in society.

An efficient and smooth transition between these stages, that is, a seamless management flow of care, is more likely to have lower morbidity and mortality in the short term and optimal final function for the injured in the long term.

10.1.1 Ambulance and Paramedics

The vertebral column (axial skeleton) has two main functions. The first function is to provide a strong but flexible structure that will support the rest of the skeleton. The second function is to house the spinal cord that transmits the majority of neural impulses from the brain to the rest of the body. These two functions must constantly be kept in mind throughout the treatment of a spine injury.

When should we consider the possibility of a spine injury? Whenever somebody is found unconscious and there has been no witnesses; when an injury results from a high risk activity (such as a car, motorcycle, diving or falling traumas); or whenever an injury is followed by the person complaining of neck pain, back pain, numbness and/or weakness of the extremities. The first person who arrives at the site of such an injury should be concerned primarily with the overall safety of the injured. If there is no immediate danger to the injured, for example, no smoke, no fire, no possibility of drowning, then the injured should be left where he/she is until trained personnel (ambulance attendants, paramedics or fire fighters) arrive. The role of the paramedics is to provide life support while safely extracting the injured from the trauma site and transporting him/her to a treatment centre.

The spine must be stabilized prior to the injured being moved. This is done by placing a rigid collar on the neck and then placing a board behind the patient's back, neck and head. Log-rolling is a technique that is used frequently to move patients with an unstable or potentially unstable spine from the ground to the stiff board (or from stretcher to stretcher).[1] Four persons are the minimum required to achieve this: one controls the head and neck, one holds the legs, and the other two move the shoulder/trunk and pelvis in unity. Once the patient is on the board, safety straps are fastened to the legs, trunk, and head and, frequently, sand bags or intravenous fluid bags are placed on each side of the head to prevent rotation of the neck. A collar alone is not enough to do that. The patient is kept in this position for transportation until they reach the hospital where further evaluation can be carried out.

This elaborate set-up is always done with a goal in mind: protect the *spinal cord* from injury. Damage to the spinal cord is to a great extent irre-

---

1 McGuire RA, Neville S, Green B, Walls C. Spinal Instability and the Log Rolling Maneuver. *J Trauma*, 27:525-531, 1987.

versible even with modern day care. Nothing can be done about the damage that occurs at the time of impact. We can only prevent further damage that can occur while the bones and ligaments of the vertebral column heal.

The American College of Surgeons Committee on Trauma describes the first hour after an injury as being the "golden hour". The initial management of a patient determines the chances of survival. Transportation of the patient to a treatment facility needs to be appropriately efficient, either by land or by air.

10.1.2 Trauma Team Leader

On the arrival of a spinal injury patient, the initial duty of the trauma team leader, emergency physicians or family practitioners, is to stabilize the vital signs and assess the patient by use of history, physical examination, radiographs, and blood tests. Once the diagnosis of a spinal injury has been made, then appropriate treatment can be determined. If the injury is straightforward and the vertebral column is stable, the treatment may be symptomatic and discharge from the emergency can occur the same day. For more complex injuries, consultation is made to a spinal surgeon.

10.1.3 Spinal Surgeon

Surgeons dealing with injuries to the spinal column are usually trained in orthopaedic surgery or neurosurgery. There has always been an overlap of these two specialties with respect to the spine. Neurosurgeons deal primarily with pathology of the brain and spinal cord, and by extension the vertebral column that surrounds the cord. Orthopaedic surgeons repair bone, joints, ligaments, and muscle anywhere in the body. Historically, neurosurgeons have concentrated on the treatment of cervical spine injuries and orthopaedic surgeons on thoracic, lumbar, and sacral injuries. Today, in many parts of North America, this relationship continues to exist.

However, over the last decade, many technological developments have made spine surgery more complex, requiring surgeons to "subspecialize". Both orthopaedic surgeons and neurosurgeons alike elect to pursue additional training in spinal surgery after the completion of their formal training. This has led to the formation of spine surgeons that can deal with spinal problems from the skull to the tailbone and to the creation of integrated spine units where both orthopaedic surgeons and neurosurgeons participate or direct the care of patients with spinal injuries.

Consultation with a spinal surgeon is obtained when an opinion is required or if a patient has one or more of the following symptoms:

1. a neurologic deficit;
2. an unstable spine;
3. a deformed spine.

The duties of the spine surgeons, therefore, are to:

1. assist the emergency or trauma surgeon in assessing a patient;
2. protect the neurologic function of a patient with a spine injury;
3. improve if possible a neurologic deficit;
4. stabilize an unstable spine;
5. correct spine deformities, that is, reduce a fracture or dislocation of the vertebrae.

The spine surgeon will assume the care of the patient for at least 1 to 2 weeks until the acute problems are managed. The following 3 to 6 months will be required for the injuries to heal. During this period, the patient is mobilized with the assistance of nurses, physiotherapists, and occupational therapists.

10.1.4 Rehabilitation Specialists

Most spinal injuries will require very little rehabilitation, particularly if there is no neurologic deficit. In the event of paralysis of any kind, prolonged immobilization, multiple system injuries, or pain control problems, extensive rehabilitation may be required. This is usually coordinated by a physiatrist or rehabilitation specialist. The prime example of a patient requiring such services is a spine injury causing paraplegia or quadriplegia. A large team, consisting of physiatrists, physiotherapists, orthotists, occupational therapists, psychologists, nurses, social workers, vocational counsellors and others, is required to re-educate the patient in performing basic activities of daily living and to achieve some level of independence and mobility. Another example would be a patient who is suffering from a chronic pain condition as a result of a prior spinal injury. There is no effective treatment for this type of problem, and a multitude of different modalities must be attempted.

10.2 THE CERVICAL SPINE

10.2.1 Anatomy

10.2.1.1 Osseous Anatomy

The spine is a column of bone divided into segments called vertebrae. These are linked by intervertebral articulations which allow movements of the spine while maintaining stability to protect the spinal cord and nerves. The typical human spine consists of 33 vertebrae. The first 24 are mobile and the remaining nine are fused together to form the sacrum and coccyx.

The mobile vertebrae are further divided in three different regions which differ in anatomy, biomechanics, and function: the cervical, thoracic and lumbar regions. The cervical and lumbar spine are in lordosis, which means that they are convex anterior. [Figure 10.1] The thoracic and sacral spine are in kyphosis and are convex posterior. This alignment is established in utero but its final form and magnitude is established at the end of skeletal growth. The vertebrae are designated according to their anatomic region: C for cervical, T for thoracic, L for lumbar, and S for sacral. Each vertebra is then numbered from cranial to caudal within its respective region, that is, C1 to C7, T1 to T12, L1 to L5, and S1 to S5. The occipital condyles of the skull articulate with C1 and are therefore referred to as C0. At the distal end four or five small ossicles form the coccyx and are usually addressed as a single unit.

The vertebrae are the bony element of the spine. Each vertebra is composed of two major parts: the anterior part is called the body and the posterior elements form the vertebral arch. [Figure 10.2] The vertebral body is oval shaped and formed mostly of cancellous (spongy and soft) bone with a thin cortical outline. The upper and lower aspects of the body articulate with the intervertebral discs through a hyaline cartilage endplate. The vertebral arch or neural arch is much more complex. The arch is attached to the body by two solid posts called pedicles. Four structures attach to the dorsal aspect of the pedicle. The lamina extends medially, connects the two pedicles, and closes the osseous ring that contains the spinal cord. The lateral projection from the pedicle forms the transverse processes. The cranial projection forms the superior articular process which articulates with the vertebra above through the facet joint. The caudal projection forms the inferior articular process which articulates with the vertebra below through the next facet joint. Finally a projection from the lamina in the midline is called the spinous process. These characteristics are shared by most of the vertebrae; however, there are several unique features of the cervical vertebrae.

The first cervical vertebra, otherwise known as the atlas, is essentially a ring with two flat and oval superior articular processes which articulate with the occipital condyles of the skull and two inferior articular processes which articulate with C2. C1 does not have a vertebral body since its vertebral body fuses to C2 during the prenatal development of the skeletal system. [Figure 10.3] This forms the odontoid or dens, which forms a superior peg allowing the ring of C1 to rotate on C2. Hence C2 is also called the axis.

The C3 to C7 vertebrae follow the typical anatomic features described earlier in this section. The following are the salient features that distinguish them from the thoracic and lumbar vertebrae: 1) The transverse processes are short, broad, and form a lateral extension of both the vertebral body and the pedicle. Within this lateral bony mass runs the foramen tranversarium which contain the vertebral arteries. 2) The superior end plate of the vertebral bodies are flared laterally and articulate with the inferior end plate of the next vertebra forming two joints called the joints of Luschka (or neurocentral joints). Although small, these joints have a strategic importance since they are located just medial to the vertebral artery and just anterior to the nerve root. 3) The spinous processes of C2 to C6 are often bifid. 4) The spinous process of C7 is very large and easily palpable as a surface landmark (vertebra prominens). 5) The facet (zygapophyseal) joints lie approximately 45 degrees from the horizontal plane and are shallow. This allows for freedom of movement in all directions. 6) The intervertebral foramina face anteriorly by 45 degrees and therefore require an oblique cervical radiograph to visualize properly. They form a canal 4 to 6 mm long through which the nerve roots exit. The normal foramina is 10 mm in its vertical diameter and 5 mm in its anteroposterior diameter.[2] The size of the foramen will vary with neck movements and with pathological processes such as arthritis of the facet joint and the joint of Luschka, disc herniations, tumors, subluxations, or dislocations. 7) The vertebral canal is fairly large, especially at the upper cervical levels. It narrows down like a funnel to the thoracic spine so that at C6 75% of the canal is taken up by the spinal cord. The anteroposterior diameter of the vertebral canal may vary considerably. Numerous studies have demonstrated that the critical diameter is 13 mm. Patients with a canal diameter below this, as measured on a standard lateral radiograph of the neck, may exhibit clinical signs of spinal cord compression.

10.2.1.2 *Intervertebral Discs*

Between each vertebral bodies lies a flat, oval, soft but resilient disc which can withstand large axial loads while permitting multiplanar motion between two vertebrae. The intervertebral disc has three components. [Figure 10.4] The outer margin is called the annulus fibrosus and is formed of multiple laminated sheets of collagen. The central portion is called the nucleus pulposus and is a gelatinous mixture of proteoglycans and collagen. Because of the gel properties of the nucleus, water can be drawn in or pushed out of the disc, which affects the flexibility and the cushioning properties of the whole disc. The top and bottom of the discs are in contact with the bone of the vertebral bodies. This part of the disc is called the end plate and is made of cartilage. The discs of the cervical, thoracic, and lumbar spine all have the same general structure but the size and shape differ from one level of the spine to the other.

---

2 Cramer GD, Darby SA. *Basic and Clinical Anatomy of the Spine, Spinal Cord and ANS*. St. Louis: Mosby, 1995.

10.2.1.3 Ligaments

The ligaments of the spine are vital structures that permit motion between vertebrae while maintaining the overall alignment and stability of the spine. In the occiput to axis complex, the alar and apical ligaments attach the dens to the skull while the transverse ligament of the atlas holds the dens tightly to the anterior aspect of C1 [Figure 10.5]. Extending the whole length of the cervical spine, the anterior longitudinal ligament (ALL) lies anterior to the vertebral bodies and disc like a strip of duct tape. The posterior longitudinal ligament (PLL) extends also down the posterior aspect of the vertebral bodies and disc within the vertebral canal. Between the lamina are the ligamentum flava or yellow ligament, and just dorsal to these are the interspinous ligaments which join the spinous processes. Finally, the strongest ligaments of the neck are the fibrous capsules of the facet joints.

10.2.1.4 Muscles

A complex arrangement of muscles in the neck permits us to move and position our head for optimal use of our sensory organs. These muscles also help to maintain posture and protect the spine by counteracting various loads applied to it. Some of the major muscle groups will be mentioned here; however, a detailed analysis of the cervical musculature is beyond the scope of this chapter. In most instances, injuries to the neck will affect many muscles and it is difficult to diagnose these injuries and to establish the severity of muscle injuries.

The muscles moving the neck are divided into two major groups: those that are posterior or dorsal to the vertebral column and those that are anterior or ventral to the spine. The most superficial muscle layer of the posterior group consists of the *trapezius*. It is innervated by cranial nerve XI (accessory nerve) and originates from the occiput, ligamentum nuche, and the spinous processes of C7 and T12. It inserts on the scapula, acromion, and clavicle. These muscles can rotate and extend the neck and elevate the whole shoulder girdle. The next layer consists of several oblique muscles called *splenius capitis*, *splenius cervicis*, and *levator scapulae*. They assist in extension of the neck and rotation. The deepest layer that is still posterior to the vertebrae are collectively known as the erector spinae muscles (*semispinalis capitis and cervicis, longissimus capitis and cervicis*). They are oriented in a longitudinal direction and are mostly responsible for extending the neck or resisting the forward weight to the head.

Muscles that are anterior to the cervical spine produce forward flexion of the neck and rotation. The closest to the vertebral bodies anteriorly are the *longus colli* muscles. They originate and insert on the anterior aspect of each vertebral body of the neck. The *longus capitis* muscle is located anterior and slightly lateral to the longus colli muscle. It originates from the anterior aspect of the transverse process and inserts in the occiput. The sternocleidomastoid muscle has no attachment to the spine but has an important role in the biomechanics of the neck as well as being an important superficial landmark. It originates from the mastoid process of the skull and inserts on the clavicle. It is the only muscle that crosses the mechanical axis of the cervical spine.

10.2.1.5 Nerves and Spinal Cord

The anatomy of the neural elements of the spine is best understood by studying first the gross anatomy of the spinal cord and nerves. These structures are the ones that can be seen on most imaging techniques such as CT scans and MRIs. Secondly we must look at the microscopic anatomy and the physiology of the spinal cord and nerves in order to understand the normal function of the spine and the deficits resulting from damaged neural tissues.

10.2.1.5.1 Gross Anatomy: The spinal cord is a continuation of the brainstem. It exits the skull through the foramen magnum and runs down the bony vertebral canal of the cervical and thoracic spine down to L1–2 when it gives off a series of nerves called the cauda equina (horse's tail from its general appearance). The spinal cord is approximately 10 mm in diameter. It is surrounded by three layers of tissue: the pia mater, the arachnoid, and the dura mater. The pia mater is directly over the spinal cord. Outside the pia flows the cerebrospinal fluid (CSF) which is contained by the arachnoid and the dura mater in what is called the subarachnoid space. Approximately 140 mL of CSF surround the brain and spinal cord and it serves to support and cushion the central nervous system from trauma.

At each segmental level of the spine exits a dorsal and ventral root that join together to form the nerve root [Figure 10.6]. The nerve root then exits the vertebral canal through the spinal foramina. In the cervical spine, the roots course almost perpendicular to the spinal cord. The first nerve root, C1, leaves the vertebral canal between the skull and the atlas. Therefore, all other remaining cervical roots exit the vertebral canal above their respective vertebra, for example the C6 root will exit just above the C6 vertebra and will be affected by pathology at the C5–6 disc level. There are eight cervical roots and seven cervical vertebrae, thus the C8 root will be located between the C7 and T1 vertebra. All the other nerve roots below C8 (T1 to T12, L1 to L5 and S1 to S4) will exit the vertebral canal in the foramen of their respective vertebra but inferior to the pedicle and in the lower half of the vertebral body. These anatomic peculiarities have important implications when correlating the bone or disc injury level with the neural injury.

The nerve root forms inside the vertebral canal and then immediately enters the spinal foramen. In this location, the nerve root is bordered anteriorly by the intervertebral disc and the uncovertebral joint, and posteriorly by the facet joint.

10.2.1.5.2 Neuroanatomy: The internal anatomy of the spinal cord is very complex. It cannot be delineated by conventional imaging techniques. The most accurate way to determine the integrity of a patient's spinal cord structure is by a meticulous and inexpensive physical exam. Using a phone cable as an analogy for the spinal cord we can say that a CT scan or an MRI will show us the outside and the general shape of the cable but will not show us whether any of the lines inside the cable are working. Making a phone call is a better test of the integrity of the cable. The "lines" within the spinal cord are called tracts and are grouped in different parts of cord depending on their function.

The cord in cross section has two distinctive components: the gray matter and the white matter. The gray matter is butterfly shaped and central. Its dorsal half (horn) receives sensory input and the ventral horn is involved with motor function. The white matter is peripheral to the gray matter and contains axons (part of a neuron) from the peripheral nerves or from the cerebral cortex.

10.2.1.5.3 Motor Tracts: Also called descending tracts since the axons originate in the brain and run down the white matter as the lateral corticospinal tract. Some axons enter the gray matter at each spinal segment and synapse in the anterior horn. From there, motor fibers are sent out to the nerve root and continue into the respective peripheral nerve to the muscle. The neurons proximal to the anterior horn are called "upper motor neurons" and the ones distal are called "lower motor neurons". Injury or disease affecting the upper and lower motor neurons result in different clinical signs and symptoms which will be described elsewhere in this chapter.

10.2.1.5.4 Sensory Tracts: Also called ascending tracts because the impulses come from the stimulation of sensory end organs distributed throughout our bodies. The impulses then come up the peripheral sensory nerve and synapse in the dorsal horn of the gray matter, then up the ascending tracts of the white matter to the brain. The principle ascending tracts of the white matter are the dorsal column which carry position and vibration sense and the anterolateral tracts which carry pain, temperature, and some light touch sensation.[3]

---

3   Carpenter MB. *Core Text of Neuroanatomy*, 2nd ed. Baltimore: Williams and Wilkins, 1978.

10.2.2 Biomechanics of the Neck

10.2.2.1 The Occipito-atlanto-axial Complex (C0–C1–C2)

The atlanto-occipital joint (C0–C1) is stabilized by its cup-shaped configuration along with the anterior and posterior atlanto-occipital membranes and in a minor way by the alar and apical ligaments [Figure 10.3]. These two joints allow for 25 degrees of flexion and extension of the head on the neck therefore responsible for the nodding motion of the head. Because of its ellipsoid form, this joint does not allow much lateral flexion and almost no rotation. It is also very difficult to image clearly with standard radiographs.

The C1–C2 articulations are intrinsically unstable because of their opposed convexity and small contact area between the joint surfaces. They provide motion in all planes of motion with 40 to 50 degrees of rotation, 20 degrees of flexion-extension, and 5 degrees of side bending. The major role of C1–2 is to provide 50% of the rotation movement of the head. Stability between the atlas and axis is dependent on the transverse ligament [Figure 10.5]. The odontoid is also tethered to the occiput by two alar ligaments, the apical ligament and the superior vertical cruciate ligament.[4]

Loss of motion for head turning or nodding and/or pain when doing these movements would indicate a pathologic process occurring in the articulations of C0–C1–C2 levels. Pain and/or neurologic deficit may be symptoms or signs of instability of the upper cervical spine. The stability of the occiput to C2 complex is to a large extent dependent on the integrity of two structures: the transverse ligament of C2 and the odontoid process of C2. The evaluation of an accident victim must therefore include an assessment of these two structures.

10.2.2.2 The Subaxial Complex (C2 to T1)

No single level is responsible for a large amount of motion but rather a small amount is allowed at each level and in all direction. The total flexibility of the neck is the result of having some motion at six spinal segments. One motion segment has a greater range of movement and it is C5–6. This is thought to explain to some extent the more frequent and earlier degeneration of this disc. In the normal cervical spine the mechanical axis is at C4. The center of gravity of the skull is anterior to the neck. To counter the anterior force applied to the neck, the posterior muscles of the neck pull in the other direction. The amount of strain on the neck muscles and onto the cervical spine is not static and changes constantly with head motion. Thus, if the head is moved forward, the center of gravity moves

---

4 Kapandji IA. *Physiologie articulaire, Tronc et Rachis*, 5th ed. Paris: Maloine, 1975.

away from the central axis of the neck and the relative weight of the head increases. The neck muscles must then pull harder. The combined increase in head weight and muscle pull places more axial (downward) pressure on the vertebrae and the discs.

The condition of the discs will influence the mechanics of the neck. The intact disc has a strong annulus and a gelatinous nucleus. When axial pressure is applied to the disc the gel is compressed. It then puts pressure on the annulus in an outward fashion. Because an intact annulus is strong there is minimal decrease in the height of the disc. The more pressure there is on the disc the more rigid it becomes and it can assist the ligaments in preventing the translation of one vertebra over the other.

10.2.2.3 Concepts of Spinal Stability

There are many definitions of stability when it is related to the spine and different interpretations of each definition. The most commonly used is probably the following which has been suggested by White and Panjabi: "*clinical instability* is the loss of the ability of the spine under physiologic loads to maintain its pattern of displacement so that there is no initial or additional neurologic deficit, no major deformity and no incapacitating pain."[5] Following this definition, clinical instability, if left untreated, has a very poor prognosis. Early identification of stability of the spine after an injury is therefore vital. The criteria that are used to determine spine stability follow the premise of the worst case scenario that if a patient partakes in regular activities with a clinically unstable spine, he or she will have progressive neurologic deterioration or incapacitating pain or develop a major deformity. However, this does not mean that a patient with a clinically stable spine will be totally asymptomatic. A number of them will have a stable neurologic deficit, or a minor deformity, or significant pain. Examples of this are seen very frequently in patients with whiplash, minor disc disruptions or fractures.

The evaluation of stability is done with a history of the accident, a physical examination, and cervical radiographs. A patient may have an unstable spine as a result of a high energy injury such as a moderate-high speed motor vehicle accident, a fall from a height, a diving injury, a gunshot wound, or a sporting injury such as hockey or football. On examination, the following signs are an indication of instability of the neck: any neurologic deficit, signs of severe head injury, a "cockrobin" position of the head, a patient holding his head up, or severe muscle guarding of the neck. The radiologic evaluation of cervical stability is initially done with static radiographs which will show major fractures and displacement. If

---

5   White AA, Panjabi MM. *Clinical Biomechanics of the Spine*, 2nd ed. Philadelphia: J.B. Lippincott Company, 1990.

there is doubt as to the status of the neck then dynamic radiographs are performed (lateral flexion and extension views) with the patient alert and oriented.

10.2.2.4 Common Injury Mechanism

Direct trauma to the neck is not common and is seen only in penetrating injuries such as gunshot wounds and in blunt traumas where there has been a direct blow to the neck such as with a bat. The vast majority of cervical traumas result from indirect forces being applied to the neck when sudden movements of the head or body occur. Forces applied to the cervical spine are usually not unidirectional and have components of translation, rotation, and axial distraction, or compression. The position of the head, the direction of the force applied, and the magnitude of the force will determine the severity and type of injury sustained.

Extension force is the most common mechanism for injuries in a rear end collision.[6] This mechanism rarely causes fractures but can give a wide variety of soft tissue tears.[7] Extension of the neck occurs as the body is accelerated suddenly forward and because of head and neck inertia, these structures lag back before they, themselves are pulled forward. *Flexion* force most commonly occurs when a motor vehicle comes to a rapid stop during a head-on collision or when striking an immovable object. In this case the patient's trunk is secured by the shoulder harness of the seat belt and decelerates at the same speed as the vehicle while the head and neck moves forward. This mechanism can cause injuries that range from a fracture dislocation with quadriplegia or death to a minor clayshoveler's fracture. *Axial* force on top of the head is indirectly transmitted to the neck and occur in diving accidents. It also occurs in contact sports such as football when a player tackles another head first or lands on the turf head first, or in hockey when a player slides head first into the boards. These forces can cause Jefferson fractures of the ring of C1, burst fractures of any vertebra from C2 to T1, or disc disruptions and herniations. *Rotational* force are usually applied to the neck in conjunction with other forces. Unusual, asymmetric fracture patterns are the result of having rotation as a component to the injury. *Distraction* forces on the neck are now rare but can result in the fracture of C2 classically called a "hangman's fracture" from its association with judicial hanging.

The most common force applied to the neck are extension which causes soft tissue disruption and a combination of flexion and axial com-

---

6 Severy DM, Mathewson JH, Bechtol CO. Controlled Automobile Rear End Collisions, an Investigation of Related Engineering and Medical Phenomena. *Can Serv Med J* 11:727, 1955.

7 MacNab I. The Whiplash Syndrome. *Orthop Clin North Am*, 2:389, 1971.

pression which cause fractures and dislocations and are more likely to be associated with a neurologic deficit.

10.2.3 Evaluation of the Patient with a Cervical Injury

10.2.3.1 History

This is the starting point of the evaluation. The history is obtained from the patient, from witnesses to the accident, and from family members. The following items must be obtained during the interview in order to make the examination and interpretation of investigations more meaningful.

1. Mechanism of injury: Since the treating doctors rarely witness the accident, the mechanism of injury must be determined from the history. Details of the accident are important to determine the direction and magnitude of the force applied to the neck. In the case of a motor vehicle accident it is important to know the make and year of the vehicle, the speed at the time of the accident and whether the patient was a passenger or the driver and if a seat belt was on. For a fall or sport accident one must determine if any protective gear was used, from what height the patient fell, and on what type of surface did the patient fall.
2. Factors that influence the initial treatment: We must then determine if there are any factors that will influence the examination and treatment of the patient, such as recent alcohol or drug use, coexistent medical conditions, head injuries, and altered level of consciousness and other associated injuries.
3. Premorbid state: It is vital to know how the patient was before the accident occurred. The type of work, hobbies, or sports the patient did will help in evaluating the disability resulting from the injury. Pre-existing neck or back problems must be known to determine the effect of the injury on the patient's present function and to assess whether the pre-existing condition is worse.
4. Neurologic symptoms: the exact location of sensory disturbances, weakness, and bowel and bladder function.
5. Disability: That claimed by the patient. The examination will then corroborate this claim or raise doubt as to the extent of the disability.

The patient's history is of course entirely subjective unless a photograph or video was made of the actual injury. It provides, however, important clues about the type of injury sustained and its effect on the patient. The examinations and investigations usually do not uncover any "new" things but only prove or disprove hypotheses that are made as the result of the interview.

10.2.3.2 Physical Examination

The examination is where objective data are collected by the examiner in order to substantiate the structural, physiologic or psychological aspects of the impairment. Some aspects of the examination are subjective because they involve the participation of the patient or a response by the patient. Such is the case for eliciting tender areas, testing motor strength and sensation. A single finding on physical exam is usually irrelevant. What is more important is finding a pattern of abnormal physical signs which also correspond to the patient's history of the accident or illness.

Observation:

- subjective signs: general posture, pain response such as wincing, crying, antalgic gait.
- objective signs: structural scoliosis or kyphosis, significant asymmetry of shoulders or head position, ambulating difficulties, coordination problems. Bruises, abrasions, or signs of head injury are clues to the injury pattern and severity in the early phases.

Palpation:

- subjective signs: eliciting tenderness is not an exact science. Generally if a specific site is tender then it can be assumed that it is a major factor in pain production; for example, a tender facet joint or specific muscle. However, many injuries about the neck will produce diffuse tenderness in the neck, head, and shoulder area decreasing the usefulness of this test. Quantification of tenderness is impossible and is very much dependent on the patient's interpretation of pain and the differences between examiners.
- objective signs: bony deformities and masses can be palpated as well as gaps in ligaments and muscle.

Range of motion testing:

- subjective signs: active range of motion is performed by the patient and will vary with the effort produced and the pain elicited. It can be accurate and objective if pain is minimal and the patient is cooperative.
- Objective signs: passive range of motion is better tolerated by the patient. As described earlier, head flexion and extension occurs at occiput to C1, head rotation is half C1 to C2 and half C2 to T1, lateral flexion of the neck and flexion extension of the neck is almost all from C2 to T1.

Neurologic function:

- Subjective signs: Testing sensation with light touch, pinprick (for pain), position (the position of a joint in space usually tested with the big toe and thumb) and vibration (with the use of a tuning fork) sense can be accurate if elicited meticulously and if the deficit follows a standard anatomic distribution [Figure 10.7]. The examiner, however, is always somewhat dependent on the patient's testimony as to whether there is normal, decreased, or no sensation in an area. Motor function evaluation is influenced by the effort of the patient during the examination. Suboptimal effort is usually evidenced by initial resistance to a motion and then sudden giving way, or results that are not reproducible from one exam to the other, or weakness of several unrelated muscle groups. Often pain can inhibit the optimal performance by the patient.
- Objective signs: Sensory testing of position and vibration is objective if the patient is blinded during the examination. Two-point discrimination, especially in the hands and fingers, is a simple method for quantifying pain and touch sensation related to cervical roots and the nerves of the upper extremities. Muscle wasting and atrophy clearly indicate either denervation or disuse of the muscle. Measuring the limb circumference and comparing the symmetry to the other limb is a simple method to document and validate subacute and chronic muscle pathology. Visible spasms or fasciculation are also signs of muscle dysfunction. Muscle strength grading is done on a scale of five: 5/5 is normal strength, 4/5 is slightly decreased resistance to motion, 3/5 the muscle is unable to resist the examiner but can put the joint through a full range of motion against gravity, 2/5 the muscle can move the joint with gravity eliminated, 1/5 there is only a muscle twitch and no significant motion of the joint, and 0/5 means no evidence of voluntary muscle contraction. A wide-based or unsteady gait is sometimes a sign of cervical cord compression.

Special tests:

- Deep tendon reflexes: For cervical injuries the reflexes in the upper and lower extremities must be elicited. The more common ones are biceps (C5 function), brachioradialis (C6 function), triceps (C7 function), knee jerk (L4 function), and ankle jerk (S1 function). Grading is on a scale of 0 to 4. 0 is an absent reflex, 1 is decreased or sluggish response, 2 is a normal response, 3 is increased response, and 4 is clearly hyperactive with sustained oscillation of the joint after the stimulus is terminated (clonus).
- Cervical distraction: Gradual distraction of the neck is performed by

placing the hands under the jaw and occiput and pulling on the head. Patients with herniated discs or narrowing of the nerve foramen usually have relief of the pain.
- Cervical compression: Axial pressure is applied to the top of the patient's head and may provoke an increase in the patient's symptoms and most significantly arm pain.
- Spurling's test: Compression of the patient's head with the neck extended and rotated to the side of radiculopathy. A positive result is obtained if the radicular pain is reproduced or worsened.
- Shoulder abduction test: Passive abduction of the patient's involved arm reduces the tension in the roots and should relieve radicular pain if it is caused by extradural compression such as with a herniated disc or foraminal stenosis.
- Shimizu reflex: the outer tip of the scapular spine is struck with a reflex hammer. The reflex is elevation of the scapula and/or abduction of the shoulder. The reflex helps detect pathology in the "blind zone" of the roots of C1 to C4.[8]
- L'hermitte's sign: shock-like sensations radiating down the arms or legs with passive flexion of the neck. It is a sign of cervical myelopathy or meningeal irritation.[9]
- Babinski test: stroking the plantar aspect of the foot from the heel to the lateral sole of the foot and then across the forefoot normally elicits no motion or a downward motion of the toes. A positive response is extension of the big toe and it indicates a problem with the upper motor neuron pathways (either spinal cord or brain but not peripheral nerves).
- Hoffman reflex: The nail of the middle finger is "flicked". A positive response is seen when the thumb and index distal phalanx flex. It is indicative of an upper motor neuron lesion above the thoracic spine.
- Clonus: Rhythmic oscillation of a joint associated with spinal cord myelopathy. Usually accompanied by a babinski sign and hyperreflexia. It cannot by faked by the patient.

10.2.4 Soft Tissue Injuries

10.2.4.1 Ligament Strain

Ligaments are structures that attach to adjacent bones. The ligaments of a joint serve to stabilize joints throughout their range of motion and to

---

8   Caillet R. *Soft Tissue Pain and Disability*, 3rd ed. Philadelphia: F.A. Davis Company, 1996.
9   DeGowin EL, DeGowin RL. *Bedside Diagnostic Examination*, 3rd ed. Toronto: Macmillan Publishing, 1976.

guide the bones during that motion. Ligament injury is graded by the clinical severity of the tear. If there is tenderness or pain over a tendon but its excursion or stretch does not exceed the normal range then it is a grade I tear. This corresponds histologically to having some of the ligament fibers that are stretched or torn but there are enough intact fibers to maintain the integrity of the whole ligament. When there is pain over a ligament and it stretches farther than normal but has an endpoint then it is a grade II tear. This involves an incomplete ligament tear with biomechanical weakening of the ligament. A grade III tear is a complete disruption of the ligament and it no longer stabilizes the joint.[10] In joints such as the knee and ankle, such a classification is easily applied because of the superficial nature of these articulations. Such is not the case in the spine. Most spinal ligaments are deep structures that are difficult to palpate. They are also surrounded by muscles which make it difficult to isolate a particular structure as being the source of pain. In the spine we can only be certain of one type of ligament injury and that is the complete ligament tear. This leads to instability that can clearly be determined by physical examination and radiographs of the neck. Partial injuries to the ligaments cannot be objectively quantified or specifically identified and therefore are usually thrown into one of several diagnostic groups such as the cervical strain. For example, if a football player injures his knee and on exam has tenderness over the medial collateral ligament but no instability, he will be diagnosed as having a grade I tear of the medial collateral ligament of the knee. This is a very specific diagnosis and the prognosis and treatment is clear. If the same football player also has pain in his neck. He is tender over his neck but there are muscles, tendons and ligaments under your probing fingers. Radiographs can be done to exclude a bony injury but otherwise he could have a damaged muscle, disc, ligament, or tendon or any combination of these. His diagnosis will be of a cervical strain but the prognosis is much less certain because of the large variability of structural damage.

The topic of ligament damage will be discussed further in the sections on whiplash injuries, fractures and dislocation.

10.2.4.2 Muscle Strain

The muscle component of soft tissue function and pain is complex and not well understood. Muscular pain can result from exercise where lactic acid can accumulate in a muscle and cause pain, stiffness, and tiredness. The pain resolves quickly when the muscle is rested. Muscle pain can also result from a simple, direct blow to a muscle belly causing a local contu-

---

10 Frank C. Ligament Healing: Current Knowledge and Clinical Applications. *J Am Ac Orth Sur*, 4(2), March/April 1996.

sion.[11] In the neck this may occur with blows to the head or neck region, sporting activities, or the fall of a heavy object on the neck and shoulders. These injuries, as well as tears of the muscle substance from the neck moving suddenly beyond its normal range of motion, generally heal without intervention within 2 to 6 weeks.

Chronic pain and tenderness of the muscle may be due to primary muscle pathology, such as in fibromyalgia, or may be caused by normal muscles which overwork because they are protecting an inflamed joint. When some areas of the muscle are permanently activated they produce a small functional contracture (trigger point) and pain.[12]

10.2.4.3 Acceleration Injuries (Whiplash)

The medical entity called whiplash is well known by most physicians, lawyers, and laypeople. Doctor Harold Crowe first used the term during a presentation in 1928 when he was describing the sudden motion of the head that causes cervical strain. Despite never having published his description, the word whiplash was used widely in the medical and legal literature.[13] Unfortunately, many myths have developed with regard to this condition because of studies with design flaws and medicolegal concerns that influence the assessment of clinical outcome. Whiplash occurs frequently following motor vehicle accidents. It has also been called hyperextension-hyperflexion injury, whiplash syndrome, hyperextension injury, cervical strain, and acceleration injury.[14]

Symptoms involving the neck will be apparent in approximately 20% of patients involved in a rear-end collision. The annual incidence in the literature has varied from 0.1 to 7 per 1,000. In the population of patients with chronic pain 0.5 to 1.0% of them will have pain from an acceleration injury.[15] Approximately one-quarter of the patients sustaining an acceleration injury will develop chronic pain and one in ten will complain of severe pain. Symptoms from these injuries occur mostly in patients that are 30 to 50 years of age, and there is no clear predominance for males or females. Factors affecting a longer period off work are the female gender, older age group, marital status, and larger family units. The economic impact of these injuries is directly related to the small number of injuries that do become chronic. Patients with a disability lasting 2 to 6 months account

---

11 Garfin SR, Vaccaro AR. Orthopaedic Knowledge Update: Spine. *American Academy of Orthopaedic Surgeons*, 1997.
12 Caillet, *supra*, note 8.
13 Breck LW, Van Norman RW. Medicolegal Aspects of Cervical Spine Sprains. *Clin Orthop*, 74:124-128, 1971.
14 Barnley L, Lord S, Bogduk N. Whiplash Injury. *Pain*, 58:283-307, 1994.
15 Garfin et al. *supra*, note 11.

for 38% of the overall costs of whiplash, and patients with more than 6 months of disability account for 46% of the total costs.[16]

Patients suffering from acceleration injuries often present with subjective symptoms that are out of proportion to the objective signs. In addition they manifest behavioral and psychological changes that are a sequelae of living with chronic pain and having multiple therapeutic interventions fail.[17] There is experimental and clinical evidence that shows a definite pathophysiologic basis to the whiplash injury.[18] The clinician must therefore regard whiplash as a legitimate injury.

A rear end impact is the most common *mechanism* of this injury [Figure 10.8]. The vehicle of the injured is often immobilized. Upon rear impact, the vehicle accelerates forward, followed 100 milliseconds later by the trunk and shoulders, which are accelerated by the car seat. The shoulders travel forward under the head which is inert and the neck is forced into extension. Finally the head recoils and the neck is thrown into flexion. An impact at 8 mph (13 km/hr) will produce a peak acceleration of 5G on the head and only 2G on the vehicle whereas an impact at 20 mph (32 km/hr) can produce a peak acceleration of 12G on the head.[19] Many factors can affect the exact forces applied to the neck such as the position of the head at the time of impact, the stiffness of the seat, the position of the head rest, the speed of impact, the direction of the impact, and discrepancies between the mass of the two vehicles.

Although the pathomechanics of whiplash is well defined, the actual tissue damage that occurs is uncertain because these injuries are rarely fatal. Knowledge on the structural damage was derived from cadaveric and animal studies, which have their limitations. The most common lesions are avulsions of the intervertebral disc from the endplate of the vertebrae, tears of the annulus fibrosis of the disc, articular pillar fractures, hemarthrosis (bleeding) in the zygapophyseal joint, rupture of the zygapophyseal joint capsule, rupture of the anterior longitudinal ligament, and contusion of the intra-articular meniscus of the zygapophyseal joint. Other injuries include tears of the muscles of the anterior neck, tears of the alar and apical ligaments at C1, injuries to the brain, injuries to the temporomandibular joint and the sympathetic trunk (Horner's syndrome), perforation of the esopha-

---

16 *Ibid.*
17 Tollison CD, Satterthwaite JR. *Painful Cervical Trauma, Diagnosis and Rehabilitative Treatment of Neuromuscular Injuries.* Baltimore: Williams and Wilkins, 1992.
18 Hirsch SA, Hirsch PJ, Hiramoto H, Weiss A. Whiplash Syndrome Fact or Fiction? *Orthop Clin North Am*, 19(4):791-795, 1988. MacNab, *supra*, note 7. Pennie BH, Agambar LJ. Whiplash Injuries: A Trial of early Management. *J Bone Joint Surg*, 72B:277-279, 1990.
19 Severy et al., *supra*, note 6; White, et al., *supra*, note 5.

gus, and inner/middle ear injuries. The posterior longitudinal ligaments, ligamentum flavum, and posterior muscles are less commonly injured unless the impact is severe.[20] Magnetic resonance imaging studies of patients who have sustained a hyperextension injury of the neck identified tears of the anterior longitudinal ligament, tears of the anterior margin of the annulus, separation of the disc from the vertebra and herniated discs in 50% of the patients.[21]

The clinical presentation of whiplash is dominated by neck pain and occipital headaches in 70% of patients. The pain is usually described as dull, aching, worse with movements. It is most often felt in the back of the neck and radiates to the head, arm, upper thoracic spine and between the scapulae. The onset of pain is often a few hours to a few days after the accident. There are often other associated symptoms such as dizziness, tinnitus, dysphagia, blurred vision, weakness, and concentration and memory disturbances. The exact pain generator is still being debated. In one study, 54% of the patients with chronic post whiplash pain had pain arising from the zygapophyseal joints.[22] Disc injury can also cause pain which is felt at the back of the neck and down to the interscapular region. Neck pain after whiplash does not seem to correlate to pre-existing degenerative changes in the neck.[23] Some studies have shown a higher age-adjusted prevalence of degenerative changes in patients who have sustained a whiplash injury in the past, but other studies do not. Headaches are usually occipital and in one study were found to originate from injury to the C2–C3 facet joints. With the development of chronic symptoms we often see patients that have low back pain, depression, anxiety, anger, frustration, compensation neurosis, post-traumatic syndrome, chronic pain syndrome, marital and family disruption, and drug dependency. The clinical picture then becomes very confusing.

The natural history of acceleration injuries reveal that most of the symptoms start within 2 days of the injury. In most patients the symptoms are mild and in 57% resolve completely within 3 months. Only 8% of the patients are unable to work as a result of the injury. Depending on the studies, between 14 and 42% of patients will develop chronic neck pain which

---

20 MacNab, *supra*, note 7.
21 Davis SJ, Teresi LM, Bradley WGJr, Ziemba MA, Bloze AE. Cervical Spine Hyperextention Injuries: MR findings. *Radiology*, 180:245-251, 1991.
22 Barnsley L, Lord SM, Wallis BJ. The Prevalance of Chronic Cervical Zygapophyseal Joint Pain after Whiplash. *Spine*, 20:20-26, 1995.
23 Balla JI. The Late Whiplash Syndrome. *Australian and New Zealand Journal of Surgery*, 50:610-614, 1980. Hildingsson C, Toolanen G. Outcome after Soft Tissue Injury of the Cervical Spine: a Prospective Study of 93 Car Accident Victims. *Acta Orthopaedica Scandinavica*, 61:357-359, 1990.

reaches a steady state at 1 year post injury.[24] Ten percent will have constant, severe pain and 4% will be unable to work. Poor prognosis indicators are severe long-standing symptoms, age over 50 years, ongoing litigation, pain radiating to the upper extremities and low back pain.[25] Older studies stated that the pain resolved after legal settlement. More recent studies show that this is usually not the case and that many of the unusual symptoms the patient had are actually caused by hard-to-evaluate tissue injuries.[26] Furthermore, although many studies report that patients with chronic post-whiplash neck pain have psychological disturbances, these studies have not used strict, validated psychological questionnaires. In 1991, a prospective study by Radanov found that psychosocial factors were not predictors of the outcome of soft tissue injuries of the neck.[27] Other studies have shown that the patients were normal at the time of the accident and developed abnormal behaviour responses after 3 months of neck symptoms. These abnormal traits were therefore acquired as a result of the injury.

The treatment of acceleration injuries of the neck remains empirical since an exact cause for the pain often remains elusive, and it is difficult to predict which patient will fall into the chronic pain group. Furthermore, most of the treatments prescribed for whiplash have not been validated scientifically and have not been found to change the natural history of whiplash. The following modalities are frequently used: analgesics, muscle relaxants, nonsteroidal antiinflammatories (NSAIDs), antidepressants, neck immobilization, neck mobilization, traction, manipulations, exercises, formal physiotherapy, spray and stretch, postural alignment training, heat, ice, massage, transcutaneous electrical stimulation, acupuncture, intra-ar-

---

24 Gargan MF, Bannister GC. Long Term Prognosis of Soft Tissue Injuries of the Neck. *J Bone Joint Surg,* 72-B(5):901-903, 1990.

25 Garfin et al., *supra,* note 11. Maimaris C, Barnes MR, Allen MJ. Whiplash Injuries of the Neck: a Retrospective Study. *Injury,* 19:393-396, 1988.

26 Balla JI. The Late Whiplash Syndrome: a Study of an Illness in Australia and Singapore Culture. *Medicine and Psychiatry,* 6:191-210, 1982. Hohl M. Soft Tissue Injuries of the Neck in Automobile Accidents: Factors Influencing Prognosis. *J Bone Joint Surg,* 56A:1675-1682, 1974. Merskey H. Psychiatry and the Cervical Sprain Syndrome, *Can Med Associa J,* 130:1119-1120, 1984. Miller H. Accident Neurosis. *Br Med J,* I:992-998, 1961. Norris SH, Watt I. The Prognosis of Neck Injuries Resulting from Rear-end Vehicle Collision. *J Bone Joint Surg,* 65B:608-611, 1983. Parmar HV, Raynakers R. The Outcome after Whiplash Injury: a Retrospective Review. *J Bone Joint Surg, Proceedings of the British Orthopaedic Association,* 72B: 936, 1990. Pennie et al. *supra,* note 13. Pennie BH, Agambar LJ. Patterns of Injury and Recovery in Whiplash, *Injury,* 22(1):57-59, 1991.

27 Radanov BP, DiStefano G, Schnidrig A, Ballinari P. Role of Psychosocial Stress in Recovery from Common Whiplash. *Lancet,* 338:712-715, 1991.

ticular injections, epidural injections, ultrasound, laser, and psychosocial intervention. Surgery is seldom necessary or advisable.[28]

Intuitively, one would think that early intervention is important to prevent the development of chronic symptoms; however, no treatment applied early has been demonstrated to change the natural course of these injuries. Studies have shown that for the acute symptoms, patient education and early self-mobilization is more effective than traditional immobilization therapy and as effective as formal physiotherapy.[29] A soft collar is still prescribed empirically to many whiplash sufferers and is not harmful as long as its use is intermittent and short-lived. Long-term use has been shown to prolong disability.

Once serious injury to the neck has been excluded, initial treatment consists of application of ice for the first 24 hours, followed by self-assisted exercises in the supine position for the next 2 to 3 days. After the acute pain subsides, isometric strengthening exercises are started and more generous passive range of motion exercises in the sitting position. The Quebec Task Force on whiplash associated disorders recommends that further treatment be based on the degree of injury at presentation.[30] A patient with a grade I injury (neck pain and stiffness but no physical signs) should have immediate return to activities and no work restrictions. For a grade II injury (neck pain and musculoskeletal signs) return to activities usually within 1 week of the injury and temporary work alterations to be reassessed after 3 weeks. Non-narcotic analgesics and NSAIDs are prescribed. For grade III injuries (neck complaints and neurologic signs) return to activity as soon as possible with work modifications reassessed every 3 weeks. Narcotics are prescribed only for the acute stage. For the patients that still have symptoms after 2 months, a multidisciplinary evaluation and treatment is indicated. Patients with poor prognostic factors should, in addition, have more detailed diagnostic evaluation since they may have lesions that can be corrected surgically before chronic behavioral changes develop. In a study by Jonsson in 1994, 20% of patients with whiplash injury required surgery to resolve the symptoms.[31] This surgical rate is the highest by far of any study in the literature.

---

28 Garfin et al., *supra*, note 11.
29 McKinney LA, Dornan JO, Ryan M. Role of Physiotherapy in the Management of Acute Neck Sprains Following Road Traffic Accidents, *Arch Emerg Med*, 6:27-33, 1989. Mealy K, Brennan H, Fenelon GG. Early Mobilization of Acute Whiplash Injuries. *Br Med J*, 292:656-657, 1986. Pennie et al., *supra*, note 18.
30 Spitzer WO, Skovron ML, Salmi LR. Scientific Monograph of the Quebec Task Force on Whiplash Associated Disorder: Redefining Whiplash and its Management. *Spine*, 20(8): 1S-73S, 1995.
31 Jonsson H Jr, Cesarini K, Sahlstedt B. Findings and Outcome in Whiplash Type Neck Distortions. *Spine*, 19:2733-2742, 1994.

10.2.4.4 Disc Disruption and Herniation

Disc pathology is an important part of other soft tissue injuries of the neck [Figure 10.9]. Isolated disc disease can occur and is a distinct clinical entity with a different natural history. A disc can be damaged by a brief, high energy increase in the axial or rotational force on the disc annulus such as a blow to the head or neck. The incidence of acute disc lesions following cervical spine trauma is not known but is on the rise in the literature because of the improved resolution of neurodiagnostic techniques. Recent studies have shown that acute disc injury was found in 35 to 42% of patients with cervical trauma.[32] More commonly, however, is that a disc is disrupted by small repetitive forces which cause a gradual wear of the annulus, and microscopic tears which eventually lead to bigger defects in the annulus and herniation of the nucleus pulposus. This mechanism is also influenced by the normal degeneration of the cervical disc which starts in the third decade of life.

One must take great care to correlate the clinical signs and symptoms of the patients to the radiographic findings. Boden in 1990 studied the MRI abnormalities of 63 volunteers who had never had any symptoms indicative of cervical disease. Overall, abnormalities were found in 19% of individuals, 14% of whom were less than 40 years of age and 28% of whom were over 40 years old. The subjects that were less than 40 years of age had a 10% incidence of assymptomatic disc herniation and a 4% incidence of foraminal stenosis. Of the subjects over 40 years of age, 5% had herniated discs, 3% had bulging discs and 20% had foraminal stenosis.[33]

Cervical disc injuries are manifested by three clinical scenarios: neck pain, radiculopathy, and myelopathy. Neck pain occurs with tears of the annulus fibrosus. There are afferent nerve fibers in the periphery of the annulus which will produce pain in the neck. Intranuclear discograms have shown that the pain can also be referred posterior to both shoulders, to the interscapular area, and to the upper arms. Radicular symptoms occur when the annulus of the disc bulges sufficiently to irritate the nerve root exiting the foramen. Herniation of the nucleus through a tear of the annulus can also compress the nerve root. The symptoms are said to have a dermatomal distribution because they follow an exact pattern of sensory distribution of the compressed root and they are one-sided [Figure 10.7]. The patient will feel pain going down the arm to the hand as well as numbness and weakness. A C4–C5 disc herniation will produce pain and numbness on the

---

32 Rizzolo SJ, Piazza MR, Cotler JM, Balderston RA, Schaefer D, Flanders A. Intervertebral Disc Injury Complicating Cervical Spine Trauma. *Spine*, 16(6): S187-S189, 1991.

33 Boden SD, McCowin PR, Davis DO, Dina TS, Alexander MS, Wiesel S. Abnormal Magnetic-Resonance Scans of the Cervical Spine in Asymptomatic Subjects. *J Bone Joint Surg*, 72-A(8):1178-1184, 1990.

thumb side of the forearm and weakness of the biceps muscle. A C5–C6 disc herniation, which is the most common, will cause pain and numbness in the thumb and index finger from irritation of the C6 root and weakness of the forearm and wrist. A C6–C7 herniation will produce middle finger pain and numbness and triceps muscle weakness from irritation of the C7 root. A C7–T1 herniation will compress the C8 root and produce symptoms in the fourth and fifth finger with weakness in the flexion of the fingers. Myelopathy is produced by disc compression of the spinal cord. An acute compression of the spinal cord by a herniated disc will produce a variety of neurologic deficits similar to those seen in fracture dislocations of the cervical spine and will be described in that section of the chapter. Myelopathy otherwise is more commonly the result of spondylosis which is the gradual wear and tear of the discs and facet joint of the neck. When the spinal canal narrows and the cord is compressed the patients develop progressive weakness and numbness of the arms and legs as well as muscle spasticity, hyperreflexia, and gait difficulties.

The natural history of intervertebral disc disruption is markedly different depending on the clinical presentation. We know from autopsy studies on 4,000 spines that significant structural changes are seen in the discs as early as age 30 years. There is evidence of spondylosis in 60% of women and 80% of men by the age of 50 years and in 90% by the age of 70 years. It seems that disc degeneration is inevitable but not necessarily symptomatic. Neck pain from a tear in the annulus resolves within 4 to 6 weeks of onset and is usually benign although the exact natural history is not known since the diagnosis is difficult to distinguish from cervical strain or whiplash injuries. Lees and Turner in 1963 followed patients with cervical radiculopathy for 19 years and found that 45% had complete resolution without recurrence, 30% had mild symptoms, and 25% had persistent or worsening symptoms.[34] The cumulative literature on the natural history of patients with cervical myelopathy shows that if left untreated, 75% will worsen within a few years and 25% will remain stable. The symptoms rarely resolve spontaneously.

The treatment of cervical disc problems, whether it be neck pain, radiculopathy, or myelopathy is always the same initially. Most patients respond well to NSAIDs, the intermittent use of a soft cervical collar, and physical therapy modalities. There is rarely any reason to do surgery for discogenic neck pain. The current surgical indications for cervical radiculopathy are: 1) persistent or recurrent arm pain nonresponsive to three months of conservative treatment; 2) progressive neurologic deficit; 3) static neurologic deficit associated with significant pain; 4) the radiologic

---

34 Lees F, Aldren Turner JW. Natural History and Prognosis of Cervical Spondylosis. *Br Med J*, 2:1607-1610, 1963.

pathology must correlate to the clinical symptoms. The surgical treatment of patients with cervical myelopathy is recommended for patients who have progressive impairment of function without sustained remissions or severe disability at presentation.

10.2.5 Fractures and Dislocations

Typically a spinal column fracture dislocation occurs to young males between the ages of 15 and 35 years. The resultant impact in terms of functional and economic loss is devastating. The most common causes are motor vehicle accidents, falls, and diving accidents, and in the United States there is an increasing incidence of firearm injuries.[35] These injuries are classified by the location of the fracture and the mechanism of injury.

10.2.5.1 Atlanto-axial Fractures

Fractures of C1 are the result of an axial load injury. The classic Jefferson fracture is a four-part fracture of the atlas. If the transverse ligament is intact then it is considered stable and is treated with a stiff collar or cervical orthosis. If the transverse ligament is disrupted the injury is unstable, and the treatment changes to a halo vest immobilization for 8 weeks followed by 4 weeks with a Philadelphia collar. There is a high incidence of concomitant cervical spine fracture. Landells in 1987 described 35 cases that he followed an average of 3.5 years. Fifty-six percent of patients had persistent significant neck pain and stiffness and scalp dysesthesia. Seventy percent of patients with an unstable fracture had long-term symptoms.[36] Levine in 1991 followed 34 patients and found that there were no late instabilities but 80% of the patients still had neck pain at follow up (4.5 years post injury).[37]

Fractures on the dens of the axis can occur from flexion or extension injuries. The commonly used and known classification is that of Anderson and D'Alonzo.[38] A type I fracture is a small avulsion of the tip of the odontoid. It is extremely uncommon and is treated with a Philadelphia collar for 8 weeks. A type II fracture occurs at the junction of the odontoid process and the body of the axis. This fracture has the highest nonunion rate re-

---

35 Foy MA, Fagg PS. *Medicolegal Reporting in Orthopaedic Trauma.* New York: Churchill Livingstone, 1995.
36 Landells CD, Van Petegham PK. Fractures of the Atlas, Classification, Treatment and Morbidity. *Spine,* 13:450-452, 1987.
37 Levine AM, Edwards CC. Fractures of the Atlas. *J Bone Joint Surg,* 73A:680-691, 1991.
38 Anderson LD, D'Alonzo RT. Fractures of the Odontoid Process of the Axis. *J Bone Joint Surg,* 56A:1663-1674, 1974.

ported as high as 60%.[39] Displacement of 5 mm, angulation of more than 10 degrees and age over 40 years are poor prognostic factors. If anatomic alignment is obtained, the treatment of choice is a halo vest immobilization. The surgical alternative is either a C1–C2 posterior fusion which will cause permanent restriction in cervical rotation or anterior internal fixation with screws. The latter treatment has a better union rate and preserves atlantoaxial rotation but is technically demanding. Type III fractures extend downward into the cancellous portion of the vertebral body. The union rate is between 85 to 90% when treated with halo immobilization for 12 weeks. The outcome of odontoid fractures is directly related to the presence or absence of bony union. With bony union the spine becomes stable and minimally symptomatic whereas fibrous union leads to pain, instability and potential neurologic deterioration. The nonunion rate varies from 5% reported by Amyes in 1956[40] and 63% by Schatzker in 1974.[41]

The other common injury occurring at C2 is a traumatic spondylolisthesis, referred to as a hangman's fracture because it was first identified by Haughton in 1866 in criminals that were executed by hanging. A hypertension movement forces the occiput into extension against the atlas producing a fracture of the C2 pedicles. The classification most widely accepted separates this injury into three types.[42] A type 1 injury occurs with hyperextension and axial loading and is usually undisplaced or minimally displaced (less than 3 mm). A type 2 injury has the same mechanism but there is significant translation and angulation at C2–C3. Most of the type 1 and 2 injuries can be treated with cervical traction for reduction of the fracture and halo vest immobilization for 12 weeks. A type 3 injury is caused by flexion and posterior distraction force. There is severe displacement and angulation at C2–C3 along with unilateral or bilateral facet dislocation. A type 3 injury usually requires an open reduction and fusion either through an anterior or a posterior approach. Effendi in 1981 reviewed 131 patients.[43] Type 3 fractures were associated with a 33% mortality. Surgery was required in 27% of type 1 fractures, 46% of type 2 and 80% of type 3. There are no studies to date that describe the long-term functional outcome of these injuries.

---

39 Clark CR, White AA. Fractures of the Dens: A Multicenter Study. *J Bone Joint Surg*, 67A(9):1340-1348, 1985.

40 Amyes EW, Anderson FM. Fracture of the Odontoid Process. *Archives of Surgery*, 72:377-393, 1956.

41 Schatzker J, Rorabeck CH, Waddell JP. Fracture of the Dens: an Analysis of 37 Cases. *J Bone Joint Surg*, 53B:392-402, 1971.

42 Levine AM, Edwards CC. The Management of Traumatic Spondylolisthesis of the Axis. *J Bone Joint Surg*, 67A:217-226, 1985.

43 Effendi B, Roy D, Cornish B, Dussault RG, Laurin CA. Fractures of the Ring of the Axis. *J Bone Joint Surg*, 63B:319-327, 1981.

10.2.5.2 Flexion Instabilities

Anterior wedge compression fractures are seen as a depression of the upper end plate of the vertebral body and occur at C4–C5 and C5–C6. They are caused by a flexion-compression force to the head. These fractures generally do not affect the vertebral canal and do not involve any damage to the posterior ligament complex. Treatment is with a rigid collar for 8 to 12 weeks. A study by Mazur in 1983 reported 27 patients with stable compression fractures treated with a cervical brace. Six patients developed painful late spinal instability.[44]

Fractures of the vertebral body with canal compromise involve a more severe wedging or comminution of the vertebral body [Figure 10.12]. These are caused by severe compression-flexion or vertical compression forces on the head. In this group are the burst fractures, the tear drop fractures and the major three column injuries with dislocation of the facet joints. These injuries often involve various degrees of neurologic injury. Treatment will vary with the presence or absence of neurologic compromise but will always involve surgery. These injuries result in a very unstable cervical spine and therefore all patients must have a surgical stabilization with either an anterior or posterior fusion or both (360 degree fusion). In the neurologically intact patient, the initial treatment will be external stabilization with a collar or traction until the investigations and lifesaving management is completed, followed by cervical traction to try and obtain proper alignment of the neck, and then a surgical stabilization is performed. In the event of a neurologic deficit, similar management is done with the addition of early administration of high dose steroids[45] and surgery to decompress the spinal cord. In the treatment of bilateral facet dislocation there has been several reports of catastrophic neurologic deficits manifested after the reductions.[46] This has been attributed to frequent (40%) disruption of the intervertebral discs which herniate onto the spinal cord during the reduction maneuver. It is recommended that if a closed reduction is done the patient be awake so that his neurologic function can be monitored at all times. If a general anesthetic must be given to accomplish the reduction or if the patient is not alert then an MRI should be done to detect disc disruption or herniation. If a disc herniation is identified, a sur-

---

44 Mazur JM, Stauffer EA. Unrecognized Spinal Instability Associated with Seemingly Simple Cervical Compression Fractures. *Spine*, 8:687, 1983.
45 Bracken MB, Shepard MJ, Collins WF, et al. A Randomized Controlled Trial of Methylprednisolone or Naloxone in the Treatment of Acute Spinal-Cord Injury: Results of the Second National Acute Spinal Cord Injury Study. *N Engl J Med*, 322:1405-1411, 1990.
46 Eismont FJ, Arena MJ, Green BA. Extrusion of an Intravertebral Disk Associated with Traumatic Subluxation or Dislocation of Cervical Facets. *J Bone Joint Surg*, 73A:1555-1560, 1991.

gical discectomy is done followed by reduction and stabilization of the spine.

The long-term outcome of this group of patients is dependent on the presence or absence of neurologic injury. In the presence of a neurologic injury the functional result will vary with the level of the injury and the degree of neurologic involvement. This will be discussed further in the section dealing with neurologic injuries. The outcome of patients without neurologic injury is unclear. Of Bohlman's large series of 300 acute fractures and dislocations in 1979, 62 patients did not have a neurologic injury. Twenty-three of these were treated without surgery and 17 could be followed for a mean of 3.8 years and were assymptomatic. Thirty-nine had a surgical stabilization and 36 could be followed. They all had a solid fusion and only one had residual pain.[47]

10.2.5.3 Rotational Instabilities

Rotational instabilities are the result of motor vehicle accidents and falls from a height producing a distractive-flexion force on the head. They are common and seen mostly at C4–C5 and C5–C6. The patterns of injury include unilateral and bilateral facet dislocations, facet fractures, and lateral mass fractures. Most of the facet injuries are unstable and 50% of the patients have a neurologic injury which consists of a root injury or sometimes a partial cord injury. Once the full extent of the injury is defined, treatment consists of a closed reduction with tong traction. Only 50% of the reductions are successful using this method. An open reduction is then required if spinal alignment is not reestablished. External immobilization of simple reduced facet dislocation has lead to a high rate of recurrence and late pain.[48] After reduction, a surgical stabilization gives the best chance for a good result. Rorabeck in 1987 reviewed 26 patients with unilateral facet dislocation. The 16 patients who were reduced had an uneventful recovery but 7 of the 10 patients that healed in a dislocated position had disabling pain.[49] Beyer at the Mayo clinic reviewed 34 patients with unilateral facet injury. Of the 24 that were treated without surgery, 42% were symptomatic at an average of 9 years after the injury,

---

47 Bohlman HH. Acute Fractures and Dislocations of the Cervical Spine, *J Bone Joint Surg*, 61A:1119-1142, 1979.

48 Hadley MN, Fitzpatrick BC, Sonntag VKH, Browner CM. Facet Fracture-dislocation of the Cervical Spine. *Neurosurgery*, 31:661-666, 1992. Herkowitz HN, Rothman RH. Subacute Instability of the Cervical Spine. *Spine*, 9:348-357, 1984. Norrell H. Traumatic Unilateral Facet Locking in the Cervical Spine. *J Fla Med Assoc*, 63:880-883, 1976.

49 Rorabeck CH, Rock MG, Hankin RJ, Bourne RD. Unilateral Facet Dislocation of the Cervical Spine: an Analysis of the Results of Treatment in 26 Patients. *Spine*, 12:23-27, 1987.

whereas only one of the ten patients treated surgically had symptoms at an average of 6.5 years from the injury.[50]

10.2.5.4 Extension Instabilities

The mechanism of hyperextension most frequently causes injuries to the soft tissues as those seen in acceleration injuries of the neck. In the event that the ligament and disc disruption spans all three columns, the spine is unstable. The spine often recoils back and spontaneously reduces thereby making the radiologic diagnosis much more difficult. Dynamic tests (flexion-extension radiographs or MRI) as well as close attention to prevertebral swelling on the lateral radiographs prevent missing these injuries.

10.2.5.5 Clay Shoveler's Fracture

These fractures are an avulsion of the spinous processes at the base of the neck and are caused by sudden contraction of the muscles. These were described in workers whose shovels would hit clay and the forceful contraction of the shoulder and neck muscles would fracture the spinous processes of C6 or C7. Since the spine remains stable, patients are treated symptomatically only. Care must be taken at the time of diagnosis to establish that the avulsed spinous process are not from a flexion injury since this would represent an unstable fracture pattern.

10.2.5.6 Gunshot Injuries

Spinal cord injuries resulting from firearms is an increasing problem, particularly in the United States. High velocity missiles from military weapons or large game hunting rifles strike the spine with such impact that they cause complete neurologic deficits (tetraplegia) and gross instability because of the destruction of bony elements of the spine. Low velocity missiles such as those from handguns or .22 caliber rifles hit with less impact and may not destabilize the spine. They frequently cause incomplete neurologic injuries.[51] Removal of the bullet fragments is not necessary unless there is a partial neurologic deficit and the fragment is impinging on the spinal cord. Pharyngeal and esophageal perforation must be explored, debrided and closed to prevent infection.[52]

---

50 Beyer CA, Cabanela ME. Unilateral Facet Dislocations and Fracture-Dislocation of the Cervical Spine: A Review. *Orthopaedics*, 15(3):311, 1993.

51 Stauffer ES, MacMillan M. Fractures and Dislocations of the Cervical Spine. *Rockwood and Green's Fractures in Adults*, 4th ed. Philadelphia: Lippincott-Raven, 1996.

52 Kupcha PC, An HS, Cotler JM. Gunshot Wounds to the Cervical Spine. *Spine*, 15:1058-1063, 1990. Yoshon D, Jane JA, White RJ. Prognosis and Management of Spinal Cord and Cauda Equina Bullet Injuries in Sixty Five Civilians. *J Neurosurg*, 32:163-170, 1970.

10.2.5.7 Seat Belts and Airbags

The effectiveness of seat belts in protecting the occupants of a motor vehicle from injury has been well documented. There are some studies, however, that suggest an increase in the incidence of neck and chest injury since the introduction of seat belt legislation[53] while others do not.[54] The shoulder harness of the seat belt can effectively immobilize the chest therefore transferring the forces applied to the car more directly to the unprotected neck. Also, an increase in the number of neck injuries may be seen as more people survive high energy crashes because of effective restraints and other safety features added to modern vehicles.

Airbags have been added to cars and trucks in order to reduce fatalities in frontal crashes. There is a growing number of reports documenting specific injuries caused by airbag deployment. Unrestrained drivers have sustained flexion injuries of the cervical and thoracic spine and direct impaction fractures of the face and sternum. There is a report of a restrained driver who sustained a hyperextension injury to the upper cervical spine.[55]

10.2.5.8 Treatment of Fractures and Dislocations

10.2.5.8.1 Brace Treatment: Cervical orthoses provide external support to the neck. Complete immobilization with this form of treatment is not possible since one cannot mold an orthosis tightly around the neck. Instead these braces hold the mandible/occiput and trunk and maintain the general alignment between the two. This decreases the extremes of motion of the cervical vertebrae. Braces are used either as temporary protection until further management is given, or as definitive treatment of stable cervical injuries, or as an adjunct to surgery. The most common braces used in order of stability provided are: minerva brace, four and two poster cervical orthoses, SOMI brace (sub-occipital mental immobilization), rigid cervical collar, Philadelphia collar, and a soft collar. Complications of brace treatment include loss of cervical position, skin breakdown at the points of contact of the brace and temporomandibular joint dysfunction from the brace pushing up on the mandible.

10.2.5.8.2 Halo Vest Treatment: This is still an external method of spine immobilization but the anchoring points are more stable. In the adult

---

53 Allen MJ, Barnes MR, Bodiwala GG. The Effect of Seat Belt Legislation on Injuries Sustained by Car Occupants. *Injury*, 16:471-476, 1985. Deans GT, Magalliard JN, Kerr M, Rutherford WH. Neck Sprain—A Major Cause of Disability Following Car Accidents. *Injury*, 18:10-12, 1987.

54 Olney DB, Marsden AK. The Effect of Head Restraints and Seat Belts on the Incidence of Neck Injury in Car Accidents. *Injury*, 17:365-367, 1986.

55 Blacksin MF. Patterns of Fracture after Air Bag Deployment. *J Trauma*, 35(6):840-843, 1993.

four pins are introduced through a metal or graphite ring and onto the outer table of the skull. This is the proximal fixation. The ring is then connected by bars to a large vest that extends from the waist to the shoulders. The mandible and neck are left free which provides more patient comfort and even access to the neck in the event that further surgery is required. A halo is used as definitive treatment for injuries that are potentially unstable or unstable injuries that have a good chance of healing well without surgery for example a type III fracture of the odontoid. Halo vests are also often used as a form of postoperative immobilization if internal stability is felt to be insufficient. Complications of halo vest treatment are numerous. Unless applied under a general anesthetic, there is significant pain with the application of the pins. Misplaced pins can impinge on the supraorbital nerves and cause numbness and pain of the forehead. Patients feel pressure around the head for 24 hours after which the treatment is painless. Since the pins must remain for 3 months they can loosen or get infected. This requires changing pin sites and there are patients that have had deep infections, osteomyelitis of the skull and intracranial abscesses. Decubitus ulcer can occur on the trunk, usually over the bony prominences of the clavicle and the scapula from the pressure of the halo vest. This is more frequent in quadriparetic patients that have no sensation below the shoulders. A short term sequela of halo treatment is stiffness and weakness of the neck after halo removal. This generally resolves within a few months and rarely causes long-term sequelae. Some patients develop large scars on the forehead which may require further surgery for correction.

10.2.5.8.3 Surgical Treatment: There are numerous surgical techniques in the armamentarium of the spinal surgeon to treat cervical spine trauma. There are no set rules as to which technique is used for a particular injury. The choice of which technique is used will depend on the injury pattern, the general condition of the patient, the surgeons training and experience, the equipment available to the surgeon, and what is in vogue at any particular time. When all is said and done, surgeons can only accomplish three things: 1) decompress neural element, 2) realign the spine, 3) stabilize the spine. They do this either through an anterior approach or a posterior approach which refers to access of the vertebra from the front side of the spinal cord or the back side. Generally the surgeon, like the bank robber, goes where the money is. If the spinal cord compression and the fractured elements are from the vertebral body or disc then an anterior approach provides direct access to the pathology. If the posterior ligament complex is torn and there is facet pathology, a posterior approach is chosen.

An anterior decompression is done through either a longitudinal or transverse incision on the front of the neck. A surgical plane between the carotid sheath and the esophagus and trachea is developed and the spine is reached. To decompress the spinal cord or nerve roots one or more discs and vertebral bodies are removed. An anterior fusion is done by taking a structural bone graft from the fibula or the pelvis and inserting it between two vertebrae in the gap left where the excised disc and vertebral bodies were. Anterior stabilization is done by fixing a plate over the vertebra and fixing it with screws. The implants must be low profile as they lie close to the esophagus. Advantages to the anterior approach are that it causes less postoperative pain, it minimizes the movements of an unstable spine since the patient is positioned supine on the table, and the blood loss is minimal. The disadvantages are that it is technically more demanding to work around vital organs (trachea, esophagus, laryngeal nerve, thoracic duct, carotid and vertebral arteries, and jugular veins) and the stabilization is less stable than posterior constructs.

Posterior decompressions involve a laminectomy or a foraminotomy (enlargement of the foramen of the nerve root) and is done through a longitudinal midline incision at the back of the neck. The paraspinal muscles are separated from the spinous processes, lamina and facet joint to access the spine. A fusion is done by decortication (gouging of the hard cortical bone) of the lamina and facets and applying cancellous bone from the pelvis over the levels that need to be fused. Stabilization can be done with clamps, wires, cables or plates and screws. Advantages of the posterior surgeries are greater access to multiple levels and a larger choice of implants.

10.2.6 Neurologic Injuries

10.2.6.1 Assessment

A detailed neurologic exam is required as soon as possible after a trauma so that neurologic deficits can be identified, defined and treated quickly. It will also provide the most valuable information to determine the patient's short- and long-term prognosis. The neurologic and musculosketal exam is described in section C of this chapter. In addition to the specific tests mentioned in that section, the bulbocavernosus reflex is an important test for a patient with severe spine trauma. It is the most distal reflex of the spinal cord and is performed by pulling or squeezing the penis or clitoris or pulling on a urinary catheter while doing a rectal exam. The reflex is positive if contraction of the rectal sphincter occurs. Because an injured spinal cord stops functioning (spinal shock) the reflex can be absent after an injury. If the reflex returns within the first 24 to 48 hours after the injury *without* the return of any voluntary motor function then the cord injury is complete and irreversible. The prognosis for neurologic recovery is very poor. Another important sign is sacral sparring. This is manifested by preservation of voluntary toe flexion and perianal sensation.

The presence of sacral sparring in a patient with paralysis is favourable to a good return of neurologic function since the cord injury is partial.

The most commonly referred to grading system for neurologic function is the Frankel grading system.[56] Frankel A patients have total absence of motor and sensory function distal to the injury, Frankel B patients have sensation that is present but motor function that is absent, Frankel C patients have present sensation and motor function that is not useful (grade 2-3/5), Frankel D patients have present sensation and motor function that is useful (grade 4-5/5), and Frankel E patients have normal motor and sensory function.

10.2.6.2 Classification

10.2.6.2.1 Root Injuries: A nerve root may be damaged or compressed within the foramen by either a fracture or dislocation of the facet or by a herniated disc. Since a nerve root is essentially a peripheral nerve, the lesion is in the lower motor neuron and may recover. Traction of the nerve root may occur with brachial plexus injuries of the shoulder. If the root is avulsed (pulled off) of the spinal cord the damage is irreversible.

10.2.6.2.2 Incomplete Cord Lesions: Partial loss of spinal cord function can result in many different combinations of motor and sensory loss. The lesion is incomplete if there is some motor and sensory function distal to the cord damage. The following are the most common patterns of incomplete cord lesions.

- Brown-Sequard syndrome: Half of the spinal cord is damaged, either right or left and results in ipsilateral (same side) paralysis and loss of vibration and position sense and contralateral (opposite side) loss of pain, touch and temperature sensation. The cause is frequently a unilateral fracture or dislocation of the facet and the prognosis for recovery is good. More than 90% of patients will recover bowel and bladder control and will be able to walk.[57]
- Central cord syndrome: This is the most common form of incomplete cord lesion and radiographs are often normal since the cord injury is produced by osteophytes (bone spurs) striking the neural element with hyperextension of the neck. There is quadriplegia which is profound and flaccid (lower motor neuron) in the arms and hands and less severe and spastic in the legs (upper motor neuron). There is usually

---

56 Frankel HL, Hancock DO, Hyslop G. The Value of Postural Reduction in the Initial Management of Closed Injury of the Spine with Paraplegia and Tetraplegia. *Paraplegia*, 7:179-192, 1969.
57 Bosch A, Stauffer ES, Nickel VL. Incomplete Traumatic Quadriplegia: A Ten Year Review. *JAMA*, 216:473-478, 1971.

sacral sparing with preservation of toe flexion, sphincter control and perianal sensation. The prognosis is fair since half of the patients will recover sufficiently to have bowel and bladder control and to walk with a spastic gait. Hand and arm paralysis, however, remains significant and permanent.[58]
- Anterior cord syndrome: Manifested by complete motor paralysis and sensory loss except for proprioception (vibration, position and deep pressure sense). Only 10 to 15% of patients have functional recovery and this is manifested early by the return of perianal sensation and some motor function in the first 24 hours.[59]
- Posterior cord syndrome: This is a rare injury where the patients lose proprioception and deep pressure sensation only. They will remain with an unsteady gait.

10.2.6.2.3 Complete Cord Lesions: Complete paralysis and absence of any type of sensation distal to the cord lesion indicates a complete cord injury or a complete disruption of the neural communication between the brain and the limbs. It may take a few days before a complete cord injury is confirmed because of the presence of "spinal shock". Spinal shock is a condition where there is transient interruption of the transmission of impulses through the normal cord because of a recent trauma. It results in complete loss of motor and sensory function in addition to the loss of reflexes. Spinal shock can last up to 24 hrs. The first sign of spinal shock resolving is return of reflex action. The reflex most distal to the injury will recover first and is the bulbocavernosus reflex. The presence of a bulbocavernosus reflex in the *absence* of motor function return is a very bad prognostic sign. It indicates that the cord damage is complete, irreversible and permanent.

10.2.6.3 Treatment and Rehabilitation

10.2.6.3.1 Initial Treatment: The initial treatment consists of keeping the patient alive since there are often other injuries that may be life threatening and there may be severe arterial hypotension causes by the neural injury. Further treatment will then be tailored to the neural injury. Nerve roots are resilient and clinical recovery is not dependent on immediate treatment. The spinal cord, however, is very sensitive to changes in its environment and damage to the cord is presently irreversible, therefore rapid, early treatment is important. Based on a randomized controlled trial published in 1990,[60] high dose methylprednisolone is given to the patients as

---

58 Stauffer et al., *supra*, note 51. Stauffer ES. Neurologic Recovery Following Injuries to the Cervical Spinal Cord and Nerve Roots. *Spine*, 9:532-533, 1984.
59 Bosch et al., *supra*, note 57.
60 Bracken et al. *supra*, note 45.

early as possible within 8 hours of the injury. The recommended dose is 30 mg/kg infused intravenously in the first hour then 5.4 mg/kg/hr for the next 23 hours. A study on GM1 ganglioside given within 72 hours of the injury also showed improved motor function recovery compared to placebo;[61] however, this protocol is not widely used. Simultaneous use of methylprednisolone and GM1 ganglioside is not recommended and no studies have compared methylprednisolone to GM1 ganglioside.

After the institution of pharmacologic agents, the mechanical component of the cord irritation or damage can be addressed. Realignment of the spinal canal must be done early by reducing the fracture or dislocation. If, after reduction of the spinal column, there is still compression of the neural elements by bone or disc material, then a surgical decompression is performed. The surgery will not reverse the damage that has already occurred but it will provide an environment that will permit maximal recovery of the cord. Bohlman and Anderson reported long-term improvement of motor function after anterior decompression and fusion of the cervical spine. A significant number of patients with complete cord lesions had significant root recovery improving their function in a wheelchair. Twenty-nine of 58 patients with incomplete cord injuries became functional community ambulators after the surgery.[62]

10.2.6.3.2 Definitive Treatment: This consists of stabilization of the cervical spine so that the rehabilitation stage can be initiated. If we wait for the bone or ligaments to heal then stability will be restored in 3 to 4 months. Valuable rehabilitation time is lost and further injury to the cord can occur during this time. To maximize and accelerate recovery, definitive stabilization of the spine is initiated within 2 weeks of the injury if it is medically safe to do so. Stabilization is by either external methods such as a halo vest and ring or internal methods with surgical instrumentation of the spine.

10.2.6.3.3 Rehabilitation and Long-Term Management: "The delivery of proper rehabilitation care to a person with a new spinal cord injury involves the establishment of a continuum of services that extend from the

---

61 Geisler FH, Dorsey FC, Coleman WP. Recovery of Motor Function after Spinal Cord Injury—a Randomized Placebo Controlled Trial with GM-1 Ganglioside. *N Eng J Med*, 324:1829-1838, 1991.

62 Anderson PA, Bohlman HH. Anterior Decompression and Arthrodesis of the Cervical Spine: Long Term Motor Improvement. Part II—Improvement in Complete Traumatic Quadriplegia. *J Bone Joint Surg*, 74A:683-692, 1992. Bohlman HH, Anderson PA. Anterior Decompression and Arthrodesis of the Cervical Spine: Long Term Motor Improvement Part I—Improvement in Incomplete Traumatic Quadriparesis. *J Bone Joint Surg*, 74A:671-682, 1992.

emergency medical system through the acute and rehabilitation hospital stay and into a programme for life-long medical care".[63] The concept of rehabilitation can be said in various ways but the above captures the essentials of a continuum of care from the time and place of the injury through to reintegration to home and one's community.

Depending on the level of the lesion, respiratory function will be a major concern early on as well making certain there is good skin care, turning every 2 hours, bladder empty (Foley catheter to begin with), adequate nutritional intake, and caring for any other associated injuries.

The goal of rehabilitation is to allow for maximal independence, taking into account the severity of the lesion. The following shows the approximate level of function depending on the injury type or level.

Optimal Function in Motor Complete Quadriplegia

Function	C1-C4	C5	C6	C7,C8,T1
Self-care				
Eating	dependent; drinks with long straw; can use mechanical feeder	independent using balanced forearm orthoses, splints and adapted utensils after setup	independent with splints	and adapted utensils
Bathing	dependent	dependent	independent with equipment	independent
Grooming	dependent	some facial grooming possible with equipment	independent with equipment	independent

---

63 Frost F. Role of Rehabilitation after Spinal Cord Injury. *Urology Clin North Am*, 20(3):551, 1993.

Optimal Function in Motor Complete Quadriplegia (cont'd.)

Function	C1-C4	C5	C6	C7,C8,T1
Self-care				
Dressing	dependent	partial assistance for upper extremities; dependent for lower extremities	independent for upper extremities; assistance for lower extremities	independent with adaptations to clothing
Toileting	dependent	dependent	independent with bowel management; assistance for bladder management	independent
Pressure relief	dependent in bed and manual wheelchair; independent with power recline wheelchair	as for C1-C4	independent	independent
Communication				
Reading	needs page turner or mouthstick	as for C1-C4	independent	independent
Writing	unable	as for C1-C4	needs hand splint	independent
Typing (electric typewriter or computer)	access with mouth or breath control or voice activation	as for C1-C4	needs hand splint	independent

Optimal Function in Motor Complete Quadriplegia (cont'd.)

Function	C1-C4	C5	C6	C7,C8,T1
Communication				
Telephone	using environmental control unit, can operate phone and other appliances	as for C1-C4	independent	independent
Mobility				
Bed	dependent	assistance, even with electric bed	independent with equipment; electric bed helpful	independent; electric bed helpful
Transfers	dependent	dependent	independent with sliding board	independent; may need sliding board
Wheelchair	independent with power wheelchair with chin or mouth control	independent with power wheelchair with hand control	independent with manual wheelchair with adapted rims; assistance outdoors	independent with manual wheelchair

Teresa L. Massagli and Kenneth M. Jaffe. Pediatrics Spinal Cord Injury; Treatment and Outcome. *Pediatrician*, 17:244-254, 1990.
(Reproduced with permission of S. Karger AG, Basel)

Optimal Function in Motor Complete Quadriplegia (cont'd.)

Function	C1-C4	C5	C6	C7,C8,T1
Mobility				
Transportation	unable to drive; travel by accessible van with lift	unable to drive (new technology may permit driving using joystick control); travel by accessible van with lift	independent driving with hand controls; assistance to load wheelchair into car	independent driving with hand controls; independent in loading wheelchair into car

Optimal Mobility in Motor Complete Paraplegia

Mobility	T2-T10	T11-L2	L3-S2
Manual wheelchair	independent indoors and in community	independent indoors and in community	may not need wheelchair except for long distances (or recreation)
Ambulation	exercise only; needs long leg braces and forearm crutches or walker; not really practical for T2-T6; needs at least standby assistance	indoor ambulation with long leg braces and forearm crutches possible; some can climb stairs with railing	indoor and community ambulator with short leg braces and forearm crutches or canes; prolonged standing may be difficult

Optimal Mobility in Motor Complete Paraplegia (cont'd.)

Mobility	T2-T10	T11-L2	L3-S2
Driving	needs hand controls; independent in loading wheelchair into car	needs hand controls; independent in loading wheelchair into car	can drive automatic transmission although hand controls may be preferred

Teresa L. Massagli and Kenneth M. Jaffe. Pediatrics Spinal Cord Injury; Treatment and Outcome. *Pediatrician*, 17:244-254, 1990.
(Reproduced with permission of S. Karger AG, Basel)

Prognosis for incomplete cord injuries;

- Anterior cord syndrome: poor for any functional return
- Central cord syndrome: variable return of upper extremity, spasticity remains
- Brown Sequard syndrome: significant return of function
- Posterior cord syndrome: unknown prognosis because of rarity of injury
- Conus medullaris (T12 to L1): usually not much improvement
- Cauda equina (L1 to L5): usually significant return of motor function

Prognosis for complete cord injuries

- C1 to C3: respirator dependant, blink or head control wheelchair, environmental control unit, computer, mouth stick
- C4: dependant, electric wheelchair with chin control
- C5: partial independance with proper equipment, electric wheelchair with arm control
- C6: Independant with equipment, driving with hand control, manual wheelchair with pegs
- C7: Independent transfers and activities of daily living (ADL), standard manual wheelchair
- C8: Independent ADL without splints, independent transfers
- T1 to T10: Manual wheelchair, independent for living
- T11 to T12: Standing in long leg braces
- L1 to L2: household ambulation with long leg braces
- L3 to L4: community ambulation with long or short leg braces
- L5 to S1: community ambulation with short leg braces
- S2 to S5: community ambulation without braces

Aside from motor function, rehabilitation of the spinal cord-injured patient will look at issues of activities of daily living (eating, dressing, bathing). It will involve developing a programme for the neurogenic bowel and bladder to reduce the risk of severe health problems and developing a programme for good skin care to reduce the risk of decubital ulcers.

It will necessitate being aware of medical complications that can arise both in the short term and long term for different systems of the body. These include the respiratory system, cardiovascular problems, including deep vein thrombosis and pulmonary embolism, autonomic hyper reflex, and urinary tract problems (urine infections, calculi, reflex with its associated biding problem). Also it will be important to be aware of possible gastric stress ulcers early on and or paralytic items. Fecal impaction has to be watched for as well. There are metabolic issues and included here are endocrine problems such as hypercalcimia.

With regards to the musculoskeletal system, thinning of the bones, heterotopic ossification (deposition of new bone in periarticular soft tissue) and spasticity are all potential problems. Spasticity is an exceedingly common and sometimes very difficult problem to deal with. Treatment is usually with different types of antispastic medications and more lately botulism toxin and/or baclafen pump have become part of the armamentarium.

After spinal cord injury, the issue of fertility and fatherhood has been a significant problem for injured males. However, over the last decade there have been significant advances in allowing spinal cord injured men to become fathers. Presently vibratory stimulation, electrostimulation by rectal probe, vas deferans aspiration and implantation of an artificial spermatocele are possible ways of collecting semen for artificial insemination into a female partner. The first two are considered the most successful to date in having a pregnancy.[64]

Another aspect of rehabilitation of spinal cord-injured patients is the integration back into their community. This may entail return to their family or it may be looking to resources to allow them to live independently in the community. The concern for family support and a community agency support is paramount in enabling the injured person to return to the community; suffice it to say that this is true of any individual who has suffered an insult/disease leading to a long-term disability and not just a spinal cord injured person.

In an article by Fuhrer et al., the aspect of life satisfaction associated with spinal cord injury was investigated.[65] They found greater life satisfac-

---

64 Seager SWJ, Halstead L. Fertility Options and Success after Spinal Cord Injury. *Urologic Clin North Am*, 20(3):542-548, 1993.
65 Fuhrer M et al. Relationship of Life Satisfaction to Impairment Disability and Handicap among Persons with Spinal Cord Injury Living in the Community. *Arch Phys Med Rehab*, 73:552-557, 1992.

tion with individuals doing more to maintain solid integration, spending more time in a working environment and being able to be out and about. It is reasonable to assume that suffering a spinal cord injury will have an emotional-psychological effect on the individual. It is common for people to react with disbelief and an element of denial at the beginning that a tragedy has occurred. The individual will need a great deal of support and counselling to adjust to the disability but the majority make a good adjustment.[66] Suicide was 6.3% of all observed deaths in a study of 9,135 spinal cord-injured patients.[67]

Quality of life concerns are always of interest in dealing with spinal cord-injured patients. Studies tend to take a subjective approach or an attempt at objectivity. Evans et al. provide an excellent review of the topic.[68] While Moreau and Shepherd have shown how many different types of physical activity leading to improved physical fitness show positive effects on cardiac, pulmonary and metabolic activities,[69] they also suggest activities of daily living and locomotion are helped by a regular exercise program.

10.2.6.4 Complications

Complete quadriplegia has a high morbidity and a significant mortality rate. In a large Canadian study of in-hospital stay of patients with complete traumatic quadriplegia, a mortality rate of 13% and a morbidity rate of 85% was seen. Pulmonary complications were the most frequent at 57%. There was a lower mortality in the patients that were treated with surgery and the morbidity rate was influenced by surgery, neurologic level, and the treatment centre.[70]

The long-term complications of quadriplegia are different and are listed here:

10.2.6.4.1. Decubitus Ulcers (Pressure Sores): Because of the loss of protective sensation of the skin, prolonged pressure may cause skin ne-

---

66 Krause JS. Longitudinal Changes in Adjustment after Spinal Cord Injury: A 15 year Study. *Arch Phy Med Rehab*, 73:514-519, 1992.
67 Devivoms et al. Suicide following Spinal Cord Injury. *Paraplegia*, 20:620-627, 1991.
68 Evans RL, et al. Quality of Life after Spinal Cord Injury: A Literature Critique and Meta Analysis. *J Am Paraplegia Soc*, 17:60-66, 1994.
69 Moreau L, Shepard R. Spinal Cord Injury Exercise and Quality of Life. *Sport Med*, 20(4):226-250, 1995.
70 Desjardins AL, Bouchard JA, Cayer DH, Bornais S. Morbidity and Mortality in Complete Traumatic Quadriplegic Patients. *Proceedings of the 52nd Annual Meeting of the Canadian Orthopaedic Association*, Hamilton, Ontario, June 2nd, 1997.

crosis and the formation of ulcers. These occur over bony prominences such as the heels, ischium of the buttocks and the hips. Ulcers are difficult to heal, slow to treat and may keep a para or quadriplegic out of his/her wheelchair for months. Attentive nursing care and frequent (every 2 hours) change of position is the most important preventative measure in addition to special beds, mattresses and cushions.

10.2.6.4.2 Pulmonary: Pulmonary complications such as atelectasis and pneumonia are frequent because of the presence of associated injuries and the frequent need to immobilize these patients in bed and to submit them to surgery and general anesthetics. In addition, quadriplegic patients will lose motor function of the intercostal muscles and some of the accessory breathing muscles making it difficult to cough or take deep breaths. In the event that the paralysis is above C4, the diaphragm is paralyzed and the patient requires a mechanical respirator to breathe.

10.2.6.4.3 Contractures: These occur if a joint is not moved through its full range of motion. Active motion does not occur with complete paralysis therefore all the joints in the paralyzed limb must be moved passively by the physiotherapist and family members to prevent permanent contractures.

10.2.6.4.4 Osteoporosis: This is inevitable with disuse of the limbs. In the long term, patients with paralysis are at risk for fractures of the pelvis and lower extremities with minimal trauma such as falling out of a wheelchair.

10.2.6.4.5 Infection of the Urinary Tract: Bladder catheterization must be done several times daily by the patients and this leads to seeding of bacteria in the bladder. Urinary tract infections and kidney stones are frequent. They must be treated aggressively since renal failure is thought to be the major factor in the shorter life expectancy of patients with complete cord injuries.

10.2.6.4.6 Bowel Obstruction: A high fiber diet and manual disimpaction must be maintained to prevent bowel obstruction.

10.2.6.4.7 Deep Vein Thrombosis: Spinal cord injury patients are at very high risk for developing venous thrombosis because of prolonged immobilization, long surgical procedures, use of high dose steroids, presence of paralyzed limbs and altered coagulation. Prophylaxis is recommended to decrease the incidence of pulmonary embolism. Prophylaxis is done with pneumatic compression devices, elastic stockings, early mobilization and pharmocologic agents such as heparin, warfarin, or low molecular weight heparin products.

10.2.6.4.8 Autonomic Dysreflexia: It is an exaggerated response of the autonomic (involuntary) nervous system to stimuli which are normally only mildly noxious. It occurs in about 30% of quadriplegic patients and only if the neural injury is above T6. It occurs rarely before 12 to 16 weeks from the injury. The offensive stimulus can be bladder distention (73%), colorectal (fecal impaction 12%, suppository or enema 4%), decubitus ulcer (4%), deep vein thrombosis, or tight clothing. The patients present with pounding headaches, hypertension, unexplained anxiety, sweating, increased pulse and spasticity, redness in the face, goosebumps (piloerection) and blurred vision.[71]

10.2.6.4.9 Heterotopic Ossification: Periarticular ossification of the soft tissues can occur in 20% of patients with spinal cord injury and may lead to swelling, pain and contractures.

10.2.6.5 Life Expectancy

The survival of spinal cord-injured patients has improved tremendously over the last 50 years. In the early part of the century a patient with complete paralysis of two or four limbs could only expect to live a few weeks to a few years. Most patients died of pressure sores or renal failure. Improved survival has occurred through a better understanding of the cause and prevention of complications and the establishment of specialized treatment centres. Canadian studies of paraplegics and tetraplegics have shown an increased mortality compared with the general population.[72] Predictions of the exact life expectancy is difficult and controversial because of the many conflicting factors such as the level of the injury, the age of the patient at the time of the injury, the care of the patient at the time of his initial hospitalization and at home after discharge and the motivation of the family and the patient.

The outcome of a spinal cord injury in a patient over the age of 50 years is less favourable according to Alander and coworkers. Ten of 13 patients with complete cervical cord lesions died within 1 year of the injury (13% survival rate) and the others had a life expectancy of 3.5 years. The survival of patients with an incomplete cord injury was 93% at 1 year. Seventy-eight percent of these patients improved their neurologic status. Forty-six percent became independent ambulators and 21% were able to

---

71 Erickson RP. Autonomic Hyperreflexia—Pathophysiology and Medical Management. *Arch Phys Med Rehabil*, 61:431-440, 1980. Kewalramani LS, Orth MS. Autonomic Dysreflexia in Traumatic Myelopathy, *Am J Phys Med*, 59:1-21, 1980.

72 Geisler WO, Jousse AT, Wynne-Jones M, Breithaupt D. Survival in Traumatic Spinal Cord Injury. *Paraplegia*, 21:364-373, 1983.

ambulate with moderate assistance. Most patients with moderate and severe cord injury required placement in an extended care facility.[73]

10.3 THE THORACOLUMBAR SPINE

10.3.1 Anatomy

10.3.1.1 Osseous Anatomy

The major bony components of the vertebrae in the thoracic and lumbar spine are similar to those in the cervical spine described earlier in this chapter. As we progress down the spine, the vertebrae and discs get bigger in size to accommodate the increased weight they must carry, much like the pyramids of Egypt or the Eiffel tower.

The thoracic vertebra has articulations on the vertebral body and transverse processes from which the ribs of the chest originate. Since the ribs are connected posteriorly to the thoracic spine and anteriorly to the sternum, a protective cage is formed to protect vital organs such as the heart and lungs. It also stiffens the thoracic spine so that there is much less motion through these spinal segments compared to the cervical and lumbar segments. The thoracic spine is in kyphosis therefore convex posterior.

The lumbar spine is in lordosis and is therefore convex anterior. The lumbar spine starts with the first vertebra that does not have a rib on it. Most humans have five lumbar vertebrae. There are congenital variations where the last vertebra of the lumbar spine will be partially or completely fused to the sacrum and this may affect the number of lumbar vertebrae. The lumbar vertebrae have the same features as the thoracic and cervical spine except that they are coarse and stout with larger bodies, pedicles, facets and lamina. They do not have neurocentral joints, articulations for ribs, or a foramen transversarium.

The sacrum is a group of vertebrae that are fused together [Figure 10.13]. They form a bony structure which is crescent-shaped when visualizing it from the side and triangular when looking at it from the front. The sacrum is a strong base or pedestal over which the rest of the spine stands. It is also the main structure that connects the upper skeleton to the pelvis and lower skeleton. It is thus built for strength and stability and not for motion.

The coccyx is composed of three to four fused rudimentary vertebrae. It is the human's vestigial elements of the tail. It articulates with the sa-

---

73 Alander DH, Parker J, Stauffer ES. Intermediate Term Outcome of Cervical Spinal Cord-injured Patients Older than 50 Years of Age. *Spine*. 22(11):1189-1192, 1997.

crum. It has very little biomechanical function but does serve as part of the origin of the gluteus maximus muscle and the pelvic floor muscles.

10.3.1.2 Intervertebral Discs

The discs of the thoracic and lumbar spine have the same general morphology as in the cervical spine. The adult lumbar discs are large and take up about 35% of the volume of the lumbar spine. There are three components: the annulus fibrosus, the nucleus pulposus, and the cartilaginous end plates [Figure 10.14]. The discs are avascular but not inactive. There is a low but significant rate of tissue turnover. Nutrition is accomplished through the cartilage end plate by diffusion and mechanical pumping of nutrients.

Numerous factors will lead to changes in the nutrition and composition of the lumbar intervertebral discs.

- Exercise: when load is applied to a disc, fluid gradually seeps out. It is estimated that a disc loses 10% of its height in a 16 hour day and therefore the average person is 1-3% shorter at the end of the day. Swelling of the disc at rest is faster and it takes 8 hours for the disc height to be restored at night. Moderate exercises have been shown to increase the nutrition of the discs whereas strenuous exercise can cause accelerated disc degeneration.[74] It is presently not known which exact exercise regimen is best for the intervertebral disc.
- Fusion: a fusion of the motion segment decreases the movements across the disc. It has been shown that there is a decrease in the metabolic activity of the disc in the fused segment and an increase in the activity of the adjacent discs.[75]
- Vibration: Studies on porcine specimens have shown a decrease in the glucose permeability of the vertebral endplate and a decrease in the water content of the disc.[76] In addition, several epidemiological studies have demonstrated that subjects exposed to vibrations have increased incidence of low back pain.[77]

---

74 Nachemson AL. The Lumbar Spine: an Orthopaedic Challenge. *Spine*, 1:59, 1976.
75 Holm S, Nachemson A. Nutrition Changes in the Canine Intervertebral Disc after Spinal Fusion. *Clin Orthop*, 169:243-258, 1983. Taylor TKF, Ghosh P, Braund KG et al. The Effect of Spinal Fusion on Intervertebral Disc Composition: an Experimental Study. *J Surg Res*, 21:91-104, 1976.
76 Hansson T, Holm S. Clinical Implications of Vibration Induced Changes in the Lumbar Spine. *Orthop Clin North Am*, 22:247-254, 1991. Holm S, Nachemson A. Nutrition of the Intervertebral Disc: Effects Induced by Vibrations. *Orthop Trans*, 9:451, 1985.
77 Sandover J. Dynamic Loading as a Possible Source of Low Back Pain Disorders. *Spine*, 8:652-658, 1983. Seidel H, Bluethner R, Hinz B. Effects of Sinusoidal Whole Body Vibration on the Lumbar Spine: the Stress-Strain Relationship. *Int Arch Occup Eviron Health*, 57:207-223, 1986.

- Smoking: Cigarette smoking has clearly been shown to affect the circulatory system around the disc, reduce the transport of nutrients into the disc and waste products out of the disc. This is thought to produce a metabolic degenerative process.[78]
- Diabetes: Similar to smoking, diabetes affects the small vessels around the disc and impairs its nutrition. This leads to accelerated degeneration.[79]

10.3.1.3 Ligaments of the Thoracolumbar Spine

The anterior and posterior longitudinal ligaments are a continuous strip lying at the front and the back of the vertebral bodies and discs along the whole length of the spine. The anterior longitudinal ligament is attached more firmly to the vertebra whereas the posterior longitudinal ligament has fibers attaching to the annulus fibrosus of the disc [Figure 10.15].

The capsular ligaments are short and attach to either sides of the facet joint. They are more taut in the thoracic and lumbar spine than in the cervical spine and therefore do not allow a great excursion of the facet joints.

The ligamentum flavum connects one border of the lamina to the next. These ligaments are composed of a large amount of elastic fibers and can deform more than other ligaments in the spine.

The interspinous ligaments and supraspinous ligaments join adjacent spinous processes. These are quite thick in the lumbar region of the spine.

Testing of the failure strength of ligaments has demonstrated that the strongest ligament in the lumbar spine is the anterior longitudinal ligament followed in order by the posterior longitudinal ligament, the ligamentum flavum, the capsular ligaments, the interspinous ligaments, and the supraspinous ligaments. In the thoracic spine the strongest ligament is the supraspinous ligament, followed by the anterior longitudinal ligament, ligamentum flavum, capsular ligaments, posterior longitudinal ligaments, and the interspinous ligaments. With the exception of the supraspinous ligaments, all of the ligaments are much stronger in the lumbar spine than in any other location in the spine.

Other noteworthy ligaments are the iliolumbar ligaments which join the ileum of the pelvis to the L5 transverse process and the sacro-iliac ligaments which form a strong capsule to the sacroiliac joints.

---

78 Holm S, Nachemson A. Immediate Effects of Cigarette Smoke on Nutrition of the Intervertebral Disc of the Pig. *Orthop Trans*, 8:380, 1984.

79 Holm S. Does Diabetes Induce Degenerative Processes in the Lumbar Intervertebral Disc? *Proceedings of the International Society for the Study of the Lumbar Spine*, Kyoto, Japan, 1989.

10.3.1.4 Muscles of the Thoracolumbar Spine

The posterior muscles of the spine can be subdivided into as many as six different layers. For the purposes of this chapter these muscles will be divided into two layers: the superficial muscles and the deep muscles. The superficial muscle layer mostly attaches the arm and scapula to the spine and they consist of the inferior half of the trapezius, the rhomboid major and minor, the latissimus dorsi, and the serratus posterior superior and inferior. The fibers of these muscles run either perpendicular or oblique to the axis of the spine. The latissimus dorsi muscle is large and originates at the thoracolumbar fascia. This structure is important as it spans a large area of the posterior lower back and attaches to the spinous processes in the midline and the iliac wing of the pelvis. It is also a strong membrane covering the deeper muscles of the lumbar spine. The deep layer of muscles have fibers that course in the same direction as the axis of the spine. This group is collectively known as the erector spinae muscles and consist of the iliocostalis, the longissimus, and the spinalis muscles. In addition, several shorter and deep muscles assist in posture of the spine. These are the multifidus lumborum and the rotatores muscles.

The muscles anterior to the thoracolumbar spine can also be divided into two groups: the deeper muscles that have direct attachments to the spine and the superficial group which do not originate or insert on the spine but their action greatly influences its biomechanics. The deeper layer consists of the diaphragm, which is a large parachute-shaped muscle that controls breathing, the iliopsoas muscle, which originates from L1 to L5 and pelvis and inserts on the femur to produce flexion of the hip, and the quadratus lumborum, which attaches to the transverse processes of the spine and help laterally flex the lumbar spine. The superficial layer of muscle lies 20 to 30 cm anterior to the spine and consists of the abdominal muscles. These are the rectus abdominis, the external oblique, the internal oblique, and the transversus abdominis muscles. They originate on the lower ribs and sternum and insert on the pelvis and to the thoracolumbar fascia. They greatly influence the lumbar spine because they function away from the spine and therefore generate more force for flexion and rotation of the spine.

There are other muscles which affect the lumbar spine by affecting the position of the pelvis. The gluteus maximus extends the hip and is vital in humans to maintain an upright stance. The hamstring muscles also extend the hip and can rotate the pelvis if they are contracted or tight. The pyriformis muscle has no influence on spine mechanics, however, since it comes out of the pelvis through the sciatic notch and crosses over the sciatic nerve. It is thought to be a cause of entrapment of the sciatic nerve and is always included in the differential diagnosis of sciatica.

10.3.1.5 Neuroanatomy of the Thoracolumbar Spine

The spinal cord is continuous from the cervical into the thoracic spine and down to the L1–L2 level. Thus, the cross-sectional anatomy is similar to the neuroanatomy of the cervical region. At each vertebral level two nerve roots exit, one on each side. Since the last cervical root is C8 and it exits just above the first thoracic vertebra, all the other roots distal to this exit below the pedicle of the vertebra from which it is numbered. For example, the T1 root will exit just below the T1 vertebra pedicle and so on down to the lumbar and sacral spine. In the thoracolumbar junction, the spinal cord becomes smaller and gives off numerous roots which will course down vertically in the dural sac until they reach their respective vertebral foramen to exit the spine. The end of the spinal cord is called conus medullaris because of its shape and the collection of nerve roots arising from the conus are called cauda equina since it looks like a horse's tail [Figure 10.6]. The spinal cord and conus medullaris contain neural tissues that are part of the upper motor neuron system, and damage to these tissues is generally irreversible. The cauda equina is a group of nerves in the peripheral neural system that are lower motor neurons. They are more resilient to injury and have a greater capacity for recovery. Neurologic injuries in the thoracic spine tend to produce symptoms of the upper motor neurons since the cord is easily damaged. It is more frequent to have complete paralysis in the thoracic spine because the cross section of the spinal canal is smaller and the cord more vulnerable. It is unusual to see partial cord injuries such as those described with cervical spine injuries. The functional deficit from a complete cord injury in the thoracic spine causes paralysis and loss of sensation in the lower extremities, bladder and bowel dysfunction, and spasticity. The upper extremities are not affected since their innervation is proximal to T1. In the T12 to L2 region a combination of upper and lower motor neuron lesions can occur because of the presence of both conus medullaris and cauda equina. One might see flaccid paralysis of some of the muscles of the legs while other muscles and the bladder are spastic. From L2 to S1 the neurologic injury is to the cauda equina. It carries a much better prognosis for recovery. The muscles, reflexes, sphincters and bladder will be flaccid rather than spastic.

10.3.1.6 Location of Pain Fibers in the Spine

The exact pathophysiology of back pain is complex. In order to understand the exact cause for the pain, we must first review which structures are capable of sending painful stimuli to the brain.

The facet joints are richly innervated, having both proprioceptive fibers (nerve endings that tell the brain what position the joint is in) and nociceptive fibers (nerve endings that transmit pain). Most of these fibers are within the joint capsule and ligaments and are stimulated by mechanical factors such as joint distention, excursion beyond the normal range of motion, direct trauma or ligamentous instability, or by chemical factors such as those produced by inflammation or infection. The synovium of the joint have recently been found to contain a great number of small diameter nerve fibers.

Bone is a tissue that responds to internal and external pressure changes, physical distortion, inflammation, and periosteal injury. In a fractured vertebra, pain is initially produced by the disruption of intramedullary nerve fibers, by stretched and torn fibers in the periosteum, and by pressure over the adjacent muscles and ligaments. With bleeding and swelling the pressure intensifies and this triggers further pain receptors. Chronic pain from bone origin can occur. A spondylolysis with a fibrous union of a pars defect may be painful, and in such patients it has been found that the fibrous tissue that fills the gap in the pars interarticularis is extensively innervated by nociceptive free nerve endings.[80]

In the intervertebral disc, fine nerve endings are seen in the outer third of the annulus fibrosus. The innervation comes from the sinuvertebral nerve which also supplies the posterior longitudinal ligament and the ventral dura. Some fibers are thought to also supply part of the vertebral body periosteum.[81] There is considerable overlap of the innervation of the ascending and descending branches of these nerves and therefore pain can radiate to other levels making the exact determination of the offending level difficult. Discogenic back pain from internal disc disruption is felt to be caused by radial tears of the disc which expose the nerve endings in the periphery of the annulus to chemical and mechanical irritants. Another source of pain from the disc is its proximity to the dorsal root ganglion (part of the nerve root that exits in the intervertebral foramen). The dorsal root ganglion is extremely sensitive to irritation and produces radicular pain.

The posterior longitudinal ligament (PLL) is richly innervated by nerve endings and in addition is closely attached to the posterior aspect of the annulus fibrosus. It is thought to be an important contributor to back pain from disc protrusion or ruptures.

Muscles and tendons around the spine also contain a variety of different nerve endings. Some transmit pain directly, and others are mechanore-

---

80 MacNab, *supra*, note 7. Schneiderman GA, McLain RF, Hambly MF, et al. The Pars Defect as a Pain Source: A Histologic Study. *Spine*, 20:1761-1764, 1995.

81 Bogduk N, Tynan W, Wilson AS. The Nerve Supply to the Human Lumbar Intervertebral Discs. *J Anat*, 132:39-56, 1981. Bogduk N. The Innervation of the Lumbar Spine. *Spine*, 8:286-293, 1983.

ceptors that may transmit painful impulses under stretch, pressure, or disruption. Chemonociceptors respond to metabolic changes in the muscle such as the accumulation of metabolites during anaerobic exercise, ischemia, and the presence of chemical irritants such as serotonin, bradykinin, and potassium.

10.3.2 Biomechanics and Pathophysiology of Thoracolumbar Injuries

10.3.2.1 The Three-column Concept

Thoracolumbar spine fractures have been classified in many different ways by a variety of authors and so-called new classifications are constantly being developed by various authors. Holdsworth in 1963 classified fractures of the spine based on a two-column concept with the anterior column being the vertebral body and discs and the posterior column being the pedicles, lamina, and facet.[82] With the development of computerized tomography, more information about the tissue damage was made available to the clinician, and the two-column classification was found to be inadequate in differentiating certain fracture type. In 1983, Francis Denis put forward a three-column concept and a classification based on this concept and on the radiologic and tomographic appearance of the fracture.[83] Because of its simplicity and usefulness, this classification was widely accepted and is still in use today.

The *anterior column* is composed of the anterior half of the vertebral body, the anterior half of the intervertebral disc, and the anterior longitudinal ligament [Figure 10.16]. The *middle column* includes the posterior half of the vertebral body, the posterior half of the intervertebral disc, and the posterior longitudinal ligament. The *posterior column* includes the pedicles, lamina, facet joints, ligamentum flavum, interspinous ligaments, and spinous processes. By definition, the spine is stable if it can withstand normal physiologic stresses without deforming or producing excessive pain or neurologic deficit. The thoracolumbar spine is considered stable if at least two columns remain intact.

The load-carrying capacity of the damaged spine has been studied by Haher.[84] The load-carrying capacity of the thoracolumbar spine decreased

---

82 Holdsworth FW. Fractures, Dislocations and Fracture-Dislocations of the Spine. *J Bone Joint Surg*, 45B:6-20,1963.

83 Denis F. The Three Column Spine and its Significance in the Classification of Acute Thoracolumbar Spinal Injuries. *Spine*, 8:817-831, 1983 and also Spinal Instability as Defined by the Three Column Spine Concept in Acute Spinal Trauma. *Clin Orthop*, 189:65-76, 1984.

84 Haher TR, Bergman M, O'Brien M, Felmy W, Choueka J, Welin D, Chow G, Vassilou A. The Effect of the Three Columns of the Spine on the Instantaneous Axis of Rotation in Flexion and Extension. *Spine*, 16:S312-S318, 1991. Haher TR, Felmy W, Baruch H, Devlin V, Welin D, O'Brien M, Ahmad J, Valenza J, Parish S. The Contribution of the Three Columns of the Spine to Rotational Stability. *Spine*, 14:663-669, 1989.

by 30% if the anterior column was ablated, by 70% if the anterior and middle column were ablated, by 65% if the middle and posterior column were ablated and by 25% if the posterior column was ablated. By ablating the annulus fibrosus of the disc, the thoracolumbar junction lost 80% of its rotatory stability while ablation of the facets only decreased the stability by 20%

10.3.2.2 Mechanism of Injury and Classification

Most of the fractures and dislocation patterns in the thoracolumbar spine can be grouped in the following categories. A *compression fracture* occurs when there is acute flexion of the spine and the anterior portion of the vertebral body fractures. Since there is only damage to the anterior column, this fracture pattern is considered stable. When there is flexion and axial compression of the vertebra, the middle and anterior column are disrupted causing a *burst fracture*. Because two columns of the spine are disrupted, the fracture is unstable but only to axial compression. There is usually not any translation of the vertebra. Flexion and distraction placed on the spine usually disrupts all three columns and is called either a *flexion distraction* fracture-dislocation, a seat belt fracture or a Chance fracture. The most common mechanism for this injury is a frontal collision with the occupant of the vehicle having a taut lap belt. The occupant's upper body is thrown forward while the pelvis and lower spine are firmly fixed to the car seat. This injury is unstable in all directions because of the disruption of all three columns. The other injury which causes a three-column injury is a *fracture dislocation* of the spine. This is produced by flexion of the spine with compression and/or rotation. These are the most unstable spine injuries and severe neurologic deficits are frequently associated with them.

10.3.3 Evaluation of the Patient

10.3.3.1 History

Fractures and dislocations of the thoracic spine require significant force to produce and the patients are often severely injured. Because life threatening injuries must be treated with haste, the history sometimes is brief. At the very least the pertinent history should include 1) Allergies, 2) Medications (and drugs and alcohol), 3) Past illnesses, 4) Last meal, and 5) Events preceding the injury (A.M.P.L.E. history).

When the patient is stabilized, a thorough history is taken, as is the case whenever the patient is reevaluated months or years after the injury. The information sought after will be the same as that described in the evaluation of the patient with a neck injury.

10.3.3.2 Physical Examination

With his or her physical exam, the clinician should be able to answer the following questions:

- Does this patient have a spinal injury?
- What is the nature of the spinal injury?
- What is the disability caused by this injury? (neurologic deficit, pain level, stiffness).
- Are there other injuries that affect spine function or the patient's overall functional capacity?

The thoracolumbar spine has a very important role in the skeleton as it bridges the upper and lower body. As such, examination of this part of the spine must also include examinations of the neck, shoulders, chest, abdomen, pelvis, hips, and lower extremity.

Observation:

- subjective signs: general posture, observation of the patient moving about in the examination room, pain response such as crying and grimacing. The patient is observed throughout the history taking. If the patient is distracted by the questions they must answer and they feel the examination has not started then a more accurate portrayal of their usual function is obtained. If at all possible the patient is observed entering and exiting the clinic or office. It is often useful to obtain information on the patient's condition on the day of the exam. The patients can tell the physician whether they are having a "good day" or a "bad day" with respect to their symptoms. Also, the amplitude of the subjective physical signs will take on a different meaning based on the patient's activities that day. For example, two patients may appear to be relatively comfortable while they are being examined but one just spent the weekend in bed because of back pain and the other one just drove 3 hours to come to the clinic, parked 10 blocks from the hospital to save on parking and waited 1 hour in the waiting room. Similar back symptoms in these two patients does not equate to the same back disability.
- objective signs: structural deformities such as scoliosis, kyphosis, lordosis, and spondylolisthesis. If seen early, bruising, seat belt marks, or abrasions can be detected. Gait evaluation will reveal leg length discrepancies, hip and knee problems, muscle weakness, or imbalance such as a foot drop and spinal deformities. A cursory examination of the muscle strength can be done by having the patient walk on his toes, on his heels and squat.

Palpation:

- subjective signs: tenderness of various structures in the lumbar spine and pelvis can be useful in determining the origin of the pain but is dependent on the patient's response to the probing finger. Specific areas of tenderness can be found over the spinous processes and the iliac crests of the pelvis. These are the only bony structures that are not covered by muscle and readily palpable. Deep pain can sometimes be elicited from the facet joints, sacroiliac joints, and coccyx. Since the L5–S1 facet joints are very close to the sacroiliac joints, it is often difficult on palpation to differentiate the two. Palpation can reveal tenderness of the erector spinae muscle or the thoracolumbar fascia.
- objective signs: palpation of edema (swelling), muscle spasms, bony deformities, and masses cannot be influenced by the patient or examiner differences. Unusual gaps in the ligaments and muscles are important determinants of the integrity of these structures.

Range of motion testing:

- subjective signs: active range of motion is performed by the patient and will vary with the effort produced and the pain elicited. It can be accurate and objective if pain is controlled and the patient is cooperative.
- objective signs: passive range of motion is controlled by the examiner. This modality, however, is almost impossible to do in its pure form for the thoracic and lumbar spine, since this area of the spine is examined with the patient standing and therefore the muscles of the spine are never completely inactive. The range of motion can be recorded in many different ways. The American Medical Association recommends the use of inclinometers to measure the motion of the thoracic and lumbar spine. Using this method, the normal range of motion of the thoracic spine is 60 degrees of flexion, and 30 degrees of left and right rotation. The normal range of motion of the lumbar spine is considered to be 60 degrees or more of flexion, 25 degrees of extension, and 25 degrees of right and left lateral rotation.[85]

Neurologic function:

- subjective signs: Sensation is tested for pain (pinprick), light touch, vibration (tuning fork) and position. In the cooperative patient an accurate determination of the neurologic involvement can be derived from this result, but the examiner must rely on the sensation reported

---

85 Doege TC, ed. *Guides to the Evaluation of Permanent Impairment*, 4th ed. American Medical Association, 1995.

by the patient. Testing of muscle strength is also dependent on the effort provided by the patient.
- objective signs: In testing sensation, two-point discrimination (the minimum distance between two points that the patient can feel separately) can be useful to quantify sensation. This is often used in the examination of the hand but not often in the examination of the lower extremities. Motor examination of the lower extremity is objectively measured by looking for muscle wasting or hypertrophy, measuring thigh and calf circumferences for asymmetries, and looking for fasciculations or spasms of the muscle. Muscle strength grading is described in 10.2.2.3, Concepts of Spinal Stability, *supra*. Normal strength is suggested if the patient has a normal gait, can heel and toe walk without difficulty and can do a deep knee bend. A trendelenberg gait (drop of the pelvis on one side) suggests weakness of the gluteus medius and L5 dysfunction. A drop foot gait suggests weakness of the foot dorsiflexors which are mostly an L4 root function and partially an L5 root function. If the patient has difficulty toe walking it suggests an S1 motor root problem.

Special tests:

- Deep tendon reflexes: The knee jerk is representative of L4 root function. The ankle jerk tests the function of the S1 root. There is no easy reflex that can be elicited for L5 in the normal patient; however, if a patient has hyperactive reflexes, then a medial hamstring jerk can be detected for L5. Reflexes are independent of the patient's voluntary control, but a patient can eliminate a reflex by keeping a specific muscle contracted. Grading is on a scale of 0 to 4 with 0 being an absent reflex, 1 a sluggish response, 2 normal, 3 hyperactive, and 4 hyperactive with clonus.
- Straight leg raising (SLR): With the patient supine, the leg is lifted with the knee in extension. This flexes the hip. By keeping the knee extended and flexing the hip, the sciatic nerve is stretched. Normally, there is enough slack in the nerve to tolerate this without any pain, and the test is limited by the muscle flexibility. If there is irritation or entrapment of the nerve either in the spinal canal or outside, the patient will have pain in the back radiating down the leg into the foot. The test result is considered positive only if the pain radiates down the leg. A positive SLR test result indicates irritation of the L4, L5, S1, or S2 nerve roots which supply the sciatic nerve [Figure 10.17].

- Lasegue sign: A positive SLR test result is further substantiated by dorsiflexing the ankle. This should aggravate the pain as it stretches the nerve even more. Plantarflexion of the ankle or flexion of the knee relieves the pain.[86]
- Crossover sign: This sign is specific to nerve root irritation from a herniated disc. A SLR test is performed on the nonpainful side and it produces pain down the other leg.
- Bowstring sign: A SLR test is performed. When the patient reports pain down the back of the leg, the knee is flexed slightly. This relieves the pain. Then the nerve is pushed on in the popliteal fossa (back of the knee). A positive bowstring is when the sciatic pain is reproduced by this.
- Kernig's sign: This test also stretches the sciatic nerve but the hip and knee are flexed to 90 degrees, then the knee is extended. A positive test result reproduces pain down the leg. If the pain shoots up the spine and into the neck, it is indicative of generalized meningeal irritation.[87]
- Tripod sign: Experienced patients have undergone numerous examinations and are aware of the response they should give to the classic SLR test. The tripod test distracts the patient into thinking that his knee or leg is being examined. The patient is sitting on the side of the examining table with the legs dangling. The hip and knee are therefore flexed and the sciatic nerve relaxed. As the physician examines the knee, it is gradually extended. In essence, this is a Kernig's test with the patient sitting. A positive test result, which is pain in the back of the leg along the sciatic nerve, will make the patient lunge back to extend the hip. In placing his hands and arms backwards for support he forms a "tripod".
- Femoral stretch test (FST): This test is to the femoral nerve what the SLR test is to the sciatic nerve. The patient is positioned prone. The hip and knee are resting in extension. The first maneuver is to flex the knee. This starts stretching the femoral nerve. With the knee flexed the hip is extended to maximize the stretch on the femoral nerve. If a patient feels pain along the anterior thigh and knee and pins and needles or numbness during this maneuver, the test result is positive. Pain in the back is not considered a feature of this test. It is a frequent occurrence because the patient is positioned prone and the lumbar spine extension is accentuated. A positive FST is indicative of irritation of the L2, L3, and L4 roots which supply the femoral nerve. Note that the L4 nerve is shared by the sciatic nerve and the femoral nerve. If

---

86 DeGowin EL et al., *supra*, note 9.
87 *Ibid.*

there is pathology of the L4 nerve then both the SLR and FST should be positive.
- Graenslen's test: The patient holds the opposite knee and hip flexed against the abdomen and chest. The other leg is extended over the side of the examining table. Pain on that side of the back is suggestive of sacroiliac pathology.
- FABER test (Patrick's test): F for flexion of the hip, AB for abduction of the hip and ER for external rotation. Pain in the groin is indicative of hip pathology and pain in the back is suggestive of sacroiliac joint pathology.
- Magnuson's test: When a patient indicates a painful spot in the lower back, it is marked with a pen. The examiner proceeds with other aspects of the examination as a diversion and then again palpates the back. A patient with organic disease identifies the same point each time whereas the malingerer will identify different painful sites.[88]
- Rectal exam: When unusual pathology is suspected, a rectal exam can provide an enormous amount of information. It may help detect aneurysms or pelvic tumors that can present as back pain or sciatica. The determination of rectal sphincter tone provides insight on the function of the sacral roots. In addition, direct osseous palpation of the coccyx, sacrum, and ischium is possible. Palpation of the ischium permits the examiner to determine if there is ischiogluteal bursitis (weaver's bottom) which sometimes mimics sciatica.
- Peripheral pulses: the femoral (anterior hip), popliteal (back of the knee), dorsalis pedis (top of the foot) and posterior tibialis (ankle) pulses are determinants of the arterial blood supply to the legs. Pain and cramping in the legs (claudication) can have a vascular etiology and must be separated from lumbar stenosis which causes a neurogenic claudication.
- Abdominal skin reflex: stroking the skin of the abdomen normally causes a retraction of the abdominal wall or the umbilicus towards the area that is stroked. The upper abdomen tests T5 to T8, the mid abdomen tests T9 to T11 and the lower abdomen tests T11 to T12.
- Cremasteric reflex: in males stroking the inner thigh causes contraction of the cremaster muscle and elevation of the testis on that side. This tests L1 to L2.
- Superficial anal reflex: stroking the skin of the perianal region causes a contraction of the sphincter on that side and tests L1 to L2.

10.3.3.2.1 Nonorganic Physical Signs: In 1984 Waddell's publication in the *British Medical Journal* distinguished the signs and symptoms of

---

88   *Ibid.*

physical disease compared to abnormal illness behaviour. These characteristics are now widely quoted in textbooks and medicolegal reports. Symptoms that correlate to abnormal illness behaviour are whole leg pain, tailbone pain, giving way of the whole leg, numbness of the whole leg, never any periods free of pain, intolerance to treatment, and emergency admissions to hospital. Physical signs associated with abnormal illness behaviour are superficial and widespread nonanatomic tenderness, lumbar pain to axial loading, lumbar pain to simulated rotation, straight leg raising that improves with distraction, regional sensory loss, and regional, jerky giving way on muscle testing.[89]

10.3.3.3 Investigations

Plain radiographs of the spine are the basis of all investigational tools available in spinal trauma. Anteroposterior and lateral views of the spine provide important information on the location of the injury, the alignment of the spine, and determine the initial stability of the spine. Radiographs will not only guide the clinician in staging further investigations, but will also determine how the patient will be handled by the nursing staff and whether the patient will be treated surgically.

Computerized tomography gives better visualization of the vertebral arches, the facet joints, and the status of the vertebral canal. It is the best modality for defining the bony elements. Its weakness is that the neural elements often cannot be distinguished from the soft tissues and intervertebral disc unless it is combined with a myelogram. Myelograms are used frequently in degenerative diseases, scoliosis, spondylolisthesis, and disc disease. Myelography in the acute trauma situation is used infrequently since it is an invasive procedure and patient positioning may not be possible if the spine is unstable or the patient's medical condition does not permit it.

Magnetic resonance imaging (MRI) is the investigation of choice for the study of the spinal cord and nerves.[90] Soft tissue definition can also show edema and haematoma formation and provides insight into the long-term prognosis for the patient. Presently, the main limitation of MRI is limited availability in some centres, particularly after regular working hours.

---

89 Waddell G, McCulloch JA, Kummel E, et al. Nonorganic Physical Signs in Low-back Pain. *Spine*, 5:117, 1979. Waddell G, Bircher M, Finlayson D, et al. Symptoms and Signs: Physical Disease or Illness Behavior? *Br Med J*, 289: 739-741, 1984. Waddell G, Sommerville D, Henderson I, Newton M. Objective Clinical Examination of Physical Impairment in Chronic Low Back Pain. *Spine*, 17:617-628, 1992.
90 Modic MT, Masaryk TJ, Ross JS. *Magnetic Resonance Imaging of the Spine*, 2nd ed. St. Louis: Mosby, 1994.

As in the cervical investigations, the radiologic findings of the thoracolumbar spine must be correlated to the clinical findings. There can be frequent false positive findings. On plain radiographs it is sometimes difficult to determine whether a compression fracture is new or old. MRI of the lumbar spine in asymptomatic individuals has shown that 20% of individuals less than 60 years of age have disc herniations and 36% of those over 60 years of age have disc herniation. Ninety percent of individuals over the age of 80 years have MRI evidence of disc degeneration.[91]

10.3.3.4 Missed Spine Fractures

The rate of missed spine fractures in the cervical spine is up to 33% and in the lumbar spine is approximately 5%.[92] Many of the delays in diagnosis occur even after arrival to the tertiary care centre. The main reason for missed fractures is a low level of suspicion as indicated by radiographs not being made or not being interpreted properly. Other factors which influence the rate of delay is a physician's not suspecting a second or third fracture when one has already been identified, an uncooperative, comatosed, or intoxicated patient, or patients not seeking medical attention. Polytrauma patients are often overwhelming and some injuries are often overlooked initially.

10.3.4 Fractures and Dislocations of the Thoracolumbar Spine

10.3.4.1 Classification

10.3.4.1.1 Compression Fractures: Flexion of the thoracolumbar spine produces a failure of the anterior column and on radiographs is delineated by a fracture of the anterior half of the upper end plate of the vertebra and compression of the trabecular (spongy) bone of the anterior vertebral body [Figure 10.18]. Because only the anterior column of the spine is damaged this injury is considered stable. It sometimes leads to kyphosis, especially in the elderly with osteoporosis. They are rarely associated with any neurologic compromise.

10.3.4.1.2 Burst Fractures: Axial loading applied to the vertebrae of the thoracolumbar spine produces an explosion of the vertebral body. The

---

91 Boden SD, Davis DO, Dina TS, Patronas SJ, Wiesel SW. Abnormal Magnetic Resonance Scans of the Lumbar Spine in Asymptomatic Patients: A Prospective Investigation. *J Bone Joint Surg*, 72-A:403-408, 1990.
92 Ergaz Z. Spinal Cord Injury in the United States: A Statistical Update. *Cent Nerv Syst Trauma*, 2:19-32, 1985. Keenen TL, Antony J, Benson DR. Noncontiguous Spinal Fractures. *J Trauma*, 30:489-491, 1990. Kewalramani LS, Taylor RG. Multiple Noncontiguous Injuries to the Spine. *Acta Ortho Scand*, 47:52-58, 1976.

typical mechanism of this fracture is a fall from a height. The classic radiologic findings are a loss of height of the whole vertebral body, a widening of the pedicles on the anteroposterior radiograph, a fracture of the lamina, and a retropulsed fragment of bone in the vertebral canal [Figure 10.19]. Five subtypes of burst fracture have been described, depending on whether one or both end plates are fractured and on the amount of rotation or lateral flexion that occurs with axial loading.[93] These fractures damage the middle and anterior column of the spine and are unstable to axial loading. Neurologic deficits can occur because of the fragment which is pushed back into the spinal canal.

10.3.4.1.3 Flexion-distraction Injuries: Otherwise known as seat belt injuries or Chance fractures.[94] The distraction disrupts bone, ligaments, and discs of the three columns. This injury is difficult to image radiologically because it sometimes has minimal involvement of the osseous elements. The Chance fractures involve primarily bone and are seen on radiographs as a split in the vertebra going through the vertebral bodies, pedicles, transverse processes and spinous process [Figures 10.20 and 10.21]. Despite involving the three columns, this injury is relatively more stable because of the interdigitations of bone. Most of the seat belt injuries involve significant damage to the disc and ligaments rather than bone. These are very unstable and are difficult to define on radiographs because the spine recoils back to a fairly normal alignment. A high index of suspicion must be maintained to make the diagnosis. This fracture is frequently associated with ruptures of the duodenum.

10.3.4.1.4 Fracture-dislocation: This is a catastrophic disruption of all three columns of the spine by compression and shearing mechanisms. This injury is highly unstable and is usually accompanied by a significant degree of neurologic impairment and dural tears. The radiographs demonstrate a disruption of the alignment of the spine with one vertebra translated over the other [Figures 10.22 and 10.23].

10.3.4.2 Treatment

10.3.4.2.1 Initial: The initial treatment is to not worsen the neurologic status or spinal deformity. This is done by extricating, transporting, and evaluating the patient by not manipulating or moving the spine. For protection of the thoracolumbar spine the patient is positioned on a stiff board, and when the patient is moved, spine alignment is maintained by a tech-

---

93 Denis, *supra*, note 83, at *Clin Orthop*, 189:65-76, 1984.
94 Chance GQ. Note on a Type of Flexion Fracture of the Spine. *Br J Rad*, 21:452-453, 1948.

nique called log rolling. It is safest to use a backboard when doing this maneuver. The initial treatment also consists in treating the life-threatening injuries as outlined by the Advanced Trauma Life Support principles. A thorough evaluation of the patient's general condition, of the soft tissue injury, of the osseous injury and of the neurologic status will then guide the definitive treatment.

10.3.4.2.2 Pharmacologic Treatment: If there is neurologic deficit, the patient is given high dose methylprednisolone within 8 hours of the injury. If the patient is to undergo a surgical procedure, pre-operative antibiotics are given.

10.3.4.2.3 Nonoperative Treatment: The indications for surgical and nonsurgical treatment of thoracolumbar fractures have changed over the last few decades and still vary from one continent to the other. Much controversy still exists as to which patient should undergo surgery and therefore the following treatments are what is recommended presently in North America in the 1990s. The future will certainly provide us with many modifications to the treatment of these fractures.

The nonsurgical treatment of thoracolumbar fractures used to be the standard in the past. Patients were kept in bed for months at a time waiting for the healing of soft tissues and bone. Many devices were used to do this such as special frames and beds which could rotate the patient from the supine to the prone position every few hours (e.g., Stryker frame). There were major disadvantages to this: the hospital length of stay and cost was enormous, the spine was not realigned and many valuable months of rehabilitation were lost. Bed rest is now used only as an initial treatment while planning definitive management. Three fracture types are, still, very effectively treated with nonoperative measures: 1) the compression fractures; 2) the burst fractures without significant neurologic deficit; and 3) the bony flexion-distraction injury (Chance fracture). A Chance fracture responds well to a body cast for 2 to 3 months. Mild compression fractures can often be treated symptomatically without the use of any external bracing or activity restrictions. More severe compression fractures, multiple compression fractures, and burst fractures can be treated effectively with a well molded body cast in extension. Well molded braces (TLSO=thoracic-lumbar-sacral orthosis) are an alternative but are much more expensive, and a noncompliant patient can easily take the brace off. The duration of treatment will depend on the age and medical condition of the patient, but averages 3 months before the brace or cast can be removed and physiotherapy started.

10.3.4.2.4 Operative Treatment: Thoracolumbar spine fractures that are treated surgically are the ligamentous flexion-distraction injuries, the fracture-dislocations, the burst fractures with significant neurologic deficit, and some of the burst and compression fractures that are thought to be unstable or where it is felt the patient will not tolerate cast treatment.

A flexion distraction injury is treated with a compression system where hooks or screws hold the vertebra above and below and rods connecting the hooks or screws compress them together.

Fracture-dislocations are grossly unstable in all directions and the patient is usually paraplegic. A decompression of the neural elements involves realignment of the spine and spinal canal. The spine is then stabilized with rods and either hooks or screws. Pedicle screws have the advantage of having purchase on all three columns of the spine and can stabilize the spine with less vertebrae incorporated in the construct. There is a 1 to 3% risk of neurologic injury using the screws as opposed to the hooks. Hook fixation requires three vertebra above the injury and three below to be fixed to provide leverage for the reduction.

Burst fractures with a significant neurologic deficit are treated with a decompression of the neural canal by reducing or removing the fragment of vertebral body that is retropulsed. This can be accomplished through either an anterior or posterior approach to the spine. Most surgeons favour an anterior approach since it permits a more thorough decompression. The spine is then fused and instrumented for stability. In patients that have neurologic deficits, a major benefit of surgery is the immediate spine stability that is provided by modern implants. Patient mobilization and rehabilitation can be started very soon after the surgery. Burst fractures without neurologic deficits are the most confusing fracture to treat since there are no universally accepted guidelines to determine which patient should have surgery and which patient should have a cast. Outcome studies have been limited so far and have not helped patient selection. A well designed, randomized, prospective study has yet to be published on the treatment of these burst fractures. The most common indications for operating on patients with a burst fracture without neurologic deficit are: 1) greater than 50% loss of vertebral body height; 2) kyphosis of greater than 20 degrees; 3) canal compromise of greater than 50%; 4) a scoliosis of greater than 10 degrees. Surgical reduction and stabilization is done through a posterior approach. Pedicle screws have revolutionized the treatment of these fractures by enabling the surgeon to realign the spine and build a solid construct by immobilizing only three vertebrae (including the fractured one).

In most operations for spinal fractures a fusion is done in addition to the decompression and the instrumentation. This is to assure solid healing of the spine by having bone bridge the injured area to connect the adjacent intact vertebrae. A posterior fusion involves using cancellous bone chips and placing them laterally and anterior to the instrumentation after making the transverse processes and facets raw (decortication, removal of cortical bone to expose easy to heal cancellous bone). An anterior fusion involves a structural graft. This graft will be a composite of hard cortical bone and rapidly healing cancellous bone, which is placed as a strut between the end plates of the intact, adjacent vertebra.

10.3.4.3 Outcome

One of the first detailed studies on outcome of thoracolumbar fractures was reported by Nicol in 1949 after he studied 152 miners with this injury. He found that 58% complained of residual pain; 60% at the injury level and 40% in the lower back area. He did not find a good correlation between the functional and radiologic results since the patients with perfect functional results had residual deformity in 48% and good alignment in 52%.[95]

Young in 1973 reviewed 116 patients with thoracolumbar fractures who had claims with the Ontario Worker's Compensation Board. Twenty-six percent had an excellent result, 52% had a good result and 22% had a fair to poor result. Patients with persistent symptoms had restriction in their range of motion, had received more courses of treatment, and required extensive rehabilitation. There were no specific differences in the fracture pattern or healing between the patients that remained symptomatic and the ones that did not. The severity of the fracture and late degenerative changes did not correlate to the final result.[96]

Day in 1977 reviewed 142 patients of the Worker's Compensation Board of British Columbia who had a fracture of the thoracolumbar spine.[97] Most were manual labourers and only the patients with intact neurologic function were included in the study. Forty-nine percent had an excellent or good result, 24% had a fair result, and 27% had a poor result. Severe comminution and compression was associated with a poor result. Most of the patients had been treated nonoperatively.

Aglietti reviewed 222 patients with compression or burst fractures with a follow-up of 5 to 21 years.[98] Thirty-three percent of patients had an excellent result, 26% good, 32% fair and 9% poor. Eighty-two percent returned to their previous occupation after about 6 months, 15% changed their employment, and 3% remained permanently disabled. There was significantly better results in the non-compensable injuries. There were no

---

95 Nicol EA. Fractures of the Dorso-Lumbar Spine. *J Bone Joint Surg*, 31-B: 376-394, 1949.

96 Young MH. Long-term Consequences of Stable Fractures of the Thoracic and Lumbar Vertebral Bodies. *J Bone Joint Surg*, 55-B:295-300, 1973.

97 Day BD, Kokan P. Compression Fractures of the Thoracic and Lumbar Spine from Compensable Injuries. *Clin Orthop Rel Res*, 124:173-176, 1977.

98 Aglietti P, Muria GV, Taylor TKF, et al. Conservative Treatment of Thoracic and Lumbar Vertebral Fractures. *Italian Journal of Orthopaedics and Traumatology*, 9(suppl): 83-105, 1984.

significant differences between the light and heavy manual labour. Compared to the normal population there was significantly increased incidence of degenerative changes following burst and compression fractures, but these changes did not correlate to the presence of symptoms.

Hu et al. used the provincial database of the Manitoba health care system to identify all patients in that province who sustained a spinal fracture and compared their medical care utilization and survival to a control group matched for age, sex, and place of residence. They found a significantly higher use of health care services and an increase in mortality over the 10 years of the study in the group that had a spinal fracture. The reasons for this difference are unknown but it appears that a spinal fracture has prolonged widespread long-term effects on a person's health.[99]

These reviews tend to show that there is a wide variation of outcomes and that no specific factor has been found useful in predicting the prognosis of a patient with a compression or burst fracture. Generally, one-third of patients will be asymptomatic, one-third will have to restrict sports or physically strenuous activity and one-third will have to change their work as a result of the fracture.

Denis in 1984 studied patients who specifically had a burst fracture without initial neurologic deficits. Of 48 patients he found that all those treated surgically returned to their previous employment, whereas 25% of those treated without surgery were unable to return to full time work. Neurologic complications ensued in 17% of the patients treated without surgery.[100]

McEvoy and Bradford in 1985 reported the results of burst fractures in 53 patients. Thirty-eight patients had a neurologic deficit and 68% improved their neurologic status after surgery. The surgically treated patients were less likely to have disabling back pain at 3-year follow up.[101]

Kraemer and Schemitsch retrospectively studied 24 patients who sustained a thoracolumbar burst fracture without neurologic deficit from 1987 to 1992.[102] Validated functional outcome instruments were used. There were no significant differences in outcomes between those treated opera-

---

99 Hu RW, Mustard C, Mayer T. Ten-Year follow up of Spinal Fractures in the Province of Manitoba: A Population Based Study. *Proceedings of the 52nd Annual Meeting of the Canadian Orthopaedic Association*, Hamilton, Ontario, June 1, 1997.
100 Dennis, *supra*, note 83, at *Clin Orthop*, 189:65-76, 1984.
101 McEvoy RD, Bradford DS. The Management of Burst Fractures of the Thoracic and Lumbar Spine. *Spine*, 10:631-637, 1985.
102 Kraemer WJ, Schemitsch EH, Lever J, McBroom RJ, McKee MD, Waddell JP. Functional Outcome of Thoracolumbar Burst Fractures Without Neurological Deficit. *Grand Rounds in Orthopaedics*, Smith and Nephew, Winter 1996.

tively versus nonoperatively. Only 33% of patients could return to their previous employment and 8% could return to their pre-injury level of sport.

There are numerous studies on burst fractures; however, they are all retrospective and inherently biased, since the surgical indications are not standardized. Furthermore, the outcome instruments utilized and study methodologies are not strict and are subject to much criticism. Until a well-designed study is performed, the treatment of burst fractures will remain empirical and the prognosis variable.

Flexion-distraction injuries are less common. Reports with few patients indicate that 1) motor vehicle accidents cause the majority of these injuries; 2) they occur at the thoracolumbar junction; 3) 50% will have an associated intraabdominal injury; 4) 25% will have a poor functional outcome; and 5) facet joint involvement and kyphosis greater then 20 degrees will be associated with a poor prognosis unless the patient is treated surgically.[103]

The Scoliosis Research Society embarked on a prospective study from 1986 to 1988 of patients with thoracolumbar fractures. The patients were followed for 2 years. Sixty-four physicians in 12 countries participated and 1,019 spinal fracture patients were recruited in the study. Gertzbein, the study coordinator, reported the results in 1992 and the main findings were the following: 1) the incidence of severe neurologic injury was reduced by the use of seat belts; 2) neurologic injuries were more frequent in the fracture dislocation group; 3) there was a higher incidence of complete neurologic deficit if the spinal injury was at the level of the cord compared to the cauda equina; 4) for burst fractures the amount of canal compromise correlated weakly to the neurologic deficit; 5) surgical intervention led to a greater degree of neurologic improvement than nonoperative treatment; 6) anterior surgery was only slightly better than posterior surgery for neurologic improvement (dependent on scale used), but anterior surgery was more beneficial than posterior for improvement of bladder function; 7) bladder function was associated to fracture type with absent bladder function in fracture dislocations, impaired bladder function associated to burst fractures and intact bladder function with compression fractures and flexion-distraction injuries; 8) a kyphotic deformity of greater than 30 degrees, 2 years post injury was associated with an increased incidence of significant back pain; 9) patients who had surgery complained of less severe pain than those who were treated without surgery.[104]

---

103 Gumley G, Taylor TKF, Ryan MD. Distraction Fractures of the Lumbar Spine. *J Bone Joint Surg*, 64-B:520-525, 1982. LeGay DA, Petri DP, Alexander DI. Flexion-Distraction Injuries of the Lumbar Spine and Associated Abdominal Trauma. *J Trauma*, 30:436-444, 1990.

104 Gertzbein, SD. Scoliosis Research Society Multicenter Spine Fracture Study. *Spine*, 17(5):528-540, 1992.

Post-traumatic kyphosis is often quoted as a reason to consider operative treatment and as a cause for long-term pain. This is very poorly documented in the literature. Most kyphotic deformities will stabilize 6 to 12 months after the injury and will not progress. A kyphotic deformity of 30 degrees or more seems more often associated with more back pain, particularly lower lumbar pain because of compensatory accentuation of the lumbar lordosis. Kyphosis in the lumbar spine is less well tolerated because there is limited potential for compensation.

Overall, 70 to 90% of patients who have had a thoracolumbar fracture will have long-standing back pain to some degree. About 20 to 40% have to modify their activities because of the pain and 8 to 20% are severely disabled because of the pain.[105]

10.3.5 Soft Tissue Injuries

10.3.5.1 Disc Disruption and Herniation

Back pain has been a problem that has affected the human race probably since we became biped, although there is only documentation dating back to the Bible and to the writings of Hippocrates. In 1934, an association was finally made between disc herniation, back pain, and sciatica.[106] It has been estimated that 80% of humans at some point in their adult life will have significant back pain. We know now that, to a large degree, low back pain is caused by derangement of the intervertebral disc.

The economic impact of low back pain is enormous. In Sweden it is estimated that 53% of persons doing light physical activity and 64% of those involved in heavy labour seek medical attention for back pain.[107] In the United States, impairment due to back pain is the most frequent cause of activity limitation in patients less than 45 years of age.[108] Thirty-five percent of sedentary workers and 45% of heavy labourers visited their respective medical department for complaints of back pain. A study by McGill revealed that only 25% of patients missing work for 1 year because of back pain returned to work, and if the absence was 2 consecutive years, the likelihood of returning to work was dismal.[109]

---

105 Stauffer ES. Thoracolumbar Spine Fractures without Neurologic Deficit. *American Academy of Orthopaedic Surgery Monograph Series*, Illinois, 1993.
106 Mixter WJ, Barr JS. Rupture of the Intervertebral Disc with Involvement of the Spinal Canal. *N Engl J Med*, 211:210, 1934.
107 Hult L. The Munkfors Investigation. *Acta Orthop Scand.* Suppl 16:5, 1954.
108 Kelsey J, White AA. Epidemiology and Impact of Low Back Pain. *Spine*, 5:133, 1980.
109 McGill CM. Industrial Back Problems, a Control Program. *J Occup Med*, 10:174, 1968.

Back pain from disc derangement can develop gradually or can have a sudden onset. Many studies have demonstrated that most patients who eventually have documented disc pathology that leads to surgery have had chronic low grade back pain for many years prior to the onset of radicular pain.[110] Many labourers describe an event where they develop back pain which later intensifies over the course of hours or days. The mechanism for disc injury often involves rotation of the lower back while lifting or carrying a heavy object. Discs can withstand a large amount of stress applied in an axial direction. The nucleus pulposus then flattens and widens and places the annulus in a stretched position. It is thought that the annulus is weakest when rotational forces are applied to it. This creates tears in the annular fibers and stimulates the nociceptive nerve endings in the peripheral layers of the annulus and causes pain. If the tear is severe, a herniation of the nucleus pulposus will occur and may cause sciatica [Figure 10.24].

The diagnostic process involves obtaining a history of pain in the lower back, usually of sudden onset, worse with coughing, sneezing, activity, and bending forward. Lying down relieves the pain. A history of pain radiating down the leg and into the foot (sciatica) is indicative of a disc disruption. Examination may reveal a decreased range of flexion of the lumbar spine, muscle spasm of the lumbar spine, and clinical signs of nerve root irritation (SLR test, Lasegue sign, bowstring sign, Kernig's sign, tripod sign). Radiographs of the lumbar spine are not helpful in the diagnosis of an acute disc disruption. They are done to eliminate other conditions in the differential diagnosis such as infections, tumors, and fractures. Myelography, computerized tomography and MRI will reveal a disc that is herniated [Figure 10.25]. A disc that is disrupted but not herniated is more difficult to document radiologically. An MRI or a discogram may be necessary if the diagnosis has not been reached. Approximately 2% of all disc herniations result in cauda equina syndrome. In this condition, a large central disc herniation applies pressure diffusely on the nerves of the cauda equina and causes pain and neurologic impairment of both legs, buttocks, perianal area and sphincter, and urinary bladder function.[111]

The natural history of lumbar disc disease has been studied extensively although many studies have looked at all causes of low back pain without a firm diagnosis of disc derangement. Sixty to 80% of us in our lifetime will have significant back pain. Only about 14% will have back pain lasting 2 weeks, 1.6% will have back pain and sciatica for 2 weeks

---

110 Garfin SR, Glover M, Booth RE, et al. Laminectomy: A Review of the Pennsylvania Hospital Experience. *J Spinal Dis*, 1:116, 1988. Spangfort EV. The Lumbar Disc Herniation. A Computer-aided Analysis of 2,504 Operations. *Acta Orthop Scand*, Suppl 142:61, 1972.

111 *Ibid.*

and 1 to 2% will have spine surgery.[112] Weber did a prospective, well-controlled study on 280 patients with 10-year follow-up.[113] All patients had a myelographically proven lumbar disc herniation. They were initially treated conservatively for 14 days. Those that did not improve after this period were randomly assigned to either surgery or continued nonoperative treatment. At the 1 year follow-up the surgery group was superior for relief of back pain and radicular pain. At the 4-year follow-up the conservative group had improved to the extent that they were not significantly different to the surgery group. There was also no loss in the quality of surgical result even if the symptoms had lasted more than three months. Beyond 12 months from the onset of leg pain there was a deterioration of the surgical results.

The treatment of lumbar disc disease is still empirical because there are major design flaws to most of the studies reporting the results of nonoperative treatment. Since the natural history of disc disease is that most will improve within several weeks of onset regardless of the treatment given, then surgery is not contemplated early unless there is severe neurologic deficit such as a cauda equina syndrome. In the first 2 months of symptoms, the following nonoperative measures are used:

- *Bed rest:* Used to minimize pain in the first few days of onset of symptoms. Two days of bed rest has been shown to be just as good as longer regimens and prevent disuse osteoporosis and muscle atrophy.[114]
- *Analgesics:* Pain control is important in order for the patient to heal without requiring inpatient admission. Strong analgesia is given for short periods of time and may involve prescribing short courses of narcotics.
- *Antiinflammatory drugs:* There are several groups of antiinflammatories which act as analgesics and also reduce inflammation in the injured area. Side effects are common and may limit their use.
- *Oral corticosteroids:* These have been demonstrated to improve the symptoms and signs of herniated disc and if given for a short course can be safe. They are presently not commonly used.
- *Muscle relaxants:* Used in the event of severe muscle spasm. These agents may cause drowsiness. Baclofen is one of the many agents that

---

112 Deyo RA, Loeser J, Bigos S. Herniated Lumbar Intervertebral Disc. *Ann Intern Med*, 112:598-603, 1990.

113 Weber H. Lumbar Disc Herniation: a Controlled, Prospective Study with Ten Years of Observation. *Spine*, 8:131, 1983.

114 Deyo RA, Diehl AK, Rosenthal N. How Many Days of Bedrest for Acute Low Back Pain? *N Engl J Med*, 315:1064-1070, 1986.

has been found to be more effective than placebo in the treatment of back pain.
- *Antidepressants:* Patients with chronic low back pain and patients with severe leg pain show mood disturbances and altered sleep patterns thought to be mediated by serotonin depression in the brain. A trial of tricyclic antidepressant therapy may be useful.[115]
- *Injection therapy:* Epidural steroids have been found to be moderately effective in reducing the radicular pain of lumbar disc disease.[116] Since the complication rate is very low, this form of treatment is often included as part of a multidisciplinary management. Facet joint injections are sometimes also used since numerous studies show that the facet joints are an important source of back and referred leg pain.
- *Exercise therapy:* This is arguably the most important aspect of the treatment of low back pain. Exercise is well known to exert a positive impact on patient's health. It has been shown, in well-designed studies, to minimize the risk of back injury and to improve existing back pain. Many programs have been described and used. Flexion exercises (Williams exercise) are designed to flex the spine to enlarge the intervertebral foramina and strengthen the abdominal muscles.[117] Extension exercises (McKenzie exercises) are designed to decrease the intranuclear pressure of the disc.[118] Other types of exercises feature range of motion, stretching, isometric exercise, isotonic exercise, isokinetic exercise, and aerobic exercise.
- *Orthotics:* External supports are commonly used as an adjunct in the treatment of low back pain, but there are no rigorous studies supporting their efficacy. They may be useful in mobilizing the patients more rapidly. Patients must only use it sporadically and wean themselves quickly, otherwise dependence on the brace leads to muscle weakness.
- *Physical therapy:* Ultrasound, laser, heat, and cold are used for short-term pain relief.
- *Traction:* Theoretically, traction distracts the disc and reduces the intradiscal pressure. Several forms of traction have been designed, in-

---

115 Dapas F, Hartman S, Martinez L. Baclofen for the Treatment of Acute Low Back Pain Syndrome. *Spine*, 10:345, 1985.
116 Dilke TWF, Burry HC, Grahame R. Extradural Corticosteroid Injection in the Management of Lumbar Nerve Root Compression. *Br Med J*, 2:635-637, 1973. White AH. Injection Techniques for the Diagnosis and Treatment of Low Back Pain. *Orthop Clin North Am*, 14:553-567, 1983.
117 Williams PC. Lesions of the Lumbosacral Spine. *J Bone Joint Surg*, 19:690, 1937.
118 McKenzie RA. *The Lumbar Spine: Mechanical Diagnosis and Therapy.* Waikanae, New Zealand: Spinal Publications, 1981.

cluding inversion therapy. None of the different forms of traction have been found to change the natural history of disc disease.
- *Spinal manipulation:* Manipulations have been effective in providing short-term pain relief for patients with low back pain but has not been found to change the long-term outcome of back pain. Most of the patients require several weeks of treatment followed by maintenance treatments. As with other modalities it should be used as part of a more global multidisciplinary treatment plan.[119]
- *Counter irritation techniques:* This includes acupuncture, biofeedback, transcutaneous electrical stimulation (TENS), and self-hypnosis. These treatments have all been found to be effective in the short term but beyond 2 months their efficacy is lost. They appear to function through a mechanism of overloading the fast conducting sensory fibers to block the conduction of pain stimuli to the brain.

It is apparent by the number of treatment modalities for disc problems and low back pain that no single treatment method is markedly better over the other. The best results are obtained from a multidisciplinary approach to discogenic back pain.[120] All patients who demonstrate a tendency towards chronicity should have a referral to such a program within 3 to 4 months of the onset of symptoms.

Surgical treatment for disc disease is considered for patients who have symptoms and signs of a disc herniation for which the pain has lasted for more than 2 months, has had a pattern of multiple recurrence, and is associated with a progressive or a severe neurologic deficit. The gold standard for surgical disc excision is the open discectomy where a 6- to 8-cm incision is performed in the back, the nerve root is exposed and retracted and the extruded part of the disc is excised. Favourable results are reported in more than 95% of carefully selected patients. Microscope-assisted discectomy has a 92% success rate and is essentially the same technique as an open discectomy, but the use of a microscope permits better visualization and performance of the procedure through a 3-cm incision. Several methods have been developed to perform minimally invasive or percutaneous discectomies. These involve insertion of a trochar obliquely into the disc and then excision or ablation of the nucleus pulposus with mechanical tools, automated nucleotomes, or laser. These techniques are less invasive

---

119 Breen AC. Chiropractors in the Treatment of Back Pain. *Rheumatol Rehabil*, 16:46, 1977. Hochler FK, Tobias JS, Buerger AA. Spinal Manipulation for Low Back Pain. *JAMA*, 245:1835-1838, 1981.

120 Mayer TG, Gatcher RJ, Mayer H, Kishino ND, Keeley J, Mooney V. A Prospective Two Year Study of Functional Restoration in Industrial Low Back Injury. An Objective Assessment Procedure. *JAMA*, 258:1763-1767, 1987.

but are only applicable to a select group of patients with disc pathology. Despite rigid selection criteria, the success of these procedures are in the range of 40 to 70%. Another percutaneous method of disc ablation is the injection of chymopapain, so-called chemonucleosis, into the disc. The proteoglycans in the nucleus are broken down or dissolved. In well-controlled studies, favourable results were seen in 75% of patients. This technique is much less popular now because of the serious side effects and allergic reactions to chymopapain.

Surgical fusions are sometimes used in the treatment of disc disruption. There is great controversy as to the benefits of spinal fusions. Favourable results are dependent on patient selection rather than on any particular fusion technique. Presently, the indications for spinal fusion in disc disease are: 1) acute disc herniations with severe, long-standing back pain component; 2) chronic disc degeneration with severe, long-standing back pain; 3) neural arch defect with disc disease; 4) disc disease with segmental instability; 5) disc disease and associated scoliosis or spondylolisthesis; and 6) iatrogenic instability (instability produced in the process of performing a decompression).

10.3.6 Spondylolysis and Spondylolisthesis

Spondylolysis is a lesion of the vertebrae located in the pars interarticularis portion of the posterior elements [Figure 10.26]. It is not seen at birth and the prevalence of spondylolysis starts to increase at the age of 5 years and reaches a plateau at the age of 18 years. Approximately 6% of adults have a spondylolysis but the lesions are often asymptomatic and not detected unless a radiograph is done. The cause of spondylolysis is felt to be traumatic. A disruption or separation of the pars interarticularis occurs because of repetitive stresses on the posterior arch. It seems that the lordotic position of the human spine, bipedal motion, or repetitive hyperextension of the lumbar spine have an influence in the production of the defect. Spondylolysis is more common in men, Caucasians, gymnasts, and football linemen, and there are family groupings.[121]

Spondylolisthesis is a condition where there is forward translation of one vertebra over another. The widely accepted classification for spondylolisthesis is that of Wiltse's.

- *Type I — Congenital:* congenital anomalies of the posterior elements such as a dysplastic (elongated) pars interarticularis.
- *Type II — Isthmic:* This spondylolisthesis is the result of a pars inter-

---

121 Fredrickson BE, Baker D, McHolick WJ, Yuan HA, Lubicky JP. The Natural History of Spondylolysis and Spondylolisthesis. *J Bone Joint Surg*, 66-A:699-707, 1984.

articularis defect (spondylolysis) or a spondylolysis that has healed in a stretched position. This is the most common form of spondylolisthesis and occurs most frequently at L5–S1.
- *Type III — Degenerative:* degenerative processes of the disc and facets cause a segmental instability and result in a spondylolisthesis without a bone defect. It is the second most common cause of spondylolisthesis and is most common at the L4–L5 level.
- *Type IV — Traumatic:* essentially a fracture dislocation in the lower lumbar spine with bone and ligament disruption other than the pars interarticularis. It is a rare form of spondylolisthesis and a severe trauma to the spine is required to produce this.
- *Type V — Pathologic:* generalized or localized bone disease which weakens the posterior elements and allows them to lengthen or break, for example, osteoporosis, tumors, osteomyelitis.
- *Type VI — Iatrogenic:* Postsurgical spondylolisthesis resulting from aggressive bone resection for the purpose of decompressing the spine or excising tumors or discs.

In addition to establishing the spondylolytic type, a grade is also determined. Grading is based on the degree of slip of the superior vertebra on the inferior one. The vertebral body is divided into four equal parts on lateral radiographs. If the superior vertebra is displaced less than 25% it is a grade I, 25 to 50% a grade II, 50 to 75% a grade III, 75 to 100% a grade IV and if the superior vertebra is completely dislocated anterior to the inferior vertebrae it is a grade V or also called a spondyloptosis. A so-called high grade slip implies a grade III, IV, or V slip.

The diagnosis of spondylolisthesis is often made in the third and fourth decade of life when a radiograph is done after a minor trauma or a lifting injury. There is a tendency to attribute the back pain to the spondylolisthesis since there are no other abnormalities evident on the radiograph. It is important to emphasize that the spondylolisthesis was there since youth and was asymptomatic until the recent trauma occurred. Traumatic spondylolisthesis in the adult requires a severe trauma and there are a few reports in the literature.[122] Frederickson et al. studied 500 school children and found that the development of pars interarticularis defects was asymptomatic and occurred between the ages of 5 and 18 years. The spondylolisthesis could progress during adolescence but not after the age of 16 years.[123] Most adults therefore have spondylolisthesies that are stable and that do not cause symptoms. Even when significant trauma to the spine is

---

[122] Cope R. Acute Traumatic Spondylolisthesis: A Report of a Case and Review of the Literature. *Clin Orthop Rel Res*, 230:162-165, 1988.

[123] Fredrickson et al., *supra*, note 121.

applied there is little effect on the isthmic spondylolisthesis. Floman et al. reviewed 200 patients with thoracolumbar spinal fractures. Five patients had pre-existing L5–S1 isthmic spondylolisthesis. Two patients had pre-existing back pain and three had old spondylolisthesis felt to be unchanged by the recent trauma.[124]

Adult patients with isthmic spondylolisthesis may become symptomatic because of accelerated degeneration of the L5–S1 disc and the onset of back pain and radiculopathy because of increasing instability at this level. Compression of the nerve roots (usually L5) occurs through bulging of the disc and from the excessive motion at the pars interarticularis, irritating the nerve root. It has been shown that in patients with severe pain, the fibrous tissue that fills the spondylolysis gap is extensively innervated by nociceptive free nerve endings.[125] Clinically selected patients can obtain marked relief of their pain from injection of the pars interarticularis with local anesthetics. The density of this innervation is variable and may explain why these lesions are minimally painful in some patients and in others cause severe, disabling pain.

In patients older than 60 years of age, degenerative spondylolisthesis is a frequent cause of back pain. As the spinal canal is narrowed by this type of spondylolisthesis it is a frequent cause of spinal stenosis and bilateral leg pain, since the posterior elements of the vertebra also slip forward and "strangle" the dural sac and cauda equina. The most common location is L4–L5.

Patients with spondylolisthesis are treated successfully with exercise programs. Those who require surgery are usually type II isthmic spondylolisthesis or type III degenerative spondylolisthesis that have had leg pain for over 6 months. The surgical treatment involves a decompression of the neural elements and a fusion of the involved vertebrae. A patient satisfaction rate of over 90% has been obtained from such surgery on carefully selected patients.[126]

---

124 Floman Y, Margulies JY, Nyska M, Chisin R, Libergall M. Effect of Major Trauma on Preexisting Lumbosacral Spondylolisthesis. *J Spinal Dis*, 4:353-358, 1991.

125 Harris IE, Weinstein SL. Long Term follow up of Patients with Grade III and IV Spondylolisthesis: Treatment with and without Posterior Fusion. *J Bone Joint Surg*, 69-A:960-969, 1987. Yuan HA, Garfin SR, Dickman CA, et al. A Historical Cohort Study of Pedicle Screw Fixation in Thoracic, Lumbar and Sacral Spinal Fusions. *Spine*, 19 (suppl 20):2279S-2296S, 1994.

126 Eisenstein SM, Ashton IK, Roberts S, et al. Innervation of the Spondylolysis "ligament". *Spine*, 19:912-916, 1994.

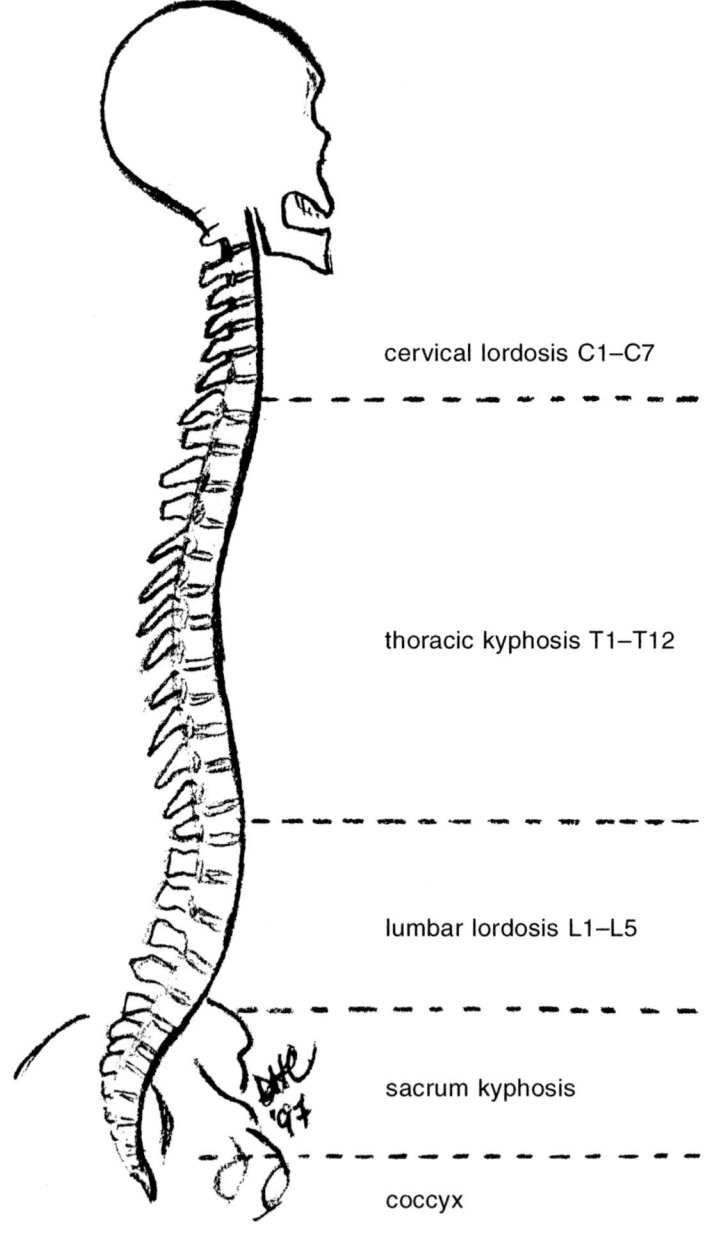

Figure 10.1
Sagittal representation of the normal spinal alignment. The cervical and lumbar spines are lordotic because the convexity is anterior, whereas the thoracic and sacral spines are kyphotic because the convexity is posterior.

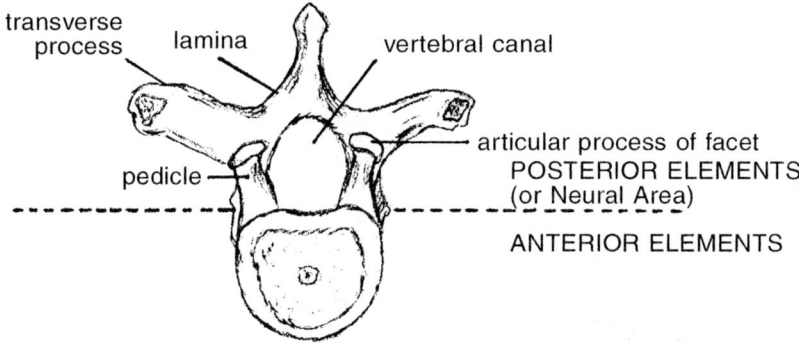

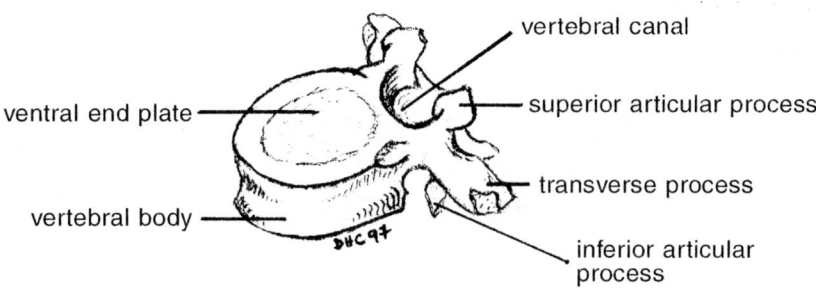

Figure 10.2
Transverse and oblique views of the typical vertebra.

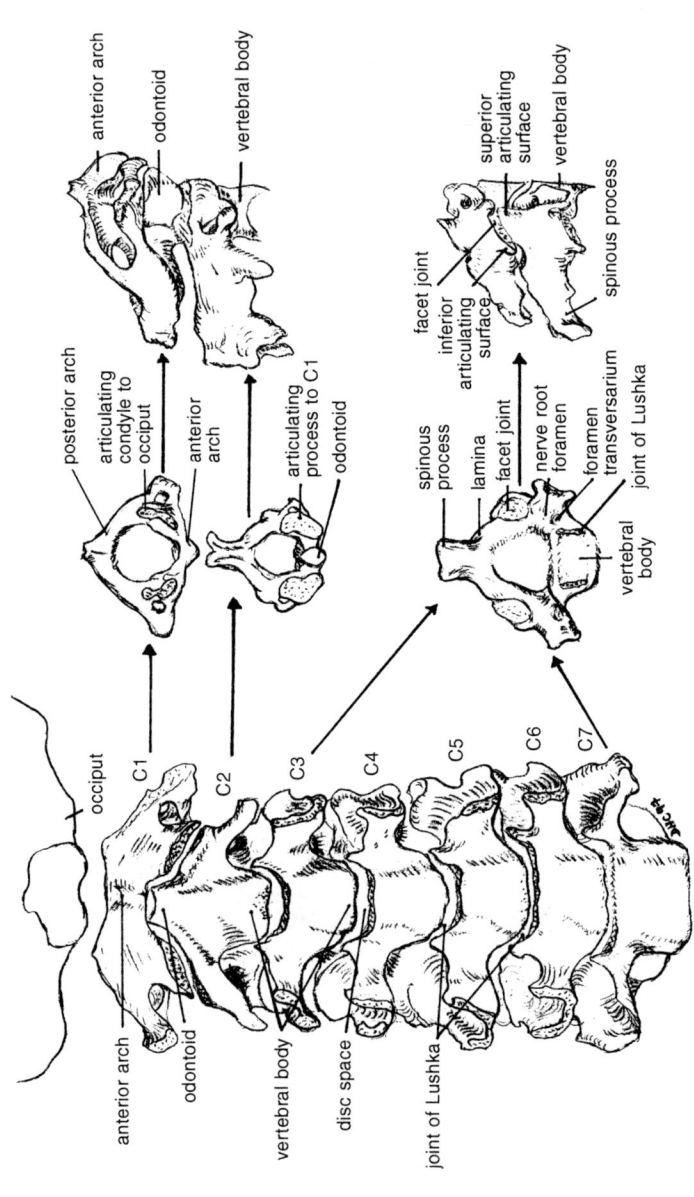

Figure 10.3
Osseous anatomy of the cervical spine from an anterior coronal view, a transverse view, and a sagittal view. The occiput to C2 vertebrae are markedly different from the C3 to C7 vertebrae.

SPINAL INJURIES   445

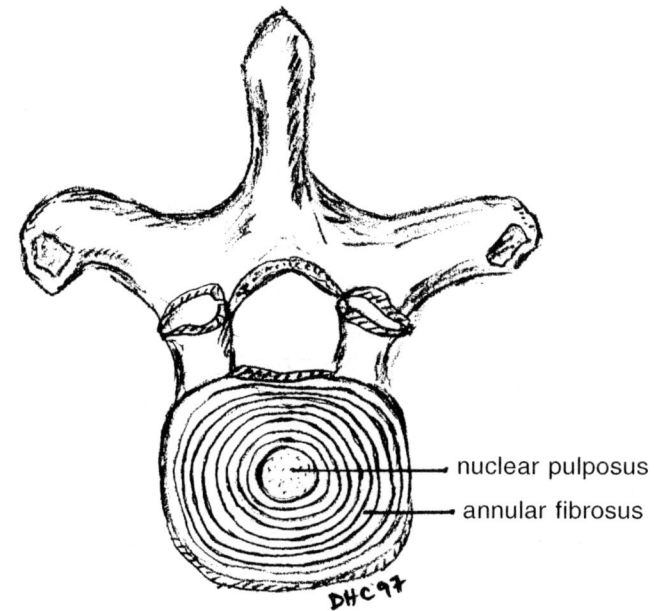

Figure 10.4
Anatomy of the intervertebral discs.

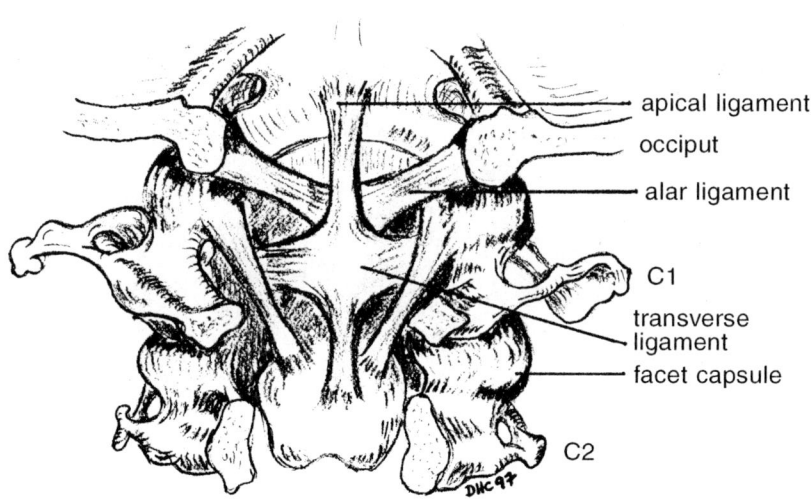

Figure 10.5
Ligament attachment of the occiput, C1 and C2 vertebra.

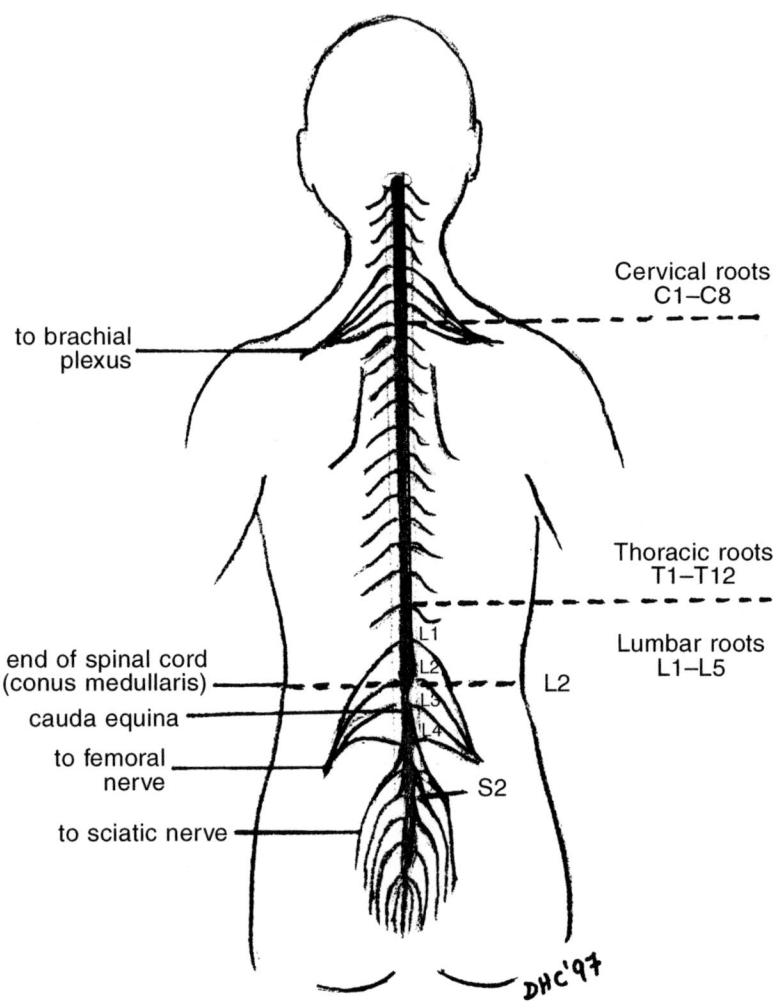

Figure 10.6
The spinal cord and the nerve roots.

SPINAL INJURIES 447

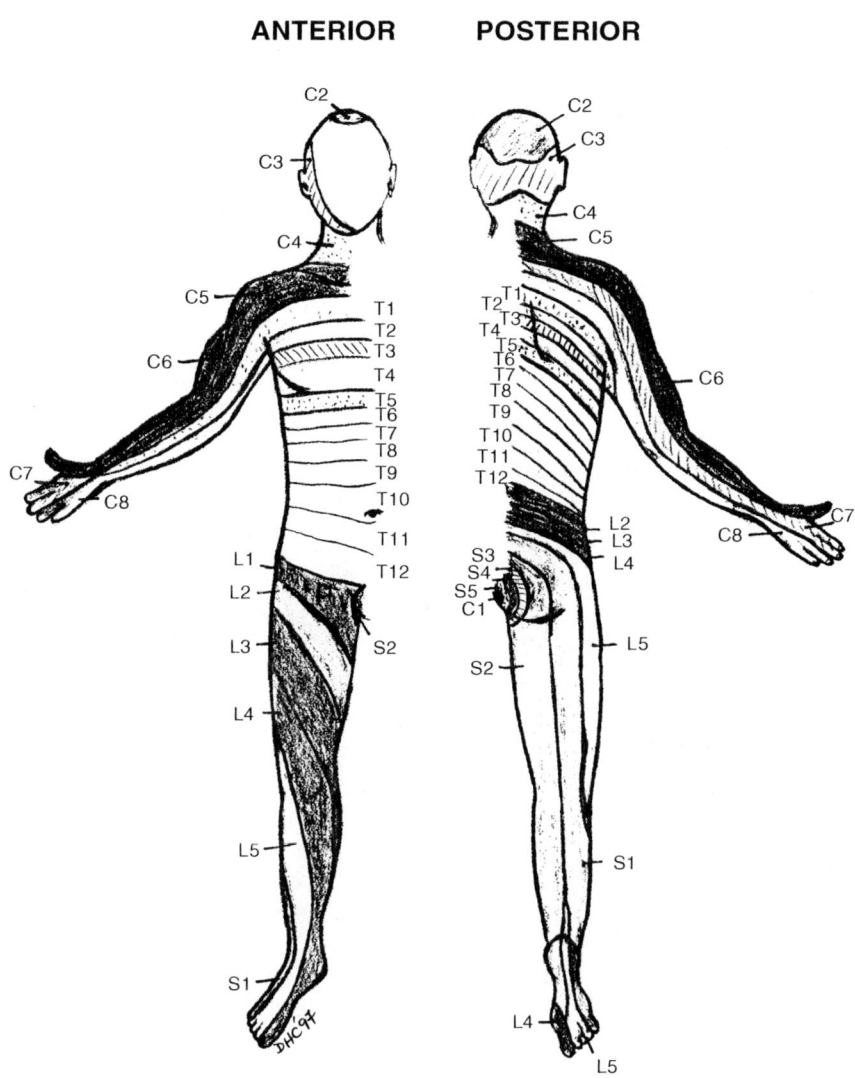

Figure 10.7
The dermatomes of the body. Sensory distribution of the nerve roots on the skin.

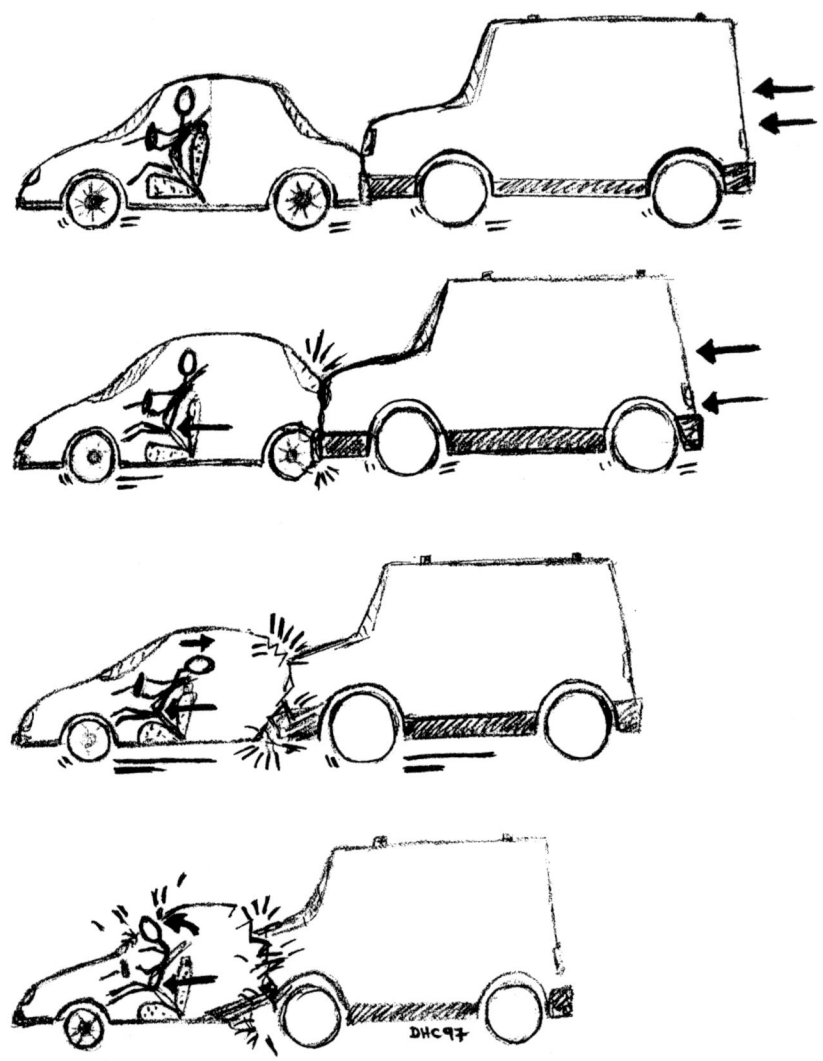

Figure 10.8
Acceleration injury of the neck. A vehicle rear-ends an immobile car. The car is suddenly pushed forward. The seat of the driver moves forward with the car. The chest and shoulders are propelled forward with the seat. The unrestrained head and neck stay in their original position because of inertia. The neck is then hyperextended. Rebound flexion of the neck occurs when the head velocity matches the car and there is recoil of the neck.

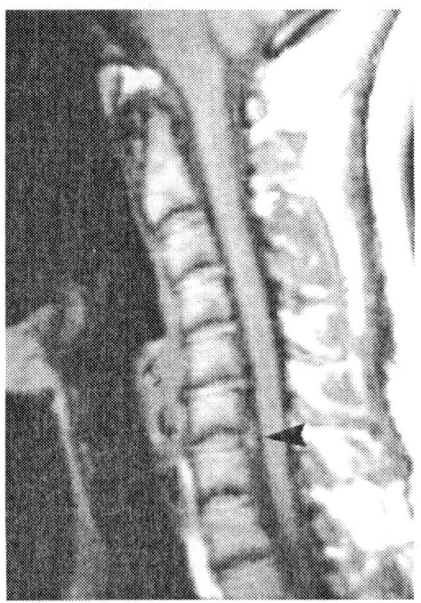

Figure 10.9
Sagittal section of an MRI of the cervical spine is showing a disc herniation at C6-C7 in a 55-year-old female.

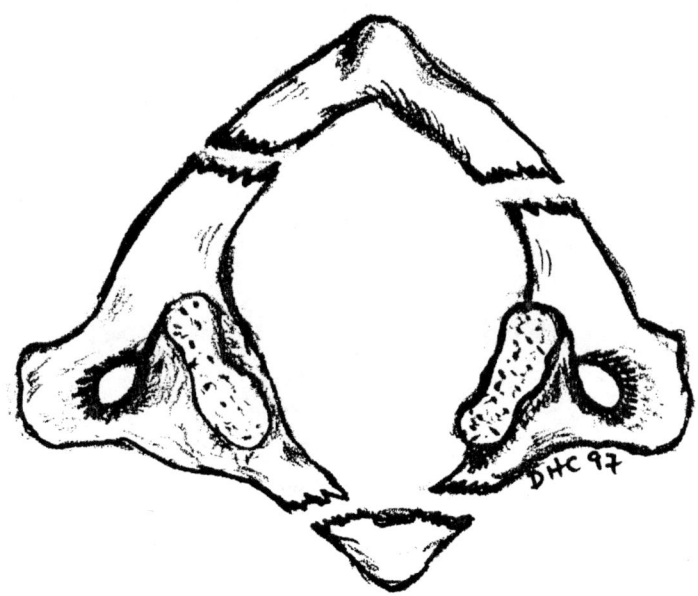

Figure 10.10
Fracture of the C1 vertebra (Jefferson fracture).

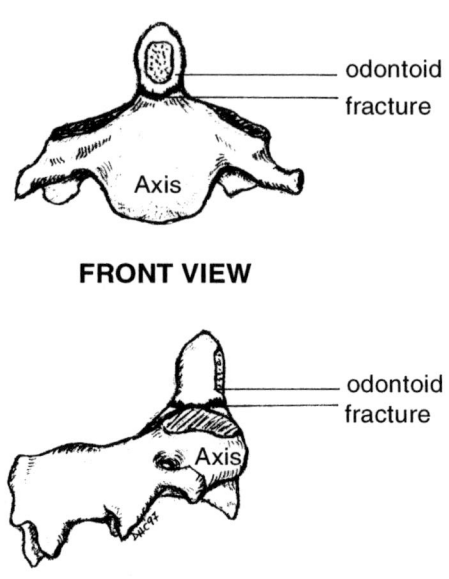

Figure 10.11
Fracture of the odontoid process of C2.

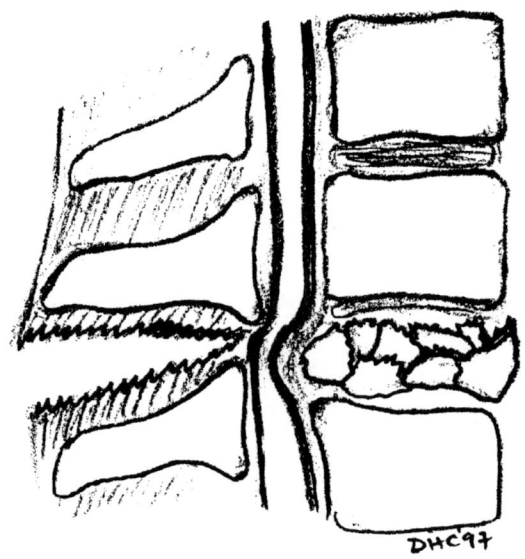

Figure 10.12
Fracture dislocation of the cervical spine with compression of the spinal cord.

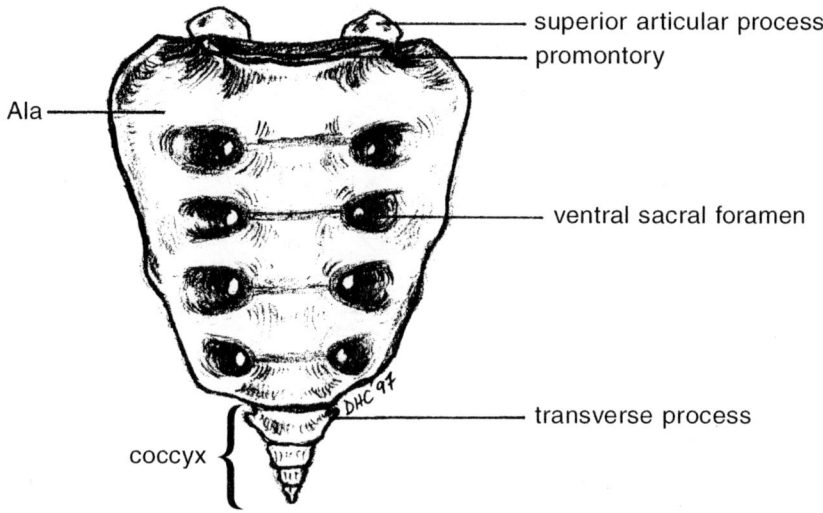

Figure 10.13
Osseous anatomy of the sacrum.

Figure 10.14
Lumbar intervertebral disc. The annulus is formed of lamellar layers of collagen, which can withstand strong tensile forces. The central gelatinous nucleus pulposus, when compressed, spreads evenly and applies tension on the annulus.

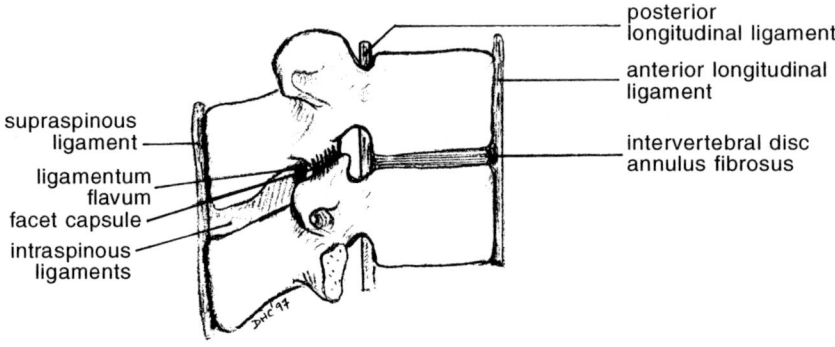

Figure 10.15
Ligaments of the thoracolumbar spine.

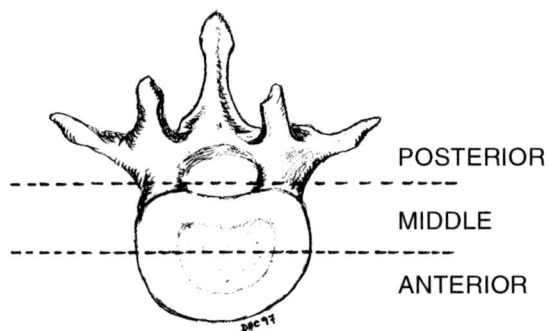

Figure 10.16
The three-column concept of the spine. For a better biomechanical understanding of the stability of the spine, the vertebra and its ligaments are divided into three columns. The anterior column is formed by the anterior half of the vertebral body and disc and the anterior longitudinal ligament. The middle column is formed by the posterior half of the vertebral body and disc and the posterior longitudinal ligament. The posterior column includes the bony elements of the posterior neural arch (pedicles, lamina, transverse and spinous processes, and the facet joints) and the facet capsule, ligamentum flavum, the intertransverse ligament, and the supraspinous ligament.

Spinal Injuries   453

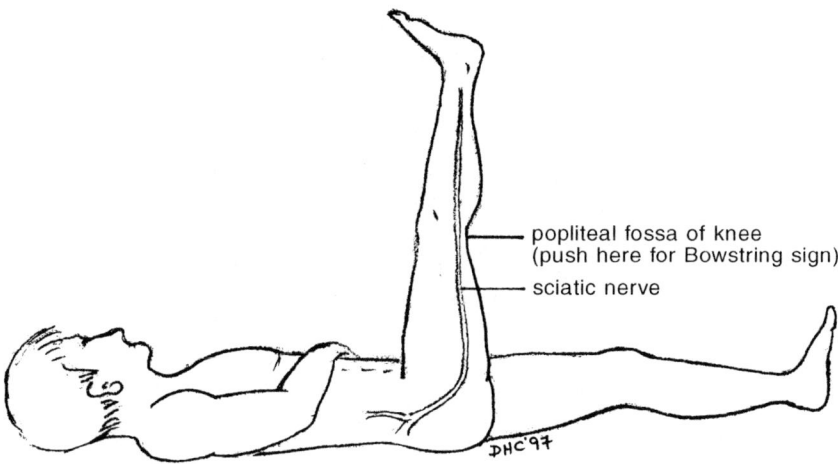

Figure 10.17
Straight leg raising test (SLR). With the knee in extension and the ankle dorsiflexed the hip is flexed gradually. This stretches the sciatic nerve and with irritation of the nerve roots in the back. This maneuver will cause pain coursing down the back of the leg.

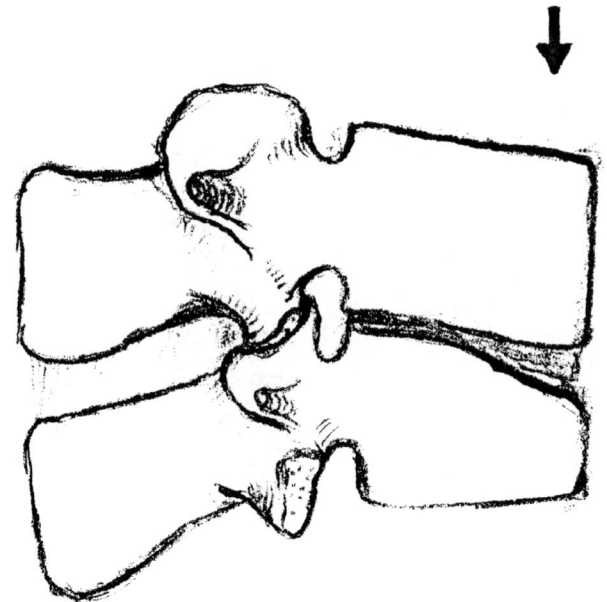

Figure 10.18
Compression fracture of the lumbar spine.

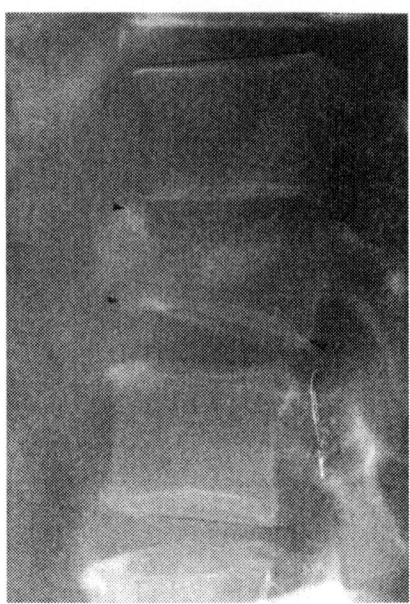

Figure 10.19A
Lateral radiograph showing loss of vertebral body height at the front and the back.

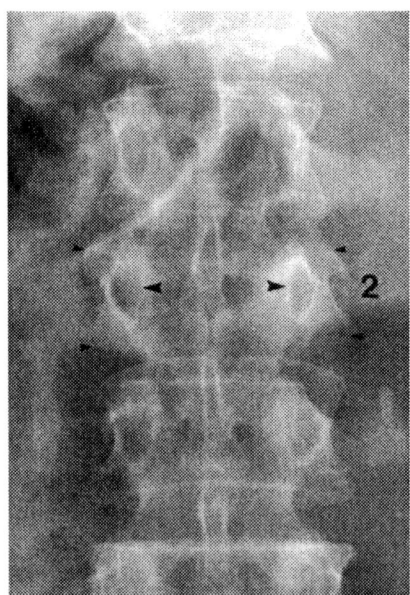

Figure 10.19B
Anteroposterior radiographs showing the classic widening of the pedicles (large arrows) in a burst fracture.

SPINAL INJURIES 455

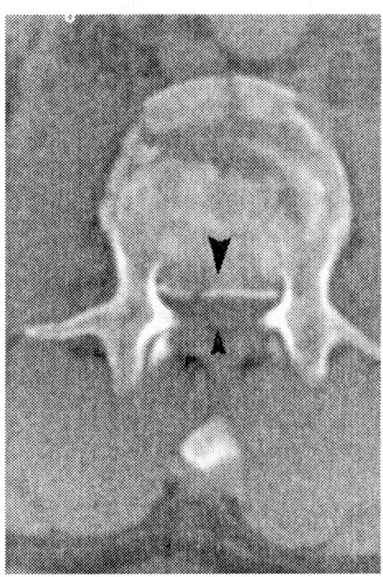

Figure 10.19C
Transverse CT scan view of the fragment of bone retropulsed into the vertebral canal. In this situation, at least 60% of the canal volume was taken up by the fragment but the patient had normal neurologic function.

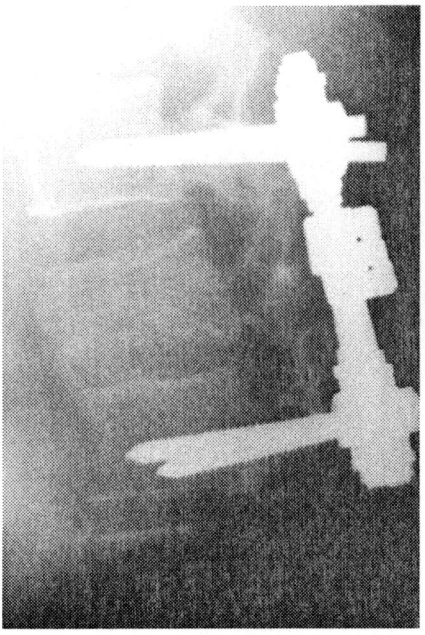

Figure 10.19D
Lateral radiographs after surgical reduction and stabilization.

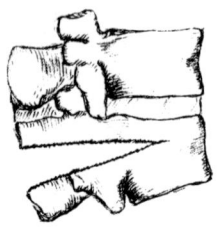

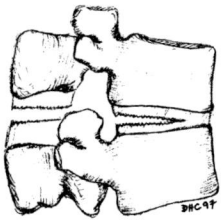

Figure 10.20
A - Thoracolumbar flexion distraction injury (Chance type). The injury extends mostly through bone.
B - Same mechanism of injury but the tissue damage is mostly through disc and ligaments.

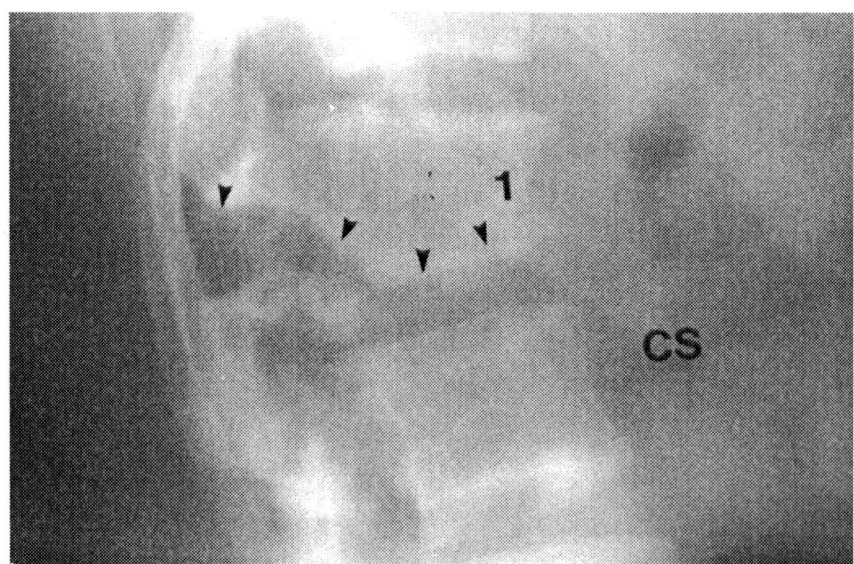

Figure 10.21A
Extension of a flexion distraction injury extending through the disc and vertebral body (follow arrows). Sagittal view.

SPINAL INJURIES 457

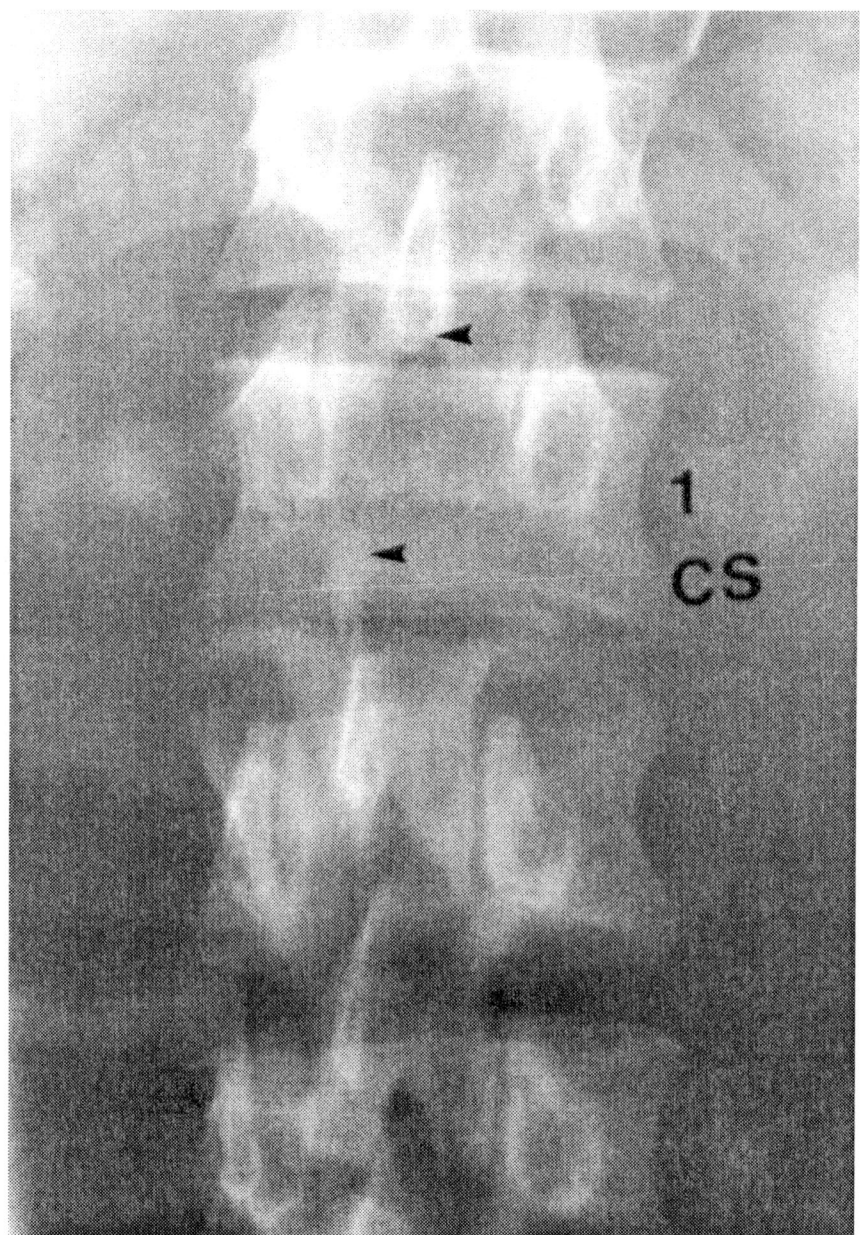

Figure 10.21B
Antero-posterior view of the same injury. The arrows demonstrate the split in the spinous process and marked displacement.

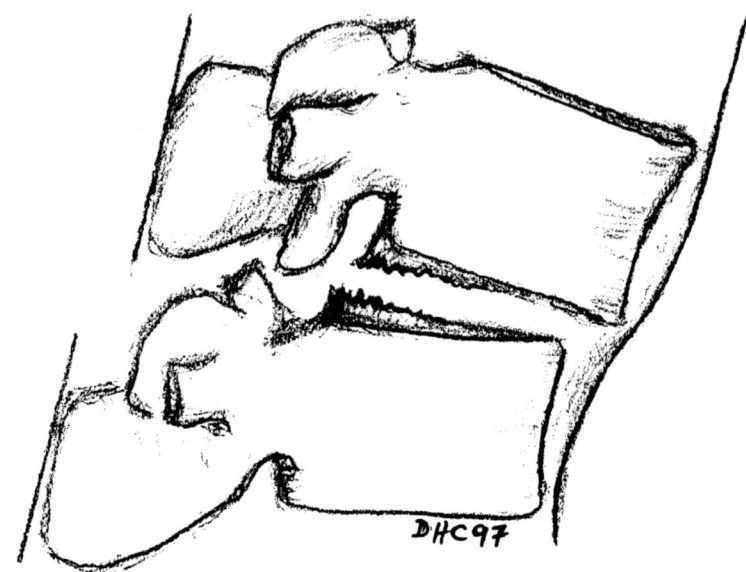

Figure 10.22
Fracture dislocation of the thoracolumbar spine with disruption of structures in all three columns.

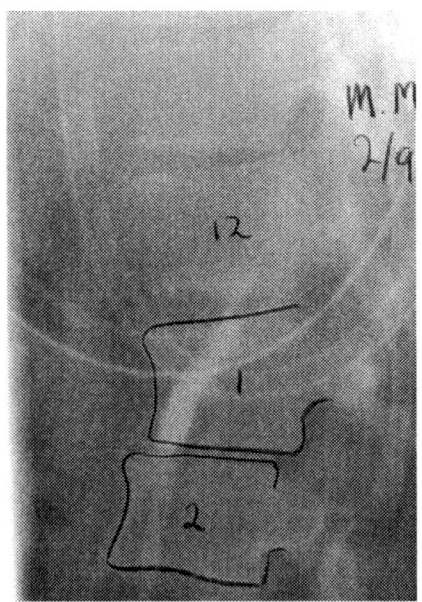

Figure 10.23A
Fracture dislocation of the thoracolumbar spine. Lateral radiographs showing translation of L1 over L2.

SPINAL INJURIES   459

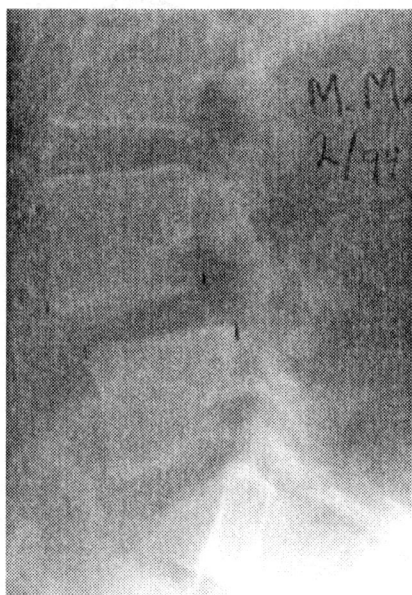

Figure 10.23B
Radiograph of the same patient showing a translation of L4 on L5. This patient had a two level fracture dislocation and was completely paraplegic.

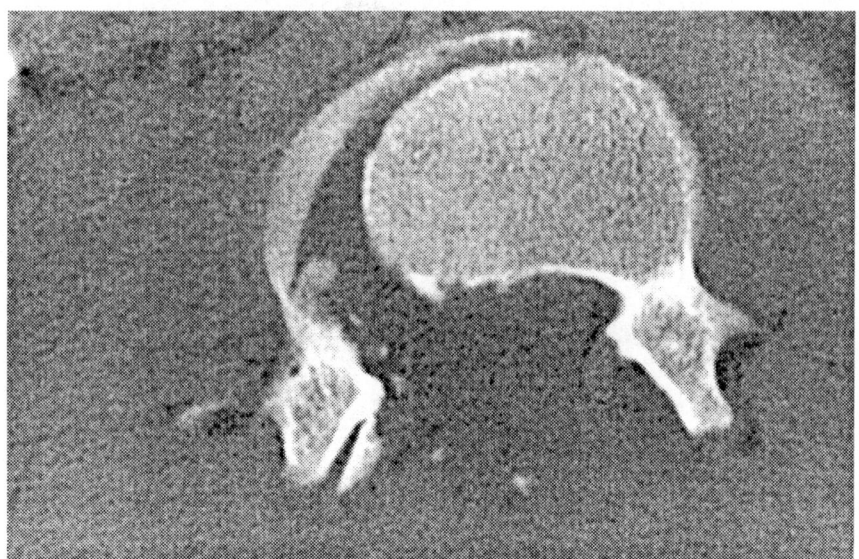

Figure 10.23C
Transverse cut of a CT scan in a fracture dislocation showing two adjacent vertebral bodies overlapping on the same image. There is also marked distortion of the vertebral canal.

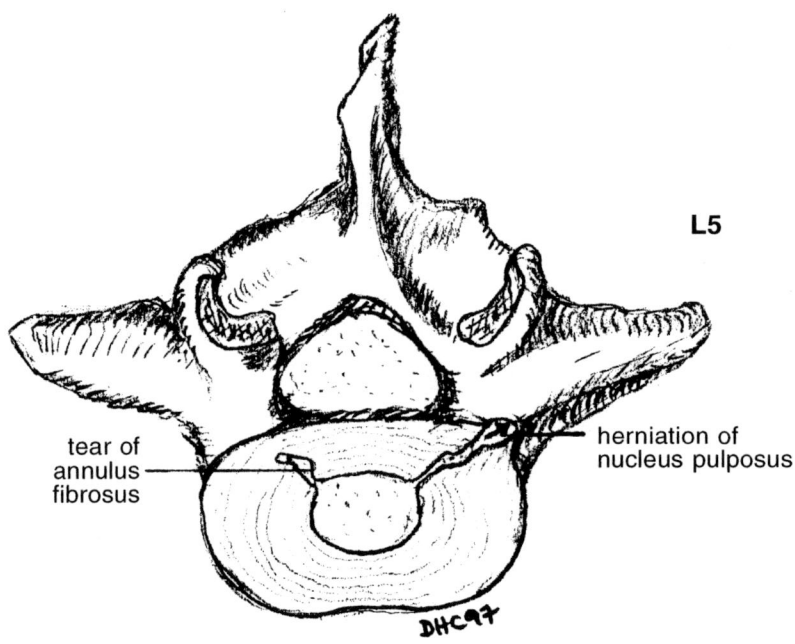

Figure 10.24
Disc disruption: Tears of the annulus fibrosus can be partial thickness or full thickness. Extrusion of the nucleus pulposus through a complete tear in the annulus is what is commonly called a disc herniation or "slipped disc".

SPINAL INJURIES   461

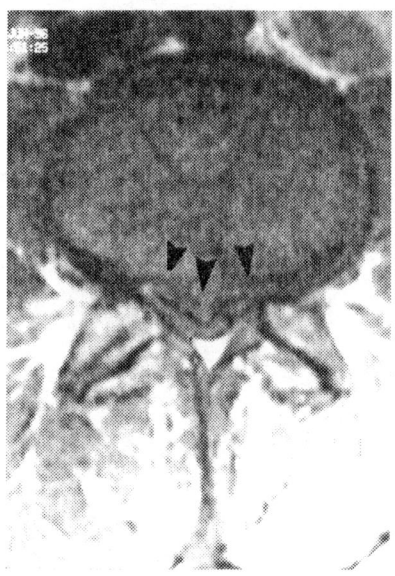

Figure 10.25
Transverse section of the MRI of a 19-year-old male with pain down both legs. The larger arrows show a disc herniation into the vertebral canal. The smaller arrows indicate the dural sac containing the nerve roots.

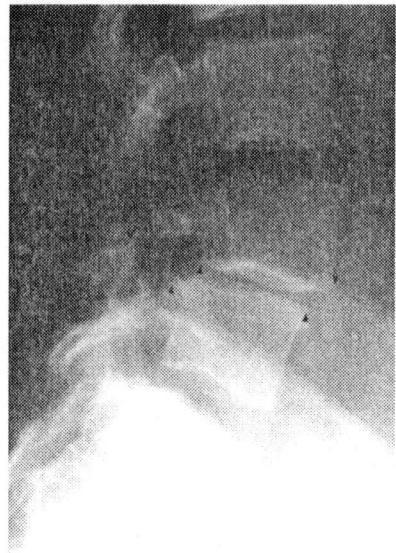

Figure 10.26
Lateral radiograph of a type II (isthmic) spondylolisthesis. The large arrows indicate the defect of the pars interarticularis and the slippage of the L4 vertebral body on L5.

Chapter 11

Injuries to the Extremities and Pelvis

by Jacques A. Bouchard, M.D., F.R.C.S.C.[*]
Geoff Dervin, M.D., F.R.C.S.C.[*]
Jacques A. Brunet, M.D., F.R.C.S.C.[*]
Alan Giachino, M.D., F.R.C.S.C.[*]
Robert J. Feibel, M.D., F.R.C.S.C.[*]

11.1 General Principles
    11.1.1 Description of the Fracture
        11.1.1.1 Location
        11.1.1.2 Displacement
        11.1.1.3 Pattern
        11.1.1.4 Angulation
        11.1.1.5 Closed versus Open
    11.1.2 Principles of Immobilization
        11.1.2.1 Casts
        11.1.2.2 Braces
        11.1.2.3 Traction
        11.1.2.4 Bedrest
        11.1.2.5 Surgical Fixation
11.2 Injuries to the Pelvis and Lower Extremities
    11.2.1 Pelvic Injuries

---

[*] Jacques A. Bouchard, M.D., F.R.C.S.C., Associate Professor, Division of Orthopaedic Surgery, University of Ottawa, is author of parts 11.1 to 11.2.4.4.5, inclusive; Geoff Dervin, M.D., F.R.C.S.C., Assistant Professor, Division of Orthopaedic Surgery, University of Ottawa, is author of parts 11.2.5 to 11.2.6, inclusive; Jacques A. Brunet, M.D., F.R.C.S.C., Associate Professor, Division of Orthopaedic Surgery, University of Ottawa, is author of parts 11.2.7 to 11.2.8.10, inclusive, 11.2.8.12 to 11.2.8.16.3, inclusive, and parts 11.3 to 11.3.1.9.5, inclusive; Alan Giachino, M.D., F.R.C.S.C., Chairman, Division of Orthopaedic Surgery, University of Ottawa, is author of parts 11.2.8.11 to 11.2.8.11.4, inclusive, and parts 11.3.2 to 11.3.4.4, inclusive; Robert J. Feibel, M.D., F.R.C.S.C., Assistant Professor, Division of Orthopaedic Surgery, University of Ottawa, is author of parts 11.4. to 11.4.3.7, inclusive.

            11.2.1.1 Anatomy
            11.2.1.2 Biomechanics of Pelvic Ring Injuries
            11.2.1.3 Classification
            11.2.1.4 Treatment
                    11.2.1.4.1 Stable Pelvic Injuries
                    11.2.1.4.2 Open Book Injuries
                    11.2.1.4.3 Lateral Compression Injuries
                    11.2.1.4.4 Vertical Shear Fractures
                    11.2.1.4.5 Open (Compound) Pelvic Fractures
                    11.2.1.4.6 Treatment of Hemorrhage Associated
                              with Pelvic Injuries
            11.2.1.5 Prognosis and Outcome
      11.2.2 Fractures of the Acetabulum
            11.2.2.1 Anatomy
            11.2.2.2 Mechanism of Injury
            11.2.2.3 Classification
            11.2.2.4 Diagnosis
            11.2.2.5 Treatment
            11.2.2.6 Prognosis
                    11.2.2.6.1 Return to Work
      11.2.3 Fractures and Dislocations of the Hip
            11.2.3.1 Introduction
            11.2.3.2 Anatomy
            11.2.3.3 Dislocations of the Hip
                    11.2.3.3.1 Anterior Dislocations of the Hip
                    11.2.3.3.2 Posterior Dislocations of the Hip
            11.2.3.4 Fractures of the Femoral Neck
                    11.2.3.4.1 Outcome of Femoral Neck Fractures
            11.2.3.5 Intertrochanteric Fractures of the Hip
                    11.2.3.5.1 Outcome
            11.2.3.6 Subtrochanteric Fractures of the Hip
      11.2.4 Fractures of the Femoral Shaft
            11.2.4.1 Classification
            11.2.4.2 Diagnosis
            11.2.4.3 Treatment
            11.2.4.4 Prognosis
                    11.2.4.4.1 Union Rate and Delayed Union
                    11.2.4.4.2 Nonunion
                    11.2.4.4.3 Deformities
                    11.2.4.4.4 Knee Range of Motion
                    11.2.4.4.5 Return to Work
      11.2.5 Injuries about the Knee
            11.2.5.1 Fractures of the Distal Femur

     11.2.5.1.1 Principles of Treatment
   11.2.5.2 Fractures of the Proximal Tibia
     11.2.5.2.1 Principles of Treatment
   11.2.5.3 Ligament Injuries of the Knee
     11.2.5.3.1 Collateral Ligaments
     11.2.5.3.2 Cruciate Ligaments
   11.2.5.4 Knee Dislocations
   11.2.5.5 Meniscal Injuries
 11.2.6 Fractures of the Tibia
 11.2.7 Fractures and Injuries of the Ankle Joint
   11.2.7.1 Anatomy
   11.2.7.2 Mechanisms of Injury
   11.2.7.3 Classification of Ankle Fractures
   11.2.7.4 Treatment of Ankle Fractures
   11.2.7.5 Complications of Ankle Fractures
   11.2.7.6 Vertical Compression Fractures
   11.2.7.7 Ligamentous Injuries to the Ankle
     11.2.7.7.1 Injuries to the Syndesmotic Ligaments
 11.2.8 Injuries to the Foot
   11.2.8.1 Introduction
   11.2.8.2 Anatomy
     11.2.8.2.1 Osteology
     11.2.8.2.2 The Tarsus
     11.2.8.2.3 The Metatarsus
     11.2.8.2.4 The Phalanges
     11.2.8.2.5 Sesamoid and Accessory Bones
   11.2.8.3 Joint, Ligaments and Aponeurosis of the Foot
     11.2.8.3.1 Ankle Joint
     11.2.8.3.2 The Subtalar Joint
     11.2.8.3.3 Talonavicular Joint
     11.2.8.3.4 The Calcaneocuboid Joint
     11.2.8.3.5 The Cuneo-Navicular Joint
     11.2.8.3.6 The Tarsometatarsal Joints (Joint of Lisfranc)
     11.2.8.3.7 The Metatarsophalangeal Joints
     11.2.8.3.8 The Interphalangeal Joints
     11.2.8.3.9 The Plantar Aponeurosis (Plantar Fascia)
   11.2.8.4 Muscles of the Foot
     11.2.8.4.1 Extrinsic Muscles
     11.2.8.4.2 Intrinsic Muscles
   11.2.8.5 The Nerves of the Ankle and Foot
   11.2.8.6 Vascular System
     11.2.8.6.1 Arteries

11.2.8.6.2 Veins
11.2.8.7 Biomechanics
11.2.8.8 Evaluation of Foot Injuries
11.2.8.9 Fractures of the Talus
    11.2.8.9.1 Blood Supply of the Talus
    11.2.8.9.2 Talar Head Fractures
    11.2.8.9.3 Talar Neck Fractures
    11.2.8.9.4 Prognosis and Complications of Talar Neck Fractures
    11.2.8.9.5 Fractures of the Body of the Talus
    11.2.8.9.6 Other Less Common Talar Fractures
11.2.8.10 Dislocations, Subluxations about the Talus
11.2.8.11 Fractures of the Calcaneus
    11.2.8.11.1 Assessment
    11.2.8.11.2 Special Tests
    11.2.8.11.3 Treatment
    11.2.8.11.4 Prognosis
11.2.8.12 Midtarsal Fractures
    11.2.8.12.1 Navicular Fractures
    11.2.8.12.2 Cuboid Fractures
    11.2.8.12.3 Cuneiform Fractures
11.2.8.13 Injuries to the Tarsometatarsal (Lisfranc's) Joints
    11.2.8.13.1 Anatomy
    11.2.8.13.2 Mechanisms of Injury and Classification
    11.2.8.13.3 Clincial Presentations
    11.2.8.13.4 Radiographic Findings
    11.2.8.13.5 Treatment
    11.2.8.13.6 Prognosis
11.2.8.14 Metatarsal Fractures
11.2.8.15 Dislocations of Metatarsophalangeal Joints
11.2.8.16 Fractures and Dislocations of the Toes
    11.2.8.16.1 Fractures of the Great Toe (Hallux)
    11.2.8.16.2 Fractures of the Lesser Toes
    11.2.8.16.3 Dislocations of the Lesser Toe Joints

11.3 Injuries to the Upper Extremities
  11.3.1 Injuries to the Shoulder
    11.3.1.1 Introduction
    11.3.1.2 Subluxations and Dislocations of the Glenohumeral Joint
        11.3.1.2.1 Pathomechanics
        11.3.1.2.2 Diagnosis
        11.3.1.2.3 Treatment

11.3.1.3 Injuries to the Acromioclavicular Joint
    11.3.1.3.1 Anatomy
    11.3.1.3.2 Mechanisms of Injury
    11.3.1.3.3 Injury Types and their Management
    11.3.1.3.4 Complications
11.3.1.4 Injuries to the Sternoclavicular Joint
    11.3.1.4.1 Anatomy
    11.3.1.4.2 Mechanisms of Injury, Diagnosis
    11.3.1.4.3 Treatment
11.3.1.5 Fractures of the Clavicle
    11.3.1.5.1 Anatomy
    11.3.1.5.2 Diagnosis and Classifications
    11.3.1.5.3 Treatment
    11.3.1.5.4 Complications
    11.3.1.5.5 Neurovascular Problems
11.3.1.6 Fractures of the Scapula
    11.3.1.6.1 Incidence
    11.3.1.6.2 Diagnosis
    11.3.1.6.3 Treatment
11.3.1.7 Fractures of the Proximal Humerus
    11.3.1.7.1 Introduction
    11.3.1.7.2 Classification
    11.3.1.7.3 Diagnosis
    11.3.1.7.4 Treatment
    11.3.1.7.5 Prognosis
    11.3.1.7.6 Complications
11.3.1.8 Fractures of the Humeral Shaft
    11.3.1.8.1 Anatomy
    11.3.1.8.2 Diagnosis
    11.3.1.8.3 Treatment
    11.3.1.8.4 Complications
11.3.1.9 Rotator Cuff Tears
    11.3.1.9.1 Introduction
    11.3.1.9.2 Pathomechanics
    11.3.1.9.3 Investigations
    11.3.1.9.4 Treatment
    11.3.1.9.5 Results of Surgical Treatment

11.3.2 Injuries to the Elbow and Forearm
    11.3.2.1 Anatomy and Biomechanics
    11.3.2.2 Fractures about the Elbow in Adults
    11.3.2.3 Injuries to the Mid-Forearm
        11.3.2.3.1 Anatomy
        11.3.2.3.2 Injuries to the Forearm

                11.3.2.3.3 Assessment
                11.3.2.3.4 Treatment
        11.3.3 Injuries to the Distal Forearm and Wrist
                11.3.3.1 Anatomy and Biomechanics
                11.3.3.2 Fractures of the Distal Radius
                        11.3.3.2.1 Treatment of Distal Radial Fractures
                11.3.3.3 Fractures of the Scaphoid
        11.3.4 The Hand
                11.3.4.1 Anatomy
                11.3.4.2 Flexor Tendon Injuries
                11.3.4.3 Extensor Tendon Injuries
                11.3.4.4 Fractures of the Hand
11.4 Special Injuries and Complications
        11.4.1 The Multiply Injured Patient
        11.4.2 The Open Fracture and the Mangled Extremity
                11.4.2.1 Open Fractures
                11.4.2.2 Mangled Extremities
                11.4.2.3 Type III B Open Tibia Fractures
        11.4.3 Complications of Injuries to the Musculoskeletal System
                11.4.3.1 Thromboembolism
                11.4.3.2 Pulmonary Embolism
                11.4.3.3 Fat Embolism and Adult Respiratory Distress
                        Syndrome
                11.4.3.4 Leg Length Discrepancy and Fracture Malunion
                        11.4.3.4.1 Leg Length Discrepancy
                        11.4.3.4.2 Malunion
                11.4.3.5 Nonunion (Pseudoarthrosis)
                        11.4.3.5.1 Classification
                11.4.3.6 Infection
                        11.4.3.6.1 Osteomyelitis
                        11.4.3.6.2 Gas Gangrene (Clostridial Myonecrosis)
                        11.4.3.6.3 Necrotizing Fasciitis
                11.4.3.7 Compartment Syndrome
Tables
    Table 1: Injury Severity Score
    Table 2: Gustilo Classification
    Table 3: Mangled Extremity Severity Score (MESS)
    Table 4: Cierny Clinical Staging System for Osteomyelitis
    Table 5: Treatment of Chronic Osteomyelitis of the Lower Extremity
            by Debridement and Microvascular Transplantation
Glossary
Figures

11.1 GENERAL PRINCIPLES

11.1.1 Description of the Fracture

You have just received a medicolegal report, which states in the diagnosis section that the patient has an open, displaced, comminuted, intra-articular fracture of the distal femoral metaphysis. In one sentence the writer has conveyed the exact injury of the patient. An orthopaedic surgeon reading this will know from these few words that an extensive surgical procedure was needed to treat this patient, followed by 3 months of walking without bearing weight, 1 year of therapy, and a prognosis that will likely involve a change of career and arthritis of the knee.

Once a fracture is defined a common nomenclature must be used to describe the injury. This will permit everyone consulting the medical record to understand the exact injury of the patient even many years after the fact. An accurate description of the fracture is important in many ways: it allows for ease of communication amongst the various specialists treating the patient, it facilitates the understanding of the injury by nonmedical professionals, and it permits scientists to differentiate injuries for various research protocols.

After reading the following sections on location, displacement, pattern, angulation, and type of fracture you should be able to construct a mental picture of the patient's injury from a verbal or written description of the fracture.

11.1.1.1 Location

The fracture is first located in the body by stating which bone is broken. Then we must specify which part of the bone is fractured. The long bones have an epiphysis, a physis, a metaphysis, and a diaphysis [Figure 11.1]. The diaphysis is the tube-like portion of strong cortical bone in the middle of a long bone. The epiphysis is the bulbous end of the long bone, which is covered with articular cartilage. The flare between the epiphysis and the diaphysis is the metaphysis, which is formed mostly of cancellous or spongy bone. Between the metaphysis and the epiphysis, in children, is the physis, also commonly known as the growth plate. The growth plates close during adolescence, which terminates growth. The bone structure is different in each of the regions of the long bone and therefore the fracture patterns, healing patterns, treatment, and prognosis is different for each.

Finally a statement must be made as to the involvement of a joint. Fractures through the physis of the bone often extend into the articular surface and disrupt the joint geometry. These fractures are described as intra-articular. If the alignment of the bones within a joint is disrupted then the articulation is subluxated or dislocated.

A complete description of the location of a fracture will therefore include the name of the bone, the part of the bone that is broken and whether a joint is disrupted or not.

11.1.1.2 Displacement

Many patients ask if they have a break, a crack, or a fracture. These terms all mean the same thing: they all imply a disruption of the bone structure. All the patients know, however, is that there is a difference between a fracture that is displaced and one that is not. The undisplaced fracture is what is commonly known as a hairline fracture or a crack in the bone. The soft tissue covering of the bone is unlikely to be disrupted and these fractures are generally stable, are easy to treat and have a good prognosis. Displacement of the fracture is generally not measured in millimeters since bones and patients are of different size and x-ray magnification changes from one radiograph to the other. Displacement is best measured as a percentage of the width of the bone diaphysis [Figure 11.2]. Thus a fracture displaced by 100% implies that there is no contact between the two ends of the fracture. The acceptable displacement between two bone fragments will vary with the bone that is fractured and the age of the patient. For example, a 10% displacement of a femoral neck fracture in a 30-year-old is unacceptable whereas a 100% displacement of a femoral shaft fracture in a 5-year-old is acceptable as long as other criteria for reduction are met.

The other dimensions of displacement are axial and rotational. Axial displacement is the shortening or distraction of the fracture. This is documented in millimeters but is subject to the inaccuracies of changing x-ray technique. Rotation of the bone is especially hard to quantify. Effort is made to restore the limb's rotation by comparing to the uninjured side. If a malunion has occurred the malrotation is measured in degrees by physical examination and sometimes by computerized tomography.

11.1.1.3 Pattern

The fracture pattern is a good indicator of the mechanism of the fracture. It is especially useful for reconstructing the events that led to the fracture and may be extremely important to the patient. Many cases of child abuse are diagnosed because there is a discrepancy between the parent or guardian's description of the events and the fracture pattern. There are four major patterns: transverse, oblique, spiral, and comminuted [Figure 11.3]. A *transverse* fracture has a short course across the bone at right angle to the cortex. It is caused by an acute bend to the bone or a direct blow on the side of the bone. An *oblique* fracture runs obliquely across the bone and can be long or short depending on the angle of the fracture with respect to the cortex. It is caused by an acute bend of the bone with axial compression. A *spiral* fracture is caused by severe rotation of the limb. The angle of the fracture changes within the fracture site. A fracture is *comminuted* when there are more then two bone fragments in the fracture. Comminuted fractures are caused by high energy trauma.

11.1.1.4 Angulation

Angulation of a fracture is measured in degrees at the apex of the fracture. The direction of the angulation is by definition the direction of the apex of the fracture. This is opposite to the tilt of the fracture which is the direction that the distal fragment is going. Taking a Colles fracture of the distal radius as an example, the classic fracture will angulate volar and tilt dorsally [Figure 11.4].

11.1.1.5 Closed versus Open

The most important factor for the prognosis of a fracture is the condition of the soft tissues overlying it. A closed fracture does not communicate with ambient air. If there is a wound anywhere near a fracture it is considered compound or open until the wound can be surgically explored. It is not uncommon to find wounds that are fairly distant from the fracture site still communicate with it. During impact and maximal displacement of the fracture a spike of bone can disrupt the skin and then recoil back to its original position.

Open fractures are further classified into the Gustilo grades.[1] A *grade I* open fracture is produced from within, by bone piercing the skin. The wound is less than 1 cm in size and contamination is minimal. A *grade II* open fracture has a wound that is between 1 to 10 cm in size and no significant contamination. A *grade III* fracture has wounds greater than 10 cm in size or severe contamination, or comminution of the bone. A grade IIIA fracture has a large wound but good muscle coverage. A grade IIIB fracture has significant degloving of the bone and loss of muscle and skin tissue. A grade IIIC fracture has severe loss of soft tissue and bone and loss of blood circulation to the limb.

11.1.2 Principles of Immobilization

Definitive treatment of a fracture initially includes restoration of the anatomy of the bone or joint followed by some form of stabilization to al-

---

1   Gustilo RB, Anderson JT. Prevention of Infection in the Treatment of One-thousand-and-twenty-five Open Fractures of Long Bones. *J Bone Joint Surg*, 58A:453, 1976.

low for bone and soft tissue healing to occur. Restoring the original configuration of the bone is called a reduction. A closed reduction is done through outside manipulation of the limb. Traction is often an excellent method of reduction or at least a component of the reduction maneuver. An open reduction is when the bone fragments are exposed and manipulated directly. A more precise and often anatomical reduction can be obtained by open methods and there has been a gradual decline in the use of closed reduction of fracture in the treatment of patients. Once the reduction is felt to be satisfactory then the bones must be held in this position for the time it takes that bone to heal (generally 6 to 16 weeks depending on the bone, fracture type, age, and health of the patient). There are many methods for immobilizing bones and these are summarized in the following section.

11.1.2.1 Casts

This consists of a roll of muslin with starch and calcium sulfate. When water is added an exothermic (heat producing) reaction occurs and the calcium sulfate crystallizes and solidifies. The application of a cast appears superficially to be an easy technique; however, knowledge of the anatomy of the limb as well as the behavior of the injury is mandatory to prevent complications of cast treatment. First a tube-like stocking called a stockinette is applied over the limb, followed by layers of sheet wadding to provide a cushion between the skin and the rigid plaster. The plaster is then applied wet and is molded and trimmed while it hardens.

Common casts are the below knee cast which can be non weight bearing or weight bearing in which case a rubber heel is added to the sole of the cast. These casts incorporate the base of the toe all the way up to just below the knee. They allow free movement of the knee. A PTB cast is a patellar tendon bearing cast. This cast extends to the knee and is molded to the anterior of the tibia and front of the knee and patellar tendon. The weight of the body is partially transmitted to the knee instead of through the ankle. It also better controls rotation of the lower leg. A long leg cast extends from the toe to the groin. It provides better immobilization of the knee and ankle but is uncomfortable and impedes the patient's activities of daily living. The general principle of external fixation by casting is that the joint above and the joint below the fracture need to be immobilized. For example a tibia fracture normally requires the use of a long leg cast to immobilize the knee and the ankle. Other common casts are the short arm cast (or SAC) and long arm cast (or LAC). The SAC stops short of the elbow and immobilizes only the wrist. The fingers are free to move. The LAC extends up the arm to also immobilize the elbow.

Plaster of Paris can be used to make splints. These provide partial immobilization and are especially useful before and after surgery for the comfort of the patient. They allow expansion to occur in the bandage when the limb swells. Maximal swelling occurs usually within 2 to 3 days of the injury.

Most recently, synthetic casts have gained wider acceptance. These are made of fiberglass and a polyurethane resin that hardens when immersed in water. The advantage of these casts is that they are lighter, more resilient, harden more quickly, and they do not soften when subjected to humidity or water. The disadvantage is that this material is more difficult to mold, is more expensive and may irritate the contralateral limb because of its abrasive surface.

Absolute immobilization is impossible with a cast. The thicker the soft tissue envelope is around the bone the less effective the cast will be in immobilizing that bone. Furthermore, the cast fits the limb perfectly immediately after application; however, the limb will change shapes and sizes. The limb can swell from the injury and from dependency, thus a cast will be loose in the morning and as the day progresses it will become more and more tight as the limb swells. Because of the immobilization and inactivity the muscles will atrophy and consequently the limb will get smaller. Cast immobilization therefore only maintains the general alignment of the limb and is most appropriate for intrinsically stable injuries.

11.1.2.2 Braces

Braces function in ways similar to casts. The distinction is that they are removable by the patient, they are reusable, and they often allow some motion of a joint through hinges. Braces protect an injured limb and unload it but do not prevent the limb from functioning. They are used most often to protect a joint that has had ligament damage such as the knee joint of an athlete.

11.1.2.3 Traction

Traction has been used for the treatment of fractures, dislocations, and deformities for thousands of years. Traction as a definitive treatment is now seldom used because of prolonged immobilization and hospitalization, joint stiffness, and extreme vigilance and supervision required by the treating physician. There are many configurations of traction but the most frequently used are skin traction and skeletal traction. Skin traction is only used with 2–5kg of weight and is a temporary measure to relieve pain and muscle spasm until definitive treatment is initiated. Skeletal traction is done through a pin (Steinman pin) passed through a bone. Large weights can be applied to the limb without danger to the soft tissue. Skeletal traction was used for the treatment of long bone fractures, especially the femur and fractures of the pelvis. In the 1990s traction is still used for the treatment of certain pelvis fractures but most other long bone fractures are treated with internal fixation in the adult. Traction is more frequently used in children since they heal the fractures faster, are less subject to stiff joints and have growth plates (physis) which interfere with placement of internal fixation devices.

11.1.2.4 Bedrest

This form of immobilization is especially useful for certain pelvic fractures and spine fractures. These fractures are often stable but located in the axial skeleton making these bones less amenable to cast treatment. Bedrest is often an adjunct to many types of fractures and can be used for pain control or to allow some healing of the fracture before the patient stresses the limb by mobilizing.

11.1.2.5 Surgical Fixation

The surgical fixation of bones can be done with external or internal implants. An external fixator uses long pins that are screws into the bone and connected to an outside frame. These are especially useful in open fractures. Soft tissue and skin cover internal fixation. It consists of either plates and screws or intramedullary rods that are inserted inside the bone. Internal fixation of the bone allows for strong, precise and direct immobilization of the bone fragments without immobilizing the adjacent joints. The patient can mobilize quickly and often can resume some or all of their regular activities before the fracture is healed. Internal fixation does not accelerate the healing of bone but allows it to happen in a more predictable way.

11.2　INJURIES TO THE PELVIS AND LOWER EXTREMITIES

11.2.1　Pelvic Injuries

11.2.1.1 Anatomy

The pelvis is formed by two innominate bones. The innominate bones are formed by the fusion of the ilium, the ischium, and the pubis, and at the confluence of these three bones is the acetabulum (or hip socket) [Figure 11.5]. An understanding of injuries to the pelvis requires us to consider the pelvic ring as a whole rather than just the two innominate bones forming the pelvis. The pelvic ring consists of the two innominate bones attached anteriorly at the pubic bone through the symphysis pubis [Figure 11.6]. Posteriorly the innominate bones (ilium portion) are attached to the sacrum by strong ligaments around the sacro-iliac joints. The ischium participates in the ring by contributing to the anatomy of the acetabulum and by providing muscle attachment to the hamstring muscles and to the adductors of the hip.

The ilium is a large flat part of the innominate bone with the iliac crest separating the anterior and posterior superior iliac spines and the inferior iliac spines. The medial part of the ilium articulates with the sacrum and the postero-inferior aspect of the ilium borders the sciatic notch. The pubis is formed by the upper and lower pubic rami and by the body of the pubis, which articulates with the symphysis pubis. The ischium is the part of the pelvis that we sit on and it has an ischial spine and a tuberosity. Together with the pubis it forms a large foramen called obturator foramen.

The soft tissues of the pelvis are complex and can be divided into the ligaments, the muscles, the neurovascular structures and the visceral organs. 1) Ligaments of the pelvis: The strongest groups of ligaments are those joining the sacrum to the ilium. They are found anterior and posterior to the sacro-iliac joint. The sacrotuberous ligament attaches the sacrum to the tuberosity of the ischium and has some fibers going to the ischial spine. The sacrospinous ligament is another large ligament between the sacrum and the ischial spine. Finally, the ligaments of the symphysis pubis allow some motion to occur but also maintain the integrity of the pelvic ring. 2) The muscles of the pelvic ring: Can broadly be divided into three groups: the muscles forming the floor of the pelvis, the muscles of the trunk that insert onto the pelvis, and the muscles of the legs that originate from the pelvis. The muscles of the floor of the pelvis maintain the integrity of the perineum, which includes the urethra, vagina, and rectal sphincter. 3) Neurovascular structures: The lumbar plexus arising from the nerve roots of L2 to L4 enter the pelvis and gives off several branches. The lateral femoral cutaneous nerve exits the pelvis close to the anterior superior iliac spine, the obturator nerve exits the pelvis through the obturator foramen and the remainder joins the roots of L5 to S3 to form the lumbosacral plexus, which then becomes the sciatic nerve. The sciatic nerve exits the pelvis through the sciatic notch, which is bordered by the ileum and the sacrotuberous ligament. Other important structures run through this notch in addition to the sciatic nerve: the inferior and superior gluteal nerves, the inferior and superior gluteal artery, the pudendal nerve, and the internal pudendal artery. The primary arterial supply of the pelvis is the internal iliac artery. It contributes blood to most of the viscera inside the pelvis, to the genitalia, and to the adductor and abductor muscles of the hip. The veins of the pelvis are numerous and form a rich plexus that drain into the internal iliac veins. 4) Visceral organs: The urinary bladder and urethra lie posterior to the pubis and symphysis pubis. The rectum lies anterior to the sacrum. In females, the vagina and uterus are in the centre of the pelvis between the bladder and the rectum.

11.2.1.2 Biomechanics of Pelvic Ring Injuries

As is the case for many other orthopaedic injuries, knowing the mechanism of the injury to the pelvis is important to define the injury and to determine treatment. Knowing the direction and magnitude of the force applied to the pelvis and the position of the body when the force is applied helps us understand the type of fracture or dislocation incurred by the patient.

The magnitude of the force can be arbitrarily grouped into low velocity injuries such as falls, or high velocity injuries such as motor vehicle accidents. Low velocity injuries produce individual fractures of various bones in the pelvis but no disruption of the pelvic ring. An example is of a fall causing a fracture of the pubic ramus.

High velocity injuries disrupt the pelvic ring and are further categorized by the direction of the force. The force can be applied to the pelvis in a frontal, lateral or vertical direction or a combination of these such as in crush injuries. More than half of these fractures are caused by motor vehicle accidents. The others are from pedestrian trauma, motorcycles, falls from a height or crush injury.[2] In motor vehicle accidents a frontal or oblique collision will open the pelvis by forcibly rotating the innominate bones. A side impact produces a lateral vector force and tends to implode or close the pelvic ring. A vertical shear fracture can occur if the occupant submarines underneath the seat belt or is ejected from the vehicle.[3] Motorcyclists tend to sustain either an open book injury of the pelvis when they are projected forward and their pelvis strikes the gas tank or a vertical shear injury when an extended extremity strikes the ground at high speed.[4] Pedestrians impact their pelvis on the hood or front of the car in a frontal or lateral direction causing either an open book injury or a lateral compression fracture.[5] Falls will cause vertical shear fractures if the victim lands vertically and the pelvis injury is often associated with other fractures of the same extremity such as a calcaneal fracture and spinal burst fractures. If they fall sideways the injury produced is that of a lateral compression.

---

2   Dalal SA, Burgess AR, Siegel JH, et al. Pelvic Fracture in Multiple Trauma: Classification by Mechanism is Key to Pattern of Organ Injury, Resuscitative Requirements, and Outcome. *J Trauma*, 29:981-1002, 1989.

3   Gokcen EC, Burgess AR, Siegel JH, Mason-Gonzalez S, Dischinger PC, Ho SM. Pelvic Fracture Mechanism of Injury in Vehicular Trauma Patients. *J Trauma*, 36:789-796, 1994.

4   Viano DC, Lau IV, Asbury C, King AI, Bergman P. Biomechanics of the Human Chest, Abdomen and Pelvis in Lateral Impact, *Accid Anal. Prev*, 21:553-574, 1989.

5   McCarroll JR, Braunstein PW, Cooper W, et al. Fatal Pedestrian Automotive Accidents. *JAMA*, 180:127-133, 1962.

11.2.1.3 Classification

Fractures of the pelvis have been classified in many ways. A commonly used classification scheme is the one proposed by Pennal and Tile and it is based on stability of the pelvis and the mechanism of injury.[6] Type A fractures are stable and do not involve the whole pelvic ring or have minimal displacement [Figure 11.7A]. Type B injuries are rotationally unstable but vertically stable and they include the open book injuries and the lateral compression injuries [Figure 11.7B). Type C injuries are vertically and rotationally unstable and include the vertical shear injury (e.g., the classic Malgaigne fracture dislocation) [Figures 11.7C and D].

Classification and initial treatment is based on the history of the injury, the physical exam, and vital signs of the patient and simple anteroposterior radiographs of the pelvis. Definitive treatment is based on more exhaustive investigations such as inlet and outlet radiographs of the pelvis, oblique views, and computerized tomographic scans.

11.2.1.4 Treatment

Pelvic ring injuries may be life-threatening or are associated with life-threatening injuries and therefore a complete evaluation of the patient must be done and emergency resuscitation initiated. Blood loss with pelvic fracture is always underestimated because it is internal into the retroperitoneal space. It often can be massive. The injury is not as obvious as extremity fractures and therefore if there is any doubt the pelvis and spine will be relatively immobilized by placing the patient on a spine board. No further stabilization is necessary unless the patient is hemodynamically unstable. The best way to control massive blood loss is to stabilize the pelvis by compressing it. In the field this can be done by the application of pneumatic compression pants. In the hospital setting, early application of pelvic clamps[7] or external fixators are usually effective. Once the patient is stabilized and all his injuries have been documented then a treatment plan can be elaborated.

11.2.1.4.1 Stable Pelvic Injuries: Approximately one-third of pelvic injury involve only one side of the ring although with modern imaging method many of these pelvic fractures have been associated to other minimally displaced fractures of the pelvic ring.[8] These injuries heal reliably

---

6   Pennal GF, Tile M, Waddell JP, Garside H. Pelvic Disruption: Assessment and Classification. *Clin Orthop*, 151:12-21, 1980.

7   Ganz R, Krushell RF, Jakob RP, et al. The Antishock Pelvic Clamp. *Clin Orthop*, 267:71-78, 1991.

8   Burgess AR, Eastridge BJ, Young JWR, et al. Pelvic Ring Disruptions: Effective Classification System and Treatment Protocols. *J Trauma*, 30:848-856, 1990.

within 6 to 8 weeks and are treated with short-term bedrest for relief of pain then gradual mobilization. Activity modifications are required for 8 to 12 weeks after which the patients may return to their usual activities. Surgery is not required nor is bracing.

11.2.1.4.2 Open Book Injuries: The symphysis pubis is disrupted and opens. Surgical fixation is required if the symphysis is open by more than 2 cm [Figures 11.7 A and B]. The injury of the posterior part of the pelvic ring consists of a widening of the sacro-iliac joint or by having a fracture of the sacrum. The posterior pelvis is not completely disrupted and may have intrinsic stability. Therefore, definitive treatment is aimed at closing the book either by the application of an external fixator on the iliac crest and performing a closed reduction or by doing an open reduction and internal fixation of the symphysis pubis with plates and screws.

11.2.1.4.3. Lateral Compression Injuries: Undisplaced injuries do not require surgery. A displaced lateral compression will cause the hemipelvis to "bucket handle" and rotate. This produces significant leg length discrepancy [Figure 11.7C]. If the leg length difference is greater than 1.5 cm, the pelvis should be reduced. Fixation of the anterior pelvis is done with either an external fixator on the iliac wings or plating of the symphysis or pubic rami. Posterior stabilization may require plating of an iliac wing fracture or screw fixation of the sacrum or sacro-iliac joint.

11.2.1.4.4 Vertical Shear Fractures: These pelvic injuries are associated with violent impacts and thus cause massive soft tissue and visceral injuries [Figure 11.7D]. Initial treatment mandates resuscitation and stabilization of the patient. The pelvis is quickly stabilized by the application of an external fixator anteriorly and the involved leg is placed in traction to reduce the hemipelvis. Once the life threatening injuries are dealt with, definitive treatment can be planned. If an external fixator-traction combination achieves an excellent reduction, consideration can be given to pursue this line of treatment. It does, however, involve keeping the patient on strict bedrest for 6 to 8 weeks. If this is not desirable or if the pelvis injury is not in a satisfactory position then open reduction of the anterior and posterior pelvic ring injury is recommended.

11.2.1.4.5 Open (Compound) Pelvic Fractures: A fracture of the pelvis is considered open or compound if there is any contamination of the bone. This can occur if the pelvis injury communicates with an outside wound (like any other open fractures of long bones) or if the pelvis perforates the bowel, the vagina, or the bladder. This type of injury requires urgent attention with thorough irrigation and debridement of the pelvis. Other specialists also intervene: the general surgeon will do a diverting colostomy and repair the bowel, the urologist must repair the bladder and/or urethra and a gynecologist should assess and repair vaginal tears.

11.2.1.4.6 Treatment of Hemorrhage Associated with Pelvic Injuries:

- Fluid resuscitation and transfusions
- Application of antishock compressive pants
- Application of an external fixator to the pelvis
- Angiogram and embolization of arterial bleeders
- Open reduction and internal fixation of the pelvis. Avoid decompression of the retroperiteal space as this can lead to uncontrolled hemorrhage.
- Laparotomy and ligation of bleeders. Rarely effective in blunt trauma since the majority of the hemorrhage comes from the plexus of veins and is difficult to control. In salvage situation the pelvis is packed with sponges to tamponade the bleeding. The packing is removed a few days later.

11.2.1.5 Prognosis and Outcome

The prognosis of undisplaced and stable pelvic injuries is excellent. The complication rate is low and most patients are able to return to full activities and function within 3 months. The prognosis for unstable pelvic fractures is more complicated to establish. Factors that will influence the prognosis are the magnitude of the original impact, the presence of associated injuries, the position of the pelvis at union and the development of complications.

Neurologic injuries are frequently missed initially because of the difficulties in assessing the neurologic status of a severely injured patient. There can be compression or traction of the nerve roots of L4 to S2. Most of the neurologic injuries are from traction of the nerve and there is no specific treatment for this. One must wait for nerve recovery to occur before (often months) the final function is determined.

Thromboembolism can develop in patients with pelvic fractures. In one study of 60 patients with pelvic fractures 15% developed a deep vein thrombosis and one patient had a pulmonary embolism.[9] They recommend serial screening with duplex ultrasound for the high-risk pelvic fractures.

The long-term prognosis appears to be related to the residual deformity of the pelvis. In a review by MacLaren with more than 5-year follow

---

9 White RH, Goulet JA, Bray TJ, Daschbach MM, McGahan JP, Hartling RP. Deep-Vein Thrombosis After Fracture of the Pelvis: Assessment with Serial Duplex-Ultrasound Screening. *J Bone Joint Surg*, 72A:495-500, 1990.

up, the patients who had less than 1 cm of displacement at the end of the healing period had significantly less pain and disability than the patients with a malunited pelvis. Eighty-eight percent had no pain and 82% had normal function whereas in the malunited group only 30% had no significant pain and normal function.[10] Matta and his colleagues showed that internal fixation of unstable pelvic injuries produced superior anatomic position, healing rates, and functional results.[11] Tile also recommends surgical fixation of unstable pelvic fractures but also emphasizes that even in a tertiary care centre most pelvic fractures are stable. His review of 494 pelvis injuries at Sunnybrook Hospital in Toronto revealed that only 19% needed stabilization and only 5% needed internal fixation.[12] Miranda performed a more detailed study of long-term function after pelvic injury. They found that even mild pelvic fractures could result in an unfavorable outcome. Thirty-three percent of the patients had altered sexual activity and 36% of patients had to change their occupation as a result of the injury.

Nonunion of pelvic fractures is unusual. When it does occur it is associated with severe disabling symptoms and requires surgical management.[13]

The mortality of pelvic fractures for the patients requiring admission to hospital has been reported to be about 10%.[14] Open pelvic fractures have a higher mortality and morbidity rate. Brenneman studies 1,179 pelvic fractures from Sunnybrook hospital and found that 44 (4%) were open fractures. Eleven (25%) of the patients with an open pelvic fracture died.[15] Patients with open pelvic fractures were on average 9 years younger, were more likely to be males and were more likely to have been involved in a motorcycle accident. In addition they required more transfusions. They had very significant long-term disability of physical functioning. Most were unable to return to gainful employment.

---

10 McLaren AC, Rorabeck CH, Halpenny J. Long-Term Pain and Disability in Relation to Residual Deformity after Displaced Pelvic Ring Fractures. *Can J Surg*, 33:492-494,1990.
11 Matta JM, Merritt PO. Displaced Acetabular Fractures. *Clin Orthop*, 230:83-97, 1988.
12 Tile M. Pelvic Ring Fractures: Should they be Fixed? *J Bone Joint Surg*, 70B:1-12, 1988.
13 Pennal GF, Massiah KA. Nonunion and Delayed Union of Fractures of the Pelvis. *Clin Orthop*, 151:124-129, 1980.
14 Chong KH, DeCoster T, Osler T, Robinson B. Pelvic Fractures and Mortality. *Iowa Orthop J*, 17:110-114, 1997. Wubben RC. Mortality Rate of Pelvic Fracture Patients. *Wis Med J*, 95(10):702-4, 1996.
15 Brenneman FD, Katyal D, Boulanger BR, Tile M, Redelmeier DA. Long Term Outcomes in Open Pelvic Fractures. *J Trauma*, 42(4):773-777, 1997.

11.2.2 Fractures of the Acetabulum

11.2.2.1 Anatomy

The acetabulum is the socket of the hip joint. Its bony structure is formed from contributions of the pubis, ischium, and ilium of the innominate bone. Before skeletal maturity the triradiate cartilage separates these three bones. The acetabulum is shaped by the growth in the triradiate cartilage. Although the acetabulum is entirely in the pelvis and makes up half of the hip joint it is addressed separately when it comes to fractures because of the unique behavior and treatment of this type of injury. The innominate bone, when viewed in the lateral direction, is likened to an inverted Y. The acetabulum is cradled in the axilla of the Y. The roof of the acetabulum is formed by the superior dome, which is part of the ilium. The posterior column is the thick and strong bone of the ischium and sciatic notch. The anterior column extends from the iliac crest to the symphysis pubis. The anterior and posterior column are further subdivided into smaller components, that is the anterior and posterior wall respectively [Figure 11.8].

Thorough knowledge of the anatomy of the pelvis and surrounding soft tissues is required for a surgeon to embark in the operative treatment of these fractures. Such an in depth study of anatomy is not in the scope of this book however the complexity of pelvic and acetabular anatomy must always be taken into consideration when dealing with individuals who have had acetabular fractures.

11.2.2.2 Mechanism of Injury

Forces transferred to the hip socket by the femoral head produce acetabular fractures. The fracture pattern will be representative of the position of the hip at the time of impact [Figure 11.9A]. If the femur and femoral head are rotated internally, the posterior wall will fracture [Figure 11.9B], and if rotated externally, the anterior wall will be involved [Figure 11.9C]. If the femoral head is adducted, the superior portion of the dome will fracture. If the femur is abducted or if the impact is lateral on the greater trochanter of the femur, the medial wall or inferior part of the dome will fracture. Most of these injuries are caused by high energy trauma such as automobile and motorcycle accidents or falls from a height. There is often comminution of the bone.

11.2.2.3 Classification

Much of the concepts dealing with the understanding and treatment of acetabular fractures were developed by Judet and Letournel in Paris in the

1960s and are still applicable today.[16] Subsequent work by Tile, Letournel, and Matta has led to an international classification. Type A fractures involve a single wall or column [Figure 11.10A], type B fractures involve both columns (transverse or T type) [Figure 11.10B] and type C fractures involve both columns and the roof (floating acetabulum) [Figure 11.10C].

11.2.2.4 Diagnosis

Because of the high-energy nature of this injury it is vital to do a thorough physical examination of the patient. In particular, the function of the sciatic and femoral nerves must be determined. Up to 40% of posterior acetabular fractures can involve sciatic nerve injury. Because of the complex three-dimensional shape of the hemipelvis and acetabulum, special investigations are required. Radiographs are taken in antero-posterior and lateral directions and also in an oblique direction. These so-called Judet views of the hip provide anatomical information of different parts of the acetabulum and pelvis. The anterior column and posterior wall are best visualized by the obturator oblique view and the posterior column and anterior wall by the iliac oblique view. Further determination of the anatomy of the fracture is made with a CT scan and sometimes with 3D reconstruction of CT images.

11.2.2.5 Treatment

Conservative treatment of fractures of the acetabulum involved bed rest and traction on the femur and was advocated for all fractures until the mid 1960s. It was then that Judet and Letournel published results which indicated that patients where the acetabulum healed in an anatomic position had a 90% chance of good to excellent results.[17] Surgical reduction and fixation was often required to achieve an adequate reduction. Premature osteoarthritis developed in the patients where a perfect reduction was not achieved. These results have since been confirmed and reproduced by other authors such as Pennal, Tile, and Matta.[18] Most authors have also found that 25% of the fractures could not be reduced anatomically despite

---

16 Judet R, Judet J, Letournel E. Fractures of the Acetabulum: Classification and Surgical Approaches for Open Reduction. *J Bone Joint Surg*, 46A-1616-1647, 1964.

17 *Ibid.*

18 Matta JM. Fractures of the Acetabulum: Accuracy of Reduction and Clinical Results in Patients Managed Operatively within Three Weeks after the Injury. *J Bone Joint Surg*, 78A:1632-1645, 1996. Pennal GF, Davidson J, Garside H, Plewes J. Results of Treatment of Acetabular Fractures. *Clin Orthop*, 151:115-123, 1980. Tile M, Kellam J, Joyce M. Fractures of the Acetabulum: Classification, Management Protocol and Results of Treatment. *J Bone Joint Surg*, 67B:324-325, 1985.

open reductions done by expert surgeons. This can be explained by the complexity of some of these injuries and by the delay in surgery that can occur because of concomitant injuries or distance of the patient from a treatment centre.

The current recommendation for treatment of acetabular fracture is to obtain an anatomic reduction. If the fracture is undisplaced or minimally displaced the patient can be treated with bed rest and traction. All other fractures require surgical reduction and fixation. Type A fractures can be reduced with classic approaches to the hip and are relatively straightforward. Type B and C fractures require complex dissection of tissues to expose the fracture and are usually performed at tertiary health care facilities and frequently with several surgeons participating.

Regardless of the type of fracture or treatment, the patient must avoid bearing weight on the leg for three months. They usually require another 3 to 6 months of rehabilitation to complete their treatment.

11.2.2.6 Prognosis

All the studies in the literature support the concept that the most important determinant of long-term results of acetabular fracture is residual displacement at the end of the treatment. The hip joint does not tolerate articular gaps or steps of more than 3 mm. Regardless of the fracture type or what treatment is given, if the reduction is near anatomical then good results are seen in 85% of patients. The risk of arthritis is lower and the functional hip scores are higher.[19] Matta reported a large review of 259 patients with acetabular fractures that were displaced at least 5 mm. All were treated surgically and 71% were reduced anatomically. Overall, 76% had a good to excellent result, however those with an anatomic reduction had an 83% chance of a good result whereas those with imperfect reduction only had a good result 68% of the time. Most of the imperfect reductions were in the very complex fractures and a small number had a good reduction that was lost in the post-operative period because of complications or lack of compliance from patients.[20]

The incidence of osteoarthritis for all acetabular fractures has been as high as 43% to 56%.[21] This rate can increase to 84% if the acetabular dome is comminuted.[22] The actual incidence is likely higher than reported because most reports have limited follow-up time.

---

19 Matta, *ibid.* Pennal et al., *ibid.* Letournel E. The Treatment of Acetabular Fractures through the Ilioinguinal Approach. *Clin Orthop*, 292:62-76,1993. Matta JM, Mehne DK, Roffi R. Fractures of the Acetabulum: Early Results of a Prospective Study. *Clin Orthop*, 205:241-250, 1985.
20 Matta, *supra*, note 18.
21 Pennal, *supra*, note 18. Letournel, *supra*, note 19.
22 Pennal, *supra*, note 18. Tile M et al., *supra*, note 18.

Many complications can occur following severe traumas to the pelvis and hip. A few complications are specific to fractures of the acetabulum and their treatment. Periarticular heterotopic ossification occurs in 17% to 20% of acetabular fractures treated surgically[23] and 5% of hips treated conservatively. In Letournel's study, of the patients who develop heterotopic ossification, 64% had no symptoms, 13% had mild limitation of movement and 23% had severe limitation of range of motion. Avascular necrosis of the femoral head is not common after acetabular fractures. Matta found only 3% of hips and Letournel 4% of 492 hips developed avascular necrosis. Sciatic nerve palsy can occur as a result of acetabular fracture because the femoral head often dislocates posteriorly. Most large studies on acetabular fractures report rates of sciatic nerve palsies of 10% to 15%.[24] It is unclear what influence surgery has on this complication. Many palsies have been detected postoperatively in patients who had poor documentation of the function of the sciatic nerve before the surgery. It is therefore imperative that all patients with acetabular fracture have a careful neurologic assessment of that extremity. The residual disability of patients with sciatic palsies is unclear.

11.2.2.6.1 Return to Work: Few studies specifically deal with the issue of return to work because they include it in an overall functional score. Approximately 70% of patients are able to return to their previous occupation. The time to return to work is on average 12 months with a range of 3 to 24 months irrespective of the treatment.

11.2.3 Fractures and Dislocations of the Hip

11.2.3.1 Introduction

The hip joint is formed by the acetabular part of the pelvis on one side and the femur on the distal side of the articulation. Fractures of the hip however commonly refer only to the fractures of the proximal femur. Hip fractures are an enormous problem because they have a devastating impact on the patient and on the health care system. It is estimated that there are 250,000 hip fractures per year in the United States and most of these will require surgical treatment and hospitalization.[25] In Ontario the hip fracture

---

23 Tile et al., *supra*, note 18. Letournel, *supra*, note 19.
24 Tile et al., *supra*, note 18. Letournel, *supra*, note 19. Fassler PR, Swiontkowski MF, Kilroy AN, Routt ML. Injury of the Sciatic Nerve Associated with Acetabular Fracture. *J Bone Joint Surg*, 75A:1157-1166.
25 Koval KJ, Zuckerman JD. Functional Recovery after Hip Fracture. *J Bone Joint Surg*, 77:751-758, 1994. Koval KJ, Zuckerman JD. Hip Fractures; II. Evaluation and Treatment of Intertrochanteric Fractures. *J.A.A.O.S.*, 2:150-156, 1994.

rate between 1981 and 1992 was 3.3 per 1000 population. In actual numbers there were 8490 hip fractures in 1990 and the projected number of hip fractures in the year 2010 will be 16,963 because of the increasing age of the population.[26]

There are many patterns and variations of hip fractures. The main ones that will be discussed are dislocations of the hip, femoral neck fractures, intertrochanteric fractures and subtrochanteric fractures.

11.2.3.2 Anatomy

The femur is the largest and strongest bone of the body. The proximal aspect is spherical in shape and articulates with the acetabulum of the pelvis. The femoral head is almost completely contained within the acetabulum. It is attached to the main part of the femur by the cylindrical femoral neck. At the junction of the femoral neck and femoral shaft are the greater and lesser trochanters, which serve as the attachment point of numerous muscles [Figure 11.11]. The proximal 10 cm of the femoral shaft is called the subtrochanteric area and is dealt with separate from the femoral shaft because of many differences in the biomechanics, treatment and prognosis.

The capsule and hip ligaments attach at the junction of the femoral neck and the intertrochanteric area of the proximal femur. Thus the femoral head and femoral neck are intra-articular and are surrounded by synovial fluid. This is significant since the femoral neck and head do not have the capacity to heal by callous formation and must rely on primary bone healing (endosteal union) for the fractures to unite.[27] The other implication is that the blood supply of the femoral head is almost all from the femoral neck and is very vulnerable if the femoral neck is fractured [Figure 11.12]. The vascular anatomy of the femoral head starts with an extracapsular arterial ring at the base of the femoral neck. The ring obtains its blood posteriorly from a large branch of the medial femoral circumflex artery and anteriorly by branches of the anterior circumflex artery. From the basal arterial ring the ascending cervical branches make their way up proximally on the surface of the femoral neck. These cervical branches form the subsynovial intracapsular arterial ring at the junction of the femoral neck and head. Epiphyseal arterial branches then enter the femoral neck and head in the subcapital region.[28] Fractures of the femoral neck in this

---

26 Jaglal SB, Sherry PG, Schatzker J. The Impact and Consequences of Hip Fracture in Ontario. *Can J Surg*, 39(2):105-11, 1996.
27 Pankovich AM. Primary Internal Fixation of Femoral Neck Fractures. *Arch Surg*, 110:20-26, 1975. Phemister DB. The Pathology of Ununited Fractures of the Neck of the Femur with Special Reference to the Head. *J Bone Joint Surg*, 21A:681-693, 1939.
28 Crock HV. An Atlas of the Arterial Supply of the Head and Neck of the Femur in Man. *Clin Orthop*, 152:17-27, 1980.

subcapital region may disrupt the blood flow to the femoral head and lead to avascular necrosis. The other vascular supply to the femoral head comes from the obturator artery in the pelvis and enters the femoral head through the ligamentum teres. This blood supply is usually inadequate to maintain the viability of the femoral head after a fracture.[29]

11.2.3.3 Dislocations of the Hip

Considerable force is required to dislocate the hip joint because of the ball and socket configuration of the bones. When the femoral head dislocates it often also involves a disruption of the osseus elements such as a fracture of the acetabular rim or femoral head itself. Two anatomic features of the hip joint will dictate the treatment and prognosis of this injury: the proximity of the sciatic nerve[30] and the tenuous blood supply of the femoral head.[31]

Numerous classification systems exist for hip dislocations. There is also a crossover with fractures of the acetabulum and femoral head because of their frequent association. The dislocation is described with respect to the position of the femoral head with respect to the acetabulum. Simply, the femoral head can dislocate anterior or posterior to the acetabulum. The anterior dislocations and further divided into the anterosuperior dislocations, the anteroinferior dislocations and dislocations associated with a fracture of the anterior rim of the acetabulum or the femoral head.

---

29 Howe WW, Lacey T, Schwartz RP. A Study of the Gross Anatomy of the Arteries Supplying the Proximal Portion of the Femur and the Acetabulum. *J Bone Joint Surg*, 32A:856-866, 1950.

30 Aufranc OE, Jones WN, Turner RH, Thomas WH. Fracture of the Acetabulum with Dislocation of Hip and Sciatic Palsy. Fracture of the Month. *JAMA*, 201:690-691, 1967. Derian PS, Bibighaus AJ. Sciatic Nerve Entrapment by Ectopic Bone after Posterior Fracture Dislocation of the Hip. *South Med J*, 67:209-210, 1974. Hirasawa Y, Oda R, Nakatani K. Sciatic Nerve Paralysis in Posterior Dislocation of the Hip. *Clin Orthop*, 126:172-175, 1977. Kleinman SG, Stevens J, Kolb L, Pankovich A. Late Sciatic Nerve Palsy Following Posterior Fracture Dislocation of the Hip. *J Bone Joint Surg*, 53A:781-782, 1971.

31 Banks SW. Aseptic Necrosis of the Femoral Head Following Traumatic Dislocation of the Hip. *J Bone Joint Surg*, 23:753-781, 1941. Duncan CP, Shim SS. Blood Supply of the Head of the Femur in Traumatic hip Dislocation. *Surg Gynecol Obstet*, 144:185-191, 1977. Phemister DB. Fractures of Neck of Femur, Dislocations of Hip, and Obscure Vascular Disturbances Producing Aseptic Necrosis of Head of Femur. *Surg Gyneco Obstet*, 59:415-440, 1934. Potts FN, Obletz BE. Aseptic Necrosis of Head of Femur Following Traumatic Dislocation. *J Bone Joint Surg*, 21:101-110, 1939. Stewart MJ. Aseptic Necrosis of the Head of the Femur Following Traumatic Dislocation of the Hip Joint: Case Report and Experimental Studies. *J Bone Joint Surg*, 15:413-438, 1933.

Posterior dislocations are most common and are either seen in isolation or accompanied with fractures of the posterior rim or wall of the acetabulum or of the femoral head.[32] When there is a fracture of the femoral head, the injury is further subclassified by the Pipkin method.[33] This has important ramifications for treatment and eventual outcome of the patient.

11.2.3.3.1 Anterior Dislocations of the Hip: About 15% of traumatic dislocations of the hip are anterior.[34] The mechanism of injury is when the knee strikes the dashboard of a car with the hip abducted and externally rotated or in a fall from a height. The dislocation is inferior if the hip is flexed and superior if the hip is extended.[35]

The diagnosis of an anterior hip dislocation is usually evident. The patient is in obvious severe discomfort and the leg is externally rotated and abducted (frog leg position). Before proceeding to the radiographic investigations, the patient must be assessed for other injuries and the status of the femoral nerve and artery must be ascertained. Only the superoanterior dislocations and open anterior dislocations have been known to cause injuries to the femoral nerve and artery.[36] The diagnosis is confirmed with routine radiographs. Post-reduction CT scans of dislocated hips are very important since they allow detection of small fragments of bone, which may become interposed between the acetabulum and the femoral head after reduction.[37]

The treatment of choice is early diagnosis and prompt closed reduction under a general anesthetic. It is not recommended to attempt more

---

32 Epstein HC. Posterior Fracture Dislocations of the Hip. *J Bone Joint Surg*, 43A:1079-1098, 1961.

33 Pipkin G. Treatment of Grade IV Fracture Dislocation of the Hip. *J Bone Joint Surg*, 39:1027-1042, 1957.

34 Epstein HC, Harvey JP. Traumatic Anterior Dislocations of the Hip. Management and Results. An Analysis of Fifty Five cases. *J Bone Joint Surg*, 54A:1561-1562, 1972. Scham SM, Fry LR. Traumatic Anterior Dislocation of the Hip with Fracture of the Femoral Head. *Clin Orthop*, 62:133-135, 1969.

35 Pringle JH. Traumatic Dislocation of the Hip Joint. An Experimental Study on the Cadaver. *Glasgow Med J*, 21:25-40, 1943.

36 Bonnemaison MFE, Henderson ED. Traumatic Anterior Dislocation of the Hip with Acute Common Femoral Occlusion in a Child. *J Bone Joint Surg*, 50A:753-756, 1968. Hampson WGJ. Venous Obstruction by Anterior Dislocation of the Hip Joint. *Injury*, 4:69-73, 1972. Nerubay J. Traumatic Anterior Dislocation of the Hip Joint with Vascular Damage. *Clin Orthop*, 116:129-132,1976. Niloff P, Petrie JG. Traumatic Anterior Dislocation of the Hip. *Can Med Assoc J*, 62:574-576, 1950. Schwartz DL, Haller JA. Open Anterior Hip Dislocation with Femoral Vessel Transection in a Child. *J Trauma*, 14:1054-1059, 1974.

37 Baird RA, Schobert WE, Pais MJ. Radiographic Identification of Loose Bodies in the Traumatized Hip Joint. *Radiology*, 145:661-665, 1982.

than two or three closed reduction before resorting to an open reduction.[38] Another indication for open reduction is the presence of bone debris in the joint or instability of the hip after the reduction is completed. After the reduction controlled range of motion and traction is recommended for 1 to 6 weeks.

The prognosis of anterior hip dislocations is guarded even in the absence of neurovascular compromise. Long-term studies have shown that even though many patients do well initially the incidence of post-traumatic arthritis is 30 to 50%.[39] Degenerative arthritis is especially a problem when there has been an impression fracture of the femoral head.[40] Aseptic necrosis of the femoral head occurs in 8% of anterior dislocations[41] and can appear up to 5 years after the dislocation.[42] The extent of the original injury is the most important determining factor in the occurrence of avascular necrosis followed by delay in reduction or repeated attempts at closed reduction.[43] Recurrent dislocations have been reported but are rare.[44]

11.2.3.3.2 Posterior Dislocations of the Hip: Posterior dislocations of the hip are the result of a high speed injury with the knee colliding, usually with the dash of a car, when the hip is flexed and adducted.[45] It is sometimes called the dashboard dislocation.[46]

Clinically the diagnosis is made when the patient complains of severe pain in the hip and has a short, flexed and internally rotated leg. Associated musculoskeletal injuries are frequent and include the following:

---

38 DeLee JC, Evans JA, Thomas J. Anterior Dislocation of the Hip and Associated Femoral Head Fractures. *J Bone Joint Surg*, 62A:960-964, 1980. Hougaard K, Thomsen PB. Coxarthrosis Following Traumatic Posterior Dislocation of the Hip. *J Bone Joint Surg*, 69A:679-683, 1987.

39 Epstein et al., *supra*, note 34. Delee et al., *ibid*. Epstein HC, Harvey JP. Traumatic Anterior Dislocations of the Hip. *Orthop Rev*, 1:33-38, 1972.

40 DeLee et al., *supra*, note 38. Funsten RV, Kinser P, Frankel CJ. Dashboard Dislocation of the Hip. *J Bone Joint Surg*, 20:124-132, 1938.

41 Brav EA. Traumatic Dislocation of the Hip. *J Bone Joint Surg*, 44A:1115-1134, 1962. Epstein HC. Traumatic Dislocation of the Hip. *Clin Orthop*, 92:116-142, 1973.

42 Nicoll EA. Proceedings and Reports of Councils and Associations: Traumatic Dislocation of the Hip Joint. *J Bone Joint Surg*, 34B:503-505, 1952.

43 Banks, *supra*, note 31. Epstein HC. *Traumatic Dislocation of the Hip*. Baltimore: Williams and Wilkins, 1980. Morton KS. Traumatic Dislocation of the Hip: A Follow up Study. *Can J Surg*, 3:67-74,1959.

44 Schwartz et al., *supra*, note 36. Dall D, MacNab E, Gross A. Recurrent Anterior Dislocation of the Hip. *J Bone Joint Surg*, 52A:574-576, 1970.

45 Reigstad A. Traumatic Dislocation of the Hip. *J Trauma*, 20:603-606, 1980.

46 Funsten et al., *supra*, note 40.

- Sciatic nerve injury in 10 to 14% of cases[47]
- Ligament injury to the ipsilateral knee[48]
- Femoral head fractures[49]
- Femoral shaft fractures[50]

Radiographs and CT scans are made to confirm the direction of the dislocation as well as to scrutinize the acetabulum and femoral head for fractures. Post-reduction radiographs are necessary. If there is persistent widening of the joint one must suspect that a fragment of bone or soft tissue is interposed in the joint and open reduction is then mandated.[51]

The treatment of posterior dislocations of the hip is controversial. Two different approaches can be used. Many advocate performing a closed reduction under general anesthetic and performing an open reduction only if the closed reduction is not successful or if the hip is unstable after reduction or if there are bone fragments trapped in the joint after reduction. Others recommend a primary open reduction, debridement of the joint and fixation of the fractures.[52] Most authors agree that whatever method is utilized it must be done as soon as possible after the injury, to optimize the patient's recovery.

The prognosis of posterior fracture dislocations of the hip is directly related to the occurrence of a number of complications. *Sciatic nerve palsy* can occur in 8 to 19% of cases.[53] The injury is usually a direct contusion

---

47   Epstein, *supra*, note 43. Hunter GA. Posterior Dislocation and Fracture Dislocation of the Hip: A Long term Follow up Study. *Clin Orthop*, 214:249-262, 1987. Stewart MJ, Milford LW. Fracture Dislocation of the Hip. *J Bone Joint Surg*, 36A:315-342, 1954. Thompson VP, Epstein HC. Traumatic Dislocation of the Hip. *J Bone Joint Surg*, 33A:746-778,1951.

48   Hunter, *ibid*. Gillespie WJ. The Incidence and Pattern of Knee Injury Associated with Dislocation of the Hip. *J Bone Joint Surg*, 57B:376-378, 1975.

49   Pipkin, *supra*, note 33. Butler JE. Pipkin Type II Fractures of the Femoral Head. *J Bone Joint Surg*, 63A:1292-1296, 1981. Kelly RP, Yarbrough SH. Posterior Fracture Dislocation of the Femoral Head with Retained Medial Head Fragment. *J Trauma*, 11:97-108, 1971. Roeder LF, DeLee JC. Femoral Head Fractures Associated with Posterior Hip Dislocations. *Clin Orthop*, 147:121-130, 1980.

50   Ehtisham SMA. Traumatic Dislocation of the Hip Joint with Fracture of Shaft of Femur on the Same Side. *J Trauma*, 16:196-205, 1976. Fina CP, Kelly PJ. Dislocations of the Hip with Fractures of the Proximal Femur. *J Trauma*, 10:77-87,1970. Stewart MJ. Management of Fractures of the Head of the Femur Complicated by Dislocation of the Hip. *Orthop Clin North Am*, 5:793-798, 1974.

51   Epstein HC, Wiss DA, Cozen L. Posterior Fracture Dislocation of the Hip with Fractures of the Femoral Head. *Clin Orthop*, 201:9-17, 1985.

52   Epstein et al., *ibid*. Epstein, *supra*, notes 32 and 41.

53   Stewart MJ, McCarroll HR, Mulhollan JS. Fracture Dislocation of the Hip. *Acta Orthop Scand*, 46:507-525, 1975.

of the nerve and rarely a laceration. The presence of a nerve deficit makes a posterior dislocation an acute surgical emergency so that the sciatic nerve can be decompressed. The peroneal branch of the sciatic nerve is most frequently affected resulting in a foot drop. The patient must be fitted early with the appropriate brace and passive dorsiflexion of the ankle is started early. Functional recovery of the nerve occurs in 60 to 70% of cases.[54] *Knee injury* occurs in one third of patients with posterior dislocations. Some patients have fractures of the patella, femur or tibia or have a more occult contusion of the hyaline cartilage of the patella. Other patients have injuries to the posterior cruciate ligament and the posterolateral ligaments. The diagnosis is sometimes delayed by many months because the patients are not weight bearing on the limb. *Recurrent posterior dislocations* are rare and occur in 0.3 to 1.2% of cases. The occurrence of this complication has multiple factors including inadequate immobilization, neurovascular insufficiency and malunion of acetabular fractures.[55] *Myositis ossificans* is reported to occur in 2% of posterior dislocations[56] and is related to the degree of initial injury. *Avascular necrosis* can occur in 6 to 40% of posterior dislocations.[57] Delay in the reduction of the hip influences the incidence of this complication. Hougaard found that reductions done within 6 hours of the injury decreased the incidence of AVN whereas Brav found that the AVN rate was affected only if the hip was dislocated for more than 12 hours.[58] The *post-traumatic arthritis* rate is difficult to establish because of the overlap between avascular necrosis and pure arthritis. The incidence is reported to be 17 to 71%. The severity of the initial trauma is the most determinant factor in the occurrence of arthritis followed by delay in diagnosis and treatment.[59] Epstein recommends a primary open reduction of posterior dislocations since he found that the incidence of post-traumatic arthritis was only 17% with surgical reductions.[60]

---

54 Epstein, *supra*, note 43. Hunter, *supra*, note 47. Stewart et al., *supra*, note 47.
55 Lutter LD. Post-traumatic Hip Redislocation. *J Bone Joint Surg*, 55A:391-394, 1973. Townsend RG, Edwards GE, Bazant FJ. Post-Traumatic Recurrent Dislocation of the Hip without Fracture. *J Bone Joint Surg*, 51B:194, 1969.
56 Epstein, *supra*, note 41.
57 Epstein, *supra*, note 43. Upadhyay SS, Moulton A. The Long Term Results of Traumatic Posterior Dislocation of the Hip. *J Bone Joint Surg*, 63B:548-551, 1981.
58 Hougaard et al., *supra*, note 38. Brav, *supra*, note 41.
59 Brav, *supra*, note 41. Morton, *supra*, note 43. Upadhyay et al., *supra*, note 57.
60 Epstein, *supra*, note 43.

11.2.3.4 Fractures of the Femoral Neck

Fractures of the femoral neck are uncommon in patients with normal bone. It is a fracture associated with osteoporosis or osteomalacia.[61] The rate of these fractures is highest in white females followed by white males, black females, and black males.[62]

For most fractures of the femoral neck, the traumatic event is trivial, involving an external rotation of the hip torquing the femoral neck or a direct fall on the greater trochanter. A fracture in the younger patient involves a more severe impact on the femur, which is transmitted to the femoral neck.[63]

The majority of femoral neck fractures are subcapital at the junction of the femoral head and neck. The Garden classification is frequently used, and it is based on the amount of displacement of the fracture.[64] A Garden I fracture is incomplete or impacted. A Garden II fracture is complete but undisplaced. A Garden III fracture is displaced but there is still contact between the femoral neck and head. A Garden IV fracture is completely displaced with dissociation of the head from the neck. The reproducibility of this classification has been found to differ from one observer to the next.[65] However, the classification is useful to determine the treatment, union rate, and the incidence of avascular necrosis. In cases of impacted fractures or stress fractures a bone scan or an MRI will help in making the diagnosis when a fracture is suspected but not seen on plain x-rays.

Patients with an undisplaced fracture will have pain in the groin radiating to the medial thigh and knee. They may be able to walk with a limp and have normal alignment of the hip. Patients with a displaced fracture will have diffuse pain of the hip, will not be able to bear weight on the leg and will have a shortened, externally rotated leg.

The age and function of the patient and the amount of displacement of the femoral neck will determine the treatment of subcapital fractures of the

---

61   Charnley RM, Bickerstaff DR, Wallace WA, Stevens A. The Measurement of Osteoporosis in Clinical Practice. *J Bone Joint Surg*, 71B:661-663, 1989. Hofeldt F. Proximal Femoral Fractures. *Clin Orthop*, 218:12-18, 1987.
62   Hinton RY, Smith GS. The Association of Age, Race and Sex with The Location of Proximal Femoral Fractures in the Elderly. *J Bone Joint Surg*, 75:752-759, 1993.
63   Protzman RR, Burkhalter WE. Femoral Neck Fractures in Young Adults. *J Bone Joint Surg*, 58A:689-695, 1976.
64   Garden RS. Malreduction and Avascular Necrosis in Subcapital Fractures of the Femur. *J Bone Joint Surg*, 53B:183-197, 1971. Garden RS. The Structure and Function of the Proximal End of the Femur. *J Bone Joint Surg*, 43B:576-589, 1961.
65   Frandsen PA, Andersen PE, Madsen F Skjodt T. Garden's Classification of Femoral Neck Fractures. *J Bone Joint Surg*, 70B:588-590, 1988.

hip. Unless there are severe medical contraindications for surgery, all fractures of the femoral neck are treated with surgical fixation or hip replacement. For the undisplaced and/or impacted fracture, the goal of treatment is to fix the fracture fragments surgically before any displacement can occur. This is done by inserting three to four screws up the femoral neck and into the femoral head. This compresses and stabilizes the fracture. Even impacted fractures have been found to displace if treated conservatively.[66] Patients treated surgically have a higher healing rate, no difference in the avascular necrosis rate and earlier return to maximal functional status.[67]

Displaced fractures of the femoral neck (Garden III and IV) are treated surgically because of an unacceptably high rate of nonunion and deformity when treated in traction or in a cast.[68] Only severe associated medical conditions in non-ambulatory patients with impaired mentation will occasionally steer the treatment towards a nonoperative approach (so called "skillful neglect" of the fracture). For most previously healthy patients the treatment will consist of a closed reduction under a general or spinal anesthetic followed by internal fixation of the fracture. If an acceptable position of the fracture is not obtained by closed manipulation then the hip joint must be opened; the fracture reduced open and then internally fixed. Banks demonstrated that the union rate of the fracture and the rate of avascular necrosis is better with an anatomic open reduction than a suboptimal closed reduction.[69] Open reduction of a displaced femoral neck fracture is one of the most difficult operations done about the hip because of the limited access to the femoral neck and the inherent instability of the fracture. Because of this, the procedure is limited to young (variable definition) patients where preserving their original femoral head is paramount.[70] Patients over the age of 65 with a displaced femoral neck fracture are considered candidates for hemiarthroplasty surgery instead of an open reduction. The long-term results of femoral head replacement surgery in this group of patients are excellent, the patient can weight bear almost im-

---

66 Pankovich, *supra*, note 27. Fielding JW, Displaced Femoral Neck Fractures. *Orthop Rev*, 2:11-17,1973. Raaymakers EL, Marti RK. Non-operative Treatment of Impacted Femoral Neck Fracture; Prospective Study of 170 Cases. *J Bone Joint Surg*, 73B:950-954, 1991.

67 Bentley G. Treatment of Nondisplaced Fractures of the Femoral Neck. *Clin Orthop*, 152:93-101, 1980.

68 Fielding JW, Wilson HJ, Zickel RE. A Continuing End Result Study of Intra-capsular Fracture of the Neck of the Femur. *J Bone Joint Surg*, 44A:965-974, 1962.

69 Banks HH. Factors Influencing the Result in Fractures of the Femoral Neck. *J Bone Joint Surg*, 44A:931-964, 1962.

70 Keller CS, Laros GS: Indications for Open Reduction of Femoral Neck Fractures. *Clin Orthop*, 152:131-137, 1980. Lowell JD. Results and Complications of Femoral Neck Fractures. *Clin Orthop*, 152:162-172, 1980.

mediately after surgery and the risk of nonunion or avascular necrosis which would necessitate a second surgical procedure is eliminated.[71]

11.2.3.4.1 Outcome of Femoral Neck Fractures: Mortality: The mortality rate in the first post-fracture year is reported to be between 14% and 36% and is about 20% in the first 6 months after the fracture irrespective of the treatment given.[72] Age and impaired mental status at the time of the fracture have been associated with a higher mortality rate.[73] Patients with at least four pre-existing medical conditions or with end stage renal disease are at higher risk for dying.[74]

Functional recovery: restoration of ambulation, self-care and independence is the goal of treatment of femoral neck fractures. Unfortunately up to 60% of patients will require institutionalization after having a hip fracture.[75] The best predictors to independent function in society are pre-fracture activity level, mental status, and absence of medical conditions, which can impair rehabilitation.[76]

Thromboembolic disease: Reported to occur in 40% of patients with fractures of the proximal femur.[77] It is now recommended to give some

---

71 Eftekhar NS. Status of Femoral Head Replacement in Treating Fracture of Femoral Neck. Hemiarthroplasty vs Total Arthroplasty. *Orthop Rev*, 2:15-23, 1973. Gingras MB, Clarke J, Evarts CM. Prosthetic Replacement in Femoral Neck Fractures. *Clin Orthop*, 152:147-157, 1980. Moore AT, Bohlman HR. Metal Hip Joint: A Case Report. *J Bone Joint Surg*, 25:688-692, 1943. Thompson FR. Two and a Half Years' Experience with a Vitallium Intramedullary Hip Prosthesis. *J Bone Joint Surg*, 36A:489-500, 1954.
72 Kenzora JE, McArthy RE, Lowell JD, Sledge CB. Hip Fracture Mortality: Relation to Age, Treatment, Preoperative Illness, Time of Surgery, and Complications. *Clin Orthop*, 186:45-56, 1984. Koval KJ, Zuckerman JD. Functional Recovery after Hip Fracture. *J Bone Joint Surg*, 77:751-758, 1994.
73 Kenzora et al. and Koval et al., *ibid.*
74 Kenzora, *supra*, note 72. Tierney CS, Goulet JA, Greenfield ML, Port FK. Mortality after Fracture of the Hip in Patients who have End Stage Renal Disease. *J Bone Joint Surg*, 76A:709-712,1994.
75 Cumming RG, Klineberg R, Katelaris A. Cohort Study of Risk of Institutionalisation after Hip Fracture. *Aust N Z J Public Health*, 20(6):579-582, 1996. Fitzgerald JF, Dittus RS. Institutionalized Patients with Hip Fractures. *J Gen Intern Med*, 5:298-303, 1990.
76 Svensson O, Stromberg L, Ohlen G, Lindgren U. Prediction of the Outcome after Hip Fracture in Elderly Patients. *J Bone Joint Surg*, 78B:115-118, 1996.
77 Culver D, Crawford JS, Gardiner JH, Wiley AM. Venous Thrombosis after Fractures of the Upper End of the Femur. *J Bone Joint Surg*, 52B:61-69, 1970. Moskovitz PA, Ellenberg SS, Feffer HL, et al. Low Dose Heparin for Prevention of Venous Thromboembolism in Total Hip Arthroplasty and Surgical Repair of Hip Fractures. *J Bone Joint Surg*, 60A:1065-1070, 1978. Snook GA, Chrisman OD, Wilson TC. Thromboembolism after Surgical Treatment of Hip Fractures, *Clin Orthop*, 155:21-24, 1981.

form of prophylactic anticoagulation regimen to patients with such fractures; either adjusted dose heparin or warfarin or low molecular weight heparin.[78]

Nonunion: Nonunion is rare for undisplaced femoral neck fractures treated surgically. Displaced femoral neck fractures have a healing rate of 85 to 95% in most recent studies.[79] Union is achieved within 6 to 12 months. Multiple factors influence the healing rate. The most notable ones are the degree of initial displacement, the amount of comminution of the neck and the quality of reduction and fixation of the fracture.[80]

Aseptic necrosis of the femoral head: This complication affects the long-term outcome when it leads to late segmental collapse of the femoral head. This occurs in 10 to 20% of undisplaced fractures and 15 to 35% of displaced fractures.[81]

Complications of hemiarthroplasty: The dislocation rate is less than 1%.[82] Infection is in the 1 to 2% range, which is significantly higher than the infection rate for similar procedures performed electively. This is probably a reflection of the patient coming into hospital urgently, dehydrated and sometimes malnourished. Pain is the most common problem after a hemiarthroplasty and can be caused by wear of the acetabular cartilage, loosening of the femoral stem or infection.[83] The incidence of pain is lower when a bipolar prosthesis is used or a total hip arthroplasty is done but these procedures also tend to have higher complication rates and prosthetic costs are higher.

---

78 Turpie AGG, Levin MN, Hirsh J, et al. A Randomized Controlled Trial of Low-Molecular Weight Heparin (Enoxiparin) to Prevent Deep Vein Thrombosis in Patients Undergoing Elective Hip Surgery. *N Eng J Med*, 315:925-928, 1986.
79 Asnis SN, Wanek-Sgaglione L. Intracapsular Fractures of the Femoral Neck. Results of Cannulated Screw Fixation. *J Bone Joint Surg*, 76A:1793-1803, 1994.
80 Barnes R, Brown JT, Garden RS, Nicoll EA. Subcapital Fractures of the Femur. *J Bone Joint Surg*, 58B:2-24, 1976. Compton EH. Accuracy of Reduction of Femoral Subcapital Fractures. *Injury*, 9:71-73, 1977. Fielding JW, Cochran GVB, Zickel RE. Biomechanical Characteristics and Surgical Management of Subtrochanteric Fractures. *Orthop Clin North Am*, 5:629-649, 1974.
81 Garden, *supra*, note 64. Asnis et al., *supra*, note 79. Barnes et al., *supra*, note 80. Fielding et al., *supra*, note 80.
82 Hinchey JJ, Day PL. Primary Prosthetic Replacement in Fresh Femoral Neck Fractures. *J Bone Joint Surg*, 46A:223-240, 1964.
83 D'Arcy J, Devas M. Treatment of Fractures of the Femoral Neck by Replacement with the Thompson Prosthesis. *J Bone Joint Surg*, 58B:279-286, 1976.

11.2.3.5 Intertrochanteric Fractures of the Hip

Intertrochanteric fractures are fractures located in the proximal femur at the line between the greater and lesser trochanter [Figure 11.13]. This fracture is outside the capsule of the hip joint and involves cancellous bone, which has excellent blood supply and usually heals uneventfully. Half of all the fractures of the proximal femur are located in this region.[84]

The mechanism of injury is almost always a fall. The patient presents with pain in the hip region, an inability to bear weight and a shortened externally rotated leg. Plain radiographs are sufficient to identify the fracture and plan the treatment.

The treatment of this fracture is surgical reduction and fixation [Figure 11.14]. Some studies suggest that the mortality rate increases if the surgery is delayed by more than 48 hours for non-medical reasons.[85] The fixation of undisplaced fractures allows for rapid mobilization and weight bearing on the leg in addition to alleviating pain from the fracture. Displaced, unstable fractures must first be reduced and then internally fixed. Mobilization and weight bearing will depend on the quality of the bone, the accuracy of the reduction, and the pre-fracture condition of the patient. The most frequent method of fixation is with a sliding hip screw and side plate or with intramedullary devices.[86]

11.2.3.5.1 Outcome: Mortality: There is a 10 to 30% mortality rate for the first year after fracture followed by a return to the age adjusted rate.[87] The mortality rate is the same as that for femoral neck fractures after age adjustments are made. The incidence of infection and thromboembolic disease is also the same as for femoral neck fractures.

Fracture malunion: Malunion occurs when the proximal femur heals in varus and is caused by failure of the implant or failure to obtain stable fixation because of osteoporotic bone or fracture comminution.[88] Varus dis-

---

84 Koval et al., Hip Fractures; II . . . *supra*, note 25.
85 McNeill DH. Hip Fractures: Influence of Delay in Surgery on Mortality. *Wis Med J*, 74:129-130, 1975.
86 Koval et al., Hip Fractures: II . . . *supra*, note 25. Hunter GA. The Results of Operative Treatment of Trochanteric Fractures of the Femur. *Injury*, 6:202-205, 1975. Katsamouris AN, Steriopoulos K, Katonis P, Christou K, Drositis J, Lefaki T, Vassilakis S, Dretakis E. Limb Arterial Injuries Associated with Limb Fractures. Clinical Presentation, Assessment and Management. *European J Vascular Endovascular Surg*, 9(1): 64-70, 1995.
87 Kyle RF, Gustilo RB, Premer RF. Analysis of Six Hundred and Twenty Two Intertrochanteric Hip Fractures. *J Bone Joint Surg*, 61A:216-221, 1979.
88 Dimon JH. The Unstable Intertrochanteric Fracture. *Clin Orthop*, 92:100-107, 1973. Wolfgang GL, Bryant MH, O'Neill JP. Treatment of Intertrochanteric Fracture of the Femur Using Sliding Screw Plate Fixation. *Clin Orthop*, 163:148-158, 1982.

placement is not associated with pain, hip weakness and a short leg unless it is less than 120 degrees (135 degrees being normal).[89]

Nonunion: The incidence of nonunion is 1 to 2%. Most of the nonunion occur in unstable comminuted fractures. Other fractures in the intertrochanteric region heal well because of good blood supply and the presence of cancellous bone.[90]

Aseptic necrosis: The incidence of this complication is 0.8% because of the extracapsular nature of this injury.[91]

11.2.3.6 Subtrochanteric Fractures of the Hip

Subtrochanteric fractures are fractures that occur from the lesser trochanter to a point down the femoral shaft that is 5 cm distal to the trochanter [Figure 11.15]. These fractures are treated separately from intertrochanteric fractures or shaft fractures because the mechanical forces acting on this part of the femur are different as is the healing and method of treatment. Subtrochanteric fractures are notorious for having a low rate of union and a high rate of malunion. The slow union of this part of the femur is due to the cortical nature of the bone and to the frequent comminution of this fracture. The frequent malunions are caused by failure of the internal fixation devices, which are subject to severe loading for prolonged periods.[92]

The Seinsheimer classification is frequently quoted and accurately predicts the fracture patterns that will lead to complications.[93] Although many authors describe the treatment of subtrochanteric fractures with traction, this often leads to malunion and delayed union. The extended hospitalization, prolonged bed rest and potential for knee stiffness also does not favour this method of treatment. Most subtrochanteric fractures are treated surgically with an open reduction of the fracture and internal fixation. Two types of fixation devices are used. Either a plate on the lateral side of the femur with a blade or a sliding screw or an intramedullary nail. If the frac-

---

89 Taylor GM, Neufeld AJ, Nickel VL. Complications and Failures in the Operative Treatment of Intertrochanteric Fractures of the Femur. *J Bone Joint Surg*, 37A:306-316, 1955.

90 Mariani EM, Rand JA. Subcapital Fractures after Open Reduction and Internal Fixation of Intertrochanteric Fractures of the Hip. *Clin Orthop*, 245:165-168, 1989. Wilson HJ, Rubin BD, Helbig FEJ, Fielding JW, Unis GL. Treatment of Intertrochanteric Fractures with Jewett Nail: Experience with 1,015 Cases. *Clin Orthop*, 148:186-191, 1980.

91 Kyle et al., *supra*, note 87.

92 Fielding et al., *supra*, note 80. Hanson GW, Tullos HS. Subtrochanteric Fractures of Femur Treated with Nail-Plate Devices: A Retrospective Study. *Clin Orthop*, 131:191-194, 1978.

93 Seinsheimer F. Subtrochanteric Fractures of the Femur. *J Bone Joint Surg*, 60A:300-306, 1978.

ture is amenable to being fixed by an intramedullary device then its use has the theoretical advantage of decreasing the load stresses on the implant and implant failure becomes less likely.[94] The rate of nonunion with modern implants is less than 5%.[95] Nail-plate devices have a failure rate of 17%.[96]

11.2.4 Fractures of the Femoral Shaft

The femur is the largest, longest and strongest bone in the body and it has a thick covering of soft tissues. To fracture the femur in its mid-portion requires a violent force such as those seen in motor vehicle accidents, pedestrians struck by vehicles, motorcycle accidents, falls from a height or gunshot wounds. A fracture of the femoral shaft is a life-threatening injury because of the frequency of other associated injuries and of complications such as fat embolism, adult respiratory distress syndrome, thromboembolism, septicemia from open wounds or severe blood loss.

11.2.4.1 Classification

There are many ways to classify femoral shaft fractures. The most important for patient survival is whether the fracture is an isolated injury or is part of multiple other injuries. In the latter case, the Injury Severity Scale (ISS) is a commonly used scale to objectively grade the degree of injury of the patient. The median lethal score for patients 15 to 44 years of age is 40, and drops to 29 for patients 45 to 64 years of age and to 20 for patients over the age of 65.[97] Femoral shaft fractures are also classified as open versus closed, simple versus complex (comminuted or segmental) and finally for the purpose of surgical fixation they are classified as to their location in the femur (proximal, middle or distal third) [Figure 11.16]. The comminution of the fracture affects the fixation method and

---

94 Tencer AF, Johnson KD, Johnston DWC, Gil K. A Biomechanical Comparison of Various Methods of Stabilization and Subtrochanteric Fractures at the Femur. *J Orthop Res*, 2:297-305, 1984.

95 Bergman GD, Winquist RA, Mayo KA, Hanson SE. Subtrochanteric Fracture of the Femur: Fixation Using the Zickel Nail. *J Bone Joint Surg*, 69A:1032-1040, 1987.

96 Villar RN, Thomas G. Subtrochanteric Fractures: Zickel Nail or Nail Plate? *J Bone Joint Surg*, 68B:255-259, 1986.

97 Baker S, O'Neill B, Haddon W, Long W. The Injury Severity Score: A Method for Describing Patients With Multiple Injuries and Evaluating Emergency Care. *J Trauma*, 14:187-196, 1974. Copes W, Champion H, Sacco W, et al. The Injury Severity Score Revisited. *J Trauma*, 28:69-77, 1988. Greenspan L, McLellan B, Griag H. Abbreviated Injury Scale and Injury Severity Score: A Scoring Chart. *J Trauma*, 25:60-64, 1985.

the union rates. The Winquist classification is widely used: Type I is minimal or no comminution, type II has at least 50% of the circumference of the major fracture intact, type III has 50 to 100% of the fracture cortices that are comminuted and type IV where there is complete loss of cortical contact.[98]

11.2.4.2 Diagnosis

Diagnosis of a femoral shaft fracture is not difficult since there is marked pain and swelling of the thigh, a visible deformity and inability to bear weight. Careful examination must also include examination of the pelvic ring, the hip and knee on the same side. Injury to the ligaments of the knee is common with fractures of the femur.[99] Examination of the knee must often be delayed until the femur is stabilized. Completion of the workup involves radiographs and generally a simple anteroposterior and lateral radiograph of the femur are sufficient information to initiate treatment as long as the radiographs are of good quality and include the hip and knee.

11.2.4.3 Treatment

The treatment of femoral shaft fractures has changed dramatically in the last half century. Five hundred years ago, skin traction was used to maintain alignment of the thigh. The main disadvantage was that there is strong muscular attachment to the femur and the pull of these muscles accentuated the shortening and deformity of the fracture. It is not feasible to apply sufficient forces on the skin for prolonged periods of time to counteract the muscles of the thigh. Skin traction has now been relegated to be used only as a temporary measure until definitive stabilization is performed. Skeletal traction with a pin in the tibia or distal femur can be used effectively to align a fractured femur and was used routinely until 1970. There are several problems with this type of treatment. Firstly, it takes 3 to 6 months to heal a femur fracture and therefore the hospital stay is very

---

98 Winquist RA, Hansen ST Jr. Comminuted Fractures of the Femoral Shaft Treated by Intramedullary Nailing. *Orthop Clin North Am*, 11:633-647,1980.

99 Moore TM, Patzakis MJ, Harvey JP Jr. Ipsilateral Diaphyseal Femur Fractures and Knee Ligament Injuries. *Clin Orthop*, 232:182-189, 1988. Pederson H, Serra J. Injury to the Collateral Ligaments of the Knee Associated with Femoral Shaft Fractures, *Clin Orthop*, 60:119-121, 1968. Shelton ML, Neer CSII, Grantham SA. Occult Knee Ligament Ruptures Associated With Fractures. *J Trauma*, 11:853-856, 1971. Vanganess C, DeCampos J, Merritt P, Wiss D. Meniscal Injury Associated with Femoral Shaft Fractures. An Arthroscopic Evaluation of Incidence. *J Bone Joint Surg*, 75:207-209, 1993.

long and expensive, in addition to the time lost to family and work. Maintaining proper alignment with traction is time consuming and requires daily adjustments. The union rate with skeletal traction is reported to be around 97%[100] but has been as low as 70%.[101] Shortening of the fracture by up to 3 cm is common.[102] Knee stiffness is common after prolonged traction and never returns to normal.[103] Because of these complications, traction as a method for definitive treatment of femoral shaft fractures has been replaced by operative internal fixation methods.

The femur is ideally suited for intramedullary fixation devices [Figure 11.17]. The femur is a straight tubular bone. Fixation methods within the endosteal canal are closer to the axis of motion of the body and therefore provide more stable fixation while sharing the load with the remainder of the femur. Another advantage of intramedullary nailing is that it can often be done without exposing the fracture. This minimizes damage to the surrounding muscles, to the periosteum and does not disturb the early stages of fracture healing. The overall advantages of intramedullary nailing are that skeletal anatomy is predictably restored and maintained until fracture healing, that the healing rate is faster and higher than other methods and that early functional return is possible. Most patients are mobilized out of bed within 24 hours of the surgery and discharged home within a few days. The disadvantages of intramedullary rod fixation is that it requires specialized surgical and radiological equipment to perform and that some complex fractures in the past were not amenable to rodding. With modern intramedullary devices, increased experience by surgeons and the possibility of locking nails proximal and distal to the fracture most of the femoral shaft fractures can be treated with this method of fixation. Union rates of 97 to 100% are reported for intramedullary rodding of the femur.[104]

Many studies have demonstrated that early stabilization of long bone

---

100 Buxton RA. The Use of Perkins' Traction in the Treatment of Femoral Shaft Fractures. *J Bone Joint Surg*, 63B:362-366, 1981.
101 Carr CR, Wingo CH. Fractures of the Femoral Diaphysis. A Retrospective Study of the Results and Costs of Treatment by Intramedullary Nailing and by Traction in a Spica Cast. *J Bone Joint Surg*, 55A:690-700, 1973. Obletz BE. Vertical Traction in the Early Management of Certain Compound Fractures of the Femur. *J Bone Joint Surg*, 28:113-116, 1946.
102 Dencker H. Shaft Fractures of the Femur. A Comparative Study of the Results of Various Methods of Treatment in 1,003 Cases. *Acta Orthop Scand*, 130:173-184, 1965.
103 Buxton, *supra*, note 100. Dencker, *ibid*. Winant EM. The Use of Skeletal Traction in the Treatment of Fractures of the Femur. *J Bone Joint Surg*, 31A:87-93, 1949.
104 Winquist et al., *supra*, note 98. Alho A, Stromsoe K, Ekeland A. Locked Intramedullary Nailing of Femoral Shaft Fractures. *J Trauma*, 31:49-59, 1991. Christie J, Court-Brown C, Kinninmonth AW, Howie C. Intramedullary

fractures in the multiply injured patients increase their survival, decrease pulmonary complications and their length of stay in the intensive care unit and in hospital.[105] Intramedullary fixation of the femur has made feasible early stabilization of the femur even in open fractures. Immediate nailing of Gustilo grade I and II fractures have been safely done.[106] For grade III fractures many can still be fixed immediately but the surgeon needs to assess the degree of contamination, the loss of other tissues surrounding the femur and also the overall condition of the patient.

In cases of massive contamination of the femur fracture then external fixation may be advisable. It is not used often to stabilize a femur because there is a thick envelope of muscle and subcutaneous tissue that must be passed through with the transfixing pins, the stabilization is not strong and it often leads to delayed union of the fracture. The other option in severe open fractures of the femur is to do a major wound debridement, place the patient in skeletal traction for 7 to 10 days and then rod the femur.[107] Plate and screw fixation has been utilized historically but does not provide as stable a fixation or as reliable a healing rate than intramedullary fixation.

Locking Nails in the Management of Femoral Shaft Fractures. *J Bone Joint Surg*, 70B:206-210, 1988. King KF, Rush J. Closed Intramedullary Nailing of the Femoral Shaft Fractures. A Review of One Hundred Twelve Cases Treated by the Kuntscher Technique. *J Bone Joint Surg*, 63A:1319-1323, 1981. Klemm KW, Borner M. Interlocking Nailing of Complex Fractures of the Femur and Tibia. *Clin Orthop*, 212:89-100, 1989. Winquist RA, Hansen ST Jr, Clawson DK. Closed Intramedullary Nailing of Femoral Fractures. *J Bone Joint Surg*, 66A:529-539, 1984.

105 Bone LB, Johnson KD, Weigelt J, Scheinber R. Early Versus Delayed Stabilization of Femoral Fractures. A Prospective Randomized Study. *J Bone Joint Surg*, 71A:336-340, 1989. Bone LB, McNamara K, Shine B, Border J. Mortality in Multiple Trauma Patients with Fractures. *J Trauma*, 37 (2):262-4, 1994. Goris RJA, Gimbrere JSF, Van Niekerk JLM, Schoots FJ, Booy LHD. Early Osteosynthesis and Prophylactic Mechanical Ventilation in the Multitrauma Patient. *J Trauma*, 22:895-903, 1982. Johnson KD, Cadambi A, Seibert GB. Incidence of Adult Respiratory Distress Syndrome in Patients with Multiple Musculoskeletal Injuries: Effect of Early Operative Stabilization of Fractures. *J Trauma*, 25:375, 1985. Meek RN, Vivida A, Crichton A, Pirani S. Comparison of Mortality of Patients with Multiple Injuries According to Method of Fracture Treatment. *J Bone Joint Surg*, 63B:456, 1981. Meek RN, Vivoda EE, Pirani S. Comparison of Mortality of Patients with Multiple Injuries According to Type of Fracture Treatment—A Retrospective Age and Injury matched Series. *Injury*, 17:2-4, 1986. Riska EB, Von Bonsdorff H, Hakkinen S, Jaroma H, Kiviluoto O, Paavilainen T. Primary Operative Fixation of Long Bone Fractures in Patients with Multiple Injuries. *J Trauma*, 17:111-121,1977.

106 Winquist et al., *supra*, note 98.

107 Chapman MW. The Role of Intramedullary Fixation in Open Fractures. *Clin Orthop*, 212:26-34, 1986.

11.2.4.4 Prognosis

11.2.4.4.1 Union Rate and Delayed Union: With intramedullary fixation of the femur Winquist showed that 87% of the fractures were healed by 3 months.[108] Cameron showed a mean union time of 20 weeks.[109] There is argument as to the definition of delayed union. The most commonly used figure is that fracture healing should occur by 8 months. The overall incidence of delayed union is 7%.

11.2.4.4.2 Nonunion: The cumulative incidence of nonunion is around 1%.[110]

11.2.4.4.3 Deformities: Less frequent with the advent of operative fixation although they still may occur. Shortening of less than 2 cm has not been shown to be clinically significant as the patients remain with a normal gait. Most studies reported prior to 1980 had 10 to 11% of patients with greater than 2 cm of shortening. There are no recent studies on this topic but in the 1990s there has been much greater use of proximal and distal locking screws with intramedullary nails. This minimizes shortening of the fracture. Nevertheless, any medicolegal assessment for femoral shaft fractures should include a determination of leg lengths. Angular deformities of 10 degrees (varus-valgus) occur in approximately 18 to 20% of patients treated in traction and 6% of patients treated with rods. These deformities, as well as recurvatum deformities, are asymptomatic in the short term but long term may affect the biomechanics of the knee and accelerate degeneration. Rotational deformities are rarely symptomatic unless they exceed 20 degrees however they are a source of concern for patients because their feet are not pointing in the same direction. In the early days of intramedullary nailing, rotational deformities were more common.[111] With modern nails rotation is controlled by proximal and distal locking. One would think that the incidence of rotational malunion would decrease; however a recent report by Braten in 1993 found that 19% of patients had rotational deformities and this number was equal in the locked and unlocked nails.[112]

---

108 Winquist et al., Closed Intramedullary . . ., *supra*, note 104.
109 Cameron CD, Meek RN, Blachut PA, O'Brien PJ, Pate GC. Intramedullary Nailing of the Femoral Shaft: A Prospective Randomized Study. *J Orthop Trauma*, 6:448-451, 1992.
110 Dencker, *supra*, note 102. Carr et al., *supra*, note 101. Winquist, Hansen, Clawson, *supra*, note 104.
111 Rokkanen P, Slatis P, Vankka E. Closed or Open Intramedullary Nailing of Femoral Shaft fractures? A Comparison with Conservatively Treated Cases. *J Bone Joint Surg*, 51B:313-323, 1969.
112 Braten M, Terjesen T, Rossvoli I. Torsional Deformity after Intramedullary Nailing of Femoral Shaft Fractures: Measurement of Anteversion Angles in 110 Patients. *J Bone Joint Surg*, 75B:799-803,1993.

11.2.4.4.4 Knee Range of Motion: Normal knee flexion is approximately 135 to 140 degrees. Normal function of the knee has been shown to require 125 degrees of knee flexion. A minimum range of 93 degrees is required for sitting, 100 degrees for climbing stairs, 106 degrees for tying shoelaces and 117 degrees to bend and pick up an object.[113] Laros and Spiegel studied over 1000 femoral shaft fractures and found that with intramedullary nailing of the fracture, 85% of patients had normal knee function (>120 degrees flexion) and 15% had some impairment of function (91 to 120 degrees of flexion).[114] Similar results were obtained with plating of the fractures. Cast and traction treatment resulted in significantly worse knee function with 45 to 60% of patients with normal function, 25-37% of patients with some impairment of function and 17% with severe impairment of function (<90 degrees flexion).

11.2.4.4.5 Return to Work: The mean time for return to work following a femoral shaft fracture is 9 months with a range of 2 to 24 months depending on the fracture type, the work type, the treatment given.[115] In open or severely comminuted fractures of the femur the mean time to return to work is 14 months. There is not much information in the capacity of patients to return to their previous occupation. It appears that about 1% of patients will not be able to return and 3% had to change jobs because of the injury. Associated injuries markedly reduce the chances of the patient to return to his/her previous occupation.

11.2.5 Injuries about the Knee

11.2.5.1 Fractures of the Distal Femur

Fractures of the distal femur [Figure 11.18] can be grouped into two broad clinical settings, reflecting differences in underlying bone quality and susceptibility to fracture. Patients of normal bone stock who are victims of high-energy trauma can sustain fractures with considerable comminution and intra-articular extension. Patients with diminished bone stock (osteopenic) such as the elderly and paraplegic may also suffer from these fractures from relatively trivial trauma [Figure 11.19]. Several patterns of fractures are observed and generally classified into categories, which reflect the severity of the fracture configuration and act as a general guide to

---

113 Laubenthal RN, Smidt GL, Kettelkamp DB. A Quantitative Analysis of Knee Motion During Daily Living. *Physical Therapy*, 52:32, 1972.
114 Laros GS, Spiegel PG. Femoral Shaft Fractures: Editorial Comment and Comparative Results. *Clin Orthop Rel Res*, 138:5-9, 1979.
115 Cameron et al., *supra*, note 109. Rokkanen et al., *supra*, note 111. Carr et al., *supra*, note 101.

methods of treatment. These categories include extra-articular, intra-articular, or combined extra- and intra-articular. As with all fractures, life saving and limb saving measures are addressed and specific treatment of the fracture is predicated upon achieving a satisfactory reduction, maintaining that reduction until union, and eventually optimizing function of the limb after union has occurred. In most instances, the treatment must be individualized taking into account the personality of the fracture which is in turn characterized by quality of the bone, fracture configuration, demands of the patient and general state, and associated injuries of the lower limb.[116]

11.2.5.1.1 Principles of Treatment: High energy fractures are often associated with other significant visceral injuries, many of which require precedence in terms of their treatment. Nevertheless, the leg should be temporarily splinted, preferably with traction to minimize pain caused by muscle spasm, avoid further damage to muscle and other soft tissues, and remove extrinsic pressure on the major neurovascular structures about the knee. Definitive treatment must ensure a satisfactory reduction of the fracture. In general, one should strive for anatomical reduction although precise guidelines have not objectively correlated with long-term function. Nevertheless, the American Medical Association's Guides to Permanent Impairment (American Medical Association, 1995) describes angulation greater than 5° as being significant and accords a level of lower limb impairment as a result. Closed methods of treatment with traction which were once the standard often fail to achieve or even maintain an appropriate reduction as described, and often are complicated by conditions which result from prolonged immobility such as pressure sores, thromboembolic disease, and pneumonia. Those fractures with intra-articular extension are particularly difficult to reduce anatomically and usually require open reduction and internal fixation. Other advantages of rigid internal fixation include the benefits of early motion for articular cartilage nutrition[117] and a decreased risk of stiffness. Several devices are available for treatment of this fracture; buttress and blade plates and intramedullary devices are most popular.[118] In many instances, sufficient bone loss will have occurred such that an autogenous or autologous bone graft or substitute will be required to fill a defect. The treating surgeon must pass judgement on the immediate stability of the fracture fixation in deciding whether the reduction is stable enough to withstand this early motion. In some situations the sur-

---

116 Schatzker J, McBroom R, Bruce D. The Tibial Plateau Fracture: The Toronto Experience. *Clin Orthop*, 138:94-104, 1979.

117 Salter R, Harris D: The healing of intraarticular fractures with continuous passive motion. *AAOS Lecture Series*, 28:102, 1979.

118 Mize R. Treatment options for the distal femur. *Instructional Course Lectures* 43:109-117, 1994.

geon may decide that bone stock is insufficient to allow internal fixation, and therefore closed treatment will be recommended. This may be particular to significant cases of osteopenia as found in the very elderly patient, or the non-ambulatory patient such as in quadriplegia or paraplegia.

Complications include neurovascular injury, which can be associated with the injury or result from manipulation of fracture fragments required for their reduction given the proximity of the popliteal nerve and vessel in the posterior part of the knee. Knee stiffness is common secondary to extra-articular scarring between the femur and quadriceps, or intra-articular as a result of synovial adhesions particularly if a period of postoperative immobilization has been deemed necessary. Infection is also a risk particularly in open fractures of which many of the high-energy fractures are. It is a challenging problem to address as union will likely be delayed or prevented if the sepsis cannot be controlled. Arthrosis and pain can occur and they are more likely in cases of intra-articular malunion or significant articular cartilage damage at the time of injury. Other complications include failure of fixation and knee instability, which may require additional surgical management.

The outcome of distal femoral fractures has improved steadily over the years. The rate of acceptable results in the literature has gone from 31% in 1967[119] to 100% in 1979.[120] Overall, studies show good results of treatment in 60 to 70% of patients. Egund in 1982 determined that the most significant predictor of osteoarthritis was a step in the articular cartilage greater than 3 mm. In his study, the patellofemoral joint was more susceptible to developing osteoarthritis than the tibiotalar joint.[121]

In summary, many of these fractures are high energy ones in patients who have been significantly injured as a result of high velocity trauma. Their management is often associated with the treatment of other life-threatening injuries. Ultimately, the function of the limb will be best restored if anatomic reduction and early motion can be achieved, and if minimal extra-articular damage has occurred.

11.2.5.2 Fractures of the Proximal Tibia

Fractures of the proximal tibia, otherwise known as tibial plateau fractures, usually arise from significant compressive or shearing forces sustained in direct trauma about the knee [Figure 11.20]. The potential for

---

119 Neer CS, Granthan SA, Shelton ML. Supracondylar fractures of the adult femur: a study of 110 cases. *J Bone Joint Surg*, 49A:591-693, 1967.
120 Schatzker J, Lambert D. Supracondylar Fractures of the Femur. *Clin Orthop*, 138:77-83, 1979.
121 Egund N, Kolmert L. Deformities, gonoarthrosis and function after distal femoral fractures. *Acta Ortho Scand*, 53:963, 1982.

post-traumatic arthrosis is very real for those fractures with intra-articular extension. These fractures must be suspected in all cases of blunt trauma about the knee, particularly in association with knee effusion and/or proximal leg ecchymosis.

11.2.5.2.1 Principles of Treatment: As in other high energy blunt trauma to the knee, primary consideration is always given to the neurovascular status of the leg and foot, and must be documented in the immediate phase. Emergent fracture involves splinting the injured leg with a long-leg rigid splint, especially if the patient is being transferred to another facility for definitive care. High-energy fractures with dubious circulation to the foot should be evaluated on an urgent basis by a vascular surgeon. Angiography, a radiographic technique to image blood vessels, may be required in some cases to define the injury unless the impairment in circulation is so apparent that emergent vascular exploration is required.

Definitive fracture treatment is planned after appropriate imaging is complete. Plain film radiographs in the anteroposterior, lateral, and oblique planes will identify most fracture fragments, although plain tomography is often ordered to supplement the information for decision making in directing the method of treatment. This latter radiographic technique provides sequential images at small intervals (3 to 5 mm) in the lateral and coronal plane and permits the surgeon to visually interpret the fracture in a third dimension which is often invaluable for preoperative surgical planning. Schatzker's classification of these fractures has helped define treatment alternatives and facilitated comparative methods of treatment.[122] The classification is ordered in terms of ascending complexity and potential difficulty with anatomy restoration.

Principles of treatment are as for any periarticular fracture: anatomic reduction and early movement contingent on adequate fracture stability until union. Several alternatives are available, and these are usually operative for higher energy fractures. Any low-energy undisplaced fractures can indeed be treated conservatively with plaster immobilization. Reduction of fragments and internal fixation can be performed by open surgery, arthroscopically aided, and possibly combined with external fixation. A greater respect for the soft tissue envelope about the knee has emerged following case reports of skin slough and wound necrosis which can precipitate infection in fractures treated by open reduction and internal fixation. This may then deteriorate into osteomyelitis, which becomes extremely difficult to control and may even lead, in some instances, to amputation. Many surgeons choose to delay definitive operative treatment of these fractures for up to two weeks if immediate fixation is prohibited by extreme soft tissue injury. The fracture can be temporarily controlled with longitudinal skele-

---

122 Schatzker et al., *supra*, note 116.

tal traction distally based with the transfixion pin in either the distal tibia or the calcaneus, or a long-leg splint if there is no significant displacement as a result of the muscle forces. Thromboembolic prophylaxis is usually ordered to prevent deep venous thrombosis and potential harmful sequelae.

As in the distal femur, the proximal tibia possesses a large amount of cancellous (spongy) bone as a structural support for the articular surface at the joint. This spongy bone is more vulnerable to the deleterious resorptive consequences of osteoporosis, which is so endemic in the elderly. As a result, injuries of relatively less energy can create fractures in this weakened bone in this population. These fractures may have considerable comminution and create a treatment challenge, but the lower energy absorbed usually results in a less severe injury to the soft tissue envelope, which is characterized in the high-energy fractures previously described.

Associated injuries can parallel the level of energy absorbed in the injury. Neurovascular injuries and compartment syndromes of the leg are occasional associated injuries more commonly seen in high-energy fractures. Their diagnosis and management are discussed in another chapter. Collateral ligament sprains, medial for valgus directed lateral plateau fractures, and lateral for varus directed medial plateau fractures are a common occurrence. The concept of pseudoligamentous laxity is frequently used in instances where the examiner believes that residual collateral laxity in the knee is secondary to depressed articular surface and not from ligamentous pathology. Frequently though, a combination of inherent ligament laxity resulting from the injury and pseudolaxity from the resulting bone depression can occur in combination and are difficult to distinguish. Plain film stress radiography with comparative views could serve to delineate the contribution of each. Though the patient ultimately deals with the resultant laxity, the distinction is of interest for the clinician who must consider alternatives for its management.

Complications can include knee joint arthrosis, stiffness, and pain secondary to damage to articular cartilage and joint incongruity. The contributors to arthrosis are many. It may result from direct trauma to the articular cartilage, or as a consequence of excessive loading in the involved compartment of the knee as a result of permanent incongruity at the joint surface, or ultimately from residual lower limb mechanical malalignment. It is the most common sequelae of such injuries with a latency to clinical symptoms influenced by injury severity, general activity level, or patient weight.

The incidence of osteoarthritis of the knee is statistically correlated to the severity of the fracture (bicondylar 42%, medial condyle 21%, lateral condyle 16%), to the final alignment of the knee (normal 13%, valgus 31%, and varus 29%) and the stability of the ligaments (stable 14%, unstable 46%).[123] The results of undisplaced fractures have universally been good to excellent (100%) when treated in plaster.[124]

11.2.5.3 Ligament Injuries of the Knee

Optimal joint function requires a balance of pain-free stability and mobility. The knee has evolved over thousands of years to provide both stability and mobility, and withstand the repetitive cycles from normal life spans. The structure of articular cartilage is a marvel that has yet to be reproduced in a laboratory setting, and allows for a near frictionless movement while protecting the underlying subchondral bone from repetitive weight bearing cycles.[125] The synovial lining generates the lubricant of the joint that is responsible for articular cartilage nutrition. Muscle-tendon units work dynamically to power the lower limb through the knee and dissipate the forces of locomotion through active and reflex mechanisms. Ligaments provide the inherent static restraints to excessive joint translation and rotation from angular and shearing forces and generally span a joint [Figure 11.21]. For description, they are defined by a point of origin on one bone and an insertion on another. They sustain injury when applied forces overcome their elastic properties and create an irreversible amount of deformation which can ultimately lead to consequences of altered joint kinematics, lower limb malalignment, and subjective instability for the patient. Ligaments about the knee are divided into collateral ligaments, which are the primary restraints to varus and valgus forces (to the side); and cruciate ligaments, which resist anteroposterior (front and back) forces and are most responsible for coordinating the coupled motions of normal knee movement. Injuries to these ligaments are traditionally graded along three subdivisions with Grade I injuries generally representing a strain with no static elongation but represented by tenderness in the patient. Grade II injuries create some static deformation, which is not recoverable, but still provide a functional restraint to the primary direction for which they oriented. Grade III injuries usually denote a complete rupture, which, by definition, is a non-functional ligament in providing its normal restraints.

11.2.5.3.1 Collateral Ligaments: The *medial collateral ligament* is a fan-shaped ligament with a superficial and deep component to provide the

---

123 Rasmussen PS, Sorensen SE. Tibial condylar fractures. *Injury*, 4:265, 1973.
124 Schatzker et al., *supra*, note 116. Hohl M, Luck JV. Fracture of the Tibia Condyle, a Clinical and Experimental Study. *J Bone Joint Surg*, 38A:1001-1018, 1956.
125 Buckwalter J, Mankin H. Articular cartilage. *J Bone Joint Surg*, 79-A:600-632, 1997.

most important restraint to valgus angulation. It originates from the medial femoral epicondyle and inserts about 5 cm distal to the joint line on the tibia. It is largely extraarticular and as such has a greater propensity for healing following injury by virtue of a luxurious blood supply. This healing phase occurs through the production and subsequent remodeling of scar tissue.[126] Controlled motion appears to improve the healing and protected mobilization is usually prescribed. Most isolated medial collateral sprains respond very well to this conservative approach, and operative treatment is rarely required in the acute setting. Combination injuries, which include further damage to the posterior oblique ligament and posteromedial capsule may require repair and may have a less favorable prognosis to conservative treatment.

The *lateral collateral ligament* is a tubular extraarticular ligament, which originates in the lateral epicondyle of the femur and inserts on the fibular head. It is the primary restraint to varus rotation and joins with the popliteal tendon and arcuate ligament to form the posterolateral corner of the knee and the major restraint to external rotation and varus.[127] It is rarely injured in isolation, but rather usually with rupture of either or both of the cruciate ligaments.[128] Isolated injuries without gross instability are treated conservatively, though complete Grade III injuries are generally treated operatively as conservative management does not yield as predictable satisfactory results as for the medial collateral ligament (MCL).

11.2.5.3.2 Cruciate Ligaments: The cruciate ligaments, so named because they cross each other in the knee, are the central pivots by which essential elements of knee kinematics are dependent. Together with their insertions they form a four-bar linkage whereby tibial motion is guided on the femur in flexion and extension. Consequences of these isolated ruptures provide significantly different consequences for the patient. Occasionally both may be torn simultaneously in the special case of knee dislocation.

The *anterior cruciate ligament (ACL)* originates in the posterior aspect of the lateral femoral condyle and inserts broadly anterior to the anterolateral spine of the tibia. It is the primary restraint to anterior tibial

---

126 Frank C, Amiel D, Akeson W. Healing of the medial collateral ligament of the knee. A morphological and biomechanical assessment in rabbits. *Acta Orthop Scand*, 54:917-923, 1983.

127 Hughston JC, Andrews JR, Cross MJ, Moschi A. Classification of knee ligament instabilities Part II. The Lateral Compartment. *J Bone Joint Surg*, 58-A:173-179, 1976.

128 Hughston JC, Jacobson KE. Chronic posterolateral instability of the knee. *J Bone Joint Surg*, 67-A:351-359, 1985. Baker CL, Norwood LA, Hughston JC. Acute posterolateral instability of the knee. *J Bone Joint Surg Am*, 65-A:614-618, 1983.

translation. Injuries to it are generally indirect as a result of strong quadriceps contraction forces as when the knee is planted and pivots in athletics such as basketball and soccer. Direct blows, which primarily injure collateral ligaments, can, if excessive, rupture the cruciate as well providing another mechanism of injury. Partial tears can also occur, though these are less common than complete ruptures, and many of these will eventually progress to full complete tears.

The diagnosis of ACL tear is primarily made on clinical grounds:

1. Mechanism of injury: usually occurs with vigorous sport, a pop is felt or heard and the patient is unable to pursue the activity.
2. Hemarthrosis: or sudden accumulation of blood in the joint. Noyes found that 72% of patients with traumatic hemarthrosis of the knee had ACL tears.
3. Lachman test: with the knee flexed 25 degrees the examiner translates the tibia anteriorly over the femur. This test is positive in 85 to 90% of ACL tears.
4. Anterior drawer test: also measures the anterior translation of the tibia but with the knee flexed at 90 degrees to test different ligament fibers.
5. Pivot shift test: This evaluation is most useful for chronic ACL laxity and demonstrates a subluxation of the tibiofemoral joint.

Confirmation of an ACL or PCL tear is made by arthroscopy or by MRI.

The natural history of the ACL deficient knee has long been the subject of considerable debate. Especially controverial is whether the ACL deficient knee is predestined for earlier onset of arthritic change. It is of some interest that the animal model for osteoarthritis is to transect the anterior cruciate ligament in the dog whereby rapid development of arthritis ensues. Nevertheless, natural history studies in adults have been few, and most studies are flawed by including only those patients who have sought medical attention because of instability. There are obviously large cohorts of ACL injured patients who never do seek medical attention and who may function very well. The late Dale Daniel of Kaiser Permanante in San Diego conducted a detailed study whereby all patients were diagnosed at inception of hemarthrosis, and those with anterior cruciate ligament diagnosed immediately and followed.[129] Patients eventually chose their own treatment whether it be conservative or surgical, and were followed closely for evidence of clinical instability and radiographic evidence of osteoarthritis. Interestingly, the authors could not demonstrate a reduction

---

129 Daniel D, Stone M, Dobson B, Fithian D, Rossman D, Kaufman K. Fate of the ACL-injured Patient. A Prospective Outcome Study. *Am J Sports Med*, 22:632-644, 1994.

of osteoarthritis in ACL reconstructed knees somewhat dismissing the notion of a protective effect of reconstruction. However, many feel that other issues in association with ACL injury such as the articular cartilage damage, bone bruise, and meniscal injury may be more important in determining the ultimate fate of the knee than the torn ligament itself [Figure 11.22].[130]

Proponents of ACL reconstruction note improved subjective stability for those patients who present with unstable pivoting with activities of daily living and also a protective effect on further meniscal injury when compared to conservatively treated ACL patients. In fact, the evidence for the perils of meniscectomy on the knee are more well documented and less controversial as first outlined by Fairbank nearly 50 years ago.[131] The intra-articular synovial environment is not conducive to stable scar formation and significant ACL repair, and therefore reconstructive techniques using a graft are generally required to restore the stability. Several choices of graft are now available, the most popular being autogenous hamstring or patellar tendon grafts, followed by allogeneic patellar, Achilles, or quadriceps tendon, and finally synthetics which are still available in Canada.

The *posterior cruciate ligament (PCL)* originates from the medial femoral condyle and inserts in the posterior aspect of the tibia approximately 1 cm below the posterior articular surface. It is considerably larger and stronger than the ACL, and is the primary restraint to posterior translation. As with the ACL, it may sustain an indirect injury by hypertension mechanisms, or directly through an anterior direct blow such as a dashboard against the flexed knee in vehicular trauma.

Manifestations of the injuries include a posterior sag as detected by the clinical examiner with the knee flexed at 90 degrees. Complaints of instability are uncommon in isolated PCL injuries although they are much more prominent with multiple ligament injuries. The isolated Grade I and II PCL is generally treated conservatively because of favorable natural history. The isolated Grade III injury is somewhat more contentious as some people will go on to develop medial and patellofemoral arthritic changes which are irreversible.[132] The difficulty is in predicting those patients who are destined for this change, and many authors suggest serial bone scans as a way to early detect worrisome changes in the involved medial and patel-

---

130 Drongowski RA, Coran AG, Wojtys EM. Predictive value of meniscal and chondral injuries in conservatively treated anterior cruciate ligament injuries. *Arthroscopy*, 10:97-102, 1994. Thompson WO, Fu FH. The Meniscus in the Cruciate-Deficient Knee. *Clin Sports Med*, 12:771-796, 1993.

131 Fairbank TJ. Knee joint changes after meniscectomy. *J Bone Joint Surg*, 30:644-670, 1948.

132 Covey CD, Sapega AA. Injuries of the Posterior Cruciate Ligament. *J Bone Joint Surg*, 75:1376-1386, 1993.

lofemoral compartments. More fundamental is the lack of proof that PCL reconstruction can prevent these osteoarthritic changes in these cases. As with the ACL, PCL reconstructive techniques can only simulate the original ligament function and have never been shown to completely restore the normal kinematics of the knee. Combined injuries to the posterolateral compartment also fare less well with nonoperative management and may require surgical repair or reconstruction.[133]

11.2.5.4 Knee Dislocations

Knee dislocations are the ultimate expression of catastrophic ligament disruption about the knee. As implied by the disruption, considerable energy is often required to yield such an injury, though it may result from what is perceived as trivial trauma from hyperextension injuries. Dislocations are described by the resulting position of the tibia as reference to the femur, and anterior dislocations are the most common [Figure 11.23]. These injuries are notorious for associated vascular and neurologic injury, and as such require urgent reduction of the dislocation after a complete neurovascular assessment has been made. Afterward, the neurovascular assessment is repeated to see if the vascular status has improved as often the reduction alone will reverse the kinking on popliteal vessels and may restore circulation. Nevertheless, a low threshold exists for definitive vascular imaging in the form of angiogram or, more recently, MRI angiography to detect vascular lesions. The concern is not only academic, as many instances of below-knee amputation have followed the dislocation because of a dysvascular lower limb. Vascular repair is often accompanied by leg fasciotomies which may result from reperfusion injuries.

The principles of treatment therefore are first to save the limb by ruling out vascular disorders; and secondly the limb is splinted in extension and in a reduced position so as not to allow a chronically subluxed knee. Occasionally an external fixator may be required to maintain this reduction. Thirdly, definitive surgery is entertained.This is the subject of considerable debate as many authors prefer immediate reconstructive efforts within the first two weeks while others allow the knee to be splinted for 4 to 6 weeks with early mobilization. They feel that much of the capsular scar tissue will heal and scar down and provide a functional knee.[134] Unfortunately, as with many aspects of knee ligament injuries, one is often unable to predict which patients will successfully form sufficient scar tissue to provide them a stable knee with this conservative treatment. This

---

133 Veltri DM, Warren RF. Operative Treatment of Posterolateral Instability of the Knee. *Clin Sports Med*, 13:615-627, 1994.
134 Taft T, Alkeminders L. The Dislocated Knee. In: Fu F, Harner C, Vince K, eds. *Knee Surgery*. Baltimore: Williams & Wilkins, 1994: 837-858.

has led some authors to advocate a more aggressive reconstructive approach for all of these patients. Ultimate function really will depend on the ultimate ligament stability that is achieved following these chosen avenues of treatment.

11.2.5.5 Meniscal Injuries

The menisci are fibrocartilaginous structures within the knee joint which serve several functions. The medial meniscus is smaller but more firmly attached to the adjacent capsule, which presumably accounts for the greater incidence of tears as seen in the medial meniscus versus the lateral side where the meniscus is more oval, larger, and mobile. Histologically, circumferential collagen fibres dominate the extracellular architecture and are linked by radial "tie" fibers. These fibers act by resisting hoop strains generated by joint compression during loading activities. The blood supply of the meniscus is most abundant in utero, and gradually decreases until it reaches a fairly stable level after age 30. The important consequence of the sparse blood supply, which is primarily located in the outer third of the meniscus, is that most tears of the meniscus fail to heal.

The menisci function by increasing the contact area of the tibiofemoral joint, and therefore dissipating peak stresses on the femoral and tibial articular cartilage. Fairbank first described pathologic changes which followed a complete open medial meniscectomy.[135] He reported squaring of the condyles and osteophytic spurring of the tibial spines as a long-term response to the medial meniscectomies. Menisci also function by increasing stability of the knee by acting as bumpers to excessive translation and rotation.

Menisci are prone to injury, particularly with weight bearing and flexion activity, by virtue of their mobility. As mentioned previously, they, for the most part, do not heal unless they are partial thickness tears, which generally do not become symptomatic. Symptoms usually include locking, clicking, and fairly localized discomfort related to their location on the joint line. Many of these symptoms can be avoided by resisting flexion and twisting activities and for the most part some patients can compensate by doing this.

The natural history of untreated meniscal tears is recurrent symptoms with this twisting and squatting activity. It is conceivable that small tears can propagate into bigger tears if left and not addressed surgically. The diagnosis of a meniscal injury is usually made clinically by combining the historical features of sudden injury with the clinical features of pain localized to the joint line and often exacerbated by provocative maneuver such as the McMurray test. This test aims to provoke meniscal symptoms by

---

135 Fairbank, *supra*, note 131.

flexing and rotating the knee under load to try and simulate symptoms. If the clinical findings are not conclusive, additional testing, usually in the form of magnetic resonance imaging, can be done to confirm and locate the type of tear. This latter modality has an accuracy of about 90%.

Treatment is aimed at controlling symptoms by avoiding provocative maneuvers. If this is not satisfactory to the patient, an arthroscopy is generally recommended for diagnosis and evaluation [Figure 11.24]. Most tears are resected back to a stable rim of meniscus with efforts aimed at preserving as much meniscal tissue. Because of the poor response to complete meniscectomy, efforts have recently focused on attempts at meniscal repair, particularly those located in the peripheral one-third of the meniscus, which is endowed with sufficient blood supply to permit healing. This has both been demonstrated in animal studies and clinical studies.[136] Whether or not function is completely restored in a healed meniscus is somewhat debatable, but the theoretical presumption is that it is which does lend some impetus to attempt a repair if the surgeon deems the tear is reparable.[137]

11.2.6 Fractures of the Tibia

Fractures of the tibia and fibula shaft are very common injuries seen in a general orthopaedic clinic. They arrive from either direct trauma which generally causes more soft tissue contusion with considerably more high energy, or the common injury is that of an indirect torsional twisting injury which can cause a spiral or short oblique fracture type pattern [Figure 11.25]. Low energy fractures are generally conducive to closed reduction where acceptable position can generally be obtained and closed treatment carried out with casting. There are some general criteria that are used to define an acceptable reduction of the bone, and, although there are some minor variations within a couple of degrees, in general one does strive for less than 5 degrees of varus or valgus, or anterior-posterior angulation. One would also try to achieve less than 10-degree difference in rotational alignment, although admittedly this is quite difficult to measure, and this is about as sensitive as one can detect in terms of the change in rotation. Deformities such as the ones mentioned become more significant the closer they are to the articular surface of either the ankle or the tibia, and therefore may be slightly less forgiving. This is based on joint alignment and

---

136 Arnoczky SP, Warren RF. The Microvasculature of the Meniscus and its Response to Injury. An Experimental Study in the Dog. *Am J Sports Med*, 11:131-141,1993. Cipolla M, Cerullo G, Puddu G. Microvasculature of the human medial meniscus: operative findings. *Arthroscopy*, 8:522-525, 1992.

137 Newman AP, Daniels AU, Burks RT. Principles and decision making in meniscal surgery. *Arthroscopy*, 9:33-51, 1993. O'Meara PM. The basic science of meniscus repair. *Orthop Rev*, 22:681-686, 1993.

pressure studies with respect to malalignment.[138] Associated injuries may include significant contusion to the soft tissue envelope from a direct trauma which may progress to fully open contamination of the fracture which should be treated as a very different entity with all the appropriate precautions of open fracture treatment that will be discussed later. Nonetheless, some high energy closed fractures show a significant damage to local vascularity and periosteal nutrition of a fracture site which may make such a fracture prone to delayed union.

In general, emergent urgent treatment is to splint the extremity and prevent further damage to the soft tissue surrounding the fracture. Efforts for immobilization and splinting, as in most fractures, are to immobilize the joint above and below the fracture site, in this case the ankle and the knee. Appropriate anterior, posterior and lateral radiographs are obtained to document both the fracture pattern, fracture location, fracture displacement and fracture angulation. These four parameters will sufficiently define a fracture and help to guide its treatment.

In general, the trend for orthopaedic care of tibial fractures has been to use closed treatment whenever possible. The ideal situation would be a stable fracture whereby a good acceptable reduction by the parameters previously defined could be obtained, and thereby allow early weight bearing with functional cast bracing as suggested and popularized by Sarmiento.[139] This allows for weight bearing stimulus and promotes healing. Most stable fractures that can be successfully reduced and are amenable to early weight bearing should unite at an average of about 12 weeks.[140] When fractures are more comminuted and cannot be reduced appropriately, then this ideal is usually not achieved, and decisions must be obtained as to how this reduction will be obtained.

The general treatment paradigm for a tibial shaft fracture again, as in most fractures, is to first reduce the fracture into an acceptable position, and then maintain that position through the period of healing until the fracture is stable enough to be self-supported without any immobilization. Ultimately the goal is to restore good function to the limb which allows for painless range of motion in both the knee and the ankle and a stable limb. The first aspect of obtaining reduction is generally obtained by a simple longitudinal traction and some gentle manipulation of the fracture while an

---

138 Paley D, Maar DC, Herzenberg JE. New concepts in high tibial osteotomy for medial compartment osteoarthritis. *Orthop Clin North Am*, 25:483-498, 1994.

139 Sarmiento A, Sobol P, Sew Hoy A, Ross S, Racette W, Tarr R. Prefabricated Functional Braces for the Treatment of Fractures of the Tibial Diaphysis. *J Bone Joint Surg*, 66-A:1328-1339, 1984.

140 Nicoll EA. Fractures of the Tibial Shaft: A Survey of 705 Cases. *J Bone Joint Surg*, 46B:373-87, 1964.

assistant will apply plaster to try and maintain the reduction for a closed fracture. Often this can be achieved in the Emergency Department with some sedation and analgesia, although not uncommonly this maneuver can be best carried out in the Operating Room under complete general anesthesia and image intensifier control where several attempts may be made to achieve an optimal reduction. Once a satisfactory reduction is achieved by the criteria described then maintenance of that reduction is the next feature of fracture care. Again, most commonly, plaster cast immobilization is the treatment of choice to maintain the reduction, usually with immobilization to the foot and above the knee obeying the principles of immobilizing the joint above and below the fracture. Occasionally the fracture is so unstable that appropriate position will not be maintained by plaster cast immobilization, and one will have to resort to some method of internal fixation or, less commonly, external fixation to maintain the position. This, therefore, does become one of the indications for internal fixation of a closed tibial fracture which is the failure either to obtain an appropriate reduction, or the failure to maintain that reduction if it was obtained.

Benefits of the closed tibial fracture treatment are that, in those cases where the fracture is stable and the patient can be managed successfully onto fracture union, there has not been a risk of infection and there are no side effects of operative treatment. The potential pitfalls of cast treatment are so-called "cast disease" which is the disuse atrophy of ligaments and muscles about the ankle and the knee which requires considerable time to restore after fracture union has been achieved. Most commonly, stiffness at the subtalar joint of the ankle can be very difficult to regain after plaster cast immobilization on the order of 12 weeks and longer that is required for many of these fractures. In many instances, this range of motion at the subtalar joint does not return to normal on long-term follow-up. Proponents of immediate internal fixation, usually with intramedullary devices if possible, site the advantage of early mobilization of the knee and ankle with less opportunity for subtalar joint stiffness. The limb becomes functional more quickly with, in many instances, no requirement for plaster immobilization subsequent to this type of fixation. The generally reported incidence of infection for closed treatment of fractures should be about on the order of 1% whether it is for open plating or intramedullary nailing. In most instances, the decision of treatment is left to the attendant surgeon based on fracture characteristics, although there are significant trends toward one type of treatment or another depending on trends of the local orthopaedic community.

Complications of closed tibial fractures include delayed union which is defined as a union having not occurred at more than 20 weeks. A frank nonunion is very difficult to quantify as the different fracture varieties denote different times to fracture union. Thereby a strict time definition is probably not appropriate. One working definition has been to assign a diagnosis of nonunion to a fracture which has not shown any progression in union at two successive 4-week intervals in similar radiographic planes of AP, lateral, and oblique. The treatment of delayed or nonunion is multifold and can include fibular osteotomy to increase axial load across the tibial fracture site or some method of internal fixation if stability seems to be the problem. The topic of nonunions is best covered in another chapter of this manual. The most common complication of closed fracture treatment is stiffness of the knee and ankle, which generally can resolve, although subtalar joint stiffness often may not completely recover.

The treatment of open tibial fractures is a separate subject onto itself as these fractures are quite common by virtue of the tibia's location and vulnerability to fracture, and more importantly, its subcutaneous location and high propensity to lacerate skin and muscle at impact. Gustillo's classification is commonly used to define the severity of the injury into grades which have been described in this text elsewhere.[141] There has been some disagreement as to the classification of these fractures as previously described by Brumback.[142] It is therefore generally felt that more adequate classification would be to group the fractures into high grade or low grade compound fractures. The low grade fractures are the grade I, II, and possibly IIIA; whereas the high grade fractures are the traditional grade IIIB fracture which means that there has been a requirement for an additional soft tissue coverage procedure and given the large extent of the open wound. Implications for fixation of the fracture and principles of treatment open tibial fractures have been well elucidated by Sanders and Burgess.[143] In general, immediate bony stabilization, either by means of external fixation or intramedullary device is generally recommended as a means of splinting the bone so that the soft tissue can heal. A recent trend has been toward substituting external fixation for intramedullary devices. Most surgeons tend to favour unreamed nails on the theoretical basis that there is less disruption to the intramedullary blood supply, and therefore less chance of rendering the fragments avascular and susceptible to infection.[144]

---

141 Gustilo RB, Mendoza RM, Williams DN. Problems in the Management of Type III (severe) Open Fractures: A new Classification of Type III Open Fractures. *J Trauma*, 24:742-746,1984.

142 Brumback RJ, Jones A. Interobserver Agreement in the Classification of Open fractures of the Tibia. *J Bone Joint Surg*, 76-A:1162-1166, 1994.

143 Burgess AR, Poka A, Brumback RJ, Bosse MJ. Management of Open Grade III Tibial Fractures. *Orthop Clin North Am*, 18:85-93, 1987. Sanders R, Swiontkowski MF, Nunley J, Spiegel PG. The Management of Fractures with Soft-Tissue Disruptions. *J Bone Joint Surg*, 75-A:778-789, 1993.

144 Schemitsh EH, Kowalski M, Senft DC, Swiontkowski MF. Acute Effects of Reamed Versus Unreamedlocked Nailing on Blood Flow in a Fractured Sheep Model [abstract]. *Journal of Orthopaedic Trauma*, 7:161-162, 1993.

The reported advantage of this intramedullary stabilization is that it may permit easier dressing change to the soft tissue wound and care of the soft tissue wound in the immediate perioperative period. In general, the successive treatment of these open tibial fractures probably lies mostly with the success in treating the soft tissue injury. Generally, failure to have adequate soft tissue closure within one week of the injury[145] seems to put the patient at higher risk of subsequent wound breakdown and infection and eventual osteomyelitis which can become very intractable and difficult to treat. Newer techniques are microvascular free tissue transfer, either in the form of fascia cutaneous or, more commonly, muscular free flaps. These have converted many of these previous devastating injuries into ones that can be salvaged with very acceptable function. If successful soft tissue closure can be achieved in a very sterile environment then there are probably several alternatives for the ultimate skeletal fixation method, although no definite method exists which is an appropriate method of treatment.[146]

Complications associated with open fracture treatment are, most importantly, infection and infection rates vary depending on the degree of contamination and energy of the fracture as well as the time to eventual debridement. Efforts to contain and reduce the role of infection include antibiotics administered as soon as possible after the injury, and an immediate urgent debridement, preferable within six to eight hours following the injury with aggressive resection of all non-viable soft tissue about the fracture. Other very common complications with open fracture include delayed union and nonunion vis-à-vis two similar fracture patterns in closed injuries because of the significant soft tissue injury. Another complication of both closed and open fractures is the potential for compartment syndrome. This is a scenario whereby pressures within an enclosed osteofascial compartment rise above that of the perfusion pressure of the capillaries. Tissue hypoxia occurs and subsequent necrosis of muscle and nerve go on to occur unless urgent decompression is carried. Tibial fractures are the most commonly implicated for compartment syndrome.

11.2.7 Fractures and Injuries of the Ankle Joint

11.2.7.1 Anatomy

The ankle joint is a complex composed of 3 bones and several supportive ligaments. The muscles that act across this hinge joint produce dorsiflexion or plantar flexion. The lower end of the tibia with its (medial)

---

145 Godina M. Early Microsurgical Reconstruction of Complex Trauma of the Extremities. *Plastic Recons Surgery*, 78:285-292, 1986.
146 Dervin GF. Skeletal Fixation of Grade IIIB Tibial Fractures. The Potential of Metaanalysis. *Clin Orthop*, 332:10-15, 1996.

malleolus and the fibular (lateral) malleolus together form a mortise configuration in which fits the talar body that is shaped like a tenon. The articular surface of the tibia at the level of the ankle joint complex is often referred to as the tibial plafond (meaning ceiling).

The medial and lateral collateral ligaments join the malleoli to the medial and lateral aspect of the hindfoot bones [Figure 11.26]. While the medial deltoid ligament is fan shaped, double layered, broad and very strong, the lateral ligament composed of three separate smaller ligaments is less resilient and less supportive and thus frequently injured (i.e., in the context of ankle fractures or sprains). The 3 components of the lateral collateral ligament are the anterior talofibular ligament, posterior talofibular ligament, and the calcaneofibular ligament. Each of these different components of the lateral collateral ligament tightens or relaxes at different positions of the ankle (i.e., dorsiflexion or plantar flexion).

The lower tibia and fibula are bound together at the ankle joint by the anterior and posterior distal tibiofibular syndesmotic ligaments, the interosseous ligament and the inferior transverse ligament. The interosseous ligament is the strongest bond between the tibia and fibula.

11.2.7.2 Mechanisms of Injury

The directions of the forces that cause injury to the ankle region are either external rotation (outward rotation of the foot), abduction (i.e., movement away from the body), adduction (i.e., movement towards the body), or vertical compression.

11.2.7.3 Classification of Ankle Fractures

Several classifications exist but are either unnecessarily complicated or add little to our understanding of the mechanisms of injuries, and thus are of little practical value. In everyday clinical practice, ankle fractures are usually characterised according to the classification of Danis-Weber (AO classification)[147] [Figure 11.27] in which the severity of the fracture is based on the position of the fibular malleolar fracture. In general, the more proximal the fibular break, the more significant the associated syndesmotic injury and the greater the chances for disruption of the mortise and subsequent displacement of the talus.

Type A ankle fractures are caused by internal rotation and adduction mechanisms and result in a transverse fracture of the fibula at or below the joint line with a possible shear fracture of the medial malleolus. Type B fractures result from external rotation and produce an oblique fibular frac-

---

147 Müller ME, Allgower M, Schneider R, Willenegger H. *Manual of Internal Fixation*, 2nd ed. New York: Springer-Verlag, 1979.

ture at the level of the joint line in an anteroposterior plane, and a medial injury (either a medial malleolar fracture or a medial collateral ligament tear). Type C fractures can be produced from either abduction alone (C1 type, which causes an oblique medial-to-lateral fibular break above a ruptured tibiofibular ligament), or from a combination of abduction and external rotation (C2 type in which more extensive tearing of the syndesmotic ligaments produces a similar but more proximal fibular fracture). Both types of C fractures may be associated with either deltoid ligament ruptures or medial malleolar fractures [Figure 11.27].

11.2.7.4 Treatment of Ankle Fractures

Closed reduction treatment of malleolar fractures consists of either cast immobilisation of undisplaced fractures, or else closed manipulative reduction of displaced malleolar fractures to achieve exact or near exact alignment, followed by cast immobilisation. Open reduction treatment is indicated when closed treatment does not yield either anatomic or near anatomic reduction, or if reduction cannot be maintained over the ensuing weeks, and whenever the fracture pattern suggests significant joint instability that is unlikely to be corrected with a cast. In general, the criteria used for proceeding with operative treatment are up to 2 mm of displacement of the malleoli and 1 to 2 degrees of talar tilt in the mortise.[148]

Conventional operative approaches of single or bimalleolar ankle fractures involve internal fixation with devices such as plates or screws but occasionally with wires or pins or small intramedullary rods [Figure 11.28]. A trimalleolar fracture (in which the posterior tibial lip is termed the third malleolus), is treated just as a bimalleolar fracture unless the tibial lip fragment involves 25% or more of the tibial articular surface and is displaced more than 2 mm. In this instance, the third malleolus must be internally fixated usually from a posterior approach.

11.2.7.5 Complications of Ankle Fractures

Complications relate in part to the severity of the fractures but may occur secondary to the type of management selected. *Infection* of the surgical wound presents early on and it may be a consequence of either an open injury or it may start de novo in a closed injury. *Nonunion* is more likely to occur following non-operatively treated fractures of the medial malleolus.[149] Nonunion of a lateral or posterior malleolus fracture is un-

---

148 Chapman MW. Fractures and Fracture-Dislocations of the Ankle. In: Mann RH, Coughlin MJ, eds. *Surgery of the Foot and Ankle.* St. Louis: Mosby, 1992.

149 Magnuson R. On the Late Results in Non-Operated Cases of Malleolar Fractures. *Acta Chir Scand* [Suppl], 90: 1-136, 1944.

common; however radiographic evidence of fibular union is very slow to appear.[150] *Malunion* of either the medial or lateral malleoli results in late clinical deformity and in the development of post-traumatic arthritis.

In most cases, irrespective of the type of treatment received, some degree of *residual loss of motion* occurs at the ankle joint and frequently at the subtalar joint. This ankylosis of the ankle and often of the subtalar joints relates to scarring of the damaged joint capsular ligaments damaged by the injury and occasionally aggravated by the surgical manipulation of the soft tissues. It is also caused by the need to immobilise the lower limb in a cast for long periods of time. Thus, despite otherwise good clinical and radiographic results of well managed ankle fractures; there is frequently some degree of residual joint ankylosis, which for some patients may be imperceptible, but for others functionally annoying or disabling.

Patients may complain of symptoms of irritation of the skin overlying the plate or screws used for internal fixation of their fractures, especially over the fibular malleolar fracture. Removal of the implants is indicated when the discomfort is very bothersome or frankly painful, or in young patients in order to prevent the development of disuse osteoporosis or weakening of the bone under the plate.

Some patients complain about more than just mild residual aches or pain or some stiffness. They may have developed *post-traumatic arthritis*, which affects between 20 to 40% of patients who sustain ankle fractures.[151] Arthritic degeneration of the joint can develop regardless of the treatment selected and despite expert realignment of the fractures. Some of the predisposing factors are inaccurate reduction of the talus in the mortise, comminution of the tibial plafond (a multi-fragmented fracture), and advancing age.[152] Early symptoms of significant pain and joint stiffness may be noted before the radiographic changes of joint incongruity are noted. The treatment of the arthritic complaints depends on the severity of the symptoms and on the extent of arthritic damage noted on plain radiographs. The management may vary from a conservative approach consisting of mild analge-

---

150 Wilson FC. Fractures and Dislocations of the Ankle. In: Rockwood CA, Green DP, eds. *Fractures in Adults*. Philadelphia: JB Lippincott, 1984.
151 Burwell HN, Charnley AD. The Treatment of Displaced Fractures at the Ankle by Rigid Internal Fixation and Early Joint Movement. *J Bone Joint Surg*, 47B: 634-660, 1965. Mast JW, Teipner WA. A Reproducible Approach to the Internal Fixation of Adult Ankle Fractures: Rationale, Technique, and Early Results. *Orthop Clin North Am*, 11: 661-679, 1980. Vasli S. Operative Treatment of Ankle Fractures. *Acta Chir Scand [Suppl]*, 226: 1-74, 1957. Wilson FC, Skilbred LA. Long-Term Results in the Treatment of Displacement Bimalleolar Fractures. *J Bone Joint Surg*, 48A: 1065, 1078, 1966.
152 Wilson et al., *ibid*.

sics, shoe modifications and weight loss, to surgical management in the form of a joint fusion or replacement arthroplasty.

11.2.7.6 Vertical Compression Fractures

These are produced typically by a fall from a height or by a sudden impact against the foot as in a deceleration motor vehicle injury in which the vehicle's floor is suddenly crumpled against the foot. The upward impaction of the talus against the tibial plafond producing minor or often extensive fracturing of the metaphyseal section of the lower tibia is often accompanied by hyper-dorsiflexion of the ankle [Figure 11.29]. The injury sustained is often designated as a tibial plafond (from the French word meaning "ceiling") fracture or as a tibial pilon (from the French word meaning "rammer" or "hammer") when the fracture involves not only the tibial metaphysis but also the lower tibial diaphysis.

The physical examination reveals severe swelling and occasionally extensive damage to the skin, i.e., abrasions and contusions. Imaging of the injury includes standard radiographic views to establish a diagnosis, but often the details of the comminution and of the degree of bony disruption and malalignment must be assessed further with plain tomography or computed tomography.

From the treatment standpoint, a successful outcome is largely dependent on the condition of the soft tissues, i.e., the ligaments, the muscles and tendons, and the skin envelope. Dirty abrasions over the injury site become colonised with bacteria quickly and may thus produce wound sepsis or osteomyelitis if early surgery is carried out through or close to the damaged skin. Unfortunately, when surgery must be delayed for several days or weeks, it is difficult or occasionally impossible to completely reduce the fractures. An open injury carries a poor prognosis with not only a high probability of infection but is also associated with a high incidence of late amputation of the lower leg and foot.

Severe tissue swelling, edema or blister formation about the injury site may prohibit an early operative intervention because of the risk of not being able to close these swollen tissue layers after internal fixation has been carried out; partial or incomplete wound closure increases the risk of wound bacterial contamination. Massive swelling of the leg muscles occasionally occurs along with the tibial plafond fracture, a complication that can lead to compartment syndromes of the foot and leg.

Nonoperative treatment is selected for undisplaced fractures or when the bone quality is poor (e.g., in an elderly or a minimally active or nonambulatory patient). Most tibial plafond fractures, however, are displaced and need to be treated by open methods.

Open treatment can consist of limited exposure of the fracture with minimal internal fixation with pins or screws, combined with the application of an external fixator apparatus spanning the tibia to the foot [Figure 11.30]. This type of open approach, which is usually applicable to minimally or moderately displaced injuries, has several advantages that relate to the fact that extensive dissection about compromised skin tissues can be avoided. The other kind of open approach involves exposing both the fibular and the tibial plafond fractures, and realigning and internally fixating these [Figure 11.31]. Often a bone grafting procedure must also be done to fill in a bone defect that may have been produced at the time of the injury by crushing of the bone tissue. Early motion is important to help reduce the degree of limited ankle mobility that often occurs.

The outcome of these injuries depends on several factors, including the condition of the skin envelope, the quality of reduction, and the fracture type. Overall, 65% have a good functional result,[153] but only 50% of the type III have an acceptable result.[154] In a large series of over 100 cases, about 50% required more than one operation. Types I and II injuries do well in 80 to 84% of cases.[155] Possible complications include infection, reflex sympathetic dystrophy, malunion, nonunion, delayed union, reduced ankle joint range of motion, and avascular necrosis of the distal tibia. Less than 70% return to their previous occupation. Rehabilitation lasts for at least 3 months after fracture healing.

11.2.7.7 Ligamentous Injuries of the Ankle

Injuries that produce a sprained ankle in essence cause a partial or complete tearing of the ligaments that support the ankle joint. They are almost exclusively produced by sudden inversion (twisting inwards) of the foot and ankle. These ligamentous injuries may occur within the substance of the ligament, at its bone attachment, or through the bone itself (this is termed avulsion fracture of a small fragment or shell of bone). The importance of ligamentous injuries of the ankle relates to whether joint stability is preserved or lost after the trauma. With increasing severity of injury, the talus can be displaced anteriorly more easily, producing a positive anterior drawer sign.

In almost every ankle sprain, the lateral collateral ligament complex is injured; isolated deltoid ligament tears are very rare. Of the three ligaments comprising the lateral complex, the anterior talofibular ligament is

---

153 Ovadia DN, Beals RK. Fractures of the Tibial Plafond. *J Bone Joint Surg*, 68A: 543-550, 1986.
154 Kellam JF, Waddell JP: Fractures of the Distal Tibial Metaphysis with Intra-Articular Extension—The Distal Tibial Explosion Fracture. *J Trauma*, 19: 593-601, 1979.
155 Kellam et al., *ibid.* Bourne RB, Rorabeck DH, MacNab I. Intra-articular Fractures of the Distal Tibia: The Pilon Fracture. *J Trauma*, 23: 591-595, 1983.

the one most often affected. One method of categorizing the severity of injury is practical based on the likelihood of late problems, with mild sprains being unlikely to lead to late problems and severe sprains usually causing late problems. On the other hand the more traditional and still popular classification is the following:

- Grade I: no ligamentous tear (tenderness over the injured ligament)
- Grade II: only anterior talofibular ligament tear
- Grade III: anterior talofibular and calcaneofibular ligament tears

It has been stated that Grade I and II injuries do not lead to late problems of ankle instability, however Brostrum has shown that isolated tears of the anterior calcaneofibular ligament can lead to chronic symptoms.[156]

Clinical assessment will help diagnose the severity of the ankle sprain by establishing which ligaments are tender and how much swelling is present. A more severe injury is present if there is significant ecchymosis, if a positive anterior drawer sign can be demonstrated, and if there is deltoid ligament tenderness. Plain radiographs are useful in demonstrating avulsion fractures and also for ruling out more significant injuries such as hindfoot or ankle fractures and osteochondral fractures of the talus. Stress radiographs (which involve stretching the ligaments and then obtaining radiographic assessments of the ankle joint when stress is applied) help to assess whether the talus is unstable in its mortise. Stress radiographs are indicated when the clinical severity of the injury is not clear or if it is surmised that the results of stress radiographs may change the treatment plans.

In terms of treatment, minor sprains require elevation of the limb to decrease swelling, early weight bearing and peroneal muscle strengthening to improve the lateral support. More severe ankle sprains are best managed with a weight bearing cast or brace immobilisation for approximately 3 weeks, followed by peroneal muscle strengthening.

11.2.7.7.1 Injuries to the Syndesmotic Ligaments produce separation (diastasis) of the distal fibula from the distal tibia secondary to tearing of the anterior and posterior distal tibiofibular ligaments and of the interosseus membrane secondary to a strong abduction or external rotation force [Figure 11.32]. Diagnosis rests on clinical assessment and on the radiographic findings of either a fracture of the fibula above the tibial plafond (which indicates that the tibiofibular ligament is torn) or a frank separation of both bones with lateral displacement of the talus and foot out of the ankle mortise (known as talar shift). Treatment is surgical, and involves correcting the fibular instability by means of internal fixation just

---

156 Brostrom LA, Stark A, Svartengren G. Acute Compartment Syndrome in Forearm Fractures. *Acta Orthop Scand*, 61(1): 50-53, 1990.

proximal to the syndesmotic tibiofibular ligaments. Commonly one or two screws are placed for 2 to 3 months to achieve approximation of the torn ligaments. No attempt is made to repair the torn ligaments as they heal spontaneously with scar tissue.

11.2.8 Injuries to the Foot

11.2.8.1 Introduction

The foot is uniquely suited to its tasks of distributing body weight, carrying the body forward over different surfaces, and breaking the shock that results from running, walking and jumping. Its two structural arches, the transverse and the longitudinal, permit absorption and transmission of ground reaction and body forces [Figure 11.33]. Precisely congruent articulations and numerous strong ligaments ensure static stability, with added dynamic support provided by intrinsic and extrinsic muscle groups. A rich nerve sensory and motor supply and an extensive vascular supply are contained within it. Finally the entire structure is enveloped by thick, protective skin that is nevertheless thin and flexible enough to allow for sensitivity and motion.

11.2.8.2 Anatomy

In this section, the relevant anatomy will be presented to facilitate the understanding of the nature of foot injuries and the rationale of their treatment.

11.2.8.2.1 Osteology: Twenty-six bones comprise the foot, related to each other so as to form 30 articulations [Figures 11.34, 11.35, 11.36]. These bones are divided anatomically into three segments: the tarsus, the metatarsus, and the phalanges. The tarsus consists of seven large bones whose shape and structure are adapted to their function of weight bearing. The metatarsus consists of five metatarsal bones. The phalanges are the fourteen bones of the toe digits.

The plantar surfaces of the tarsus and proximal metatarsus form a *transverse arch*. The *longitudinal arch* is formed by the plantar surfaces of the tarsal bones, the tarsometatarsal articulations and the metatarsus; its stability is maintained by strong supportive ligaments and aponeuroses, and is enhanced by several intrinsic and extrinsic muscle-tendon groups.

When viewing the foot from the functional standpoint, clinicians divide the foot into three regions: the hindfoot (calcaneus and talus), the midfoot (navicular, cuboid, cuneiform bones) and the forefoot (metatarsal and phalanges) [Figure 11.37].

11.2.8.2.2 The Tarsus: The *talus* (also known as astragalus) connects the foot to the leg at the level of the ankle joint. It has three parts, namely the body, the neck and the head. Hyaline articular cartilage covers approximately 60% of this bone. It articulates with the lower tibial articular surface (also termed tibial plafond) at the level of the ankle joint and with the calcaneus on its plantar (or inferior) surface through three facets of the subtalar joint, and with the navicular bone at the talonavicular joint [Figure 11.35]. Other points of contact of the talar body with the ankle joint occur through articulations with the medial and lateral malleoli of the ankle. The broad medial projection of bone from the tibia (known as the medial malleolus) thus articulates with the medial aspect of the body of the talus while the terminal extension or malleolus of the fibula articulates against the lateral surface of the talus. The resulting configuration of the ankle joint resembles that of a mortise in which sits the tenon which is the body of the talus.

Stability of the talus in the ankle joint is particularly good because of the convex dome shape of the body that fits securely in the concavity of the mortise of the ankle joint, and because of the large malleolar structures that stabilize it medially and laterally. Strong collateral and capsular ligaments also brace the articulation.

The plantar surface of the talus is thus partly covered with articular cartilage but the exposed bone in the region of the neck has a deep groove in which many important small blood vessels enter to supply the talus, especially the talar body. In the context of a fracture of the talar neck, an interruption of blood supply to this bone leads to death of all or part of the body of the talus (a pathologic condition known as aseptic necrosis) and eventual collapse of part or all of this section of the talus. The head of the talus is round, mostly covered with hyaline articular cartilage, and is directed against the convexly shaped navicular bone.

The *calcaneus* is the large bone positioned under the talus and constituting the heel of the foot. Although it carries most of the weight transmitted from the talus, it remains a relatively fragile bone with a high proportion of cancellous to cortical bone, and so it can easily fracture and compress as a result of a fall. The posterior portion of the calcaneus receives the insertion of the calf muscles by means of the Achilles tendon. The three calcaneal articular facets (posterior, anterior, and the middle facet which is also known as the sustentaculum tali) articulate with the three corresponding articular facets of the talus to form the subtalar joint [Figure11.38]. The medial aspect of the calcaneus has a bony extension, the sustentaculum tali under which courses the tendon of the flexor hallucis longus (the long flexor of the great toe), and over which rests part of the talus. The distal aspect of the calcaneus contacts the cuboid bone through a concavo-convex articulation [Figures 11.35, 11.36].

The boat-shaped *navicular* bone articulates with the round talar head on its proximal surface, and through concavo-convex surfaces with the medial, middle and lateral cuneiform bones on its distal surface. A small facet also exists for articulation with the cuboid bone. A prominent medial plantar projection (which sometimes develops as a separate or accessory navicular bone) termed the tuberosity is the principal attachment of the posterior tibial tendon (which is an important dynamic supporting structure of the longitudinal arch).

The *cuboid bone* articulates with the calcaneus on its proximal surface and the bases of the fourth and fifth metatarsal bones on its distal surface. The medial aspect usually has two surfaces for articular contact, one always with the lateral cuneiform bone and another less constant one with the navicular bone. There is a groove on its plantar lateral aspect in which courses the tendon of the peroneus longus.

The *three cuneiform* bones articulate with the navicular bone proximally and the bases of the first, second, and third metatarsal bones distally. Their dorsal surfaces are convex while their plantar surfaces are concave. The shape of the articulations of each pair of these bones is wedge shaped, and thus as a group they are shaped and assembled in an intrinsically stable configuration that helps to create the transverse arch of the foot. The medial cuneiform bone is shaped not as long as the other two to create a bony recess into which fits securely the second metatarsal base.

11.2.8.2.3 The Metatarsus: Five metatarsal bones connect the tarsus to the phalanges of the toes. Their bases articulate with each other. The wider base portions of each metatarsal become more narrow at midsection (the shaft) and then taper at the level of the metatarsal neck to end in a head section which articulates with the proximal phalanx of its respective toe. Usually the first metatarsal is shortest, largest and thus the sturdiest. Its large head has two articulations for two (or more) small accessory bones (known as sesamoids) contained within the tendon slips of the flexor hallucis brevis. The second metatarsal is longest and the least mobile because of its secure proximal fit in the tongue and groove articulation provided by the three cuneiforms. The second metatarsal constitutes the axis through which abduction and adduction of the other rays are related. The fifth metatarsal shape has a lateral prominence or styloid process on the dorsal surface to which is attached to the tendon of the peroneus brevis; fractures of this styloid process may masquerade as a sprain of the ankle.

11.2.8.2.4 The Phalanges: The great toe has two phalanges and the lesser four toes have four each. The proximal expansion of each phalanx is known as the base while the distal rounded articular surface is composed of a medial and lateral condyle. The distal phalanges have no condyles but a wide tuberosity or tuft which helps absorb pressure.

11.2.8.2.5 Sesamoid and Accessory Bones: There are usually two small ovoid sesamoid bones contained in the medial and lateral tendon slips of the flexor hallucis brevis, but the medial one can be multifragmented or multipartite. They are positioned under the head of the first metatarsal bone. Other sesamoids can be found under the other metatarsal bones or in the tendons of peroneus longus, tibialis posterior or tibialis anterior. Common accessory bones that occasionally develop in the foot are the accessory navicular (os tibiale externum), an ossicle at the base of the fifth metatarsal (os vesalanium), and the os trigonum at the posterior plantar aspect of the talus.

11.2.8.3 Joint, Ligaments and Aponeurosis of the Foot

11.2.8.3.1 Ankle Joint: The ankle joint consists of a mortise-like articulation created by the body of the talus with the distal tibia and its medial malleolus and with the fibular malleolus (situated laterally). It is more stable when positioned in dorsiflexion because of the wider aspect of the anterior body of talus that wedges itself in the ankle mortise. The strong ligaments that ensure stability of the ankle joint consist of the medial collateral deltoid ligaments, the lateral collateral ligament and the thin and less resilient anterior and posterior capsular ligaments [Figure 11.26]. The deltoid ligament, the strongest of all, has a deep layer joining the medial malleolus to the body of the talus and a superficial portion spanning from the medial malleolus to the navicular and calcaneal bones but also to the more posterior aspect of the talus. The three lateral collateral ligament components are the anterior talofibular, the calcaneofibular and the posterior talofibular ligaments.

11.2.8.3.2 The Subtalar Joint: This joint has two (sometimes three) pairs of matching articular facets on the inferior surface of the talus and on the superior surface of the calcaneus. These are the posterior, the anterior, and (when present) the medial [Figure 11.38] facets. A strong interosseous talocalcaneal ligament helps to prevent excessive eversion (i.e., sideways movement of the heel) while the cervical ligament tightens to prevent excess inversion (i.e., inward movement of the heel). The calcaneo-navicular (spring) ligament [Figure 11.39B] spanning the interval between the anterior calcaneal process and the sustentaculum tali of the os calcis to the deep surface of the navicular bone helps to support the talar neck and head. The bifurcate ligament is composed of the spring ligament along with a ligamentous slip from the calcaneus to the cuboid ligaments.

11.2.8.3.3 Talonavicular Joint: The round head of the talus is firmly seated in the concavity of the navicular bone by strong talonavicular capsular ligaments which are strengthened on the plantar surface by the spring (calcaneo-navicular) ligament.

11.2.8.3.4 The Calcaneocuboid Joint: Along with the talonavicular joint, the calcaneocuboid joint compresses the midtarsal joint of Chopart, a joint complex that moves in concert with the subtalar joint. The calcaneocuboid capsular ligaments stabilize the joint, but on the plantar surface the long and short ligaments provide further support. The bifurcate ligament provides considerable support to the midtarsal joint of Chopart [Figure 11.40].

11.2.8.3.5 The Cuneo-Navicular Joint: Three separate facets of the navicular bone face the three cuneiform bones but only one joints exists. Dorsal and plantar capsular ligaments ensure stability of the cuneo-navicular joint.

11.2.8.3.6 The Tarsometatarsal Joints (Joint of Lisfranc): These are the articulations at the interval between the metatarsal bases and the cuneiform and cuboid bones [Figures 11.39 A and B]. The shape of the metatarsal bases and the recessed position of the second metatarsal bone surrounded by the cuneiform bones confers intrinsic stability to this articulation. However, there are some individuals who have variable motion (dorsiflexion, plantarflexion and rotation) due to ligamentous laxity at the joint between the base of the first metatarsal and the medial cuneiform. Although the dorsal capsular ligaments also stabilize all the tarsometatarsal articulations, the thicker and broad plantar capsular ligaments and the intermetatarsal and interosseous cuneo-metatarsal ligaments add exceptional stability to these joints. When the plantar capsular ligaments are ruptured, the midfoot joints tend to collapse and eventually the longitudinal arch flattens.

11.2.8.3.7 The Metatarsophalangeal Joints: These are the intrinsically stable articulations between the rounded metatarsal heads and the concave proximal portions of the proximal phalanges. Stability is enhanced by plantar (also known as the plantar plate), collateral, and deep transverse metatarsal ligaments.

11.2.8.3.8 The Interphalangeal Joints: These are reinforced by collateral ligaments and the plantar capsular ligament that includes a ligamentous and fibrous plate.

11.2.8.3.9 The Plantar Aponeurosis (Plantar Fascia) [Figure 11.41]: This is an extremely strong fibrous structure, composed of one thick calcaneal (medial) tuberosity attachment and six bands that attach to the metatarsophalangeal joint plantar ligament (plantar plate).

11.2.8.4 Muscles of the Foot

11.2.8.4.1 Extrinsic Muscles [Figure 11.42A]: All innervated by the deep peroneal nerve, the extrinsic muscles arise in the leg from the tibia and fibula to attach at different sites on the foot. The extensor (dorsiflexor) muscles are situated anteriorly; they are composed of the tibialis anterior and the extensor digitorum longus, and the extensor hallucis longus. While the tibialis anterior muscle assists in inversion (deviation of the foot inwards), the other two are responsible for ankle and toe dorsiflexion. The peroneal muscles (peroneus longus and brevis) are situated laterally and are innervated by the superficial peroneal nerve; they help to evert (deviation of the foot outwards) the foot.

The flexor group of muscles is situated posteriorly, and all are innervated by the posterior tibial nerve. They are composed of three deeper muscles, the posterior tibial muscle, the flexor hallucis longus, the flexor digitorum longus, and two more superficial ones, the gastrocnemius and the soleus. The flexor group is responsible for ankle plantar flexion and toe flexion. The tibialis posterior muscle inverts the foot (i.e., deviation of the foot inwards) and dynamically supports the longitudinal arch of the foot.

11.2.8.4.2 Intrinsic Muscles: These are the small short muscles situated in the foot. The extensor digitorum brevis, innervated by the terminal branches of the deep peroneal nerve is the only intrinsic muscle on the dorsal surface of the foot. Its tendons attach to the dorsal surfaces of the proximal phalanges of the first, second, third and fourth toes.

The plantar intrinsic muscles [Figure 11.42B], arranged in four layers are:

first layer: the abductor hallucis, the flexor digitorum brevis, the abductor digiti minimi;
second layer: the quadratus plantae, the lumbricals;
third layer: the flexor hallucis brevis, the adductor hallucis, the flexor digiti minimi;
fourth layer: the interossei.

These muscles are furthermore grouped into compartments. In the context of severe foot injuries with significant bleeding into the compartments, these muscles may suffer irreversible ischemic damage and become replaced by scar tissue. They are innervated by the medial and lateral plantar nerves which are the terminal two branches of the posterior tibial nerve.

11.2.8.5 The Nerves of the Ankle and Foot [Figure 11.43]

Knowledge of the sensory and motor supply to the foot and ankle is important because of the frequent concomitant occurrence of nerve injuries with bone and soft tissue injuries to the foot and ankle. In the buttock region exits the large sciatic nerve which separates into two major nerves, the peroneal division and the posterior tibial division. The common peroneal nerve will divide in the proximal 1/3 of the leg into the deep peroneal nerve and a superficial peroneal nerve, while the posterior tibial nerve divides just beyond the medial malleolus into medial and lateral plantar nerves.

Terminal branches of the superficial peroneal nerve provide sensation to the dorsal aspect of the foot and ankle while the sensory supply of the medial aspect of the ankle is supplied by the saphenous nerve (the terminal branch of the femoral nerve in the thigh). Sensation to the lateral aspect of the ankle and foot is provided by the sural nerve (arising from branches of both the common peroneal and posterior tibial nerve). Sensory supply to the web space between the great toe and the second toe is provided by the terminal branches of the deep peroneal nerve. Finally, further branching of the sural and superficial peroneal nerve gives rise to pairs of dorsal digital sensory nerves.

On the plantar surface, the medial and lateral plantar nerves, both arising from the posterior tibial nerve, give sensory supply to the sole of the foot and end as pairs of plantar digital sensory nerves to the toes. They also provide motor supply to the intrinsic muscles of the foot. Other small calcaneal sensory nerves arise from the posterior tibial nerve to supply the heel pad. These are frequently injured in the context of blunt injuries of the foot and calcaneal fractures.

11.2.8.6 Vascular System

11.2.8.6.1 Arteries: [Figures 11.44 and 11.42A] Three arteries provide the blood supply to the foot. The anterior tibial artery in the lower leg becomes the dorsalis pedis artery as it enters the foot alongside the extensor tendons; it then enters the sole of the foot to form the first plantar metatarsal artery. The larger posterior tibial artery courses with the posterior tibial nerve behind the medial malleolus before terminating as the medial and lateral plantar arteries. The larger lateral plantar artery joins with the plantar terminal branches of the dorsalis pedis to form the plantar vascular arch. The toes receive their arterial blood supply from the plantar arch. Owing to the deep location of the plantar arch, surgical exposure in the event of uncontrollable bleeding can be very difficult.

Finally, a peroneal artery is present just posterior to the distal tibiofibular joint, giving off many small calcaneal branches and other branches that join with branches of the anterior tibial artery.

11.2.8.6.2 Veins: Superficial veins lie under the skin while deep veins accompany the arteries. The great saphenous vein (situated subcutaneously, just anterior to the medial malleolus) constitutes the main drainage receptacle of the dorsum of the foot. The smaller saphenous vein (situated midline in the posterior calf) drains the lateral portion of the foot. The deep veins of the foot drain into the deep plantar venous arch, which in turn empties into venous networks that surround the peroneal, anterior and posterior tibial arteries. These eventually drain into the popliteal vein at the back of the knee.

11.2.8.7 Biomechanics

Weak calf muscles, loss of joint mobility and bony malalignment will each produce gait abnormalities. Gait alterations put excessive stress on other components of the lower extremity and this in turn may eventually cause rapid deterioration of injured parts. A brief review of some of the pertinent mechanical aspects of gait is presented in order to understand how foot injuries described later in this chapter affect the foot's ability to function in moving the body and absorbing energy to arrest the body's momentum.

The gait cycle consists of two phases, one being the *swing phase* during which the foot is moved forward off the ground until it contacts the ground again to begin the other phase of stance. *Stance phase* can be divided into heel-strike, flat-foot and toe-off portions. The foot acts as a rigid lever at toe-off and becomes a flexible shock absorber at heel strike. The ankle functions as a hinge joint allowing only dorsiflexion and plantar flexion of the foot within the ankle mortise. Limitation of ankle range of motion will impair progression of normal gait.

The subtalar joint is the most important foot joint, allowing foot inversion and eversion (i.e., medial inward deviation, and lateral or outward deviation) and thus helping the foot adjust itself to uneven or inclined surfaces (e.g., walking sideways on a hill, or on a country trail). Loss of the accommodative function of the subtalar joint causes the talus to bind in the ankle mortise and decreases the efficiency of gait.

The heel pad is composed of specialized fat cells, that by design help absorb the shock at heel strike. Damage to this hydraulic cushion is usually irreversible, causes significant pain on weight bearing, and thus impairs gait mechanics.

At heel strike, the hindfoot everts and thus unlocks the foot, relaxing the midtarsal joint complex and thus creating a flexible midfoot to allow accommodation of the foot to the ground and better absorption of the energy of the ground reaction forces at impact. At push-off, the subtalar joint inverts thus "locking" the midtarsal joints to create a rigid lever at the midfoot for forward propulsion.

During gait, from midstance to toe-off, contraction of the extrinsic muscles, intrinsic muscles and passive dorsiflexion of the metatarsophalangeal joints causes elevation of the longitudinal arch of the foot. Combined with locking of the midtarsal joints, elevation of the arch creates a stable lever arm for push-off.

11.2.8.8 Evaluation of Foot Injuries

A general history and physical examination is fundamental when managing patients who have suffered a foot injury. The general medical condition and the presence of certain systemic disorders (e.g., diabetes, peripheral vascular disease, arthritis) must be identified since they may influence the selection of treatment and the outcome. Finally, the patient's vocational and avocational requirements must be known as treatment may also need to be modified accordingly.

Knowledge of the mechanism of injury will assist a clinician in determining the extent of injury and in suspecting injury to other body structures. The specifics of the injury (e.g., fall from a height onto tiptoes, sudden foot inversion, direct blunt trauma, etc.) must be recorded as they are obviously important.

Initial physical examination of the foot consists of an inspection for lacerations, punctures, swelling and deformity secondary to injury. Discoloration and pallor signifying circulation impairment are noted. Next, the foot is palpated gently over bone, tendon and joint surface landmarks to locate areas of sensitivity, deformity and soft tissue tension. Occasionally joint manipulations and stress tests are carried out and if circumstances are appropriate the patient's gait is assessed. An examination of the neurological and vascular functions of the foot must always be done.

After splinting and elevating the injured foot, *special tests* relative to the suspected foot injury are then ordered. These will include standard or conventional radiographic views and possibly additional special radiographic projections as well. Plain tomography (i.e., thin section multiplane radiographic cuts) are useful for visualizing the degree of fragmentation or displacement of fracture fragments. Computerized tomography (CT scanning) provides the same information as plain tomography but in great detail; but unfortunately it is not necessarily more useful when applied to every kind of foot and ankle injury. Bone scanning techniques using bone seeking radioisotopes are helpful when suspecting an occult fracture that is not evident on standard radiographs. Finally, in the context of foot trauma, magnetic resonance imaging is sometimes used to evaluate the injuries to the soft tissues, especially those involving tendons.

11.2.8.9 Fractures of the Talus

Typically, fractures of the talus occur either through the head, body or neck regions of the bone [Figure 11.45]. Each of these types of fractures are discussed separately because they each must be managed in different ways.

11.2.8.9.1 Blood Supply of the Talus: A brief review of the blood supply of the talus is relevant in the preamble to a discussion of talar fractures because the most harmful complication that can arise from these injuries is a concomitant traumatic interruption of the blood supply of that bone. The extra-osseous circulation, which is greater than the intra-osseous blood supply, forms a vascular ring around the talar neck and in the sinus tarsi.[157] The sinus tarsi is a tunnel-like space on the lateral aspect of the subtalar joint where several small arterial branches enter the talar neck through foramina. With serious damage to part or all of the blood supply to the talus, a condition of avascular necrosis may occur leading to collapse deformity of the talar body.

11.2.8.9.2 Talar Head Fractures: These constitute 5 to 10% of all talar injuries. They are usually produced by ankle and foot hyperdorsiflexion compressive forces at the joint. Since the blood supply to the head is very good, avascular necrosis is uncommon, however the concern with the injury is obtaining excellent realignment of the fracture so as to avoid talonavicular joint incongruity leading to the late development of post-traumatic arthrosis of that articulation.

These fractures are well seen on standard radiographs but may need more accurate appraisal by means of computerized tomography. In the case of displaced talar head fractures, the goal is to obtain and maintain fracture reduction usually with screws, less often with K-wires, as wires do not provide sufficient stability to the realigned fracture. Non displaced fractures are treated with cast immobilisation for approximately 6 to 8 weeks.

Complications that can occur include: midtarsal joint instability from nonunion, late post-traumatic talonavicular joint arthrosis, fracture nonunion, and rarely osteonecrosis. If complications occur and the fracture fragments cannot be securely realigned, a talonavicular joint fusion (i.e., surgically obtained obliteration of the articulation) should be carried out. Most current fusion techniques employ screw fixation and a bone graft (obtained from the patient's pelvis or lower leg) slotted into the talar head and navicular and thus placed across the talonavicular joint interval.

11.2.8.9.3 Talar Neck Fractures: These fractures represent 50% of all talar injuries. The mechanism of injury is one of hyperdorsiflexion of the

---

157 Haliburton RA, Sullivan CR, Kelly PJ, et al. The Extraosseous and Intraosseous Blood Supply of the Talus. *J Bone Joint Surg*, 40A: 1115-1120, 1958. Kelly PJ, Sullivan CR: Blood Supply of the Talus. *Clin Orthop*, 30: 37-44, 1963. Mulfinger GL, Trueta J. The Blood Supply of the Talus. *J Bone Joint Surg*, 52B: 160-165, 1970.

foot against the tibia with impingement of the neck against the lower anterior tibial surface. With further force, the talar neck breaks and the talar and subtalar joint capsular ligaments disrupt; with added torsional forces the subtalar joint subluxes (i.e., partially dislocates) or dislocates.[158]

Hawkins has devised a classification of talar neck fractures that has practical significance.[159] A *type I* injury is a nondisplaced fracture with no accompanying joint subluxation. A *type II* injury involves a displaced talar neck fracture with subluxation or dislocation of the subtalar joint. In a *type III* injury, the body of the talus is displaced from the neck segment and dislocated from both the subtalar and ankle joints. A *type IV* injury is a type I or type III injury with talonavicular joint dislocation.[160] As the displacement of the talar neck increases, so does the incidence of fracture malunion, post-traumatic osteoarthritis, and osteonecrosis.[161]

Clinically, there are signs of severe foot and ankle pain, and occasionally foot deformity is present. Due to the high energy of trauma responsible for producing talar neck fractures, concomitant foot or ankle fractures occur frequently. Radiographic evaluation is necessary to confirm the diagnosis and to plan surgical strategy. Treatment varies according to the type of fracture sustained. Type I injuries are usually managed by means of a non weight bearing cast that is worn until radiographic evidence of fracture healing is evident (2 to 3 months). A displaced fracture needs operative reduction, employing either an anteromedial, or anterolateral or posterolateral approach.[162]

Type II injuries require open treatment when there is 3 mm or more of dorsal displacement or rotational deformity. Post-operative care is the same as in type I injuries with no weight bearing in general for approximately 3 months. At regular intervals, radiographs are obtained to evaluate bone healing but also to see if at 8 weeks there are signs of re-vascularization of the body of the talus, i.e., evidence of a Hawkins' sign.[163]

---

158 Daniels TR, Smith JW. Talar Neck Fractures. *Foot Ankle*, 14: 225-234, 1993.
159 Hawkins LG. Fractures of the Neck of the Talus. *J Bone Joint Surg*, 52A:991-1002, 1970.
160 Canale ST, Kelly FB Jr. Fractures of the Neck of the Talus: Long-Term Evaluation in Seventy-One Cases. *J Bone Joint Surg*, 60A: 143-156, 1978. Daniels TR, Smith JW. Talar Neck Fractures. *Foot Ankle*, 14: 225-234, 1993.
161 Daniels et al., *supra*, note 158. Gilquist J, Oretrop N, Stenstrom A, et al. Late Results after Vertical Fracture of the Talus. *Injury*, 6. 173-179, 1974. Kenwright J, Taylor RG. Major Injuries of the Talus. *J Bone Joint Surg*, 52B: 36-48, 1970.
162 Trillat A, Bousquet G, Lapeyre B. Displaced Fractures of the Neck or of the Body of the Talus. Value of Screening by Posterior Surgical Approach. *Rev Chir Orthop Reparatrice Appar Moteur*, 56: 529-536, 1970.
163 Hawkins, *supra*, note 159.

Several type III injuries are open (up to 50%)[164] or else cause severe tension on the skin. They are true surgical emergencies in need of immediate debridement of the ruptured skin and damaged tissue and prompt realignment of the disrupted subtalar joint and the fracture itself. This surgery is typically difficult to perform because of the usually secure displacement of the talar body that is surrounded by unyielding soft tissues. Approaches to realign the talus include the temporary insertion of a calcaneal traction pin or the application of an external fixator to distract the soft tissues and thus help disengage the talar body, or a medial malleolar osteotomy to access the fracture easily and to thus realign the displaced body of talus. Internal fixation is achieved with large or small size screws or with Kirshner wires if this is not feasible [Figure 11.46, 11.47B and 11.47C]. Post-operative care requires prolonged immobilization in a below knee cast until Hawkins' sign is seen on subsequent radiographs, after which further care includes partial weight bearing in a weight relieving brace (patellar tendon bearing brace), followed by full weight bearing once the radiographs confirm fracture healing.

11.2.8.9.4 Prognosis and Complications of Talar Neck Fractures: These include delayed or nonunion, subtalar and ankle post-traumatic arthritis, osteonecrosis, skin necrosis and infection. *Osteonecrosis* has been shown to increase with severity of injury, from 0 to 13% for Type I fractures, to 20 to 50% for type II fractures, and up to 83 to 100% in type III fractures.[165] The earliest radiographic sign of re-vascularization is Hawkins' sign of patchy subchondral bone resorption in the talar body, seen six to eight weeks post trauma. It suggests re-vascularization of the body of the talus. An MRI of the talus is another useful test to detect this vascular complication, provided the internal fixation used was titanium and not the usual stainless steel screws which produce image artifact and distortion. Bone scan with a bone seeking radioisotope is also helpful. Osteonecrosis can take up to 2 years to heal.[166] Ideally the talus should be protected from weight bearing stress until it has fully re-vascularized; however, sometimes the osteonecrotic talus collapses despite lack of weight bearing.[167] Most patients with avascular necrosis of the talus are significantly disabled because of pain, limping and partial or complete ankylosis of the ankle or subtalar joints. However, there is no direct relationship between the development of avascular necrosis and permanently

---

164 Adelaar RS. Surgical Treatment of Fractures of the Talus. In: Gould JS, ed. *Operative Foot Surgery*. Philadelphia: WB Saunders, 1994: 377-398.
165 Hawkins, *supra*, note 159. Canale et al., *supra*, note 160.
166 Adlaar, *supra*, note 164.
167 Heckman JD. Fractures and Dislocations of the Foot. In: Rockwood CA, Green DP, eds. *Fractures in Adults*. Philadelphia: JB Lippincott, 1984.

disabling symptoms.[168] When osteonecrosis is symptomatic, reconstructive surgery is indicated. While the description of the details of these operations is beyond the scope of this book, it is important to list these. They include: fusion of the ankle joint; fusion or the subtalar joint; tibial-calcaneal fusion after excision of the collapsed necrotic body of talus; a triple fusion (subtalar, talonavicular, calcaneal cuboid joint fusions); and occasionally pantalar joint fusion (i.e., a triple fusion with an ankle fusion).

Problems related to fracture healing are somewhat less serious. *Delayed union* is common, but *nonunion* is uncommon. Delayed union can occur if there has been extensive damage by the fracture to the blood supply to the bone; healing can be slow in general because bone consolidation of talar fractures occurs from inside (i.e., from the endosteal network of blood vessels). The fracture should be protected from weight bearing stresses until there is evidence of healing but in the absence of bone healing at one year, a bone grafting procedure should be done. *Malunion* is another potential complication, and usually results in the foot being deviated into a varus (turned in) position; when this is severe, the resulting functional problems and pain require corrective surgery.

Post-traumatic arthritis of the ankle and subtalar joint may result despite competent fracture management. The symptoms of local ankle or hindfoot pain aggravated by prolonged standing or walking, especially over uneven ground suggest this complication which is caused by severe damage to the smooth articular cartilage that lines the articular surface of the talus. The symptoms and radiographic signs may be mild or much more severe, but they are usually more disabling if avascular necrosis with collapse of the talar body has occurred. If medical management (physical therapy, anti-arthritic or pain relief medications, shoe modifications, braces that partially relieve body weight) of this complication is unsuccessful, then a fusion is usually required to effectively and permanently block the painful ankle or the painful subtalar joint motion.

Finally in the case of type III injuries or in those with severe tension on the skin produced by the severely displaced talar body, skin necrosis and infection can occur; this complication is the harbinger of a poor result.

11.2.8.9.5 Fractures of the Body of the Talus: These comprise 20% of all talar fractures. A variety of fracture configurations have been described but most occur as a result of compressive or shearing forces.[169] Diagnosis from standard radiographs is usually adequate but considerable information regarding amount of displacement or comminution (number of fracture fragments) can be obtained from tomograms (thin cut multi-plane

---

168 Canale et al., *supra*, note 160.
169 Heckman, *supra*, note 167.

radiographs) or CT scans. Although some fractures are undisplaced and can be managed conservatively with a cast until fracture healing occurs, any displaced fracture requires open reduction and internal fixation to restore congruity of the ankle and subtalar joints, a goal which is absolutely necessary given the critical functions of these articulations in gait. Often because of the inaccessible location of the fracture under the tibial plafond it is necessary to carry out a malleolar osteotomy (sectioning of the lateral or medial malleolus) to gain access to the fracture for the purpose of realignment and internal fixation. In order to avoid complications of avascular necrosis and ankle or subtalar arthritis it is imperative to achieve perfect or the best possible reduction of the body's articular surface. Should osteonecrosis or degenerative arthritis develop, the principles of treatment are the same as those mentioned following the development of the sequelae after talar neck fractures.

11.2.8.9.6 Other Less Common Talar Fractures: Other fractures of the talus include fractures of the lateral or posterior process (medial and lateral processes) [Figure 11.47A]. They are uncommon, usually undisplaced and may be difficult to diagnose and to image with conventional radiographs. Conservative treatment is most often effective but displaced fractures require fixation if technically feasible.

11.2.8.10 Dislocations, Subluxations about the Talus

The subtalar joint is the articulation responsible for the side-to-side movement of the hindfoot that is necessary for walking on uneven ground or on inclines.

A subtalar joint dislocation involves a simultaneous dislocation of both the subtalar and talonavicular joints. Most commonly (85% of the time) the foot is displaced medially, secondary to a strong inversion force that pulls the calcaneus medially.[170] The talus remains in the ankle joint while the navicular bone comes to rest on the neck of the talus. A strong eversion force produces the less common lateral subtalar joint dislocation in which the calcaneus moves laterally. Athletic injuries and also high-energy injuries such as falls from a height and motor vehicle accidents can produce subtalar joint dislocations. Additional shearing injuries to the dis-

---

170 DeLee JC, Curtis R. Subtalar Dislocation of the Foot. *J Bone Joint Surg*, 64A: 433-437, 1982. Dunn AW. Peritalar Dislocation. *Orthop Clin North Am*, 5: 7-18, 1974. Grantham SA. Medial Subtalar Dislocation: Five Cases with a Common Etiology. *J Trauma*, 4:845-849, 1964. Heppenstall RB, Farahrar H, Balderstron R, Lotke P. Evaluation and Management of Subtalar Dislocations. *J Trauma*, 20:494-497, 1980. Mac SS, Kleiger B. The Early Complications of Subtalar Dislocations. *Foot Ankle*, 1: 270-274, 1981.

located articular surfaces can occur in up to 45% of subtalar joint dislocations but may be difficult to see on the radiographs.[171]

Treatment consists of prompt and gentle reduction under anaesthesia so as to achieve muscular relaxation and thus minimize damage to the articular surfaces during the realignment manipulations. When joint reduction can't be achieved by closed methods, an open reduction must be done not only to realign the joint but also to remove any obstructing osteochondral debris that may be preventing the reduction. After reduction, cast immobilization is needed for three to four weeks followed by progressive weight bearing and physical therapy to restore subtalar and ankle joint motion, particularly subtalar motion.

The *prognosis* relates in part to the direction of injury. The force required to produce a medial subtalar injury is less than that for a lateral dislocation, and thus it is not surprising that lateral dislocations tend to fare worse. However, lateral subluxations of dislocations have a higher incidence of concomitant fractures to adjacent foot bones and frequent osteochondral subtalar joint debris, two facts that account for more residual subtalar joint stiffness and a worse prognosis. With prompt reduction, patients with simple uncomplicated subtalar joint dislocation do well at long-term follow up, but almost all have partial or complete limitation of subtalar joint mobility. Some patients, however, continue to experience pain and difficulties when walking on uneven ground.[172]

11.2.8.11 Fractures of the Calcaneus

The calcaneus, also called Os calcis, is the heel of the foot. It is the bone that strikes the ground first when walking and occupies the bulk of the hindfoot. It is a bone with multiple functions. On the plantar surface the calcaneus provides a solid base for attachment of the firm fibro-fatty septae connected to the skin. This provides a cushioned non-mobile pad for weight bearing. Multiple areas are present on the surface of the calcaneus for the attachment of muscles, ligaments, retinacular slings and most importantly, the Achilles' tendon posteriorly [Figure 11.40]. The attachment of this tendon on the posterior aspect of the calcaneus places it away from the centre of rotation of the ankle joint thus enhancing its biomechanical leverage. Also associated with the calcaneus are grooves and passageways to allow tendons, arteries and veins to enter the foot in a

---

171 Delee, *ibid*.
172 Grantham, *supra*, note 170. Buckingham WW Jr. Subtalar Dislocation of the Foot. *J Trauma*, 13: 753-765, 1973. Larson HW. Subastragalar Dislocation (Luxatio Pedis Sub Talo). A Follow-up Report of Eight Cases. *Acta Chir Scand*, 113: 380-392, 1957. Smith H, Sage FP. Medullary Fixation of Forearm Fractures. *J Bone Joint Surg*, 39A: 9198, 1957.

partially protected manner. Since the calcaneus connects the hindfoot to talus and midfoot it interacts at a number of locations and each interaction is a joint [Figure 11.34]. Each of these articulations have similar characteristics in that they are synovial joints with hyaline cartilage and allow unique and limited range of motions restricted by the joint configuration, the surrounding capsule, the ligaments and the supporting musculotendinous units. Distally, the calcaneus articulates with the cuboid bone and proximally, it articulates with the talus bone superiorly. The talus articulates with the tibia and fibula to form the ankle joint. The joint between talus and calcaneus is called the subtalar joint. This joint is divided into three aspects; an anterior facet, a middle facet, and the larger posterior facet [Figure 11.48]. It is this joint that allows the motion of inversion and eversion of the hindfoot.[173] The plane of motion is therefore more in a medial-lateral direction as opposed to the joint proximal to it, the ankle joint, which allows motion in the anterior-posterior direction. The main function of the subtalar joint is to transmit the weight borne by the calcaneus to the talus and to allow some motion that will accommodate walking on uneven ground—more particularly, uneven ground that would cause the heel to invert or evert. The function of the calcaneal-cuboid joint is to allow transmission of forces from the midfoot to the hindfoot and to allow a small degree of rotation and sidewards motion of the midfoot.[174] The consistency of bony architecture of the calcaneus is rather uniform. It has a very thin periosteal outer shell, quite different from the strong thick cortex of long bones, and an internal supporting structure of thin beams of bone. These beams, called trabeculae, are oriented to best counter the applied forces. The calcaneus is therefore a structure consisting mainly of cancellous bone and not dense cortical bone.

Fractures of the calcaneus are complicated injuries and must be subdivided into two main categories with additional subcategories;

1. Fractures that occur as a result of tension forces
2. Fractures that occur as a result of compression forces.

Fractures can occur in any bone as a result of tension or pulling and in the cortical region of a long bone this frequently is a result of a rotational stress. In the metaphyseal-epiphyseal region or in an epiphysioid bone like the calcaneus, a fracture that occurs from tension is called an avulsion fracture and is related to the attachment of either ligaments or tendons. This type of fracture in the calcaneus is frequent for small ligaments yet

---

173 American Academy of Orthopaedic Surgeons, *Atlas of Orthotics, Biomechanical Principles and Applications*. St. Louis: Mosby, 1975: 258-264.
174 *Ibid.*

rarely does the Achilles tendon produce such a fracture. More frequently the calcaneus fractures as a result of a compressive force such as a fall from a height onto the heel. In this instance the thin external shell and the trabecular internal bony architecture is involved. Depending upon the severity of the injury, the fracture may be displaced or not. In this category it is important to subcategorize this compression fracture as to whether damage has occurred to the articular surfaces of the calcaneus and the degree to which these joints have been involved.[175] The injury to the joint may be one in which only the hyaline cartilage is damaged and no fracture is seen on radiographic examination. It may be one in which various degrees of disruption of the articular surface has occurred. In addition, only the subtalar joint may be damaged or both the subtalar and the calcaneocuboid joint may be involved. When the fracture involves the subtalar joint, the anterior and middle facets are usually spared the consequences of the fracture and the posterior facet is usually either depressed or split and/or comminuted and rotated [Figure 11.49]. The remaining pieces may be deformed to the extent that anatomical reconstitution may be impossible [Figure 11.49]. In addition, for both subcategories of extra-articular fractures (those that do not involve the joint) and intra-articular fractures, it is usual that the displacement that accompanies the crushing of the cancellous bone will distort the architecture of the calcaneus in multiple planes. The crushing will often change the leverage moment, which the Achilles tendon exerts, on the calcaneus. More importantly, the widening of the heel caused by the explosion of the trabecular bone and splintering of the thin periosteal shell on the lateral cortex may press on neighbouring structures such as the peroneus brevis and longus tendons, the distal tip of the fibula and Sural nerve producing pain and disability [Figure 11.40].

Classifications of calcaneal fractures:

> Fractures that occur in tension (avulsion fractures)
> Fractures that occur in compression

Extra-articular Fractures:

- Non-displaced

---

175 Essex-Lopresti P. The Mechanism, Reduction, and Results in Fractures of the Os Calcis, *British J Surg*, 39:395-419, 1952. Giachino AA, Uhthoff HK. Intra Articular Fractures of the Calcaneus. *J Bone Joint Surg*, 71A:784-787, 1989. Mittler BE, Notari MA, Gudeon A, Norman SY. Joint Depression Calcaneal Fracture. *J Foot Surg*, 24:366-369, 1985. Rowe CR, Sakellarides HT, Freeman PA, Sorbie C. Fractures of the Os Calcis. *J Am Med Assn*, 184:920-923, 1963. Wilkins J, Patzakis M. Choice and Duration of Antibiotics in Open Fractures. *Orthop Clin North Am*, 22(3): 433-437, 1991.

- Displaced with/without lateral tendon/nerve compression

Intra-articular Fractures:
- Subtalar joint—non displaced
- displaced
  with/without lateral
  tendon/nerve involvement
- both subtalar and calcaneocuboid joints
  —non displaced
  —displaced
    with/without lateral tendon/nerve involvement

11.2.8.11.1 Assessment: The standardized approach consists of an orderly assessment of the patient's history of injury, a complete physical examination, and special diagnostic procedures. The typical history of a patient with a calcaneus fracture is one of a fall from a height onto the feet. Specific questions must be directed towards the spinal region as frequently the force that produces a calcaneal fracture is also transmitted to the spine and the cancellous vertebral bodies located in the thoracolumbar junction may also be fractured. The physical examination also must include the whole body. The expected findings locally in the involved hindfoot include; gross swelling, ecchymosis, pain to palpation, limitation in the range of motion of the subtalar joint and inability to bear weight. An injury to the thoracolumbar spine may reveal mild kyphosis, local tenderness to deep palpation of the spinous process, and possibly signs of a neurological deficit if the spinal cord or nerve roots are damaged.

11.2.8.11.2 Special Tests: Plain radiographs of the calcaneus should include; a lateral view [Figure 11.50A], to assess the general shape, internal architecture, and outline of the subchondral bone of the posterior facet of the calcaneus, and oblique views. In addition, a tangential view to access the degree of widening and lateral displacement should be requested.[176] Even with excellent positioning and proper radiographic techniques, plain radiography is at best an incomplete radiographic assessment and computerized tomography scanning (CT scanning) is mandatory to evaluate the incidence and degree of involvement of the articular surfaces [Figures 11.50B and C].[177] Frequently plain radiographs do not sug-

---

176 Giachino et al., *ibid*. Broden B. Roentgen Examination of the Subtaloid Joint in Fractures of the Calcaneus. *Acta Radiol*, 31:85-91, 1949.
177 Rowe et al., *supra*, note 175. Giachino et al., *supra*, note 175. Gilmer PW, Herzenberg J, Frank JL, Silmerman P, Martinez S, Goldner JL. Computerized Tomographic Analysis of Acute Calcaneal Fractures. *Foot and Ankle*, 6:184-193, Feb. 1986. Guyer BH, Levinsohn EM, Frederickson BE, Bailey GL, Formikell M. Computer Tomography of Calcaneal Fractures. Anatomy,

gest the presence of an intra-articular fracture that is well demonstrated on CT scanning. In addition, the amount of damage seen on CT scan may provide useful guidance in the treatment decision making process and help with predicting a final outcome status.[178]

11.2.8.11.3 Treatment: There are a large variety of treatment modalities used in calcaneal fractures.[179] Undisplaced extra-articular and intra-articular fractures are usually treated with avoidance of weight bearing and physiotherapy to maintain joint mobility. Displaced extra-articular fractures may be treated by non-weight bearing and the displacement accepted or attempts made to reduce the displacement. The most difficult of calcaneal fractures is the displaced intra-articular fracture and these continue to be managed by both operative and non-operative methods.[180] Open re-

---

Pathology, and Clinical Relevance, *Am J Radiol*, 145:911-919, 1985. Heger L, Wulff K, Seddiqi MS. Computed Tomography of Calcaneal Fractures. *Am J Radiol*, 145:131-137, 1985. Herzenberg JE. Computerized Tomography of Calcaneal Fractures [letter]. *Am J Radiol*, 146:644-645, 1986. Lowrie IG, Finlay DB, Brenkel IJ, Gregg PJ. Computerized Tomographic Assessment of the Subtalar Joint in Calcaneal Fractures. *J Bone Joint Surg*, 70B(2): 247-250, 1988. Pablot SM, Danemen A, Stringer DA, Carroll N. The Value of Computed Tomography in the Early Assessment of Comminuted Fractures of the Calcaneus: A Review of Three Patients. *J Pediat Orthop*, 5:435-438, 1985. Sanders R, Fortin P, Di Pasquale T, Walling A. Operative Treatment in 120 Displaced Intra Articular Calcaneal Fractures Results Using a Prognostic Computed Tomography Scan Classification. *Clin Orthop*, 290:87-89, 1993. Segal D, Marsh JL, Leiter B. Clinical Application of Computerized Axial Tomography (CAT) Scanning of Calcaneus Fractures. *Clin Orthop*, 199:144-123, 1985. Zayer M. Fracture of the Calcaneus. A Review of 110 Fractures. *Acta Orthop Scand*, 40:530-542, 1969. Zirna H, Akino MD. The CAT Scan: An Aid in Evaluating Calcaneal Fractures. *J Foot Surg*, 25:270-272, 1986.

178 Pablot et al., *ibid*. Sanders et al., *ibid*.
179 Giachino et al., *supra*, note 175. Rowe et al., *supra*, note 175. Kyle et al., *supra*, note 87. Zayer, *supra*, note 177. Arnesen A. Fracture of the Os Calcis and its Treatment. *Acta Chir Scandinavica*, Supplementum, 234, 1958. Cotton FJ. Os Calcis Fracture. *Ann Surg*, 64:480-488, 1916. Gray CH. Crush Fractures of the Os Calcis, *Lancet*, 242:106-108, 1942. Jarvoholm U, Korner L, Thoren O, Wiklund LM. Fractures of the Calcaneus, A Comparison of Open and Closed Treatment. Acta Orthop Scandinavica, 55:652-656, 1984. Lindsay WRN, Dewar FP. Fractures of the Os Calcis, *Am J Surg*, 95:555-576, 1958. McAuley JP, Alexander DI. Results of Treatment for Severe Calcaneal Fractures. In: Proceedings of the Canadian Orthopaedic Association, 67B(2):326, 1985. Nade S, Monahan PRW. Fractures of the Calcaneum: A Study of the Long-Term Prognosis, *Injury*, 4:200-207, 1972-1973. Widen A. Fractures of the Calcaneus, *Acta Chir Scand Supp*, 188, 1954.
180 Giachino et al., *supra*, note 175. Rowe et al., *supra*, note 175. Guyer et al., *supra*, note 177. Bertelsen A, Hasner E. Primary Results of Treatment of Fracture of the Os Calcis by "Foot-Free Walking Bandage" and Early Movement. *Acta Orthop Scandinavica*, 21:140-154, 1951. Geckeler EO. Comminuted Fractures of the Os Calcis. Choice of Treatment. *Arch Surg*, 61:469-476, 1950. Harding D, Waddell JP. Open Reduction in Depressed

duction and internal fixation is gaining in popularity in the last decade. On occasion, the radiographs and surgical exposure reveal a joint so damaged that re-constitution is impossible. In this situation, fusing the joint may be warranted. Although immediate fusion, that done within the first few weeks of injury on occasion may be the treatment of choice[181] allowing the fracture to heal and assessing outcome before fusing the joint tends to be the more popular course of action when a fusion of the subtalar joint is considered a possibility. In addition to directing attention to the displaced fracture, decompression of neighbouring structures (peroneal tendons and sural nerve) may be necessary.[182]

11.2.8.11.4 Prognosis: The poorest results for calcaneal fracture lies in the category of displaced comminuted intra-articular fractures.[183] Even with a perfect anatomical reduction and stable internal fixation, normalcy

---

Fractures of the Os Calcis. *Clin Orthop.* 199:124-131, 1985. Hazlett JW. Open Reduction of Fractures of the Calcaneum. *Can J Surg*, 12:310-317, 1969. Lance EM, Carey EJ, Wade PA. Fractures of the Os Calcis: Treatment by Early Mobilization. Clin. Orthop, 30:76-90, 1963. Maxfield JE, McDermott FJ. Experiences with the Palmer Open Reduction of Fractures of the Calcaneus. *J Bone Joint Surg*, 37A:99-106, Jan. 1955. Maxfield JE. Os Calcis Fractures: Treatment by Open Reduction. *Clin Orthop*, 30:91-99, 1963. McReynolds IS. Trauma to the Os Calcis. In: Jahss M, ed. *Disorders of the Foot*. Philadelphia: W.B. Saunders, 1982: 1497-1542. Paley D, Hall H, McMurtry R, Green J. Operative Treatment of Calcaneal Fractures: A Long Term Follow-up; Calcaneal Protocol Score, and Factors that Affect Outcome. *Orthop Trans*, 11:484, 1987. Palmer I. The Mechanism and Treatment of Fractures of the Calcaneus. Open Reduction with the Use of Cancellous Grafts. *J Bone Joint Surg*, 30A:2-8, 1948. Parks JC. The Nonreductive Treatment for Fractures of the Os Calcis. *Orthop Clin North Am*, 4:193-195, 1973. Pozo JL, Kirwan EOG, Jackson AM. The Long Term Results of Conservative Management of Severely Displaced Fractures of the Calcaneus. *J Bone Joint Surg*, 66B(3):386-390, Jan. 1973. Ross SDK, Sowerby MRR. The Operative Treatment of Fractures of the Os Calcis. *Clin. Orthop*, 199:132-143, 1985. Salama R, Benamara A, Weissman SL. Functional Treatment of Intra-Articular Fractures of the Calcaneus. *Clin Orthop*, 155:236-240, 1976. Slatis P, Kiviluoto O, Santavirta S, Laasonen EM. Fractures of the Calcaneum. *J Trauma*, 19:939-943, 1985. Soeur R, Remy R. Fracture of the Calcaneus with Displacement of the Thalamic Portion. *J Bone Joint Surg*, 57B(4):413-421, 1975. Stephenson JR. Displaced Fractures of the Os Calcis Involving the Subtalar Joint. The Key Role of the Superomedial Fragment. *Foot and Ankle*, 4:91-101, Sept.-Oct. 1983.

181 Giachino et al., *supra*, note 175. Sanders et al., *supra*, note 177. Zayer, *supra*, note 177. Dick IL. Primary Fusion of the Posterior Subtalar Joint in the Treatment of Fractures of the Calcaneum. *J Bone Joint Surg*, 35B:375-380, 1953. Noble J, McQuillan WM. Early Posterior Subtalar Fusion in the Treatment of Fractures of the Os Calcis. *J Bone Joint Surg*, 61B(1):90-93, 1979. Thompson KR. Treatment of Comminuted Fractures of the Calcaneus by Triple Arthrodesis. *Orthop Clin North Am*, 4:189-191, 1973.

182 Giachino et al., *supra*, note 175. Herzenberg, *supra*, note 177.

183 Sanders et al., *supra*, note 143.

will never be obtained.[184] The damage done at the time of injury of necessity produces an injury to the articular cartilage and obtaining a normal subtalar range of motion and normal hindfoot function is not expected.

11.2.8.12 Midtarsal Fractures

This region of the midtarsal joint is composed of the navicular, the cuboid, and cuneiform bones [Figure 11.37]. The talonavicular and calcaneal cuboid portions of the midtarsal joint complex become mobile when the heel is everted and relatively fixed when the heel is inverted. It is important to understand that when isolated fractures, dislocations, or sprains occur in this region that the clinician must search for associated injuries in the midtarsal region and elsewhere in the foot. In other words, isolated injuries of the midtarsal region are very uncommon.

11.2.8.12.1 Navicular Fractures: Avulsion fractures (i.e., fractures produced from a severe and abrupt pulling force of a tendon or ligament on its bone attachment) are usually treated with symptomatic treatment (i.e., analgesics, light compression bandage, foot elevation and rest, crutches), including a walking cast in some cases. Fractures involving the medial (tuberosity) portion of the navicular are most often the result of sudden increased tension on the posterior tibial tendon and are usually undisplaced; cast immobilization usually suffices in ensuring sound healing, but if this does not occur then usually excision of the ununited fracture fragment is carried out along with suturing of the posterior tibial tendon to the bed of bleeding navicular bone. Fractures of the body of the navicular, unless undisplaced, require anatomical reduction that is usually achieved by open methods. Internal fixation of these fractures is technically difficult in part because of the curved banana shape of the navicular bone but also because of the fact that fractures of the body of this small bone tend to be multifragmented.

---

184 Geckeler, *supra*, note 180. Gray, *supra*, note 179. Harding D, Waddell JP. Open Reduction in Depressed Fractures of the Os Calcis. *Clin Orthop.* 199:124-131, 1985. Hazlett, *supra*, note 180. Lance EM, Carey EJ, Wade PA. Fractures of the Os Calcis: A Follow-up Study. *J Trauma*, 4:15-56, 1964. Lance et al., *supra*, note 180. Magnuson R. On the Late Results in Non-Operated Cases of Malleolar Fractures. *Acta Chir Scand* [Suppl], 90: 1-136, 1944. Maxfield et al., *supra*, note 180. Mizuno K, Hirohata K. The Long Term Results of Open Reduction in the Os Calcis Fractures, *Orthop Trans*, 11:484, 1987. Paley D et al., *supra*, note 180. Palmer I, *supra*, note 180. Ross et al., *supra*, note 180. Soeur et al., *supra*, note 180. Stephenson, *supra*, note 180. Sanders et al., *supra*, note 143. Magnuson, *supra*, note 149. Giachino et al., *supra*, note 175. Widen, *supra*, note 179. Bertelson et al., *supra*, note 180.

11.2.8.12.2 Cuboid Fractures: The most common type of fracture of this bone has been termed the "nutcracker" fracture and it is often accompanied by a tarsometatarsal joint injury, either a sprain or a fracture dislocation. As minimal bone impaction usually occurs, cast immobilization for 6 to 8 weeks usually ensures a good result unless associated with a tarsometatarsal joint injury.

11.2.8.12.3 Cuneiform Fractures: Injuries to these bones rarely occur as isolated injuries and usually are associated with tarsometatarsal joint injuries. Thus, careful physical examination and scrutiny of the foot radiographs will often reveal other important concomitant injuries that require special attention and treatment that encompasses the management of cuneiform fractures.

11.2.8.13 Injuries to the Tarsometatarsal (Lisfranc's) Joint

11.2.8.13.1 Anatomy: As discussed previously, intrinsic stability of these articulations is provided primarily by the trapezoidal shape of the middle three metatarsal bases, forming a Roman arch configuration and also by the recessed locked position of the second metatarsal base between the medial and lateral cuneiform bones [Figures 11.34, 11.35, 11.36]. Besides the strong and thick plantar ligamentous structures that brace these joints, there are also ligaments between the bases of the metatarsal and one very strong one between the medial cuneiform and the base of the second metatarsal bone [Figure 11.39]. This last one, known as Lisfranc's ligament, is very important: in severe sprains or disruptions of the tarsometatarsal joint, a radiographic tell-tale sign that points to the diagnosis of a tarsometatarsal injury is the small chip of bone pulled off at the base of the second metatarsal (which is exactly where attaches Lisfranc's ligament).

11.2.8.13.2 Mechanisms of Injury and Classification: Lisfranc (a military surgeon during the Napoleonic wars) treated many fallen calvarymen who had sustained tarsometatarsal joint injuries. Nowadays, high-energy trauma, or injuries related to falls or severe sprains during athletic pursuits produce these injuries. One can classify the injuries as sprains, joint fracture-subluxations, and joint fracture-dislocations.

Two broad mechanisms of trauma, direct and indirect, can produce these injuries. Direct trauma to the dorsum of the foot produce a tarsometatarsal joint disruption from the crushing effect sustained; an example of this injury is when an individual's foot is crushed under a fallen wall or under a car wheel. The more common indirect mechanisms involve twisting or axial loading of the fixed foot. Axial loading as a mechanism of injury can be in a heel-to-toe or in a toe-to-heel (i.e., falls with ankle maintained in maximal plantar flexion or equinus) direction. The three common patterns of tarsometatarsal joint disruptions (i.e., either subluxations or dislocations) are the homolateral, isolated and divergent [Figure 11.51]. A comprehensive and broadly accepted elaboration of this classification has been devised by Hardcastle.[185]

11.2.8.13.3 Clinical Presentations: These injuries are often overlooked and underdiagnosed because they masquerade as severe foot or ankle sprains. Thus a high degree of suspicion is needed in many cases to make the diagnosis. Aside from severe foot pain and inability to bear weight, the patient usually presents with severe swelling on the dorsum of the foot in the region of the tarsometatarsal joint and exquisite sensitivity when the midfoot joint intervals are palpated. Forefoot malalignment or deformity is evident only in the case of a fracture dislocation or with some fracture subluxations. Attempts to gently stress the articulations are usually not tolerated because of severe pain. In severe disruptions seen late, especially those secondary to a direct mechanism, the circulation may be compromised (the dorsalis pedis pulse on the dorsum of the foot is not palpable), and possibly sensation may also be reduced because of a developing or a full-blown compartment syndrome of the foot.

11.2.8.13.4 Radiographic Findings: Each of the three standard radiographic views of the foot is essential to confirm the presence and the severity of the injury. The oblique view is particularly helpful in showing any subtle displacement of the metatarsal bases not seen on the AP (anteroposterior) view in which the middle metatarsal bases often appear stacked on each other because of their trapezoidal shape and arch configuration.

Most disruptions to the tarsometatarsal joint can be readily diagnosed from the standard radiographs, which would reveal one of the three common patterns of injury and associated fractures of the metatarsal bases. However, in several instances, the injuries have realigned themselves spontaneously[186] and so no gross radiographic abnormality is noted. However, two tell-tale signs may be present on these films thus confirming that a significant injury has occurred. These are an avulsion injury of the base of the second metatarsal (produced by the sudden pull of Lisfranc's ligament) and a partial crushing or shearing injury to the distal cuboid articular surface (known as a nutcracker fracture) [Figure 11.52]. Furthermore, careful scrutiny of the oblique views may reveal lack of precise alignment of the metatarsal bases with their corresponding cuneiform and cuboid bones. Finally, in equivocal cases, tomography or CT scanning is often very helpful.

---

185 Hardcastle PH, Reschauer R, Kutscha-Lissberg, et al. Injuries to the Tarsometatarsal Joint. *J Bone Joint Surg*, 64B: 349-359, 1982.
186 Anderson LD. Injuries of the Forefoot. *Clin Orthop*, 122: 18-27, 1977.

11.2.8.13.5 Treatment: Sprains should be treated for up to 6 weeks with cast immobilization to ensure complete ligament healing. Subluxations or dislocations require precise reduction, even though adequate function often results from incomplete joint reduction[187] and though anatomic or near anatomic reduction does not always prevent the development of post-traumatic arthritis.[188] When the patient presents late with massive foot swelling, it is better to wait a few days before attempting joint reduction as the foot swelling may prevent all attempts to perfectly realign the joint disruption.

While closed reductions and casting of subluxed tarsometatarsal joints may appear to be initially successful, often the deformity is lost as soon as the swelling subsides during the first few weeks. Consequently, it is recommended to place at least one or usually several temporary percutaneous K wires across the realigned tarsometatarsal joint to prevent any loss of alignment. Furthermore, as the goal is to obtain anatomical alignment, the currently popular treatment approach favours joint realignment by opening the displaced tarsometatarsal joints and securing the reduction with several smooth pins or screws if necessary. Associated displaced fractures of cuneiform, navicular or other foot bones may also necessitate open reduction and internal fixation. The adequacy of reduction should be confirmed intra-operatively with radiographs. Immobilization in a cast and delayed weight bearing at approximately eight to ten weeks are recommended to ensure adequate healing of the disrupted ligaments and of the fractures. Often a moulded arch support worn for one year assists in relieving symptoms during the several months' duration of the rehabilitation phase.

11.2.8.13.6 Prognosis: There is substantial disagreement in the literature on the long-term effects of injury to the Lisfranc's joint. Some authors have presented several cases of incompletely realigned tarsometatarsal joint disruptions where the patients had no or few functional problems or pain related to their foot injury.[189]

On the other hand the current treatment standard is to *obtain* and

---

187 Brunet JA, Wiley JJ. The Late Results of Tarsometatarsal Joint Injuries. *J Bone Joint Surg*, 69B: 437-440, 1987. Gilmer PW, Herzenberg J, Frank JL, Silmerman P, Martinez S, Goldner JL. Computerized Tomographic Analysis of Acute Calcaneal Fractures. *Foot and Ankle*, 6:184-193, Feb. 1986. Wilppula E. Tarsometatarsal Fracture-Dislocation: Late Results in 26 Patients. *Acta Orthop Scand*, 44: 335-45, 1973.
188 Heckman, *supra*, note 167.
189 Aitken A, Poulson D. Dislocations of the Tarsometatarsal Joint. *J Bone Joint Surg*, 45A: 246-260, 1963. Brunet JA, Wiley JJ. The Late Results of Tarsometatarsal Joint Injuries. *J Bone Joint Surg*, 69B: 437-440, 1987. Wilson DW. Injuries of the Tarsometatarsal Joints. Etiology, Classification and Results of Treatment. *J Bone Joint Surg*, 54B: 677-686, 1972. Wilppula, *supra*, note 187.

maintain anatomical joint realignment. The favoured open treatment of these injuries with permanent (usually) screw fixation appears to yield better results as tarsometatarsal joint realignment is assured. The biomechanical function of the tarsometatarsal joint in providing a fixed joint complex and stable lever during the toe-off portion of the gait cycle is thus restored, and to a greater degree than when temporary transarticular fixation pins are used. However, no long-term comparative studies exist to validate this currently popular approach, and furthermore, other long-term studies have shown satisfactory relief or improvement of pain and function in the majority of cases when the joint disruptions were reduced and pinned.[190] Although proponents of the open approach with screw fixation of the realigned Lisfranc joint cite the late development of arthritis of the joint as justification for their management, it is known that many patients, despite accurate joint reductions, develop arthritis which in some cases is symptomatic but often not in others. Finally, the late development of arthritis may be primarily determined by the damage sustained by the articular cartilage at the time of injury and less so by the severity or type of joint displacement.[191]

11.2.8.14 Metatarsal Fractures: Fractures involving the metatarsal bases should arouse suspicion of a concomitant injury to the adjacent joint tarsometatarsal injury. The exception is a fracture of the fifth metatarsal styloid process. Isolated fractures of the metatarsal shaft may be treated with simple cast immobilization for 4 to 6 weeks when the fracture is undisplaced or minimally displaced, or operatively if significantly displaced in a plantar or dorsal direction. Operative fixation of selected displaced metatarsal fractures is achieved by either K wire or plate and screw fixation.

Metatarsal neck fractures should be realigned by closed or by open methods if displaced plantarly or significantly angulated. Malunion of one or more displaced metatarsal neck fractures will lead to mal-distribution of body weight on the forefoot and the development of painful plantar keratoses (callosities).

Fractures of the first metatarsal are very special in that any significant displacement will severely impact on forefoot comfort and affect its weight bearing function. Thus, these fractures are often addressed surgically with plates and screws (or external fixators in some instances) to restore length and alignment.

Fractures of the *fifth metatarsal bone* deserve special attention if in-

---

190 Brunet JA et al., *supra*, note 187. Wilppula E., *supra*, note 187.
191 Jeffreys TE. Lisfranc's Fracture-Dislocation. A Clinical and Experimental Study of Tarso-metatarsal Dislocations and Fracture-Dislocations. *J Bone Joint Surg*, 45B: 546-551, 1963.

volving the proximal 1/3 of the shaft (the so-called "Jones" fracture) or the styloid process. In the proximal diaphyseal (shaft) section, the bone tissue is primarily composed of thick compact cortical bone, which once fractured produces a slow and limited healing response over the small surface area of the fracture. (In some instances, healing may be significantly delayed or absent). These fractures require prolonged cast immobilization (up to 10 weeks approximately) before clinical and radiographic signs of union are noted, and if union appears to be delayed or absent then open fixation and grafting are indicated.[192]

The very common *avulsion fracture of the styloid process of the fifth metatarsal* is produced by sudden inversion of the foot by the peroneus brevis (whose tendon attaches to the styloid process). The diagnosis is easy to establish as the area is locally tender and because stretching and passively inverting the foot produce pain. Radiographs (especially the oblique views) clearly demonstrate the injury. Sometimes the fracture extends into the articulation with the cuboid, or occasionally it is significantly displaced (greater than 1 cm). In terms of the radiographic differential diagnosis, it is important to distinguish the jagged edges of the fracture from the smooth outline of a relatively common accessory bone (the Os vesalanium) that is situated next to the fifth metatarsal styloid process. Treatment of the fracture varies, depending on surgeon and patient preference and on the degree of disability that is apparent at the time of injury.[193] Thus one can apply either a tensor or a tape bandage, or a walking cast for 3 to 6 weeks until the fracture area is no longer tender. Significant displacement may result in a nonunion; however most nonunions are asymptomatic because at least firm tenacious fibrous tissue bridges the fracture gap. If a nonunion is symptomatic, one treatment option for a small fragment of united bone is to excise it and to re-attach the peroneus brevis tendon to the metatarsal base[194] and another approach is to realign and fixate the fragment with a pin and wire.

11.2.8.15 Dislocations of the Metatarsophalangeal Joints

These are either very uncommon injuries or are infrequently reported. A discussion of these injuries is beyond the scope of this book, but two

---

192 Dameron TB. Fractures and Anatomical Variations of the Proximal Portion of the Fifth Metatarsal. *J Bone Joint Surg*, 57A: 788-792, 1975. Kavanaugh JH, Brower TD, Mann RV: The Jones Fracture Revisited. *J Bone Joint Surg*, 60A: 776-782, 1978. Zeldo RR, Torg JS, Rachun A. Proximal Diaphyseal Fractures of the Fifth Metatarsal—Treatment of the Fractures and their Complications in Athletes. *Am J Sports Med*, 7: 95-101, 1979.

193 Heckman, *supra*, note 167.

194 Heckman, *supra*, note 167.

references that contain all the current relevant details are listed at the end of this chapter.[195]

11.2.8.16 Fractures and Dislocations of the Toes

11.2.8.16.1 Fractures of the Great Toe (Hallux): Direct or indirect (e.g., "stubbing of the toes") blows may fracture a phalanx of the hallux. Most often splinting or casting will effectively relieve pain and lead to sound healing of an undisplaced or minimally displaced fracture. Significantly displaced fractures of the shaft or of the intra-articular portion of the phalanx should be addressed with an open reduction and internal fixation. All types of fractures, especially those with intra-articular extensions into the metatarsophalangeal or interphalangeal joints lead to at least some joint stiffness and possibly to painful post-traumatic arthritis.

11.2.8.16.2 Fractures of the Lesser Toes: These fractures are common and are quite painful until 2 or 3 weeks later when they have begun to consolidate. Minimally displaced or non-displaced fractures only require gauze and tape splinting to the adjacent toe ("buddy taping"). Significantly displaced fractures need to be reduced by closed means (rarely by open methods).

11.2.8.16.3 Dislocations of the Lesser Toe Joints: These are very uncommon. The pertinent references are listed at the end of this chapter.[196]

11.3 INJURIES TO THE UPPER EXTREMITIES

11.3.1 Injuries to the Shoulder

11.3.1.1 Introduction

The shoulder girdle is a complex of four joints that includes the glenohumeral, the scapulothoracic, the acromioclavicular, and the sternoclavicular joints. Several small and large muscles stabilize and activate these articulations, while strong ligaments brace them and assist in suspending the upper limb. Through the shoulder region pass large blood vessels and the network of sensory and motor nerves (known as the brachial plexus) that supply the entire upper limb [Figure 11.66].

The bones of the shoulder consist of the proximal (upper) portion of the humerus, the scapula and the clavicle [Figure 11.53]. The proximal

---

195 Brunet JA, Tubin S. Traumatic Dislocations of the Lesser Toes. *Foot Ankle*, 18: 406-411,1997. Brunet et al., *supra*, note 187.
196 Brunet and Tubin, *ibid.* Jahss MH. Chronic and Recurrent Dislocations of the Fifth Toe. *Foot Ankle*, 1: 275-278. 1981.

humerus whose round articular surface faces the small oval shaped glenoid cavity of the scapula has 2 large bony prominences (tuberosities) on which are inserted the tendons of the rotator cuff tendons and between which pass one of the two tendons (the long head tendon) of the biceps muscle.

The blood supply to the humeral head is critical and may be disrupted as a result of a trauma. The main arterial contribution to the humeral head is the anterior humeral circumflex artery, the terminal portion being the arcuate artery which has an interosseous course and which perfuses the entire humeral head [Figure 11.54].

Normal shoulder function depends on the integrity of the four joints: the glenohumeral, the sternoclavicular (S.C.), the acromioclavicular (A.C.), and the scapulothoracic [Figure 11.53]. The glenohumeral articulation is that formed by the round humeral head and the shallow glenoid socket of the scapula. The scapulothoracic joint consists of the articulation that takes place when the plate-like body of the scapula glides and rotates on the posterior lateral surface of the rib cage. The sternoclavicular and acromioclavicular joints and their joint capsular ligaments play a role in maintaining the shoulder girdle solidly braced and supported at the side of the body.

With almost all upper limb activities, all four joints of the shoulder complex move synchronously with the majority of the motion occurring at the glenohumeral joint. With advancing age shoulder motion decreases, but in general the glenohumeral joint contributes about two-thirds of the total range of flexion or abduction (movement of arm away from side of body) while the scapulothoracic joint provides the remainder.[197] With the arm at the side, the normal range of rotation is as much as 170 degrees.[198] During shoulder flexion, the clavicle rotates up to 10 degrees at the acromioclavicular joint and up to 50 degrees at the sternoclavicular joint.[199]

From a biomechanical standpoint, the role of the scapulothoracic joint is to complement the movements of the glenohumeral joint. It primarily helps with positioning, stabilization and suspension of the upper limb. The suspensory muscles of the scapular bone are the levator scapulae, the trapezius and the serratus anterior, while the suspensory ligaments are the coracoclavicular ligaments [Figure 11.55]. Scapulothoracic motion involves complex muscle coupling or combinations of muscles that work together to assist in adjusting the plane of the glenoid socket so that it faces the humeral head with all the positional changes of the upper limb.

---

197 Neer CS II. Anatomy of Shoulder Reconstruction. In: Neer CS II, ed. *Shoulder Reconstruction*. Philadelphia: WB Saunders, 1990.

198 *Ibid.*

199 Near, *supra*, note 197. Rockwood CA. Subluxations and Dislocations about the Shoulder. In: Rockwood CA, Green, DP, eds. *Features in Adults*. Philadelphia: JB Lippincott Co., 1984.

The glenohumeral joint is intrinsically unstable by virtue of the mismatch of the large humeral head and the shallow glenoid that measures approximately one-third the size of the humeral head. Joint stability is enhanced by the glenoid labrum (which is an annular ligament which deepens the glenoid socket), the capsular ligaments and the three anterior glenohumeral ligaments (the superior, middle and inferior glenohumeral ligaments) [Figure 11.56]. Additional stability is ensured by the rotator cuff group of tendons which attach on the greater and lesser tuberosities; along with their role as a humeral head rotator and abductor, they maintain the humeral head centred in the centre of the glenoid cavity[200] with all activities or positions of the upper limb [Figure 11.58 and 11.59]. The tendon of the long head of the biceps that runs between the tuberosities to attach just above the glenoid helps to steer the humeral toward the glenoid during various work or sport activities. The subacromial-subdeltoid bursa, a large thin walled sac containing lubricating fluid covers the rotator cuff and a portion of the long head of the biceps and permits smooth gliding of these structures under the coracoacromial arch [Figure 11.57].

Finally, the deltoid muscle is the large, thick, triangular muscle that forms a cape over the shoulder girdle [Figure 11.60]. It receives its motor innervation from the axillary nerve, a nerve that can be injured from stretching or transection at the time of shoulder fracture or dislocation, or at surgery. The deltoid works synchronously with the rotator cuff muscles, providing considerable power for those activities involving the use of the upper limb at chest level or higher. The pectoralis major inserts just below the surgical neck of the shoulder; it provides stability to the upper limb movements, acts as a powerful arm adductor (i.e., movement of the arm against the side of the body), and also assists in internal rotation (i.e., rotation towards the body) of the shoulder.

In summary, normal shoulder motion requires that all four joints of the shoulder complex be freely mobile. The rotator cuff tendons and its muscles stabilize the humeral head in the glenoid cavity and assist in rotational and abduction movements of the shoulder. Full elevation of the arms is accomplished by a 2:1 ratio of glenohumeral and scapulothoracic motion, with the supraspinatus muscle being responsible for initiating that movement [Figures 11.61 and 11.62].

11.3.1.2 Subluxations and Dislocations of the Glenohumeral Joint

Despite the evident mismatch between the humeral head and the glenoid socket, the glenohumeral articulation is a very stable joint by vir-

---

200 Saha AK. Dynamic Stability of the Glenohumeral Joint. *Acta Orthop Scand*, 42: 491-505, 1971.

tue of the several ligamentous and tendon structures that surround the humeral head and maintain it securely in the shallow glenoid socket.

Instability of the glenohumeral joint can be secondary to trauma or it can develop insidiously in individuals with lax ligaments. In this book, only the post-traumatic variety will be discussed.

11.3.1.2.1 Pathomechanics: Usually the force that produces shoulder instability is applied to the arm and indirectly to the shoulder region. Minor trauma to the glenohumeral articulation can result in a sprain or a subluxation. If the trauma is more significant, the shoulder joint may displace posteriorly, anteriorly or inferiorly. In this case, not only can the humeral head remain displaced and require medical attention to have it repositioned (reduced) in the glenoid cavity, but often subsequent smaller traumas to the shoulder may produce a chronically unstable articulation. Recurrent shoulder dislocations or subluxations may stem from one major injury to either the glenoid labrum or to the glenohumeral (capsular) ligaments, or to all of these structures together. Frequent dislocations and subluxations can further stretch or damage these soft tissue joint restraints and can also damage the bone portions of the articulation leading to glenoid rim fractures and humeral head impaction fractures or dents (known as Hill-Sachs lesions) [Figure 11.63].

11.3.1.2.2 Diagnosis: The vast majority (98%) of shoulders dislocate anteriorly, i.e., with the humeral head displaced in front of the glenoid socket.[201] The diagnosis of shoulder instability can often be established by reviewing the history of the injury, which includes complaints of severe shoulder pain or unreliability when positioning the arm a certain way, or symptoms of the arm going numb or dead when throwing an object overhand. These symptoms in conjunction with the physical findings of pain or uneasiness with certain shoulder provocative tests usually cinch the diagnosis.

In the acute setting, plain radiographs are diagnostic; these views consist of the anteroposterior or AP view and a lateral view, either the tangential scapular or "Y" view, or the axillary lateral view. In the case of chronic instabilities, bone injury to the glenoid or humeral head can be demonstrated on the plain radiographs or with computed tomography scans, while the soft tissue labrum tears can be imaged either with a CT scan-arthrography test (thin computer cuts of the joint that has been pre-injected with radiographic contrast medium) or with MRI.

11.3.1.2.3 Treatment: In acute traumatic shoulder dislocations, urgent treatment is required as the pain is quite severe and shoulder function is completely impaired. Reduction of the glenohumeral joint should be car-

---

201 Rockwood, *supra*, note 199.

ried out quickly after radiographic assessment has been done to rule out any fracture and to establish the direction of the humeral head displacement. Most often, joint reduction can be carried out by closed means. Pre-reduction and post-reduction assessments of the upper limb's neurologic and vascular status should be done focusing particularly on the axillary nerve function (motor supply to the deltoid muscle and sensory supply to the skin overlying it) that often is affected because of stretching produced by the sudden, traumatic, displacement of the humeral head. Radiographs are needed post-reduction to confirm anatomic realignment and to rule out the possibility of a fracture caused by the reduction technique. After reduction, a brief period of immobilization in a sling is required (to permit the damaged tissues to form reparative scar) followed by a program of physical therapy to enhance shoulder stability and endurance for use of the arm in the position known to produce instability.

Surgical repairs are indicated when instability persists despite a structured supervised program of physical therapy performed over several months to improve muscular support for the joint. While a discussion on the surgical technical alternatives is beyond the scope of this book, in general a surgical procedure is selected to correct the specific anatomic lesion discovered at the time of surgery. For example, if a glenoid labral detachment has occurred, then that structure must be secured to the glenoid rim; if the glenohumeral ligaments are detached or stretched, then they must be reattached or shortened; if the glenohumeral capsule has become quite lax, then it must be adjusted to a smaller size. Occasionally other procedures are selected, such as tendon reinforcement of the joint capsule or bone blocks to buttress an unstable humeral head. If a large deep humeral head Hill-Sachs lesion has occurred, then a joint replacement, a humeral shaft derotation osteotomy, or a joint fusion may be required; small Hill-Sachs lesions that accompany soft tissue capsulolabral tears can be ignored.

Surgical correction of the glenohumeral instability can be accomplished by either the traditional open or by recently perfected arthroscopic techniques. The success rates of any operative repair depends on several factors including age, the direction of instability (anterior or posterior), the severity of the anatomic lesion and the ease of surgical repair, the patient's occupation and avocational interests, and in the case of arthroscopic repairs the surgeon's technical abilities and experience. However in general, the success rates are better with anterior instabilities, with open approaches (unless the surgeon's experience with arthroscopic surgery is extensive) and in patients above age 30 years.

Potential complications of traumatic anterior dislocations of the shoulder include injuries to the bones (glenoid rim or humeral head or humeral tuberosities), tears of the rotator cuff produced by excessive stretching of these tendons at the time of injury, injury to the axillary artery or to its branches, and injuries to the axillary nerve which may be stretched by the dislocated humeral head.

11.3.1.3 Injuries to the Acromioclavicular Joint

11.3.1.3.1 Anatomy: The function of the clavicle is to securely maintain the shoulder and arm at the side of the body. This bone articulates with the axial skeleton at its medial end at the sternoclavicular joint and with the shoulder at the lateral end at the acromioclavicular joint. At the acromioclavicular (AC) joint, the thin capsular ligaments and the overlying deltoid and trapezius muscles stabilize the AC joint, but it is the contribution of the 2 coracoclavicular ligaments (the conoid and trapezoid ligaments) that significantly enhances the stability of the AC articulation [Figure 11.56]. The coracoacromial ligaments are important as they function as important suspensory ligaments of the upper extremity.

11.3.1.3.2 Mechanisms of Injury: The typical AC joint sprain, subluxation or dislocation is caused by a direct blow to the shoulder region sustained from a fall. This mechanism of injury results in the arm being pushed down from downward pressure exerted on the acromion during the fall. If the force is severe, the capsular ligaments of the AC joint are torn, and then possibly the coracoclavicular ligaments as well. If the force is very severe, then the deltoid and trapezius muscular attachments that cover the AC joint will also tear resulting in a significant loss of ligamentous support to the upper extremity which then tends to sag downward. In all types of AC joint injuries, the normally smooth articular surfaces of the acromion and clavicle may be significantly injured and thus may eventually develop late degenerative osteoarthritis.

11.3.1.3.3 Injury Types and their Management: Figure 11.64 illustrates the three common injuries to the AC joint, type I being a sprain; type II a subluxation with disruption of the AC joint ligaments and type III a dislocation produced by disruptions of both the AC joint capsular ligaments and the coracoclavicular ligaments. A type I injury produces local tenderness and usually resolves within 2 weeks with treatment consisting of complete upper extremity rest in a sling and analgesics as required. A type II injury is more painful and thus rest in a sling is required for approximately 2 to 3 weeks, followed by gradual exercises of the shoulder and return to activities by 6 weeks.

The appropriate management of type III AC joint disruptions remains controversial. Generally speaking, the results of conservative and non-operative treatment of these complete dislocations are equally good in terms of recovery of shoulder function and comfort. However, compared to the results of surgically treated lesions, several clinical trials of conservatively managed cases have shown that shoulder movement and function are recovered more quickly and that patients resume sports and work much earlier. Some surgeons have advocated early repair of acute type III injuries in selected cases (athletes or heavy labour workers) believing that an open repair withstands better to repetitive stresses and heavy loads.[202] Although clinical experience suggests that considerably displaced lesions (i.e., those with over 2 cm elevation of the distal clavicle) do better with surgical correction,[203] in general it appears that most patients who suffer the usual type III injury recover shoulder function without surgical intervention. A reasonable compromise may be to treat type III lesions expectantly, resorting to secondary reconstructive procedures for those patients who remain significantly symptomatic several months after injury despite an intensive program of active rehabilitation.

If surgical management is chosen, there are several types of AC joint reconstructive techniques. They include primary ligament reconstruction, acromioclavicular joint fixation with pins, coracoclavicular fixation with a screw or with synthetic graft material or with tendon or fascial tissue, and finally by means of a dynamic muscle transfer to the elevated unstable clavicle.[204]

11.3.1.3.4 Complications: Several complications can develop following all types of AC joint injuries or as a consequence of one treatment approach or the other. First of all, with any type of AC joint injury, associated fractures to other parts of the shoulder girdle often occur and may mitigate against a good outcome regardless of the treatment chosen. Coracoclavicular ossification may occur after a Type III injury but may not affect the treatment outcome.[205] Late erosive changes (osteolysis) of the distal end of the clavicle may develop secondary to the damage received to the articular surface, producing a dull ache over the AC joint along with general shoulder weakness and pain; usually these symptoms resolve within a year, if not decompression of the AC joint by excision of the lateral 1 cm segment of the clavicle improves the symptoms in approximately 85% of cases.[206]

Common complications of nonoperative treatment include shoulder

---

202 Rockwood CA, Young DC. Disorders of the Acromioclavicular Joint. In Rockwood CA, Matsen FA, eds. *The Shoulder*. Philadelphia: WB Saunders, 1990.
203 Richards RR. Disorders of the Acromioclavicular Joint. In: Richards RR, ed. *Tissue Reconstruction in the Upper Extremity*. New York: Churchill Livingstone, 1995.
204 Rockwood and Young, *supra*, note 202.
205 Rockwood CA. Disorders of the Sternoclavicular Joint. In: Rockwood CA, Matsen FA, eds. *The Shoulder, supra*, note 202.
206 Schneider T, Strauss JM, Fink B, et al. *Open Mumford Procedure for AC Joint Pathology*. Presented at the Sixth International Congress on Surgery of the Shoulder (ICSS), Helsinki, Finland, 1995.

girdle stiffness secondary to immobilization, skin irritation with improper use of a harness used to achieve closed reduction of Type III dislocations, residual displacement and deformity of the AC joint (sometimes producing a significant cosmetic problem) and late degenerative post-traumatic arthritis of the AC joint.

There are several possible complications that can arise from operative treatment of type III AC joint disruptions. They include wound infection, osteomyelitis, late post-traumatic acromioclavicular joint arthritis, soft tissue calcification (between the coracoid and the clavicle, erosion of the bones (clavicle, coracoid) by the metal or suture internal fixation, late fracturing of the bone through which were implanted fixation pins or through the screw holes in the bones, migration of the pins and wires, inadequate reduction of the AC joint and loss of reduction. Finally, though not a complication of the treatment itself, a second operation to remove the fixation devices is usually necessary.

11.3.1.4 Injuries of the Sternoclavicular Joint

11.3.1.4.1 Anatomy: Considerable forces are transmitted through the sternoclavicular (SC) joint on account of its important functional role as the connection between the upper extremity and the axial skeleton. Strong ligaments (interclavicular, costoclavicular and capsular anterior, posterior ligaments) and an intra-articular disc [Figure 11.65] ensure strength of the articulation. The joint functions as a ball and socket articulation because it moves in almost all planes. Given its location just anterior to several vital structures (the large vessels entering and exiting the heart, the heart, the lungs and the trachea), injuries to the SC joint (and their management) can have very serious and potentially life threatening consequences.

11.3.1.4.2 Mechanisms of Injury, Diagnosis: Most often sports injuries (for example, piling on in football) and motor vehicle accidents produce sternoclavicular joint sprains, subluxations, and dislocations or else fractures of the medial end of the clavicle. The joint disruptions result in the more common anterior displacement or the less common posterior displacement of the clavicle. Physical findings are helpful in determining the direction of the displacement of the clavicle, but in the case of posterior displacement, the patient may present with breathing difficulties, a choking sensation, or venous congestion of the neck and upper extremity due to compression of the clavicle against underlying vital structures. Careful radiographic assessment (plain radiographs, 40° cephalic tilt view, and if necessary AC joint tomography or CT scans) is mandatory for establishing the diagnosis and for decision making treatment.

11.3.1.4.3 Treatment: Most SC joint injuries consist of sprains of subluxations. Joint sprains become asymptomatic in a matter of days, while joint subluxations, which are usually managed with a padded "figure of 8" harness and sling become comfortable after 2 to 3 weeks; ultimately, shoulder function is not affected. Dislocations on the other hand are rare. Complete anterior dislocations are best treated symptomatically and with skilful neglect, accepting the residual cosmetic deformity and chronic joint achiness, mainly because of the frequent difficulties and significant risks associated with open reduction and internal fixation. Acute traumatic posterior dislocations must be reduced by closed methods (rarely by open methods) and become stable when the shoulders are held back in a "figure of 8" harness or body cast worn for 3 to 4 weeks.[207]

11.3.1.5 Fractures of the Clavicle

11.3.1.5.1 Anatomy: Despite being the strong connection between the upper extremity to the axial skeleton, the "S" shaped clavicle is frequently fractured.[208] This nevertheless strong structure contributes to power and stability to the arm and shoulder girdle, assists in all motions of the shoulder girdle, acts as a frame for insertions and origins of muscles of the neck and upper extremity, and finally by virtue of its shape and strength protects the adjacent underlying neurovascular structures (brachial plexus, axillary and subclavian vessels) [Figure 11.66].

11.3.1.5.2 Diagnosis and Classification: Falls on the outstretched hand, or lateral compression to the shoulder region, or a direct blow are the chief causes of fractures of the clavicle in adults. Most of the time, the diagnosis is strongly suspected from the physical findings but radiographic assessment is necessary to determine the precise location of the fracture, for evaluating the number of fracture fragments, and to identify associated (local) fractures of the shoulder girdle.

Although complete and complex classifications of clavicle fractures exist, for therapeutic reasons almost all clinicians prefer to classify them according to whether they involve the middle, proximal (or medial) or distal (or lateral) one-third segments of the clavicle.

11.3.1.5.3 Treatment: It may appear redundant yet it is important to point out that the goals of treatment of clavicle fractures are to achieve rapid bone healing with a minimum loss of shoulder girdle mobility and

---

207 Rockwood CA. Disorders of the Sternoclavicular Joint. In: Rockwood CA, Matsen FA, eds. *The Shoulder, supra*, note 202.
208 Craig EV. Fractures of the Clavicle. In: Rockwood CA, Matsen FA, eds. *The Shoulder, supra*, note 202.

with a minimum amount of residual deformity. Unfortunately, most fractured clavicles cause a fair amount of inconvenience and discomfort during the healing period, and lead to the production of a visible fracture bump that may be large.

The majority of fractures (82%), involve the middle one-third segment [Figure 11.67]. The majority of these are amenable to a successful outcome by means of closed reduction treatment.[209] This consists of immobilization of the shoulders upward, outward and backward by applying a "figure of 8" harness or a plaster spica cast that is worn for a period of 6 to 8 weeks, followed by a sling for 3 to 4 weeks. Occasionally an open reduction is necessary. These uncommon circumstances include compromise or injury to the underlying neurovascular structures that fails to improve with closed treatment, severe comminution with severe angulation and tenting of the skin that fails to respond to closed treatment, an open fracture that requires debridement, multiple trauma in which case closed treatment is impractical or impossible, and in other instances of neuromuscular imbalances (Parkinsonism, seizure disorders) that render the patient unable to tolerate closed reduction treatment with the traditional figure of 8 harness. Internal fixation of middle one-third clavicle fractures is usually accomplished by means of a contoured plate and screws or a threaded intramedullary pin.

Fractures of the distal third of the clavicle include those at the very end of the clavicle which can be treated effectively with a sling for 3 to 4 weeks followed by a program of gradual shoulder mobilization exercises. The outcome of managing these types of clavicle fractures is almost always sound bone healing and complete recovery of shoulder function and strength. Those fractures that occur just medial to the coracoclavicular ligaments [Figure 11.68] are managed as if they were middle one-third fractures (with the traditional figure of 8 harness). Union is often delayed and shoulder stiffness develops because of the need for prolonged immobilization. Thus, in these cases, another reasonable treatment approach is to reduce and internally fix the fracture. Finally, fractures of the tip of the clavicle extending into the AC joint are treated symptomatically with a sling and analgesics. If these lead to symptomatic late degenerative osteoarthritis of the clavicle (usually evident 2 years post injury), then an excisional arthroplasty of the distal 1 cm of the clavicle may need to be carried out.

Fractures of the medial third segment require symptomatic treatment (sling, analgesics) unless they cause severe neurovascular compromise, in which case open reduction must be considered. Fractures extending into or

---

209 Rowe CR. The Clavicle. In: Rowe CR, ed. *The Shoulder*. New York: Churchill Livingstone, 1988.

very close to the sternoclavicular joint are discussed under Injuries of the Sternoclavicular Joint.

11.3.1.5.4 Complications: *Nonunion* occurs in 0.1% to 0.8% of all cases.[210] Possible causes of nonunion include inadequate period of immobilization, refracture due to premature (within 3 months of injury) return to contact sports or heavy work, and because of the severity of the trauma (50% are related to severe trauma which produces more bone displacement and stripping of the soft tissue envelope that initiates fracture healing). Older clinical series have revealed that following open reduction and internal fixation of clavicle fractures there is a 3 to 5% incidence of nonunion, however with modern techniques it is surmised that the incidence is much lower.

In about 85% of cases, the nonunion involves the middle one-third segment. Most often (75%) nonunions are painful, cause the shoulder to sag, and may also produce vascular or neurologic symptoms in the upper limb due to traction on these structures as the arm sags. Nonunions may be repaired using various reconstructive techniques that include internal fixation and a bone graft followed by prolonged shoulder immobilization and rest to ensure union.

11.3.1.5.5 Neurovascular Problems: These may occur either secondary to exuberant fracture callus producing encroachment on these structures, or because of fracture nonunion causing stretching of the neurovascular structures as the arm sags to the side of the body. When symptoms are severe, decompression of these neurovascular structures, removal of the excessive bone tissue under the clavicle followed by reconstruction of the clavicle fracture is needed. Concomitant acute laceration of the underlying subclavian vessel injuries presents uncommonly and requires an immediate (and often life-saving or limb-saving) intervention by a vascular surgeon. Concomitant acute brachial plexus lacerations are also uncommon, and need to be explored and repaired if technically possible by a neurosurgeon or a microvascular surgeon.

The subcutaneous position of the clavicle and its great mobility in the upper chest region are such that non-anatomic fracture alignment is often quite noticeable. In many instances, it may be argued that a *malunion* has resulted from the usual management consisting of non-operative treatment. Although it is virtually impossible and functionally unnecessary to restore perfect alignment of clavicle fracture fragments by closed methods, some patients will be disappointed because of the visible enlargement at the

---

210 Jupiter JB, Leffert RD. Nonunion of the Clavicle: Surgical Management and Associated Complications. *J Bone Joint Surg*, 69A: 753-760, 1987. Neer CS II. Nonunion of the Clavicle. *JAMA*, 172: 1006-1011, 1960.

fracture site secondary to either the production of a large amount of fracture callus or because of some degree of overlapping or angulation of the fracture fragments. In these cases, often retrospective analysis does not reveal any degree of substandard treatment. Occasionally, a better looking result would have been obtained had surgery been offered for the severely displaced or angulated fractures; however, an open approach has recognized risks, including visible scar, the possibility of fracture nonunion, a longer postoperative morbidity, and the need to ultimately remove the internal fixation.

The last among the common complications resulting from clavicle fractures is *arthritis* of the sternoclavicular or acromioclavicular fractures which occurs when these fractures extend into these articulations; discussion of these specific entities appears in 11.3.1.5.3, Treatment, *supra*.

11.3.1.6 Fractures of the Scapula

11.3.1.6.1 Incidence: The incidence of scapular fractures is low (1% of all fractures, 5% of all shoulder fractures) probably because it is protected by several layers of muscle and the rib cage but also because the energy of trauma to the shoulder can usually be dissipated by movement of the scapula on the rib cage.

11.3.1.6.2 Diagnosis: In terms of *distribution of the fractures*, approximately 50% involve the body of the scapula, 25% the neck portion, 10% the glenoid articular surface, 7% the coracoid, 7% the acromion [Figure 11.69]. In 90% of cases the fracture occurs in the context of a polytrauma with high energy direct force applied to the shoulder region; in the remainder, scapular fractures are caused by indirect muscular forces producing avulsion fractures (e.g., coracoid or acromial fractures). *Diagnosis* may be easy to establish when symptoms of pain and signs of swelling and ecchymoses point to the scapular region as the site of injury. However, in cases of polytrauma the fracture may be suspected and diagnosed later on when the more important injuries (i.e., the more clinically obvious and the life- or limb-threatening ones) have been treated. *Imaging of the fracture* is done with plain radiographs (A-P, lateral and axillary views) and if needed, with CT scans which help to assess the amount of disarray of the fracture fragments and congruity of the humeral head in the glenoid cavity.

11.3.1.6.3 Treatment: In over 90% of cases, the amount of fracture fragment displacement is minimal so treatment is symptomatic (sling for 3 to 6 weeks and analgesics) followed by shoulder rehabilitative therapy. By 6 weeks, the fracture usually is healed and by 6 months, full functional recovery has occurred.

There is little enthusiasm for operative treatment of these fractures because without intervention, most fractures heal well with a full return of shoulder function. Also, operative approaches are difficult and the bone stock of the scapula is not suited for the application of conventional stable fixation techniques. However, open treatment is called for in the case of significantly displaced fractures of the glenoid rim or socket that produce at least 5 mm of displacement, and when the displaced scapular fractures occur concurrently with a type III acromioclavicular joint disruption, or with a significantly displaced clavicular, acromial or coracoid fracture leading to disruption of the superior shoulder suspensory complex of the upper limb.[211] Other indications for open reduction and internal fixation include displaced glenoid neck fractures with at least 10 mm of displacement or over 40 degrees angulation with reference to the body of the scapula, and in the case of severely displaced coracoid and acromial fractures. Finally, if the fracture callus entraps the suprascapular nerve and appears to be producing paralysis of the supraspinatus and infraspinatus muscles of the rotator cuff, then early exploration of the nerve and open management of the fracture are indicated. Following operative treatment, most patients require 6 to 12 months of rehabilitative therapy before reaching a stable plateau of recovery.[212] In postoperative cases, shoulder function is usually not completely restored because of residual partial ankylosis of the glenohumeral joint and because of injury to and scarring of the periscapular and rotator cuff muscles.

11.3.1.7 Fractures of the Proximal Humerus

11.3.1.7.1 Introduction: These fractures (which account for 4 to 5% of all fractures) affect elderly patients more frequently because their bones are more fragile (osteoporotic) and thus more susceptible to break. In younger patients, these injuries are often the result of high-energy trauma. Most often, the fracture occurs through the surgical neck of the proximal humerus [Figure 11.70] as a result of falls on the outstretched arm or from a blow to the lateral side of the arm. The majority (80%) are relatively undisplaced and thus amenable to brief immobilization in a sling or to simple closed management and early functional exercises. The remainder however require reduction (open or closed) because the fracture fragments are significantly displaced and thus unstable, or because malunion would seriously compromise shoulder function and comfort.

---

211 Goss TP. Scapular Fractures and Dislocations: Diagnosis and Treatment. *J Am Acad Orthop Surg*, 3: 22-33, 1995.
212 *Ibid.*

11.3.1.7.2 Classification: Assessment of these fractures and treatment approaches are most often based on a popular classification that determines the number of fractured segments or "parts", and the angulation or separation of these parts.[213] Figures 11.71 and 11.72 illustrate the four major segments and the muscles that insert on two of these segments, the lesser and the greater tuberosities. These parts consist of the head or articular segment (or anatomic neck level), the lesser tuberosity, the greater tuberosity, and the shaft (surgical neck level). *Guidelines* for significant displacement of these segments are defined as separation of 1 cm or more, or angulation of 45 degrees or more of the segments.[214] Thus a fracture with minimal displacement could be called a one-part fracture. A two-part fracture is one in which only one segment (first part) is displaced at least 1 cm or angulated 45 degrees or more in relationship to the other segment (second part).

In the young and the athletically inclined, guidelines for the management of these fractures may differ.[215] Some surgeons have recommended that the threshold for operative reduction should be 5 mm of displacement or 30 degrees of angulation. Their contention is that even moderate fracture malalignment in young patients and in athletes is unacceptable because it produces measurable losses of shoulder and upper extremity performance, strength and mobility that seriously compromise the athlete's career.

Other fracture patterns that do not fall into this classification are fracture-dislocations in which the articular segment is outside of the joint space, and the "impression fracture" or "head splitting" fractures.

11.3.1.7.3 Diagnosis: Diagnosis and characterization of these fractures are established from the history, the physical findings and with the help of two radiographs taken at right angles to each other. Associated injuries to the upper limb neurovascular structures sometimes occur and should be documented before initiating treatment. Tomography and CT scans provide essential information in instances when details are required about the number and position of severely comminuted fracture fragments, when there appear to be glenoid or humeral head articular defects.

11.3.1.7.4 Treatment: *Conservative (Closed Treatment):* In the majority of cases (80% of the time, approximately), displacement of the fracture

---

213 Neer CS II. Displaced Proximal Humeral Fractures: Part I. Classification and Evaluation. *J Bone Joint Surg,* 52A: 1077-1089, 1970a.

214 *Ibid.*

215 Powell SE, Chandler RW. Fracture of the Proximal Humerus. In: Jobe FW, ed. *Operative Techniques in Upper Extremity Sports Injuries.* St. Louis: Mosby Year Book, 1996.

fragments is minimal, i.e., less than 1 cm of separation or less than 45 degrees of angulation. In these instances, perfect anatomic realignment is not necessary in order to obtain a good functional and a comfortable result. Since these minimally displaced fractures are held together by the intact tissues of the periosteum and the rotator cuff tendons, treatment comprises of immobilization for 3 or 4 weeks in a sling until clinical union is apparent, which is when the fracture fragments can be passively mobilized as a unit without pain. Thereafter, a program of active and active-assisted exercises is instituted until a maximum level of recovery has been reached.[216]

Although significantly displaced fractures have the potential to unite, they inevitably lead to considerably reduced joint mobility, pain and functional impairment. However, for selected patients who are medically unfit or who are unable to participate in the required long rehabilitation program, accepting the deformity of the displaced fracture may be a reasonable treatment alternative.

Closed or Open Reduction Treatment: Significantly displaced proximal humeral fractures (see above discussion on the criteria for displacement) require either closed or open reduction approaches. In selected cases of three-part fractures and in most four-part fractures, prosthetic replacement of the humeral head with repair of the tuberosity fragments to the humeral shaft and to the prosthesis are better alternatives to internal fixation of the severely displaced osteoporotic fracture fragments. Fixation of these pieces of weak osteoporotic bone may be technically impossible and because the injury may have completely stripped the blood supply of the humeral head jeopardizing the chances of achieving fracture union.

Operative intervention is also needed when the proximal humeral fracture is associated with a dislocated articular head segment. Large, deep "impression" or "head splitting" fractures are best managed by prosthetic replacement.

Operative fixation of proximal humeral fractures can be accomplished with a variety of implants, which are selected based on the amount of bone fragment comminution, size or degree of osteoporosis. In some instances, stable fixation cannot be achieved and thus supplementary external support with a sling or body spica cast is required for a few weeks, in order to ensure adequate bone healing in the early stages. Rehabilitation exercises are instituted as soon as possible not only to promote early mobility and endurance but to reduce the chances of developing significant joint ankylosis and shoulder muscle atrophy or weakness. Often, the internal fixation devices are large relative to the size of the patient's bones and thus impede

---

216 Young TB, Wallace WA. Conservative Treatment of Fractures and Fracture-Dislocations of the Upper End of the Humerus. *J Bone Joint Surg*, 67B:373-377, 1985.

shoulder movements in flexion and in abduction; in these cases, removal of the implants after fracture union has occurred permits more progress to be achieved.

11.3.1.7.5 Prognosis: Virtually all types of proximal humeral fractures are clinically solid by 3 to 4 weeks but may not appear radiologically healed until 3 months after injury. On the other hand, recovery of motion, function and pain requires several more months. Residual mild to moderate joint ankylosis, pain at the extremes of motion, and shoulder weakness often persist despite many months of rehabilitative therapy.[217]

Following prosthetic replacement, usually performed for three- and four-part fractures, rehabilitation (i.e., formal physical therapy in a rehabilitation unit) in conjunction with an exercise program performed by the patient can produce tangible results even beyond 1 year; hence the need for ongoing rehabilitative care, patient encouragement and patient cooperation.

11.3.1.7.6 Complications: The common complications specifically related to the proximal humeral neck fractures include joint stiffness, malunion of the fracture fragment, avascular necrosis of the humeral head, myositis ossificans of the pericapsular tissues, and less commonly nonunion. Reduced joint mobility or stiffness or tightness at the extremes of motion may respond to physical therapy (i.e., local anti-inflammatory modalities and stretching), but nevertheless some degree of painful stiffness frequently persists despite the best rehabilitative efforts. Often stiffness improves after removal of the internal fixation, which may be compromising the space for unrestricted movement of the rotator cuff tendons in the subacromial inlet.

Malunion involving the tuberosities of a mild degree is usually compatible with a very good and comfortable functional result; however, more severe malunion (e.g., when impingement occurs at the rotator cuff inlet or when retraction of the tuberosities has occurred) may require technically difficult reconstructions. Three or four part fracture malunions require prosthetic replacement of the proximal humerus, an operative intervention that is much more difficult to perform weeks or months later than in the acute setting.

Avascular necrosis of the humeral head may occur if the blood supply to the humeral head has been interrupted as a result of the fracture plane that severs the anterior humeral circumflex artery [Figure 11.73] or because of extensive soft tissue stripping produced by the injury or at the time of surgical reconstruction. The incidence ranges from 3 to 25% for

---

217 Powell et al., *supra*, note 215.

three-part fractures, to as much as 90% for four-part fractures.[218] Sometimes avascular necrosis is suspected at the time of injury because of the severe disarray of the fracture fragments (and especially if there is concomitant glenohumeral dislocation), but at other times it becomes obvious only on follow-up radiographs where the humeral head begins to collapse. If and when this complication is painful, then it can only be managed with prosthetic replacement of the humeral head.

Pericapsular callus formation (myositis ossificans) usually is produced in the context of fracture-dislocations of the proximal humerus and their management; this extra bone formation in the juxta-articular tissues significantly impairs shoulder mobility and comfort and therefore function.

Fracture *nonunion* may occur if muscle or tendon tissue remains interposed between the fracture fragments or if there is too much separation between the fracture fragments; repair or reconstruction of this complication is technically difficult and is best managed with prosthetic replacement of the proximal humerus.

Finally, concomitant *vascular injuries* may occur. They occur at the time of injury by impaling of the axillary artery by a bone fragment by severe stretching and tearing of an inelastic atherosclerotic vessel by the trauma of the injury. Axillary artery injuries accompanying proximal humeral fractures must be diagnosed without delay and managed expeditiously.[219]

Brachial plexus injuries also occur; most are temporary and are due to stretching of the nerve (neuropraxia).

Complications arising directly or indirectly from the operative management of these injuries include wound infection and osteomyelitis, injury to the axillary nerve, painful loosening of the fixation implants when fracture nonunion occurs, and avascular necrosis of the humeral head secondary to the extensive soft tissue dissection required at open reduction.

11.3.1.8 Fractures of the Humeral Shaft

11.3.1.8.1 Anatomy: The humeral shaft occupies the arm section of the upper limb. Anatomically, it extends from the humeral neck to the supracondylar ridges of the elbow. Important landmarks (that are not well seen radiographically) include the deltoid tuberosity (to which is attached

---

[218] Hagg O, Lundberg BJ. Aspects of Prognostic Factors of Comminuted and Dislocated Proximal Humeral Fractures. In: Bateman JE, Welsh RP, eds. *Surgery of the Shoulder.* Philadelphia: BC Decker, 1984. Neer CS II. Displaced Proximal Humeral Fractures. Part II. Treatment Three-Part and Four-Part Displacement. *J Bone Joint Surg*, 52A: 1090-1103, 1970b.

[219] Brunet JA. Axillary Artery Injuries Associated with Humeral Neck Fractures. In: Post M, Morrey BF, Hawkins RJ, eds. *Surgery of the Shoulder.* St. Louis: Mosby Year Book, 1990.

the deltoid muscle tendon), and the spiral groove (in which course the radial nerve and the profunda brachii vessels). The muscles, which cloak this bone (in the anterior compartment of the arm), are the biceps, the coracobrachialis and the brachialis, whereas only the broad triceps muscle (the single muscle occupying the entire posterior compartment of the arm) covers its posterior surface [Figure 11.74]. The important neurovascular structures in the anterior compartment consist of the brachial artery and vein, and the median, musculo-cutaneous and ulnar nerves. Only the radial nerve and its accompanying profunda brachii artery course in the posterior compartment.

11.3.1.8.2 Diagnosis: Fractures of the humeral shaft are most often the result of direct trauma. The clinical diagnosis is usually obvious, and the radiographs are confirmatory. Important soft tissue injuries accompany the humeral shaft fractures and hence it is fundamental to carry out at the time of injury a detailed examination of the neurovascular status of the entire upper limb.

11.3.1.8.3 Treatment: The vast majority of closed humeral fractures can be treated non-operatively. Good alignment and fracture union can be achieved using the currently popular closed methods of a hanging cast, coaptation or "U" shaped splints, or by the means of so-called functional bracing. Each method has advantages and specific indications. The first method, though inconvenient for the patient during the first 4 to 6 weeks of treatment achieves fracture alignment by dependency traction and by frequent adjustments of the cast. The U splint is used when the surgeon chooses to remove a hanging cast early. Functional bracing is selected for reliable and cooperative patients once the swelling and pain have decreased; the brace is then applied and early motion of the shoulder and elbow joints are encouraged.[220]

Very few closed fractures require open reduction. It has been shown that function of the upper extremity is not affected by as much as 20 degrees of fracture anterior angulation, 30 degrees of varus angulation, and 3 cm of shortening of the shaft.[221] Operative treatment with internal fixation is thus indicated when acceptable alignment cannot be maintained or obtained. Operative stabilization can be achieved with either compression plating or intramedullary fixation. While the latter method of fixation has until recently been very popular because of the ease of its application, many patients develop chronic shoulder pain and weakness after this type of fixation has been used because the intramedullary nail is inserted

---

[220] Gregory PR, Sanders RW. Comparison Plating Versus Intramedullary Fixation of Humeral Shaft Fractures. *J Am Acad Orthop Surg*, 5: 215-223, 1997.
[221] *Ibid.*

through the rotator cuff at the level of the shoulder. Compression plating provides a more reliable construct that may be more technically difficult to apply, requires much more soft tissue dissection through the posterior or through the anterior compartment via the anterolateral approach, and risks injury to the radial nerve.[222]

11.3.1.8.4 Complications: One complication commonly associated with distal one-third humeral shaft fractures is *injury to the radial nerve* [Figure 11.75]. This nerve injury leads to the clinical syndrome of wrist drop in which the muscles of the forearm innervated by the radial nerve do not function. In this instance, the patient is unable to extend the fingers or thumb or move the wrist in extension and in radial (towards the thumb side) deviation. Over the years, there has been considerable debate on whether in the context of an acute humeral fracture a palsy (paralysis) of the radial nerve should be explored in order to verify its integrity and to be sure that it has not been severed or become trapped at the fracture interface. However, most radial nerve injuries are the result of stretching or bruising and are thus incomplete palsies that usually recover within 3 to 4 months.[223] Thus it is recommended that a concomitant radial nerve palsy be observed since most (94%) recover spontaneously. The notable exception to the rule is in open fractures of the humerus, where concomitant radial nerve palsy could be due to transection of the radial nerve; in this case there is a clear indication for immediate exploration of the radial nerve with repair of the fracture site.[224]

Nonunion or delayed union of humeral fractures occurs most commonly in widely displaced transverse fractures, and sometimes after open reduction and internal fixation, and if an inappropriately heavy hanging cast is used. Highly successful (94% union rate) treatment follows removal of avascular fibrous tissues that cover the fracture ends, bone grafting, and the application of rigid internal fixation.[225]

Other complications include *myositis ossificans* of the muscles that surround the fracture and some residual *joint stiffness* and loss of function of the elbow or shoulder joints secondary to prolonged immobilization of the fracture. A fortunately less common complication is that of a concomi-

---

222 Gregory et al., *supra*, note 220.
223 Pollock FH, Drake D, Bovill EG, et al. Treatment of Radial Neuropathy Associated with Fractures of the Humerus. *J Bone Joint Surg*, 63A: 239-243, 1981. Stewart MI. Fractures of the Humeral Shaft. In: Adams JP, ed. *Current Practice in Orthopedic Surgery*. St. Louis: Mosby, 1964.
224 *Ibid.*
225 Boyd HB, Lipinski SW, Wiley AH. Observation on Nonunion of the Shaft of the Long Bones with a Statistical Analysis of 842 Patients. *J Bone Surg*, 43A: 159, 1961. Campbell WC. Ununited Fractures of the Shaft of the Humerus. *Ann Surg*, 105: 135, 1937.

tant *vascular injury*. This true emergency situation requires prompt diagnosis, blood replacement, and then arterial repair after the fracture has been stabilized by internal fixation.[226]

11.3.1.9 Rotator Cuff Tears

11.3.1.9.1 Introduction: The rotator cuff is a broad tendinous structure which envelops the humeral head and which receives contributions from the tendons of the supraspinatus, the infraspinatus, the subscapularis, and the teres minor muscles [Figure 11.76]. The functions of the rotator cuff are to actively maintain the humeral head centered in the glenoid cavity and to assist in the fine rotational and abduction (motion of the arm away from the side of the body) movements of the shoulder [Figure 11.77].

Apart from injuries to the shoulder bones and joints, trauma to the shoulder region can affect the rotator cuff tendons. Occasionally, injuries to these tendons are unrecognized at the time of the accident because of the more urgent and often more obvious bone or joint trauma to the shoulder girdle or to other parts of the body. Rotator cuff injuries may affect shoulder function, strength, endurance and comfort.

Throughout life the rotator tendons undergo progressive changes consisting of fiber disruption and thinning (known as degeneration) as a result of normal age-related processes. A complete discussion of these complex changes and of their etiological theories is beyond the scope of this book, but suffice it to state that thinning and even rupture of part or of all of the cuff occurs as a normal evolutionary phenomenon beyond the age of 40 years.[227]

11.3.1.9.2 Pathomechanics: Regardless of age, trauma to the shoulder region, as mentioned above, can produce a rotator cuff injury consisting of either stretching of the tendons, or partial or complete tearing. In the case of young patients (i.e., below age 40 years), the cuff tissue is quite resilient to most types of trauma and usually suffers a stretching injury from which it recovers completely. However, the same degree of trauma to older patients (i.e., above age 40 years) will produce partial tears or full thickness

---

226 Rich NM, Baugh JH, Hughes CW. Acute Arterial Injuries in Vietnam, 1000 Cases. *J Trauma*, 10: 359, 1990. Rich NM, Metz CW, Hutton HE, et al. Internal Versus External Fixation of Fractures with Concomitant Vascular Injuries in Vietnam. *J Trauma*, 11: 463-473, 1971.

227 DePalma AF. *Surgery of the Shoulder*. Philadelphia: 1950. Lohr JF, Uhthoff HK. The Pathogenesis of Degenerative Rotator Cuff Tears. *Orthop Trans*, 11: 237, 1987. Matsen FA, Arntz CT. Rotator Cuff Failure. In Rockwood CA, Matsen FA, eds. *The Shoulder*. Philadelphia: WB Saunders, 1990.

tears of the one or of all of the components of the cuff, and in some cases convert a partial tear into a complete tear, or extend the size of a partial or complete tear. Rotator cuff tears (complete or incomplete types) can still occur in younger patients if the shoulder trauma is severe.

Injuries to the supraspinatus and to the subscapularis portions of the rotator cuff can occur by means of avulsion injuries (i.e., severe pulling apart of a bone fragment with its attached tendon) of the greater or lesser tuberosities. These injuries should be investigated and treated as outlined in the section on the management of two- and three-part proximal humeral fractures. Other rotator cuff tendons injuries that are not associated with avulsion of their bone attachment may be much more difficult to recognize initially and are often interpreted as simple shoulder sprains. When shoulder function in this subset of patients fails to improve after 4 to 6 weeks of rehabilitative therapy, one should become suspicious of an underlying full thickness (complete) or significant partial thickness (incomplete) of one or of all of the components of the rotator cuffs.

11.3.1.9.3 Investigations: Appropriate investigations of suspected complete cuff tears should include plain shoulder radiographs (to rule out tuberosity avulsion fractures and to assess the position of the humeral head with reference to the overlying acromion), and an arthrogram (dye injection study of the shoulder to outline the presence or absence of an intact rotator cuff), or an MRI. Suspected partial cuff tears are best visualized with an MRI.

11.3.1.9.4 Treatment: The presence of a complete cuff tear in an older individual does not in itself imply the need for an immediate operative repair, as it is known that approximately 20 to 40% of shoulder cuffs in autopsy cases have tears that are presumably asymptomatic.[228] Furthermore, many patients with complete traumatic tears are mildly or only occasionally inconvenienced by the associated pain and weakness of the shoulder. Therefore, in the setting of an injured shoulder, appropriate management of a recently diagnosed complete tear in an older individual should include a trial of active rehabilitative therapy consisting of a structured program of exercises with the realistic goal being to obtain a fully mobile, comfortable and strong but perhaps less enduring shoulder.

Surgical intervention is indicated in younger patients with a complete traumatic cuff tear, or in older patients with the same lesion that fails to respond to conservative treatment (i.e., disabling and severe functional loss). At surgery, repair of complete tears of all sizes may not always be technically possible. In general, repair techniques involve mobilizing the ruptured cuff and reattaching it to its bony insertion and to adjacent cuff

---

228 *Ibid.*

tendons. Following a brief period of immobilization in a sling (or occasionally in a shoulder plaster spica cast), a program of formal rehabilitative therapy is begun and continued for up to 5 months if necessary. Maximum level of recovery may not be attained until 1 year after surgery.[229] A successful result, as determined subjectively by the patient, would include complete or near complete pain relief and the return of almost all mobility and strength.

11.3.1.9.5 Results of Surgical Treatment: Over the past 25 years, the results of rotator cuff repairs have improved such that at 1 year post-surgery, pain is alleviated in over 90% of patients, strength improved in 80 to 90% of cases, and overall shoulder function improved in 75 to 95% of cases.[230]

Generally the results of surgical treatment are better if the tear is small, and if the repair is carried out early as opposed to several months or a few years after injury. Tuberosity avulsion injuries that heal with moderate displacement may lead to a painful syndrome of impingement at the subacromial inlet. This occurs as the enlarged tuberosity fracture fragment and the humeral head are made to rotate under the narrow space of the coracoacromial arch, producing impingement and pain secondary to subacromial bursitis, and ultimately leading to reduced shoulder function.

Operative repair is not always successful for a variety of reasons. Technical reasons include poor quality of the damaged tissues of the rotator cuff tendon, the massive size of some of the tears, poor bone stock for reattachment of the tendon, and inadequate or excessive decompression of the subacromial space. In the postoperative period, explanations for a failed repair include insufficient external support of the shoulder and arm, improper or inadequate rehabilitation by an inexperienced physical therapist, and finally patient non-compliance for the necessarily long rehabilitation. The success rate of revision rotator cuff repair (carried out almost exclusively for pain relief) is approximately 50%.[231]

---

229 Harryman DT, Mack LA, Wang K, et al. Repairs of the Rotator Cuff. Correlation of Functional Results with Integrity of the Cuff. *J Bone Joint Surg*, 73A: 982-989, 1991.

230 Connor PM, Bigliani LU. Rotator Cuff Repair. In: Copeland SA, ed. *Shoulder Surgery*, London: WB Saunders, 1997.

231 Bigliani LU, Cordasco FA, McIlveen SJ, et al. Operative Treatment of Failed Repairs of the Rotator Cuff, *J Bone Joint Surg*, 74A: 1505-1515, 1992.

11.3.2 Injuries to the Elbow and Forearm

11.3.2.1 Anatomy and Biomechanics

The elbow joint connects the single arm bone with the two forearm bones [Figure 11.78]. The main plane of function is flexion and extension through the ulno-humeral joint. The radial head abuts against the capitellum and also articulates with the proximal radio-ulnar joint (radial notch). Rotation of the radius is allowed by these two articulations.[232] The elbow flexes through a single centre of rotation located in the humeral condyles much like the action of a hinge.[233] The joint surface is a complex configuration with ridges and valleys interacting precisely with one another. This irregular joint surface is in marked contradistinction to the shoulder joint where a wide range of controlled sloppiness is possible. These exact interdigitations suggest that in addition to the ligamentous support[234] [Figure 11.79], a degree of joint stability is afforded by the bony contours.[235] It

---

232 London JT. Kinematics of the Elbow. *J Bone Joint Surg*, 63A: 529-530, 1981. Morrey BF, Adkew LJ, An KN, Chao, EY. A Biomechanical Study of Normal Elbow Motion. *J Bone Joint Surg*, 63A: 872-877, 1981. Morrey BF. Applied Anatomy and Biomechanics of the Elbow Joint. *Instr Course Lect XXXV*, 59-68, 1986. Morrey BF. Biomechanics of the Elbow. In: Morrey, BF, ed. *The Elbow and Its Disorders*, vol. L. Philadelphia: W.B. Saunders, 1985: 43-61.

233 London, *ibid*. Morrey BF, Chao EY. Passive Motion of the Elbow Joint. A Biomechanical Analysis. *J Bone Joint Surg*, 58A: 501-508, 1976. Morrey BF. Applied Anatomy and Biomechanics of the Elbow Joint, *ibid*. Morrey, BF, An KN. Functional Anatomy of the Ligaments of the Elbow. *Clin Orthop*, 201: 84-90, 1985. Volz RB. Biomechanics Update #2. Basic Biomechanics: Lever Arm, Instant Center of Motion, Moment Force, Joint Reactive Force. *Orthop Rev*, 15: 677-684, 1986.

234 Funk DA, An KN, Morrey BF, Daube JR. Electomyographic Analysis of Muscles Across the Elbow Joint Joint. *J Orthop Res*, 5: 529-538, 1987. Hotchkiss RN, Green DP. Fractures and Dislocations of the Elbow. *Fractures in Adults*, 3rd ed., J.P. Lippincott: 739-841, 1991. Hotchkiss RN, Weiland AJ. Valgus Stability of the Elbow. *J Orthop Res*, 5: 372-377, 1987. Morrey BF, An KN. Articular and Ligamentous Contributions to the Stability of the Elbow Joint. *Am J Sports Med*, 11: 315-319, 1983. Morrey BF. Biomechanics of the Elbow. In: Morrey, BF, ed. *The Elbow and Its Disorders*, vol. L: 43-61, *supra*, note 232. Schwab GH, Bennett JB, Woods GW, Tullos HS. Biomechanics of Elbow Instability: The Role of the Medial Collateral Ligament. *Clin Orthop*, 146: 42-52, 1980. Sojbjerg JO, Ovensen J, Neilsen S. Experimental Elbow Instability After Transection of the Medial Collateral Ligament. *Clin Orthop*, 218: 186-190, 1987. Tullos HS, Schwab G, Bennett JB, Woods GW. Factors Influencing Elbow Stability. *Instr Course Lect VIII*, 185-199, 1982.

235 An KN, Morrey BF, Chao EYS. The Effect of Partial Removal of the Proximal Ulna on the Elbow Constraint. *Clin Orthop*. 209: 270-279, 1986. Gartsman GM, Sculo TP, Otis JC. Operative Treatment of Olecranon Fractures Excision or Open Reduction with Internal Fixation. *J Bone Joint Surg*, 63A: 718-721, 1981.

also warns that a disruption of the architecture will greatly influence joint motion. In addition to the joint surface interactions are recesses, which intimately interact with prominent areas. In flexion the coronoid process would impact upon distal humerus were it not for the recession of the coronoid fossa. Similarly, in extension, the olecranon fits into the olecranon fossa. Muscles originate about the elbow [Figure 11.80], providing the basis for motion of the elbow as well as the shoulder, wrist and hand. The orchestration of the muscles, ligaments and joint surface control elbow motion. Morrey has shown that most activities of daily living require a relatively large range of motion in contradistinction to the small functional range required by the wrist joint. The elbow requires 30 degrees to 130 degrees of flexion and extension and 50 degrees each of pronation and supination.[236] Any loss of motion will require adaptation by either using the opposite upper limb or changing shoulder, neck, or body position.[237] Crossing the elbow joint are the neurovascular structures as they proceed distally [Figure 11.81].

11.3.2.2 Fractures about the Elbow in Adults

Fractures can involve one, two or three bones of the elbow, with and without intra-articular involvement, joint dislocations, and muscle, ligamentous and neurovascular injury.[238]

Fractures in the distal humerus not involving the condyles or involving the joint surface are called supracondylar fractures. If displaced, these fractures can often be treated by non-operative methods including closed reduction[239] and olecranon traction.[240] On occasion the operative methods

---

236 Morrey et al., *supra* note 232.
237 Hotchkiss and Green, *supra*, note 234.
238 Miller JH. The Mechanisms of Elbow Fractures: An Investigation Using Impact Tests in Vitro. *Injury*, 26(3): 163-168, 1995.
239 Böhler L. *The Treatment of Fractures*, vol 5. New York: Grune & Stratton, 1956. Conn, J, Wade PA. Injuries of the Elbow (A Ten Year Review). *J Trauma*, 1: 248-268, 1961. DePalma AF. *The Management of Fractures and Dislocations*. Philadelphia: W.B. Saunders, 1959. Hoyer A. Treatment of Supracondylar Fractures of the Humerus by Skeletal Traction in an Abduction Splint. *J Bone Joint Surg*, 34A: 623-637, 1952. Keon-Cohen BT: Fractures of the Elbow. *J Bone Joint Surg*, 48A: 1623-1639, 1966. King D, Secor C. Bow Elbow (Cubitus Varus). *J Bone Joint Surg*, 33A: 572-576, 1951. Mann TS. Prognosis in Supracondylar Fractures. *J Bone Joint Surg*, 45B: 516-522, 1963. Roberts JB, Kelly JA. *Treatise on Fractures*, 2nd ed. Philadelphia: J.B. Lippincott, 1921. Sisk TD. Fractures of the Distal End of Humerus. In: Crenshaw AH, ed. *Campbell's Operative Orthopaedics*, 6th ed. St. Louis: Mosby, 1980: 674-683. Smith FM. *Surgery of the Elbow*, 2nd ed. Philadelphia: W.B. Saunders, 1972. Smith L. Deformity Following Supracondylar Fracture of the Humerus. *J Bone Joint Surg*. 42A: 235-252, 1960. Speed K. *A Textbook of Fractures and Dislocation*. Philadelphia: Lea & Febiger, 1935.
240 Böhler *ibid*. Conn *ibid*. Smith FM, *ibid*. Smith L, *ibid*. Decoulx P, Ducloux

of percutaneous pin fixation[241] or open reduction and internal fixation[242] may be preferable, especially when there is an unacceptable result from closed reduction, a vascular injury, or other fractures in the arm or forearm.[243]

Intercondylar fractures of the distal humerus involve the articular surface [Figure 11.82]. Displaced comminuted T or Y fractures of the distal humerus [Figure 11.83] are some of the most difficult fractures to treat successfully. The fracture is caused by the impact force on the ulna, transmitted to the trochlear groove and forcing the condyles apart. Open reduction and internal fixation tends to be the preferred method of treatment[244]

M, Hespeel J, Coulx J. Les Fractures de l'Extremite Inferieure de l'Humerus Chez l'Adulte. *Rev Chir Orthop*, 50:263-273, 1964. MacAusland WR, Wyman ET. Fractures of the Adult Elbow. *A.A.O.S. Inst Course Lect XXLV*, 169-181, 1975. Merle D'Aubigne R, Meary R, Carlioz J. Fractures sus et intercondyliennes recentes de l'adulte. *Rev Chir Orthop*, 50: 279-288, 1964. Siris IE. Supracondylar Fractures of the Humerus. *Surg Gynecol Obstet*, 68: 201-222, 1939.

241 Anderson L. Fractures. In: Crenshaw A.H., ed. *Campbell's Operative Orthopaedics*, 5th ed. St. Louis: Mosby, 1971. Childress HM. Transarticular Pin Fixation in Supracondylar Fractures of the Elbow in Children, *J Bone Joint Surg*, 54A: 1548-1552, 1972. Fowles JV, Kassab MT, Said K. Supracondylar Fractures in Children, Stabilization by Two Lateral Percutaneous Pins. Presented at the Canadian Orthopaedic Association Annual Meeting, Winnipeg, Manitoba, 1973. Jones KG. Percutaneous Pin Fixation of Fractures of the Lower End of the Humerus. *Clin Orthop*, 50: 53-69, 1967. Swenson AL. Treatment of Supracondylar Fractures of the Humerus by Kirschner-Wire Transfixation. *J Bone Joint Surg*, 30A: 993-997, 1948.

242 Müller et al., *supra*, note 147. Conn et al., *supra*, note 239. Bryan RS. Fractures About the Elbow in Adults. *A.A.O.S. Inst Course Lect*, 30: 200-223, 1981.

243 Sisk, *supra*, note 239. Anderson, *supra*, note 241. Bryan, *ibid.*.

244 Müller et al., *supra*, note 147. Bryan, *supra*, note 242. Bryan RS, Bickel WH. T Condylar Fractures of the Distal Humerus. *J Trauma*, 11: 830-835, 1971. Bryan RS, Moorey BF. Fractures of the Distal Humerus. In: Morrey BF, ed. *The Elbow and Its Disorders*, vol. 1. Philadelphia: W.B. Saunders, 1985: 302-339. Bush LF, McClain EJ. Operative Treatment of Fractures of the Elbow in Adults. *Instr Course Lect*, XVI: 265-277, 1959. Heim U, Pfeiffer KM. *Elbow. Internal Fixation of Small Fractures*, vol. 3: 107-109. Henley MB. Intra-articular Distal Humeral Fractures in Adults. *Orthop Clin North Am*, 18: 11-23, 1987. Knight RA. Fractures of the Humeral Condyles in Adults. *South Med J*, 48: 1165-1173, 1955. Willenegger H. Problems and Results in the Treament of Comminuted Fractures of the Elbow. *Reconstr Surg Traumatol*, 11: 118-127, 1969. Zagorski JB, Jennings JJ, Burkhalter WE, Uribe, JW. Comminuted Intraarticular Fractures of the Distal Humeral Condyles. Surgical vs Nonsurgical Treatment. *Clin Orthop*, 202: 197-204, 1986. Cassebaum WH. Open Reduction of T and Y Fractures of the Lower End of the Humerus. *J Trauma*, 9:9115-925, 1969.

although on occasion closed reduction and traction[245] or total elbow arthroplasty may be appropriate for the most severe cases.

Radial head fractures, may not only represent an injury to the articular surface but may indicate that the joint had become unstable and there also exists associated ligamentous and interosseous membrane injuries. Displaced radial head fractures are generally treated by open reduction and internal fixation although excision of the radial head may be appropriate in those with irreparable fractures and the elderly low demand patient.

Fractures of the olecranon may occur from a direct blow,[246] a failure of the bone in compression, an angulatory force, or, rarely, an avulsion fracture caused by the tension of the triceps tendon. Open reduction internal fixation is generally accepted as the treatment of choice for displaced olecranon fractures.[247] Non-operative treatment tends to be associated with a higher number of complications.[248]

The parameters that effect the functional outcome of fractures about the elbow are many. Seekamp felt the late functional outcome of elbow fractures depends less on the fracture than on the presence of a nerve lesion. He suggests that the method of primary treatment should facilitate early mobilization.[249]

11.3.2.3 Injuries to the Mid-forearm

11.3.2.3.1 Anatomy: The forearm consists of the unit between the arm and wrist and in this discussion has been broken into artificial segments of which the most proximal aspect of the forearm is discussed with the elbow and the most distal aspect discussed with the wrist. The remaining large

---

245 DePalma, *supra*, note 239. Keon-Cohen, *supra*, note 239.
246 Hotchkiss and Green, *supra*, note 234.
247 Deane M. Comminuted Fractures of the Olecranon. An Appliance for Internal Fixation. *Injury*, 2:103-106, 1970. Horne JG, Tanzer TL. Olecranon Fractures: A Review of 100 Cases. *J Trauma*, 21:469-472, 1981. Muller C, Rahn BA, Pfister U, Meinig RP. The Incidence, Pathogenesis, Diagnosis, and Treatment of Fat Embolism. *Orthopaedic Review*, 23 (2): 107-17, 1994. Muller ME, Allgower M, Schneider R, Willenegger H. *Manual of Internal Fixation*. New York: Springer-Verlag, 1991. Perkins, G. Fractures of the Olecranon. *Br Med J*, 2: 668-669, 1936.
248 Perkins, *ibid.* Willenegger, *supra*, note 244. Eriksson E, Sahlen O, Sandahl U. Late Results of Conservative and Surgical Treatment of Fracture of the Olecranon. *Acta Chir Scand*, 113: 153-166, 1957. Simon MM. Complete Anterior Dislocation of Both Bones of the Forearm and the Elbow (Review of Recorded Cases and Literature With Report of a Case), *Ned J Rec*, 133: 333-336, 1931.
249 Seekamp A, Regal G, Blauth M, Klages U, Kleeme R, Tscherne H. Long-Term Results of Therapy of Open and Closed Fractures of the Elbow Joint. *Unfallchirurg*, 100 (3): 205-211, 1997.

middle segment consists of a complex anatomy of two bones; the radius and the ulna, and multiple soft tissue structures [Figure 11.81]. The muscles serve to either rotate the forearm bones, (most specifically rotate the radius about the ulna), palmar flex or dorsiflex the wrist, flex or extend the fingers, and those muscles that cross the elbow flex, extend, and stabilize that joint. The two main arteries, the radial and ulnar arteries, originate from the brachial artery just distal to the elbow joint and pass distally on either side of volar aspect of the forearm to enter the hand. Three major nerves enter the forearm; the radial nerve, the ulnar nerve, and the median nerve. The radial nerve soon divides into a superficial branch, which supplies sensation to the dorsal radial aspect of the hand and a more important branch the posterior interosseous nerve (deep radial nerve). The radial and posterior interosseous nerves together supply the muscles that extend the wrist, thumb and fingers and abduct the thumb in addition to innervating the supinator and brachioradialis muscles. Most of the important functions of this nerve are therefore involved with the innervation of muscles in the proximal half of the forearm and damage to the distal forearm would only involve the limited dorso-radial sensory contribution. Although the median and ulnar nerves also innervate proximal forearm muscle bellies, they both pass by the wrist and into the hand where they have important motor and sensory functions.

11.3.2.3.2 Injuries to the Forearm: Injuries to the forearm are common and result from a number of mechanisms—rotatory torque, angulatory bending, penetrating and compression forces. The type and amount of damage done to each structure, the presence of bacterial contamination, and the delay and type of treatment are major factors influencing the end result. When injured, a structure will either not perform its specialized function or do so to a variable degree and usually with the consequence of influencing other structures in the vicinity. A simple displaced transverse fracture of both bones in the mid forearm with no other associated injuries will result in an unstable forearm with intact sensation and blood supply but one in which muscles cannot contract properly as a result of pain and instability. A lacerated artery may result in diminished blood flow distally and effect healing or lead to death of tissue. An injured nerve may cause lack of distal sensation and loss of motor power to the area served by that nerve. An open injury introduces bacterial contamination and may be the cause of an acute infection. Damage to the skin may produce a situation in which the wound cannot be converted to a closed environment. Some injuries involve only one structure and other more severe injuries involve multiple structures and multiple different types of soft tissue injuries. A closed fracture of the distal third of the radius is an example of the former. A farmyard compression injury in which both bones of the forearm are comminuted, skin is lost, muscles are torn, one or both major arteries and nerves are ruptured and the wound is contaminated with manure is an example of the latter.[250]

11.3.2.3.3 Assessment: The history of the accident, including mechanism of injury, time and location of injury, is necessary to understand the degree and type of damage. The history must also rule-out involvement of other areas in the body and then concentrate on the chief complaints. The historical evaluation should also include the past health of the patient and a systematic review of systems. The physical examination must also include the whole involved limb paying particular attention to assessing the function of each of the structures present in the forearm. Is the skin intact? Is bony stability present? Is there local pain to light and deep palpation? Do each of the nerves have normal sensory, motor and autonomic function? Is the blood supply intact? Can a pulse be felt distally and if not is there a pulse proximally and on the opposite limb and how does the ability to feel a pulse relate to the systemic blood pressure? One must ascertain whether there is a disruption in the arterial inflow at a point or whether the general blood pressure is so low that a pulse can not be perceived. Are the muscles alive and working properly? Are they soft and will they contract normally and produce the expected result? Is a compartment syndrome present?[251]

11.3.2.3.4 Treatment: In most instances, anatomical structures which are damaged are generally repaired.[252] On occasion, because of good collateral circulation, one may not repair an injury to either a radial or an ulnar artery.[253] If there is evidence of diminished blood supply to the hand, repair may be recommended.[254] Injuries to nerves can be complex. On oc-

---

250 Gustilo, RB, Gruniger RP, Davis T. Classification of Type III (severe) Open Fractures Relative to Treatment and Results. *Orthopaedics*, 10(12): 1781-1788, 1987. Merritt K, Dowd JD. Role of Internal Fixation in Infection of Open Fractures: Studies with Staphylococcus Aureus and Proteus Mirabilis. *J Orthop Res*, 5(1): 23-28, 1987.
251 Brostrom et al., *supra*, note 156.
252 Katsamouris et al., *supra*, note 86. Bardot J, Legre R, Tranier T, Aubert JP. Coverage of Arterial Repair of the Upper Limb. Choice of a Technique Apropos of 24 Cases. *Ann Chir Plast*, 39(3):46-355, 1994. Pillai L, Luchette FA, Romano KS, Ricotta JJ. Upper Extremity Arterial Injury. *American Surgeon*, 63(3): 224-227, 1997.
253 Aftabuddin, M. Islam N, Jafar MA, Haque E, Alimuzzaman M. Management of Isolated Radial or Ulnar Arteries at the Forearm. *J Trauma*, 38(1): 149-151, 1995. Soucacos PN, Beris AE, Xenakis TA, Malizos KN, Vekris MD. Open Type IIIB and IIIC Fractures Treated by an Orthopaedic Microsurgical Team. *Clin Orthop*, (314): 59-66, 1995.
254 Eastcoot HHG. *Arterial Surgery*, 3rd ed. New York: Churchill Livingstone, 1992: 398.

casion the injury is a clean cut whereas at other times it is ripped and stretched with injury to the nerve occurring over a long distance. For the clean cut injury the repair may be a direct suture but for the latter case an excision of the damaged tissue and then interposition cable graft with nerve taken from elsewhere to fill the gap is frequently necessary[255] Fractures need accurate reduction[256] and maintenance of reduction. Usually this demands open reduction and internal fixation[257] and a review of the historical landmarks in the treatment of radius and ulnar fractures supports this conclusion. In 1949 Knight and Purvis[258] showed that nonunion developed in 12% of those treated with close reduction and that many of the others that did unite had a malunion and resulting poor function. Later studies explained why malunion produced a disability.[259] Tarr, Garfinkel and Sarmiento[260] showed that angular and rotatory deformities of 10% or less result in minimal limitation of pronation and supination but that 15 degrees of total deformity resulted in a loss of motion. Mathews showed that stiffness and a loss of rotation would occur when the deformity reached 20 degrees, especially in the mid forearm.[261] Accurate internal fixation therefore was considered necessary but the early methods proved to be inadequate. Nonunion developed in 46% of those treated with open reduction and internal fixation in 1949 because of inadequate fixation.[262] In 1957

---

255 Pillai et al., *supra*, note 252. Crenshaw AH, ed. *Campbell's Operative Orthopaedics*, 7th ed. St. Louis: Mosby, 1987, vol. 1:514-518.
256 Eastcoot, *supra*, note 254. Crenshaw AH, *ibid.*, vol. 3.
257 Smith et al., *supra*, note 172. Anderson LD, Bacartow TW. Treatment of Forearm Shaft Fractures with Compression Plates. *Contemp Orthop*, 8: 17-25, 1984. Anderson LD, Sisk TD, Tooms RE, et al. Compression Plate Fixation in Acute Diaphyseal Fractures of the Radius and Ulna. *J Bone Joint Surg*, 57A: 287-297, 1975. Jinkins JW Jr, Lockhard LD, Eggers GWN. Fractures of the Forearm in Adults. *South Med J*, 53: 669-679, 1960. Knight RA, Purvis GD. Fractures of Both Bones of the Forearm in Adults. *J Bone Joint Surg*, 31A: 755-764, 1949. Sage FP. Medullary Fixation of Fractures of the Forearm: A Study of the Medullary Canal of the Radius and a Report of Fifty Fractures of the Radius Treated with a prebent Triangular Nail. *J Bone Joint Surg*, 41A: 1489-1516, 1959.
258 Knight et al., *ibid.*
259 Langkamer VG, Ackroyd CE. Internal Fixation of Forearm Fractures in the 1980s: Lessons to be Learnt. *Injury*, 22(2): 97-102, 1991.
260 Tarr RR, Garfinkel AI, Sarmiento A. The Effects of Angular and Rotational Deformities of Both Bones of the Forearm. *J Bone Joint Surg*, 66A:65-70, 1984.
261 Matthews LS, Kaufer H, Graver DF, Sonstegard DA. The Effect on Supination — Pronation of Angular Malalignment of Fractures of Both Bones of the Forearm: An Experimental Study. *J Bone Joint Surg*, 64A:14-17, 1982.
262 Knight et al., *supra*, note 257.

Smith and Sage reported a 38% nonunion rate when Kirschner wires or Steinmann pins were used for intramedullary fixation and a 14% nonunion rate when the then available intramedullary nails were used.[263] A new fixation device, a pre-bent triangular nail introduced by Sage in 1959, was associated with an improved 6% nonunion rate.[264] In 1960 Jinkins reported a 4% nonunion rate with Eggers plates.[265] Following this a Swiss A-O (Arbeitsgemeinshaft Fuër Osteosynthesefragen) group introduced a compression plate with a 2 to 3% nonunion rate.[266] Anderson and Bacastow reported 1.4% nonunion rate with D.C.P. (dynamic compression plates).[267] Along with the improved rates of non-union has come, in most instances, improved soft tissue function as fingers can move sooner when the bones have been stabilized and stiffness is less likely to occur. The benefit of modern open reduction and internal fixation treatment of displaced forearm fractures in the adult usually outweigh the low risk of infection (usually less than 1% in closed injuries), and the re-fracture rate associated with plate removal, the scar, and the risks of anaesthesia.[268] In spite of this there may be times when a closed reduction combined with maintenance of an adequate reduction is acceptable. Open fractures need emergent cleansing, soft tissue debridement and reconstruction[269] intravenous antibiotics,[270] tetanus immune status assessment, stabilization,[271] and wound

---

263 Smith et al., *supra*, note 172.
264 Sage, *supra*, note 257.
265 Jinkins et al., *supra*, note 257.
266 Anderson and Bacartow, *supra*, note 257. Anderson, Sisk, Tooms, et al., *supra*, note 257.
267 Anderson and Bacartow, *supra*, note 257.
268 Knight et al., *supra*, note 257. Boyd HB, Anderson LD, Johnston DS. Changing Concepts in the Treatment of Non-union. *Clin Orthop*, 43: 37-54, 1965. Hertel R, Pisan M, Lambert S, Ballmer FT. Plate Osteosynthesis of Diaphyseal Fractures of the Radius and Ulna. *Injury*, 27(8): 545-548, 1996. Hidaka S, Gurtilo RB. Refracture of Bones in the Forearm after Plate Removal. *J Bone Joint Surg*, 66A:1241, 1984. Suedkamp NP, Barbey N, Beuskens A, Tempka A, Haas NP. The Incidence of Osteitis in Open Fractures: An Analysis of 948 Open Fractures (A Review of Hannover Experience). *J Orthop Trauma*, 7(5): 473-482, 1993.
269 Katsamouris et al., *supra*, note 86. Hou SM, Sun JS, Liu TK. Management of Bony Defects in Open Grade III Fractures. *J Formosan Medical Assoc*, 91(3): 315-322, 1992. Sadove RC, Vasconez HC, Arthur KR, Draud JW, Burgess RC. Immediate Closure of Traumatic Upper Arm and Forearm Injuries with the Latissimus Dorsi Island Myocutaneous Pedicle Flap. *Plastic and Reconstructive Surgery*, 88(1): 115-120, 1991. Seligson D, Henry SL. Treatment of Compound Fractures. *Am J Surg*, 161(6): 693-701, 1991.
270 Wilkins et al., *supra*, note 175.
271 Young et al., *supra*, note 216. Seligson et al., *supra*, note 269. Yokoyama K, Shindo M, Itoman M, Yamamoto M, Sasamoto N. Immediate Internal Fixation for Open Fractures of the Long Bones of the Upper and Lower Extremities. *J Trauma*, 37(2):230-6, 1994.

management.[272] Stabilization of the open fracture is still not managed uniformly. There is a trend towards internal fixation of those open fractures not associated with arterial injury.[273] As the severity of the injury increases, so does the number and severity of complications. One study of open fractures associated with arterial injury requiring vascular repair reported a 41.6% amputation rate and a wound infection rate of 13.9%.[274] The best method of stabilizing these fractures is still unclear. Internal plate fixation, internal intramedullary rod fixation, and external fixation are examples of methods used.[275] Some injuries are so severe that salvage is impossible. As each patient presents a different degree of involvement, the choice of reconstruction or amputation is occasionally unclear. To help with the decision, the mangled extremity severity score (MESS) was developed to help determine which mangled limbs will eventually come to amputation.[276]

The prognosis in compound open fractures is mainly related to the bony comminution and bone loss, the amount and type of bacterial contamination, the degree of devitalized tissues, and the length of time the wound has been left without treatment. Some systemic factors such as malnutrition, increasing age, diabetes mellitus, and use of medications, which interfere with the immune response, may also be important.

---

272 Ostermann PA, Henry SL, Seligson D. The Role of Local Antibiotic Therapy in the Management of Compound Fractures. *Clin Orthop*, (295): 102-111, 1993. Ostermann PA, Henry SL, Seligson D. Timing of Wound Closure in Severe Compound Fractures. *Orthopaedics*, 17(5): 397-399, 1994. Ostermann PA, Seligson D, Henry SL. Local Antibiotic Therapy for Severe Open Fractures. A Review of 1085 Consecutive Cases. *J Bone Joint Surg*, 77B(1): 93-97, 1995.
273 Duncan R, Geissler W, Freeland AE, Savoie FH. Immediate Internal Fixation of the Forearm. *J Orthop Trauma*, 6(1) 25-31, 1992.
274 Soucacos et al., *supra*, note 253. Seligson D, Ostermann PA, Henry SL, Wolley T. The Management of Open Fractures Associated with Arterial Injury Requiring Vascular Repair. *J Trauma*, 37(6): 938-940, 1994.
275 Sadove et al., *supra*, note 269. Morgan WJ, Breen TF. Complex Fractures of the Forearm. Review. *Hand Clinics*, 10(3): 375-390, 1994.
276 Gregory RT, Gould RJ, Peclet M, Wagner JS, Gilbert DA, Wheeler JR, Snyder SO, Gayle RG, Schwab CW. The Mangled Extremity Syndrome (M.E.S.): a Severity Grading System for Multisystem Injury of the Extremity. *J Trauma*, 25(12):1147-50, 1985. Helfet D, Howey T, Sanders R, Johansen K. Limb Salvage Versus Amputation: Preliminary Results of the Mangled Extremity Severity Score. *Clin Orthop*, 256:80-86, 1990. Levin, LS, Goldner RD, Urbaniak JR, Nunley JA, Hardaker WT Jr. Management of Severe Musculoskeletal Injuries of the Upper Extremity. *J Orthop Trauma*, 4(4): 432-440, 1990. Slauterbeck JR, Britton C, Moneim MS, Clevenger FW. Mangled Extremity Severity Score: An Accurate Guide to Treatment of the Severely Injured Upper Extremity. *J Orthop Trauma*, 8(4): 282-285, 1994.

11.3.3 Injuries to the Distal Forearm and Wrist

11.3.3.1 Anatomy and Biomechanics

The distal forearm and wrist comprise a complex unit of multiple small joints designed to allow liberal motion in three planes whilst maintaining stability and providing for the transmission of forces from the fingers and the hand proximally.

The wrist, or carpus, consists of eight bones of which seven are true carpal bones and one, the pisiform bone, is located in the vicinity of the carpus but does not participate in the weight bearing, nor the stability aspects of the wrist [Figure 11.84]. It is a sesamoid bone located in the tendon of the flexor carpi ulnaris and is similar in concept to the patella (kneecap) located in the quadriceps mechanism at the knee. The pisiform bone articulates with the triquetrum, moves the line of pull of the flexor carpi ulnaris further from the centre of rotation of the wrist thereby improving the mechanical advantage, and partially protects the ulnar nerve and artery as they enter the hand [Figure 11.85]. Short intrinsic ligaments connect the seven true carpal bones to each other and at the area of contact there exists a smooth complimentary shaped articular surface of hyaline cartilage. These seven bones are positioned between the two forearm long bones, the radius and ulna and the five metacarpal bones that support the fingers and thumb [Figure 11.86].

The carpal bones each have a different shape from one another and unique functions. The proximal support system consists of the sloped distal articular surface of the radius [Figure 11.84] divided into two facets; one for the proximal pole of scaphoid and one for the lunate [Figure 11.87]. In addition, the proximal support system also includes the soft fibrocartilage tissue covering the distal end of the ulna (the triangular fibrocartilage—TFC).[277] This proximal supporting system therefore has a very firm base (the radius) and a softer hammock or trampoline like support ulnarly, the triangular fibro-cartilage [Figure 11.88]. This ulnar aspect dynamically varies in the amount of support offered. The two sloped facets of the radius have hyaline cartilage resting on a firm subchondral bone plate supported by the trabecular bone of the epiphysis and metaphysis. At its ulnar edge the radial surface continues into the triangular fibrocartilage but deep to this junction and nearly at 90 degrees to the lunate fossa is another articular surface on the radius—the sigmoid notch. This notch articulates with the head of the ulna as the forearm moves through the rotation arc of pronation (palm down) and supination (palm up) [Figure 11.89]. This joint

---

277 Cooney WL, Linscheid RL, Dobyns JH. *The Wrist: Diagnosis and Operative Treatment*. St. Louis: Mosby, 1998. Ekenstam, F. Anatomy of the Distal Radioulnar Joint. *Clin Orthop*, 275:14-18, 1992.

is called the distal radioulnar joint (DRUJ) and does not participate in the normal wrist joint (radiocarpal) movements of dorsiflexion and palmar flexion, nor radial or ulnar deviation. Because the ulna proximally articulates with the end of the humerus by means of grooved surfaces and a distal anterior process (coronoid) and a proximal anterior portion (the tip of olecranon), it firmly holds the distal articular end of the humerus and will allow flexion and extension but no rotation. Therefore all pronation and supination occurs as a result of the radius moving the concave platform of the articular cartilage in the sigmoid notch over the convex articular surface of the ulnar head. This articular surface occupies approximately 215 degrees of the ulnar head.[278] The remaining part of the ulnar head has ligamentous attachments and an area dedicated to stabilizing the extensor carpi ulnaris tendon. Multiple anatomical structures actively and passively orchestrate pronation and supination. Since it is the radius that rotates about the ulna [Figure 11.89], the muscles that attach to the radius and actively produce this rotation must be normal with an intact nerve and blood supply. The configuration of the DRUJ surface, the anterior and posterior periphery of the TFC (the dorsal and volar radioulnar ligaments) the DRUJ capsule and interosseous membrane control the passive movement of the radius about the ulnar head.[279] The bow of the mid radius passively allows pronation to occur without bony contact against ulna. A non-contracted intraosseous membrane allows the bowed mid radius to passively move further away from the ulna into full supination [Figure 11.89] and a normal elbow joint—more specifically the proximal radioulnar joint and radiocapitellar joint, passively control radial head rotation. In supination the radius and ulna are nearly parallel to each other whereas in pronation the radius crosses the ulna and this oblique path of the radius of necessity brings the distal supporting surface of the radius more proximal than when the bones are parallel in supination. It is this proximal-distal movement of the distal articular surface of the radius accompanied by the lack of such an occurrence by the ulnar head that produces a variation in support provided to the ulnar side of the carpus by the TFC and ulnar head. This dynamic change in the relative lengths of radius and ulna (called ulnar variance) may be 2 mm [ref. for dynamic ulnar variance] in a normal individual. On the sloped firm radial platform and the bouncy and varying ulnar platform rests the proximal carpal row. From the radial side to the ulnar side the bones are; the scaphoid, the lunate and the triquetrum [Figure 11.84] with the scaphoid and lunate articulations bearing most of the

---

278 Cooney et al., *ibid.*
279 Cooney et al., *supra*, note 277. Short WH, Palmar AK, Werner FW, et al. A Biomechanical Study of Distal Radial Fractures. *J Hand Surg [AM]*, 12: 529-534, 1987.

weight. This articulation is called the proximal radiocarpal joint. These bones also articulate distally in the midcarpal joint with four carpal bones, which in turn articulate with the metacarpal bones in the hand [Figure 11.84]. These four bones in the distal row have very firm ligamentous attachments to the metacarpals and minimal motion occurs at this carpometacarpal joint. The distal row tends to function as a unit. The proximal row is much more mobile. The scaphoid lies in line with axis of the thumb and in both palmar flexion of the carpus and radial deviation it flexes. Because it is securely attached to the lunate with short ligaments (scapholunate ligaments), the lunate also flexes when the scaphoid flexes and likewise for the triquetrum. In a similar fashion, with carpal dorsiflexion and ulnar deviation the contour of the articular surfaces and ligaments cause the proximal row to move into dorsiflexion [Figure 11.90]. Palmar and dorsiflexion occurs at the radiocarpal and midcarpal joints, whereas radial and ulnar deviation occurs mainly at the radiocarpal joint.[280] The slope of the distal radius is such that it projects distally and ulnarly approximately 24 degrees [Figure 11.84] and volarly 12 degrees. No muscles, by way of tendons, attach to any of the carpal bones therefore extrinsic ligaments attaching to the very distal rim of radius and to a lesser degree the ulna are necessary to maintain this group of carpal bones (held to each other by intrinsic ligaments) from slipping off this sloped platform [Figure 11.91].

Two major arteries cross the wrist region. The ulnar artery passes on the volar ulnar side staying radial to the pisiform while the radial artery begins volar and radial before coursing obliquely dorsally and distally deep to the first dorsal compartment to enter the hand between the first and second metacarpals [Figure 11.81]. Both major arteries give off branches and contribute to the superficial and deep carpal arches and digital arteries. The bones of the carpus receive their blood supply from branches of these major vessels. The scaphoid, lunate and to a lesser degree capitate bones have unique blood supply patterns with vessels supplying the proximal parts entering distally.[281]

The tendons in the distal forearm and wrist region have proximal muscle bellies and cross the carpus without inserting into it [Figures 11.81 and 11.92]. Only the long tendon of the brachioradialis muscle fails in this respect in that it inserts into the distal radial aspect of radius without crossing the carpus. On the palmar side of the wrist exists a tunnel, a carpal tunnel bounded by a floor and two walls made of bone and a thick fibrous roof. The floor and walls merge into each other forming a semicircle and

---

280 Short et al., *ibid.*
281 Cooney, W.P. Vascular and Nuerologic Anatomy of the Wrist at 106-125. In: Cooney et al., *supra*, note 277.

the thick fibrous roof, the flexor retinaculum, connects both sides of the bony semicircle. Nine tendons, two to each finger and one to the thumb plus the median nerve make up the contents of the carpal tunnel. Note that the palmar branch of the Median nerve separates proximal to the carpal tunnel and enters the hand superficial to the carpal tunnel. The ulnar nerve and artery lie just outside the carpal tunnel ulnarly [Figure 11.85]. The tendons on the palmar side are large, round and have a thin loose covering called tenosynovium [depicted as blue in Figure 11.93]. The tendons that cross the wrist dorsally are thin, flat, and maintained closely to the bony plane by retinacula that form six compartments [Figure 11.92]. In addition to the median and ulnar nerves, the radial nerve traverses the region of the wrist on the dorsal radial aspect. This nerve is purely a sensory nerve at the distal location and plays a part, along with sensory branches of the ulnar nerve and median nerve in supplying sensation to the region.

11.3.3.2 Fractures of the Distal Radius

A fall onto the outstretched hand is the usual situation that results in a fracture of the distal radius. If the fracture is one in which the distal articular surface tilts dorsally and when viewed from the side of the forearm has a face down dinner fork deformity, it is called a Colles' fracture. Shearing type fractures are frequently called Barton fractures and fractures associated with palmar displacement of the distal fragment are referred to as Smiths' fractures.[282] Since the forces that produce this injury are quite varied and of markedly different magnitudes; and since the age, health, and gender of the individuals also vary (thereby associated with different physical characteristics of the distal radius), many different fracture patterns occur. When assessing a patient with this injury, one must firstly insure by history (in an intellectually competent and alert individual) that no other area of the body has been injured. The pain from the fracture site may mask other injuries, especially those in the vicinity of the fracture and these injuries may involve bony structures or soft tissue structures not easily diagnosed on plain radiography. Many different classifications exist for fractures of the distal radius and none is universally accepted.[283] Most importantly, one must understand why the classifications differ and what features should be included when assessing an injury to the distal radius. Important is a clear diagnosis of the extent of the injury; the location of the fracture, the direction of displacement, and the amount of displacement. Does the fracture enter the radiocarpal joint and is therefore an intra-ar-

---

282 Cooney WL. *Fractures of the Distal Radius*. New York: Springer-Verlag, 1996: 310-355.

283 Fernandez DL, Jupiter JB. *Fractures of the Distal Radius*. New York, Springer Verlag, 1996: 23-52.

ticular fracture? If so, is it displaced? Two millimetres of displacement may be tolerable.[284] Displacement direction distally into the joint space is worse than a gap. Is the fracture comminuted or one or two major pieces? A comminuted fracture indicates damage to a large area of the surface and probable hyaline cartilage damage. It also indicates great difficulty in surgically restoring anatomical congruity. Single large fragments suggest less damage and, if necessary, generally allow for easier repositioning and fixation. Is the fracture extra-articular and thereby not involving the articular surface of either the radiocarpal joint or distal radio-ulnar joint? Is this extra-articular fracture displaced? Which direction and to what degree is it displaced or tilted, and is it associated with, and with what amount of, proximal migration or translation? Is the radius shortened? If the radius is shortened, is it shortened on the radial side, the ulnar side or both? Generally one describes the distal fragments position when discussing displacement. A dorsal tilt with the apex of the angle of the fracture volarly is what one refers to as a Colles' fracture. A final result with an excessive dorsal tilt as viewed on a lateral radiograph that leaves the longitudinal axis of the capitate bone no longer co-linear with the longitudinal axis of the radius causes the carpal bones to line up in a zigzag fashion [Figure 11.94]. Since no muscles or tendons attach to the carpal bones this alignment inherently is unstable in compression. The zigzag position is only maintained by ligamentous support and will result in a weakened grip and abnormally located joint compression forces that may with time produce excess wear on some aspects of the hyaline cartilage surfaces.[285] Generally one would attempt to restore the volar and anatomical tilt of the distal radial articular surface and avoid a dorsal tilt of 20 degrees.[286] A volar tilt, especially if associated with volar translation does not usually produce a zigzag collapse pattern of the carpus but it does frequently interfere with supination.[287] Shortening of the radius occurs mainly on the radial aspect with loss of the normal inclination. Shortening is a major cause of the clinical deformity and disability. If shortening occurs to a great amount on the ulnar side this indicates that the ulnar support structures have been torn and instability of the DRUJ may exist.[288] In addition, any residual shortening, even two millimetres on the ulnar side, may in certain individuals cause the non-injured and non-shortened ulna to be relatively long and

---

284 Cooney et al., *supra*, note 277.
285 Khirk JL, Jupter JB. Intra-Articular Fractures of the Distal End of the Radius in Young Adults. *J Bone Joint Surg*, 68A: 647-659, 1986.
286 *Supra*, note 282.
287 Fernandez et al., *Supra*, note 283.
288 Aro, HT, Koivunen T. Minor Axial Shortening of the Radius Affects Outcome of Colles' Fracture Treatment. *J Hand Surg [AM]*, 16: 392-398, 1991.

may cause the TFC and ulnar head deep to it to exert excessive pressure against the lunate and triquetrum producing ulnocarpal impaction dorsal ulnar pain especially with dorsiflexion and ulnar deviation and may also result in ulnar sided wrist pain and a weak grip—especially in pronation as in this position the amount of ulnar variance is at its greatest. Does the fracture enter the sigmoid notch of the radius and is it comminuted or displaced? A damaged sigmoid notch especially one with a residual articular surface incongruity will likely limit forearm rotation. Even a fracture that just misses the articular surface of the sigmoid notch may be associated with a joint fibrosis reaction that causes a limitation of forearm rotation. Is there a fracture of the ulnar head or neck? Is there a fracture of the ulnar styloid and is it displaced distally or radially? The significance of ulnar styloid fractures is still not fully appreciated but on occasions a distally displaced ulnar styloid fracture may produce late symptoms of ulnostyloid-triquetral impaction, and a radially displaced ulnar styloid may indicate that the peripheral attachment of the TFC is anchored to its base and thereby suggests an injury to the supporting system of the DRUJ. Is there a widening of the DRUJ and loss of its ligamentous supports? What combination of these injuries has occurred and are there complicating issues such as median nerve compression or tendon rupture? The ubiquitous "Colles" fracture may in fact be an injury to many structures.

11.3.3.2.1 Treatment of Distal Radial Fractures: The goal of treatment of these injuries is to achieve an acceptable result. What is acceptable for a 90-year-old female patient's non-dominant forearm may not be acceptable for a 23-year-old male plumber. All treatment methods have their own success rates and incidence of complications. Treatment can be categorized into: 1. obtaining an acceptable reduction, 2. maintaining an acceptable reduction, 3. preventing complications, 4. rehabilitation.

Obtaining an acceptable reduction may be as simple as a manual manipulation and application of Plaster of Paris or it may require open operative reduction and internal fixation. Between these two extremes are a number of treatment modalities including; bone grafting, external fixation, percutaneous fixation, and a combination of external and internal fixation. Obtaining an anatomical reduction is most difficult and usually impossible in severely comminuted displaced intra-articular fractures. Maintaining an acceptable reduction demands the creation of a system that will counteract deforming forces until bony healing provides stability. A snug, well-moulded plaster that is changed as the swelling diminishes often is sufficient. On occasion external fixation, percutaneous pin fixation, bone grafting and internal fixation is necessary to maintain a reduction. Fractures frequently become difficult to successfully manipulate manually after 3 weeks; therefore, if a change in the treatment plan is to occur, it should be undertaken before the fracture consolidates. Patients should be seen on a weekly basis for 3 weeks, and then depending upon the fracture pattern, one may allow a longer interval between visits.

The three factors that have been shown to correlate with a poor clinical result are; loss of radial length, excessive dorsal tilt, and articular damage.[289] One should strive to avoid radial shortening more than 5 mm, a displacement in the articular surface of more than 2 mm, and a dorsal tilt more than 20 degrees.[290] Complications of the injury include those that occur at the moment of impact, those that result from swelling and disuse, and those associated with treatment. Hyaline cartilage once damaged is never normal. Swelling within a confined space may compress the median nerve and produce a carpal tunnel syndrome or a compartment syndrome. Cooney has classified complications into early, intermediate and late categories.[291]

In the early subcategory he includes; unstable reduction, non-anatomic articular reduction, median or ulnar nerve injury, compartment syndrome, tendon and peripheral nerve damage. Intermediate stage complications may include loss of reduction and secondary deformity, nerve compression syndromes and symptoms related to wrist instability. Late complications include nerve compression syndromes, arthritis affecting the radiocarpal or DRUJ, reflex sympathetic dystrophy, tendon adhesions or rupture, and mal-union or nonunion.

The final result is likely related to the amount of damage done at the time of the accident, the success in restoring the distal radius and involved structures to an anatomical configuration, the success in maintaining the reduction, unknown factors which may produce complications such as reflex sympathetic dystrophy, and the amount of rehabilitation effort expended by the patient.

11.3.3.3 Fractures of the Scaphoid

Although any of the carpal bones can be fractured, by far the scaphoid bone is involved most frequently. In addition, its unique location, and blood supply pattern make the consequences of fracture in this bone more serious than the same injury in other bones. Patients frequently think that only a sprain of the wrist has occurred[292] and may not seek medical care for months at which time a pseudoarthrosis of the scaphoid has been established. Also of concern is the difficulty in radiographic identification of

---

289 Aro et al., *ibid.* Fernandez et al., *supra*, note 283. Cooney et al., *surpa*, note 277.
290 Fernandez et al., *supra*, note 283.
291 Cooney et al., *supra*, note 277.
292 Gutterrez, G. Office Management of Scaphoid Fractures. *Physical and Sports Medicine*. 24:8, August 1996.

acute non-displaced scaphoid fractures.[293] This inability to clearly demonstrate all undisplaced scaphoid fractures on radiographs[294] has created a diagnosis of "clinical scaphoid fracture". When the history and physical suggest a scaphoid fracture and radiographic examination does not support the clinical impression, the recommended course of action is to immobilize the wrist in a plaster and wait approximately two weeks and repeat the radiographic examination searching for a fracture line that has become obvious, or secondary signs of a fracture. An alternative course, if considered necessary, may be computed tomography (CT) at the time of initial assessment. This would more clearly demonstrate the bony trabecular pattern of the scaphoid bone and obviate the need for plaster immobilization in those scaphoids not found to be fractured.

Since the scaphoid is oriented in the plane of the thumb and since it spans the midcarpal joint and is under compression, any fracture in its substance if not treated will frequently cause the distal pole to angulate volarly[295] (bend towards the palm) leaving a gap dorsally. This is most common in midscaphoid fractures. The collapse of the scaphoid into a humpback deformity will result in a shortened scaphoid and this bony strut will therefore not support the distal carpus to same extent, allowing the distal row to approach slightly towards the distal radius.[296] For this to happen the midcarpal joint between capitate and lunate must angle slightly in a zigzag collapse deformity.[297] In addition the distal half of the scaphoid often repeatedly strikes the radial styloid and with time produces a localized arthritis and bony spurs on the opposing bone surfaces. Movement at the pseudoarthrosis results in a fibrous cyst formation, a shortened scaphoid[298] and a dense sclerotic bony cortex that will not heal even if immobilized.

In addition, to these consequences of abnormal biomechanics a fracture in the scaphoid is often associated with diminished or no blood supply to the proximal fragment. The blood supply to the scaphoid is such that the arterial entry point is distal near the mid section and once inside the bone

---

293 Compton, *supra*, note 80.
294 Gutterrez, *supra*, note 292.
295 Belsol RJ, Hilbelank DR, Llewellyn A, Dale M, Greene TL, Rayhack JM. Computed Analysis of the Pathomechanics of Scaphoid Waist Non-Union. *J Hand Surg.* 16A:899-906, 1991. Fernandez DL. A Technique for Anterior Wedge-Shaped Graft for Scaphoid Non-Unions with Carpal Instability. *J Hand Surg*, 9A:733-7, 1984. Trumble TE, Clarke T, Kreder HJ. Non-Union of the Scaphoid. *J Bone Joint Surg*, 78A:1829-1937, 1996.
296 Nattras GR, King GJW, McMurtry RY, Brant RF. An Alternative Method for Determination of Carpal Height Ratio. *J Bone Joint Surg*, 76A:88, 1994 L.
297 Belsol et al., *supra*, note 295.
298 *Ibid*.

it curves and proceeds proximally.[299] This unusual method of nourishment from distal to proximal predisposes the proximal scaphoid to ischemia and resultant avascular necrosis (death of bone as a result of a lack of blood supply). This is more likely when a fracture traverses the mid aspect of the scaphoid and especially when the fracture is more proximal.

Treatment of undisplaced scaphoid fractures demands immobilization.[300] Acute undisplaced scaphoid fractures treated with immobilization usually heal. Treatment of displaced scaphoid fractures usually requires open reduction and internal fixation.[301] Unrecognized acute undisplaced scaphoid fractures, if not immobilized, will likely not heal and will likely progress to a pseudoarthrosis.

Treatment of established nonunions (pseudoarthrosis) requires treatment that is individualized and must incorporate the pseudoarthrosis type, the symptoms and documented rate of progression of arthritis, the age and the demands of the patient, and a discussion with the patient concerning the expected results. The reported natural history of an individual with a scaphoid pseudoarthrosis is one of slow progression to localized wrist arthritis and a wrist with a diminished grip strength, diminished range of motion and pain when the wrist is moved to its limits.[302] Some individuals appear to have a stable fibrous pseudoarthrosis that does not always progress to localized arthritis and may be discovered incidently on radiographs.[303] Since the progression to symptomatic arthritis is usually slow, elderly, low demand individuals may, on occasion, be observed but younger high demand patients would benefit from surgery to obtain a normal scaphoid height and bone union. Surgery usually demands bone graft interposition[304] and internal fixation[305] and the success rate varies with the

---

299 Taleisnik J, Kelly PJ. The Extraosseus and Interosseous Blood Supply of the Scaphoid Bone. *J Bone Joint Surg*, 48A:1125, 1966.

300 Belsol et al., *supra*, note 295. Daly K, Gill P, Magnussen PA, Simonis RB. Established Non-Union of the Scaphoid Treated by Volar Wedge Grafting and Herbert Screw Fixation. *J Bone Joint Surg*, 70B: 530-534, 1996. Herbert TJ, Fisher WE. The Management of the Fractured Scaphoid Using a New Bone Screw. *J Bone Joint Surg*, 66B:114-123, 1984. Mack GR, Bosse MJ, Gelberman RH, Yu E. The Natural History of Scaphoid Non-Union. *J Bone Joint Surg*, 66A: 504, 1984.

301 Filin SL, Herbert TJ. Herbert Screw Fixation of Scaphoid Fractures. *J Bone Joint Surg*, 78B:519-29, 1996.

302 Mack et al., *supra*, note 300. Ruby LK, Stinson J, Belsky MR. The Natural History of Scaphoid Non-Union: A Review of 55 Cases. *J Bone Joint Surg*, 67A: 438, 1985.

303 Stark HH, Rickard TA, Zemel NP, Ashworth CR. Treatment of Un-united Fractures of the Scaphoid by Iliac Bone Grafts and Kirschner-Wire Fixation. *J Bone Joint Surg*, 70A:982-990, 1988.

304 Belsol et al., *supra*, note 295.

305 Filin et al., *supra*, note 301. Shaw JA. A Biomechanical Comparison of Scaphoid Screws. *J Hand Surg*, 12A:347-53, 1986.

location of the fracture in the scaphoid, the amount of degeneration present in the wrist and the presence or absence of avascular necrosis of the proximal pole of the scaphoid.[306] A literature review shows that the success rate of bone grafting scaphoid pseudoarthrosis is quite variable ranging from 47% to 97%.[307] The biomechanical compressive forces that angulate the fractured scaphoid, the unusual blood supply pattern that predisposes to avascular necrosis, the progression to localized wrist arthritis, carpal collapse,[308] diminished wrist function and pain, and the inability to guarantee a successful result with bone graft and internal fixation of scaphoid nonunions makes the early diagnosis and treatment of scaphoid fractures a necessity.

11.3.4 The Hand

11.3.4.1 Anatomy

The human hand is an appendage, which permits a most efficient interaction between environment and organism. It is richly supplied with sensory end organs to identify light touch, pain, temperature and spatial orientation. It has numerous bones and joints to allow mobile and stable platforms as well as forearm musculotendinous units to both apply power and large excursions to these platforms. Small hand motor units produce precision work. In addition there are two main sources of blood supply [Figure 11.81] and a padded firm palmar aspect for grasping. The carpal bones support the five metacarpals [Figure 11.95]. The thumb first metacarpal rests in the saddle joint of the trapezium and has a complimentary shaped surface which allows the thumb metacarpal to flex and extend, adduct across the palm towards the little finger, abduct, and rotate (circumduct). The thumb has only two bones distal to the metacarpal; the proximal and distal phalanges and these two bones have intervening synovial joints, which permit only flexion and extension. Collateral ligaments protect both these joints and permit only a small amount of side to side movement that is not in the plane of flexion nor extension [Figure 11.96]. Long tendons originating in the forearm abduct the first metacarpal (APL or abductor pollicis longus), extend the first metacarpal (EPB or extensor pollicis brevis), extend the interphalangeal joint (EPL or extensor pollicis longus) and flex the interphalangeal joint (FPL or flexor pollicis longus) [Figure

---

306 Stark et al., *supra*, note 303. Trumble et al., *supra*, note 295. Hebert et al., *supra*, note 300. Baton NJ. Experience with Scaphoid Grafting. *J Hand Surg*, 22B:2:153-160, 1997. Filin et al., *supra*, note 301.

307 Baton, *ibid*. Filin et al., *supra*, note 301. Hebert et al., *supra*, note 300. Stark et al., *supra*, note 303. Trumble et al., *supra*, note 295.

308 Fernandez, *supra*, note 295.

11.92]. In addition, the muscles of the thenar eminence and adductor pollicis add fine motor control. The second, third, fourth and fifth metacarpals articulate with the distal carpal row and are the supporting structures for each of the four digits. The second and third carpal metacarpal joints are firmly attached and allow little movement. The fourth and fifth carpometacarpal joints allow some flexion and extension and thus create an increase in the transverse arch of the hand in a cupping effect. Each of the digits contains three phalanges. These bones articulate by means of a synovial joint with hyaline cartilage and are stabilized by capsule and ligaments. The shape of the metacarpophalangeal articulations and the location of the collateral ligaments are such that sideward motion of these joints is possible when the digits are fully extended. When the metacarpophalangeal joint is fully flexed the collateral ligaments are tight and no sideward motion is possible. The proximal and distal interphalangeal joints do not demonstrate that feature and are equally stable through all sections of the flexion-extension arch. Musculotendinous units in the forearm provide gross motor function to the digits. Each digit has two long flexor tendons (FDS, FDP) and variable number of extensor tendons [Figure 11.93]. The index finger has two (EIP, EDC), the little finger has two (EDM, EDC), and the third and fourth digits have a variable number of extensions from the extensor digitorum communis [Figure 11.92]. In addition, small musculotendinous units in the hand, the interossei muscles and the abductor digit minimi, and the lumbrical muscles originating on each of the flexor digitorum profundus tendons provide fine motor control [Figure 11.93]. To prevent bowstringing, a fibrous retinacular sheath begins at the neck of the metacarpal and ends at the distal phalanx [Figures 11.97 and 11.93].

Whenever a tendon passes through a fibro-osseous tunnel and is enclosed, it is surrounded by a two layered sheath [each layer is separated by a thin layer of lubricating fluid—depicted as blue in Figure 11.93] called a synovial sheath or tenosynovium. This prevents the direct abrasion of the tendon substance against the walls of the restraining fibro-osseous tunnel. This protective synovial sheath projects on either side of the restraining fibro-osseous tunnel and the distance that it extends on either side is related to the total excursion of the tendon. The fibrous retinacular sheath system is only present on the palmar aspect. Dorsally, the flat extensor tendons are restrained by retinaculum as they cross the wrist [Figure 11.92]. They lie in relatively free and loose areolar tissue as they proceed distally. The blood supply to the hand is by two main sources; the radial and ulnar arteries [Figure 11.81]. These arteries enter the hand on the volar aspect and feed the superficial and deep carpal arches. Each digit has two digital arteries. The sensory nerve supply to the hand is by three nerves; the radial, the ulnar, and median nerves [Figure 11.98]. The fine motor supply to the thenar muscles is mainly from the median nerve. The digits obtain fine motor control from the interossei and lumbrical muscles. All of these muscles are innervated by branches from the ulnar nerve except for the two lumbricals to the index and long fingers.

11.3.4.2 Flexor Tendon Injuries

Flexor tendons are injured in a multitude of ways and often injuries to neighboring structures complicate the presentation. The compact unique anatomy coupled with the limited blood supply and limited healing ability may turn even a clean tendon laceration into a permanent disability. The flexor tendons travel through many different environments [Figures 11.97 and 11.99] and each zone presents its own challenges and complications. When one must repair one or two tendons lacerated in the mid aspect of the finger (zone 2) one is faced with the problems of retrieval, exposure, repair, dehiscence, adhesions, and joint stiffness. Frequently the proximal end of the lacerated tendon is retracted into the palm. It is necessary to expose the distal end. This will necessitate opening the tendon sheath. This must be accomplished in such a way that its function of restraining the flexor tendons close to the phalanx and preventing bow stringing is not lost. The proximal end must be retrieved and threaded distally to the repair site. This must be accomplished with little damage or irritation to the outside of the tendon so as to prevent future tendon adhesions. The repair must be secure and non-bulky as the space is confined. The reaction to injury causes changes in the tendon at the site of injury and in less than a week the suture may not hold well in this softened edematous area.[309] If movement is unprotected, there is a great risk of the suture pulling through this softened tissue and allowing the repair to separate. The junction starts to become firm at about three weeks. If the digit is immobilized to prevent this dehiscence, the healing process may not only cause the tendon to heal but healing or adhesions can occur between the tendon sheath and the tendon, between the two tendon sheaths and on to the fibro-osseous tunnel wall. To counter this dilemma, better suturing techniques[310] and controlled motion programs have been developed. Any added injury such as phalangeal fractures, large dirty wounds with tissue loss and crush injuries,

---

309 Mason ML, Allen HS. The Rate of Healing Tendons: Experimental Study of Tensile Strength. *Ann Surg.* 113: 424-459, 1941.

310 Ikuta Y, Tsauge K. Postoperative Results of Looped Nylon Suture Used in Injuries of the Digital Flexor Tendons. *J Hand Surg*, 10-B:67-72, 1985. Kessler I, Nissim F. Primary Repair Without Immobilization of Flexor Tendon Division Within the Digital Sheath. *Acta Orthop Scand* 40: 587-601, 1969. Kessler, I. The AGrasping Technique for Tendon Repair. *The Hand* 5: 253-255, 1973. Ketchum LD. Suture Materials and Sutures Techniques Used In Tendon Repair. *Hand Clin*, 1: 43-54, 1985. Savage R, Risitano G. Flexor Tendon Repair Using a Standard Method of Repair and Early Active

will have deleterious effect on this process. In uncomplicated situations, good to excellent results may be expected in 69 to 90% of patients.[311]

11.3.4.3 Extensor Tendon Injuries

Extensor tendons travel in different anatomical areas as they proceed distally and these have been classified into zones [Figure 11.100].[312] Injuries in the four proximal zones tend to have better results than those in the distal zones.[313] Newport reported that two thirds of all extensor tendon lacerations were associated with concomitant injury to bone, skin or joint.[314] Tendon injuries associated with a fracture had poor results.[315] Treatment modalities include static splinting, dynamic splinting, and tendon repair. Results very according to location of injury, associated injuries and the method of treatment.[316]

11.3.4.4 Fractures of the Hand

Fractures of the distal phalanx are often caused by crush injuries with concomitant involvement of the nail bed or finger pulp. If the articular surface is not involved, treatment is usually directed only to the soft tissue. Cleansing and loose splinting is usually all that is necessary. Avulsion fractures occasionally occur. When the fracture is dorsal it is related to an extensor mechanism force and conversely when it is volar, it has resulted

---

Immobilization. *J Hand Surg*, 14-B:396-399, 1989. Tonkin M. Lister G. Results of Primary Tendon Repair with Closure of the Tendon Sheath. *Aust NZJ Surg*, 60: 947-952, 1990. Tsauge M, Ikuta Y, Matsuishi Y. Intra-tendinous Tendon Suture in the Hand: A New Technique. *The Hand*, 7: 250-255, 1975.

311 Savage et al., *ibid.* Ikuta et al., *ibid.* Kettelkamp DB, Flatt AE, Moulds R. Traumatic Dislocation of the Long Finger Extensor Tendon: A Clinical, Anatomical, and Biomechanical Study. *J Bone Joint Surg*, 53A: 229-240, 1971.

312 Kleinert HE, Verdan C. Report of the Committee on Tendon Injuries. *J Hand Surg*, 8A:794-798, 1983.

313 Hung LK, Chan A, Chang J, et al. Early Controlled Active Mobilization with Dynamic Splintage for Treatment of Extensor Tendon Injuries. *J Hand Surg Am*, 15:251-257, 1990. Lovett WL, McCalla MA. Management and Rehabilitation of Extensor Tendon Injuries. *Orthop Clin North Am*, 14: 811-826, 1983. Newport ML, Blair WF, Steyers CM Jr. Long-Term Results of Extensor Tendon Repair. *J Hand Surg*, 15A:961-966, 1990.

314 Newport ML. Extensor Tendon Injuries in the Hand. *J Am Acad Orthop Surg*, 5:59-66, 1997.

315 Newport et al., *supra*, note 313. Hauge MF. The Results of Tendon Suture of the Hand: A Review of 500 Patients. *Acta Orthop Scand*, 24:258-270, 1954. Kelly AP Jr. Primary Tendon Repairs: A Study of 789 Consecutive Tendon Severances. *J Bone Joint Surg*, 41A:581-598, 1959.

316 Newport, *supra*, note 314.

from a pull of the flexor digitorum profundus tendon. Dorsal avulsion injuries usually involve a small fragment of bone and these are usually treated with immobilization.[317] Only a small percentage of patients regain normal function.[318] Abouna and Brown listed factors which lead to a poor outcome: age over 60 years, a delay in treatment, a short period of immobilization, a large initial extensor lag and patients with short stocky fingers.[319]

Flexor digitorum profundus avulsion injuries may or may not have a segment of the proximal phalanx attached to it. Early operative repair is mandatory if one is to restore active flexion of the distal inter-phalangeal joint.

Displaced fractures of the proximal and mid phalanges usually require open reduction and internal fixation if an intra articular component is present. If no articular fracture is present the fracture treatment is individualized. Closed reduction with immobilization, closed reduction and protected early active motion, closed reduction and traction, closed reduction and percutaneous pin fixation and open reduction internal fixation are all acceptable treatment modalities. Factors that influence the results include the presence of crush injury, tendon damage, skin loss, more than one fracture in a finger,[320] the age of the patient,[321] and the skill of the sur-

---

317 Abouna JM, Brown H. The Treatment of Mallet Finger. The Results in a Series of 148 Consecutive Cases and a Review of the Literature. *Br J Surg*, 55: 653-667, 1968. Brooks, D. Splint for Malette Fingers. *Br Med J*, 1(2): 1238, 1964. Crawford, GP. The Molded Polythene Splint for Mallet Finger Deformities. *J Hand Surg*, 9A: 231-237, 1984. Elliott RA. Injuries to the Extensor Mechanism of the hand. *Orthop Clin North Am*, 1: 335-354, 1970. Hillman FE. New Technique for Treatment of Mallet Fingers and Fractures of the Distal Phalanx. *JAMA*, 161: 1135-1138, 1956. Kinninmonth AWG, Holburn F. A Comparative Controlled Trial of a New Perforated Splint and a Traditional Splint in the Treatment of Mallet Finger. *J Hand Surg*, 11B: 261-262, 1986. Lord, RD. Intramedullary Fixation of Metacarpal Fractures. *JAMA*, 164: 1746-1749, 1957. Magnuson PB. *Fractures*. Philadelphia: J.B. Lippincott, 1942. Manktelow RT, Mahoney JL. Step Osteotomy: A Precise Rotation Osteotomy to Correct Scissoring Deformities of the Fingers. *Plast Reconstr Surg*, 68: 571-576, 1981. Mansoor IA. Fractures of the Proximal Phalanx of Fingers: A Method of Reduction. *J Bone Joint Surg*, 51A: 196-198, 1969. Margles SW. Intra-articular Fractures of the Metcarpo-phalangeal and Proximal Interphalangeal Joints. *Hand Clin*, 4: 67-74, 1988. Mikic Z, Helal B. The Treatment of the Mallet Finger by Oakley Splint, *Hand*, 6: 76-81, 1974.
318 Mikic et al., *ibid.*
319 Abouna et al., *supra*, note 317.
320 Huffaker WH, Wray RC, Weeks PM. Factors Influencing Final Range of Motion in the Fingers after Fractures of the Hand. *Plast Reconstr Surg*, 63: 82-87, 1979.
321 Dobyns JH, Linscheid RL, Cooney WP. Fractures and Dislocations of the Wrist and Hand, Then and Now. *J Hand Surg*, 8: 687-690, 1983.

gery.[322] Fractures of the metacarpal neck are frequent in the fifth metacarpal and typically are associated with the metacarpal head tilted volarly. Treatment is aimed at preventing post injury sequelae and frequently a moderate amount of displacement is accepted.[323] Metacarpal shaft fractures must be assessed for proper rotation and frequently can be treated with closed reduction and immobilization. Some fractures may need percutaneous pin fixation or open reduction and internal fixation.[324]

Injury to the median or ulnar nerve in the hand results in a major disability involving fine motor function and sensation. Repair of these injured structures is necessary yet a permanent disability will always remain.[325]

11.4 SPECIAL INJURIES AND COMPLICATIONS

11.4.1 The Multiply Injured Patient

The goal of treatment of the multiply injured patient is restoration of the patient to full function. This is dependent on the nature of the initial injury, the initial resuscitation as well as subsequent treatment of injuries. The immediate priorities in the emergency room are to treat life-threatening problems such as airway obstruction, chest injury and hemorrhage. Resuscitation begins in the field and continues in hospital under the direction of a trauma team leader. The patient is assessed for neurologic disability and is exposed to facilitate examination. Trauma series screening x-rays of the cervical spine, chest and pelvis are obtained and the trauma team leader then proceeds with a careful head to toe secondary survey. Further radiographs are obtained and the management plan formulated. Inability to successfully resuscitate the patient or maintain ventilation and blood pressure may require immediate surgical intervention. These life-threatening injuries take priority over others yet further injury can be prevented by

---

322 Green DP, Rowland SA. *Fractures in Adults*, 3rd ed. Philadelphia: JB Lippincott, 1991: 442-561.
323 *Ibid.*
324 Green et al., *supra*, note 322.
325 De Medinaceli L, Prayon M, Merle M. Percentage of Nerve Injuries in Which Primary Repair Can Be Achieved by End to End Approximation: Review of 2,181 Nerve Lesions. *Microsurgery*, 14(4): 244-246, 1993. Hudson DA, de Jager LT. The Spaghetti Wrist. Simultaneous Laceration of the Median and Ulnar Nerves with Flexor Tendons at the Wrist. *J Hand Surg Br*, 18(2): 171-173, 1993. Kallio PK, Vastamaki M. An Analysis of The Results of Late Reconstruction of 132 Median Nerves. *J Hand Surg Br*, 18(1): 97-105, 1993. Novak CB, MacKinnon SE, Kelly L. Correlation of Two Point Discrimination and hand Function Following Median Nerve Injury. *Ann Plast Surg*, 31(6): 495-498, 1993. Trevett MC, Tuson C, de Jager LT, Juon JM. The Functional Results of Ulnar Nerve Repair. Defining the Indications for Tendon Transfer. *J Hand Surg* Br, 20(4): 444-446, 1995.

gently realigning a fractured or dislocated extremity and applying appropriate splints. This is especially important when deformity results in distortion of vessels and obstruction of the blood supply to the extremity.

In the multiply injured patient, the presence of blunt chest or abdominal trauma does not prevent further surgical procedures from being performed. It must be expected that lung contusions will continue to worsen and that the patient's general condition will deteriorate over the ensuing 3 to 4 days. The orthopaedic surgeon has an opportunity to proceed with extremity stabilization. The presence of an unstable pelvic fracture should be dealt with early in the resuscitation phase since the control of bleeding by the application of a pelvic external fixator represents the control of hemorrhage. Similarly, the early stabilization of facial fractures can facilitate upper airway management and potentially decrease the period of mechanical ventilation required. Many patients require surgery for 8 to 12 hours when multiple injuries are present. The presence of an associated closed head injury is a concern but with intracranial pressure (ICP) monitors now available, brain resuscitation measures can be instituted and monitored during anesthesia when clinical examination is not possible.

The treatment priorities for extremity injuries are to: manage joint dislocations; recognize and repair vascular injury; irrigate and debride open fractures; stabilize fractures which may contribute to ongoing hemorrhage such as pelvic fractures; and stabilize femur, unstable spine and humerus fractures. Studies by Bone and Johnson[326] have documented decreased mortality, significantly fewer pulmonary complications, especially ARDS (adult respiratory distress syndrome), and shortened length of stay in the intensive care unit when major musculoskeletal problems are stabilized within the first 48 hours of the injury in polytrauma patients. Border attributed this reduction in mortality to a more rapid mobilization of the patient such that the patient could sit up, cough and participate in pulmonary toilet. Patients treated in traction for a fractured femur may have the head of the bed elevated to 45 degrees for short periods of time but for the most part these patients remain supine. In addition, mobilization of the patient from side to side in bed usually results in some fracture site motion, pain and the need for narcotic analgesics.

The injury severity score (ISS) takes into consideration injuries in 6 major body regions: head or neck; face; chest; abdominal or pelvic con-

---

326 Bone, Johnson, Weigelt, Scheinber; Bone, McNamara, Shine, Border; and Johnson et al., *supra*, note 105. Border JR, LaDuca J, Seibel R. Priorities in the Management of the Patient with Polytrauma. *Prog Surg*, 14:84, 1975. Fakhry SM, Rutledge R, Dahners LE, Kessler D: Incidence, Management, and Outcome of Femoral Shaft Fracture: A Statewide Population-based Analysis of 2,805 Adult Patients in a Rural State. *J Trauma*, 37(2):255-61, 1994.

tents; extremities and pelvis and external.[327] Injuries are scored from 1 (minor) to 5 (critical) and the three most severe scores squared and then summed to yield the ISS. The ISS is a useful guide to trauma surgeons in predicting the potential for mortality (Table 1). There is evidence from a number of randomized controlled trials that early fracture fixation (EFF) of *all* long bone fractures leads to a reduction in mortality and morbidity in multiple trauma patients. Bone compared a group of 676 patients treated with EFF to a similar group of 906 patients from the American College of Surgeons Multiple Trauma Outcome Study (MTOS).[328] In patients less than 50 years of age and with injury severity scores (ISS) of 18–34 and 35–45 mortality was reduced from 11.8% to 5.1% and from 25.8% to 11.5%, respectively. Similar reductions in mortality were noted for patients older than 50 years with a reduction from 26.4% to 8% for ISSs of 18–24 and from 42.3% to 18.4% for ISSs of 35–45. Most deaths that occur in the first 24 hours are as a result of severe hemorrhage or head injury. Within the first 7 to 10 days following injury and after 24 hours most deaths are due to pulmonary complications including ARDS. Late deaths usually result from multi-system organ failure, which is usually precipitated by a focus of infection either pulmonary, intra-abdominal, urologic or other.

At times, the nature of the patient's injuries are such that final function is difficult to predict. Severe injury to the brain is an example of such a situation. If the patient also has multiple long bone fractures, the approach to management for the patient should not necessarily be pessimistic to avoid excessive shortening, displacement or union of fractures in unacceptable alignment. The recent introduction of automobile supplemental restraint systems (SRS), side impact protections systems (SIPS) and increased seat belt use has resulted in a reduction in serious facial, chest and abdominal injuries. While the airbag will provide protection against internal injury, automobile passengers are more likely to sustain multiple extremity fractures or multiple fractures in one extremity due to passenger compartment intrusion. A patient with a displaced fracture of the mid-shaft humerus and of the femur will most likely require surgical management of the humeral fracture to facilitate the use of crutches or a walker during convalescence. A patient with a similar but isolated humeral shaft fracture might have the option of being treated by splint immobilization.

Management of a closed fracture is more likely to include operative fixation in the multiply injured patient. For open fractures, the risks and potential benefits of EFF must be carefully considered. Yokoyama reported the results of immediate open reduction with internal fixation of 66 open fractures (54 patients) of the long bones in the upper and lower extrem-

---

327 Baker et al., *supra*, note 97.
328 Bone, McNamara, Shine, Border, *supra*, note 105.

ity.[329] Using the Gustilo classification there were 13 (20%) type I, 30 (45%) type II, 11 (16%) type IIIA, 6 (9%) type IIIB, and 6 (9%) type IIIC soft tissue injuries. There were three late deep infections (4.5%), all at the sites of type III fractures. Nonunion occurred in four open fractures (6.1%). If a complete and timely debridement can be accomplished, immediate internal fixation of open fractures can result in a decrease in mortality in patients with multiple trauma. Careful attention to the general status of the patient is required in addition to the severity of the soft tissue wound at the fracture site.[330] For patients with Type III open fractures, the surgeon must weigh the risk of deep bone infection arising at the site of the open fracture against the risk of death for a trauma patient due to incomplete EFF.

11.4.2 The Open Fracture and the Mangled Extremity

11.4.2.1 Open Fractures

The goals of treatment of an open fracture are prevention of infection, healing of the fracture, and restoration of function to the extremity. Open fractures are those where the skin is disrupted, resulting in communication between the fracture site and the outside environment. The initial treatment of an open fracture can affect the final outcome. The surgical component of treatment consists of immediate, thorough and repeated debridement; stabilization of the fracture; coverage of the wound; and early bone grafting.[331] Effective antibiotic therapy is also a major factor in the prevention of infection. Since approximately 30% of patients with open fractures have multiple-system injuries, life-threatening problems must be recognized and treated before operative management of the open fracture is initiated.[332]

Open fractures are most commonly classified into three types according to mechanism of injury, degree of soft tissue damage, configuration of the fracture and the level of wound contamination (Table 2). In a Type-I open fracture, the wound is less than 1 cm long, reasonably clean, has little associated soft tissue damage and no crush injury. This type of fracture is most commonly seen in the tibia where a sharp spike of bone penetrates the skin, creating a small puncture wound. Type-II open fractures have a laceration which is greater than 1 cm in length. There is no extensive soft tissue damage, skin flap or avulsion. There is a slight or moderate crush in-

---

329 Yokoyama et al., *supra*, note 271.
330 Yokoyama et al., *supra*, note 271. Lhowe DW, Hansen ST. Immediate Nailing of Open Fractures of the Femoral Shaft, *J Bone Joint Surg*, 70A:812-20, 1988.
331 Gustilo RB, Merkow RL. Current Concepts Review: The Management of Open Fractures. *J Bone Joint Surg*, 72A:299, 1990.
332 *Ibid.*

jury, moderate fragmentation of fracture and moderate contamination [Figure 11.101]. The Type-III fracture is characterized by extensive damage to soft tissue, including muscle, skin, nerve and/or vessels and a high degree of contamination. This group includes high-velocity gunshot wounds, farm injuries, and segmental or comminuted fractures due to high velocity trauma. Type-III fractures have been divided into three subtypes. In Type III-A fractures, large lacerations or skin flaps are present but the soft tissue coverage is adequate. This subtype includes segmental or severely comminuted fractures due to high-energy trauma, *regardless of the size of the wound*.[333] The Type III-B open fracture is associated with extensive soft tissue loss with exposed bone and periosteal stripping. The wound is massively contaminated and severe comminution or bone loss present at the fracture site [Figure 11.102]. Type III-C open fractures or dislocations involve an arterial injury that must be repaired, regardless of the degree of soft tissue injury.[334] The amputation rates for these types of very serious open fractures range from 25 to 90%.[335] Early amputations occur due to an inability to restore perfusion due to wide zone of injury or technical difficulties with arterial or venous repair [Figure 11.103]. Successful restoration of blood flow may be complicated by thrombosis or clot formation at the site of the vascular repair. Gustilo advocates arterial repair with interpositional vein graft and adequate muscle compartment fasciotomy within 4 to 6 hours of the injury.[336] The incidence of infection increases proportionately with the severity of the soft tissue injury. For Type-I fractures, the infection rate ranges between 0 and 2%; for Type II, from 2 to 7%; Type IIIA, 7%; Type IIIB, from 10 to 50%; and for Type IIIC, from 25 to 50%.[337] The Gustilo and Anderson classification system is widely used to categorize open fractures, yet Kappa analysis studies demonstrate only moderate agreement among surgeons. Although useful, the classification does have limitations yet there does not appear to be a better or more practical alternative. In addition, the Gustilo classification has been in world-

---

333 Gustilo et al., *supra*, note 331.
334 Gustilo et al., *supra*, note 331.
335 Gustilo et al., *supra*, note 331. Caudle RJ, Stern PJ. Severe Open Fractures of the Tibia. *J Bone Joint Surg*, 69A:801-7, 1987. Lange RH, Bach AW, Hansen ST Jr., Johansen KH. Open Tibial Fractures With Associated Vascular Injuries. Prognosis for Limb Salvage. *J Trauma*, 25:203-8, 1985.
336 Gustilo et al., *supra*, note 331. Lange et al., *ibid.*
337 Gustilo et al., *supra*, note 331. Dellinger EP, Miller SD, Wertz MJ, Grypma M, Droppert B, Anderson PA. Risk of Infection After Open Fracture of the Arm or Leg. *Arch Surg*, 123:333-9, 1988. Pratzakis MJ, Wilkins J, Moore TM. Considerations in Reducing the Infection Rate in Open Tibial Fractures. *Clin Orthop*, 178:36-41, 1983. Rittmann P, Schibli M, Matter P, Allgower M. Open Fractures. Long-term Results in 200 Consecutive Cases. *Clin Orthop*, 138:132-40, 1979.

wide use for over 2 decades and is now engrained in the medical literature.[338]

When treating an open fracture, the attending physician will follow an organized step-wise approach and treat the problem as an acute emergency. A thorough initial assessment is carried out to diagnose other life-threatening injuries. Compression sterile bandages are applied to any areas of active bleeding. Tourniquets and vessel clamps should be avoided. Deformity of the limb is reduced by gentle traction and an appropriate splint applied to protect the limb from further injury. Appropriate antibiotic therapy is initiated in the emergency department or as soon as possible and continued for 2 to 3 days. The patient's tetanus immunization status is evaluated and updated if necessary. Arrangements are made for debridement and irrigation of the wound in the operating room under appropriate anesthetic. Wounds are extended to improve visualization of the fracture [Figure 11.104]. For Type II and Type III fractures, repeat debridement in 24 to 72 hours is carried out. The fracture is stabilized and the wound left open for 5 to 7 days. The surgeon should consider whether the nature of the fracture is such that early cancellous bone grafting may be required to promote fracture union. The injured extremity is then rehabilitated.[339] Initial cultures obtained from open fracture wounds reveal predominantly normal skin flora such as staphyloccocus epidermidis and propionibacterium acnes or environmental contaminants (bacillus and clostridium species) which do not commonly cause infection. Certain bacteria are associated with specific types of environmental exposure. Clostridium perfringens, the causative organism for gas gangrene can follow farm injuries. Fresh water-related injuries are commonly associated with Pseudomonas aeruginosa and aeromonas hydrophilia infection. Pseudomonas and Staphylococcus aureus are infrequently cultured from initial wounds yet are frequently cultured from patients while in hospital. The prominence of these hospital-acquired bacteria in open fracture care emphasizes the importance of early coverage of the open fracture wound.[340] The fracture may be stabilized with an external fixator, plates and screws, intramedullary nail, splint, cast or traction. A plaster splint may be used for a stable, isolated Type I fracture until the wound is healed. The limb may then be placed in a plaster cast.[341] For open fractures of the femoral shaft, initial debridement and ir-

---

[338] Horn, BD, Rettig ME. Interobserver Reliability in the Gustilo and Anderson Classification of Open Fractures. *J Orthop Trauma*, 7(4):357-60, 1993.

[339] Gustilo et al., *supra*, note 331.

[340] Godina, *supra*, note 145. Gustilo et al., *supra*, note 331. Caudle et al., *supra*, note 335. Cierny G III, Byrd HS, Jones RE. Primary Versus Delayed Soft Tissue Coverage for Severe Open Tibial Fractures. A Comparison of Results. *Clin Orthop*, 178:54-63, 1983.

[341] Gustilo et al., *supra*, note 331.

rigation may be followed by temporary skeletal traction through the proximal portion of the tibia.

Open tibial fractures, particularly those with more severe grades of soft tissue injury have been associated with high rates of malunion, nonunion and infection.[342] The use of plaster casts for open tibial shaft fractures has been associated with an infection rate in excess of 15% and malalignment rates as high as 70%.[343] Reamed intramedullary nailing remains a reliable method of treatment for open tibial shaft fractures. In a prospective comparison between plate and external fixation, Bach and Hansen reported deep infection rates of 19% and 3%, respectively.[344] Dervin attempted a meta-analysis of 2 prospective studies comparing external fixation and intramedullary nail fixation.[345] There was no statistical difference between the two groups although there did appear to be a slight trend towards higher infection in the nail group but better alignment. For Type I, II and IIIA fractures soft tissue coverage can be achieved by delayed primary closure of the skin edges. If skin loss has occurred or if skin apposition is tight due to soft tissue swelling, meshed split thickness skin grafts may be applied 5 to 7 days following the injury. Type IIIB and IIIC fractures are associated with extensive soft tissue loss and usually require repeated debridements to obtain a clean wound. Early soft tissue coverage, preferably with muscle reduces the risk of infection, permits the delivery of blood to the field with associated oxygen, white blood cells to fight bacteria and deliver antibiotics [Figure 11.105].[346] An additional advantage is that bone healing has been shown to be biomechanically stronger in animal studies comparing skin versus muscle coverage.[347] Stable soft tissue coverage is

---

342 Keating JF, O'Brien PI, Blachut PA, Meek RN, Broekhuyse HM. Reamed Interlocking Intramedullary Nailing of Open Fractures of the Tibia. *Clin Orthop*, 338:182, 91, 1997.

343 Keating et al., *ibid*. Brown PW, Urban JG. Early Weight-bearing Treatment of Open Fractures of the Tibia: An End-result of Sixty-three Cases. *J Bone Joint Surg*, 51A:59-75, 1969. Puno RM, Teynor JT, Nagano J, Gustilo RB. Critical Analysis of Results of Treatment of 201 Tibial Shaft Fractures. *Clin Orthop*, 212:113-21, 1986.

344 Bach AW, Hansen ST. Plates Versus External Fixation in Severe Open Tibia Fractures: A Randomized Trial, *Clin Orthop*, 241:89-94, 1989.

345 Dervin, *supra*, note 146.

346 Gustilo et al., *supra*, note 331. Caudle et al., *supra*, note 335. Cierny et al., *supra*, note 340. Lowenberg D, Feibel RJ, Eshima I, Louie K. Combined Muscle Flap and Ilizarov Reconstruction for Bone and Soft Tissue Defects. *Clin Orthop*, 332:37-51, 1996.

347 Richards RR, McKee MD, Paitich CB, et al. A Comparison of the Effects of Skin Coverage on the Early Strength of Union at the Site of the Osteotomy after Devascularization of a Segment of Canine Tibia. *J Bone Joint Surg*, 73-A:1323, 1991.

also necessary to permit the placement of cancellous iliac crest bone grafts to promote bone healing [Figure 11.105].[348]

11.4.2.2 Mangled Extremities

The severely mangled extremity remains a management problem. Modern methods of open fracture management, skeletal fixation, and soft tissue and bone reconstruction have dramatically improved the potential for limb salvage.[349] The surgeon is faced with the need to make a decision regarding salvage of the extremity or proceed with early amputation. If early amputation is selected as treatment, the patient and family may call the decision into question. Similarly, a mangled limb, which is salvaged but remains with nerve and other deficits may leave the patient with a severe and prolonged impairment or require amputation years after the initial injury. The upper extremity can function with minimal sensation and may be able to provide substantial function as an assistive limb despite serious impairment. The upper limb is also a non-weight-bearing extremity. Salvage of the upper extremity is better than almost any prosthesis to some patients. In the lower extremity, the goal is to provide a limb which is able to allow full weight-bearing, has protective sensation and possesses durable soft tissue coverage.[350]

Velazco examined the medical and economic impact of delayed versus primary amputations following open fractures of the tibia. All patients were taken to the operating room for consideration of limb salvage procedures including debridement, fasciotomy, revascularization, or rigid fixation. Forty-three patients ultimately had amputations of a total of 263 patients treated. Fourteen of the 43 patients had primary amputations: the average hospital stay was 22.3 days and on average 1.6 surgical procedures were required. The 29 patients with delayed amputations had an average of 53.4 days hospitalization and 6.9 surgical procedures. Six of the delayed amputation patients developed infection secondary to the injured extremity and died. No patient in the primary amputation group developed infection or died.[351]

In an attempt to clarify this situation, multiple scoring systems have been developed as a *guide* to the decision-making process. One of the earliest examined injuries according to involvement of the skin, nerve, artery and bone.[352] This was later updated to become a simple rating scale based

---

348 Blick SS, Brumback RJ, Lakatos R, et al. Early Prophylactic Bone Grafting of High-energy Tibial Fractures. *Clin Orthop*, 220:21-40, 1989.
349 Velazco A, Whitesides TE Jr., Fleming LL. The Medical and Economic Impact of Severely Injured Lower Extremities. *J Trauma*, 28(8):1270-3, 1988.
350 Gustilo et al., *supra*, note 331.
351 Velazco et al., *supra*, note 349.
352 Gregory et al., *supra*, note 276.

on skeletal/soft tissue injury, limb ischemia, shock, and age.[353] A Mangled Extremity Severity Score (MESS) greater than or equal to 7 predicted amputation with 100% accuracy.[354] McNamara observed that a MESS score (Table 3) of 4 or higher was 100% sensitive; a value of 7 or higher was most specific and the positive predictive value was 100%. More recent studies have been critical of the MESS score and other scoring scales by way of poor interobserver reliability.[355] McNamara addressed these criticisms by modifying the MESS to include nerve injury and by separating the bone and soft tissue injury into different categories (NISSSA). The new score was found to be more sensitive (81.8% versus 63.6%) and more specific (92.3% versus 69.2%) when compared to the MESS.[356]

The accuracy of any scale will probably never reach 100% because of the great homogeneity of injuries and injury patterns. The MESS and NISSSA are not in general use although a trained orthopaedic surgeon will evaluate and consider all factors contained in the scales to arrive at the best treatment plan for the patient. The general guidelines remain preservation of life, limb and function. A patient with normal foot function and sensation and a MESS score of 4 may not wish to proceed with a series of extensive surgical reconstructions and period of prolonged disability. After thorough pre-operative discussions, the patient may elect to proceed with early amputation.

An absolute indication for immediate amputation is a Type IIIC open fracture with a warm ischemia time of longer than 6 hours with posterior tibial nerve disruption. This nerve injury would result in absence of sensation on the plantar aspect or sole of the foot. Relative indications for primary amputation are: serious associated polytrauma; severe foot injuries on the same side of the open tibial fracture; and anticipated protracted course to salvage. Studies have shown that the functional abilities of amputees are comparable with those of healthy controls.[357] Pain was present

---

353 Helfet et al., *supra*, note 276.
354 Helfet et al., *supra*, note 276. Robertson PA. Prediction of Amputation After Severe Lower Limb Trauma. *J Bone Joint Surg*, 73B(5):816-8, 1991.
355 Bonanni F, Rhodes M, Lucke JF. The Futility of Predictive Scoring of Mangled Lower Extremities. *J Trauma*, 34(1):99-104, 1993.
356 McNamara MG, Heckman JD, Corley FG. Severe Open Fractures of the Lower Extremity: a Retrospective Evaluation of the Mangled Extremity Score (MESS). *J Orthop Trauma*, 8(2):81-7, 1994.
357 Lerner RK, Esterhai JL, Polomano RC, Cheatle MD, Heppenstall B. Quality of Life Assessment of Patients with Post-traumatic Fracture Nonunion, Chronic Refractory Osteomyelitis, and Lower-extremity Amputation. *Clin Orthop*, 295:28-36, 1993. Marsh JL, Prokuski L, Biermann JS. Chronic Infected Tibial Nonunions with Bone Loss. Conventional Techniques Versus Bone Transport. *Clin Orthop*, 301:139, 1994.

in 75% of patients with persistent nonunion, chronic osteomyelitis of bone or lower extremity amputations studied by Lerner.[358] Eighty-five percent of the amputee patients believed they had been significantly mentally scarred by their orthopaedic problem. Despite this, the amputee had minimal restriction of lifestyle and activity in contrast to the patient with osteomyelitis. Eventually, many chronic osteomyelitis patients are faced with the treatment decision of amputation. Patients who were able to attempt to salvage their limbs initially and then participate in the decision to proceed with amputation were more pleased with the outcome than those having immediate amputation [Figure 11.106]. No significant spouse-related psychosocial maladjustments were observed among the study groups.[359]

11.4.2.3 Type IIIB Open Tibia Fractures

These very severe tibial fractures are frequently associated with bone loss, massive contamination and loss of covering soft tissues. Hence the difficulty of the reconstruction rises dramatically. Christian reconstructed Type IIIB open tibial fractures and severe bone loss with external fixation, antibiotic bead spacers to maintain the soft tissue pocket, free tissue transfer and massive cancellous bone grafting. Two to four iliac crest grafts were harvested per patient and all fractures were healed in an average of 9 months.[360] Therefore, the total volume of cancellous bone graft available for segmental defect reconstruction remains a limiting factor.

The harvesting of autogenous iliac crest bone graft is a frequently performed orthopaedic procedure. When the anterior iliac crest is used, the lateral femoral cutaneous (LFC) nerve is at risk.[361] In 10% of normal persons, the nerve exits the pelvis by crossing the iliac crest 2 cm posterolateral [Figure 11.107] to the anterior superior iliac spine (ASIS). This normal variation places the nerve at risk when the iliac crest is exposed near the ASIS.[362] The nerve is tethered to deep tissues as it exits the pelvis and may also be injured by stretching if excessive stretching is necessary for exposure of the inner table.[363] The nerve may also become entrapped in scar tissue following surgery. Injury to the LFC nerve or meralgia paresthetica results in symptoms of pain, paresthesias and numbness over the

---

358 Lerner et al., *ibid.*
359 Lerner et al., *supra*, note 357.
360 Christian EP, Bosse MJ, Robbe G. Reconstruction of Large Diaphyseal Defects, Without Free Fibular Transfer, in Grade IIIB Tibial Fractures. *J Bone Joint Surg*, 71-A:994, 1989.
361 Fowler BK, Dall BE, Rowe, DE. Complications Associated with Harvesting Autogenous Iliac Bone Graft. *Am J Orthopaedics*, 12:895-903,1995.
362 *Ibid.*
363 Kurz LT, Garfin SR, Booth RE. Harvesting Autogenous Iliac Bone Grafts: a Review of Complications and Techniques. *Spine*, 14(12)1324-31, 1989.

anterolateral aspect of the thigh. Symptoms usually resolve after 3 months without treatment but local nerve blocks or resection of a painful neuroma may be necessary.[364] A neuroma results from the repair tissue generated by a completely or partially transected peripheral nerve. The ilioinguinal nerve has rarely been injured and supplies sensation to the scrotum or labia and inner aspect of the thigh.[365] The superior cluneal nerves innervate the skin in the buttock region and are at risk of injury when bone graft is harvested from the posterior iliac crest. Injury to the superior gluteal artery can result in massive bleeding which is difficult to control since the lacerated vessel tends to retract into the pelvis.[366] Urgent exposure and ligation of pelvic vessels or arteriographic embolization may be necessary. Injury to other arteries in the region can result in excessive bleeding with haematoma formation in 1 to 10% of patients. Hernia formation, cosmetic deformity and chronic donor-site pain can result as well. The incidence of chronic pain ranges from 1.5 to 29%.[367]

Treatment of segmental bone loss with free vascularized fibular or iliac crest grafts obviates some of the problems associated with simple iliac crest bone grafting. The technique establishes immediate vascularity to the bony bed but these transplants[368] require compensatory hypertrophy prior to unprotected weight-bearing. This usually requires 12 to 18 months and is not often feasible. There remains a high rate of refracture[369] when large segmental vascularized bone transfers are used in the lower extremity. The Papineau technique remains an alternative for reconstruction of lower extremity defects or osteomyelitis but requires prolonged hospitalization and intensive wound care.[370]

---

364 Fowler et al., *supra*, note 361. Kurz et al., *supra*, note 363. Massey EW. Meralgia Parasthetica Secondary to Trauma of Bone Graft. *J. Trauma*, 20:342-3, 1980. Weikel AM, Habal MB. Meralgia Parestheica: A Complication of Iliac Bone Procurement. *Plast Reconstr Surg*, 60:572-4, 1977.
365 Fowler et al., *supra*, note 361.
366 Fowler et al., *supra*, note 361.
367 Fernyhough JC, Schimandle JJ, Weigel MC, et al. Chronic Donor-site Pain Complicating Bone-graft Harvesting from the Posterior Iliac Crest for Spinal Fusion. *Spine*, 17(12):1474-80, 1992. Hutchinson MR, Dall BE. Midline Fascial Splitting Approach to the Iliac Crest for Bone Graft — A New Approach. *Spine*, 19(1):62-64, 1994.
368 Banio A, Hertel R. Double Vascularized Fibulas for the Reconstruction of Large Tibial Defects. *J Reconstr Microsurg*, 9:421, 1993. Shapiro MS, Endrizzi DP, Cannon RM, Dick HM. Treatment of Tibial Defects and Nonunions Using Ipsilateral Vascularized Fibular Transposition. *Clin Orthop*, 296:207, 1993.
369 Weiland AJ, Moore JR, Daniel RK. Vascularized Bone Autografts. Experience with 41 Cases. *Clin Orthop*, 174:87, 1983.
370 Papineau LJ. Osteocutaneous Resection-reconstruction in Diaphyseal Osteomyelitis. *Clin Orthop*, 101:306, 1974.

The Ilizarov technique of bone formation by distraction osteosynthesis has revolutionized fracture care. This technique of distraction osteosynthesis involves the controlled fracture of the tibia most commonly at a normal site. The osteotomy is low-energy and usually performed through multiple drill holes and carefully completed using an osteotome. After a latent interval of 5 to 14 days the bony repair tissue is gradually pulled apart or distracted at a rate of 0.25 to 1 mm per day depending on the bony site and age of the patient.[371] Shortening or segmental bone loss can be addressed [Figure 11.108] to avoid or reduce the number of iliac crest bone grafts required [Figure 11.109]. Vasconez advocates the use of Ilizarov bone lengthening technique for defects of greater than 2 cm.[372] Approximately 15 mL of cancellous bone graft can be obtained from an anterior iliac crest—40 ml from the posterior.[373] Calculation of the volume of the cylindrical tibial shaft (approx. 30 mm diameter) yields 2 cm as the maximum estimated segmental bone loss as the limit reconstructible using one iliac crest. Combined soft tissue coverage and Ilizarov reconstruction have shown considerable promise for complex Type IIIB open tibia fractures with extensive bone loss.[374]

Impairment scores for 17 patients with Gustilo Type III open tibia fractures were examined retrospectively[375] by using the Guides to the Evaluation of Permanent Impairment. Fractures were graded as type IIIA, 7; type IIIB, 5; and IIIC, 5 patients. The average impairment scores of the three groups were: IIIA, 7.1%; IIIB, 19%; and IIIC, 18.4%. Each of these impairment scores was less than the impairment scores for below knee (28%) or through knee (36%) amputation. The decision to salvage a limb can be a difficult one.[376] Williams evaluated the total cost of limb salvage utilizing the Ilizarov method versus amputation.[377] Hidden costs for the

---

371 Green SA, Jackson JM, Wall DM, et al. Management of Segmental Defects by the Ilizarov Intercalary Bone Transport Method. *Clin Orthop*, 280:136, 1992. Ilizarov GA, Ledyaev VI. The Replacement of Long Tubular Bone Defects by Lengthening Distraction Osteotomy of One of the Fragments. *Clin Orthop*, 280:7, 1992.
372 Vasconez HC, Nicholls PJ. Management of Extremity Injuries with External Fixator or Ilizarov Devices. *Clin Plast Surg*, 18(3):505-13, 1991.
373 Evarts CM. *Surgery of the Musculoskeletal System*, 2nd ed. New York: Churchill Livingstone, 1990.
374 Lowenberg et al., *supra*, note 346.
375 Kemp AG, van Niekerk JL, van Meurs PA. Impairment Scores of Type III Open Tibial Fractures. *Injury*, 24(3):161-2, 1993.
376 Bowen CVA, Botsford DJ, Hudak PL, Evans, PJ. Microsurgical Treatment of Septic Nonunion of the Tibia. Quality of Life Results. *Clin Orthop*, 332:52-61, 1996.
377 Williams MO. Long-Term Cost Comparison of Major Limb Salvage Using the Ilizarov Method Versus Amputation. *Clin Orthop*, 301:156, 1994.

amputee were factored in, including the lifetime projected prosthetic cost. The amputation group represented a nearly seven-fold increase in cost over the life of the patient as compared to limb salvage utilizing the Ilizarov method of limb reconstruction. The Ilizarov method has provided the most reliable way to restore bony continuity in a long segmental defect and maintain equal limb lengths.[378]

11.4.3 Complications of Injuries to the Musculoskeletal System

11.4.3.1 Thromboembolism

Thromboembolic disease is a common and potentially very dangerous complication of injuries to the musculoskeletal system. The formation of clots within the deep veins of the lower extremities, or thrombosis can result from trauma to the veins at the time of the initial injury or following retraction for exposure during surgery to stabilize a fracture. Venous stasis due to decreased mobility contributes to the potential for propagation or enlargement of the thrombus within the vein. When a thrombus dislodges embolism results with passage of the clot into the lungs. Risk factors for thromboembolism include: age, obesity, extent of surgery and degree of injury, immobilization and past history of thromboembolic disease. The true incidence of thromboembolism is difficult to determine but prevention rather than detection remains the cornerstone of treatment. Clinical signs and symptoms are notoriously unreliable. Symptoms of leg swelling, calf tenderness or pain, shortness of breath, rapid breathing or heart rate or fever should initiate a search for a potential cause.

Venography remains the gold standard for investigation.[379] A venogram is performed by a radiologist by inserting an intravenous cannula into a dorsal foot vein or the saphenous vein. A radio-opaque contrast dye is injected and the venous system inspected for nonfilling defects or diversion of venous blood flow. Venography is not useful or practical as a screening test since it can induce thrombosis in approximately 1% of cases. Iodine 125-labelled fibrinogen scanning has been used for detection of venous clots in the lower extremity. This latter method has largely been replaced by Duplex ultrasound examination which uses the Doppler effect to detect blood flow.

---

378 Green et al., *supra*, note 371. Ilizarov, *supra*, note 371. Feibel RJ, Oliva A, Jackson RL, et al. Soft Tissue Reconstruction in Orthopaedic Surgery. Secondary Procedures. *Orthop Clin North Am*, 24:537, 1993.
379 Culver et al., *supra*, note 77.

11.4.3.2 Pulmonary Embolism

Pulmonary embolism occurs when a venous thrombus or clot dislodges, usually from the lower extremity. The venous circulation carries the clot back to the heart. The clot enters and passes through the first two of 4 chambers in the heart. The clot is then ejected into the pulmonary artery which carries blood from the heart to the lungs. The presence of a large clot or a saddle embolus can obstruct the two main branches of the pulmonary artery and result in cardiac arrest and sudden death. Smaller clots may travel into smaller side branches of the pulmonary artery and injure lung tissue, a condition known as pulmonary infarction. These smaller clots are responsible for the classic signs of dyspnea, chest pain, hypotension and hemoptysis. The common triad of chest pain, dyspnea and cyanosis occurs in less than 3%.[380] Most cases of pulmonary embolism are not identified by symptoms, physical findings, electrocardiography or chest film.[381] Decrease in the arterial oxygen tension or pO2 is a very important diagnostic sign.

When pulmonary embolism is suspected, most patients are investigated by means of a radioisotope-labelled ventilation-perfusion lung scan. The radioisotope technitium ^{99m}Tc is injected into a peripheral vein and a perfusion image obtained of the pulmonary arterial circulation. The lung ventilation scan involves inhalation of radioisotope and improves the predictive value of the study. The presence of maintained ventilation to a segment of lung with a discrete perfusion defect is suggestive of pulmonary embolism [Figure 11.110]. These scans are usually interpreted as low, intermediate or high probability for pulmonary embolism. The risks of anticoagulation must then be weighed against the probability of a pulmonary embolism being present. When the ventilation-perfusion scan is indeterminate, a pulmonary angiogram may be obtained to directly visualize a segmental filling defect or clot in the pulmonary vascular tree [Figure 11.111].

Prevention of thromboembolic disease: Early mobilization of the patient and ankle, knee and hip as well as active range of motion is important in the prevention of thromboembolic disease. Graded compression stockings are also of benefit but cannot be used alone in high-risk patients.[382] Intermittent calf compression pumps[383] involve the use of a small air com-

---

380 Coon WW, Willis PW. Deep Venous Thrombosis and Pulmonary Embolism—Prediction, Prevention and Treatment. *Am J Cardiol*, 4:611, 1959.
381 Hildner FJ, Ormond RS. Accuracy of the Clinical Diagnosis of Pulmonary Embolism. *JAMA*, 202:567, 1967.
382 Sigel B, Edelstein AL, Savitch L, et al. Type of Compression for Reducing Venous Stasis. *Arch Surg*, 110:171, 1975.
383 Nicolaides AN, Fernandes e Fernandes J, Pollock AV. Intermittent Sequential Pneumatic Compression of the Leg in the Prevention of Venous Stasis and Post-operative Deep Vein Thrombosis. *Surgery*, 87:69, 1980.

pressor to cyclically inflate small plastic or rubber bladders which act in sequence to compress venous blood out of the extremity and towards the heart. Retrograde flow of blood back into the extremity is prevented by the presence of normal venous valves.

Prevention may be directed towards the arterial or venous circulation. Antiplatelet agents such as aspirin and dextran are used to prevent arterial thrombosis in microsurgical procedures and in the field of vascular surgery. These agents do not have a primary role in the prevention of venous thromboembolism. Antithrombotic drugs such as warfarin (coumadin) and heparin have been shown to dramatically reduce the incidence of thromboembolic disease. Warfarin is given in tablet form and changes in the coagulation times are usually not seen until 2 to 3 days after the first dose. Warfarin has the disadvantage of usually requiring the transfusion of homologous or banked fresh frozen plasma to administer clotting factors when anticoagulation must be discontinued. This may be necessary if postoperative bleeding occurs or if the patient must be returned on an urgent basis to the operating room. Heparin must be administered by continuous intravenous drip and has a relatively short half-life of action. It may be discontinued 45 minutes to 1 hour prior to a planned surgical procedure without risk of excessive intra-operative bleeding. A newer family of drugs known as low-molecular weight heparins (enoxiparin, tinziparin, fragmin) have recently been introduced and offer the advantage of once or twice daily subcutaneous injection. Daily monitoring of the patient's coagulation profile is not necessary although platelet counts must be checked weekly.

Treatment must be initiated as soon as the diagnosis is certain. For patients with a high probability of pulmonary embolism based on clinical presentation and arterial blood gas analysis, anticoagulation may need to be initiated prior to confirmatory ventilation-perfusion scans. Patients are normally anticoagulated for 3 months or until after any residual risk factors have resolved. The usual initial therapy is heparin followed by conversion to coumadin anticoagulation 5 to 7 days thereafter. Once an appropriate level has been established by way of the coumadin, the intravenous infusion of heparin is discontinued.

In patients who are unable to tolerate systemic anticoagulation, a transvenous inferior vena cava filter can be considered. This device, also known as a Greenfield filter or umbrella is placed in the inferior vena cava, the large vein which drains blood from the lower body into the heart. A patient with a cerebral hemorrhage or intra-abdominal bleeding is an example of the type of patient who may require this form of treatment. If a clot is dislodged from a lower extremity vein, it becomes lodged in the filter and is prevented from passing up into the pulmonary vessels. Surgical removal of a large clot from the pulmonary artery may be indicated for patients with persistent hypotension and severe, persistent hypoxemia.[384] In a review of 9,721 trauma patients, Winchell identified 36 patients (0.4%) who suffered a clinically evident pulmonary embolus (PE) despite a policy of routine prophylaxis against deep vein thrombosis that included use of prophylactic inferior vena caval filters.[385] Eight of these patients died. Using both univariate and multivariate analyses four high risk patient categories were derived: Head and spinal cord injury with neurologic deficit; head injury with associated long bone fracture; severe pelvic fracture and associated long bone fracture; and multiple long bone fractures. These patient groups have an absolute risk of PE despite prophylaxis ranging from 1.5% to 3.8%. Work by Winchell and Rogers suggests that patients with an estimated risk of PE despite prophylaxis of greater than 2-5% are reasonable candidates for prophylactic vena caval filter placement.[386] The exact role of such filters is not yet fully understood since the main risk factor with placement is thrombosis or clotting of the inferior vena cava (IVC).

11.4.3.3 Fat Embolism and Adult Respiratory Distress Syndrome

Fat embolism syndrome is a potentially serious and life threatening complication of long bone trauma, blunt trauma and intramedullary manipulation.[387] Clinical signs and symptoms of fat embolism are encountered in 0.9 to 2.2% of patients with long bone fractures and up to 10% of multiple fracture patients with associated unstable pelvic fractures.[388] FES has also been described following joint arthroplasty. The mortality rate ranges from 5 to 15%.[389]

Signs and symptoms of FES usually begin within 24 to 48 hours after trauma. The classic triad involves pulmonary changes, cerebral dysfunc-

---

384 MacLean LD, Shibata HR, McLean APH, et al. Pulmonary Embolism: the Value of Bedside Scanning, Angiography and Pulmonary Embolectomy. *Can Med Assoc J*, 97:991, 1967.
385 Winchell RJ, Hoyt DB, Walsh JC, Simons RK, Eastman AB. Risk Factors Associated with Pulmonary Embolism Despite Routine Prophylaxis: Implications for Improved Protection. *J Trauma*, 37(2):600-6, 1994.
386 Rogers FB, Shackford SR, Wilson J et al. Prophylactic Vena Caval Filter Insertion in Severely Injured Trauma Patients: Indications and Preliminary Results. *J Trauma*, 35:637, 1993.
387 Muller et al., *supra*, note 247.
388 Gossling HR, Pellegrini VD Jr. Fat Embolism Syndrome: A Review of the Pathophysiology and Physiological Basis of Treatment. *Clin Orthop*, 165:68, 1982.
389 Fuschsig P, Brucke P, Blumel G, et al. A New Clinical and Experimental Concept on Fat Metabolism. *N Engl J Med*, 276:1192, 1967. Peltier LF. An Appraisal of the Problem of Fat Embolism. *Inst Obstet Surg*, 104:313, 1957. Sevitt S. Fat Embolism in Patients with Fractured Hips. *Br Med J*, 2:257, 1972.

tion such as confusion, and petechial rash. Mental status alteration can consist of drowsiness, confusion, restlessness, and even seizures. The patient must be carefully evaluated to rule out head injury as a potential cause of these symptoms. Respiratory failure is secondary to the evolving effects of vasoactive substances on the lung and the conversion of neutral fats to toxic free fatty acids. A decrease in arterial oxygen saturation is a hallmark finding in FES and frequently the only lab abnormality in mild cases. Oxygen desaturation, fever and rapid heart rate represents a triad of symptoms which signal onset of the syndrome. Clinical diagnosis is important since laboratory and radiographic diagnosis is not specific. Petechial rash is seen in approximately half of patients as are retinal hemorrhages which can be seen on fundoscopic examination of the eyes with a standard ophthalmoscope. The rash is characteristically located in the axillae, upper chest and conjuctivae of the eyelids. The rash is frequently transient. Microcirculatory disturbance affecting the kidney filtration system can result in the release of fat globules into the urine.[390]

The classic laboratory finding in FES is the presence of a diminished arterial oxygen concentration (pO2). Chest x-ray changes are not always present. Minor changes can occur on electrocardiogram examination of the heart and a fall in the platelet count seen on a complete blood count. A high index of clinical suspicion must be maintained, particularly in patients with severe or multiple fractures of the lower extremities. Baseline arterial blood gas measurement when the patient arrives in the emergency department are useful in detecting early and subtle changes. Treatment consists of early stabilization of fractures, careful volume resuscitation, analgesia, respiratory support and perhaps steroids. Central nervous system symptoms do not necessarily resolve immediately with the institution of oxygen therapy. This is felt to be due to microemboli and microhemorrhage formation in the brain rather than hypoxemia. The vast majority of patients today survive FES without permanent sequelae.[391]

Charesh, in a retrospective analysis of 138 multiply injured patients (ISS > 18) noted a trend towards greater mortality rate, length of stay (LOS), LOS in the critical care unit, and duration of mechanical ventilation in patients undergoing femur fracture fixation greater than 24 hours following injury. In patients without associated chest injury a pneumonia rate of 38% for the delayed group was noted, compared to 10% for the early group (p = 0.07). Chest injured patients had a pneumonia rate of 48% for delayed femur fixation compared with 14% for the early group. The overall rate of complications of pneumonia, adult respiratory syndrome, fat embolism syndrome, and pulmonary embolus was 56% in the

---

390 Evarts, *supra*, note 373.
391 Evarts, *supra*, note 373.

delayed chest-injury group compared to 16% in the early chest-injury patients.[392] Several other investigators have demonstrated similar beneficial effects of early fracture fixation.[393]

11.4.3.4 Leg Length Discrepancy and Fracture Malunion

11.4.3.4.1 Leg Length Discrepancy: Shortening can occur following fracture and more commonly becomes a problem in the lower extremity. Up to 3 or 4 cm of shortening can be permitted in the humerus without becoming functionally or cosmetically important. When shortening in the lower extremity is excessive, an increase in energy expenditure for gait results, gait is cosmetically disturbing and an orthotic or shoe lift may be required. Other concerns relate to scoliosis, premature onset of low back degenerative problems and late degenerative arthritis in the longer leg. All children with a significant leg length inequality (LLI) have scoliosis as pelvic obliquity tilts the lumbosacral junction. The scoliosis is flexible and correctable when the patient lies down.

In general, a limb-length inequality of greater than 2.0 cm (3.7%) results in gait asymmetry (limp) that is greater than that observed in the general population.[394] Patients with up to 2.0 cm of LLI do not require a shoe lift or orthotic within the shoe, although most seem to prefer a 5 to 8 mm lift to correct approximately half of the LLI. Giles and Taylor studied 1309 patients between 19 and 77 years of age presenting with low back pain, and 50 volunteers ages 20 to 67 years without previous history of back pain.[395] They noted that 18.3% of patients with chronic low back pain and 21.9% of those with acute low back pain had a discrepancy of greater than 9 mm. In the control group of patients, only 8% of patients had an LLI of greater than 9 mm. Therefore, leg length inequality of 1.0 cm or more is observed more frequently in patients complaining of low back pain than in the normal population. Inequality of 2 to 5 cm may be treated with a shoe or heel lift, although the age and lifestyle activities of the patient must be carefully considered. Heel lifts of 5 cm or greater are poorly tolerated because of the weight of the heel and shoe as well as balance and cosmetic

---

392 Charash WE, Fabian TC, Croce MA. Delayed Surgical Fixation of Femur Fractures is a Risk Factor for Pulmonary Failure Independent of Thoracic Trauma. *J Trauma*, 37 (2):667-672, 1994.

393 Johnson et al., *supra*, note 105. Talucci R, Manning J, Lampard S, et al. Early Intramedullary Nailing of Femoral Shaft Fractures: A Cause of Fat Embolism Syndrome. *Am J Surg*, 146:107, 1983.

394 Kaufman KR, Miller LS, Sutherland DH: Gait asymmetry in patients with limb-length inequality. *J Pediatr Orthop*, 16(2):144-50, 1996.

395 Giles LGF, Taylor JR. Low Back Pain Associated with Leg Length Inequality. *Spine*, 6:510, 1981.

concerns. Options for surgical management include: open or closed femoral shortening of the opposite side; lengthening of the involved tibia or femur; or appropriately timed growth arrest of the long leg in skeletally immature patients.

Holm performed isokinetic knee tests to assess thigh muscle function in 10 patients before and after femoral shortening for leg length discrepancy. Isokinetic tests at 2 years showed a significant reduction in quadriceps and hamstring function. Holm concluded that long-term loss of muscle force should be expected after a midshaft shortening of the femur of more than 10%.[396] For patients with 4 to 6 cm of shortening through a healed femur fracture, shortening of the opposite leg is an option. Based on Holm's work, between 3.2 and 4.4 cm of femoral shortening can be achieved safely although reports outline up to 6 or 8 cm shortenings. Contralateral femoral shortening usually involves a 3 to 4 months time to healing of the osteotomy. The technique is less acceptable when performed for tibial shortening since uneven knee heights can result in a unusual cosmetic appearance.

11.4.3.4.2 Malunion: Malunion is defined as an unacceptable position of a healed fracture. Malunion may occur as a result of excessive shortening, rotation or angulation in either the sagital or coronal plane. Most malunion concerns arise when the angulation deformity alters the alignment of the knee and ankle. It is widely accepted that excessive angulation of the tibia, for example, may predispose the ankle and knee to osteoarthritic degeneration.[397] Merchant and Dietz reviewed 37 patients with an isolated tibial shaft fracture an average of 29 years following the injury. Angulation of greater than 5 degrees was associated with radiographic changes in the ankle consistent with early arthritis, but no difference was noted between proximal and distal third fractures.[398] The concept of the weight-bearing axis is termed the *mechanical axis* [Figure 11.112]. The mechanical axis is depicted as the line passing from the centre of the ankle to the centre of the hip, and represents the path of transmission of forces along the lower extremity.[399]

---

396 Holm I, Nordsletten L, Steen H, Folleras G, Bjerkreim I. Muscle Function After Midshaft Femoral Shortening. A Prospective Study with a Two-Year Follow-up. *J Bone Joint Surg*, 76B:143-6, 1994.

397 Kettelkamp DB, Hillbery BM, Murrish DW, Heck DA. Degenerative Arthritis of the Knee Secondary to Fracture Malunion. *Clin Orthop*, 234:159-69, 1988. McKellop HA, Llinas A, Sarmiento A. Effects of Tibial Malalignment on the Knee and Ankle Joint. *Orth Clin North Am*, 25(3):415-23, 1994.

398 Merchant TC, Dietz FR. Long-term Follow-up After Fractures of the Tibial and Fibular Shafts. *J Bone Joint Surg*, 71A:599-606, 1989. Tetsworth K, Paley D. Malalignment and Degenerative Arthropathy. *Orthop Clin North Am*, 25(3):367-377, 1994.

399 Tetsworth et al., *ibid*.

In order to understand what is acceptable alignment, it is important to review the results of closed tibial fracture management. Sarmiento reported the results of one thousand consecutive tibial shaft fractures treated with prefabricated functional below-knee braces. In 95% of the fractures, the final shortening was less than or equal to 12 mm. The mean final shortening was 4.0 mm, compared with mean initial shortening of 4.25 mm. Final angulatory deformity in any plane was less than or equal to 6 degrees in 90% of patients. Sarmiento felt that the presence of an intact fibula was a relative contraindication to functional bracing because angulatory deformity was more likely to develop. The incidence of nonunion was 1.1%.[400]

There is no general agreement regarding the acceptable limits of angulation.[401] Johnson felt that any deviation from normal alignment was detrimental.[402] Graehl recommends performing a corrective osteotomy of the distal tibia immediately above the ankle joint when significant angular deformity involves the lower two thirds of the tibia.[403] Rosemeyer recommends corrective tibial osteotomy for varus deformities exceeding 6 degrees and valgus osteotomies exceeding 12 degrees.[404] In contrast, Brown[405] and Sarmiento[406] note that 5 degrees of varus or valgus at any level are cosmetically and functionally acceptable. Dehne[407] and Nicoll[408] note no significant problems with function or comfort with up to 10 degrees of angulation.[409] Malunion criteria established by Zucman and Maurer[410] are: 10 degrees or more of varus or flexion; 15 degrees of valgus

---

400 Sarmiento A, Sharpe FE, Ebramzadeh E, Normand P, Shankwiler J. Factors Influencing the Outcome of Closed Tibial Fractures Treated with Functional Bracing. *Clin Orthop*, 315:8-24, 1995.
401 McKellop et al., *supra*, note 397.
402 Johnson KD. Management of Malunion and Nonunion of the Tibia. *Orthop Clin North Am*, 18(1):157-171, 1987.
403 McKellop et al., *supra*, note 397. Graehl PM, Hersch MR, Heckman JD. Supramaleolar Osteotomy for the Treatment of Symptomatic Tibial Malunion. *J Orthop Trauma*, 1:281-92, 1987.
404 Rosemeyer B, Pforringer W. Basic Principles of Treatment in Pseudarthroses and Malunion of Fractures of the Leg. *Arch Orthop Traumat Surg*, 95:57-64, 1979.
405 Brown PW. The Early Weight-bearing Treatment of Tibial Shaft Fractures. *Clin Orthop*, 105:167-78, 1974.
406 Sarmiento et al., *supra*, note 400.
407 Dehne E, Deffer PA, Hall RM, et al. The Natural History of the Fractured Tibia. *Surg Clin North Am*, 41:1495-1513, 1961.
408 Nicolaides et al., *supra*, note 383.
409 McKellop, *supra*, note 397.
410 Zucman J, Maurer P. Two-level Fractures of the Tibia: Results in Thirty-six Cases Treated by Blind Nailing. *J Bone Joint Surg*. 51B:686-93, 1969.

or recurvatum; 10 degrees of internal rotation; or with 20 degrees of external rotation.[411] Puno defined malunion as a deformity greater than 10 degrees in varus or valgus, or greater than 20 degrees of procurvatum or recurvatum.[412]

In a cadaver study, McKellop examined knee and ankle joint contact areas and pressures with varying positions of malunion.[413] Varus and valgus angulations increased the pressure in the medial and lateral compartments of the knee, respectively. This effect was minimal for malunions of up to 5 degrees except for valgus alignment of the upper third of the tibia where contact pressures rose in a linear manner. For fractures of the distal third, valgus angulation of as much as 20 degrees resulted in only a 25% increase in contact pressure. For various loading conditions at the ankle, the contact area was most affected by fractures located in the distal third of the tibia. The greatest decrease in ankle joint contact area (45%) was noted with recurvatum of 15 degrees and the ankle loaded in plantarflexion.[414] The results of this study must be carefully considered since Kristensen found no evidence of arthritis of the ankle 20 to 39 years following injury in patients with residual angulation exceeding 10 degrees.[415]

In summary, shortening of greater than 2 cm and rotational deformity greater than 5 degrees in internal rotation or more than 10 to 15 degrees of external rotation should not be accepted. Attempts should be made to align tibial fractures and accept less than 5 degrees of medial, lateral, anterior, or posterior angulation.[416] When osteotomy is selected as treatment for tibial malunion, the procedure can be carried out as an opening or closing wedge. Most patients with tibial malunion benefit from the additional lengthening obtained from an opening wedge osteotomy. The osteotomy is performed with as little soft tissue dissection as possible and the triangular defect is usually filled with cancellous iliac crest bone graft [Figure 11.113]. Plate or intramedullary rod fixation may be selected, depending on the location of the deformity. Occasionally, when performing an oblique osteotomy of the tibia and fibula to correct rotation or angular deformity, a small amount of length can be obtained and locked intramedullary rod fixation performed. Careful monitoring for compartment syndrome is necessary following an acute lengthening of this type.[417] Pa-

---

411 McKellop et al., *supra*, note 397.
412 Puno et al., *supra*, note 343.
413 McKellop et al., *supra*, note 397.
414 McKellop et al., *supra*, note 397.
415 Kristensen KD, Kiaer T, Blicher J. No Arthrosis of the Ankle 20 Years After Malaligned Tibial-shaft Fracture. *Acta Orthop Scand*, 60:208-9, 1989.
416 Johnson, *supra*, note 402.
417 Johnson, *supra*, note 402.

tients with an atrophic soft tissue envelope may benefit from Iizarov angular deformity correction with or without lengthening.

11.4.3.5 Nonunion (Pseudoarthrosis)

Most cases of nonunion occur in the tibia, usually as a result of an open fracture with disruption of the soft tissue envelope. The most important factors affecting the healing of fractures are the local anatomy, blood supply and the extent of local soft tissue disruption. The greater the energy absorption, the more severe the soft tissue injury and the higher the incidence of nonunion. In the tibia, endosteal blood vessels coursing through the marrow cavity provide blood supply to the inner two thirds of the bone. Periosteal blood vessels provide blood supply to the outer third from outside the bone via the soft tissues.[418] Systemic factors such as the age of the patient, associated medical problems, cigarette smoking, and the method of treatment effect the potential for nonunion but the underlying biology of the initial injury is the most important factor.

Delayed union is difficult to precisely define since there are varying ranges of normal for a given fracture. A severe open tibial shaft fracture may take as long as 9 to 12 months to heal even with subsequent surgical interventions. The presence of very little bone healing at 3 months following the injury would not generate as much concern as the same situation in a closed fracture. Nonunion for tibial shaft fractures is defined as a fracture which has not healed after 9 months of adequate treatment. Union of a fracture is defined as bridging bone formation across the fracture site. This is associated with absence of pain when the fracture site is stressed on physical examination, during weight-bearing as well as absence of motion.

11.4.3.5.1 Classification: Nonunions are classified based on the amount of blood supply at the bone interface: hypertrophic, atrophic, or oligotrophic [Figure 11.114]. Hypertrophic nonunions are characterized by the "elephant's foot" appearance on radiographs with exuberant periosteal bone formation. The local biology of such nonunions is good in that there is sufficient blood supply to permit healing but instability and micromotion at the fracture site exist. The gap is narrow and the bone has made an attempt to unite. Oligotrophic nonunions have a lesser amount of bone formation. Bone which is laid down is usually seen in areas of muscle coverage and areas of skin and subcutaneous tissue have little or no callus.

---

418 MacNab I, DeHaas WG. The Role of Periosteal Blood Supply in the Healing of Fractures of the Tibia. *Clin Orthop*, 105:27, 1974. Rhinelander FW. Tibial Blood Supply in Relation to Fracture Healing. *Clin Orthop*, 105:34, 1974.

Atrophic nonunions may have diminished bone vascularity at the fracture site.

Vascularity at the nonunion site and the potential presence of infection must be determined prior to formulating a surgical plan. The presence of true synovial pseudarthrosis or "false joint" formation requires thorough resection for contact of healthy bleeding bone without intervening soft tissues. The general principles of management of nonunions are: to provide stability; consider the introduction of bone graft to the site; rule out infection; assess the soft tissue envelope and resect any infected nonviable bone. In some cases the surgeon recognizes that this may result in segmental loss of a portion of the bone and that more complicated reconstructions may become necessary.[419] If the soft tissues overlying a nonunion site are deficient the result is inadequate blood supply to the bone. When a local bone graft is required the soft tissues may lack sufficient compliance to permit them to stretch out and allow the placement of the bone graft. The simplest approach is to perform local skin advancement flaps, if possible. Local skin and subcutaneous flaps or fasciocutaneous flaps may also be selected. The workhorse flaps are muscle flaps since these flaps have been shown to have superior blood supply and a much greater ability to deal with residual local infection.[420] Free muscle flaps or microvascular transplants are harvested from a remote donor site and the arteries and veins repaired to restore blood supply to the muscle in the recipient site. Some patients with bulky muscle flaps may wish to undergo revision surgery to facilitate footwear use but debulking of free flaps is usually not necessary.[421]

There has been an increasing trend to avoiding posterolateral bone grafting although this certainly remains accepted treatment. The posterolateral bone graft involves placement of bone graft on the posterior surface of the tibia. Its main advantage and reason for success is that it results in union of the tibia above the nonunion site to the fibula and below. An area of poor quality soft tissue is therefore bypassed and the potential for skin breakdown avoided. Advocates of anterior bone grafting feel that the posterior procedure strips the important remaining blood supply from the bone and that the local soft tissue envelope anteriorly must be improved first before embarking on a bone grafting procedure.

Compression plating with or without bone grafting may be performed with application of the plate to the tension side of the bone. Decortication

---

419 Lowenberg et al., *supra*, note 346.
420 Calderone W, Chang N, Mathes SJ. Comparison of the Effect of Bacterial Inoculation in Musculocutaneous and Fasciocutaneous Flaps. *Plast Reconstr Surg*, 70:1, 1982.
421 Feibel et al., *supra*, note 378.

or "petalling" of the exposed bone surfaces is important to allow adequate integration of cancellous bone graft. Rotational correction may sometimes be necessary. Osteotomy of the fibula is required in most cases to permit compression across the nonunion site. Since plates are load-bearing devices the patient must be treated by protected weight-bearing until fracture union is seen to be progressing on follow-up radiographs. The main risk with plate management is the conversion of a non-infected nonunion to an infected nonunion. This method is best reserved for patients with a soft-tissue envelope that is reasonably normal and permits coverage of the plate.

For aseptic nonunion of the tibia with shortening, Ilizarov distraction treatment may be necessary.[422] Closed intramedullary nailing may also be performed for hypertrophic nonunion. When an atrophic nonunion arises in a previously rodded tibial shaft fracture, the surgeon must consider infection as a possible cause. In the absence of infection, reamed exchange nailing may be performed if the initial nail was placed using unreamed technique.[423] If the initial nail was reamed and the nonunion remains atrophic, open cancellous bone grafting may be performed. In this latter situation, the nail may require exchange as well depending on the potential risk of fatigue failure as judged by the activity of the patient.

11.4.3.6 Infection

11.4.3.6.1 Osteomyelitis: Osteomyelitis is the infection of bone marrow and/or bone structures, usually by a bacterium which produces pus. Hematogenous or blood-borne osteomyelitis arises as a result of spread from a distant site. This type is seen most commonly in children. In the adult population, direct local contamination of bone by way of an open fracture is the most common cause of osteomyelitis. The diagnosis usually requires the presence of the following criteria: (1) exposed and infected bone present; (2) positive bacterial cultures from the bone and (3) microscopic evidence on laboratory examination of the bone tissue.[424] Diagnosis begins with a careful and complete history of the problem including assessment of the patient's overall medical condition. On examination, the limb is carefully evaluated for deformity, old scars, previous flap or skin grafting procedures, drainage, redness, and odour. Range of motion in all of joints as

---

422 Cattaneo R, Catagni M. Classification and Treatment of Nonunions. In: Maiocchi AB, Aronson J, eds. *Operative Principles of Ilizarov*. Baltimore: Williams and Wilkins, 1991: 190-198.

423 Templeman D, Thomas M, Varecka T, Kyle R. Exchange Reamed Intramedullary Nailing for Delayed Union and Nonunion of the Tibia. *Clin Orthop*, 315:169-175, 1995.

424 Gayle LB, Lineaweaver WC, Oliva A, Siko PP, et al. Treatment of Chronic Osteomyelitis of the Lower Extremities with Debridement and Microvascular Muscle Transfer. *Clin Plast Surg*, 19(4):895-903, 1992.

well as the nerve and vascular status of the involved extremity is assessed.[425] Baseline bloodwork includes a complete blood count for assessment of possible anemia and to examine the white blood cell count. Active infection will be associated with elevation of the white count as well as the erythrocyte sedimentation rate (ESR).

Plain radiographs are obtained of the involved region of the limb. Long leg length x-ray films may be required especially when malalignment is evident. The previous films should also be carefully examined chronologically and areas of potential sequestrum formation identified. A sequestrum is a fragment of dead bone, which has become separated from the surrounding healthy bone. Tomograms or CT scans may provide additional information regarding possible concealed sequestra even in the presence of retained metallic internal fixation devices.[426] In situations where deep infection is suspected by history, physical examination or blood work yet not clearly proven, radionucleotide scans may be useful. A technitium (Tc 99m) scan is performed initially to record the baseline uptake of isotope at the fracture site. Technitium is a radioactive isotope, which is avid for areas of active bone turnover such as in degenerative arthritis or remodelling fracture (usually less than 2 years). An indium chloride In 111 or gallium citrate Ga 67 scan is performed within the next 24 to 48 hours.[427] Scans are interpreted as being supportive of the diagnosis of osteomyelitis when either the gallium or indium uptake is greater than that noted on the technitium baseline scan. Magnetic resonance imaging (MRI) scans with gadolinium enhancement are also useful in such cases but will not provide an image in the presence of a ferrous-based metallic implant. This phenomenon is referred to as a signal void.

Once assessment of the patient and the osteomyelitic area has been completed, the infection is staged. Staging is useful as a guide to treatment. Patients with cancer or severe malnutrition may be candidates for chronic suppressive therapy or deferral of the definitive treatment. The Cierny classification divides (Table 4) the host into three physiologic classes: normal, compromised host, and treatment deferred. The osteomyelitis is classified according to the extent of bone involvement: medullary, superficial, localized, and diffuse [Figure 11.115]. In medullary involvement, the marrow cavity is involved while superficial osteomyelitis affects only the outer portion or cortex. Localized osteomyelitis involves a combination of medullary and cortical involvement. Diffuse osteomyelitis is permeative, circumferential or through-and-through disease which usu-

---

425 Evarts, *supra*, note 373.
426 Evarts, *supra*, note 373.
427 *Ibid.*

ally requires resection of a segment of tissue for adequate debridement.[428] Figure 11.116 shows the clinical appearance of a 69-year-old male with diabetes mellitus. Symptoms of purulent drainage had persisted for 3 years after treatment for an open tibia fracture. Initial staging revealed a mixed cortical-medullary osteomyelitis and, therefore, clinical stage IIIB disease.

The treatment principles of osteomyelitis include: resection of non-viable and infected soft and hard tissues; conversion of the infected wound to a healthy contaminated wound; provision of adequate drainage; administration of antibiotics and obliteration of dead space. Osteomyelitis more commonly occurs in bones such as the tibia which have little surrounding muscle coverage. Early soft tissue coverage with rotation or free muscle flaps is widely accepted as the best means of preventing deep infection for patients with high grade open fractures of the tibia.[429] Since Stark's report in 1946 of his experience with the use of pedicled muscle flaps in the treatment of chronic osteomyelitis, the use of muscle flap coverage following debridement has proven to be the most successful and widely adapted treatment modality.[430] Although the mechanisms by which muscle flaps potentiate healing in chronic wounds are not clearly established, the tissue malleability of muscle flaps make them especially suited for obliterating complex wound spaces.[431] Several authors have reported favourable experience with the use of microvascular transplantation in the treatment of chronic osteomyelitis (Table 5). Experimental data have demonstrated the specific antibacterial role of a flap in an infected wound, including enhanced bacterial clearance and increased oxygen delivery.[432] There is no such data to support flap coverage in the presence of a major infected, non-viable segment of bone, known as a sequestrum.[433] The primary advantage of muscle transfer is that it allows an almost unrestricted approach to debridement [Figure 11.117], not unlike the approach taken in cancer resection surgery.

Open cancellous bone grafting or Papineau technique is uncommonly used largely due to improved microsurgical success rates. The technique

---

428 *Ibid.*
429 Godina, *supra*, note 145. Byrd HS, Cierney G III, Tebbetts JB. The Management of Open Tibial Fractures with Associated Soft Tissue Loss: External Pin Fixation with Early Flap Coverage. *Plast Reconstr Surg*, 68:73, 1981. Ger R. Muscle Transposition for Treatment and Prevention of Chronic Post-traumatic Osteomyelitis of the Tibia. *J Bone Joint Surg*, 59A:784, 1977.
430 Gayle et al., *supra*, note 424. Stark WJ. The Use of Pedicled Muscle Flaps in the Surgical Treatment of Chronic Osteomyelitis Resulting from Compound Fractures. *J Bone Joint Surg*, 28:343, 1946.
431 Gayle et al., *supra*, note 424.
432 Daly et al., *supra*, note 300.
433 Gayle et al., *supra*, note 424.

may be necessary for a patient who is unable to tolerate other treatment modalities. Resection of soft tissue and bone to healthy, viable bleeding surfaces is carried out. The wound is then allowed to granulate, a stage of wound healing characterized by the proliferation of inflammatory tissue and new capillary buds. Cancellous bone graft is laid over the defect. The deepest layer of bone graft incorporates and the necrotic, nonviable superficial bone graft is removed and a further bone graft carried out approximately 2 weeks later. Eventually, the granulation tissue is covered with split thickness skin graft but instability of the overlying resultant skin is a major disadvantage.[434] Free vascularized fibular, iliac crest and rib grafts have largely been replaced by Ilizarov technique.[435]

Marsh compared the results of resection and bone transport versus less extensive debridement, external fixation, bone grafting, and soft tissue coverage for the treatment of infected tibial nonunions with segmental defects.[436] Results were similar except for significantly less limb length discrepancy in the transport group.

Bowen studied the quality of life results for patients with post-traumatic infected nonunion of the tibia treated by microsurgical reconstruction. Patients were treated by wound excision followed by soft tissue and skeletal reconstruction. Despite relatively low scores on follow-up questionnaires, most patients were either very or completely satisfied with the outcome of surgery. Patients often reported that satisfaction was related to preservation of the limb.[437]

11.4.3.6.2 Gas Gangrene (Clostridial Myonecrosis): Gas gangrene is one of the most serious complications of open wounds. The bacterial nature of the disease was recognized in 1871 by Bottini. By World War II the term *gas gangrene* was limited to invasive anaerobic infections of muscle characterized by profound toxicity, extensive edema, massive tissue necrosis, and gas production. The clostridial species are responsible for producing gas gangrene and are ubiquitous within the environment. The most common offending organism is Clostridium perfringens, a nonmotile, gram-positive, anaerobic bacillus. The organism proliferates in contaminated wounds where there is associated tissue necrosis, body fluids, and low oxygen tension. The exact modern-era incidence is not known. In almost all cases, the wound involves injury to muscle such as with a deep, penetrating wound of the thigh or buttock. The incubation period for clostridial organisms is 12 to 24 hours. Patients note rapid swelling, tissue

---

434 Papineau, *supra*, note 370. Cabanela ME. Open Cancellous Bone Grafting of Infected Bone Defects. *Orthop Clin North Am*, 15:427, 1984.
435 Lowenberg et al., *supra*, note 346.
436 Marsh, *supra*, note 357.
437 Bowen et al., *supra*, note 376.

thickening, and drainage of thin, dark fluid. The patient's heart rate becomes elevated but temperature is not elevated until the infection advances. Clinical deterioration proceeds quickly to a state of obtundation, coma, and profound shock. Clinical examination of the extremity reveals bronze discoloration in the wound, a musty odour and crepitus on palpation of the soft tissues. Diagnosis is made on clinical grounds since the presence of gas within the tissues is not specific for gas gangrene. Gram stain identification of gram-positive bacilli is useful when the diagnosis is suspected. Treatment involves aggressive debridement, multiple incisions for fasciotomy and excision of necrotic tissues although open amputation is frequently required.[438] At surgical exploration, the muscle is dark red or grey, does not contract or bleed and frothy gas bubbles invade the muscle fibres. Repeat debridement is carried out at 24 to 48 hours and delayed closure of the open amputation wound performed when the wound appears clean. High dose antibiotic therapy as well as careful fluid resuscitation, central venous pressure and urinary output monitoring are important additions to surgical therapy. Hyperbaric oxygen therapy may also be useful if the clinical condition of the patient permits.

11.4.3.6.3 Necrotizing Fasciitis: Necrotizing fasciitis is a rapidly progressive, extremely aggressive infection of the subcutaneous and fascial tissue planes, which has a high mortality rate. Most patients have some form of underlying condition such as peripheral vascular disease or diabetic neuropathy, which predisposes them to the infection. The initial injury may be quite minor such as a small cut on the toe of a diabetic individual. The infection usually involves multiple organisms although peptostreptococcus, bacteroides and gram negative bacilli are most commonly cultured. The clinical appearance of the patient may be very similar to gas gangrene except that there is no underlying infection of muscle. The treatment is primarily surgical and involves the excision of infected, nonviable tissues. Appropriate antibiotic therapy is important as is volume replacement. Hyperbaric oxygen therapy may also be indicated if the clinical condition of the patient permits. Once the acute infection has been treated, exposed muscle may be covered by split thickness skin grafts, in the same way burn patients are treated.

11.4.3.7 Compartment Syndrome

Compartment syndrome is a potentially serious and life-threatening complication of trauma to the extremities. Increases in compartment pressures may occur due to bleeding from fracture, edema or swelling from

---

[438] DeHaven KE, Evarts CM. The Continuing Problem of Gas Gangrene: A Review and Report of Illustrative Cases. *J Trauma*, 11:983-91, 1971.

prolonged venous outflow obstruction or after prolonged arterial obstruction to the extremity. Whatever the initiating event, the result is an increase in the total volume of the muscle compartment. The muscle compartment is enveloped by fascia, a firm fibrous membrane, which does not readily expand. As volume within the compartment expands, pressure increases. A secondary effect is the occlusion of veins and venules, which have thinner, less muscular walls than the arteries delivering blood to the compartment. This results in an increase in the pressure across the capillary bed of the compartment and the delivery of further edema fluid into the compartment. As further fluid accumulates, pressure in the affected compartment climbs even higher until even the arteries are occluded. Therefore, tissue pressures are helpful in monitoring or establishing the diagnosis. Recent studies have suggested that determination of the difference between mean arterial and compartment pressures is more useful than the absolute tissue-pressure measurement.[439]

Patients presenting with late manifestations of compartment syndrome have a high potential for secondary amputation. Shaw emphasized the importance of repeat examination under anesthetic of the affected limb following fasciotomy [Figure 11.118], even if apparently healthy granulation tissue is forming.[440]

---

[439] Mabee JR, Bostwick TL. Pathophysiology and Mechanisms of Compartment Syndrome. *Orthopaedic Review*, 22(2): 175-81, 1993.

[440] Shaw CJ, Spencer JD. Late Management of Compartment Syndromes. *Injury*, 26 (9):633-5, 1995.

TABLES

Table 1: Injury Severity Score

A previously healthy female is admitted to hospital with a cerebral contusion, ruptured spleen, closed femur fracture, and multiple arm lacerations following a motor vehicle accident.

Injury Severity Score	Severity Scale
Cerebral contusion	3
Ruptured spleen	2
Femur fracture	3
Forearm lacerations	2
Flail chest	4

Injury Severity Score (ISS) = $(3)^2 + (3)^2 + (4) = 22$ (The three most severely affected systems used)

LD_{50}* (ISS)

Age	ISS
15-44	40
45-65	29
>65	20

Source: Baker SP, O'Neill B, Haddon Jr, W, et al. The Injury Severity Score: A method for describing patients with multiple injuries and evaluating emergency care. *J. Trauma* 14:187, 1974.

---

* LD_{50}: The lethal dose for 50% of the population.

Table 2: Gustilo Classification

I	Wound less than 1 cm long, clean, little soft tissue damage and no crush injury
II	Laceration greater than 1 cm in length, no extensive soft tissue damage, no skin flaps or avulsions, moderate crush injury to skin, moderate fragmentation of fracture, moderate contamination.
III	Extensive damage to soft tissues, including muscle, skin and possibly nerve and/or vessels, high degree of contamination includes gunshot wounds, farm includes, segmental and comminuted fractures due to high velocity trauma.
	A: Large laceration or skin flaps but sufficient for soft-tissue coverage at the fracture site.
	B: Extensive soft tissue loss with exposed bone, periosteal stripping, massive contamination, severe comminution or bone loss.
	C: Any open fracture with arterial injury that *must be repaired* regardless of the degree of injury.

Data from: Gustilo RB, Anderson JT. Prevention of infection in the treatment of one thousand and twenty-five open fractures of long bones. *J Bone Joint Surg* 58A(4):453-8, 1976.

Table 3: Mangled Extremity Severity Score (MESS)

Skeletal/Soft Tissue Injury	Points
Low energy (stab, simple fracture, civilian gunshot wound	1
Medium energy (open or multiple fractures, dislocations)	2
High energy (close-range shotgun, military gunshot wound, crush injury	3
Very high energy (above with gross contamination, soft tissue avulsion	4
Limb Ischemia	
Pulse reduced or absent but perfusion normal	1*
Pulseless, diminished capillary refill, paresthesias	2*
Cool, paralyzed, insensate, numb	3*
*score doubled for ischemia time greater than 6 hours	
Shock	
Systolic blood pressure always above 90 mm Hg	0
Transient hypotension	1
Sustained hypotension	2
Age	
<30	0
30-50	1
>50	2

From: Johansen K, Daines M, Howey T et al. Objective criteria accurately predict amputation following lower extremity trauma. *Trauma* 30:569, 1990; with permission.

Table 4: Cierny Clinical Staging System for Osteomyelitis *

Anatomic Type	Physiologic Class	Clinical Stage
I Medullary	A Normal	
II Superficial +	B Compromised =	IIIB**
III Localized	C Treatment deferred	
IV Diffuse		

From: Bowen CVA, Botsford DJ, Hudak PL, Evans PJ. Microsurgical treatment of septic nonunion of the tibia. Quality of life results. *Clin Orthop* 332:52-61, 1996, with permission.

---

* The anatomic type of bone involvement is combined with physiologic class of patient to determine the clinical stage of the disease.

** Given as an example.

Table 5: Treatment of Chronic Osteomyelitis of the Lower Extremity by Debridement and Microvascular Transplantation

Author	No. Patients Reported	% Success	Follow-up Time (mean years)
Mathes (1982)	11	100	1.8
May (1982)	18	100	1.6
Weiland (1984)	33	80	3.5
Gordon (1988)	14	86	3.9
Anthony (1991)	27	96	7.4
Gayle (1992)	55	91	5.8

From: Gayle LB, Lineaweaver WC, Oliva A, Siko PP, et al. Treatment of chronic osteomyelitis of the lower extremities with debridement and microvascular muscle transfer. *Clin Plast Surg* 19(4):895-903, 1992, with permission.

GLOSSARY

Abduction: Movement away from the midline.
Abductor digiti minimi: Muscle that moves the small finger away from the hand.
Abductor pollicis longus: Muscle of the forearm that moves the thumb away from the hand.
Abscess: A cavity formed within a solid tissue. Often refers to pus containing cavity.
Acetabulum: Part of the pelvis that forms the hip socket.
Achilles tendon: Tendon, which joins the gastrocnemius and soleus, muscles to the calcaneus. Also called tendo-calcaneus. Strong plantar flexor of the ankle joint.
Acromioclavicular: Joint between the acromion part of the shoulder blade (scapula) and the clavicle (collar bone).
Adduction: Movement toward the midline.
Adductor pollicis: Muscle that moves the thumb towards the hand.
Afferent: Going towards a centre.
Alar: Winged.
Allogenic: Graft provided by a different donor of the same species.
Aneurysm: Dilatation of an artery.
Angiogram: Radiologic evaluation where radio-opaque contrast is injected in arteries to visualize them.
Angulation: Abnormal bend in a joint or bone.
Ankylosis: Stiffening of a joint.
Annulus fibrosus: Peripheral ring like structure of the intervertebral disc. Composed mostly of collagen (hence fibrous in nature).
Anterior drawer test: Clinical sign of an anterior cruciate ligament deficient knee.
Anterior superior iliac spine: Small bony prominence anterior to the pelvis which is easily palpable and used as a landmark.
Apical: Located at or near the apex of a structure.
Aponeurosis: A fibrous sheet acting as an origin or insertion of a flat muscle.
Arachnoid mater: Resembling a cobweb, denotes the thin covering of the brain and spinal cord.
Articulations: Place of union, usually moveable between two bones, also called a joint.
Arcuate artery: Terminal portion of the anterior humeral circumflex artery, supplying blood to the humeral head.
Arcuate ligament: Ligament stabilizing the posterolateral aspect of the knee joint.
ARDS: Adult respiratory distress syndrome.

Arteriographic embolisation: Insertion of arterial catheters guided radiologically into specific vessels.
Arthrogram: Radiographs of a joint after injection of radio-opaque fluid.
Arthroplasty: Reconstruction of a joint. Often refers to a joint replacement surgery.
Arthroscopy: Visual examination of the internal anatomy of a joint.
Arthrosis: Degeneration of a joint.
Articular cartilage: Hyaline, smooth cartilage, which covers the bones of a joint.
Atelectasis: Collapse or closure of small alveoli in the lung.
Atlas: In the Greek mythology was a titan who supported the earth. The atlas is the first cervical vertebra supporting the head.
Atrophy: Wasting of a tissue.
Autonomic Dysreflexia: Exaggerated response of the autonomic (involuntary) nervous system.
Autonomic: Related to the involuntary nervous system.
Avascular necrosis: Death of a section of bone (e.g., femoral head, talar body, humeral head, lunate) because of an interruption in blood supply.
Avulsion: Forcible tearing away.
Axial: Related to forces transmitted along the straight line around which a body revolves.
Axillary artery: Artery located in the shoulder and axilla, which supplies blood to the arm.
Axillary nerve: Nerve coursing around the proximal humerus and innervating the deltoid muscle and a patch of skin on the shoulder.
Axis: A straight line around which a body revolves. In the case of the second cervical vertebra the straight line is the odontoid around which the atlas rotates.
Axon: It is a process extending out of the neuron (cell of nervous system) which conducts nervous impulses from the body of the neuron to the synapse.
Biceps muscle: Muscle of the upper arm, which flexes the elbow.
Blade plate: Stainless steel plate used for fixation of some fractures of the femur.
Botulism toxin: toxin produced by the bacteria *Clostridium botulinum* found in spoiled food.
Bowstring: Physical sign associated with irritation of the nerve roots supplying the sciatic nerve. Palpated in the popliteal fossa of the knee with the hip flexed.
Brachial plexus: A network of nerve proximal to the shoulder innervating the arm.
Brachialis: Muscle of the upper arm and elbow, which flexes the elbow.
Brachioradialis muscle: Muscle of the forearm.

Bradykinin: One of the many polypeptides (protein) in the body which acts on the involuntary muscles and circulatory system.
Buddy taping: Joining an injured digit to an adjacent healthy one, which will serve as a splint.
Bursa: A sac containing fluid found in areas prone to friction.
Bursitis: Inflammation of a bursa.
Burst fracture: Fractured vertebra where an axial force is applied to the vertebra causing it to "explode".
Buttress plate: Plate that supports a fractured bone and prevents it from shortening or collapsing.
Calcification: Deposition of insoluble calcium salts in tissues.
Callus: Accumulation of bone at the ends of a fracture.
Cancellous: Spongy part of the bone also known as spongiosa.
Capillaries: Very fine blood vessels between the arteries and veins. Vessels where the red blood cells exchange oxygen and nutrients with the tissue cells.
Capitate: One of the bones of the wrist articulating with the lunate.
Capitellum: Distal end of the humerus at the elbow articulating with the radial head.
Capsule: Dense structure that envelops an organ or a body part. In the musculoskeletal system usually refers to the envelope of a joint.
Carotid: Major artery in the neck (from Karoo meaning to put to sleep, which occurs if the carotid artery is compressed).
Carpus: Bones of the wrist.
Cartilage: A connective tissue, which is nonvascular and firm. There are three kinds: hyaline, elastic and fibrocartilage.
Catheter: A hollow tube passed in a body's orifice, usually in the urethra to the bladder.
Cauda equina: Group of nerves in the vertebral canal of the spine, which have the appearance of a horse's tail.
Caudal: Toward the tail end of the organism.
Cephalic: Related to the head or towards the head.
Chance fracture: Flexion-distraction fracture of the vertebra usually at the thoracolumbar junction.
Chopart: Francois Chopart, a Paris surgeon who described the joints of the mid foot.
Clavicle: Collarbone, S shaped bone connecting the sternum to the shoulder girdle.
Coagulation: The process of clotting where the blood changes from liquid to solid.
Collateral ligaments: Ligaments on either side of many joints which limit varus-valgus (side to side) motion.

Colles fracture: A common pattern of distal radius fracture named after the Irish surgeon who described it.
Colostomy: Surgical formation of an artificial anus by opening the colon to the skin of the abdomen.
Comminution: Breaking into several small fragments.
Common peroneal nerve: One of two components of the sciatic nerve. Responsible for the innervation of muscles which dorsiflex the foot and provides sensation to the top of the foot.
Compartment syndrome: Increase in pressure within the fascial compartments of a muscle in response to swelling from an injury.
Condyles: A rounded articular surface at the end of a bone.
Contralateral: The opposite side.
Conus medullaris: Conical end of the spinal cord at L1–L2 in adults.
Coracobrachialis: Muscle of the upper arm originating from the coracoid process of the scapula.
Coracoclavicular ligaments: The conoid and trapezoid ligaments maintaining the relationship between the coracoid process and the clavicle.
Coracoid: Bony prominence projecting anteriorly from the scapula.
Coronal: Related to a frontal radiologic view.
Coronoid process: Bony prominence of the proximal ulna at the elbow where attaches the capsule of the elbow and the brachialis muscle.
Cortex: The outer portion of an organ. Here mostly referring to the outer portion of the bone which is very dense and strong.
Cortical: Relating to a cortex.
Corticospinal: Long tract of axons, which connect the cerebral cortex to the spine.
Coumadin: Or warfarin. Commonly used agent to prevent coagulation of blood.
Cruciate: Shaped like a cross.
CT scan: Or CAT scan, for computerized axial tomography. Imaging technique where a computer reconstructs an image from radiographs taken from 360 degrees around the body part.
Cuboid: Bone of the lateral midfoot.
Cuneiform: Bone of the medial midfoot.
Cyanosis: Dark blue coloration of the skin and mucous membrane generally caused by a deficiency of oxygen.
Debridement: Excision of devitalized tissues from a wound.
Decortication: Removal of the external layer of the bone.
Decubitus ulcer: Skin ulcer caused by pressure (pressure sore).
Deep peroneal nerve: A branch of the common peroneal nerve.
Deltoid ligament: Ligament on the medial side of the ankle joining the medial tibia to the talus and calcaneus.
Deltoid muscle: Muscle of the shoulder, which abducts the arm.

Dens: A toothlike process projecting upward from the body of the axis; also odontoid.
Dermatome: The area of the skin where sensory impulses go to a single spinal nerve root.
Diaphragm: Parachute shaped muscle separating the chest and abdominal cavity, whose function is to inflate and deflate the lungs.
Diaphysis: The shaft of a long bone formed mostly of cortical bone.
Diastasis: Separation of bones or muscles that are normally joined.
Differential diagnosis: A list of possible diagnoses, which will then be shortened to one single diagnosis.
Discogram: Invasive procedure, which involves injecting radio-opaque dye into the disc. The radiographic appearance of the disc and dye is apparent and the pain response of the patient to the injection may be an indication as to the source of the back pain.
Dislocation: (Dis = apart and locatio = location or placement) Usually refers to a joint where there is disruption of the normal arrangements of the bones. The dissociation is complete in a dislocation and partial in a subluxation.
Distal: Most distant to the referred location (e.g., fracture).
Distraction: To separate objects such as bone fragments or a joint.
Dorsalis pedis artery: Dorsal artery on the foot with a pulse easily palpable.
DRUJ: Distal Radio-Ulnar joint (at the wrist).
Duodenum: First portion of the small bowel where the stomach empties.
Dura mater: A tough outer membrane forming the outer envelope of the brain and spinal cord.
Dynamic: (dynamis = force) Involves motion and/or force. Opposite of static.
Dysesthesia: Impairment of sensation, often an unpleasant sensation produced by ordinary stimuli.
Dysphagia: Impaired swallowing.
Dyspnea: Shortness of breath.
Ecchymosis: Bruise or accumulation of blood under the skin.
Edema: Swelling, accumulation of fluid in tissues.
Efferent: Going away from the centre.
Embolism: Obstruction of a vessel usually by a blood clot, fat or air.
Embolization: To obstruct a blood vessel from within.
Endosteum: Membrane lining the inner surface of the bone.
Endplate: The ending of a motor nerve fiber onto a muscle or in the vertebra, a hyaline cartilage surface separating the bony cortex of the vertebra and the disc.
Epicondyle: Bony prominence adjacent to a condyle, *kondylos* = knuckle.
Epiphysis: Part of a long bone closest to a joint, or the end of a long bone.

Erector spinae: Group of muscles running the length of the spine, posterior, close to the midline.
Esophagus: The gullet, portion of the digestive tract between the mouth and the stomach.
Extensor digitorum brevis: Muscle, which straightens the fingers or toes.
Extensor digitorum communis: Group of muscles and tendons in the forearm, which extend the fingers.
Extensor pollicis brevis: Short muscle, which extends the thumb.
Extensor pollicis longus: Long muscle, which extends the thumb.
External fixator: Apparatus outside the body, which maintains the relationship of two bone fragments. Fixed to the bone by pins that protrude through the skin and soft tissues.
Facet: Small smooth area on a bone. When the superior and inferior articular facets join they for the zygoapophyseal joints or more commonly called the "facet joints".
Fascia: A sheet of fibrous tissues that envelops groups of muscles.
Fasciculation: Involuntary contraction of the muscle or twitching.
Fasciotomy: Incision in the fibrous tissue around muscle. Usually performed to allow the muscle to expand during a compartment syndrome.
Fat embolism: Phenomenon occurring mostly after long bone fracture where fat droplets are deposited in the lungs and cause an inflammatory reaction.
Fibrous: Connective tissue formed by fibroblasts.
Flaccid: Without tone.
Flaps: A tongue of soft tissue transferred on a pedicle to an adjacent skin and/or muscle defect.
Free flap: A flap that is completely detached and transferred to a distant defect in the body. A vascular pedicle is anastamosed to the recipient's limb's blood supply.
Flat foot phase: Middle part of the stance phase of the gait cycle where there is maximal surface contact of the foot to the floor.
Flexor carpi ulnaris: Muscle of the forearm, which assists the wrist in palmar flexion.
Flexor digitorum profundus: Deep tendon and muscle of the hand and forearm, which flex the fingers.
Flexor hallucis brevis: Short flexor of the big toe.
Flexor hallucis longus: Long flexor to the big toe
Flexus digitorum longus: long flexors of the toes or fingers.
Foot drop: Paralysis of the muscle, which controls the dorsiflexion of the foot.
Foramen magnum: The large opening at the base of the skull which permits the spinal cord to exit the skull.
Foramen: A perforation or opening in a bone.

Forefoot: Portion of the foot distal to the tarso-metatarsal joint.
Free tissue transfer: Grafting of tissue from one body part to the other, usually restoring the vascular supply.
Functionnal bracing: Bracing which allows motion of the joints.
Gait: Manner of walking.
Ganglion: (= knot in Greek) A group of nerve cell bodies in the peripheral nervous system. Also a cyst containing gelatinous tissues within fibrous tissue, tendons, muscles, cartilage or bone.
Ganglioside: Glycosphingolipid found in nerves.
Gastrocnemius: Muscle of the calf.
General anesthetic: Anesthesia involving deep sedation and ventilatory support.
Glenohumeral: The "ball and socket" part of the shoulder joint.
Glenoid: Socket of the shoulder, part of the scapula.
Gluteus maximus: Large muscle of the buttock responsible for hip extension.
Granulation tissue: Granular tissue formed of nodular inflammatory tissue. Normal stage of healing of soft tissues and skiing.
Gray matter: Nonmyelinized portion of the central nervous system.
Hamstring muscle: Three muscles at the back of the thigh, which extend the hip and flex the knee.
Hawkins sign: Radioluscent line of the talar body seen on radiographs after injury. It is a radiologic sign indicating preservation of the blood supply of the talus.
Heel pad: Skin of the heel with its underlying fat cells separated by fibrous septae.
Heel strike: First part of the stance phase of gait.
Hemarthrosis: Bleeding or accumulation of blood inside a joint.
Hematoma: An accumulation of blood outside of the vascular system, often coagulated or in various stages of organization and resorption.
Hemiarthroplasty: Joint replacement of one side of the joint only.
Hemoptysis: Spitting blood from the lungs or bronchial passages.
Hemorrhage: Profuse bleeding.
Heparin: Intravenous agent preventing coagulation of blood.
Herniation: Protrusion of an organ or part of an organ through the wall of the cavity usually containing it.
Heterotopic ossification: Formation of bone in soft tissues. Most common around the hip joint.
Heterotopic: Any material not in its normal location or misplaced.
Hill-Sachs lesion: Defect of the humeral head caused by an impaction fracture when the shoulder dislocates.
Hindfoot: Portion of the foot formed by the talus and calcaneus.

Horner's syndrome: Dilated pupil, dry eye, and droopy eyelid due to paralysis of the cervical sympathetic ganglion.
Humerus: Long bone of the upper arm.
Hyaline: A glassy, homogenous, translucent appearance. Refers to a type of cartilage found in moving joints.
Hypertension: High arterial blood pressure.
Hypertrophic: Overgrowth of bone.
Hyperbaric oxygen: Oxygen over one atmospheric pressure.
Hypotension: Low blood pressure.
Hypoxemia: Subnormal oxygenation of the blood.
Hypoxia: Decreased level of oxygen in tissues.
Iatrogenic: Resulting from the professional activities of the physician or surgeon.
Ileum: The third portion of the small intestine.
Ilium: The winged portion of the pelvic bone.
Iliopsoas: Muscle, which flexes the hip, originates on the lumbar spine and inserts on the lesser trochanter of the femur.
Ilizarov: A method of external fixation which allows for bone lengthening and deformity correction.
Image intensifier: Instrument providing fluoroscopic radiographic images on a TV type screen or monitor.
Impacted: Fractured bone fragments that are wedged together.
In utero: Within the womb, not yet born.
Infarction: An area of tissue necrosis from interruption of arterial blood supply.
Inlet: Superior passage or entry of the pelvis.
Innominate bone: Bone formed by the ilium, pubis and ischium, half of the pelvis.
Intercostal: Between the ribs.
Interossei muscles: Small intrinsic muscles of the hand and feet.
Interosseus: Said of a membrane or ligament joining two bones.
Interphalangeal joint: Small joints of the fingers and toes between phalanges. DIP=distal interphalangeal joint and PIP=proximal interphalangeal joint.
Intertrochanteric: Between the lesser and greater trochanters of the proximal femur.
Intramedullary: Within the bone marrow or the spinal cord.
Ipsilateral: Same side of the body.
Ischemia: Lack of blood supply to an area.
Ischeum: Portion of the innominate bone of the pelvis.
Isokinetic: Muscle contraction with the limb in motion at constant speed.
Isometric: Muscle contraction without motion of the joint or change in the length of the muscle.

Isotonic: Contraction of the muscle where the limb is allowed to move and the tone of the muscle is constant but the velocity of movement changes.
Judet views: Oblique views of the hemipelvis helpful in delineating fractures of the acetabulum.
K wires: Kirshner wires. Straight stainless steel wires used for bone fixation.
Kyphosis: Hump-back, an abnormal curvature of the spine with the convexity posterior.
Labrum: The lip of the acetabulum and glenoid.
Lachman test: Physical sign, which demonstrates laxity or deficiency of the anterior cruciate ligament.
Lamina: A flat layer on the posterior part of the vertebra, covers the neural elements.
Laparotomy: Opening of the abdomen for visual and tactile exploration of internal organs.
Lateral femoral cutaneous nerve: Sensory nerve of the anterior thigh.
Latissimus dorsi: Broad, flat muscle of the flank and back.
Levator scapulae: Muscle of the back, which elevates the scapula (shoulder blade).
Ligaments: A band of fibrous tissue connecting two or more bones.
Ligamentum flavum: The yellow ligament, elastic structure connecting the lamina of adjacent vertebrae.
Lisfranc: Jacques, French surgeon. Name given to the tarso-metatarsal joint.
Longitudinal: Running lengthwise along the axis of the body.
Lordosis: Hollow back or saddle back, curvature of the spine with the convexity anterior.
Lumbrical muscles: Small muscles of the fingers.
Lunate: Bone of the carpus articulating with the radius, scaphoid, and capitate.
Lushka: German anatomist, his name associated to many structures. In the cervical spine the joints of Lushka are adjacent to the disc and are also referred to as neurocentral joints.
Malleolus: Rounded bony prominence on either side of the ankle.
Malunion: Union of bone in a deformed, faulty position.
Mastoid: Breast shaped process.
Median nerve: One of the major nerves of the arm supplying sensation to the palmar aspect of the thumb, index and middle finger.
Meniscus: Crescent shaped cartilage within a joint.
MESS: Mangled extremity scoring system.
Metabolic: Related to the chemical activity of a tissue.

Metaphysis: Part of a long bone situated between the diaphysis and the epiphysis. It is mostly formed of cancellous bone.
Metatarsus: Bones of the forefoot articulating with the toes.
Methylprednisolone: Synthetic cortico-steroid with potent anti-inflammatory properties.
MRI: For magnetic resonance imaging; noninvasive, nonradiating imaging technique that provides excellent morphologic accuracy and also provides information on the biochemical and pathophysiologic changes within a structure.
Muscle free flap: Muscle transferred with its vascular pedicle to cover a soft tissue defect.
Musculo-cutaneous nerve: Nerve of the upper arm.
Myelogram: Radiographs of the spinal cord and nerves after injection of radio-opaque substance in the subarachnoid space where the cerebrospinal fluid flows.
Myelomalacia: Softening of the spinal cord.
Myelopathy: Disease or damage of the spinal cord.
Myositis ossificans: Inflammation of a muscle leading to intramuscular bone formation.
Nail: A device inserted into the intramedullous cavity of bone to stabilize it. Known also as I.M. rod.
Navicular: Small banana shaped bone of the medial side of the midfoot.
Necrosis: Irreversible damage or death of parts of an organ
Necrotizing fasciitis: Severe bacterial infection of the subcutaneous tissue causing tissue death.
Neurocentral joint: See joint of Lushka.
Neuroma: Tumor arising from cells of the nervous system although most traumatic neuromas are disorganized regeneration of a nerve arranged in a fibrous bundle.
Neuron: The nerve cell.
Neurapraxia: Paralysis from an injury to a nerve but that recovers quickly because of the lack of neuronal degeneration.
Nociception: Mechanism for the appreciation of painful stimuli.
Nonunion: Fracture that failed to heal, pseudarthrosis.
Nucleus pulposus: The central, gelatinous part of the intervertebral disc. It is this portion of the disc that generally herniates through the annulus fibrosus.
Obturator: Large opening of the pubic bone.
Odontoid: See dens.
Olecranon: Proximal end of the ulna where the triceps tendon inserts.
Oligotrophic: Deficient nutrition.
O.R.I.F.: Open reduction and internal fixation. It is applied to a fracture or

dislocation that is treated surgically and stabilized with internal implants.
Orthosis: In Greek means making straight. Commonly used term for a brace which can either be corrective or which stabilizes a body part.
Ossicles: Small bone.
Ossification: The formation of bone.
Osteochondral fracture: Fracture in a joint, which causes injury to the bone and cartilage.
Osteolysis: Absorption or destruction of bone.
Osteomalacia: A disease causing bones to soften and deform. In children called rickets.
Osteomyelitis: Infection of the bone.
Osteonecrosis: Bone death.
Osteophytes: A bony outgrowth.
Osteoporosis: Reduction in the quantity of bone.
Osteosynthesis: Bringing and maintaining fractured bones in close apposition.
Osteotome: Chisel.
Osteotomy: Cutting a bone usually to correct a deformity.
Outlet: Exit of the pelvis.
Palsy: Paralysis.
Paralysis: Loss of power or voluntary movement of a muscle through injury of its nerve supply.
Pars interarticularis: Area of the posterior elements of the vertebra that joins the superior and inferior articular process.
Patellar tendon: Ligament that attaches the patella to the tibia.
Patellofemoral joint: Articulation between the patella and femur.
Pathology: The structural and functional changes that result in an abnormal condition.
Pedicles: A bony tubed stalk extruding from the posterior aspect of the vertebral bodies and connecting them to the posterior neural arch.
Perfusion: Supply of nutrients or chemicals to the tissues.
Periosteal: Located just outside the bone. Periosteum is a fine layer of tissue covering all bones and which participates in the metabolism and production of bone.
Peroneal muscle: Muscle of the lateral aspect of the calf.
Petechia: Small hemorrhagic spots in the skin.
Phalanges: Small bones of the toes and fingers.
Physis: Growth plate of long bones.
Pia mater: Pius or tender, a thin envelope covering the brain and spinal cord.
Pisiform bone: Pea sized bone of the wrist.
Pivot shift test: Clinical sign of an anterior cruciate deficient knee.

Plantar keratosis: Callosities of the skin of the foot.
Plexus: Network of nerve or vessels.
Pneumonia: Infection of lung tissue.
Polytrauma: Accident victim with multiple injuries.
Popliteal: Back of the knee.
Posterior tibial artery: Main artery of the back of the leg, supplying the foot.
Posterior tibial nerve: One of two main branches of the sciatic nerve.
Premorbid: Preceding the onset of disease.
Processes: A projection or outgrowth.
Profunda brachii artery: Brachial artery of the shoulder and arm.
Pronation: Rotation of the forearm so that the palm of the hand faces down or backwards.
Prone: Position of the body when lying face down.
Proprioception: The capacity to feel the position of joints in space.
Prospective: Refers to a study or research, which is established before the patients are treated.
Proximal: Before the referenced area (e.g., fracture, joint).
Pseudoarthrosis: A false joint following a failure of the bone to unite.
Pseudolaxity: Laxity of a ligament caused by pathology of the joint rather than the ligament itself.
Pubic rami: Upper and lower cylindrical portion of the pubis.
Pubis: Anterior portion of the pelvis.
Pulmonary artery: Artery bringing blood from the heart to the lungs.
Pulmonary embolism: Blood clot that travels from the legs to the lungs and obstructs the pulmonary valculature.
Pyriformis: Small muscle posterior to the hip. Anatomically crosses over the sciatic nerve.
Quadratus lumborum: Muscle of the back joining the ribs, lumbar spine and iliac crest.
Quadriceps: Group of four muscles inserting into the patella and functions to extend the knee.
Quadriplegia: Or tetraplegia. Paralysis of all four limbs.
Radial head: Proximal end of the radius.
Radial nerve: Nerve of the arm supplying muscles that extend the wrist, fingers and thumbs.
Radicular: Related to the nerve root.
Radiculopathy: Disease of the spinal nerve roots.
Radius: Bone of the forearm.
Ramus: One of the primary divisions of a nerve or artery.
Randomized controlled trial: Study where the patients are randomly allocated to different treatments. The control group is a group of patients

undergoing no treatment or standard treatment and is used to compare to the experimental group.
Rectum: Terminal portion of the digestive tract.
Rectus abdominis: Muscle of the outer wall of the abdomen.
Recurvatum: Bending backward of a joint, hyperextension.
Reduction: Manoeuvre to restore the alignment of a bone or joint. "Closed" if done by external manipulation of the limb. "Open" if the bone or joint is exposed surgically.
Retinaculum: A retaining ligament.
Retroperitoneum: Space behind the peritoneum of the abdomen.
Retrospective: Refers to a study or research that is performed after treatment of the patient.
Rhomboid: Muscle of the back attaching the spine to the scapula.
Root: The foundation or the beginning of a part.
Rotator cuff: Four tendons joining together and forming a cuff around the humeral head.
Saddle embolus: Large clot caught at the intersection of the pulmonary arteries.
Saphenous nerve: Sensory nerve of the lower leg.
Saphenous vein: Long vein of the medial leg often used for graft.
Scaphoid: Bone of the wrist.
Scapula: Shoulder blade.
Scapulothoracic: Movement of the scapula relative to the thoracic cage.
Sciatica: Neuralgia of the sciatic nerve.
Sclerotic: Induration, hardening of the bone.
Sepsis: Presence of bacteria and their toxins in the blood.
Septicemia: Systemic disease caused by the multiplication of microorganisms in the blood.
Serotonin: A vasoconstricting substance found in high concentration in platelets and in parts of the central nervous system.
Serratus: Muscle joining the scapula to the rib cage.
Sesamoid: A bone entirely contained within a tendon.
Sinus tarsi: Tunnel-like space on the lateral aspect of the subtalar joint where several small arterial branches enter the talar neck through foramina.
Soleus: Muscle of the calf, where the gastrocnemius plantar flexes the ankle.
Spasms: An involuntary, painful muscle contraction, a cramp.
Spastic: Increase in muscle tone.
Spermatocele: A cyst of the epidydimis.
Spica cast: Spica=ear of wheat. Bandage or cast that is wrapped to look like an ear of wheat. Most commonly a cast immobilizing the thumb, shoulder or hip.

Spinal anesthetic: Injection of a local anesthetic in the spine causing transient complete motor and sensory paralysis of the legs.
Split thickness skin graft: Superficial layers of the skin are harvested and grafted elsewhere.
Spondylolisthesis: (Greek spondylos = vertebra and olisthesis = slipping and falling) Forward movement of one vertebral body over the other.
Spondylolysis: (Greek spondylos = vertebra and lysis = loosening) The breakage of part of the vertebra, usually the pars interarticularis.
Spondylosis: General term applied to lesions of the spine that are degenerative in nature.
Spring ligament: Ligament joining the calcaneus and the navicular bone of the foot.
Stance phase: Part of the gait cycle where the foot is in contact with the floor.
Stasis: Sluggish flow.
Static: Without movement or force, opposite to dynamic.
Steinman pins: Large straight metallic bars inserted into a bone for stabilization or skeletal traction.
Stenosis: A narrowing or stricture of any canal.
Sternoclavicular: Articulation between the sternum and the collarbone.
Steroids (corticosteroids): Large family of chemicals which may be natural, for example glucocorticoid produced by the adrenal glands, or synthetic such as prednisone or methylprednisolone.
Stress radiographs: Radiograhs taken while the joint is being pushed on to open the ligaments.
Subcapital: Distal to the femoral head.
Subchondral: Bone under articular cartilage.
Subclavian vessels: Blood vessels of the shoulder located underneath the collarbone.
Subluxation: Partial disruption of the normal relationship between two bones. See also dislocation.
Subscapularis: Muscle of the shoulder joining the scapula to the humerus. A component of the rotator cuff.
Subtalar: Articulation between the talus and the calcaneus.
Superficial peroneal nerve: One of two branches of the peroneal nerve in the anterior aspect of the lower leg and ankle.
Superior cluneal nerve: Small sensory nerve of the buttock lying over the iliac crest and susceptible to injury when harvesting bone graft.
Superior gluteal artery: Artery of the buttock exiting the pelvis through the sciatic notch.
Supination: Rotation of the forearm so that the palm of the hand faces upwards or anterior.
Supine: Is said of the body when lying face up.

Supraspinatus: Muscle of the rotator cuff of the shoulder.
Sural nerve: Sensory nerve of the posterolateral side of the lower leg.
Sustentaculum tali: Lateral projection of the calcaneus, which supports the talus.
Swing phase: Part of the gait cycle where the foot is off the ground and swinging forward towards heel strike.
Sympathetic chain: Nerves of the sympathetic part of the autonomic (involuntary) nervous system.
Symphysis pubis: Joint that links the two halves of the pelvis through the pubic bone.
Synapse: Membrane-to-membrane contact of a nerve cell with another. Location for transmission of the nerve impulses.
Syndesmosis: Fibrous joint held by strong ligaments.
Synovial fluid: Lubricating fluid of the joint formed by the synovial cells lining the joint cavity.
Synovium: Membrane lining the inside of a joint.
Systemic: Related to the entire organism.
Talus: Bone of the foot articulating with the tibia to form the ankle joint.
Tarsus: Collective names for the bones of the hind and midfoot.
Tear drop fracture: Fracture of the vertebral column, usually the cervical spine where a small corner of the vertebral body is avulsed and shaped like a tear drop.
Tenosynomium: Membrane forming a sleeve around the tendons to protect them from friction.
Tetanus: A disease caused by the toxin of *Clostridia tetani* and marked by sustained muscular contractions.
TFCC: Triangular Fibrocartilage Complex. Meniscus of the wrist.
Thenar eminence: Small muscles of the palm of the hand.
Thromboembolism: A blood clot that migrates and obstructs arteries usually in the lungs or the brain.
Thrombosis: The formation of a thrombus.
Thrombus: A clot within a blood vessel or the chambers of the heart.
Tibia plafond: Distal end of the tibia that forms the ceiling of the ankle joint.
Tibia plateau: Proximal end of the tibia supporting the femoral condyles.
Tibialis anterior: Muscle and tendon anterior to the lower leg and ankle which dorsiflexes the ankle.
Tibialis posterior: Muscle and tendon posterior to the ankle which supports the arch of the foot and plantar flexes the ankle.
Tinnitus: Ringing or noises in the ear.
Toe-off: Final portion of the stance phase of gait where the foot leaves the ground.

Trabeculae: Supporting beams or fibers within an organ. Forms the spongy or cancellous portion of the bone.
Trachea: Windpipe.
Translation: To move across.
Trapezium: Small bone of the wrist articulating with the thumb.
Trapezius: Large muscle of the neck and shoulder.
Triceps muscle: Muscle of the back of the upper arm. Extends the elbow.
Triquetrum: Small bone of the wrist.
Trochanter: Bony prominence of the proximal femur.
Tuberosity: Bony prominence of the proximal humerus.
Ulcers: Superficial loss of tissue at the surface of an organ, generally the skin or a mucous membrane.
Ulna: Long bone of the forearm.
Ulnar nerve: Large nerve of the arm better known for its subcutaneous course on the medial side of the elbow.
Unreamed: Said of intramedullary nails that are inserted without reaming or shaping the medullary canal.
Urethra: Canal from the bladder to the perineum.
Valgus: Bent or tilted away from the body.
Varus: Bent or tilted towards the body.
Vas deferans: Canal conveying semen.
Vena cava: Large vein of the abdomen and thorax returning blood from the lower extremities and trunk to the heart.
Venography: Radiologic study of veins.
Viscera: Internal organs.
Vital signs: Refers usually to the pulse, blood pressure, respiratory rate, and temperature.
Volar: On the palm side of the hand and the plantar side of the foot.
Warfarin: Coumadin, strong oral anticoagulant.
White matter: Myelinated portion of the central nervous system.
Wrist drop: Inability to actively extend the wrist because of a radial nerve palsy.
Zygapophyseal: Facet joints.

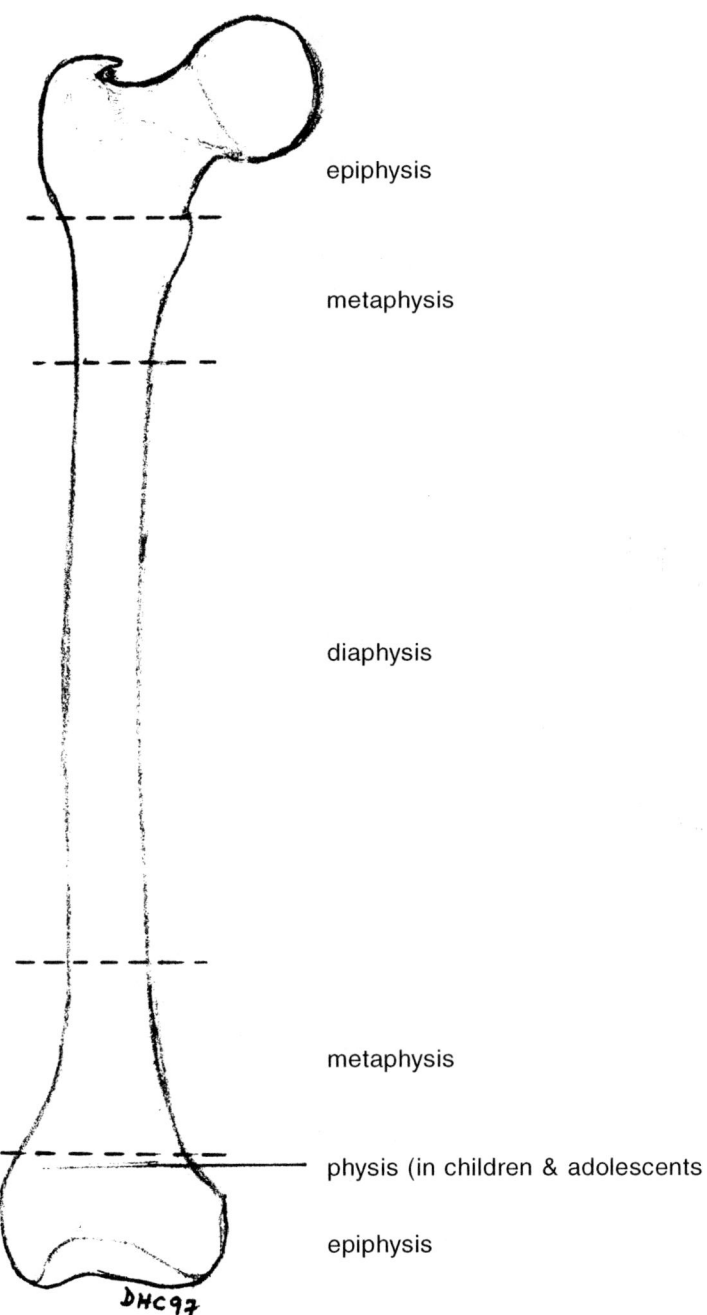

Figure 11.1
The femur and the anatomic divisions of a long bone.

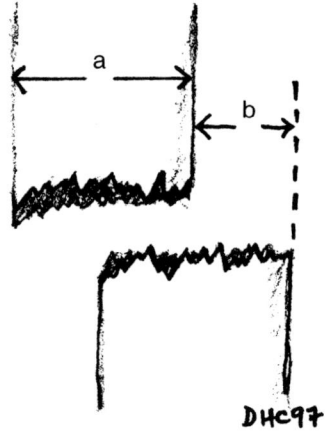

Figure 11.2
Displacement of a fracture.

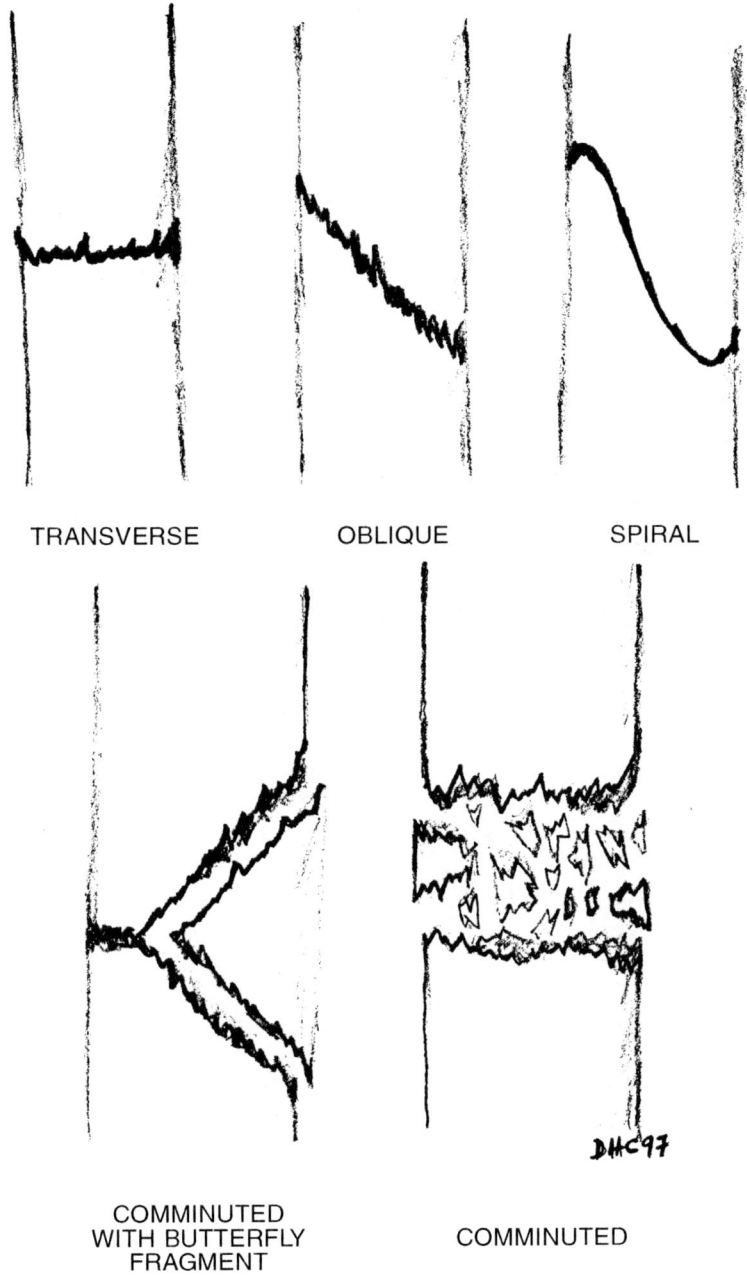

Figure 11.3
Fracture patterns.

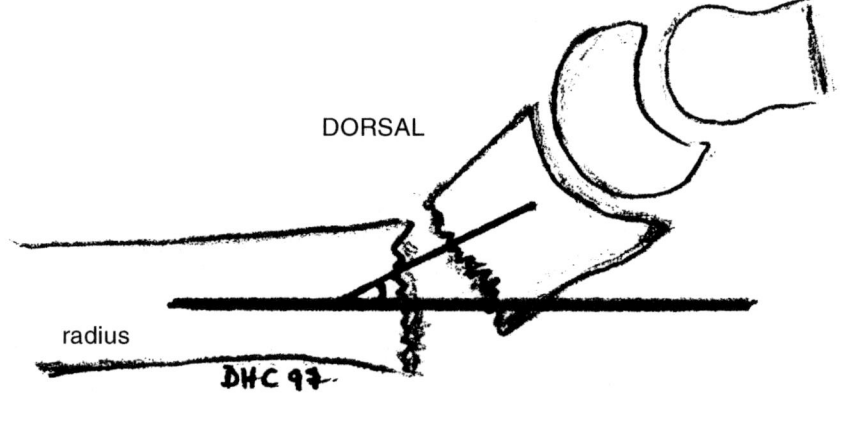

Figure 11.4
Angulation of a fracture.

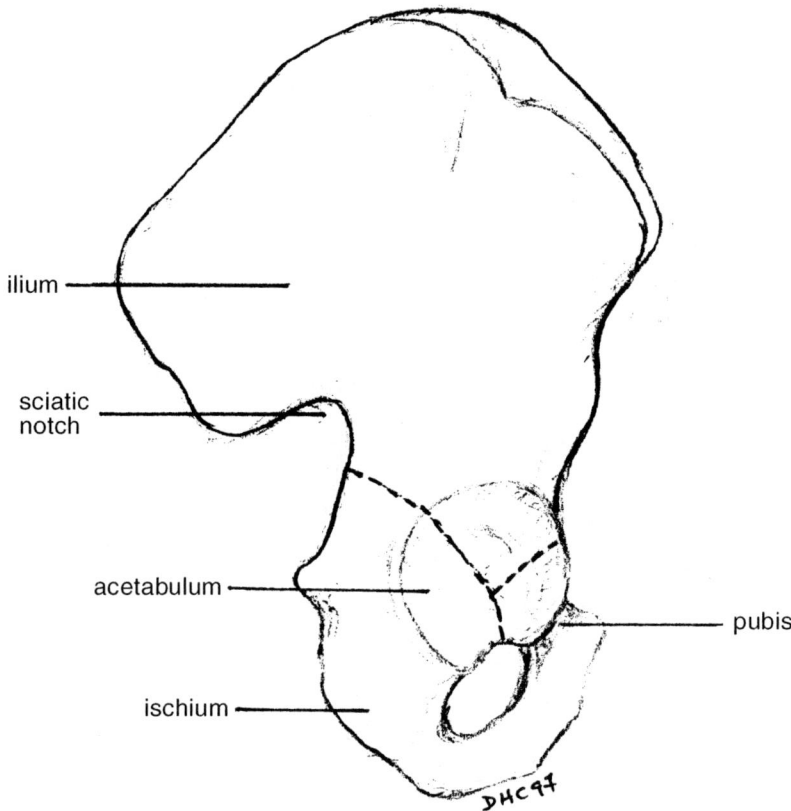

Figure 11.5
The innominate bone or half of the pelvis. It is formed by the ilium, pubis, and ischium. The confluence of these three portions forms the acetabulum.

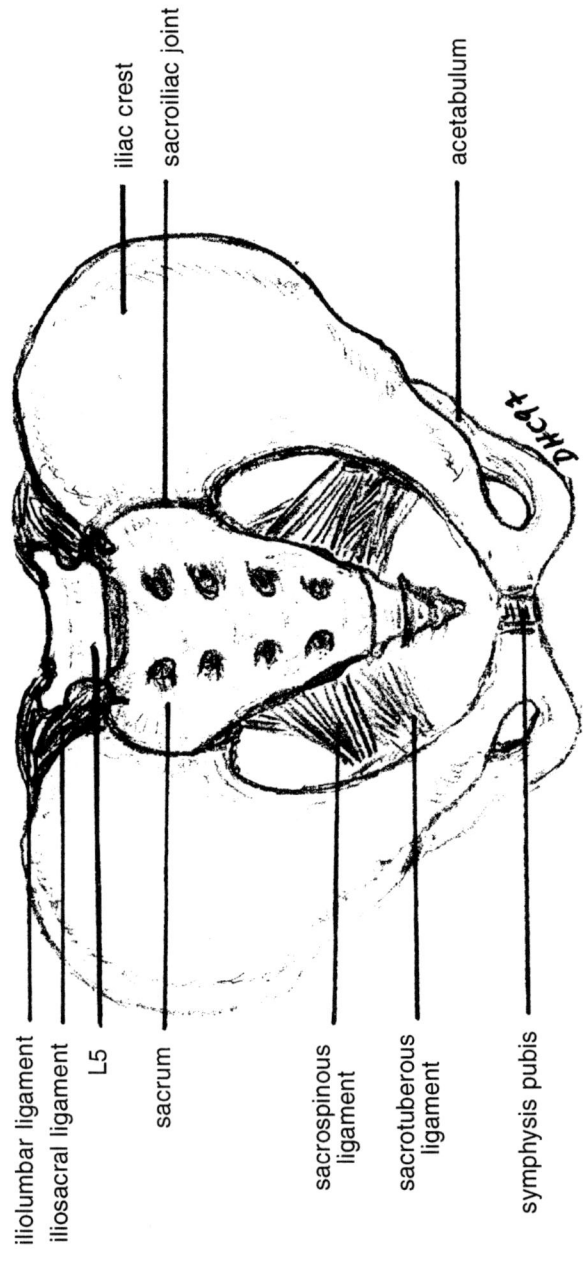

Figure 11.6
Anatomy of the pelvis.

INJURIES TO THE EXTREMITIES AND PELVIS 651

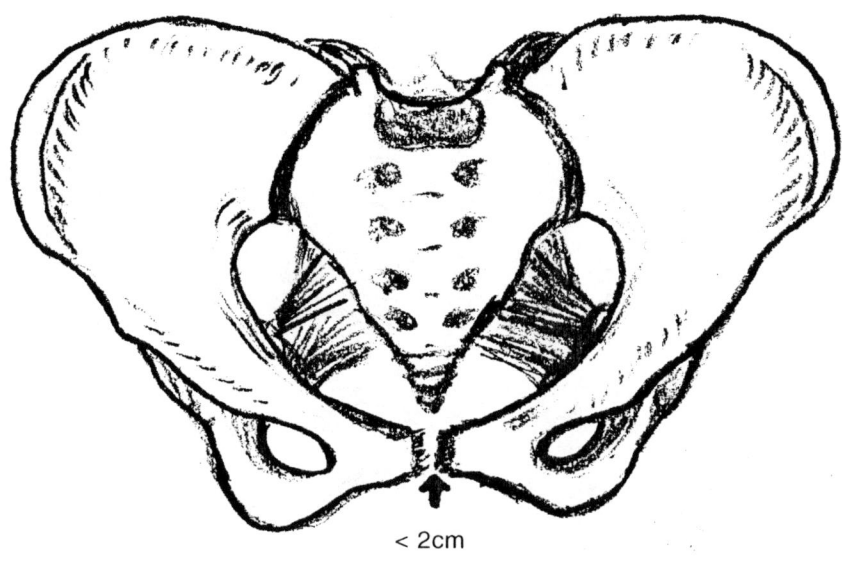

Figure 11.7A
Pelvic injuries — Stable pelvic injury. Disruption of the symphysis pubis with minimal displacement.

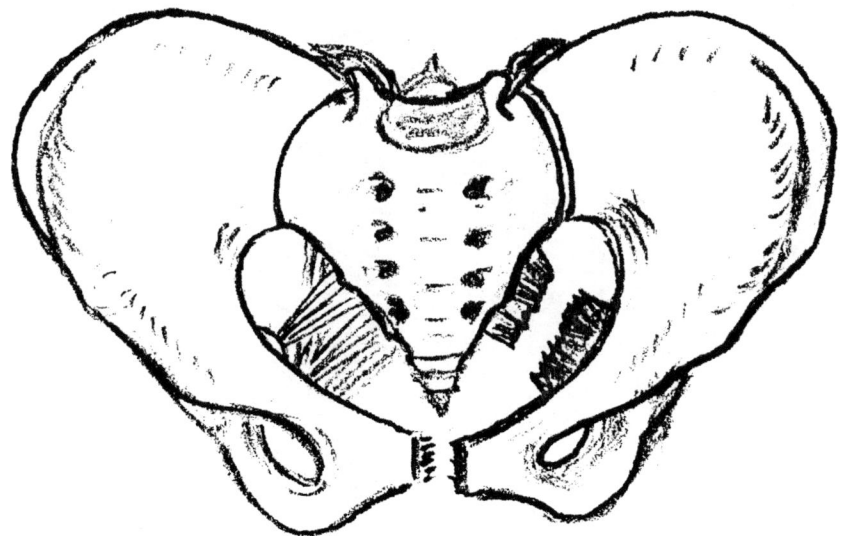

Figure 11.7B
Pelvic injuries — Disruption of the symphysis pubis in addition to the sacrospinous and sacrotuberous ligaments and widening of the left sacroiliac joint.

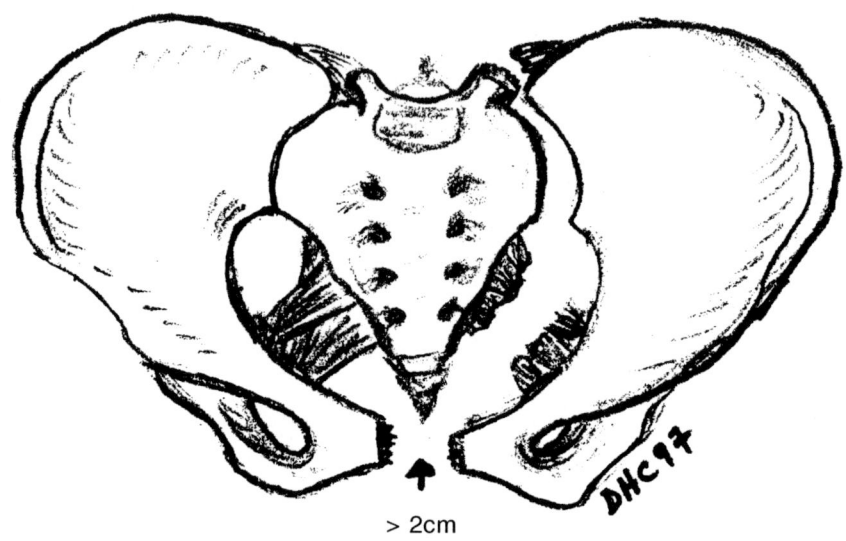

Figure 11.7C
Pelvic injuries — Complete disruption of all the ligaments holding the left innominate bone.

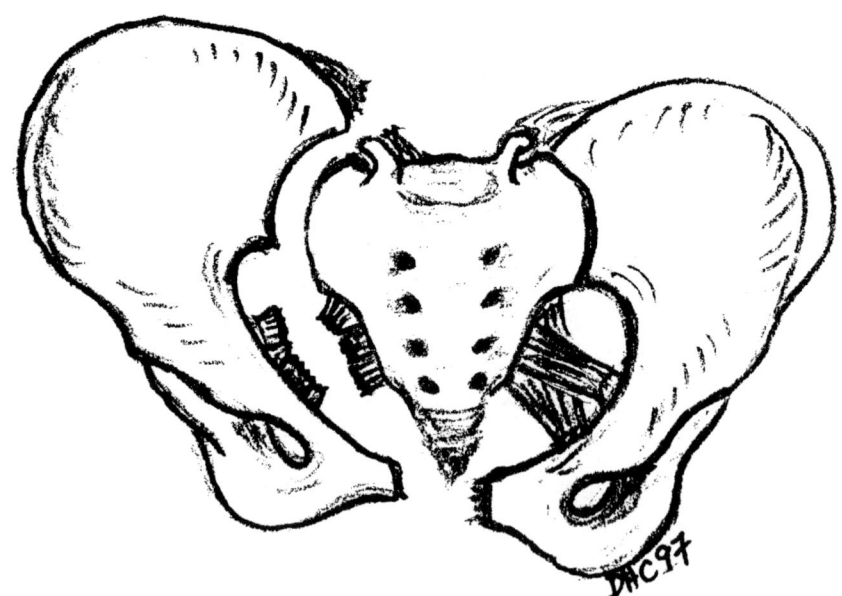

Figure 11.7D
Pelvic injuries — Malgaigne fracture: vertical shear injury.

INJURIES TO THE EXTREMITIES AND PELVIS 653

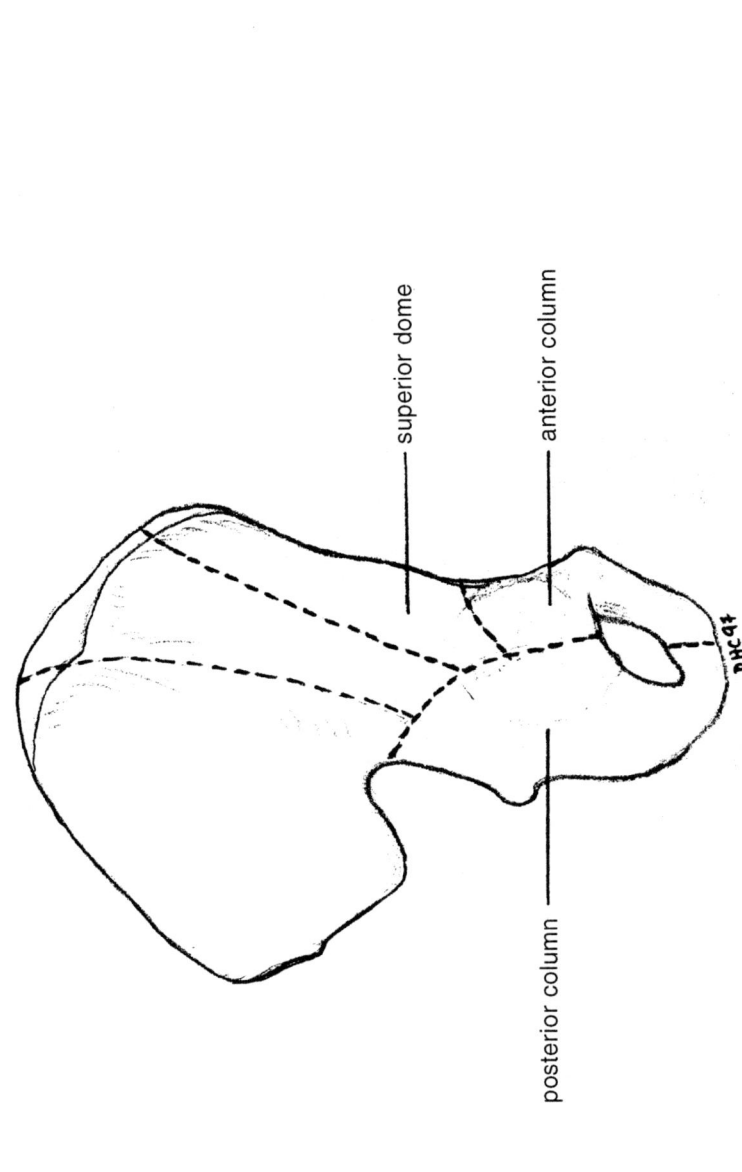

Figure 11.8
The acetabulum is part of the ilium, pubis, and ischium. The fracture type and mechanism is determined by the injuries to the superior dome, anterior or posterior column.

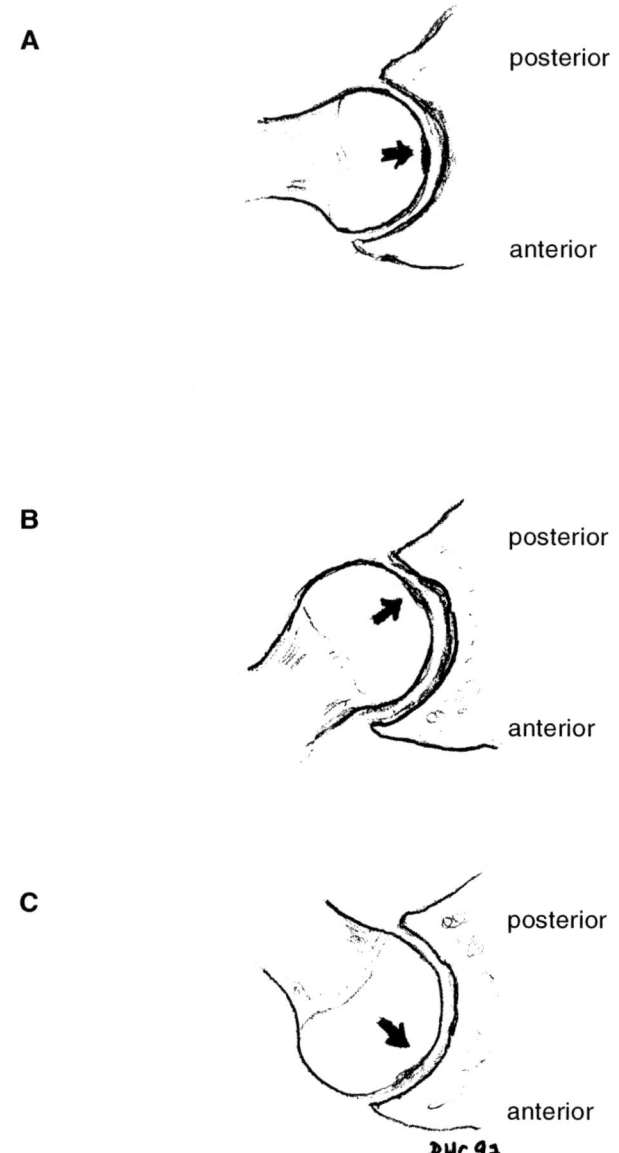

Figure 11.9
Fractures of the acetabulum: mechanism — **A:** *The hip in neutral position is driven into the acetabulum causing a central fracture of the medial wall and/or superior dome.* **B:** *The hip is rotated internally, causing a fracture of the posterior column.* **C:** *The hip is rotated externally, causing a fracture of the anterior column.*

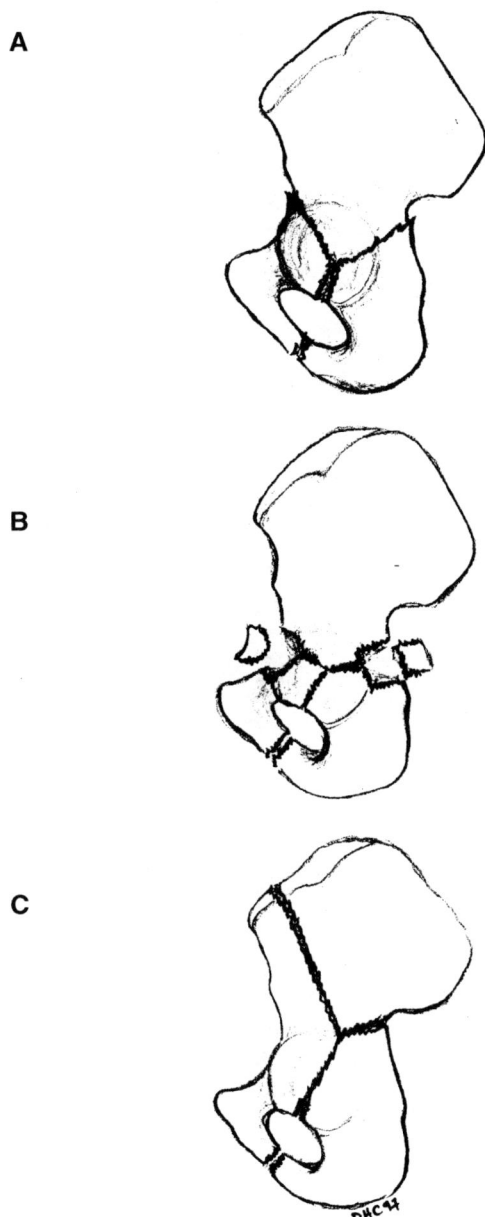

Figure 11.10
Fractures of the acetabulum — **A:** *Type A: fractures involving either the anterior or the posterior column.* **B:** *Type B: fractures involving both the anterior and posterior column.* **C:** *Type C: fractures involving the superior dome of the acetabulum.*

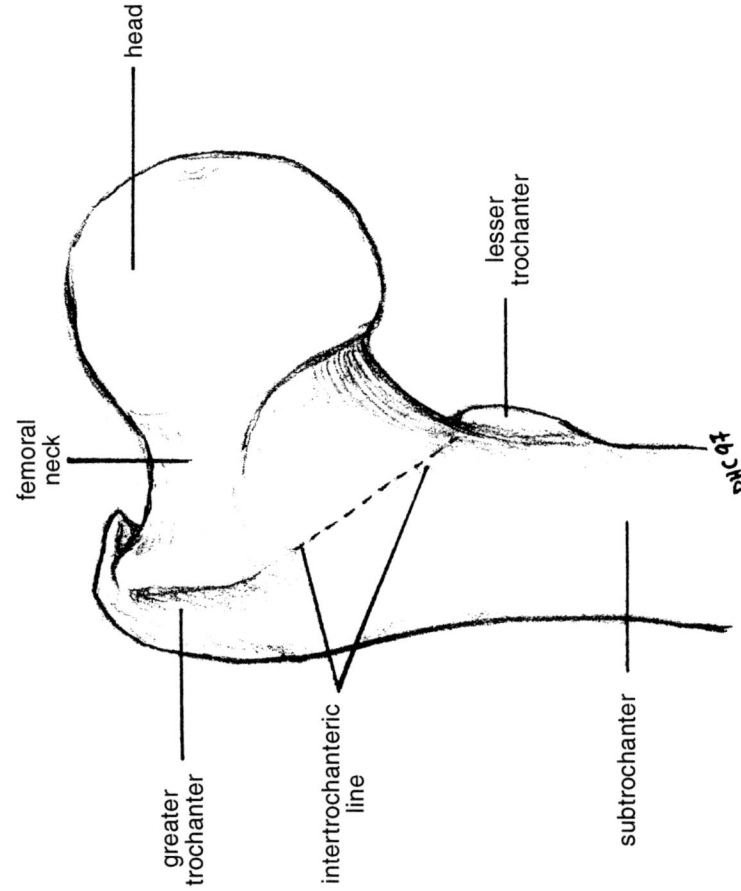

Figure 11.11
Anatomy of the proximal femur.

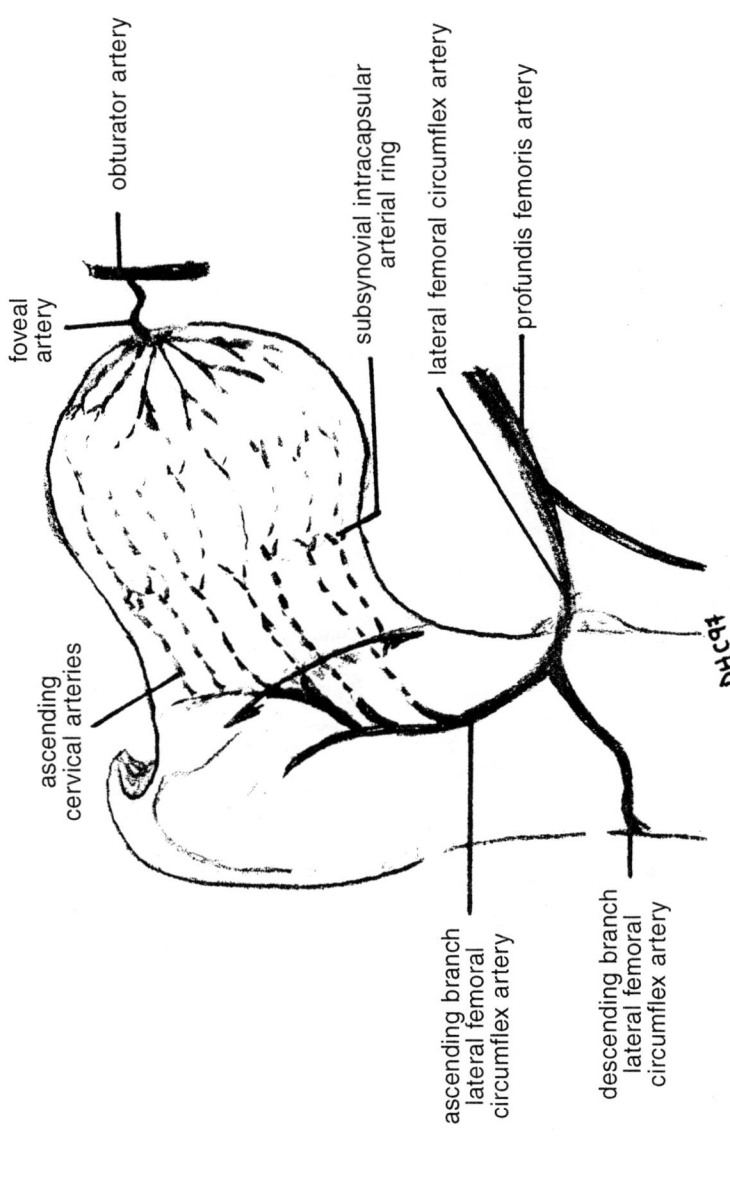

Figure 11.12
Blood supply to the femoral head.

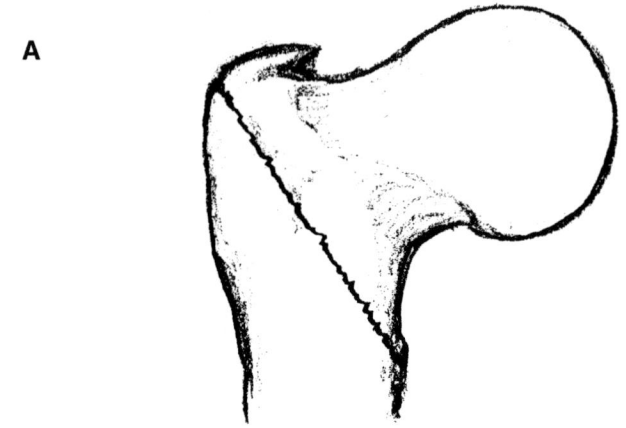

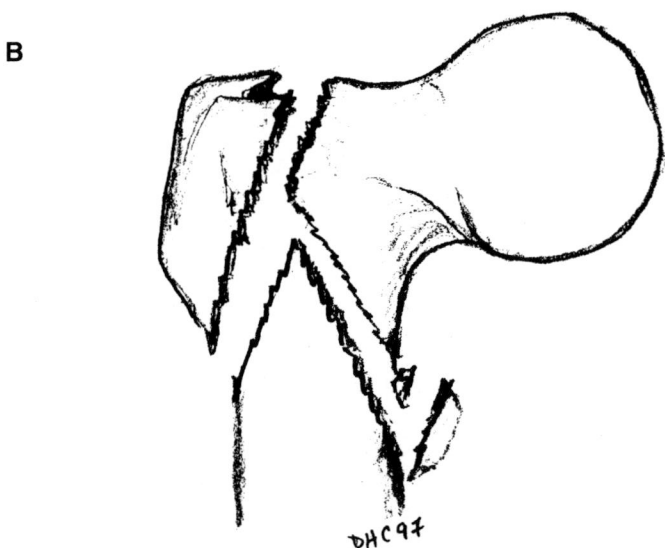

Figure 11.13
*Intertrochanteric fractures of the femur — **A:** Undisplaced. **B:** Comminuted.*

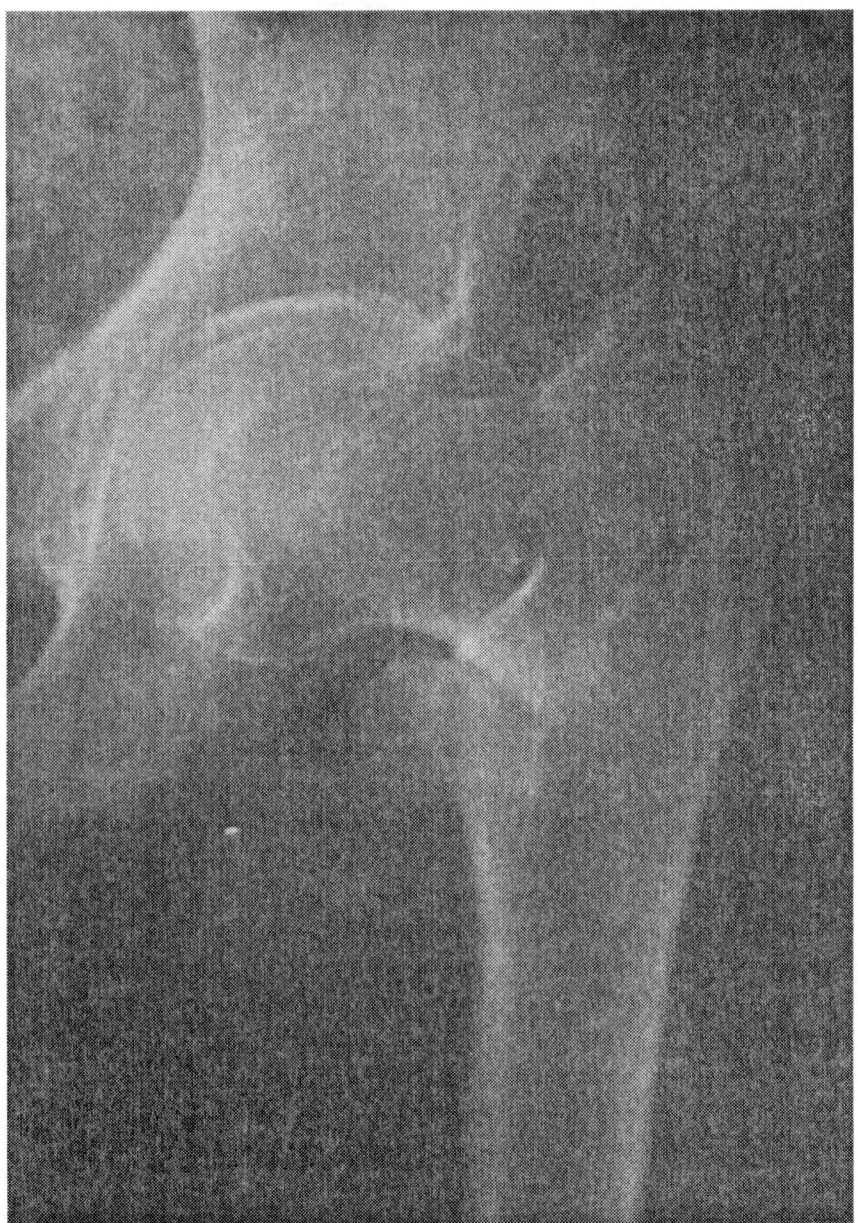

Figure 11.14
Radiograph of a comminuted intertrochanteric fracture of the proximal femur.

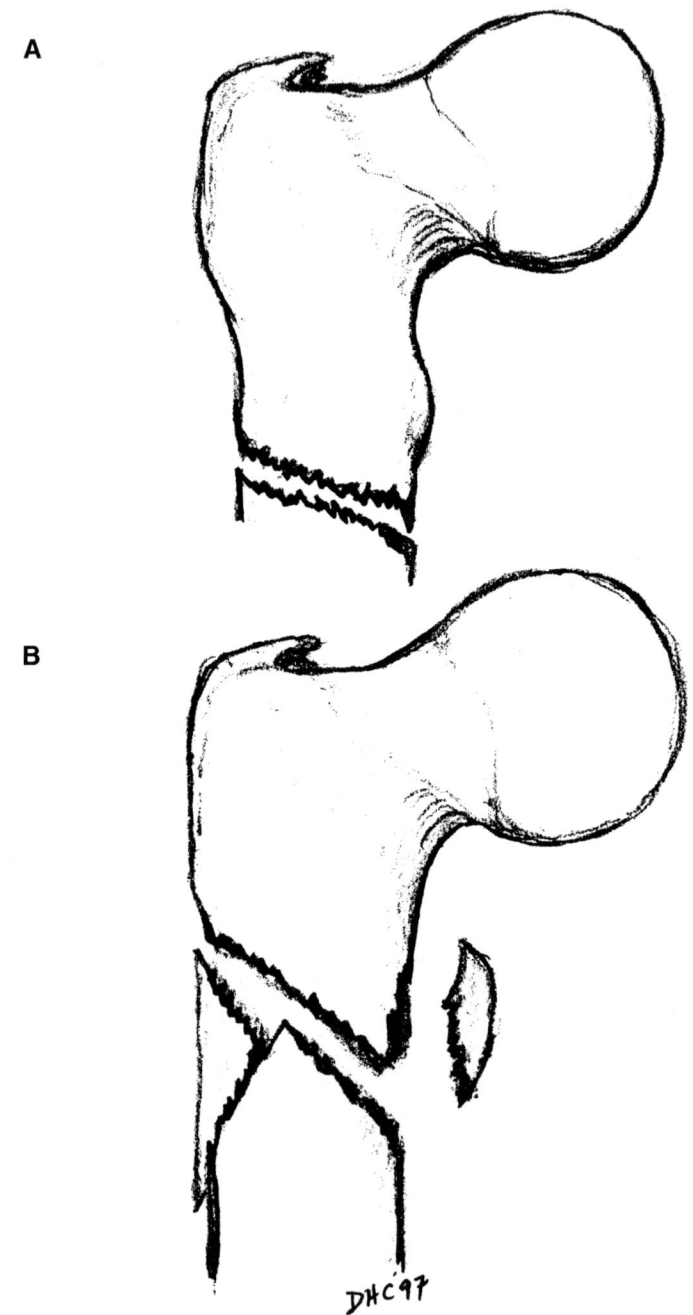

Figure 11.15
A: *Simple oblique.* **B:** *Comminuted.*

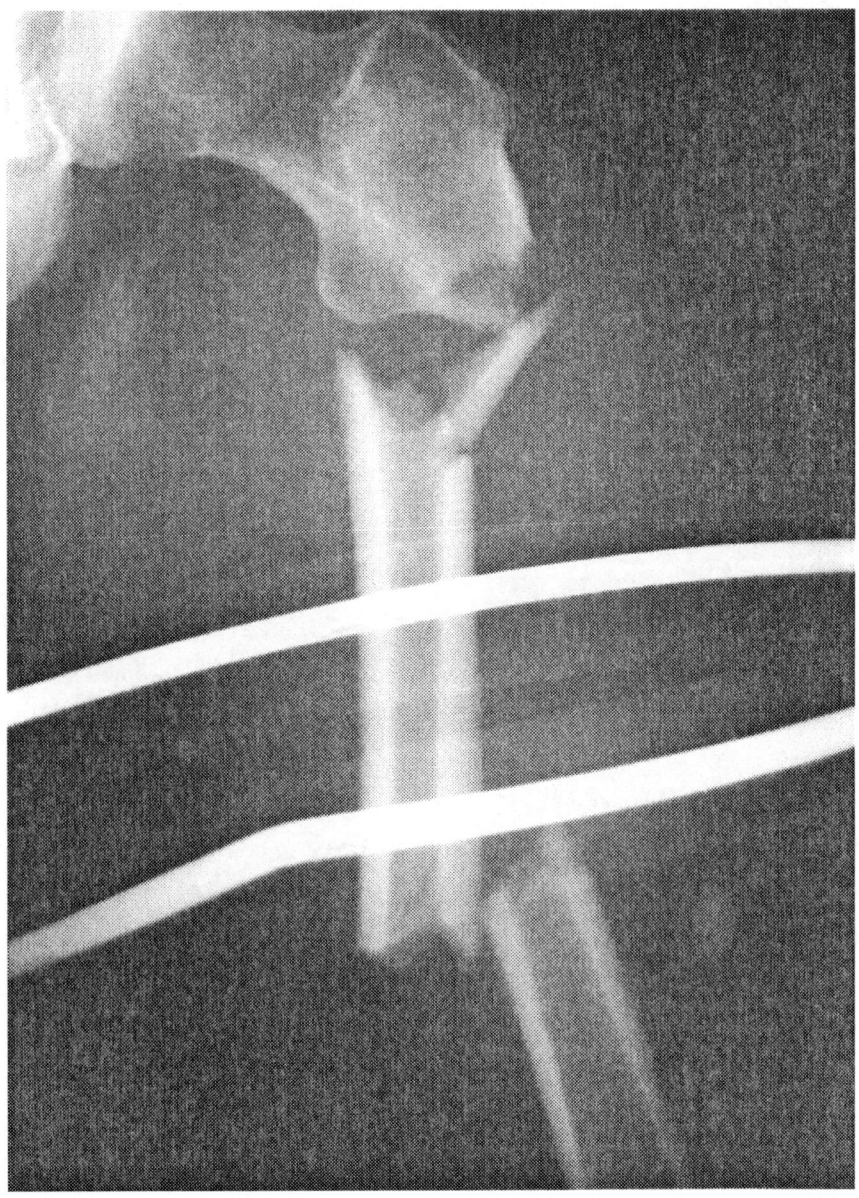

Figure 11.16
Radiograph of a femoral shaft fracture.

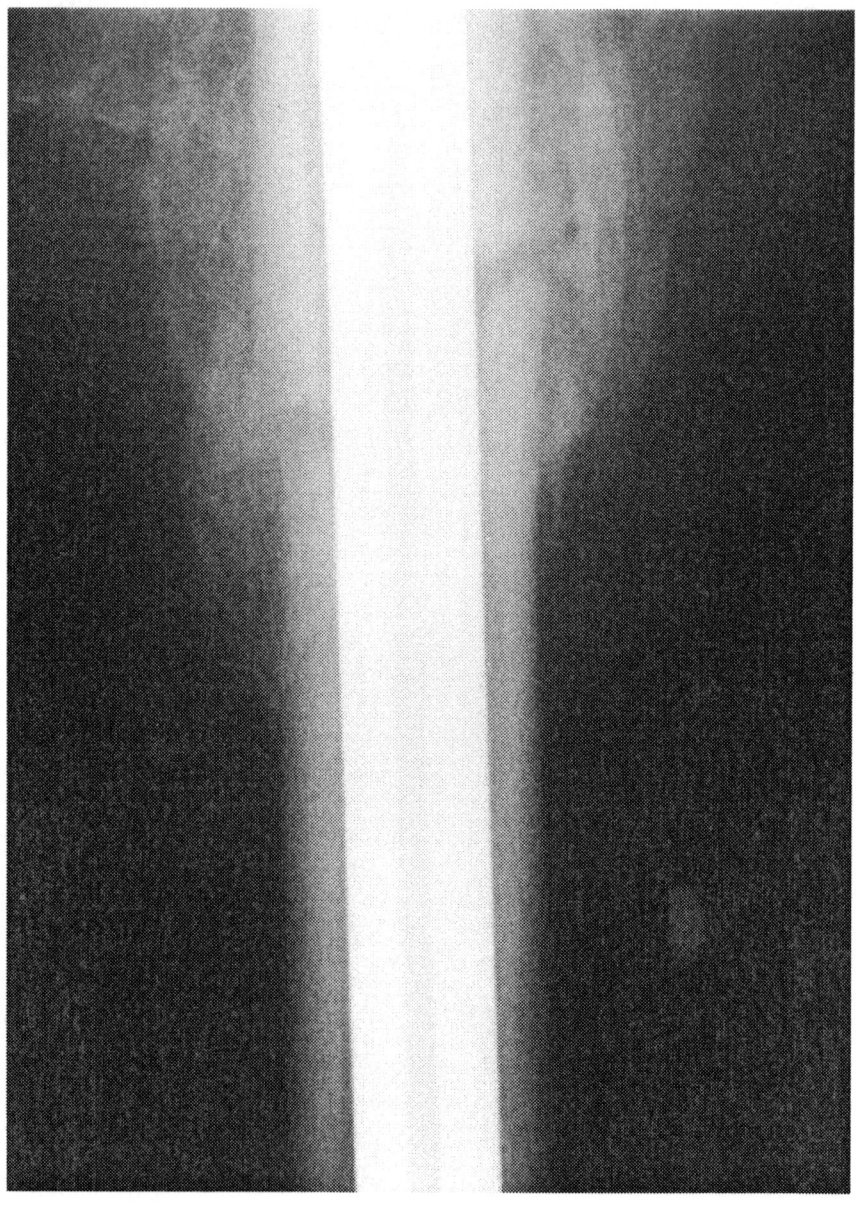

Figure 11.17
Femoral shaft fracture treated with an intramedullary nail.

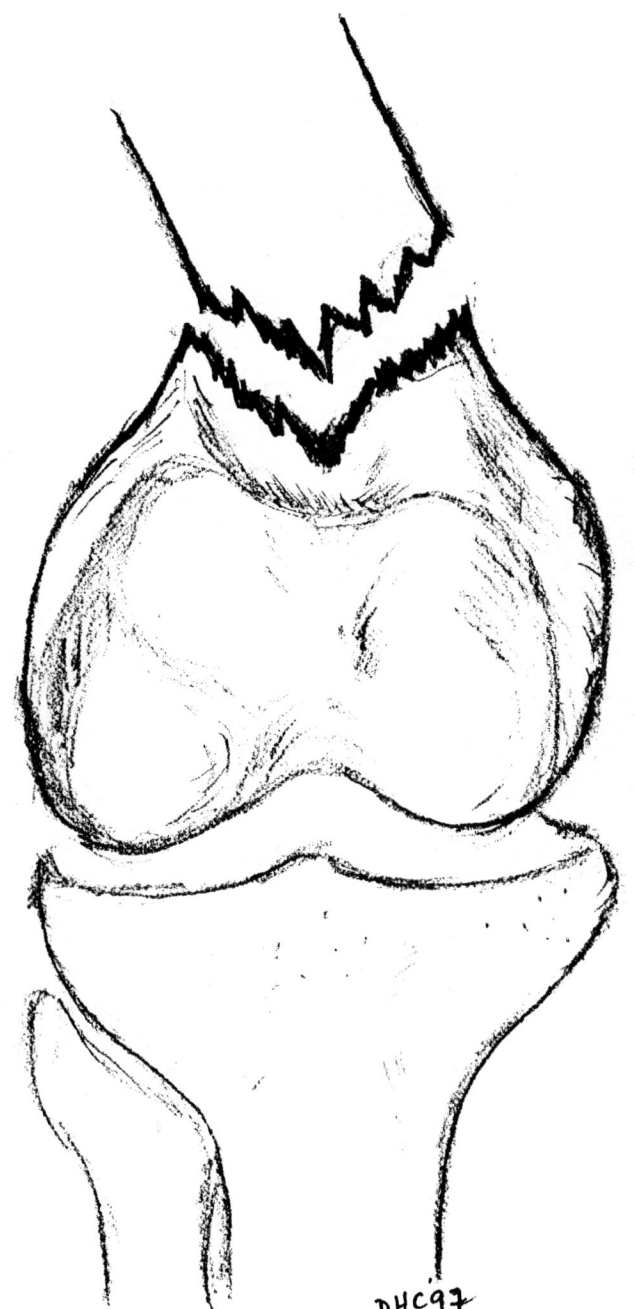

Figure 11.18
Supracondylar fracture of the distal femur (anteroposterior view).

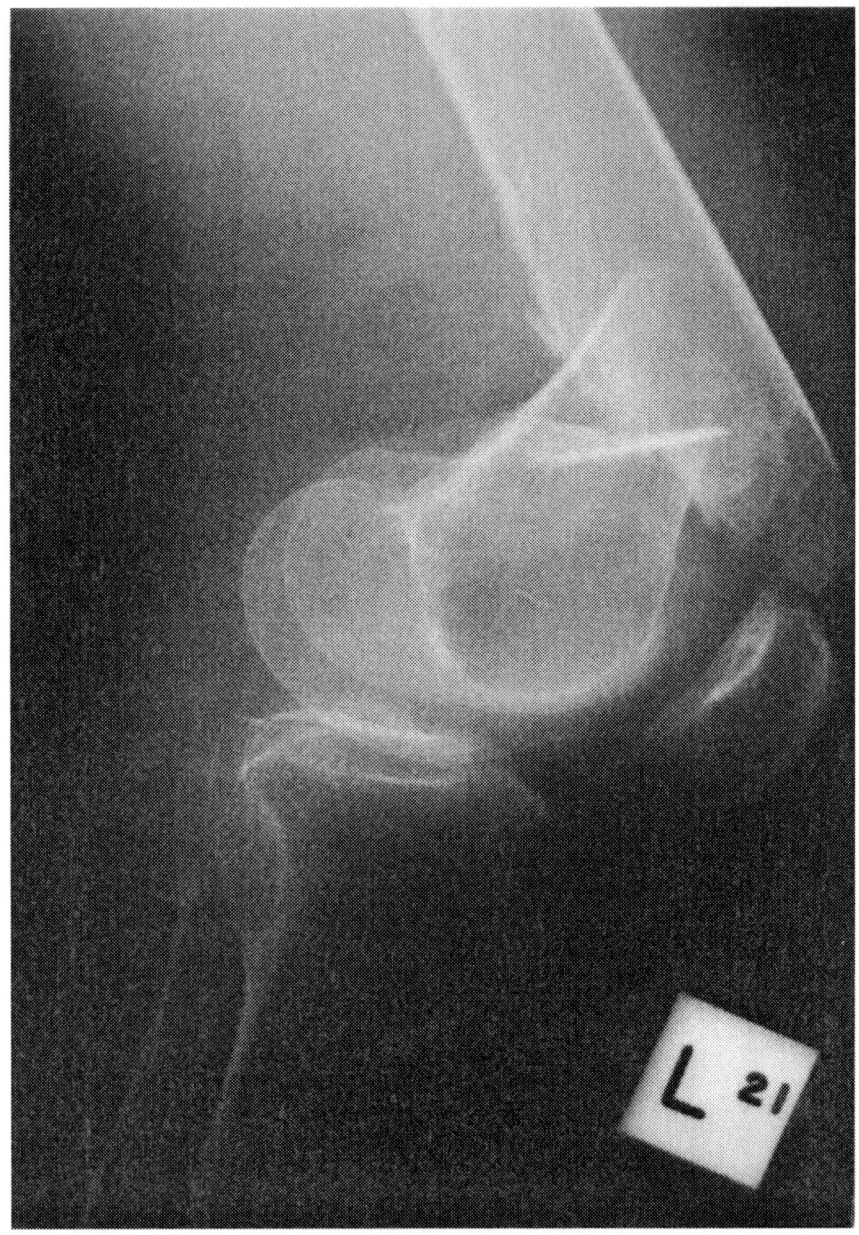

Figure 11.19
Lateral radiograph of a distal femoral fracture.

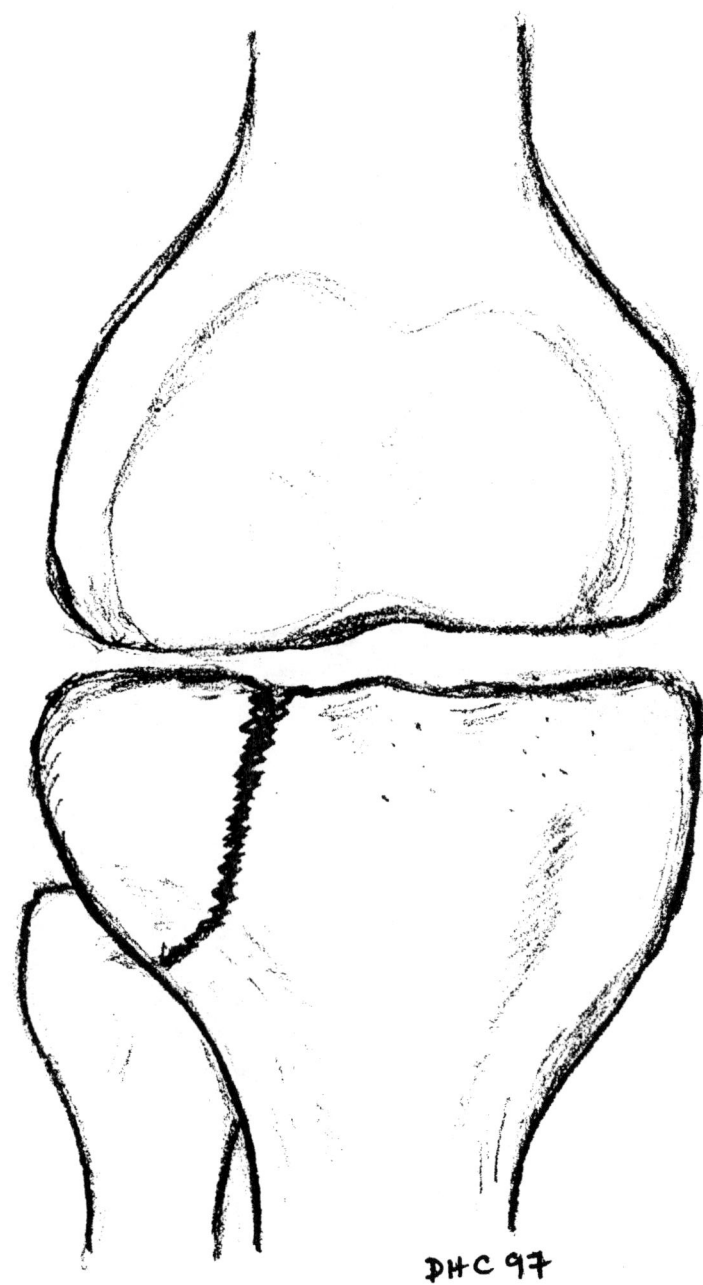

Figure 11.20
Fracture of the lateral tibia plateau. Note the intra-articular component of the fracture in the weight-bearing surface of the tibia.

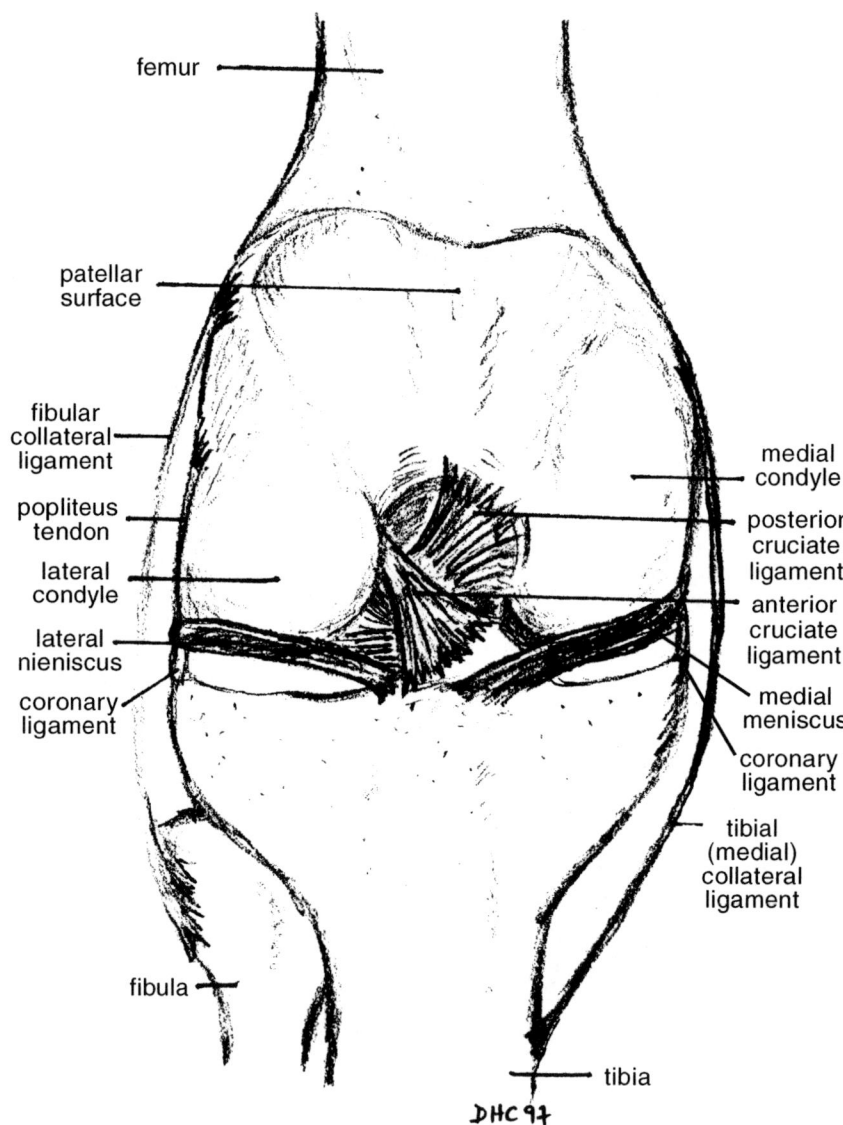

Figure 11.21 (continued on next page)
Anatomy of the knee (front or coronal view).

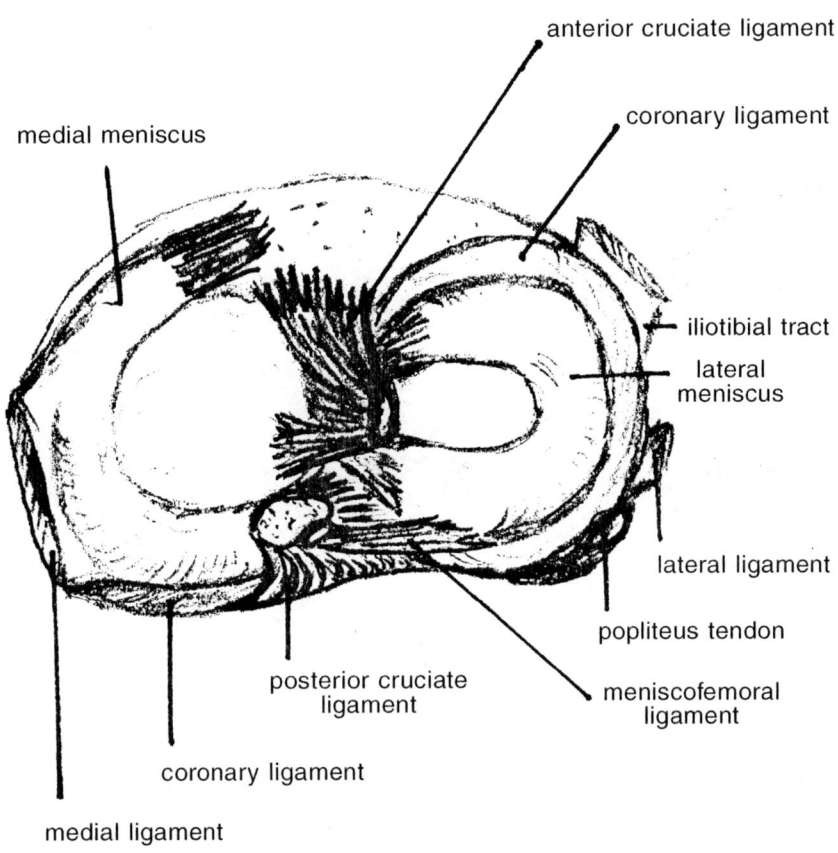

Figure 11.21 (continued from previous page)
Anatomy of the knee (transverse view).

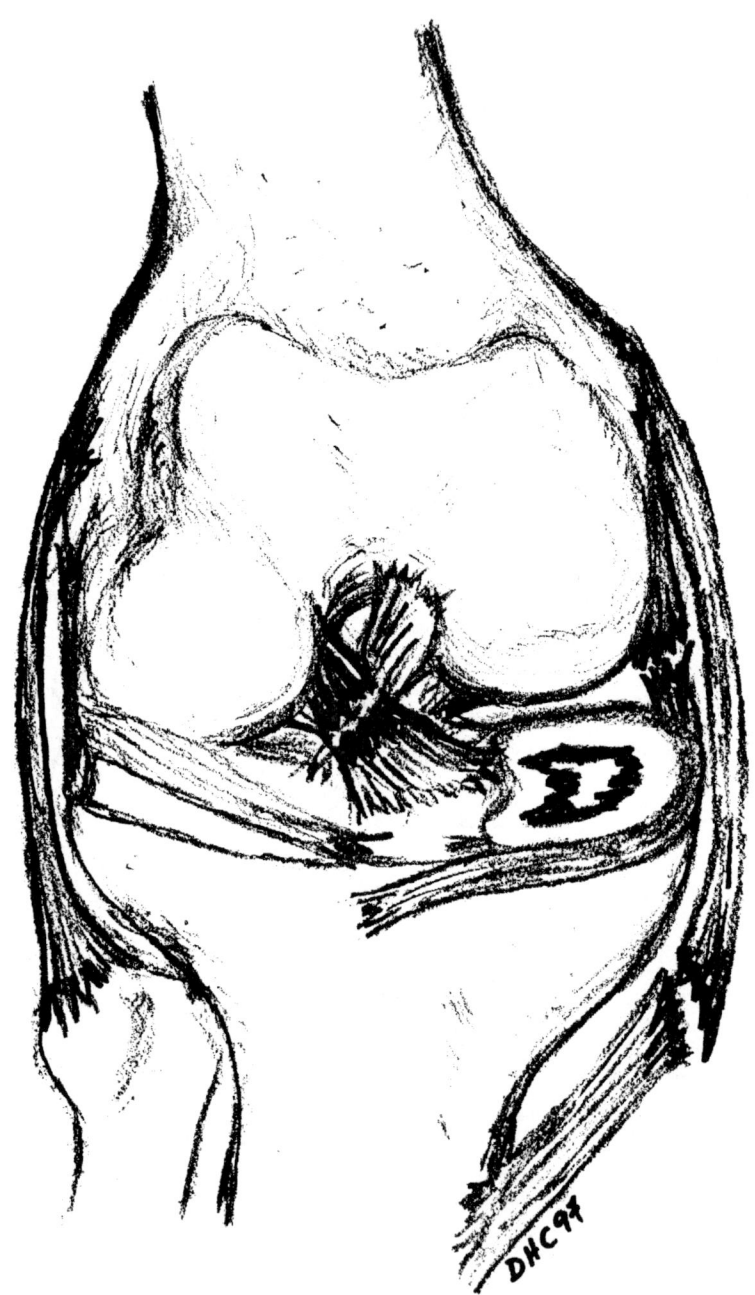

Figure 11.22
Anterior cruciate ligament tear associated with a tear of the deep and superficial medial collateral ligament and the medial meniscus.

INJURIES TO THE EXTREMITIES AND PELVIS   669

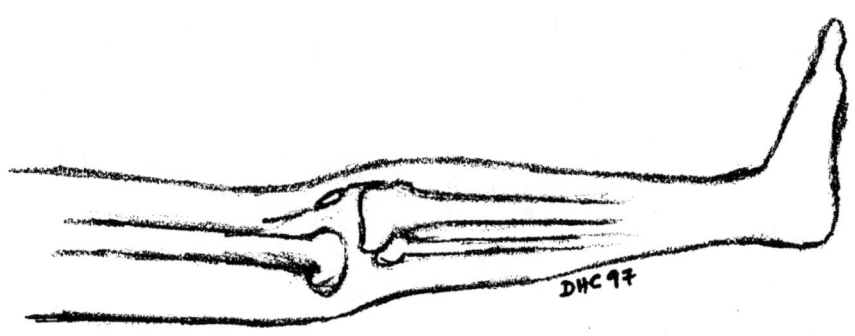

Figure 11.23
Anterior dislocation of the knee. The tibia is displaced anterioroly, relative to the femur.

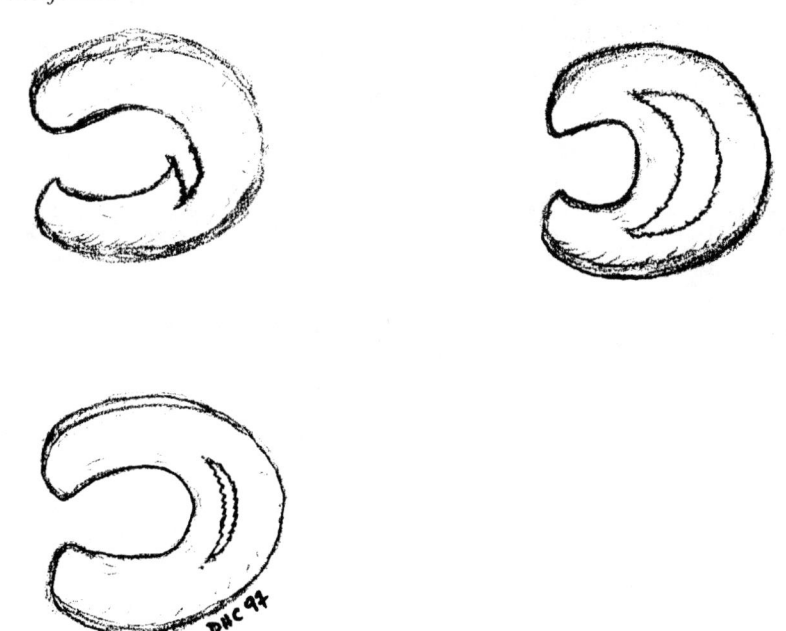

Figure 11.24
Patterns of knee meniscus tears.

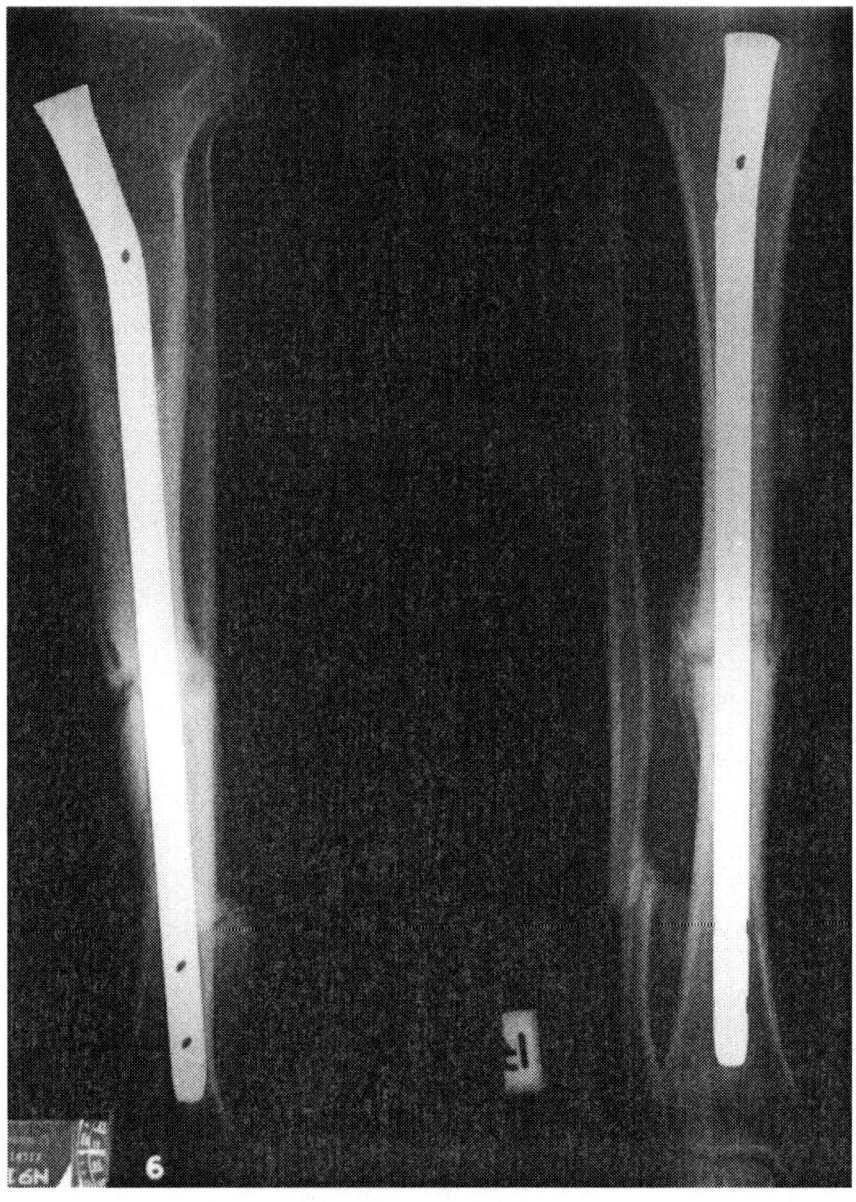

Figure 11.25
Fracture tibia shaft (diaphysis).

INJURIES TO THE EXTREMITIES AND PELVIS 671

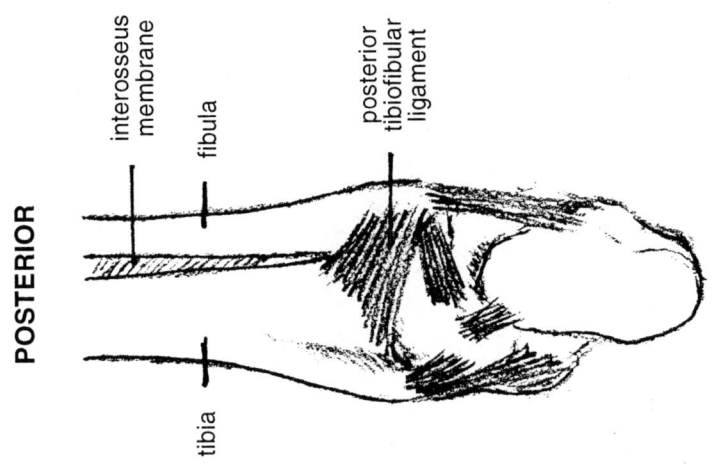

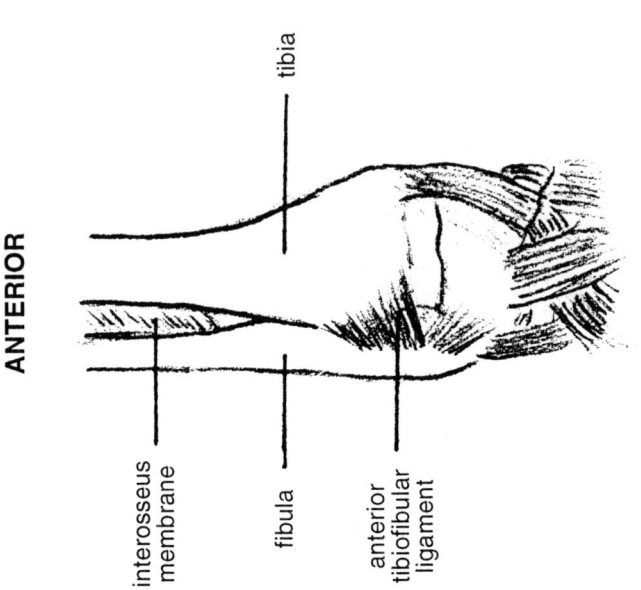

Figure 11.26 (continued on next page)
Ligamentous anatomy of the ankle and subtalar joint.

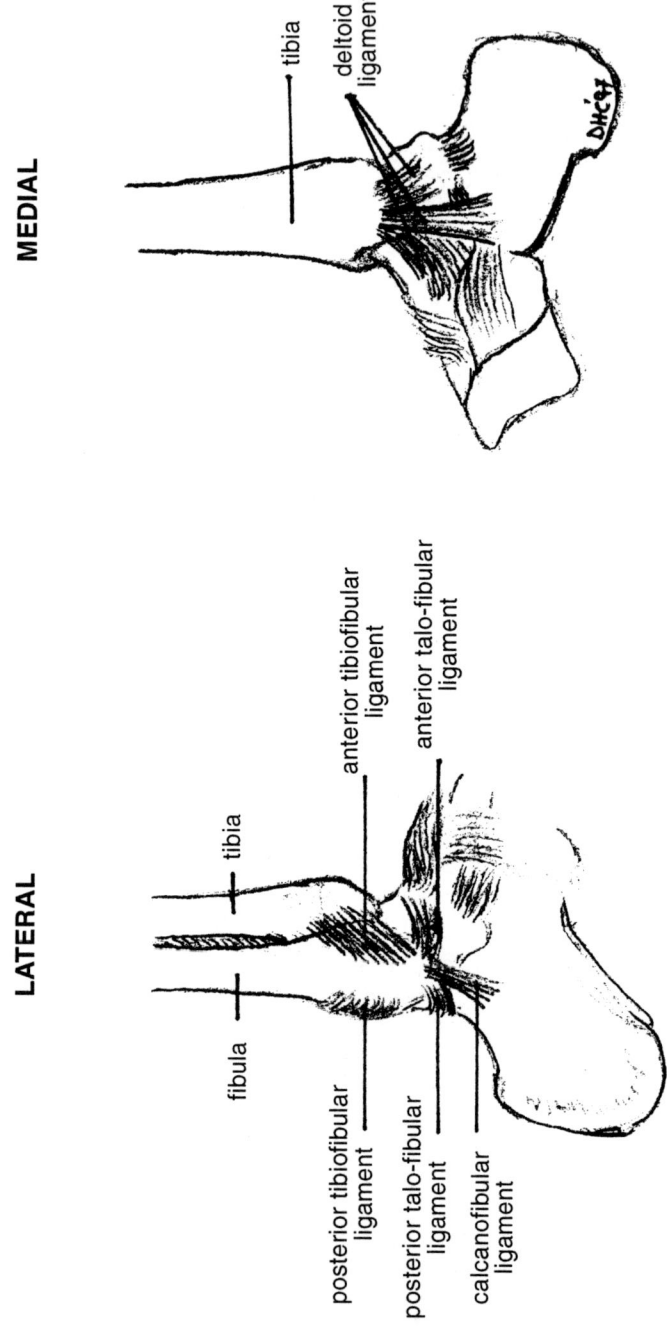

Figure 11.26 (continued from previous page)
Ligamentous anatomy of the ankle and subtalar joint.

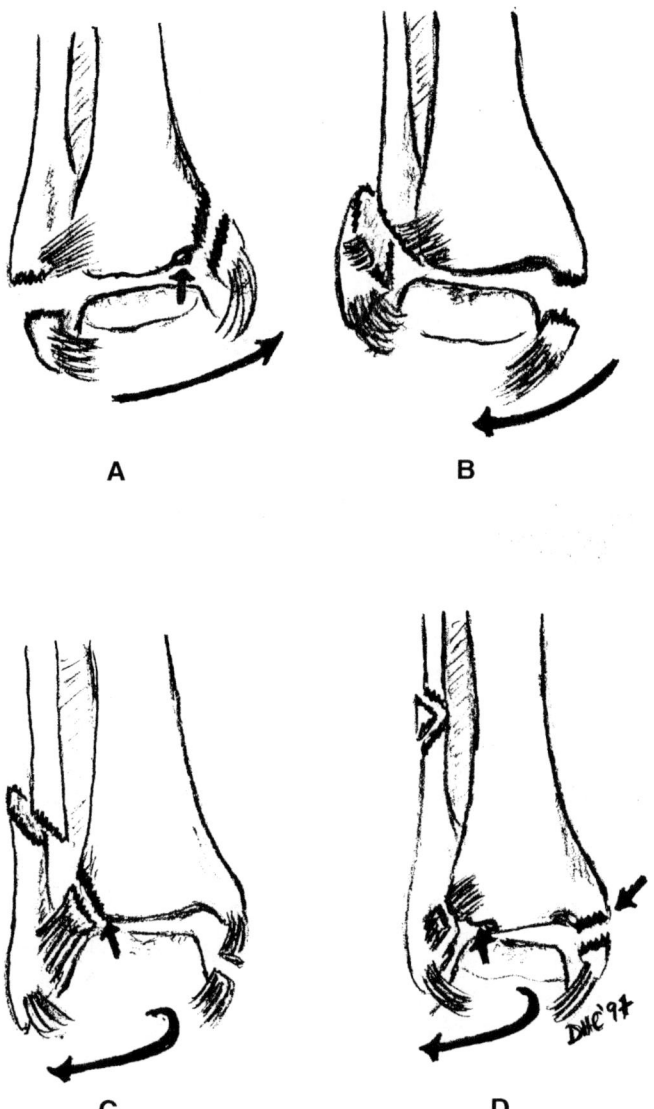

Figure 11.27
*Weber classification of ankle fractures — **A:** Type A: An inversion injury, the fibula is fractured below the tibiofibular ligaments. **B:** Type B: An eversion and external rotation injury. The fracture of the fibula is spiral and is at the level of tibiofibular joint. **C:** Type C: The ligament disruption is more severe because of a tear of the medial ligaments, the tibiofibular ligaments, and the interosseus membrane. **D:** An impaction fracture of the tibia plafond articular surface.*

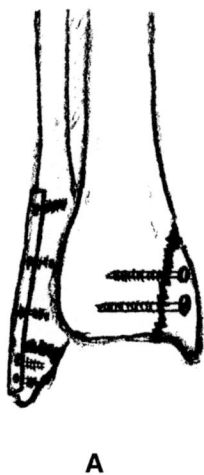

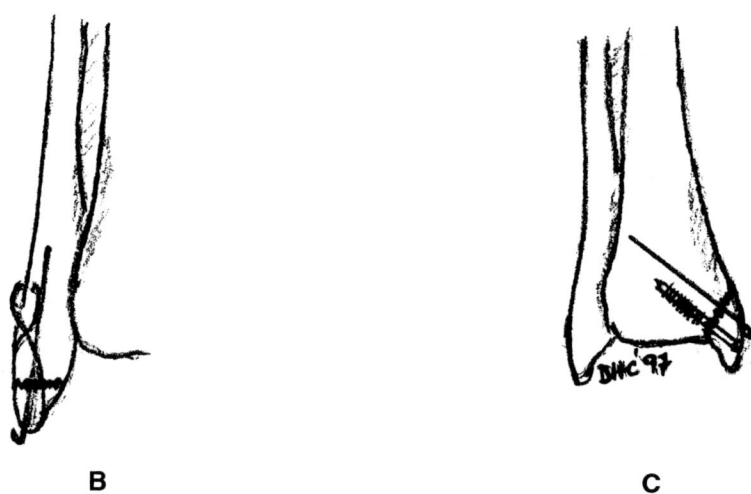

Figure 11.28
Various methods of internal fixation of the ankle.

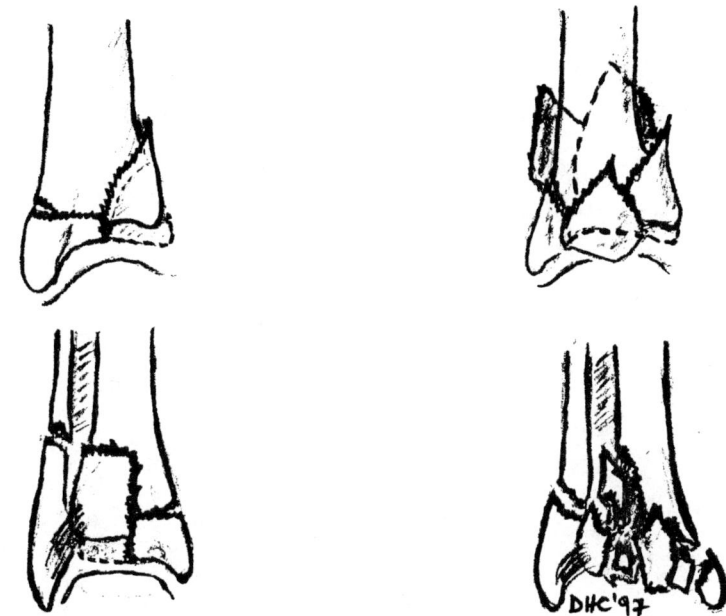

Figure 11.29
Fractures of the tibia plafond or pilon fractures.

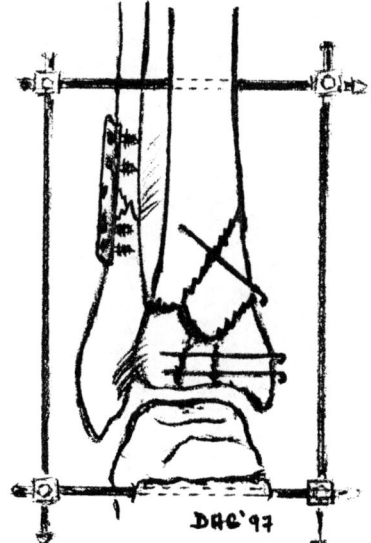

Figure 11.30
Tibia plafond fracture and fibula fracture treated with a combination of limited internal fixation and external fixation. The articular anatomy is restored in addition to the length of the tibia.

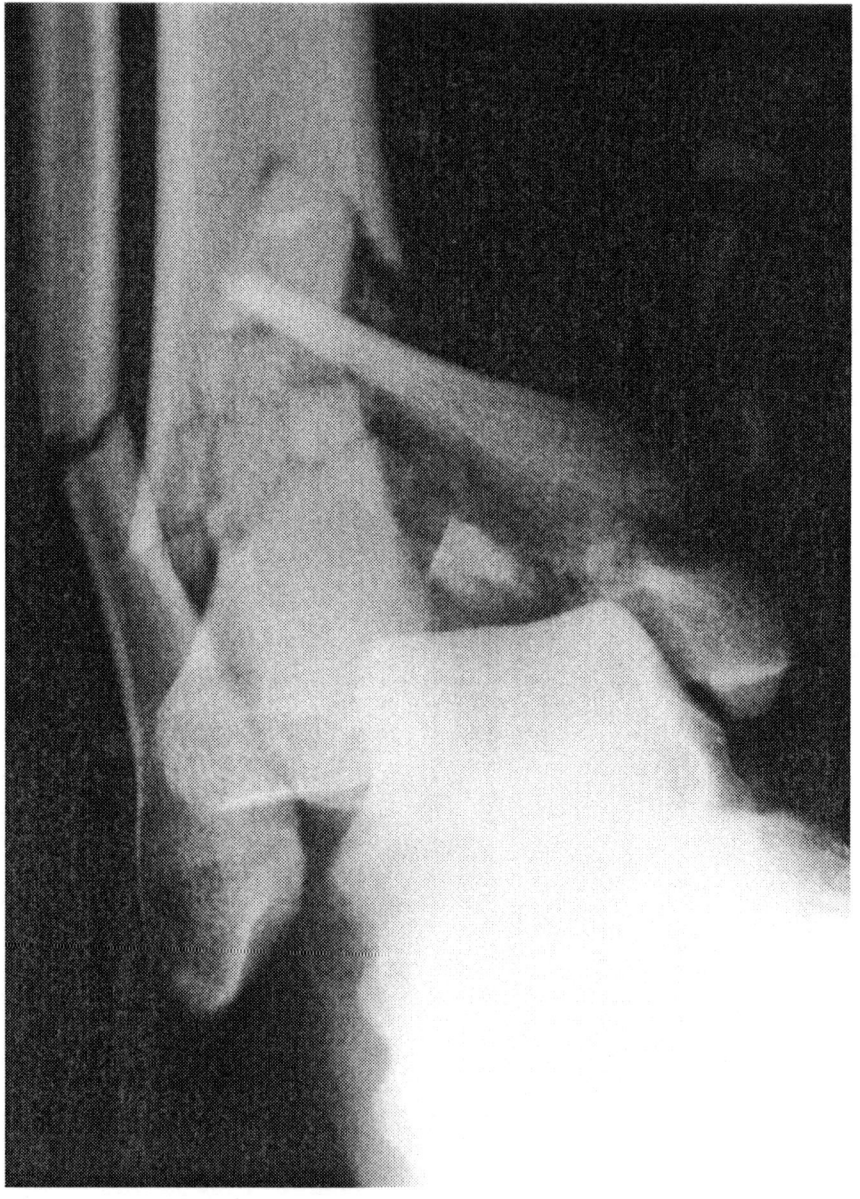

Figure 11.31
Radiograph of a young male with a severely comminuted distal tibia fracture.

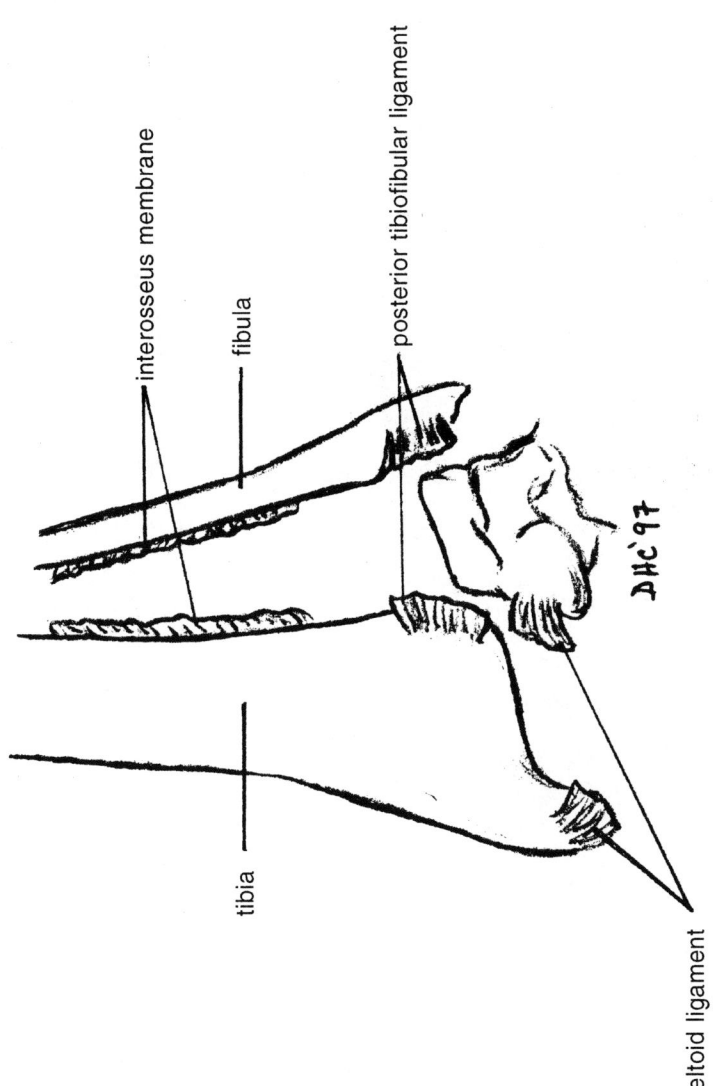

Figure 11.32
Tibio-talar dislocation. Note the extensive ligamentous disruption.

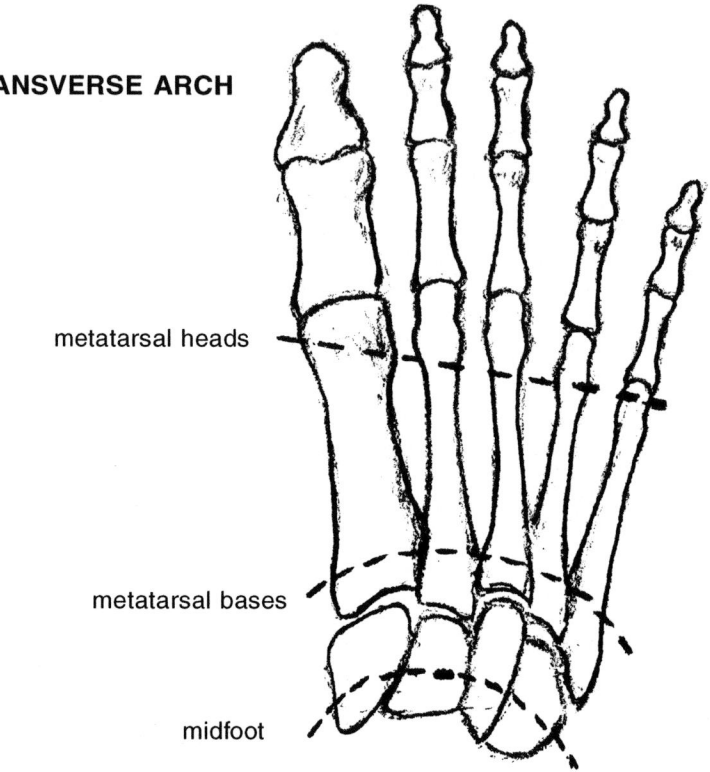

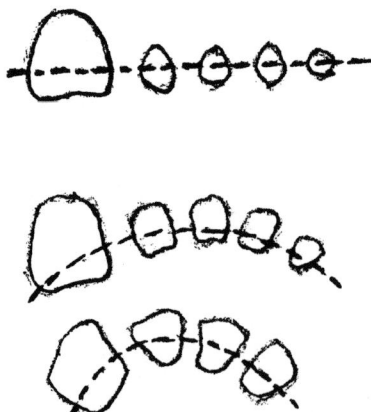

Figure 11.33 (continued on next page)
Transverse and longitudinal arches of the foot.

Injuries to the Extremities and Pelvis 679

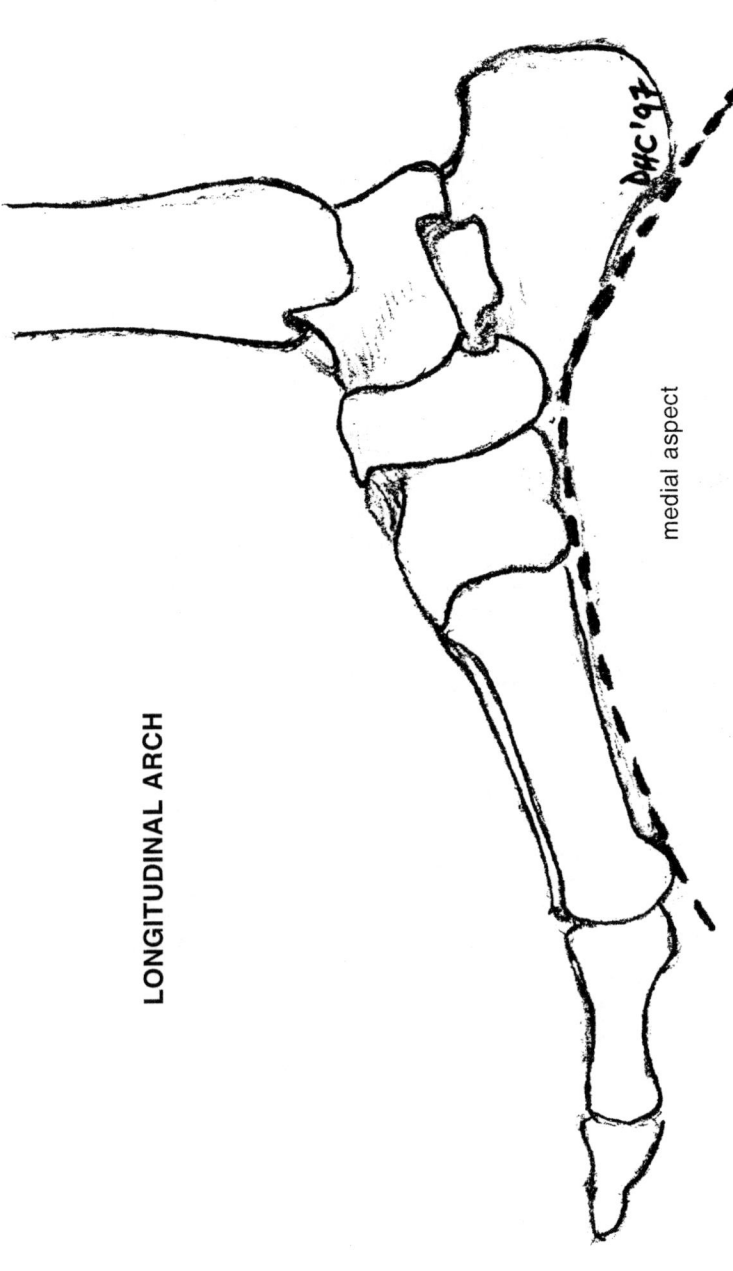

Figure 11.33 (continued from previous page)
Transverse and longitudinal arches of the foot.

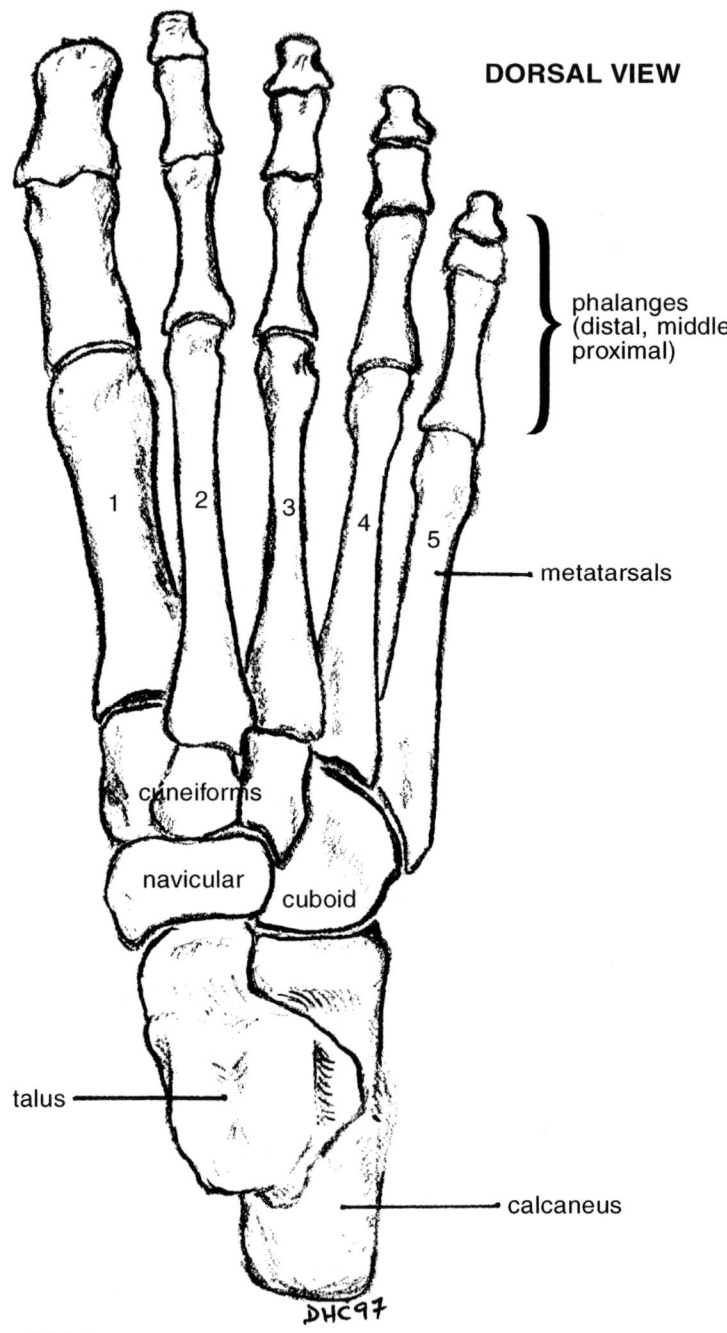

Figure 11.34
Osseus anatomy of the foot (dorsal view).

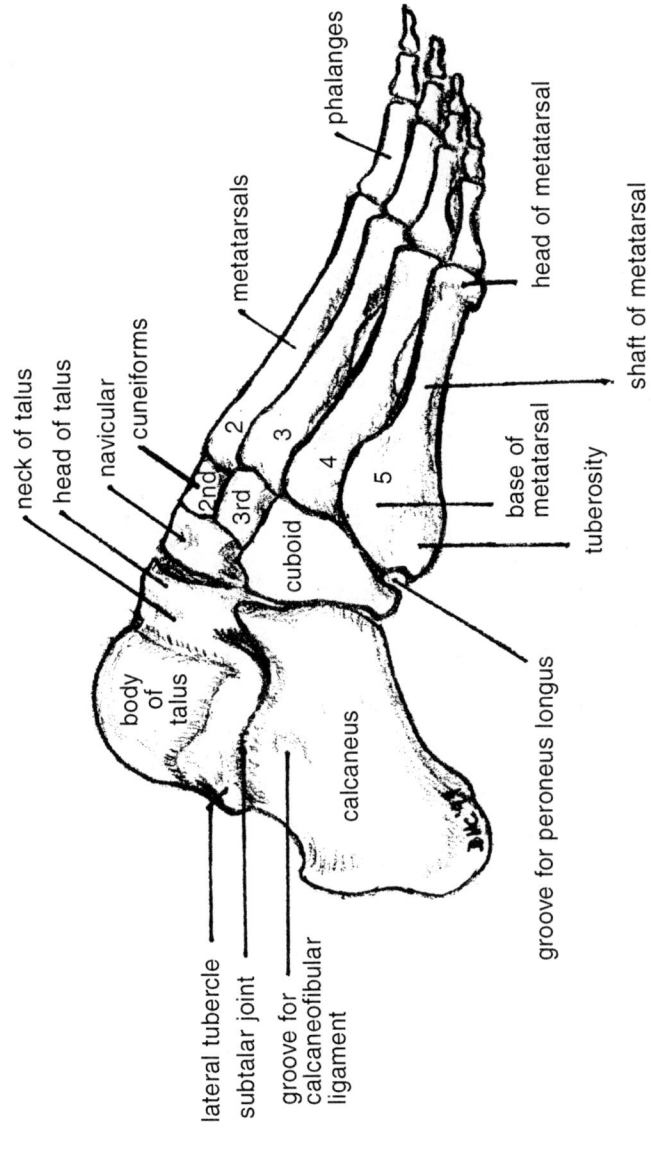

Figure 11.35
Osseus anatomy of the foot (lateral view).

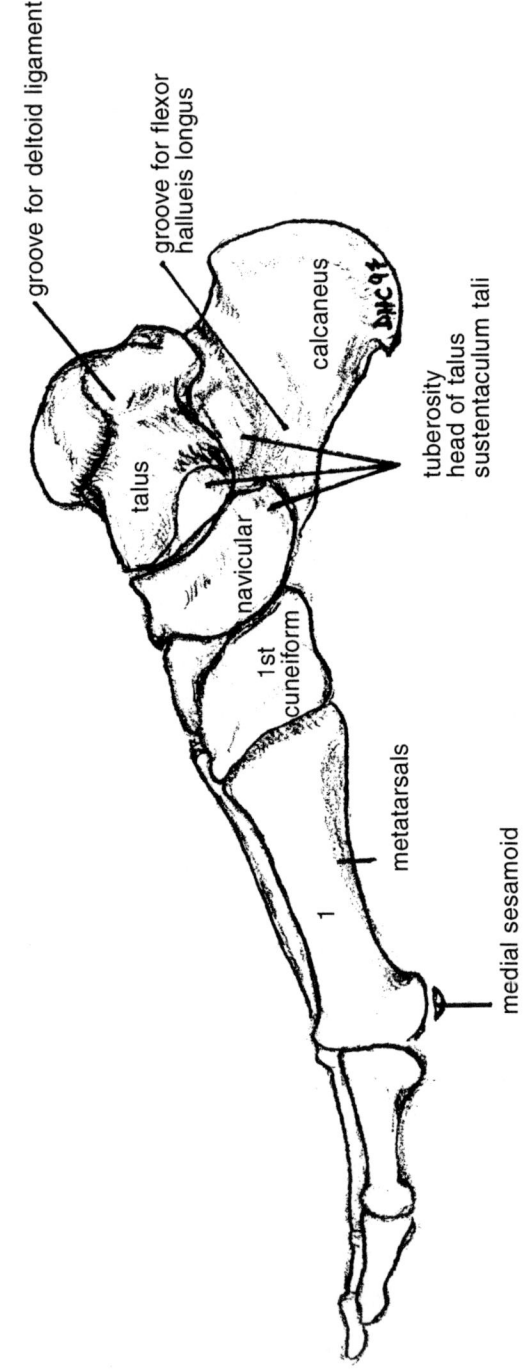

Figure 11.36
Osseus anatomy of the foot (medial view).

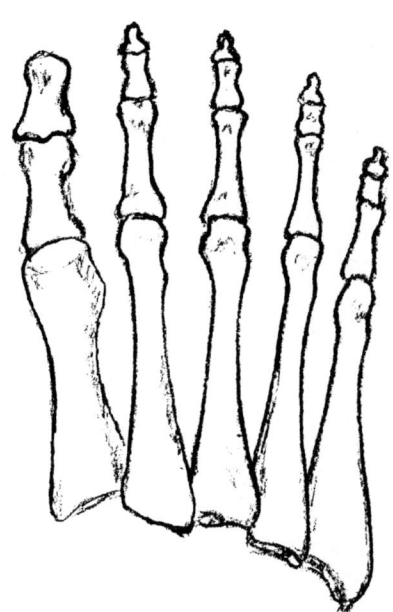

Figure 11.37
The joints of the Chopart and Lisfranc. Chopart's joints are the calcaneocuboid and the talonavicular articulations. Lisfranc's joints are the tarsometatarsal joints (between the cuneiforms and cuboid and the metatarsals).

FOREFOOT

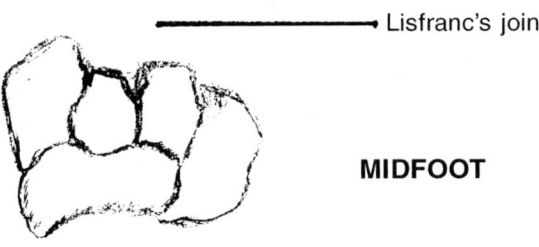

Lisfranc's joint

MIDFOOT

Chopart's joint

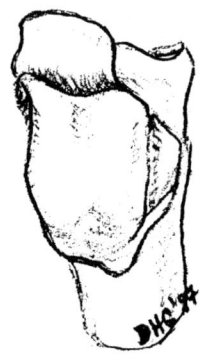

HINDFOOT

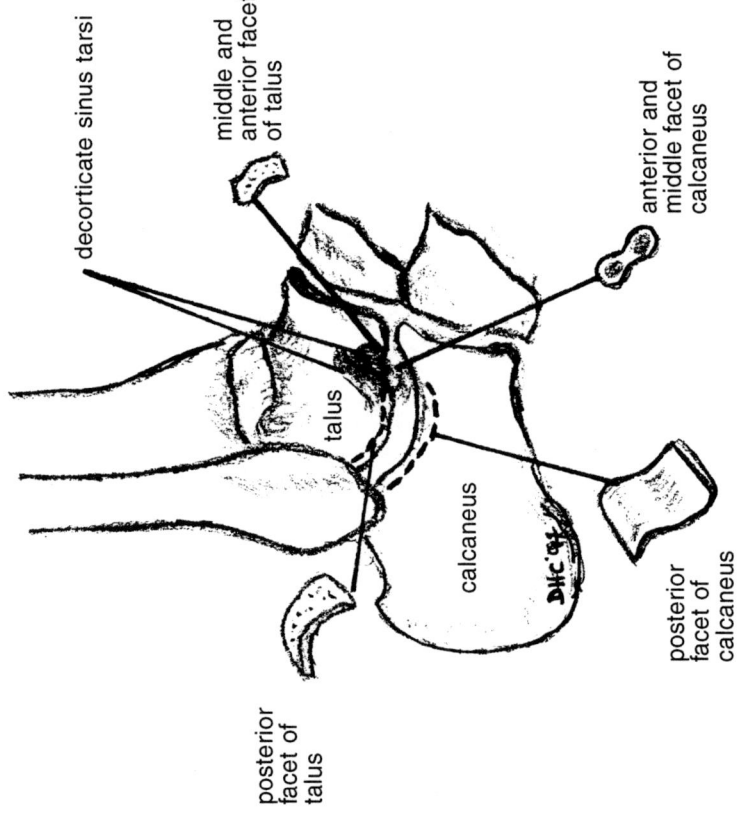

Figure 11.38
The subtalar joint (talo-calcaneal joint).

INJURIES TO THE EXTREMITIES AND PELVIS 685

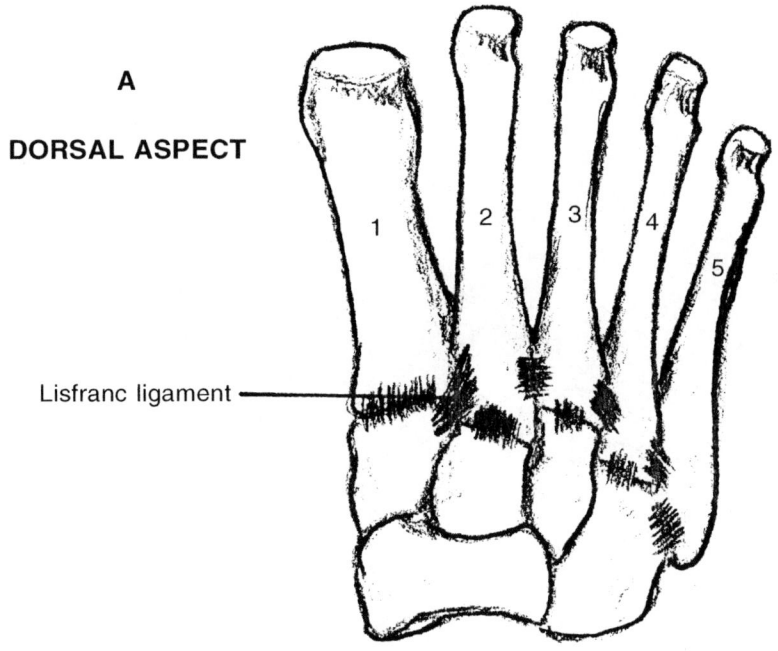

Figure 11.39 (continued on next page)
A: The Lisfranc joints joining the five metatarsals of the foot to the cuneiform and cuboid.

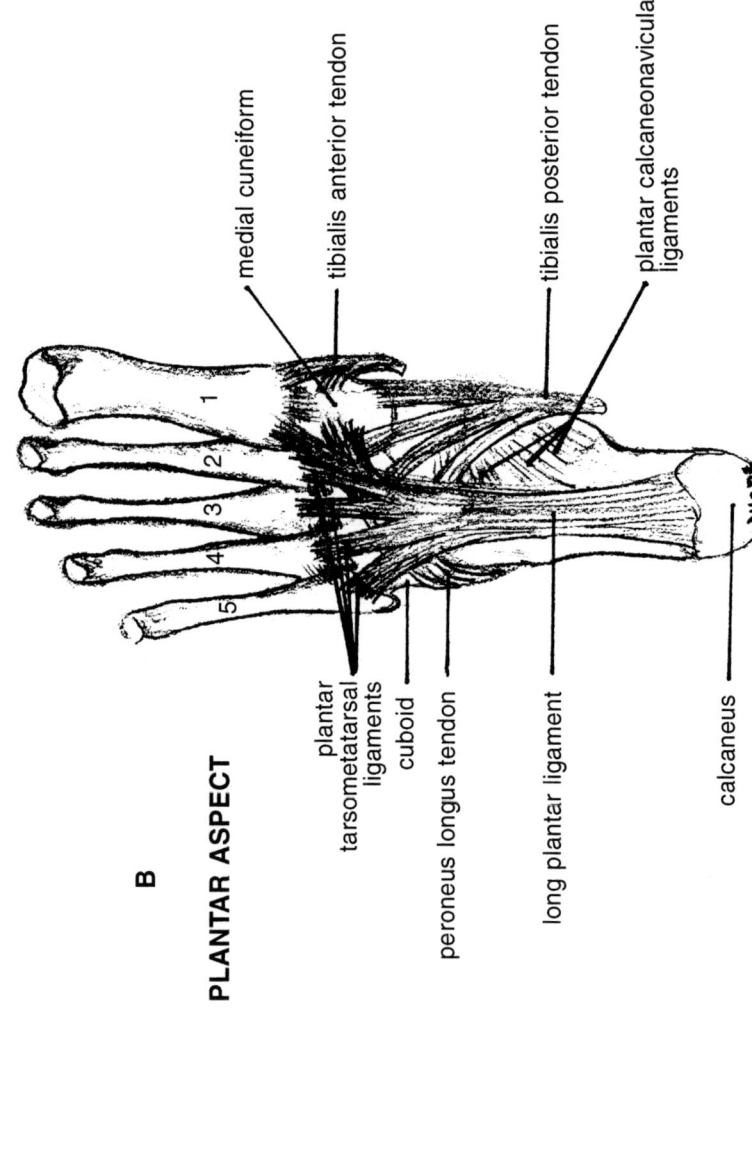

Figure 11.39 (continued from previous page)
B: The plantar calcaneo navicular ligament (spring ligament) and other plantar ligaments of the foot.

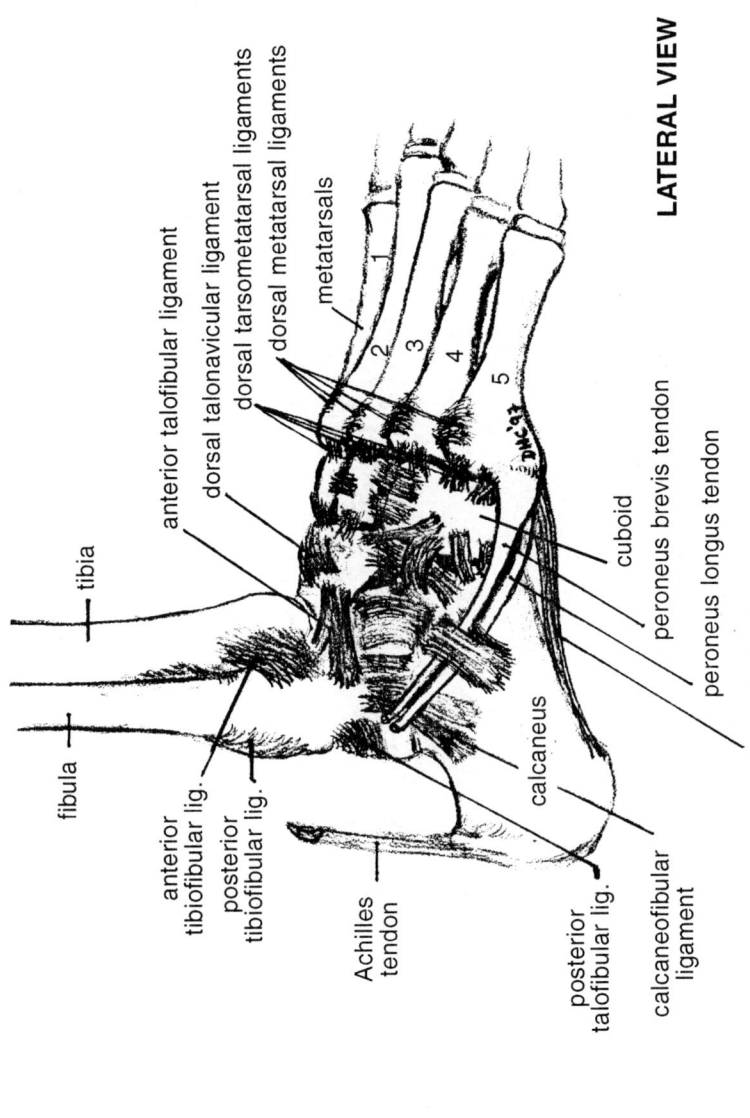

Figure 11.40
The dorsal and lateral ligaments of the foot, ankle and subtalar joints.

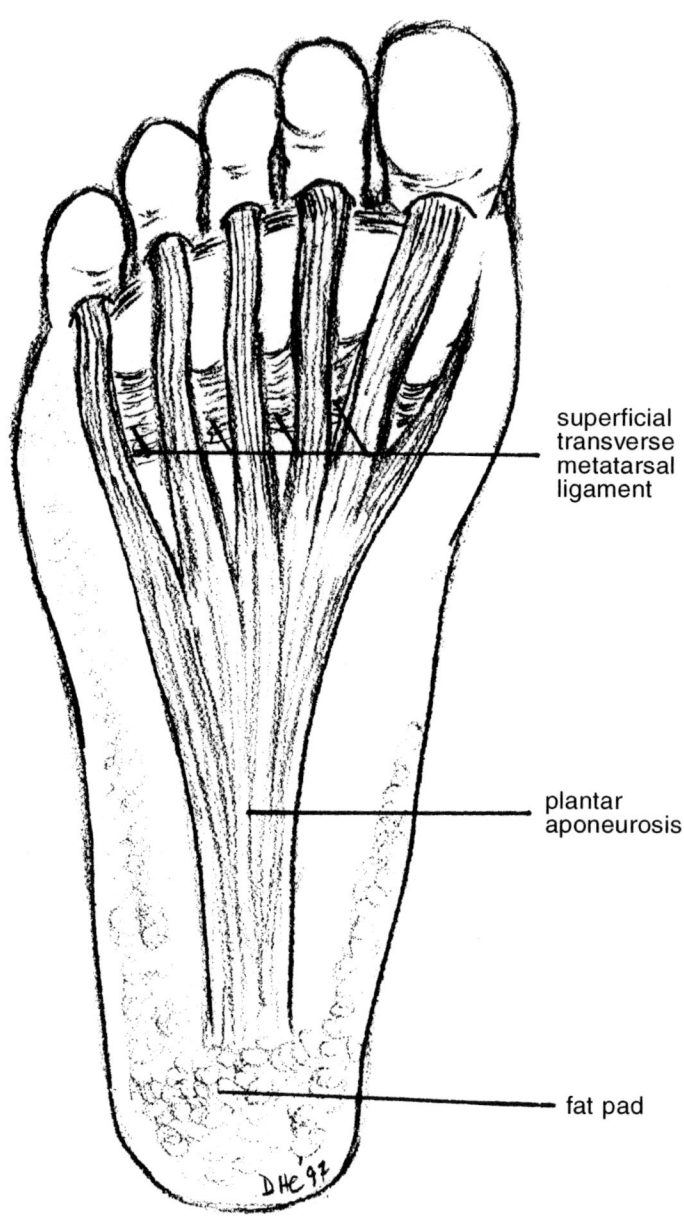

Figure 11.41
The plantar fascia (plantar aponeurosis).

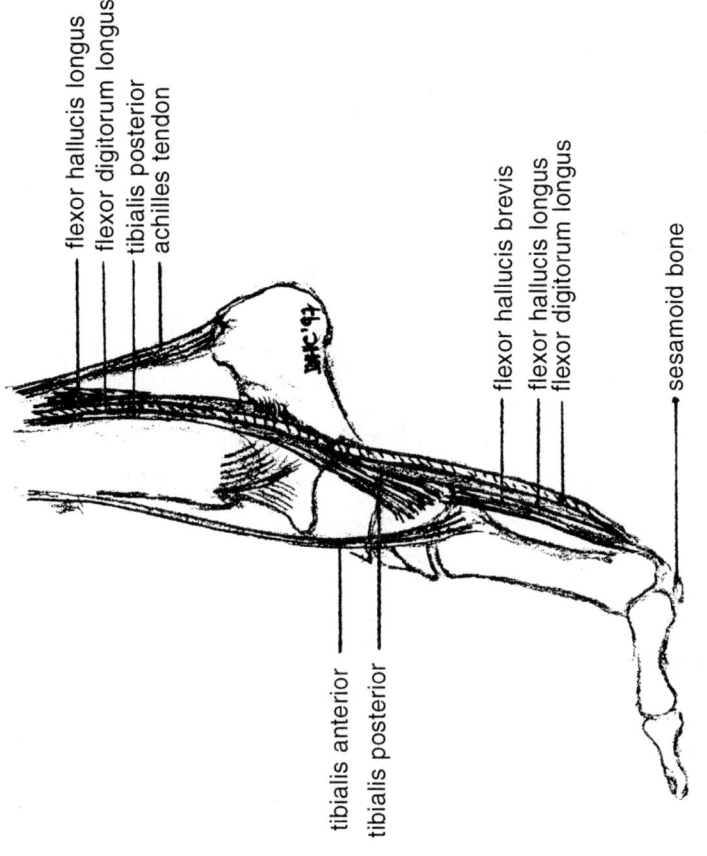

Figure 11.42A (continued on next page)
Extrinsic muscles and tendons of the foot.

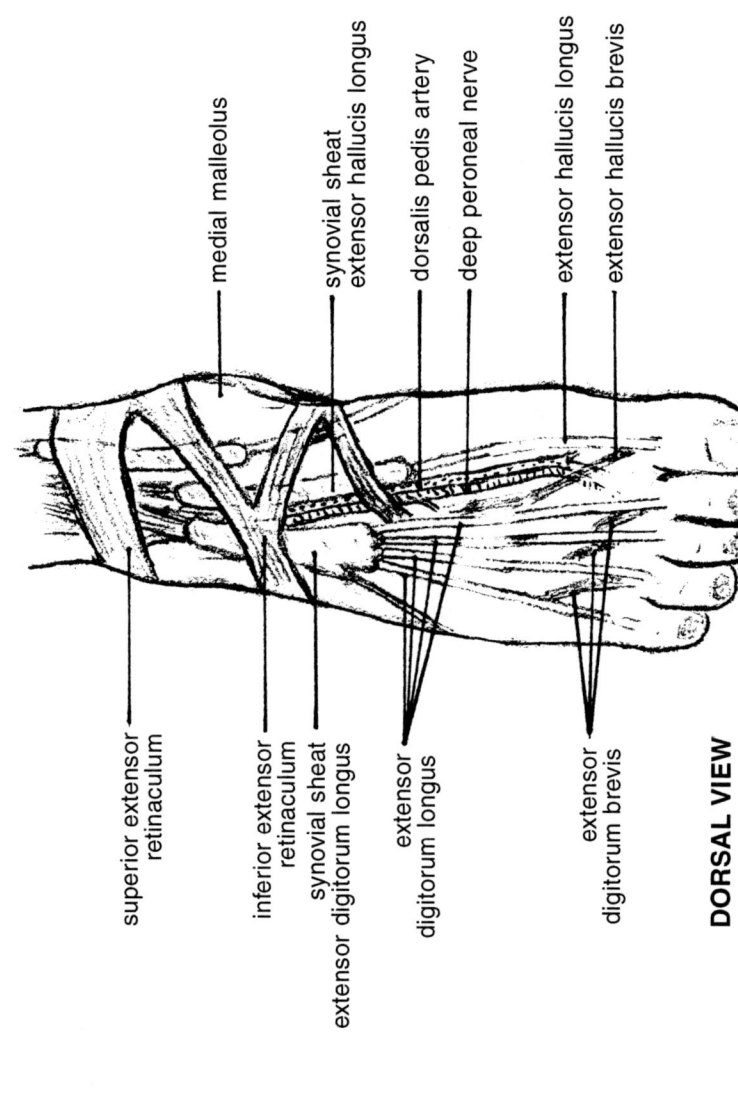

Figure 11.42A (continued from previous page)
Extrinsic muscles and tendons of the foot.

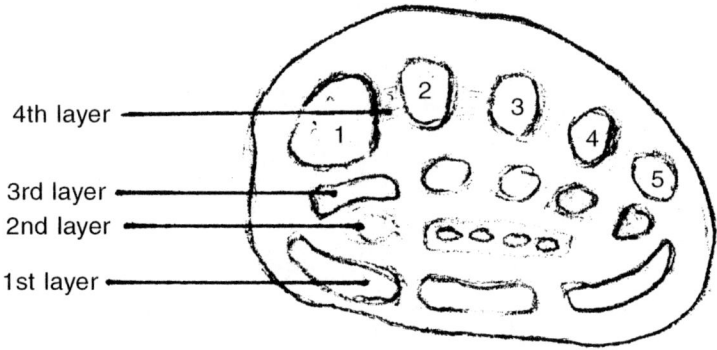

Figure 11.42B
Intrinsic muscles of the foot.

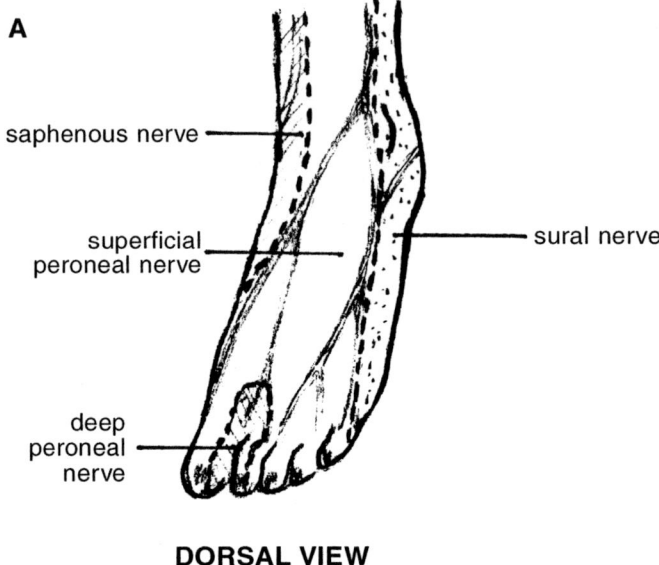
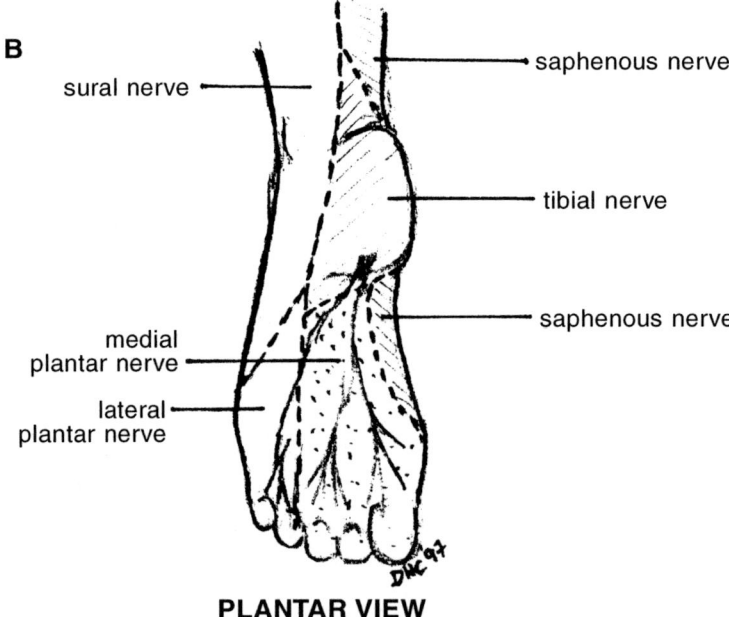

Figure 11.43
Nerve supply of the foot.

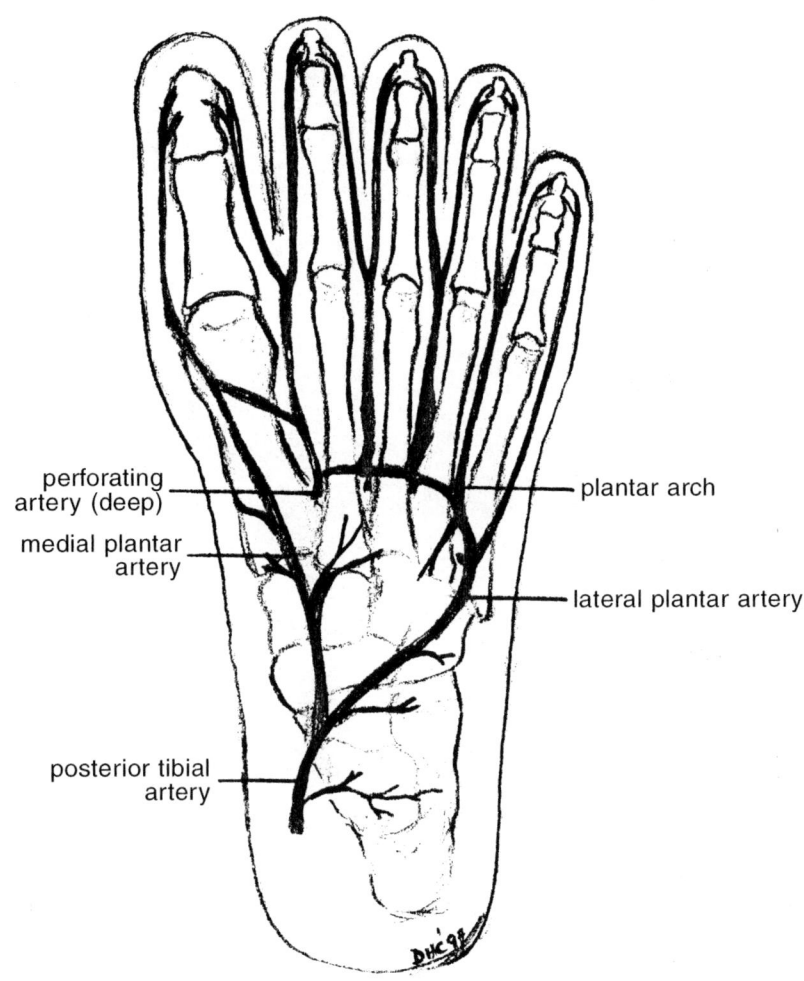

Figure 11.44
Arterial network of the foot.

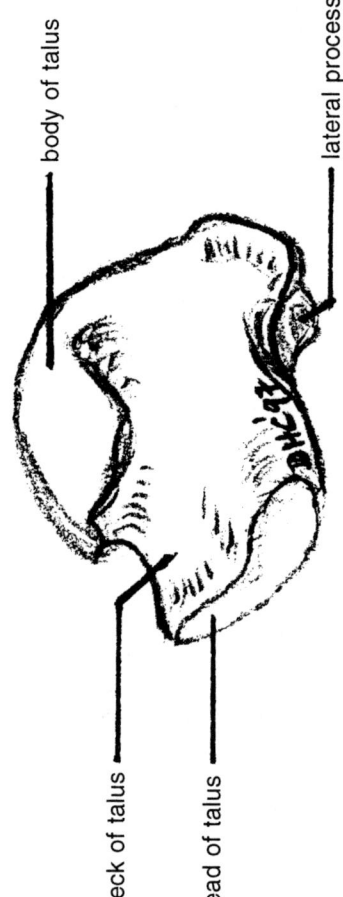

Figure 11.45
Osseus anatomy of the talus. View from the medial side.

INJURIES TO THE EXTREMITIES AND PELVIS 695

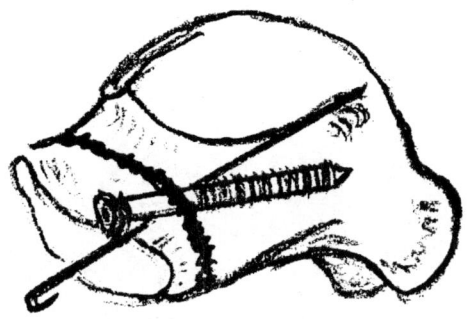

MEDIAL VIEW

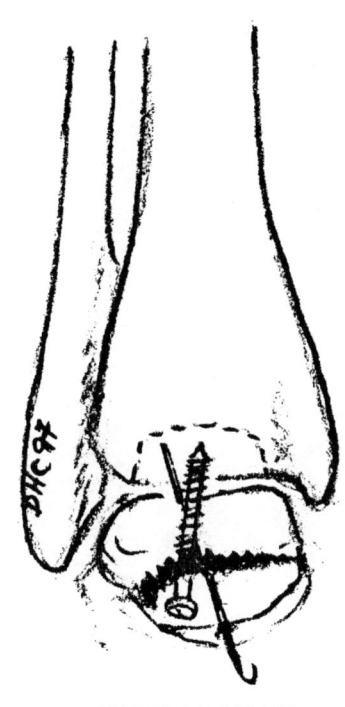

DORSAL VIEW

Figure 11.46A
Fracture of the neck of the talus. Schema of the location of the fracture and one form of internal fixation.

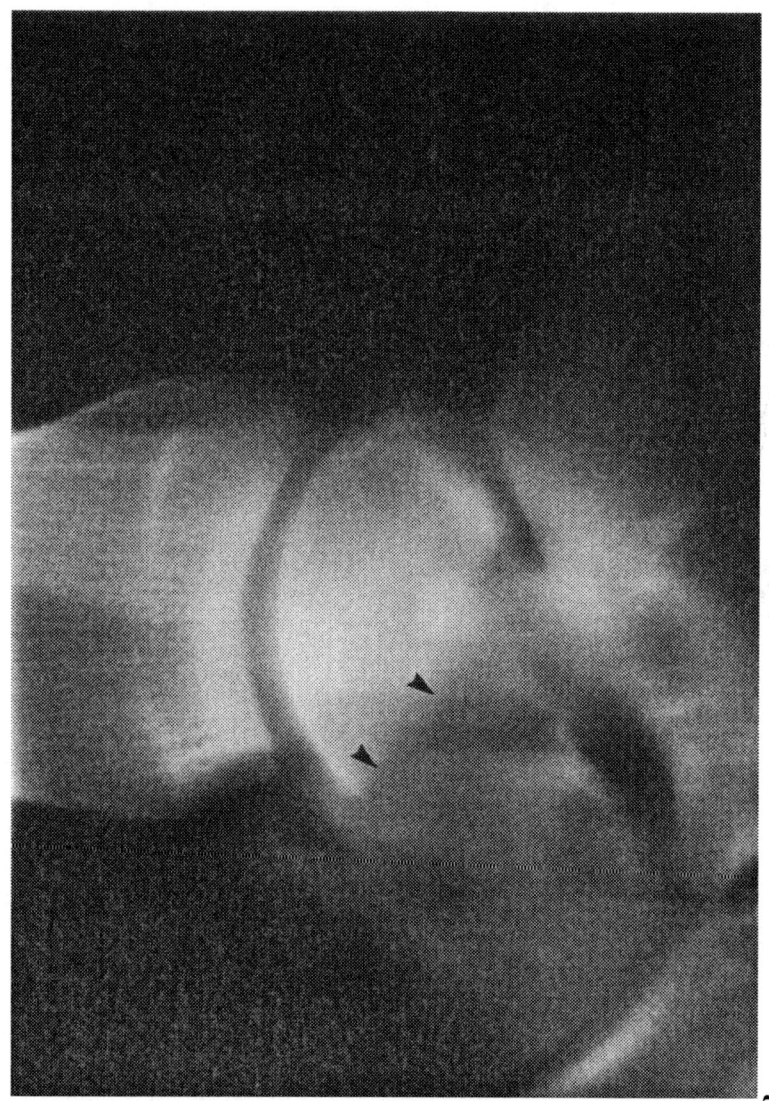

Figure 11.46B
Lateral radiographs of the foot showing a displaced fracture of the talar neck (arrows) and the body of the talus which is at risk for avascular necrosis.

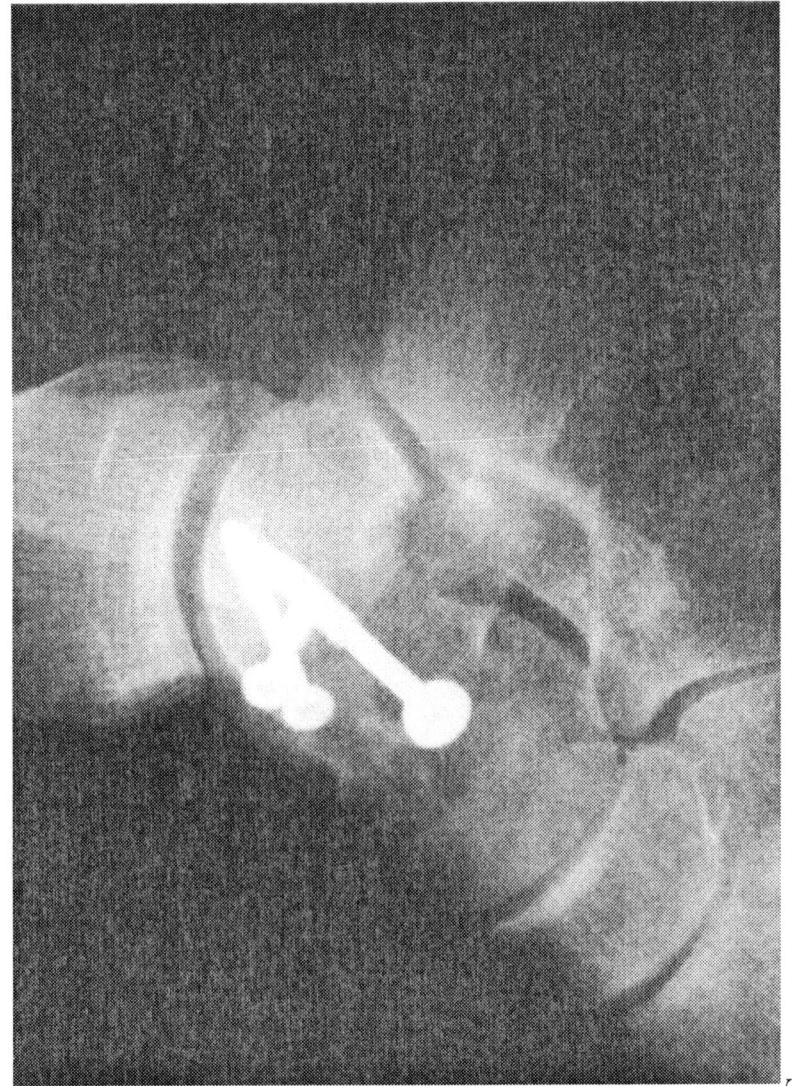

Figure 11.46C
The fracture was reduced and fixed with three screws.

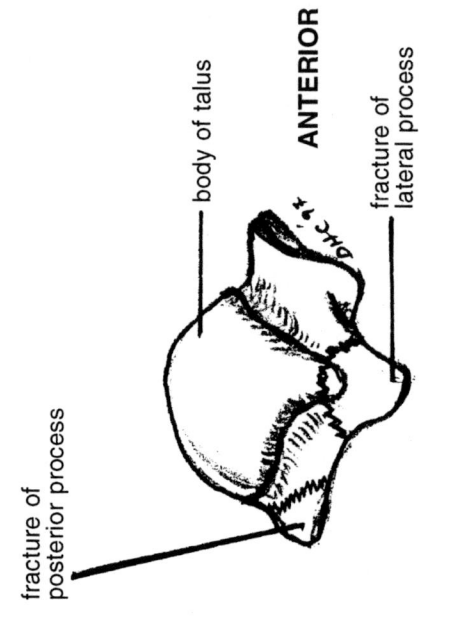

Figure 11.47A
Fractures of the talus.

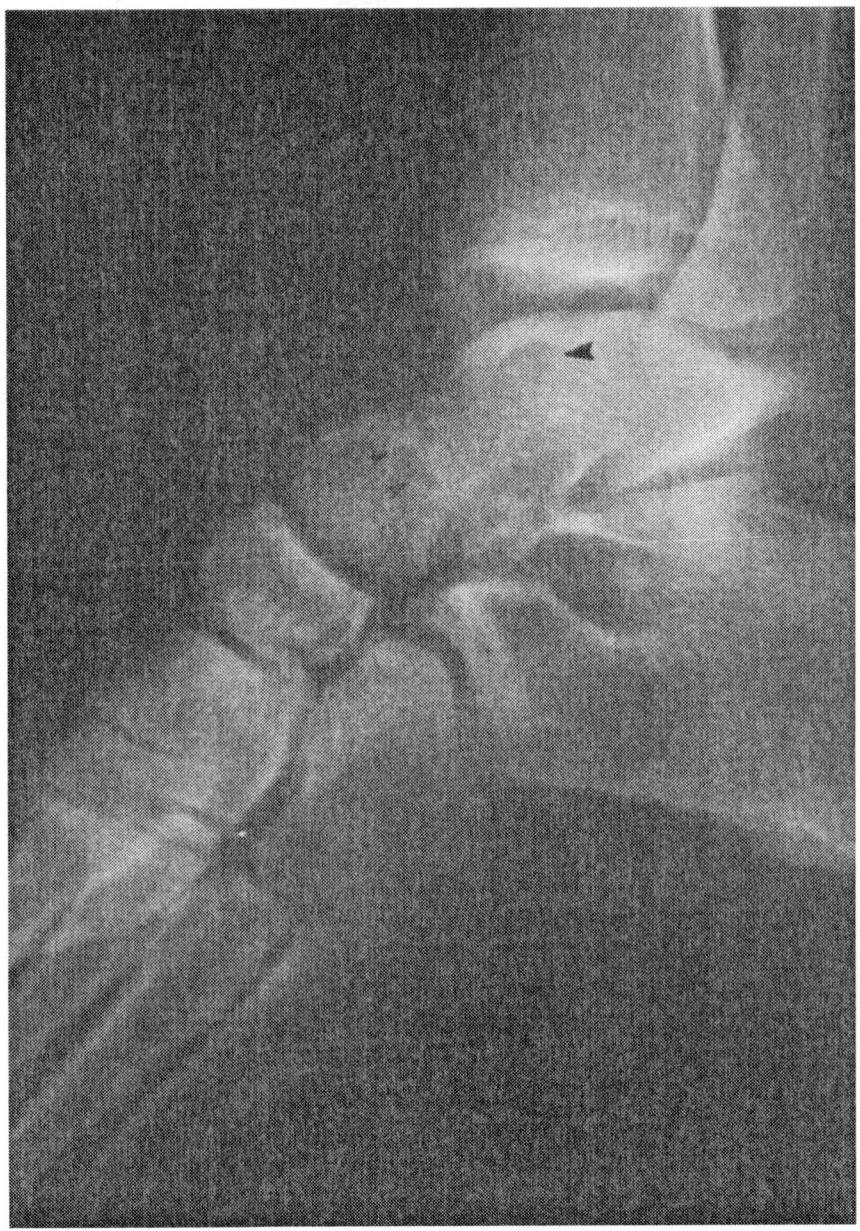

Figure 11.47B
Fracture of the talus.

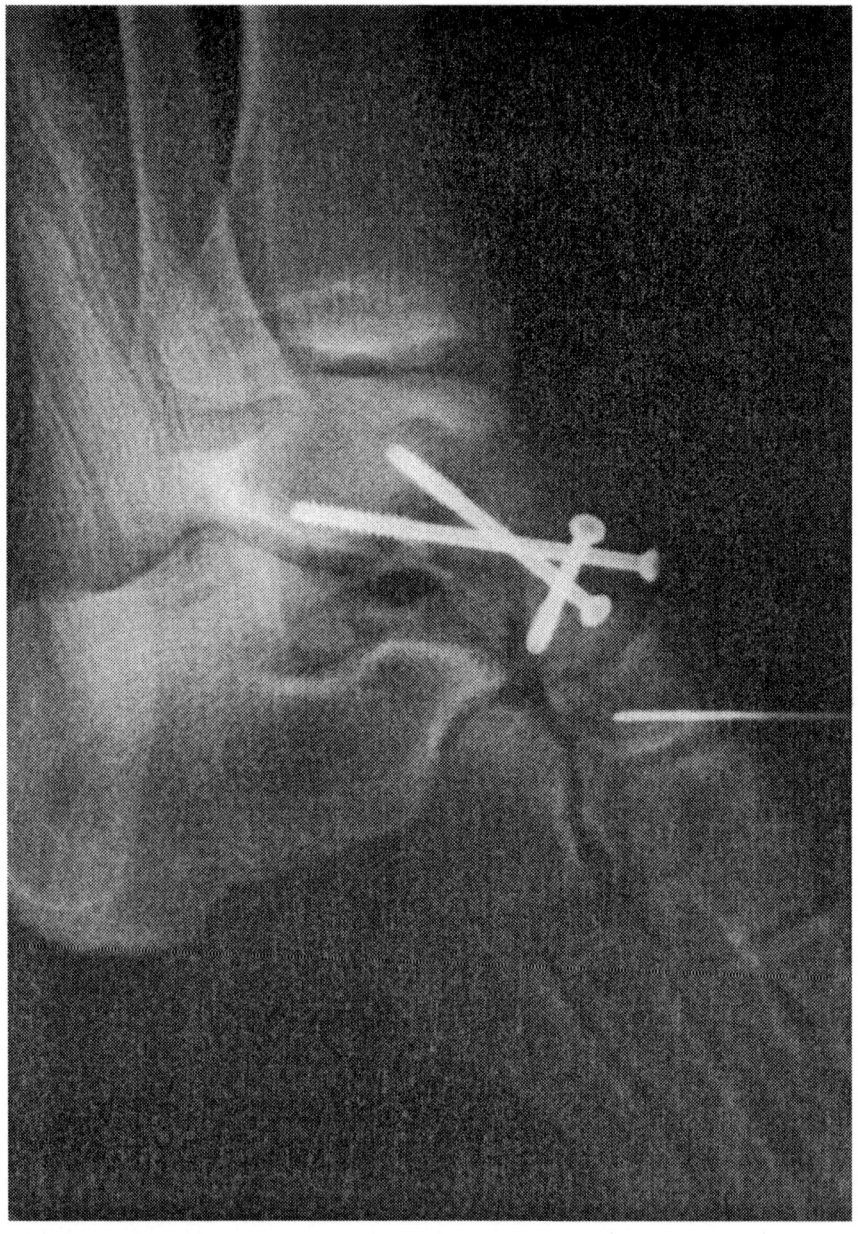

Figure 11.47C
Fracture of the talus.

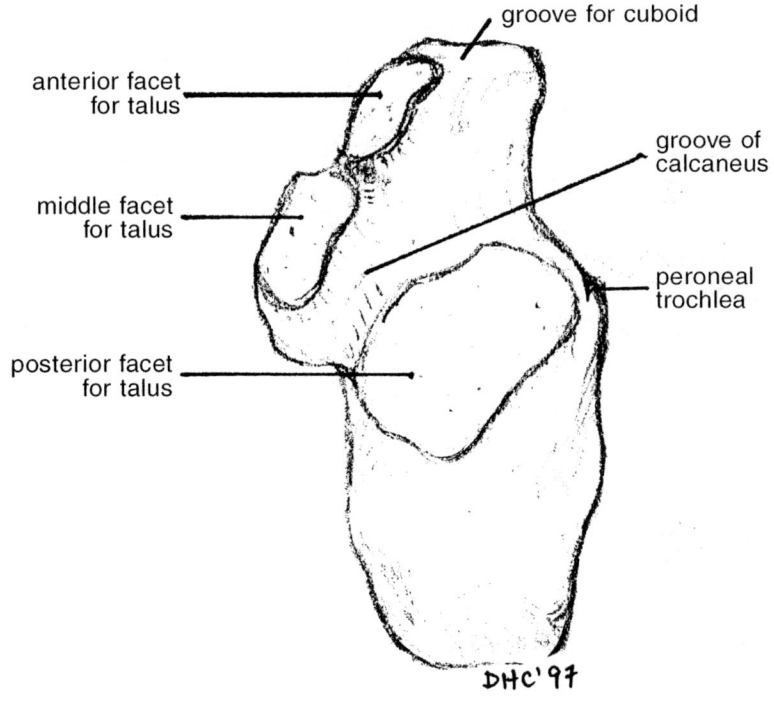

Figure 11.48
Superior view of the calcaneus.

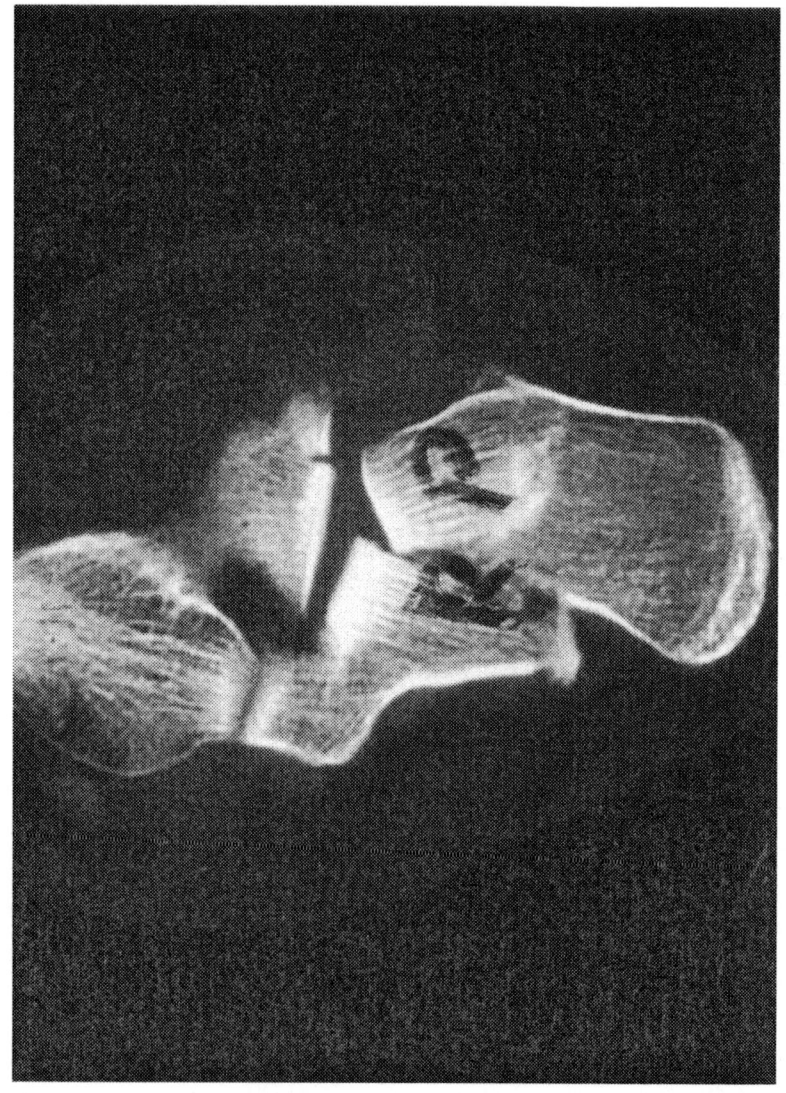

Figure 11.49
C.T. of subtalar joint showing the anterior and middle facets intact but the posterior facet split, depressed and rotated.

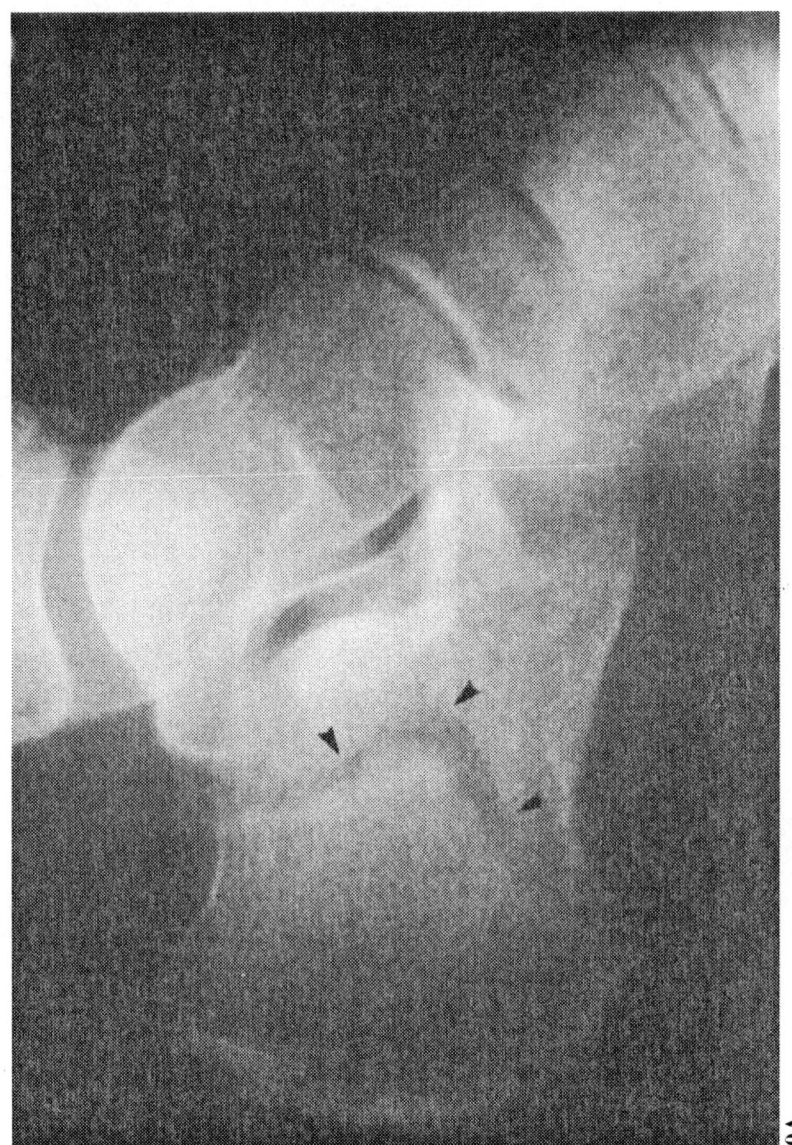

Figure 11.50A
Young female who fell from a height. Lateral view demonstrates a fracture. C.T. imaging is necessary to better define the fracture.

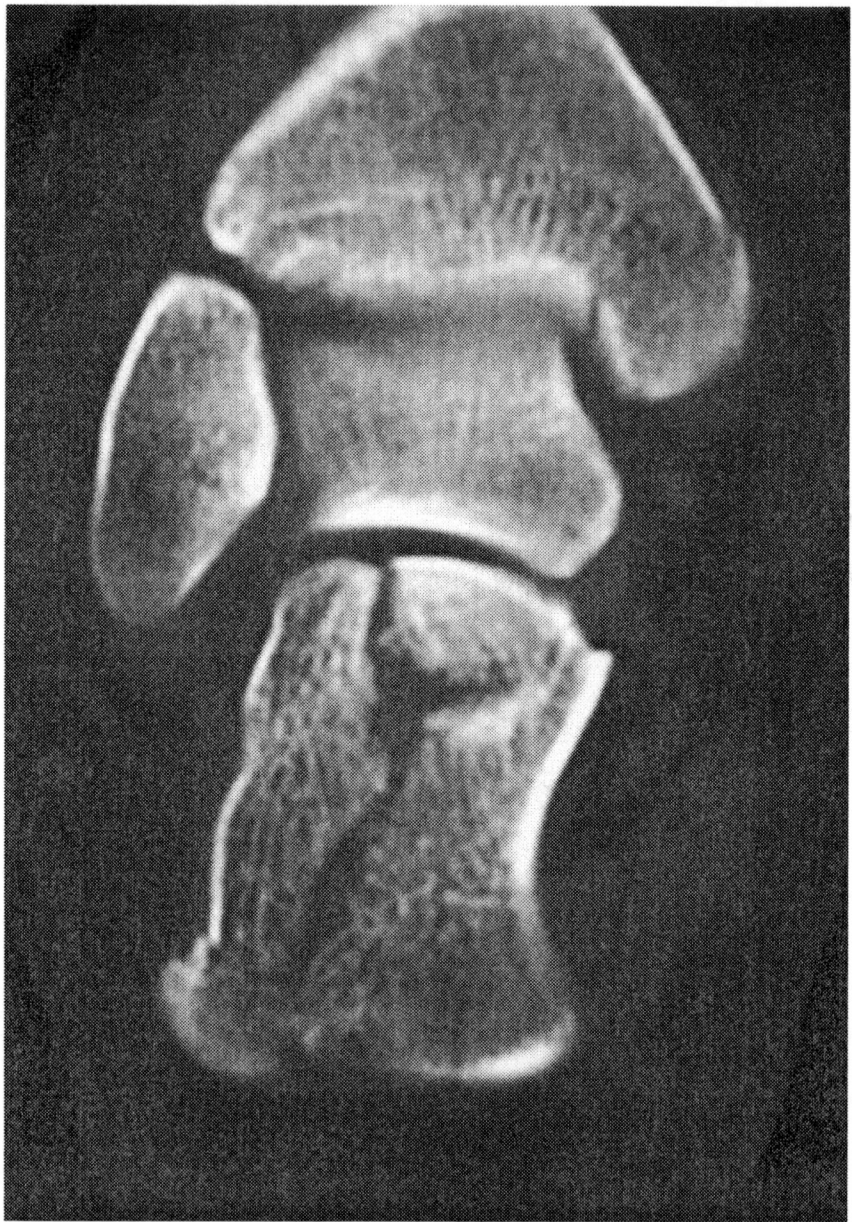

Figure 11.50B
Young female who fell from a height. Coronal CT scan showing the fracture extending into the subtalar joint and displacement of the posterior facet. Note also a fracture of the medial malleolus of the ankle.

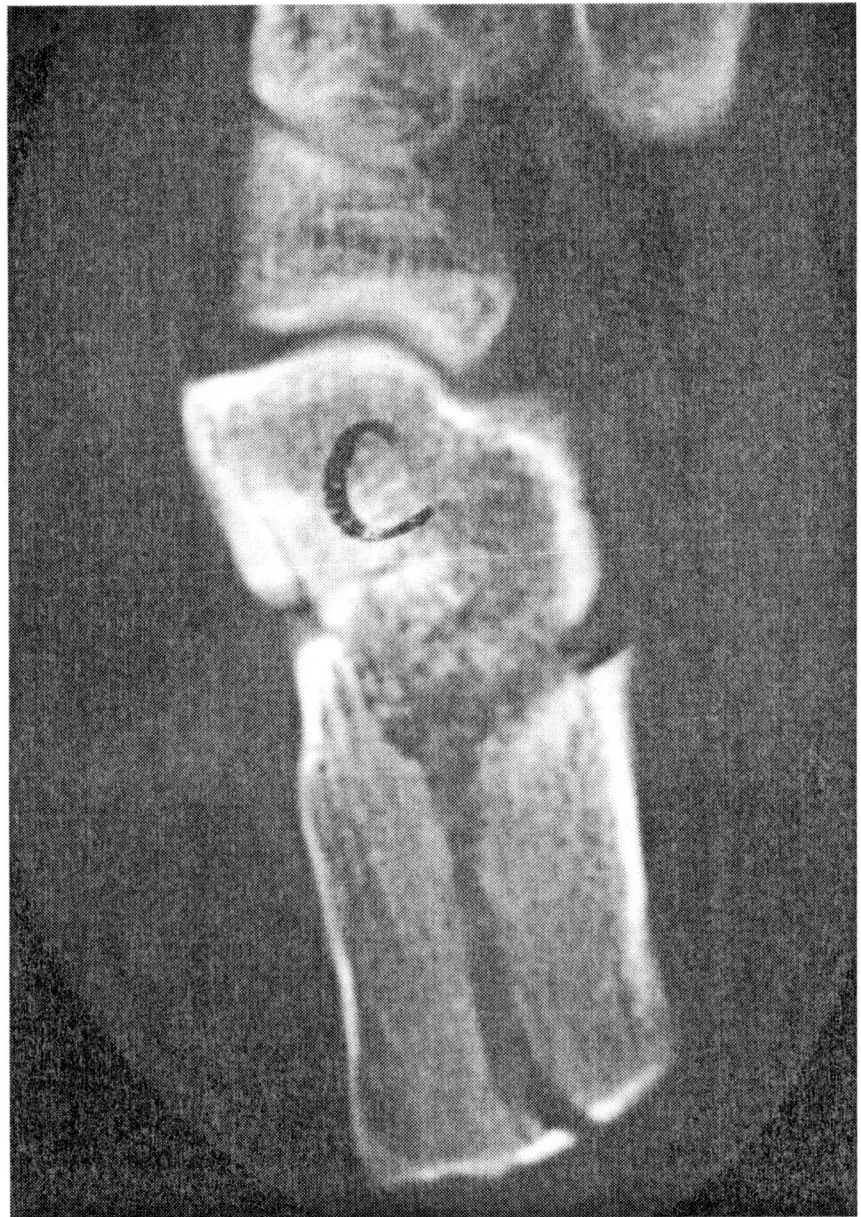

Figure 11.50C
Young female who fell from a height. Transverse cut of the CT scan illustrating the major fracture component and an intact calcaneo cuboid joint.

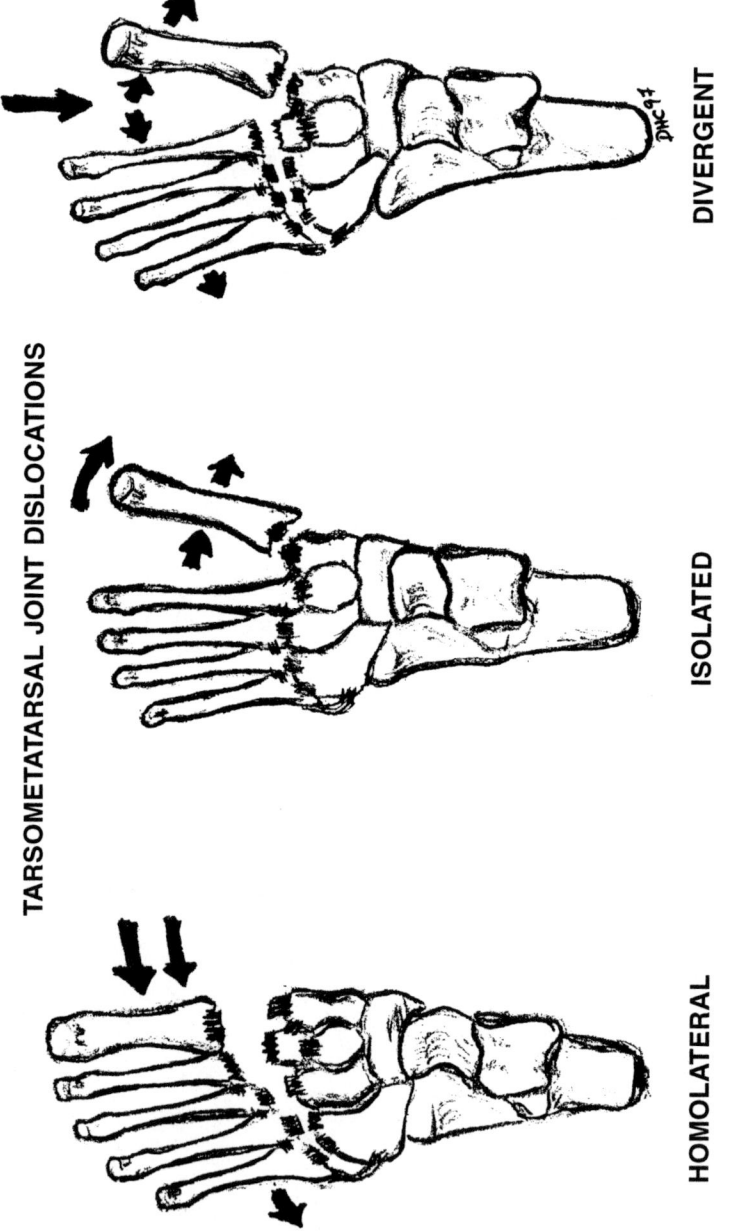

Figure 11.51
Tarso-metatarsal joint fracture-dislocation (Lisfranc injuries).

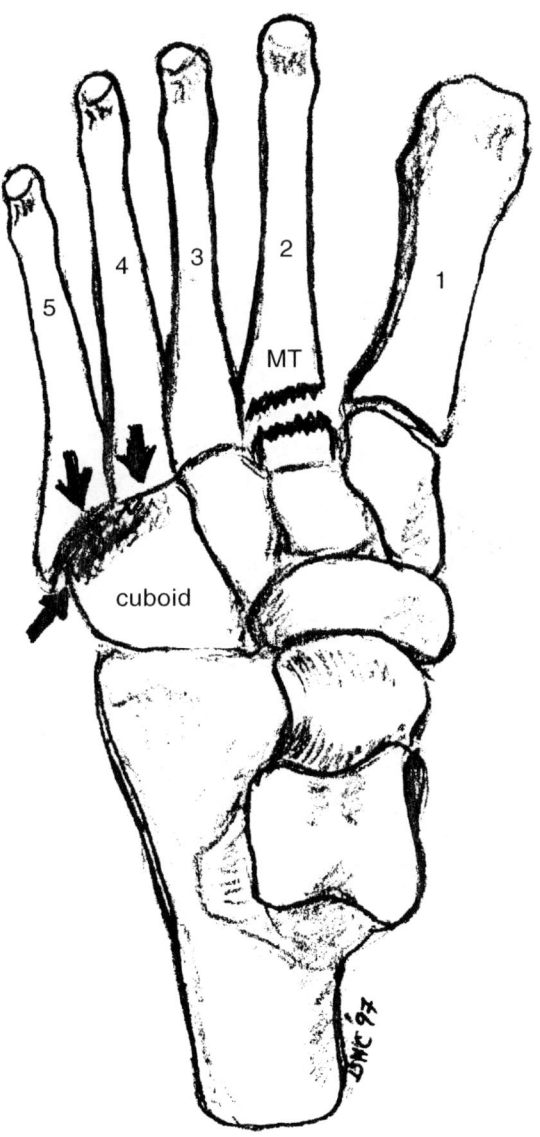

Figure 11.52
Lisfranc injury with a "nutcracker" fracture of the cuboid.

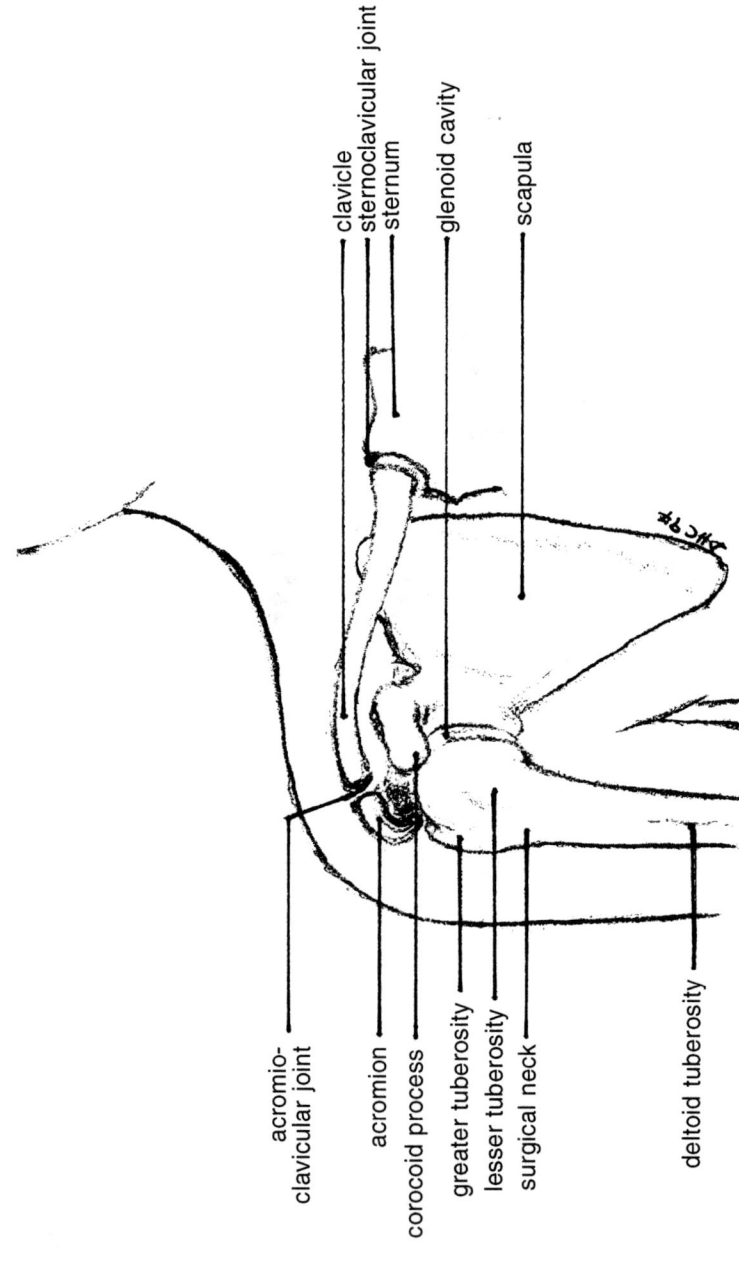

Figure 11.53
Osseus anatomy of the shoulder.

INJURIES TO THE EXTREMITIES AND PELVIS 709

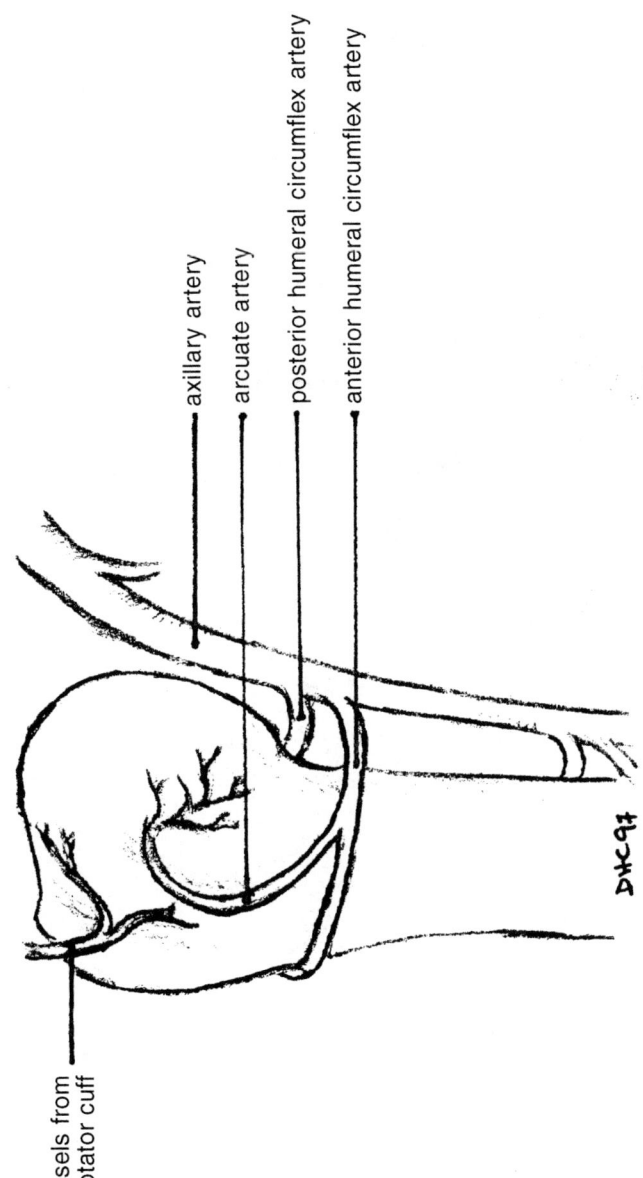

Figure 11.54
Blood supply to the humeral head.

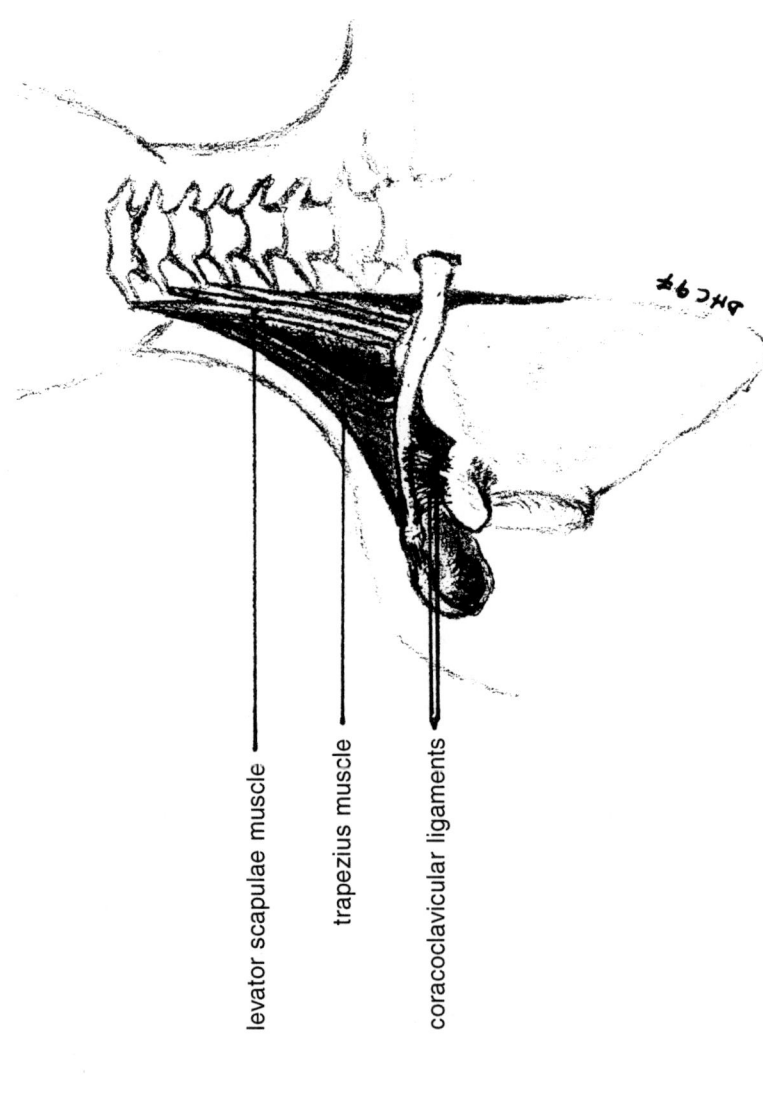

Figure 11.55
The suspensory muscles and ligaments of the scapula.

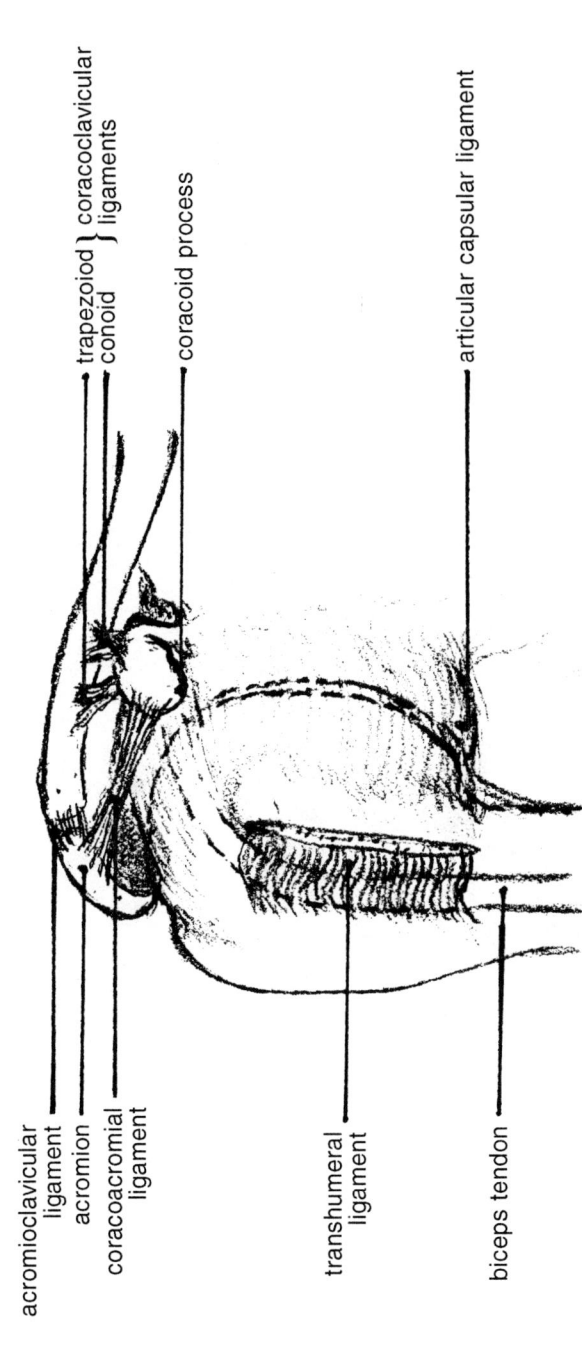

Figure 11.56A
The shoulder joint is composed of the glenohumeral joint and the acromioclavicular joints. The glenohumeral joint is a ball and socket type of articulation but it has a very shallow socket requiring strong tendons (the rotator cuff) and capsular ligaments for stability. Anteroposterior view.

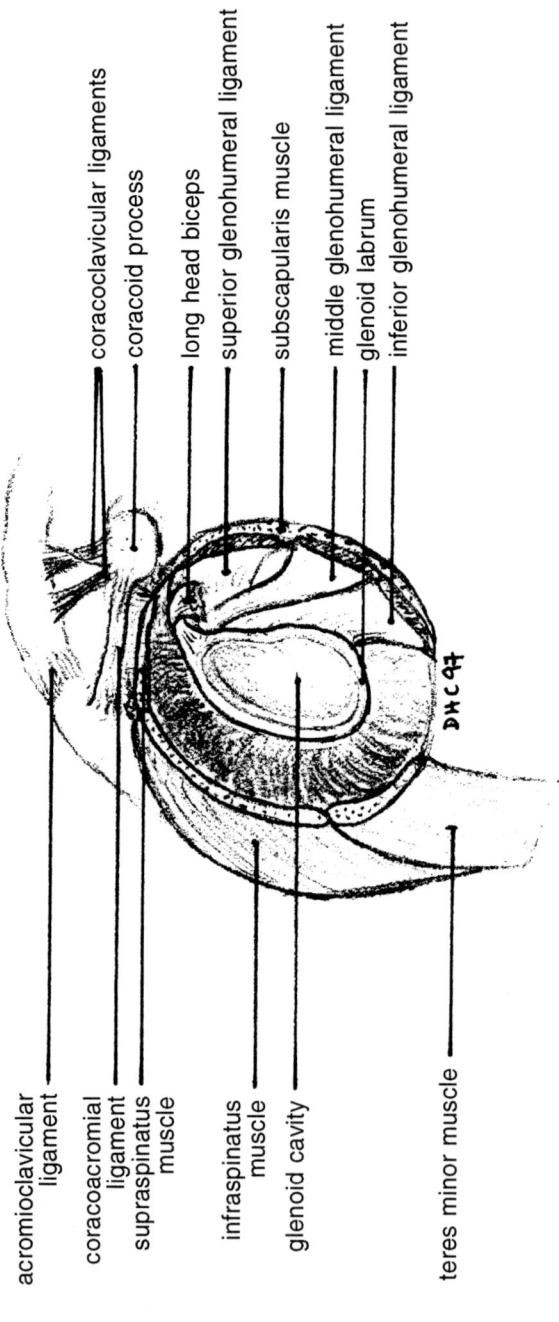

Figure 11.56B
The shoulder joint is composed of the glenohumeral joint and the acromioclavicular joints. The glenohumeral joint is a ball and socket type of articulation but it has a very shallow socket requiring strong tendons (the rotator cuff) and capsular ligaments for stability. End on view of the glenoid with the humeral head removed.

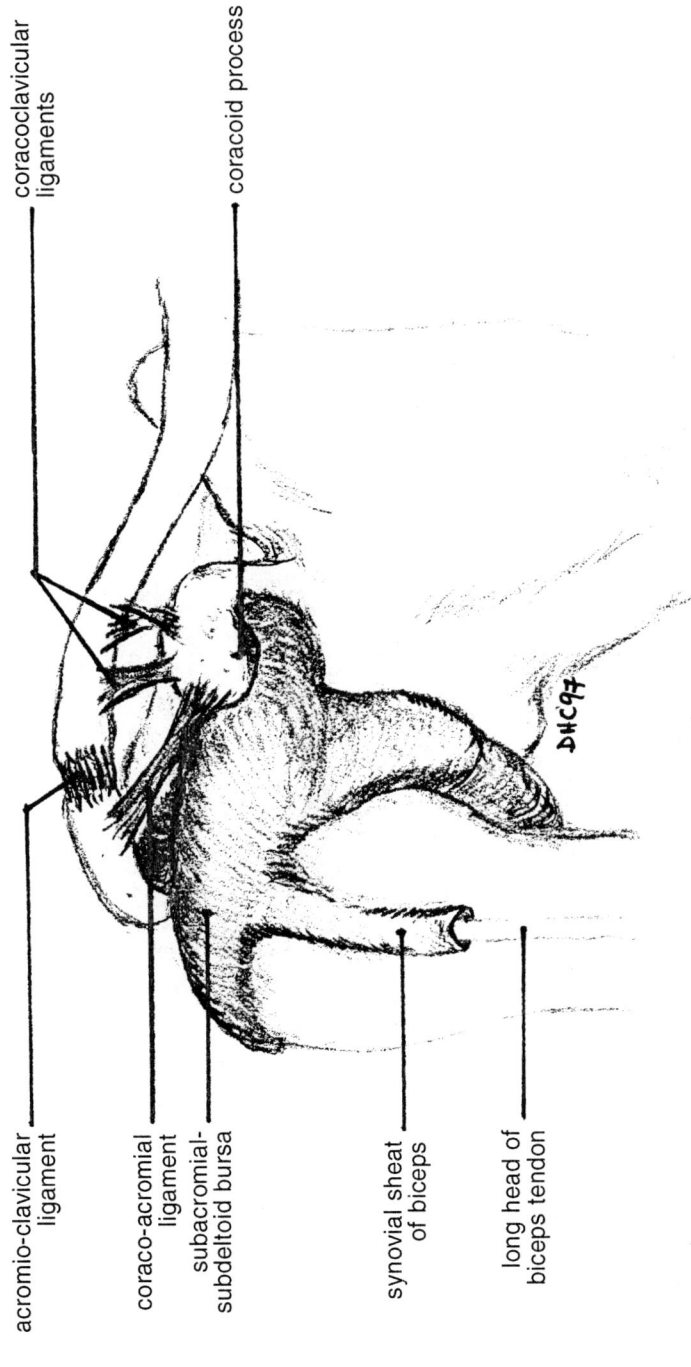

Figure 11.57
The subacromial-subdeltoid bursa.

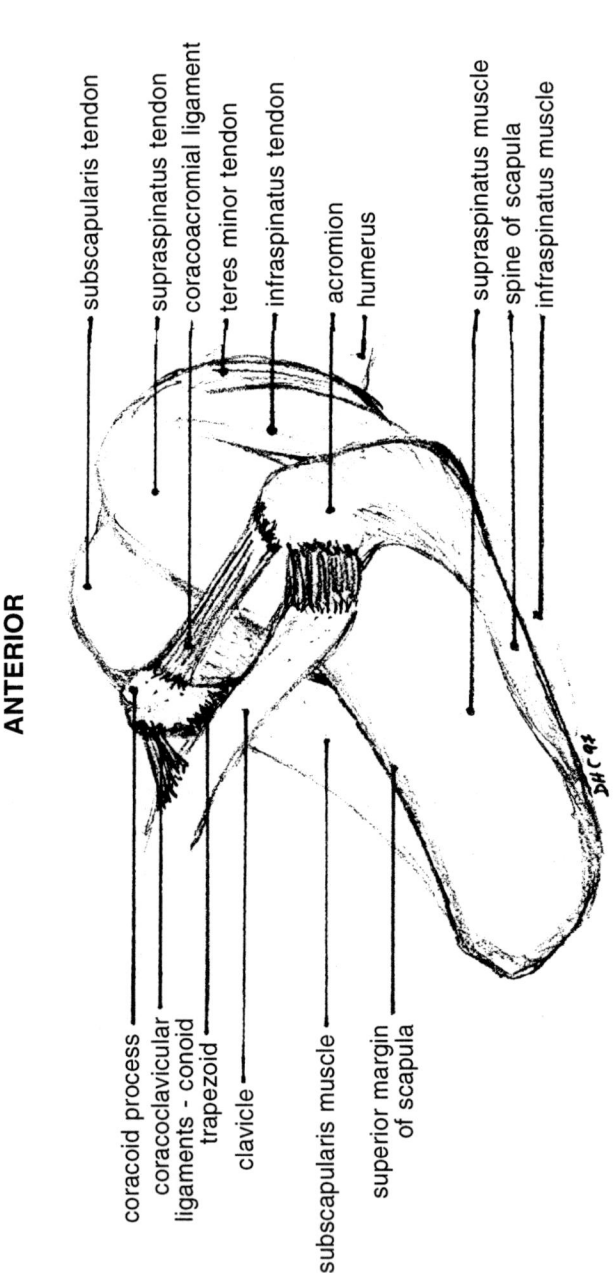

Figure 11.58
The rotator cuff (subscapularis + supraspinatus + infraspinatus + teres minor) viewed from above. Relationship to the scapula, clavicle, acromion and coracoid.

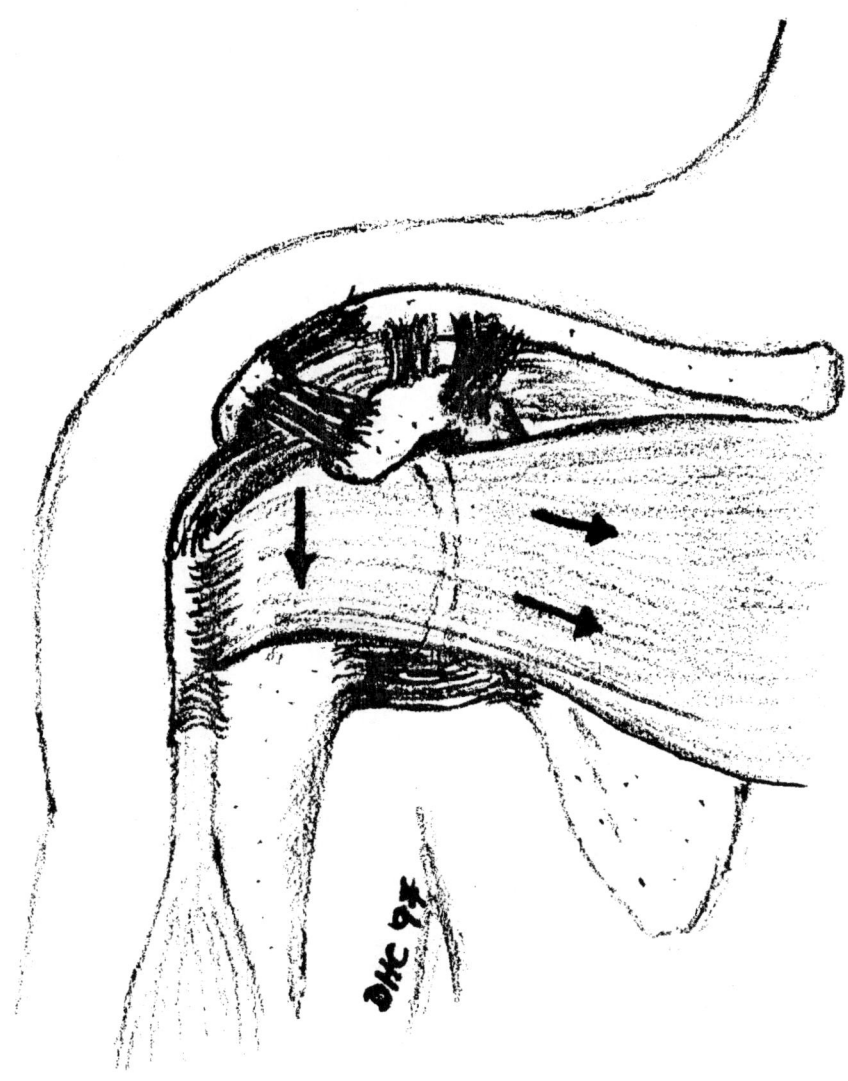

Figure 11.59
The subscapularis tendon of the rotator cuff anterior to the glenohumeral joint.

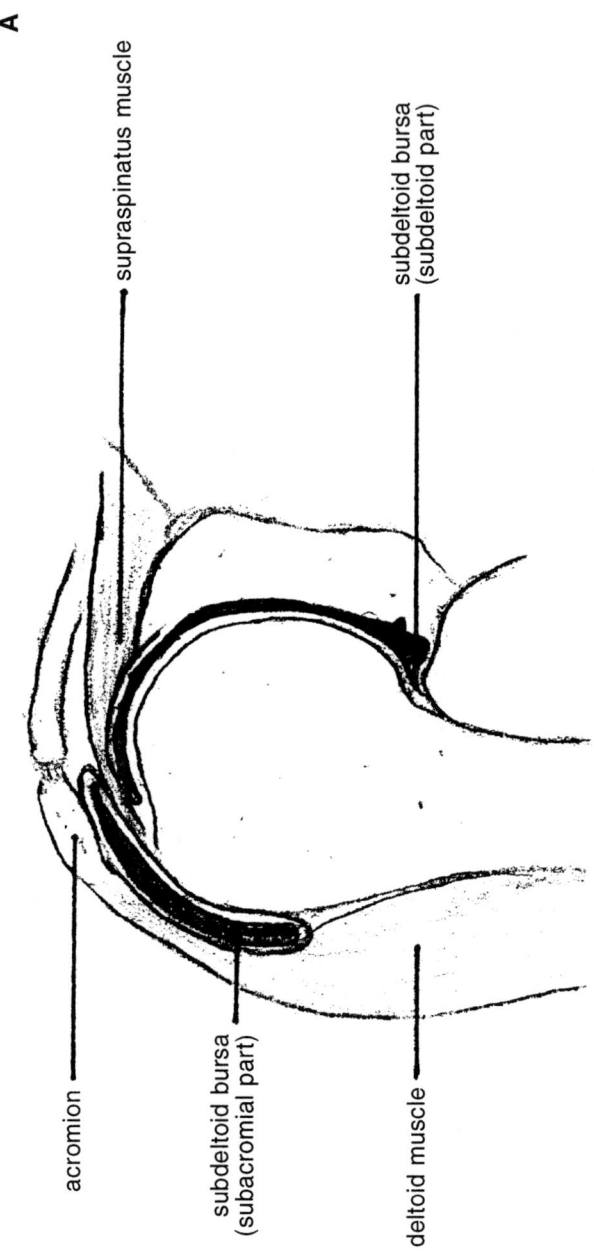

Figure 11.60 (continued on next page)
The deltoid muscle: anteroposterior view.

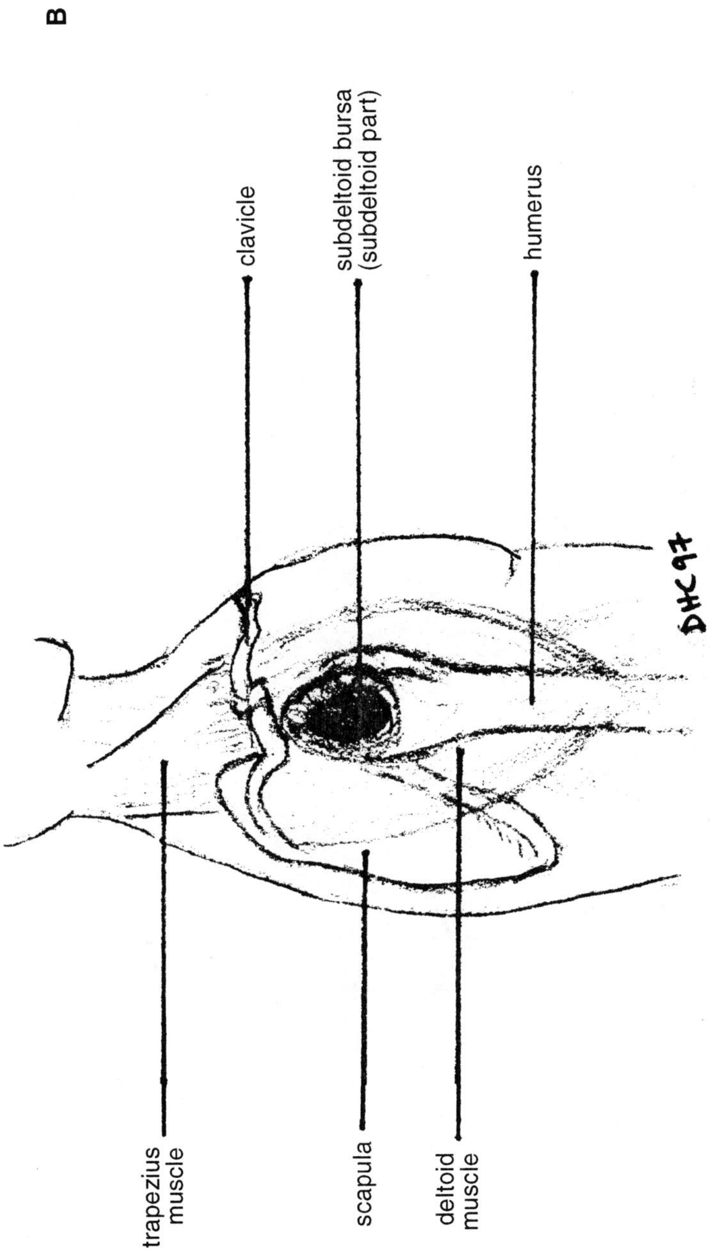

Injuries to the Extremities and Pelvis 717

Figure 11.60 (continued from previous page)
The deltoid muscle: lateral view.

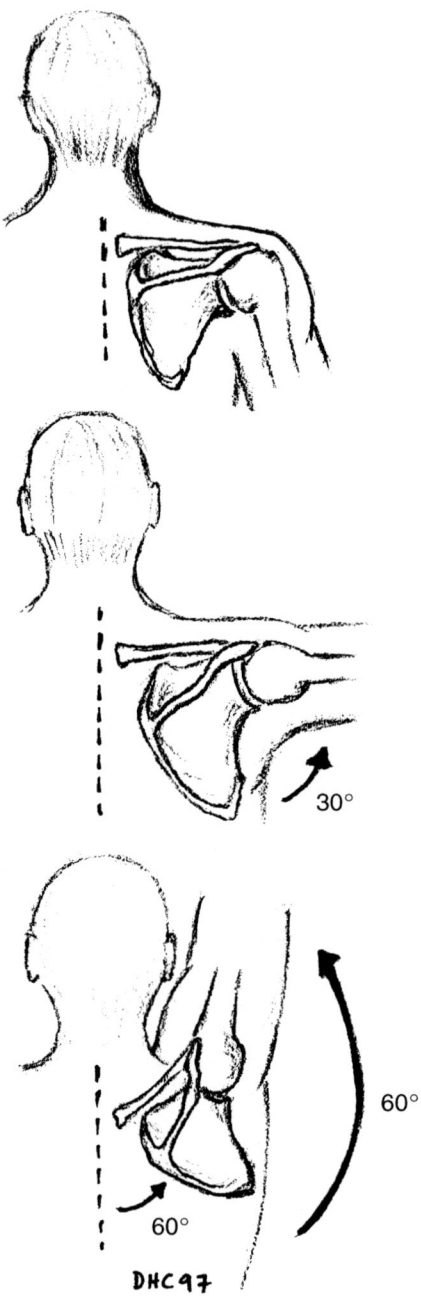

Figure 11.61
Elevation of the arm (abduction): proportion of scapulothoracic and glenohumeral motion.

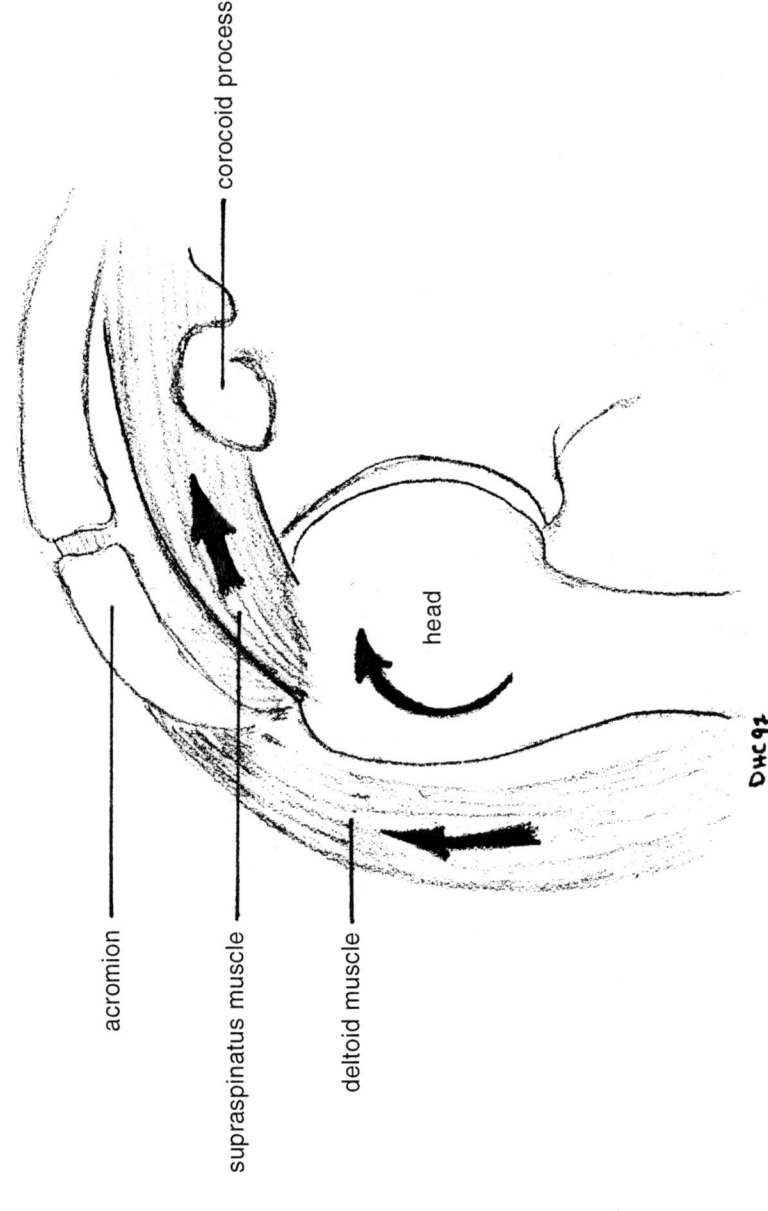

Figure 11.62
Abduction of the glenohumeral joint is done by the supraspinatus and the deltoid muscles.

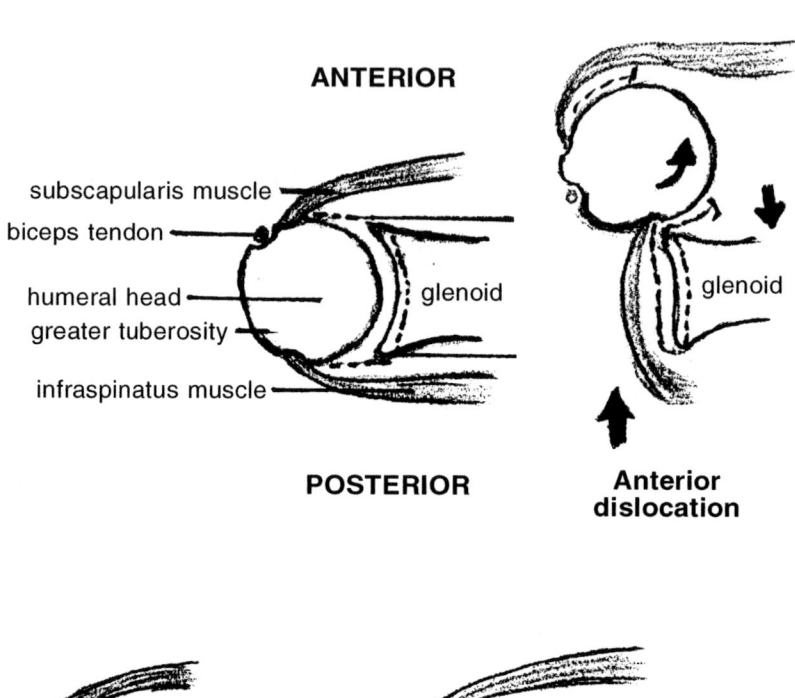

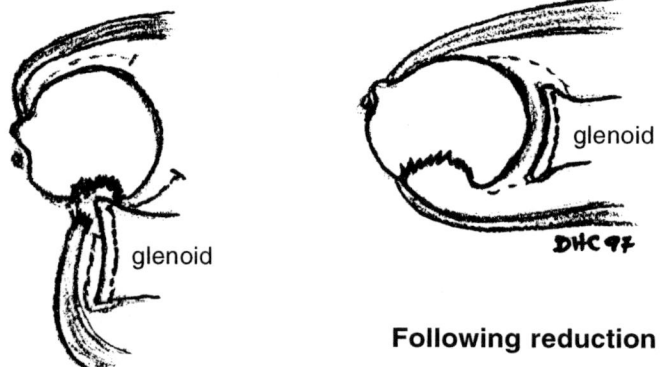

Figure 11.63
Hill-Sachs lesion of the humeral head. Caused by the impaction of the humeral head against the corner of the glenoid when the head is dislocated.

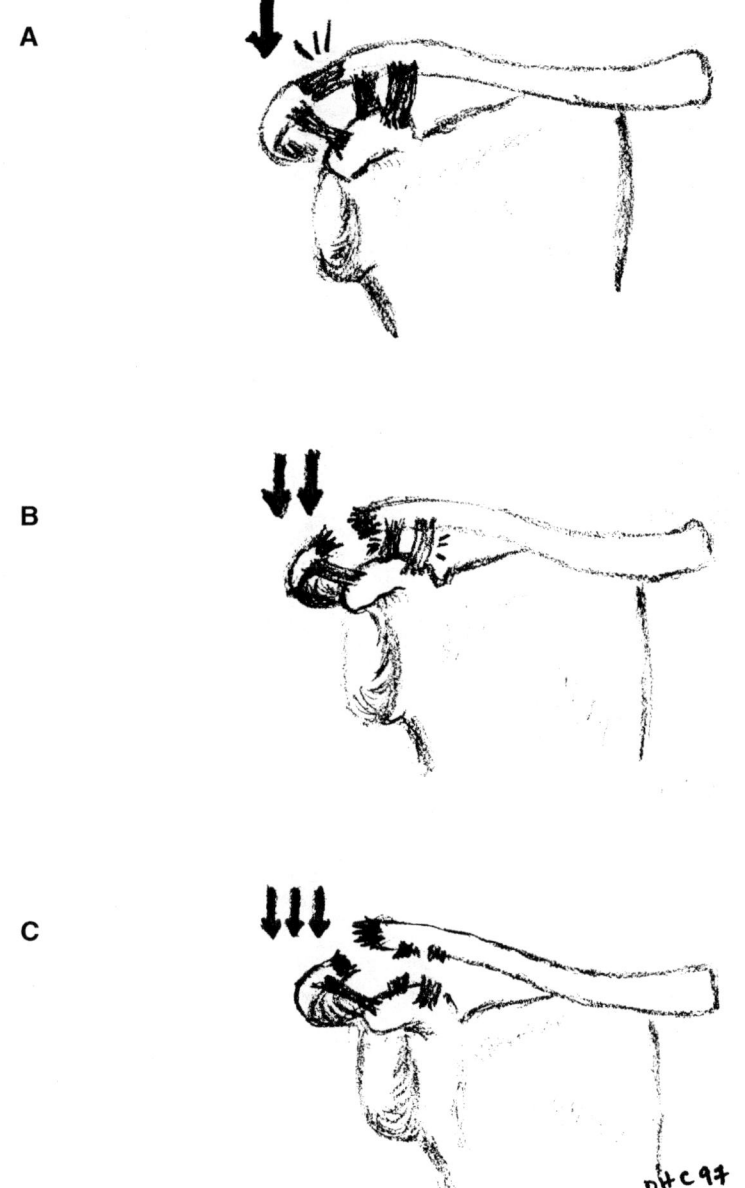

Figure 11.64
Acromio-clavicular joint disruption ("shoulder separation"). **A:** *Grade I: strain of the AC ligaments.* **B:** *Grade II: tear of the AC ligaments.* **C:** *Grade III: tear of the AC ligaments and the coracoclavicular ligaments allowing the clavicle to rise.*

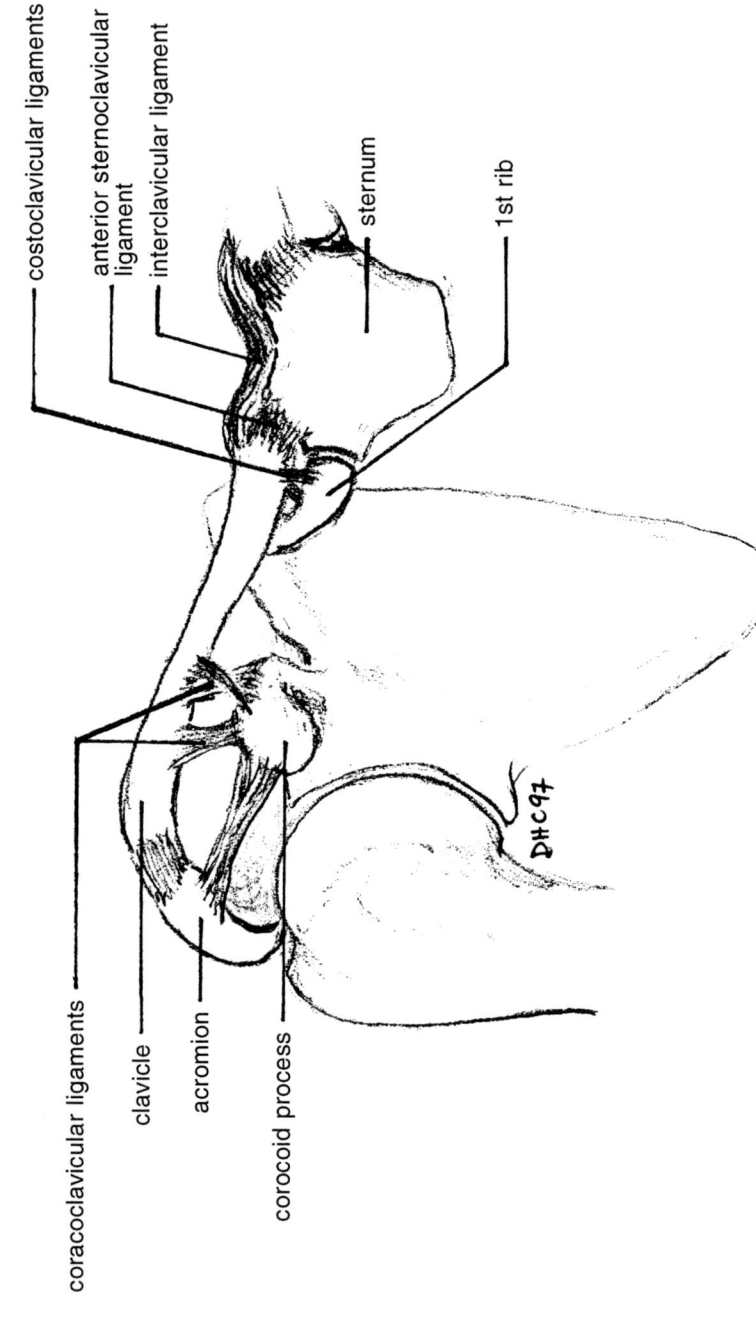

Figure 11.65
The sternoclavicular joint.

Injuries to the Extremities and Pelvis 723

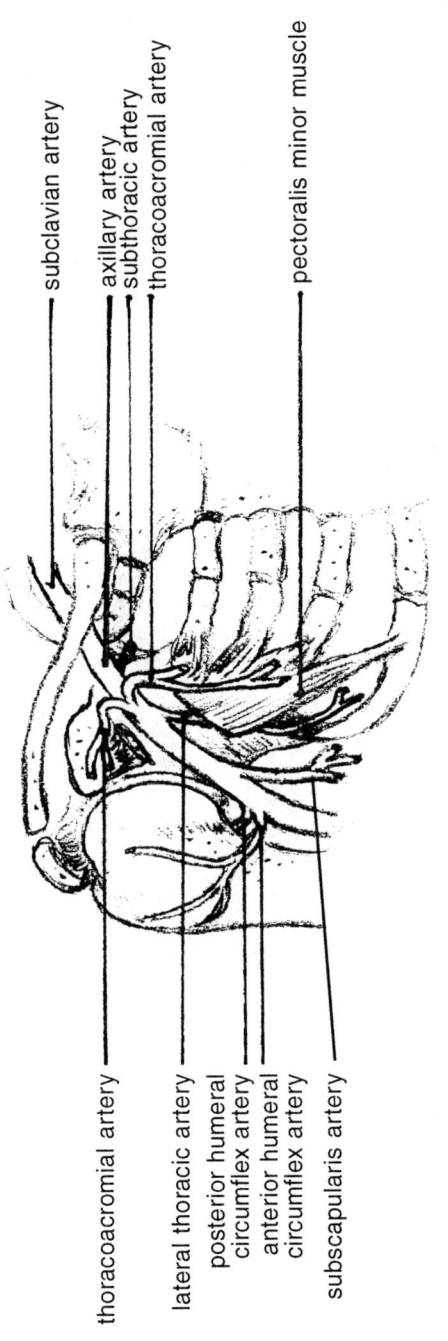

Figure 11.66A
Major arteries of the shoulder.

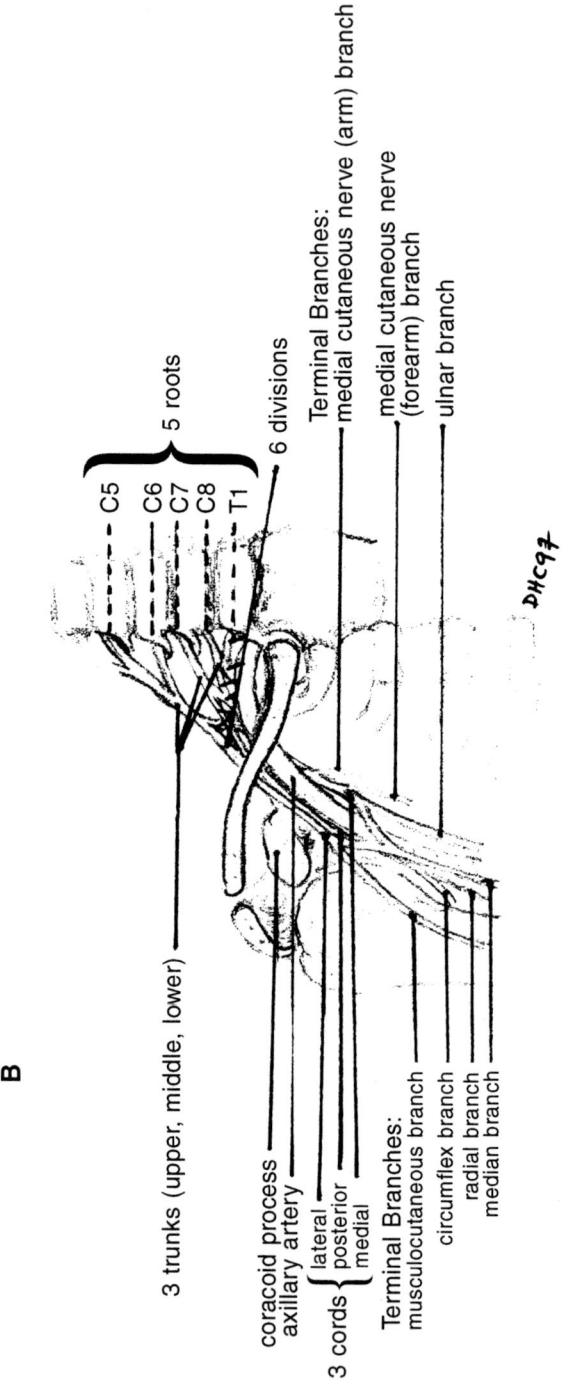

Figure 11.66B
The brachial plexus of nerves.

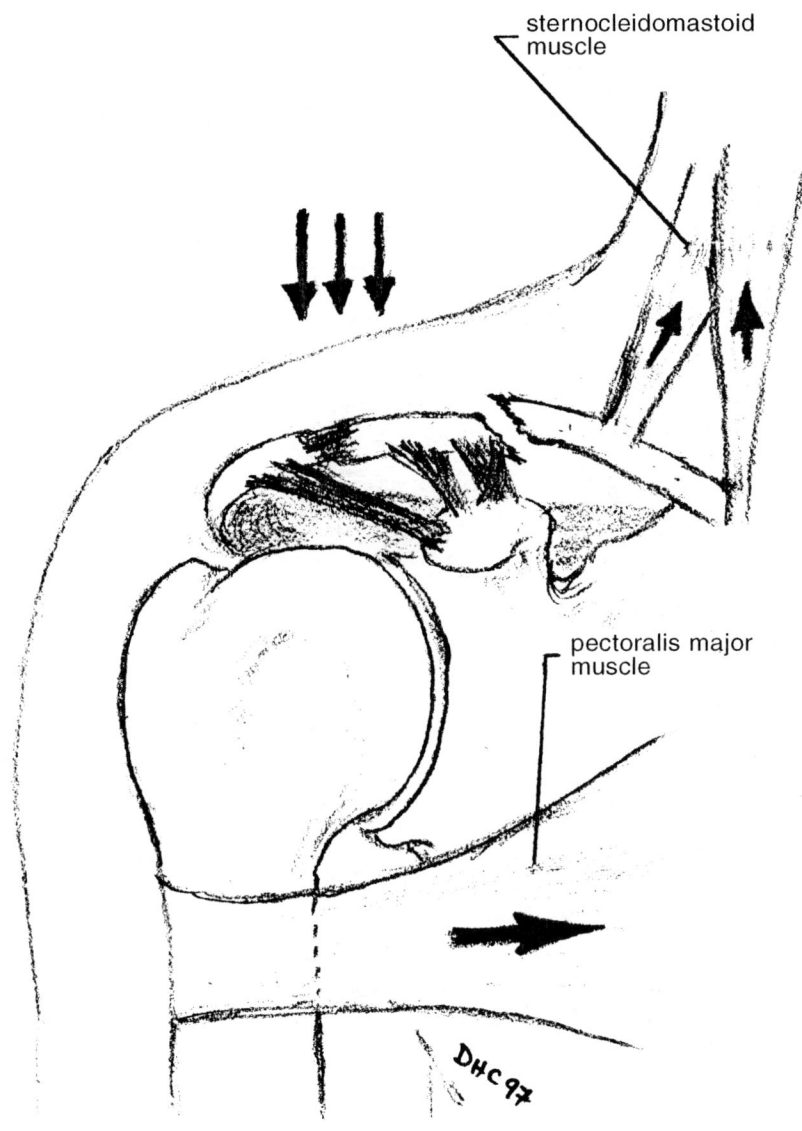

Figure 11.67
Fractures of the clavicle (middle third).

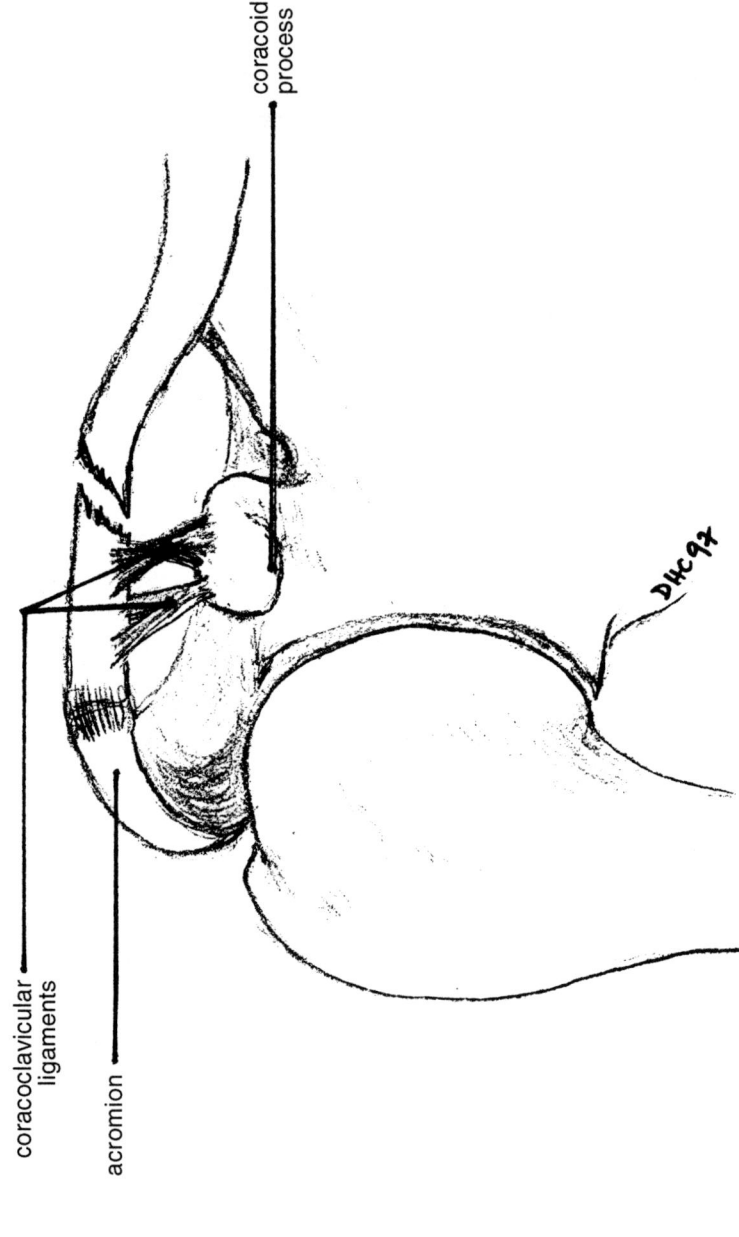

Figure 11.68
Fracture of the lateral third of the clavicle just medial to the ligaments.

INJURIES TO THE EXTREMITIES AND PELVIS 727

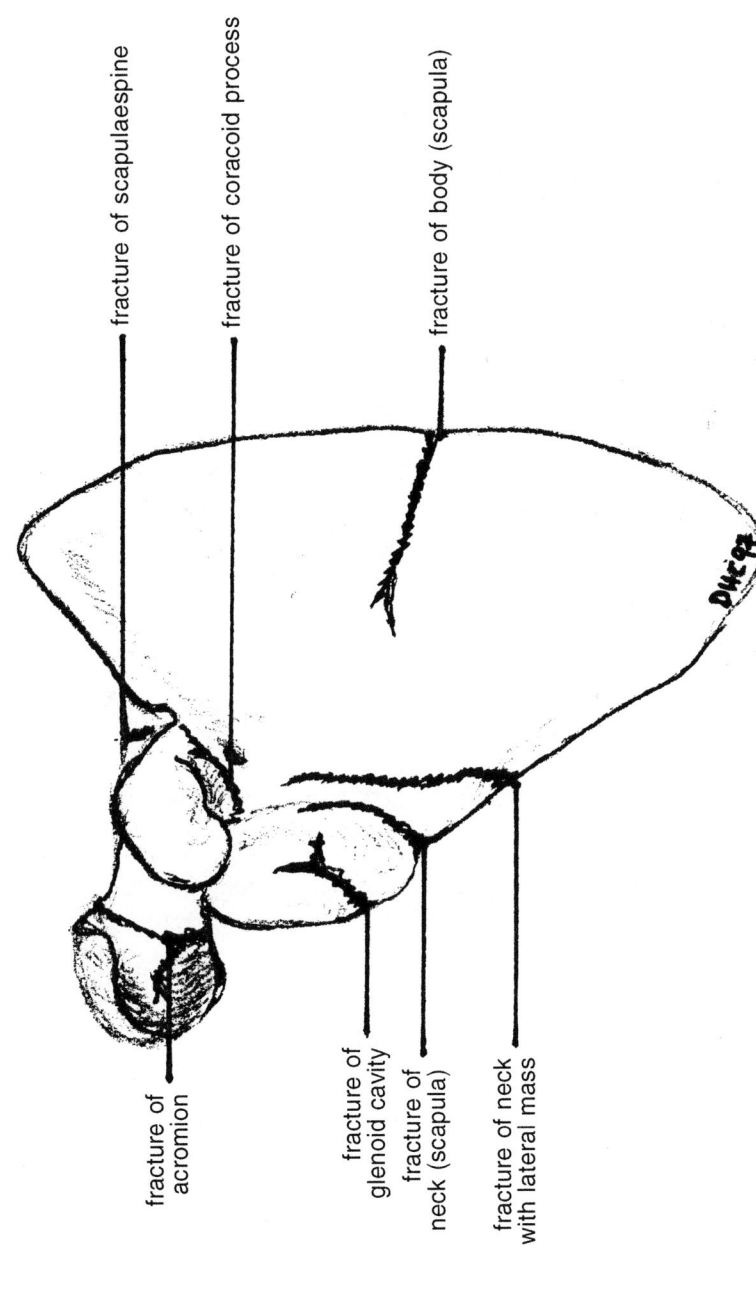

Figure 11.69
Fractures of the scapula.

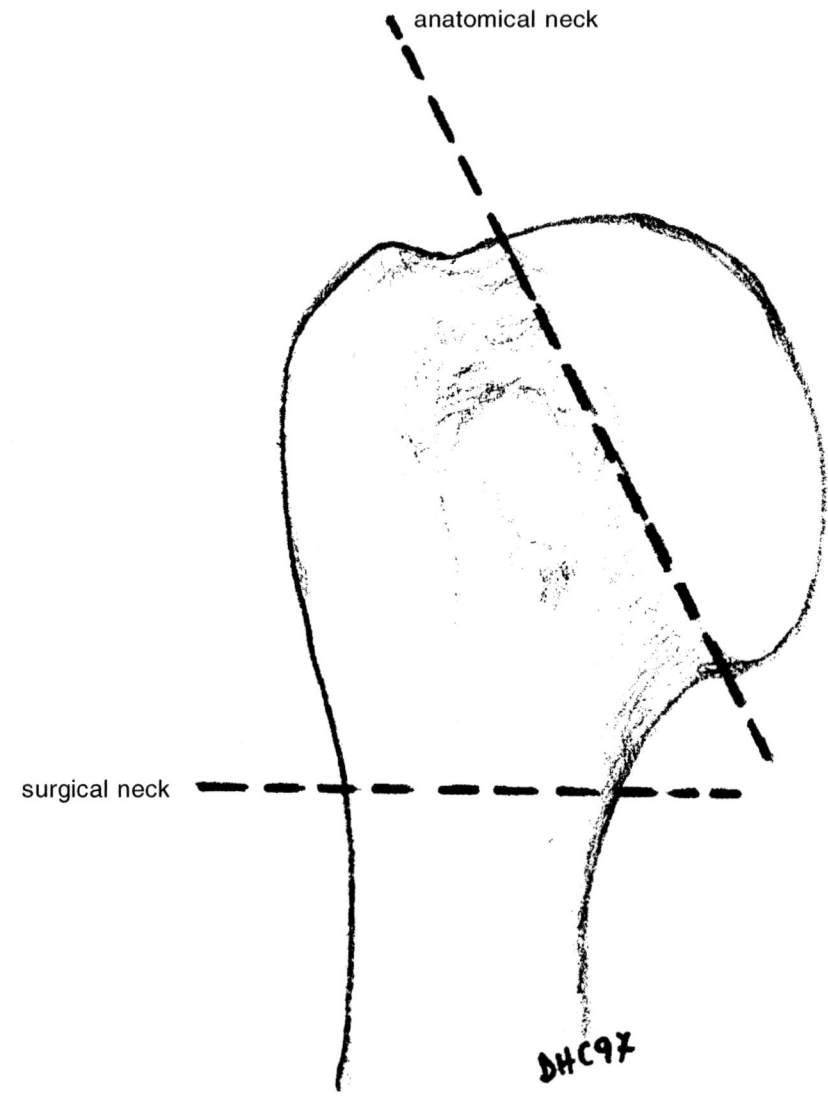

Figure 11.70
The surgical and anatomic neck of the humerus.

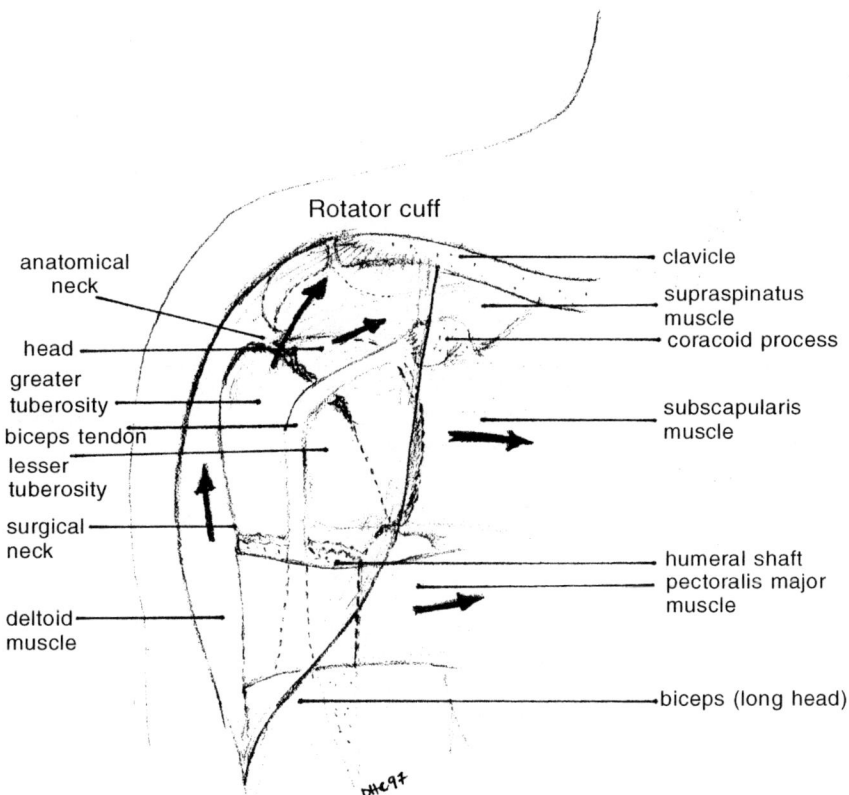

Figure 11.71
Muscles inserting of the greater tuberosities of the humeral head.

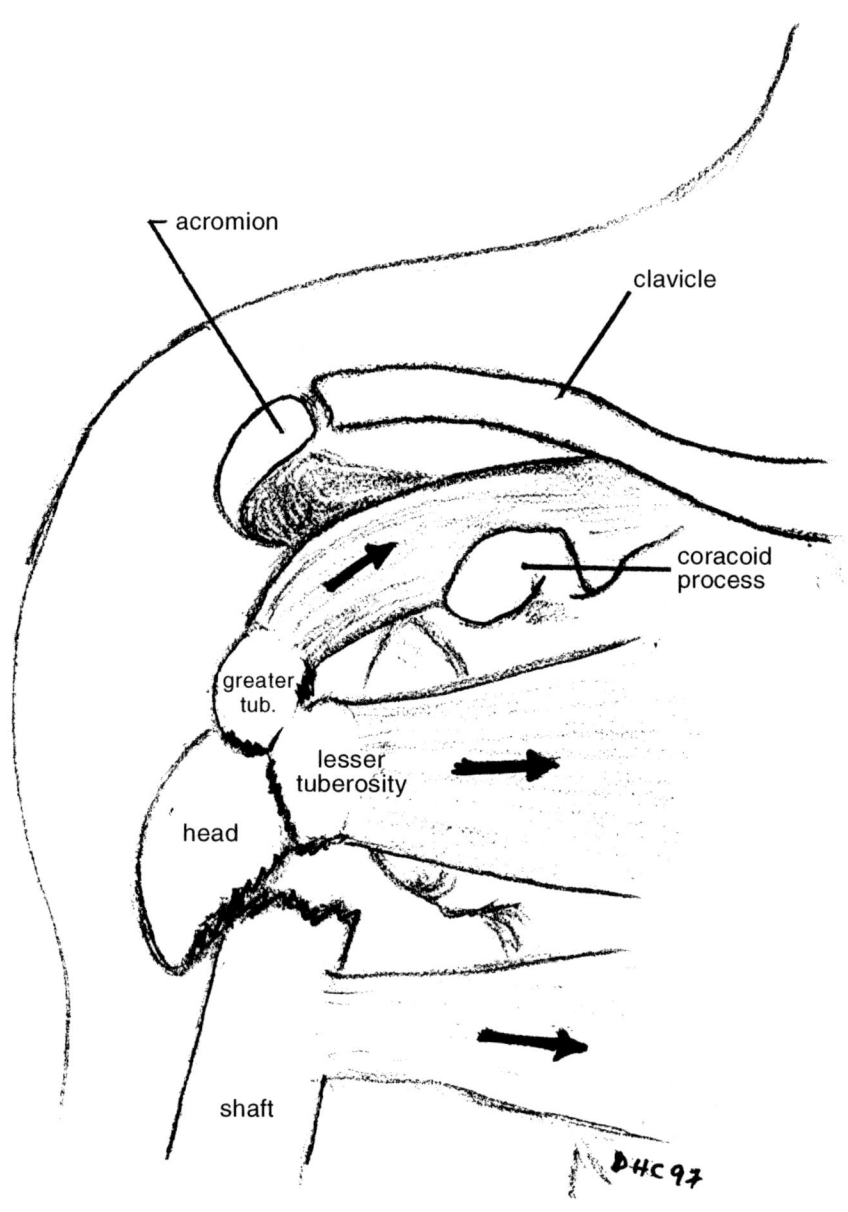

Figure 11.72
Comminuted fractures of the humeral head.

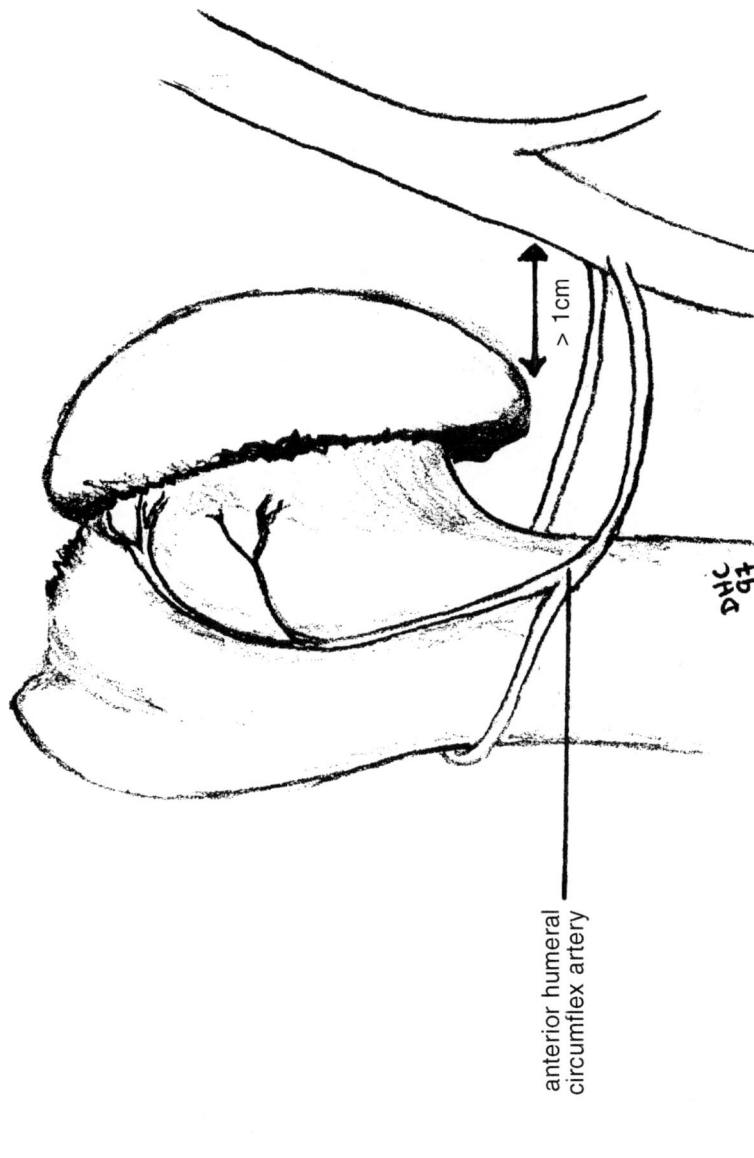

Figure 11.73
Fracture of the anatomic neck of the humerus with disruption of the blood supply to the humeral head.

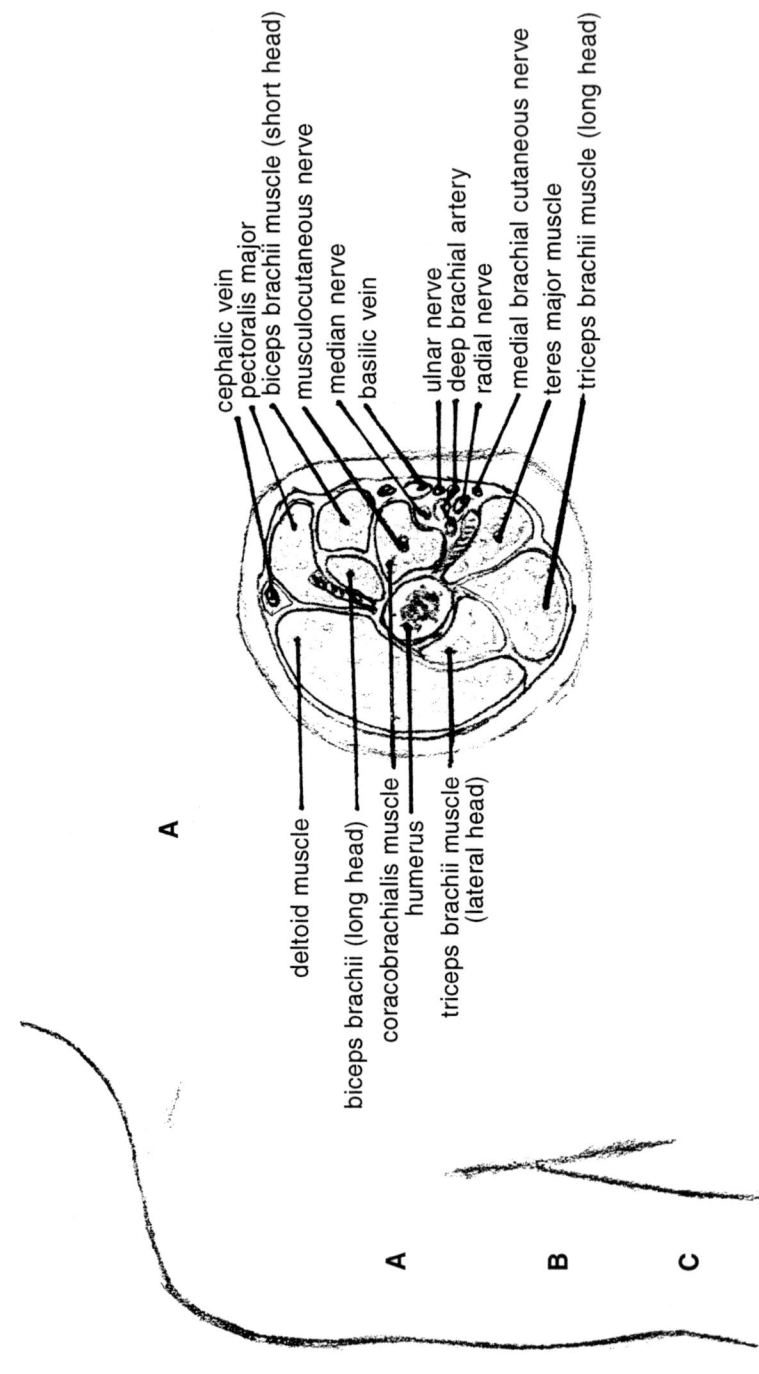

Figure 11.74 (continued on next page)
Compartments of the arm and the neurovascular structures.

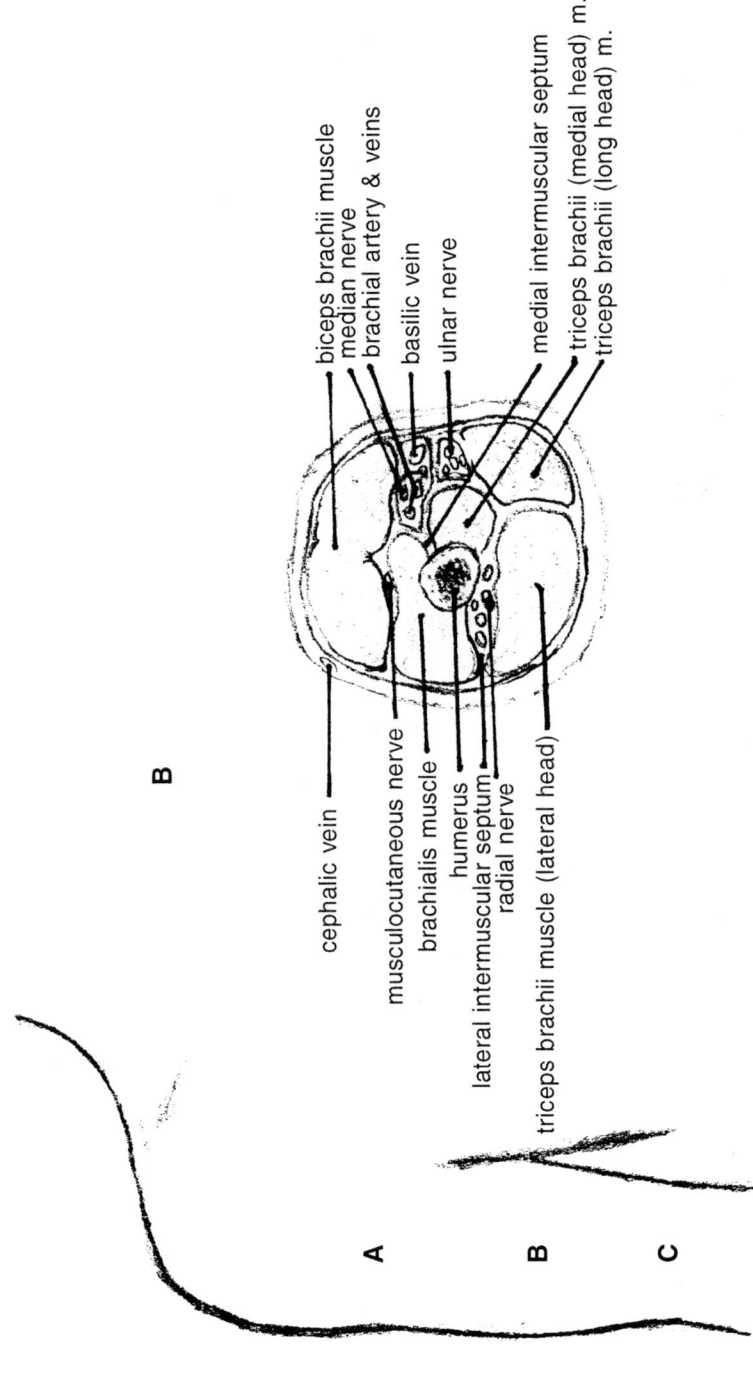

Figure 11.74 (continued from previous page; see also next page) *Compartments of the arm and the neurovascular structures.*

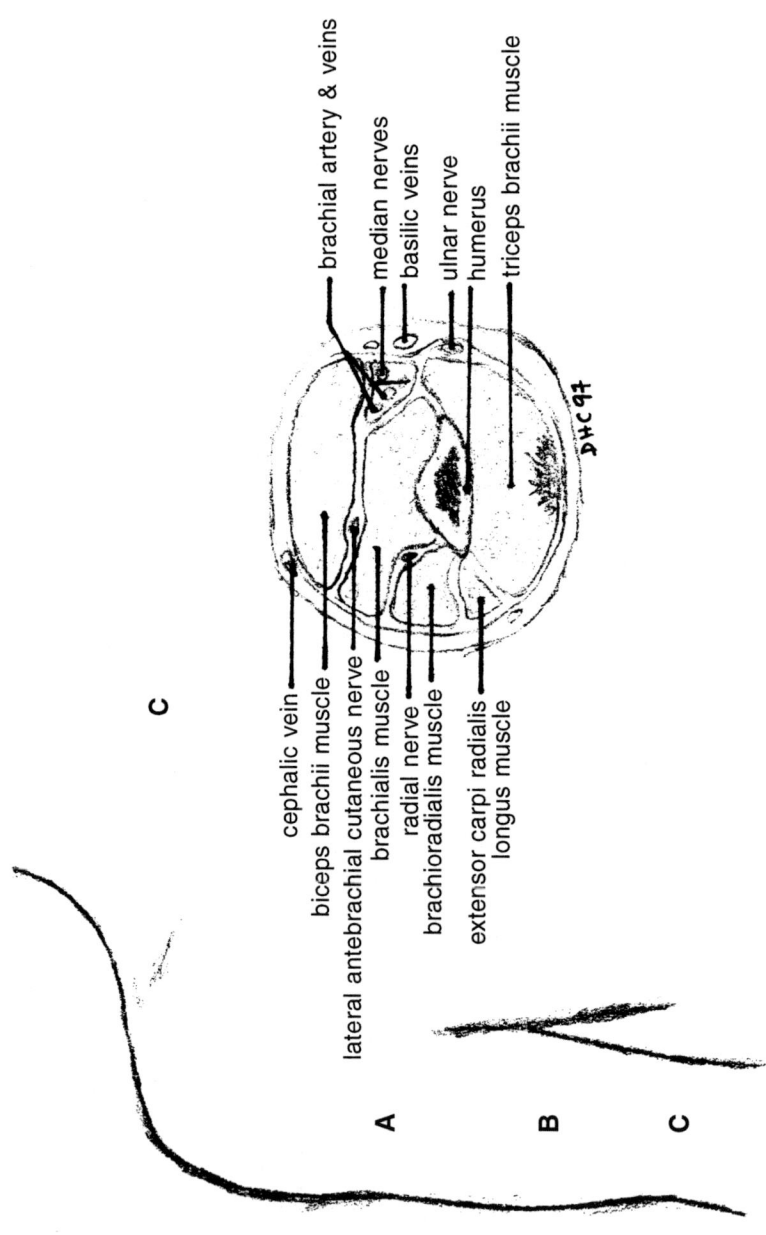

Figure 11.74 (continued from previous pages)
Compartments of the arm and the neurovascular structures.

INJURIES TO THE EXTREMITIES AND PELVIS 735

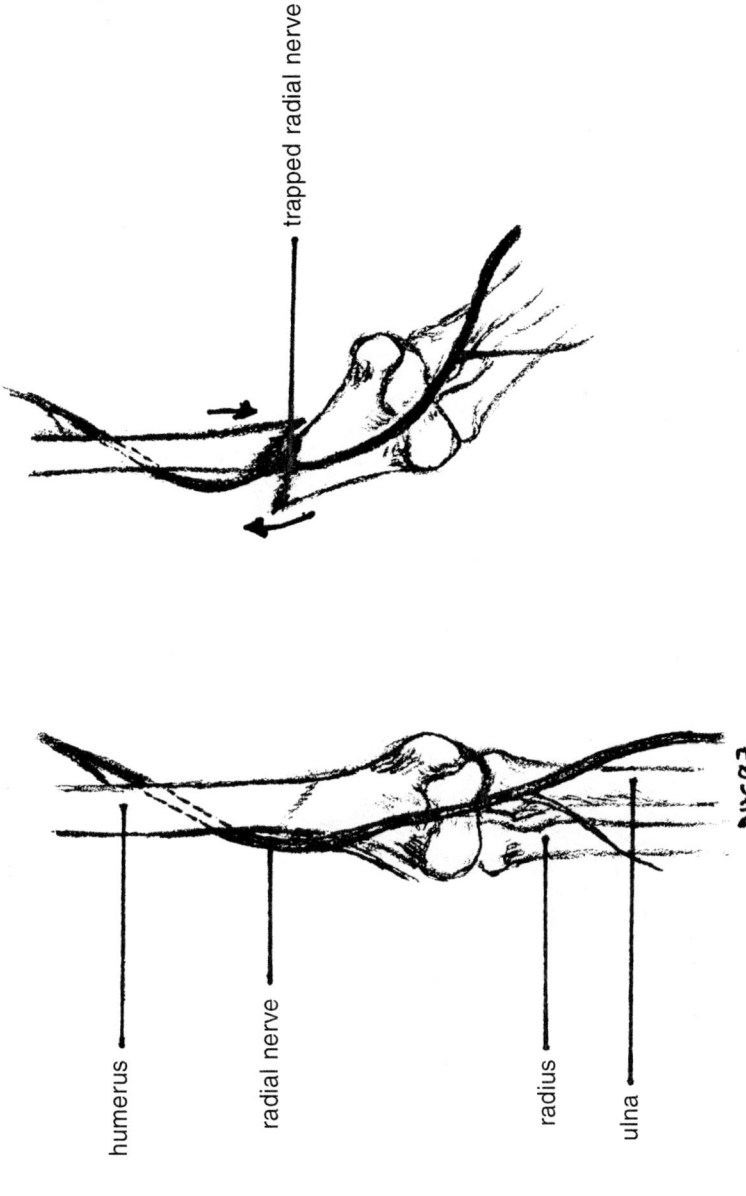

Figure 11.75
The radial nerve and a frequent site of injury with a fracture of the distal third of the humerus.

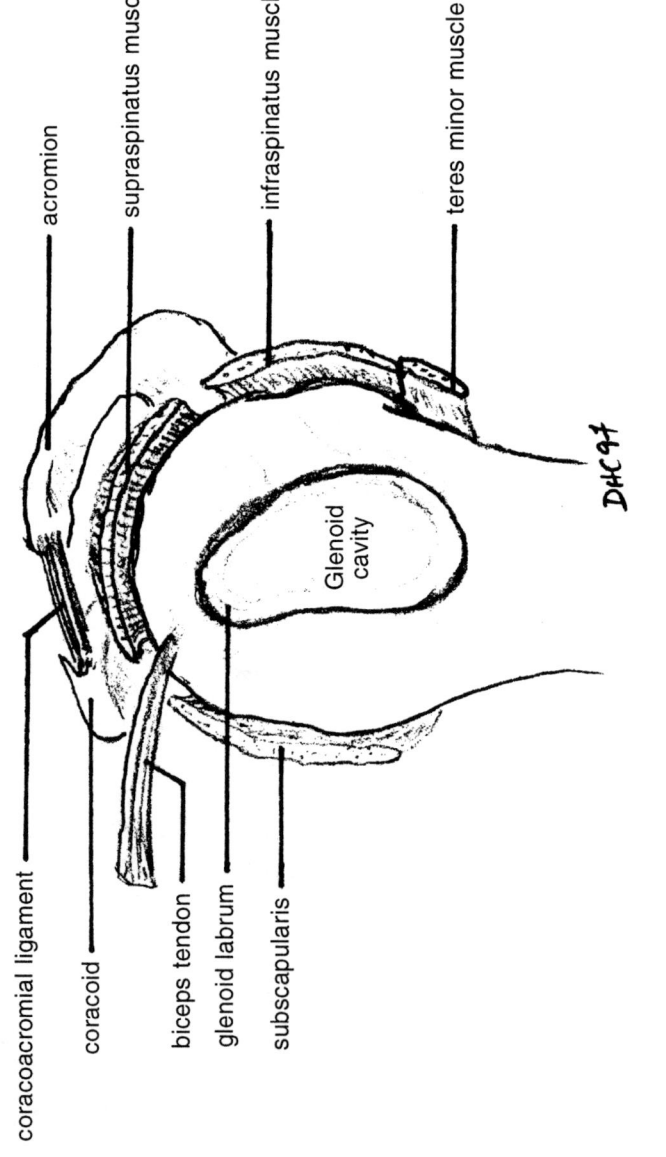

Figure 11.76
Cross section of the rotator cuff (subscapularis, supraspinatus, infraspinatus, teres minor).

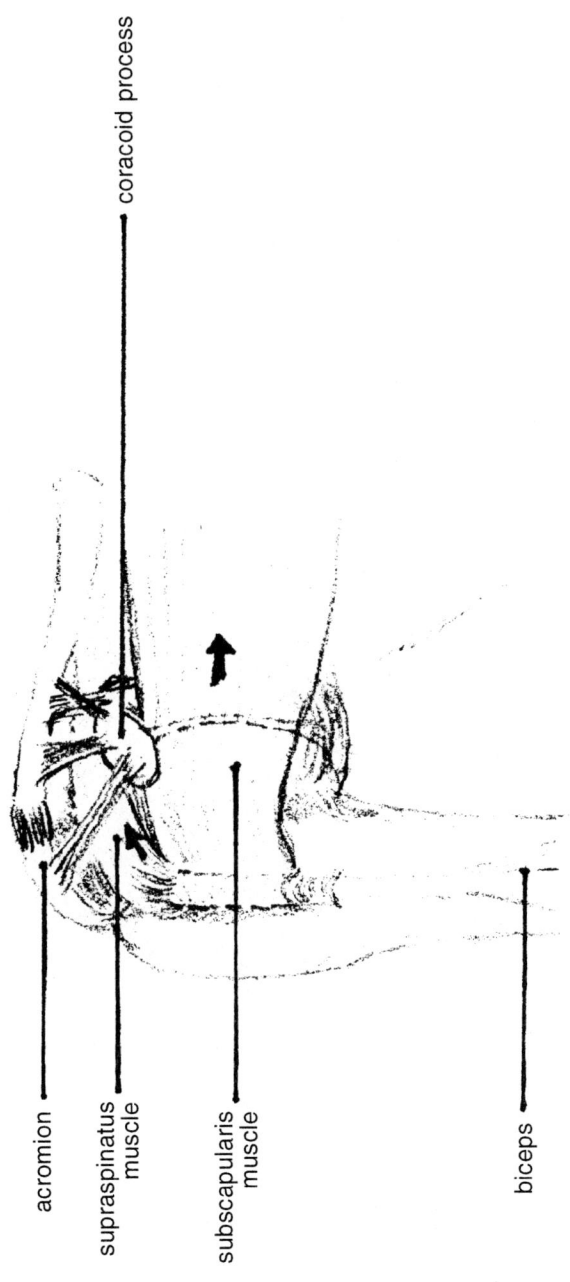

Figure 11.77 (continued on next page) *Function of the rotator cuff.*

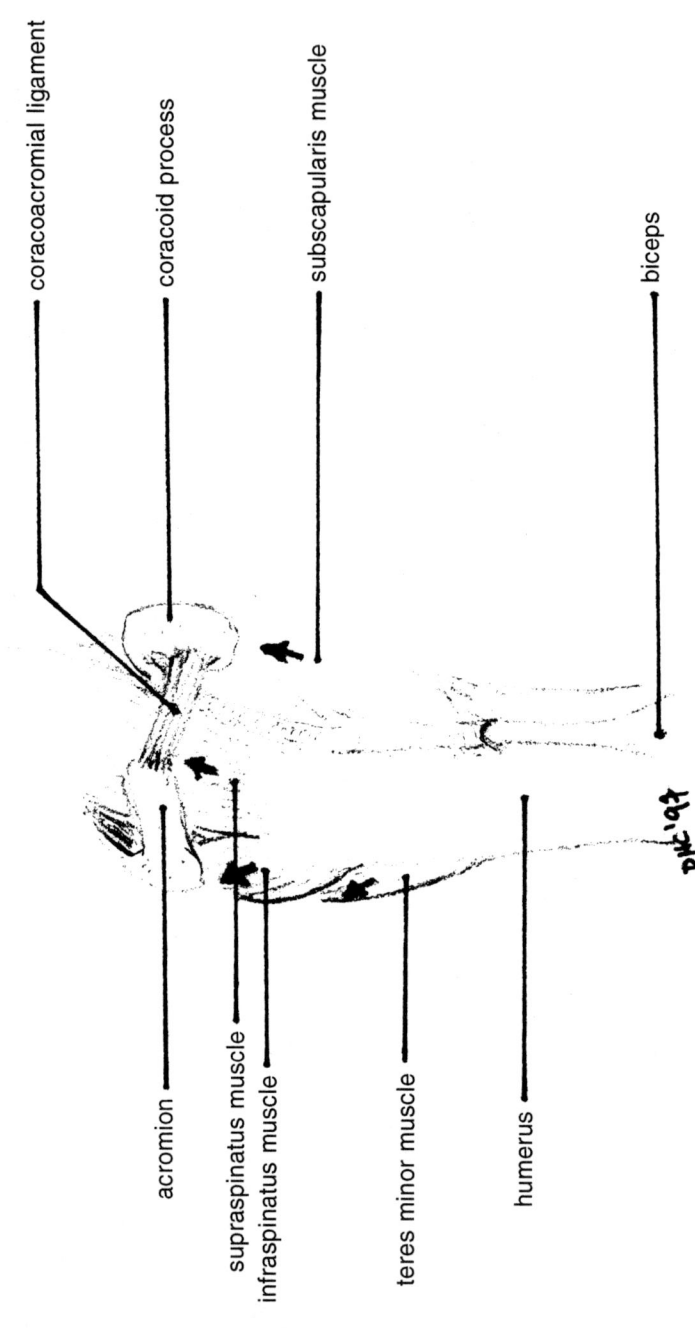

Figure 11.77 (continued from previous page)
Function of the rotator cuff.

INJURIES TO THE EXTREMITIES AND PELVIS   739

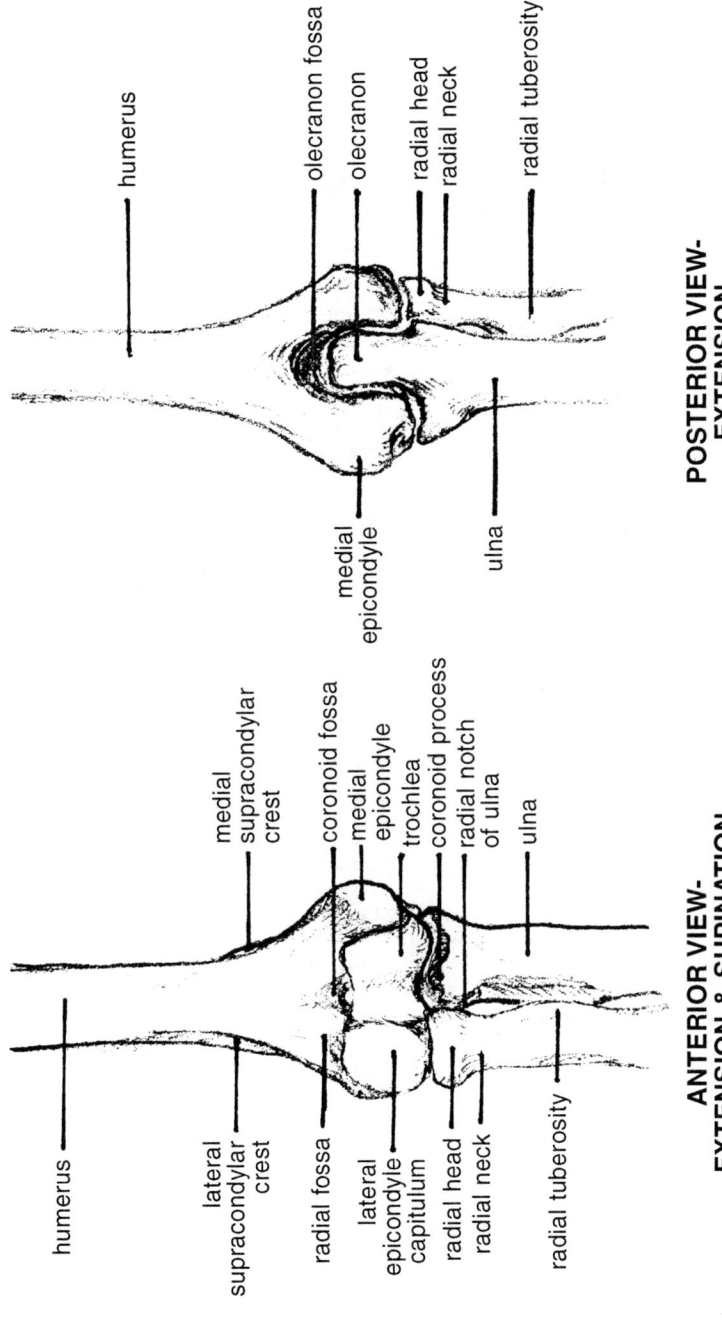

Figure 11.78A
Osseus anatomy of the elbow. Antero-posterior view.

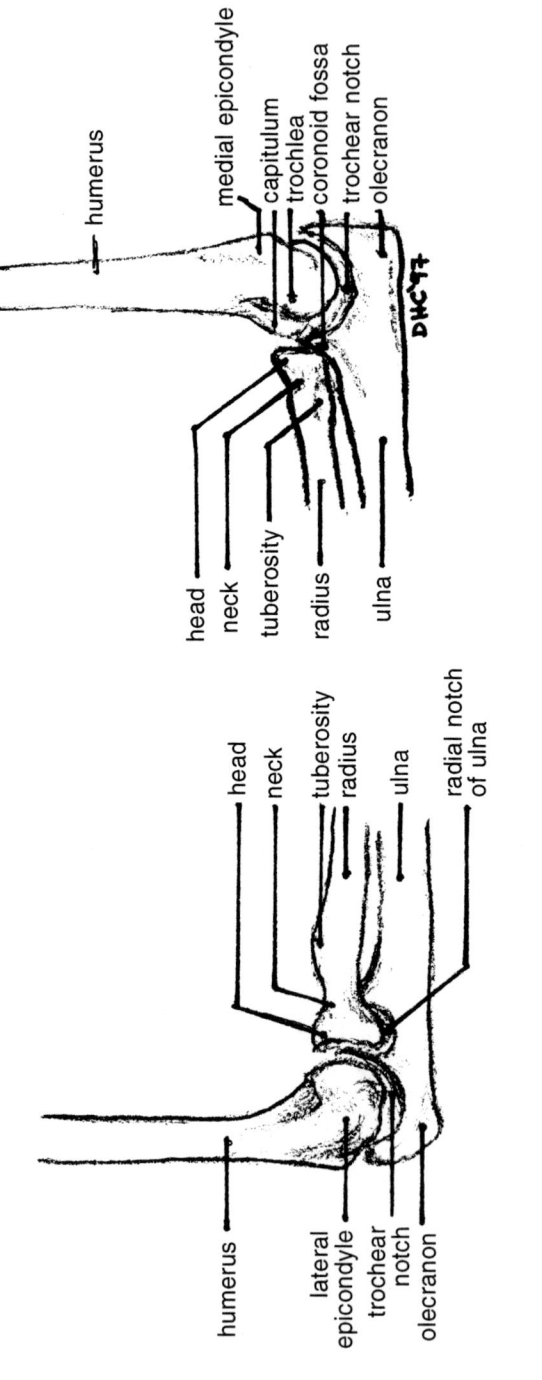

Figure 11.78B
Osseus anatomy of the elbow. Lateral view.

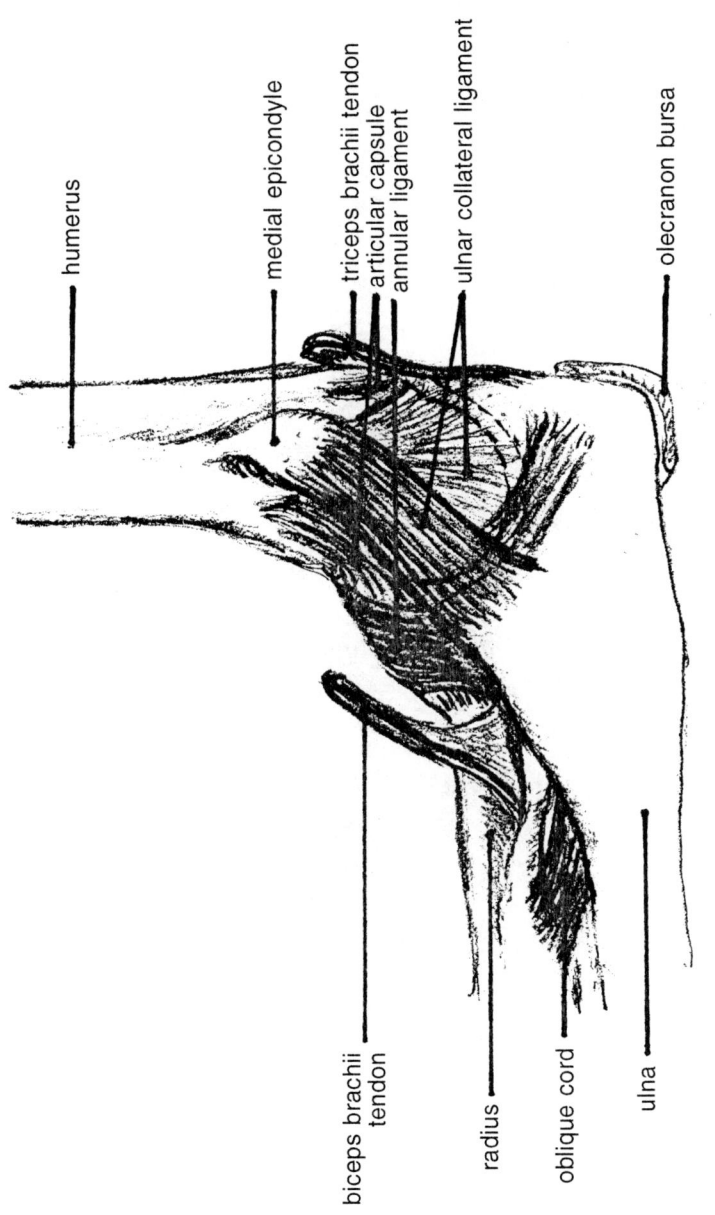

Figure 11.79 (continued on next page)
Ligamentous support of the elbow joint.

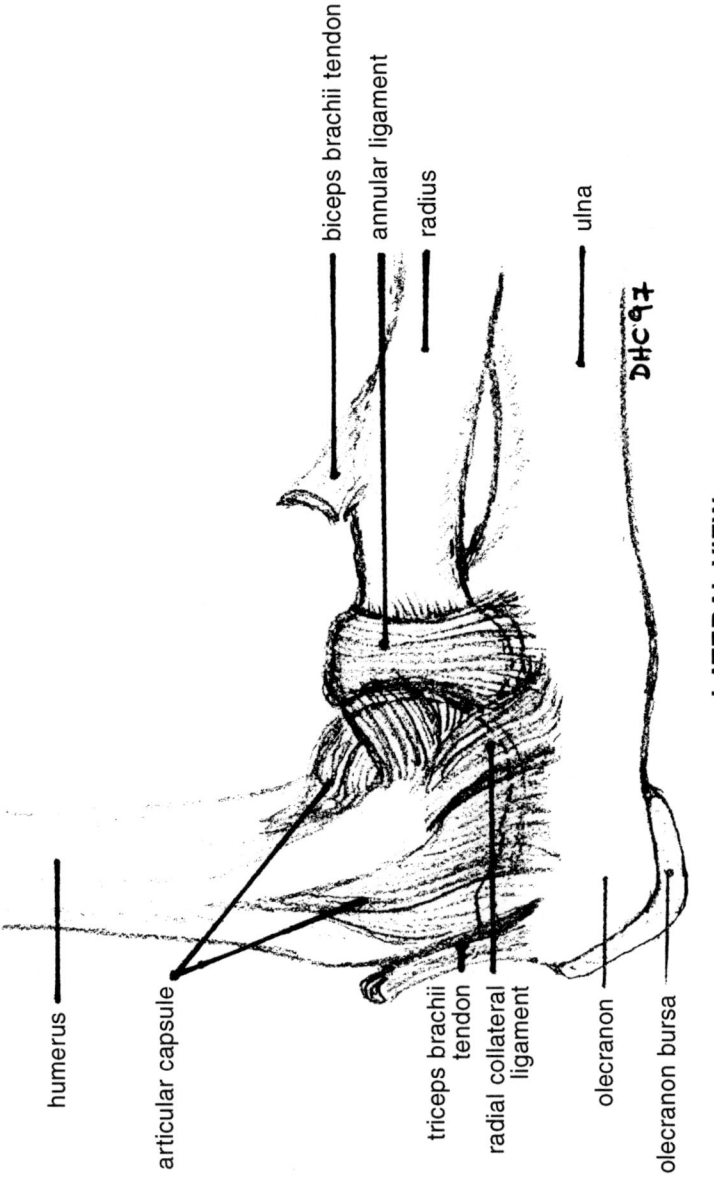

Figure 11.79 (continued from previous page)
Ligamentous support of the elbow joint.

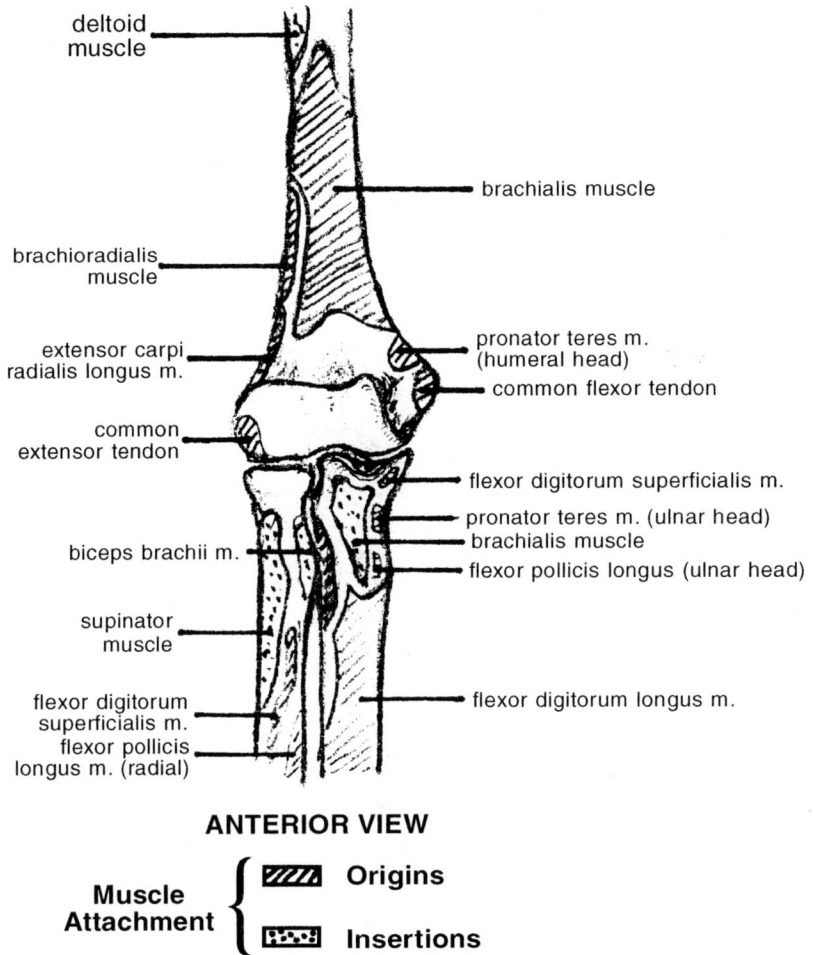

Figure 11.80 (continued on next page)
Muscles originating and inserting around the elbow.

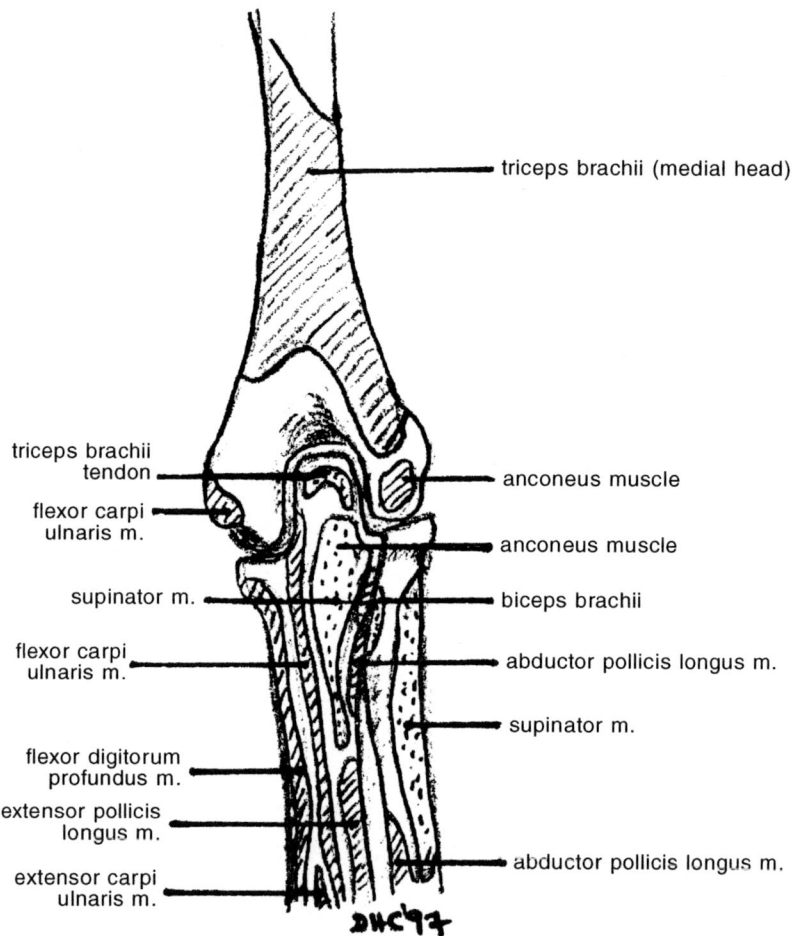

Figure 11.80 (continued from previous page)
Muscles originating and inserting around the elbow.

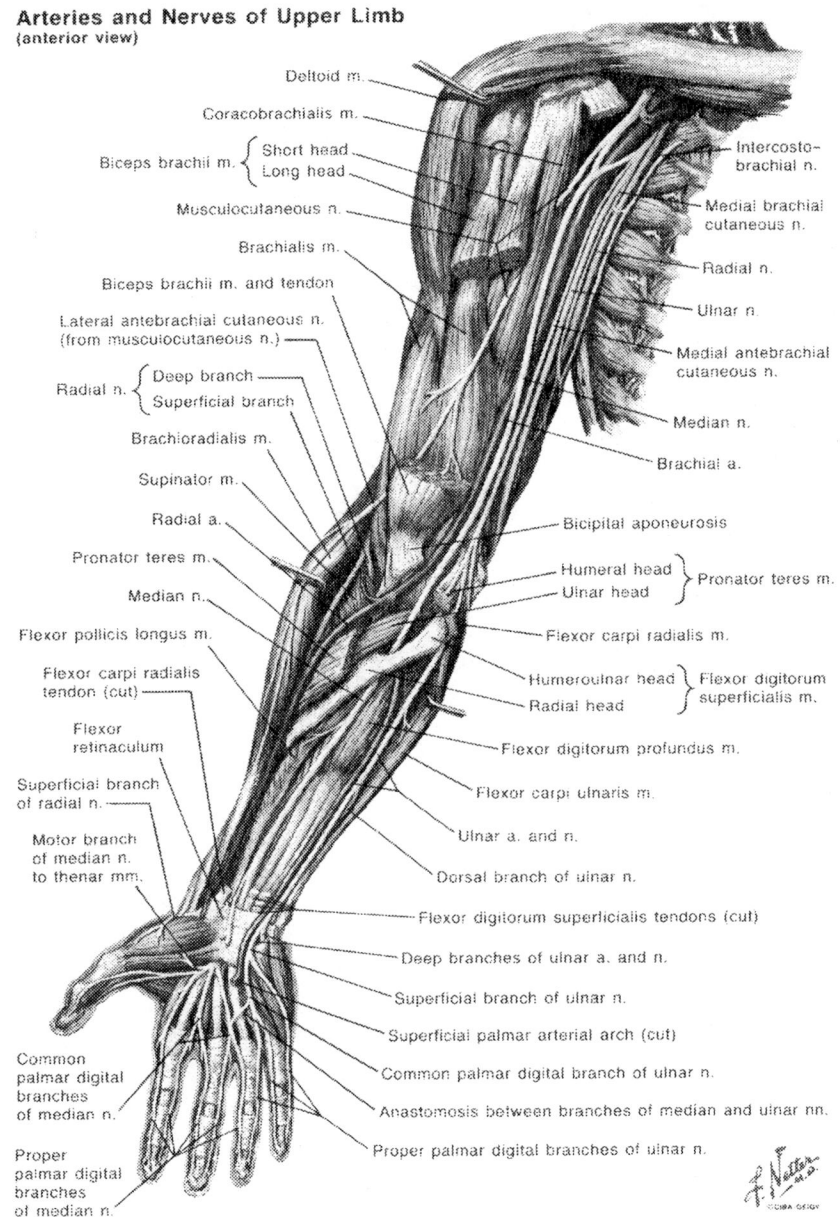

Figure 11.81
Neurovascular structures of the arm.
Copyright 1987. Novartis. Reprinted with permission from The Ciba Collection of Medical Illustrations, Vol. 8, Part I, Sec. I, illustrated by Frank H. Netter, MD. All rights reserved.

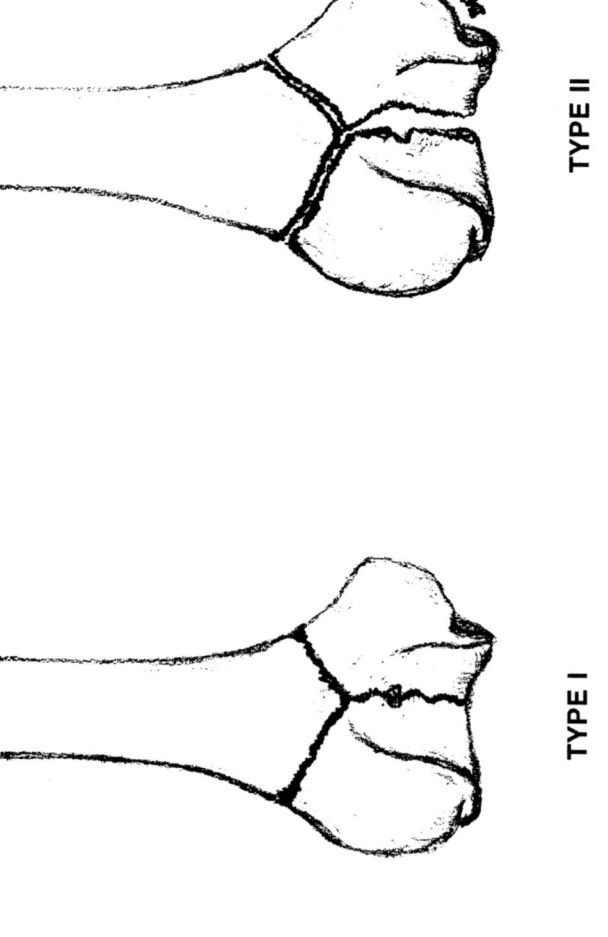

Figure 11.82
Intercondylar fracture of the distal humerus: type I and II.

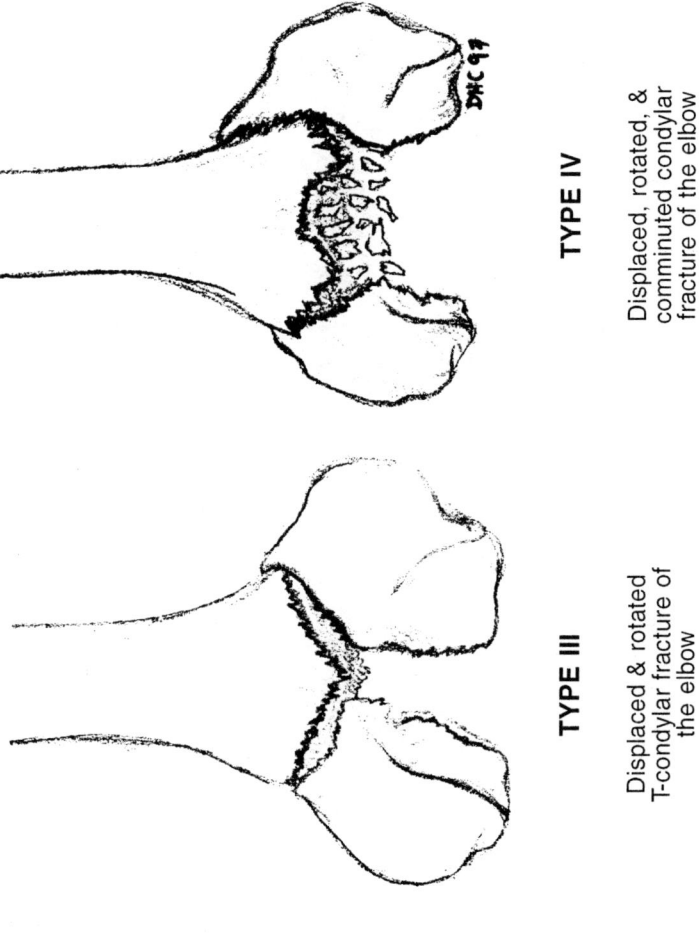

Figure 11.83
Intercondylar fracture of the distal humerus: type III and IV.

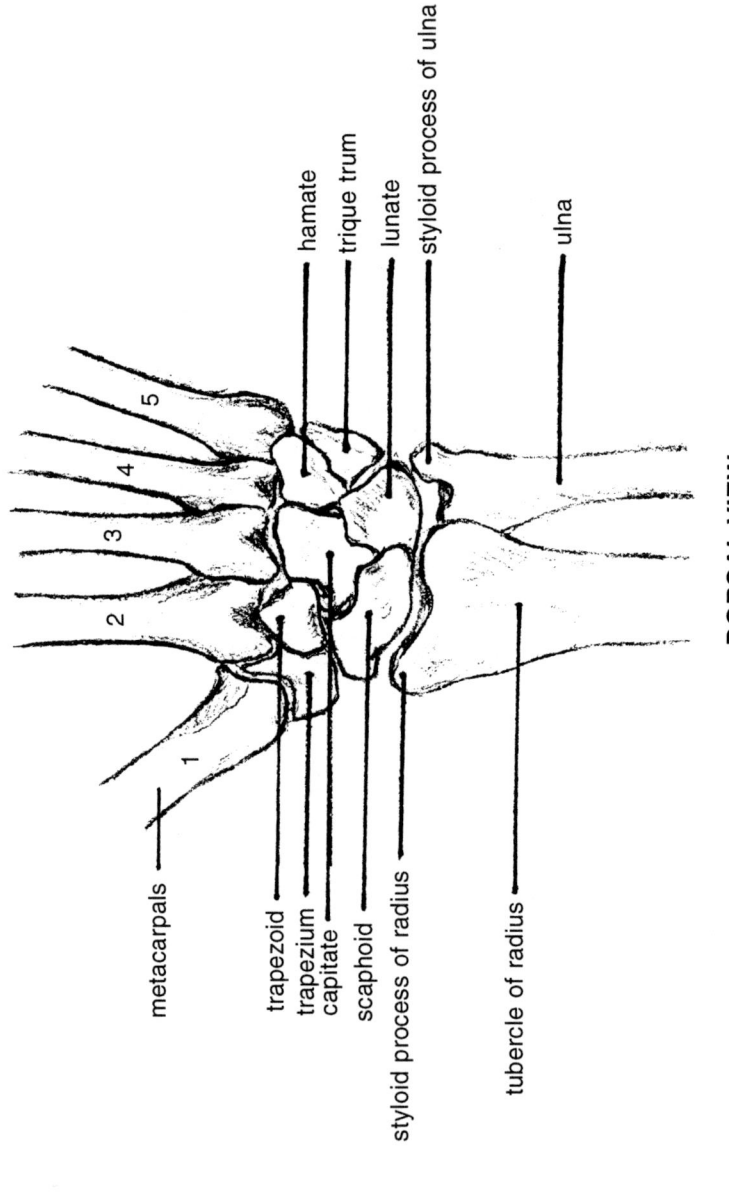

Figure 11.84 (continued on next page)
Osseus anatomy of the wrist.

Injuries to the Extremities and Pelvis 749

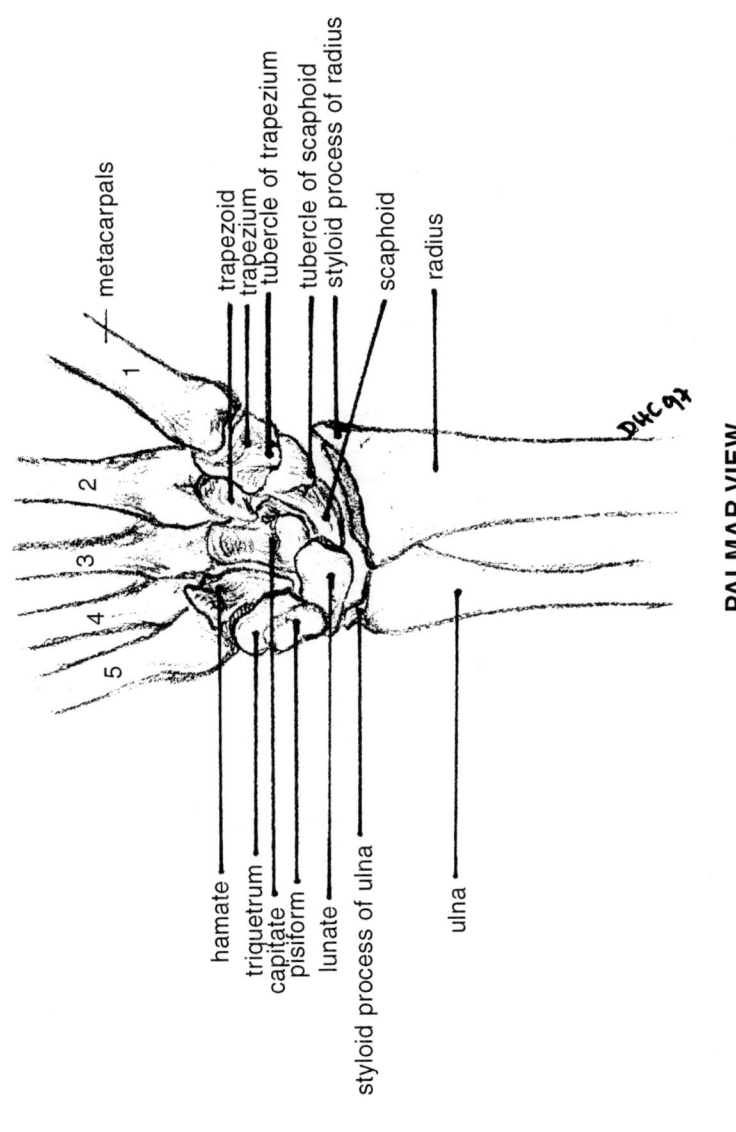

Figure 11.84 (continued from previous page)
Osseus anatomy of the wrist.

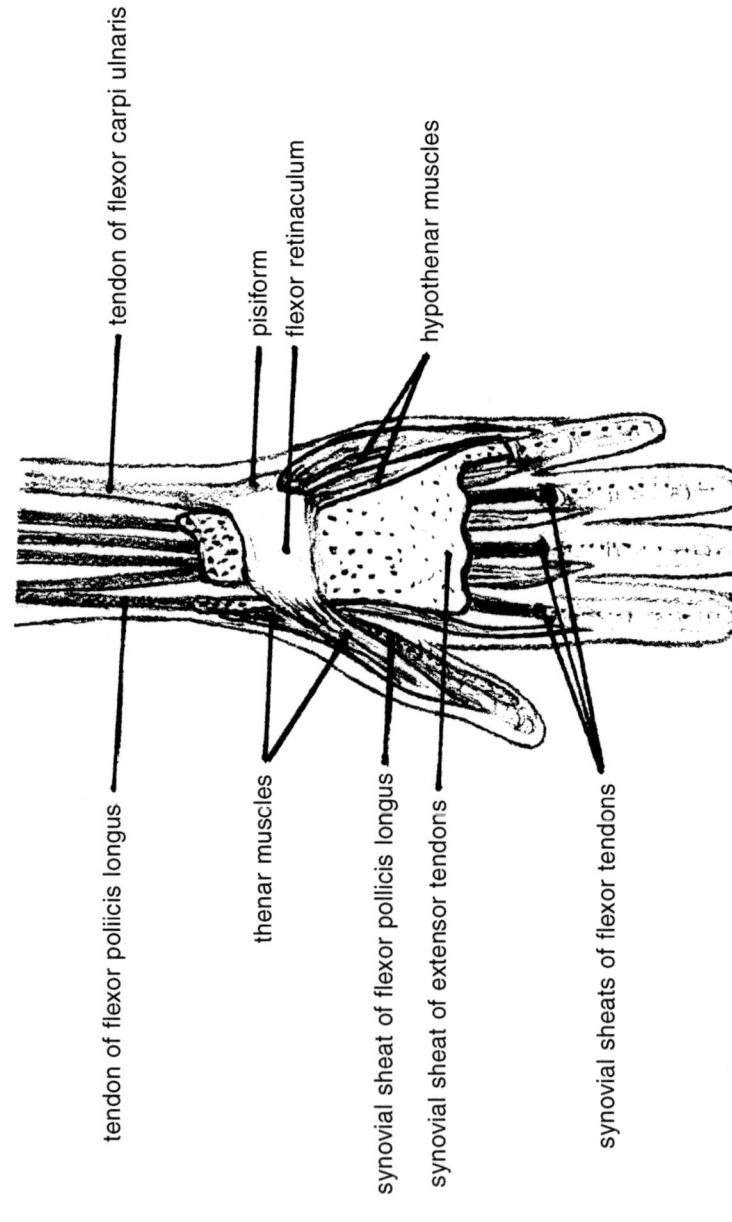

Figure 11.85 (continued on next page)
Tendons and synovial sheaths of the hand.

Injuries to the Extremities and Pelvis 751

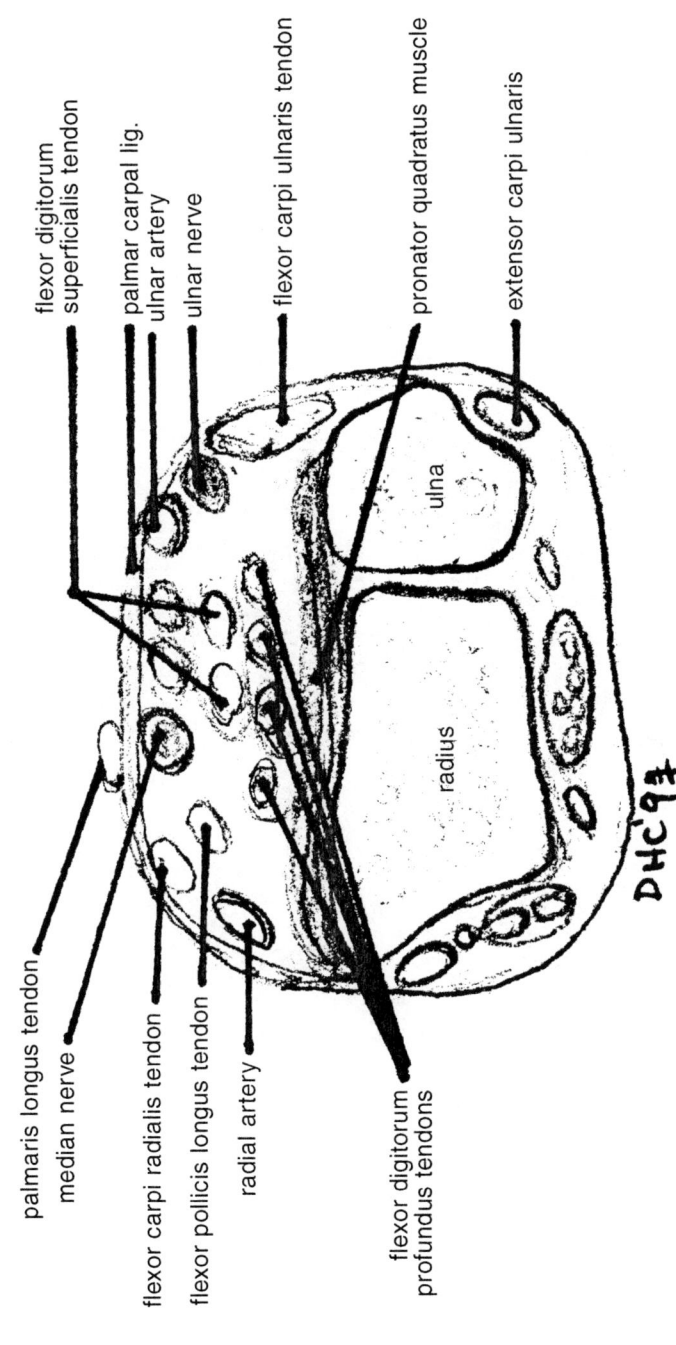

Figure 11.85 (continued from previous page; see also next page)
Tendons and synovial sheaths of the hand.

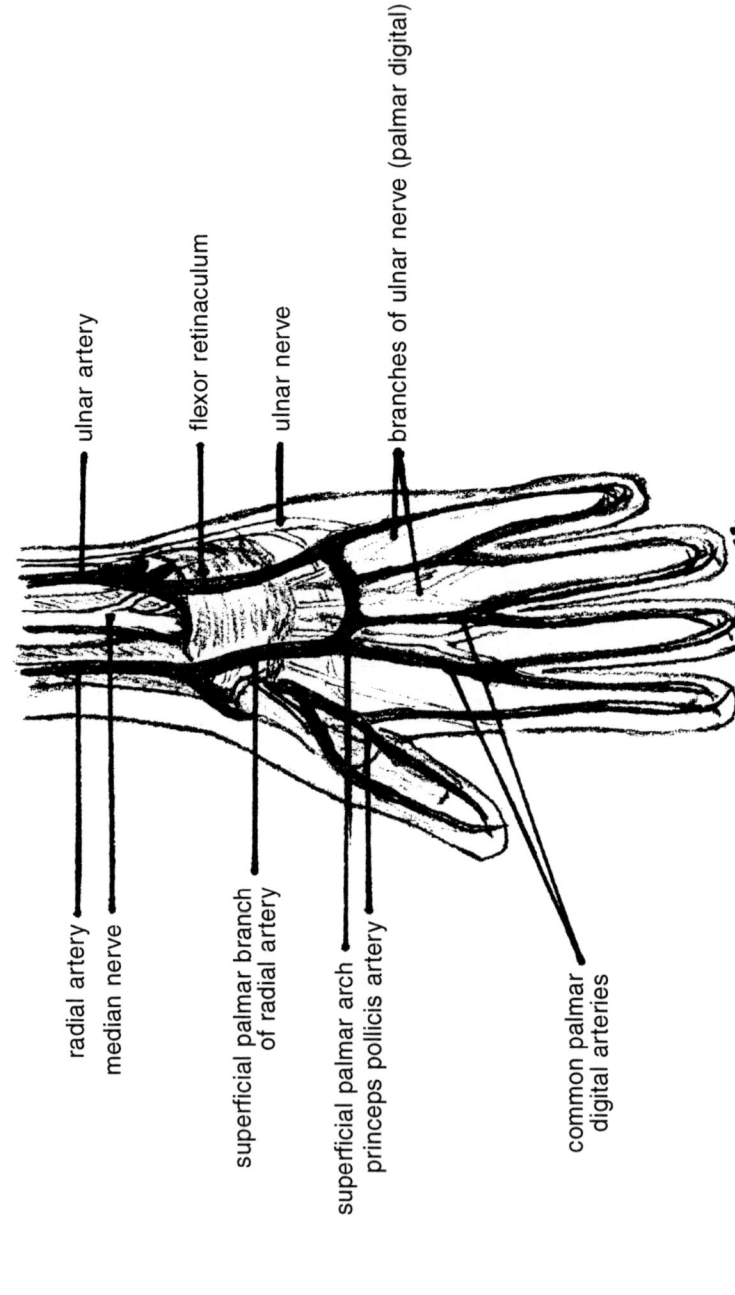

Figure 11.85 (continued from previous pages)
Tendons and synovial sheaths of the hand.

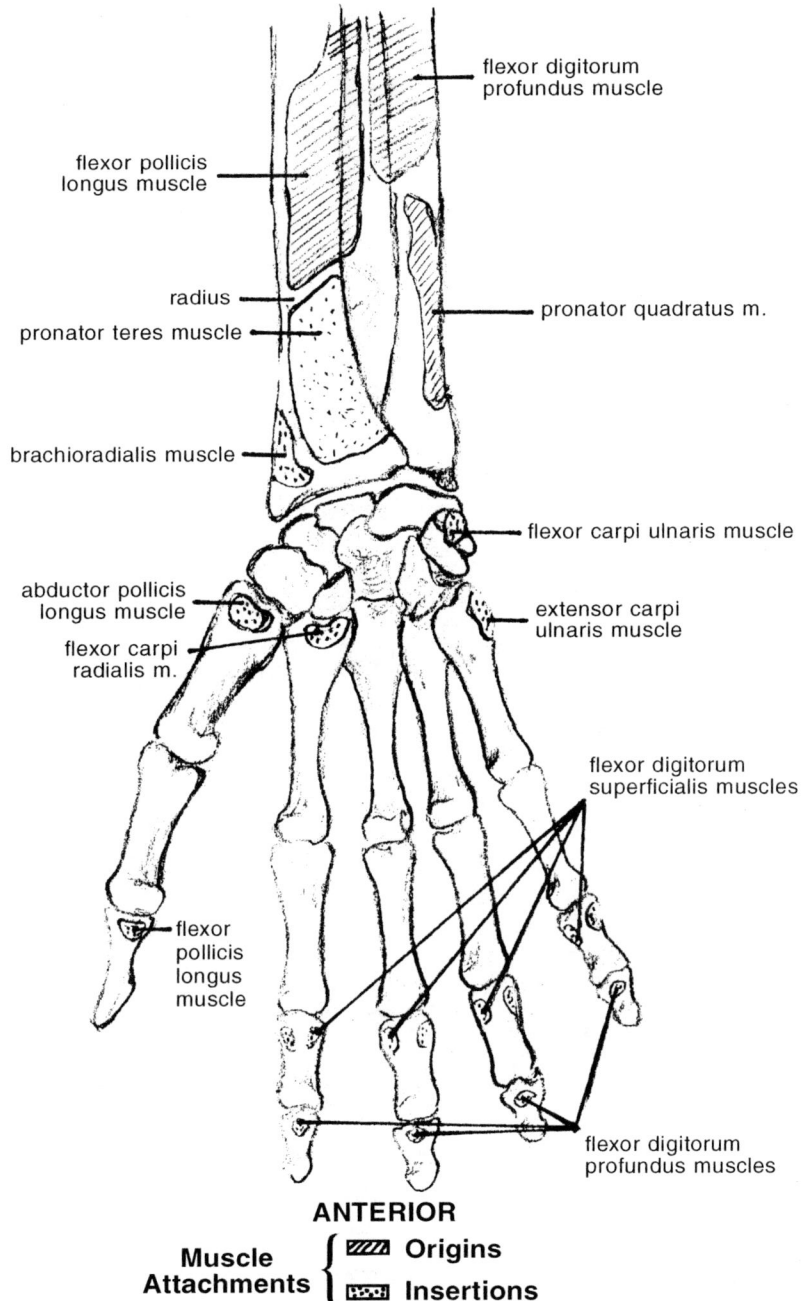

Figure 11.86 (continued on next page)
Bones of the hand and wrists with the origin and insertions of muscles.

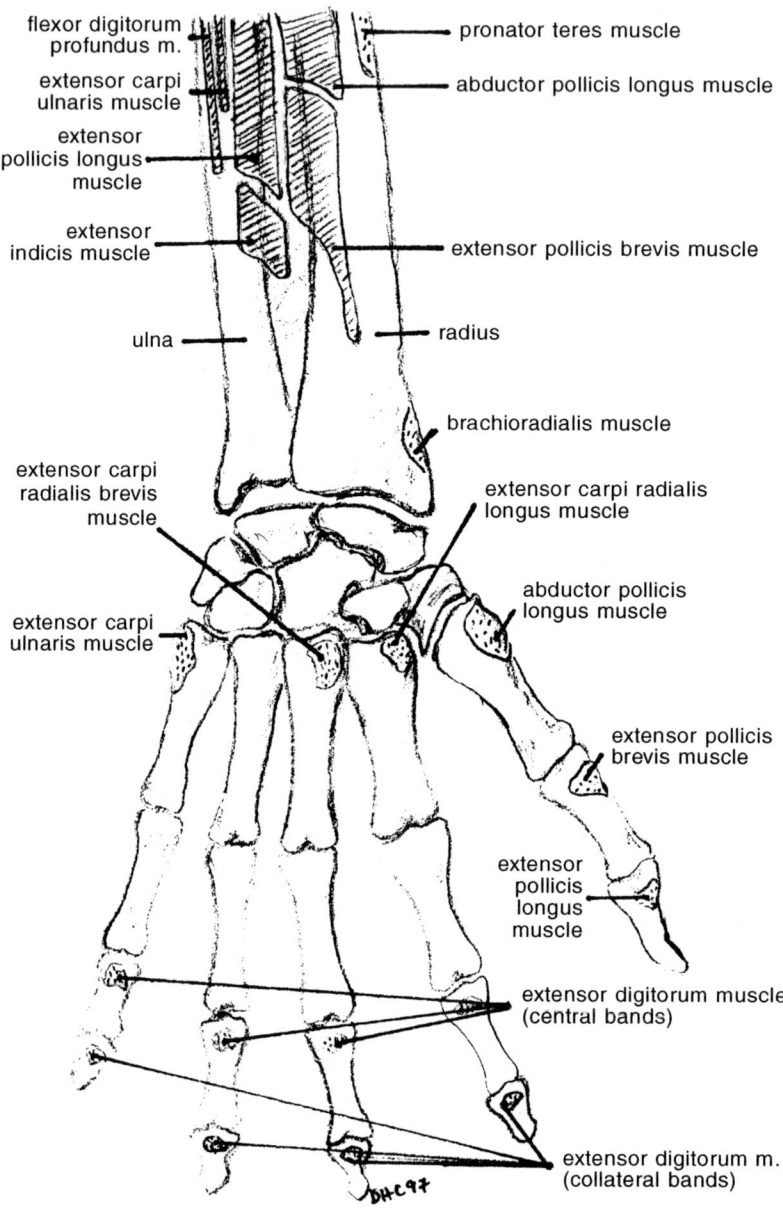

Figure 11.86 (continued from previous page)
Bones of the hand and wrists with the origin and insertions of muscles.

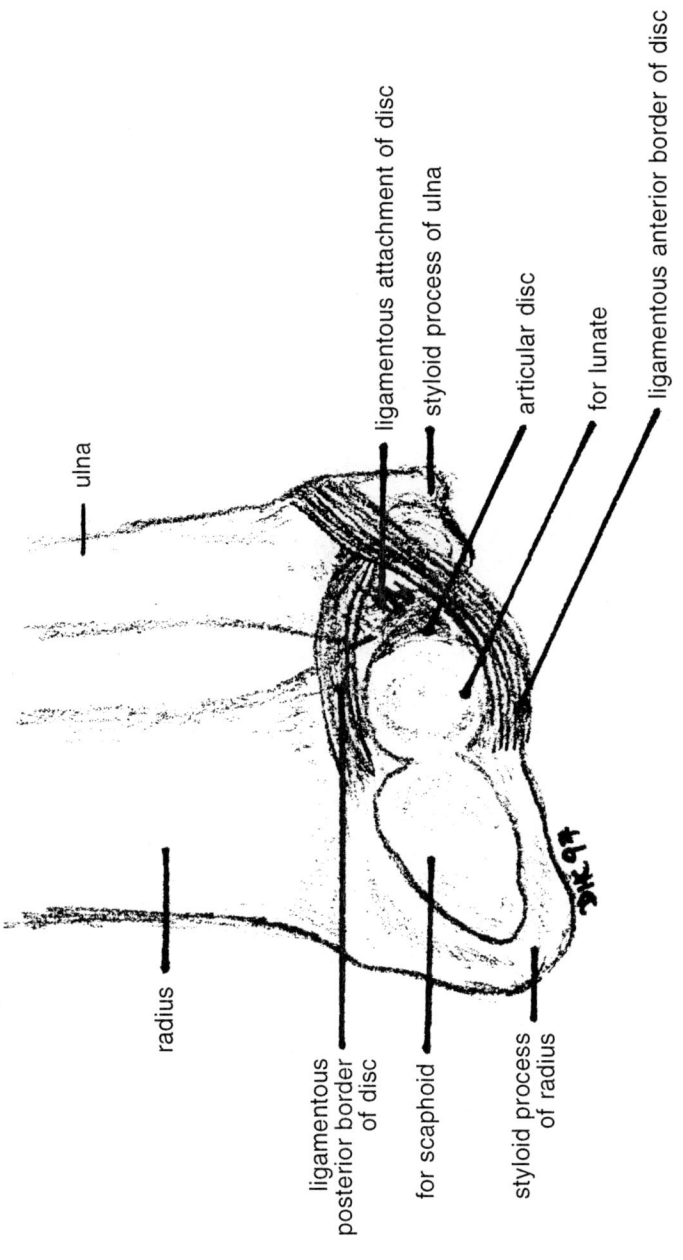

Figure 11.87
The two facets of the distal radius: one for the scaphoid and one for the lunate.

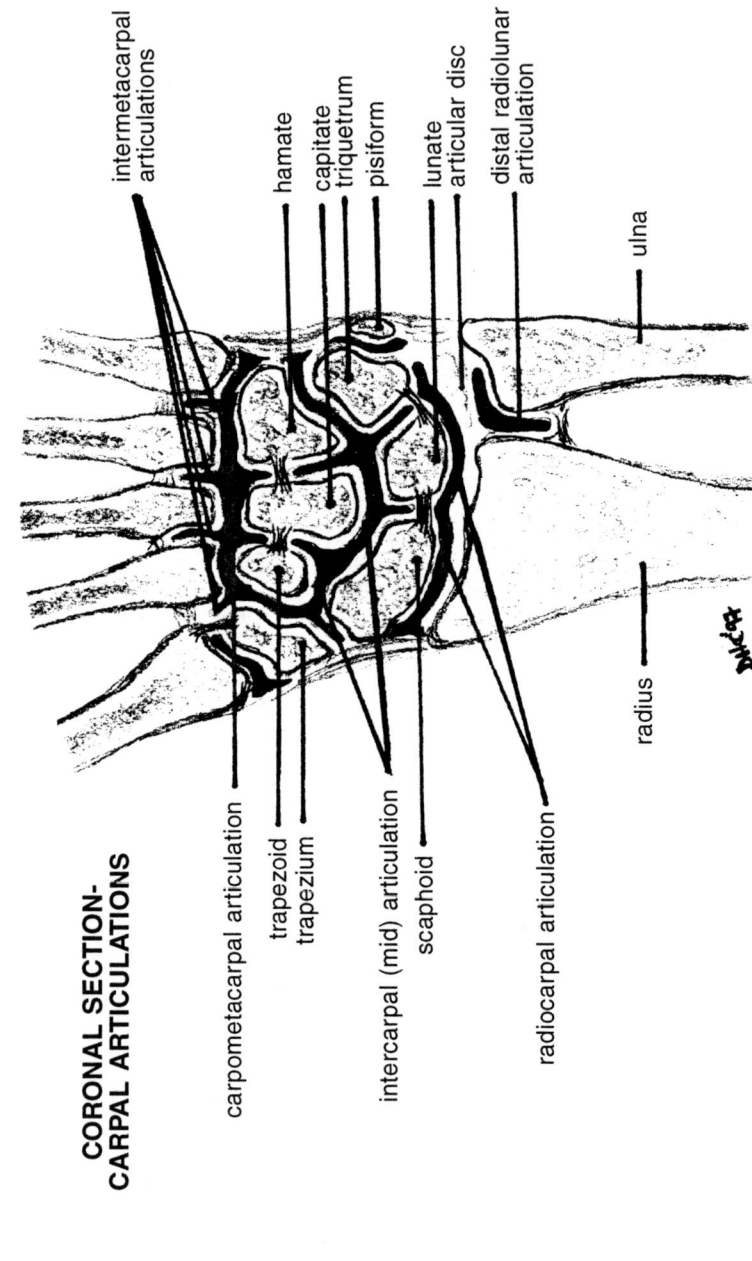

Figure 11.88
The articulations of the wrist.

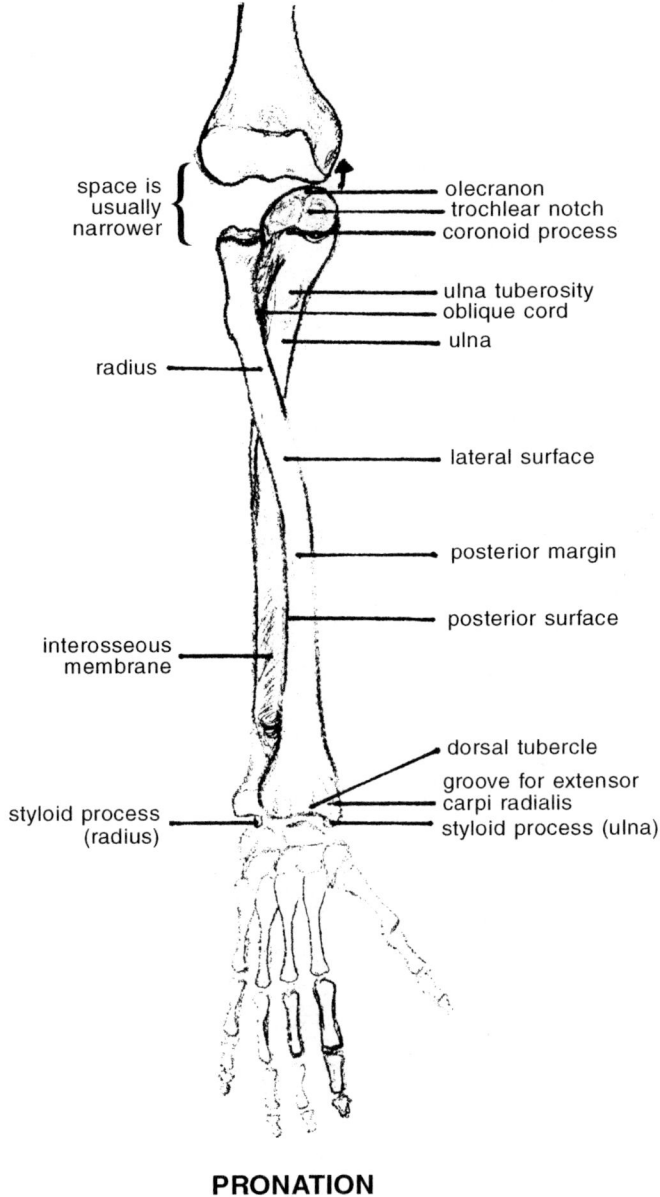

**PRONATION
ANTERIOR VIEW**

Figure 11.89 (continued on next page)
Pronation and supination of the forearm. Note how the radius crosses over the ulna in pronation.

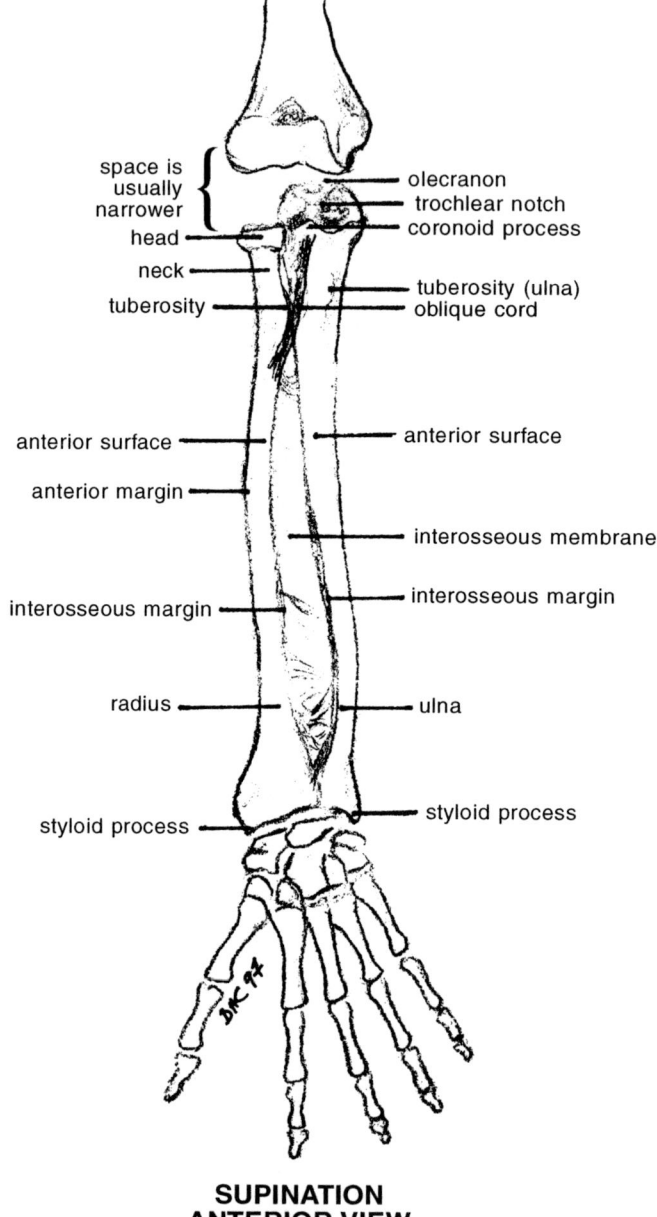

Figure 11.89 (continued from previous page)
Pronation and supination of the forearm. Note how the radius crosses over the ulna in pronation.

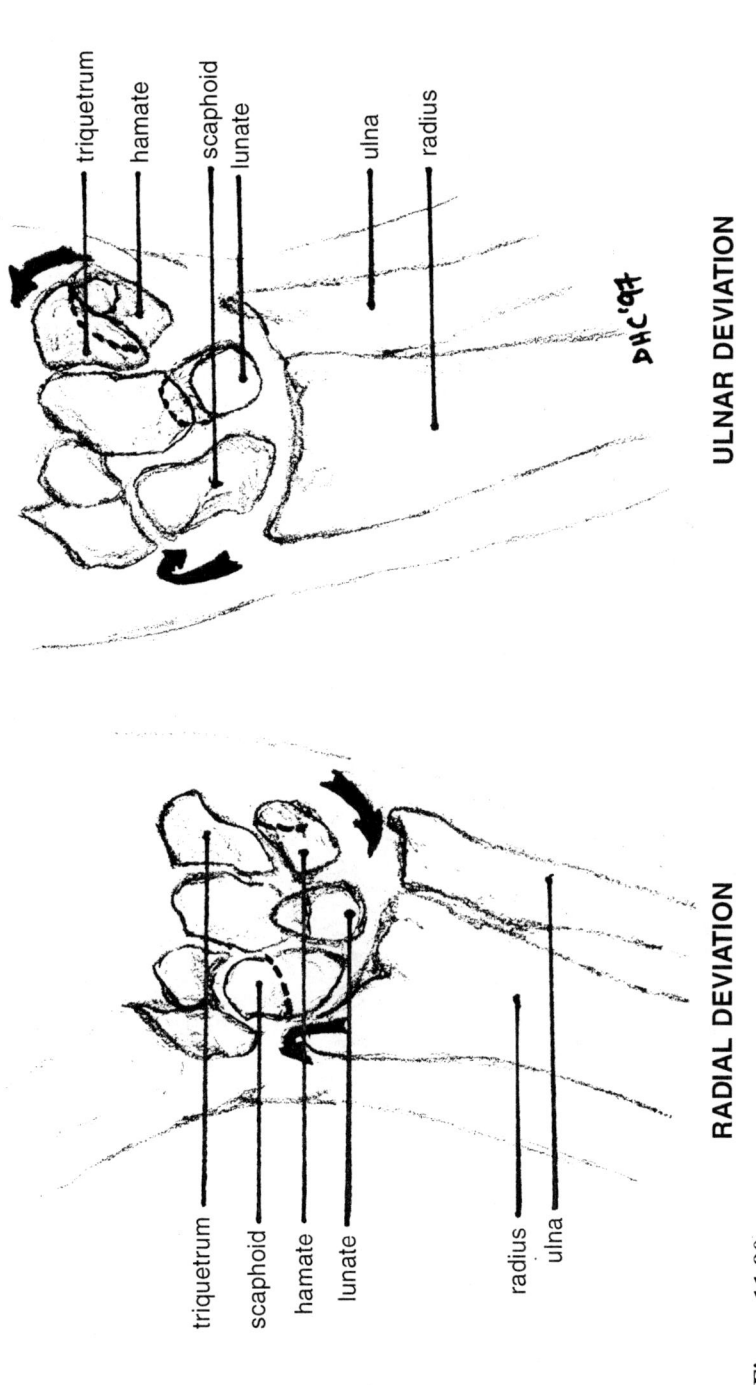

Figure 11.90
Radial deviation of the wrist causes the scaphoid and lunate to flex down. Palmar and dorsiflexion occur at the radiocarpal as well as the midcarpal joint whereas radial and ulnar deviation occur mostly at the radiocarpal joint.

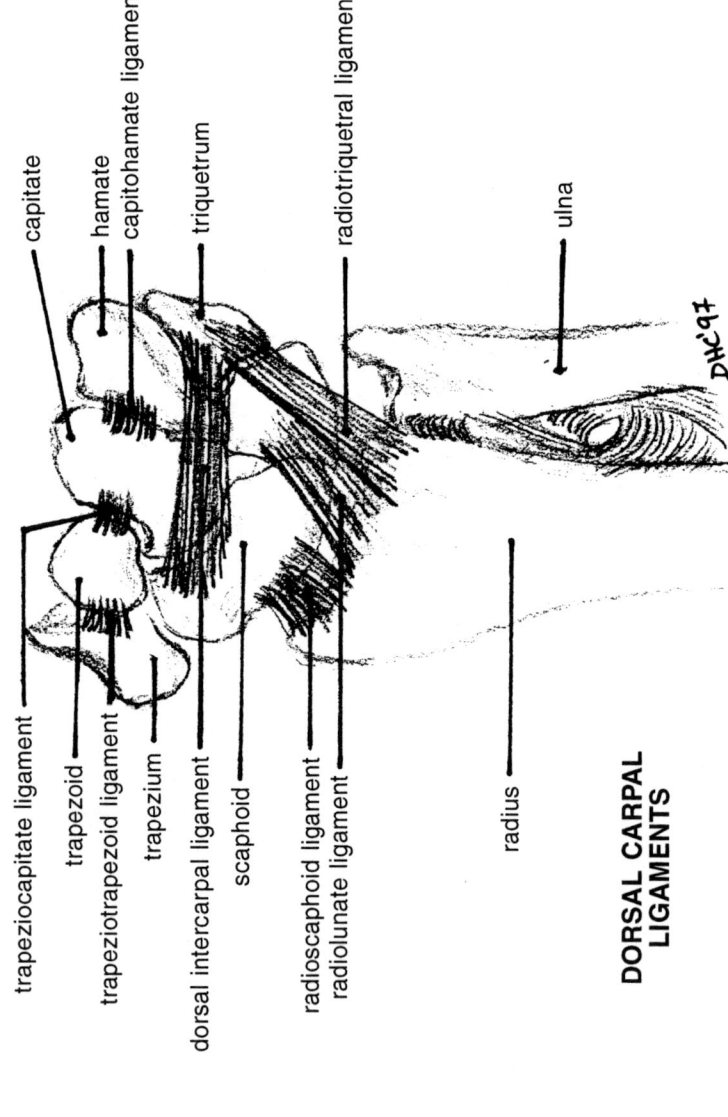

Figure 11.91
Radiocarpal and radioulnar ligaments.

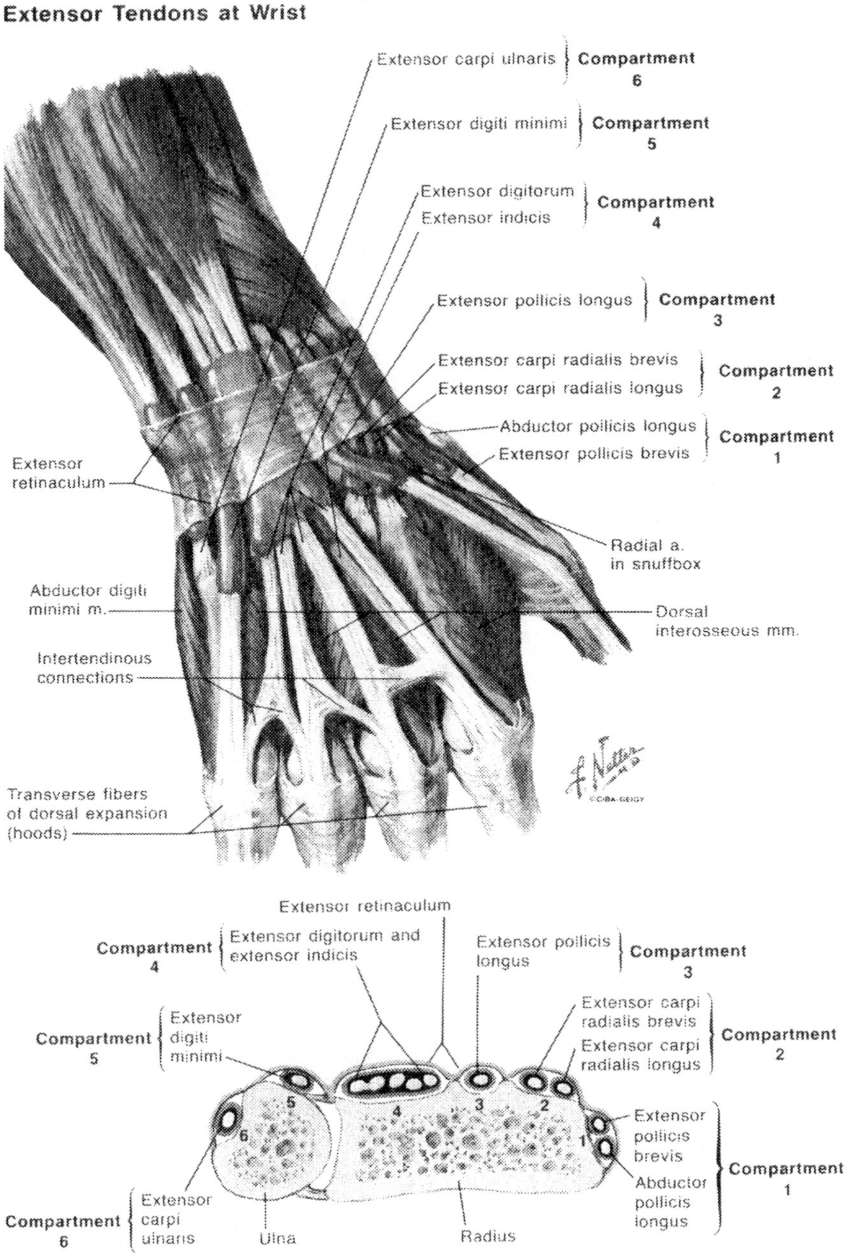

Figure 11.92
Tendon compartments of the wrist.
Copyright 1987. Novartis. Reprinted with permission from The Ciba Collection of Medical Illustrations, Vol, 8, Part I, Sec. I, illustrated by Frank H. Netter, MD. All rights reserved.

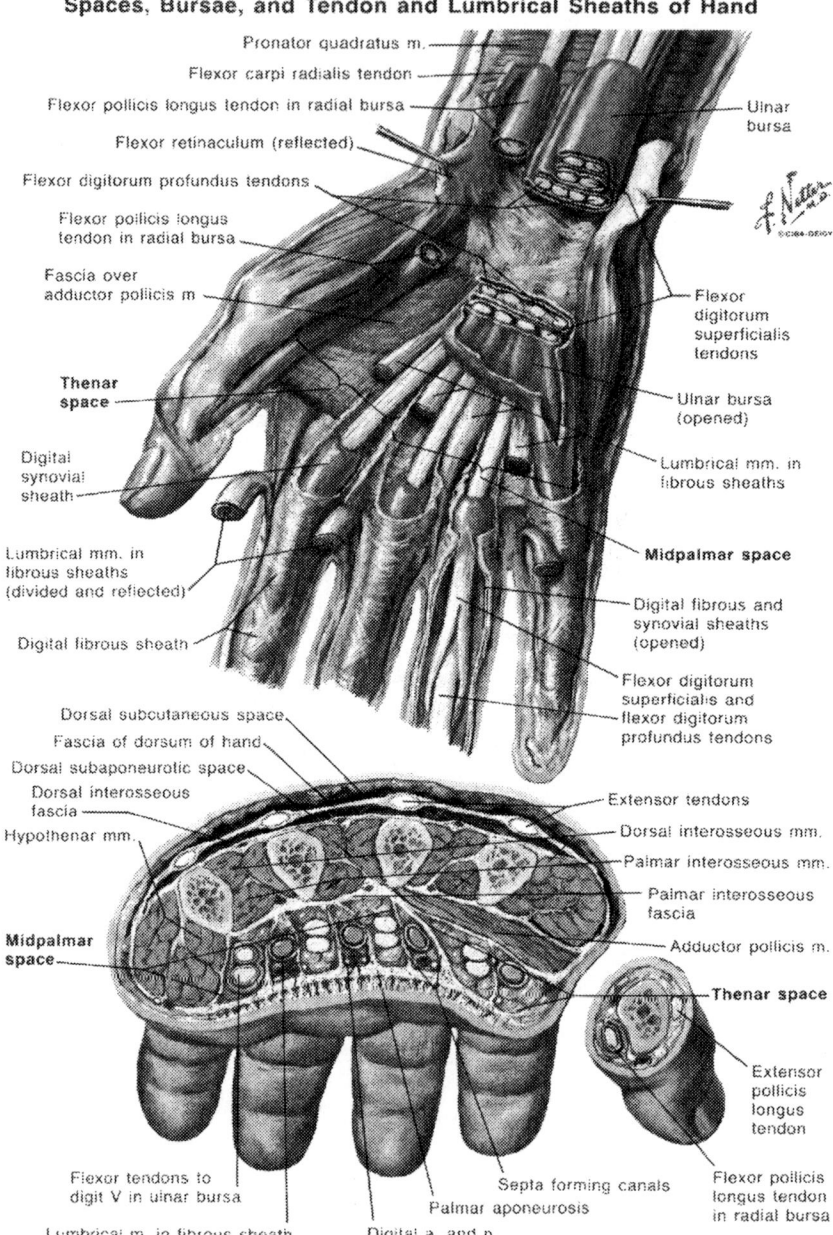

Figure 11.93 (continued on next page)
Palmar tendons and tenosynovium of the hand.
Copyright 1987. Novartis. Reprinted with permission from The Ciba Collection of Medical Illustrations, Vol, 8, Part I, Sec. 1, illustrated by Frank H. Netter, MD. All rights reserved.

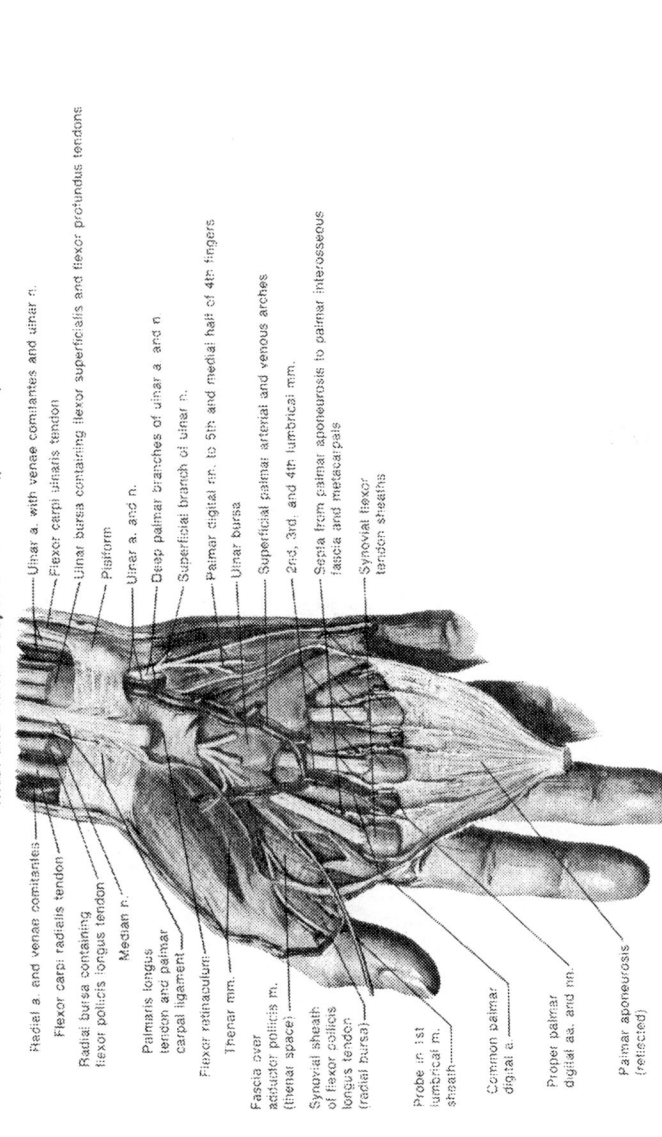

Figure 11.93 (continued from previous page; see also next page)
Palmar tendons and tenosynovium of the hand.
Copyright 1987. Novartis. Reprinted with permission from The Ciba Collection of Medical Illustrations, Vol. 8, Part I, Sec. I, illustrated by Frank H. Netter, MD. All rights reserved.

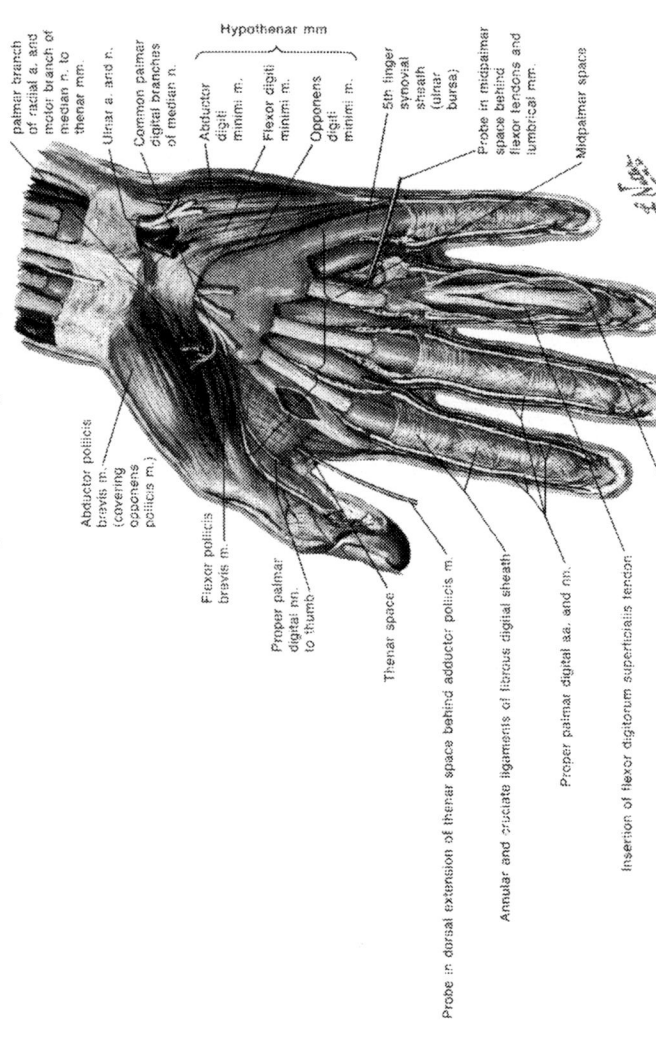

Figure 11.93 (continued from previous pages)
Palmar tendons and tenosynovium of the hand.
Copyright 1987. Novartis. Reprinted with permission from The Ciba Collection of Medical Illustrations, Vol. 8, Part I, Sec. I, illustrated by Frank H. Netter, MD. All rights reserved.

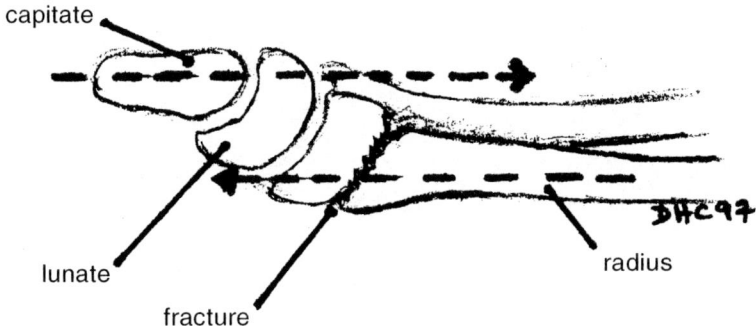

Figure 11.94
Dorsal tilt of the radius causes the lunate and capitate to collapse in a zigzag fashion and become nonlinear.

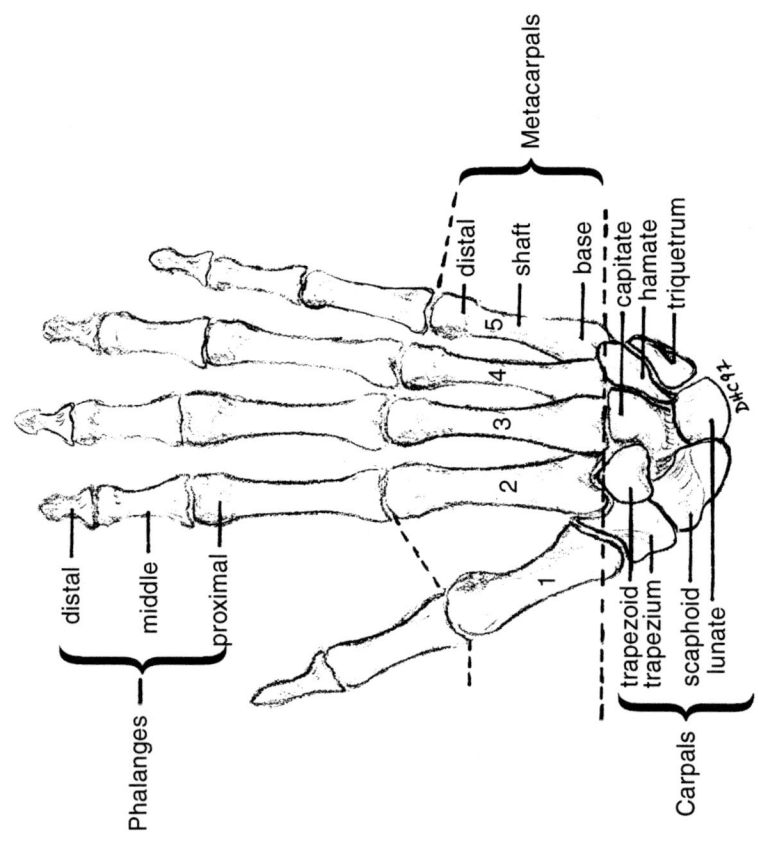

Figure 11.95
Osseus anatomy of the hand.

Injuries to the Extremities and Pelvis 767

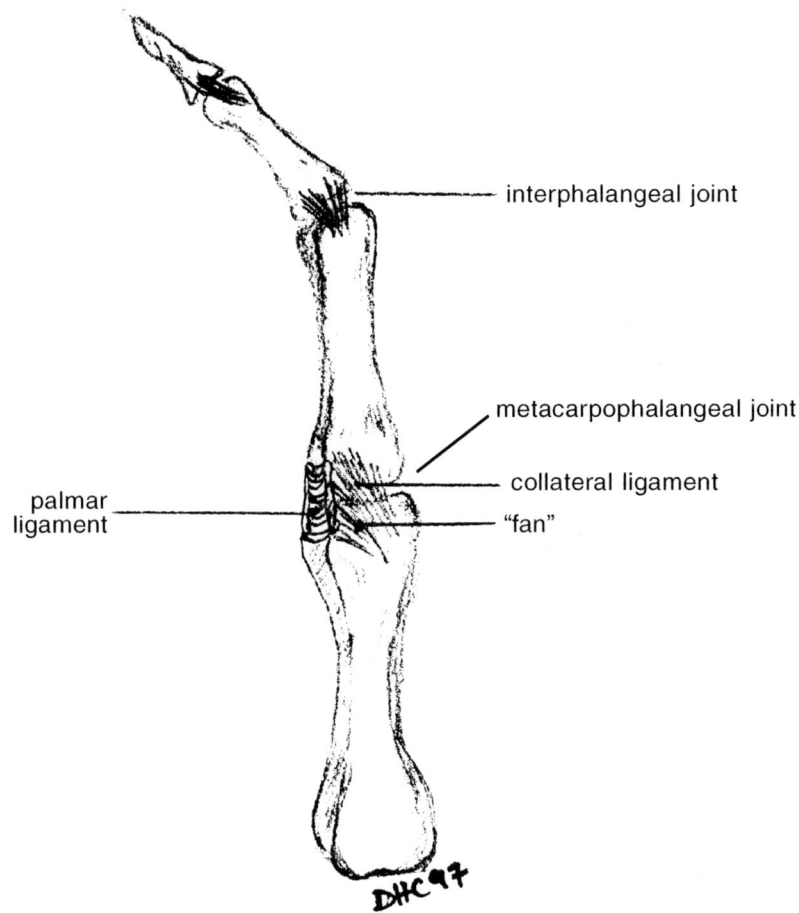

Figure 11.96
Lateral view of the bones of the finger. The collateral ligaments stabilize the interphalangeal joints and the metacarpophalangeal joints.

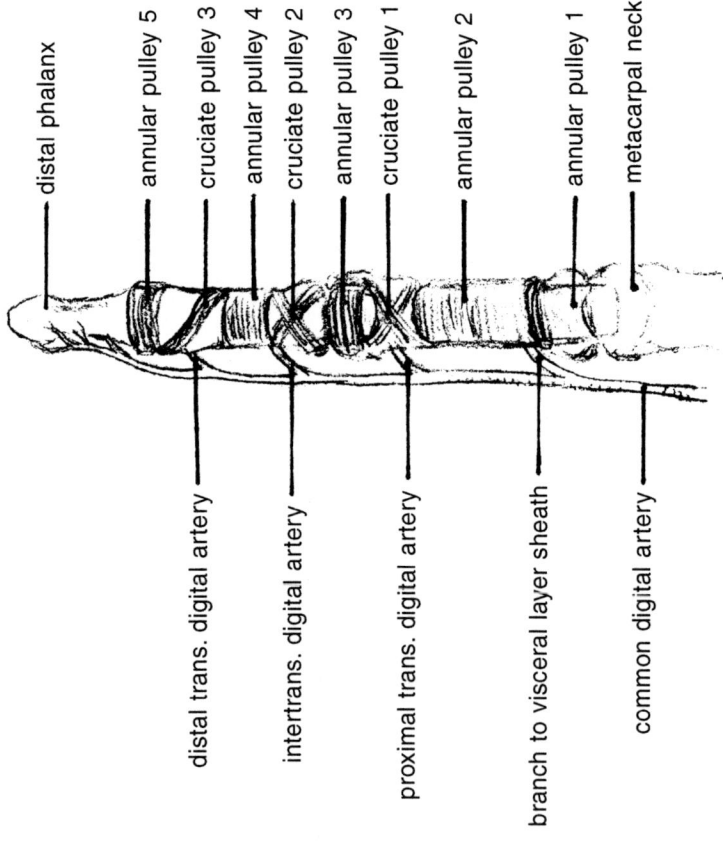

Figure 11.97
Fibrous retinacular sheaths (pulleys) of the finger, preventing bowstringing of the tendons.

Injuries to the Extremities and Pelvis

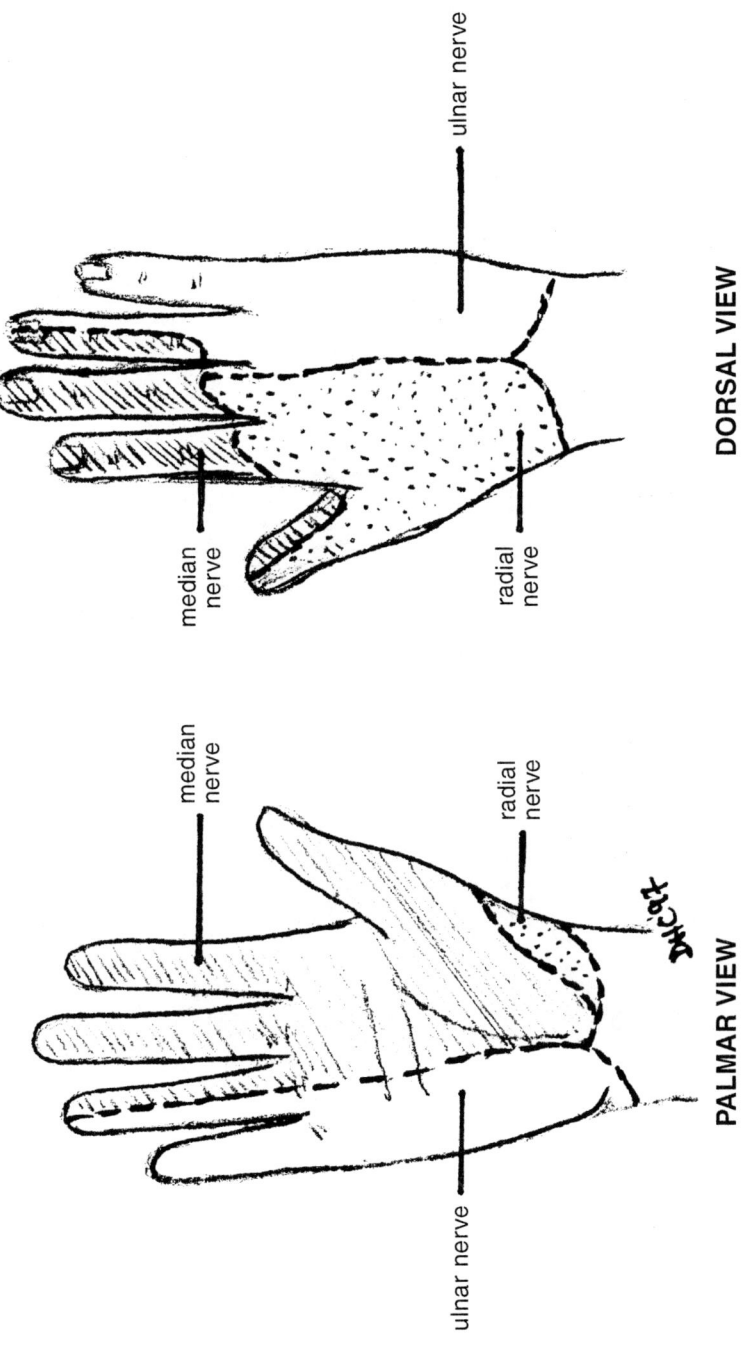

Figure 11.98
Sensory nerve supply to the hand.

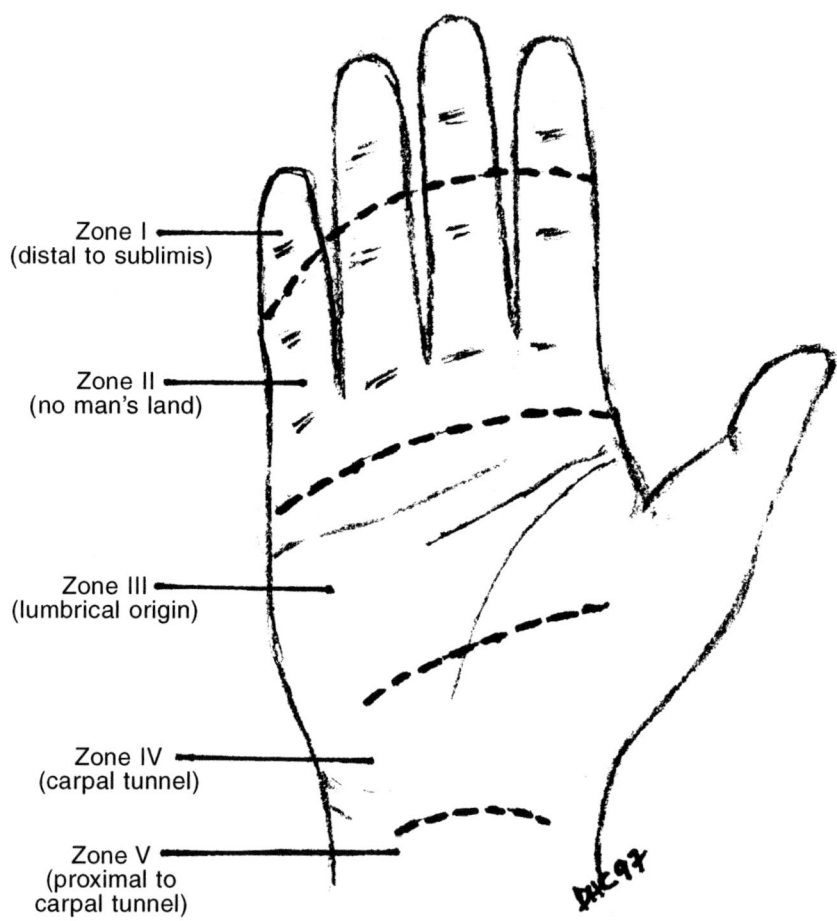

Figure 11.99
Zones of the extensor tendons.

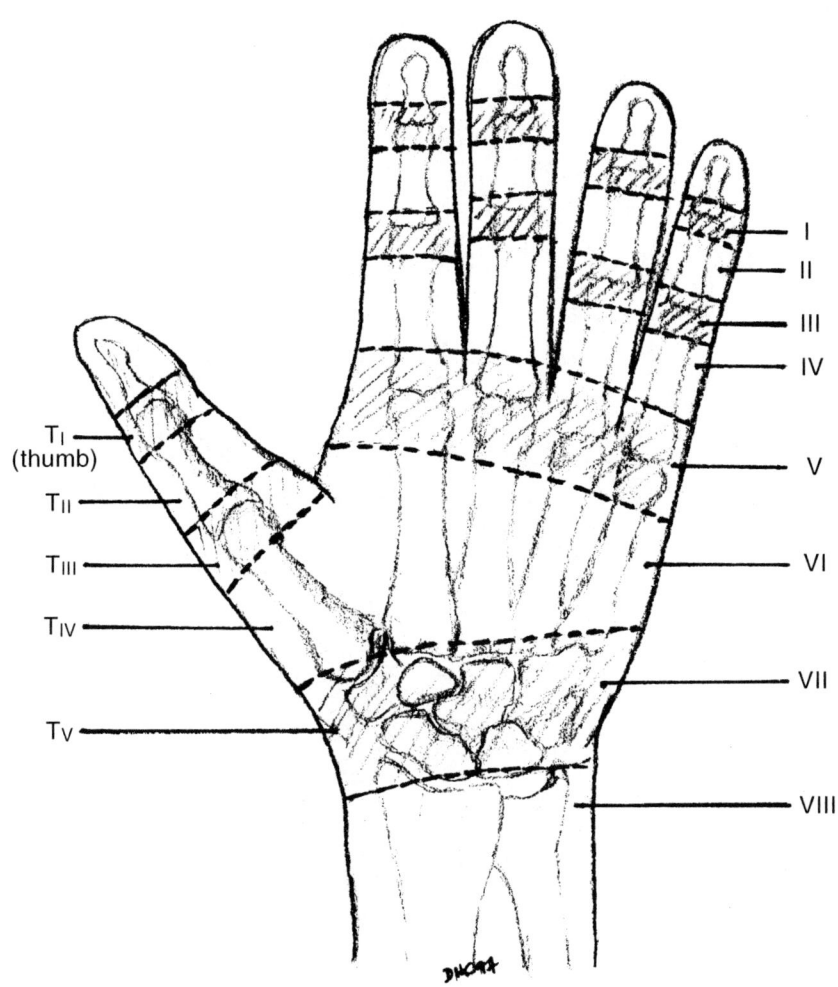

EXTENSOR TENDON ZONES

Figure 11.100
Zones of the extensor tendons.

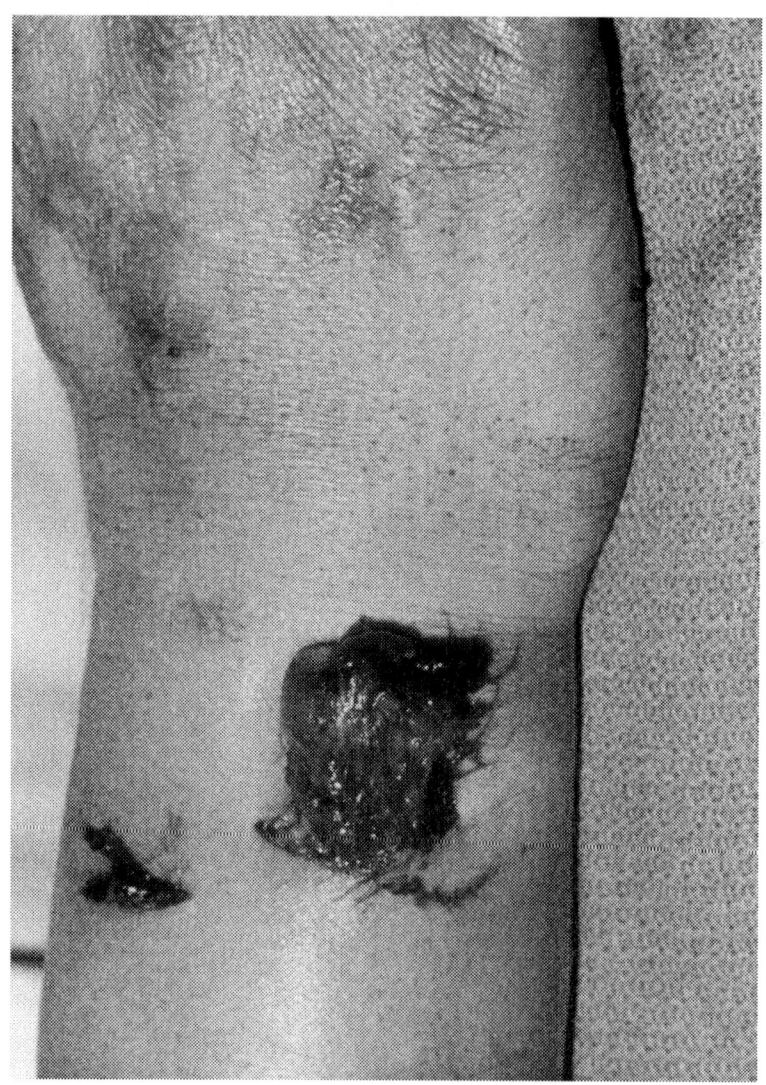

Figure 11.101
Gustilo type II open fracture. Distal ulna protrudes through a 2-cm transverse laceration at the wrist. A second smaller wound is noted at a separate fracture site.

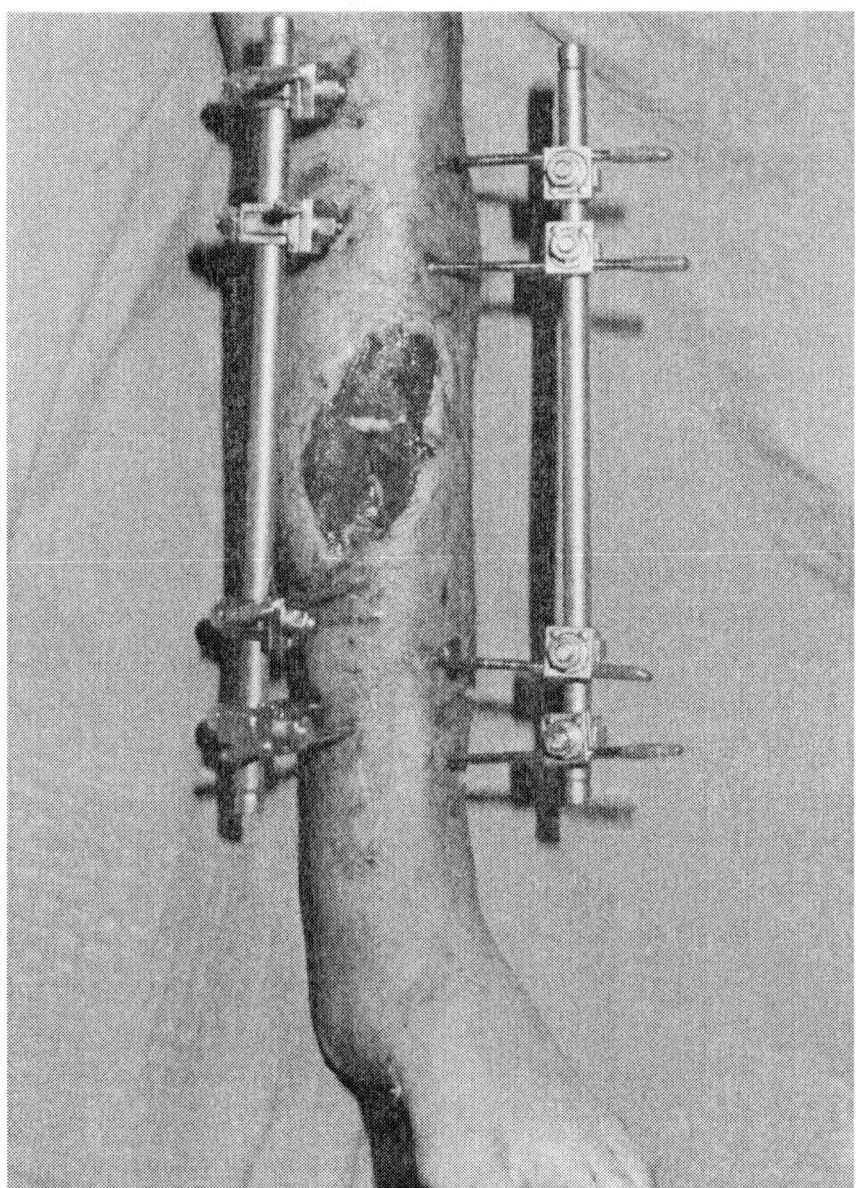

Figure 11.102
Gustilo type IIIB open tibia fracture. Extensive loss of soft tissue as well as bone. The exposed surfaces of bone are nonviable and required further resection prior to reconstruction.

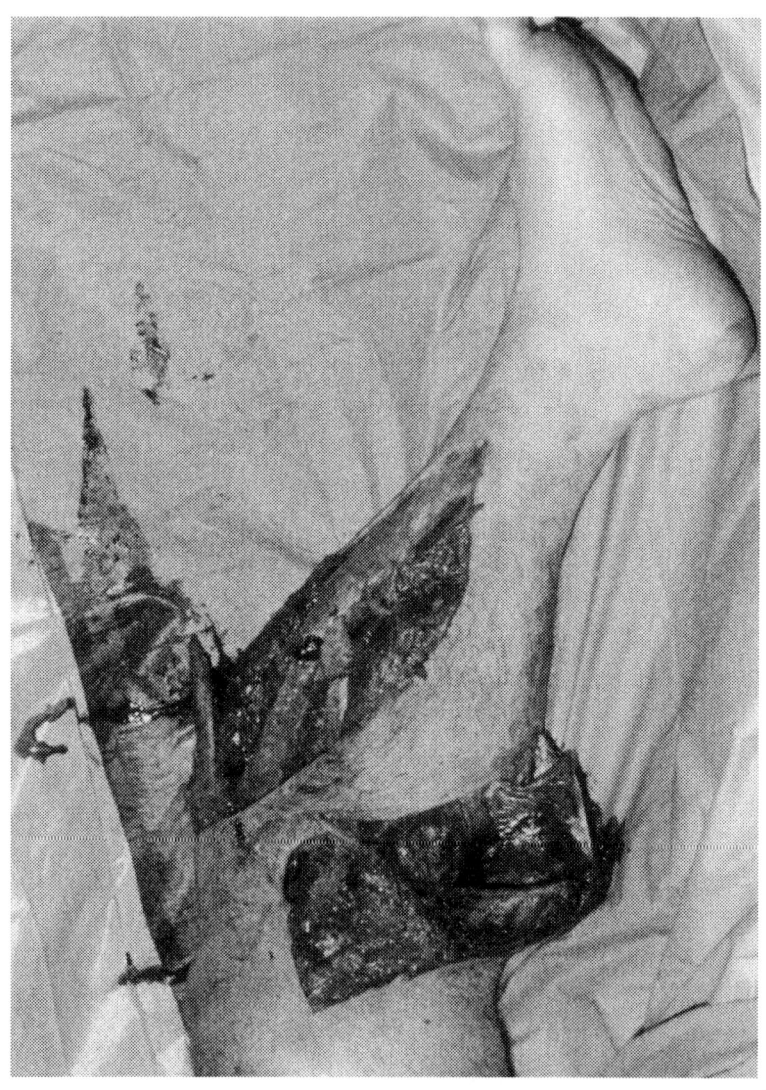

Figure 11.103
Gustilo type IIIC open tibia fracture. Crush injury with vascular injury. Note the pale appearance of the foot and ankle region of the non-perfused, pulseless lower leg.

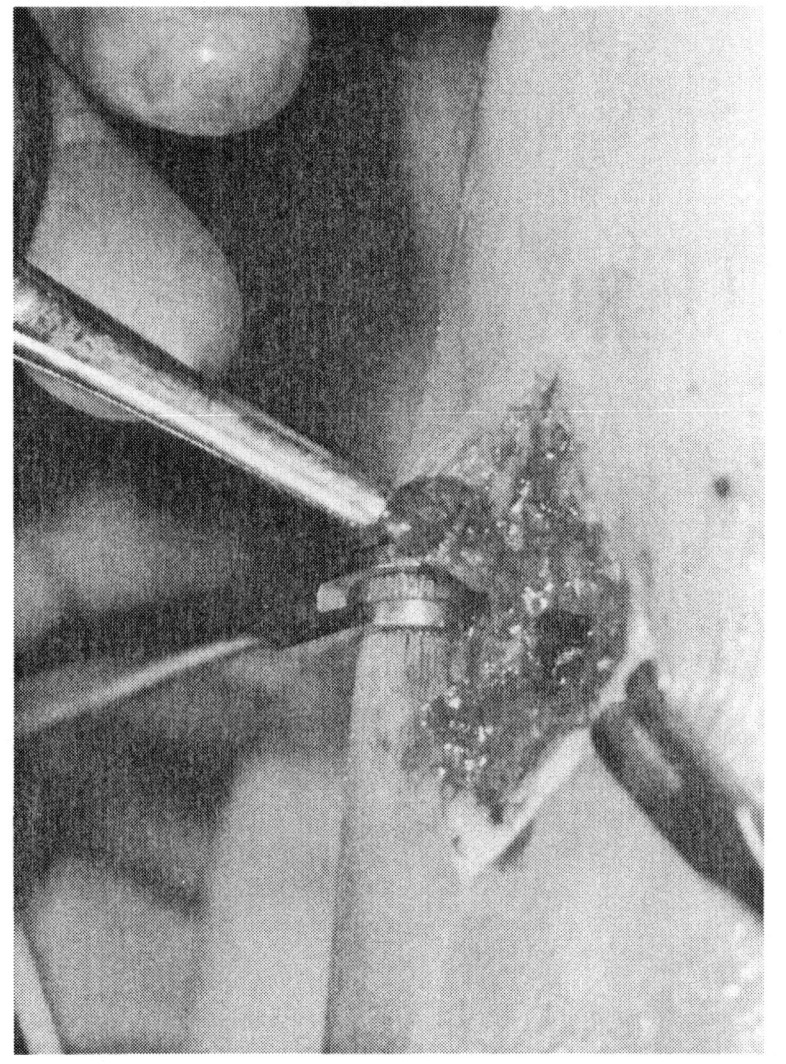

Figure 11.104
Gustilo type I open fracture with a wound measuring 3 mm in size has been extended through a longitudinal incision to permit meticulous debridement and irrigation of the wound.

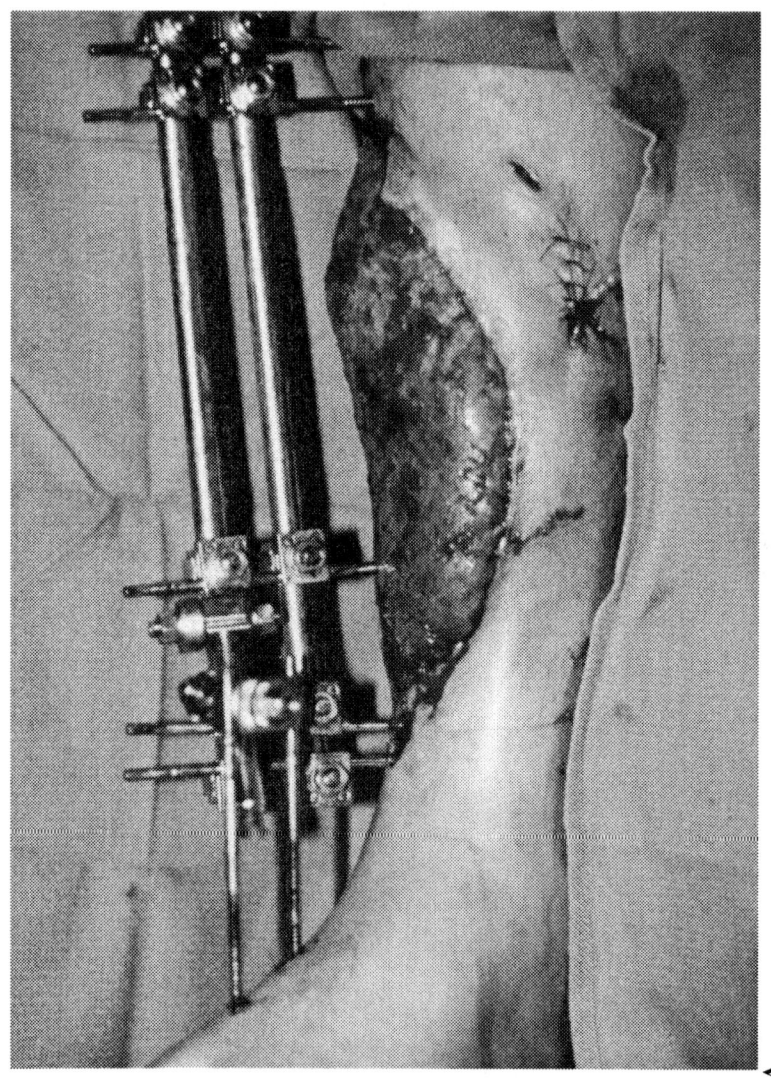

Figure 11.105A
Gustilo type IIIB open tibia fracture. Soft tissue defect has been covered with rectus abdominis muscle transplant. Appearance prior to placement of split thickness skin graft.

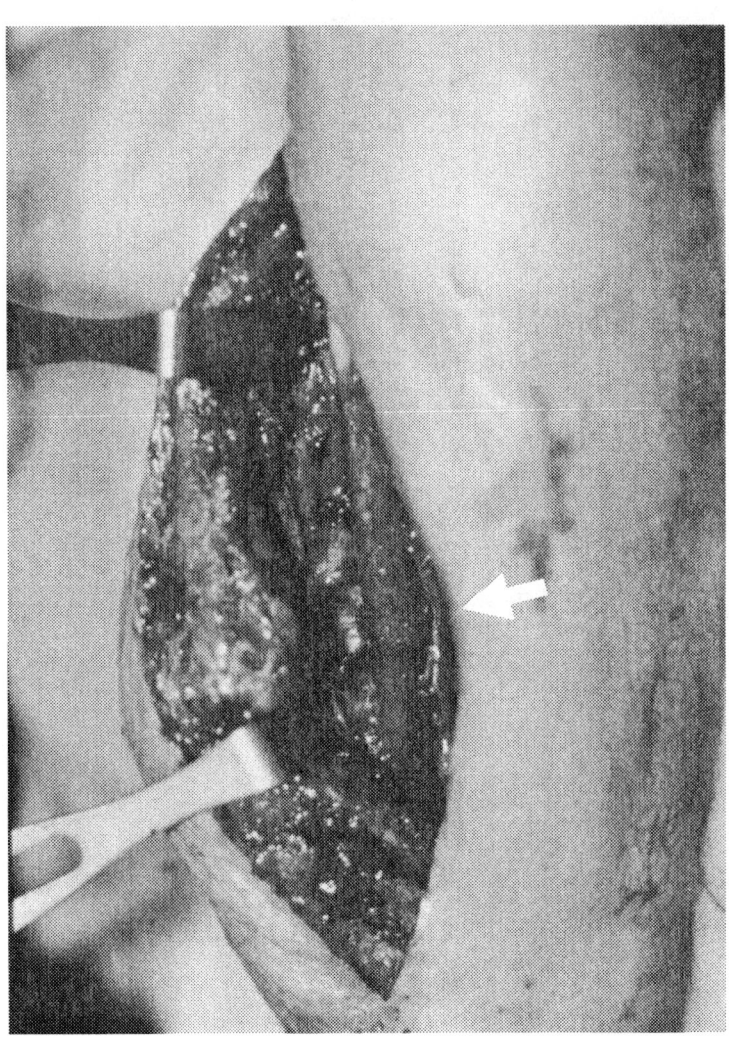

Figure 11.105B
Six weeks later, muscle flap elevated to permit placement of cancellous iliac crest bone graft along tibial shaft fracture (arrow). (From: Feibel RJ, Oliva A, Jackson RL, et al. Soft tissue reconstruction in orthopaedic surgery. Secondary procedures. Orthop Clin N Am 24:537, 1993, with permission.)

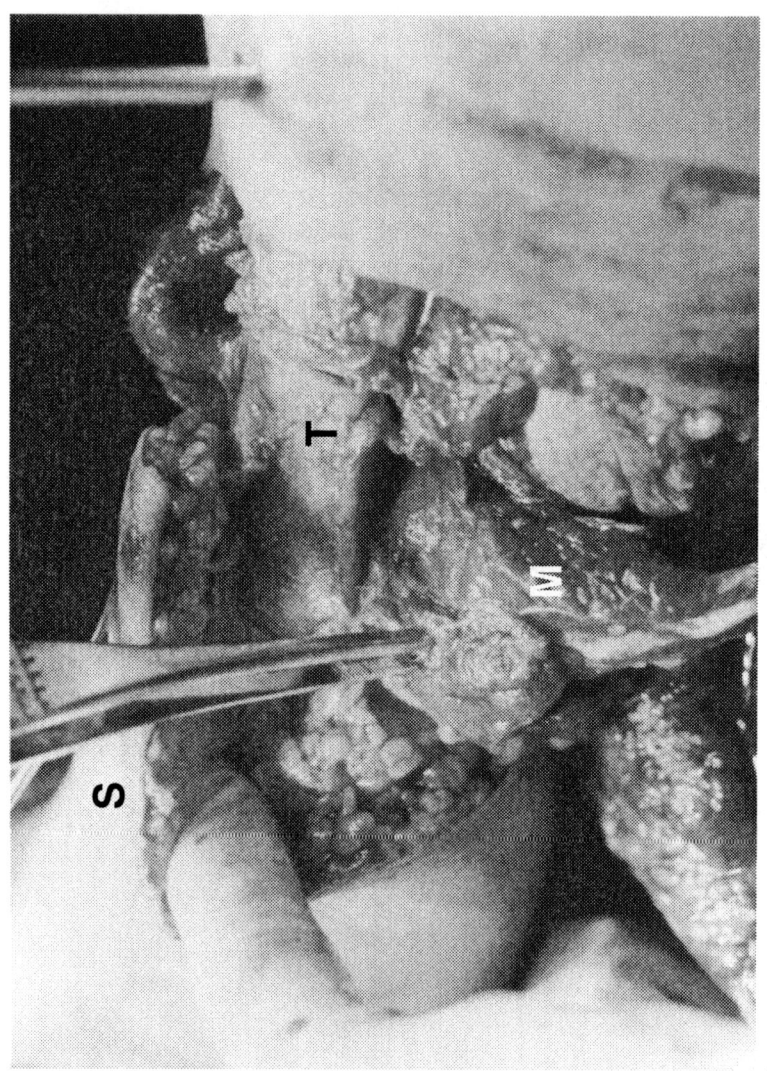

Figure 11.106A
Twenty-year-old female pedestrian struck by an automobile. Intra-operative photo of Gustilo type IIIC open tibia fracture. Note extensive skin (S) and muscle (M) avulsion with exposed tibia (T). Revascularization was performed.

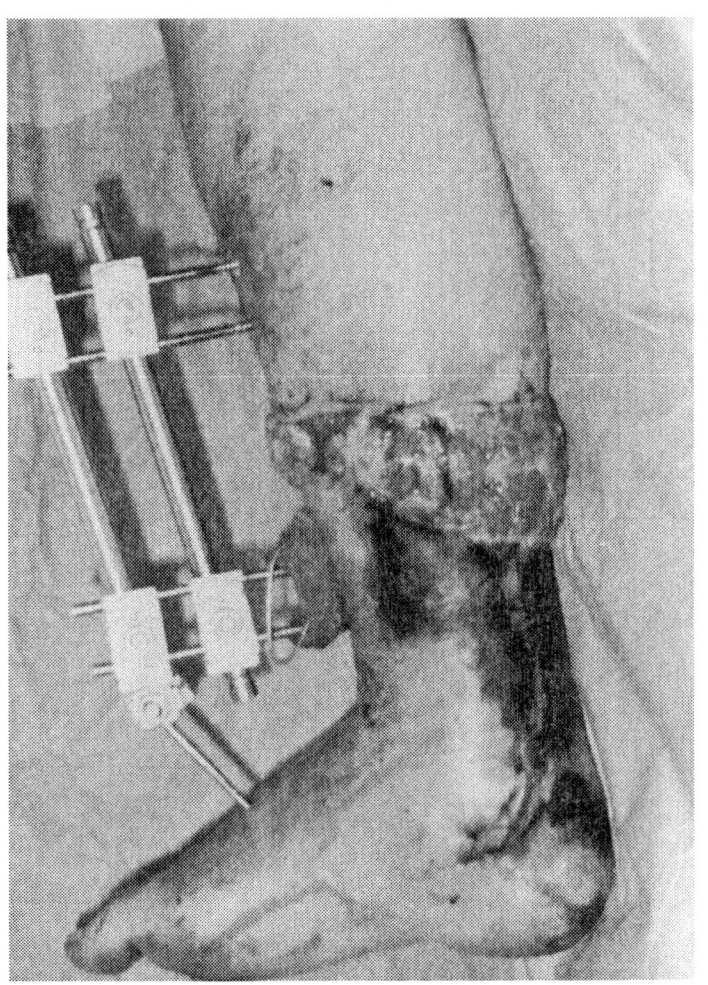

Figure 11.106B
Extensive skin necrosis (black region) and absence of sensation on the sole of the foot due to 13 cm. loss of the posterior tibial nerve. The patient had sustained a brain concussion at the time of injury but by one week following injury was improved, off the ventilator, and was able to begin participating in discussion regarding treatment of her severe injury. Appearance 14 days following injury, immediately prior to below knee amputation.

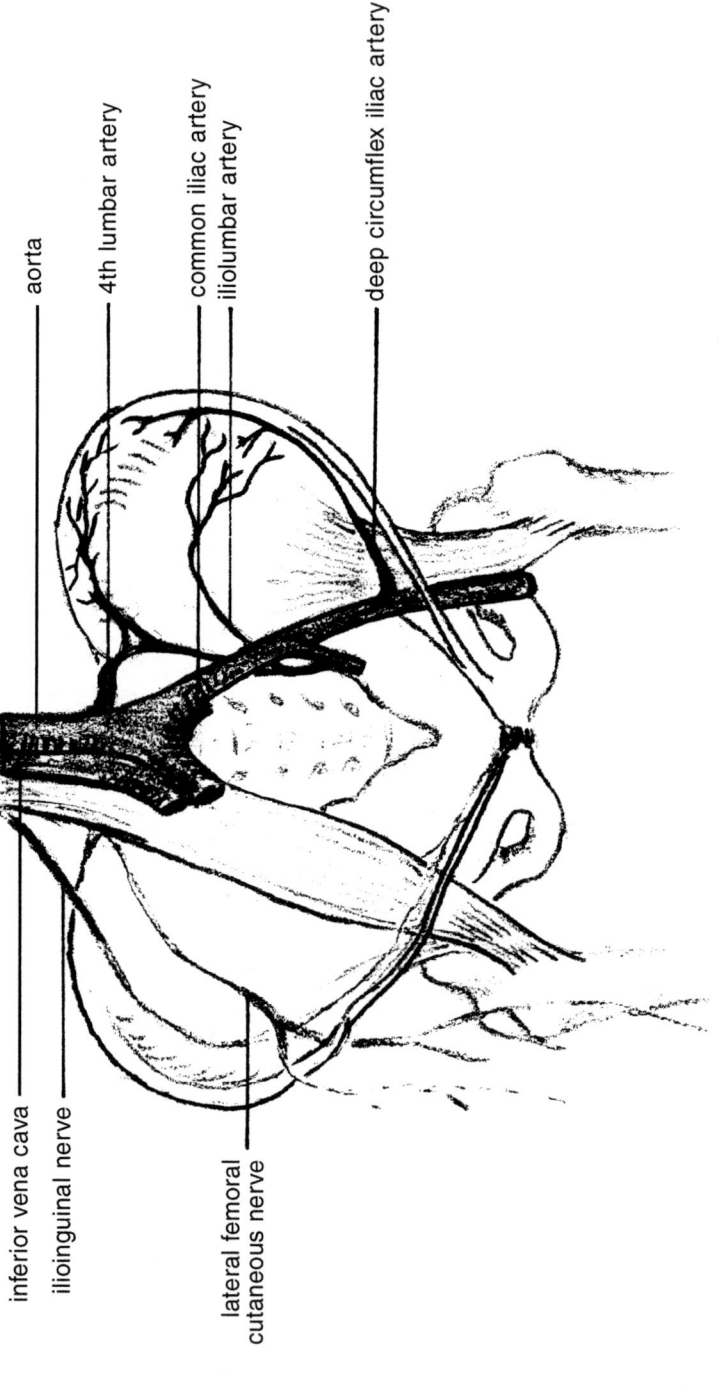

Figure 11.107A
Anatomic structures at risk when harvesting bone graft from the anterior iliac crest (excluding the inferior vena cava and aorta).

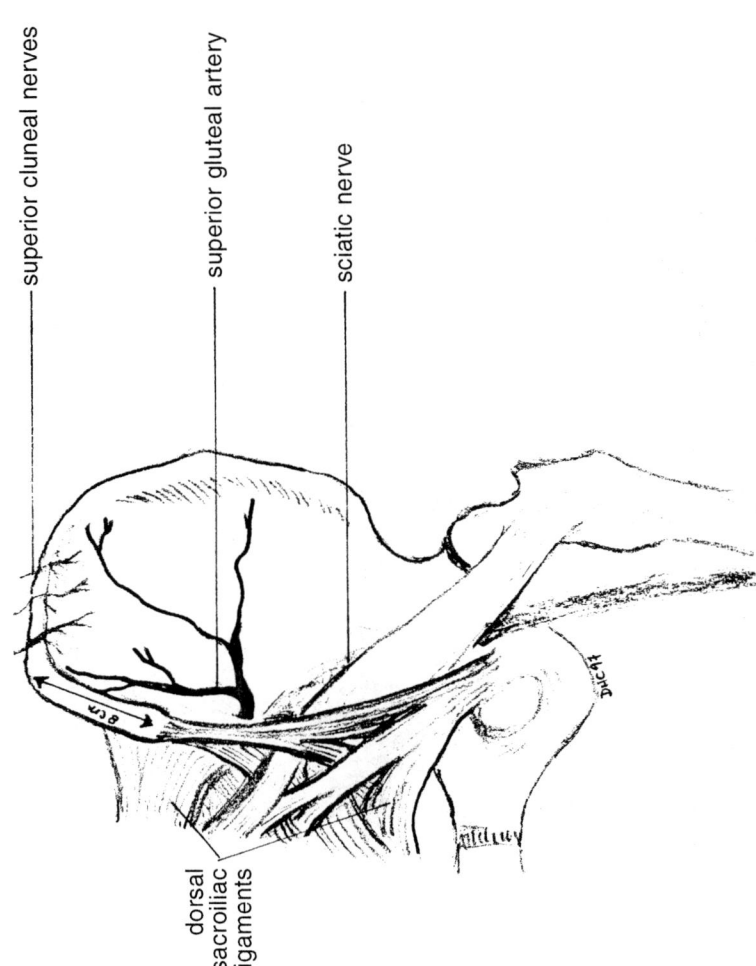

Figure 11.107B
Anatomic structures at risk when harvesting bone graft from the posterior iliac crest.

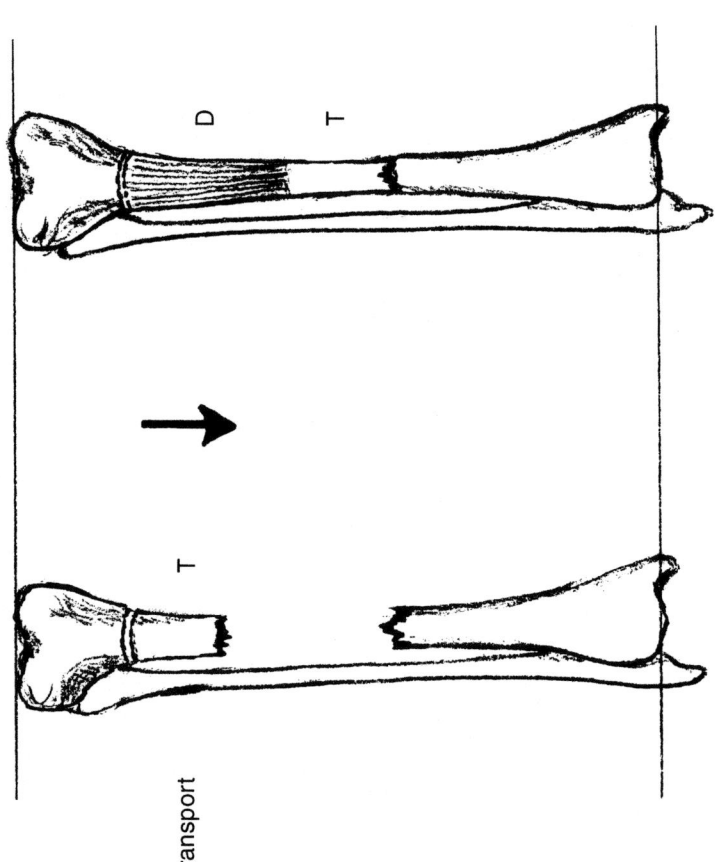

Figure 11.108A
Ilizarov technique for reconstruction of bone defects of the tibia. Bone transport: Tibia is maintained at original length. Corticotomy (osteotomy) of the proximal tibia is performed and the transport fragment (T) is gradually drawn inferiorly or "transported". Distraction bone fills the gap (D).

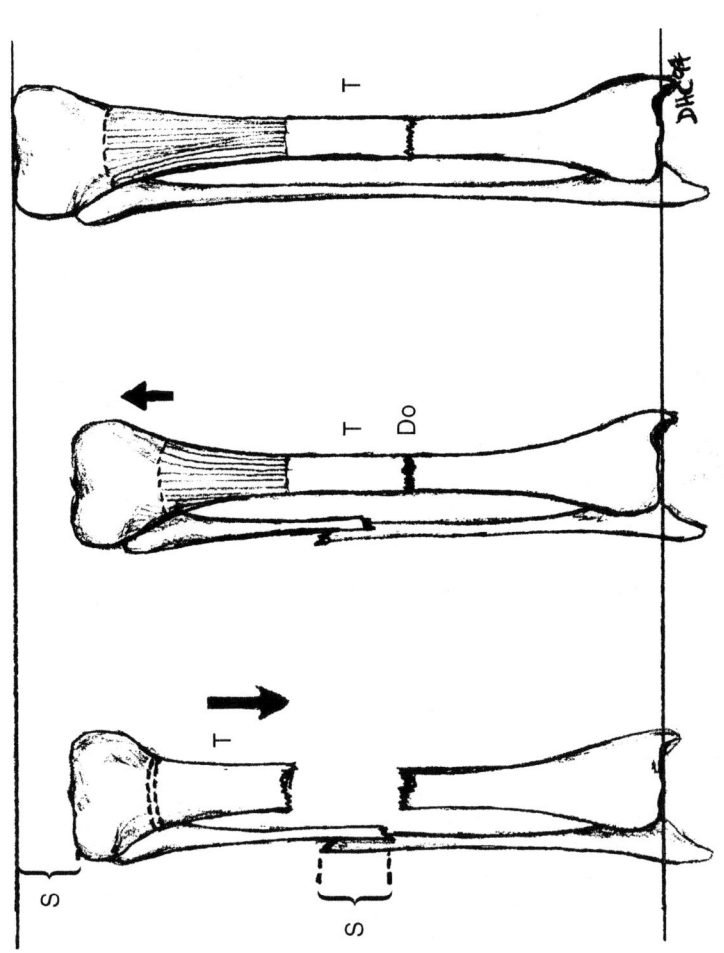

Figure 11.108B
Ilizarov technique for reconstruction of bone defects of the tibia. Bone transport with lengthening: Segmental bone loss in a tibia which has already shortened with previous treatment. The extent of shortening is indicated by "S" at the tibia and fibula. Lengthening continues after "docking" (Do) of the transport fragment (T) with the distal tibia.

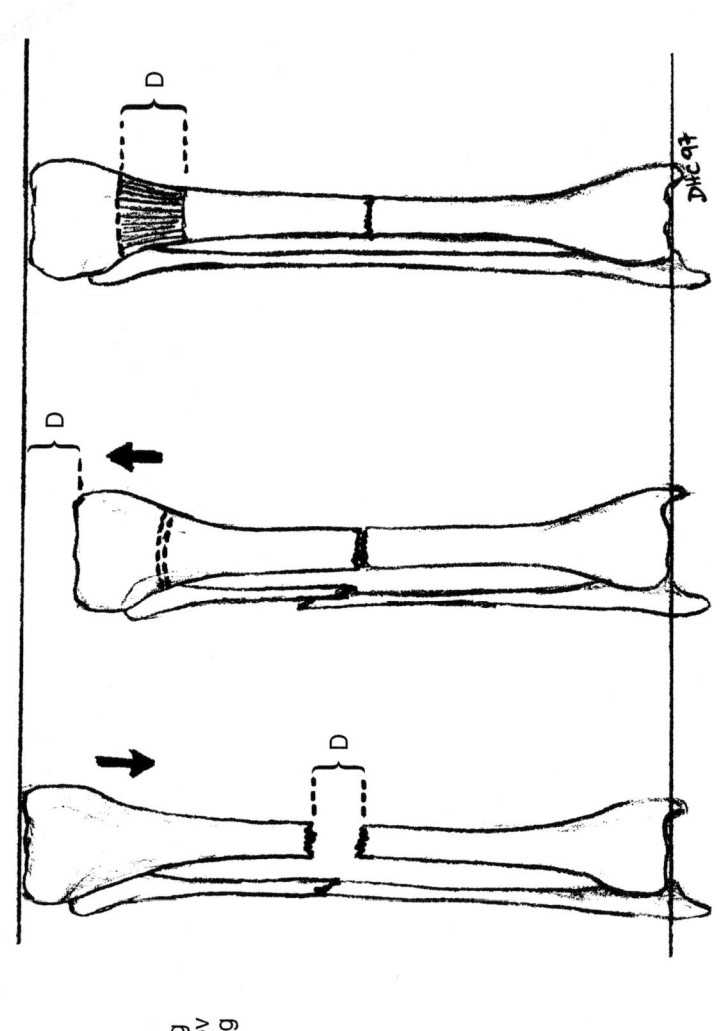

Figure 11.108C
Ilizarov technique for reconstruction of bone defects of the tibia. Acute shortening with secondary lengthening: Patients with bone loss of up to 2.5 to 3 cm. (D) and associated soft tissue defects may be managed by acute shortening at the fracture site. Secondary lengthening restores the tibia to original length.

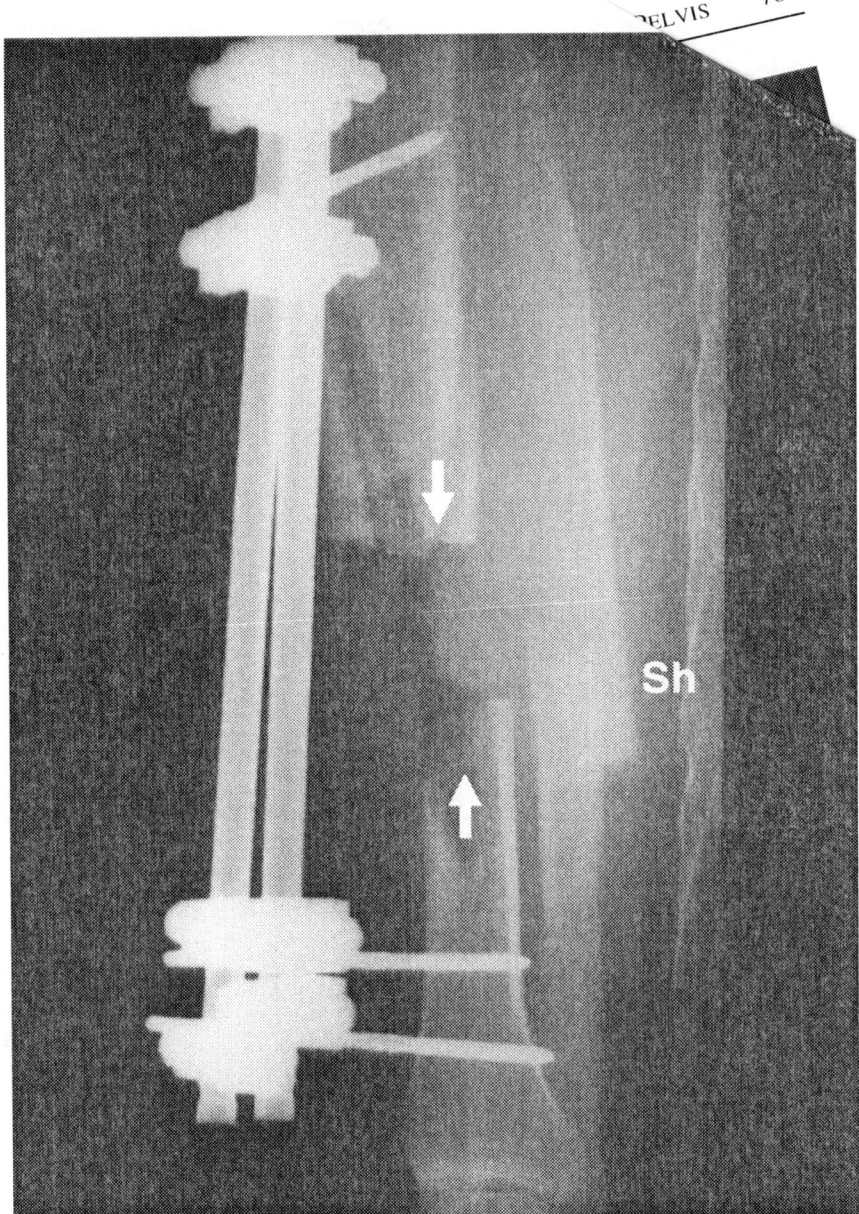

Figure 11.109A
Ilizarov management of Gustilo type IIIB open tibia fracture. A 29-year-old male referred with marked shortening (Sh) of the tibia after a saw mill accident. The extent of the bone loss was 8 cm. Note segmented bone loss (gap) at arrows and residual shortening as noted by fibular overlap (Sh).

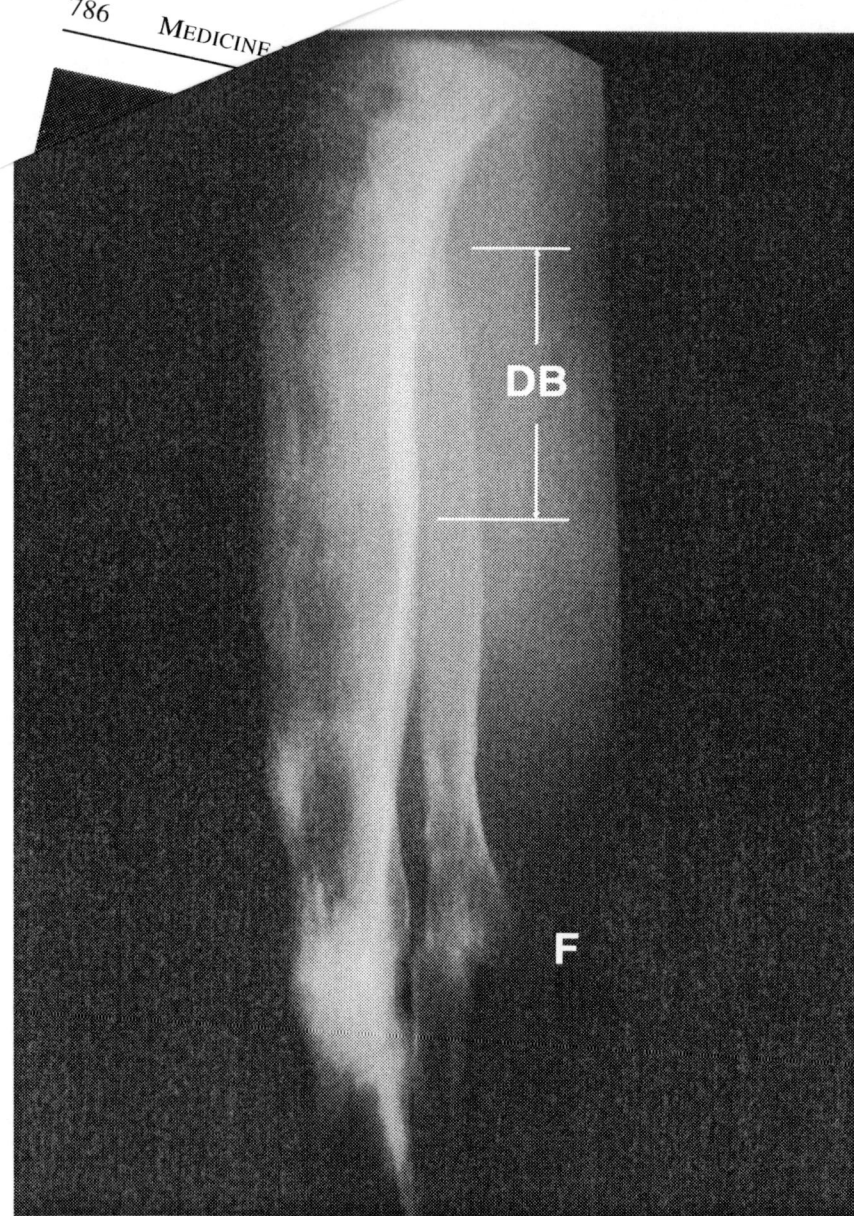

Figure 11.109B
Ilizarov management of Gustilo type IIIB open tibia fracture. Lateral x-ray film at one year demonstrating mature distraction bone (DB) in the proximal tibia. The patient returned to his original work but declined the employer's request that he return to the same machine where the injury occurred. Note fibular length (overlap) has been restored (F).

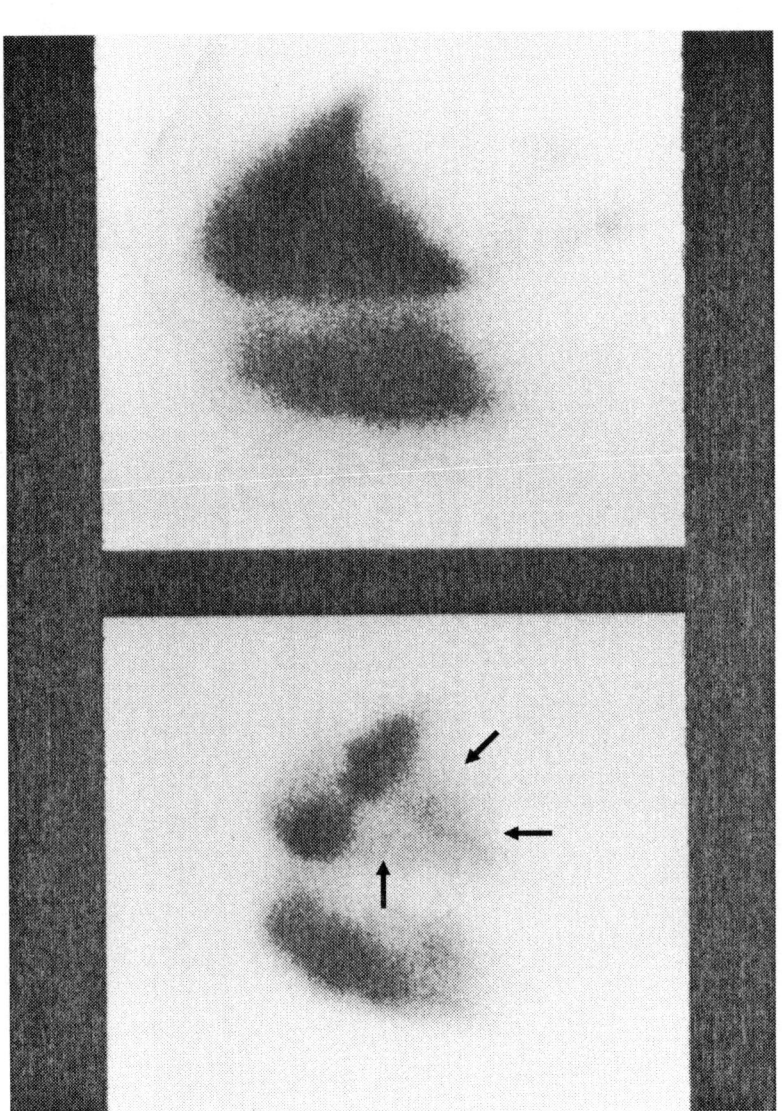

Figure 11.110
Perfusion lung scan showing perfusion defect consistent with pulmonary embolus. Perfusion scan at left, ventilation scan right.

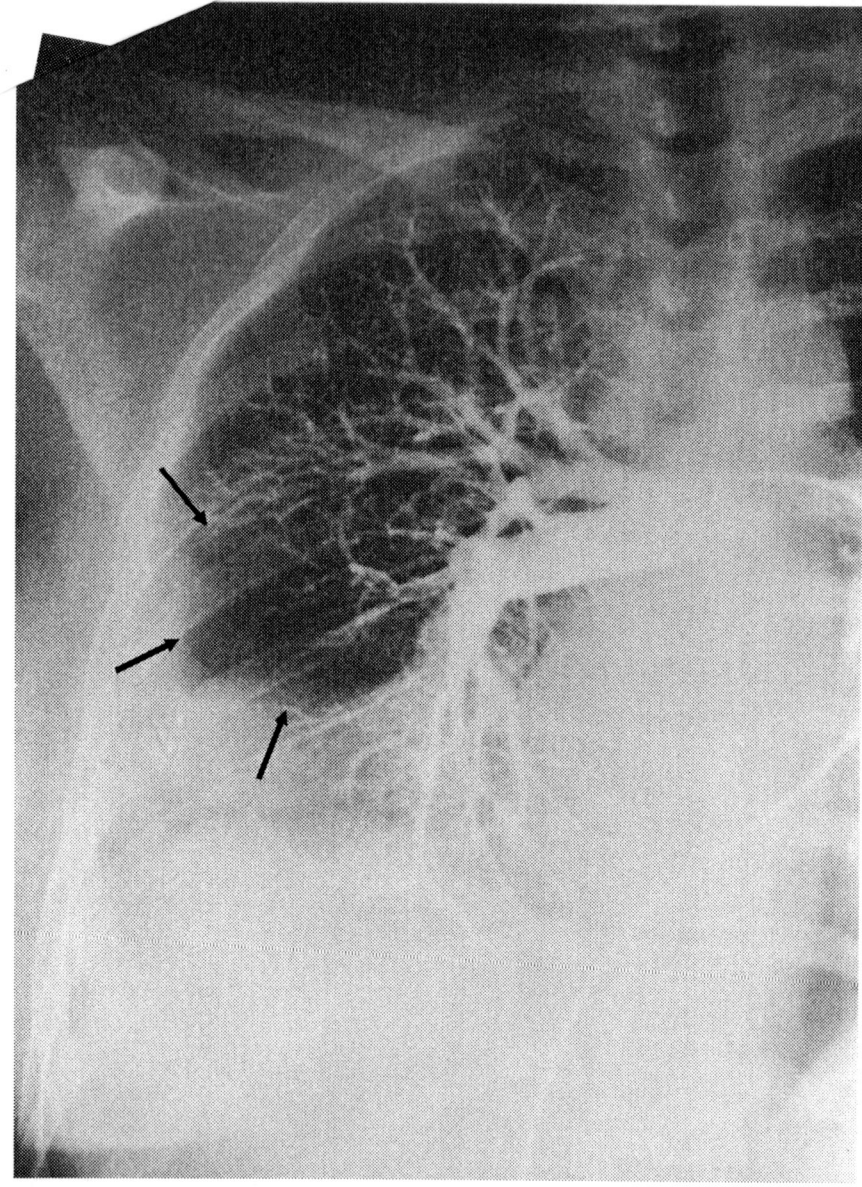

Figure 11.111
Pulmonary angiogram with perfusion defect (arrows). (Photo courtesy of Dr. Gordon French)

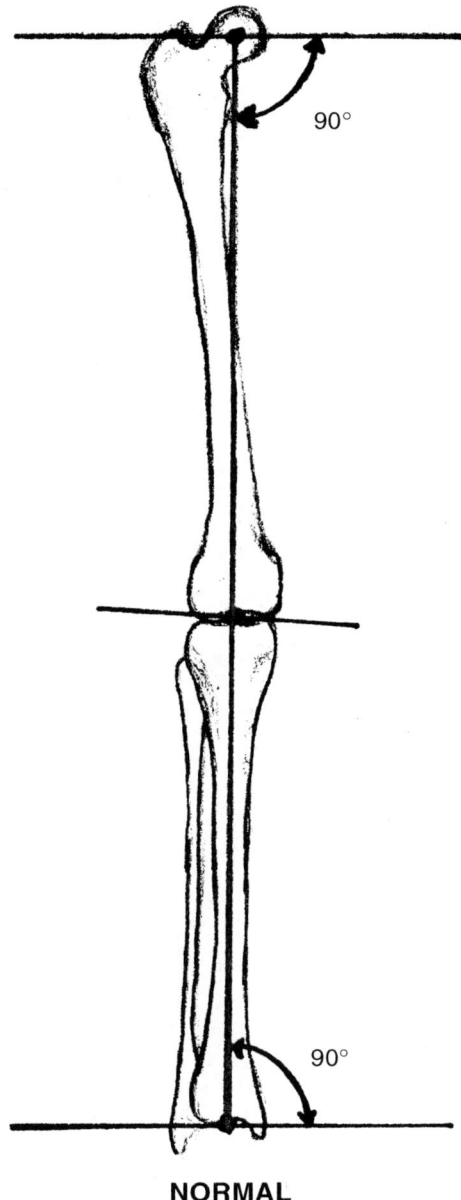

Figure 11.112A
Mechanical axis. The mechanical axis is depicted as the line passing from the centre of the ankle to the centre of the hip and represents the path of transmission of forces along the lower extremity.

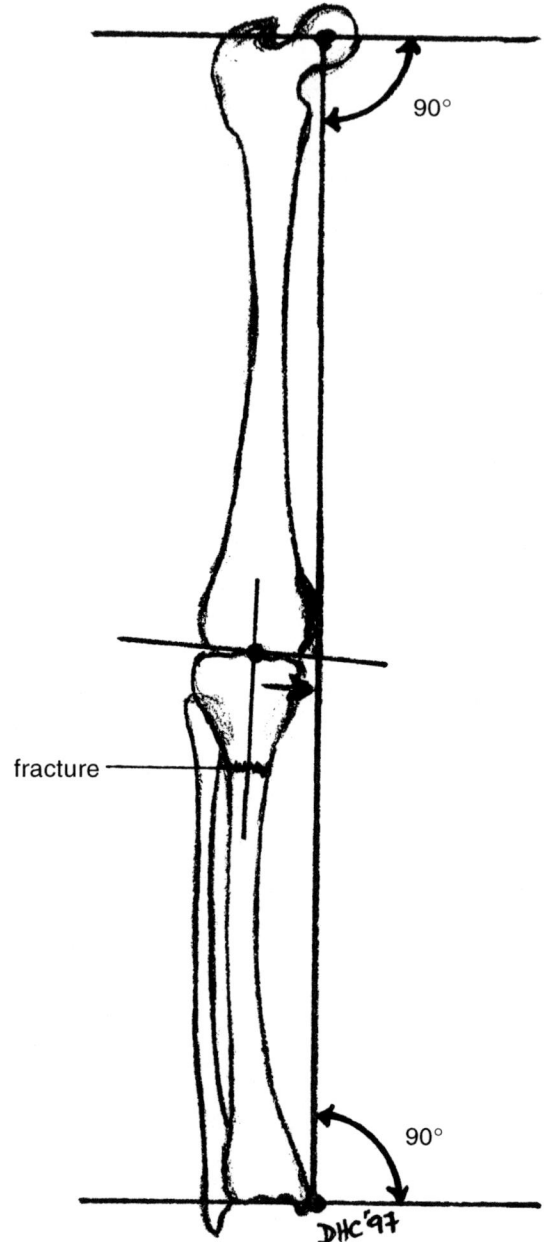

Figure 11.112B
Mechanical axis. With varus deformity of the tibia, the mechanical axis shifts medially, placing increased stress on the medial compartment of the knee.

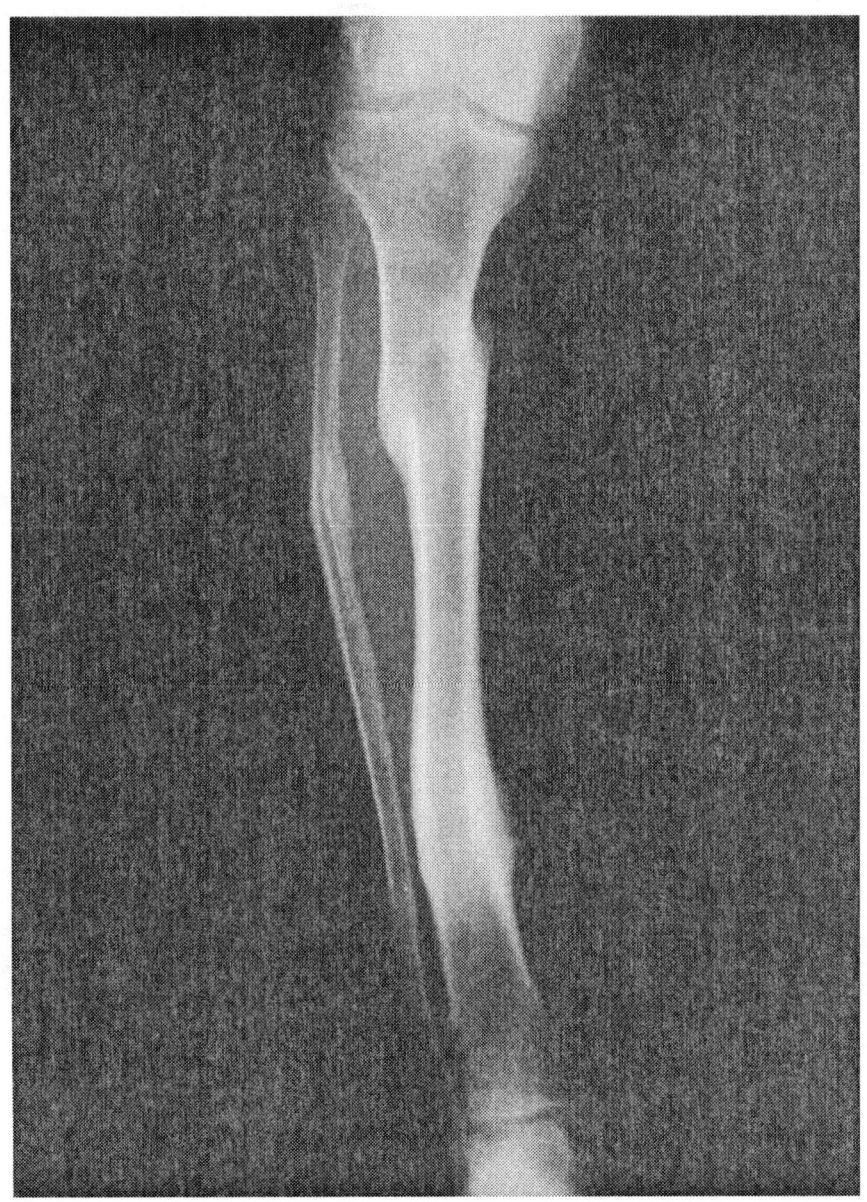

Figure 11.113A
Varus malunion of segmental tibia fracture with 1.8 cm. of shortening.

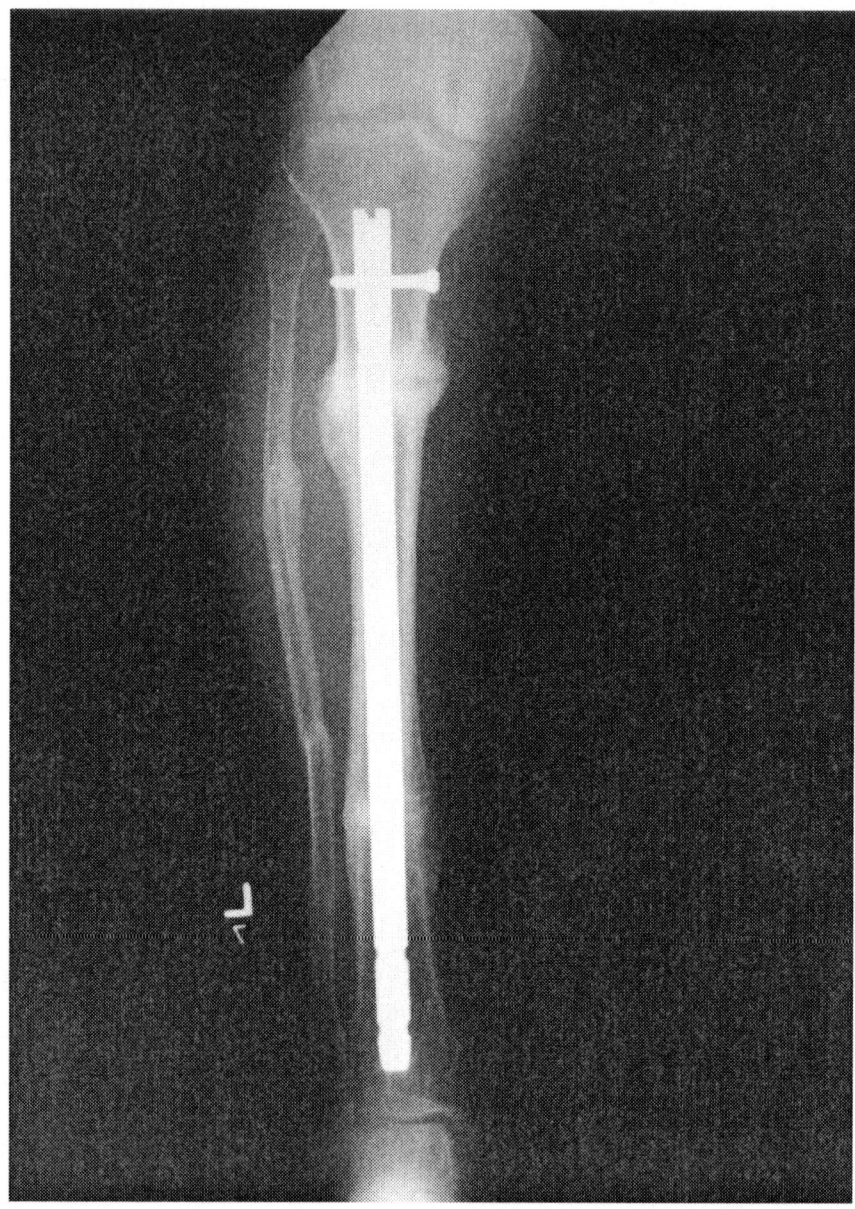

Figure 11.113B
Two level opening wedge osteotomy and intramedullary rod fixation.

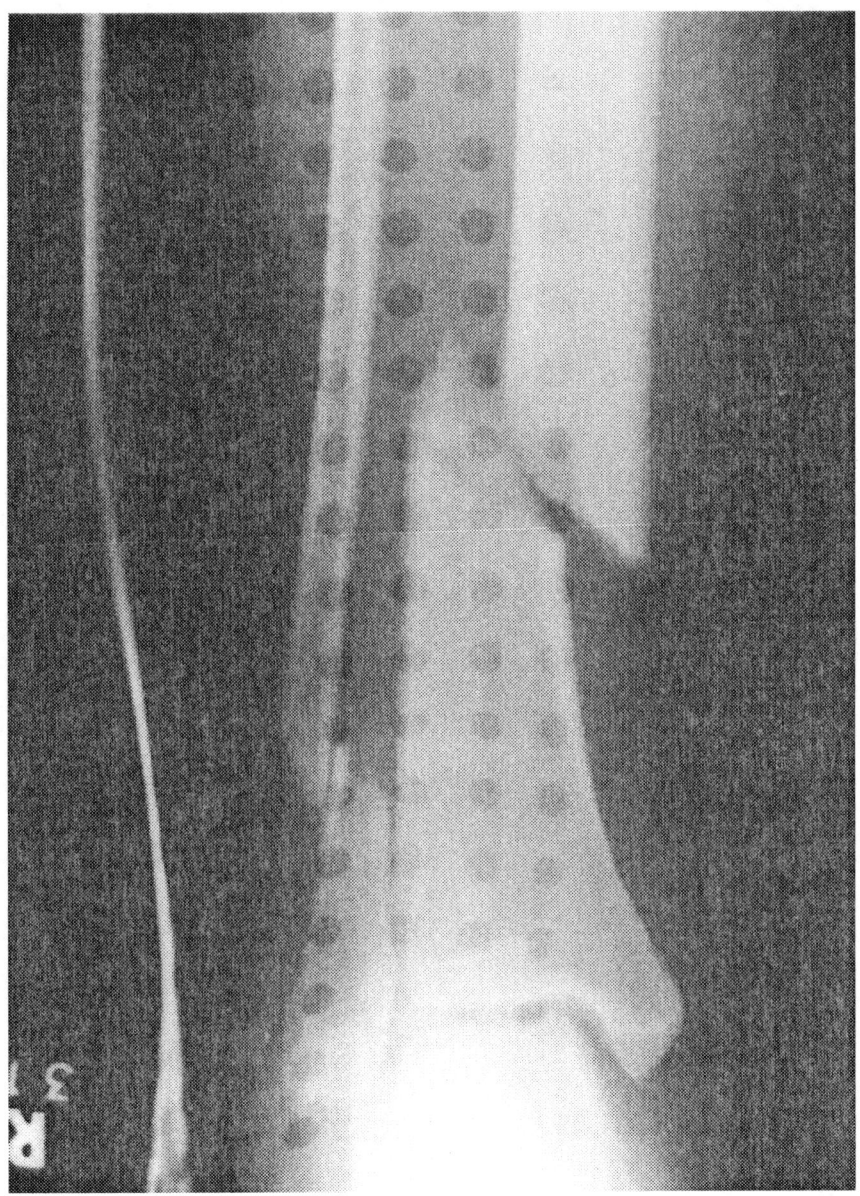

Figure 11.114A
Open fracture of the tibia treated initially by debridement and irrigation.

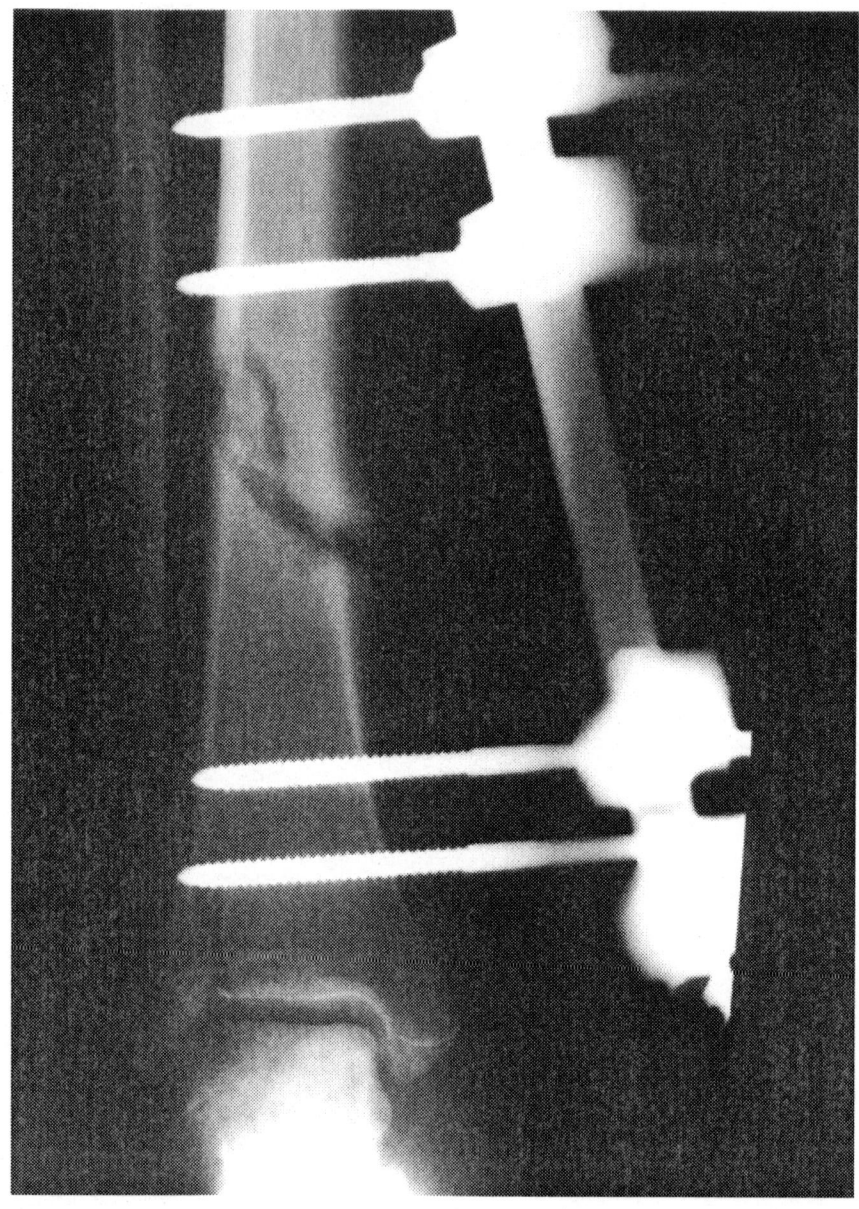

Figure 11.114B
Appearance immediately following debridement and external fixation. Alignment is excellent.

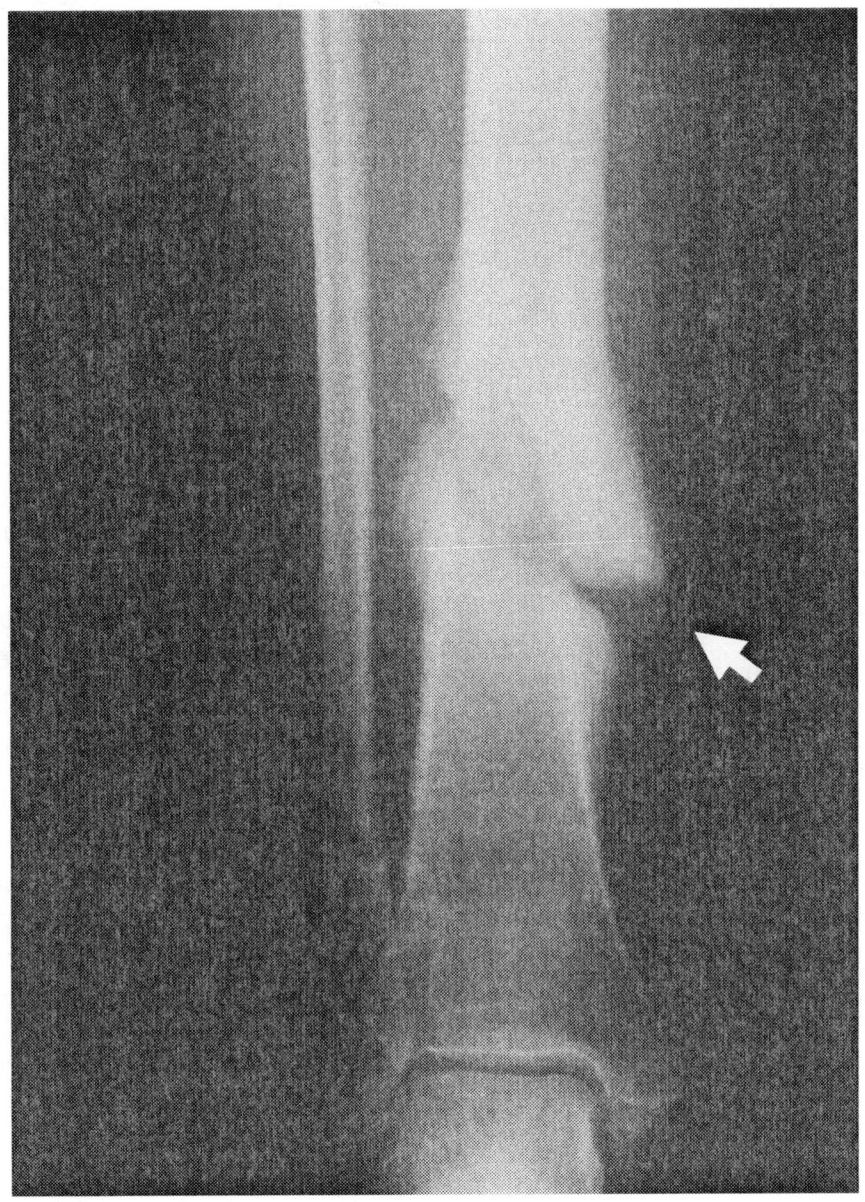

Figure 11.114C
Despite exhuberant bone formation, a hypertropic nonunion developed (arrow).

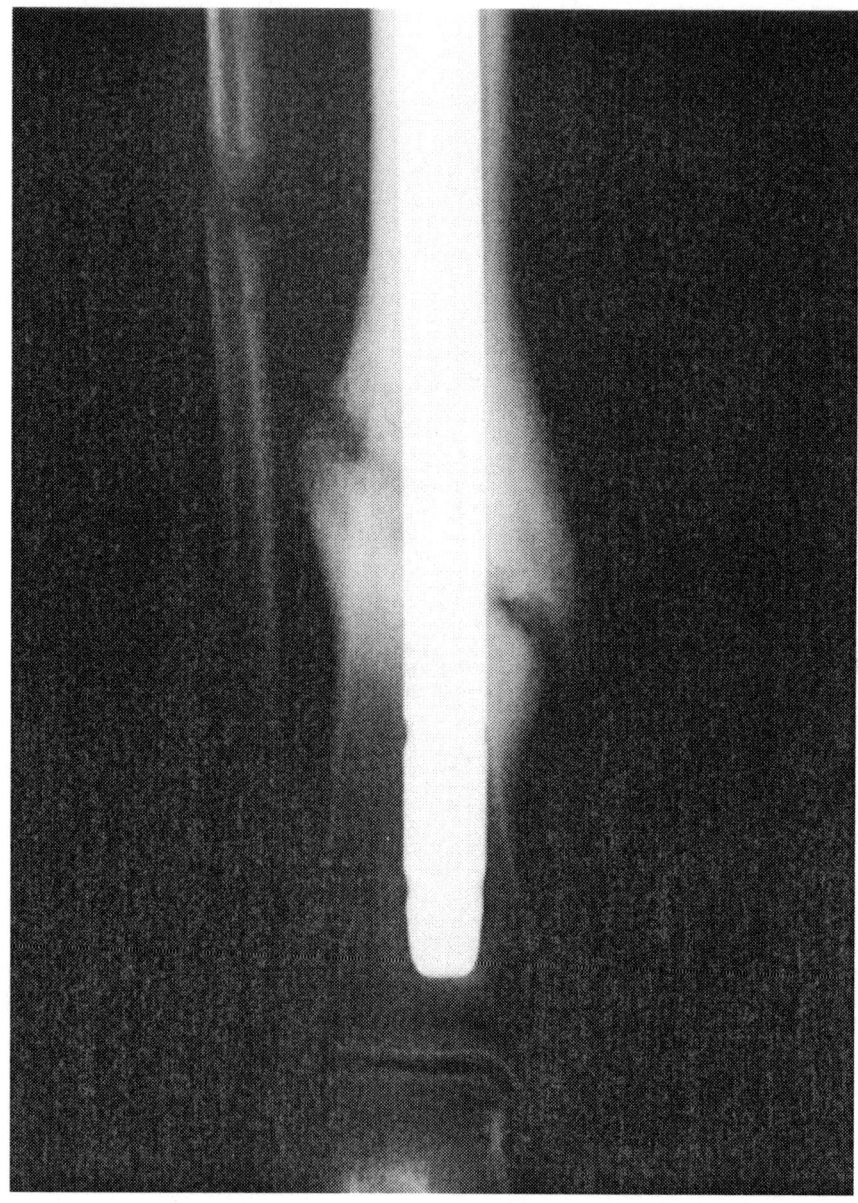

Figure 11.114D
Stabilization of the nonunion by intramedullary rod fixation resulted in union of the fracture.

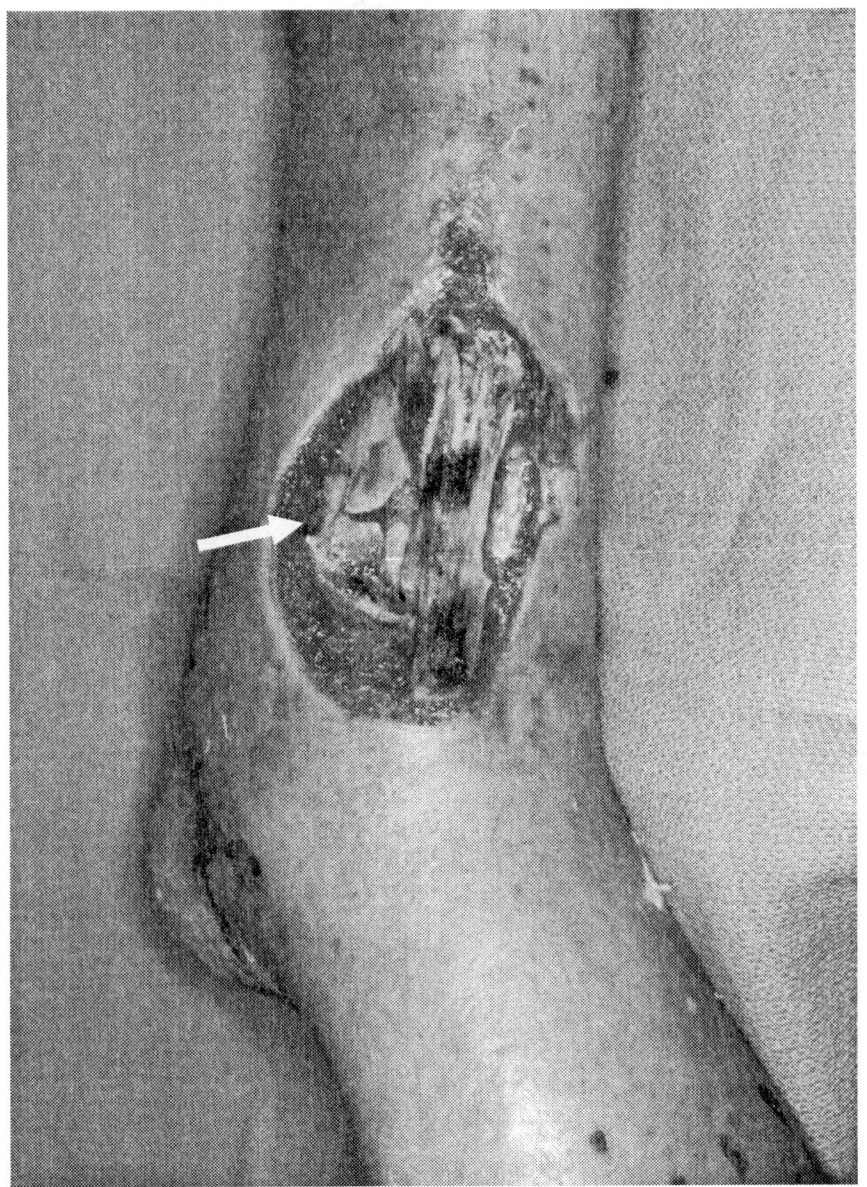

Figure 11.115A
Cierny superficial (II) osteomyelitis following open reduction and internal fixation of an open distal tibia-fibula fracture. Note necrotic bone (arrow) and dissicated tibialis anterior tendon (black, at centre of wound).

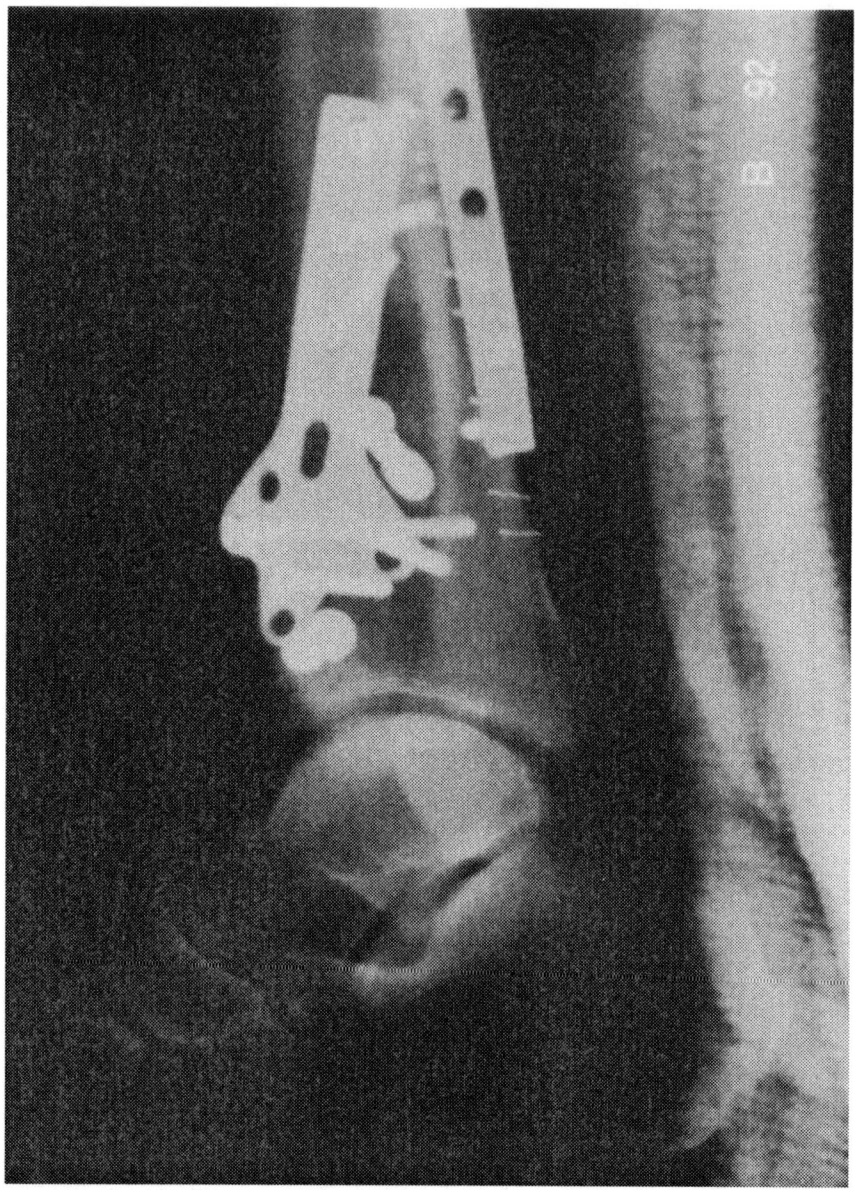

Figure 11.115B
Lateral radiograph reveals excellent position of fracture fragments which does not hint at the potentially limb-threatening nature of the soft tissue envelope problem.

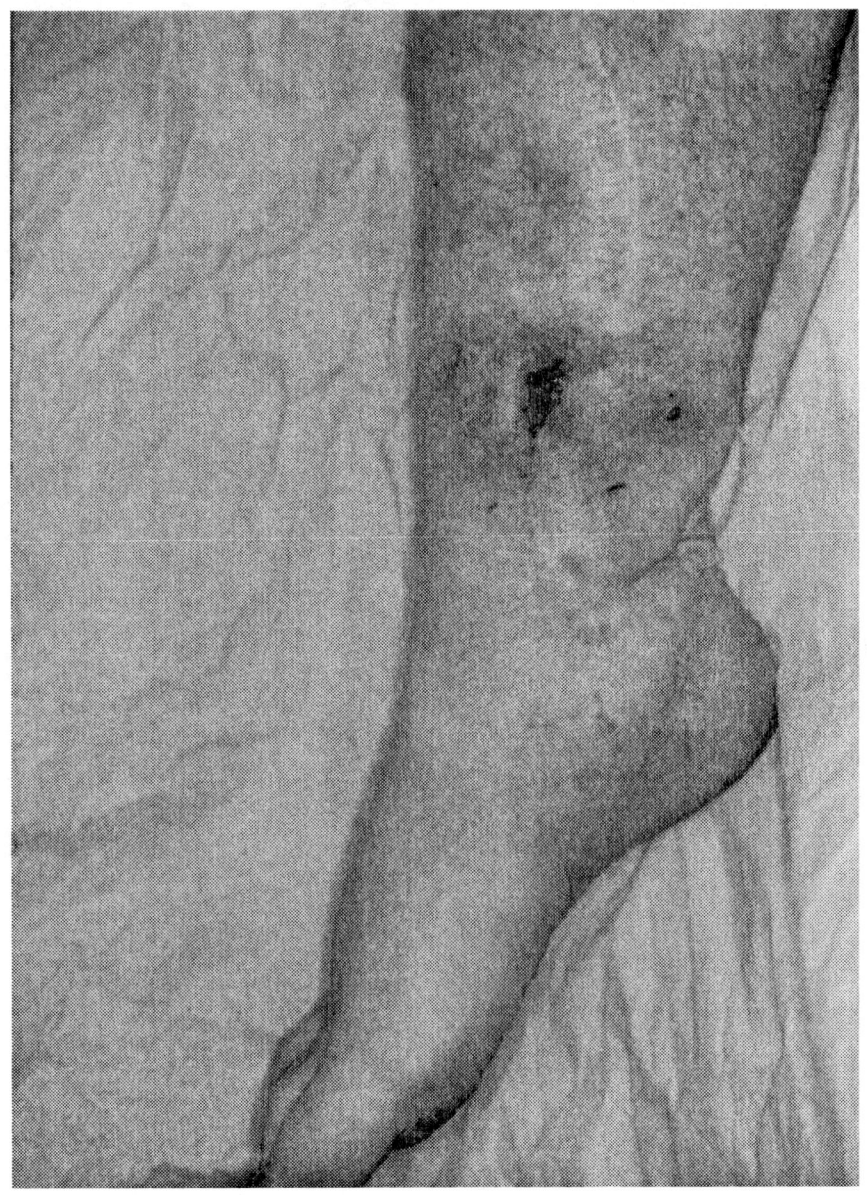

Figure 11.116A
Cierny localized (III) osteomyelitis. A 69-year-old man with chronic infection and drainage from the lower tibia following an open fracture.

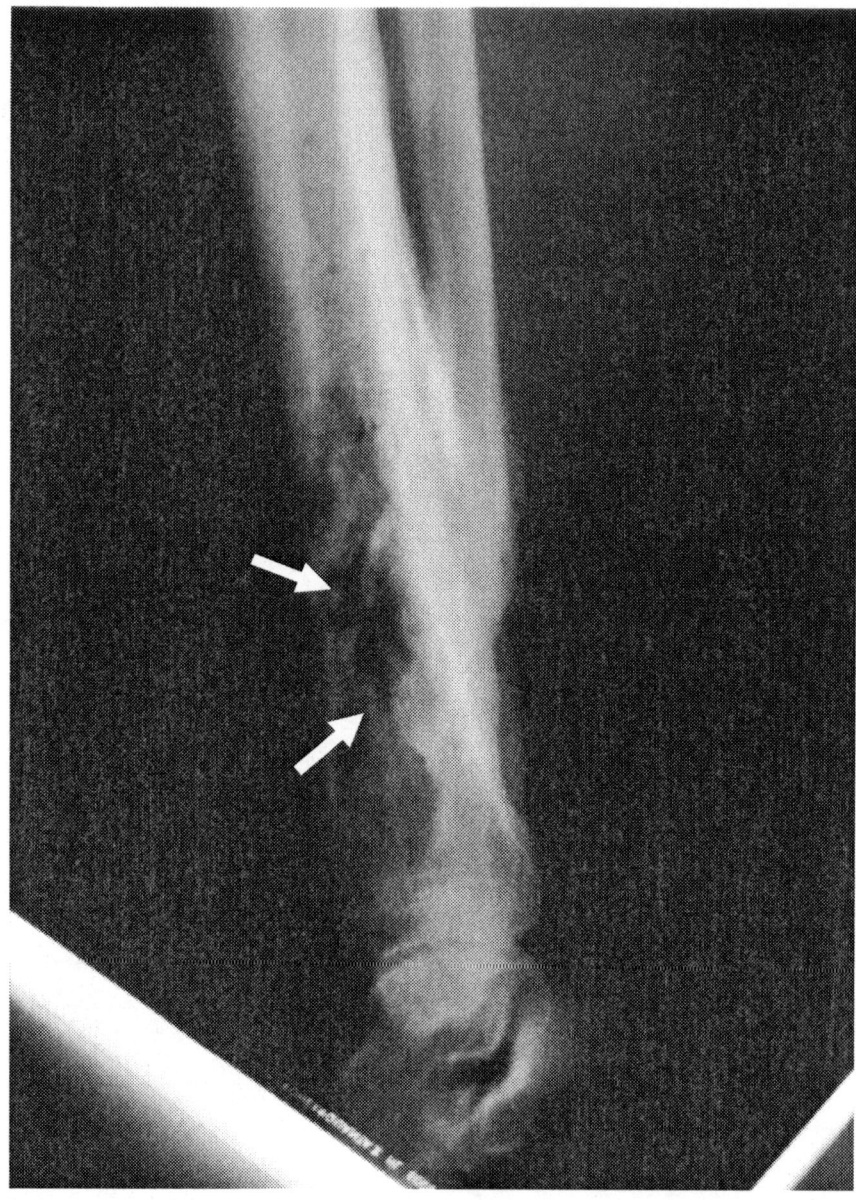

Figure 11.116B
Cierny localized (III) osteomyelitis. Lateral x-ray film demonstrates lytic area consistent with osteomyelitic involvement of cortex and medullary bone (arrows).

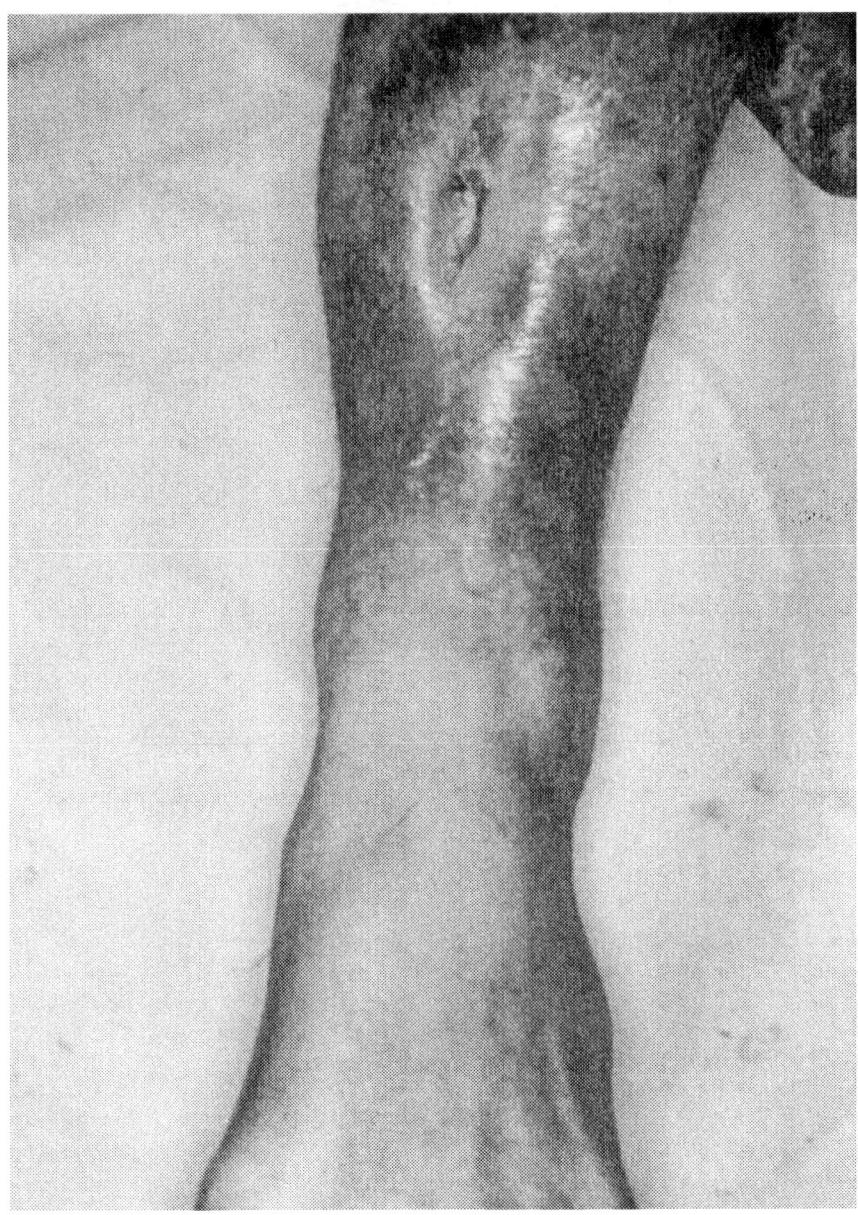

Figure 11.117A
Cierny diffuse (IV) osteomyelitis. Brawny induration of skin and soft tissue scarring surrounding area of exposed, infected tibia.

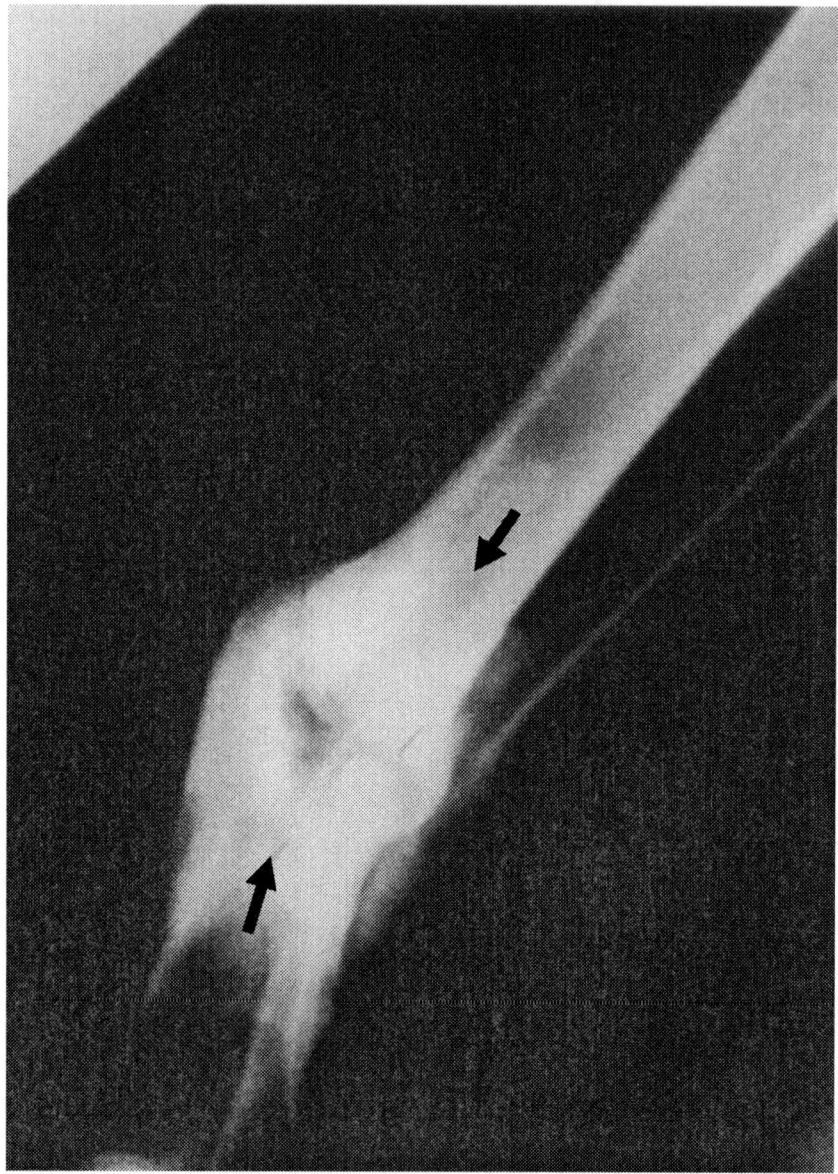

Figure 11.117B
Cierny diffuse (IV) osteomyelitis. Mixed sclerotic lytic appearance on preoperative radiograph of the multiply-operated tibia. The sclerotic region (arrows) was a nonviable sequestrum which required resection. (From: Feibel RJ, Oliva A, Jackson RL et al. Simultaneous free-tissue transfer and Ilizarov distraction osteosynthesis in lower limb salvage: Case report and review of the literature. J Trauma 37: 322-327, 1994, with permission.)

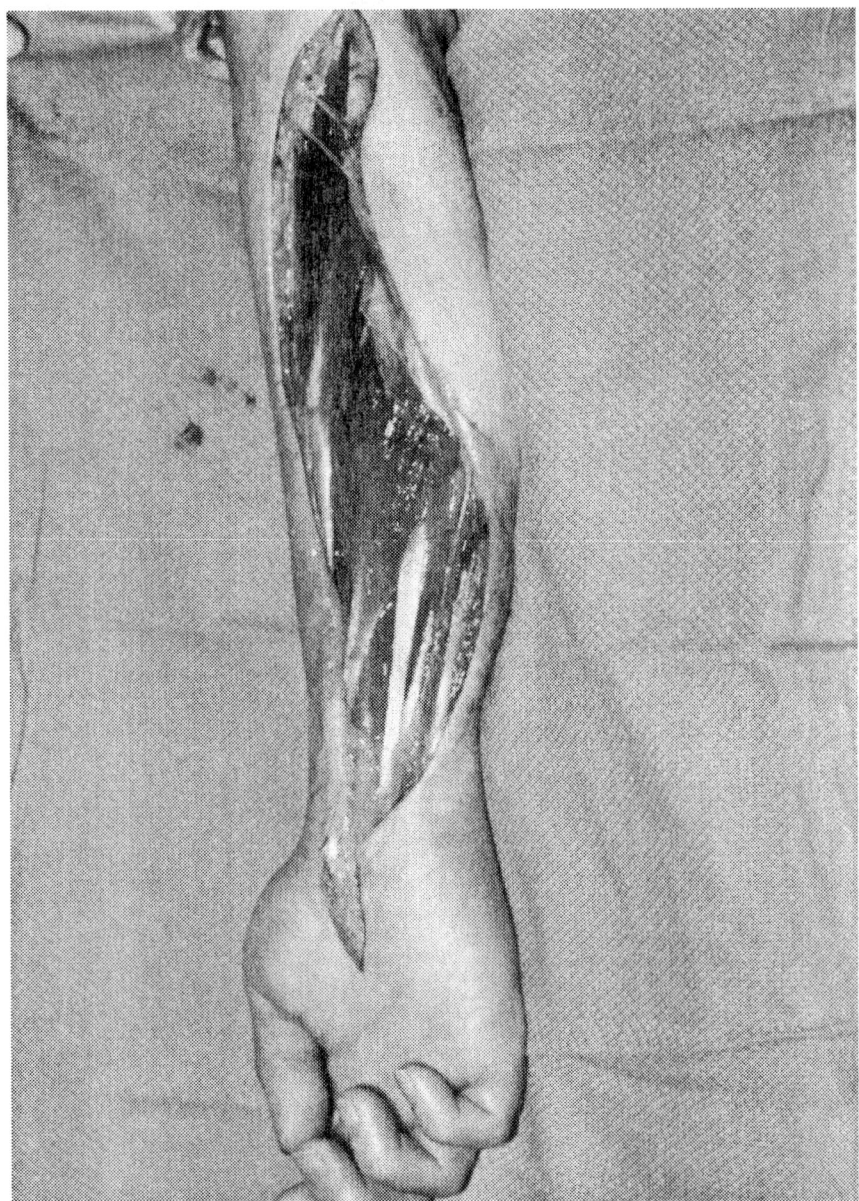

Figure 11.118
Forearm compartment syndrome. Appearance following volar and dorsal fasciotomy.

Chapter 12

Chronic Pain Disorders

by Robert W. Teasell, M.D., F.R.C.P.C.[*]
and Manfred Harth, M.D., F.R.C.P.C.[*]

12.1 Introduction
    12.1.1 The Problem
    12.1.2 Defining Chronic Pain
    12.1.3 Clinical Classification Controversies
12.2 Specific Clinical Entities
    12.2.1 Whiplash Injuries
        12.2.1.1 Mechanisms of Injury
        12.2.1.2 Clinical Picture
    12.2.2 Nonspecificity of Chronic Soft Tissue Pain Disorders
    12.2.3 Myofascial Pain
    12.2.4 Fibromyalgia
        12.2.4.1 Clinical Criteria
        12.2.4.2 Questioning Clinical Criteria
    12.2.5 Relationship Between Fibromyalgia and Trauma
        12.2.5.1 The Argument Against
        12.2.5.2 The Argument For
12.3 Recovery and Pathophysiology
    12.3.1 Recovery After Trauma
    12.3.2 Evidence for an Organic Basis for Chronic Pain
        12.3.2.1 Evidence of a Central Neurological Origin for Regional Pain
        12.3.2.2 Evidence of a Mechanical Origin for Chronic Whiplash Injury Pain
        12.3.2.3 Conclusions
    12.3.3 Are Psychological Factors Causative?
12.4 Disability Secondary to Chronic Pain Disorders
    12.4.1 Definitions: Impairment, Disability and Handicap
    12.4.2 The Rise in Chronic Pain Disability Claims
    12.4.3 The Acute Medical Model and Chronic Pain Disorders

---

[*] Departments of Physical Medicine and Rehabilitation, and Medicine, (Division of Rheumatology), London Health Sciences Centre and University of Western Ontario, London, Ontario, Canada.

12.4.3.1 The Search for Structural Abnormalities
12.4.4 Discordance Between Pain, Impairment, and Disability
12.4.5 Assessment of Disability in Chronic Pain Disorders
12.4.6 Acceptance of Chronic Pain and Disability
12.4.7 Compensation and Secondary Gain in Disability
    12.4.7.1 Compensation and Chronic Pain
    12.4.7.2 Secondary Gain
    12.4.7.3 Secondary Losses
12.4.8 Socioeconomic Factors and Disability
    12.4.8.1 Lower Socioeconomic Status and Risk of Disability
12.4.9 The Work Environment
    12.4.9.1 Heavy Physical Work
    12.4.9.2 Job Dissatisfaction
12.4.10 The Shift to Managing Chronic Pain Disability Only
12.4.11 The Trend Towards Rejecting Chronic Pain Disability
    12.4.11.1 The Report on Back Pain in the Workplace
    12.4.11.2 Quebec Task Force on Whiplash Associated Disorders
12.5 Future Conflict: Chronic Pain, Disability, and Society

12.1 INTRODUCTION

This chapter is designed to look specifically at the issue of chronic pain, and its relationship to disability, following trauma. Chronic pain, an entity where pain persists well beyond the generally accepted healing time of a particular injury, is being increasingly recognized as a common cause of impairment and disability. Few issues in medicine are as fraught with more conflict and controversy than that of chronic "soft tissue" pain. "Soft tissue" pain appears to arise from muscle, ligaments, tendons, and joint capsules. The pathophysiology or biologic mechanisms by which pain is perceived in these "soft tissues" has not been adequately elucidated. This has led to the paradox whereby these chronic pain conditions, which are the most prevalent and costly for society, are also the least well understood and accepted.

12.1.1 The Problem

Chronic pain is estimated to be the third largest health problem in the world and in 1982 affected approximately 65 million Americans.[1] Of pa-

---

1   National Institutes of Health. Chronic Pain: Hope Through Research. Publication no. 82-2406. Bethesda, MD: 1982. Latham J, Davis BD. The Socioeconomic Impact of Chronic Pain. *Disability and Rehabilitation* 1994; 16(1):39-44.

tients suffering from chronic pain, 6–10% are work disabled.[2] The vast majority of chronic pain is directly related to musculoskeletal disorders. Musculoskeletal disorders affecting articular structures such as rheumatoid arthritis, ankylosing spondylitis, and osteoarthritis are chronic, painful and potentially disabling; however, they are well recognized and accepted even if disability assessments are not always well performed and satisfactory.[3] The other major group of musculoskeletal pain disorders, the so-called "soft tissue" pain disorders, suffer from lack of wide recognition and/or acceptance, and the issues of evaluation and treatment of disability have proven to be highly controversial. These chronic "soft tissue" pain disorders have been the source of increasing attention because of concerns about the rising costs of disability claims and the inability of the medical system to contain these costs. It is these chronic "soft tissue" pain disorders and their resultant disability which is the focus of this chapter.

12.1.2 Defining Chronic Pain

The International Association for the Study of Pain (IASP) defines pain as "an unpleasant sensory and emotional experience associated with actual or potential tissue damage or described in terms of such damage."[4] This definition does allow for the distinction between nociception, which represents a stimulus from a peripheral receptor, and pain, which is regarded as subjective and experiential in nature.

Chronic pain is best defined as pain which persists for longer than 6 months. Unfortunately, there is of yet no universally accepted taxonomy for chronic pain syndromes. Difficulties which arise in defining or classifying the various chronic pain states are legion and are described later in this chapter.

The pain experienced by individuals is described in a variety of ways (e.g., sharp, aching, burning) and in a range of patterns. Intensity of the

---

2   Van Korff M, Ormel J, Keefer FJ, Dworkin SF. Grading the Severity of Chronic Pain. *Pain* 1992; 50:133-149. Spitzer WO, LeBlanc FF, Dupuis M. Scientific Approach to the Assessment and Management of Activity-Related Spinal Disorders. *Spine* 1987; 12:51-559. Crombie IK, Davies HT, McRae WA. The Epidemiology of Chronic Pain: Time for New Directions. *Pain* 1994; 57:1-3. Sanders SH. Why do Most Patients with Chronic Pain not Return to Work? In: Cohen MJM, Campbell JN, eds. *Pain Treatment Centers at a Crossroads: A Practical and Conceptual Reappraisal, Progress in Pain Research and Management*. Seattle: IASP Press, 1996, vol. 7: 193-201.

3   Liang MH, Daltroy LH, Larson MG, et al. Evaluation of Social Security Disability in Claimants with Rheumatic Disease. *Ann Intern Med* 1991; 115:26-31. Hadler NM. Disability Determination and the Social Consciousness. *Arthritis Care Res* 1996; 9:163-169.

4   Merskey H, Bogduk N, eds. *Classification of Chronic Pain Syndromes and Definitions of Pain Terms*, 2nd ed. Seattle: IASP Press, 1994.

pain varies between individuals and over time. Intensity of pain can be measured by a verbal numerical scale or the visual analogue scale. Pain is most often exacerbated by physical activity which involves the affected region but is also typically aggravated by inactivity or immobility, weather changes and emotional stress. Sleep disturbance and psychosocial difficulties are common. Findings on physical examination are generally limited to characteristic areas of tenderness in musculoligamentous structures and often restricted range of motion. Varying degrees of physical limitations and disability are common.

12.1.3 Clinical Classification Controversies

Chronic pain disorders are generally diagnosed on the basis of clinical criteria. Some of them, such as whiplash injuries and chronic low back pain (CLBP), have readily recognizable presentations. Classification criteria for the fibromyalgia syndrome have been proposed by the American College of Rheumatology[5] but have been recently questioned in the face of compensation or work injury. Other entities such as repetitive strain injury or myofascial pain syndrome have proven more difficult to define.[6] Where definitions exist they are often met with incredulity.[7] Skepticism has largely developed because the pathophysiology of these conditions remains largely unknown. For instance, a patho-anatomic or pathophysiologic explanation cannot be offered in over 85% of cases of low back pain.[8] The term repetitive (or repetition) strain injury (RSI) has been criticized because it fails to define repetition or strain,[9] whereas injury implies

---

5 Wolfe F, Smythe HA, Yunus MB, et al. The American College of Rheumatology 1990 Criteria for the Classification of Fibromyalgia Report of the Multicenter Criteria Committee. *Arthritis Rheum* 1990; 33:160-172.

6 Diwaker HN, Stothard J. What Do Doctors Mean by Tenosynovitis and Repetitive Strain Injury? *Occup Med* (Oxf) 1995; 45:97-104. Wolfe F, Simons DG, Fricton J, et al. The Fibromyalgia and Myofascial Pain Syndromes: A Preliminary Study of Tender Points and Trigger Points in Persons with Fibromyalgia, Myofascial Pain Syndrome and No Disease. *J Rheumatol* 1992; 19:944-951.

7 Ochoa JL. Guest Editorial: Essence, Investigation, and Management of "Neuropathic" Pains: Hopes from Acknowledgement of Chaos. *Muscle and Nerve* 1993; 997-1008. Loesser JD, Sullivan M. Disability in the Chronic Low Back Pain Patient may be Iatrogenic. *Pain Forum* 1995; 4(2):114-121. Bohr TW. Fibromyalgia Syndrome and Myofascial Pain Syndrome: Do They Exist? *Neurol Clin* 1995; 13:365-384. Bohr TW. Problems with Myofascial Pain Syndrome and Fibromyalgia Syndrome. *Neurology* 1996; 45:593-597.

8 Spitzer et al., *supra*, note 2. White AA, Gordon GC. Synopsis: Workshop on Idiopathic Low Back Pain. *Spine* 1982; 7:141-149.

9 Cleland LG. "RSI". A Model of Social Iatrogenesis. *Med J Aust* 1987; 236:238-239. Brooks P. Repetitive Strain Injury. *Br Med J* 1993; 307:1298.

"damage to tissues which has never been shown."[10] This skepticism is embodied in the Back Pain Report by Fordyce et al.[11] in their recommendation that nonspecific low back pain be reconceptualized "as a problem of activity intolerance, not a medical problem" or the Quebec Task Force's recommendation that the period for compensation and rehabilitation for whiplash associated disorders be restricted to 27 days.[12] It has even been suggested that these entities are examples of recurrent social and cultural phenomena which have assumed a new guise in the twentieth century.[13]

12.2 SPECIFIC CLINICAL ENTITIES

Before discussing issues of pathophysiology and disability, it would be worthwhile describing three clinical entities commonly associated with trauma, namely whiplash, myofascial pain, and fibromyalgia, as well as problems in terms of specificity in terms of distinguishing between the latter two.

12.2.1 Whiplash Injuries

The Quebec Task Force adopted the following definition of whiplash: "Whiplash is an acceleration-deceleration mechanism of energy transfer to the neck. It may result from rear-end or side-impact motor vehicle collisions, but it can also occur during diving or other mishaps. The impact may result in bony or soft tissue injuries (whiplash injuries), which in turn may lead to a variety of clinical manifestations (Whiplash-Associated Disorders)." In British Columbia and Saskatchewan, two Canadian provinces with single-payer motor vehicle insurance programs, 68% and 85% respectively, of all claims paid out, were for whiplash injuries.[14]

12.2.1.1 Mechanisms of Injury

Typically the injured individual is the occupant of a stationary vehicle

---

10 Brooks, *ibid.*
11 Fordyce WE, ed. *Back Pain in the Workplace.* Seattle: IASP Press, 1995.
12 Spitzer WO, et al. Quebec Task Force on Whiplash-Associated Disorders. *Spine* 1995; 20(85):1S-73S.
13 Pearce JMS. New Diagnoses for Old Disease: Dangers and Distractions. *QJ Med* 1994; 87:253-258. Shorter E. The Borderland between Neurology and History. *Neurol Clin* 1995; 13:229-239.
14 Spitzer et al., *supra*, note 12. Giroux M. Les Blessumes a la Colonne Cervicale; Importance du Probleme. *Le Medicin du Quebec*, Sept 22-26, 1991. Sobeco, Ernst and Young. Saskatchewan Government Insurance Automobile Injury Study. Report to the Saskatchewan Government Insurance Office, March 1989.

which is struck from behind,[15] although injury frequently occurs following side-on and head-on collisions.[16] Injury is thought to occur when neck musculature is unable to compensate for the rapidity of head and torso movement resulting from the acceleration forces generated at the time of impact.[17] When the physiologic limits of cervical structures are exceeded, anatomical disruption of the "soft tissues" of the neck (including muscles, ligaments and joint capsules) results.

12.2.1.2 Clinical Picture

The clinical syndrome of whiplash is dominated by head, neck, and upper thoracic pain and often is associated with a variety of poorly explained symptoms such as tinnitus and blurred vision. The symptom complex is remarkably consistent from patient to patient and is frequently complicated by psychological sequelae such as anger, anxiety, depression, and concern over litigation or compensation. Typical physical and psychosocial complaints in chronic whiplash are listed in Table 1 (below).

Table 1. Physical and Psychosocial Complaints Associated with Whiplash Injuries

- Neck and shoulder pain
- Headache
- Arm pain/parasthesia/weakness
- Dizziness
- Tinnitus
- Fatigue
- Low back pain
- Sleep disturbance
- Temporomandibular joint pain
- Depression
- Anger and frustration
- Anxiety

---

15 Bogduk N. The Anatomy and Pathophysiology of Whiplash. *Clin Biomech* 1986; 1:92-101. Deans GT. Incidence and Duration of Neck Pain Among Patients Injured in Car Accidents. *Br Med J* 1986; 292:94-95. Frankel VH. Pathomechanics of Whiplash Injuries to the Neck. In: Morley TP, ed. *Current Controversies in Neurosurgery*. Philadelphia: W.B. Saunders, 1976: 39-50. Macnab I. The "Whiplash Syndrome". *Orthop Clin North Amer* 1971; 2:389-403. LaRocca H. Acceleration Injuries of the Neck. *Clin Neurosurg* 1978; 25:205-217.

16 Deans, *ibid.*

17 Hohl M. Soft Tissue Neck Injuries. In: The Cervical Spine Research Society Editorial Committee, eds. *The Cervical Spine*, 2nd ed. Philadelphia: J.B. Lippincott Company, 1989: 436-441.

- Loss of job and income
- Marital and family disruption
- Drug dependency

Women appear to experience whiplash injuries more often than men.[18] A delay in onset of symptoms of several hours following impact is characteristic of whiplash injuries.[19] Most patients feel little or no pain for the first few minutes following injury after which symptoms gradually intensify over the next few days.

12.2.2 Nonspecificity of Chronic Soft Tissue Pain Disorders

Tunks[20] notes that, "when blind clinical examination of fibromyalgia and myofascial patients is used, examiners are not able to distinguish between myofascial and chronic fibromyalgia conditions by using bedside clinical examinations for tenderness threshold, tender point counts, or trigger points and referred pain."[21] One of the difficulties in distinguishing between myofascial pain and fibromyalgia is that there is considerable overlap between these two conditions. It is not uncommon to see patients who initially suffer from localized myofascial pain go on to develop more generalized fibromyalgia. Many believe these two entities to represent a continuum of muscle or musculoligamentous pain disorders. We will next look at each of these entities in turn.

12.2.3 Myofascial Pain

Myofascial pain remains a poorly understood clinical entity which nevertheless appears to be quite common. The "trigger point" is regarded as the characteristic feature of myofascial pain.[22] Myofascial trigger points

---

18 Spitzer et al., *supra*, note 12. Balla JI. The Late Whiplash Syndrome. *Aust NZ J Surg* 1980; 50:610-614.
19 Deans GT, McGailliard JN, Kerr M, Rutherford WH. Neck Pain — A Major Cause of Disability Following Car Accidents. *Injury* 1987; 18:10-12. Dunsker SB. Hyperextension and Hyperflexion Injuries of the Cervical Spine. In: Youmans JR, ed. *Neurological Surgery*, 2nd ed. Philadelphia: WB Saunders, 1982: 2332-2343. Evans RW. Some Observations on Whiplash Injuries. In: Evans RW, ed. *The Neurology of Trauma*. Neurologic Clinics 1992; 10(4):975-995.
20 Tunks E. Nonspecificity of Chronic Soft Tissue Pain Syndromes. *Pain Res Manage* 1997; 2(3):176-180.
21 Wolfe et al., *supra*, note 6. Tunks E, McCain GA, Hart LE, Teasell RW, et al. The Reliability of Examination for Tenderness in Patients with Myofascial Pain, Chronic Fibromyalgia and Controls. *J Rheumatol* 1995; 22:944-952.
22 Travell JG, Simons DG. *Myofascial Pain and Dysfunction: The Trigger Point Manual*. Baltimore: Williams and Wilkins, 1983.

are circumscribed, 2-5 mm in diameter, self-sustaining, hyperirritable foci of tenderness reported to be located within a taut band of skeletal muscle or its associated fascia. Compressing this trigger point is locally painful and may give rise to characteristic referred pain, tenderness and autonomic phenomena.

Although the diagnosis of myofascial pain requires the presence of these palpable trigger points, it is often difficult to reliably establish the presence or absence of these trigger points on physical examination. Empirical support for myofascial pain derives primarily from experimental studies involving mechanical irritation of deep tissues (i.e., muscles, deep fascia, etc.) which resulted in poorly localized aching or burning often associated with muscle soreness and tenderness over bony prominences.[23] This referred pain, although often delayed in onset, was reproducible and often accompanied by autonomic phenomena. Tunks notes, "Although the concept of myofascial pain has wide currency, these criteria have never been tested for test-retest and inter-rater reliability, or sensitivity and specificity in a properly controlled trial." Where chronic fibromyalgia and myofascial pain criteria have been blindly assessed, specificity has been poor, although sensitivity has remained good.[24]

12.2.4 Fibromyalgia

12.2.4.1 Clinical Criteria

Fibromyalgia syndrome is a condition of chronic, diffuse, musculoskeletal pain, of unknown etiology, usually associated with fatigue and non-restorative sleep. The American College of Rheumatology[25] has developed criteria for the clinical diagnosis of fibromyalgia which are the most widely used:

- There is persistent widespread (diffuse) pain of at least three months' duration.

---

23 Croft AC. Soft Tissue Injury: Long-Term and Short-Term Effects. In: Foreman SM, Croft AC, eds. *Whiplash Injuries. The Cervical Acceleration Deceleration Syndrome*. Baltimore: Williams & Wilkins, 1988: 293. Feinsten B, Langton JNK, Jameson RM, Schiller F. Experiments of Pain Referred from Deep Somatic Tissues. *J Bone Joint Surg* (Am) 1954; 36:981-997. Inman VH, Saunders JB. Referred Pain from Skeletal Structures. *J Nerve Ment Dis* 1944; 99:660-697.

24 Tunks, *supra*, note 20. Tunks et al., *supra*, note 21. Wolfe et al., *supra*, note 6. Tunks E. Clinical Experimental Investigations in Fibromyalgia and Myofascial Pain. In: Vaeroy H, Merskey H, eds. *Progress in Fibromyalgia and Myofascial Pain*, Amsterdam: Elsevier, 1993: 161-172.

25 Wolfe et al., *supra*, note 5.

- This widespread pain includes at least three sites, one of which must be above the waist, one below the waist, one in the centre of the body, and one on each side of the body.
- Pain is evoked by palpation with 4 kg of pressure in at least 11 of 18 prescribed tender points.

Wolfe et al.[26] noted that, "In 1990 the American College of Rheumatology (ACR 1990) Criteria for the Classification of Fibromyalgia were published and have become the 'de facto' standard for diagnostic classification.... Although the ACR 1990 criteria were proposed as classification criteria they also appear to be quite useful for diagnosis. Classification of the patient as having fibromyalgia occurs regardless of my other concomitant medical diagnosis. Thus fibromyalgia is not a disorder of exclusion."

The robustness of these criteria can be judged by noting that they had a sensitivity, specificity and overall accuracy of 88%, 81% and 85% when compared with patients with similar chronic rheumatic pain disorders. The ACR Committee originally selected 30 tender points through physical examination training sessions, analyzed and reviewed the data, and used independent and blinded assessments; both dolorimetry and digital palpation were used.[27] The percentage of patients positive for tender points was compared between both fibromyalgia patients and controls; it is important to recall that these controls had a variety of musculoskeletal conditions including rheumatoid arthritis, low back pain, and psoriatic arthritis.[28] The accuracy of various combinations of tender points and symptoms was tested. It is possible that other tender point and symptom combinations could give better accuracy, or that the combination of criteria used by the ACR might yield lower accuracy in another independent pool sample; however, this remains to be demonstrated.

12.2.4.2 Questioning Clinical Criteria

Tunks[29] has noted, "When the ACR criteria for fibromyalgia[30] are used to compare chronic fibromyalgia patients with nonpainful controls, the criteria perform well, showing acceptable specificity and sensitivity. However, when these criteria are used in a design comparing chronic

---

26 Wolfe F and the Vancouver Fibromyalgia Consensus Group. The Fibromyalgia Syndrome: A Consensus Report on Fibromyalgia and Disability. *J Rheumatology* 1996; 23(3):534-539.
27 Wolfe et al., *supra*, note 5.
28 Wolfe et al., *supra*, note 5.
29 Tunks, *supra*, note 20.
30 Wolfe et al., *supra*, note 5.

fibromyalgia with other chronic pain categories, sensitivity and specificity remain good with respect to distinguishing patients from normals, but specificity in distinguishing between pain categories is very poor."[31] Others have questioned the very validity of the diagnosis of fibromyalgia. Bohr[32] considers the evidence for fibromyalgia syndrome as profoundly flawed and refers to it as "junk science." Others have called it an illusory entity,[33] or trivialized it as a "medicalization of the syndrome of being out of sorts."[34]

Criticism of the methodology of the ACR Committee on the basis that the classification criteria were based on tautological methodology neglect three important considerations. The first is that there is frequently in medicine, and certainly in rheumatology, no true "gold standard." In the area of diagnosis and classification, the gold standard implies a standard which is relevant, absolute, perfect and immutable. There is no such thing in medicine. There are standards which have a very high degree of accuracy, that is, very high specificity, sensitivity, positive and negative predictive values. There are standards which are less accurate. There is none that is perfect. This is true of most rheumatic diseases.

The second point, arising as a result of the above considerations, is that ACR Committees concerned with classification have established criteria using the same methodology. These criteria are designed to have a reasonably high sensitivity and specificity, using characteristics from a group of patients seen in various clinics, and believed to have a certain condition by physicians experienced in treating these conditions; two instances are the American Rheumatism Association (ARA is the former name for ACR) criteria for rheumatoid arthritis and systemic lupus erythematosus.[35]

Thirdly, there is at least one interesting piece of negative evidence which suggests blinded examination on pre-selected patients does not inevitably lead to criteria for a condition; this is a study where experts on the myofascial pain syndrome could find little agreement among themselves in detecting trigger points.[36]

---

31 Tunks et al., *supra*, note 21.
32 Bohr (1995), *supra*, note 7. Bohr (1996), *supra*, note 7.
33 Ochoa, *supra*, note 7.
34 Hadler NM. The Danger of the Diagnostic Process. In: Hadler NM, ed. *Occupational Musculoskeletal Disorders*. New York: Raven, 1993: 16-33.
35 Arnett FC, Edworthy SM, Bloch DA, et al. The American Rheumatism Association 1987 Revised Criteria for the Classification of Rheumatoid Arthritis. *Arthritis Rheum* 1988; 31:315-324. Tan EM, Cohen AS, Friess JF, et al. 1982 Revised Criteria for the Classifications of Systemic Erythematosus. *Arthritis Rheum* 1982; 25:1271-1277.
36 Wolfe et al., *supra*, note 6.

12.2.5 Relationship between Fibromyalgia and Trauma

12.2.5.1 The Argument Against

Wolfe et al.[37] note that, "While the association between work disability or compensation and fibromyalgia is well established, data regarding causality are largely absent. The clinical dilemma, whether an injury or workplace stress caused the patient's fibromyalgia, a retrodictive (or It Did) causal proposition[38] can rarely be determined to be certainly true or certainly false.[39] Evidence that trauma can cause fibromyalgia, a potential (or It Can) causal proposition,[40] comes from a few case series or case reports[41] and is insufficient to establish causal relationships. That trauma might cause fibromyalgia sometimes, a predictive (or It Will) causal proposition,[42] can only be addressed by epidemiology studies that measure the risk of potential exposures on the development of fibromyalgia. Epidemiologic studies of trauma and fibromyalgia needed to address potential or predictive causality are currently not available."[43]

12.2.5.2 The Argument For

Yunus et al.[44] in response to this consensus document by Wolfe et al.,[45] noted that, "With regard to injury and fibromyalgia syndrome, the Report[46] emphasizes scientific causality and becomes involved in the jargons of retrodictive and predictive causal propositions. Causal propositions are

---

37 Wolfe et al., *supra*, note 26.
38 Kramer MS, Lane DA. Causal Propositions in Clinical Research and Practice. *J Clin Epidemiol* 1992; 45:639-649.
39 *Ibid.*
40 *Ibid.*
41 Moldovsky H, Wong MTH, Lue FA. Litigation, Sleep, Symptoms and Disabilities in Post-Accident Pain (Fibromyalgia). *J Rheumatol* 1993; 20:1935-1940. Greenfield S, Fitzcharles MA, Esdaile JM. Reactive Fibromyalgia Syndrome. *Arthritis Rheum* 1992; 35:678-681. Romano TJ. Clinical Experiences with Post-Traumatic Fibromyalgia Syndrome. *WV Med J* 1990; 86:198-202. Saskin P, Moldofsky H, Lue FA. Sleep and Posttraumatic Rheumatic Pain Modulation Disorder (Fibrositis Syndrome). *Psychosom Med* 1986; 48:319-323.
42 Kramer et al., *supra*, note 38.
43 Wolfe et al., *supra*, note 26.
44 Yunus MB, Bennett RM, Romano TJ, Russell J, et al. Fibromalgia Consensus Report: Additional Comments. *J Clinical Rheumatology.* 1997; 3(6): 324-327.
45 Wolfe et al., *supra*, note 26.
46 Wolfe F, Potter J. Fibromyalgia and Work Disability. Is Fibromyalgia a Disabling Disorder? *Rheum Dis Clin North Am* 1996; 22:369-391.

rarely established with absolute certainty in the realm of medicine.[47] An alternative (and better known) model is the consideration of consistency of association, strength of association, dose-response relationship, and biologic plausibility.[48] In the context of a legal setting (where the Consensus Report is likely to be used), causality entails only 51% certainty, usually stated in terms of reasonable medical probability. Based on a consistent clinical pattern,[49] case-control or descriptive studies,[50] and biologic plausibility of central nervous system plasticity,[51] it seems more than 51% likely that trauma does play a causative role in some fibromyalgia syndrome patients, as agreed by other independent observers.[52] That trauma can cause localized or regional musculoskeletal pain is not arguable, rather the question is: can regional pain and tenderness become widespread? The biologic plausibility of such a spread of pain and tenderness is now supported by changes in the central nervous system (neuroplasticity), as well documented in animals[53] (that have no obvious secondary gain!) and in humans."[54] It is interesting to note that in a large series of cases of whiplash

---

47 Kramer et al., *supra*, note 38.
48 Hulley SB, Cummings SR. *Designing Clinical Research: An Epidemiologic Approach.* Baltimore: Williams & Wilkins, 1988: 108-109.
49 Moldovsky et al., *supra*, note 41. Romano, *supra*, note 41. Bennett RM. Disabling Fibromyalgia: Appearance versus Reality. *J Rheumatol* 1993; 20(11):1821-1824. Pellegrino MJ. *Post-Traumatic Fibromyalgia: A Medical Perspective.* Columbus, OH: Andem Publishing, 1996. Wolfe F. Post-traumatic Fibromyalgia: A Case Report Narrated by the Patient. *Arthritis Care Res*; 1994; 7:161-165.
50 Greenfield et al., *supra*, note 41. Bengtsson A, Henriksson KG, Jorfeldt L, Kagedal B, Lennmarken C, Lindstrom F. Primary Fibromyalgia. A Clinical and Laboratory Study of 55 Patients. *Scan J Rheumatol* 1986; 15:340-347. Yunus MB, Aldag JC. Clinical and Psychological Features of Regional Fibromyalgia: Comparison with Fibromyalgia Syndrome (abstr). *Arthritis Rheum* 1993; 36:S221. Buskila D, Neumann L, Vaisberg G, Alkalay D, Wolfe F. Increased Rates of Fibromyalgia Following Cervical Injury. *Arthritis Rheum* 1997; 40:446-452.
51 Yunus MB. Towards a Model of Pathophysiology of Fibromyalgia: Aberrant Central Pain Mechanisms with Peripheral Modulation. *J Rheumatol* 1992; 19:846-850. Coderre TJ, Katz J, Vaccarino AL, Melzack R. Contribution of Central Neuroplasticity to Pathological Pain: Review of Clinical and Experimental Evidence. *Pain* 1993; 52:259-285. Dubner R, Ruda MA. Activity-Dependent Neuronal Plasticity Following Tissue Injury and Inflammation. *Trends Neurosci* 1992; 15:96-103.
52 Wolfe F. The Fibromyalgia Problem. *Arthritis Rheum* 1997; 24:1247-1249.
53 Coderre et al., *supra*, note 51. Dubner et al., *supra*, note 51.
54 Yunus et al., *supra*, note 44. Torebjork HE, Lundberg LER, Lamotte RH. Central Changes in Processing of Mechanoreceptive Input in Capsaicin-induced Secondary Hyperalgesia in Humans. *J Physiol* (Lond) 1992; 448:765-780.

syndrome followed for 1 year 20% developed fibromyalgia syndrome versus 1.7% of controls who had lower limb injuries.[55]

12.3 RECOVERY AND PATHOPHYSIOLOGY

The debate on whether chronic pain states such as fibromyalgia can develop following trauma is driven by arguments about whether all soft tissue injuries heal, the uncertain pathophysiology of chronic pain disorders and the role of psychological factors. We will explore each of these in turn.

12.3.1 Recovery After Trauma

Many chronic pain disorders begin with a trauma. A critical element of the debate regarding persistent pain revolves around the normal anticipated time for musculoligamentous healing to occur. The Quebec Task Force on Whiplash Associated Disorders[56] noted, "Apart from anatomic studies, much of the scientific understanding of soft tissue injury and healing is derived from animal models, and there is little information on the normal recuperation period. In the animal model of soft tissue healing, there is a brief period (less than 72 hours of acute inflammation and reaction), followed by a period of repair and regeneration (approximately 72 hours to up to 6 weeks), and finally by a period of remodelling and rematuration that can last up to one year." Although animal studies suggest complete tissue repair should occur, in humans a significant number continue to suffer chronic pain, raising questions as to the applicability of such animal data to pain. As well, chronic musculoligamentous injuries about the shoulder joint (i.e., rotator cuff), ankle joint (lateral ligamentous instability) or knee joint (cruciate ligamentous tears) to name a few, are well accepted and yet defy the above models of healing in those individuals who go on to chronicity. Nevertheless, the concepts that *all* soft tissue injuries heal or that there are normal expected healing times has become entrenched in the minds and treatment protocols of a diverse group of treating clinicians. It is important to recognize that the vast majority of soft tissue injuries do heal relatively pain-free and without disability. It is the minority who continue to suffer chronic pain and even disability who are at the centre of a raging debate.

12.3.2 Evidence for an Organic Basis for Chronic Pain

It is not sufficient to suggest an organic source for chronic pain on the basis that some injuries may not recover pain-free. However, recent re-

---

55 Buskila et al., *supra*, note 50.
56 Spitzer et al., *supra*, note 12.

search has revealed increasing evidence which suggests that chronic pain has some organic basis.

12.3.2.1 Evidence of a Central Neurological Origin for Regional Pain

A compelling literature regarding changes to the central nervous system in chronic pain has emerged over the last decade. Mense[57] has recently reviewed the theoretical and experimental basis for referred pain arising from muscle. According to this review, unlike cutaneous pain which is very accurately localized, muscle pain is difficult to localize and often referred to regions remote from muscle.[58] Regional pain syndromes refer to conditions in which painful areas extend beyond a single dermatome or musculoligamentous structure and tend to involve wider regions of the body. Mense[59] describes animal experiments in which persistent nociceptive input from muscle (in the form of an experimental myositis or muscle irritation) results in an expansion of rat spinal cord dorsal horn neurons responding to electrode stimulation of peripheral nerves. The dorsal horn of the spinal cord receives and processes pain signals from peripheral nociceptors or pain receptors. This indicates that the population of spinal cord neurons which can be activated by afferents (painful input) from that muscle increases in size over time. The spread of excitability or central sensitization to adjacent neuron populations in the dorsal horn of the spinal cord may then result in the sensation of spreading or radiating pain. This mechanism appears to involve release of neurotransmitters from the spinal cord terminals of nociceptive muscle afferent or sensory nerve fibers.[60]

Along the same line, in experimental work where substance P, a well-known pain neurotransmitter, has been administered at high concentrations into the dorsal horn of the spinal cord of animals, activation of nociceptive neurons at low concentration occurs and leads to long lasting depolarization of the cell membrane.[61] In contrast to amino acid neurotransmitters,

---

57 Mense S. Referral of Muscle Pain. *Amer Pain Soc J* 1994; 3(1):10-12.
58 Inman et al., *supra*, note 23. Hockaday JM, Whitty CWM. Patterns of Deferred Pain in the Normal Subject. *Brain* 1967; 90:481-496. Kellgren JH. Observations on Referred Pain Arising from Muscle. *Clin Sci* 1938; 3:175-190. Sinclair DC, Wedell G, Feindel WH. Referred Pain and Associated Phenomena. *Brain* 1948; 71:184-211.
59 Mense, *supra*, note 57.
60 Molander C, Ygge I, Dalsgaard C-J. Substance P, Somatostatin- and Calcitonin Gene-Related Peptide-like Immunoreactivity and Fluoride Resistant Acid Phosphatase-Activity in Relation to Retrogradely Labelled Cutaneous, Muscular and Visceral Primary Sensory Neurons in the Rat. *Neurosci Lett* 1987; 74:34-42.
61 Sastry BR. Substance P Effects on Spinal Nociceptive Neurones. *Life Sci* 1979; 24:2169-2178. Zieglgansberger W, Tulloch IF. Effects of Substance P on Neurones in the Dorsal Horn of the Spinal Cord of the Cat. *Brain Res* 1979; 166:273-282.

substance P is regarded as a volume neurotransmitter[62] which is capable of influencing large populations of spinal cord neurons in the vicinity of the release site. This property may help explain the induction of widespread changes in spinal cord dorsal horn excitability during experimental myositis or muscle irritation and may further serve to explain the phenomenon of regional pain syndromes whereby muscle tenderness and pain appears to spread beyond the original site of injury. It may also have particular relevance for clinical conditions such as fibromyalgia, which is characterized by generalized muscle tenderness and pain.

In this regard, three independent studies of patients with clinical diagnosis of fibromyalgia[63] have demonstrated levels of substance P in the cerebrospinal fluid which is two to three times that of normal controls. Substance P is not the only neurotransmitter that may induce the observed effects. Other neuropeptides and excitatory amino acids capable of causing similar changes in dorsal horn excitability have been described.[64] It is also interesting to note that in patients with fibromyalgia syndrome, blood and cerebrospinal fluid levels of serotonin percursors and serotonin are lower than controls.[65] Serotonin has been implicated in a large number of psychophysiologic processes such as the regulation of sleep, perception, memory, and anxiety.[66] All of these data suggest that there are objective and measurable changes which occur in the central nervous system, leading to neurochemical abnormalities that may account for chronic pain.

---

62   Agnati LF, Fuxe K, Zoli M, et al. A Correlation Analysis of the Regional Distribution of Central Enkephalin and Beta-Endorphin Immunoreactive Terminals and of Opiate Receptors in Adult and Old Male Rats: Evidence for the Existence of Two Main Types of Communication in the Central Nervous System: The Volume Transmission and the Wiring Transmission. *Acta Physiol Scan* 1986; 128:201-207.

63   Vaeroy H, Helle R, Forre O, Kass E, Terenius L. Elevated CSF Levels of Substance P and High Incidence of Raynaud's Phenomenon in Patients with Fibromyalgia: New Features for Diagnostics. *Pain* 1988; 32:21-26. Russell IJ, Orr MD, Littman B, et al. Elevated Cerebrospinal Fluid Levels of Substance in Patients with Fibromyalgia Syndrome. *Arthritis Rheum* 1994; 37:1593-1601. Bradley RA, Alberts KR, Alarcon GC, Alexander MT, Mountz JM, et al. Abnormal Brain Regional Cerebral Blood Flow (RCBF) and Cerebrospinal Fluid (CSF) Levels of Substance P (SP) in Patients and Non-Patients with Fibromyalgia (FM). *Arthritis & Rheumatism* 1996; 39(9S):S212.

64   Coderre et al., *supra*, note 51.

65   Yunus, *supra*, note 51. Russell IJ, Vaeroy H, Javors M, Nyberg F. Cerebrospinal Fluid Biogenic Amine Metabolites in Firbromyalgia/Fibrositis Syndrome and Rheumatoid Arthritis. *Arthritis Rheum* 1992; 35:550-556. Sambrosk W, et al., Biochemical Changes in Fybromyalgia. *J Rheumatology* 1996; 55:168-173.

66   Roth BL. Multiple Serotonin Receptors: Clinical and Experimental Aspects. *Ann Clin Psychiatry* 1994; 6:67-78.

12.3.2.2 Evidence of a Mechanical Origin for Chronic Whiplash Injury Pain

Macnab outlined a mechanism of injury involving neck hyperextension; subsequently governments mandated the use of head rests to reduce injury. Animal studies, in particular Macnab's work with anesthetized monkeys, demonstrated an impressive series of injuries on autopsy including haematomas in muscles, ligamentous tearing, partial separation of discs on the ligament, and damage to the zygapophyseal or facet joints.[67] Taylor and Twomey[68] did careful autopsy studies of the cervical spines of younger subjects who died of major trauma and compared these to subjects who died of natural causes. In the trauma subjects, discogenic and facet joint lesions were abundant but absent in the nontrauma group.

Barnsley et al.[69] provided the most impressive evidence of facet joint involvement in many whiplash injuries utilizing placebo-controlled injections of local anesthetics. Twenty-seven of 38 patients studied obtained complete relief of pain following two blocks of the symptomatic joint and each obtained longer lasting relief with the longer-acting drug (bupivacaine) than the shorter-acting medication (lignocaine). A variety of other studies had come to similar conclusions based upon identification of tears of joint capsules at operation, post mortem examinations, cadaver studies, and animal experiments. Finally, although studies of treatment are still limited, there are indications that radiofrequency coagulation may effectively relieve cervical zygapophyseal joint pain for periods in excess of 6 months when compared to sham-treated controls.[70] Sturzenegger et al.[71] studied whiplash patients at 1 week post-accident and again at 1 year. They noted that the accident mechanism and initial findings suggestive of a more severe injury at 1 week were significantly related to persistence of symptoms.

12.3.2.3 Conclusions

Although these studies are by no means definitive, the emerging data

---

67 Macnab, *supra*, note 15.
68 Taylor JR, Twomey LT. Acute Injuries to Cervical Joints. *Spine* 1993; 18(9):1113-1122.
69 Barnsley L, Lord S, Bogduk N. Comparative Local Anaesthetic Blocks in the Diagnosis of Cervical Zygapophyseal Joint Pain. *Pain* 1993; 55:99-106.
70 Lord SM, Barnsley L, Wallis BJ, McDonald GJ, Bogduk N. Percutaneous Radiofrequency Neurotomy for Chronic Cervical Zygapophyseal Joint Pain. *NEJM* 1996; 335(23):1721-1726.
71 Sturzenegger M, Radanov BP, DiStefano G. The Effect of Accident Mechanisms and Initial Findings on the Long Term Course of Whiplash Injury. *J Neurol* 1995; 242:443-449.

suggests there may be an organic basis for what has long been regarded as idiopathic chronic pain. It therefore appears to be presumptuous to assume that our current technology and knowledge are perfect, that all injured patients should get better based on experimental animal studies, that current research does not point to an organic basis for pain and that there are no further discoveries to be made about the pathogenesis of pain. As our understanding of pain, and in particular chronic pain, continues to expand, the concept that all soft tissue injuries should heal or that there is no pathophysiologic basis for continuing symptoms has become somewhat dubious.

12.3.3 Are Psychological Factors Causative?

There is an appropriate trend in the current literature towards understanding pain within a biopsychosocial framework. In other words, pain is seen as being a multidimensional experience with nociceptive (biochemical), psychological and social factors all influencing the final perception of pain. However, within this framework there needs to be a determination as to whether a particular psychological feature is causative of the pain or occurs as a consequence. Gamsa[72] in a study of large numbers of patients with chronic pain in different centres provided evidence that psychological changes were more a consequence of pain than attributable to premorbid characteristics. Dworkin[73] has asserted that despite exhaustive research we still "know nothing" about how emotional and behavioral factors contribute to chronic pain.

The vast majority of literature linking chronic pain and psychological factors is correlational based on specialty-based practices with all of their inherent referral biases. Crook and Tunks[74] have shown that patients in pain clinics differ significantly from patients in the general population. They are more likely to have been injured, report more intense and more constant pain, have more difficulties with activities of daily living, are more depressed and withdrawn socially, and show more long-term consequences due to unemployment, litigation, and substance abuse. Nevertheless, a substantial volume of correlational evidence generated from pain clinics or specialty practices is often regarded as proof that chronic pain is a consequence of psychological factors or "less effective repertories".[75] Psychosocial factors continue to be regarded by some as critical to the

---

72 Gamsa A. Is Emotional Status a Precipitator or a Consequence of Pain? *Pain* 1990; 42:183-195.
73 Dworkin RH. What Do We Really Know about the Psychological Origins of Chronic Pain. *APS Bull* 1991; 1:7-11.
74 Crook J, Tunks E. Defining the "Chronic Pain Syndrome": An Epidemiological Method. In: Fields HL, Dubner R, Cervero F, eds. *Advances in Pain Research and Therapy*. 1986, vol. 9: 871-877.
75 *Supra*, note 11.

transition from acute to chronic pain disorders.[76] Because premorbid psychopathology has not been shown to be a strong predictor of chronic pain or chronic pain disability, there has been increasing emphasis on looking at coping styles and social reinforcers as being important in development of chronic pain disability. We will explore the relationship between some of these factors and chronic pain disability after first discussing the issue of disability seen following chronic pain.

12.4 DISABILITY SECONDARY TO CHRONIC PAIN DISORDERS

12.4.1 Definitions: Impairment, Disability and Handicap

The World Health Organization (WHO) differentiates between impairment and disability. *Impairment* is defined as a loss or abnormality of psychological, physiologic, or anatomic structure or function; these disturbances are at the organ or system level, such as problems with hearing, vision, or specific musculoskeletal movements.[77] An assessment of impairment is frequently what is being sought in examinations requested by third-party agencies.[78] *Disability* is defined as "any restriction or lack ... of ability to perform an activity in the manner or within the range considered normal for a human being".[79] Disability is a multifactorial phenomenon which is determined not only by impairment but also by psychological, social, and economic factors. *Handicap* is regarded as a disadvantage that limits or prevents the fulfilment of a normal role.[80] It is well known that employers may be reluctant to hire or offer continuing employment to handicapped individuals.[81]

---

76 Sauter S, Swanson N. The Relationship Between Work Place Psychosocial Factors and Musculoskeletal Disorders in Office Work: Suggested Mechanisms and Evidence. In: Gordon S, Blair S, Fine L, eds. *Repetitive Motion Disorders of the Upper Extremity*. Rosemont, IL: AAOS, 1994: 65-76.
77 World Health Organization. *The International Classification of Impairments, Disabilities and Handicaps*. World Health Organization, Geneva, 1980.
78 Carey TS. Disability Determination: The Challenge of Back Ache. In Hadler NM, ed. *Clinical Concepts in Regional Musculoskeletal Illness*. Orlando, FL: Grune & Stratton, 1987: 247-261.
79 World Health Organization, *supra*, note 77.
80 *Ibid*.
81 White KP, Harth M, Teasell RW. Work Disability Evaluation and the Fibromyalgia Syndrome. Seminars in Arthritis and Rheumatism 1995; 24(6):371-381.

12.4.2 The Rise in Chronic Pain Disability Claims

The last 4 decades have seen a significant rise in the number of disability claims/awards for patients complaining of chronic pain disorders.[82] This increase in disability claims has not been fully accounted for; it cannot be entirely attributed to a similar increase in the incidence of chronic pain disorders. Although there is no evidence that the actual incidence of LBP has increased,[83] back-related disability expenditures in the United States grew an average of 14.3% per year from 1970 through 1986.[84] It is not clear how much these figures have been corrected for other factors.

For chronic low back pain (CLBP) less than 50% of persons disabled from working with pain for over 6 months return to work. After 2 years of disability return to work is uncommon.[85] Hazard[86] has observed that an estimated $85 billion is spent annually on LBP sufferers in the United States and as much as 80% goes to the minority of CLBP patients who are disabled by their pain.[87] It has been suggested that the system designed to care for disabled patients with chronic pain disorders may actually be exacerbating the problem[88] through an expectation of compensation.[89]

12.4.3 The Acute Medical Model and Chronic Pain Disorders

Current health care is dominated by the science of objective assessment and treatment of disease, generally referred to as "the acute medical model." The acute medical model relies upon the determination of symp-

---

82 Hadler, *supra*, note 34. Weisman J, Deyo R. Back Pain: Epidemiological Data. *APS Bulletin* 1993; 3(1):14-23. Feuerstein M. Testimony before the New York Assembly Joint Hearings on Workers' Compensation, University of Rochester Medical Center, Rochester, New York, 1993 — quoted in Fordyce (1995), *supra*, note 11.

83 Waddell G. A New Clinical Model for the Treatment of Low Back Pain. *Spine* 1987; 12:632-644.

84 Berkowitz M, Greene C. Disability Expenditures. *Am Rehab* 1985; 15:7-15. Hazard RG. Occupational Low Back Pain: The Critical Role of Functional Goal Setting. *American Pain Society Journal* 1994; 3(2):101-106.

85 Hazard, *ibid*. Waddell, *supra*, note 83. Beals RK, Hickman NW. Industrial Injuries of the Back and Extremities: Comprehensive Evaluation — An Aid in Prognosis and Management. A Study of One Hundred and Eighty Patients. *J Bone Joint Surg* 1972; 54A:1593-1601.

86 *Supra*, note 84.

87 White et al., *supra*, note 8. Spitzer et al., *supra*, note 2. Spengler DM, Bigos ST, Martin NA, et al. Back Injuries in Industry: A Retrospective Study. *Spine* 1986; 11:241-245.

88 Fordyce, *supra*, note 11.

89 Schrader H, Obelieniene D, Bovim G, Surkiene D, Mickevicience D, Miseviciene I, Sand T. Natural Evolution of Late Whiplash Syndrome outside the Medicolegal Context. *Lancet* 1996; 347:1207-1211.

toms and physical signs, diagnostic tests, where necessary, leading to a diagnosis which guides appropriate treatment. The goal is cure or amelioration of the disease state.

Difficulties arise with chronic pain disorders because they do not readily lend themselves to diagnoses (as a disease) and treatment through the acute medical model. There are few objective signs and none are universally viewed as reliable. Diagnostic tests generally fail to confirm or demonstrate structural abnormalities. Treatment is ineffective in the majority of cases and there is too often a paucity of treatment efficacy data.[90] Hence, the physician is confronted with a patient where the acute medical model is obviously inadequate.

Problems arise when physicians then attribute symptoms not associated with obvious physical pathology to associated psychosocial factors (referred to as "mind-body" dualism) and inadvertently blame the patients for their own symptoms. This blame may come in the form of diagnoses such as malingering, hysteria, somatoform pain disorder, secondary gain, or litigation neurosis. Cassell[91] summarizes this approach as, "no cause, no relief, no problem."

12.4.3.1 The Search for Structural Abnormalities

Cassell[92] clearly identifies a weakness in the acute medical model of disease in "its dependence on the idea that all changes in the function of an organism or its parts are referable to changes in its structure. In the everyday medical world this has made the search for a diagnosis essentially the search for altered structure." The concept that altered structure must account for alterations in function (illness) is artificial and clinically lacks utility; identification of altered structure does not always indicate why a particular patient has chronic pain. Advances in technology have only emphasized the failings of the altered structure approach to chronic pain.[93] For instance, MRI scanning of the cervical and lumbosacral spine frequently demonstrates structural abnormalities in asymptomatic individuals and is often normal in symptomatic individuals.[94]

---

90 Spitzer et al., *supra*, notes 2, 12.
91 Cassell EJ. *The Nature of Suffering*. Oxford: Oxford University Press, 1991.
92 *Ibid.*
93 Hitselberger WE, Witten RM. Abnormal Myelograms in Asymptomatic Patients. *J Neurosurg* 1968; 28:204-206. Holt EP. The Question of Lumbar Discography. *J Bone Joint Surg* 1968; 50A:720-726. Wiesel SW, Tsormas N, Feffer HL, Citrin CM, Patronas N. A Study of Computer-Assisted Tomography 1. The Incidence of Positive CAT Scans in an Asymptomatic Group of Patients. *Spine* 1984; 9:549-551.
94 Boden SD, Davis DO, Thomas SD, Patronas NJ, Weisel SW. Abnormal Magnetic-Resonance Scans of the Lumbar Spine in Asymptomatic Subjects. *J Bone Joint Surg* 1990; 72-A(3):403-408.

Cassell[95] has observed that technology too often "defines the values that represent good or bad, success or failure. . . . Its power to oversimplify the inherently complex and produce certainty where doubt is necessarily present has proven irresistible not only to medicine but to the whole culture." This problem was demonstrated in a recent monograph by Fordyce et al.[96] where "specific" low back pain is characterized by radiographic evidence of a known cause of pain. In contrast, "nonspecific" low back pain (NSLBP), characterized by lack of a known radiographic cause, is regarded as an entirely different entity, because it fails to meet the criteria for a medical disorder. In this conceptual model, the patient with NSLBP is not considered disabled.[97] Although this model simplified the criteria for disability, it failed to deal with clinical realities. For instance, the clinical presentation of a patient with NSLBP may be virtually identical to that of another individual disabled with a recognizable radiologic abnormality. Moreover, as mentioned previously, the relationship between pain and radiographic abnormalities for many of these clinical entities is tenuous at best. Defining impairment based only upon specific radiographic abnormalities[98] means those patients with complaints of pain who do not meet these narrow criteria are not regarded as legitimate. This approach has led to the extreme concept that permanent compensation for disability should not be awarded to patients with chronic pain disorders.[99] It also sidesteps the thorny issue of what the patient is actually experiencing when he or she complains of pain.[100] Nevertheless, the requirement for structural abnormalities to "legitimize" illness or chronic pain is frequently seen in insurance and WCB claims or in no-fault, "threshold" auto accident legislation.

12.4.4 Discordance between Pain, Impairment, and Disability

Bennett[101] notes that, "it is increasingly evident that dysfunction in chronic pain states is poorly correlated with the severity of pain."[102]

---

95 Cassell, *supra*, note 91.
96 Fordyce, *supra*, note 11.
97 Fordyce, *supra*, note 11.
98 Fordyce, *supra*, note 11.
99 Fordyce, *supra*, note 11. Schroder et al., *supra*, note 89. Clifford JC. Successful Management of Chronic Pain Syndrome. *Can Fam Physician* 1993; 39:549-559.
100 Gamsa A, Vikis-Feibergs V. Psychological Events are Both Risk Factors in, and Consequences of, Chronic Pain. *Pain* 1991; 44:271-277.
101 *Supra*, note 49.
102 Tait RC, Margolis RB, Krause ST, Liebowitz E. Compensation Status and Symptoms Reported by Patients with Chronic Pain. *Arch Phys Med Rehab* 1988; 1027-1029. Dekker J, Boot B, Van der Woude LH, Bijlsma JW. Pain and Disability in Osteoarthritis: A Review of Biobehavioral Mechanisms. *J Behav Med* 1992; 15:189-214. Anonymous. Report of the Commission on the Evaluation of Pain. *Soc Secur Bull* 1987; 50:13-44.

Gatchel[103] notes in chronic low back pain that although there are correlations between the categories of pain, impairment, and disability, "there is usually not a 1:1:1 relation among them." Most troublesome has been the inability to "develop an algorithm or model to help guide and predict the therapeutic process, on the basis of measurement of these various components".[104] Gatchel[105] notes that these constructs of impairment, disability and pain defy objective and reliable assessment.

12.4.5 Assessment of Disability in Chronic Pain Disorders

Steig[106] argues that in the United States disability is ultimately a legal and not a medical determination, and that psychosocial factors are more important than physical factors in determination of disability in some patients, such as those with chronic soft tissue pain disorders. He notes, "simply applying knowledge of a person's medical problems via history, records review, and analysis of laboratory data and adding data from physical examinations (no matter how sophisticated) cannot suffice to accurately determine disability in many cases." He also notes that, "attempts to simplify disability assessment in complex cases by the application of physical test data alone may be unethical and may do both patients and society an injustice." He then notes, "that proper assessment of complex disability case requires a careful multidisciplinary assessment including, when appropriate, employers and family members."

Physicians are often asked to assume multiple roles in dealing with chronic pain and disability. These roles include that of diagnostician, therapist, advocate, and disability assessor. There has been an increasing debate on this subject within the context of fibromyalgia, a generalized chronic pain disorder.[107] Bennett[108] noted that, "There are no validated instruments for assessing disability in fibromyalgia syndrome patients. The most practical resource is the American Medical Association's Guide to the

---

103 Gatchel RJ. Occupational Low Back Pain Disability. Why Function Needs to "Drive" the Rehabilitation Process. *American Pain Soc J* 1994; 3(2):107-110.
104 *Ibid.* Gamsa A. The Role of Psychological Factors in Chronic Pain. I. A Half Century of Study. *Pain* 1994; 57:5-15(a).
105 *Supra,* note 103.
106 Steig RL. The Futility of Physical Testing in the Assessments of Disability. *Am Pain Soc Journal* 1994; 3(3):187-190.
107 Wolfe et al., *supra,* note 46. Ehrlich GE, Wolfe FF. The Difficulties of Disability and its Determination. *Rheum Dis Clin North Am* 1996; 22:613-621. Bennett RM. Fibromyalgia and the Disability Dilemma: A New Era in Understanding a Complex, Multi-dimensional Pain Syndrome. *Arthritis Rheum* 1996; 39:1627-1634.
108 *Ibid.*

Evaluation of Permanent Impairment.[109] As an overview to the problem, it states that 1) pain evaluation does not lend itself to strict laboratory standards of accuracy; 2) the evaluation of chronic pain cannot be made on the basis of the degree of tissue damage — the classic medical model; 3) pain evaluation requires a thorough understanding of a multifaceted biopsychosocial model of disease;[110] and 4) the physician's judgment of impairment represents a blend of the art and science of medicine, and judgment must be characterized not so much by scientific accuracy as by procedural regularity. It acknowledges that physicians are often uncomfortable in evaluating chronic pain states, but notes that they regularly make decisions on the basis of probabilities backed up by experience and stated in terms of reasonable medical possibility.[111]

Bennett notes, "It is evident that the nature of disability in fibromyalgia syndrome is different from some other disease; for example RA or strokes. The American Medical Association Guide to the Evaluation of Permanent Impairment is commonly used by assessors of disability and relies almost exclusively on measurements of range of motion and strength to arrive at a definition of total person impairment. When applied to patients with fibromyalgia syndrome such an assessment leads to the conclusion that they have no significant impairment. Often radiographs, blood tests, and even advanced imaging techniques are used to support this judgement. Many of these issues have been carefully scrutinized in an article by Wolfe[112] and to quote him, 'The problem with functional disability in fibromyalgia is face validity. Patients with fibromyalgia syndrome don't look ill. Clinically they are not weak. They would appear to be able to do most tasks and ADL activities in ways that would appear to be their HAQ scores.' The functional disability in FMS is not so much that of a two-dimensional impairment but a three-dimensional impairment. The third dimension being time and the problem being the ability to sustain repetitive activity or other forms of a chronic workload.[113] It has often been assumed

---

109 American Medical Association. *Guides to the Evaluation of Permanent Impairment*, 4th ed. Chicago: American Medical Association, 1993.
110 Engel GL. A Clinical Application of the Biopsychosocial Model. *Am J Psychiatry* 1980; 137:535-544.
111 Bennett, *supra*, note 107.
112 Wolfe F. Disability and the Dimension of Distress in Fibromyalgia. *J Musculoskeletal Pain* 1993 (1):65-87.
113 Henriksson C, Gundmark I, Bengtsson A, Ek AC. Living with Fibromyalgia. Consequences for Everyday Life. *Clin J Pain* 1992; 8:138-144. Jacobsen S, Wildschiodtz G, Danneskiold-Samse B. Isokinetic and Isometric Muscle Strength Combined with Transcutaneous Electrical Muscle Stimulation in Primary Fibromyalgia Syndrome. *J Rheumatol* 1991; 18:1390-1393. Jacobsen S, Danneskiold-Samse B. Dynamic Muscular Endurance in Primary Fibromyalgia Compared with Chronic Myofascial Pain Syndrome. *Arch Phys Med Rehabil* 1992; 73:170-173.

that such patients have a low threshold for pain and magnify sensations of bodily discomfort which most people would ignore. A recent study by Clark et al.[114] suggest that this is probably not true for the majority of patients with fibromyalgia syndrome. When patients were exercised to volitional exhaustion on a treadmill, it was noted that 76% were able to work hard enough to achieve an anaerobic threshold (i.e., a respiratory quotient of greater than 1). Within this group 96% appropriately perceived their level of exertion. On the other hand patients not reaching an anaerobic threshold tended to overestimate their level of exertion."[115]

Physicians are often asked to provide objective evidence for disability following a traumatic event. In the case of fibromyalgia, Bennett[116] modifies guidelines suggested by Wolfe:[117] "(1) Establish that the diagnosis is present citing the 1990 American College of Rheumatology criteria.[118] (2) If there is an apparent post-traumatic initiation of the syndrome, describe the pattern of development of pain and other symptoms including sleep disturbance. In this situation, the fibromyalgia syndrome often begins as an apparent focal myofascial pain syndrome related to the initial site of trauma and, over the course of 6 to 18 months, spreads from one area to another until the patient has total body pain. The history is so consistent from patient to patient that it provides compelling prima facie evidence for a post-traumatic origin. The case is further strengthened if the patient was previously fully functional in vocation and avocation, had a good work record and their life was irrevocably altered by the development of fibromyalgia syndrome. (3) Describe the severity of the syndrome using questionnaires such as the HAQ, FIQ,[119] pain diagram, a tender point count and total myalgic score. If this data is unavailable on a longitudinal basis, it will provide especially useful data for assessment of disability. (4) To answer the question, 'Is the patient disabled?', one can cite several references indicating the prevalence of disability in patients with fibromyalgia syndrome in this and other countries.[120] It should be pointed out that there is no cure for fibromyalgia syndrome and work impairment results from an

---

114 Clark SR, Burkhardt CS, Campbell S, O'Reilly C, Bennett RM. Fitness Characteristics and Perceived Exertion in Women with Fibromyalgia. *J Musculoskeletal Pain* 1993.
115 Bennett, *supra*, note 49.
116 Bennett, *supra*, note 49.
117 *Supra*, note 112.
118 *Supra*, note 5.
119 Burkhardt CS, Clark SP, Bennett RM. The Fibromyalgia Impact Questionnaire: Development and Validation. *J Rheumatol* 1991; 18:728-733.
120 Bengtsson et al., *supra*, note 50. Cathey MA, Wolfe F, Roberts FK, et al. Demographic Work Disability, Service Utilization and Treatment Characteristics of 620 Fibromyalgia Patients in Rheumatologic Practice (abstr). *Ar-*

inability to perform repetitive muscular tasks. Also cite evidence for nonrestorative sleep and fatigue being linked to the EEG finding of alpha-delta sleep. Lastly, point out that the combination of work intolerance and excessive fatigue makes it difficult for the patient to be competitively employed."[121]

12.4.6 Acceptance of Chronic Pain and Disability

There appears to be a great deal of variability among chronic pain disorder patients in terms of their coping responses to pain and development of subsequent disability. The fact that individual coping styles can influence pain disability was illustrated in a recent study by Schmitz et al.[122] These authors, inspired by Brandstater's[123] work on aging, looked at the effect of assimilative and accommodative coping styles on chronic pain. Assimilative coping involved "active attempts (e.g., instrumental activities, self-corrective actions, compensatory measures) to alter unsatisfactory life circumstances and situational constraints in accordance with personal preferences."[124] In contrast, accommodative coping, defined as downgrading of aspirations, positive reappraisal and self-enhancing comparisons, "is directed towards a revision of self-evaluative and personal goal standards in accordance with perceived deficits and losses." The authors based their study on the assumption that chronic pain was a major source of threat or impediment to achievement of personal goals. Their results suggested that "accommodative coping functioned as a protective resource by preventing global losses in the psychological functioning of chronic pain patients and maintaining a positive life perspective."[125] The authors noted that the ability to flexibly adjust personal goals "attenuated the negative impact of the pain experience" both in terms of improved psychological well-being as well as a reduction of disability through pain-related coping strategies. Rigid premorbidly highly active individuals tend to have much greater dif-

---

thritis Rheum 1990; 33:S10. Cathey MA, Wolfe F, Kleinheksel SM, Hawley DJ. Socioeconomic Impact of Fibrositis. A Study of 81 Patients with Primary Fibrositis. *Am J Med* 1986; 81:78-84. McCain GA, Cameron R, Kennedy JC. The Problem of Long-Term Disability Payments and Litigation in Primary Fibromyalgia: The Canadian Perspective. *J Rheumatol* 1989; (suppl 19) 16:174-176.

121 Bennett, *supra*, note 49.
122 Schmitz U, Saile H, Nilges P. Coping with Chronic Pain: Flexible Goal Adjustment as an Interactive Buffer against Pain-Related Distress. *Pain* 1996; 67:41-51.
123 Brandstadter J, Renner G. Tenacious Goal Pursuit and Flexible Goal Adjustment: Explication and Age-Related Analysis of Assimilative and Accommodative Strategies of Coping. *Psychol Aging* 1992; 5:58-67.
124 Schmitz et al., *supra*, note 122.
125 Schmitz et al., *supra*, note 122.

ficulty adjusting their goals to match the limitations imposed by the pain. Other factors such as education level, flexibility of employment, etc., may also play a role in adjustment to chronic pain and may in turn interact with coping styles.

Bennett noted that, "Disabled patients with pain usually link impaired functioning to having persistent pain and cannot conceive of living a normal life as long as they are in pain.[126] Thus, they pursue a search for a cure which is never realized, and the fruitlessness of this search rationalizes their continued disability. In the process they not only remain dysfunctional, but also overutilize medical care and develop increasing personal distress. Interestingly, it is the belief that pain is the major cause of disability, rather than the absolute level of pain, that seems to determine the actual degree of dysfunction.[127] These psychosocial and behavioural issues are clearly relevant in the cases of some fibromyalgia syndrome patients seeking disability, but should not be generalized. Each patient has to be thoughtfully evaluated according to his or her unique set of circumstances."[128]

12.4.7 Compensation and Secondary Gain in Disability

12.4.7.1 *Compensation and Chronic Pain*

The issue of compensation as an important factor in chronic pain disability was first advanced by Miller[129] with respect to "minor head injury" in a carefully selected group of 50 patients (out of a series of 2,000) where he argued, based on his own follow-up of a group of claimants seen in his medico-legal practice, that in effect, they all got better after settlement of their cases. This argument was rebutted by Mendelson[130] who reviewed 10 studies conducted since 1945 and noted that all had failed to confirm Miller's reported findings with respect to several types of compensable injury, in that they failed to report a large number of patients improving after settlement. The notion that patients' pains improve and they return to work

---

126 Reesor, Craig KD. Medically Incongruent Chronic Back Pain: Physical Limitations, Suffering, and Ineffective Coping. *Pain* 1988; 32:35-45. Talo S, Hendler N, Brodie J. Effects of Active and Completed Litigation on Treatment Results: Workers' Compensation Patients Compared with other Litigation Patients. *J Occup Med* 1989; 31:265-269.
127 Riley JF, Adhern DK, Follick MJ. Chronic Pain and Functional Impairment: Assessing Beliefs about Their Relationship. *Arch Phys Med Rehab* 1988; 69:579-582.
128 Bennett, *supra*, note 107.
129 Miller HG. Accident Neurosis. *Br Med J* 1961; i:919-925, 992-998.
130 Mendelson G. Not "Cured By a Verdict". Effect of Legal Settlement on Compensation Claimants. *Med J Austral* 1982; 2:219-230.

shortly after the final settlement of compensation claims remains unfounded.[131] In those who did eventually return to work there was a trend towards less physically demanding and lower-paying jobs with the majority failing to return to pre-injury employment status.[132] More recently, Rohling et al.[133] conducted a meta-analysis of 32 studies which compared compensated patients with non-compensated patients. Compensation status accounted for only 6% of the variance in pain experience.

Mendelson[134] has noted that compensation does have some impact on presentation and duration of musculoskeletal complaints, although this is modulated by a variety of factors. Although there is no evidence that compensation actually influences the incidence of injury it has been shown to influence injury claim rates[135] as well as the injury claim duration;[136] this was similar for both "verifiable" injuries and "non-verifiable" injuries. In contrast, Violin et al.[137] found the wage/compensation ratio did not predict chronicity of pain. Compensation patients are less likely to improve after lumbar disc surgery.[138] There is consistent evidence that LBP patients receiving compensation respond less well to therapy than those receiving no compensation. However, these differences are often small and patients receiving compensation often benefited from therapy.

12.4.7.2 Secondary Gain

The controversy regarding chronic pain disorders and disability is inevitably tied to the concepts of secondary gain and the availability of compensation, two concepts which are at the heart of popular behavioral theories regarding chronic pain. The term secondary gain remains a vague

---

131 *Ibid.*
132 *Supra*, note 130.
133 Rohling ML, Binder LM, Langhinrichsen-Rohling J. Money Matters: A Meta-Analytic Review of the Association between Financial Compensation and the Experience and Treatment of Chronic Pain. *Health Psychology* 1995; 14(6):537-547.
134 Mendelson G. Compensation and Chronic Pain. *Pain* 1992; 48:121-123.
135 Robertson LS, Keeve JB. Worker Injuries: The Effect of Workers' Compensation and OSHA Inspections. *Health Politics, Policy and Law* 1983; 8:581-597. Nachemson A. Work for All. *Clin Orthop* 1983; 179:77-82.
136 Robertson et al., *ibid.* Worral JD, Appel D. The Impact of Workers' Compensation Benefits on Low Back Claims. In: Hadler NM, ed. *Clinical Concepts in Regional Musculoskeletal Illness*. Orlando: Grune and Stratton, 1987: 281-297. Sanderson P, Todd B, Holt G, et al. Compensation, Work Status, and Disability in Low Back Pain Patients. *Spine* 1995; 20:554-556.
137 Violin E. VanKoevering D, Loeser JD. Back Sprain in Industry. The Role of Socioeconomic Factors in Chronicity. *Spine* 1991; 16(5):542-548.
138 Hudgins WR. Computer-Aided Diagnosis of Lumbar Disc Herniation. *Spine* 1983; 8:604-615.

but commonly used term which suggests that the individual is somehow rewarded economically, physically and/or emotionally as a consequence of having an illness. This gain may come in the form of monetary benefits, relief from responsibilities within the family or at work, or as increased attention from friends and family members. Being "sick" (and disabled) presumably becomes the individual's solution to dealing with stressful situations, that is, a stressful workplace or an unpleasant family situation. Because secondary gain has not been well defined it has proven difficult to study.[139]

Fishbain[140] noted that one difficulty was inappropriately equating the presence of secondary gain factors and disability with malingering. Hence, any potential benefit such as disability payments or a concerned family member casts suspicion on the legitimacy of the recipient. The resultant suspicion of the chronic pain patient may then overtly or covertly interfere with treatment. Treatment failures are then blamed on secondary gain. Adaptive responses to chronic pain (i.e., accepting a certain level of disability and appropriately pacing activities) may also be misinterpreted as secondary gain. In addition, all illnesses have some associated secondary gain. The identification of presumed secondary gain "does not necessarily mean that secondary gain has an etiological or reinforcing affect on the chronic pain", an error referred to as "overinference".[141] Overinference is a common error particularly when one considers secondary gain without also measuring secondary losses.

12.4.7.3 Secondary Losses

Patients with chronic pain disorders suffer secondary losses as a consequence of being in chronic pain and disabled, a concept which is rarely discussed. The inability to work brings with it a great deal of frustration, boredom, anxiety, depression, and a significant loss of social status. In addition, individuals suffer financial losses which they rarely make up. Family and marital stressors inevitably develop. Few "win the lottery" as some would assert. Hence, the concept of secondary gain must be balanced with that of secondary loss. It has been noted that "the chronic pain patient incurs large number of secondary losses as a result of allegedly seeking secondary gain and that the patient appears to act in spite of these potential secondary losses."[142] In cases where apparent secondary losses outweigh

---

139 Fishbain DA. Secondary Gain Concept. Definition Problems and Its Abuse in Medical Practice. *American Pain Soc J* 1994; 3(4):264-273. Freeman DW. *Sick Rule Dynamics and Chronic Back Pain in the Injured Worker*. Seventh World Congress on Pain, Paris, France, Abstract 315:108, 1993.
140 Fishbain, *ibid*.
141 Fishbain, *supra*, note 139.
142 Fishbain, *supra*, note 139. Freeman, *supra*, note 139.

apparent secondary gains, the utility of the concept of secondary gain as an etiological factor in the cause of persistence of pain and disability must be viewed with skepticism.

12.4.8 Socioeconomic Factors and Disability

Socioeconomic factors are very important to chronic pain disability although the relationship between increasing chronic pain disability and a rapidly changing socioeconomic environment has not been well studied.

12.4.8.1 Lower Socioeconomic Status and Risk of Disability

Lower socioeconomic status has been shown to increase the frequency and severity of disability and the rate of progression to disability in patients with musculoskeletal disorders, including arthritic conditions.[143] Badley and Ibanez[144] have noted that several population studies have reported an increased frequency of chronic musculoskeletal disorders in individuals with lower education level and lower income.[145] The same authors note that lower socioeconomic status has been found to increase the risk of disability in those individuals with musculoskeletal disorders.[146] Low back pain is more common among those in lower socioeconomic groups,[147] a trend likely attributable in large part to more physically de-

---

143 Leigh JP, Fries JF. Predictors of Disability in a Longitudinal Sample of Patients with Rheumatoid Arthritis. *Ann Rheum Dis* 1992; 51:581-587. Leigh JP, Fries JF. Occupation Income, and Education as Independent Covariates of Arthritis in Four National Probability Samples. *Arthritis Rheum* 1991; 34:974-995(a). Pincus T, Callahan LF. Formal Education as a Marker for Increased Mortality and Morbidity in Rheumatoid Arthritis. *J Chronic Dis* 1985; 38:973-984. Deyo RA, Diehl AK. Psychosocial Predictors of Disability in Patients with Low Back Pain. *J Rheumatol* 1988; 15:1957-1964.
144 Badley EM, Ibanez D. Socioeconomic Risk Factors and Musculoskeletal Disability. *J Rheumatol* 1994; 21:515-521.
145 Pincus T, Callahan LF, Burkhauser RV. Most Chronic Diseases are Reported More Frequently by Individuals with Fewer than 12 years of Formal Education in the Age 18-64 United States Population. *J Chronic Dis* 1987; 40:865-874. Leigh JP, Fries JF. Education Level and Rheumatoid Arthritis: Evidence from Five Data Centers. *J Rheumatol* 1991; 18:24-34(b). LaVecchia C, Negri E, Pagano R, Decarli A. *Education, Prevalence of Disease, and Frequency of Health Care Utilization.*
146 Verbrugge LM, Gates GM, Ike RW. Risk Factors for Disability among U.S. Adults with Arthritis. *J Clin Epidemiol* 1991; 44:167-182.
147 Nagi SZ, Riley LE, Newby LG. A Social Epidemiology of Back Pain in a General Population. *J Chronic Dis* 1973; 26:769. Reisbord LS, Greenland S. Factors Associated with Self-Reported Back-Pain Prevalence: A Population-Based Study. *J Chronic Dis* 1985; 38:691.

manding work.[148] Gallagher et al.[149] have found that for low back pain patients the perception that a job change was difficult was associated with a reduced chance of returning to work by a factor of three.

However, as Badley and Ibanez[150] point out, musculoskeletal disorders are not unique in this association. Those with lower socioeconomic status report more chronic conditions and are more likely to report lower functional status, greater limitation of daily activities, and less good health.[151] Socioeconomic factors may also contribute to work disability. Badley and Ibanez[152] in a cross-sectional survey of Canadian households (over 16 years) found disability was independently associated with increasing age, not being married, fewer years of schooling, lower income and not being employed. These risk factors were similar for *both* musculoskeletal and non-musculoskeletal causes of disability. For instance, Krause and Anson[153] demonstrated that employment after spinal cord injury was dependent not only on the severity of the injury but also on age and education with older, more poorly educated individuals being less likely to be employed. Hence, poorer, older, less educated individuals are less likely to be able to find alternative work and are least able to handle the loss of income associated with chronic pain disability. Alternatively they are going to be more dependent on compensation payments.

12.4.9 The Work Environment

12.4.9.1 Heavy Physical Work

The nature of the job of an individual with chronic pain is an important contributor to disability. It is intuitively obvious that a manual labourer is going to have more difficulty with the heavy, physical demands of his or her job than a school teacher who has more sedentary employment. The nurse who must lift patients and who injures her back (a common occurrence) will have more difficulty than a physician with a similar

---

148 Kelsey JL, Golden AL. Occupational and Workplace Factors Associated with Low Back Pain. In: Deyo RA, ed. *Occupational Medicine, State of the Art Reviews: Back Pain in Workers*. Philadelphia: Hanley & Belfus, 1988: 7-16.
149 Gallagher R, Rauh V, Hangh L, et al. Determinants of Return to Work Among Low Back Pain Patients. *Pain* 1989; 39:55-67.
150 *Supra*, note 144.
151 House JS, Kessler RC, Herzog AR, et al. Age, Socioeconomic Status, and Health. *Milbank Q* 1990; 68:383-411. Blaxter M. Health and Social Class — Evidence on Inequality in Health from a National Survey. *Lancet* 1987; 2:30-33.
152 *Supra*, note 144.
153 Krause JS, Anson CA. Employment after Spinal Cord Injury: Relation to Selected Participant Characteristics. *Arch Phys Med Rehabil* 1996; 77:737-743.

problem. Several reviews of low back pain in workers support an association of heavy manual labour and LBP[154] and such workers are more likely to develop compensable back injuries.[155] In turn, these workers are going to be less likely to perform their job duties when compared to individuals with LBP and less physically demanding jobs. Hence, the physical requirements of the job will significantly influence the degree of disability. The availability of work and the willingness of an employer to accommodate an injured employee's needs are important and also affect the degree of disability.

Yelin et al.[156] reviewed the data regarding 3,100 adults with limitations in activities and chronic disease who had responded to the 1978 Social Security Administration Survey of Disabled and Non-Disabled Adults. They noted that nature of the work itself had the most profound impact on whether patients stopped working. Persons in white-collar occupations had much lower disability rates while those in service occupations had far higher rates. Self-employment (work autonomy) reduced the probability of lost work. Among all the work variables the authors noted that, "the interaction of the demands of the job and the limitations one experienced in performing them had the strongest effect among disability status."[157] Work disability did not correlate well with the severity of symptoms but did with the actual physical demands of the workplace.[158]

12.4.9.2 Job Dissatisfaction

Whether an individual takes time off work related to any injury has been associated with a supervisor's assessment of their ability in the work-

---

154 Kelsey et al., *supra*, note 148. Frymoyer JW, Pope MH, Clements JH. Risk Factors in Low Back Pain. *J Bone Joint Surg* 1983; 65:213. Garg A, Moore SJ. Epidemiology of Low-Back Pain in Industry. In: Moore SJ, Garg A, eds. *Occupational Medicine, State of the Art Reviews: Ergonomics: Low-Back Pain, Carpal Tunnel Syndrome, and Upper Extremity Disorders in the Workplace.* Philadelphia: Hanley & Belfus, 1992: 599-608. Snook SH. Low Back Pain in Industry: In: White AA, Gordon SL, eds. *American Academy of Orthopaedic Surgeons Symposium on Idiopathic Low Back Pain*, St. Louis: Mosby, 1982: 23-38.
155 Bergqvist-Ullman M, Larson N. Acute Low Back Pain in Industry. *Acta Orthop Scand* 1977; 170 (suppl):1-117. Jenson RC. Epidemiology of Work-Related Back Pain. Topics in Acute Care, *Trauma and Rehabilitation* 1988; 2:1-15.
156 Yelin EH, Henke CJ, Epstein WV. Work Disability among Persons with Musculoskeletal Conditions. *Arthritis & Rheumatism* 1986; 29(11):1322-1333.
157 *Ibid.*
158 Yelin et al., *supra*, note 156.

place.[159] Some authors regard job satisfaction as an important factor determining whether an individual develops chronic pain and/or returns to work.[160] This concept was strongly supported by a large prospective study of industrial workers at the Boeing Company.[161] Workers in the study were followed for approximately 4 years. Two-hundred and seventy-nine of 3,020 studied workers reported back pain in this longitudinal study. Those subjects who stated they "hardly ever" enjoyed their job tasks were 2.5 times more likely to report a job injury ($p=0.0001$) than subjects who "almost always" enjoyed their job tasks. However, there are limitations to the interpretation of this study. Only 1,569 responded and of these 136 reported back pain; of the 1,326 for whom complete data were available, 117 reported back pain. On the question "I enjoy the tasks involved in my job", 18% of those who stated "hardly ever" reported back pain over a 4-year period, compared to 14% and 7% reporting "some of the time" and "almost always" respectively. The study looked only at individuals who took time off for acute pain and did not deal with chronic disabling pain. Hales and Bernard[162] also noted that the Bigos[163] study did not investigate potentially precipitating job or task demand stressors while noting that most researchers considered job dissatisfaction to be a "stress response" to factors in the work place or from individual psychosocial stresses rather than a stress itself. The authors themselves note the effect of work perceptions

---

159 Bigos SJ, Battie MC, Spengler DM, et al. A Prospective Study of Work Perceptions and Psychosocial Factors Affecting the Report of Back Injury. *Spine* 1991; 16:1-6. Bigos SJ, Battie MC, Spengler DM, Fisher LD, Fordyce WE, Hansson T, Nachemson AL, Zeh J. A Longitudinal, Prospective Study of Industrial Back Injury Reporting. *Clin Orthop and Related Research* 1992; 279:21-34.

160 Cohen MC, Houlihan DL, Lippincott P, Pearlson TD. Long-term Impact of Intensive Inpatient Treatment and Subsequent Medical Utilization and Impairment in Chronic Benign Pain. In: American Pain Society 11th Annual Scientific Meeting, 1992: 56. Manruta T, Swanson DW, Swensen WM. Chronic Pain: Which Patients May a Pain Program Help? *Pain* 1979; 7:321-329. Mintz J, et al. Treatments of Depression and the Functional Capacity to do Work. *Arch Gen Psychiatr* 1992; 49:761-768. Magora A. Investigation of the Relationships Between Low Back Pain and Occupation. *Scan J Rehabil Med* 1973; 5:191-196. Niemcryk S, Jenkins D, Rose R, et al. The Prospective Impact of Psychosocial Variables on Rates of Illness and Injury in Professional Employees. *J Occup Med* 198; 29:645-652. Steig R. The Cost Effectiveness of Pain Treatment Centers. *Clin J Pain* 1990; 6:301-304.

161 Bigos et al., (1991 and 1992), *supra*, note 159.

162 Hales TR, Bernard BP. Epidemiology of Work-Related Musculoskeletal Disorders. *Orthopedic Clinics of North America* 1996; 27(4):679-709.

163 Bigos et al., (1991), *supra*, note 159.

and psychosocial factors were "statistically significant though clinically modest."[164]

Skovron et al.[165] in a cross-sectional study of 4,000 Belgian adults, found that work satisfaction was not associated with a first episode of LBP. However, poor work satisfaction was associated with a daily history of LBP among all working respondents with a history of LBP. The authors speculated that work satisfaction was not causally related to LBP, but rather intervened with work to lead to an altered perception of work once LBP had developed. This was notable in that the Bigos[166] study was confined to individuals who actually had sickness absence due to LBP. Hence, work dissatisfaction may lead individuals with LBP to take a few days off work but is not revealing regarding the true incidence of LBP. Apart from the Bigos[167] study, other cross-sectional studies have found an association between work dissatisfaction or workplace stress and low back pain;[168] although again, the relationship is not strong. In contrast one longitudinal study[169] and several cross-sectional studies[170] did not find an association.[171] Thus, job dissatisfaction has yet to be shown to be causative of low back pain and what data exist are conflicting. The role of job dissatisfaction in chronic disability has not been adequately studied.

---

164 Bigos et al., (1991), *supra*, note 159.
165 Skrovron ML, Szpalski M, Nordin M, Melot C, Cukier D. Sociocultural Factors in Back Pain: A Population Based Study in Belgian Adults. *Spine* 1994; 19:129-137.
166 Bigos et al., (1991), *supra*, note 159.
167 Bigos et al., (1991), *supra*, note 159.
168 Heliovaara M, Makela M, Knekt P, et al. Determinants of Sciatica and Low Back Pain. *Spine* 1991; 16:608-614. Svensson H-O, Andersson GBJ. The Relationship of Low Back Pain, Work History and Work Environment, and Stress: A Retrospective Cross-sectional Study of 38-64 Year Old Women. *Spine* 1989; 14:517-522.
169 Beiring-Sorenson F, Thomsen CE, Hilden J. Risk Indicators for Low Back Trouble. *Scan J Rehabil Med* 1989; 21:151-157.
170 Astrand NE. Medical, Psychological, and Social Factors Associated with Back Abnormalities and Self-Reported Back Pain: A Cross-Sectional Study of Male Employees in a Swedish Pulp and Paper Industry. *Br J Indust Med* 1987; 44:327-336. Skrovron ML, Mulvihill MN, Sterling RC, et al. Work Organization and Low Back Pain in Nursing Personnel. Ergonomics 1987; 30:359-366. Svensson H-O, Andersson GBJ. Low Back Pain in 40 to 47 Year Old Men: Work History and Work Environment Factors. *Spine* 1983; 8:272-276. Feyer AM, Williamson A, Mandryk J, et al. Role of Psychosocial Risk Factors in Work-Related Low Back Pain. *Scand J Work Environ Health* 1982; 18:368-375. Linton SJ. Risk Factors for Neck and Back Pain in a Working Population in Sweden. *Work and Stress* 1990; 4:41-49.
171 Hales et al., *supra*, note 162.

12.4.10 The Shift to Managing Chronic Pain Disability Only

With the failure of the medical system to reliably treat chronic pain disorders and difficulties in accurately assessing the level of disability, many rehabilitation programs have chosen to focus primarily on managing disability, with increased function as the major and often only goal.[172] Gatchel[173] has noted that this refocusing on the issue of disability is both complicated and highly stressful for both patients and health care providers. Function has proven attractive as a goal because it is observable and objectively measurable and allows the health care provider(s) to avoid or minimize subjective (and presumably unreliable) self-reports of pain and disability.[174]

The functional approach focuses on virtues of independence and self-reliance, characteristics highly valued by society. Concerns about the discordance between impairment, disability and pain are not so clear to patients and hence the functional approach leads to conflict. For patients, pain relief is a primary goal and health care professionals' focus on the lack of reliable objective measures are often seen as a repudiation of the veracity of their pain and, by inference, their own personal character. Hence, this discordance becomes a source of dispute between health care providers, patients, and eventually third-party payers. Concerns regarding this discordance have led to an increasing reluctance on the part of third-party payers to accept patient and physician reports of disability secondary to chronic pain.

12.4.11 The Trend Towards Rejecting Chronic Pain Disability

An even more ominous trend has been to reject chronic pain disability entirely in an attempt to contain costs associated with disability compensation/income replacement. This trend is epitomized by two reports, one largely American and the other Canadian.

12.4.11.1 The Report on Back Pain in the Workplace

As mentioned previously, a Task Force on Pain in the Workplace was commissioned by the International Association for the Study of Pain (IASP) to suggest solutions to the marked increase in disability related costs due to nonspecific low back pain (NSLBP) in economically developed countries. The Task Force's recommendations were based on the

---

172 Gatchel, *supra*, note 103. Clifford, *supra*, note 99.
173 Gatchel, *supra*, note 103.
174 Gatchel, *supra*, note, 103. Mayer TG, Gatchel FJ. *Functional Restoration for Spinal Disorders: The Sports Medicine Approach*. Philadelphia: Lea and Febiger, 1988.

premise that "impairment and permanent disability should be restricted to conditions for which causation has been demonstrated".[175] However, the recommendations were based on the fact that the presence of nociception was deemed determinable only if specific radiologic abnormalities were present. In essence, only potentially surgically correctable lesions were regarded as legitimate. The presumption was that pain in NSLBP (defined as pain in the absence of radiographic markers) was different and not legitimate in terms of nociception and disability. NSLBP and subsequent disability are presented as largely behavioral problems, fostered by inappropriate medicalization, and a willingness to compensate pain.[176]

The Task Force did suggest comprehensive re-evaluation, including social and vocational assessment components in cases where function had not been restored and return to work not achieved. The authors of the report recommended that pain be reconceptualized as "activity intolerance" and disability as "unemployment." This reconceptualization avoided the issue of what the patient was actually experiencing when he or she complained of pain. Designating disability as "unemployment" sets the stage for eventually denying compensation once the usual period of unemployment payments came to an end, regardless of whether the patient remained disabled or not. This report basically recommended that a time limit be placed on disability payments in order to control costs while denying the reality of chronic pain by replacing it with the term "activity intolerance."

12.4.11.2 Quebec Task Force on Whiplash Associated Disorders

Injured workers are of course not the only individuals who will suffer from such an approach. Patients injured in motor vehicle accidents who receive so called "soft tissue injuries" affecting the neck are particularly liable to develop chronic pain which in some jurisdictions (e.g., the province of Quebec in Canada) will not be compensated after a very limited time; in the case of Quebec that period is recommended as a mere 27 days.[177]

12.5 FUTURE CONFLICT: CHRONIC PAIN, DISABILITY, AND SOCIETY

Several authors have implicitly or explicitly recommended that chronic pain disorders should be addressed as psychosocial and not as biological or clinical problems.[178] The reasons cited are threefold: 1) Biologi-

---

175 *Supra*, note 11.
176 *Supra*, note 11.
177 Spitzer et al., *supra*, note 12.
178 Ochoa, *supra*, note 7. Fordyce, *supra*, note 11. Schrader, *supra*, note 89. Hadler, *supra*, note 34.

cal mechanisms offer an inadequate explanation of the pain, impairment, and disability; 2) The secondary gain inherent in compensation awards militate against a speedy resolution of the problem; 3) The current compensation system is too costly in the aggregate. Add to this the complexity of chronic pain disability and there is a great temptation to simply refuse to acknowledge and compensate individuals with chronic pain and disability.

We have previously discussed the first two points. With regard to the third point we agree that the costs involved have approached disconcerting levels. The offered solution of rejection of chronic pain rather than medical or clinical categorization is, however, questionable. It is unlikely that the search for a biological and clinical explanation for these disorders will be abandoned in individual patients, and controversy may be exacerbated rather than avoided. Lack of acceptance of a clinical categorization for chronic pain disorders will do nothing by itself in preventing disability.

The primary justification for advocating change is that the present system has left the problem unsolved and has become too costly. The concept of disability secondary to chronic pain disorders as not being worthy of permanent disability status because it is strongly influenced by psychological and environmental factors or is a consequence of "less effective repertoires" is arguably discriminatory. Worse still, it will affect those least able to deal with the withdrawal of support, that is, those in lower socioeconomic groups with limited options. If a changing socioeconomic environment has led to the epidemic of disability, withdrawing social support may simply exacerbate the problem.

The risk factors for disability in chronic pain disorders does not seem to be different from that of non-musculoskeletal disorders. It is not clear how society as a whole will gain if costs are shifted from third-party payers to unemployment or welfare agencies. Social factors are recognized as important contributors to disability in conditions which are far less controversial, and better defined. For instance, in a recent report Reisine et al.[179] pointed out that complexity of the work itself, the desire to remain employed, and reduced work hours influenced work disability in rheumatoid arthritis. Of greatest concern is that older, less educated and lower income individuals are more likely to be targeted by any changes in the compensation system. Such individuals are least able to cope with reductions in disability payments and their degree of suffering will be exacerbated.

Chronic musculoskeletal pain syndromes require further clarification and research. Future research will need to take into account the needs of the individual patient and the social costs of compensation, and to focus on issues of work structure, worker education, and incentives to stay at work.

---

179 Reisine S, McQuillan J, Fifield J. Predictors of Work Disability in Rheumatoid Arthritis Patients. A Five Year Follow-up. *Arthritis Rheum* 1995; 38:1630-1637.

Chapter 13

Reflex Sympathetic Dystrophy

by Robert W. Teasell, M.D., F.R.C.P.C.*

13.1 Defining Reflex Sympathetic Dystrophy
13.2 Role of the Sympathetic Nervous System in RSD
13.3 Concerns Regarding Definitions/Pathophysiology
13.4 The Role of Psychological Factors
13.5 Diagnosis
    13.5.1 Clinical Diagnosis
    13.5.2 Nuclear Bone Scan
    13.5.3 Radiological Studies
    13.5.4 Sympathetic Blockade
13.6 Treatment
    13.6.1 Physical Therapy
    13.6.2 Sympathetic Blockade
    13.6.3 Surgical Sympathectomy
    13.6.4 Corticosteroids
    13.6.5 Calcitonin
    13.6.6 Hydroxyl Radical Scavengers
    13.6.7 Surgically Implantable Devices
13.7 Prognosis
13.8 Summary

13.1 DEFINING REFLEX SYMPATHETIC DYSTROPHY

Reflex sympathetic dystrophy (RSD) remains an enigmatic and poorly understood clinical condition. The term was first introduced by Evans.[1] RSD is clinically characterized by distal limb pain and edema, exquisite

---

* Chief and Chair, Department of Physical Medicine and Rehabilitation; Associate Professor, University of Western Ontario.
1 Evans JA. Reflex Sympathetic Dystrophy. *Surg Clin North Am* 1946; 26:780-790.

tenderness in the form of allodynia (pain resulting from non-noxious stimuli) or hyperalgesia (increased sensitivity to noxious stimuli), protective immobility, trophic skin changes, and vasomotor instability of the involved extremity[2] (Table 1). Sometimes the diagnosis is made in the presence of allodynia and hyperalgesia alone.[3] RSD is often associated with causalgia, which occurs in association with injury to a large nerve, and many authors consider them to be the same clinical entity.

Table 1. Clinical Criteria for RSD

Definite RSD
- Pain in an extremity
- Vasomotor instability
- Edematous extremity
- Dystrophic skin changes

Probable RSD

- Pain and tenderness in an extremity
- Vasomotor instability
- Extremity swelling

Possible RSD

- Vasomotor instability
- Edematous extremity

Doubtful RSD

- Unexplained pain and tenderness in an extremity

Modified from Kozin (1976, 1976b, 1981a).

---

2   Kozin F, McCary DJ, Sims JE, Genant HK. The Reflex Sympathetic Dystrophy Syndrome I Clinical and Histologic Studies: Evidence of Bilaterality, Accentuation of Periarticular Regions and Predictable Response to Corticosteroids. *Am J Med* 1976; 60: 321-331. Kozin F, Genant HK, Bekerman C, McCarty DJ. The Reflex Sympathetic Dystrophy Syndrome II. Roentgenographic and Ocintigraphic Evidence of Bilaterality and of Periarticular Accentration. *Am J Med* 1976; 60: 332-338. Kozin F, Ryan LM, Cavvera GF, Soin JS, Wortmann RL. The Reflex Sympathetic Dystrophy Syndrome (RSD) III. Scintigraphic Studies Further Evidence for the Therapeutic Efficacy of Systemic Corticosteroids and Proposed Diagnostic Criteria. *Am J Med* 1981; 70: 23-30. Kozin F, Soin JS, Ryan LM, Carrera GF, Wortmann RL. Bone Scintigraphy in Reflex Sympathetic Dystrophy Syndrome. *Radiolography* 1981; 138:437-443.

3   Sunderland S. Pain Mechanisms in Causalgia. *J Neurol Neurosurg Psychiatry* 1976; 39: 471-480.

The Sixth World Congress on Pain Consensus statement offered the following definition of RSD:

> [A] descriptive term meaning a complex disorder or a group of disorders that may develop as a consequence of trauma affecting the limbs, with or without an obvious nerve lesion. RSD may also develop after visceral diseases, and central nervous system lesions or rarely, without an obvious antecedent event. It consists of pain and related sensory abnormalities, abnormal blood flow and sweating, abnormalities in the motor system and changes in structure of both superficial and deep tissues (trophic changes). It is not necessary that all components are present. It is agreed that the name "reflex sympathetic dystrophy" is used in a descriptive sense and does not imply specific mechanisms.[4]

As an extension and completion of the consensus statement, and to address concerns that the term RSD implied a pathophysiological role for the sympathetic nervous syndrome, a revised taxonomic system for RSD was presented.[5] All RSD/causalgia disorders are now classified under the umbrella of *complex regional pain syndrome* (CRPS), which is based entirely on clinical criteria. Inclusion criteria under the CRPS syndrome label include the presence of regional pain (spontaneous and evoked) and other sensory changes following a noxious event. The pain is associated with changes in skin colour, skin temperature, abnormal sweating, edema, and sometimes motor abnormalities. Two types of CRPS have been identified: CRPS type I, corresponding to RSD, and CRPS type II, corresponding to causalgia. Sympathetic maintained pain (SMP) is no longer considered as a separate disorder but rather as a description of a type of pain that could be found in a variety of pain disorders, including CPRS I and II.[6]

---

4   Janig W, Blumberg H, Boas RA, Campbell JN. The Reflex Sympathetic Dystrophy Syndrome: Consensus Statement and General Recommendations for Diagnosis and Clinical Research. In: Bond JE, Charlton C, Woolf J, eds. *Proceedings of the VI World Congress on Pain.* Amsterdam: Elsevier, 1991: 373-376.
5   Merskey H, Bogduk N, eds. *Classification of Chronic Pain: Descriptions of Chronic Pain Syndromes and Definition of Pain Terms*, 2nd ed. Seattle: IASP Press, 1994. Stanton-Hicks M, Janig W, Hassenbusch S, Haddoc JD, Boas R, Wilson P. Reflex Sympathetic Dystrophy: Changing Concepts and Taxonomy. *Pain* 1995; 63:127-133.
6   Janig W. The Puzzle of "Reflex Sympathetic Dystrophy": Mechanisms, Hopthesis, Open Questions. In: W. Janig, M. Stanton-Hicks. Reflex Sympathetic Dystrophy: A Reappraisal. *Progress in Pain Research and Management,* 1996; 6:1-24.

Table 2. Terminology in Reflex Sympathetic Dystrophy

Reflex sympathetic dystrophy	RSD symptom complex in absence of Trauma to major nerve (chronic regional pain syndrome type I).
Causalgia	RSD symptom complex following peripheral nerve injury, usually major mixed nerves (chronic regional pain syndrom II).
Sudek's atrophy	RSD symptom complex post soft-tissue trauma with bony atrophy.
Algoneurodystrophy	RSD symptom complex post minor trauma (European terminology).
Sympathetic independent	RSD symptom complex which fails to or dependent pain respond to sympathetic blockade.
Sympathetic maintained	RSD symptom complex which responds pain to sympathetic blockade.
Alloydnia	Pain from a non-noxious stimulus (i.e., lightly stroking skin).
Hyperalgesia	Increased pain to a noxious stimulus (i.e., pressing on MCP joints).
Complex regional pain syndrome I	RSD
Complex regional pain syndrome II	Causalgia

13.2 ROLE OF THE SYMPATHETIC NERVOUS SYSTEM IN RSD

RSD has long been regarded as a consequence of abnormalities of the sympathetic nervous system (SNS) based largely upon the presence of vasomotor instability, a frequent response to sympathetic blockade, and experimental data which strongly support the notion that efferent SNS activity can be involved in the generation of pain.[7] However, the specific role of the SNS in RSD remains unclear. Terms such as sympathetically maintained pain (SMP) are often used to describe those cases which respond to sympathetic blockade.[8] Campbell et al.[9] have gone as far as to define the pain on the basis of whether the pain is eliminated by blockade of sympathetic efferent innervation of the painful limb, i.e., sympathetic dependent or independent pain.

There is clinical evidence of involvement of the SNS in RSD. RSD is characterized by swelling, rubor, warmth, and signs of vasomotor instability in the early stages suggesting sympathetic hypoactivity. The later stages are characterized by pale cyanosis, coolness, and hyperhidrosis suggesting sympathetic hyperactivity. Bone scan, at least in the early stages, frequently demonstrates signs of increased blood flow. Sympathetic blockade

---

7   White JC, Sweet WH. *Pain and the Neurosurgeon*. Springfield: Charles C. Thomas, 1969. Wallin G, Torebjork HE, Hallin RG. Preliminary Observations on the Pathophysiology of Hyperalgesia in the Causalgic Pain Syndrome. In: Y. Zotterman, ed. *Sensory Function of the Skin in Primates*. Oxford: Pergamon, 1976: 489-499. Janig W. The Sympathetic Nervous System in Pain: Physiology and Pathophysiology. In: M. Stanton-Hicks, ed., *Pain and the Sympathetic Nervous System*. Boston: Kluwer Academic Publishers, 1990: 17-89. Stanton-Hicks M. *Pain and the Sympathetic Nervous System*. Boston: Kluwer Academic Publishers, 1990. Bonica JJ. Causalgia and Other Reflex Sympathetic Dystrophies. In: JJ Bonica, ed. *The Management of Pain*, 2nd ed. Philadelphia: Lea & Febiger, 1990: 220-243. Arner S. Intravenous Phentolamine Test: Diagnostic and Prognostic Use in Reflex Sympathetic Dystrophy. *Pain* 1991; 46:17-22. Raja SN, Treede RD, David KD, Campbell JN. Systemic Alpha-Adrenergic Blockade with Phentolamine: A Diagnostic Test for Sympathetically Maintained Pain. *Anesthesiology* 1991; 74:691-698. Campbell JN, Meyer RA, Raja SN. Is Nociceptor Activation by Alpha-1 Adrenoceptors the Culprit in Sympathetically Maintained Pain? *American Pain Society Journal* 1992; 1(1): 3-11. Blumberg H, Hoffman U, Mohadjer M, Scheremet R. Clinical Phenomenology and Mechanisms of Reflex Sympathetic Dystrophy: Emphasis on Edema. In: G.F. Gebhart, DL Hammond, TS Jensen, eds. *Proceedings of the 7th World Congress on Pain Progress in Pain Research and Management*. Seattle: IASP Press, 1994, vol. 2: 455-481.

8   Roberts WJ. A Hypothesis on the Physiological Basis for Causalgia and Related Pain. *Pain* 1986; 24: 297-311.

9   Campbell et al., *supra*, note 7.

(regional blocks, guanethidine bier block, intravenous phentolamine) is frequently used to confirm the diagnosis.

The concept of SMP is attractive because it implies that the pain of RSD may be responsive to therapeutic approaches which target efferent sympathetic activity. However, the role of the SNS in RSD has proven to be difficult to define, especially for individual patients.

Table 3. Difficulty Determining the Role of the Sympathetic Nervous System in Reflex Sympathetic Dystrophy

- Dynamic nature of RSD
- Heterogenicity of the clinical picture of RSD
- Lack of a pathophysiological mechanism linking SNS and pain
- Paradox between sympatholytic treatment being used despite clinical picture of sympathetic hypoactivity

As mentioned above, RSD is initially characterized by sympathetic hypoactivity followed by sympathetic hyperactivity. Among patients with RSD there is a significant heterogenicity to the clinical presentation. Currently there is no pathophysiological mechanism linking the SNS and pain. Finally, sympathetic blockade and sympathectomies are often paradoxically used early on in the course of RSD when the clinical picture is characterized by sympathetic hypoactivity.

Arnold[10] has demonstrated that in the RSD-affected limb there is evidence of hyperresponsiveness of the peripheral alpha-adrenoceptors. Interestingly, similar findings were found in patients with a painful diabetic peripheral neuropathy of the lower extremities.[11] However, it is unclear as to how hyperresponsive peripheral alpha-adrenoceptors influence pain or whether such a finding is even important. Recent work by Verdugo and Ochoa,[12] has called into serious question the entire concept of SMP and the role of the SNS in the pain of RSD.

---

10 Arnold JMO, Teasell RW, MacLeod AR, Brown J, Carruthers SG. Increased Venous Alpha-Adrenoceptor Responsiveness in Patients with Reflex Sympathetic Dystrophy. *Annals of Internal Medicine* 1993; 118: 619-621.

11 Capes SE, Teasell RW, Simon J, Finestone HM, Arnold JMO. Increased Alpha-Adrenoceptor Responsiveness in Painful Diabetic Neuropathy. Department of Medicine Resident Research Day, London, Ontario, May 16, 1996.

12 Verdugo RJ, Ochoa JL. Sympathetically Maintained Pain. I. Phentolamine Block Questions the Concept. *Neurology* 1994; 44: 1003-1010(a). Verdugo RJ, Campero M, Ochoa JL. Phentolamine Sympathetic Block in Painful Polyneuropathies II. Further Questioning of the Concept of Sympathetically Maintained Pain. *Neurology* 1994; 44: 1010-1014(b).

13.3 CONCERNS REGARDING DEFINITIONS/PATHOPHYSIOLOGY

Ochoa has been quite outspoken in his critique of RSD as a clinical entity and to attempts to ascribe a SNS etiology to the clinical picture, especially the pain. Concerns have included: (1) overinterpreting vasomotor changes in involved regions as indicative of abnormal sympathetic activity; (2) assigning pathophysiological significance to pain relief after sympathetic blocks in the absence of control blocks; (3) subsequently ascribing a causative role in the pain to the SNS and (4) ignoring the possibility that multiple pathophysiologic events, including psychogenic causes, may lead to the clinical picture of RSD.[13]

Although these concerns are valid, Ochoa[14] complicated the debate by assuming the etiology was psychogenic based upon anecdotal evidence that these patients often had significant emotional difficulties in the absence of determinable pathophysiology. Although it is obvious that the SNS is frequently abnormal in RSD (as witnessed by frequent vasomotor changes) it is unknown as to whether the SNS affects the pain or is responsible for the development of RSD (i.e., is it causative or secondary). Verdugo and Ochoa[15] studied patients presumably meeting criteria for RSD or causalgia and demonstrated that most patients did not respond to treatment with alpha-blockers, whereas those who did respond were as likely to respond to saline infusion (placebo) as phentolamine (an alpha-1 blocker). Phenylephrine (an alpha-1 agonist) failed to aggravate the pain.

13.4 THE ROLE OF PSYCHOLOGICAL FACTORS

Several studies have supported the concept that psychological factors play a role in the onset and persistence of RSD although most of these have been based on retrospective clinical data or anecdotal experiences.[16] Bruehl and Carlson[17] noted that studies utilizing the MMPI suggested RSD

---

13 Ochoa JL. Guest Editorial: Essence, Investigation, and Management of "Neuropathic" Pains: Hopes from Acknowledgement of Chaos. *Muscle and Nerve* 1993; 997-1008.
14 *Ibid.*
15 *Supra,* note 12.
16 Van Houdenhove B, Vasquez G, Onglhena P, Stans C, Vandeput C, et al. Etiopathogenesis of Reflex Sympathetic Dystrophy: A Review and Biopsychosocial Hypothesis. *Clin J Pain* 1992; 8: 300-306. Geertzen JHB, deBruijn H, deBruijn-Kofman AT, Arendzen JH. Reflex Sympathetic Dystrophy: Early Treatment and Psychological Aspects. *Arch Phys Med Rehabil* 1994; 75:442-446.
17 Bruehl S, Carlson CR. Predisposing Psychological Factors in the Development of Reflex Sympathetic Dystrophy. *Clin J Pain* 1992; 8:287-299.

patients tended to be depressed, somatically preoccupied and tended to use repression as a psychological defence. However, the same authors noted these same personality characteristics are often noted on the MMPI in all types of chronic pain syndromes.[18] The study has been criticized on methodological grounds. Haddox et al.[19] and Zucchini et al.[20] found they were unable to distinguish between RSD and non-RSD pain patients based on personality factors.

Hardy et al.[21] measured the psychological profile of RSD patients. They found that RSD patients were more anxious and depressed, complained of somatic distress more frequently, and had poor ability to relate interpersonally compared with a group of non-RSD patients suffering from hand injury.

Geertzen et al.[22] reported a study in which patients with RSD were compared with a control group of 42 patients who underwent elective hand surgery. Female RSD patients were more depressed, had more feelings of inadequacy, and demonstrated high psycho-neurotism scores. Eighty percent of the RSD patients had a serious social life event in 2 months before and one month after trauma compared to 20% of the controls. The authors also noted that not all individuals who developed RSD exhibited psychological abnormalities. They noted, "depression, emotional disturbances, anxiety, and/or life events together with a trauma can increase the risk of RSD. All of these factors can create stress which disturbs the autonomic nerve system and probably maintains the RSD."

Bruehl et al.[23] examined possible psychological differences between RSD and non-RSD chronic pain patients in consecutive series of 34 RSD, 50 non-RSD limb pain, and 165 low back pain (LBP) patients. RSD patients reported more somatization and phobic anxiety as well as greater coping with pain through diverting attention than LBP patients. Comparisons between RSD and non-RSD limb pain revealed no significant differences with the exception of somatization scores. The relationship between distress and pain severity was found to be strong in RSD and non-RSD

---

18 Bradley LA, Van der Heide LH. Pain Related Correlates of MMPI Profile Subgroups Among Back Pain Patients. *Health Psychol* 1984; 3:157-174.
19 Haddox JD, Abram SE, Hopwood MH. Comparison of Psychometric Data in RSD and Radiculopathy. *Reg Anesth* 1988; 13:27.
20 Zucchini M, Alberti G, Moretti MP. Algodystrophy and Related Psychological Features. *Funct Neurol* 1989; 4:153-156.
21 Hardy MA, Merritt WD. Psychological Evaluation and Pain Assessment in Patients with Reflex Sympathetic Dystrophy. *J Hand Ther* 1988; 155-164.
22 Geertzen et al., *supra*, note 16.
23 Bruehl S, Husfeldt B, Lubenow TR, Nath H, Ivankovich AD. Psychological Differences Between Reflex Sympathetic Dystrophy and Non-RSD Chronic Pain Patients. *Pain* 1996; 67:107-114.

limb pain than in LBP patients. The results provided partial support for clinical assumptions that RSD patients are more psychologically dysfunctional than other chronic pain patients.

Despite controversy as to whether individuals with a previous history of psychological disorders are more prone to developing RSD, it is generally agreed that psychologically stable patients can develop problems of emotional stability after prolonged exposure to RSD.[24] Lynch[25] reported a high incidence of a direct time-relation between the provoking physical pain and psychological dysfunction. No evidence was found that psychological factors or a specific personality characteristic made a patient more susceptible to RSD. Given the conflicting evidence, the role of psychological factors in RSD remains unclear; however, they are a prominent feature of the clinical presentation and cannot be ignored.

13.5 DIAGNOSIS

13.5.1 Clinical Diagnosis

While causalgia is generally easily identifiable, the clinical picture of RSD is not always apparent. Nevertheless, RSD is a clinical diagnosis. Kozin's criteria for RSD, established over 20 years ago, are an example of widely accepted clinical criteria (see Table 2).[26] Chronic limb pain with evidence of sympathetic involvement is common, while RSD meeting rigorous clinical criteria is fortunately uncommon. Unfortunately, too many patients are overdiagnosed with the label of RSD leading to questionable and dubious treatment.

13.5.2 Nuclear Bone Scan

The diagnostic test most frequently used to confirm the diagnosis of RSD is the three-phase technetium bone scan. Nuclear-scan studies are considered to be consistent with RSD when the blood-pool or blood-flow phase demonstrates diffuse asymmetric uptake in the involved limb, or when the 3-hour delayed image demonstrates asymmetric periarticular uptake in the affected hand or foot.[27] Kozin et al.[28] studied 50 patients with

---

24 Lynch ME. Psychological Aspects of Reflex Sympathetic Dystrophy: A Review of the Adult and Paediatric Literature. *Pain* 1992; 49:337-347.
25 *Ibid.*
26 *Supra*, note 2.
27 Davidoff G, Werner R, Cremer S, Jackson D, Ventocilla C, Wolf L. Predictive Value of the Three-Phase Technetium Bone Scan in Diagnosis of Reflex Sympathetic Dystrophy Syndrome. *Arch Phys Med Rehabil* 1989; 70:135-137.
28 Kozin et al., (1981), *supra*, note 2.

limb pain, 28 of whom met the clinical criteria for definite or probable RSD. All had technetium bone scans. Sensitivity was 67% and specificity 86%. Davidoff et al.[29] studied 119 patients with nonspecific limb pain. Twenty-five (21%) met Kozin's criteria for definite or probable RSD.[30] All went on to have technetium bone scans. Sensitivity was 44% and specificity 92%. Positive predictive value was 61% and negative predictive value was 86%.

13.5.3 Radiological Studies

Radiological studies are of limited benefit in diagnosing RSD. The most commonly seen change is Sudek's atrophy, where periatricular osteopenia is seen, usually in the hands or feet. However, to detect osteopenia there must be 30–50% demineralization[31] and even then it is not necessarily pathognomonic of RSD.

13.5.4 Sympathetic Blockade

Stellate ganglion or lumbar sympathetic blocks are frequently used to confirm the presence or absence of sympathetically maintained pain (SMP). For some authors a positive response to regional sympathetic blockade is considered essential to the diagnosis of RSD/SMP.[32] False positive results can occur when the anesthetic spreads to nearby afferent fibers, generally nerve roots, to produce a sensory somatic block.[33] Phentolamine infusions and guanethidine bier blocks have also been used diagnostically.[34] Recent work[35] suggests the response to sympathetic blockade may be no better than placebo.

13.6 TREATMENT

Treatment of RSD is evolving towards a more conservative approach. Most studies looking at treatment are anecdotal uncontrolled reports. Various treatments for RSD are available. In the case of causalgia (RSD asso-

---

29 *Supra*, note 27.
30 Kozin et al., (1981), *supra*, note 2.
31 Tepperman PS, Greyson ND, Hilbert L, Williams JI. Reflex Sympathetic Dystrophy in Hemiplegia. *Arch Phys Med Rehabil* 1981; 62:549-554.
32 Roberts, *supra*, note 8.
33 Campbell et al., *supra*, note 7.
34 Arner, *supra*, note 186. Raja et al., *supra*, note 186. Hannington-Kiff KG. Intravenous Regional Sympathetic Blockade with Guanethidine. *Lancet* 1974; 1:1019-1020. Hannington-Kiff KG. Relief of Sudek's Atrophy by Regional Intravenous Guanethidine. *Lancet* 1977; 1:1132-1133.
35 *Supra*, note 12.

ciated with nerve damage), over 60% of patients were still suffering symptoms despite aggressive therapy after over 3 years.[36]

13.6.1 Physical Therapy

Physical therapy is regarded as very important. Its value is based upon anecdotal observation.[37] Indiscriminate and overaggressive therapy may increase afferent stimulation and aggravate symptoms.[38] The greatest potential complication of RSD is contractures; passive range of motion exercises and splinting may be necessary. Contrast baths and transcutaneous electrical nerve stimulation (TENS) are commonly used.

13.6.2 Sympathetic Blockade

RSD has long been regarded as a disorder of sympathetic overactivity. The mechanism of action of sympathetic blocks is not yet clearly understood.[39] Early RSD appears to be characterized by reduced sympathetic activity but paradoxically inhibition of sympathetic activity has been reported to improve the condition.[40] Therefore, sympathetic regional (cervical stellate ganglion or lumbar sympathetic) blockade are still frequently used in the treatment of causalgia and RSD. Alternatively, reserpine or guanethedine (the latter no longer available in the U.S.) bier blocks may be tried. Guanethidine acts as a false transmitter displacing noradrenaline from storage vesicles.[41] Reserpine blocks reuptake of noradrenaline with subsequent catecholamine depletion. Given as a local block, guanethidine has been reported to relieve pain in up to 80% of cases.[42] However, there are no properly controlled studies demonstrating efficacy for any of these treatments. Nevertheless, Bonica[43] has argued that properly used early in the course of the disease, sympathetic blockade combined with vigorous physical therapy cures some 80% of RSD patients. However, without ade-

---

36 Girgis (1989).
37 Schutzer SF, Gossling HR. Current Concepts Review. The Treatment of Reflex Sympathetic Dystrophy Syndrome. *J Bone Joint Surg* 1984; 66-A(4):625-629.
38 *Ibid.*
39 Shelton RM, Lewis CW. Reflex Sympathetic Dystrophy: A Review. *J Am Acad Dermatol* 1990; 22:513-520.
40 *Supra*, note 37. Christensen K, Jensen EM, Noer I. The Reflex Sympathetic Dystrophy Syndrome. Response to Treatment with Systemic Corticosteroids. *Acta Chir Scand* 1982; 148:653-655.
41 Tabira T, Shibaski H, Kuroiwa Y. Reflex Sympathetic Dystrophy (Causalgia). Treatment with Guanethedine. *Arch Neurol* 1983; 40:430-432.
42 Jaeger SH, Singer DI, Whitenack SH. Nerve Injury Complications. Management of Neurogenic Pain Syndromes. *Hand Clin* 1986; 2:217-234.
43 *Supra*, note 7.

quately controlled studies one must question whether placebo, tourniquets, physical therapy, or simple rest would have obtained the same results.

13.6.3 Surgical Sympathectomy

Surgical sympathectomy is generally performed if the patient receives some relief from a succession of sympathetic blocks.[44] Again, there is controversy regarding the efficacy of sympathectomy. There are no controlled studies (they would be difficult to perform) demonstrating the usefulness of sympathectomy; it appears to be more useful in causalgia than in RSD.[45] Despite anecdotal reports that sympathectomy helps some patients[46] there is increasing reluctance to utilize sympathectomy in the treatment of chronic RSD with many authors now reporting that sympathectomy does not cure RSD in the absence of injury to a large somatic nerve.[47] If performed it must be done early and must be extensive (must remove all functional sympathetic nervous tissue connections). In my practice sympathectomy is no longer recommended as a standard treatment option for RSD, even in patients who respond positively to sympathetic blockade.

13.6.4 Corticosteroids

Corticosteroids have been used early in the course of RSD. Patients are generally given large doses initially (between 30–60 mg daily) for 7 to 10 days with rapid taper over the next 1 to 2 weeks.[48] Corticosteroids have been reported to be effective when given in the early phase of the disorder.[49] There are no controlled trials. However, it is still sometimes used in

---

44 Shelton et al., *supra*, note 39.
45 Mockus MB, Rutherford RB, Rosales C, Pearce WH. Sympathectomy for Causalgia. *Arch Surg* 1987; 122:668-671.
46 Nathan PW. Pain and the Sympathetic System. In: Bannister R, ed. Autonomic Failure. *A Textbook of Clinical Disorders of the Autonomic Nervous System*, 2nd ed. Oxford: Oxford University Press, 1988: 733-747.
47 Ochou et al., *supra* note 13. Mockus et al., *supra* note 45. Perl ER. Nociceptors and Primary Hyperalgesia (Discussion). In: Willis W, ed. *Hyperalgesia and Allodynia*. New York: Raven Press, 1992: 167-171.
48 Kozin F, McCary DJ, Sims JE, Genant HK, *supra*, note 2. Rosenthal AK, Wortmann RL. Diagnosis, Pathogenesis and Management of Reflex Sympathetic Dystrophy Syndrome. *Comprehensive Therapy* 1991; 17(6):46-50.
49 Kozin et al., *supra*, note 2. Kozin (1981), supra, note 2. Christensen, *supra*, note 40. DeTakats G. Sympathetic Reflex Dystrophy. *Med Clin North Am* 1965; 49:117-129. Glick EN. Reflex Dystrophy (Algoneurodystrophy): Results of Treatment by Corticosteroids. *Rheumatol Rehab* 1973; 12:84-88. Mowat AG. Treatment of the Shoulder-hand Syndrome with Corticosteroids. *Ann Rheum Dis* 1974; 33:120-123. Poplawski ZJ, Wiley AM, Murray JF. Post-traumatic Dystrophy of the Extremities. *J Bone Joint Surg* (AM) 1983; 65(5):642-655.

shoulder-hand syndrome (widely regarded as a variant of RSD) seen early in the course of a stroke.

13.6.5 Calcitonin

Calcitonin has been used, primarily in Europe, either parenterally[50] or intranasally.[51] Gobelet et al.[52] examined the efficacy of intranasal salmon calcitonin in a double-blind randomized study of 66 patients with RSD. In the group who received intranasal salmon calcitonin combined with physiotherapy, pain, range of motion, and ability to work were improved, compared with the control group who received physiotherapy alone. The effect of calcitonin appears to be primarily analgesic.[53]

13.6.6 Hydroxyl Radical Scavengers

Hydroxyl radical scavengers, namely dimethylsulfoxyde (DMSO), have been used based on the hypothesis that there is an initial inflammatory response.[54] In RSD patients, Goris et al.[55] reported good results with hydroxyl radical scavengers. Geertzen et al.[56] studied 26 patients who were randomly assigned to 3 weeks of either guanethidine blockade or DMSO. All patients were treated within 3 months of development of RSD. Significant improvement was noted in both groups after 9 weeks of treatment; the DMSO group had a tendency toward a better outcome. The negative side effects include an onion-garlic like taste and smell and the cosmetic ap-

---

50 Doury P, Dirheimer Y, Pattin S. Algodystrophy: Diagnosis and Therapy of a Frequent Disease of the Locomotor Apparatus. Berlin: Springer-Verlag, 1981. Gobelet C, Meier JL, Schaffner W, Bischof-Delaloye A, Gerster JC, Burckhardt P. Calcitonin and Reflex Sympathetic Dystrophy Syndrome. *Clin Rheumatol* 1986; 5:382-388.
51 Gobelet C, Waldburger M, Meier JL. The Effect of Adding Calcitonin to Physical Treatment of Reflex Sympathetic Dystrophy. *Pain* 1992; 48:171-175.
52 *Ibid.*
53 Doury et al., *supra*, note 50. Acquaviva P, Eisinger JB, Schiano A, Recordier AM. Traitement des algoclystrophies par la calcitonine. Marceille Med 1976; 91:33-44. Ginsberg F, Vandenabeek G, Delcourt E. Le traitement de l'algoneurodystrophic par la thyrocalcitonine. *Med Hyg* 1987; 36:2632-2633. Gennari C, Francini G, Gorvelli S, Nami R. Bone pain, Endorphins and Calcitonin. 1st Int. Workshop. The Effects of Calcitonins in Man. Florence, April 2-3, 1982, 87 (referred to in Gobelet et al., *supra*, note 51).
54 Goris RJA, Dongen LMV, Winters HAH. Are Toxic Oxygen Radicals Involved in the Pathogenesis of Reflex Sympathetic Dystrophy? *Free Rad Res Comms* 1987; 3:13-18.
55 *Ibid.* Goris RJA. Treatment of Reflex Sympathetic Dystrophy with Hydroxyl Radical Scavengers. *Unfallchirurg* 1985; 88:330-332.
56 *Supra*, note 16.

pearance of the treated hand. The positive effect is that patients can treat themselves as an outpatient.

13.6.7 Surgically Implantable Devices

In desperate cases, surgical implantables, i.e., intrathecal morphine pump, spinal cord or peripheral nerve stimulation, are becoming more popular for treatment of the lower extremities; however, technical difficulties make them less practical for treatment of the upper extremities.

13.7 PROGNOSIS

Prognosis is generally poor and worsens with the chronicity of the condition. Subbaro and Stillwell[57] reported that only 23% of 125 RSD patients were able to return to full daily activity. As mentioned earlier, in the case of causalgia over 60% of patients were still suffering symptoms despite aggressive therapy after over 3 years.[58] Accurate determination of prognosis for individual patients afflicted with RSD is hampered by the heterogenicity of the clinical picture and differences in the clinical picture over time.

13.8 SUMMARY

RSD is a clinical diagnosis with lack of agreement on clinical criteria. The cause of RSD is unknown. The role of the sympathetic nervous system is not known and is being increasingly questioned. Replacing RSD with the concepts of sympathetic maintained pain has not proven to be useful. Psychological factors are important; whether they predispose certain individuals to development of RSD has not yet been established but there is a trend toward seeing psychological disorders as a significant risk factor in the development of RSD.

Sympathetic blockade and sympathectomy are of questionable value because of a lack of proper controlled trials. If used they are more likely to be of value early in the course of the disorder. Physical exercise, analgesics, and supportive therapy appear to be the most effective treatments. Corticosteroids early in the course may be helpful, especially in RSD following stroke; here again there are no controlled trials. High tech treatments of intrathecal morphine pumps or spinal cord stimulators may become more prominent in the future. Calcitonin and DSMO are two treatments which have been reported to have some success but which have not enjoyed widespread popularity.

---

57 Subbaro J, Stillwell GK. Reflex Sympathetic Dystrophy of the Upper Extremity: Analysis of Total Outcome of Management of 125 Cases. *Arch Phys Med Rehab* 1981; 62:544-549.
58 Girgis, *supra*, note 36.

Chapter 14

Rehabilitation

by John Latter, M.D., F.R.C.P.C.[*]

14.1 Definition of Rehabilitation
    14.1.1 Impairment
    14.1.2 Disability
    14.1.3 Handicap
    14.1.4 Possible Revisions of Categorization Model
14.2 An Interdisciplinary Approach
    14.2.1 Physiatrist
    14.2.2 Physiotherapist
    14.2.3 Occupational Therapist
    14.2.4 Rehabilitation Nurse
    14.2.5 Social Worker
    14.2.6 Psychologist
    14.2.7 Speech-Language Pathologist
    14.2.8 Nutritionist
    14.2.9 Leisure/Recreational Therapist
    14.2.10 Vocational Counsellor
    14.2.11 Child Life Worker/Specialist
    14.2.12 Teacher
14.3 Treatment Modalities in Rehabilitation
    14.3.1 Therapeutic Heat and Cold
    14.3.2 Acupuncture
    14.3.3 Massage
    14.3.4 Electrical Stimulation
    14.3.5 Other Modalities

14.1   DEFINITION OF REHABILITATION

Rehabilitation is defined as the development of a person to the fullest physical, psychological, social, vocational, avocational and educational po-

---

[*]   Professor in Head, Section of Physical Medicine and Rehabilitation, University of Manitoba.

tential, consistent with his or her physiologic or anatomical impairment and environmental limitation.[1] For the most part rehabilitation consists of an interdisciplinary team approach, which provides an environment that allows for optimal functioning of an individual with a disability, be it physical or cognitive. But what do terms such as impairment and disability mean? Although there is not total unanimity with regard to the acceptance of a "definition" for these words, the World Health Organization (WHO) has published an *International Clarification of Impairments, Disabilities and Handicaps*,[2] and its definitions provide a framework from which to gain an understanding of such terms.

14.1.1 Impairment

Impairment is "any abnormality of psychological, physiological or anatomical structure of function." Examples may be a lack of full range of motion of a joint, sore throat, or blurred vision.

14.1.2 Disability

Disability is "any restriction or lack (resulting from an impairment) of ability to perform an activity in the manner or within range considered normal for a human being." An example of this may be a person's inability to comb or wash their hair because of pain, or lack of range or motion of their shoulder.

14.1.3 Handicap

Handicap is "a disadvantage for a given individual resulting from an impairment or a disability that limits or prevents the fulfilment of a role that is normal (depending on the age, sex and social and cultural factors) for that individual." In many ways, it could be described as a particular society's perception of an impairment or disability. What may be considered a handicap in one social environment may not be in another. Having an almost full range or motion of one's finger and thumb may not interfere with everyday function for many people, but for a professional pianist it would be a disaster. Amputees with protheses can manage many activities, but legislation in some jurisdictions may prevent them from legally doing some of these tasks, for example, driving machinery.

Although it is important to keep these definitions in mind as a baseline, both doctors and lawyers need to be aware that insurance companies

---

[1] Delisa J, et al. *Rehabilitation Medicine Principles and Practice*. Philadelphia: J.B. Lippincott, 1988: 3.

[2] (hereinafter ICIDH) World Health Organization International Classification of Impairments, Disabilities and Handicaps. A Manual of Classification Relative to the Consequences of Disease. Geneva, Switzerland: World Health Organization, 1980.

and different levels of government may and will have their own such definitions to fit their criteria for eligibility for financial renumeration. It often becomes a dollar and cents issue and not always what is perceived as fair and reasonable for the individual who has an insult producing a significant change in their functional abilities.

It is suggested that what is important to remember at all times in consideration of rehabilitation is the well-being of the individual and their "current functional capacity."[3]

14.1.4 Possible Revisions of Categorization Model

In 1997 the World Health Organization in collaboration with users and other experts, published a draft version of ICIDH-2, a new look into categorization[4] and, as well, Butler et al.[5] published an article using a suggested different model of disablement by the U.S. National Centre of Medical Rehabilitation Research.

14.2 AN INTERDISCIPLINARY APPROACH

An all-encompassing approach to rehabilitation of an individual is best done through an interdisciplinary team approach. This is by necessity, as well as being in the best interest of the person receiving such care. With the explosion in health care information, technology, and skills available, no one discipline can provide the expertise needed to adequately meet the needs of an individual with a disability in maximizing his or her potential. Depending on the fiscal and human resources available, the team could be quite large or relatively small. Clearly, the group needs to decide upon how best to meet the needs of the individual.

The rehabilitation team usually consists of a physiatrist (physician specialist), physiotherapist, occupational therapist, rehabilitation nurse, social worker, psychologist, speech-language pathologist, nutritionist, leisure/recreational therapist (more adult situation), vocational counsellor (adult situation), child life specialist (children rehab), teacher (children, youth and adolescence rehab). A brief description of each of these health

---

3 Basmajan J, Kirby L. *Medical Rehabilitation*. Baltimore: Williams and Wilkins, Baltimore, 1984: 17.
4 World Health Organization (1997) ICIDH-2: International Classification of Impairment Activities and Participation. Geneva, Switzerland: WHO.
5 Butler C, Chambers H, Goldstein M, Harris S, Leach J, Campbell S, Adams R, Darrah J. Evaluation Research in Developmental Disabilities: A Conceptual Framework for Reviewing Treatment Outcomes. *Development Medicine and Clinical Neurology* Jan. 1999; (41)1:55-59.

disciplines follows. It is recognized that there is overlap among team members with respect to access of training and expertise.

14.2.1 Physiatrist

A physician with specialty training in the field of physical medicine and rehabilitation. The physiatrist provides the medical guidance for the team in dealing with the individual with a disability.

14.2.2 Physiotherapist

A physiotherapist is a graduate of a recognized school of physiotherapy who plans and implements a physiotherapy programme using specialized knowledge and skills for the prevention or treatment of movement dysfunction.[6] Some of the physiotherapist's activities may include:

- joint range of motion and exercises to maintain or increase such range;
- muscle strength evaluation and quantification;
- evaluation of sitting and standing balance, transfer and ambulation including wheelchair and bipedal;
- exercises to increase strength endurance and coordination for either specific muscle groups or the entire body;
- various physical therapy modalities such as both superficial and deep heat and cold, electrical stimulation, traction and massage; and
- aid in home evaluations to make the environment barrier-free and accessible.[7]

14.2.3 Occupational Therapist

An occupational therapist is a graduate of a recognized school of occupational therapy "which utilizes the analysis and application of activities specifically related to occupational performance in the areas of self care, production and leisure. Through assessment, interpretation and intervention, the occupational therapist addresses problems impeding function or adaptive behaviour in persons whose occupational performance is impaired by illness or injury, emotional disorder, developmental disorder, social disadvantage or the aging process."[8] Some of the work done relates to:

- the assessment and planning of activities of daily living (dressing, undressing, feeding, toileting, personal hygiene, eating);
- assessment of home environment to make accessibility easier;

---

6   The Canadian Physiotherapy Association. Toronto, Canada, 1991.
7   Delisa J, et al., *supra*, note 1, at 7.
8   Canadian Association of Occupational Therapists. Ottawa, Canada, 1993.

- involvement in assessment for and prescription of wheelchair (manual/electric) or other motorized mobility aids and appropriate insert;
- driving assessment;
- environmental control assessment; and
- feeding assessment.

14.2.4 Rehabilitation Nurse

A rehabilitation nurse is a care giver whose priorities include assessing the patient's health status and helping the patient to maximize functional capacity. The rehab nurse will also:

- work with the individual in following up on other team members' recommendations when not in direct therapy;
- work with the family and team in coordinating discharge after inpatient stay;
- keep team members apprised of changes in health status of the individual;
- often coordinate training related to continence of bowel and bladder; and
- often plays the part of psychiatrist, chaplain, etc., for client as they are seen as honest broker by the patient.

14.2.5 Social Worker

This person may be involved in the following:

- helping the individual deal with the emotional effects of a disability; both as an inpatient and outpatient;
- work with the family members in learning to cope with a loved one's disability;
- aid the individual and families with financial issues resulting from the individual's disability (disability pension costs for renovations);
- aid in finding appropriate living accommodations (more often from being an inpatient but may be as an outpatient); and
- provide information about resources in the community that may aid the individual and families in allowing the disabled individual to access their community to their fullest wishes.

14.2.6 Psychologist

This person may be involved in the following:

- helping the individual and the team through cognitive assessment, to better understand their present level of cognitive function;

- work with team, families, vocational counsellor or teachers in providing recommendations for employer or schools regarding the capabilities of an individual for future planning; and
- may provide counselling regarding personal issues related to individual's disability, be they emotional, sexual, or pertaining to self-esteem.

14.2.7 Speech-Language Pathologist

This professional may be involved in:

- assessing the communication capabilities of the individual and organizing a plan to maximize that individual's abilities through time, to communicate (this may be verbal or nonverbal);
- working with the family or care givers in giving guidance on how best they can help the individual in their communication programme;
- assessing oral motor skills related to feeding and swallowing;
- helping individuals, before surgery, understand the consequences of the surgery on one's ability to communicate, and afterwards work with the individual on their specific needs (e.g., training with artificial larynx).

14.2.8 Nutritionist

This professional may be involved in:

- assessing caloric needs of the individual and making recommendations to the individual and the team on how best to meet these needs;
- helping the team and individual best meet overall nutritional needs as well as basic caloric needs;
- providing information and teaching to individual, family and/or care givers about appropriate nutrition and how to give it; this is especially so when feeding is by tube (be it nasogastric [tube through nose to the stomach] or some type of gastrotomy tube [tube into stomach]);
- providing nutritional follow up as necessary once patient is discharged; and
- may work in hospital or community agency.

14.2.9 Leisure/Recreational Therapist

This professional may be involved in:

- assessing patient recreational/leisure interests (either inpatient or outpatient);
- aiding the patient in choosing an activity that will meet his or her interests at that moment in time (taking into account physical, emotional and

cognitive concerns, this is done with the hope of improving the patient's motivation and self-esteem through the activities);
- providing information regarding leisure/recreational pursuits which are available in the individual's community and which concerns their particular disability.

14.2.10 Vocational Counsellor

With information from the team, especially neuropsychological assessment, this person may be involved in:

- assessing vocational abilities of the client;
- providing guidance as to how to pursue realistic vocational, post-secondary or avocational pursuits; and
- being a liaison with employment counselling groups in the community, with prospective employers or post-secondary education institutes regarding individual's educational or vocational aptitudes and how best to maximize these potential aptitudes.

14.2.11 Child Life Worker/Specialist

This professional may be involved in:

- helping the child, through recreational activities, regain or gain comfort in socializing skills;
- following through via play activities on aspects of therapeutic intervention as set out by the rehabilitation team (communication, fine motor activity, problem solving skills, for example);
- providing an element of normal everyday activity through play activities despite being in hospital and having significant functional change; in this way hope to maintain or improve self-esteem;
- educating parents about play activities which the team feels will improve function of the child.

14.2.12 Teacher

Especially in child rehabilitation settings, with input from the team, but most often in collaboration with speech-language pathologist and psychologist, this individual may:

- provide appropriate learning environment to help maximize educational abilities;
- provide liaison between hospital and school to which the young person attends, regarding educational abilities and strategies to maximize those abilities.

This provides an overview of some of the activities provided by some of the team members. As necessary, other health care professionals such as prothestists, arthotists, rehabilitation engineers, chiropodists, podiatrists, dance- and music therapists all may be called upon to be rehabilitation team members. It is stated as a reminder, though, that the family, significant other, or usual care giver for an individual are exceedingly important members of the rehabilitation team. They need to be encouraged to be part of the team right from the very beginning and to be party to decisions being made about an individual's rehabilitation care. These people are going to be the main coordinators of ongoing rehabilitation once the patient is discharged.

14.3 TREATMENT MODALITIES IN REHABILITATION

Many different pieces of equipment and techniques are used in modalities found in the rehabilitation field. Different forms of heat and cold have been the mainstay, but machines to reduce pain and stimulate muscles and mechanisms to relax muscles all now play a significant role.

Following is a discussion of some of the techniques and equipment used as examples of the different types of modalities available.

14.3.1 Therapeutic Heat and Cold

Heat and cold affect the body physiologically in three ways primarily. They have an impact on circulation, pain sensitivity, and neuromuscular reaction.[9] Heat increases blood flow as it causes vasodilation and increased metabolic demand. Cold leads to vasoconstriction and decreased metabolic demand. Heat increases the extensibility of soft tissues, especially the musculotendinous conjunction, and it also causes muscle relaxation. Cold decreases these muscle activities.

The effect on pain may be described as acting in a possible three ways: "direct alteration of the stimulus, alteration of the metabolic activity of the neural receptor sensitive to pain, or altered transmission of pain relevant neural firing within the central nervous system especially at the level of the spinal cord."[10] Heat and cold will be active in these different ways to various degrees.

It must be remembered that sometimes heat works for some people

---

9   Nanneemaw D. Thermal Modalities: Heat and Cold: A Review of Physiologic Effects with Clinical Applications; *Am Assoc Occup Health Nurses J* 1991; 39:70-75. Delisa, J.A. Practical Use of Therapeutic Physical Modalities. *American Farming Physician* 1983; 5(27):129-138. Terrerman PS, Divlin, M. Therapeutic Heat and Cold: Post Graduate Medicine 1983; 10 (73):69-76. Reid, David. Rehabilitation, etc.

10 Nannemaw D., *ibid.*, at 73.

where as cold works for others, especially when it comes to muscle relaxation.

Different forms of heat can be dry heat, moist heat, ultrasound, short wave diathermy (not as often used as it once was) and infrared. Application of cold is mostly through ice.

14.3.2 Acupuncture

This has been used for centuries in China to treat and prevent diseases. In North America and Western Europe, its main use has been that of relief of pain, be it manual stimulation or electrical stimulation of needles, and as a form of analgesia. Ding-Zong Wu,[11] and Sven Anderson[12] provide good reviews on the reason how it may provide pain relief and each paper does go on to explain some suggestions for how it may help in disease entities. As a modality, acupuncture is becoming more widely used and accepted in North America for its pain relief as it is in this area that physiologic explanations are more accepted.

14.3.3 Massage

It is a modality that has been used for centuries, but its physiologic and therapeutic effects are not well understood scientifically, but that is changing. "Massage is commonly seen as a therapeutic art without scientific foundation"[13] by some. It has been shown to dilate superficial blood vessels and thus allow for increased rate of blood flow, increased venous return (deep massage), reduce swelling in limbs, improved mobility of tendon ligaments and muscles, and relief or reduction of muscle spasm.[14]

It is of interest that massage therapy is beginning to show gains for preterm infants, cocaine-exposed infants and HIV-positive infants (gaining weight), as well as for some medical conditions such as eating disorders, psoriasis, and post-traumatic stress disorder.[15]

---

11 Wu Ding-Zong. Acupuncture and Neurophysiology. *Clin Neurol Neurosurg* 1990, 91(2):13-25.
12 Anderson S. The Functional Background in Acupuncture Effects. *Scan J Rehab Med* 1993 (Supp. 29):31-60.
13 Goats G. Massage: The Scientific Basis of an Ancient Art: Physiological and Therapeutic Effects. *Brit J Sports Med* 1996; 28(3):153.
14 *Ibid.*, at 153-156.
15 Field T. Massage Therapy for Infants and Children. *Development & Behaviour Paeds* 1995; vol 16(2):105-111.

14.3.4 Electrical Stimulation

This modality is used in a variety of ways in rehabilitation. It is used to help diagnostically (nerve conduction and electromyographic studies) and functionally to help muscles maintain normal strength when for various reasons they may have to rest. An example of this may be in maintaining and improving strength in the quadriceps muscle after knee surgery or injury,[16] or to help improve voluntary movement in paretic muscles after a spinal cord injury with its associated psychological effects.[17] This is done by applying electrodes to muscles and then stimulating them with an electric current. This stimulation may be continuous or intermittent. It has also been shown to decrease muscle tone to allow for normal function to take place.[18]

Another form of electrical stimulation is often used to help relieve pain. This is what is called transcutaneous electrical stimulation (TENS) and frequently is used in chronic low back pain despite evidence in some quarters that it was no more effective then treating with a placebo.[19]

14.3.5 Other Modalities

Other modalities that are used often are traction, manipulation, exercise, and rest.

For example, traction is used in cervical soft tissue injury. Manipulation is used in mobilizing facet joints (part of the vertebral column) which became tight or out of alignment.

Exercise is used a great deal in recovery of soft tissue injuries (muscle, tendon, ligament) to help repair extensibility and strength of the particular tissue injured.

Rest is a form of a modality treatment. On its own, or in combination with other modalities, this is the first line of treatment after an acute injury. The length of time one rests an injured tissue depends on the type of tissue being repaired and the type of injury that has occurred; for example, fractured bones necessitate longer rest than soft tissue sprains.

---

16 Snyder-Mackler L, et al. Strength of the Quadriceps Femoris Muscle and Functional Recovery After Reconstruction of the Anterior Cruciate Ligament. *J Bone Joint Surg* 1995; 77-F(8):1166-1173.

17 Bradley M. The Effects of Participating in a Functional Electrical Stimulation Exercise Programme on Affect in People with Spinal Cord Injuries. *Arch Physic Med Rehab* 1996; 75:671-679.

18 King II, Theodore I. The Effect of Neuromuscular Electrical Stimulation in Reducing Tone. *Am J Occ Therapy* 1996; 50(1):62-64.

19 Deyo R, et al. A Controlled Trial of Transcutaneous Electrical Nerve Stimulation (TENS) and Exercise for Chronic Low Back Pain. *N Eng J Med* 1990; 323(23):1627-1634.

Index

ACCESS TO HEALTH RECORDS
    Canadian Health Record Association (CHRA)   69-80
        code of practice for safeguarding health information   78-80
        patient access to health records, policy statement re   76-78
        principles and guidelines   69-76
            authorization for release of information   73-74
            consent to disclosure, transmittal or examination
              of health record   71-72
    confidentiality of health records   61-64
    legislation regarding access to documents containing personal
      medical information   80-83
        generally   80-81
        Long-term Care Act   81-83
    right to access own personal medical records   65-67
        waiver of right   67-69

ACETABULUM (HIP SOCKET) FRACTURES
    anatomy   481, 653
    classification   481-482, 655
    diagnosis   482
    mechanism of injury   481, 654
    prognosis   483-484
    return to work   484
    treatment   482-483

ACUPUNCTURE, 863 *See also* REHABILITATION

ANKLE JOINT FRACTURES AND INJURIES
    anatomy   517-518, 671-672
    ankle fractures
        classification of   518-519, 673
        complications of   519-521
            post-traumatic arthritis   520-521
            residual loss of motion   520
        treatment of   519, 674
    ligamentous injuries   522-524
        syndesmotic ligaments   523-524, 677
    mechanisms of injury   518

ANKLE JOINT FRACTURES AND INJURIES — *Continued*
    vertical compression fractures   521-522, 675-676

BACK PAIN, 434-439, 834-835, 837, 838-839 *See also* CHRONIC PAIN DISORDERS and SPINAL INJURIES, thoracolumbar spine, soft tissue injuries

BLOOD CLOT *See* HEAD INJURY, pathophysiology of head injury, secondary injuries

BRAIN DEAD *See* HEAD INJURY

BRAIN INJURY, NEUROPSYCHOLOGY AND TRAUMATIC *See also* HEAD INJURY
    neuropsychological procedures   354-362
        commonly used tests   357-360
            attention and concentration   358-359
            executive functions   360
            generally   357-358
            intelligence   358
            language   359
            memory and learning   359
            personality measures   360
            sensory-motor abilities   359-360
            visuospatial and visuoconstructive abilities   359
        personality variables affecting test performance   355-357
            anxiety   357
            depression   356-357
            malingering   355-356
            pain   357
        testing procedures 354-355
            interview and history   354
            test administration   355
            test behaviour   354
        test results   361-362
            test interpretation   361
            test report   361-362
    neuropsychologist,   350-351
    rehabilitation and recovery   364-366
        factors related to rehabilitation   364-365
        recovery: age severity, extent   365-366
        rehabilitation techniques   365
    sequelae of traumatic brain injury (TBI)   362-364
        cognitive sequelae   362-363
            attention and concentration   362
            executive functions   363
            learning   363
            memory   362-363
        emotional and behavioural sequelae   363-364
            anosognosia   364

BRAIN INJURY, NEUROPSYCHOLOGY AND TRAUMATIC
— Continued
        emotional lability and disinhibition   364
        fatigue   363
        insensitivity or lack of empathy   364
        irritability   364
   "traumatic brain injury" (TBI), defined   351-353
      epidemiology   353
      Glasgow Coma Scale   347, 351
      post-concussion syndrome (PCS)   352
      post-traumatic amnesia (PTA)   351
      post-traumatic stress disorder (PTSD)   353

CANADIAN HEALTH RECORD ASSOCIATION (CHRA), 69-80 *See also* ACCESS TO HEALTH RECORDS

CHRONIC PAIN DISORDERS *See also* REHABILITATION
   disability secondary to   822-839
      acceptance of chronic pain and disability   829-830
      acute medical model and chronic pain disorders   823-825
         generally   823-824
         search for structural abnormalities   824-825
      assessment of disability   826-829
      compensation and secondary gain in disability   830-833
         compensation and chronic pain   830-831
         secondary gain   831-832
         secondary losses   832-833
      definitions: impairment, disability and handicap   822
      disability claims, rise in   823
      discordance between pain, impairment, and disability   825-826
      lower back pain (LBP)   834-835, 837, 838-839
      managing chronic pain disability only, shift to   838
      rejecting chronic pain disability, trend towards   838-839
         Quebec task force on whiplash associated disorders   839
         report on back pain in workplace   838-839
      socioeconomic factors and disablity   833-834
         lower socioeconomic status and risk of disability   833-834
      work environment   834-837
         heavy physical work   834-835
         job dissatisfaction   835-837
   fibromyalgia   812-814
      assessment of disability   826-829
      clinical criteria   812-813
         American College of Rheumatology (ACR) criteria   812-813
         questioning ACR criteria   813-815
      recovery and pathophysiology   817-821
   fibromyalgia and trauma, relationship between   815-817

CHRONIC PAIN DISORDERS — *Continued*
    argument against 815
    argument for 815-817
  future conflict: chronic pain, disability, and society 839-840
  introduction 806
    classification controversies, clinical 808-809
    defining chronic pain 807-808
    the problem 806-807
  myofascial pain 811-812
  recovery and pathophysiology 817-822
    evidence for organic basis for chronic pain 817-821
      conclusions 820-821
      evidence of central neurological origin for regional pain 818-819
      evidence of mechanical origin for chronic whiplash injury pain 820
    psychological factors causative, whether 821-822
    recovery after trauma 817
  soft tissue pain disorders, nonspecificity of chronic 811
  whiplash injuries 809-811
    clinical picture 810-811
    mechanical origin for chronic whiplash injury pain, evidence of 820
    mechanisms of injury 809-810

CLAVICLE FRACTURES *See* SHOULDER INJURIES

COMA
  generally 334
  Glasgow Coma Scale 347, 351

CONCUSSION, CEREBRAL, 329-333, 352 *See also* BRAIN INJURY, NEUROPSYCHOLOGY AND TRAUMATIC and HEAD INJURY

CONFIDENTIALTY OF HEALTH RECORDS 61-64

CROSS-EXAMINATION OF EXPERTS *See* EXPERT EVIDENCE, preparing expert for trial

DEPRESSION 356-357

DISABILITY *See* CHRONIC PAIN DISORDERS, disability secondary to

DISCOVERY PROCESS, 1-2, 96-114 *See also* PRODUCTION OF HEALTH RECORDS IN PERSONAL INJURY ACTION
  affidavit of documents 96-100
  examination for discovery 100-114
  generally 1-2

DUTY TO CREATE, MAINTAIN AND PRESERVE HEALTH RECORDS
   general statutes with health record components   28-60
       Child and Family Services Act   29-33
           duty to create   30-33
           executive responsibility   29
           statute summary   29-30
       Coroners Act   34-34
           duty to create   35
           executive responsibility   34
           statute summary   34-35
       Drug and Pharmacies Regulation Act   35-38
           duty to create   37-38
           executive responsibility   35
           statute summary   35-37
       Long-term Care Act   38-42
           duty to create   41-42
           executive responsibility   38
           statute summary   38-41
       Mental Health Act   42-52
           duty to create   45-52
           executive responsibility   42
           "psychiatric facility" defined   42
           statute summary   42-44
       Vital Statistics Act   52-53
           duty to create   52-53
           executive responsibility   52
           statute summary   52
       Workers' Compensation Act   53-57
           duty to create   56-57
           statute summary   53-55
       Workplace Safety and Insurance Act   53, 58-60
           duty to create   59-60
           statute summary   58-59
   introduction   11-13
   record-keeping under Health Professions Acts   11-18
       Chiropody Act   14-15
       Massage Therapy Act   16-17
       Medicine Act   13-14
       Optometry Act   17-18
   record-keeping under medical institutions statutes   18-28
       generally   18
       Public Hospitals Act   18-28
           anaesthetic, where administer   25-26
           blood transfusion   27
           dentist, treatment by   24
           midwife, admitted by   24-25
           out-patient   20-22
           patient other than out-patient   19-20, 21-22

DUTY TO CREATE, MAINTAIN AND PRESERVE HEALTH
RECORDS — *Continued*
        problem in care or treatment   27-28
        surgical operation   26-27

DUTY TO REPORT PERSONAL MEDICAL INFORMATION
    duty to report, statutory   157-158
    duty to warn   158-160
    statutes containing "duty to report" provisions   160-183
        Charitable Institutions Act   177-178
        Child and Family Services Act   161-164
        Coroners Act   164-165
        Day Nurseries Act   178
        generally   160-161
        Health Protection and Promotion Act   166-172
            reportable and communicable diseases   158, 166-172
        Highway Traffic Act   172-174
            case law   173-174
        Homes for the Aged and Rest Homes Act   179-180
        Homes for Retarded Persons Act   178-179
        Mental Hospitals Act   180
        Nursing Homes Act   181-182
        Private Hospitals Act   182
        Public Hospitals Act   182-183
        Regulated Health Professions Act   175-176
        Vital Statistics Act   176-177

ELBOW AND FOREARM INJURIES
    anatomy and biomechanics   572-573, 739-745
    distal forearm and wrist   581-590
        anatomy and biomechanics   581-584, 748-764
            arteries   583, 745
            carpal bones   581-583
            tendons   583-584, 745, 750-752, 761-764
        distal radius fractures   584-587, 765
            treatment of   586-587
        scaphoid fractures   587-590
            treatment of   589-590
    elbow in adults, fractures about   573-575
        distal humerus
            fractures in   773-574
            intercondylar fractures of   574-575, 746-747
    mid-forearm injuries   575-580
        anatomy   575-576, 745
        assessment   577
        forearm injuries   576-577
        treatment   577-580

EPIDEMIOLOGY OF HEAD INJURY, 298-299, 353 *See also* HEAD INJURY

EVIDENCE ACT
    section 35 127-129
    section 52 129-134
        medical reports 230-236

EXPERT EVIDENCE
    admissibility of expert opinion evidence 193-199
        exclusionary rule, absence of 197
        necessity in assisting trier of fact 195-196
        properly qualified expert 197-199
            Marquard decision 198-199
        relevance 193-195
    conclusion 245
    court-appointed experts 214-217
    duties and responsibilities of expert witness 210-214, 255
    family doctor-patient relationship 244-245
    good expert report, producing 236-241
        instructing expert 236-240
    hearsay, expert opinion based on 200-201
    introduction 188
    locating expert witness 219-220
    medical reports: Evidence Act, s. 52 230-236
        generally 230-231
        good report, producing 236-241
        medical practitioner
            calling to testify at trial 232-233
                securing attendance for cross-examination 233-235
                when unavailable for cross-examination 235
        purpose of s. 52 231-232
    medico-legal reports, guidelines and detailed outline for 246-249
    novel expert opinion evidence 204-210
        battered wife syndrome 205
        child sexual abuse 206-207
        novel scientific evidence 207-210
        video reconstruction 205-206
    number of experts allowed to tesify 243-244
    opinion evidence generally 188-189
    preparing expert for trial 251-282
        basis of expert's opinion 264-274
            build expert's opinion slowly 265
            define terms 271-272
            demonstrative aids 267-271
                introducing visual aid 271
                judicial discretion not to admit 270-271
            ending on powerful note 274
            generally 264
            hypothetical question 265-267
            mainstream opinion, show that expert presenting 272

EXPERT EVIDENCE — *Continued*
   summarize each stage of expert's opinion 265
   weakness, dealing with any 272-274
  conclusion 282
  cross-examination of experts 274-282
   areas of challenge 277-280
   preparation of expert 275-277
   purposes of cross-examination 274-275
   techniques of 280-282
  direct examination 260
  expert witness, considerations for 210-214, 254-257
  general preparation 252-253
  heart of expert's opinion 264
  introduction 251-252
  preparing expert to provide expert opinion 257-260
   suggested steps 257-260
  qualifying expert witness 260-264
  theory of case 253-254
 qualifications of experts 191-192
 remuneration for expert opinion 221-223
  payment for expert's services 222-223
  professional conduct 222
 report, expert 223-230, 236-243
  disclosure of expert report, raw data and drafts 224-227
  format of report 241-242
  good report, producing 236-241
  leave to file expert's report 229-230
  review of 242-243
  service of copy of report: r. 53.03 223-224
  solicitor-client privilege versus litigation privilege 227-229
 right expert witness, approaching 217-219
 ultimate issue rule 201-204
 when to choose expert witness 220-221
 why experts needed 190-191

EXTREMITIES INJURIES AND PELVIC INJURIES GENERALLY *See also* PELVIC INJURIES and SPECIAL INJURIES AND COMPLICATIONS
 fracture, description of 469-471
  angulation 471, 648
  closed versus open 471
  displacement 470, 646
  generally 469
  location 469-470, 645
  pattern 470-471, 647
 glossary 629-644
 immobilization, principles of 471-474
  bedrest 474
  braces 473

EXTREMITIES INJURIES AND PELVIC INJURIES GENERALLY— *Continued*
    casts 472-473
    generally 471-472
    surgical fixation 474
    traction 473-474

FEMORAL SHAFT FRACTURES
    classification 497-498, 661
    diagnosis 498
    prognosis 501-502
        deformities 501
        knee range of motion 502
        nonunion 501
        return to work 502
        union rate and delayed union 501
    treatment 498-500, 662

FEMUR *See* FEMORAL SHAFT FRACTURES

FIBROMYALGIA *See* CHRONIC PAIN DISORDERS

FOOT INJURIES
    anatomy 524-527
        metatarsus 526
        osteology 524, 680-683
        phalanges 526
        sesamoid and accessory bones 527
        tarsus 524-526, 681-682
    biomechanics 531-532
    calcaneus fractures 538-544
        assessment 541
        categories 539-540, 687, 702
        classifications 540-541
        generally 538-39, 680, 687, 701
        prognosis 543-544
        special tests 541-542, 703-705
        treatment 542-543
    dislocations of metatarsophalangeal joints 549-550
    dislocations, subluxations about talus 537-538
    evaluation of injuries 532
    introduction 524, 678-679
    joint, ligaments and aponeurosis of foot 527-528
        ankle joint 527, 671
        calcaneocuboid joint 528, 687
        cuneo-navicular joint 528
        interphalangeal joints 528
        metatarsophalangeal joints 528
        plantar aponeurosis 528, 688
        subtalar joint 527, 684, 686

FOOT INJURIES — *Continued*
    talonavicular joint 527-528
    tarsometatarsal joints (Lisfranc joints) 528, 685-686
  metatarsal fractures 548-549, 707
    fifth metatarsal bone 548-549
  midtarsal fractures 544-545
    cuboid fractures 545
    cuneiform fractures 545
    navicular fractures 544
  muscles of foot 529
    extrinsic muscles 529, 689-690
    intrinsic muscles 529, 691
  nerves of ankle and foot 529-530, 692
  talus fractures 532-533, 694
    blood supply of talus 533
    body of talus 536-537
    other less common talar fractures 537, 698
    talar head fractures 533
    talar neck fractures 533-535, 695-697, 699-700
      prognosis and complications 535-536
        osteonecrosis 535-536
        post-traumatic arthritis 536
  tarsometatarsal (Lisfranc's) joint injuries 545-548
    anatomy 545, 680-682, 685
    clinical presentations 546
    mechanisms of injury and classification 545-546, 706
    prognosis 547-548
    radiographic findings 546, 707
    treatment 547
  toe fractures and dislocations 550
    great toe (Hallux) fractures 550
    lesser toe joints, dislocations of 550
    lesser toes, fractures of 550
  vascular system 530-531
    arteries 530, 689-690, 693
    veins 530-531

FOREARM INJURIES *See* ELBOW AND FOREARM INJURIES

FREEDOM OF INFORMATION AND PROTECTION OF PRIVACY ACT 151-153

GANGRENE, GAS 621-622

HAND INJURIES
  anatomy 590-592, 745, 761-764, 766-769
    tendons 590-591
  extensor tendon injuries 593, 771
  flexor tendon injuries 592-593, 768, 770

HAND INJURIES — *Continued*
    fractures of hand 593-595

HEAD INJURY *See also* BRAIN INJURY, NEUROPSYCHOLOGY AND TRAUMATIC
    acute evaluation of head-injured patient 317-320
        diagnostic imaging 319-320
        history and physical examination 318-319
        introduction 317-318
    acute management of severe head injuries 320-328
        introduction 320
        intracranial pressure monitoring 322-324
            choice of monitor 324
            indications for monitoring 323
            introduction 322-323
        intracranial pressure, treatment of elevated 325-328
            guideline for initiating treatment 325
            therapeutic measures, specific 325-328
                anti-seizure prophylaxis 328
                    post-traumatic seizures (PTS) 328
                barbiturates 327
                corticosteroids 327-328
                CSF drainage 326
                head elevation 326
                hyperventilation 326-327
                introduction 325
                mannitol 327
                sedation, analgesia, and neuromuscular blockade 325-326
        monitoring techniques, additional 324-325
            jugular venous oxygen saturation monitoring 324-325
            transcranial doppler 324
        overall management goals 322
        resuscitation, initial 321-322
    blood vessels of brain 296-298
        arteries of brain 296-297, 342
        veins of brain 297-298, 343
    brain
        blood vessels of 296-298
        brainstem 295-296
        cellular foundation of neuroanatomy 288-290
            introduction 288
            neuron 288-289, 340
            neuroglia 289-290
        cerebellum 296
        cerebral hemispheres 290-293
            basal ganglia 293
            frontal lobe 291-292

876 INDEX

HEAD INJURY — *Continued*
        introduction 290-291, 341
        occipital 293
        parietal lobe 292
        temporal lobe 293
    diencephalon 293-295
        epithalamus 294-295
        hypothalamus 294
        subthalamus 294-295
        thalamus 293-294
    divisions of brain 287-288, 340
    ventricles of brain 298, 343
  brain dead 333-336
    cessation of brain function 334-335
    guidelines 333-334
    introduction 333
    irreversibility 335
    laboratory tests 336
    special circumstances 336
  concussion, cerebral 329-333
    definitions 329-330
        Grade I concussion 330
        Grade II concussion 330
        Grade III concussion 330-331
    immediate on scene evaluation 331
    introduction 329
    management recommendations 331-333
        Grade I concussion 331
        Grade II concussion 331-332
        Grade III concussion 332-333
  epidemiology of head injury 298-299
  introduction 285
  meninges (coverings of brain) 286-287
    arachnoid mater 287, 339
    dura mater 286-287, 338-339
    introduction 286
    pia mater 287
  pathophysiology of head injury 299-317
    impact (primary) injuries 299-304
        cerebral concussion 303, 329-333
        diffuse brain injury 303-304
        gray matter contusions 303
        scalp injuries 299-300
        skull fracture 300-303
            basal skull fractures 302-303
            classification 300
            depressed skull fractures 301-302
            lineal skull fractures 300-301

HEAD INJURY — *Continued*
    introduction 299
    secondary injuries 305-317
        intracranial haematoma 305-312
            acute subdural haematoma 307-308, 345
            chronic subdural haematoma 308-310
            epidural haematoma 305-307, 344
            intracerebral haematoma 310-312, 346
            traumatic subarachnoid hemorrhage 310
        raised intracranial pressure 312-317
            consequences of 314-317
                brain shift and herniation 315-316, 347
                central transtentorial herniation 317
                cingulate herniation 316
                ischemia 314-315
                lateral transtentorial (uncal) herniation 316-317
            introduction and definitions 312-314
    skull 285-286, 337
    ventricles of brain 298, 343

HEALTH PROFESSION STATUTES
    Health Profession Acts 7-10
        format of each Act 8
        regulations 8-10
    Health Professions Board 5
    Health Professions Procedural Code 5-7, 153-155
        College for each health profession 5-7
            committees 6-7
            objects 5-6
        prescription period 7
    Health Professions Regulatory Advisory Council 4
    introduction 1-2
        cross-examination of medical witness at trial 2
            preparation of medical witness 2
        discovery 1-2
    Regulated Health Professions Act 3-4 *See also* REGULATED HEALTH PROFESSIONS ACT

HEALTH RECORDS
    access to, 61-83 *See also* ACCESS TO HEALTH RECORDS
    duty to create, maintain and preserve health records, 11-60 *See also* DUTY TO CREATE, MAINTAIN AND PRESERVE HEALTH RECORDS
    production of, in personal injury action, 85-155 *See also* PRODUCTION OF HEALTH RECORDS IN PERSONAL INJURY ACTION

HIP FRACTURES AND DISLOCATION *See also* ACETABULUM FRACTURES
    anatomy 485-486, 656-657
    dislocation of hip 486-487
        anterior dislocation of hip 487-488
        posterior dislocations of hip 488-490
            avascular necrosis (AVN) 490
            knee injury 490
            sciatic nerve palsy 489-490
    femoral neck fractures 491-493, 657
        outcome of 493-494
    intertrochanteric fractures 495-496, 658-659
        outcome 495-496
    introduction 484-485
    subtrochanteric fractures 496-497, 660

HIP SOCKET *See* ACETABULUM FRACTURES

INFECTION, 618-622 *See also* SPECIAL INJURIES AND COMPLCATIONS

KNEE INJURIES
    distal femur fractures 502-504, 663-664
        treatment, principles of 503-504
    ligament injuries 507, 666-668
        collateral ligaments 507-508
            lateral collateral ligament 508
            medial collateral ligament (MCL) 507-508
        cruciate ligaments 508-511
            anterior cruciate ligament (ACL) 508-510, 511
            posterior cruciate ligament (PCL) 509, 510-511
    proximal tibia fractures 504-507, 665
        treatment, principles of 505-507

LEG LENGTH DISCREPANCY AND FRACTURE MALUNION, 612-616 *See also* FEMORAL SHAFT INJURIES, FOOT INJURIES and KNEE INJURIES

LIGAMENT INJURIES *See* ANKLE JOINT FRACTURES AND INJURIES and KNEE INJURIES

LONG-TERM CARE ACT
    access to personal medical information 81-83
    duty to create medical records 38-42

MANGLED EXTREMITIES 602-604, 626
    Mangled Extremity Severity Score ((MESS) 603, 626

MEDICO-LEGAL REPORTS
    guidelines and detailed outline for 246-249
    Ontario Evidence Act 230-236

MULTIPLY INJURED PATIENT 595-598
    injury severity score (ISS) 596-597, 624

NEUROPSYCHOLOGY See BRAIN INJURY, NEUROPSYCHOLOGY AND TRAUMATIC

PAIN DISORDERS See CHRONIC PAIN DISORDERS

PELVIC INJURIES
    anatomy 474-475, 649-650
    biomechanics of pelvic ring injuries 476
    classification 477, 651-652
    prognosis and outcome 479-480
    treatment 477-479
        hemorrhage associated with pelvic injuries 479
        lateral compression injuries 478, 652
        open book injuries 478, 651
        open (compound) pelvic fractures 478-479
        stable pelvic injuries 477-478
        vertical shear fractures 478, 652

OPEN FRACTURES 598-602, 772-777
    Gustilo classification 598-600, 625

OSTEOMYELITIS 618-621, 627-628, 797-802

"POLICE INFORMER" PRIVILEGE 146-149

POST-TRAUMATIC SEIZURES (PTS) 328

PRODUCTION OF HEALTH RECORDS IN PERSONAL INJURY ACTION
    discovery process 96-114
        affidavit of documents 96-100
        examination for discovery of non-party 113-114
            case law 114
        examination for discovery of party 100-113
            case law 104-113
            undertakings 103-104
        generally 1-2
    introduction 86-87
    medical examination of party, court-ordered 124-126
        case law 126
    not producible in personal injury action, health records 87-96
        Child and Family Services Act 87-88
        Coroners Act 88-89
        Drug and Pharmacies Regulation Act 92-93
        Highway Traffic Act 89
        Human Rights Code 90
        Independent Health Facilities Act 90
        Mental Health Act 91-92

880   INDEX

PRODUCTION OF HEALTH RECORDS IN PERSONAL INJURY
ACTION — *Continued*
    Regulated Health Professions Act 92-93
    Workplace Safety and Insurance Act 93-96
    Workers' Compensation Act 93-96
  order for production of documents from non-party 114-124
    case law 115-123
    comment 124
  related topics
    computerized records 149-150
    Freedom of Information and Protection of Privacy Act 151-153
    incident reports 137-138
    Municipal Freedom of Information and Protection of
    Privacy Act 151, 153
    "police informer" privilege 146-149
    quality assurance programs 138-139
    Registrar of College under Health Professions Procedural
     Code information concerning health profession
     member 153-155
    spoliation of health records 141-146
      "spoliation" defined 141
    undertaking, deemed 139-141
  trial 126-137
    court-appointed expert, medical reports of 135-136
    generally 126-127
    medical records under Evidence Act
      section 35 127-129
      section 52 129-134
    medical records under Ontario Rules of Civil Procedure,
      r. 53.03 134-135, 223-224, 229-230
        case law 135
    photographic film of health records, use of 136-137

PULMONARY EMBOLISM, 608-610, 787-788 *See also* SPECIAL INJURIES
AND COMPLICATIONS

REFLEX SYMPATHETIC DYSTROPHY (RSD)
  concerns regarding definitions/pathophysiology 847
  defining reflex sympathetic dystrophy (RSD) 841-844
    clinical criteria for RSD 841-842
    complex regional pain syndrome (CRPS) 843
    terminology in RSD 844
  diagnosis 849-850
    clinical diagnosis 849
    nuclear bone scan 849-850
    radiological studies 850
    sympathetic blockade 850
    prognosis 854

REFLEX SYMPATHETIC DYSTROPHY (RSD) — *Continued*
    role of psychological factors 847-849
    role of sympathetic nervous system (SNS) in RSD 845-846
    summary 854
    treatment 850-854
        calcitonin 853
        corticosteroids 852-853
        hydroxyl radical scavengers 853-854
        physical therapy 851
        surgical sympathectomy 852
        surgically implantable devices 854
        sympathetic blockade 851-852

REGULATED HEALTH PROFESSIONS ACT *See also* HEALTH PROFESSIONS STATUTES
    duty to report personal medical information 175-176
    health records not producible in personal injury action 92-93
    introduction 3-4
    procedural code 5-7 153-155

REHABILITATION
    definition 855-857
        disability 856
        handicap 856
        impairment 856-857
        revisions of categorization model, possible 857
    interdisciplinary approach 857-862
        child life worker/specialist 861
        generally 857-858
        leisure/recreational therapist 860-861
        nurse, rehabilitation 859
        nutritionist 860
        occupational therapist 858-859
        physiatrist 858
        physiotherapist 858
        psychologist 859-860
        social worker 859
        speech-language pathologist 860
        teacher 861-862
        vocational counsellor 861
    treatment modalities 862-864
        acupuncture 863
        electrical stimulation 864
        massage 863
        other modalities 864
        therapeutic hot and cold 862-863

SHOULDER INJURIES
    acromioclavicular joint injuries 555-557

882   INDEX

SHOULDER INJURIES — *Continued*
  anatomy 555, 711-712
  complications 556-557
  injury types and their management 555-556, 721
    shoulder separation 555-556, 721
  mechanics of injury 555
 clavicle fractures 558-561
  anatomy 558, 723-724
  classifications 560
  diagnosis and classification 558
  neurovascular problems 560-561
  treatment 558-560, 725-726
 glenohumeral joint subluxations and dislocations 552-555
  diagnosis 553
  pathomechanics 553, 720
  treatment 553-555
 humeral shaft fractures 566-569
  anatomy 566-567, 732-734
  complications 568-569, 735
  diagnosis 567
  treatment 567-568
 introduction 550-552, 708-719, 723-724
  four joints, integrity of 551-552
 proximal humerus fractures 562-566
  classification 563, 729-730
  complications 565-566, 731
  diagnosis 563
  introduction 562 728
  prognosis 565
  treatment 563-565
    closed or open reduction treatment 564-565
    conservative (closed treatment) 563-564
 rotator cuff tears 569-571
  introduction 569, 736-738
  investigations 570
  pathomechanics 569-570
  surgical treatment results 571
  treatment 570-571
 scapula fractures 561-562
  diagnosis 561, 727
  incidence 561
  treatment 561-562
 sternoclavicular joint injuries 557-558
  anatomy 557, 722
  mechanics of injury, diagnosis 557
  treatment 558

SOLICITOR-CLIENT PRIVILEGE 227-229

SPECIAL INJURIES AND COMPLICATIONS
   mangled extremities 602-604, 778-779
      Mangled Extremity Severity Score (MESS) 603, 626
   multiply injured patient 595-598
      injury severity score (ISS) 596-597, 624
   musculoskeletal system, complications of injuries to 607-623
      compartment syndrome 622-623, 803
      fat embolism and adult respiratory distress syndrome 610-612
      infection 618-622
         gas gangrene (clostridial myonecrosis) 621-622
         necrotizing fasciitis 622
         osteomyelitis 618-621, 797-801
            Cierny classification 619-620, 627
            treatment of 620-621, 628
      leg length discrepancy and fracture malunion 612-616
         leg length discrepancy 612-613
         malunion 613-616, 789-792
      nonunion (Pseudoarthrosis) 616-618
         classification 616-618, 793-796
      pulmonary embolism 608-610, 787-788
      thrombeombolism 607
   open fractures 598-602, 772-777
      Gustilo classification 598-600, 625
   open tibia fractures, Type IIIB 604-607, 780-786

SPINAL INJURIES
   cervical spine 372-413
      anatomy 372-377
         discs, intervertebral 374, 445
         ligaments 375, 445
         muscles 375-376
         nerves and spinal chord 376-377
            gross anatomy 376-377
            motor tracts 377
            neuroanatomy 377
            sensory tracts 377
         osseous anatomy 372-374, 442-444
      cervical injury, evaluation of patient with,
         history 381
         physical examination 382-384
            neurologic function 383
            special tests 383-384
   fractures and dislocations 393-400
      atlanto-axial fractures 393-394
      flexion instabilities 395-396, 450
         anterior wedge compression fractures 395

884 INDEX

SPINAL INJURIES — *Continued*
    Clay Shoveler's fracture 397
    extension instabilities 397
    gunshot injuries 397
    rotational instabilities 396-397
    seat belts and airbags 398
    treatment of fractures and dislocations 398-400
        brace treatment 398
        halo vest treatment 398-399
        surgical treatment 399-400
    vertebral body with canal compromise, fractures of 395-396, 450
neck, biomechanics of 378-381
    common injury mechanism 380-381
    occipito-atlanto-axial complex (C0-C1-C2) 378, 445
    spinal stability, concepts of 379-380
    subaxial complex (C2-T1) 378-379
neurological injuries 400-413
    assessment 400-401
    classification 401-402
        chord lesions
            complete 402, 408
            incomplete 401-402, 408
        root injuries 401
    complications 410-412
        bowel obstruction 411
        contractures 411
        dysreflexia, antonomic 412
        ossification, heterotopic 412
        osteoporosis 411
        pulmonary 411
        thrombosis, deep vein 411
        ulcers, decubitus 410-411
        urinary tract, infection of 411
    life expectancy 412-413
    treatment and rehabilitation 402-410
        definitive treatment 403
        initial treatment 402-403
        prognosis 408-410
        rehabilitation and long-term management 403-410
            paraplegia, optimal mobility in motor complete 407-408
            quadriplegia, optimal function in motor complete 404-407
soft tissue injuries 384-393
    acceleration injuries 386-390, 448
        treatment 389-390
    disc disruption and herniation 391-393, 447, 440

SPINAL INJURIES — *Continued*
- ligament strain 384-385
- muscle strain 385-386
- whiplash 386-390, 448
  - treatment 389-390
- team member, role of each 369-372
  - ambulance and paramedics 370-371
  - generally 369-370
  - rehabilitation specialists 372
  - spinal surgeon 371-372
  - trauma team leader 371
- thoracolumbar spine 413-441
  - anatomy 413-419
    - discs, intervertebral 414-415, 451
    - ligaments of 415, 452
    - muscles of 416
    - neuroanatomy of 417
    - osseous anatomy 413-414
    - pain fibers in spine, location of 417-419
  - evaluation of patient 420-425
    - history 420
    - investigations 426-427
    - missed spine fractures 427
    - physical examination 421-426
      - motion testing, range of 422
      - neurologic function 422-423
      - observation 421
      - palpation 422
      - special tests 423-426
        - femoral stretch test (FST) 424-425
        - nonorganic physical signs 425-426
        - straight leg raising (SLR) 423, 424, 425, 453
  - fractures and dislocations of 427
    - classification 427-428
      - burst fractures 420, 427-428, 430, 454
      - compression fractures 427, 453
      - flexion-distraction injuries 428, 456-457
      - fracture-dislocation 428, 429-430, 458-459
    - outcome 431-434
      - burst fracture 430, 431-433
      - flexion-distraction injuries 433
      - post-traumatic kyphosis, 433-434
    - treatment 428-431
      - initial 428-429
      - nonoperative treatment 429
      - operative treatment 429-431
      - pharmacologic treatment 429
  - soft tissue injuries 434-439

SPINAL INJURIES — *Continued*
    disc disruption and herniation 434-439, 460-461
        back pain 434-436
        nonoperative treatment 436-438
        surgical treatment 438-439
    spondylolysis and spondylolisthesis 439-441, 461
    thoracolumbar injuries, biomechanics and pathophysiology of 419-420
        mechanism of injury and classification 420
            burst fracture 420
        three-column concept 419-420, 452

STATUTES *See* HEALTH PROFESSION STATUTES

THROMBOEMBOLISM 607

TIBIA FRACTURES
    open tibia fractures, Type IIIB 604-607, 780-786
    proximal tibia fractures 504-507, 665

TRAUMATIC BRAIN INJURY (TBI) *See* BRAIN INJURY, NEUROPSYCHOLOGY AND TRAUMATIC

WHIPLASH INJURIES
    chronic pain disorder 809-811
    generally 386-390, 448
    mechanical origin for chronic whiplash injury pain, evidence of 820
    Quebec task force on whiplash associated with disorders 839

WRIST INJURIES, 581-590 *See also* ELBOW AND FOREARM INJURIES, distal forearm and wrist
    anatomy and biomechanics 581-584, 748-764
    distal radius fractures 584-586, 765
        treatment of 586-587
    scaphoid fractures 587-590
        treatment of 589-590